Contents

II European driving: cut through the confusion
IV Driving regulations
VII Ski resorts

1 Route planning maps

1 Key to route planning map pages

24 Road maps

24 Key to road map pages · Distance table

201 City plans and approach maps

Alicante C	201	Luxembourg C	215
Amsterdam C U	202	Lyon C U	215
Antwerpen C	201	Madrid U C	215
Athina U C	202	Málaga C	216
Barcelona C U	203	Marseille C	216
Basel C	203	Milano C U	217
Beograd C	205	Moskva C U	218
Berlin C U	204	München C U	218
Bordeaux C U	205	Nápoli C U	219
Bruxelles U C	205	Oslo U C	219
Budapest C U	206	Paris C U	220
Dublin C U	207	Praha C U	222
Düsseldorf C U	207	Roma C U	223
Edinburgh C	207	Rotterdam C	222
Firenze Florence C	209	Sankt Peterburg U	222
Frankfurt C	209	Sevilla C	224
Genève Geneva C	209	Stockholm C U	225
Génova Genoa C	209	Strasbourg C U	224
Göteborg C	210	Stuttgart C	224
Granada C	210	Torino U C	226
Hamburg C U	210	Venézia C	226
Helsinki C U	211	Warszawa C U	227
İstanbul U	211	Wien U C	227
København C U	212	Zagreb C	228
Köln Cologne C	212	Zürich C	228
Lisboa C U	213	C City street plan	
London C U	213	U Urban area map	

229 Index to road maps

www.philips-maps.co.uk

First published in 1998 by Philip's,
a division of Octopus Publishing Group Ltd
www.octopusbooks.co.uk
Endeavour House, 189 Shaftesbury Avenue, London WC2H 8JY
An Hachette UK Company • www.hachette.co.uk

Twenty-second edition 2013, first impression 2013

Ordnance Survey® This product includes mapping
data licensed from Ordnance
Survey®, with the permission of the Controller of Her Majesty's
Stationery Office © Crown copyright 2013. All rights reserved.
Licence number 100011710.

OS is a registered Trade Mark of the Northern Ireland
Department of Finance and Personnel. This
product includes mapping data licensed from
Ordnance Survey of Northern Ireland®, reproduced with the
permission of Land and Property Services under delegated
authority from the Controller of Her Majesty's Stationery Office,
© Crown Copyright 2013.

up-to-date at the time of publication, some of this information
is subject to change and the Publisher cannot guarantee its
correctness or completeness.

The information in this atlas is provided without any
representation or warranty, express or implied and the
Publisher cannot be held liable for any loss or damage due to
any use or reliance on the information in this atlas, nor for any
errors, omissions or subsequent changes in such information.

The representation in this atlas of any road, drive or track is not
evidence of the existence of a right of way.

The mapping on page 214 and the town plans of Edinburgh and
London are based on mapping data licenced from Ordnance
Survey with the permission of the Controller of Her Majesty's
Stationery Office, © Crown Copyright 2013. All rights reserved.
Licence number 100011710.

The maps of Ireland on pages 26 to 30 and the urban area
map and town plan of Dublin are based on Ordnance Survey
Ireland by permission of the Government Permit Number 8847
© Ordnance Survey Ireland and Government of Ireland, and
Land and Property Services under delegated authority from the
Controller of Her Majesty's Stationery Office
© Crown Copyright 2013 Permit Number 120086

Cartography by Philip's, Copyright © Philip's 2013

Photographic acknowledgements: Page II top left, joyfull /
Shutterstock; top right Tjurunga / Dreamstime; bottom right
mladn61 / iStockphoto • Page III centre zstock / Shutterstock;
bottom Lya_Cattel /iStockphoto • Page VII Ingmar Wesemann /
iStockphoto.com • Page VIII Jivko Kazakov / iStockphoto.com

Printed in China

Legend to route planning

Motorway with sel…
tunnel, under const…
Toll motorway, pre-…
Main through route…
25 56 European road num… motorway number
55 National road number
56 Distances – in kilometres
International boundary, national boundary
LE HAVRE Car ferry and destination
1089 Mountain pass, international airport, height (metres)

Town – population
MOSKVA 5 million +
BERLIN 2–5 million
MINSK 1–2 million
Oslo 500000–1million
Århus 200000–500000
Turku 100000–200000

Gävle 50000–100000
Nybro 20000–50000
Ikast 10000–20000
Skjern 5000–10000
Lillesand 0–5000

The green version of the symbol indicates towns with
Low Emission Zones

Scale · pages 2–23

1:3 200 000
1 in = 50.51 miles
1 cm = 32km

0 10 20 30 40 50 60 70 80 90 100 110 miles
0 20 40 60 80 100 120 140 160 180 km

Legend to road maps pages 26–200

7 8 Motorway with junctions – full, restricted access
◇ services, rest area
tunnel, under construction
Toll Motorway – with toll barrier
Pre-pay motorway – A CH CZ H SK 'Vignette' must
be purchased before travel, see pages IV–VII
Principal trunk highway – single / dual carriageway
tunnel, under construction
Other main highway – single / dual carriageway
Other important road, other road
E25 A49 European road number, motorway number
135 National road number
Col Bayard 1248 Mountain pass
Scenic route, gradient – arrow points uphill
143 Distances – in kilometres
28 major
minor
Principal railway with tunnel
Ferry route with journey time – hours : minutes
Nápoli 15:30
Short ferry route
International boundary, national boundary
National park, natural park

✈ Airport
🏛 Ancient monument
⚲ Beach
🏰 Castle or house
⛰ Cave
✦ Other place of interest
❀ Park or garden
✝ Religious building

⛷ Ski resort
🎡 Theme park
World Heritage site
1754▲ Spot height
Sevilla World Heritage town
Verona Town of tourist interest
City or town with Low Emission Zone

Scale · pages 26–181

1:753 800
1 inch = 12 miles
1 cm = 7.5km

0 2 4 6 8 10 12 14 16 18 20 22 24 26 28 miles
0 4 8 12 16 20 24 28 32 36 40km

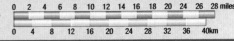

Scale · pages 182–200

1:1 507 600
1 inch = 24 miles
1 cm = 15km

0 4 8 12 16 20 24 28 32 36 40 44 48 52 miles
0 8 16 24 32 40 48 56 64 72 80km

European driving:
cut through the confusion

Stay safe with GEM Motoring Assist

- Are you confused about European driving laws? ● Do you need advice about equipment requirements and which documents to take? ● Are you new to driving on the right hand side? ● How will you know what speed limits apply? ● Who do you call if you have an accident or break down?

Millions of us drive abroad on holiday each year. Perhaps it's a long motorway trip to the Mediterranean, a selection of historic cities and sites or a gentle tour along quiet country lanes. Whatever the purpose, it makes sense to ensure that both we and our vehicles are properly prepared for the journey.

It's not easy getting to grips with the finer points of driving in other countries, however experienced you may be as a motorist. Whether you have notched up thousands of miles of European driving or are preparing to make your first journey, the chances are you will always manage to find some road sign or legal requirement that will cause confusion.

What's more, 'driving in Europe' covers such a huge area. With the inclusion of Croatia (July 2013), there are 28 countries in the European Union alone, each with its own set of road traffic laws and motoring customs. Driving in Europe can mean a spectacular and sunny coastal road that's within sight of Africa, or a snowy track amid the biting cold of the Arctic Circle, where the only others on the road are reindeer. Add to this some of the world's most congested cities, dense clusters of motorways (many with confusing numbers) and a big variation in safety standards and attitudes to risk. No wonder we often risk getting lost, taking wrong turnings or perhaps stopping where we shouldn't.

Depending on the country we're in, our errors at the wheel or our lack of familiarity with the rules of the road can sometimes bring unwelcome consequences. In any country, foreign drivers are subject to the same traffic rules as residents, enforceable in many situations by hefty on-the-spot fines and other sanctions. The situation across Europe is complex, simply because of the number of different sets of rules. For example, failure to carry a specific piece of breakdown equipment may be an offence in one country, but not in another. It's easy to see why the fun and excitement of a road trip in Europe could be spoilt by a minefield of regulations.

But we want to ensure that doesn't happen. Preparation and planning are key to a great holiday. It certainly pays to do a bit of research before you go, just to ensure you and your vehicle are up to the journey, your documents are in order and you're carrying the correct levels of equipment to keep the law enforcers happy.

BEFORE YOU GO

Some sensible planning will help make sure your European journey is enjoyable and, we hope, stress-free. So take some time before departure to ensure everything is in good shape: and that includes you, your travelling companions and your vehicle.

For you:

Try to become familiar with the driving laws of your holiday destination, including the local speed limits and which side of the road to drive on. You will be subject to these laws when driving abroad and if you are stopped by the police, it is not an excuse to say that you were unaware of them. Police officers in many countries have the power to impose (and collect) substantial on-the-spot fines for motoring offences, whether you are a resident of that country or a visitor. GEM Motoring Assist can link you direct with up-to-date information on driving in 27 different European countries. For each country, you will find a downloadable three-page PDF document containing detailed information on driving facts, traffic laws, document and equipment requirements – and even a few simple, emergency phrases to help you if you're in difficulty.
Go to www.motoringassist.com/europe

The Foreign and Commonwealth Office also gives country-specific travel and driving advice www.gov.uk/driving-abroad.

Passports

Check everyone's passport to make sure they are all valid.

Don't wait for your passport to expire. Unused time, rounded up to whole months (minimum one month, maximum nine months), will usually be added to your new passport. New passports usually take two weeks to arrive. The Passport Office (0300 222 0000, www.gov.uk/government/organisations/hm-passport-office) offers a faster service if you need a replacement passport urgently, but you'll have to pay a lot more.

Driving Licence

The new style photocard driving licence is valid in all European Union countries. However, you must ensure you carry both parts: the credit card-size photocard and paper licence. The previously used pink EU format UK licence is also valid but may not be recognized in some areas so it is advisable to carry an International Driving Permit as well. These cost £5.50 and are available from Post Offices (www.postoffice.co.uk/international-driving-permit).

Travel Insurance

Travel insurance is vital as it covers you against medical emergencies, accidents, thefts and cancellations, and repatriation. Ask for details before buying any travel insurance policy. Find out what it covers you for, and to what value. More important, check what's not covered. One of the key benefits of GEM membership is the excellent discount you can get on travel insurance.
For more details, please visit our website:
www.motoringassist.com/philipsmaps

European Breakdown Cover

Don't risk letting a breakdown ruin your European trip. Ensure you purchase a policy that will cover you for roadside assistance, emergency repair and recovery of your vehicle to the UK, wherever in Europe you may be heading. Once again, GEM members enjoy a specially discounted rate. You'll find the details at www.motoringassist.com/philipsmaps

EHIC

The E111 medical treatment form is no longer valid. Instead, you need an EHIC card for everyone travelling. These are free and cover you for any medical treatment you may need during a trip to another EU country or Switzerland. However, do check at the time of requiring assistance that your EHIC will be accepted. Apply online (www.ehic.org.uk), by telephone (0845 606 2030) or complete an application form, available from a Post office. Allow up to 14 days for the cards to arrive.

For your vehicle:

Service

It makes sense to get your car serviced before you travel. As a minimum, ensure the tyres have plenty of tread left and that water and oil levels are checked and topped up if required. Check them regularly during your time away.

Who has priority?

Make sure you keep a watchful eye on signs telling you who has priority on the road. Look for a yellow diamond sign, which tells you that traffic already on the road has priority. If you see the yellow diamond sign crossed out, then you must give way to traffic joining the road.

Priorité a droite

Despite the use of the yellow diamond signs, be aware that on some French and Belgian roads (especially roundabouts in Paris), the traditional 'priorité a droite' practice is followed, even though it may no longer be legal. In theory these days, the rule no longer applies unless it is clearly signed. In practice, though, it makes sense to anticipate a driver pulling out in front of you, even though the priority may be yours.

Stop means stop!

If you come to a solid white line with an octagonal 'STOP' sign, then you must come to a complete stop. In other words your wheels must stop turning. Adherence to the 'STOP' sign is generally more rigorously enforced in European countries than you may be used to here.

Headlight flash

Bear in mind that the practice of flashing headlights at a junction in France does not mean the same thing as it might in the UK. If another motorists flashes his headlights at you, he's telling you that he has priority and will be coming through in front of you.

Vehicle Registration Document

Police in many countries can demand that you prove you have the right to be driving your car. That means you need to show the registration document, or a suitable letter of authorization if the registration document is not in your name. Remember you should never leave the registration document in the car.

Nationality plate

Your vehicle must display a nationality plate of an approved pattern, design and size.

MOT

If your car is more than three years old, make sure you take its current MOT test certificate with you.

Insurance

If you are planning a trip to Europe, you should find that your car insurance policy provides the minimum amount of cover you need. But it's important to contact your insurer before you go, to confirm exactly what level of cover you have and how long it will be valid, especially if you plan to venture outside the EU (see also page IV).

Mechanical adjustments

Check the adjustments required for your headlights before you go. Beam deflectors are a legal requirement if you drive in Europe. They are generally sold at the ports, on ferries and in the Folkestone Eurotunnel terminal, but be warned – the instructions can be a little confusing! The alternative is to ask a local garage to do the job for you before you go. If you choose this, then make sure you shop around as prices for this simple task vary enormously.

Equipment check-list

This checklist represents GEM's suggestions for what you should take with you in the car. Different countries have different rules about what's compulsory and these rules change from time to time. So it's important to check carefully before you set out. For country-by-country guidance, visit www.motoringassist.com/europe or see page IV of this atlas.

- Fire extinguisher
- First aid kit
- High-visibility jacket – one for each occupant
- Two warning triangles
- Replacement bulbs and fuses
- Spare spectacles (if worn) for each driver
- Snow chains for winter journeys into the mountains
- Disposable camera and notebook to record any collisions or damage for insurance purposes (if it is safe).

Contact details

Make sure you have all relevant emergency helpline numbers with you, including emergency services, breakdown assistance, the local British consulate and your insurance company. There are links to embassies and consulates around the world from the Foreign Office website. (www.fco.gov.uk) For information, the European emergency telephone number (our equivalent of 999) is 112.

TOP TIPS FOR STAYING SAFE

Collisions abroad occur not just because of poor driving conditions locally, but also because we do not always take the same safety precautions as we might expect to take at home, for example by not wearing a seatbelt or by drinking and driving.

1. Plan your route before you go. That includes the journey you make to reach your destination (with sufficient breaks built in) and any excursions or local journeys.

2. Remember that you will be subject to the same laws as local drivers. Ignorance will not be accepted as an excuse.

3. Take extra care at junctions when you're driving on the 'right side' of the road. If driving in a family group, involve everyone in a quick 'junction safety check' to help reduce the risk of a collision. Having everybody in the car call out a catchphrase such as "DriLL DriLL DriLL" (Driver Look Left) on the approach to junctions and roundabouts is a small but potentially life-saving habit.

4. Take fatigue seriously. The excellent European motorway network means you can cover big distances with ease but you must also make time for proper breaks (experts recommend at least 15 minutes every two hours). If possible, share the driving and set strict daily limits to the number of hours.

5. Drink-driving limits across Europe are lower than those in the UK. The only exception is Malta, where the limit is the same (0.8mg per ml). Bear this in mind if you're flying to a holiday or business destination and plan to have a drink on the plane, as the combination of unfamiliar roads and alcohol in your bloodstream is not a safe one. It's also worth remembering that drivers who cause collisions because they were drinking are likely to find their insurance policy will not cover them.

6. Expect the unexpected. Styles of driving in your destination country are likely to different from those you know in the UK. Drive defensively and don't get involved in any altercations on the road.

7. Don't overload your car while away, however tempting the local bargains may appear. Also, make sure you have good all-round visibility by ensuring you don't pile up items on the parcel shelf or boot, and keep your windscreen clear of dirt and dust.

8. Always wear a seatbelt and ensure everyone else on board wears one. Check specific regulations regarding the carriage of children: in some countries children under the age of 12 are not permitted to travel in the front of the car.

9. Don't use your phone while driving. Even though laws on phone use while driving differ from country to country, the practice is just as dangerous wherever you are.

10. When you're exploring on foot, be wise to road safety as a pedestrian. You may get into trouble for 'jay-walking', so don't just wander across a road. Use a proper crossing, but remember that drivers may not stop for you! And don't forget that traffic closest to you approaches from the LEFT.

WORTH KNOWING

You will need a separate GB sticker in EU countries unless your car has a registration plate containing the GB euro-symbol. In non-EU countries the euro-plate is not valid so you will need the separate sticker as well.

Fuel is generally most expensive at motorway service areas and cheapest at supermarkets. However, these are usually shut on Sundays and Bank Holidays. So-called '24 hour' regional fuel stations in France seldom accept payment by UK credit card, so don't rely on them if to fill up during a night-time journey.

If you see several fuel stations in short succession before a national border, it's likely that fuel on the other side will be more expensive, so take the opportunity to fill up.

Radar speed camera detectors are illegal in most European countries.

The insurance 'green card' is no longer required for journeys in the EU but it is advisable to carry one anyway. It is also important to make sure you have contact details for your insurer in case of an accident or claim.

Speed limits in France are enforced vigorously. An additional 400 fixed cameras were installed across France in early 2012. Radar controls are frequent, and any driver (including non-residents) detected at more than 25km/h above the speed limit can have their licence confiscated on the spot. Furthermore, if you are caught exceeding the speed limit by 50km/h, even on a first offence, you will face a term of imprisonment.

New legislation introduced in France in 2012 required every driver to carry a self-breathalyser test kit. However, the imposition of a €11 fine for failing to produce a breathalyser when required has been postponed indefinitely. So, in theory, you are required to carry a breathalyser kit, but no fine can be imposed if you don't.

Luxembourg has specific rules relating to how you fix a sat nav device to your windscreen. Get it wrong and you could be fined on the spot.

Norway and Sweden have low drink-driving limits: just 20mg per 100ml of blood (compared to 80 in the UK). In Slovakia, the limit is zero.

In Hungary, the limit is also zero. If you are found to be drink-driving, your driving licence will be withdrawn by police officers on the spot.

Other laws and motoring advice to be aware of across Europe:

Austria Recent rules require the mandatory use of winter tyres between 1 November and 15 April.

Belgium You will have to pay to use most public toilets – including those at motorway service stations • You are not permitted to use cruise control on motorways when traffic is heavy • There are also specific penalties for close-following on motorways • Roadside drug-testing of drivers (using oral fluid testing devices) was introduced late in 2010 and now forms a regular part of any police controls.

Cyprus There have been important changes in how speeding and drink-driving are sanctioned. Cyprus now has a graduated system of speeding fines, ranging from one euro per km/h over the limit in marginal cases through to fines of up to €5,000 and a term of imprisonment for the most severe infringements. There are also graduated fines for drink-driving, ranging from fixed penalties for being slightly over the limit to terms of imprisonment and fines of up to 5,000 for the most severe.

Denmark Cars towing caravans and trailers are prohibited from overtaking on motorways at certain times of day.

Finland If you hit an elk or deer, you must report the collision to the police. • Speeding fines are worked out according to your income. Access to a national database allows police at the roadside to establish a Finnish resident's income and number of dependants. Officers then impose a fine based on a specific number of days' income. A 'ticket calculator' on the Finnish Police website (**www.poliisi.fi**) allows you to work out the fine before committing the offence! The minimum speeding fine is 115 euros.

France As of 1 July 2012, any driver must be in possession of a valid breathalyser (displaying a 'BF' number), either electronic or chemical, to be shown to a police officer in case of control. • The banning of radar detectors, with fines of €1500 for anyone using them • Increased penalties for driving while using a mobile phone • Legislation requiring motorcyclists and their passengers to wear high-visibility clothing may be reintroduced.

Germany Check your fuel level regularly as it's an offence to run out of fuel on a German motorway. If you run out, you face an on-the-spot fine • It's also an offence to make rude signs to other road users.

Greece has Europe's highest accident rate in terms of the number of crashes per vehicle. Take extra care at traffic light junctions, as red lights are frequently ignored. • Since 2 April 2012 all drivers detected with more than 1.10 g/l of alcohol in blood, or more than 0.60mg/l in breath will be prosecuted for the offence. • Carrying a petrol can in a vehicle is forbidden.

Ireland The alcohol limit was reduced in 2011 from 0.8 mg per ml to 0.5mg • Beware of rural three-lane roads, the middle overtaking lane is used by traffic travelling in both directions • On wider rural roads it's the accepted practice for slower vehicles to pull over to let faster traffic through.

Italy Police can impound your vehicle if you cannot present the relevant ownership documents when requested. • You will need a red and white warning sign if you plan to use any rear-mounted luggage rack such as a bike rack • Zero alcohol tolerance is now applied for drivers who have held a driving licence for less than three years, as well as to drivers aged 18 to 21, professional drivers, taxi drivers and truckers.

Norway Under new legislation, police officers can perform roadside drug impairment saliva tests. There are specific limits set for the presence of 20 common non-alcohol drugs • You'll find what amounts to a zero tolerance where drinking and driving is concerned. Only 0.1mg of alcohol per millilitre of blood is permitted • Speeding fines are high. For example, a driver caught at 25 km/h over the 80 km/h speed limit on a national road could expect a fine of around £600.

Portugal If you are towing a caravan, you must have a current inventory of the caravan's contents to show a police officer if requested.

Slovakia It is now mandatory to use dipped headlights on every road journey, regardless of the time of day, season or weather conditions.

Spain Motorway speed limits in Spain are 120km/h. • If you need glasses for driving, then the law requires you to carry a spare pair with you in the car. • It's compulsory to carry two spare warning triangles, spare bulbs for your car and reflective jackets.

Turkey Take great caution if you're driving at dusk. Many local drivers put off using their lights until it's properly dark, so you may find oncoming traffic very hard to spot • During the time of Ramadan, many people will do without food and water between the hours of sunrise and sunset. This can seriously reduce levels of alertness, especially among people driving buses, trucks and taxis.

MOTORWAY VIGNETTES

Some countries require you to purchase (and in some cases display) a vignette before using motorways.

In **Austria** you will need to purchase and display a vignette on the inside of your windscreen, they are available at border crossings and petrol stations. More details from **www.austria.info**

Bulgaria operates a vignette system for travel on all state roads. Vignettes can only be purchased in Bulgaria (not before you get there). A seven-day vignette costs €5 for a car. The penalty for not displaying is €60.

In the **Czech Republic**, you can buy a vignette at the border and at petrol stations. Make sure you write your vehicle registration number on the vignette before displaying it. The roads without toll are indicated by a traffic sign saying "Bez poplatku". More details from **www.motorway.cz**

In **Hungary** an e-vignette system was introduced in 2008. It is therefore no longer necessary to display the vignette, though you should make doubly sure the information you give on your vehicle is accurate. Vignettes are sold at petrol stations throughout the country. Buy online at **www.motorway.hu.**

In **Slovakia**, a vignette also must be purchased before using the motorways. This is sold in two kinds at the border and petrol stations. You will need to write your vehicle registration plate on the vignette before displaying it. More details from **www.slovensko.com**

In **Switzerland**, you will need to purchase and display a 'vignette' before you drive on the motorway. Bear in mind you will need a separate vignette if you are towing a caravan. Purchase the Swiss vignette in advance from **www.autobahnen.ch.**

FREQUENTLY ASKED QUESTIONS

Do I need to use dipped headlights all the time? It is currently mandatory to use dipped headlights for daytime journeys in 15 of the 27 EU countries. Additionally, an European directive now requires all new cars to be fitted with daytime running lights.

Do German motorways still not have speed limits? Speed limits apply to around 30% of German motorways. A further 10% of motorway in Germany is subject to variable speed limits, determined by motorway control rooms. Across other stretches there is a recommended speed limit of 130km/h. It is worth remembering that whereas exceeding this limit is not an offence, the penalties for a high-speed driver being involved in an accident are considerably higher.

Why do European motorways all seem to have two numbers on the map and the road signs? This is because the roads form the international network of 'E-roads'. In most countries maps and signs will have the European road number (shown in white on green) alongside the appropriate national road number. However, in Sweden and Belgium only the E-road number will be shown.

As a visitor to a country, rather than a resident, am I exempt from speeding fines? No. Different countries have different mechanisms for dealing with traffic offences committed by non-resident drivers. If, for example, you are stopped for speeding, then expect to receive a fine which you can usually pay 'on the spot' by credit card. A number of bilateral agreements exist, allowing police to obtain non-resident driver details and issue penalties for offences recorded by automatic enforcement cameras. Interestingly, 'foreign' drivers make up only about 5% of traffic on Europe's roads, yet they account for 15% of all speeding offences. A wider European cross-border enforcement directive is expected to be brought into law in 2014. This will cover not only speeding but also other offences, such as non-wearing of seatbelts and crossing red traffic lights.

If I hire a car in one country, am I allowed to take it into another country? The issue is most likely to be with insurance, so check with the hiring company before setting off. Ask to see something in writing so you are sure that you are getting the right information. Often, when hiring, you will find you have only the minimum cover required for driving in the country where you hired the car. If you plan to take it into other countries, then make sure your insurance will cover you and purchase a top-up policy if necessary.

GEM MOTORING ASSIST

Since its foundation in 1932, GEM Motoring Assist has been at the forefront of road safety in the UK. Now one of the largest member-led road safety organisations, GEM provides a wide range of discounts and benefits for its 74,000+ members, including the UK's best-value range of breakdown recovery insurance products for motorists, motorcyclists and caravanners. GEM members also benefit from discounts on European breakdown cover and travel insurance, as well as enjoying free access to GEM's Accident Management Service, which provides free-of-charge legal help following any road traffic collision. Members receive *Good Motoring*, a free quarterly magazine and access to an excellent line-up of road safety leaflets and web-based advice. Why not make GEM Motoring Assist your one-stop shop for trouble-free motoring! Visit **www.motoringassist.com/philipsmaps** today.

Driving regulations

Vehicle
A national vehicle identification plate is always required when taking a vehicle abroad.

Fitting headlamp converters or beam deflectors when taking a right-hand drive car to a country where driving is on the right (every country in Europe except the UK and Ireland) is compulsory.

Within the EU, if not driving a locally hired car, it is compulsory to have either Europlates or a country of origin (e.g. GB) sticker. Outside the EU (and in Andorra) a sticker is compulsory, even with Europlates.

Documentation
All countries require that you carry a valid passport, vehicle registration document, hire certificate or letter of authority for the use of someone else's vehicle, full driving licence/ International Driving Permit and insurance documentation/green card. Some non-EU countries also require a visa.

Licence
A photo licence (both photo and paper parts) is preferred; with an old-style paper licence, an International Driving Permit (IDP) should also be carried. In some countries, an IDP is compulsory, whatever form of licence is held. Non-EU drivers should always have both a licence and and an IDP.

Insurance
Third-party cover is compulsory across Europe. Most insurance policies give only basic cover when driving abroad, so you should check that your policy provides at least third-party cover for the countries in which you will be driving and upgrade it to the level that you require. You may be forced to take out extra cover at the frontier if you cannot produce acceptable proof that you have adequate insurance. Even in countries in which a green card is not required, carrying one is recommended for extra proof of insurance.

Motorcycles
It is compulsory for all motorcyclists and passengers to wear crash helmets. In France it may become compulsory for all motorcyclists and passengers to wear a minimum amount of reflective gear.

Other
In countries in which visibility vests are compulsory one for each person should be carried in the passenger compartment, or panniers on a motorbike, where they can be reached easily.

Warning triangles should also be carried in the passenger compartment.

The penalties for infringements of regulations vary considerably from one country to another. In many countries the police have the right to impose on-the-spot fines (ask for a receipt). Penalties can be severe for serious infringements, particularly for exceeding the blood-alcohol limit; in some countries this can result in immediate imprisonment.

In some countries, vignettes for toll roads are being replaced by electronic tags. See country details.

Please note that driving regulations often change, and that it has not been possible to cover all the information for every type of vehicle.

The publishers have made every effort to ensure that the information given here was correct at the time of going to press. No responsibility can be accepted for any errors or their consequences.

The symbols used are:

- 🏛 Motorway
- ⚠ Dual carriageway
- ⚠ Single carriageway
- 🚗 Surfaced road
- 🚙 Unsurfaced / gravel road
- 🏘 Urban area
- ⊘ Speed limit in kilometres per hour (kph). These are the maximum speeds for the types of roads listed. In some places and under certain conditions they may be considerably lower. Always obey local signs.
- 🚗 Seat belts
- 👶 Children
- 🍷 Blood alcohol level
- △ Warning triangle
- ⚕ First aid kit
- 💡 Spare bulb kit
- 🧯 Fire extinguisher
- ⊖ Minimum driving age
- 📋 Additional documents required
- 📱 Mobile phones
- LEZ Low Emission Zone
- ★ Other information

The publishers have made every effort to ensure that the information given here was correct at the time of going to press. No responsibility can be accepted for any errors or their consequences.

Andorra Principat d'Andorra AND
Area 468 sq km (181 sq miles)
Population 86,000 **Capital** Andorra la Vella (64,000)
Languages Catalan (official), French, Castilian, Portuguese **Currency** Euro = 100 cents
Website http://visitandorra.com

⊘	🏛	⚠	⚠	🏘
	n/a	90	60/90	50

- 🚗 Compulsory
- 👶 Under 10 and below 150 cm must travel in an EU-approved restraint system adapted to their size in the rear. If in front, any airbags must be deactivated.
- 🍷 0.05%
- △ Compulsory 🧰 Recommended
- 💡 Compulsory 🧯 Recommended
- ⊖ 18
- 📱 Not permitted whilst driving
- ★ Dipped headlights compulsory for motorcycles during day and for other vehicles during poor daytime visibility.
- ★ On-the-spot fines imposed
- ★ Visibility vests compulsory
- ★ Winter tyres or snow chains compulsory in poor conditions or when indicated by signs

Austria Österreich A
Area 83,859 sq km (32,377 sq miles)
Population 8,414,000 **Capital** Vienna / Wien (2,419,000)
Languages German (official) **Currency** Euro = 100 cents
Website www.austria.gv.at

⊘	🏛	⚠	⚠	🏘
	130	100	100	50
If towing trailer under 750kg / over 750 kg				
	100	100	100/80	50

- 🚗 Compulsory
- 👶 Under 12 and under 150cm cannot travel as a front or rear passenger unless they use a suitable child restraint; under 12 over 150cm must wear adult seat belt
- 🍷 0.049%; 0.01% if licence held less than 2 years
- △ Compulsory 🧰 Compulsory
- 💡 Recommended 🧯 Recommended
- ⊖ 18 (16 for mopeds)
- 📱 Only allowed with hands-free kit
- LEZ LEZ On A12 motorway non-compliant vehicles banned and certain substances banned, night-time speed restrictions; Steermark province has LEZs affecting lorries
- ★ Dipped headlights must be used during the day by all road users. Headlamp converters compulsory
- ★ Radar detectors prohibited
- ★ Snow chains recommended in winter. Winter tyres compulsory 1 Nov.–15 Apr. in poor driving conditions
- ★ To drive on motorways or expressways, a motorway sticker must be purchased at the border or main petrol station. These are available for 10 days, 2 months or 1 year. Vehicles 3.5 tonnes or over must display an electronic tag.
- ★ Visibility vests compulsory

Belarus BY
Area 207,600 sq km (80,154 sq miles)
Population 9,457,000 **Capital** Minsk (2,101,000)
Languages Belarusian, Russian (both official)
Currency Belarusian ruble = 100 kopek
Website www.belarus.by/en/government

⊘	🏛	⚠	⚠	🏘
	110	90	90	60*
If towing trailer under 750kg				
	90	70	70	

*In residential areas limit is 20 km/h • Vehicle towing another vehicle 50 kph limit • If full driving licence held for less than two years, must not exceed 70 kph

- 🚗 Compulsory in front seats, and rear seats if fitted
- 👶 Under 12 not allowed in front seat and must use appropriate child restraint
- 🍷 0.00% △ Compulsory 🧰 Compulsory
- 💡 Recommended 🧯 Compulsory
- ⊖ 18
- 📋 Visa, vehicle technical check stamp, international driving permit, green card, health insurance. Even with a green card, local third-party insurance may be imposed at the border
- 📱 Use prohibited
- ★ A temporary vehicle import certificate must be purchased on entry and driver must be registered
- ★ Dipped headlights are compulsory during the day Nov–Mar and at all other times in conditions of poor visibility or when towing or being towed.
- ★ Fees payable for driving on highways
- ★ It is illegal for vehicles to be dirty
- ★ Radar-detectors prohibited
- ★ Winter tyres and snow chains recommended

Belgium Belgique B
Area 30,528 sq km (11,786 sq miles)
Population 11,036,000
Capital Brussels/Bruxelles (1,830,000)
Languages Dutch, French, German (all official) **Currency** Euro = 100 cents
Website www.belgium.be/en

⊘	🏛	⚠	⚠	🏘
	120*	120*	90	50**
If towing trailer				
	90	90	60	50
Over 3.5 tonnes				
	90	90	60	50

*Minimum speed of 70kph may be applied in certain conditions on motorways and some dual carriageways
**Near schools, hospitals and churches the limit may be 30kph

- 🚗 Compulsory
- 👶 All under 19s under 135 cm must wear an appropriate child restraint. Airbags must be deactivated if a rear-facing child seat is used in the front
- 🍷 0.05% △ Compulsory 🧰 Recommended
- 💡 Recommended 🧯 Compulsory
- ⊖ 18
- 📱 Only allowed with a hands-free kit
- ★ Cruise control is not permitted on motorways
- ★ Dipped headlights mandatory at all times for motorcycles and advised during the day in poor conditions for other vehicles
- ★ On-the-spot fines imposed
- ★ Radar detectors prohibited
- ★ Sticker indicating maximum recommended speed for winter tyres must be displayed on dashboard if using them
- ★ Visibility vest compulsory

Bosnia & Herzegovina
Bosna i Hercegovina BIH
Area 51,197 sq km (19,767 sq miles)
Population 3,840,000 **Capital** Sarajevo (669,000)
Languages Bosnian/Croatian/Serbian
Currency Convertible Marka = 100 convertible pfenniga
Website www.fbihvlada.gov.ba/english/index.php

⊘	🏛	⚠	⚠	🏘
	130	100	80	50

- 🚗 Compulsory if fitted
- 👶 Under 12 not allowed in front seat; under 5 must use appropriate child restraint
- 🍷 0.03%
- △ Compulsory 🧰 Compulsory
- 💡 Compulsory ⊖ 18
- 📋 Visa, International Driving Permit
- 📱 Prohibited
- ★ Dipped headlights compulsory for all vehicles at all times
- ★ GPS must have fixed speed camera function deactivated; radar detectors prohibited.
- ★ On-the-spot fines imposed
- ★ Visibility vest compulsory
- ★ Winter tyres compulsory 15 Nov–15 Apr; snow chains recommended

Bulgaria Bulgariya BG
Area 110,912 sq km (42,822 sq miles)
Population 7,365,000 **Capital** Sofia (1,302,000)
Languages Bulgarian (official), Turkish
Currency Lev = 100 stotinki **Website** www.government.bg/fce/index.shtml?p?equals?0023&s?equals?001

⊘	🏛	⚠	⚠	🏘
	130	90	90	50
If towing trailer				
	100	70	70	50

- 🚗 Compulsory in front and rear seats
- 👶 Under 3s not permitted in vehicles with no child restraints; 3–10 year olds must sit in rear
- 🍷 0.05%
- △ Compulsory 🧰 Compulsory
- 💡 Recommended 🧯 Compulsory
- ⊖ 18
- 📋 Photo driving licence with translation and International Driving Permit; vehicle insurance specific to Bulgaria
- 📱 Only allowed with a hands-free kit
- ★ Dipped headlights compulsory
- ★ Fee at border
- ★ GPS must have fixed speed camera function deactivated; radar detectors prohibited
- ★ On-the-spot fines imposed
- ★ Road tax stickers (annual, monthly or weekly) must be purchased at the border and displayed prominently with the vehicle registration number written on them.
- ★ Visibility vest compulsory

Croatia Hrvatska HR
Area 56,538 km² (21,829 mi²) **Population** 4,285,000
Capital Zagreb (1,212,000) **Languages** Croatian
Currency Kuna = 100 lipa **Website** www.vlada.hr/en

⊘	🏛	⚠	⚠	🏘
	130	110	90	50
Under 24				
	120	100	80	50
If towing				
	110	80	80	50

- 🚗 Compulsory if fitted
- 👶 Children 2–12 not permitted in front seats and must use appropriate child restraint. Under 2 permitted in front only in appropriate rear-facing seat with any airbags disabled
- 🍷 0.05%, 0.00% for drivers of vehicles over 3.5 tonnes and under-25s
- △ Compulsory 🧰 Compulsory
- 💡 Compulsory ⊖ 18
- 📱 Only allowed with hands-free kit
- ★ Dipped headlights compulsory
- ★ In winter, snow chains compulsory in the mountains; snow tyres compulsory everywhere else Nov–Apr
- ★ On-the-spot fines imposed
- ★ Radar detectors prohibited
- ★ Tow bar and rope compulsory
- ★ Visibility vest compulsory

Czech Republic
Česká Republika CZ
Area 78,864 sq km (30,449 sq miles)
Population 10,513,000 **Capital** Prague/Praha (2,300,000)
Languages Czech (official), Moravian
Currency Czech Koruna = 100 haler
Website www.vlada.cz/en/

⊘	🏛	⚠	⚠	🏘
	130	130	90	50
If towing				
	80	80	80	50

- 🚗 Compulsory in front seats and, if fitted, in rear
- 👶 Children: Children under 36 kg and 150 cm must use appropriate child restraint. Only front-facing child retraints are permitted in the front in vehicles with airbags fitted
- 🍷 0.00% △ Compulsory 🧰 Compulsory
- 💡 Compulsory 🧯 Compulsory
- ⊖ 18 (17 for motorcycles under 125 cc)
- 📱 Only allowed with a hands-free kit
- LEZ Two-stage LEZ in Prague for vehicles over 3.5 and 6 tonnes. Permit system.
- ★ Dipped headlights compulsory at all times
- ★ GPS must have fixed speed camera function deactivated; radar detectors prohibited
- ★ On-the-spot fines imposed
- ★ Vignette needed for motorway driving, available for 1 year, 60 days, 15 days. Toll specific to lorries introduced 2006, those over 12 tonnes must buy an electronic tag
- ★ Visibility vest compulsory
- ★ Wearers of spectacles or contact lenses must carry a spare pair in their vehicle at all times
- ★ Winter tyres or snow chains compulsory between Nov and Apr

Denmark Danmark DK
Area 43,094 sq km (16,638 sq miles)
Population 5,580,000 **Capital** Copenhagen / København (1,954,000) **Languages** Danish (official)
Currency Krone = 100 øre **Website** www.denmark.dk/en

⊘	🏛	⚠	⚠	🏘
	130	80	80	50
If towing				
	80	70	70	50

- 🚗 Compulsory front and rear
- 👶 Under 135cm must use appropriate child restraint; in front permitted only in an appropriate rear-facing seat with any airbags disabled
- 🍷 0.05% △ Compulsory 🧰 Recommended
- 💡 Recommended 🧯 Recommended
- ⊖ 17
- 📱 Only allowed with a hands-free kit
- LEZ Aalborg, Arhus, Copenhagen, Frederiksberg and Odense. Proofs of emissions compliance/compliant filter needed to obtain sticker. Non-compliant vehicles banned.
- ★ Dipped headlights must be used at all times
- ★ Radar detectors prohibited
- ★ Tolls apply on the Storebaeltsbroen and Oresundsbron bridges.
- ★ Visibility vest recommended

Estonia Eesti EST
Area 45,100 sq km (17,413 sq miles)
Population 1,287,000 **Capital** Tallinn (543,000)
Languages Estonian (official), Russian
Currency Euro = 100 cents
Website http://valitsus.ee/en/government

⊘	🏛	⚠	⚠	🏘
	n/a	90*	70	50
If full driving licence held for less than two years				
	90	90	70	50

*In summer, the speed limit on some dual carriageways may be raised to 100/110 kph

- 🚗 Compulsory in front seats and if fitted in rear seats
- 👶 Under 12 not allowed in front seats; under 7 must have child safety seat in rear
- 🍷 0.02% △ 2 compulsory 🧰 Compulsory
- 💡 Recommended 🧯 Compulsory
- ⊖ 18
- 📱 Only allowed with a hands-free kit
- ★ A toll system is in operation in Tallinn
- ★ Dipped headlights compulsory at all times
- ★ Winter tyres are compulsory Dec–Feb but illegal from May–Sep.

Finland Suomi FIN
Area 338,145 sq km (130,557 sq miles)
Population 5,422,000 **Capital** Helsinki (1,362,000)
Languages Finnish, Swedish (both official)
Currency Euro = 100 cents
Website http://valtioneuvosto.fi/etusivu/en.jsp

⊘	🏛	⚠	⚠	🏘
	120	100	80*	30/60
If towing				
	80	80	80	30/60

*100 in summer • If towing a vehicle by rope, cable or rod, max speed limit 60 kph • Maximum of 80 kph for vans and lorries • Speed limits are often lowered in winter

- 🚗 Compulsory in front and rear
- 👶 Below 135 cm must use a child restraint or seat
- 🍷 0.05%
- △ Compulsory 🧰 Recommended
- 💡 Recommended 🧯 Recommended
- ⊖ 18 (motorbikes below 125cc 16)

- Only allowed with hands-free kit
- ★ Dipped headlights must be used at all times
- ★ On-the-spot fines imposed
- ★ Radar-detectors are prohibited
- ★ Visibility vest compulsory
- ★ Winter tyres compulsory Dec–Feb

France (F)

Area 551,500 sq km (212,934 sq miles)
Population 63,350,000 **Capital** Paris (12,162,000)
Languages French (official), Breton, Occitan
Currency Euro = 100 cents
Website www.diplomatie.gouv.fr/en/

	130	110	90	50
On wet roads or if full driving licence held for less than 2 years				
	110	100	80	50
If towing below / above 3.5 tonnes gross				
	110/90	100/90	90/80	50

50kph on all roads if fog reduces visibility to less than 50m • Licence will be lost and driver fined for exceeding speed limit by over 40kph

- Compulsory in front seats and, if fitted, in rear
- In rear, 4 or under must have a child safety seat (rear facing if up to 9 months); if 5–10 must use an appropriate restraint system. Under 10 permitted in the front only if rear seats are fully occupied by other under 10s or there are no rear safety belts. In front, if child is in rear-facing child seat, any airbag must be deactivated.
- 0.05%. If towing or with less than 2 years with full driving licence, 0.00% • All drivers/motorcyclists must carry 2 unused breathalysers to French certification standards, showing an NF number.
- Compulsory Recommended
- Recommended
- 18 (16 for motorbikes under 80 cc)
- Use not permitted whilst driving
- LEZ An LEZ operates in the Mont Blanc tunnel
- ★ Dipped headlights compulsory in poor daytime visibility and at all times for motorcycles
- ★ GPS must have fixed speed camera function deactivated; radar-detection equipment is prohibited
- ★ It is compulsory to carry a French-authority-recognised (NF) breathalyser.
- ★ On-the-spot fines imposed
- ★ Tolls on motorways. Electronic tag needed if using automatic tolls.
- ★ Visibility vests must be carried in the passenger compartment; legislation making visibility vests compulsory for motorcyclists and passengers may be reintroduced.
- ★ Winter tyres recommended. Carrying snow chains recommended in winter as these may have to be fitted if driving on snow-covered roads, in accordance with signage.

Germany Deutschland (D)

Area 357,022 sq km (137,846 sq miles)
Population 80,328,000
Capital Berlin (6,000,000)
Languages German (official)
Currency Euro = 100 cents
Website www.bundesregierung.de

	*	*	100	50
If towing				
	80	80	80	50

*no limit, 130 kph recommended

- Compulsory
- Under 150 cm and 12 or under must use an appropriate child seat or restraint. In front if child is in rear-facing child seat, airbags must be deactivated.
- 0.05%, 0.0% for drivers 21 or under or with less than two years full licence
- Compulsory Compulsory
- Recommended Recommended
- 18 (motorbikes: 16 if under 50cc)
- Use permitted only with hands-free kit – also applies to drivers of motorbikes and bicycles
- LEZ More than 60 cities have or are planning LEZs. Proof of compliance needed to acquire sticker. Non-compliant vehicles banned.
- ★ Dipped headlights compulsory in poor weather conditions and tunnels; recommended at other times
- ★ GPS must have fixed speed camera function deactivated; radar detectors prohibited
- ★ Motorcyclists must use dipped headlights at all times; other vehicles must use dipped headlights during poor daytime visibility.
- ★ On-the-spot fines imposed
- ★ Tolls on autobahns for lorries
- ★ Winter tyres compulsory in all winter weather conditions; snow chains recommended

Greece Ellas (GR)

Area 131,957 sq km (50,948 sq miles)
Population 10,815,000
Capital Athens/Athina (3,753,000)
Languages Greek (official)
Currency Euro = 100 cents
Website www.primeminister.gr/english

	120	110	110	50
Motorbikes, and if towing				
	90	70	70	40

- Compulsory in front seats and, if fitted, in rear
- Under 12 or below 135cm must use appropriate child restraint. In front if child is in rear-facing child seat, any airbags must be deactivated.
- 0.05%, 0.00% for drivers with less than 2 years full licence and motorcyclists
- Compulsory
- Compulsory
- Recommended
- Compulsory
- 17
- Not permitted.
- ★ Dipped headlights compulsory during poor daytime visibility and at all times for motorcycles
- ★ On-the-spot fines imposed
- ★ Radar-detection equipment is prohibited
- ★ Tolls on several newer motorways.

Hungary Magyarország (H)

Area 93,032 sq km (35,919 sq miles)
Population 9,938,000 **Capital** Budapest (3,285,000)
Languages Hungarian (official)
Currency Forint = 100 filler
Website www.kormany.hu/en

	130	110	90	50
If towing				
	80	70	70	50

- Compulsory in front seats and if fitted in rear seats
- Under 150cm and over 3 must be seated in rear and use appropriate child restraint. Under 3 allowed in front only in rear-facing child seat with any airbags deactivated.
- 0.00%
- Compulsory Compulsory
- Compulsory Recommended
- 17
- Only allowed with a hands-free kit
- LEZ Budapest has vehicle restrictions on days with heavy dust and is planning an LEZ.
- ★ All motorways are toll and operate electronic vignette system with automatic number plate recognition, tickets are available for 4 days, 7 days, 1 month, 1 year
- ★ During the day dipped headlights compulsory outside built-up areas; compulsory at all times for motorcycles
- ★ Electronic vignette system in use for tolls on several motorways
- ★ On-the-spot fines issued
- ★ Snow chains compulsory where conditions dictate
- ★ Visibility vest compulsory

Iceland Ísland (IS)

Area 103,000 sq km (39,768 sq miles)
Population 322,000 **Capital** Reykjavík (202,000)
Languages Icelandic **Currency** Krona = 100 aurar
Website www.government.is/

	n/a	90	80	50

- Compulsory in front and rear seats
- Under 12 or below 150cm not allowed in front seat and must use appropriate child restraint.
- 0.05%
- Compulsory Compulsory
- Compulsory Compulsory
- 18; 21 to drive a hire car; 25 to hire a jeep
- Only allowed with a hands-free kit
- ★ Dipped headlights compulsory at all times
- ★ Driving off marked roads is forbidden
- ★ Highland roads are not suitable for ordinary cars
- ★ On-the-spot fines imposed
- ★ Winter tyres compulsory c.1 Nov–14 Apr (variable)

Ireland Eire (IRL)

Area 70,273 sq km (27,132 sq miles)
Population 4,588,000
Capital Dublin (1,804,000)
Languages Irish, English (both official)
Currency Euro = 100 cents
Website www.gov.ie/en/

	120	100	80	50
If towing				
	80	80	80	50

- Compulsory where fitted. Driver responsible for ensuring passengers under 17 comply
- Children 3 and under must be in a suitable child restraint system. Airbags must be deactivated if a rear-facing child seat is used in the front. Those under 150 cm and 36 kg must use appropriate child restraint in cars with seatbelts.
- 0.05%, 0.02% for novice and professional drivers
- Compulsory Recommended
- Recommended Recommended
- 17 (16 for motorbikes up to 125cc; 18 for over 125cc; 18 for lorries; 21 bus/minibus)
- Only allowed with a hands-free kit
- ★ Dipped headlights are compulsory during daylight hours
- ★ Dipped headlights compulsory for motorbikes at all times and in poor visibility for other vehicles
- ★ Driving is on the left
- ★ GPS must have fixed speed camera function deactivated; radar detectors prohibited
- ★ On-the-spot fines imposed
- ★ Tolls are being introduced on some motorways; the M50 Dublin has barrier-free tolling with number-plate recognition.

Italy Italia (I)

Area 301,318 sq km (116,338 sq miles)
Population 60,000,000
Capital Rome / Roma (2,778,000)
Languages Italian (official)
Currency Euro = 100 cents
Website www.italia.it

	130	110	90	50
If towing				
	80	70	70	50
Less than three years with full licence				
	100	90	90	50
When wet				
	100	90	80	50

Some motorways with emergency lanes have speed limit of 150 kph

- Compulsory in front seats and, if fitted, in rear
- Under 12 not allowed in front seats except in child safety seat; children under 3 must have special seat in the back
- 0.05%, but 0.00% for professional drivers or with less than 3 years full licence
- Compulsory
- Recommended
- Compulsory
- Recommended
- 18 (14 for mopeds, 16 up to 125cc, 20 up to 350cc)
- Only allowed with hands-free kit
- LEZ Most northern and several southern regions operate seasonal LEZs and many towns and cities have various schemes that restrict access. There is an LEZ in the Mont Blanc tunnel
- ★ Dipped headlights compulsory outside built-up areas, in tunnels, on motorways and dual carriageways and in poor visibility; compulsory at all times for motorcycles
- ★ On-the-spot fines imposed
- ★ Radar-detection equipment is prohibited
- ★ Snow chains compulsory where signs indicate Nov–April
- ★ Tolls on motorways. Blue lanes accept credit cards; yellow lanes restricted to holders of Telepass pay-toll device.
- ★ Visibility vest compulsory

Kosovo Republika e Kosoves / Republika Kosovo (RKS)

Area 10,887 sq km (4203 sq miles)
Population 1,734,000
Capital Pristina (198,000)
Languages Albanian, Serbian (both official), Bosnian, Turkish, Roma
Currency Euro (Serbian dinar in Serb enclaves)
Website www.kryeministri-ks.net/?page?equals?2,1

	120	100	100	60

- Compulsory
- Under 12 must sit in rear seats
- 0.03%, 0.00% for professional, business and commercial drivers
- Compulsory
- Compulsory
- Compulsory
- Compulsory
- 18 (16 for motorbikes less than 125 cc, 14 for mopeds)
- International driving permit, locally purchased third-party insurance (green card is not recognised), documents with proof of ability to cover costs and valid reason for visiting. Visitors from many non-EU countries require a visa.
- Only allowed with a hands-free kit
- ★ Dipped headlights compulsory at all times
- ★ Winter tyres or snow chains compulsory in poor winter weather conditions

Latvia Latvija (LV)

Area 64,589 sq km (24,942 sq miles)
Population 2,070,000
Capital Riga (1,018,000)
Languages Latvian (official), Russian
Currency Lats = 100 santims (Euro from 1 Jan 2014)
Website www.mk.gov.lv/en

	90/100	90	90	50
If towing				
	90/100	90	90	50

In residential areas limit is 20kph • If full driving licence held for less than two years, must not exceed 80 kph

- Compulsory in front seats and if fitted in rear
- If under 12 years and 150cm must use child restraint in front and rear seats
- 0.05%, 0.02% with less than 2 years experience
- Compulsory
- Compulsory
- Recommended
- Compulsory
- 18 (14 for mopeds, 16 up to 125cc, 21 up to 350cc)
- Only allowed with hands-free kit
- ★ Dipped headlights must be used at all times all year round
- ★ On-the-spot fines imposed
- ★ Pedestrians have priority
- ★ Visibility vests compulsory
- ★ Winter tyres compulsory for vehicles up to 3.5 tonnes Dec–Feb, but illegal May–Sept

Lithuania Lietuva (LT)

Area 65,200 sq km (25,173 sq miles)
Population 3,043,000
Capital Vilnius (839,000)
Languages Lithuanian (official), Russian, Polish
Currency Litas = 100 centai
Website www.lrvk.lt/en

	130	110	90	50
If towing				
	n/a	70	70	50

In winter speed limits are reduced by 10–20 km/h

- Compulsory in front seats and if fitted in rear seats
- Under 12 not allowed in front seats unless in a child safety seat; under 3 must use appropriate child seat and sit in rear
- 0.04%, 0.02% for those with less than 2 years' full licence
- Compulsory
- Compulsory
- Recommended
- Compulsory
- 18 (14 for mopeds)
- Only allowed with a hands-free kit
- ★ Dipped headlights must be used at all times
- ★ On-the-spot fines imposed
- ★ Visibility vest compulsory
- ★ Winter tyres compulsory 10 Nov–1 Apr

Luxembourg (L)

Area 2,586 sq km (998 sq miles)
Population 538,000
Capital Luxembourg (94,000)
Languages Luxembourgian / Letzeburgish (official), French, German
Currency Euro = 100 cents
Website www.visitluxembourg.com

	130/110	90	90	50
If towing				
	90	75	75	50

If full driving licence held for less than two years, must not exceed 75 kph • In 20 km/h zones, pedestrians have right of way.

- Compulsory
- Children under 3 must use an appropriate restraint system. Airbags must be disabled if a rear-facing child seat is used in the front. Children 3 to 18 and / or under 150 cm must use a restraint system appropriate to their size. If over 36kg a seatbelt may be used in the back only
- 0.05%, 0.02 for young drivers, drivers with less than 2 years experience and drivers of taxis and commercial vehicles
- Compulsory
- Compulsory (buses)
- Compulsory
- Compulsory (buses, transport of dangerous goods)
- 18
- Use permitted only with hands-free kit
- ★ Dipped headlights compulsory for motorcyclists and in poor visibility for other vehicles
- ★ On-the-spot fines imposed
- ★ Visibility vest compulsory
- ★ Winter tyres compulsory in winter weather

Macedonia Makedonija (MK)

Area 25,713 sq km (9,927 sq miles)
Population 2,059,000
Capital Skopje (507,000)
Languages Macedonian (official), Albanian
Currency Denar = 100 deni
Website www.vlada.mk/?language=en-gb

	120	100	60	60
Newly qualified drivers				
	100	80	60	60
If towing				
	80	70	50	50

- Compulsory in front seats; compulsory if fitted in rear seats
- Under 12 not allowed in front seats
- 0.05%, 0.00% for business, commercial and professional drivers and with less than 2 years experience
- Compulsory
- Compulsory
- Compulsory
- Recommended; compulsory for LPG vehicles
- 18 (mopeds 16)
- International driving permit; visa
- Use not permitted whilst driving
- ★ Dipped headlights compulsory at all times
- ★ GPS must have fixed speed camera function deactivated; radar detectors prohibited
- ★ Novice drivers may only drive between 11pm and 5 am if there is someone over 25 with a valid licence in the vehicle.
- ★ On-the-spot fines imposed
- ★ Tolls apply on many roads
- ★ Visibility vest must be kept in the passenger compartment and worn to leave the vehicle in the dark outside built-up areas
- ★ Winter tyres or snow chains compulsory 15 Nov–15 Mar

Moldova (MD)

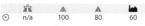

Area 33,851 sq km (13,069 sq miles)
Population 3,500,000 **Capital** Chisinau (801,000)
Languages Moldovan / Romanian (official)
Currency Leu = 100 bani **Website** www.moldova.md

⊙	90	90	90	60
If towing or if licence held under 1 year				
⊙	70	70	70	60

- Compulsory in front seats and, if fitted, in rear seats
- Under 12 not allowed in front seats
- 0.00% △ Compulsory Compulsory
- Recommended Compulsory
- 18 (mopeds and motorbikes, 16; vehicles with more than eight passenger places, taxis or towing heavy vehicles, 21)
- International Driving Permit (preferred), visa
- Only allowed with hands-free kit
- ★ Motorcyclists must use dipped headlights at all times
- ★ Winter tyres recommended Nov–Feb

Montenegro Crna Gora (MNE)

Area 14,026 sq km, (5,415 sq miles)
Population 625,000 **Capital** Podgorica (186,000)
Languages Serbian (of the Ijekavian dialect)
Currency Euro = 100 cents
Website www.gov.me/en/homepage

⊙	n/a	100	80	60

80kph speed limit if towing a caravan

- Compulsory in front and rear seats
- Under 12 not allowed in front seats
- 0.05% △ Compulsory Compulsory
- Compulsory Compulsory
- 18 (16 for motorbikes less than 125cc; 14 for mopeds)
- Prohibited
- ★ An 'eco' tax vignette must be obtained when crossing the border and displayed in the upper right-hand corner of the windscreen
- ★ Dipped headlights must be used at all times
- ★ From mid-Nov to March, driving wheels must be fitted with winter tyres
- ★ On-the-spot fines imposed
- ★ Tolls on some primary roads and in the Sozina tunnel between Lake Skadar and the sea
- ★ Visibility vest compulsory

Netherlands Nederland (NL)

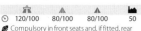

Area 41,526 sq km (16,033 sq miles)
Population 16,789,000
Capital Amsterdam 2,333,000 • administrative capital 's-Gravenhage (The Hague) 1,406,000
Languages Dutch (official), Frisian
Currency Euro = 100 cents
Website www.government.nl

⊙	120/100	80/100	80/100	50

- Compulsory in front seats and, if fitted, rear
- Under 135cm must use appropriate child restraint; if no seat belts, under 3s not permitted in vehicle; rear-facing child seat permitted in the front only if airbags deactivated
- 0.05%, 0.02% with less than 5 years experience or moped riders under 24
- △ Recommended Recommended
- Recommended Recommended
- 18
- Only allowed with a hands-free kit
- LEZ About 20 cities operate or are planning LEZs. A national scheme is planned.
- ★ Dipped headlights compulsory for motorcycles and recommended in poor visibility and on open roads for other vehicles
- ★ Radar-detection equipment is prohibited

Norway Norge (N)

Area 323,877 sq km (125,049 sq miles)
Population 5,064,000
Capital Oslo (1,442,000)
Languages Norwegian (official), Lappish, Finnish
Currency Krone = 100 øre
Website www.norway.org.uk

⊙	90/100	80	80	30/50
If towing trailer with brakes				
⊙	80	80	80	50
If towing trailer without brakes				
⊙	60	60	60	50

- Compulsory in front seats and, if fitted, in rear
- Children less than 150cm tall must use appropriate child restraint. Children under 4 must use child safety seat or safety restraint (cot)
- 0.01% △ Compulsory Recommended
- Recommended Recommended
- 18 (heavy vehicles 18/21)
- Only allowed with a hands-free kit
- LEZ Planned for Bergen, Oslo and Trondheim
- ★ Dipped headlights must be used at all times
- ★ On-the-spot fines imposed
- ★ Radar-detectors are prohibited
- ★ Tolls apply on some bridges, tunnels and access roads into Bergen, Oslo, Trondheim and Stavangar. Several use electronic fee collection only.
- ★ Visibility vest compulsory
- ★ Winter tyres or summer tyres with snow chains compulsory for snow- or ice-covered roads

Poland Polska (PL)

Area 323,250 sq km (124,807 sq miles)
Population 38,501,000 **Capital** Warsaw / Warszawa (2,666,000) **Languages** Polish (official)
Currency Zloty = 100 groszy
Website http://en.poland.gov.pl

Motor-vehicle only roads¹, under/over 3.5 tonnes				
⊙	130²/80²	110/80	100/80	n/a
Motor-vehicle only roads¹ if towing				
⊙	n/a	80	80	n/a
Other roads, under 3.5 tonnes				
⊙	n/a	100	90	50/60³
Other roads, 3.5 tonnes or over				
⊙	n/a	80	70	50/60³
Other roads, if towing				
⊙	n/a	60	60	30

¹Indicated by signs with white car on blue background. ²Minimum speed 40 kph. ³50 kph 05.00–23.00; 60 kph 23.00–05.00; 20 kph in marked residential areas

- Compulsory in front seats and, if fitted, in rear
- Under 12 not allowed in front seats unless in a child safety seat; in rear seats children under 12 and less than 150 cm must use child safety seat. Rear-facing child seats not permitted in vehicles with airbags.
- 0.02% △ Compulsory Recommended
- Recommended Compulsory
- 18 (mopeds and motorbikes – 16)
- Only allowed with a hands-free kit
- ★ Dipped headlights compulsory for all vehicles
- ★ On-the-spot fines imposed
- ★ Radar-detection equipment is prohibited

Portugal (P)

Area 88,797 sq km (34,284 sq miles)
Population 10,582,000 **Capital** Lisbon / Lisboa (2,815,000) **Languages** Portuguese (official)
Currency Euro = 100 cents
Website www.portugal.gov.pt/en.aspx

⊙	120*	100	90	50
If towing				
⊙	100*	90	80	50

*40kph minimum; 90kph maximum if licence held under 1 year

- Compulsory in front seats; compulsory if fitted in rear seats
- Under 12 and below 150cm must travel in the rear in an appropriate child restraint; rear-facing child seats permitted in front only if airbags deactivated
- 0.05% △ Compulsory Recommended
- Recommended Recommended
- 18 (motorcycles under 50cc 17)
- MOT certificate for vehicles over 3 years old, photographic proof of identity (e.g. driving licence or passport) must be carried at all times.
- Only allowed with hands-free kit
- LEZ An LEZ prohibits vehicles without catalytic converters from certain parts of Lisbon. There are plans to extend the scheme to the whole of the city
- ★ Dipped headlights compulsory for motorcycles, compulsory for other vehicles in poor visibility and tunnels
- ★ It is recommended that wearers of spectacles or contact lenses carry a spare pair.
- ★ On-the-spot fines imposed
- ★ Radar-detectors prohibited
- ★ Tolls on motorways; do not use green lanes, these are reserved for auto-payment users. Some motorways require an automatic toll device.
- ★ Visibility vest compulsory

Romania (RO)

Area 238,391 sq km (92,042 sq miles)
Population 19,044,000 **Capital** Bucharest / Bucuresti (2,200,000) **Languages** Romanian (official), Hungarian
Currency Romanian leu = 100 bani
Website www.gov.ro

Cars and motorcycles				
⊙	120/130	100	90	50
Vans				
⊙	110	90	80	50
Motorcycles				
⊙	100	80	80	50

For motor vehicles with trailers or if full driving licence has been held for less than one year, speed limits are 20kph lower than those listed above • Jeep-like vehicles: 70kph outside built-up areas but 60kph in all areas if diesel

- Compulsory in front seats and, if fitted, in rear
- Under 12 not allowed in front seats
- 0.00%
- △ Compulsory Compulsory
- Compulsory Compulsory
- 18
- Only allowed with hands-free kit
- ★ Dipped headlights compulsory outside built-up areas, compulsory everywhere for motorcycles
- ★ Electronic road tax system; price depends on emissions category and length of stay
- ★ It is illegal for vehicles to be dirty
- ★ On-the-spot fines imposed
- ★ Tolls on motorways
- ★ Visibility vest compulsory
- ★ Winter tyres compulsory Nov–Mar if roads are snow- or ice-covered, especially in mountainous areas

Russia Rossiya (RUS)

Area 17,075,000 sq km (6,592,800 sq miles)
Population 143,400,000
Capital Moscow / Moskva (11,511,000)
Languages Russian (official), and many others
Currency Russian ruble = 100 kopeks
Website www.gov.ru/index_en.html

⊙	110	90	90	60
If licence held for under 2 years				
⊙	70	70	70	60

- Compulsory in front seats
- Under 12 permitted in front seat only in an appropriate child restraint
- 0.00%
- △ Compulsory Compulsory
- Compulsory Compulsory
- 18
- International Driving Permit with Russian translation, visa, green card endorsed for Russia, International Certificate for Motor Vehicles
- Only allowed with a hands-free kit
- ★ Dipped headlights compulsory during the day
- ★ On-the-spot fines imposed
- ★ Picking up hitchhikers is prohibited
- ★ Radar detectors/blockers prohibited
- ★ Road tax payable at the border

Serbia Srbija (SRB)

Area 77,474 sq km, 29,913 sq miles
Population 7,187,000
Capital Belgrade / Beograd (1,659,000)
Languages Serbian
Currency Dinar = 100 paras **Website** www.srbija.gov.rs

⊙	120	100	80	60

- Compulsory in front and rear seats
- Age 3–12 must be in rear seats and wear seat belt or appropriate child restraint; under 3 in rear-facing child seat permitted in front only if airbag deactivated
- 0.03% △ Compulsory Compulsory
- Compulsory Compulsory
- 18 (16 for motorbikes less than 125cc; 14 for mopeds)
- International Driving Permit, green card or locally bought third-party insurance
- No legislation
- ★ 3-metre tow bar or rope
- ★ 80km/h speed limit if towing a caravan
- ★ Dipped headlights compulsory
- ★ Radar detectors prohibited
- ★ Tolls on motorways and some primary roads
- ★ Visibility vest compulsory
- ★ Winter tyres compulsory Nov–Apr for vehicles up to 3.5 tonnes. Carrying snow chains recommended in winter as these may have to be fitted if driving on snow-covered roads, in accordance with signage.

Slovak Republic Slovenska Republika (SK)

Area 49,012 sq km (18,923 sq miles)
Population 5,411,000
Capital Bratislava (660,000)
Languages Slovak (official), Hungarian
Currency Euro = 100 cents
Website www.government.gov.sk

⊙	130	90	90	60

- Compulsory in front seats and, if fitted, in rear
- Under 12 or below 150cm must be in rear in appropriate child restraint
- 0.0
- △ Compulsory Compulsory
- Compulsory Recommended
- 18 (15 for mopeds)
- International driving permit, proof of health insurance
- Only allowed with a hands-free kit
- ★ Dipped headlights compulsory at all times
- ★ On-the-spot fines imposed
- ★ Radar-detection equipment is prohibited
- ★ Tow rope recommended
- ★ Vignette required for motorways, car valid for 1 year, 30 days, 7 days; lorry vignettes carry a higher charge.
- ★ Visibility vests compulsory
- ★ Winter tyres compulsory

Slovenia Slovenija (SLO)

Area 20,256 sq km (7,820 sq miles)
Population 2,055,000
Capital Ljubljana (273,000)
Languages Slovene
Currency Euro = 100 cents
Website www.gov.si

⊙	130	100*	90*	50
If towing				
⊙	80	80*	80*	50

*70kph in urban areas

- Compulsory in front seats and, if fitted, in rear
- Under 12 and below 150cm must use appropriate child restraint; babies must use child safety seat
- 0.05%
- △ Compulsory Compulsory
- Compulsory Recommended
- 18 (motorbikes up to 125cc – 16, up to 350cc – 18)
- Only allowed with hands-free kit

- ★ Dipped headlights must be used at all times
- ★ Snow chains or winter tyres compulsory mid-Nov to mid-March, and in wintery conditions at other times
- ★ Vignettes valid for variety of periods compulsory for vehicles below 3.5 tonnes for toll roads. Write your vehicle registration number on the vignette before displaying it. For heavier vehicles electronic tolling system applies; several routes are cargo-traffic free during high tourist season.
- ★ Visibility vest compulsory

Spain España (E)

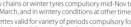

Area 497,548 sq km (192,103 sq miles)
Population 47,265,000
Capital Madrid (6,369,000)
Languages Castilian Spanish (official), Catalan, Galician, Basque
Currency Euro = 100 cents
Website www.lamoncloa.gob.es/home.htm

⊙	110	100	90	50
If towing				
⊙	80	80	70	50

- Compulsory in front seats and if fitted in rear seats
- Under 135cm and below 12 must use appropriate child restraint
- 0.05%, 0.03% if less than 2 years full licence or if vehicle is over 3.5 tonnes or carries more than 9 passengers
- △ Two compulsory (one for in front, one for behind)
- Recommended
- Compulsory Recommended
- 18 (18/21 heavy vehicles; 18 for motorbikes over 125cc; 16 for motorbikes up to 125cc; 14 for mopeds up to 75cc)
- Only allowed with hands-free kit
- ★ Dipped headlights compulsory for motorcycles and in poor daytime visibility for other vehicles.
- ★ It is recommended that wearers of spectacles or contact lenses carry a spare pair.
- ★ Radar-detection equipment is prohibited
- ★ Snow chains recommended for mountainous areas in winter
- ★ Spare tyre compulsory
- ★ Tolls on motorways
- ★ Visibility vest compulsory

Sweden Sverige (S)

Area 449,964 sq km (173,731 sq miles)
Population 9,556,000
Capital Stockholm (2,121,000)
Languages Swedish (official), Finnish
Currency Swedish krona = 100 ore
Website www.sweden.gov.se

⊙	110–120	80	70–100	30–60
If towing trailer with brakes				
⊙	80	80	70	50

- Compulsory in front and rear seats
- Under 16 or below 135cm must use appropriate child restraint; below 140cm may travel in front only if airbag deactivated; rear-facing child seat permitted only if airbag deactivated.
- 0.02% △ Compulsory Recommended
- Recommended Recommended
- 18
- No legislation
- LEZ Gothenberg, Helsingborg, Lund, Malmo, Mölndal and Stockholm have LEZs, progressively prohibiting vehicles 6 or more years old.
- ★ 1 Dec–31 Mar winter tyres, anti-freeze and shovel compulsory
- ★ Dipped headlights must be used at all times
- ★ On-the-spot fines imposed
- ★ Radar-detection equipment is prohibited

Switzerland Schweiz (CH)

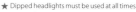

Area 41,284 sq km (15,939 sq miles)
Population 7,955,000 **Capital** Bern (126,000)
Languages French, German, Italian, Romansch (all official) **Currency** Swiss Franc = 100 centimes / rappen
Website www.admin.ch

⊙	120	80	80	50/30
If towing up to 1 tonne / over 1 tonne				
⊙	80	80	60/80	30/50

- Compulsory in front and, if fitted, in rear
- Up to 12 years and below 150 cm must use an appropriate child restraint
- 0.05%
- △ Compulsory Recommended
- Recommended Recommended
- 18 (mopeds up to 50cc – 16)
- Only allowed with a hands-free kit
- ★ Dipped headlights compulsory
- ★ GPS must have fixed speed camera function deactivated; radar detectors prohibited
- ★ Motorways are all toll and for vehicles below 3.5 tonnes a vignette must be purchased at the border. The vignette is valid for one calendar year. Vehicles over 3.5 tonnes must have an electronic tag for travel on any road.
- ★ On-the-spot fines imposed
- ★ Pedestrians have right of way
- ★ Picking up hitchhikers is prohibited on motorways and main roads
- ★ Wearers of spectacles or contact lenses must carry a spare pair in their vehicle at all times
- ★ Winter tyres recommended Nov–Mar; snow chains compulsory in designated areas in poor winter weather

Turkey Türkiye (TR)

Area 774,815 sq km (299,156 sq miles)
Population 75,627,000
Capital Ankara (4,966,000)
Languages Turkish (official), Kurdish
Currency New Turkish lira = 100 kurus
Website www.mfa.gov.tr/default.en.mfa

	120	90	90	50
If towing				
	70	70	70	40

- Compulsory in front seats
- Under 150 cm and below 36kg must use suitable child restraint. If above 136 cm may sit in the back without child restraint. Under 3s can only travel in the front in a rear facing seat if the airbag is deactivated. Children 3–12 may not travel in the front seat.
- 0.05%, 0.00% if towing
- Two compulsory (one in front, one behind)
- Compulsory
- Compulsory
- Compulsory
- 18
- International driving permit advised; note that Turkey is in both Europe and Asia, green card/UK insurance that covers whole of Turkey or locally bought insurance, visa bought at the point of entry
- Prohibited
- ★ Dipped headlights compulsory in daylight hours
- ★ On-the-spot fines imposed
- ★ Several motorways, and the Bosphorus bridges are toll roads
- ★ Tow rope and tool kit must be carried

Ukraine Ukraina (UA)

Area 603,700 sq km (233,088 sq miles)
Population 44,854,000
Capital Kiev / Kyyiv (3,648,000)
Languages Ukrainian (official), Russian
Currency Hryvnia = 100 kopiykas
Website www.kmu.gov.ua/control/en

	130	90	90	60
If towing				
	80	80	80	60

Speed limit in pedestrian zone 20 kph

- Compulsory in front and rear seats
- Under 12 and below 145cm must sit in rear
- 0.02% – if use of medication can be proved. Otherwise 0.00%
- Compulsory
- Compulsory
- Optional
- Compulsory
- 18 cars; 16 motorbikes
- International Driving Permit, visa, International Certificate for Motor Vehicles, green card
- No legislation
- ★ A road tax is payable on entry to the country.
- ★ Dipped headlights compulsory in poor daytime visibility
- ★ Tow rope and tool kit recommended
- ★ Winter tyres compulsory Nov–Apr in snowy conditions

United Kingdom (GB)

Area 241,857 sq km (93,381 sq miles)
Population 63,182,000
Capital London (15,011,000)
Languages English (official), Welsh (also official in Wales), Gaelic
Currency Sterling (pound) = 100 pence
Website www.direct.gov.uk

	112	112	96	48
If towing				
	96	96	80	48

- Compulsory in front seats and if fitted in rear seats
- Under 3 not allowed in front seats except with appropriate restraint, in rear must use child restraint if available; in front 3–12 or under 135cm must use appropriate child restraint, in rear must use appropriate child restraint (or seat belt if no child restraint is available, e.g. because two occupied restraints prevent fitting of a third).
- 0.08% (may change to 0.05% in Scotland)
- Recommended
- Recommended
- Recommended
- Recommended
- 17 (16 for mopeds)
- Only allowed with hands-free kit
- LEZ London's LEZ operates by number-plate recognition; non-compliant vehicles face hefty daily charges. Foreign-registered vehicles must register.
- ★ Driving is on the left
- ★ On-the-spot fines imposed
- ★ Smoking is banned in all commercial vehicles
- ★ Some toll motorways and bridges

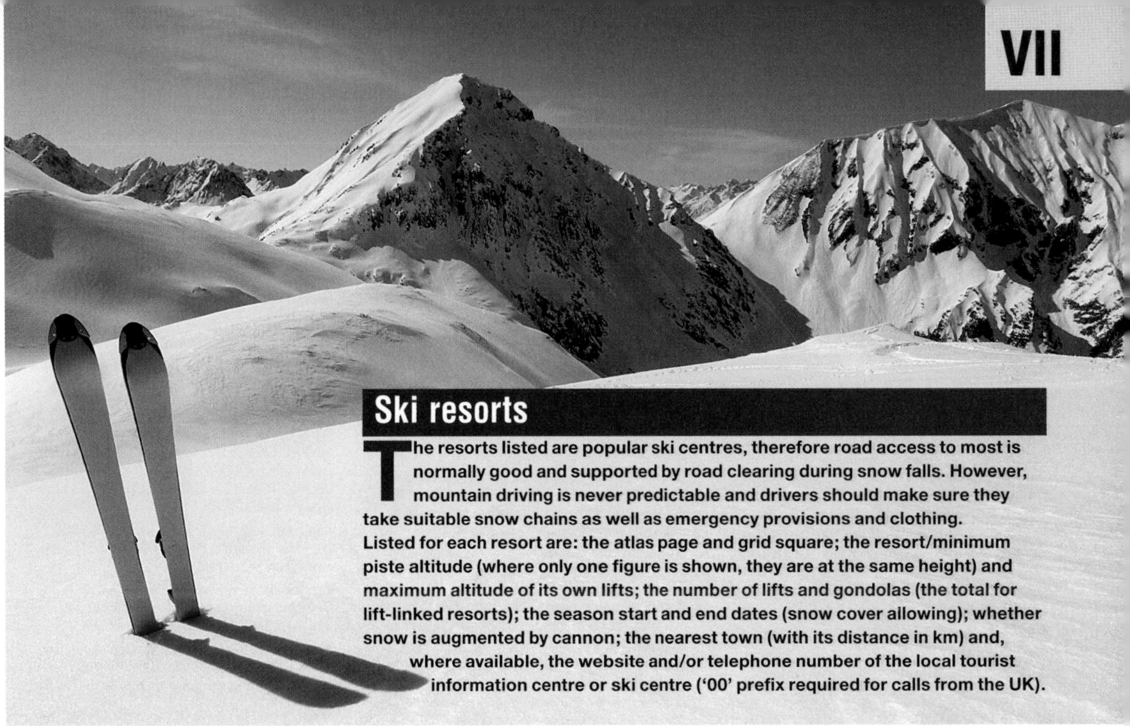

Ski resorts

The resorts listed are popular ski centres, therefore road access to most is normally good and supported by road clearing during snow falls. However, mountain driving is never predictable and drivers should make sure they take suitable snow chains as well as emergency provisions and clothing. Listed for each resort are: the atlas page and grid square; the resort/minimum piste altitude (where only one figure is shown, they are at the same height) and maximum altitude of its own lifts; the number of lifts and gondolas (the total for lift-linked resorts); the season start and end dates (snow cover allowing); whether snow is augmented by cannon; the nearest town (with its distance in km) and, where available, the website and/or telephone number of the local tourist information centre or ski centre ('00' prefix required for calls from the UK).

The ❄ symbol indicates resorts with snow cannon

Andorra

Pyrenees

Pas de la Casa / Grau Roig 146 B2 ❄ 2050–2640m 65 lifts Dec–Apr •Andorra La Vella (30km) www.pasdelacasa-andorra.com *Access via Envalira Pass (2407m), highest in Pyrenees, snow chains essential.*

Austria

Alps

Bad Gastein 109 B4 ❄ 1050/1100–2700m 50 lifts Dec–Mar •St Johann im Pongau (45km) +43 6432 3393 0 www.gastein.com

Bad Hofgastein 109 B4 ❄ 860–2295m 50 lifts Dec–Mar •St Johann im Pongau (40km) +43 6432 3393260 www.gastein.com/en/bad-hofgastein-austria

Bad Kleinkirchheim 109 C4 ❄ 1070–2310m 27 lifts Dec–Mar •Villach (35km) +43 4240 8212 www.badkleinkirchheim.at

Ehrwald 108 B1 ❄ 1000–2965m 24 lifts Dec–Apr •Imst (30km) +43 512 5351 553 www.tiscover.at/ehrwald

Innsbruck 108 B2 ❄ 574/850–3200m 78 lifts Dec–Apr •Innsbruck + 43 512 56 2000 www.innsbruck-pauschalen.com *Motorway normally clear. The motorway through to Italy and through the Arlberg Tunnel are both toll roads.*

Ischgl 107 B5 ❄ 1340/1380–2900m 42 lifts Dec–May •Landeck (25km) +43 50990 100 www.ischgl.com *Car entry to resort prohibited between 2200hrs and 0600hrs.*

Kaprun 109 B3 ❄ 885/770–3030m, 53 lifts Nov–Apr •Zell am See (10km) +43 6542 770 www.zellamsee-kaprun.com

Kirchberg in Tirol 109 B3 860–2000m 60 lifts Nov–Apr •Kitzbühel (6km) +43 5357 2000 www.kitzbuehel-alpen.com *Easily reached from Munich International Airport (120 km)*

Kitzbühel (Brixen im Thale) 109 B3 ❄ 800/1210–2000m 60 lifts Dec–Apr •Wörgl (40km) + 43 5357 2000 www.kitzbuehel-alpen.com

Lech/Oberlech 107 B5 ❄ 1450–2810m 62 lifts Dec–Apr •Bludenz (50km) +43 5583 21610 www.lech-zuers.at *Roads normally cleared but keep chains accessible because of altitude.*

Mayrhofen 108 B2 ❄ 630–2500m 75 lifts Dec–Apr •Jenbach (35km) +43 5285 6760 www.mayrhofen.at *Chains rarely required.*

Obertauern 109 B4 ❄ 1740/1640–2350m 26 lifts Dec–Apr •Radstadt (20km) +43 6456 7252 www.obertauern.com *Roads normally cleared but chain accessibility recommended. Camper vans and caravans not allowed; park these in Radstadt*

Saalbach Hinterglemm 109 B3 ❄ 1030/1100–2100m 52 lifts Nov–Apr •Zell am See (19km) +43 6541 6800 68 www.saalbach.com *Both village centres are pedestrianised and there is a good ski bus service during the daytime*

St Anton am Arlberg 107 B5 ❄ 1300–2810m 84 lifts Dec–Apr •Innsbruck (104km) +43 5446 22690 www.stantonamarlberg.com

Schladming 109 B4 ❄ 745–1900m 88 lifts Dec–Mar •Schladming + 43 36 87 233 10 www.schladming-dachstein.at

Serfaus 108 B1 ❄ 1427/1200–2820m 70 lifts Dec–Apr •Landeck (30km) +43 5476 6239 www.serfaus-fiss-ladis.at *Private vehicles banned from village. Use Dorfbahn Serfaus, an underground funicular which runs on an air cushion.*

Sölden 108 C2 ❄ 1380–3250m, 33 lifts Sep-Apr (glacier); Nov-Apr (main area) •Imst (50km) +43 572 000 200 www.soelden.com *Roads normally cleared but snow chains recommended because of altitude. The route from Italy and the south over the Timmelsjoch via Obergurgl is closed Oct-May and anyone arriving from the south should use the Brenner Pass motorway.*

Zell am See 109 B3 ❄ 750–1950m 53 lifts Dec–Mar •Zell am See +43 6542 770 www.zellamsee-kaprun.com *Low altitude, so good access and no mountain passes to cross.*

Zell im Zillertal (Zell am Ziller) 109 B3 ❄ 580/930–2410m 22 lifts Dec–Apr •Jenbach (25km) +43 5282 7165–226 www.zillertalarena.com

Zürs 107 B5 ❄ 1720/1700–2450m 62 lifts Dec–Apr •Bludenz (30km) +43 5583 2245 www.lech-zuers.at *Roads normally cleared but keep chains accessible because of altitude. Village has garage with 24-hour self-service gas/petrol, breakdown service and wheel chains supply.*

France

Alps

Alpe d'Huez 118 B3 ❄ 1860–3330m 85 lifts Dec–Apr •Grenoble (63km) +33 4 76 11 44 44 www.alpedhuez.com *Snow chains may be required on access road to resort.*

Avoriaz 118 A3 ❄ 1800/1100–2280m 35 lifts Dec–May •Morzine (14km) +33 4 50 74 02 11 www.avoriaz.com *Chains may be required for access road from Morzine. Car-free resort, park on edge of village. Horse-drawn sleigh service available.*

Chamonix-Mont-Blanc 119 B3 ❄ 1035–3840m 49 lifts Dec–Apr •Martigny (38km) +33 4 50 53 00 24 www.chamonix.com

Chamrousse 118 B2 ❄ 1700–2250m 26 lifts Dec–Apr •Grenoble (30km) +33 4 76 89 92 65 www.chamrousse.com *Roads normally cleared, keep chains accessible because of altitude.*

Châtel 119 A3 ❄ 1200/1110–2200m 41 lifts Dec–Apr •Thonon-Les-Bains (35km) +33 4 50 73 22 44 http://info.chatel.com/english-version.html

Courchevel 118 B3 ❄ 1750/1300–2470m 67 lifts Dec–Apr •Moûtiers (23km) www.courchevel.com *Roads normally cleared but keep chains accessible. Traffic 'discouraged' within the four resort bases.*

Flaine 118 A3 ❄ 1600–2500m 26 lifts Dec–Apr •Cluses (25km) +33 4 50 90 80 www.flaine.com *Keep chains accessible for D6 from Cluses to Flaine. Car access for depositing luggage and passengers only. 1500-space car park outside resort. Near Sixt-Fer-á-Cheval.*

La Clusaz 118 B3 ❄ 1100–2600m 55 lifts Dec–Apr •Annecy (32km) www.laclusaz.com *Roads normally clear but keep chains accessible for road from Annecy.*

La Plagne 118 B3 ❄ 2500/1250–3250m 109 lifts Dec–Apr Moûtiers (32km) +33 4 79 09 79 79 www.la-plagne.com *Ten different centres up to 2100m altitude. Road access via Bozel, Landry or Aime normally cleared. Linked to Les Arcs by cablecar*

Les Arcs 119 B3 ❄ 1600/1200–3230m 77 lifts Dec–May •Bourg-St-Maurice (15km) +33 4 79 07 12 57 www.lesarcs.com *Four base areas up to 2000 metres; keep chains accessible. Pay parking at edge of each base resort. Linked to La Plagne by cablecar*

Les Carroz d'Araches 118 A3 ❄ 1140–2500m 80 lifts Dec–Apr •Cluses (13km) + 33 4 50 90 00 04 www.lescarroz.com

Les Deux-Alpes 118 C3 ❄ 1650/1300–3600m 55 lifts Dec–Apr •Grenoble (75km) +33 4 76 79 22 00 www.les2alpes.com *Roads normally cleared, however snow chains recommended for D213 up from (D1091).*

Les Gets 118 A3 ❄ 1170/1000–2000m 52 lifts Dec–Apr •Cluses (18km) +33 4 50 75 80 80 www.lesgets.com

Les Ménuires 118 B3 ❄ 1815/1850–3200m 40 lifts Dec–Apr •Moûtiers (27km) +33 4 79 00 73 00 www.lesmenuires.com *Keep chains accessible for D117 from Moûtiers.*

Les Sept Laux Prapoutel 118 B3 ❄ 1350–2400m, 24 lifts Dec–Apr •Grenoble (38km) +33 4 76 08 17 86 www.les7laux.com *Roads normally cleared, however keep chains accessible for mountain road up from the A41 motorway. Near St Sorlin d'Arves.*

Megève 118 B3 ❄ 1100/1050–2350m 79 lifts Dec–Apr •Sallanches (12km) + 33 4 50 21 28 www.megeve.com *Horse-drawn sleigh rides available.*

Méribel 118 B3 ❄ 1400/1100–2950m 61 lifts Dec–May •Moûtiers (18km) +33 4 79 08 60 01 www.meribel.net *Keep chains accessible for 18km to resort on D90 from Moûtiers.*

Morzine 118 A3 ❄ 1000–2460m 67 lifts, Dec–Apr •Thonon-Les-Bains (30km) +33 4 50 74 72 72 www.morzine-avoriaz.com

Pra Loup 132 A2 ❄ 1600/1500–2500m 53 lifts Dec–Apr •Barcelonnette (10km) +33 4 92 84 10 04 www.praloup.com *Roads normally cleared but chains accessibility recommended.*

Risoul 118 C3 ❄ 1850/1650–2750m 51 lifts Dec–Apr •Briançon (40km) www.risoul.com *Keep chains accessible. Near Guillestre. Linked with Vars Les Claux*

St-Gervais Mont-Blanc 118 B3 ❄ 850/1150–2350m 27 lifts Dec–Apr •Sallanches (10km) +33 4 50 47 76 08 www.st-gervais.com

Serre Chevalier 118 C3 ❄ 1350/1200–2800m 77 lifts Dec–Apr •Briançon (10km) + 33 4 92 24 98 98 www.serre-chevalier.com *Made up of 13 small villages along the valley road, which is normally cleared.*

Tignes 119 B3 ❄ 2100/1550–3450m 97 lifts Jan–Dec •Bourg St Maurice (26km) +33 4 79 40 04 40 www.tignes.net *Keep chains accessible because of altitude.*

Val d'Isère 119 B3 ❄ 1850/1550–3450m Dec–Apr 97 lifts•Bourg-St-Maurice (30km) +33 4 79 06 06 60 www.valdisere.com *Roads normally cleared but keep chains accessible.*

Val Thorens 118 B3 ❄ 2300/1850–3200m 29 lifts Dec–Apr •Moûtiers (37km) +33 4 79 00 08 08 www.valthorens.com *Chains essential – highest ski resort in Europe. Obligatory paid parking on edge of resort.*

Valloire 118 B3 ❄ 1430–2600m 34 lifts Dec–Apr •Modane (20km) +33 4 79 59 03 96 www.valloire.net *Road normally clear up to the Col du Galbier, to the south of the resort, which is closed from 1st November to 1st June. Linked to Valmeinier.*

Valmeinier 118 B3 ❄ 1500–2600m 34 lifts Dec–Apr •St Michel de Maurienne (47km) +33 4 79 59 53 69 www.valmeinier.com *Access from north on D1006 / D902. Col du Galbier, to the south of the resort closed from 1st November to 1st June. Linked to Valloire.*

Valmorel 118 B3 ❄ 1400–2550m 90 lifts Dec–Apr •Moûtiers (15km) +33 4 79 09 85 55 www.valmorel.com *Near St Jean-de-Belleville. Linked with ski areas of Doucy-Combelouvière and St François-Longchamp.*

Vars Les Claux 118 C3 ❄ 1850/1650–2750m 51 lifts Dec–Apr •Briançon (40km) +33 4 92 46 51 31 www.vars-ski.com *Four base resorts up to 1850 metres. Keep chains accessible. Linked with Risoul.*

Villard de Lans 118 B2 ❄ 1050/1160–2170m 28 lifts Dec–Apr •Grenoble (32km) +33 4 76 95 10 38 www.villarddelans.com

Pyrenees

Font-Romeu 146 B3 ⊕ 1800/1600–2200m 25 lifts Nov–Apr •Perpignan (87km) ☎+33 4 68 30 68 30 🖳www.font-romeu.fr *Roads normally cleared but keep chains accessible.*

Saint-Lary Soulan 145 B4 ⊕ 830/1650/1700–2515m 31 lifts Dec–Mar •Tarbes (75km) ☎+33 5 62 39 50 81 🖳www.saintlary.com *Access roads constantly cleared of snow.*

Vosges

La Bresse-Hohneck 106 A1 ⊕ 500/900–1350m 33 lifts Dec–Mar •Cornimont (6km) ☎+33 3 29 25 41 29 🖳www.labresse.net

Germany

Alps

Garmisch-Partenkirchen 108 B2 ⊕ 700–2830m 38 lifts Dec–Apr •Munich (95km) ☎+49 8821 180 700 🖳www.gapa.de *Roads usually clear, chains rarely needed.*

Oberaudorf 108 B3 ⊕ 480–1850m 30 lifts Dec–Apr •Kufstein (15km) ☎+49 8033 301 20 🖳www.oberaudorf.de *Motorway normally kept clear. Near Bayrischzell.*

Oberstdorf 107 B5 815m 26 lifts Dec–Apr •Sonthofen (15km) ☎+49 8322 7000 🖳http://oberstdorf.de

Rothaargebirge

Winterberg 81 A4 ⊕ 700/620–830m 19 lifts Dec–Mar •Brilon (30km) ☎+49 2981 925 00 🖳www.winterberg.de *Roads usually cleared, chains rarely required.*

Greece

Central Greece

Mount Parnassos: Kelaria-Fterolakka 182 E4 1640–2260m 14 lifts Dec–Apr •Amfiklia ☎Kelaria +30 22340 22693–5, Fterolakka 22340 22373 🖳www.parnassos-ski.gr (Greek only)

Mount Parnassos: Gerondovrahos 182 E4 1800–1900m 14 lifts Dec–Apr •Amfiklia ☎+30 29444 70371

Peloponnisos

Mount Helmos: Kalavrita Ski Centre 184 A3 1650–2100m 7 lifts Dec–Mar •Kalavrita ☎+30 2692 2261 🖳www.kalavrita-ski.gr (Greek only)

Mount Menalo: Ostrakina 184 B3 1500–1600m 4 lifts Dec–Mar •Tripoli ☎+30 27960 22227

Macedonia

Mount Falakro: Agio Pneuma 183 B6 1720/1620–2230m 7 lifts Dec–Apr •Drama ☎+ 30 25210 23691 🖳www.falakro.gr (Greek only)

Mount Vasilitsa: Vasilitsa 182 C3 1750/1800–2113m 3 lifts Dec–Mar •Konitsa ☎+ 30 24620 26100 🖳www.vasilitsa.com (Greek only)

Mount Vermio: Seli 182 C4 1500–1900m 8 lifts Dec–Mar •Kozani ☎+ 30 23320 71234 🖳www.seli-ski.gr (in Greek)

Mount Vermio: Tria-Pente Pigadia 182 C3 1420–2005m 7 lifts Dec–Mar •Ptolemaida ☎+30 23320 44464 🖳www.3-5pigadia.gr

Mount Verno: Vigla 182 C3 1650–1900m 5 lifts Dec–Mar •Florina ☎+30 23850 22354 🖳www.vigla-ski.gr (in Greek)

Mount Vrondous: Lailias 183 B5 1600–1850m 4 lifts Dec–Mar •Serres ☎+30 23210 53790

Thessalia

Mount Pilio: Agriolefkes 183 D5 1300–1500m 5 lifts Dec–Mar •Volos ☎+30 24280 73719 🖳www.skipilio.gr (Greek only)

Italy

Alps

Bardonecchia 118 B3 ⊕ 1312–2750m 21 lifts Dec–Apr •Bardonecchia ☎+ 39 0122 99137 🖳www.bardonecchiaski.com *Resort reached through the 11km Frejus tunnel from France, roads normally cleared.*

Bórmio 107 C5 ⊕ 1200/1230–3020m 24 lifts Dec–Apr •Tirano (40km) ☎+39 342 903300 🖳www.bormio.com *Tolls payable in Ponte del Gallo Tunnel, open 0800hrs–2000hrs.*

Breuil-Cervinia 119 B4 ⊕ 2050–3500m 21 lifts Jan–Dec •Aosta (54km) ☎+39 166 949136 🖳www. cervinia.it *Snow chains strongly recommended. Bus from Milan airport.*

Courmayeur 119 B3 ⊕ 1200–2760m 21 lifts Dec–Apr •Aosta (40km) 🖳www.courmayeur.com *Access through the Mont Blanc tunnel from France. Roads constantly cleared.*

Limone Piemonte 133 A3 ⊕ 1000/1050–2050m 29 lifts Dec–Apr •Cuneo (27km) ☎+ 39 171 925281 🖳www.limonepiemonte.it *Roads normally cleared, chains rarely required.*

Livigno 107 C5 ⊕ 1800–3000m 31 lifts Nov–May •Zernez (CH) (27km) ☎+ 39 342 996379 🖳www.livigno.com *Keep chains accessible. The direction of traffic through Munt la Schera Tunnel to/from Zernez is regulated on Saturdays. Check in advance.*

Sestrière 119 C3 ⊕ 2035/1840–2840m 92 lifts Dec–Apr •Oulx (22km) ☎+39 122 799411 🖳http://www.comune.sestriere.to.it *One of Europe's highest resorts; although roads are normally cleared keep chains accessible.*

Appennines

Roccaraso – Aremogna 169 B4 ⊕ 1285/1240–2140m 39 lifts Dec–Apr •Castel di Sangro (7km) ☎+39 864 62210 🖳www.roccaraso.net (in Italian)

Dolomites

Andalo – Fai della Paganella 121 A3 ⊕ 1042/1050/2125m 19 lifts Dec–Apr •Trento (40km) 🖳www.paganella.com ☎+39 0461 585836

Arabba 108 C2 ⊕ 1600/1450–2950m 29 lifts Dec–Mar •Brunico (45km) ☎+39 436 780019 🖳www.arabba.it *Roads normally cleared but keep chains accessible.*

Cortina d'Ampezzo 108 C3 ⊕ 1224/1050–2930m 37 lifts Dec–Apr •Belluno (72km) 🖳www.cortina.dolomiti.org *Access from north on route 51 over the Cimabanche Pass may require chains.*

Corvara (Alta Badia) 108 C2 ⊕ 1568–2500m 52 lifts Dec–Apr •Brunico (38km) ☎+39 471 836176 🖳www.altabadia.it *Roads normally clear but keep chains accessible.*

Madonna di Campiglio 121 A3 ⊕ 1550/1500–2600m 72 lifts Dec–Apr •Trento (60km) ☎+39 465 447501 🖳www.campigliodolomiti.it/homepage *Roads normally cleared but keep chains accessible. Linked to Folgarida and Marilleva.*

Moena di Fassa (Sorte/Ronchi) 108 C2 ⊕ 1184/1450–2520m 8 lifts Dec–Apr •Bolzano (40km) ☎+39 462 609500 🖳www.fassa.com

Selva di Val Gardena/Wolkenstein Groden 108 C2 ⊕ 1563/1570–2450m 84 lifts Dec–Apr •Bolzano (40km) ☎+39 471 777777 🖳www.valgardena.it *Roads normally cleared but keep chains accessible.*

Norway

Hemsedal 47 B5 ⊕ 700/640–1450m 24 lifts Nov–May •Honefoss (150km) ☎+47 32 055030 🖳www.hemsedal.com *Be prepared for extreme weather conditions.*

Slovak Republic

Chopok (Jasna-Chopok) 99 C3 ⊕ 900/950–1840m 17 lifts Dec–Apr •Jasna ☎+421 907 886644 🖳www.jasna.sk

Donovaly 99 C3 ⊕ 913–1360m 17 lifts Nov–Apr •Ruzomberok ☎+421 48 4199900 🖳www.parksnow.sk/zima

Martinské Hole 98 B2 1250/1150–1456m 8 lifts Nov–May •Zilina ☎+421 43 430 6000 🖳www.martinky.com (in Slovak only)

Plejsy 99 C4 470–912m 9 lifts Dec–Mar •Krompachy ☎+421 53 429 8015 🖳www.plejsy.com

Strbske Pleso 99 B4 1380–1825m 7 lifts Dec–Mar •Poprad ☎+421 52 449 2455 🖳www.vt.sk

Slovenia

Julijske Alpe

Kanin (Bovec) 122 A2 460/1600–2389m 5 lifts Dec–Apr •Bovec ☎+ 386 5 3896444 🖳www.boveckanin.si

Kobla (Bohinj) 122 A2 512/530–1495m 6 lifts Dec–Mar •Bohinjska Bistrica ☎+386 4 5747 100 🖳www.bohinj.si/kobla

Kranjska Gora 122 A2 ⊕ 800–1210m 19 lifts Dec–Mar •Kranjska Gora ☎+386 4 5809 440 🖳www.kranjska-gora.si

Vogel 122 A2 570–1800m 8 lifts Dec–Apr •Bohinjska Bistrica ☎+386 4 5729 712 🖳www.vogel.si

Kawiniške Savinjske Alpe

Krvavec 122 A3 ⊕ 1450–1970m 10 lifts Dec–Apr •Kranj ☎ 386 4 25 25 911 🖳www.rtc-krvavec.si

Pohorje

Rogla 123 A4 1517/1050–1500m 13 lifts Dec–Apr •Slovenska Bistrica ☎+386 3 75 76 000 🖳www.rogla.eu

Spain

Pyrenees

Baqueira-Beret/Bonaigua 145 B4 ⊕ 1500–2500m 33 lifts Dec–Apr •Vielha (15km) ☎+34 973 639010 🖳www.baqueira.es *Roads normally clear but keep chains accessible. Near Salardú.*

Sistema Penibetico

Sierra Nevada 163 A4 ⊕ 2100–3300m 24 lifts Dec–May •Granada (32km) ☎+34 902 70 80 90–3 🖳http://sierranevada.es *Access road designed to be avalanche safe and is snow cleared.*

Sweden

Idre Fjäll 199 D9 590–890m 33 lifts Nov–Apr •Mora (140km) ☎+46 253 41000 🖳www.idrefjall.se *Be prepared for extreme weather conditions.*

Sälen 49 A5 360m 100 lifts Nov–Apr •Malung (70km) 🖳www.skistar.com/salen *Be prepared for extreme weather conditions.*

Switzerland

Alps

Adelboden 106 C2 1353m 55 lifts Dec–Apr •Frutigen (15km) ☎+41 33 673 80 80 🖳www.adelboden.ch *Linked with Lenk.*

Arosa 107 C4 1800m 16 lifts Dec–Apr •Chur (30km) ☎+41 81 378 70 20 🖳www.arosa.ch *Roads cleared but keep chains accessible because of high altitude (1800m).*

Crans Montana 119 A4 ⊕ 1500–3000m 34 lifts Dec–Apr, Jul–Oct •Sierre (15km) ☎+41 27 485 04 04 🖳www.crans-montana.ch *Roads normally cleared, however keep chains accessible for ascent from Sierre.*

Davos 107 C4 1560/1100–2840m 38 lifts Nov–Apr •Davos ☎+41 81 415 21 21 🖳www.davos.ch

Engelberg 106 C3 ⊕ 1000/1050–3020m 26 lifts Nov–May •Luzern (39km) ☎+41 41 639 77 77 🖳www.engelberg.ch *Straight access road normally cleared.*

Flums (Flumserberg) 107 B4 ⊕ 1400/1000–2220m 17 lifts Dec–Apr •Buchs (25km) ☎+41 81 720 18 18 🖳www.flumserberg.ch *Roads normally cleared, but keep chains accessible.*

Grindelwald 106 C3 ⊕ 1050–2950m 39 lifts Dec–Apr •Interlaken (20km) ☎+41 33 854 12 12 🖳www.jungfrauregion.ch

Gstaad – Saanenland 106 C2 ⊕ 1050/950–3000m 74 lifts Dec–Apr •Gstaad ☎+41 33 748 81 81 🖳www.gstaad.ch *Linked to Anzère.*

Klosters 107 C4 ⊕ 1191/1110–2840m 52 lifts Dec–Apr •Davos (10km) ☎+41 81 410 21 21 🖳www.klosters.ch *Roads normally clear but keep chains accessible.*

Leysin 119 A4 ⊕ 2263/1260–2330m 16 lifts Dec–Apr •Aigle (6km) ☎+41 24 493 33 33 🖳www.leysin.ch

Mürren 106 C2 ⊕ 1650–2970m 12 lifts Dec–Apr •Interlaken (18km) ☎+41 33 856 86 86 🖳www.mymuerren.ch *No road access. Park in Strechelberg (1500 free places) and take the two-stage cable car.*

Nendaz 119 A4 ⊕ 1365/1400–3300m 20 lifts Nov–Apr •Sion (16km) ☎+41 27 289 55 89 🖳www.nendaz.ch *Roads normally cleared, however keep chains accessible for ascent from Sion. Near Vex.*

Saas-Fee 119 A4 ⊕ 1800–3500m 23 lifts Jan–Dec •Brig (35km) ☎+41 27 958 18 58 🖳www.saas-fee.ch *Roads normally cleared but keep chains accessible because of altitude.*

St Moritz 107 C4 ⊕ 1856/1730–3300m 24 lifts Nov–May •Chur (89km) ☎+41 81 837 33 33 🖳www.stmoritz.ch *Roads normally cleared but keep chains accessible.*

Samnaun 107 C5 ⊕ 1846/1400–2900m 40 lifts Dec–May •Scuol (30km) ☎+41 81 868 58 58 🖳www.engadin.com *Roads normally cleared but keep chains accessible.*

Verbier 119 A4 ⊕ 1500–3330m 17 lifts Nov–Apr •Martigny (27km) ☎+41 27 775 38 88 🖳www.verbier.ch *Roads normally cleared.*

Villars-Gryon 119 A4 ⊕ 1253/1200–2100m 16 lifts Dec–Apr, Jun–Jul •Montreux (35km) ☎+41 24 495 32 32 🖳www.villars.ch *Roads normally cleared but keep chains accessible for ascent from N9. Near Bex.*

Wengen 106 C2 ⊕ 1270–2320m 39 lifts Dec–Apr •Interlaken (12km) ☎+41 33 856 85 85 🖳http://wengen.ch *No road access. Park at Lauterbrunnen and take mountain railway.*

Zermatt 119 A4 ⊕ 1620–3900m 40 lifts, all year •Brig (42km) ☎+41 27 966 81 19 🖳www.zermatt.ch *Cars not permitted in resort, park in Täsch (3km) and take shuttle train.*

Turkey

North Anatolian Mountains

Uludag 186 B4 1770–2320m 13 lifts Dec–Mar •Bursa (36km) ☎+90 224 285 21 11 🖳http://skiingturkey.com/resorts/uludag.html

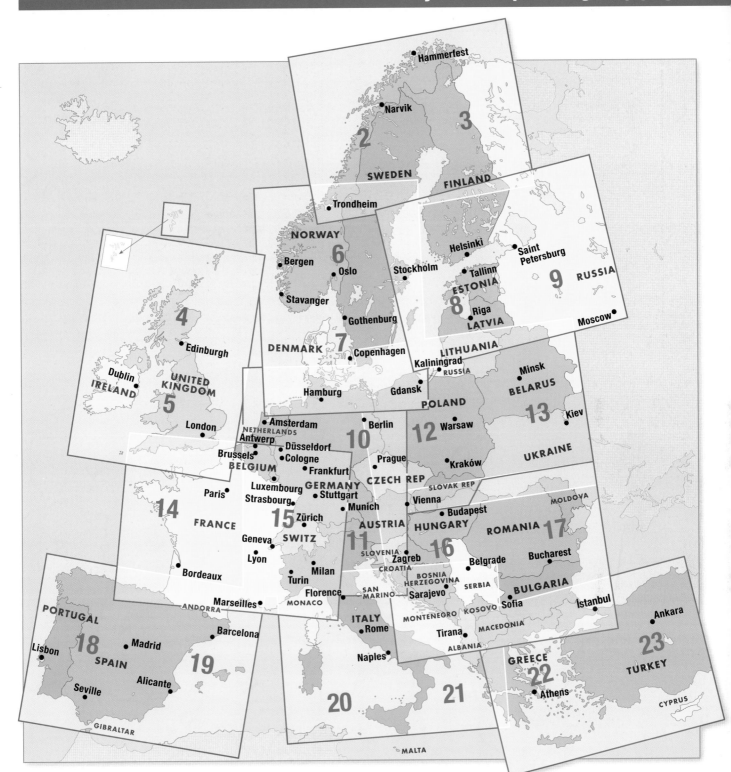

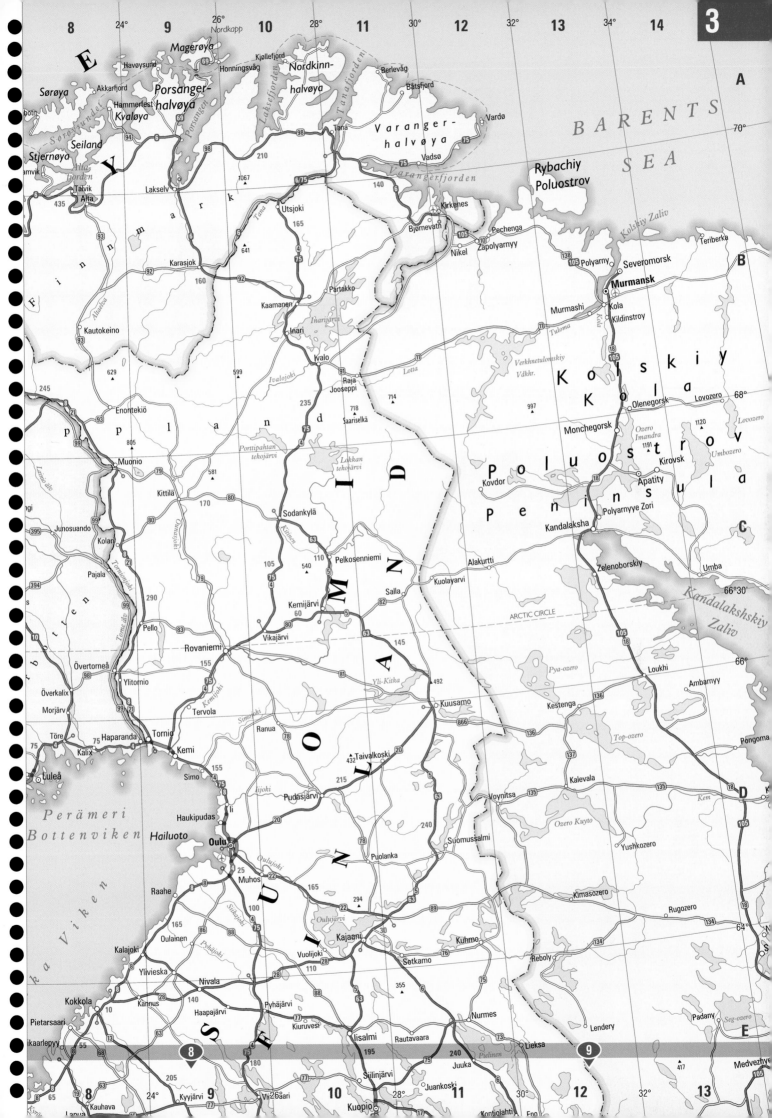

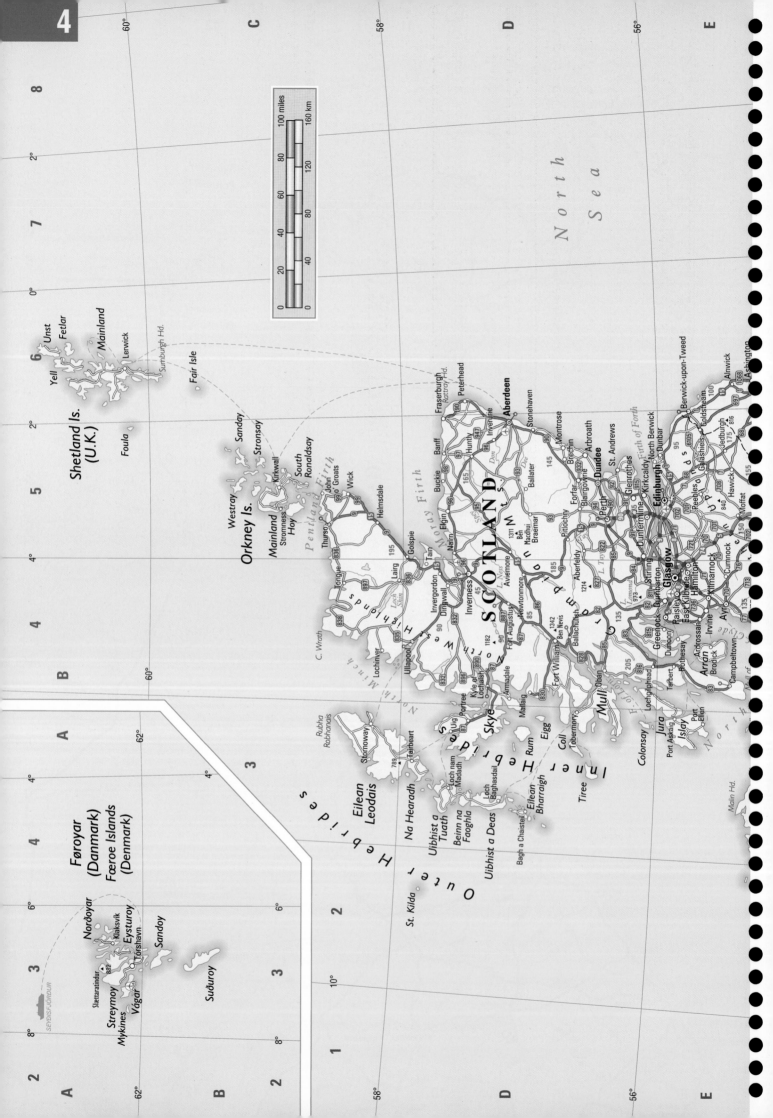

A   B   C   D   E

8   2°

7

6   2°

5   2°

4   4°

3   6°

2   8°

Shetland Is. (U.K.)

Unst
Fetlar
Yell
Mainland
Lerwick
Foula
Sumburgh Hd.
Fair Isle

Orkney Is.

Westray
Sanday
Stronsay
Mainland
Stromness
Hoy
Kirkwall
South Ronaldsay
Pentland Firth

Føroyar (Danmark)
Færoe Islands (Denmark)

Norðoyar
Klaksvík
Eysturoy
Streymoy
Mykines
Vágar
Tórshavn
Sanday
Slættaratindur 882
Suðuroy

SEYÐISFJÖRÐUR

Rubha Robhanais

Eilean Leodais

Na Hearadh

Uibhist a Tuath
Beinn na Faoghla
Uibhist a Deas

Bagh a Chaisteil

Eilean Bharraigh

St. Kilda

Outer Hebrides

789

Loch nam Madadh

Loch Baghasdail

Tiree

Stornoway
Tairbeart
Uig
Portree
Skye
Kyle of Lochalsh
Armadale
Mallaig
Rum
Eigg
Coll
Tobermory
Mull
Colonsay
Jura
Islay
Port Askaig
Port Ellen

Inner Hebrides

C. Wrath
Lochinver
Ullapool
Tongue
Lairg
Loch Shin
Durness

North Minch

North West Highlands

Thurso
John o' Groats
Wick
Helmsdale
Golspie
Tain
Dingwall
Invergordon
Inverness
Aviemore
Newtonmore
Fort Augustus
Ben Nevis 1342
Fort William
Ballachulish
Oban
Lochgilphead
Tarbert
Campbeltown
Rothesay
Dunoon
Arran
Brodick
Ardrossan
Irvine
Ayr
Cumnock
Kilmarnock
East Kilbride
Hamilton
Glasgow
Paisley
Greenock
Dumbarton
Stirling
Dunfermline
Kirkcaldy
Edinburgh
Perth
Pitlochry
Aberfeldy
Blairgowrie
Forfar
Dundee
Brechin
Arbroath
Montrose
Stonehaven
Aberdeen
Inverurie
Huntly
Banff
Buckie
Elgin
Nairn
Ben Macdhui 1311
Braemar
Ballater
Fraserburgh
Peterhead
Rattray Hd.
St. Andrews
Glenrothes
North Berwick
Dunbar
Berwick-upon-Tweed
Coldstream
Galashiels
Jedburgh
Peebles
Hawick
Moffat
Alnwick
Ashington

SCOTLAND

Moray Firth
Grampian Mts.
Firth of Forth
Firth of Clyde
Mull of Kintyre
Malin Hd.
North Channel

North Sea

Loch Ness
Loch Lomond
Loch Tay
Dee
Don

100 miles   160 km

0   20   40   60   80   100
0   40   80   120   160

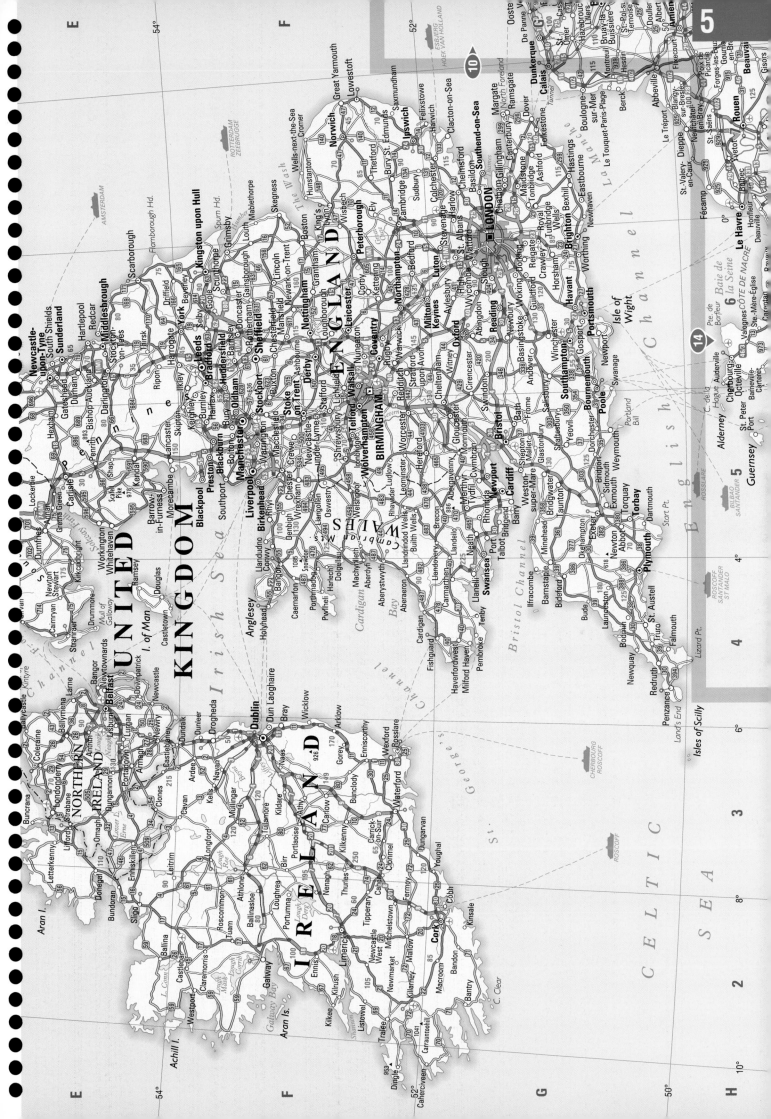

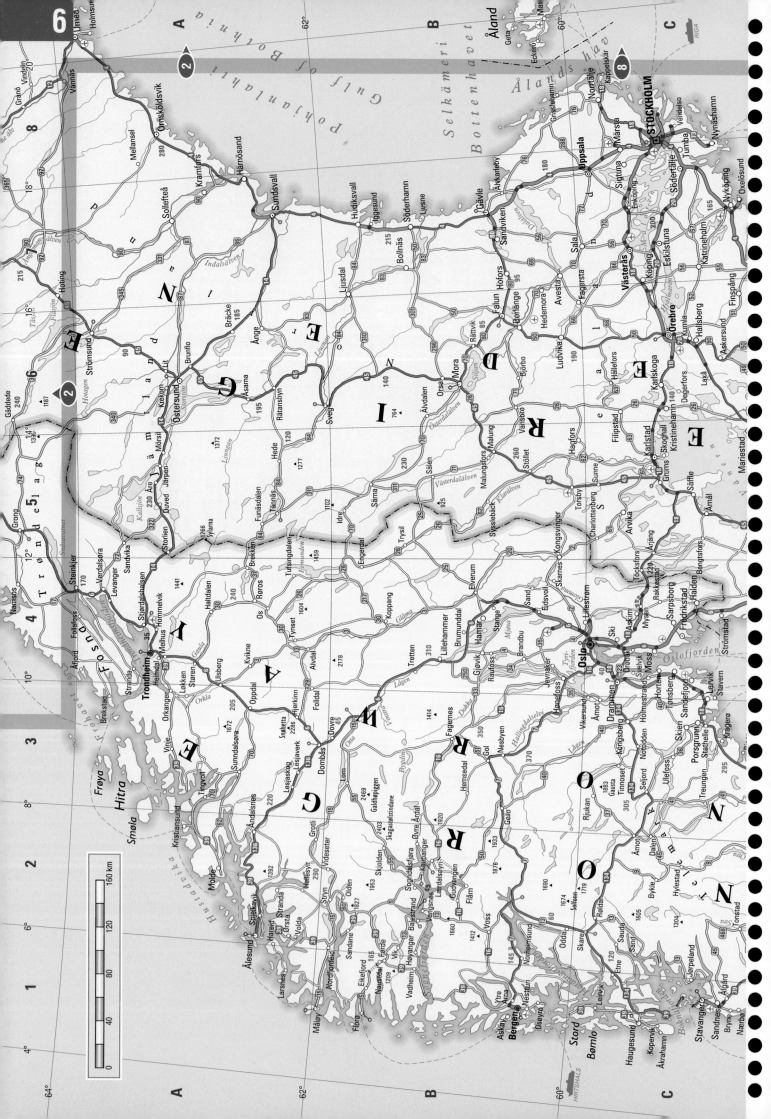

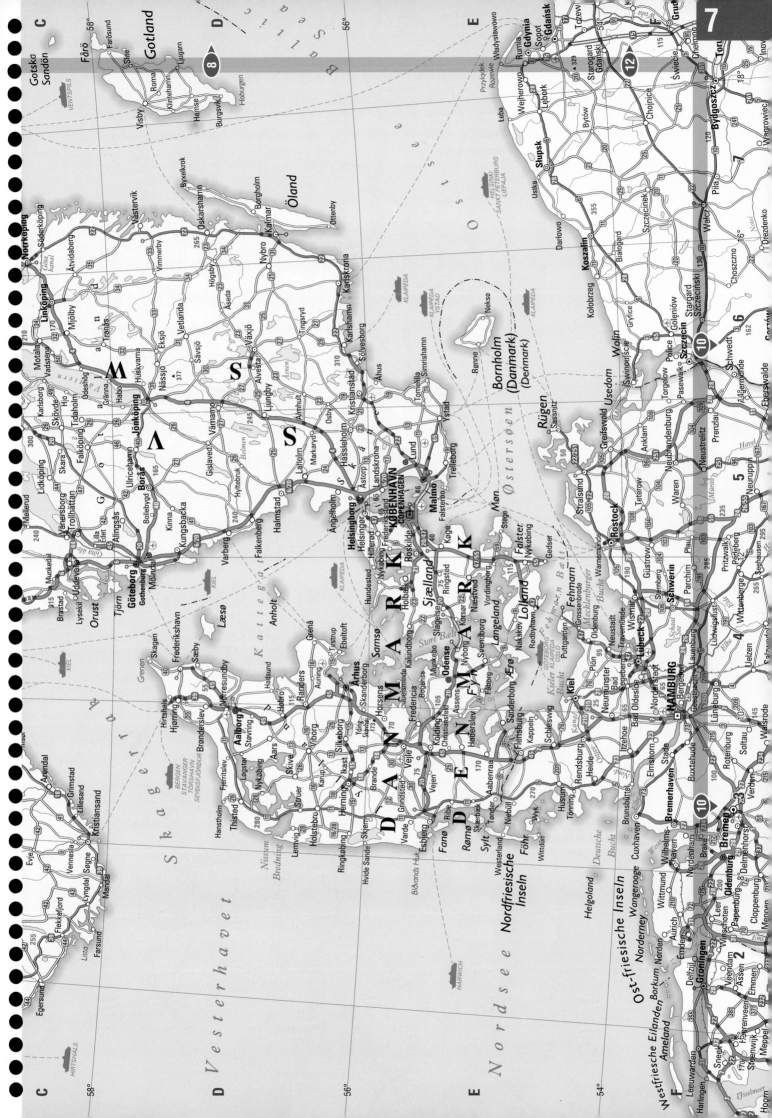

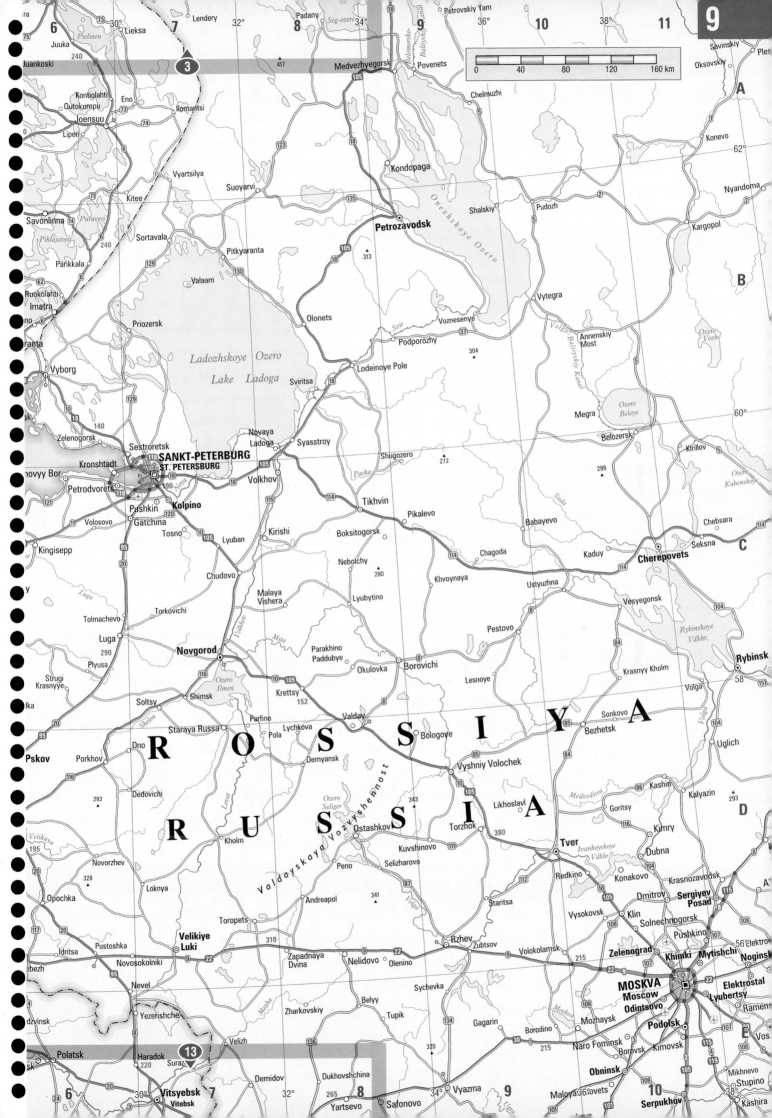

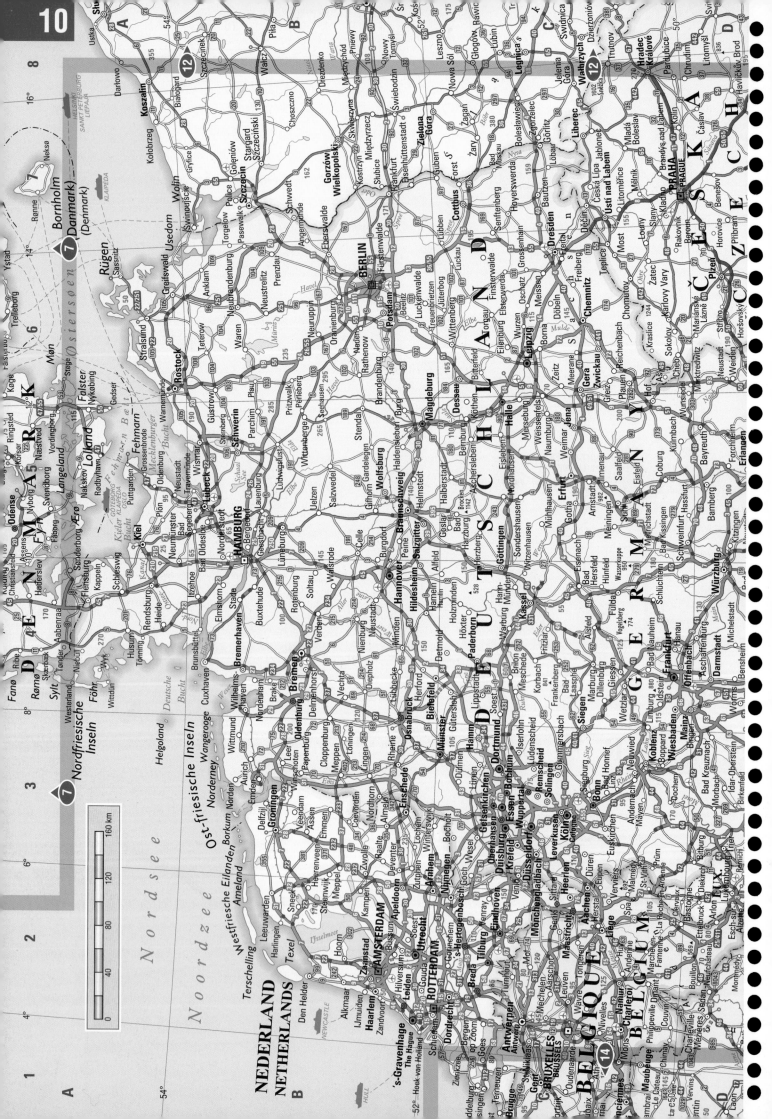

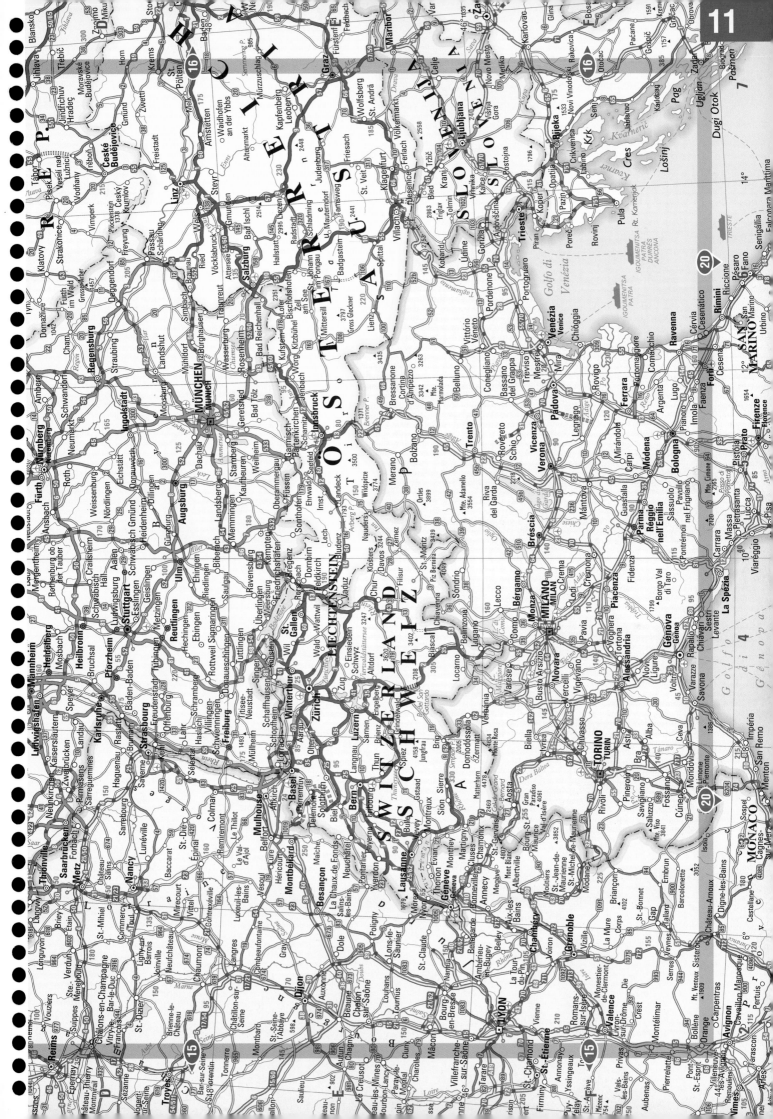

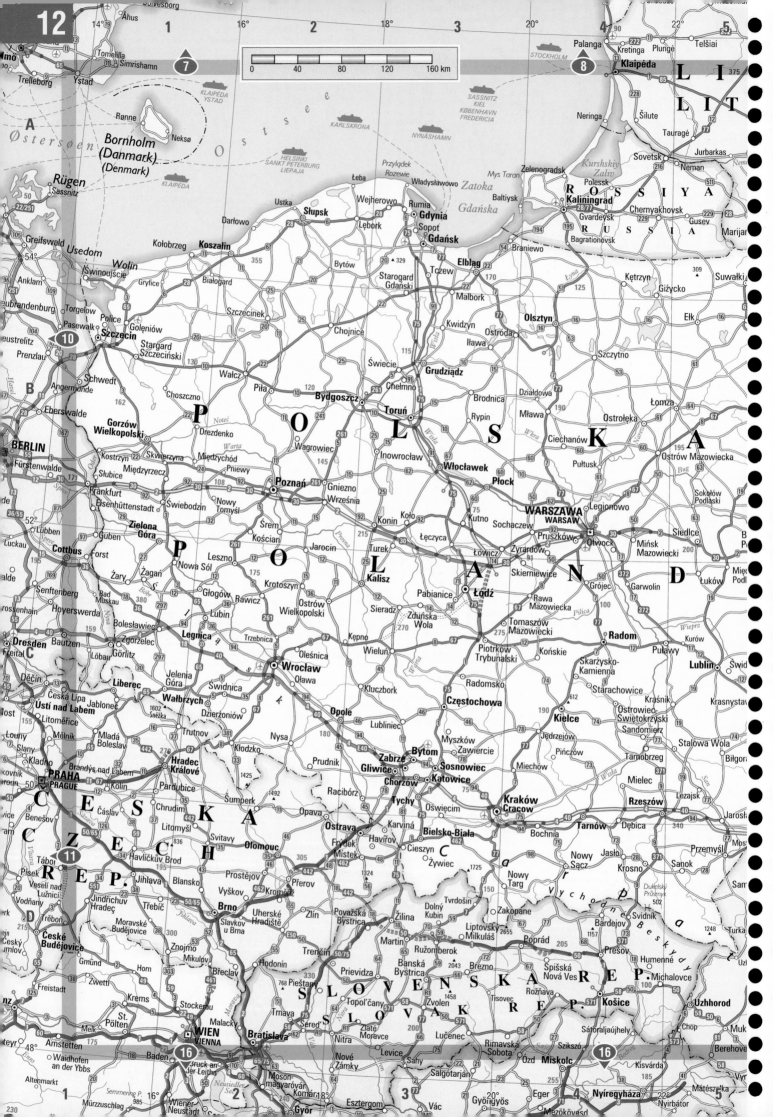

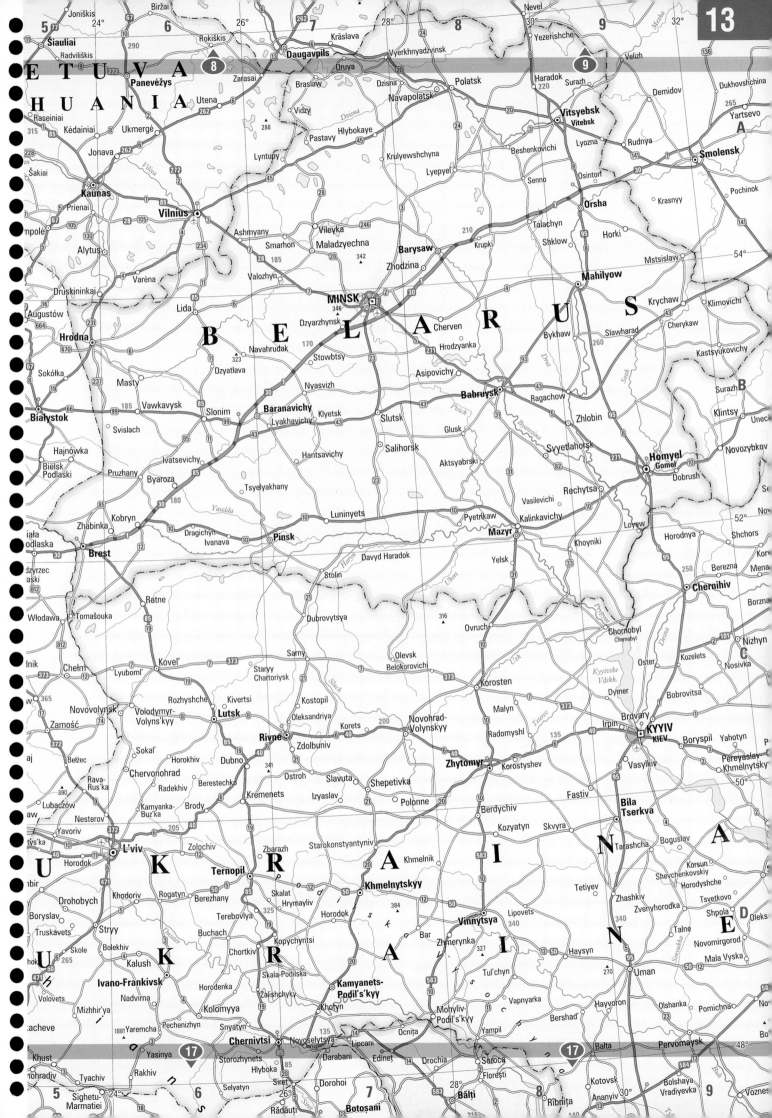

ENGLISH CHANNEL

La Manche

Channel Is. (U.K.)

Guernsey — St. Peter Port — Sark — Jersey — St. Helier — Alderney

F R A N C E

Bay of Biscay — Golfe de Gascogne

CÔTE DE NACRE — CÔTE D'EMERAUDE — CÔTE DE CORNOUAILLE — CÔTE D'AMOUR — CÔTE DE JADE — CÔTE D'ARGENT — CÔTE DES LANDES — CÔTE BASQUE

Baie de la Seine

G. de St.-Malo

Île d'Ouessant — Belle-Île — Î. de Noirmoûtier — Î. d'Yeu — Î. de Ré — Î. d'Oléron

Selected place names:

Barnstaple, Minehead, Weston-super-Mare, Frome, Andover, Basingstoke, Woking, Dorking, Canterbury, Ramsgate, North Foreland, Bideford, Bridgwater, Taunton, Glastonbury, Shaftesbury, Salisbury, Winchester, Guildford, Reigate, Royal Tunbridge Wells, Maidstone, Tonbridge, Dover, Dunkerque, Calais, De Panne, Veurne

Okehampton, Exeter, Bridport, Dorchester, Bournemouth, Poole, Gosport, Havant, Brighton, Bexhill, Hastings, Folkestone, Boulogne-sur-Mer, Lille, Béthune, Lens

Bude, Launceston, Newton Abbot, Torquay, Sidmouth, Exmouth, Weymouth, Portland Bill, Swanage, Newport, Isle of Wight, Portsmouth, Worthing, Eastbourne, Newhaven, St. Omer, Cassel, Hazebrouck, Bruay-la-Buissière, Lillers

Newquay, Bodmin, St. Austell, Plymouth, Dartmouth, Start Pt., Torbay, Le Havre, Honfleur, Deauville, Dieppe, Le Tréport, Abbeville, Amiens, Arras, Cambrai

Redruth, Truro, Falmouth, Penzance, Land's End, Lizard Pt., Rosslare, Cork

Brest, Le Conquet, Pte. St.-Mathieu, Crozon, Pte. du Raz, Audierne, Quimper, Pont-l'Abbé, Pte. de Penmarch, Concarneau, Quimperlé, Lorient, Auray, Carnac, Quiberon, Le Palais, Le Croisic, La Baule, St.-Nazaire, Pornic

Perros-Guirec, Roscoff, Lannion, Paimpol, Binic, Guingamp, Morlaix, Landivisiau, Châteaulin, Carhaix-Plouguer, Pontivy, Loudéac, St.-Brieuc, Lamballe, Dinard, St.-Malo, Dinan, Mûr-de-Bretagne, St.-Méen-le-Grand, Ploërmel, Rennes, Vitré, Laval, Mayenne, Le Mans, Vendôme, Orléans

Granville, Avranches, Le Mont-St.-Michel, Fougères, Pontorson, Coutances, Villedieu-les-Poêles, St.-Lô, Caen, Bayeux, Lisieux, Bernay, Évreux, Mantes-la-Jolie, St.-Germain, PARIS, Versailles, Créteil, Évry, Étampes, Melun, Fontainebleau, Nemours

Cherbourg-Octeville, Valognes, Carentan, Ste.-Mère-Église, Barneville-Carteret, La Haye-du-Puits, Vire, Flers, Argentan, Falaise, Gacé, L'Aigle, Verneuil-sur-Avre, Dreux, Rambouillet, Chartres, Nogent-le-Rotrou, Châteaudun, Cloyes, Blois, Amboise, Tours, Romorantin-Lanthenay, Vierzon, Bourges

Alençon, Sées, Mortagne-au-Perche, Bonnétable, Mamers, La Ferté-Bernard, Châteaudun, Artenay, Pithiviers, Montargis, Gien, Briare, Cosne-Cours-sur-Loire, La Charité-sur-Loire

Angers, Saumur, Chinon, Loudun, Châtellerault, Châteauroux, Issoudun, St.-Amand-Mont-Rond, Montluçon

Nantes, Clisson, Cholet, Thouars, Bressuire, Parthenay, Poitiers, Chauvigny, Montmorillon, Lussac-les-Châteaux, Argenton-sur-Creuse, La Châtre, Aubusson, Châtelguyon

Montaigu, Challans, La Roche-sur-Yon, Les Sables-d'Olonne, Luçon, Fontenay-le-Comte, St.-Maixent-l'École, Niort, Civray, Bellac, St.-Junien, Confolens, Guéret, Bourganeuf, La Souterraine

La Rochelle, Rochefort, Saintes, Royan, Cognac, Angoulême, Chasseneuil-sur-Bonnieure, Limoges, St.-Léonard-de-Noblat, Uzerche, Eymoutiers, Ussel, Puy-de-Dôme, Le Mont-Dore, Puy de Sancy

Le Verdon-sur-Mer, Lesparre-Médoc, Blaye, St.-André-de-Cubzac, Libourne, Bergerac, Périgueux, Brantôme, Thiviers, St.-Yrieix-la-Perche, Brive-la-Gaillarde, Terrasson-la-Villedieu, Tulle, Argentat, Mauriac, Murat, Aurillac, Chaudes-Aigues, St.-Chély-d'Apcher

Bordeaux, Arcachon, C. Ferret, Langon, La Réole, Marmande, Tonneins, Villeneuve-sur-Lot, Agen, Fumel, Cahors, Figeac, Decazeville, Rodez, Villefranche-de-Rouergue

Lacanau, Mimizan, Labouheyre, Mont-de-Marsan, Castets, Tartas, Dax, St.-Sever, Aire-sur-l'Adour, Condom, Lectoure, Castelsarrasin, Moissac, Montauban, Caussade, Gaillac, Albi, Cordes, Carmaux, Castres, Mazamet

Bayonne, Biarritz, Donostia-Irún, San Sebastián, Hasparren, Orthez, Salies-de-Béarn, Pau, Oloron-Ste.-Marie, Mauléon-Licharre, Tarbes, Auch, Mirande, L'Isle-Jourdain, Toulouse, Grisolles, Rabastens, Lavaur, Castelnaudary, Carcassonne

Santander, Torrelavega, San Vicente de la Barquera, Llanes, Laredo, Castro-Urdiales, Getxo, Bilbao, Barakaldo, Durango, Eibar, Tolosa, Beasain, Vitoria, Pamplona, Oña, Reinosa, Lourdes, Bagnères-de-Bigorre, Foix, Pamiers, Limoux

COSTA MONTAÑESA, COSTA VASCA, Pizos de Europa

Scale bar:
0 — 20 — 40 — 60 — 80 — 100 miles
0 — 40 — 80 — 120 — 160 km

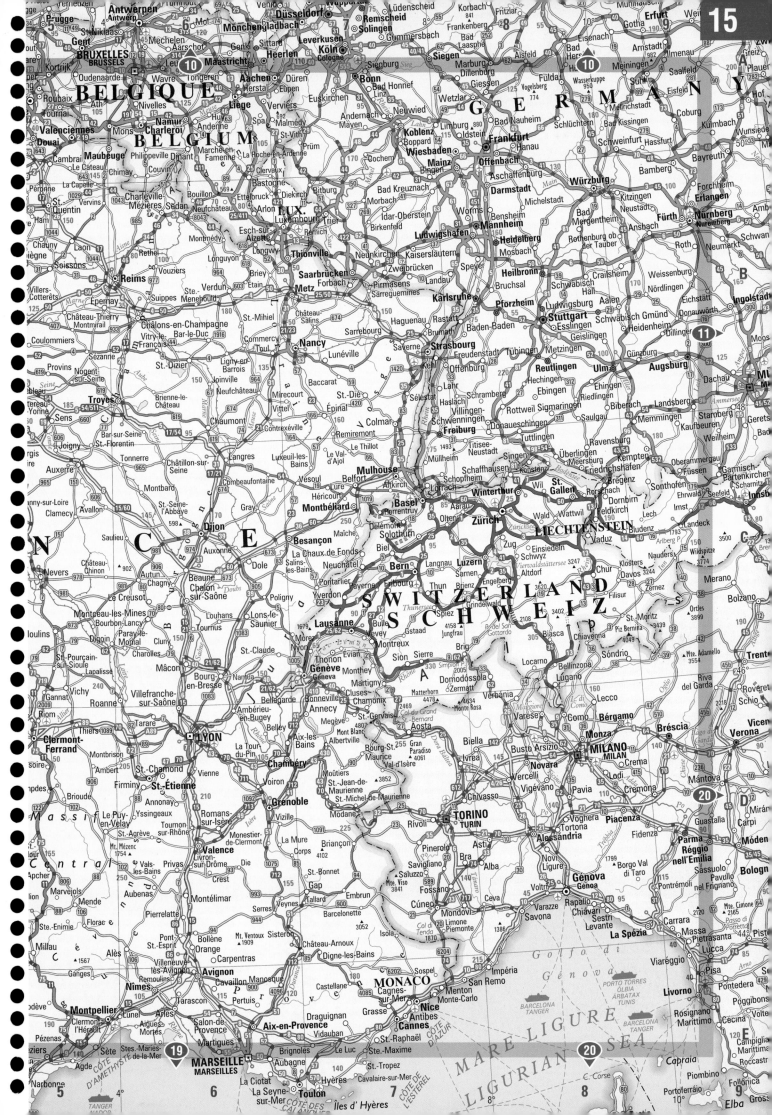

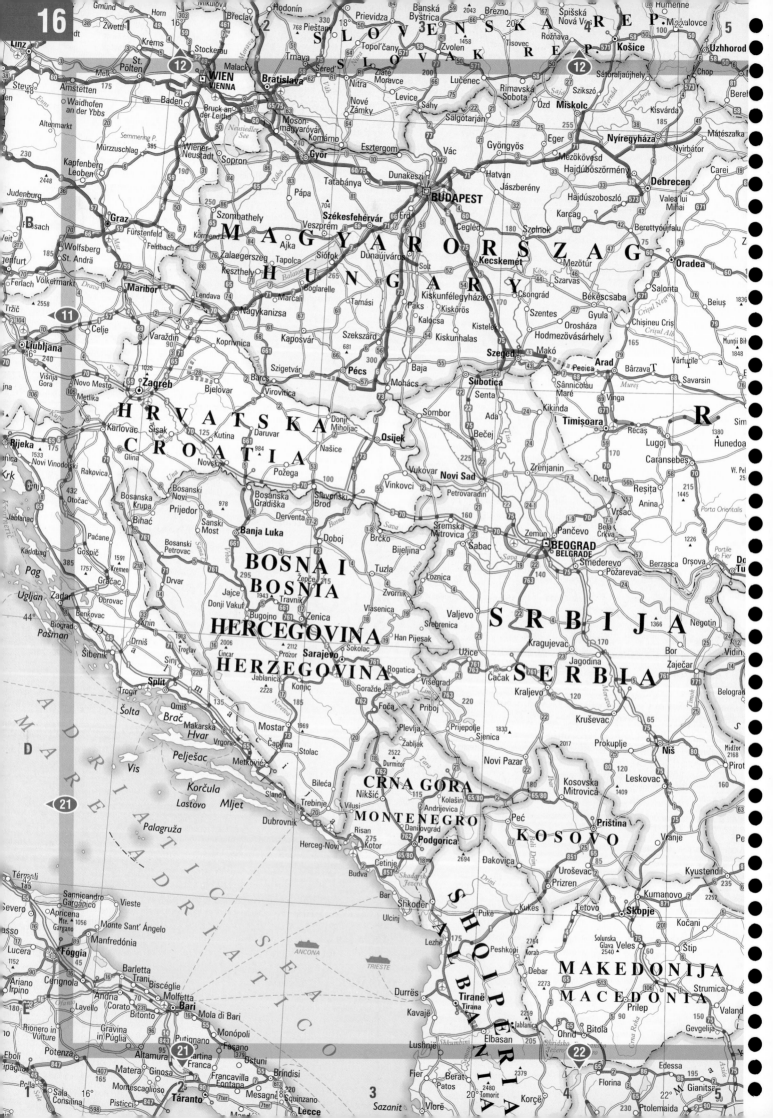

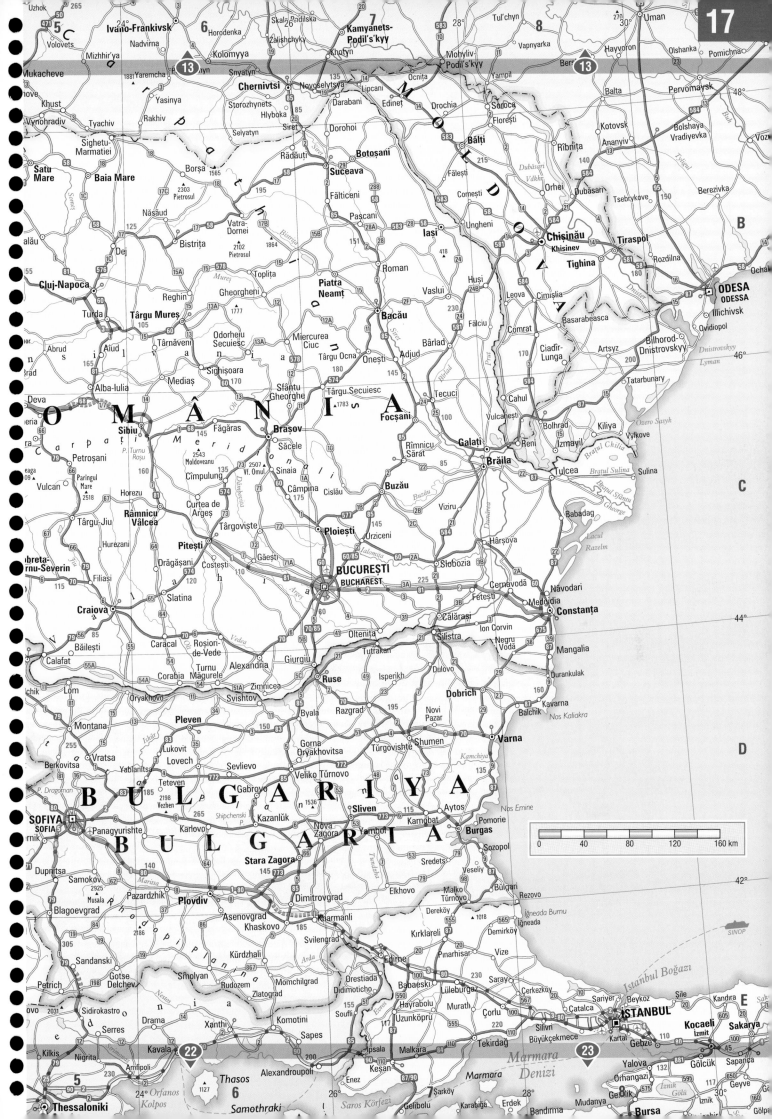

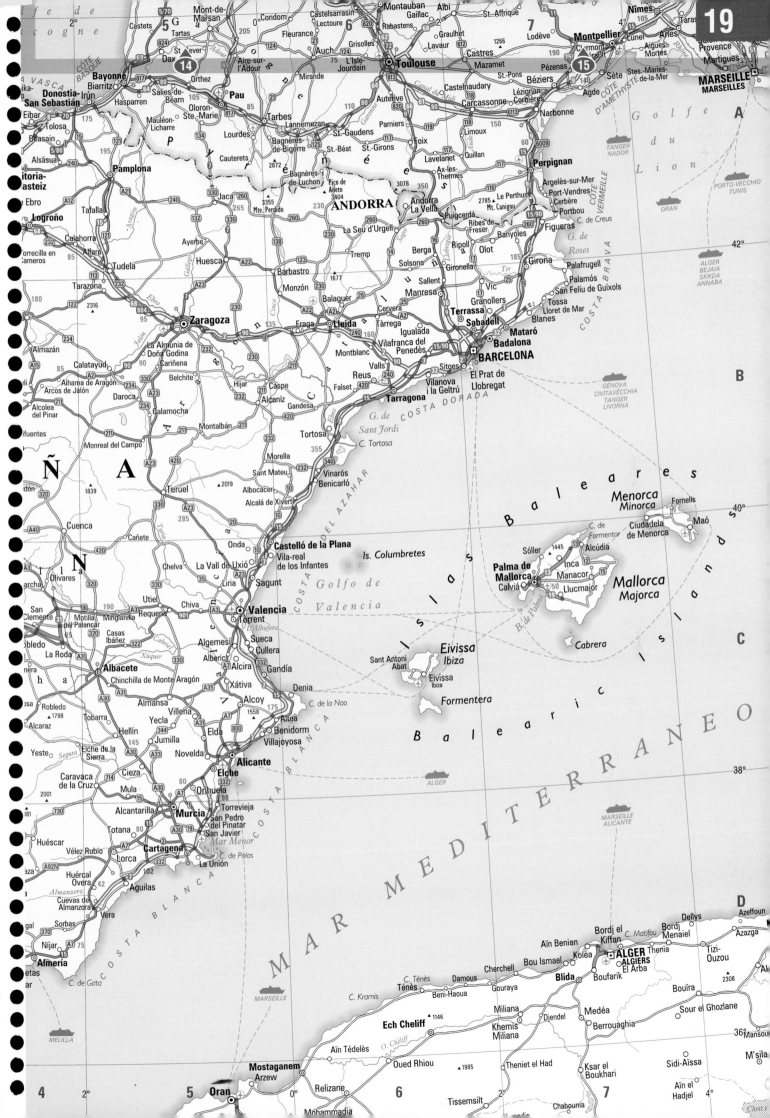

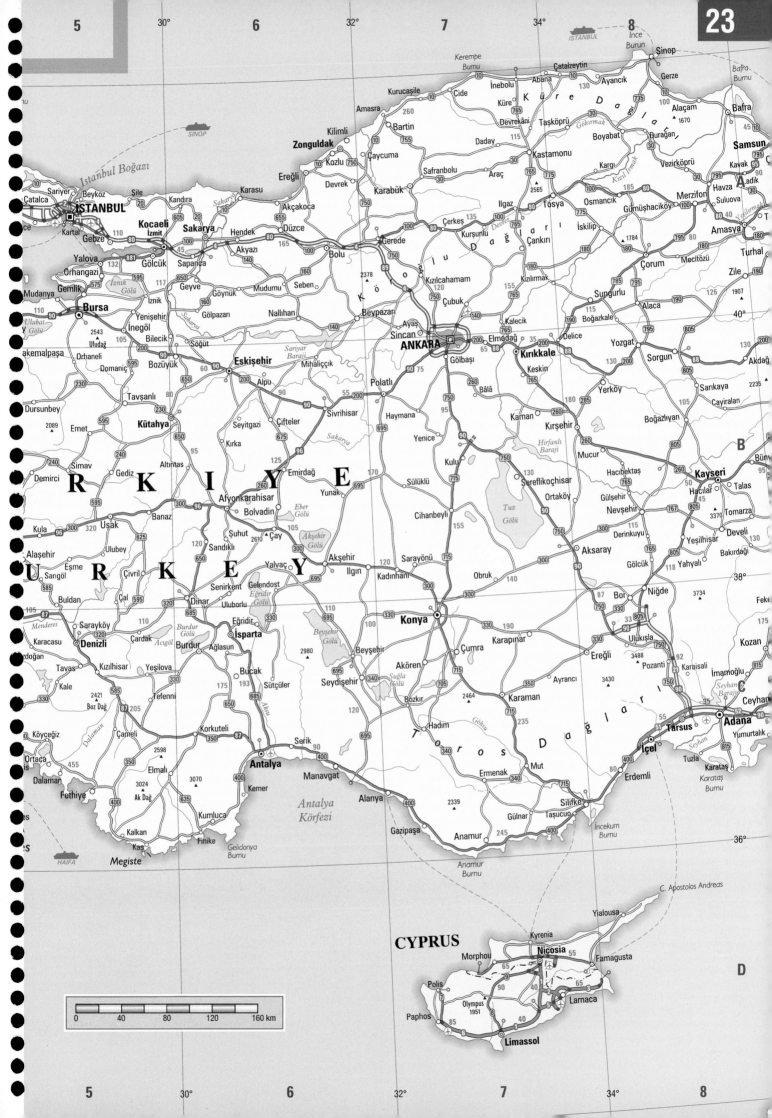

Key to road map pages

- **Florence** *Firenze* **City plan**
- **İstanbul** **City approach map**
- **Milan** *Milano* **City plan and approach map**
  See pages 201–228 for city plans and approach maps

97 **Map pages at 1 : 750 000**

182 **Map pages at 1 : 1 500 000**

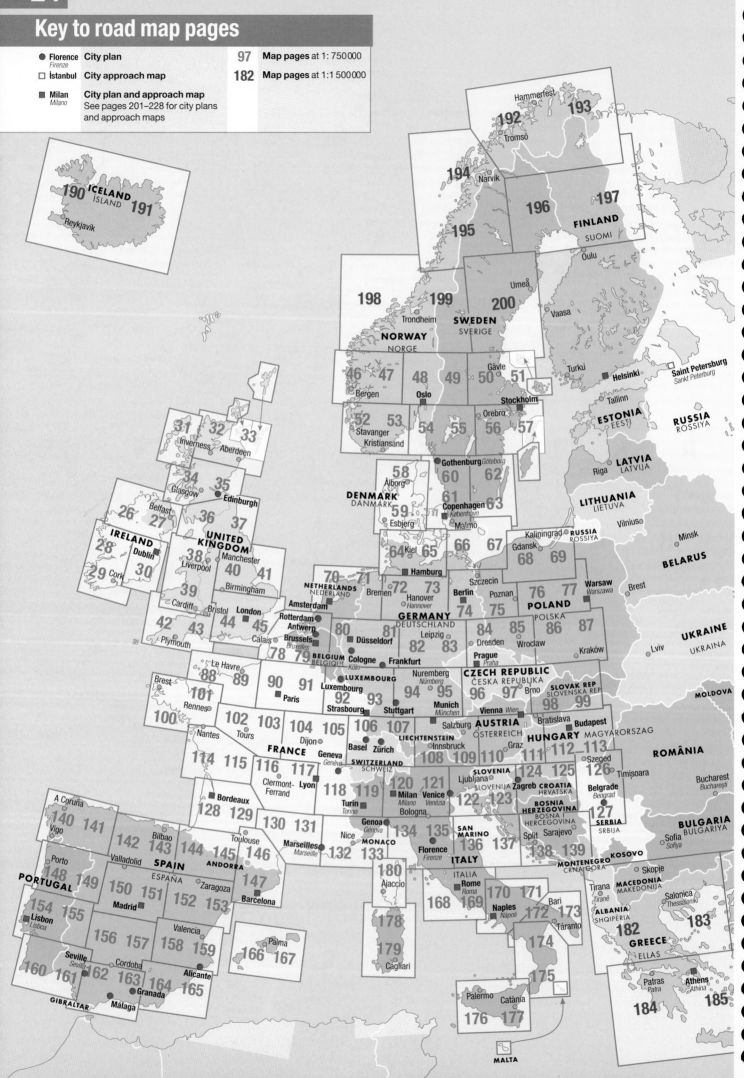

Distance table

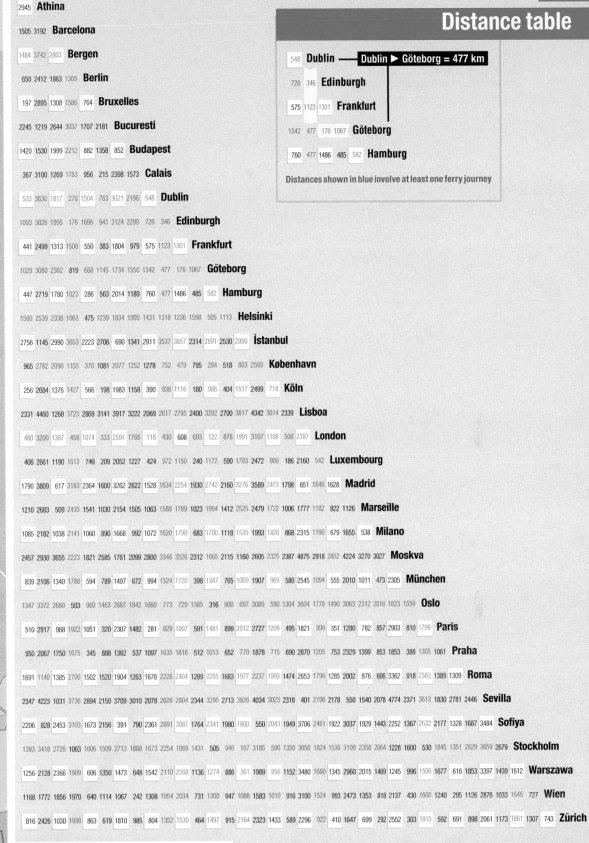

Legend box:

	Dublin	Edinburgh	Frankfurt	Göteborg
Dublin	548			
Edinburgh	726	346		
Frankfurt	575	1123	1301	
Göteborg	1342	477	176	1067
Hamburg	760	477	1486	485	582

Dublin ▶ Göteborg = 477 km

Distances shown in blue involve at least one ferry journey

Distance table:

	Amsterdam	Athina	Barcelona	Bergen	Berlin	Bruxelles	Bucuresti	Budapest	Calais	Dublin	Edinburgh	Frankfurt	Göteborg	Hamburg	Helsinki	İstanbul	København	Köln	Lisboa	London	Luxembourg	Madrid	Marseille	Milano	Moskva	München	Oslo	Paris	Praha	Roma	Sevilla	Sofiya	Stockholm	Warszawa	Wien
Athina	2945																																		
Barcelona	1505	3192																																	
Bergen	1484	3742	2803																																
Berlin	650	2412	1863	1309																															
Bruxelles	197	2895	1308	1586	764																														
Bucuresti	2245	1219	2644	3037	1707	2181																													
Budapest	1420	1530	1999	2212	882	1358	852																												
Calais	367	3100	1269	1783	956	215	2398	1573																											
Dublin	533	3630	1817	270	1504	763	3021	2196	548																										
Edinburgh	1093	3826	1995	176	1696	941	3124	2299	726	346																									
Frankfurt	441	2499	1313	1508	550	383	1804	979	575	1123	1301																								
Göteborg	1029	3080	2362	819	668	1145	1734	1550	1342	477	176	1067																							
Hamburg	447	2719	1780	1023	286	563	2014	1189	760	477	1486	485	582																						
Helsinki	1560	2539	2338	1063	475	1239	1834	1009	1431	1318	1236	1598	505	1113																					
İstanbul	2756	1145	2990	3653	2223	2706	690	1341	2911	3537	3657	2314	2891	2530	2350																				
København	965	2782	2090	1103	370	1081	2077	1252	1278	752	479	795	284	518	803	2593																			
Köln	256	2684	1376	1427	566	198	1983	1158	390	938	1116	180	986	404	1517	2499	714																		
Lisboa	2331	4460	1268	3723	2869	3141	3917	3222	2069	2617	2795	2400	3282	2700	3817	4342	3014	2339																	
London	480	3200	1387	458	1074	333	2591	1766	118	430	608	693	122	878	1991	3107	1188	508	2187																
Luxembourg	406	2661	1190	1613	749	209	2052	1227	424	972	1150	240	1172	590	1703	2472	900	186	2160	542															
Madrid	1790	3809	617	3183	2364	1600	3262	2622	1528	1634	2254	1930	2742	2160	3276	3589	2473	1798	651	1646	1628														
Marseille	1210	2683	509	2435	1541	1030	2154	1505	1063	1588	1789	1023	1994	1412	2525	2479	1722	1006	1777	1182	822	1126													
Milano	1085	2182	1038	2141	1060	890	1668	992	1072	1620	1798	683	1700	1118	1535	1993	1428	868	2315	1190	679	1655	538												
Moskva	2457	2930	3655	2223	1821	2585	1761	2099	2800	3348	3526	2312	1665	2115	1160	2605	2325	2387	4875	2918	2852	4224	3270	3027											
München	839	2106	1340	1788	594	789	1497	672	994	1524	1720	398	1347	765	1069	1907	969	580	2545	1094	555	2010	1011	473	2305										
Oslo	1347	3372	2680	503	960	1463	2667	1842	1660	773	729	1385	316	900	697	3089	590	1304	3604	1778	1490	3063	2312	2018	1823	1559									
Paris	510	2917	988	1922	1051	320	2307	1482	281	829	1007	591	1481	899	2012	2727	1209	495	1821	399	351	1280	782	857	2903	810	1799								
Praha	950	2067	1750	1675	345	888	1362	537	1097	1635	1816	512	1013	652	770	1878	715	690	2870	1205	753	2329	1399	853	1853	388	1305	1061							
Roma	1691	1140	1385	2706	1502	1520	1904	1263	1678	2226	2404	1289	2265	1683	1977	2237	1993	1474	2653	1796	1285	2002	876	606	3362	918	2583	1389	1309						
Sevilla	2347	4223	1031	3736	2894	2150	3709	3010	2078	2626	2804	2344	3295	2713	3826	4034	3023	2318	401	2196	2178	550	1540	2078	4774	2371	3613	1830	2781	2446					
Sofiya	2206	828	2453	3103	1673	2156	391	790	2361	2891	3087	1764	2341	1980	1800	550	2043	1949	3706	2461	1922	3037	1929	1443	2252	1367	2632	2177	1328	1687	3484				
Stockholm	1393	3418	2726	1063	1006	1509	2713	1888	1673	2254	1069	1431	505	946	167	3185	590	1350	3650	1824	1536	3109	2358	2064	1228	1600	530	1845	1351	2629	3659	2679			
Warszawa	1256	2128	2366	1909	606	1350	1473	648	1542	2110	2268	1136	1274	886	361	1989	956	1152	3480	1680	1345	2960	2015	1469	1245	996	1506	1677	616	1853	3397	1439	1612		
Wien	1168	1772	1856	1970	640	1114	1067	242	1308	1954	2034	731	1308	947	1088	1583	1010	916	3100	1524	993	2473	1353	818	2137	430	1600	1240	295	1126	2876	1033	1646	727	
Zürich	816	2426	1030	1938	863	619	1810	985	804	1352	1530	464	1497	915	2164	2323	1433	589	2296	922	410	1647	699	292	2552	303	1815	592	691	898	2061	1173	1861	1307	743

km

RUSSIA
ROSSIYA

Moscow
Moskva

Kiev
Kyyiv

UKRAINE
UKRAINA

MOLDOVA

İstanbul

Ankara

186   187

TURKEY
TÜRKIYE

İzmir

Antalya

188   189

181

Nicosia   CYPRUS
KYPROS

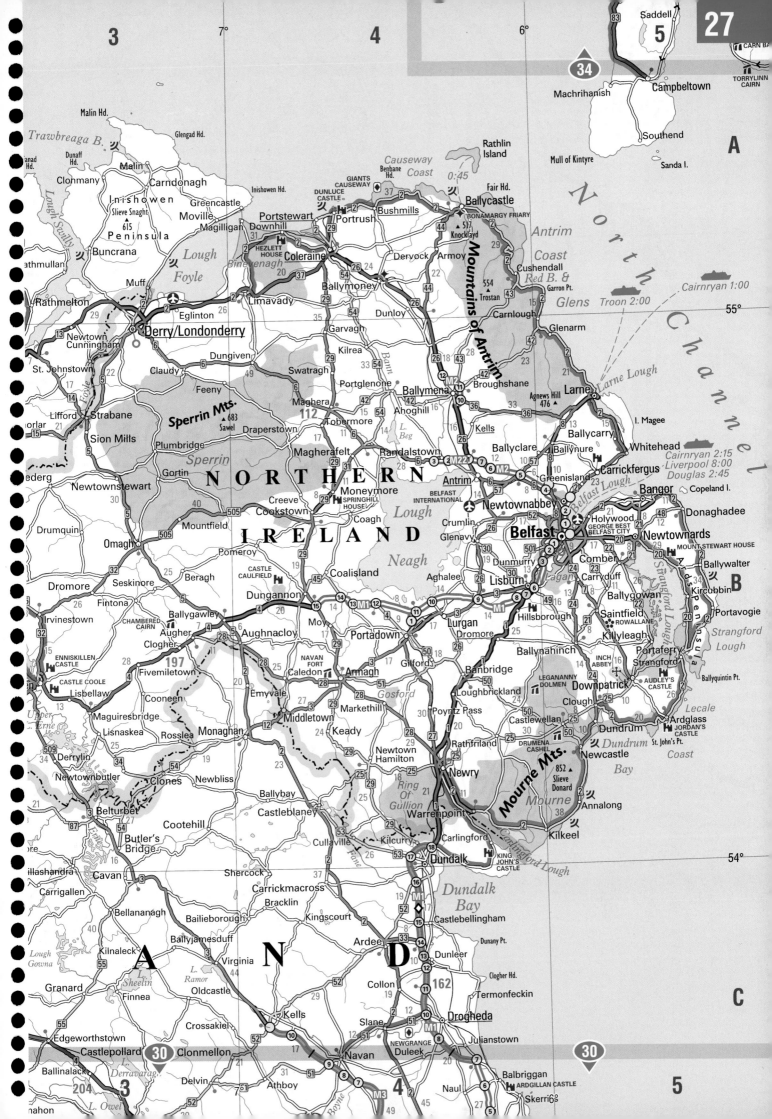

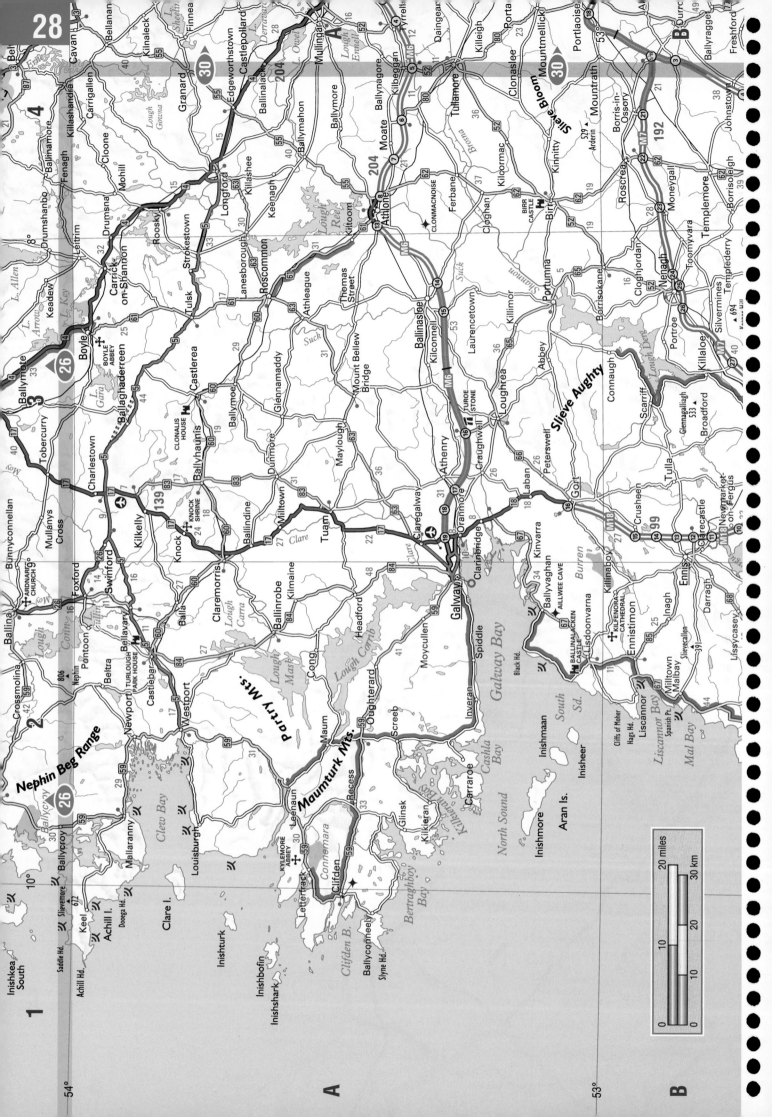

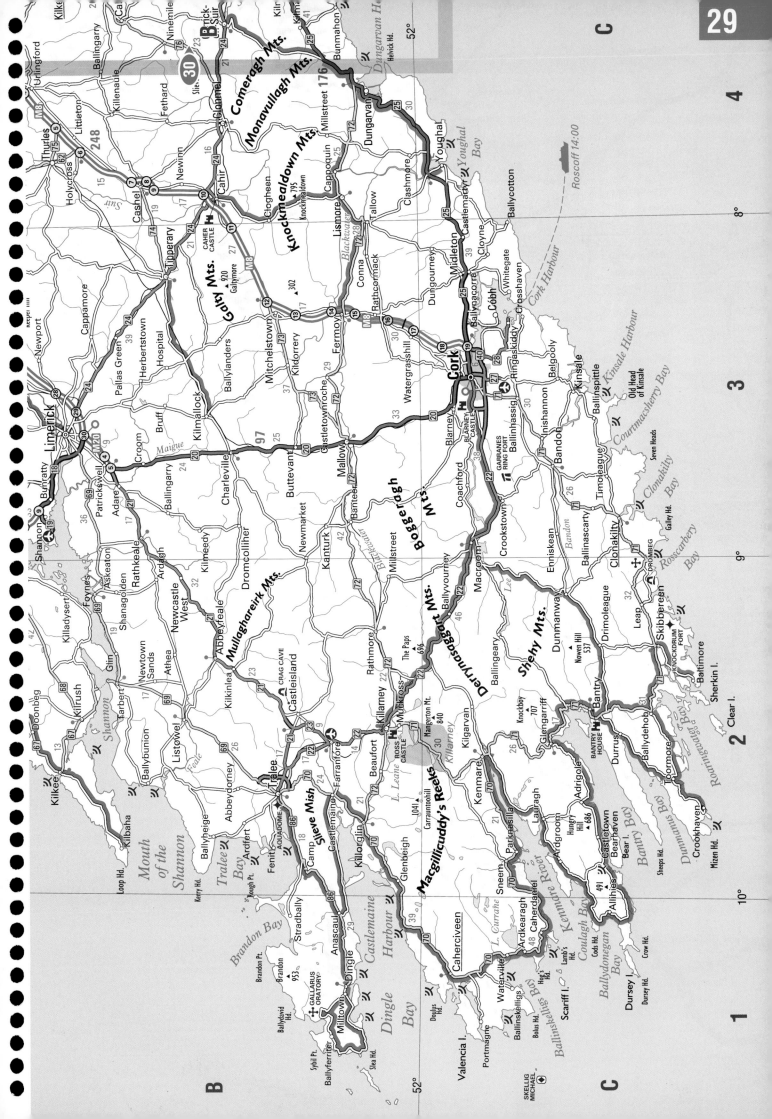

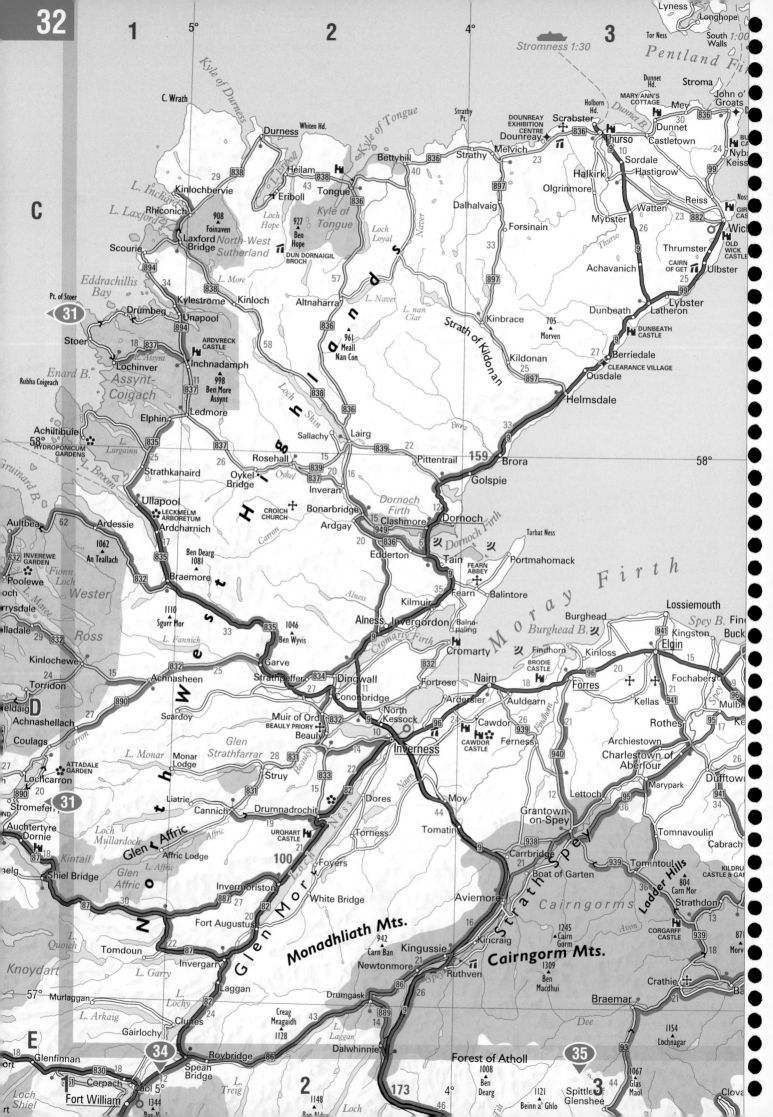

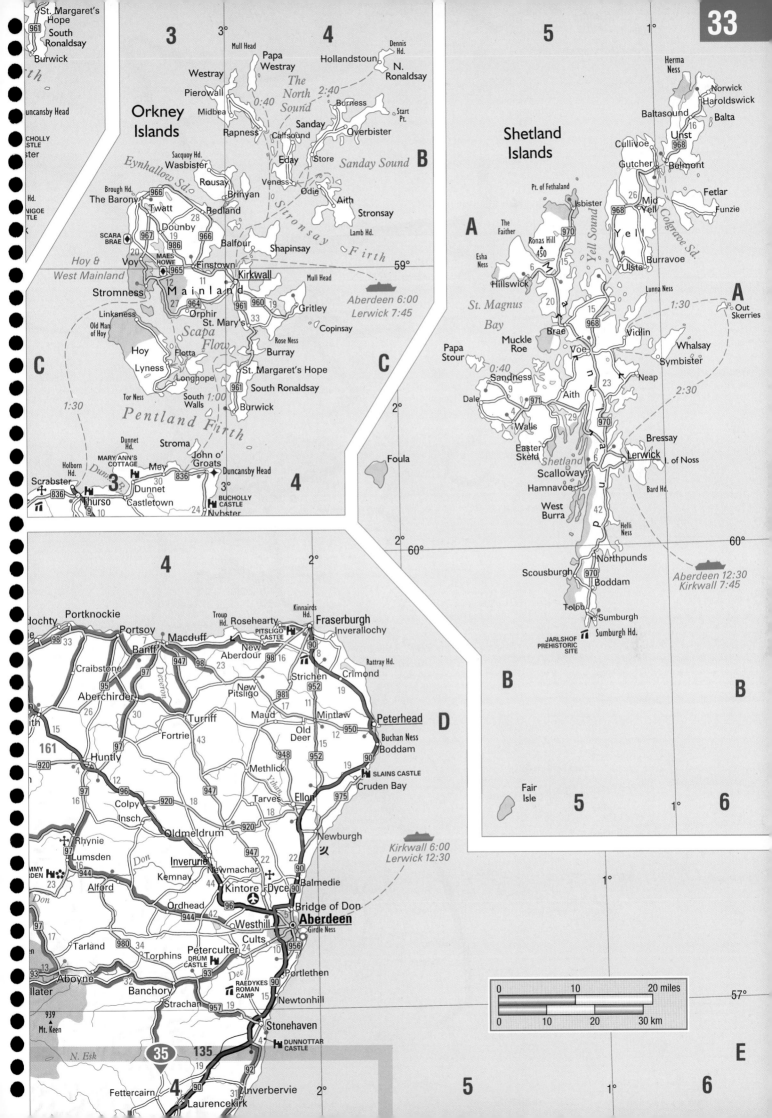

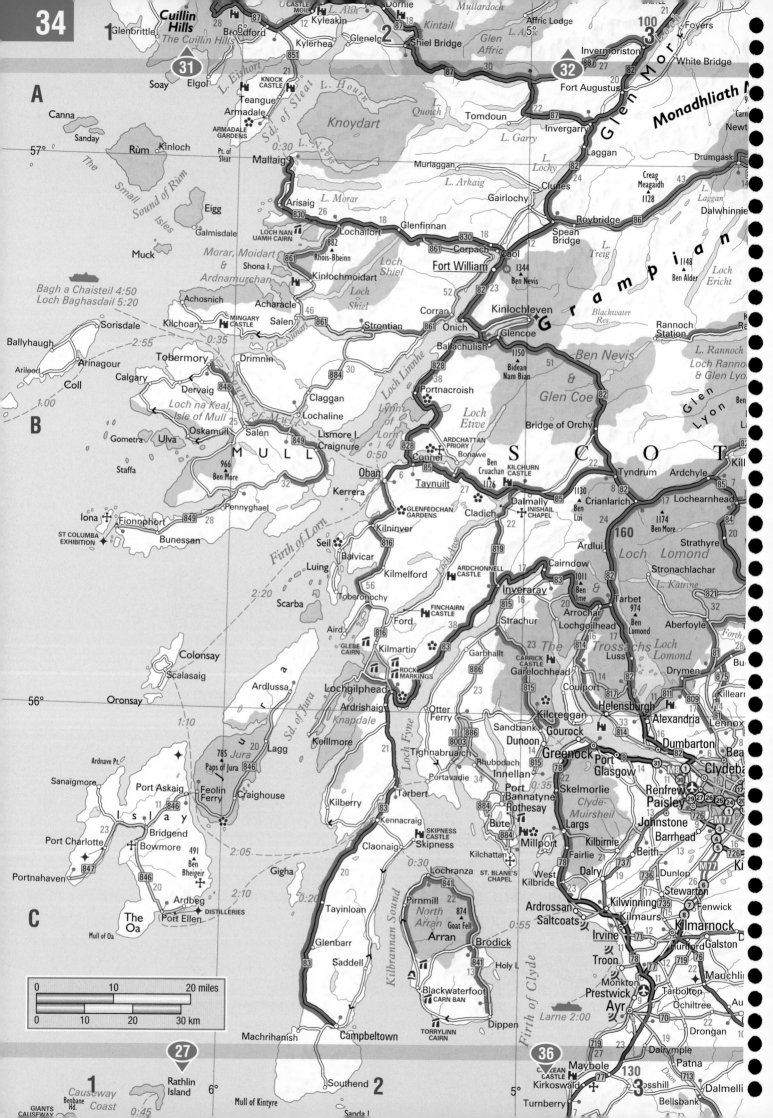

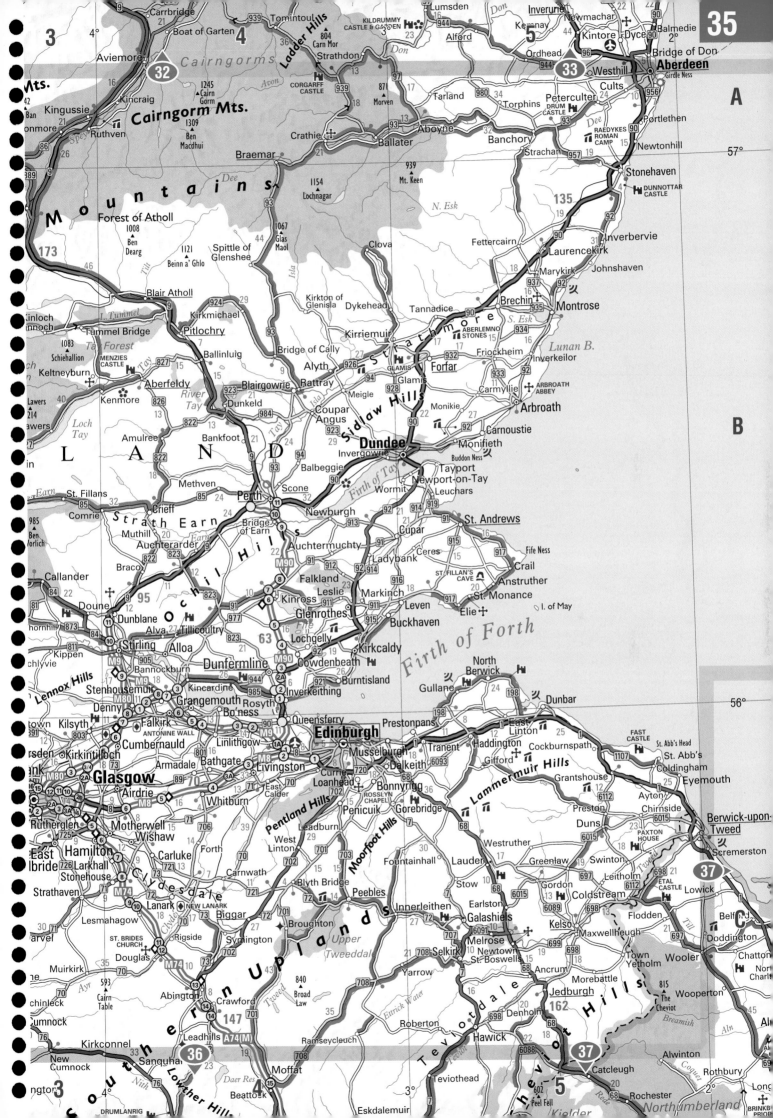

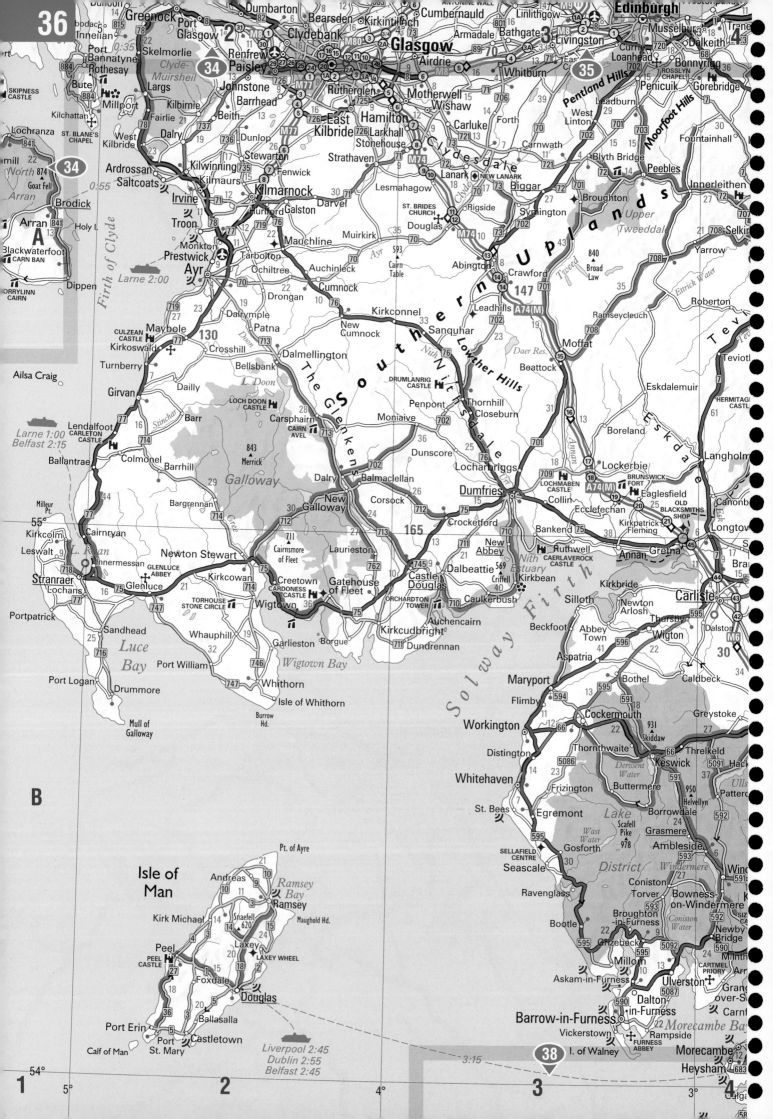

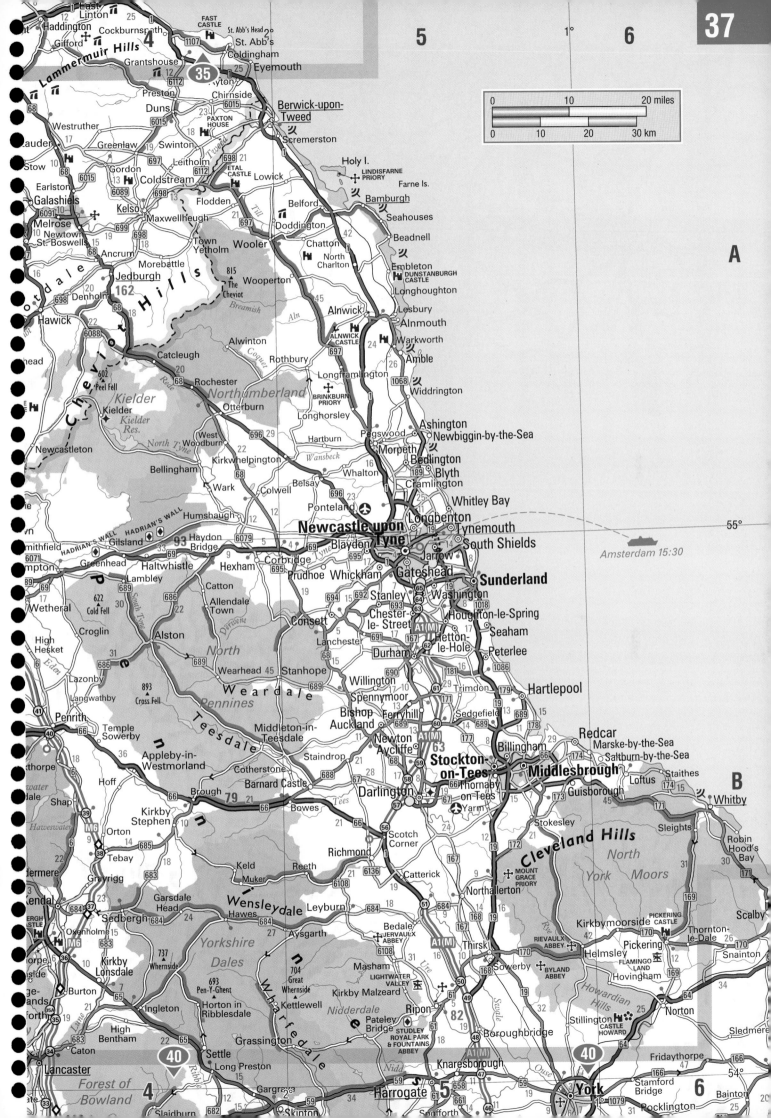

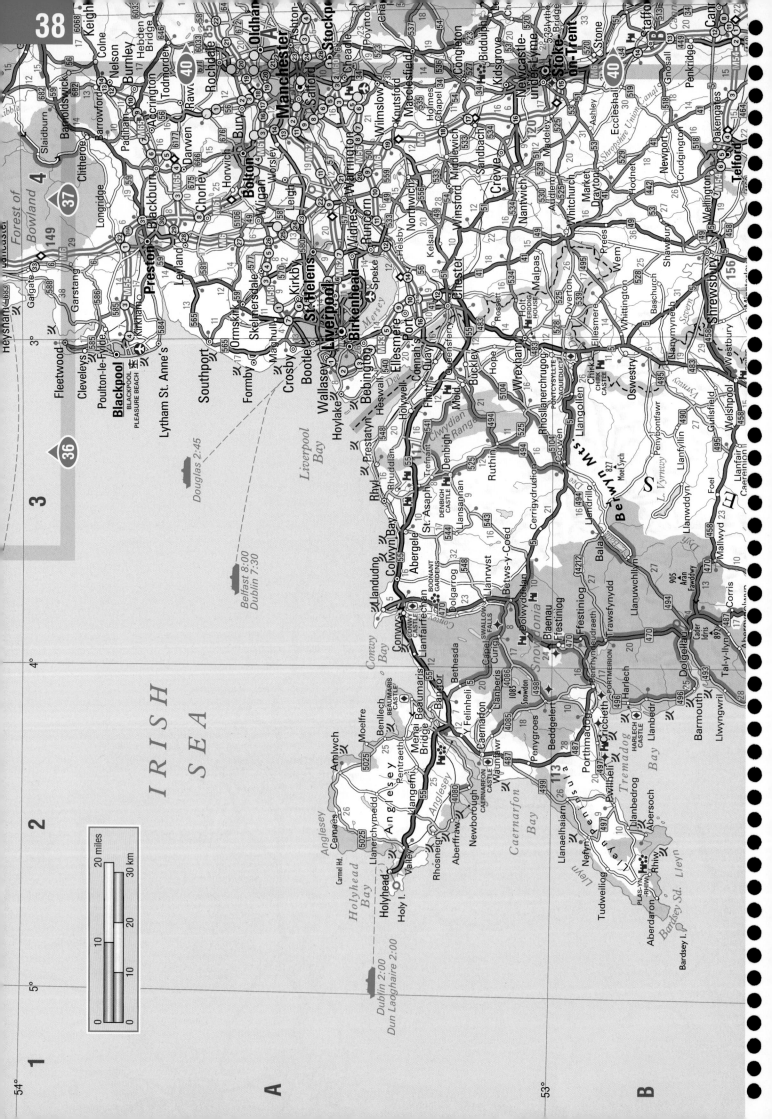

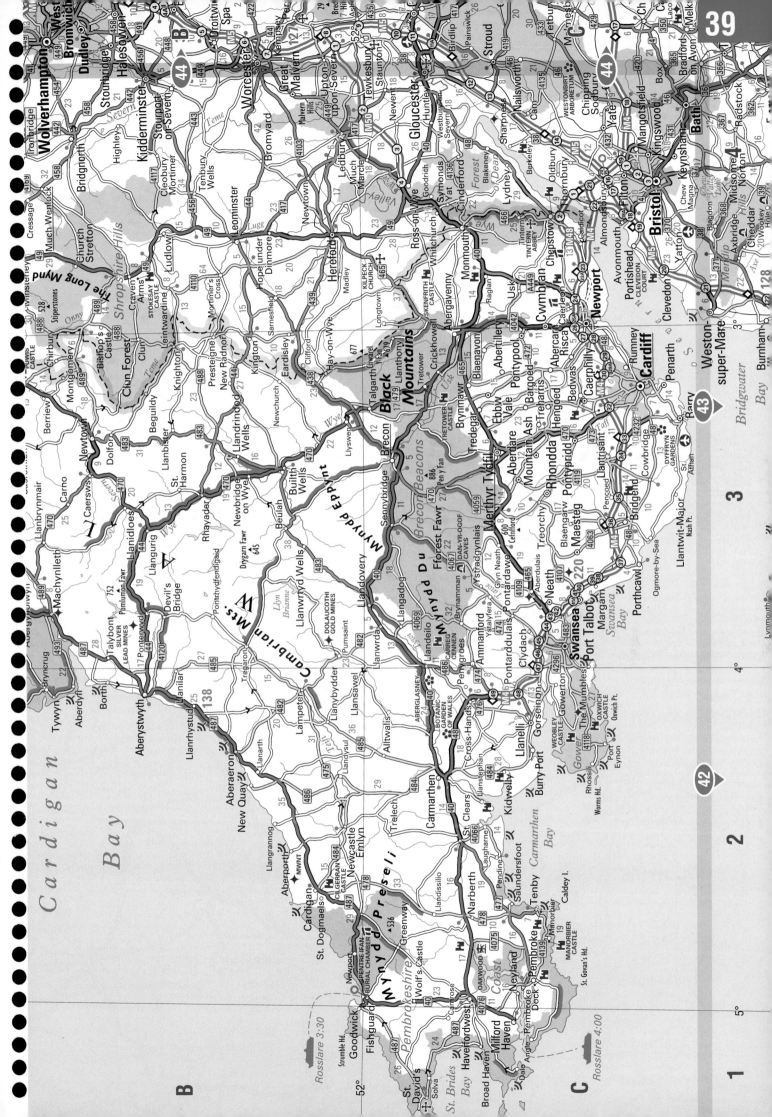

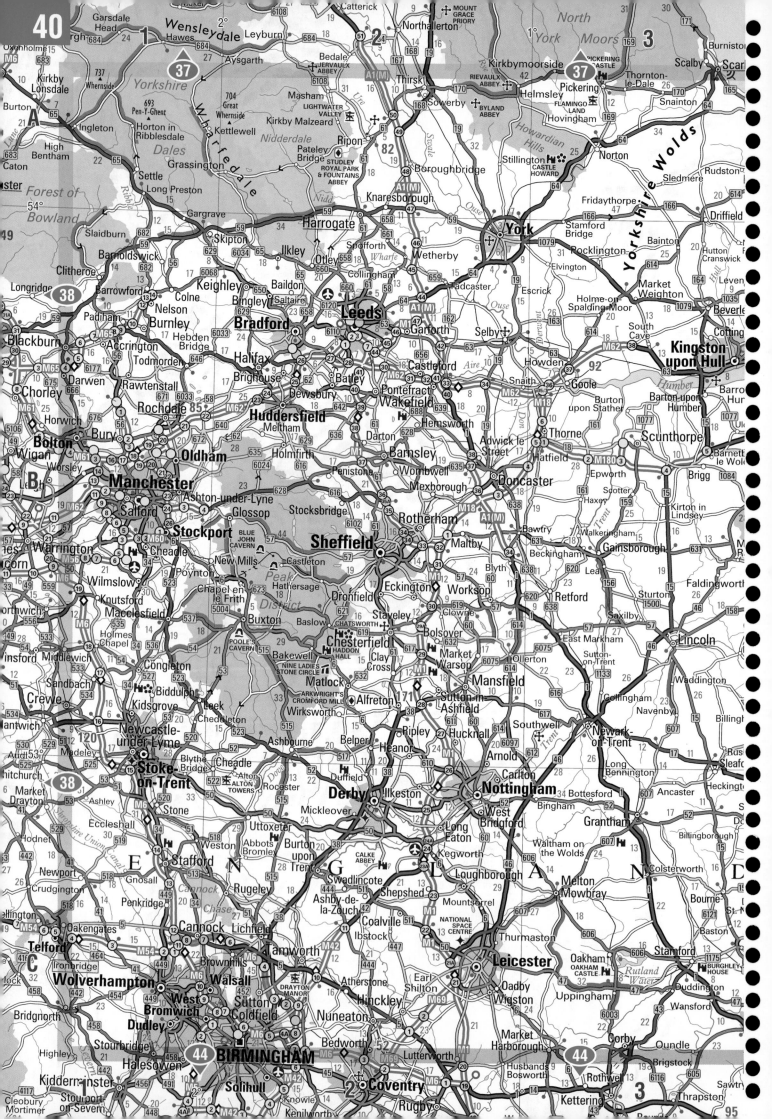

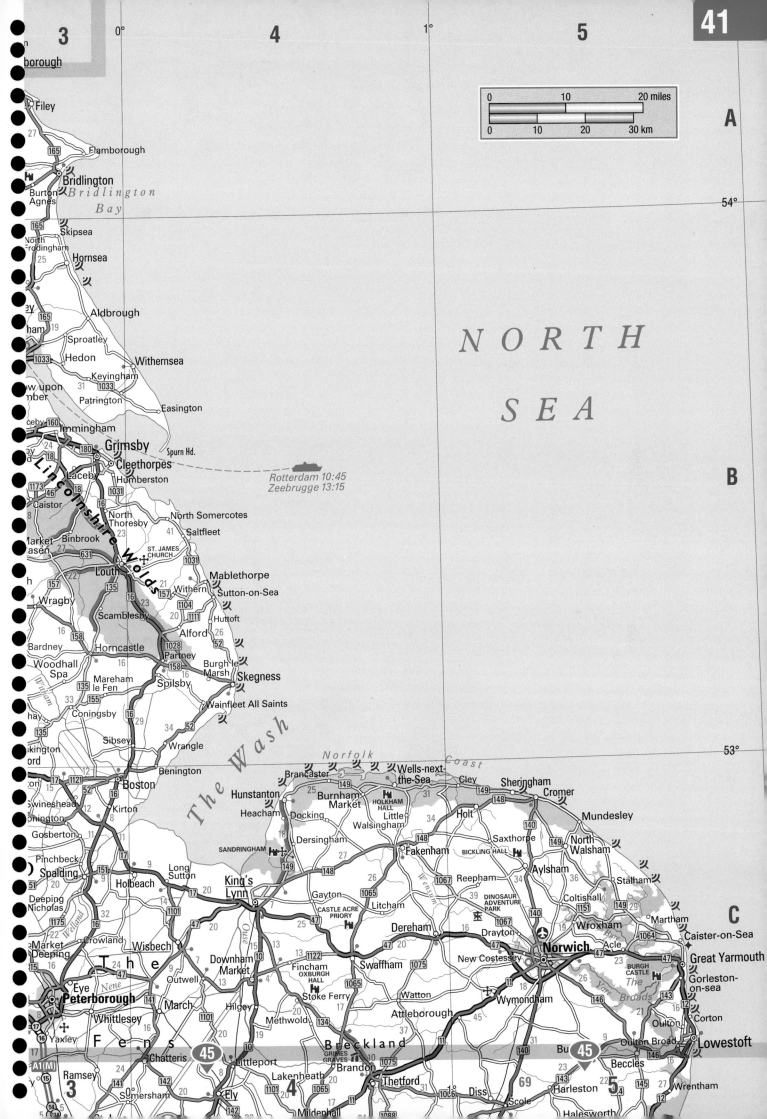

3 0° **4** 1° **5**

A

B

C

N O R T H

S E A

*Bridlington
Bay*

Filey
Flamborough
27
165
Bridlington
Burton
Agnes

165
Skipsea
North
Frodingham
25
Hornsea

165
Aldbrough
ham 19
Sproatley
1033
Hedon
Withernsea
w upon
nber
31
1033
Keyingham
Patrington
Easington
aceby
160
Immingham
Spurn Hd.
24
18
180
Grimsby
Cleethorpes
Laceby
Humberston
1173
46
18
1031
Caistor
16
North
Somercotes
16
North
Thoresby
Saltfleet
Market
asen
27
Binbrook
23
41
631
ST. JAMES
CHURCH.
1031
h
157
22
Louth
135
Mablethorpe
Wragby
21
Withern
Sutton-on-Sea
157
16
23
1104
Scamblesby
20
1111
Huttoft
16
158
Alford
26
Bardney
135
52
Woodhall
Spa
Horncastle
16
Partney
1028
158
16
Mareham
le Fen
Spilsby
Burgh le
Marsh
William
135
155
Skegness
hay
33
Coningsby
16
29
34
52
Wainfleet All Saints
135
Sibsey
Wrangle
kington
ord
Benington

The Wash

Norfolk   Coast

53°

Rotterdam 10:45
Zeebrugge 13:15

ton
17
1121
Boston
12
15
Brancaster
Wells-next-
the-Sea
Cley
Sheringham
52
16
Hunstanton
149
Burnham
Market
31
149
Cromer
wineshead
12
Kirton
8
Heacham
25
HOLKHAM
HALL
148
onington
Docking
Little
Walsingham
34
Holt
Mundesley
Gosberton
18
Dersingham
148
140
Pinchbeck
SANDRINGHAM
27
Saxthorpe
149
North
Walsham
Spalding
151
9
Long
Sutton
149
148
Fakenham
BICKLING HALL
Aylsham
51
9
Holbeach
King's
Lynn
26
Reepham
34
36
Coltishall
Stalham
Deeping
Nicholas
32
1101
17
20
9
7
Gayton
1065
39
DINOSAUR
ADVENTURE
PARK
1067
140
1151
149
29
1175
16
14
CASTLE ACRE
PRIORY
Litcham
1067
Wroxham
1064
Martham
Market
Deeping
22
Crowland
Wisbech
20
25
47
Dereham
Drayton
47
Acle
47
Great Yarmouth
Caister-on-Sea
15
24
Downham
Market
10
13
1122
Swaffham
47
20
Norwich
BURGH
CASTLE
47
Gorleston-
on-sea
Eye
Nene
141
Outwell
13
Fincham
OXBURGH
HALL
1075
New Costessey
Yare
The
Broads
143
Peterborough
March
Hilgey
Methwold
1065
Stoke Ferry
Watton
Wymondham
146
21
Oulton
Corton
16
12
8
Whittlesey
1101
134
Attleborough
45
140
Bu
Oulton Broad
Lowestoft
17
Yaxley
16
F e n s
45
GRIMES
GRAVES
10
1075
45
Beccles
146
A1(M)
Ramsey
142
Chatteris
Littleport
Brandon
Thetford
Breckland
69
Harleston
145
27
Wrentham
15
24
141
20
8
Lakenheath
1101
1065
31
Diss
5
4
Somersham
142
Ely
17
Scole
Mildenhall
1088
Halesworth

Lincolnshire Wolds

0   10   20 miles

0   10   20   30 km

54°

The

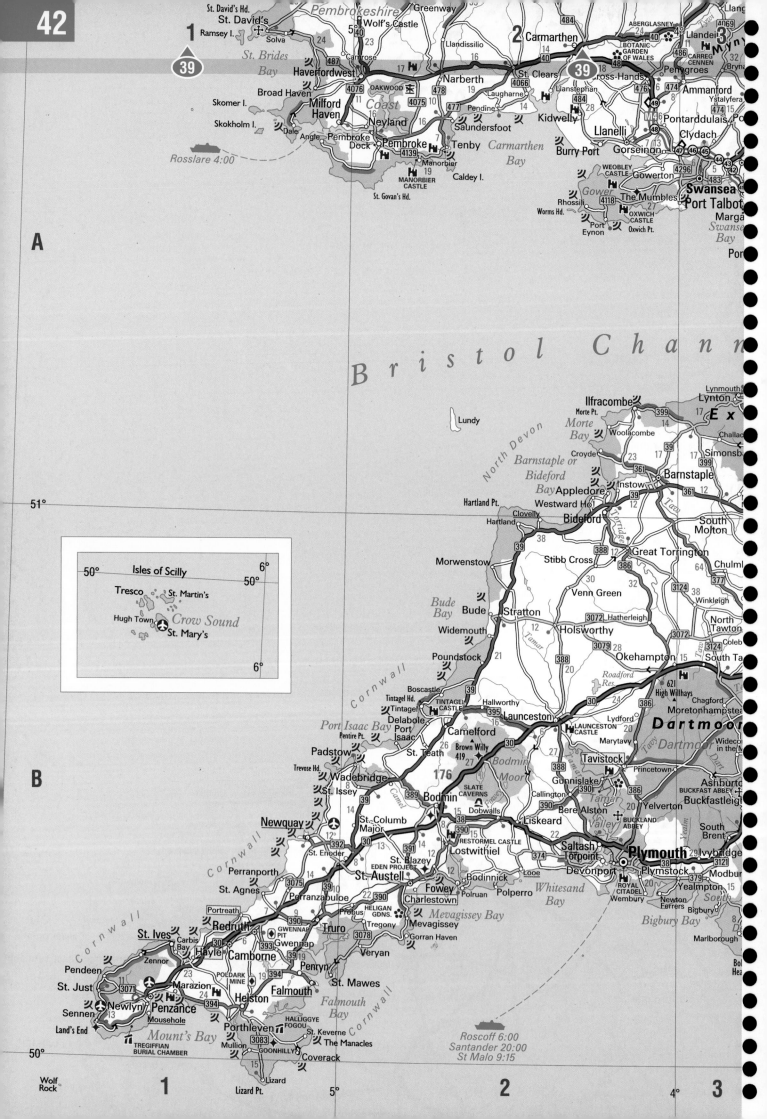

St. David's Hd.
St. David's
Ramsey I.
Solva
St. Brides Bay
Pembrokeshire
Greenway
Wolf's Castle
Camrose
Haverfordwest
Broad Haven
Milford Haven
Skomer I.
Skokholm I.
Dale
Angle
Pembroke Dock
Pembroke
Rosslare 4:00
Manorbier
MANORBIER CASTLE
St. Govan's Hd.
Caldey I.

Llandissilio
Narberth
St. Clears
Laugharne
Pendine
Saundersfoot
Tenby
Carmarthen Bay

Carmarthen
BOTANIC GARDEN OF WALES
ABERGLASNEY
Llandei
Mynydd
Penygroes
Cross-Hands
Ammanford
Ystalyfera
Pontarddulais
Llanstephan
Kidwelly
Burry Port
Llanelli
Gorseinon
Clydach

CARREG CENNEN

WEOBLEY CASTLE
Gowerton
Gower
Rhossili
The Mumbles
OXWICH CASTLE
Port Eynon
Oxwich Pt.
Worms Hd.
Swansea
Port Talbot
Marga
Swansea Bay
Por

A

Bristol Chann

Lundy

North Devon
Morte Bay
Ilfracombe
Morte Pt.
Woolacombe
Croyde
Barnstaple or Bideford Bay
Appledore
Instow
Westward Ho!
Bideford
Hartland Pt.
Clovelly
Hartland
Morwenstow

Lynmouth
Lynton
Ex
Challac
Simonsb
Barnstaple
South Molton
Chulml
Stibb Cross
Great Torrington
Venn Green
Winkleigh
North Tawton
Holsworthy
Hatherleigh
Okehampton
South Ta
Colet

51°

Isles of Scilly
50°   6°
Tresco   St. Martin's
Hugh Town   Crow Sound
St. Mary's
6°

Cornwall
Bude Bay
Bude
Widemouth
Poundstock
Boscastle
Tintagel Hd.
Tintagel
TINTAGEL CASTLE
Delabole
Port Isaac
Hallworthy
Camelford
Brown Willy 419
Bodmin Moor
SLATE CAVERNS
Stratton

Tamar
High Willhays
Roadford Res.
621
Chagford
Moretonhampstea
Dartmoor
Lydford
Marytavy
Tavistock
Princetown
Widec in the
Launceston
LAUNCESTON CASTLE

Port Isaac Bay
Pentire Pt.
Padstow
Trevose Hd.
Wadebridge
St. Issey
Newquay
St. Columb Major
St. Enoder
Bodmin
Dobwalls
Liskeard
Callington
Gunnislake
Bere Alston
BUCKLAND ABBEY
Yelverton
Ashburt
BUCKFAST ABBEY
Buckfastleig
South Brent

B

176

RESTORMEL CASTLE
St. Blazey
EDEN PROJECT
Lostwithiel
Bodinnick
Looe
Polperro
Whitesand Bay

Saltash
Torpoint
Plymouth
Devonport
ROYAL CITADEL
Plymstock
Wembury
Newton Ferrers
Ivybridge
Modbur
Yealmpton
Bigbury
South
Bigbury Bay

Perranporth
St. Agnes
Perranzabuloe
HELIGAN GDNS.
Probus
Tregony
Fowey
Charlestown
St. Austell
Mevagissey
Gorran Haven
Mevagissey Bay

Portreath
Redruth
GWENNAP PIT
Gwennap
Truro
Veryan

Roscoff 6:00
Santander 20:00
St Malo 9:15

St. Ives
Carbis Bay
Hayle
Camborne
Penryn
Falmouth
St. Mawes
Falmouth Bay
Cornwall

Pendeen
Zennor
St. Just
POLDARK MINE
Marazion
Newlyn
Penzance
Helston
Sennen
Land's End
Mousehole
Porthleven
HALLIGGYE FOGOU
St. Keverne
The Manacles
Mount's Bay
TREGIFFIAN BURIAL CHAMBER
Mullion
GOONHILLY
Coverack

Wolf Rock
Lizard
Lizard Pt.

1   5°   **2**   4°   **3**

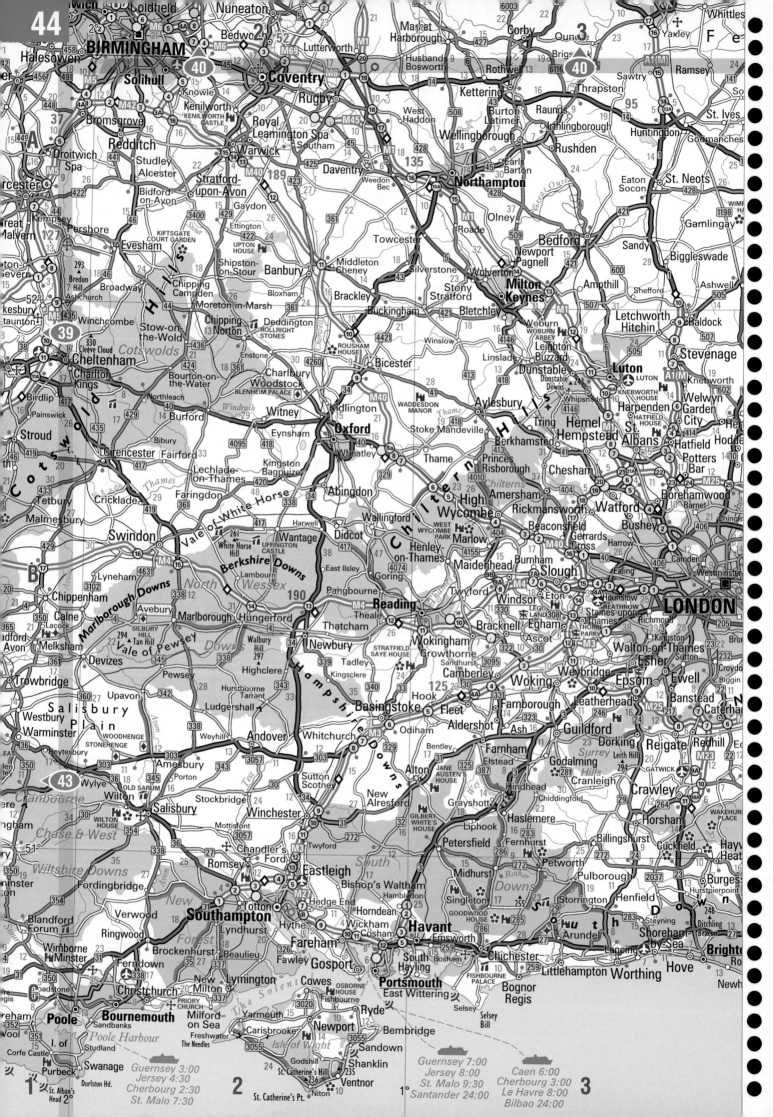

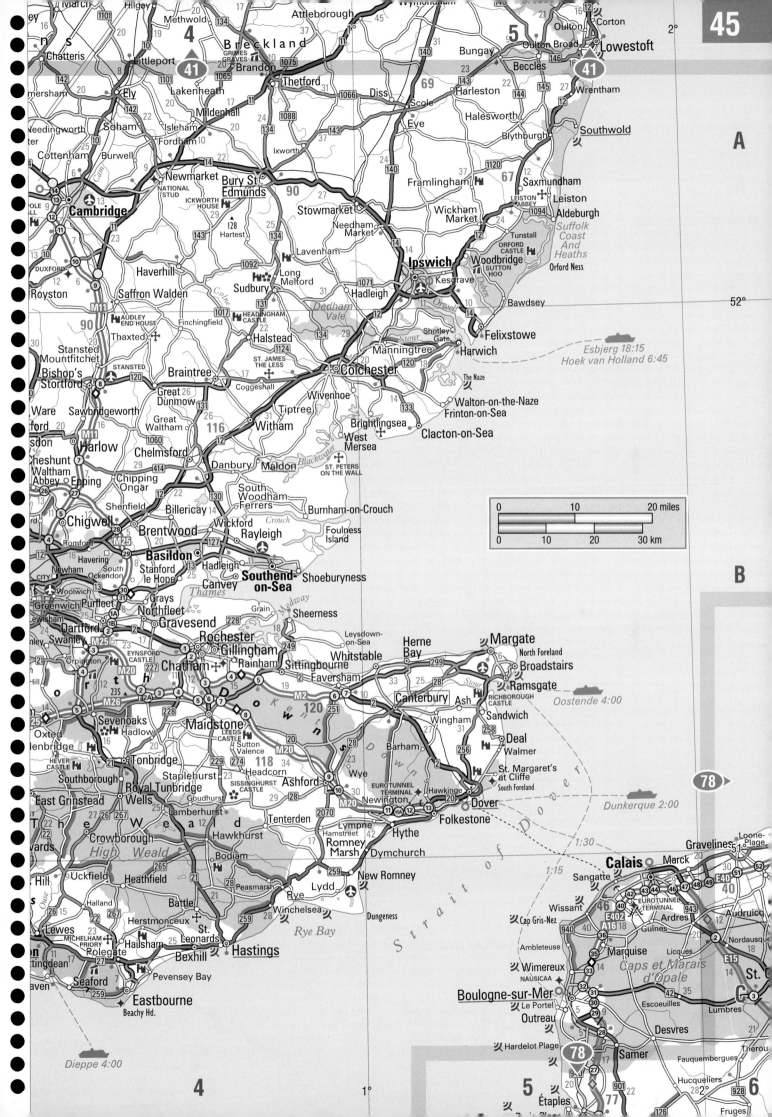

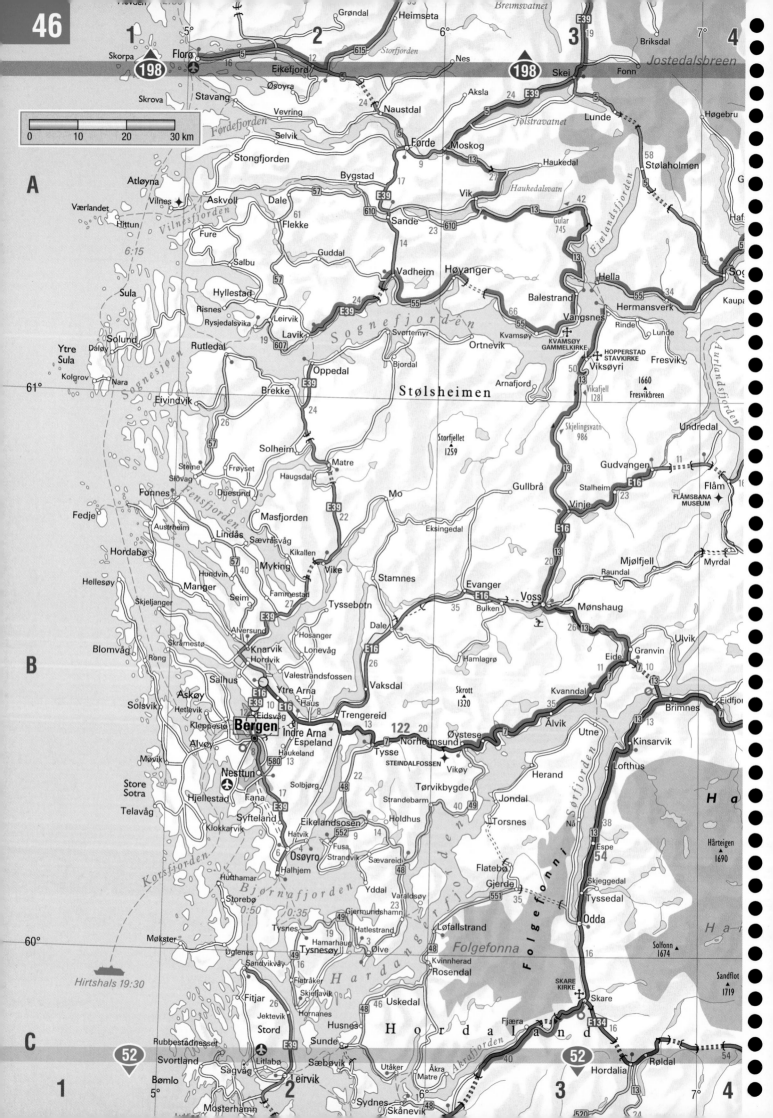

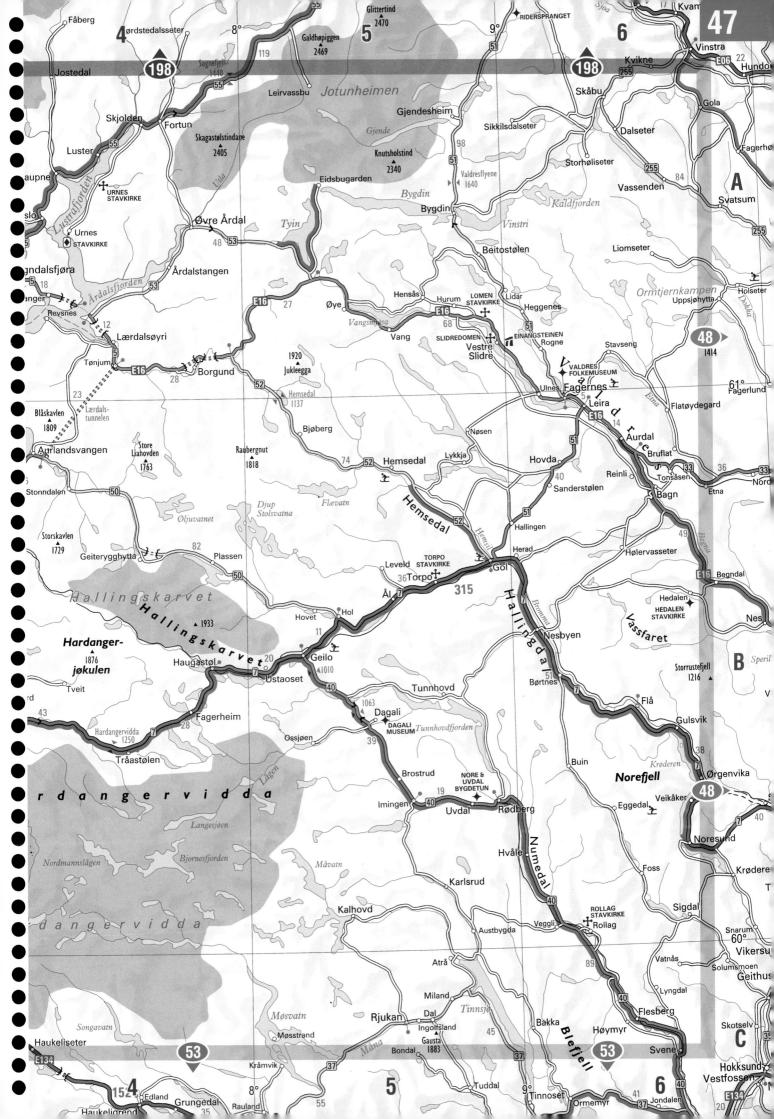

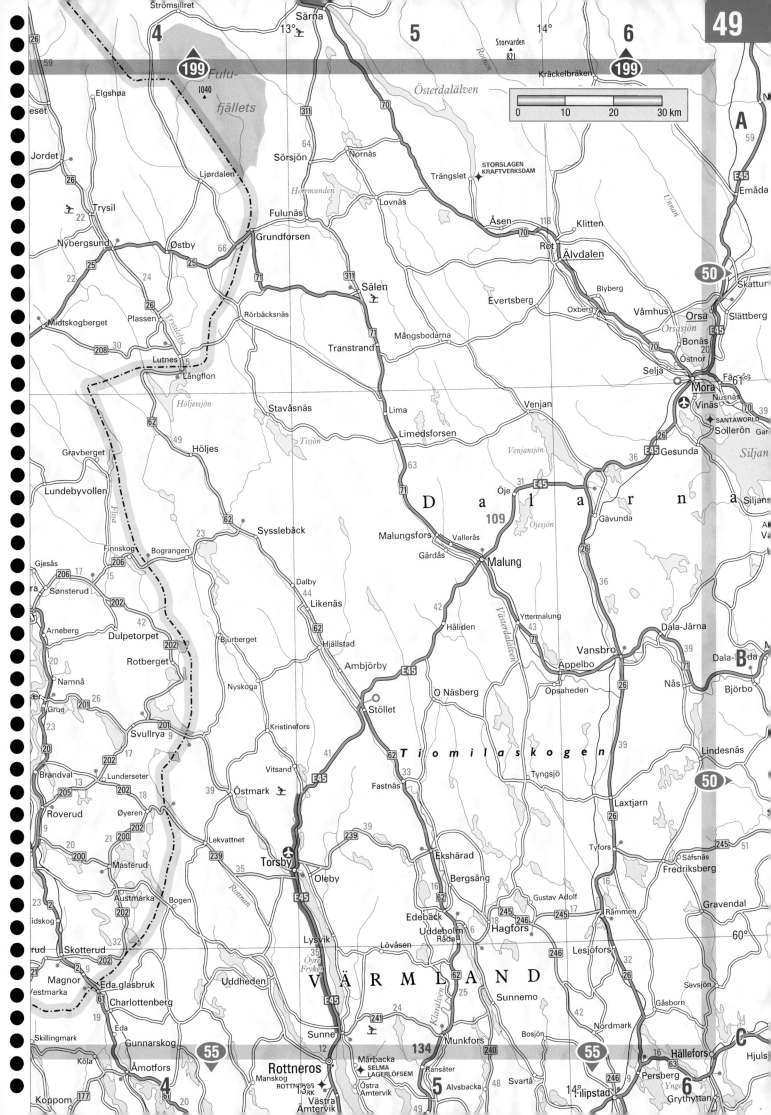

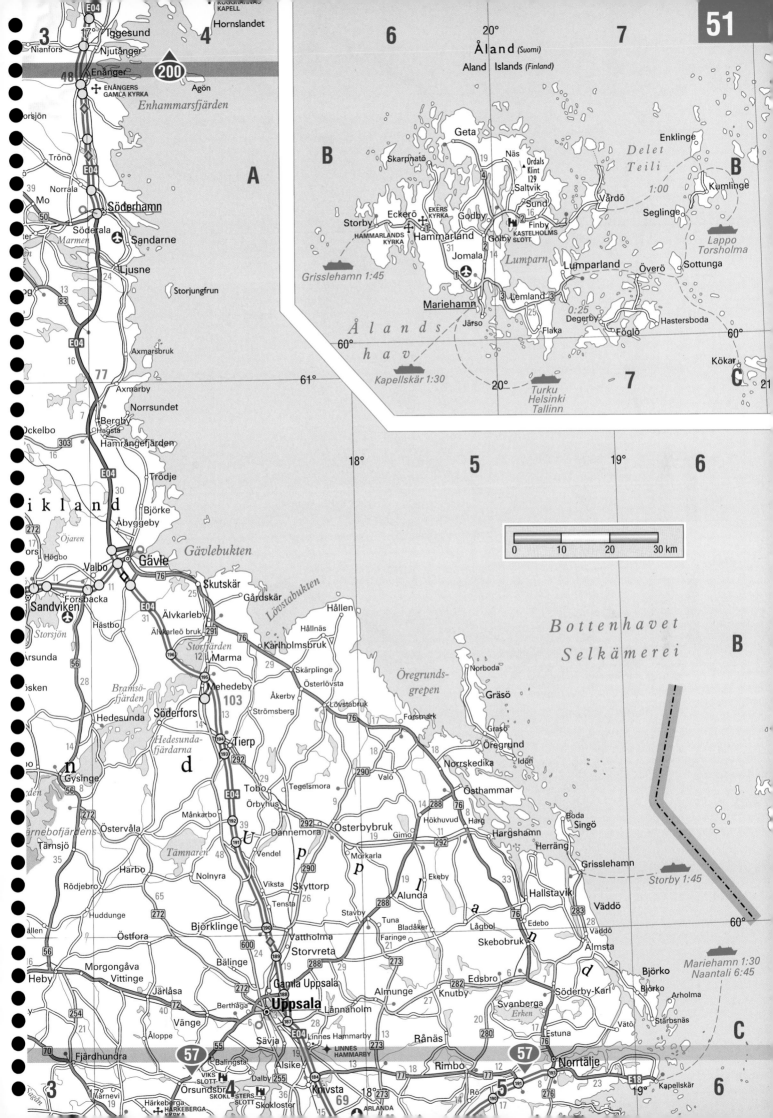

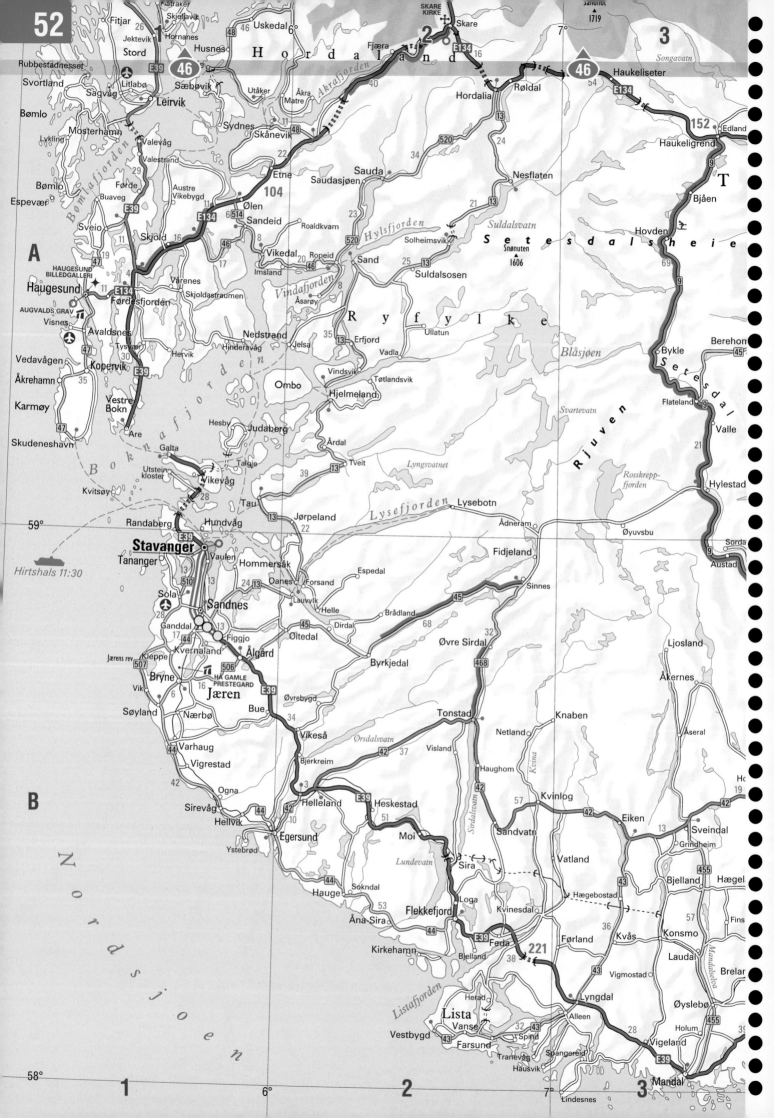

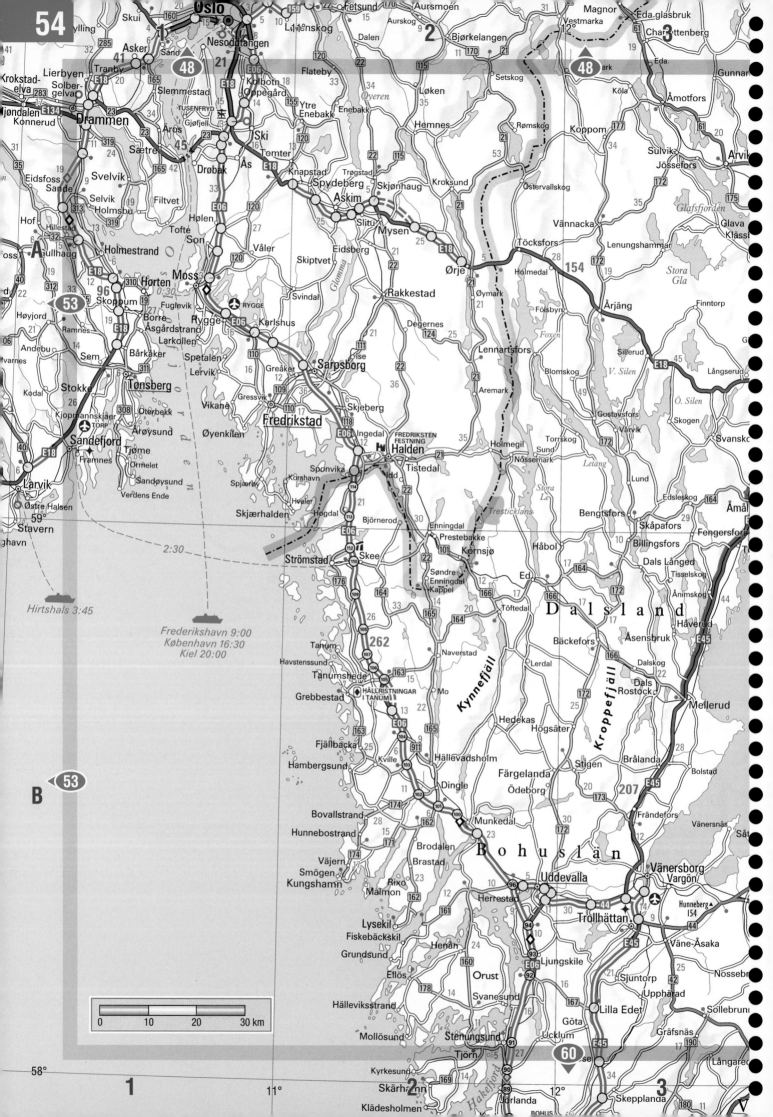

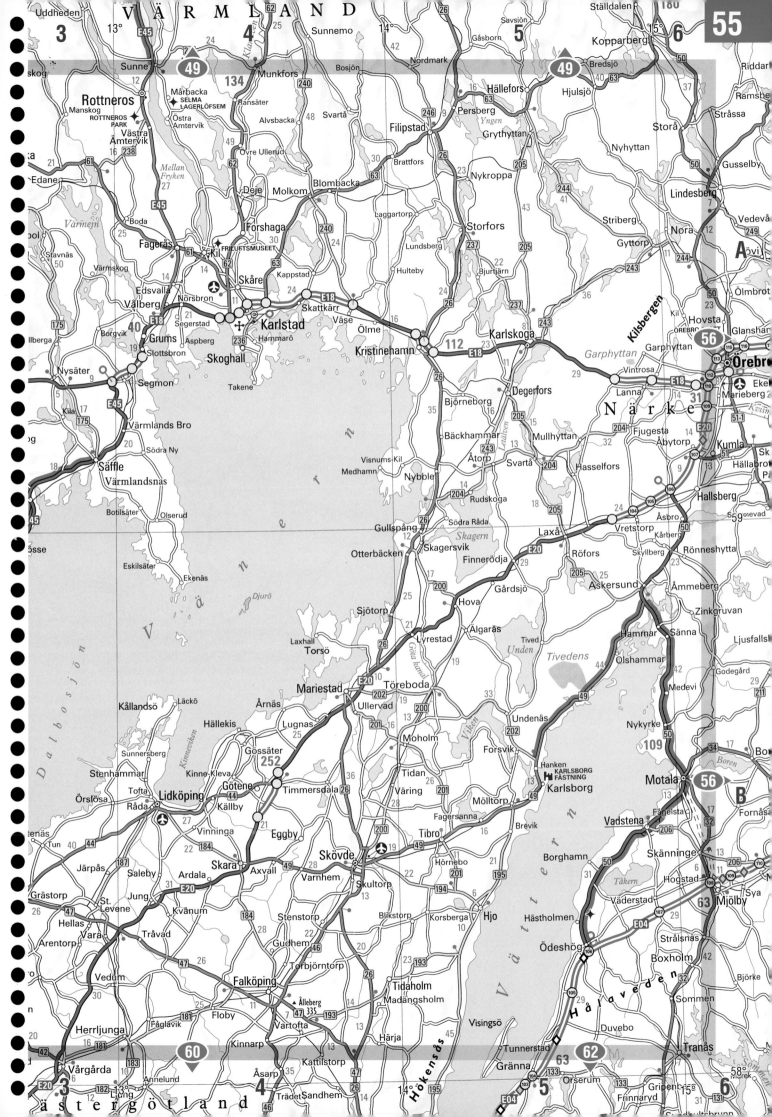

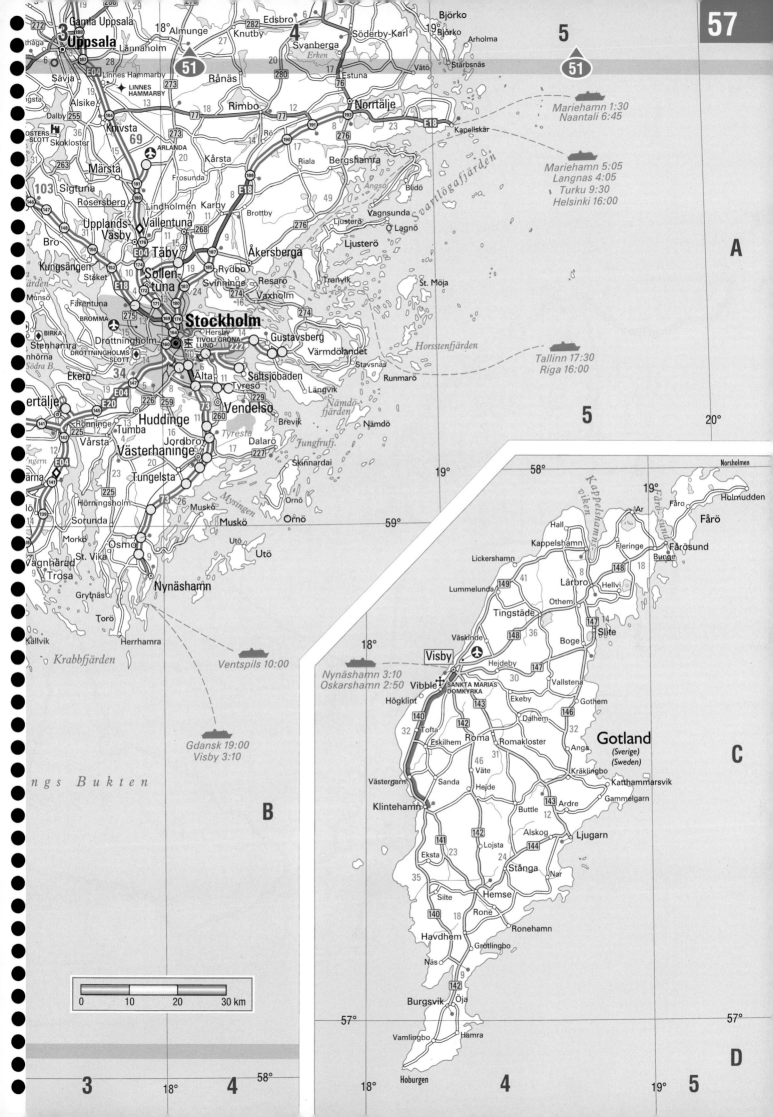

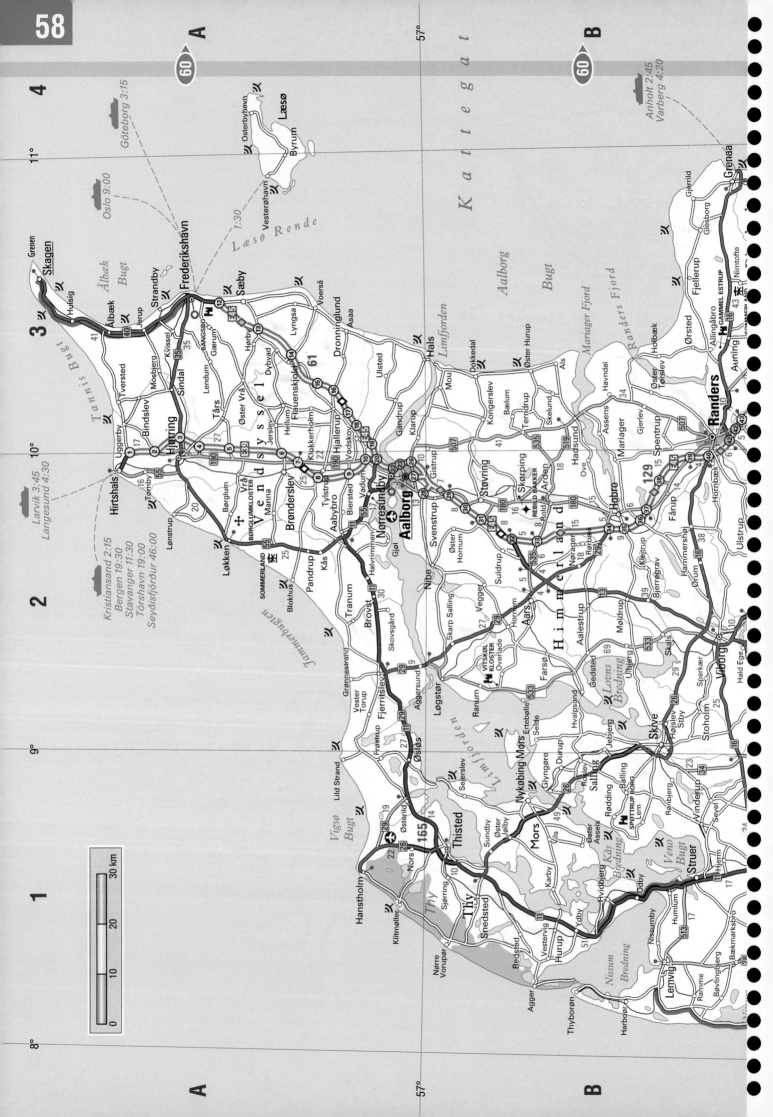

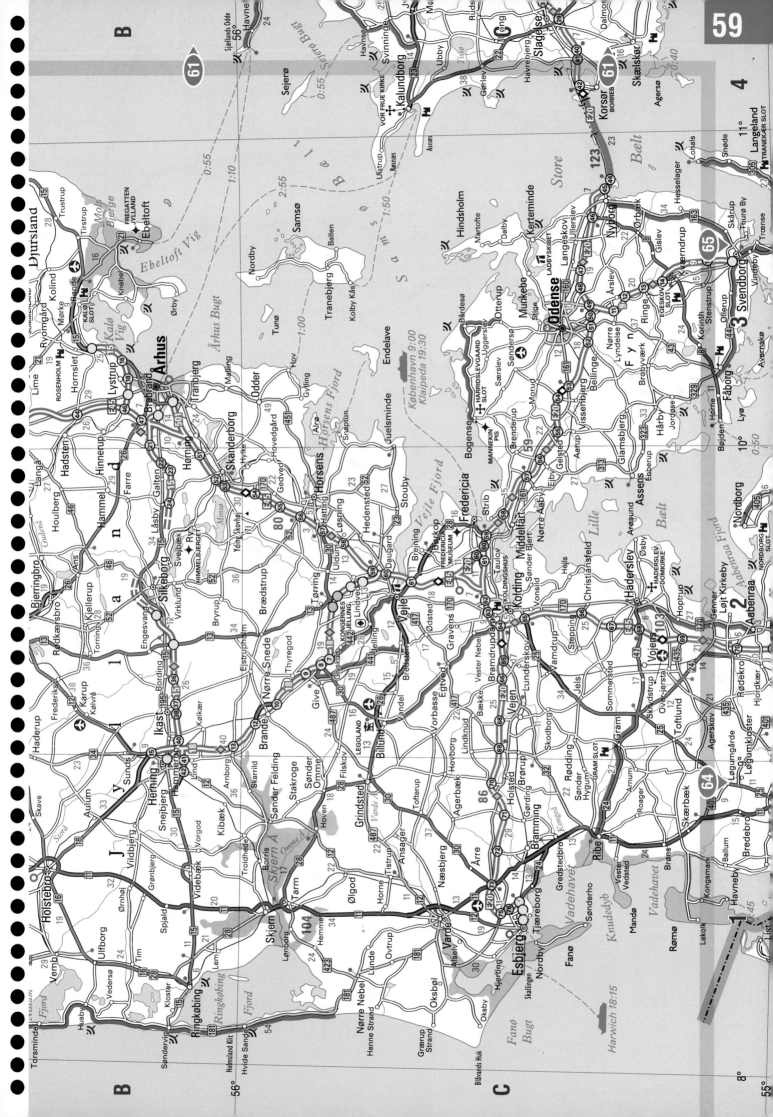

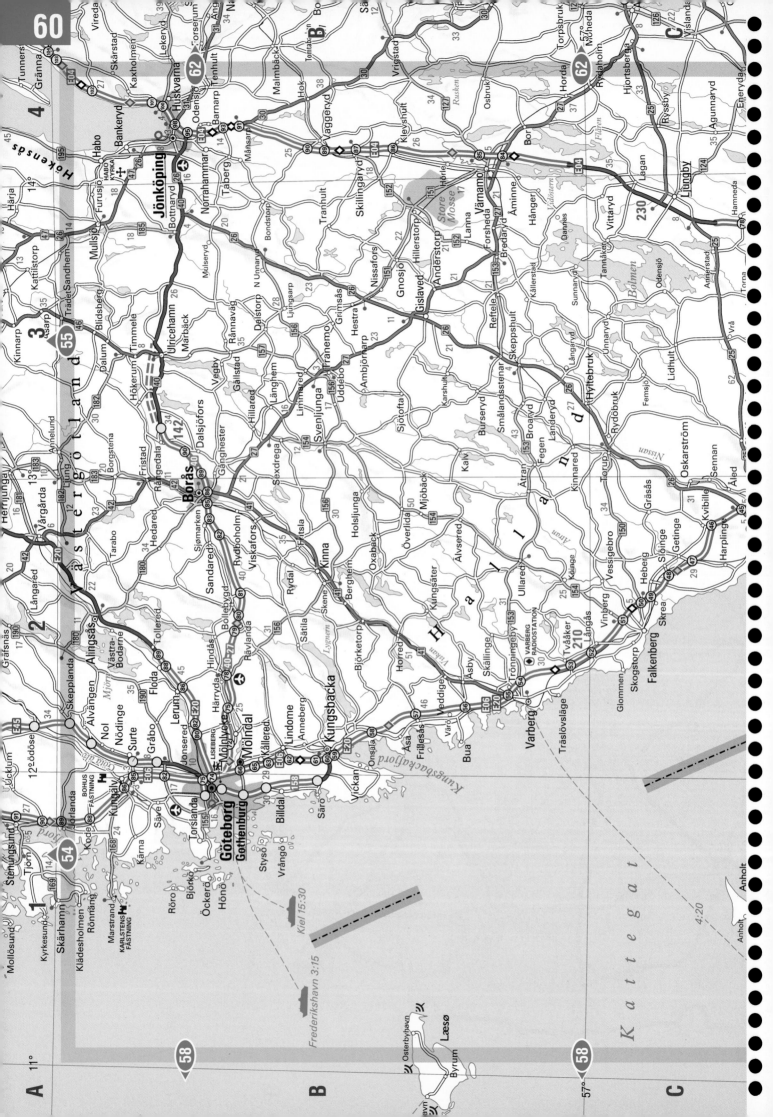

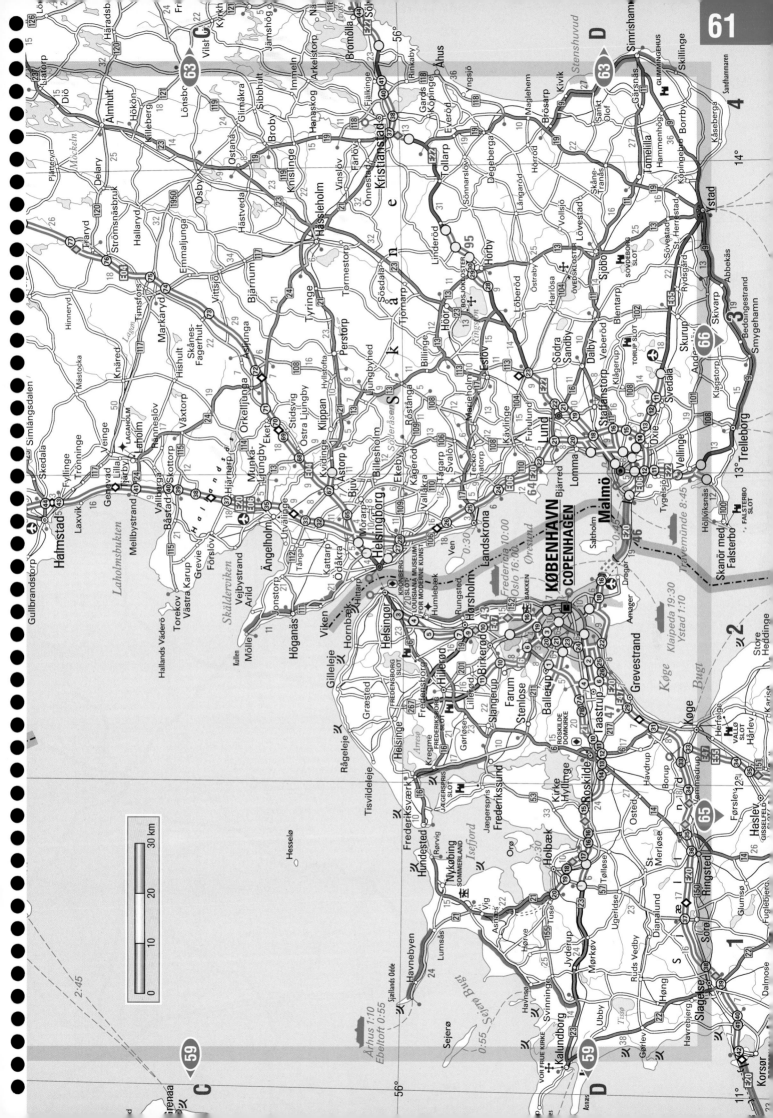

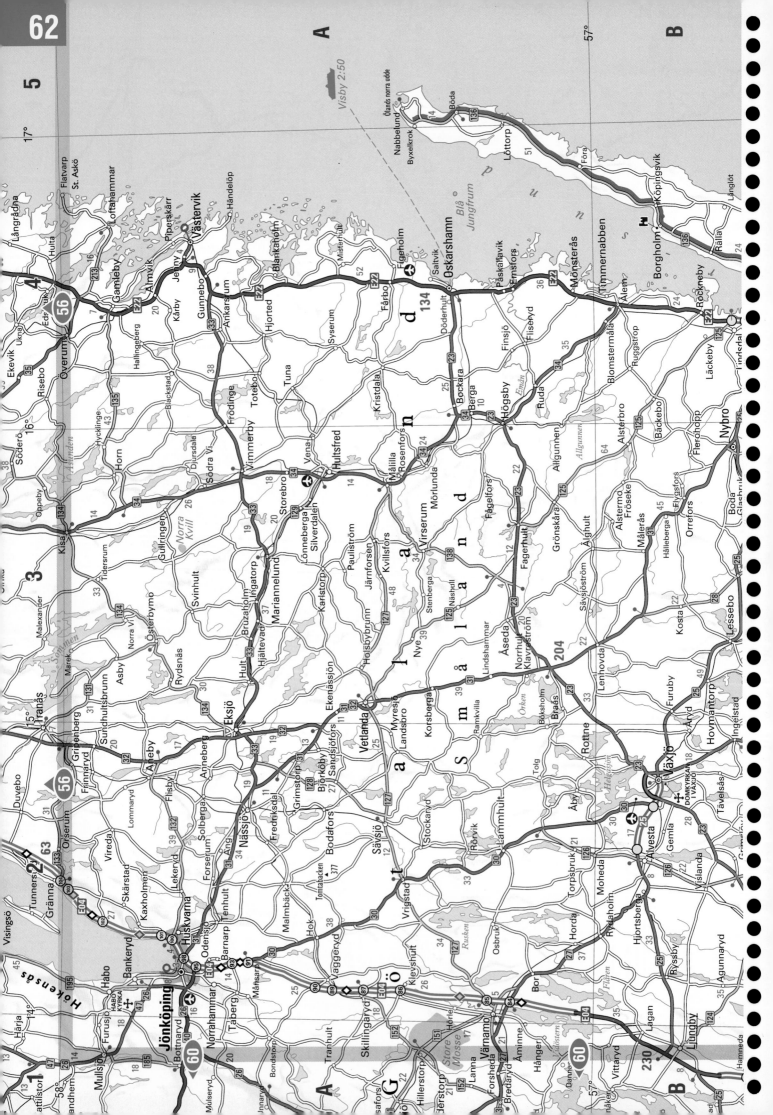

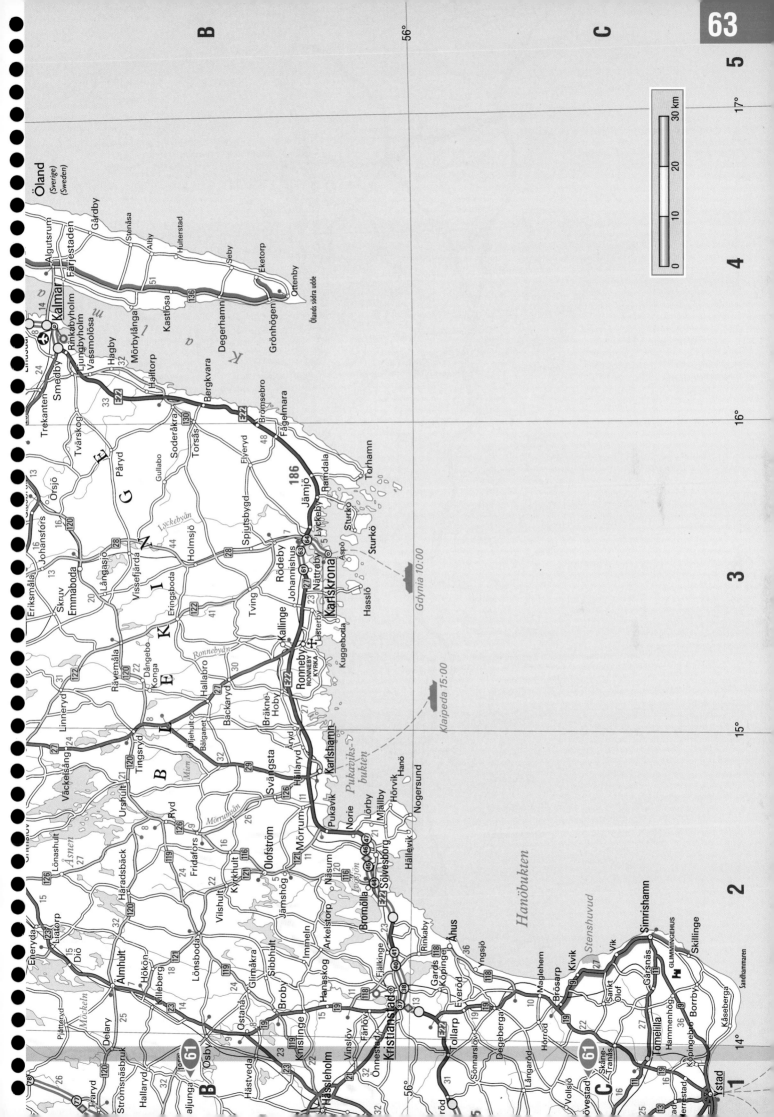

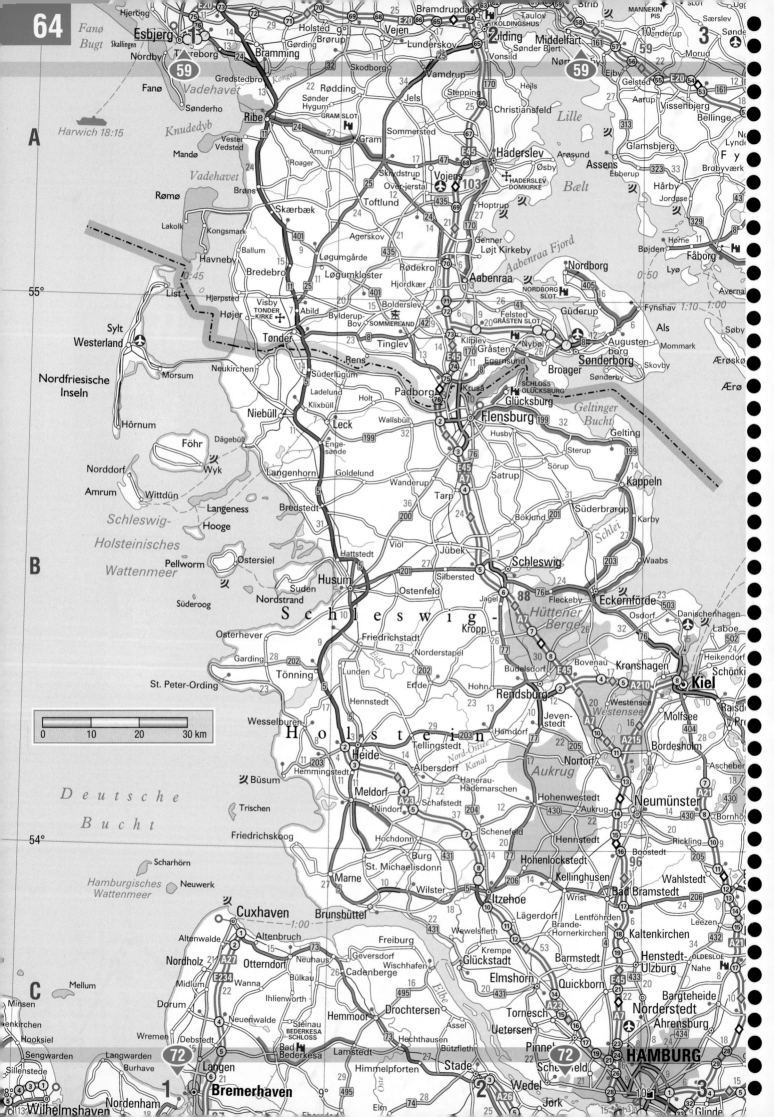

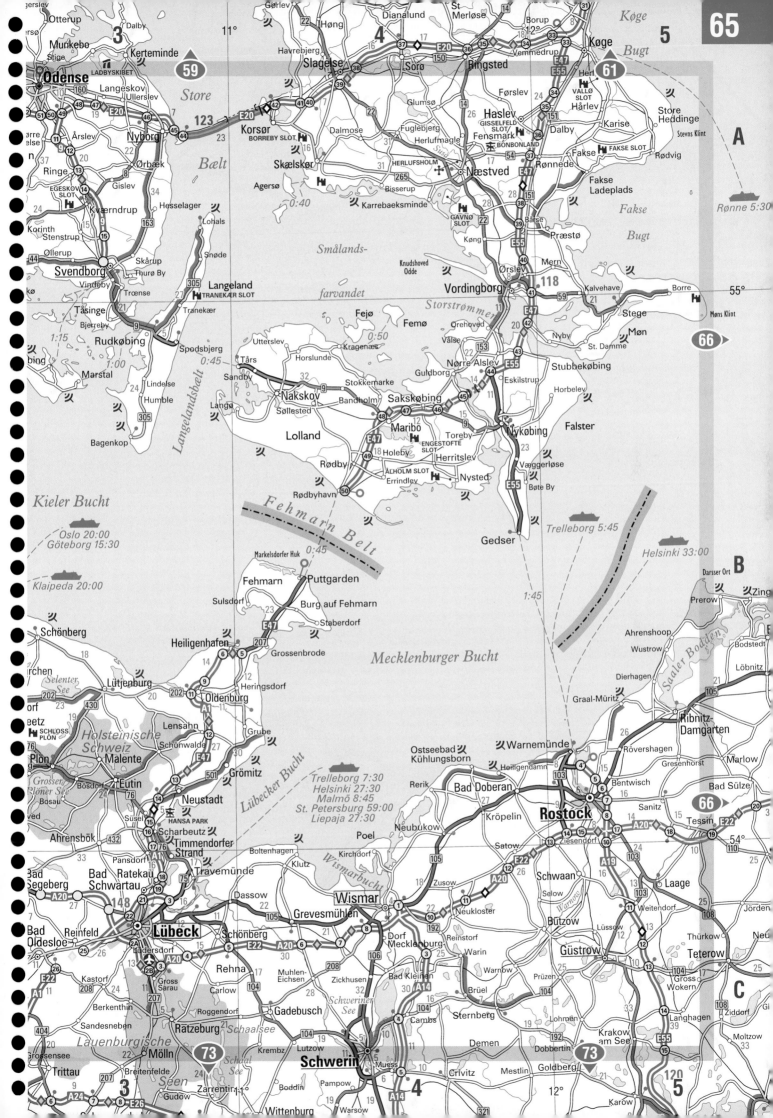

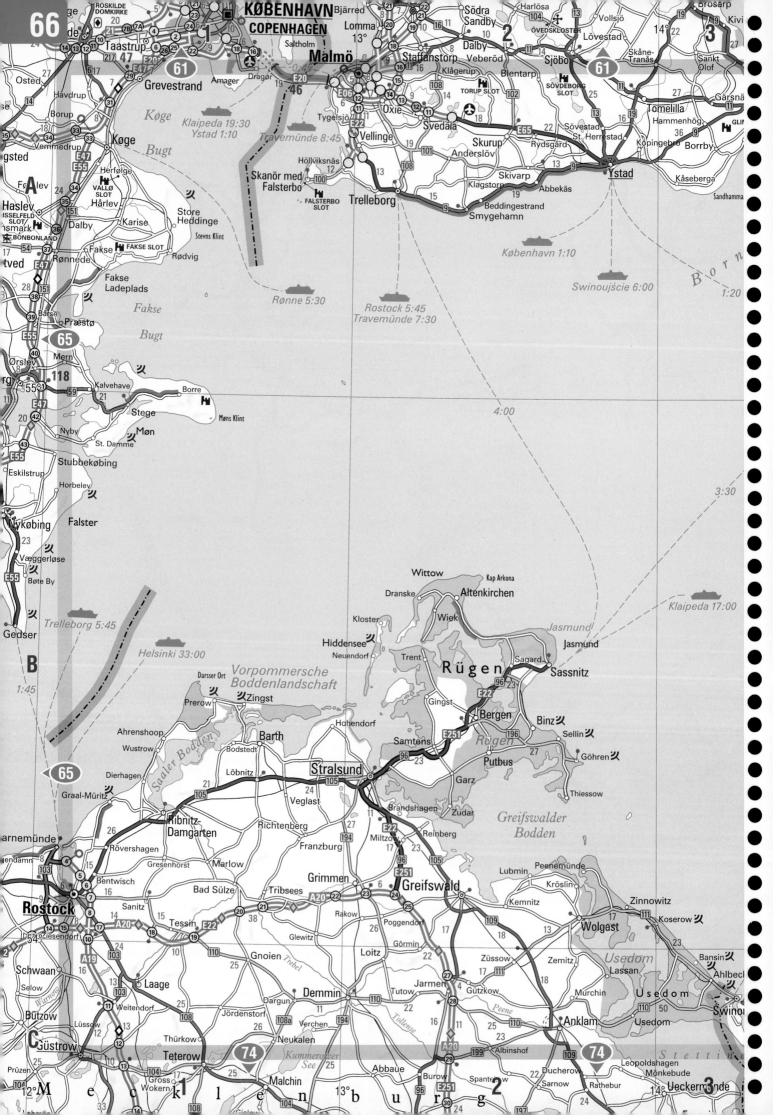

Stenshuvud

Vik

Simrishamn

MMINGEHUS

Skillinge

ren

holmsgattet

Ertholmene

Hammeren

HAMMARSHUS Sandvig-Allinge

Tejn

Bornholm
(Danmark)
(Denmark)

Rø

Gudhjem

Hasle

Klemensker

Nyker

Svaneke

Øster-marie

Køge 5:30   Rønne

Nylars 38 Åkirkeby

28

Neksø

Pedersker

Snogebaek

55°

A

Jaroslawiec

J. D

J. Kopań

B

203 64 *Wieprza*

Darłowo

Stary Jaroslaw

Dąbki

MUZEUM DARŁOWO

Sławno

Łazy

J. Bukowo

68

E28 Ostrowiec

203

Mielno

J. Jamno

Jamno

Lejkowo

Sarbinowo

Sianów

Ystad 6:00

Ustronie Morskie

42

Koszalin

206

Nacław

35

Kołobrzeg

11

Bonin

Mrzezyno

11

Dobrzyca

26

ZAMEK W KOSZALINIE

Manowo

5

Dygowo

Wrzosowo

Biesiekierz

Niechorze

102

162

163

Niedalino

Rosnowo

Mostowo

Rewal

Trzebiatów

21

Karlino

166

31

37

Radew

Pobierowo 102 31

103

Cerkwica

18

Gościno

19

Gorawino

E28

16

163

Dargiń

11

54°

Dziwnów

Swierzno

23

Rega

6

219

149

25

169

Bobolice

Międzywodzie

8

Kamień Pomorski

109

Ryman

Sławoborze

12

Tychowo

171

Wolinski

102 32

Kolczewo

12

105

Rzeszníkowo

Rabino

17

Tychówka

167

29

Grzmiąca

11

Międzyzdroje

107

Mechowo

17

33

Ząbrowo

162

Parseta

Białowąs

23

30

ujscie

3

21

15

13

Gryfice

6

Sławno

167

 r Haff

Lubin

18

Gołczewo

108

E28

Rabino

Zdrój

Barwice

24

172

Zalew Szczeciński

Wolin

E65 75

106

20 Płoty

152

Resko

Rusinowo

Sława

75

ZAMEK W POLCZYNIE

163

Ostropole

Nowe Warpno

Przybiernów

Żabowo

Staregard

35

Świdwin

16°

Bierzwnica

Drawski

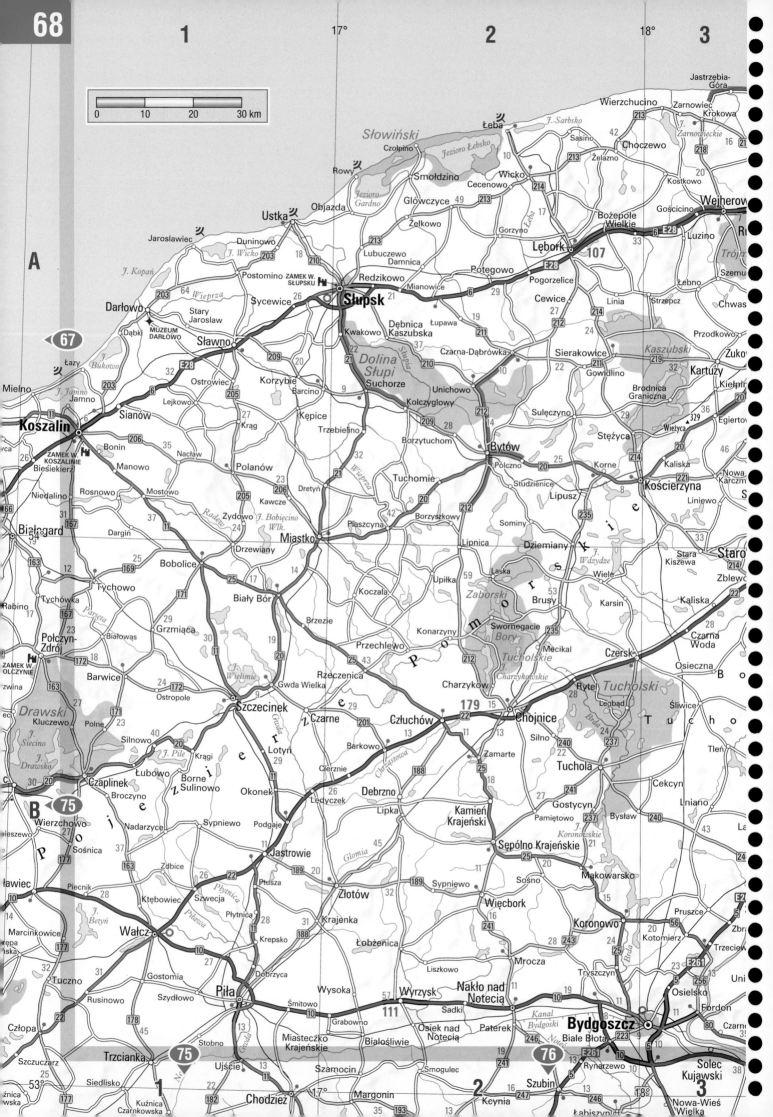

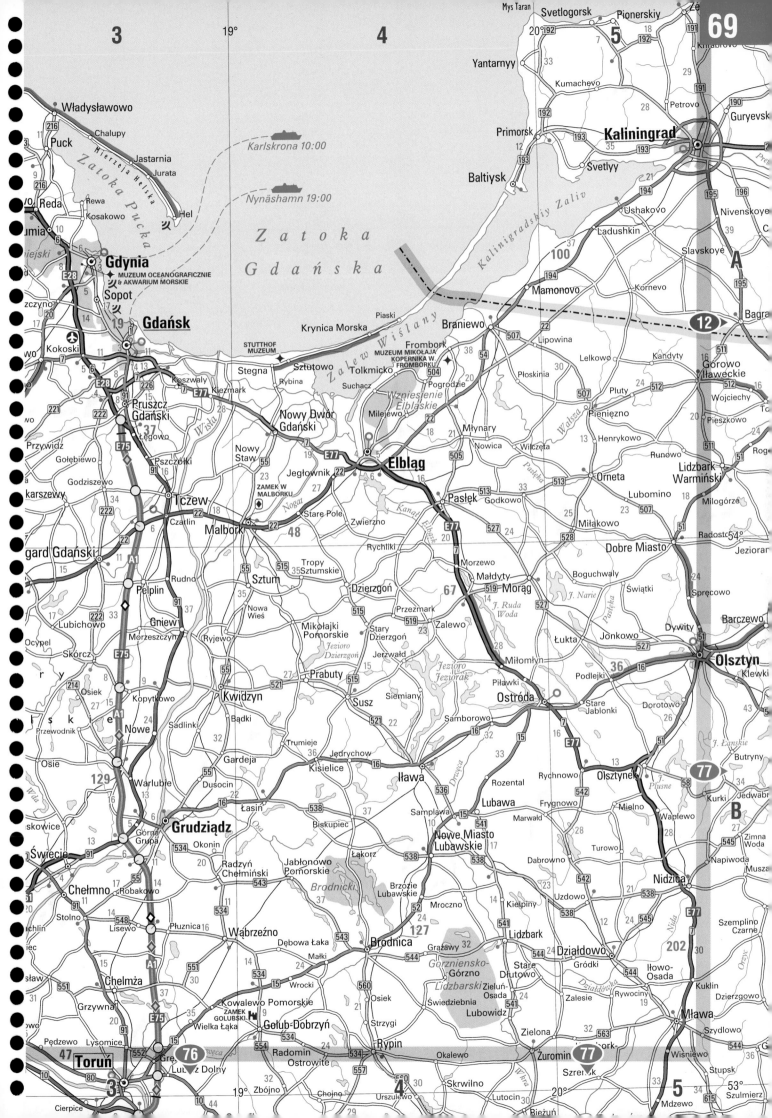

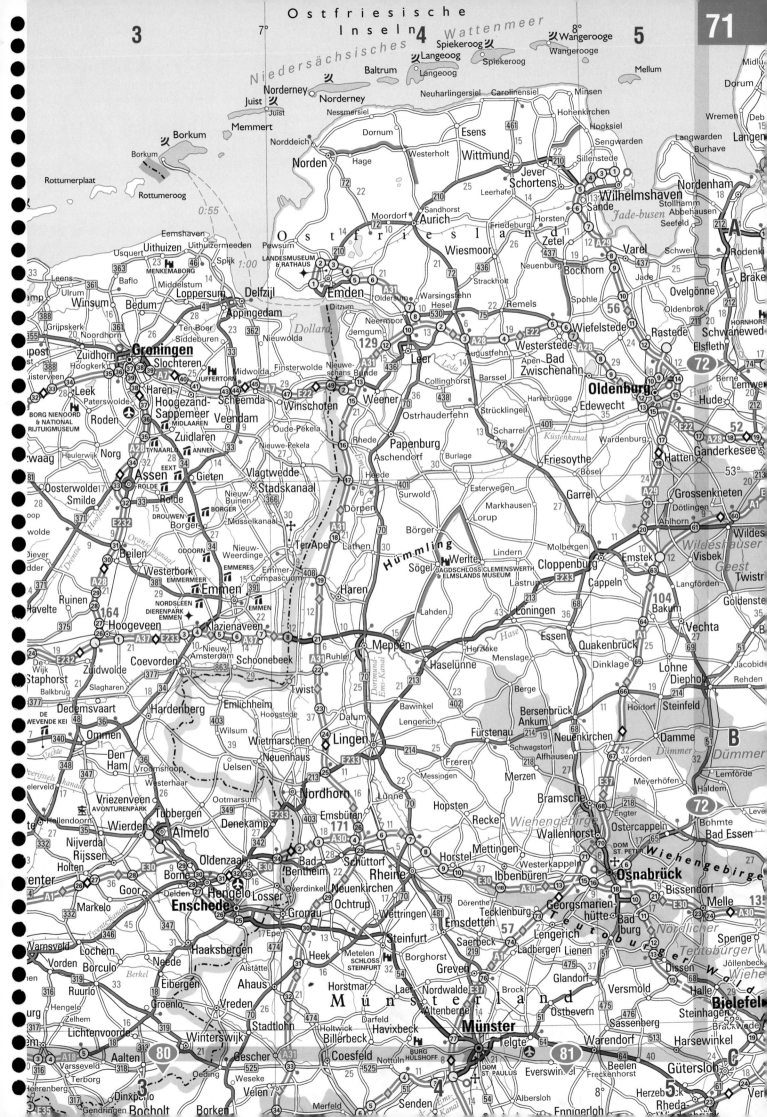

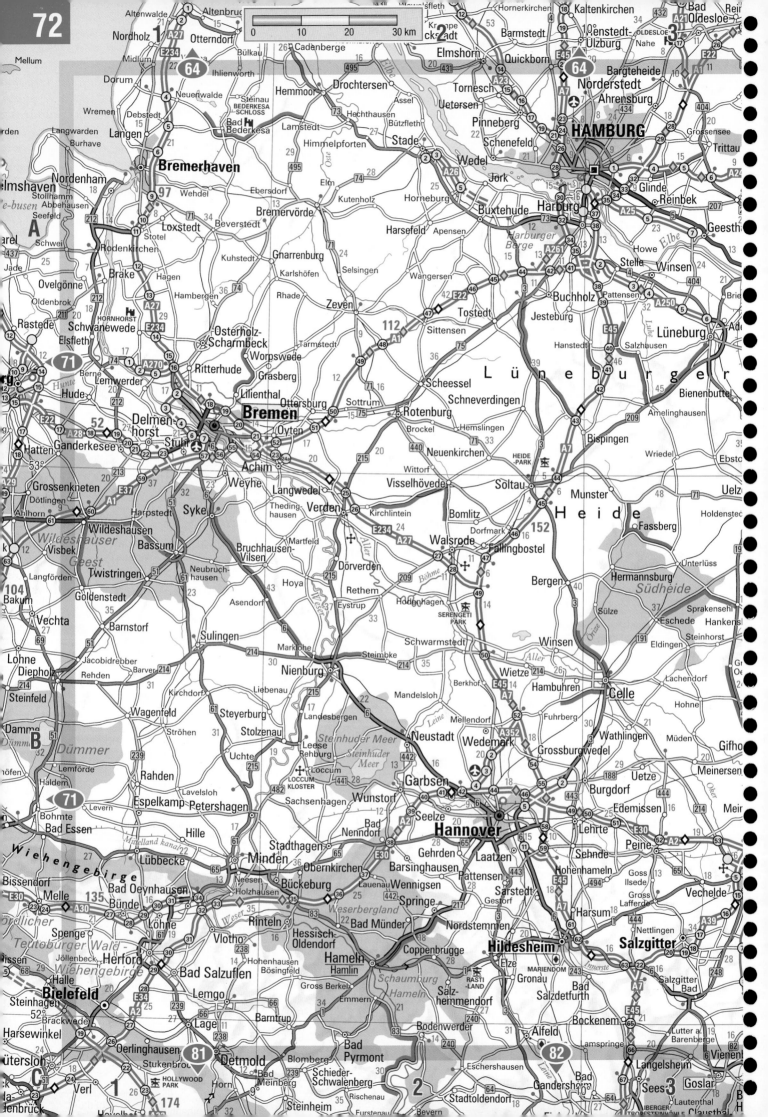

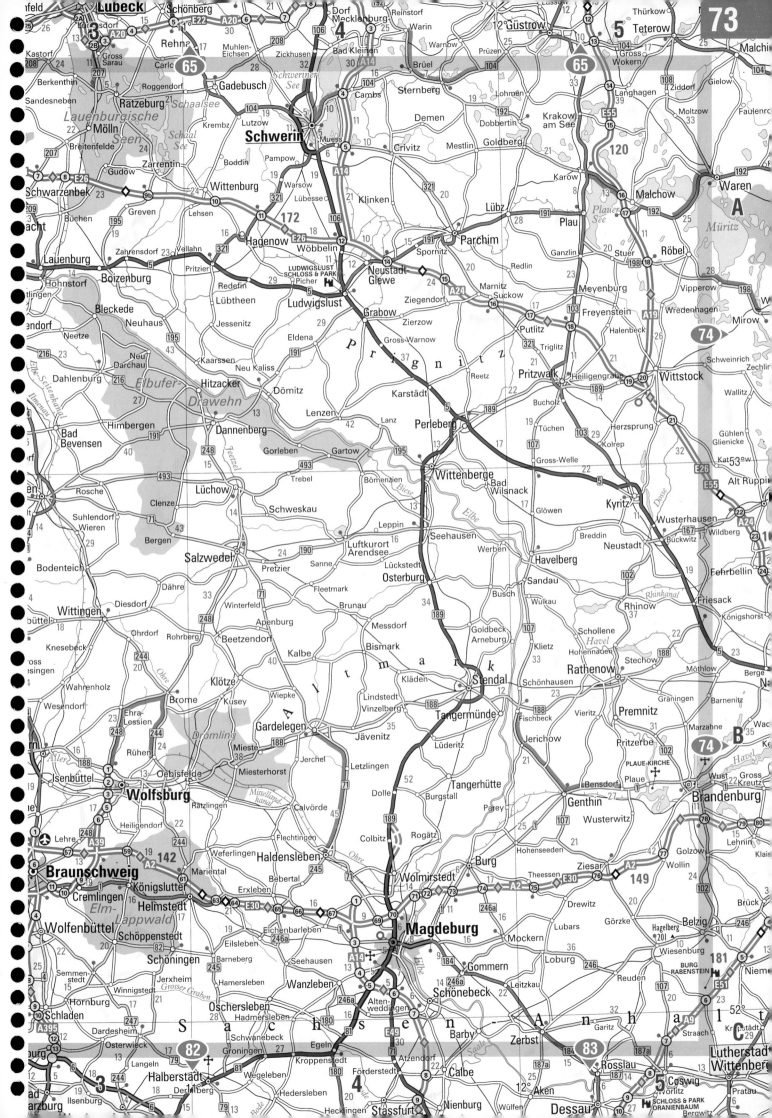

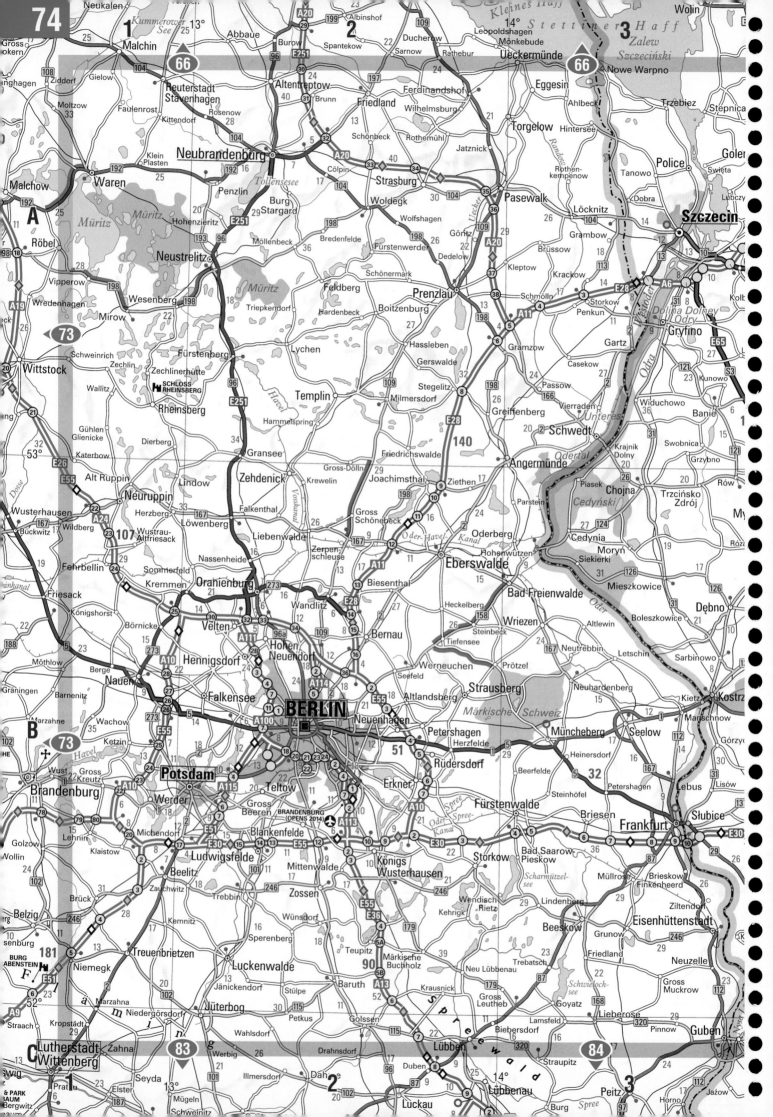

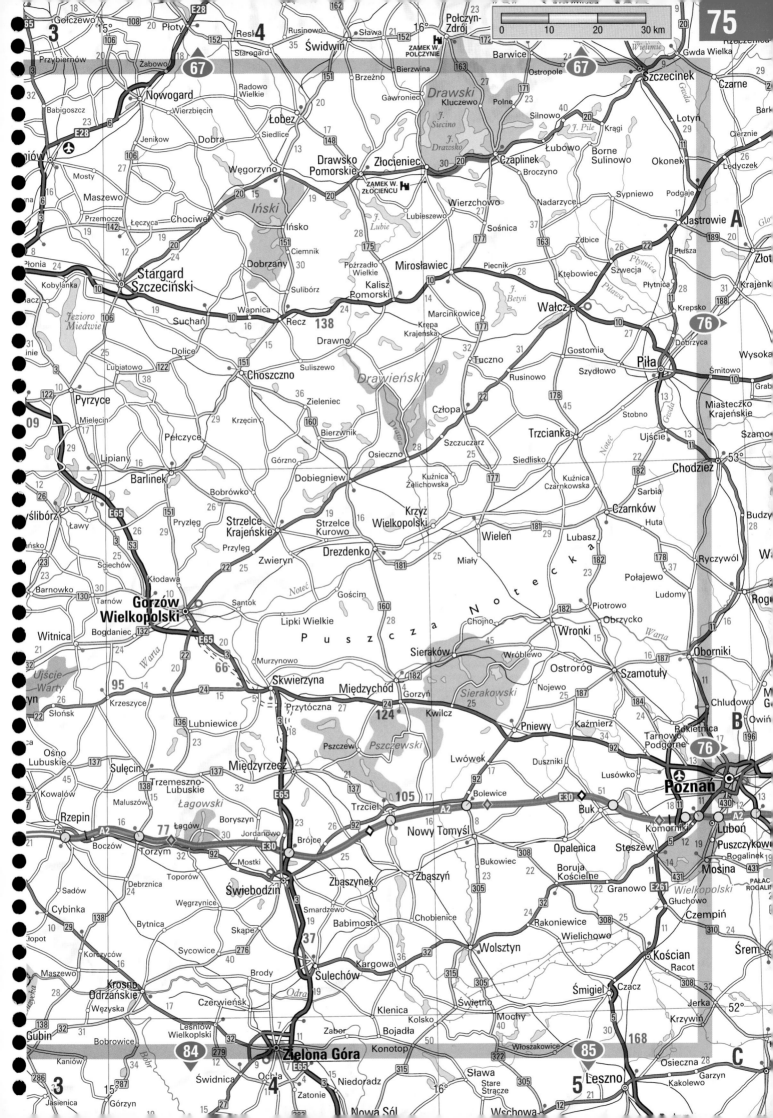

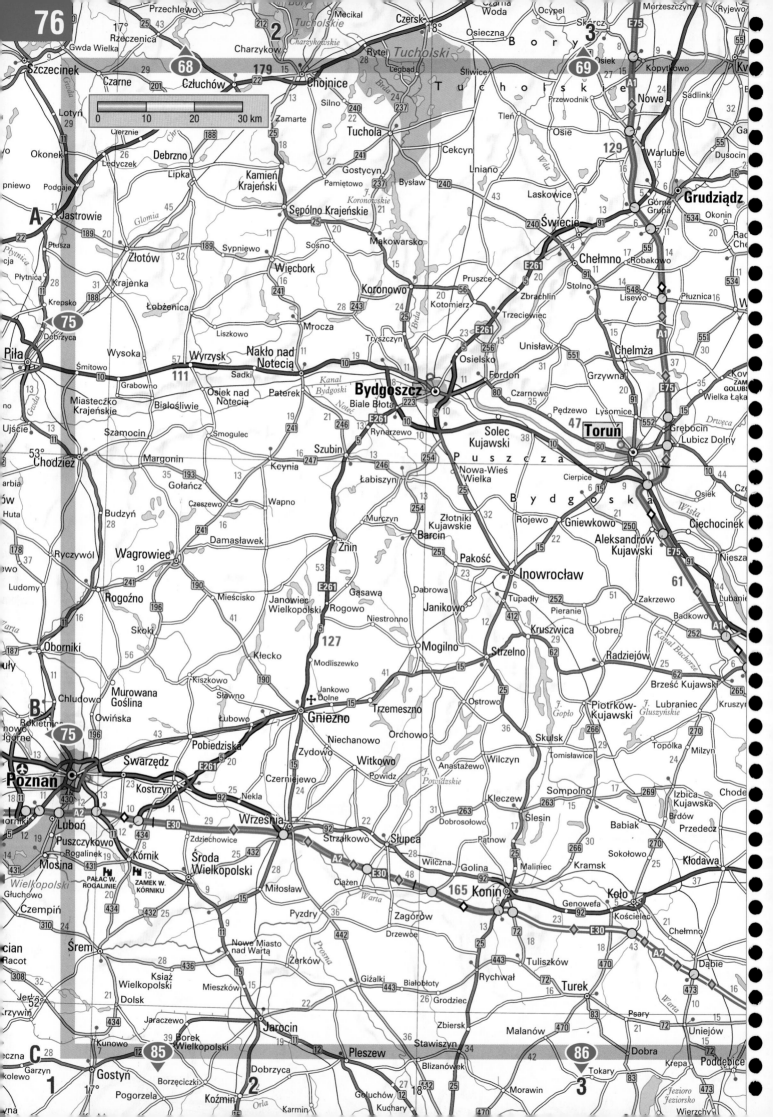

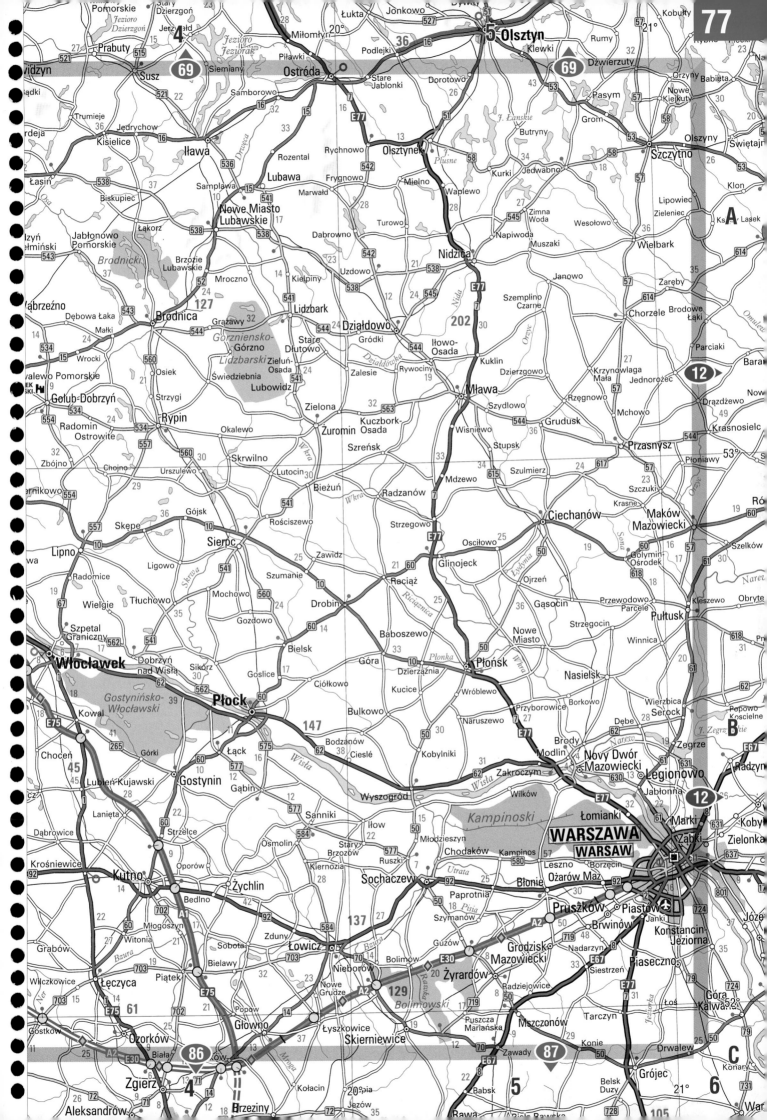

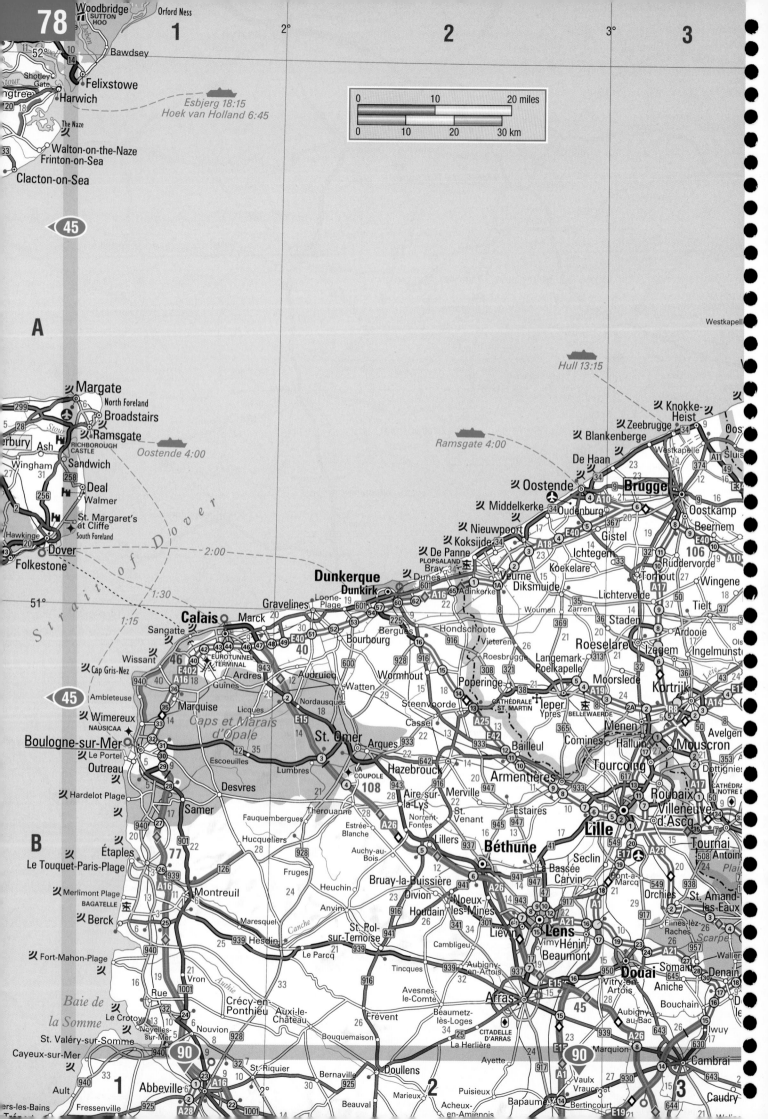

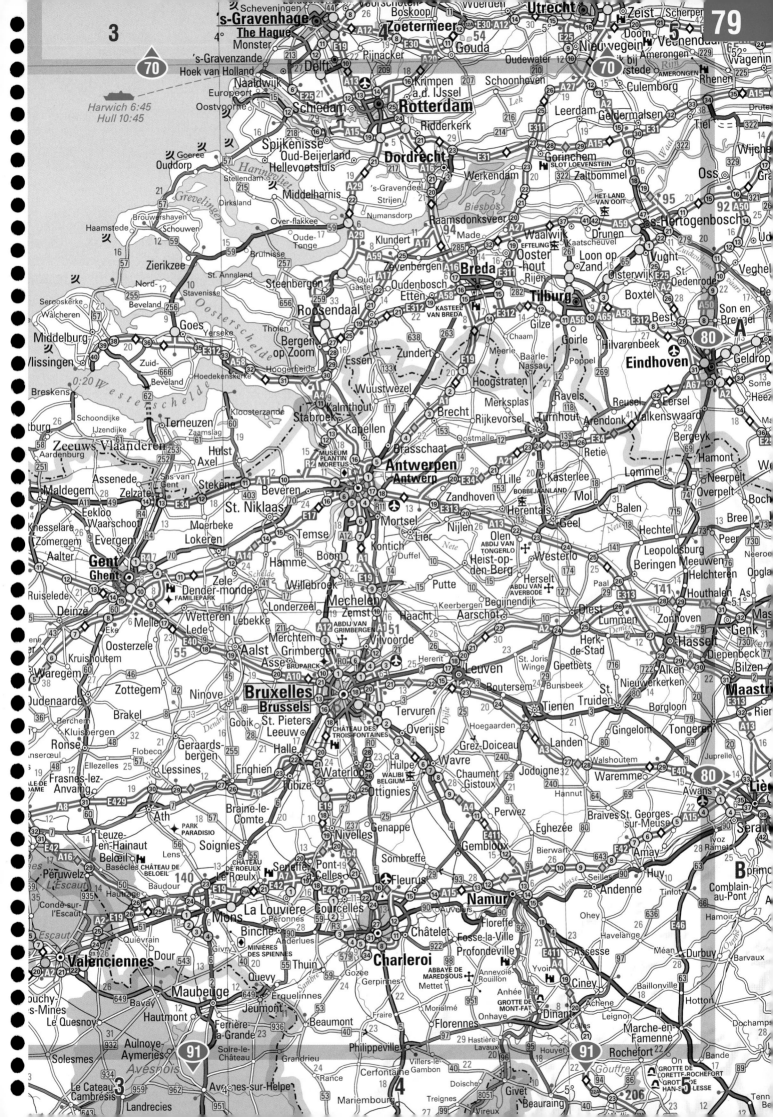

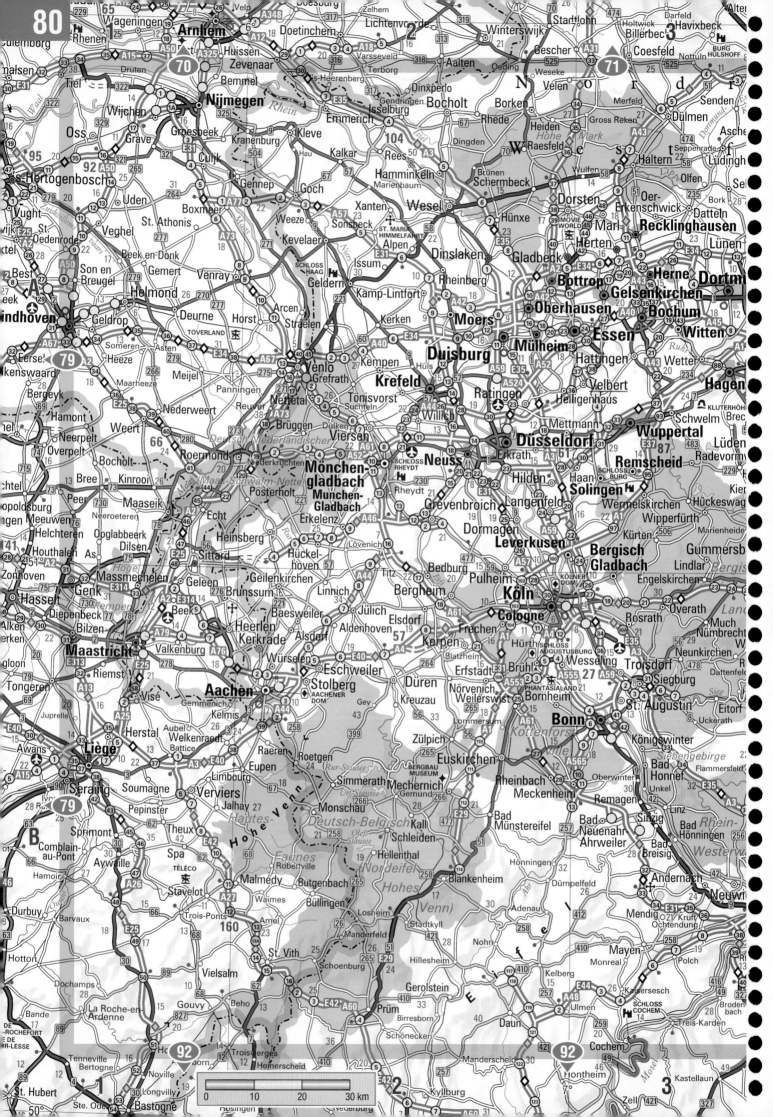

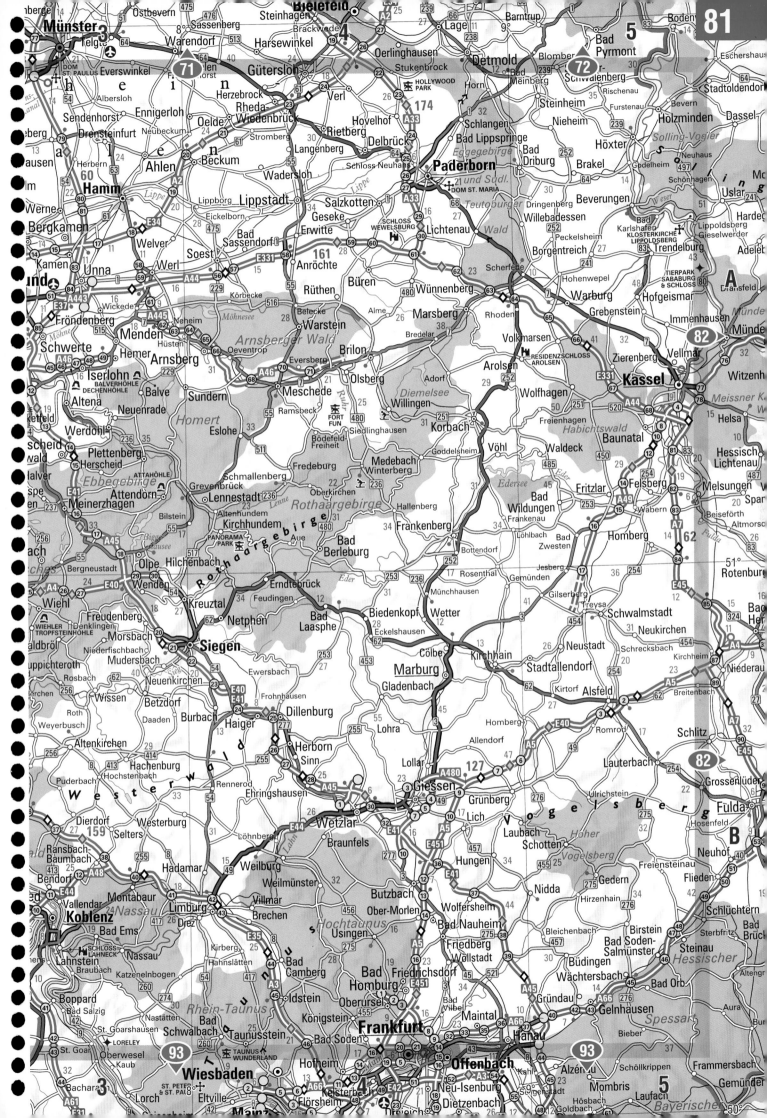

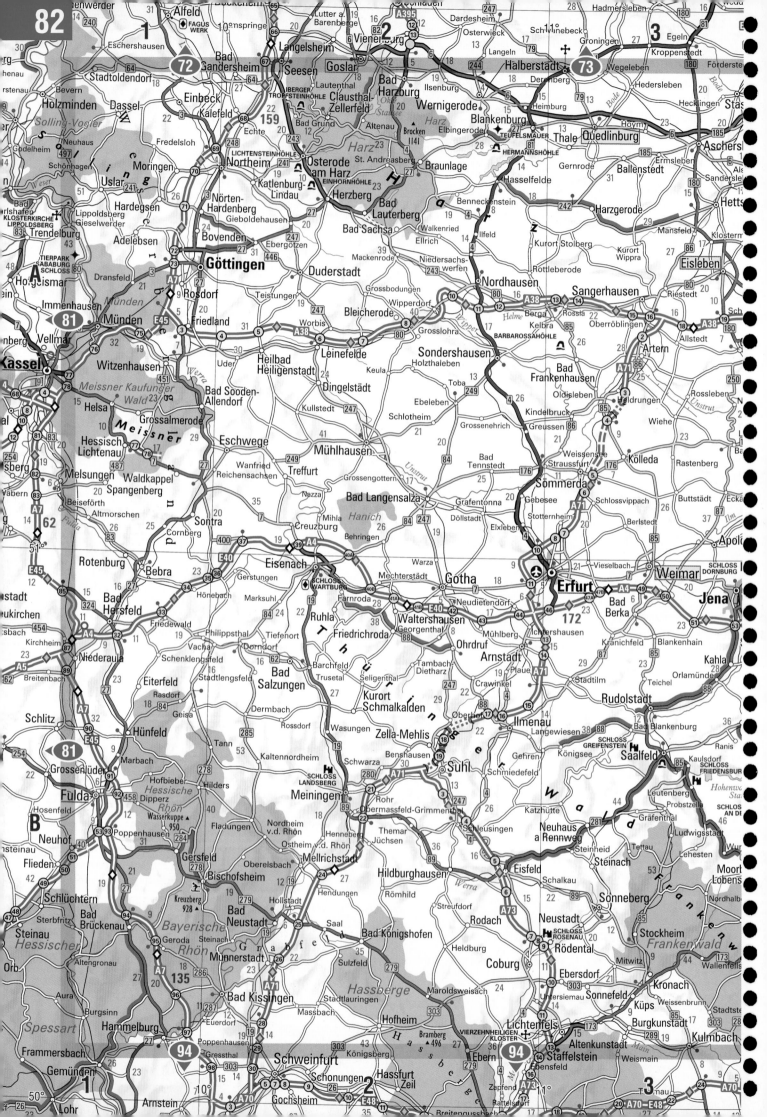

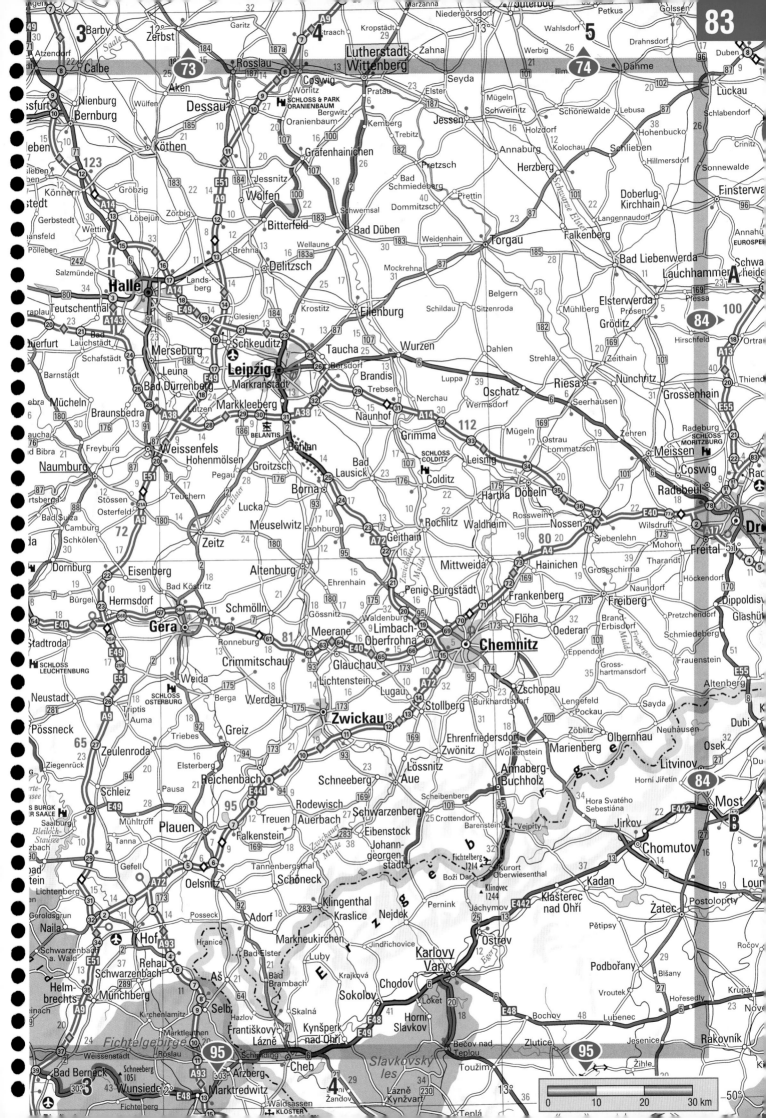

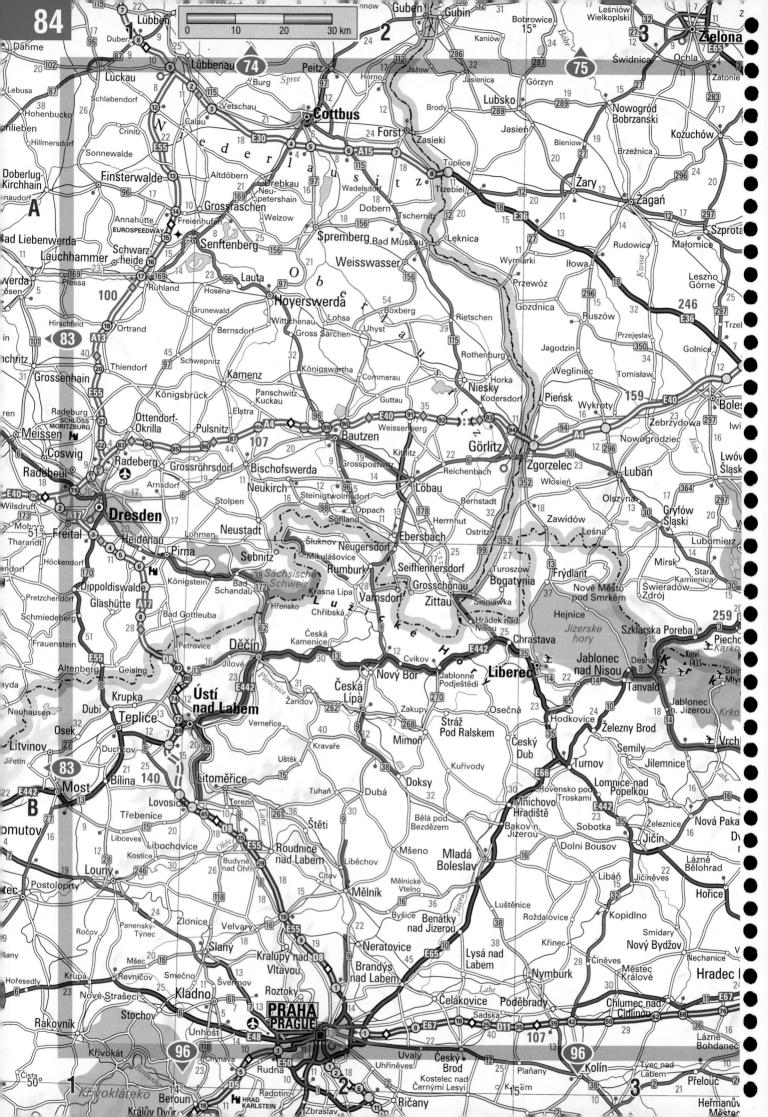

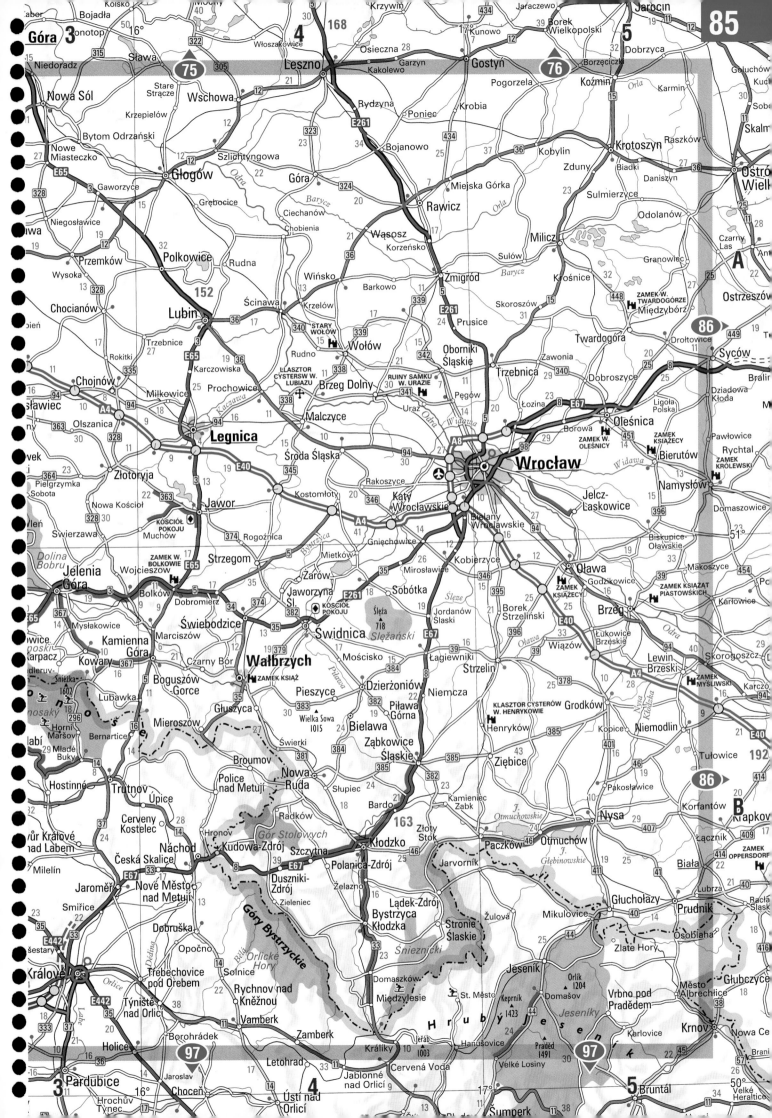

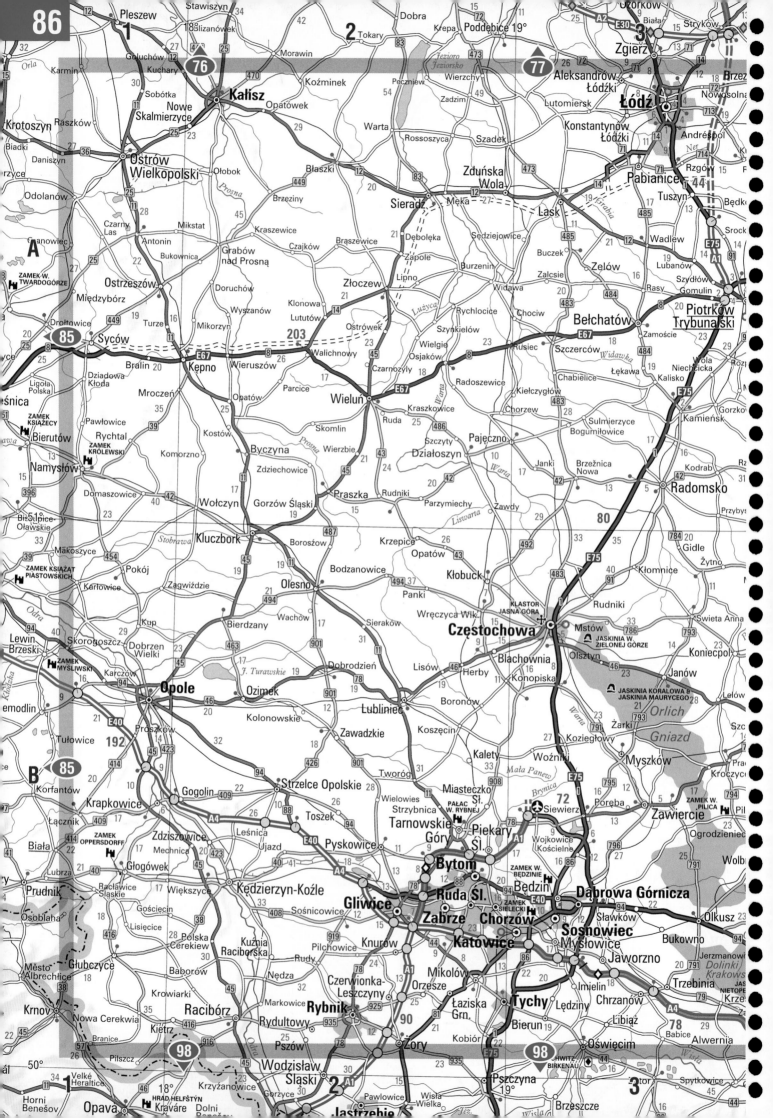

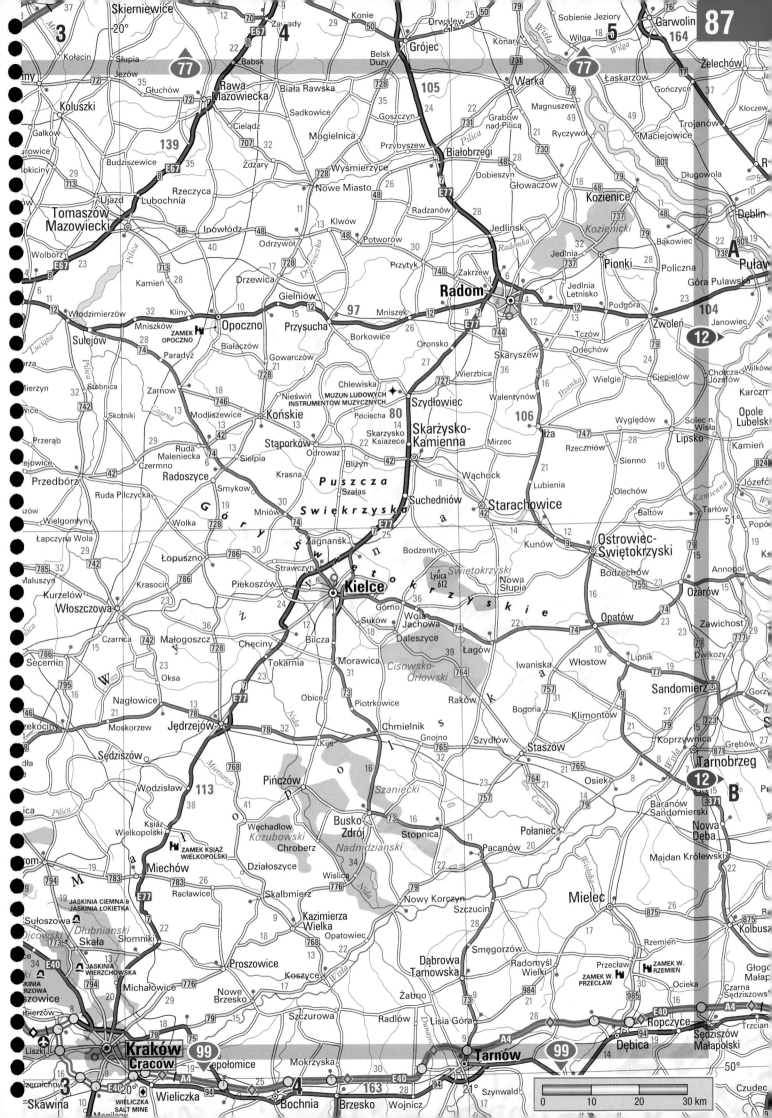

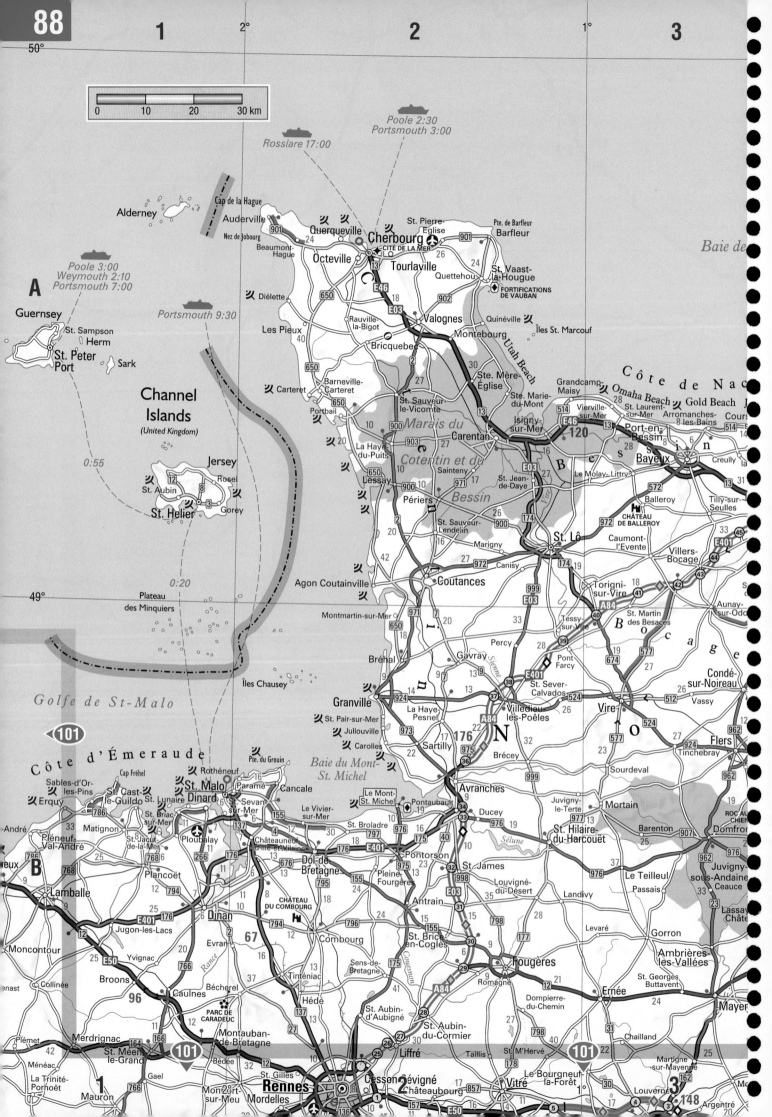

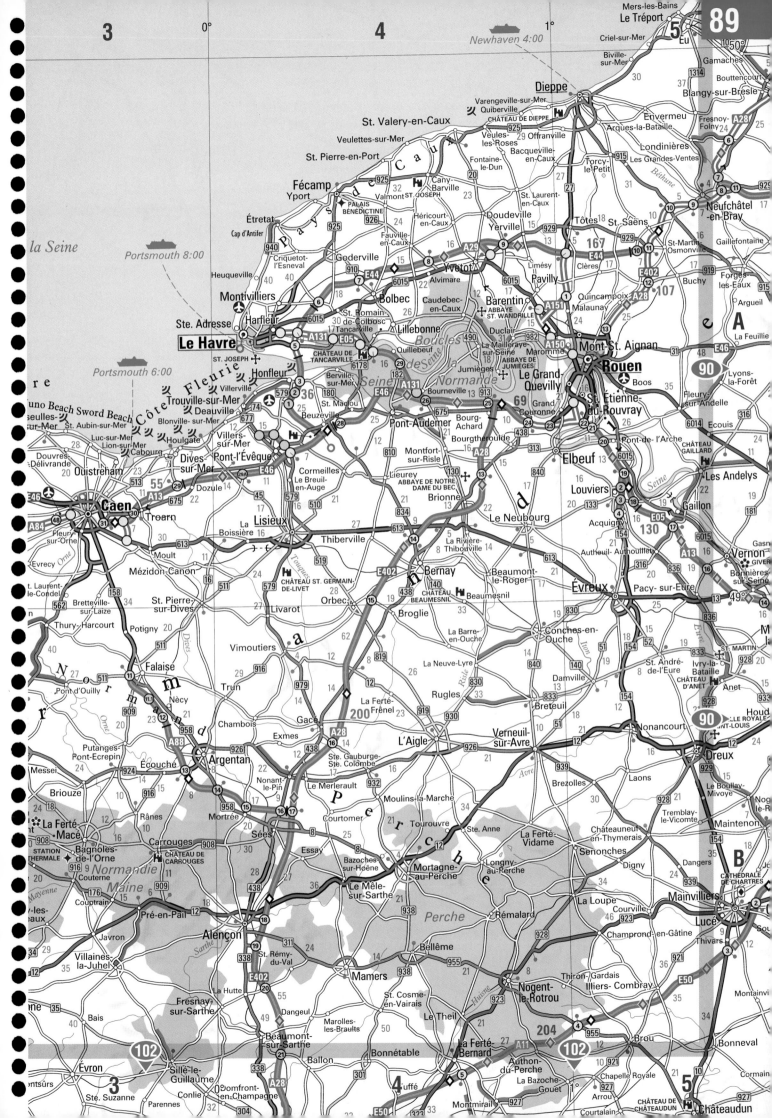

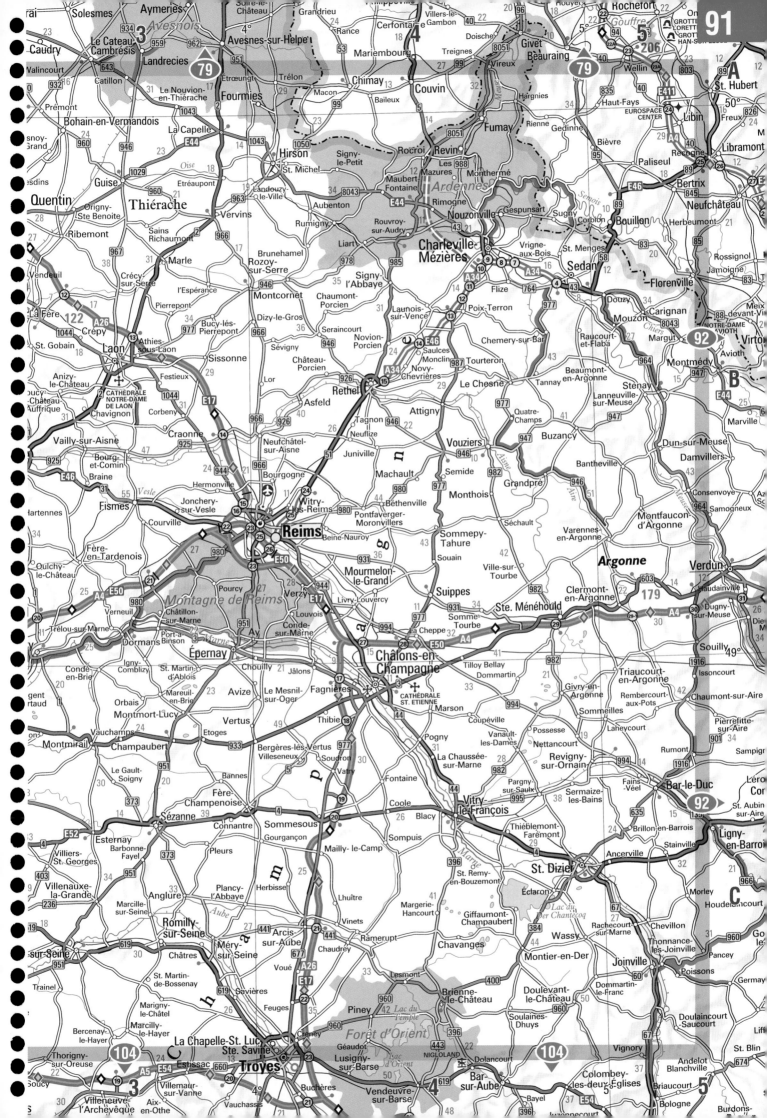

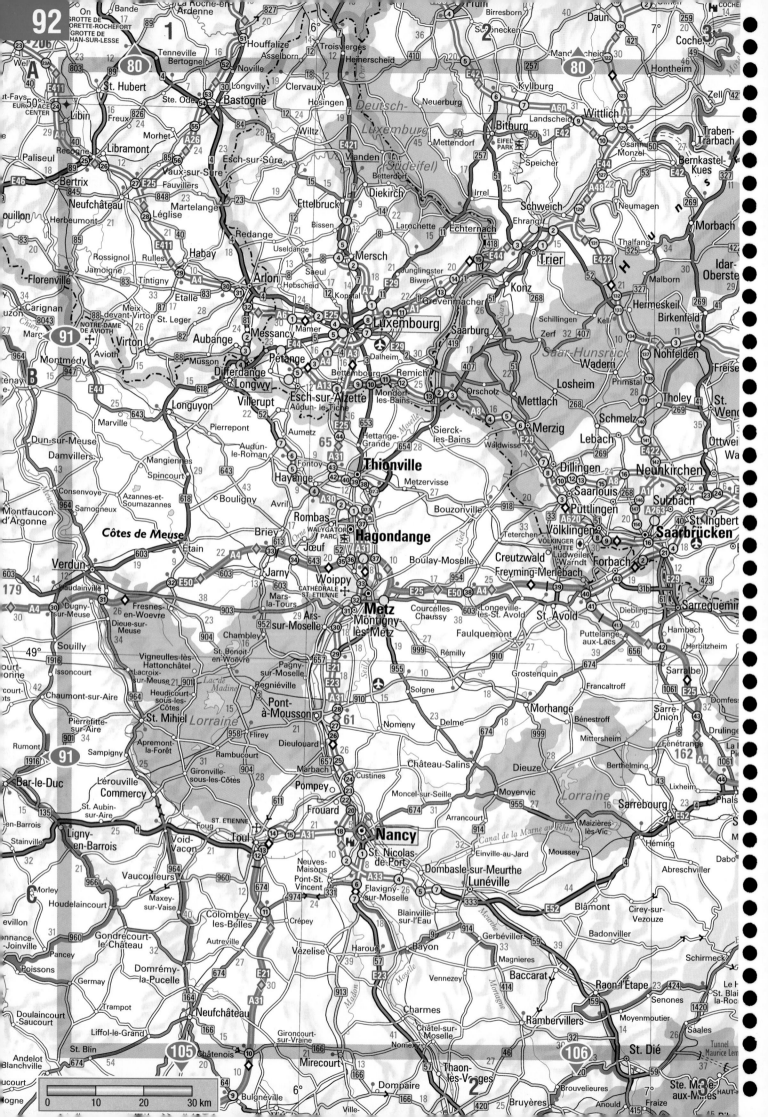

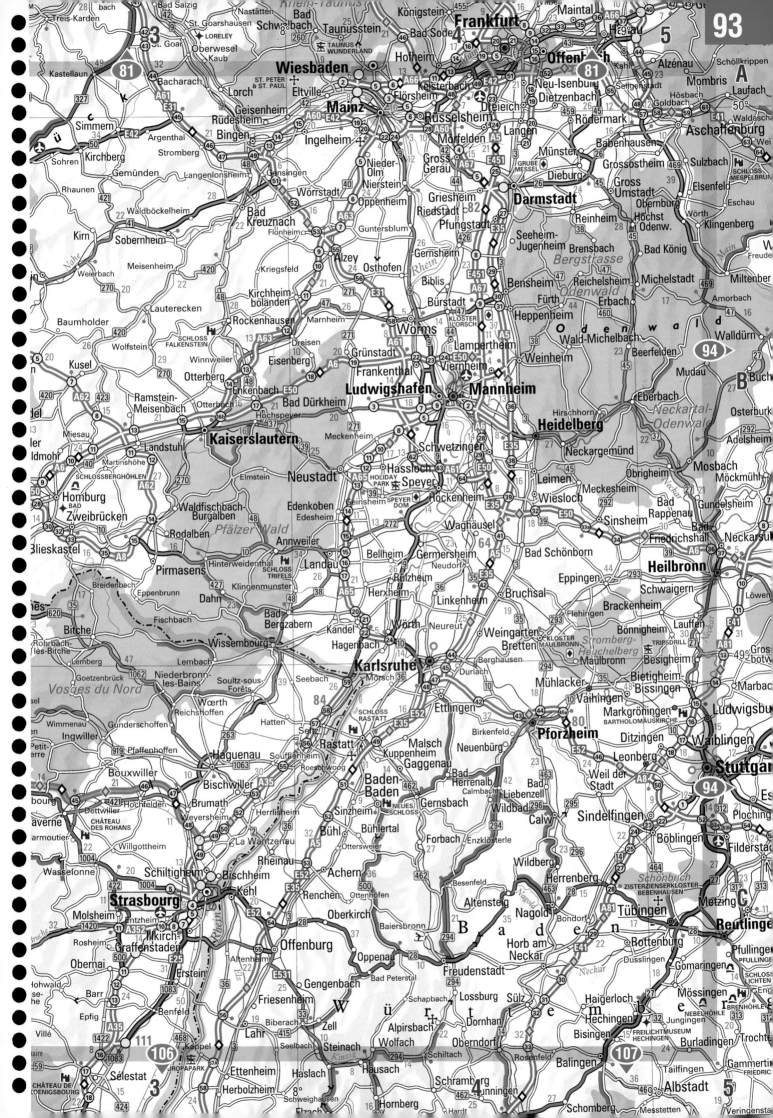

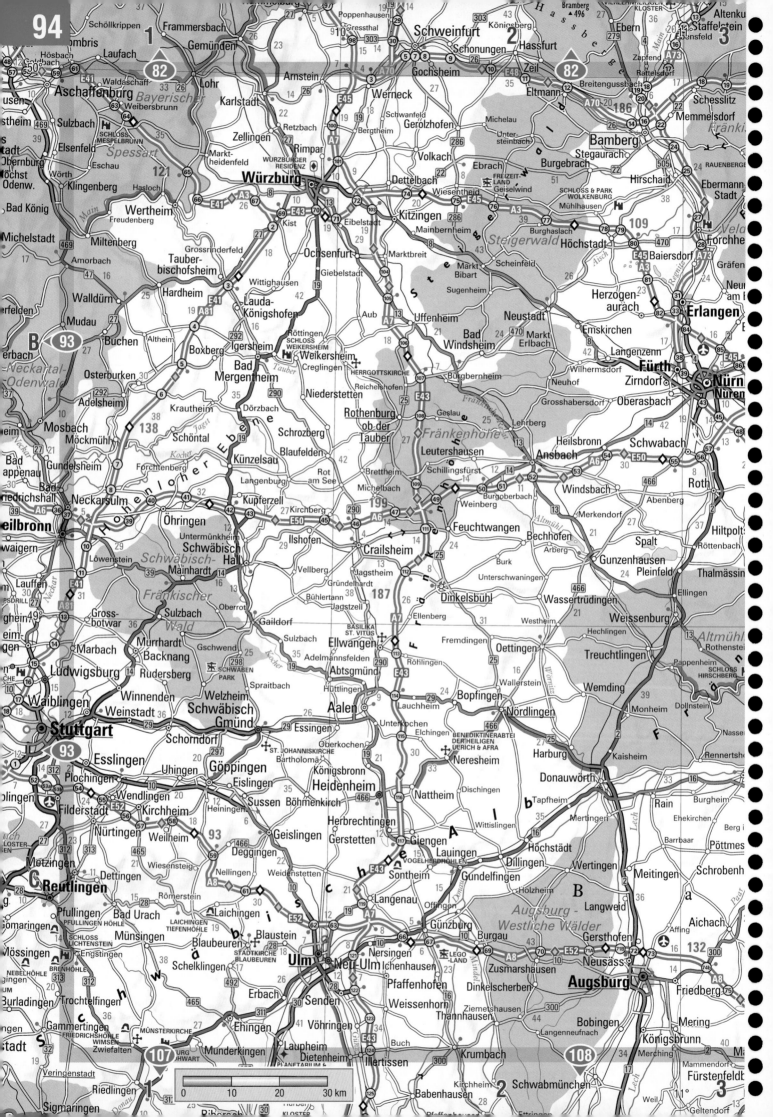

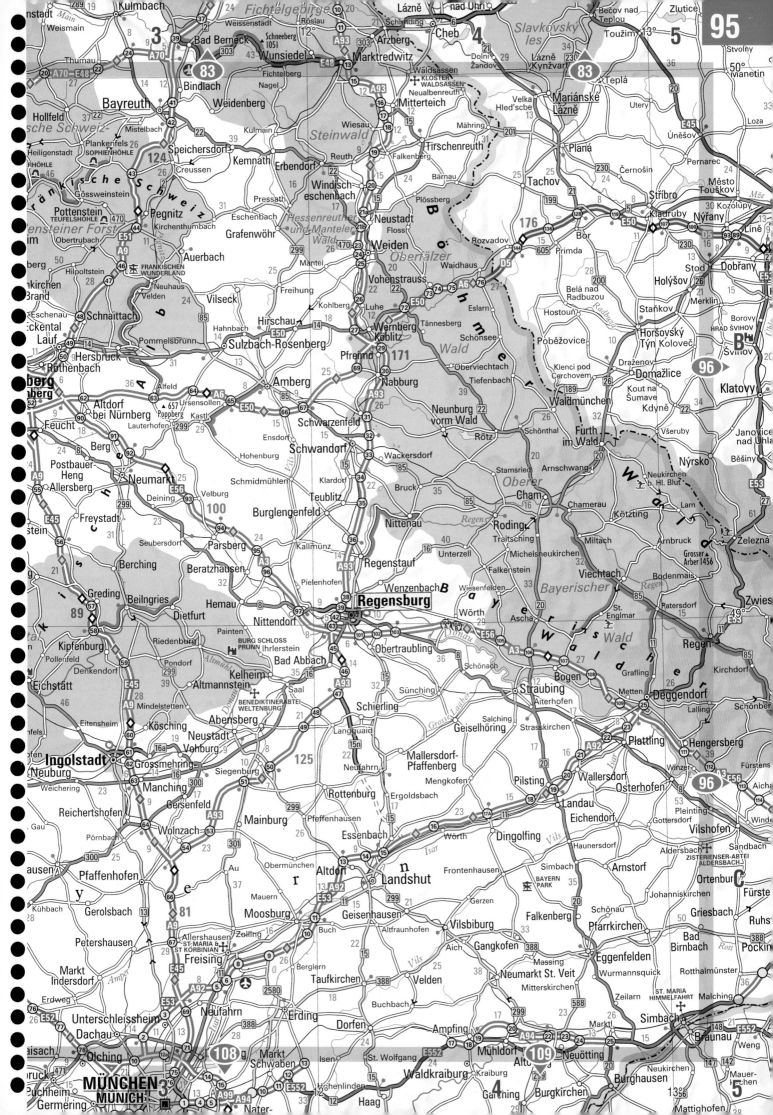

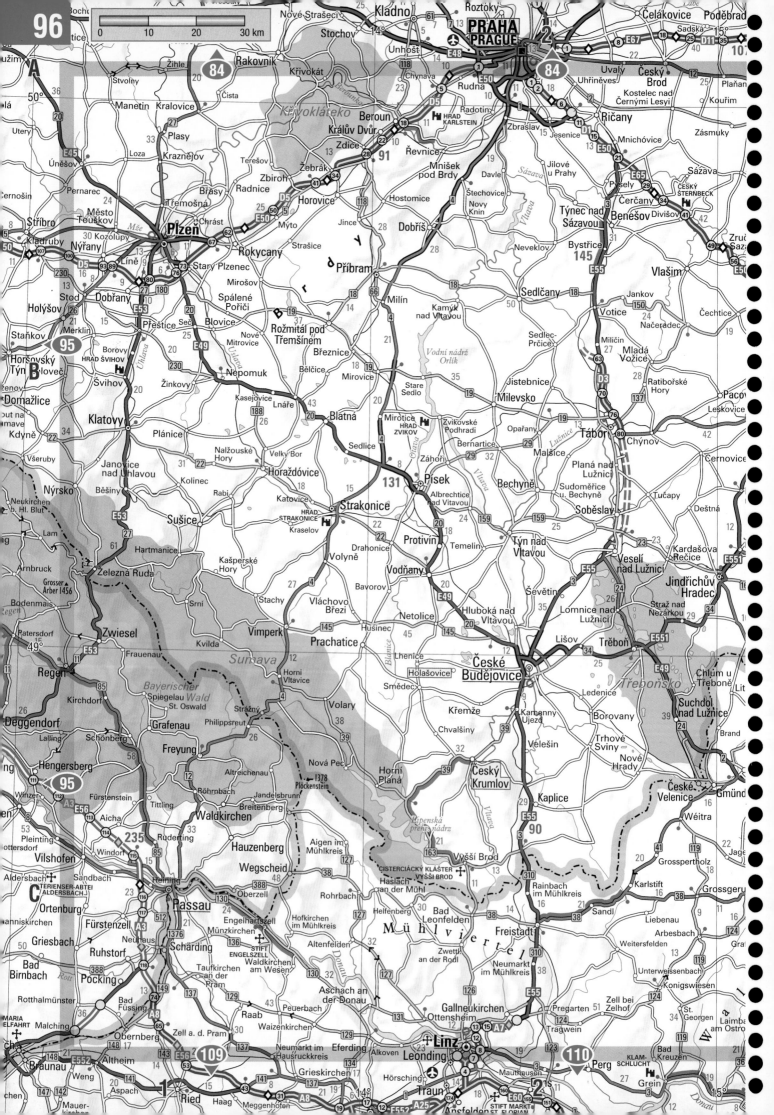

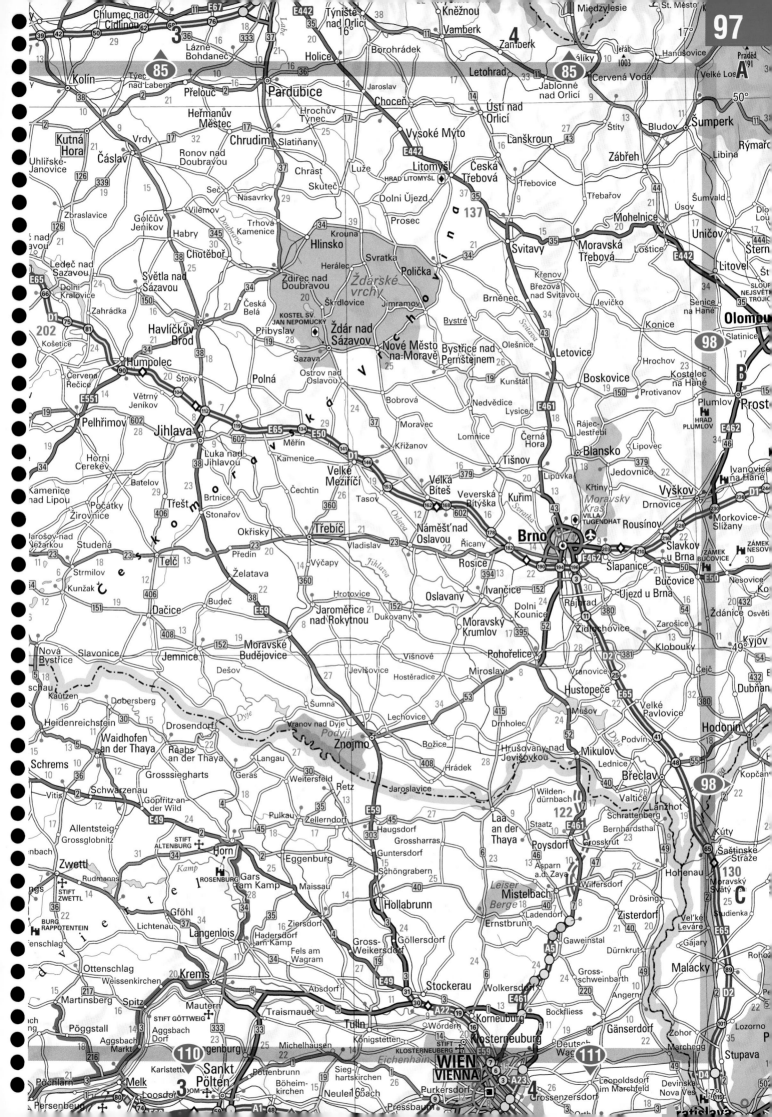

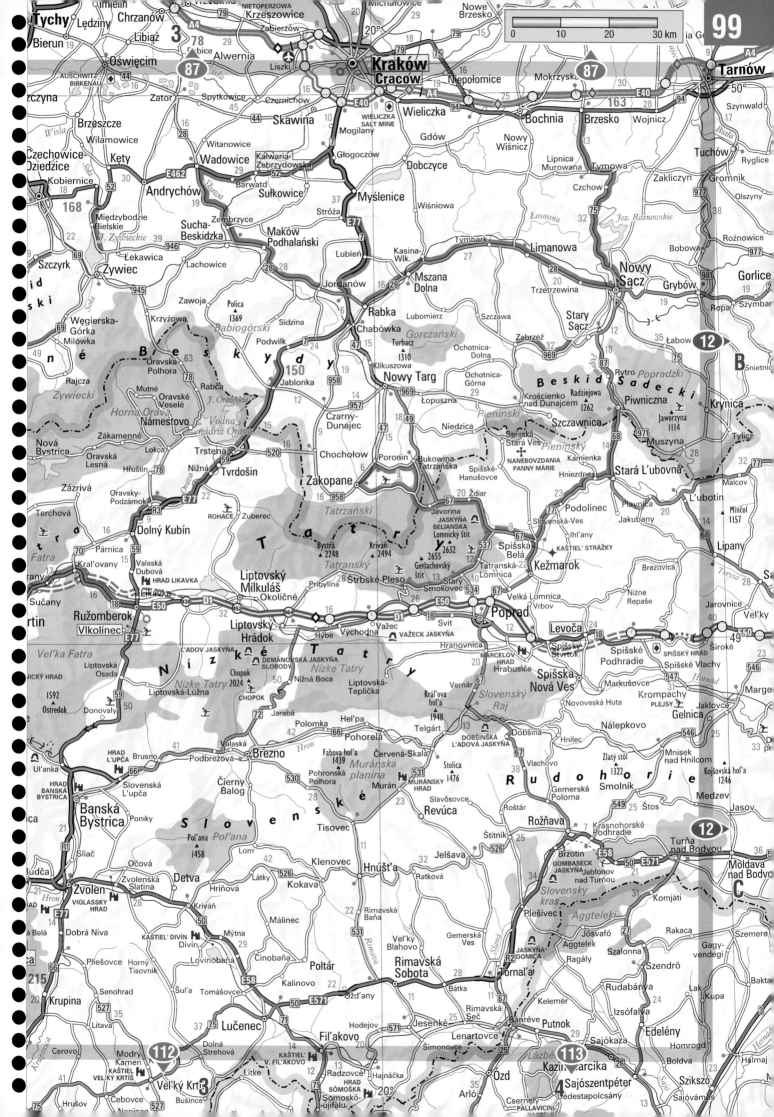

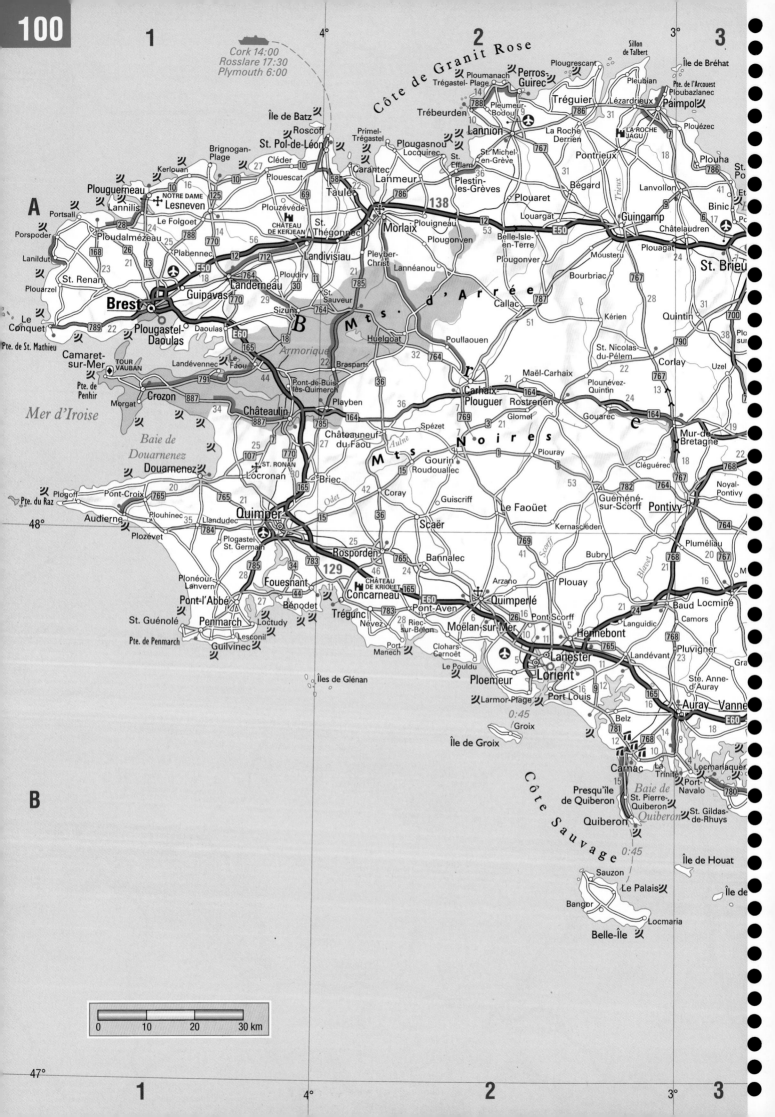

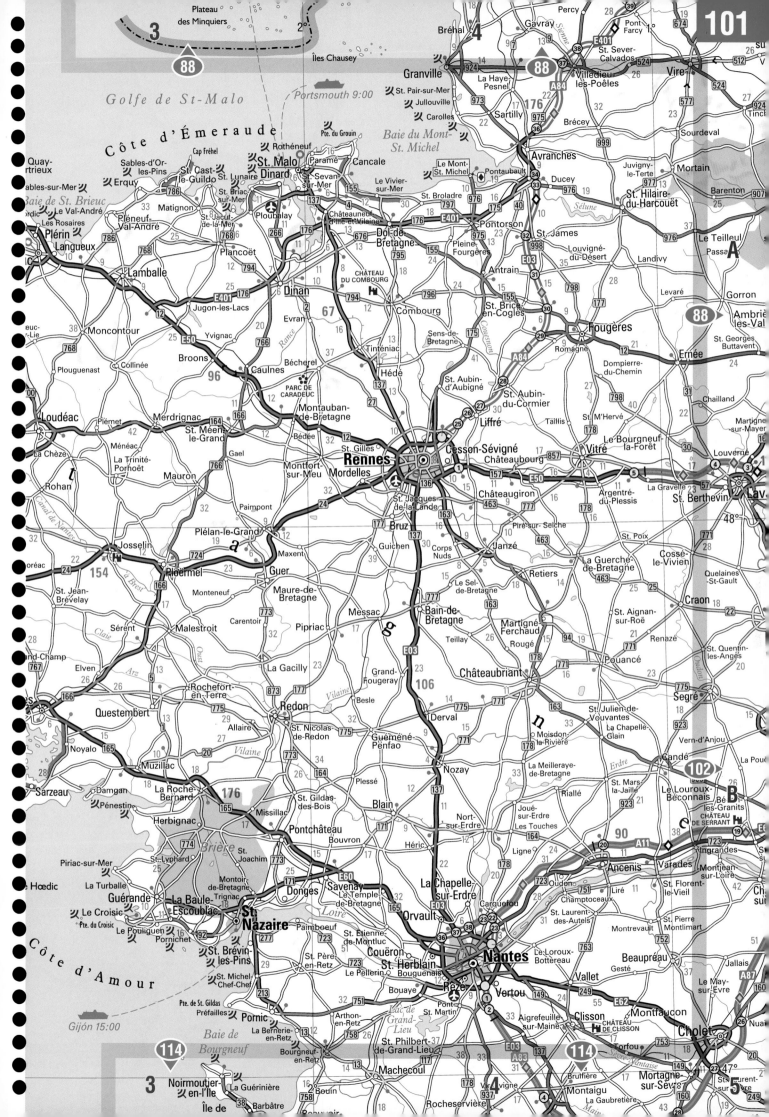

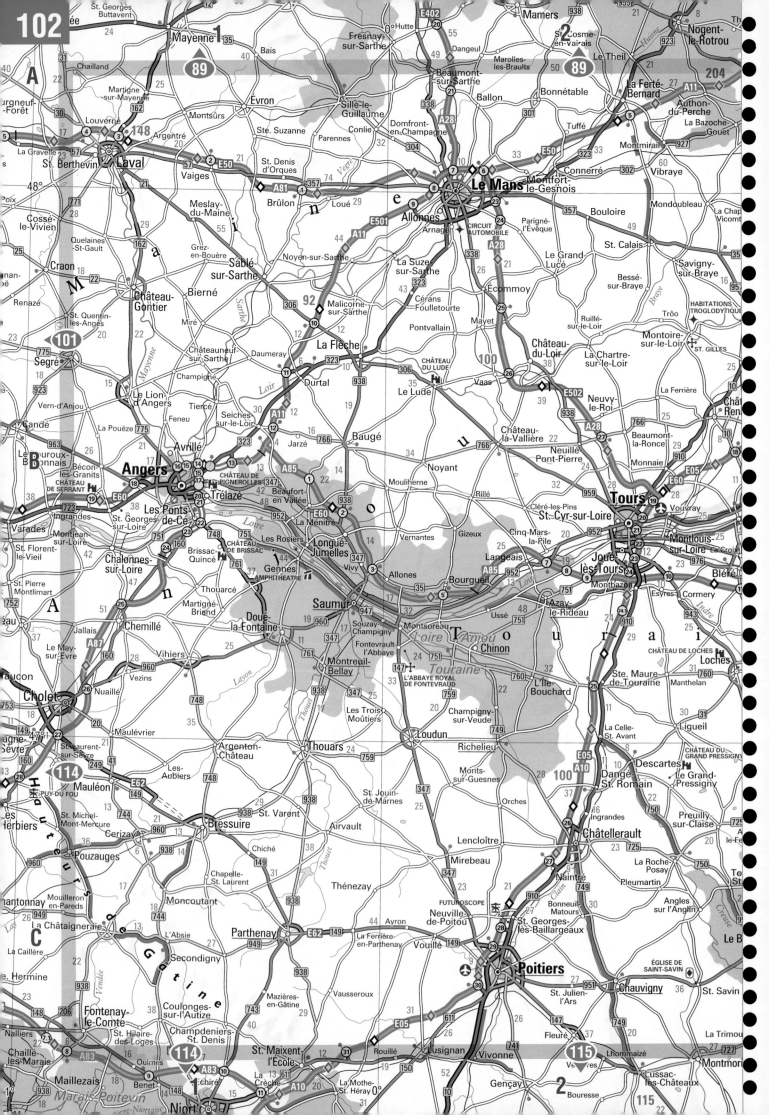

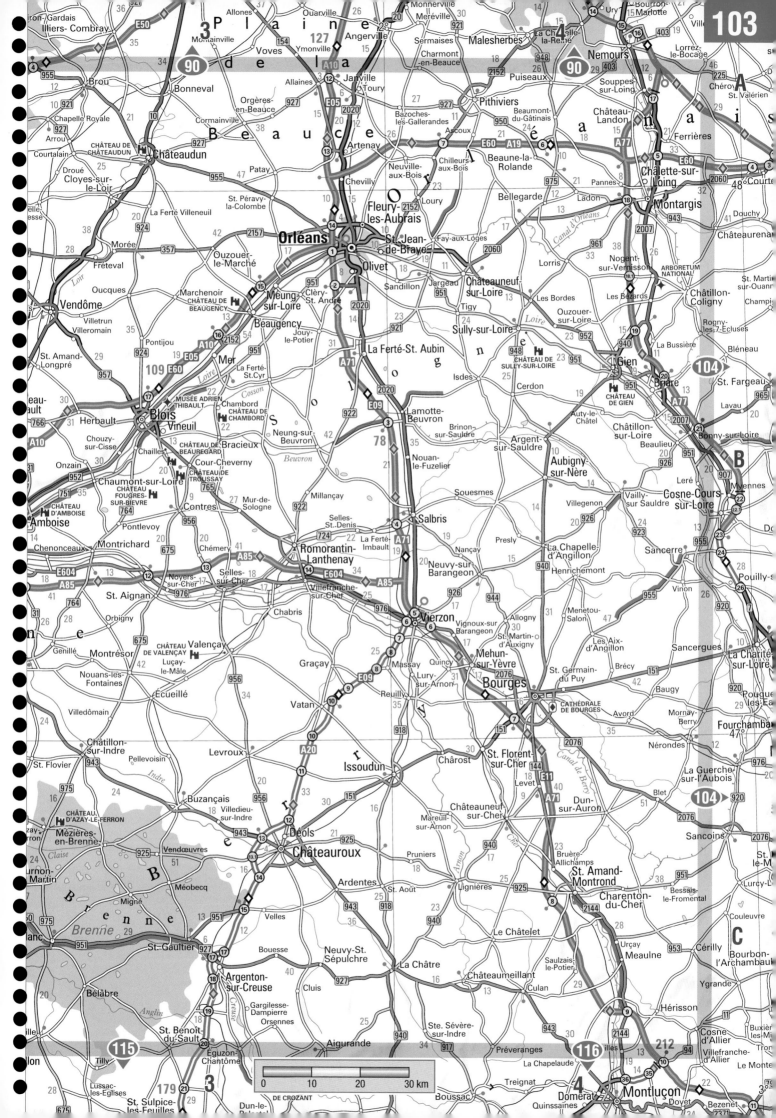

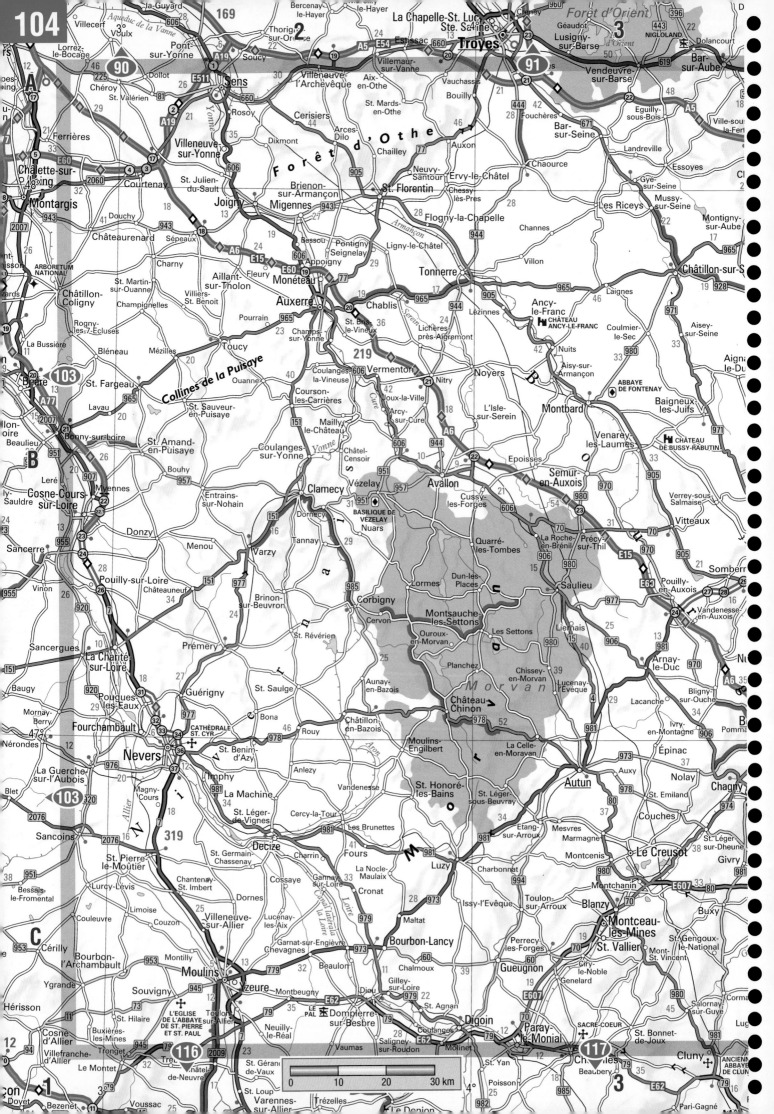

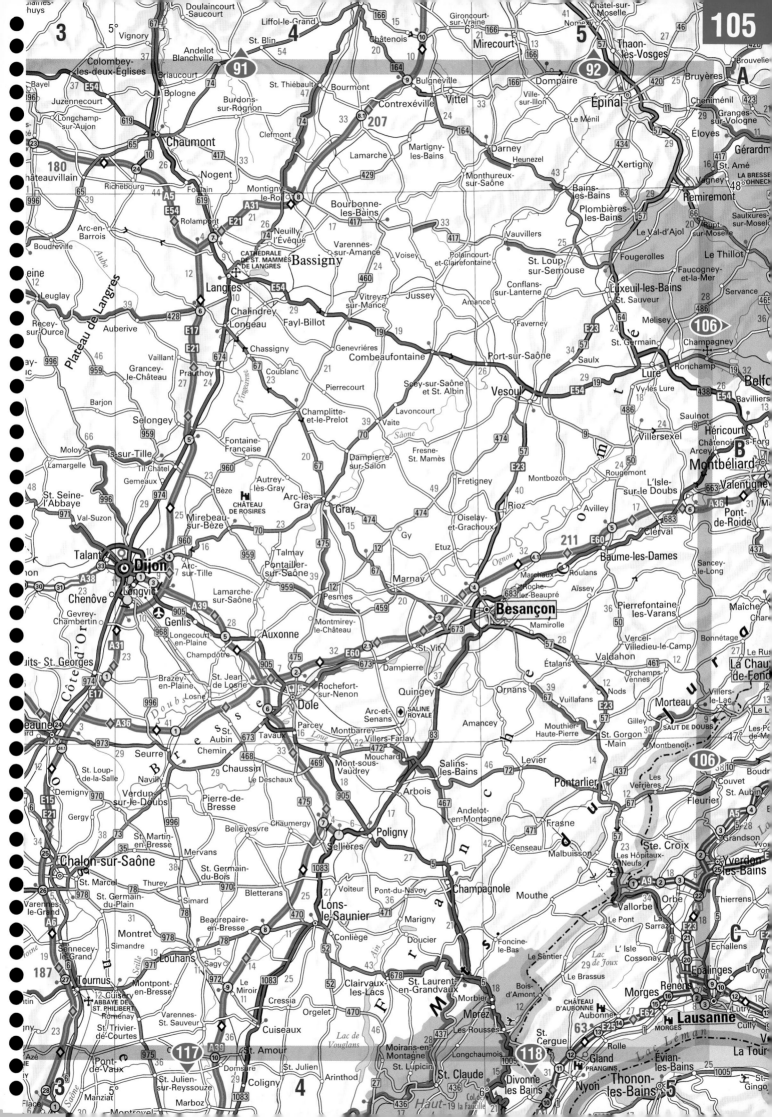

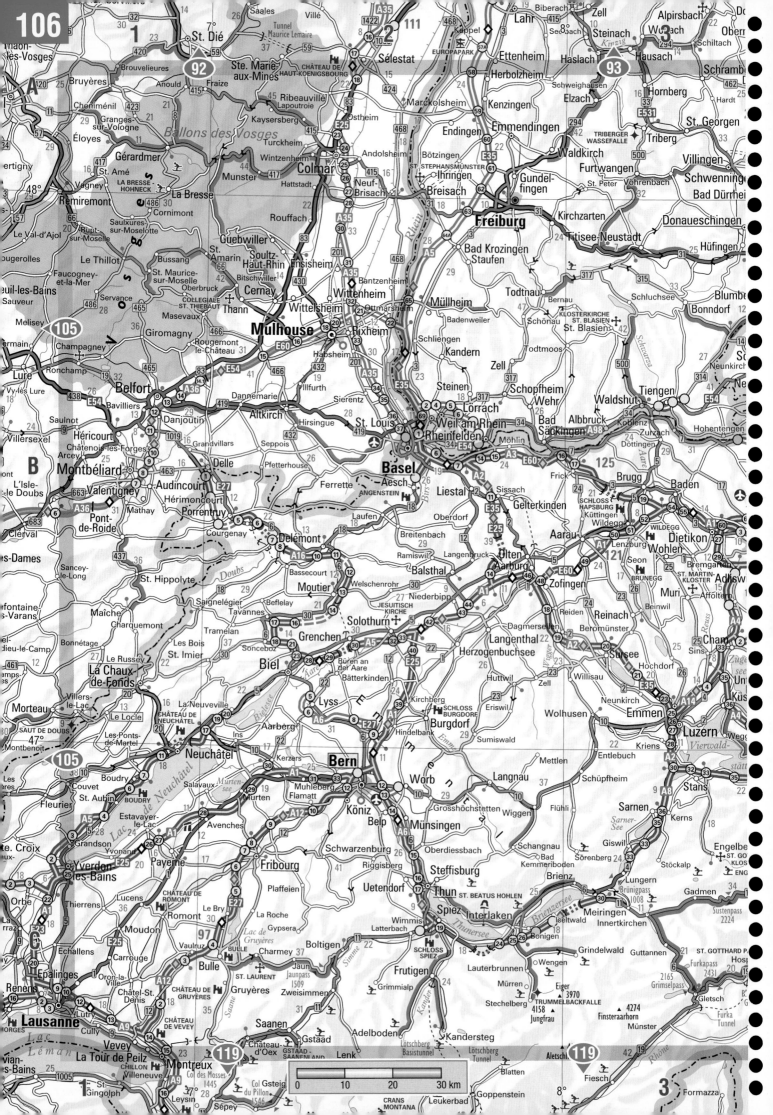

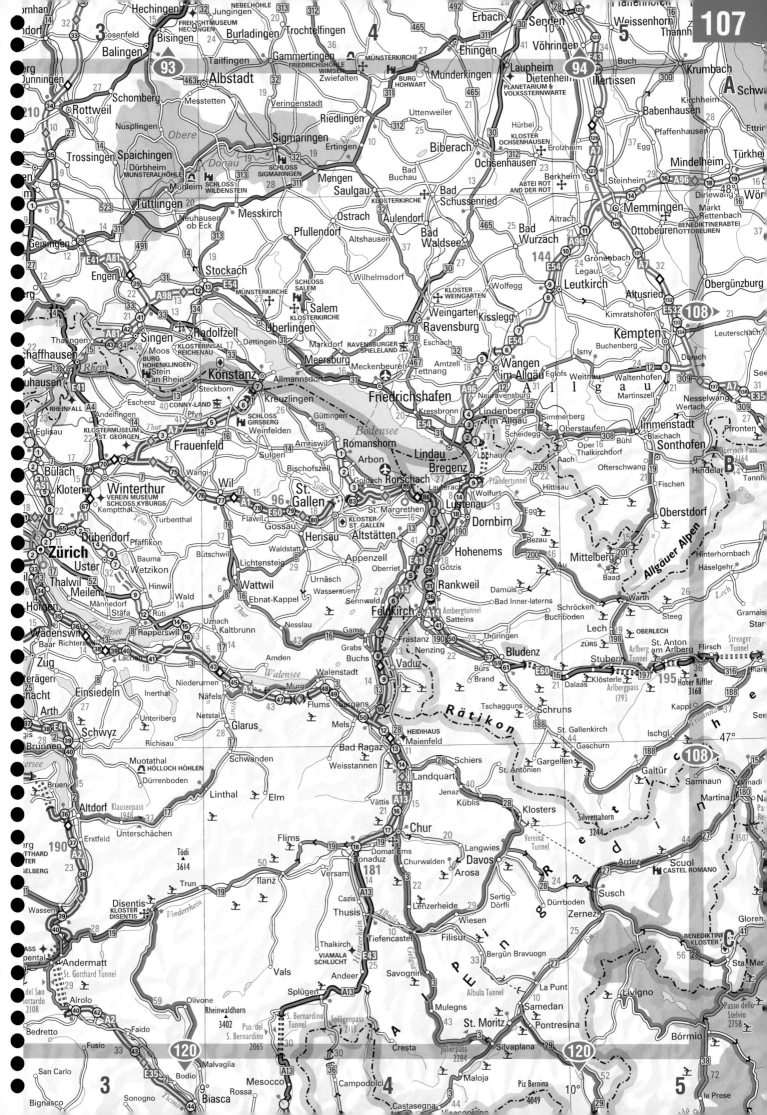

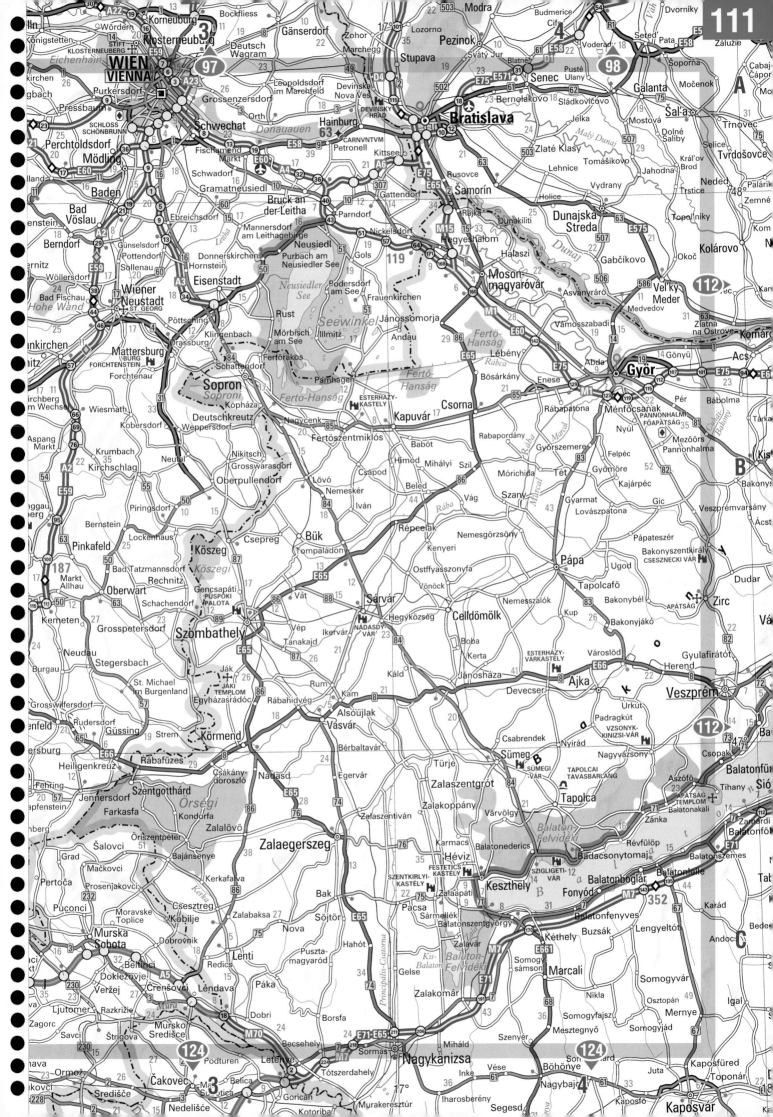

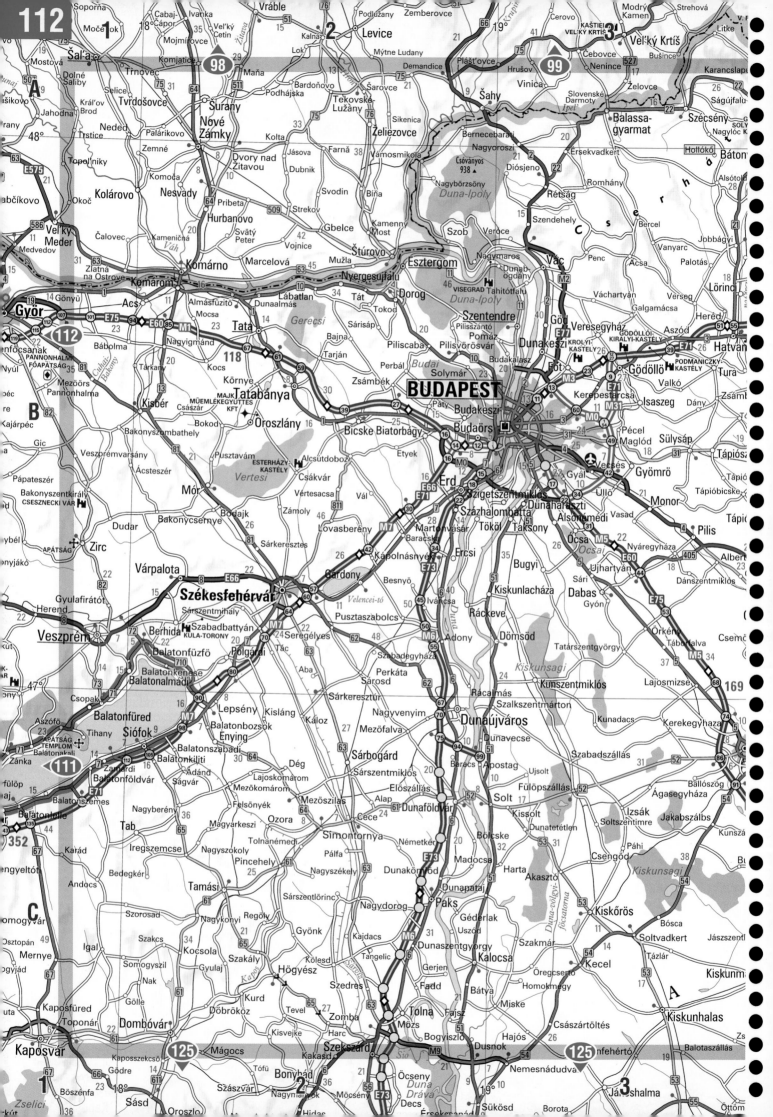

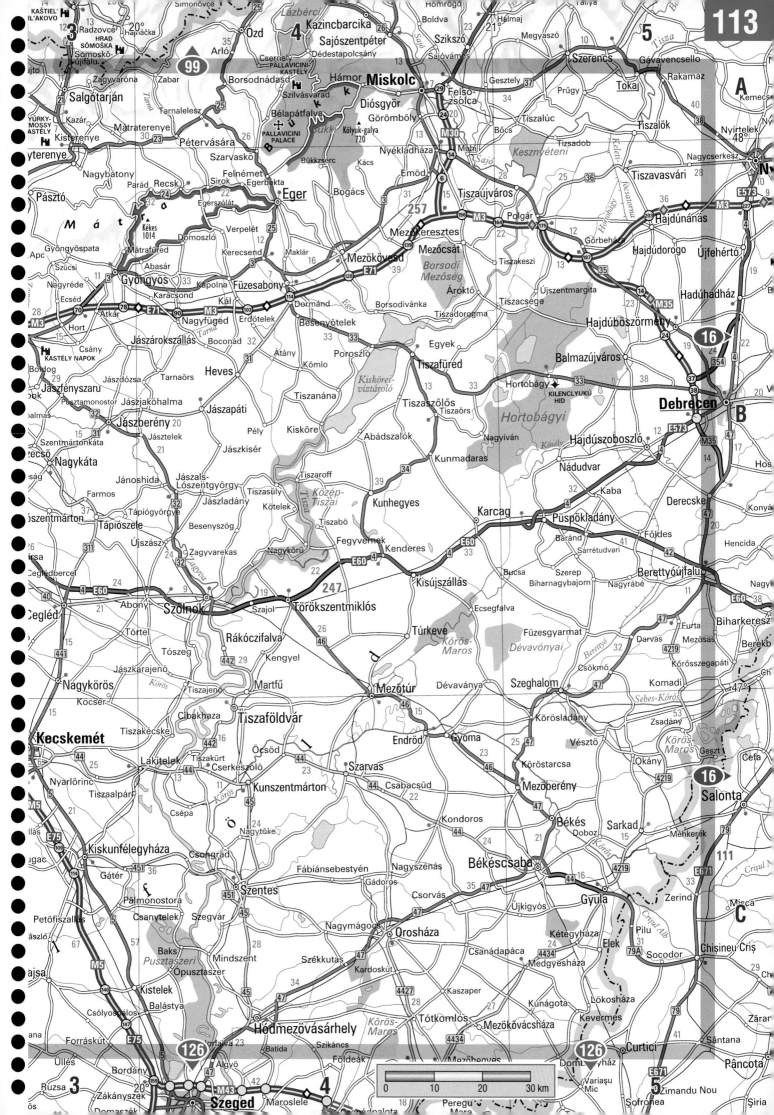

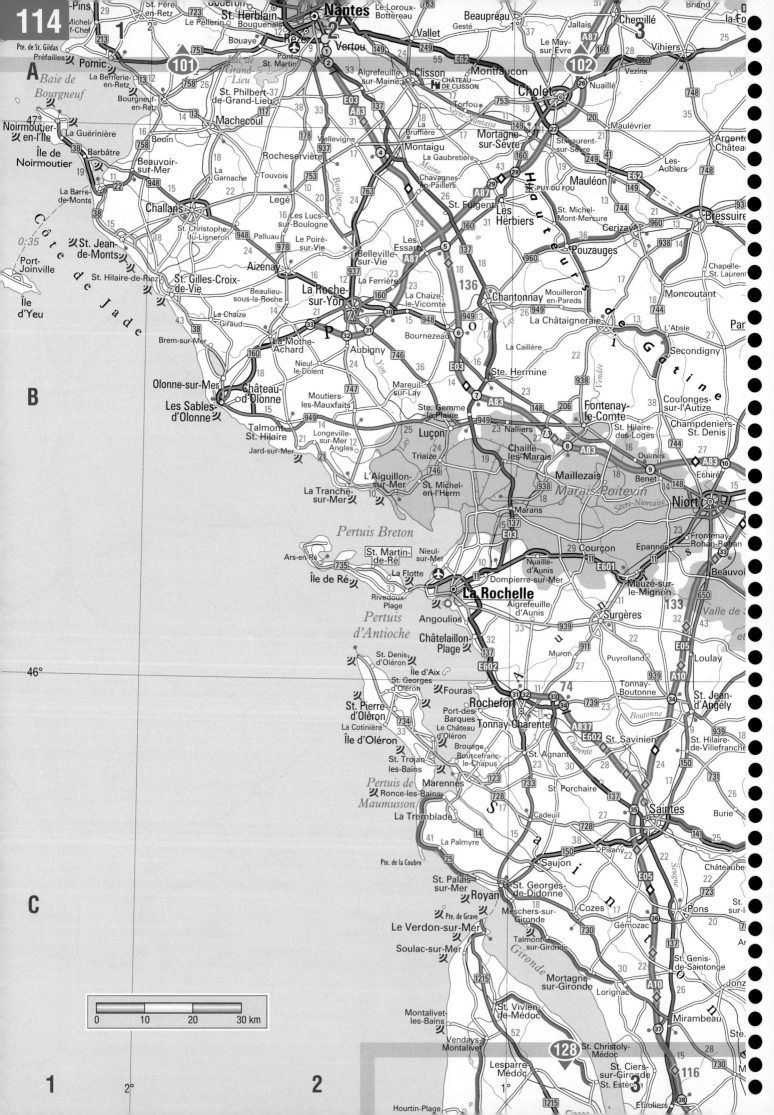

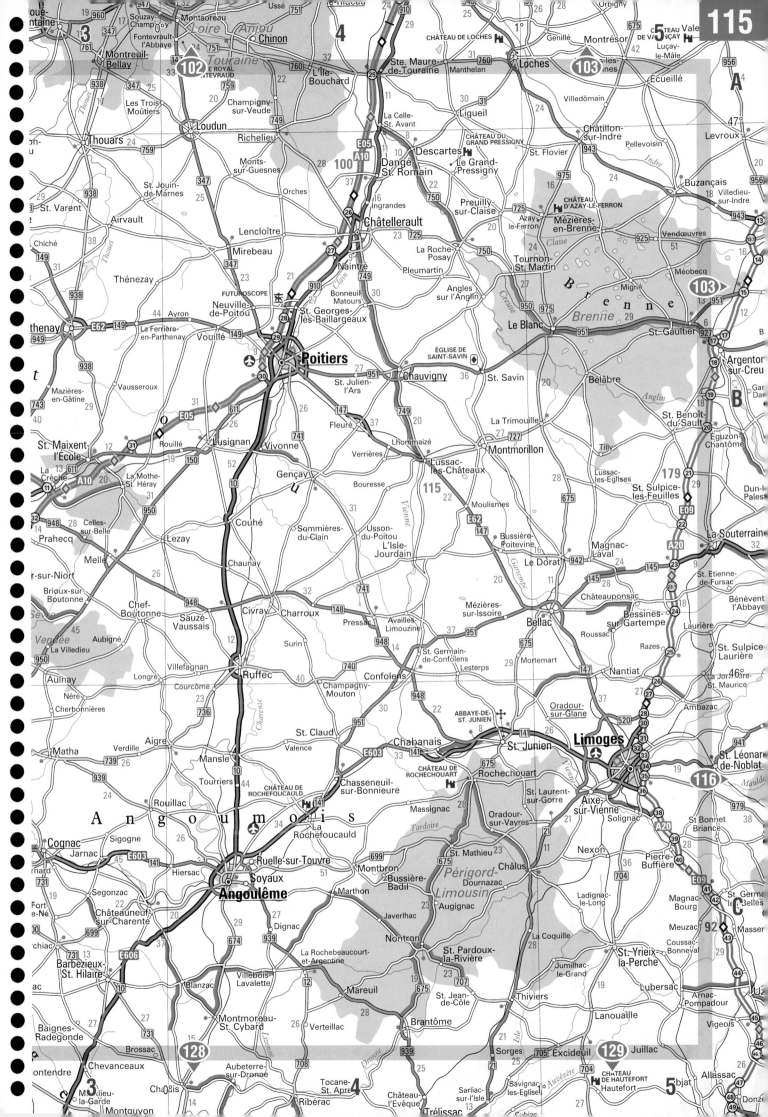

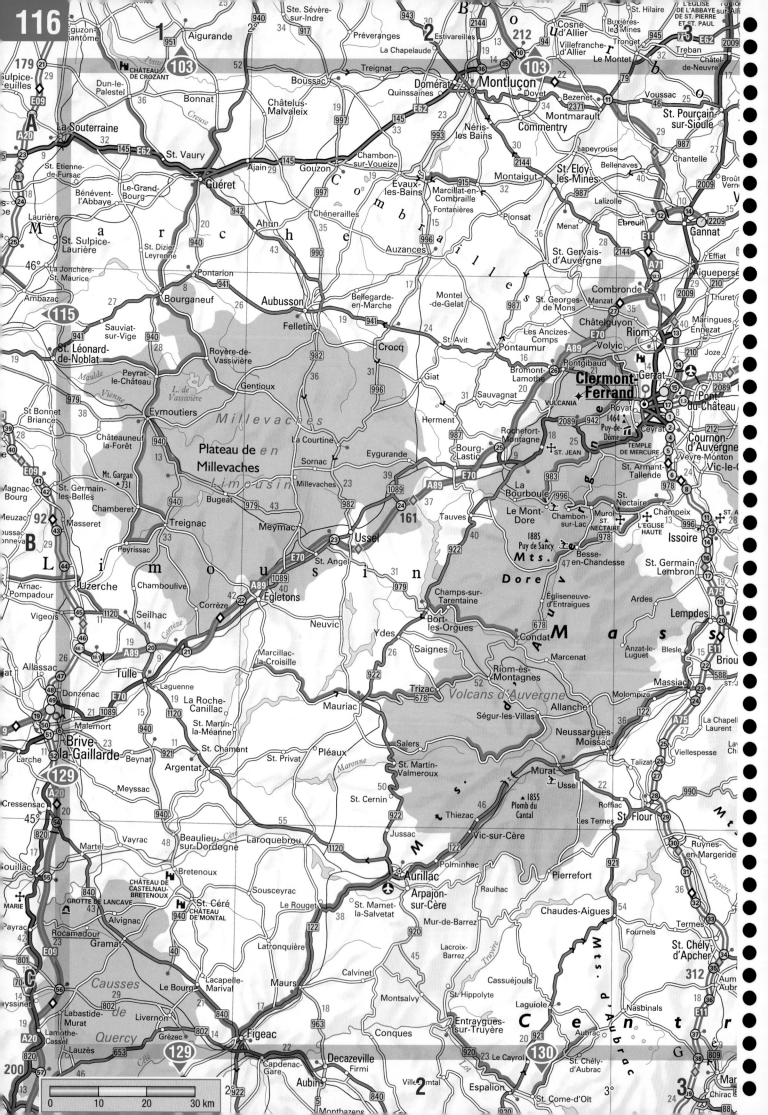

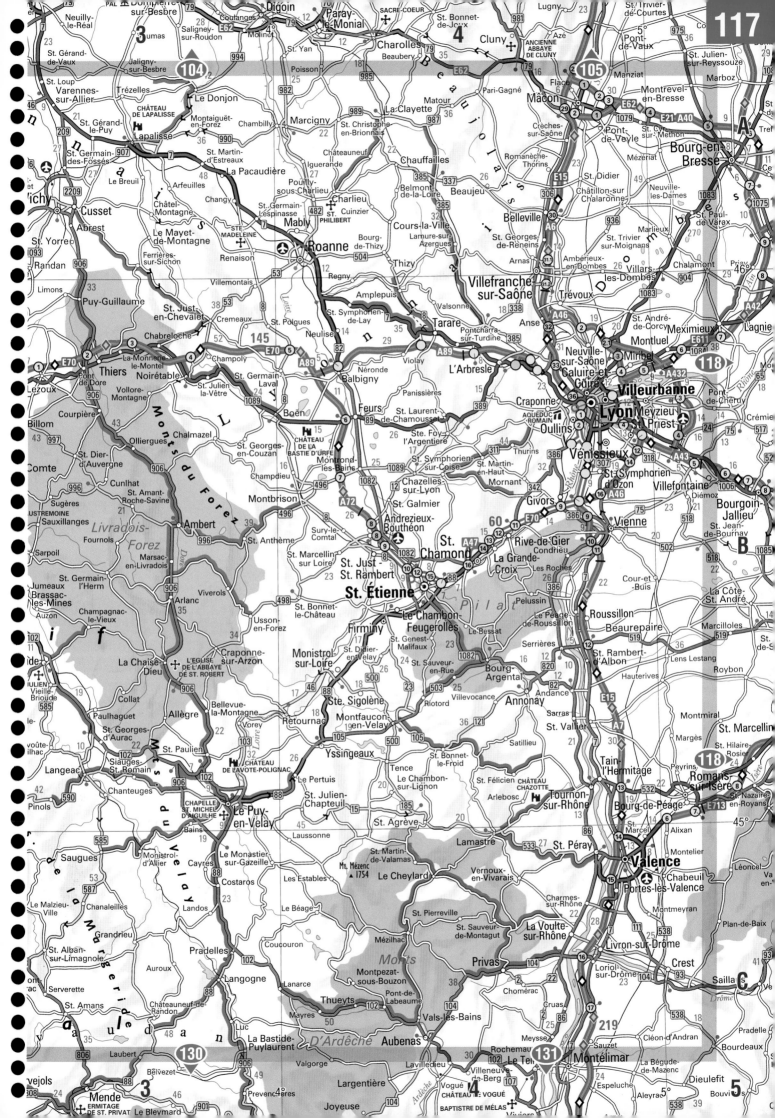

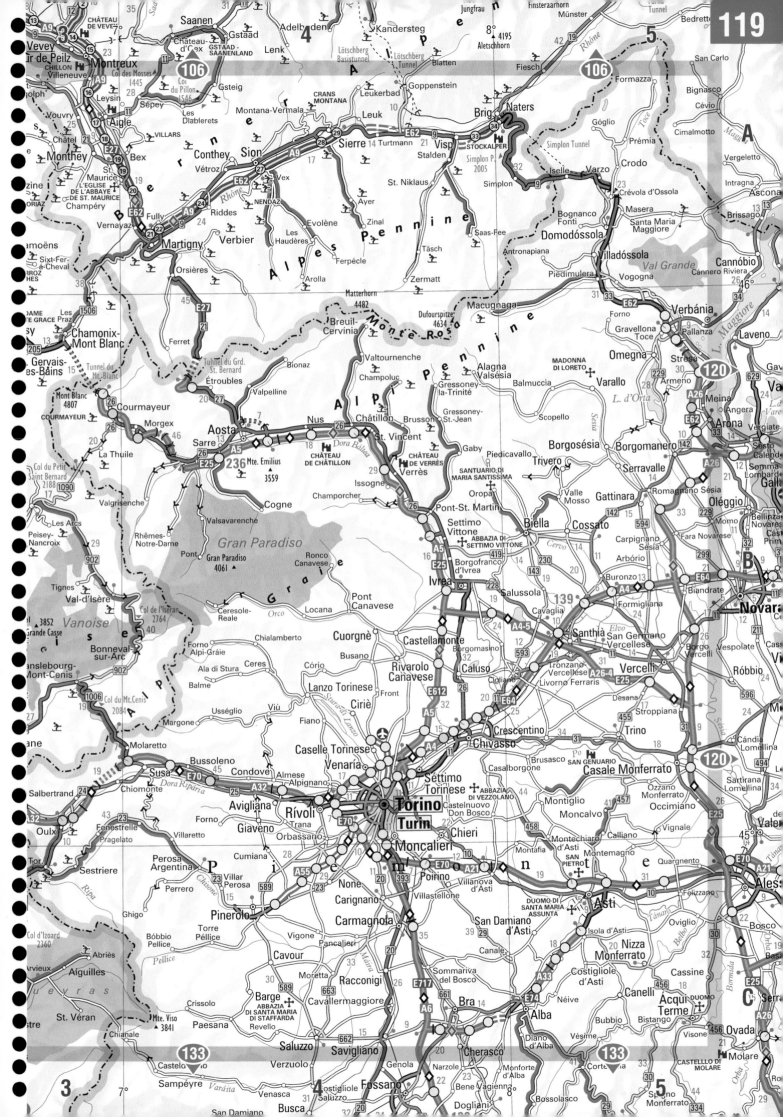

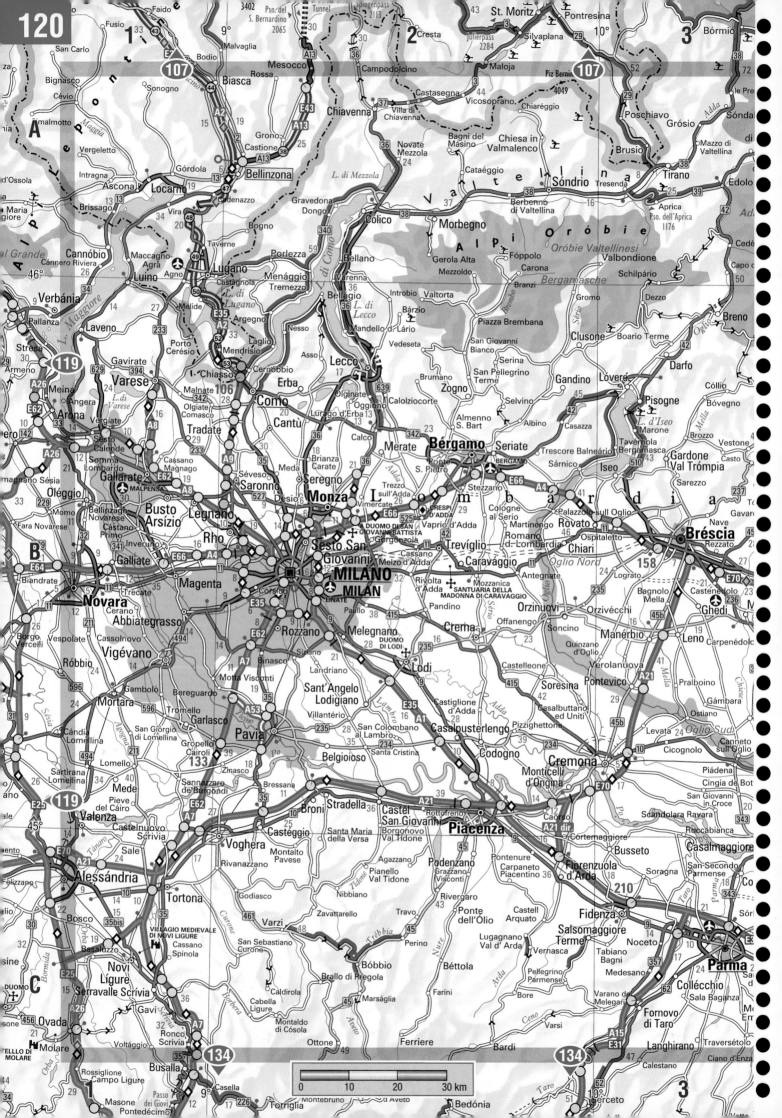

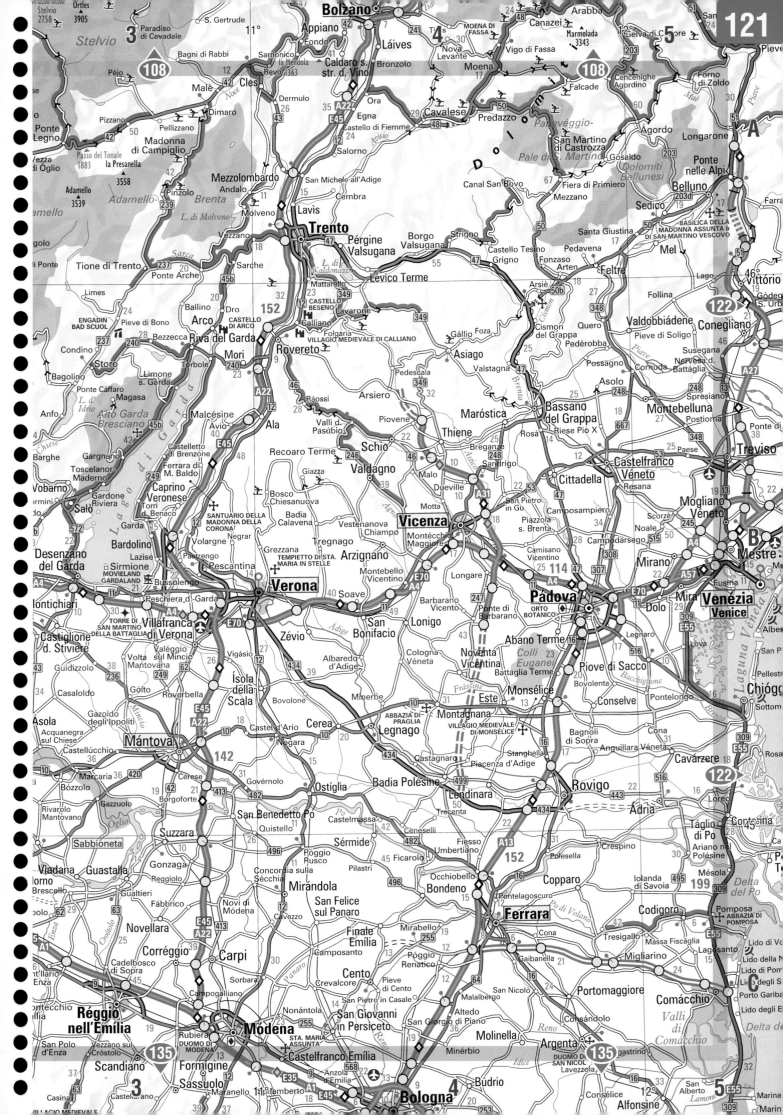

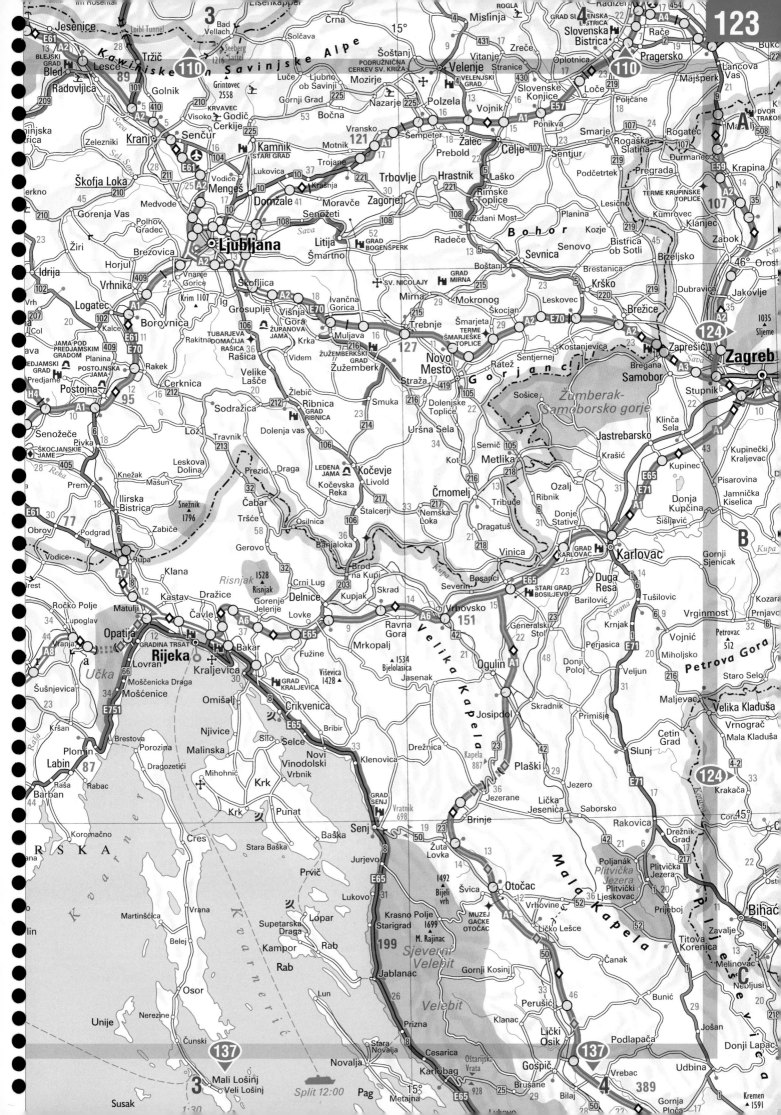

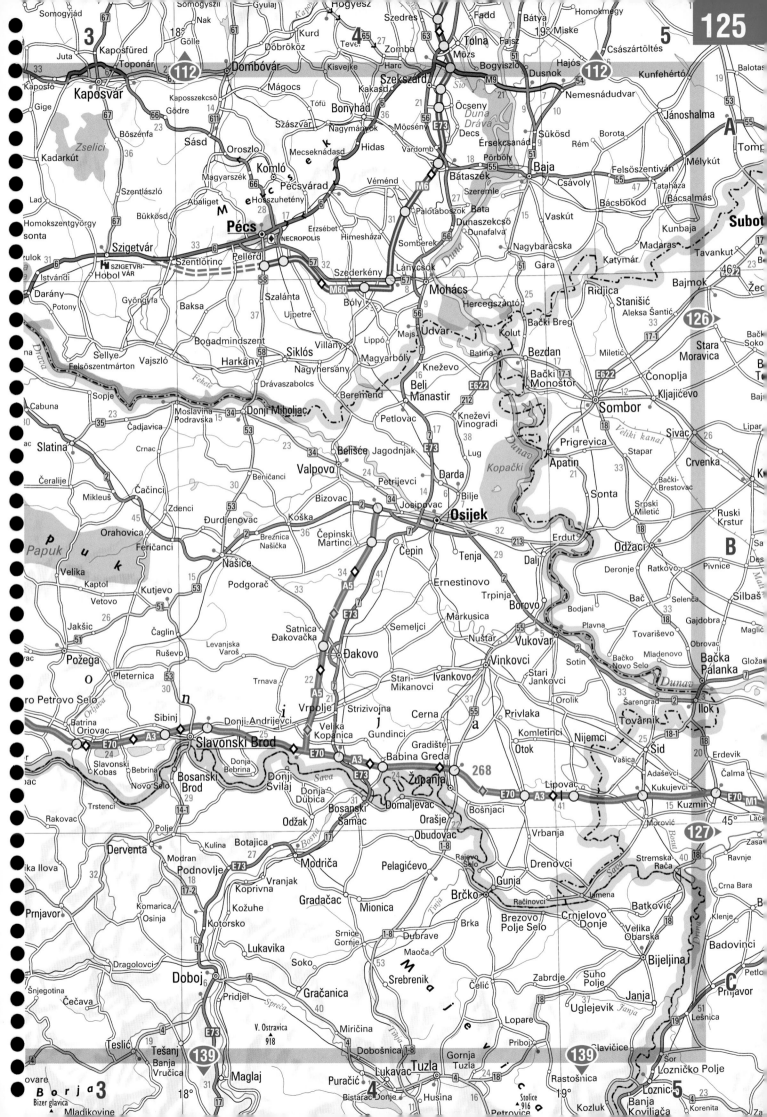

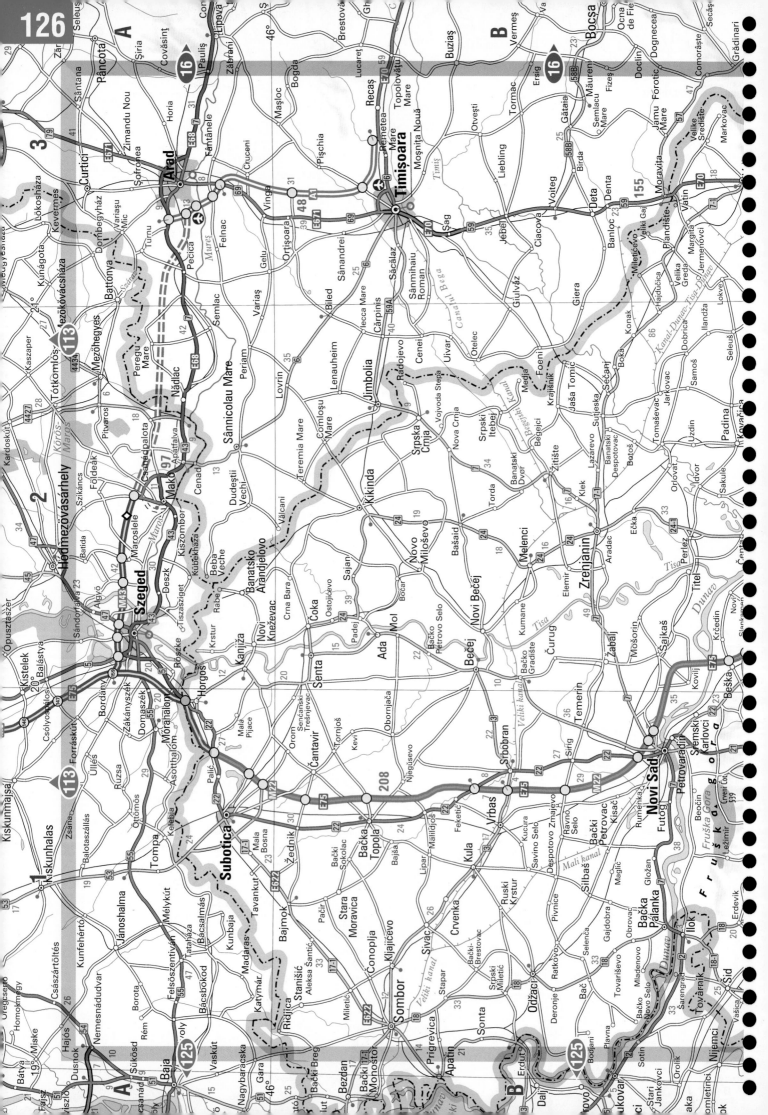

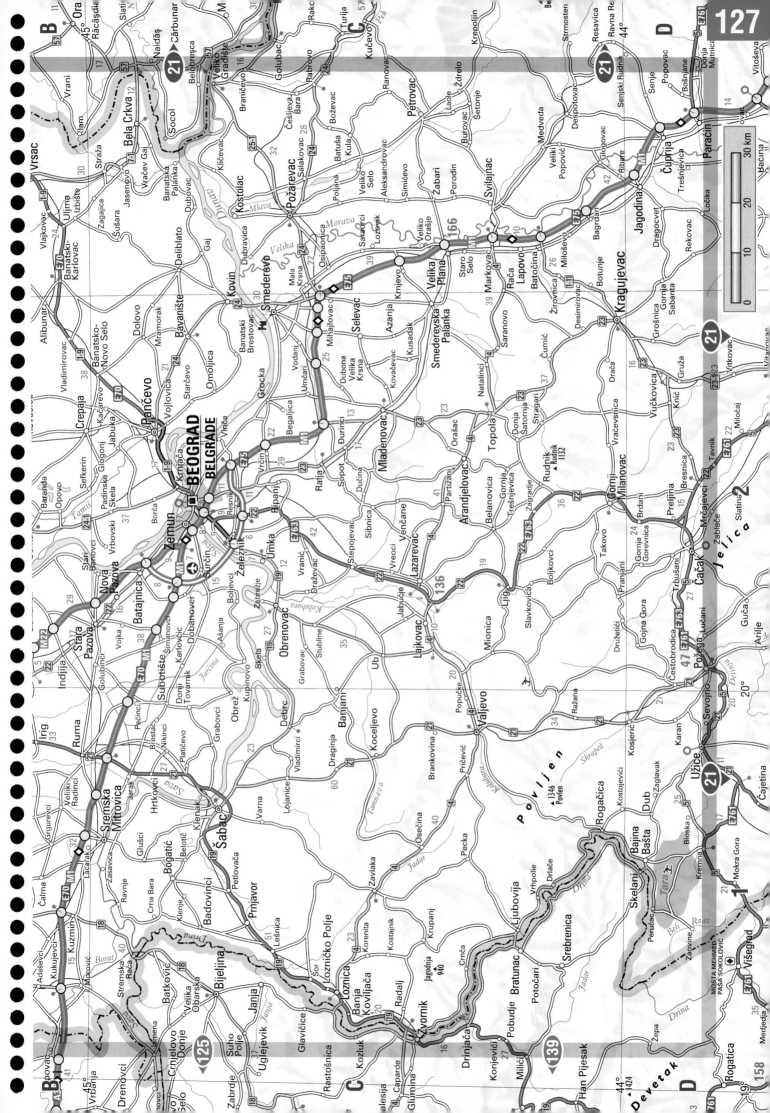

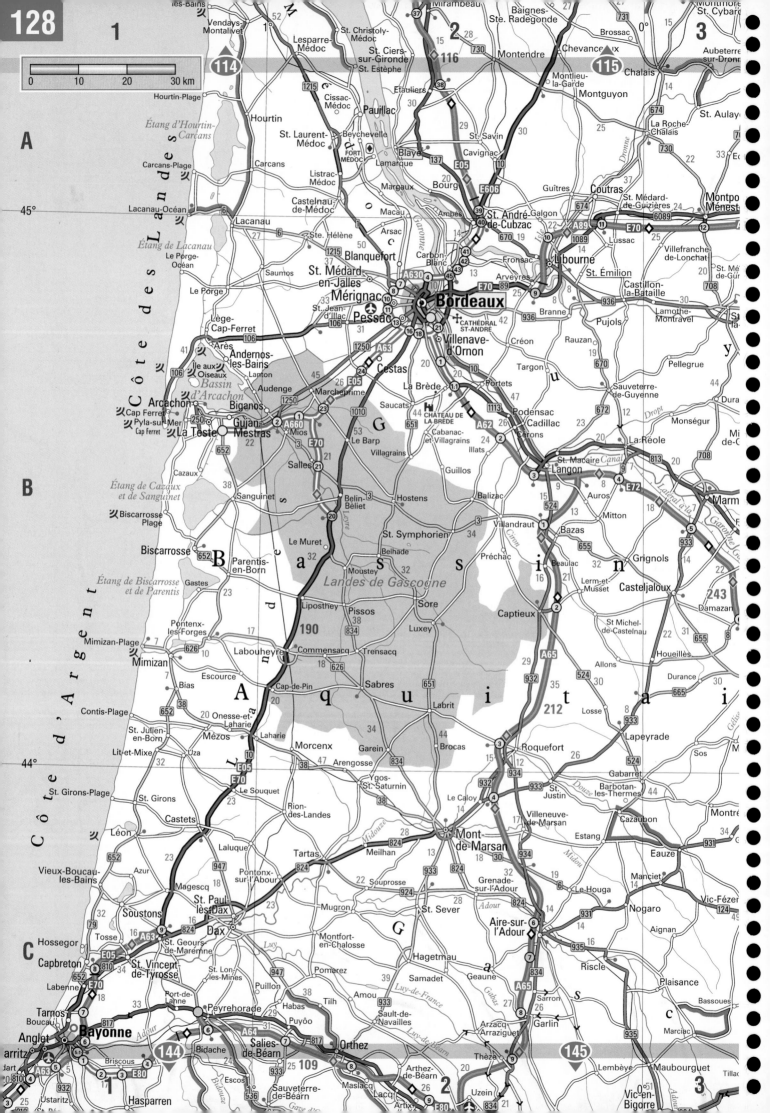

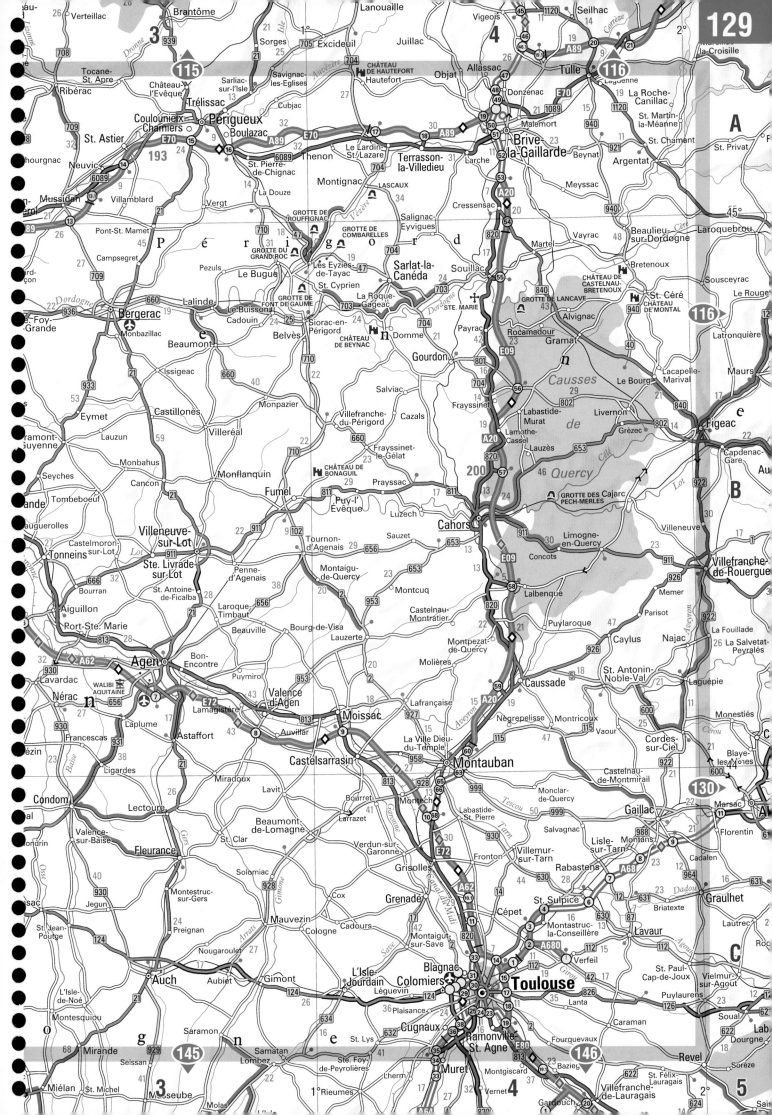

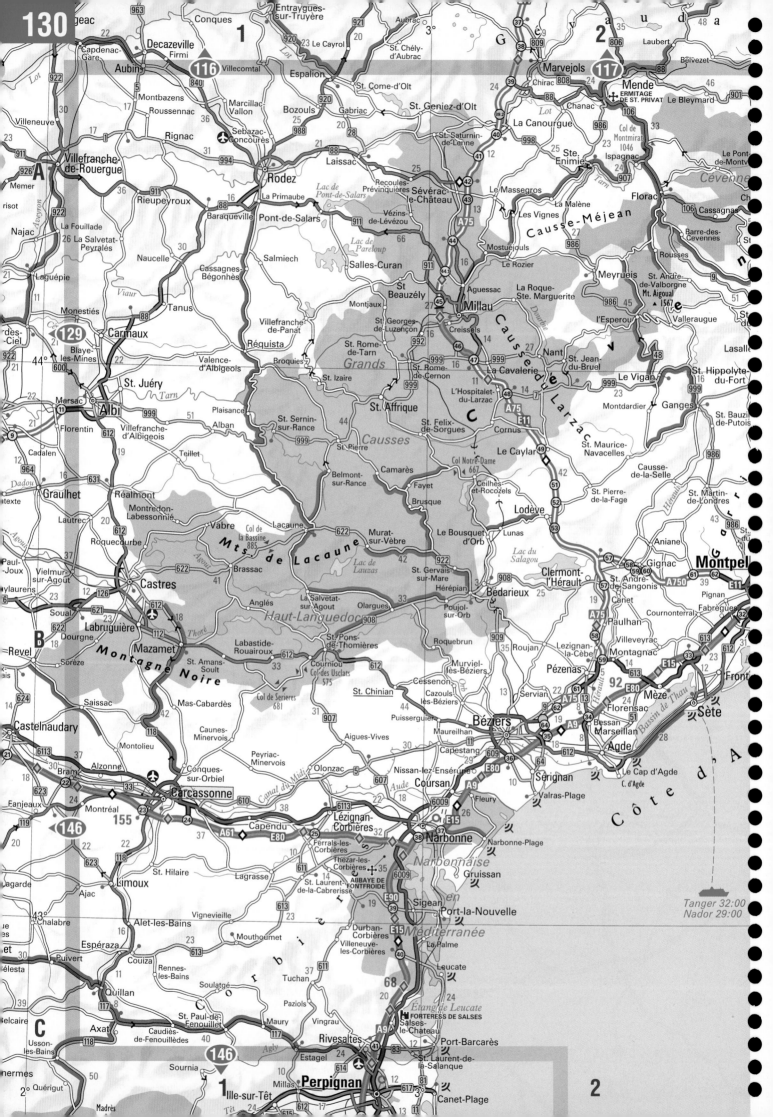

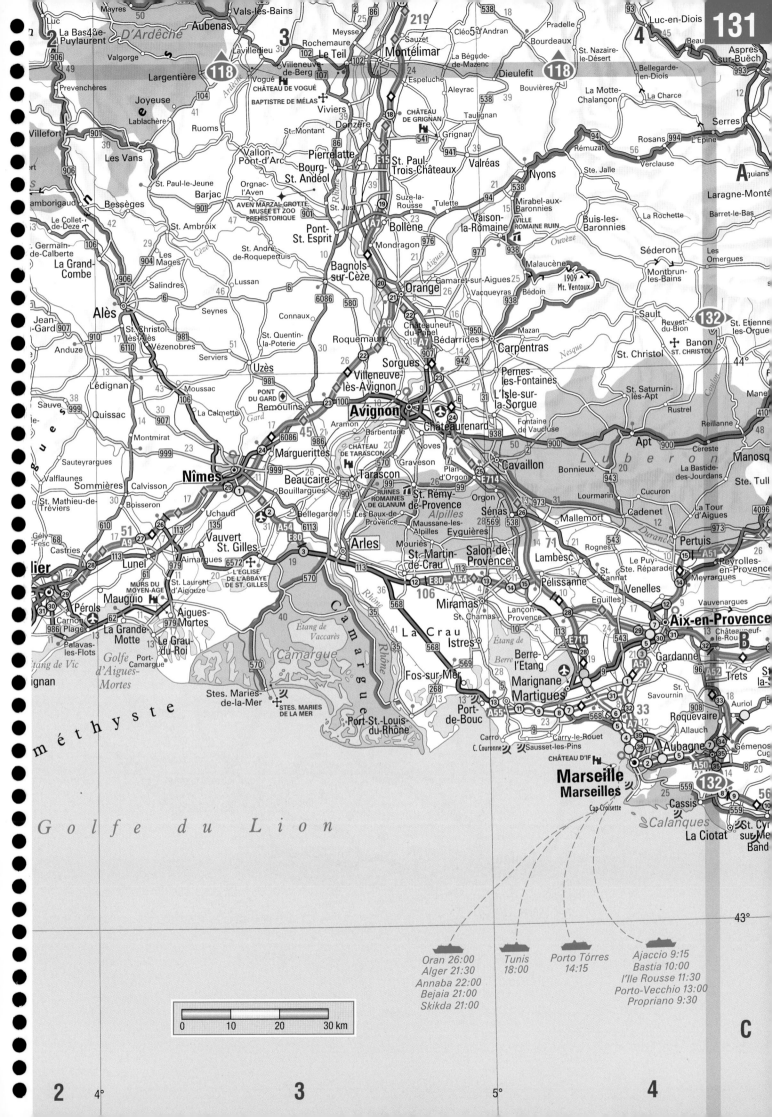

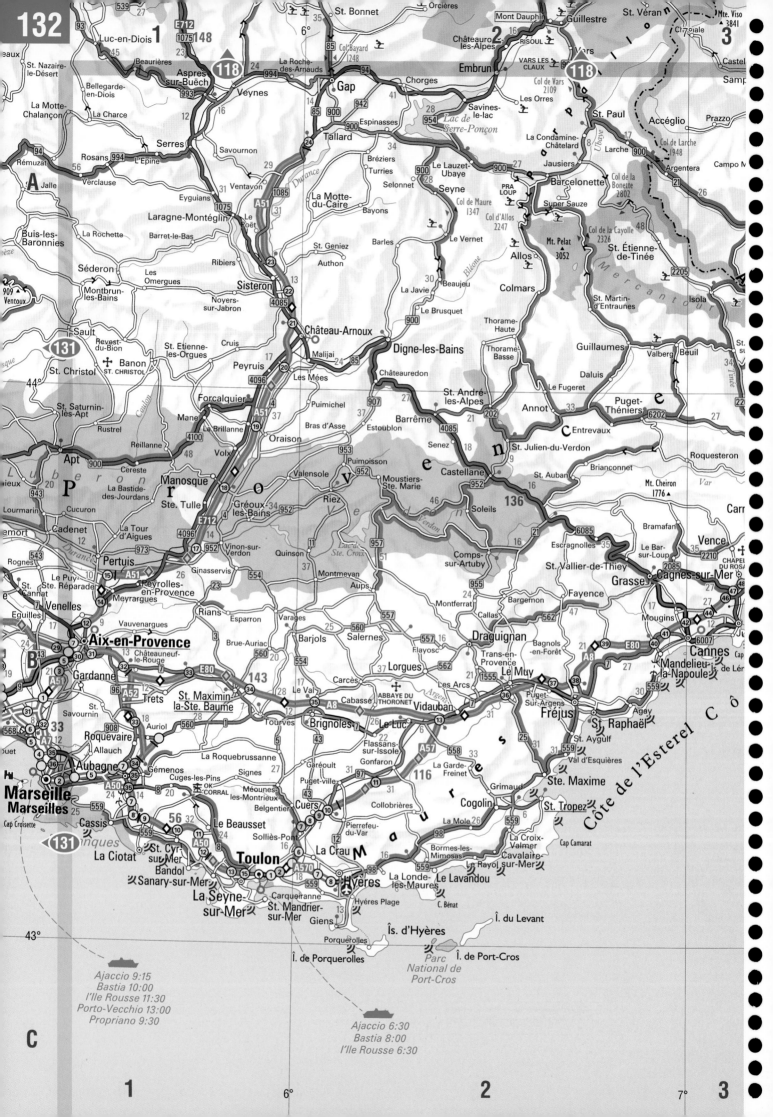

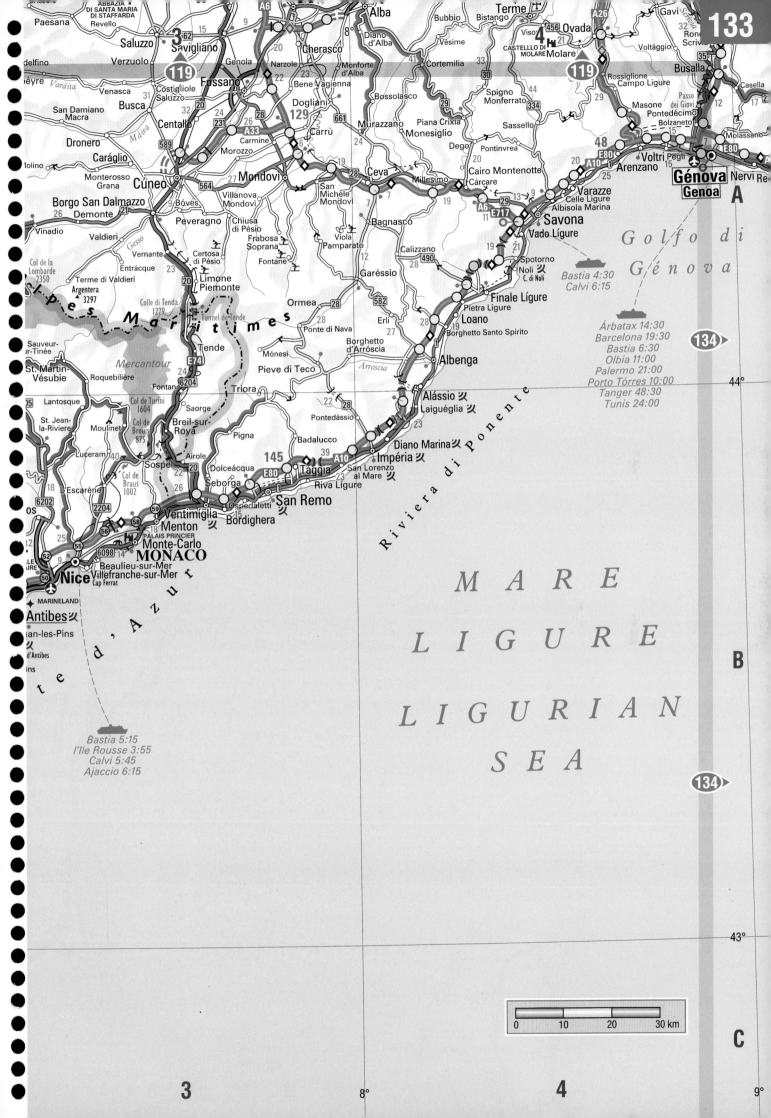

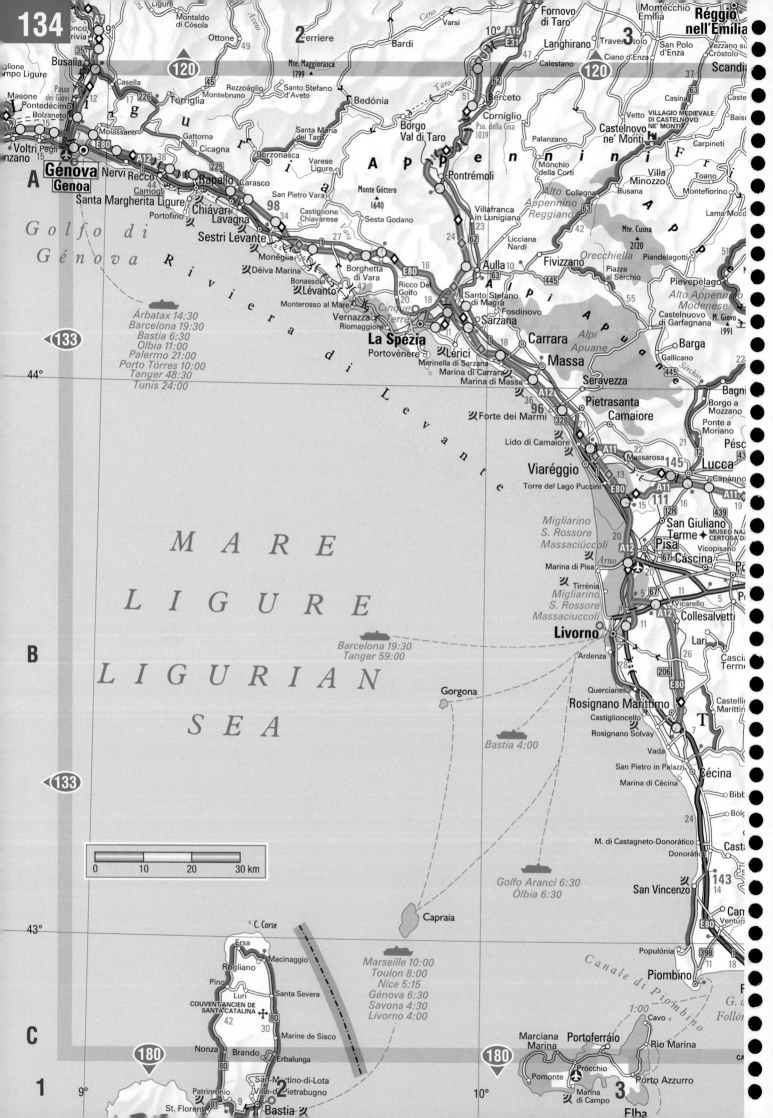

MARE

LIGURE

LIGURIAN

SEA

Golfo di Génova Riviera

Génova
Genoa

Busalla

Voltri

Nervi Recco

Santa Margherita Ligure

Portofino

Camogli

Rapallo

Chiávari

Lavagna

Sestri Levante

Monèglia

Déiva Marina

Bonassola

Lèvanto

Monterosso al Mare

Vernazza

Riomaggiore

Cinque Terre

Portovénere

La Spézia

Lèrici

Marinella di Sarzana

Marina di Carrara

Marina di Massa

Forte dei Marmi

Lido di Camaiore

Viaréggio

Torre del Lago Puccini

Árbatax 14:30
Barcelona 19:30
Bastia 6:30
Olbia 11:00
Palermo 21:00
Porto Tórres 10:00
Tanger 48:30
Tunis 24:00

Barcelona 19:30
Tanger 59:00

Gorgona

Bastia 4:00

Golfo Aranci 6:30
Ólbia 6:30

Capraia

Marseille 10:00
Toulon 8:00
Nice 5:15
Génova 6:30
Savona 4:30
Livorno 4:00

C. Corse

Ersa

Macinaggio

Rogliano

Pino

Luri

Santa Severa

COUVENT ANCIEN DE SANTA CATALINA

Marine de Sisco

Nonza

Brando

Erbalunga

Patrimonio

San Martino-di-Lota

Ville-di-Pietrabugno

St. Florent

Bastia

Appennino

Montaldo di Cósola

Ottone

Ferriere

Bardi

Varsi

Mte. Maggiorasca 1799

Santo Stefano d'Aveto

Bedónia

Borgo Val di Taro

Pontrémoli

Villafranca in Lunigiana

Licciana Nardi

Aulla

Santo Stefano di Magra

Fosdinovo

Sarzana

Carrara

Massa

Seravezza

Pietrasanta

Camaiore

Ponte a Moriano

Massarosa

Lucca

Capánno

San Giuliano Terme

Pisa

Cascina

Marina di Pisa

Tirrénia

Migliarino S. Rossore Massaciúccoli

Livorno

Ardenza

Quercianella

Rosignano Maríttimo

Castiglioncello

Rosignano Solvay

Vada

San Pietro in Palazzi

Marina di Cécina

Cécina

Bibb

Bólg

M. di Castagneto-Donorático

San Vincenzo

Populónia

Piombino

Cavo

Rio Marina

Marciana Marina

Portoferráio

Pomonte

Prócchio

Marina di Campo

Porto Azzurro

Elba

Fornovo di Taro

Montécchio Emília

Réggio nell'Emília

Langhirano

Ciano d'Enza

San Polo d'Enza

Scandia

Berceto

Corníglio

Palanzano

Castelnovo ne' Monti

VILLAGIO MEDIEVALE DI CASTELNOVO NE' MONTI

Carpineti

Alto Appennino Reggiano

Villa Minozzo

Montefiorino

Toano

Collagna

Busana

Mte. Cusna 2120

Piandelagotti

Alto Appennino Modenese

Castelnuovo di Garfagnana

M. Giovo 1991

Barga

Gallicano

Péscia

Golfo di Génova

Casella

Torriglia

Montebruno

Rezzoáglio

Santa Maria del Taro

Gattorna

Cicagna

Borzonasca

Varese Ligure

Carasco

San Pietro Vara

Castiglione Chiavárese

Sesta Godano

Ricco Del Golfo

Borghetto di Vara

Fivizzano

Piazza al Sérchio

Pievepélago

Orecchiella

Golfo di Génova

Unije
Nerezine
Čunski **3**
Pula
1:30

Klanac

Prizna
15°
Stara
Novalja
Cesarica

Lički
Osik
4 odlapača
Gošpić **389**

Jošan
Donj

Novalja
Karlobag
E65
928
25
Brušane
29
Bilaj
Bruvno
Vrebac

Udbina **123**

Mali Lošinj
Veli Lošinj **123**

Pag
Metajna

50
28
22
Gornja
Ploča
17
1
Kremen
1591
33
Mazin
Do

Pag

928

Susak

AENONA

Lukovo
Šugorje

Medak
Vaganski
vrh
1757
Raduc
7

Sveti Rok
50
21

A

Gornja

Silba

Gorica

Barič Draga
Tribanj
Kruščica

Paklenica

A1
26

Velebit **27**

Gračac

Olib

Vir

Povljana

Starigrad-
Paklenica
28

20
16

Premuda
Ist
Virsko
more

Vir

Ražanac

E65
12
Jasenice **54**
27

Zrmanja

Otrić

Molat
2:15

Privlaka
Vrsi

8
Poličnik
17
Posedarje
12

Obrovac

Kaštel
Žegarski

21

AENONA
Nin

Novigrad
13

16
18

Ervenik

Sestrunj
Petrčane
1:20

502
Murvica
8

27

23

Mokro
Polje

Ancona 6:00

Božava

Zadar
18

Zemunik Donji
56
21
10

Medvide

Brbinj

Preko
TVRĐAVA SV.
MIHOVILA
Kali

Bibinje
Sukošan
17
Benkovac
ASSERIA

BURNUM **138**
44°

Kukljica

Dugi Otok

26
Miranje
A1
27

Đevrske

Krka

Kistan

Zaglav

Pašman
Pašman

Turanj

Biograd na Moru
Pakoštane
Stankovci

49

MANASTIR
KRKA

Sali

Tkon

Vransko
Jezero
39

E65

Skradin

Telašćica

Žut

Pirovac **27**

33

Kornat

Murter
Tisno
37

Prokljansko
Jezero

8
Vodice
KATEDRALA
SV JAKOVA
Zablaće

Šibenik

Kornati

Žirje

149
Krapanj

29

Primošten

Zadar 6:00

Split 7:30
Starigrad 9:40
Durrës 19:00
Zadar 6:00
Trieste 6:30

A D R I A T I C   S E A

Jabucka

Rogoznica

B

138

Svetac

43°

el Tronto

degli Abruzzi **3**

15°
0   10   20   30 km

4

C

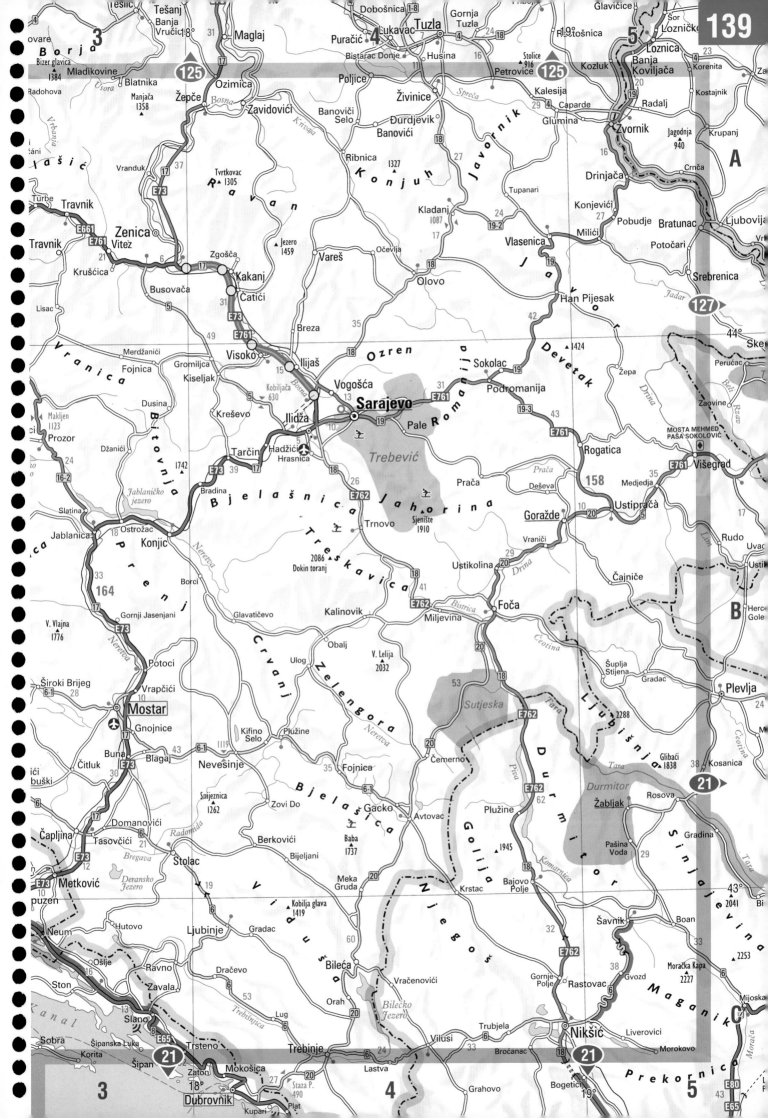

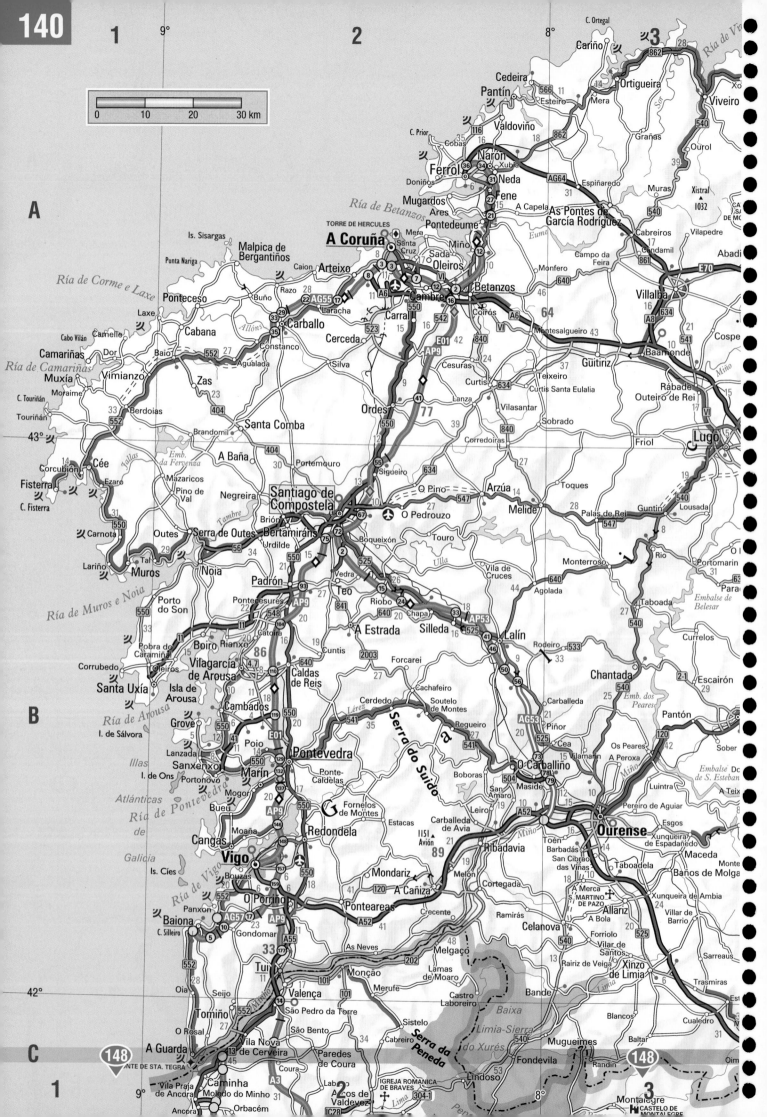

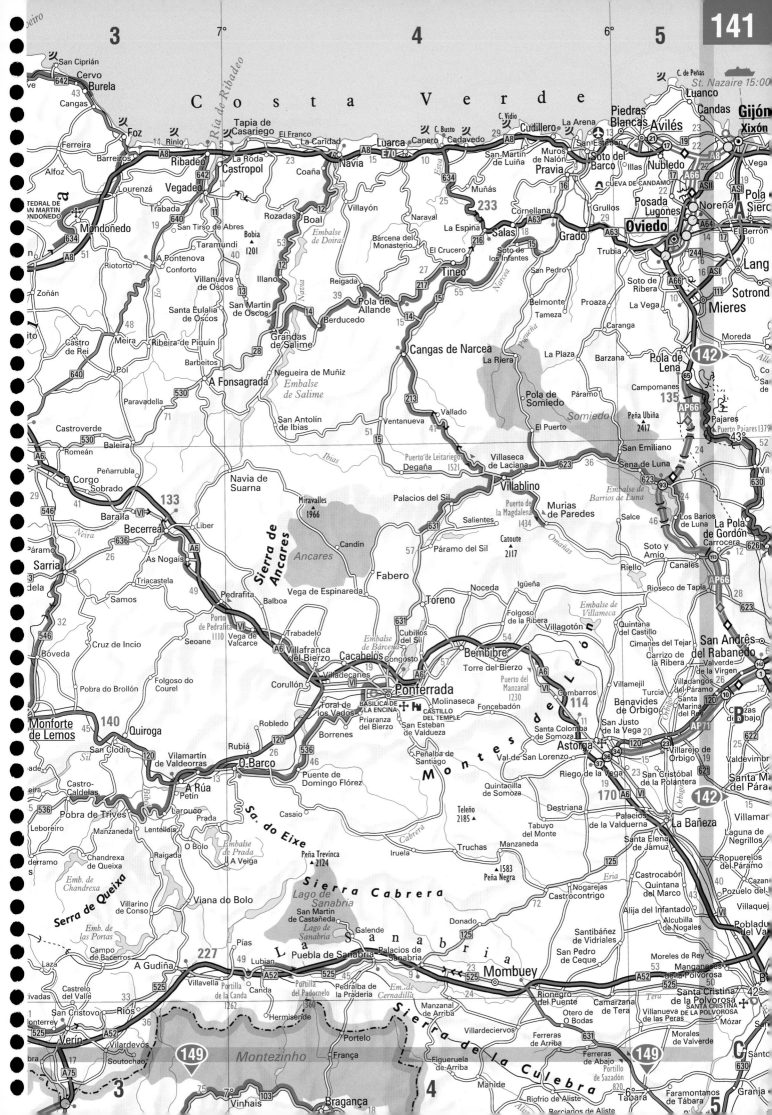

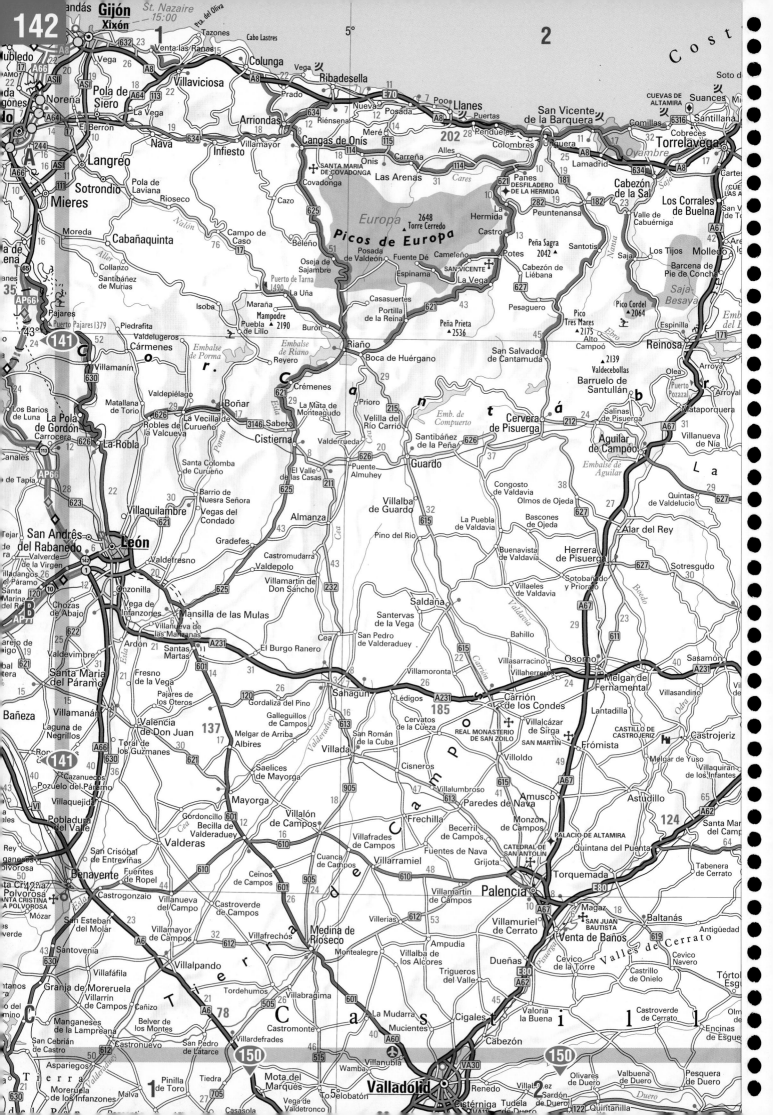

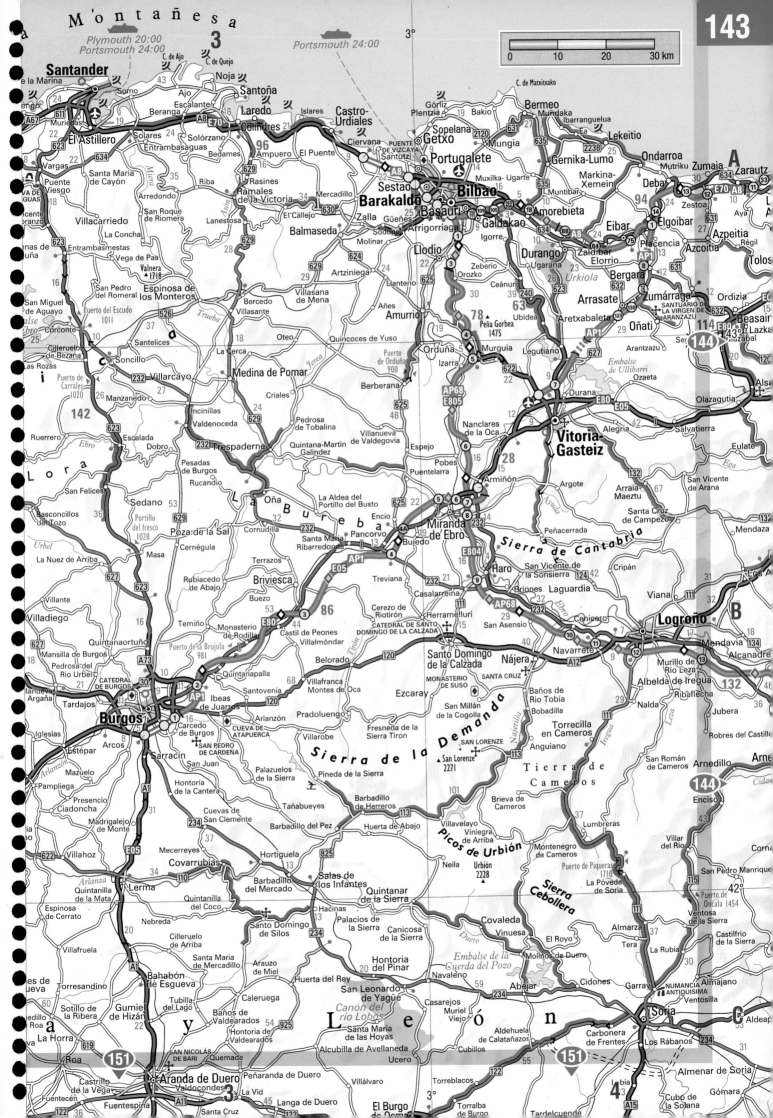

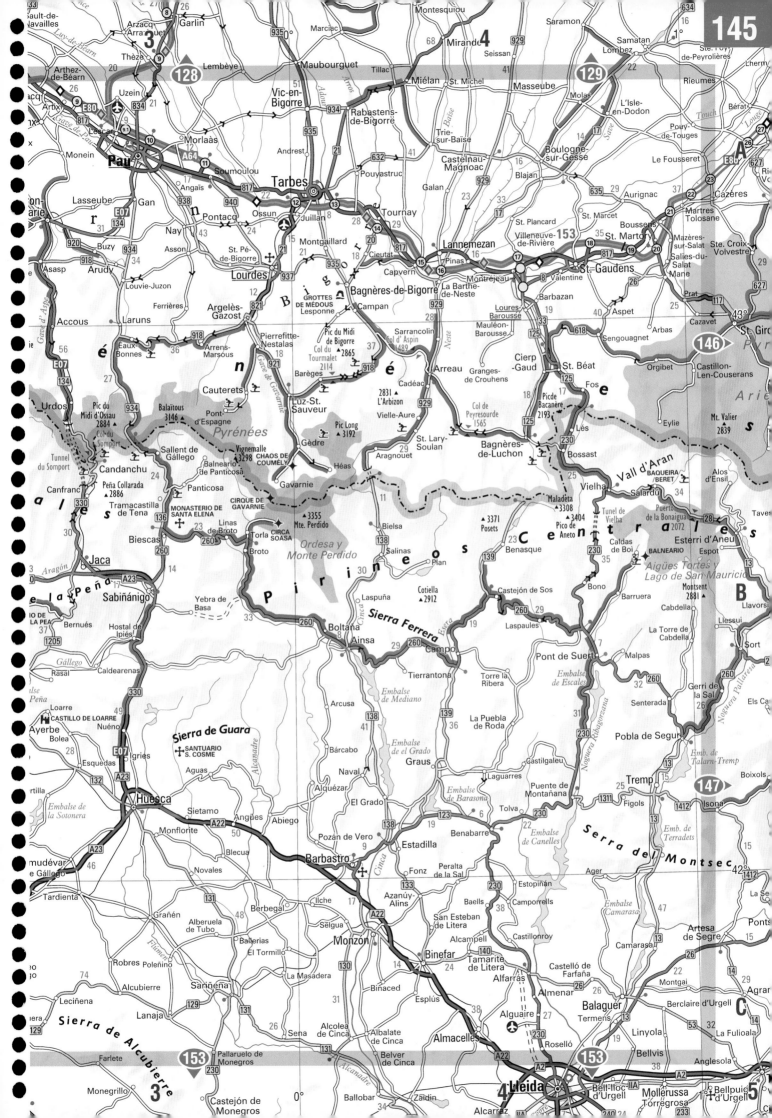

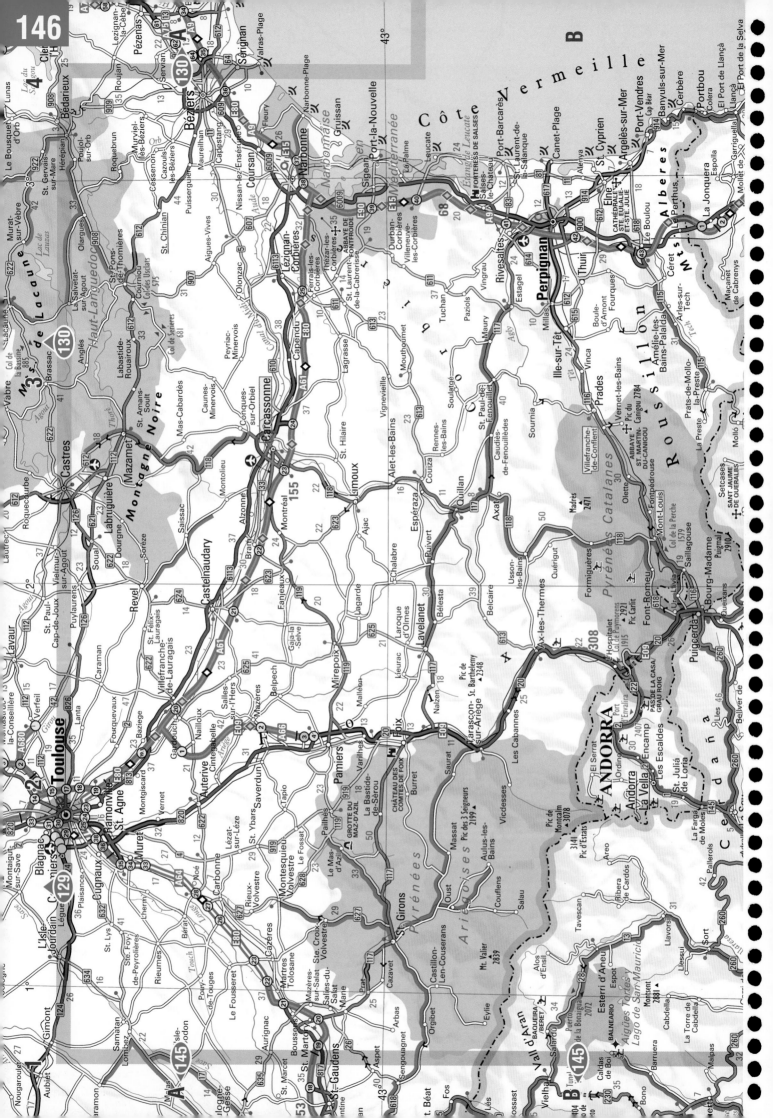

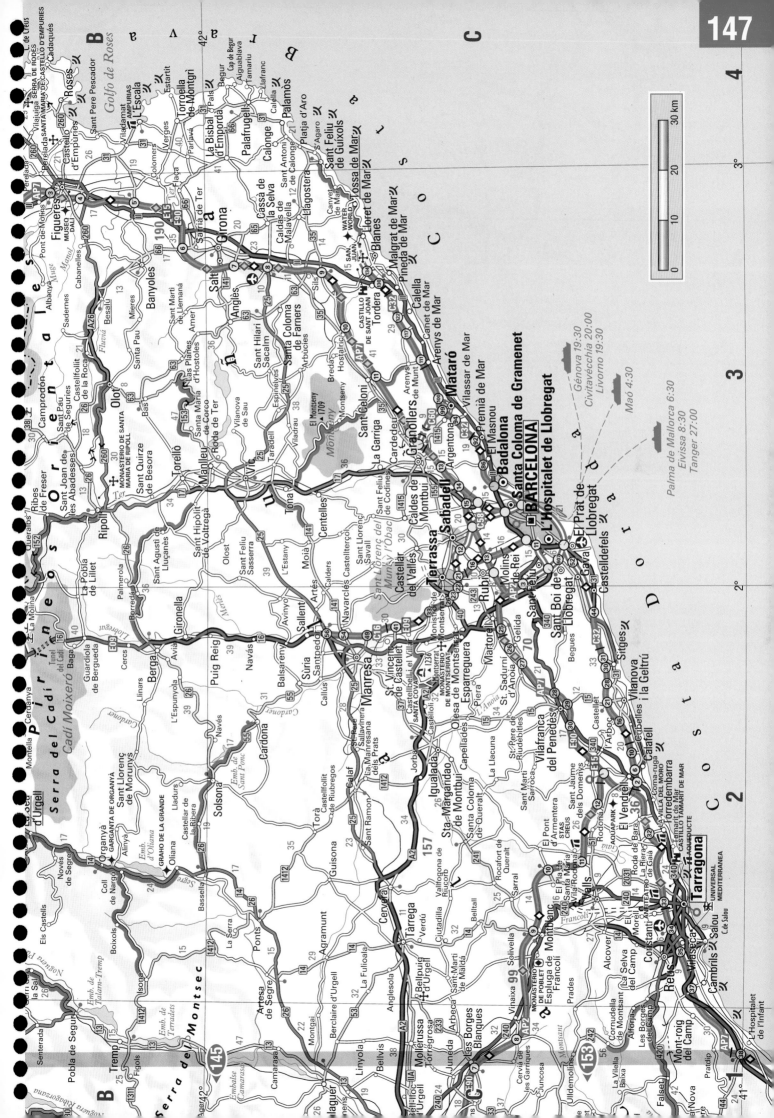

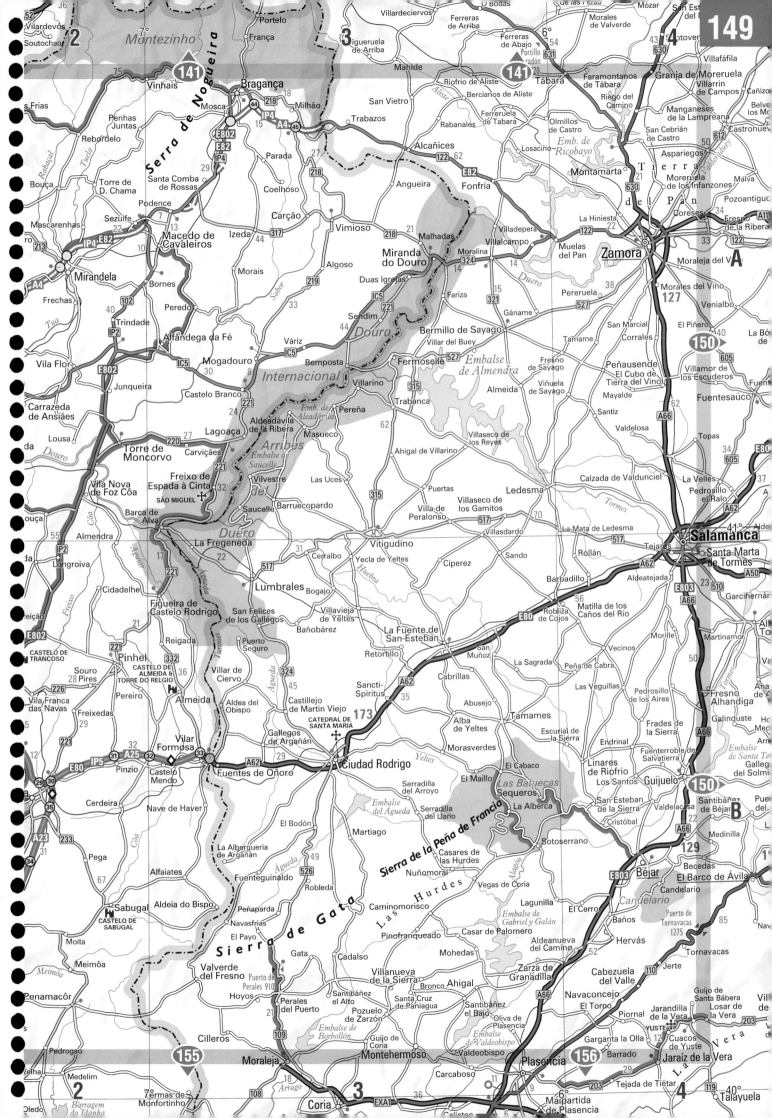

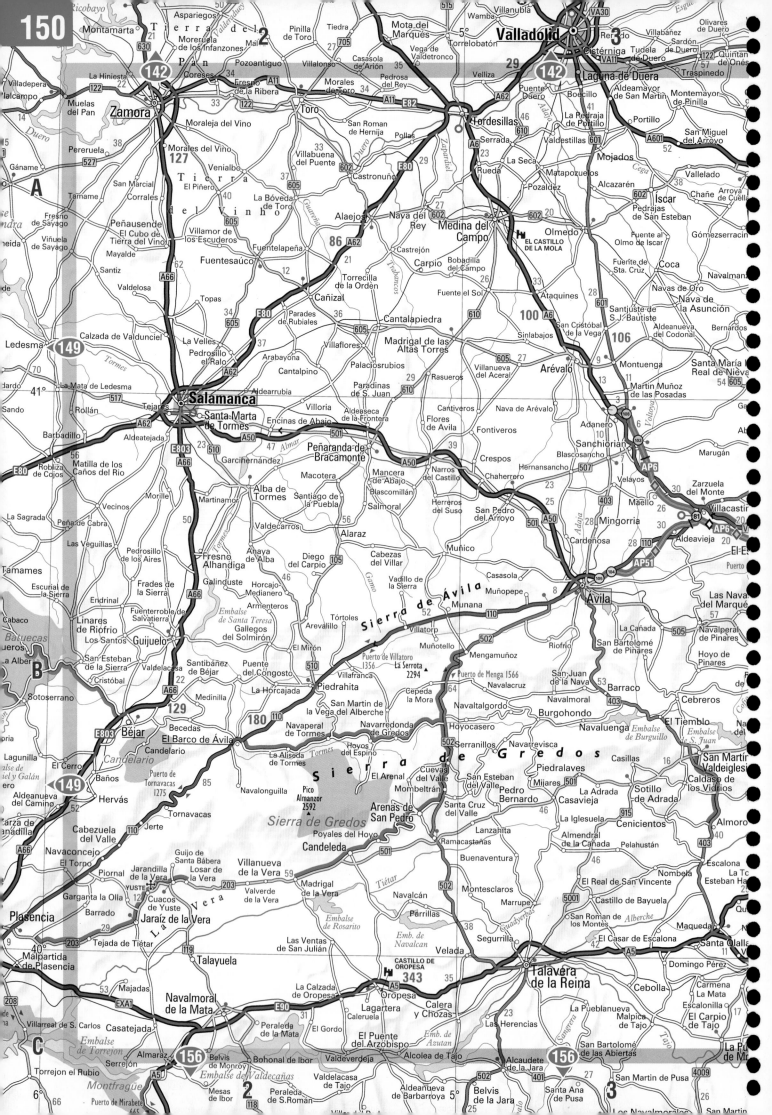

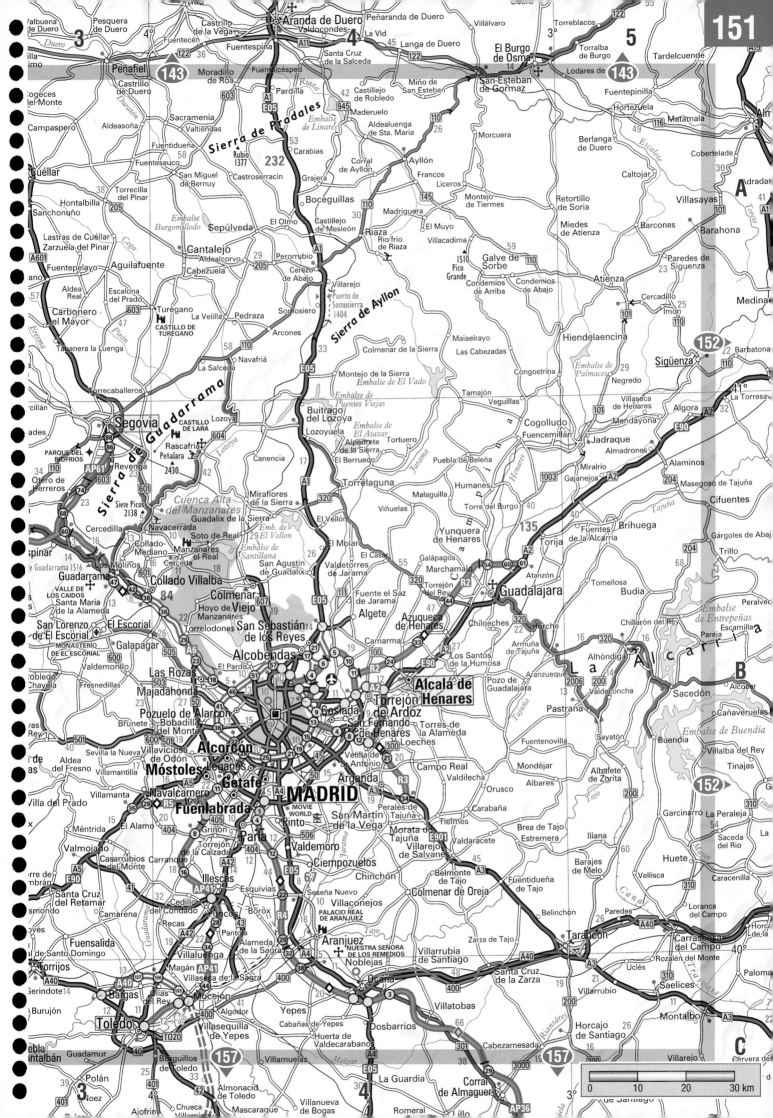

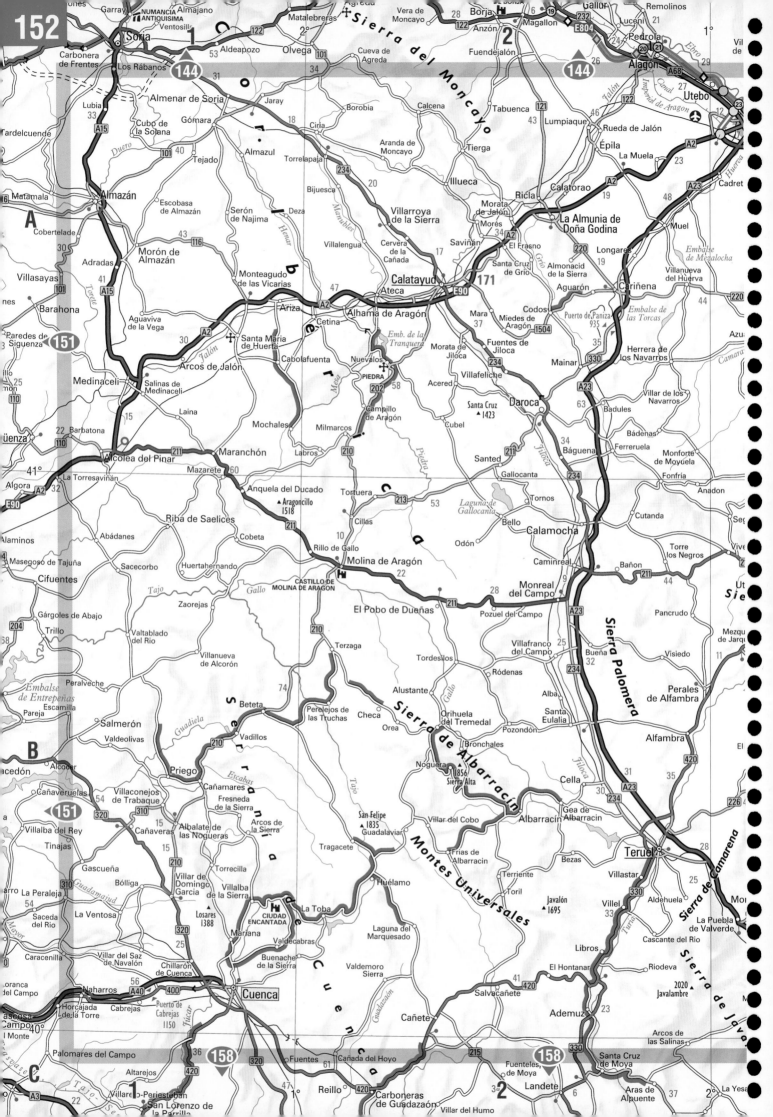

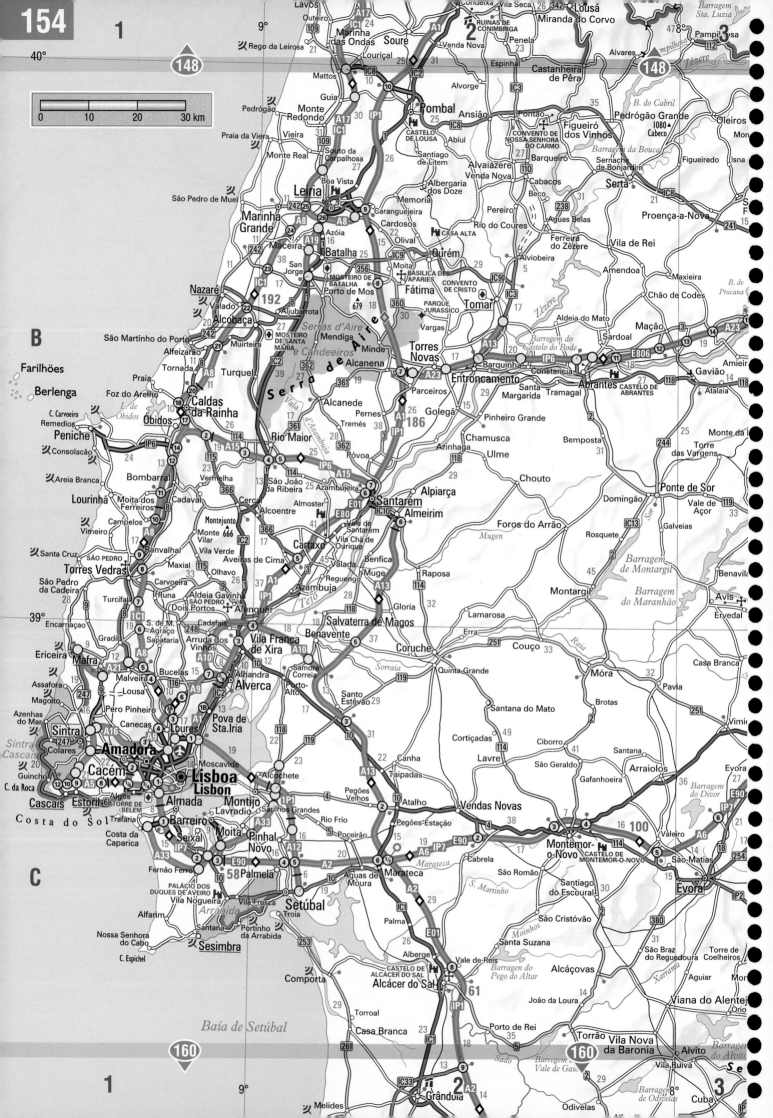

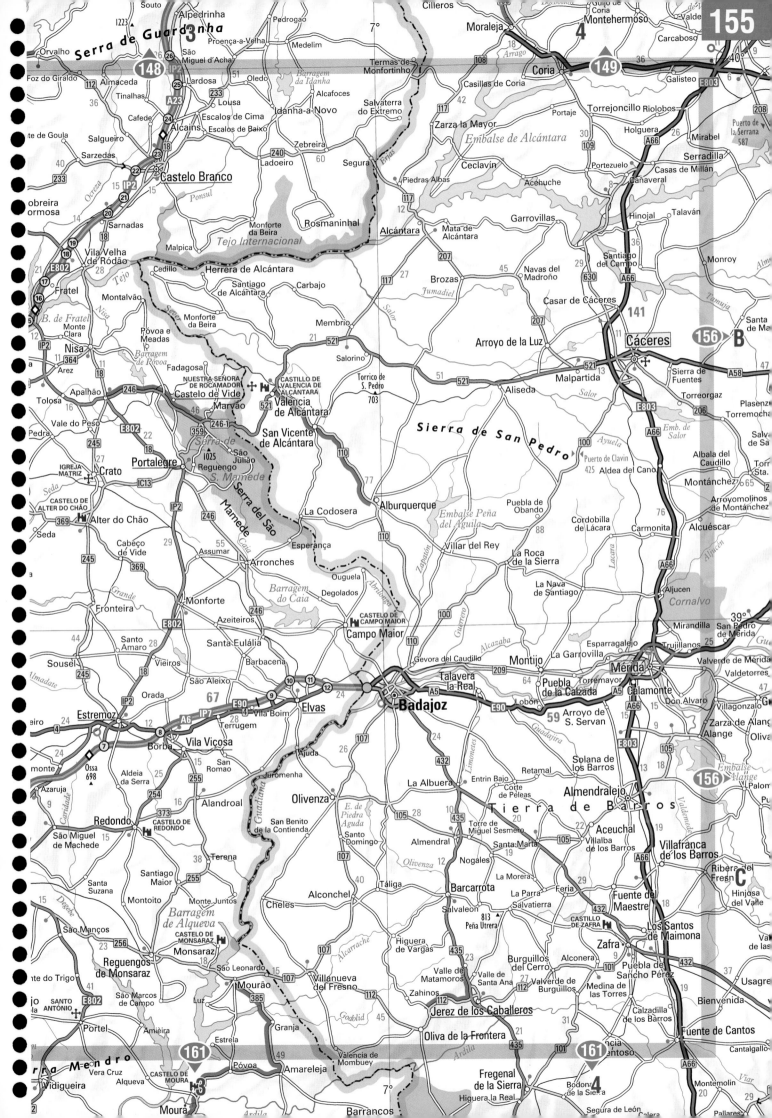

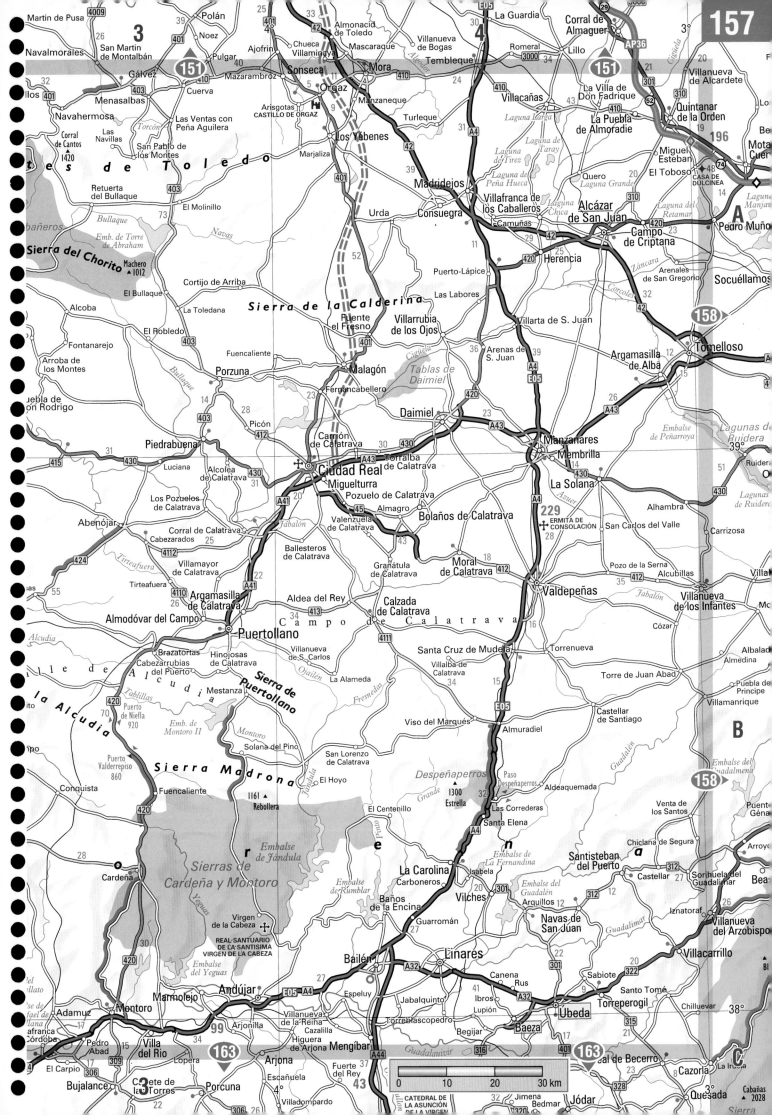

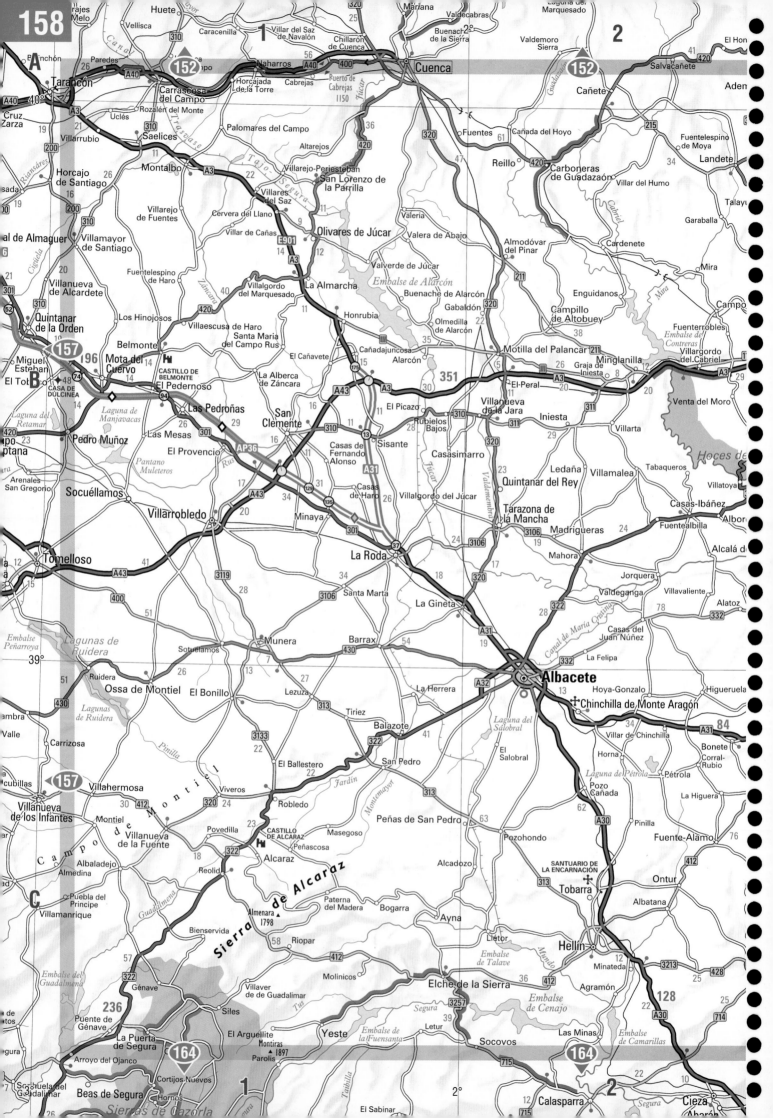

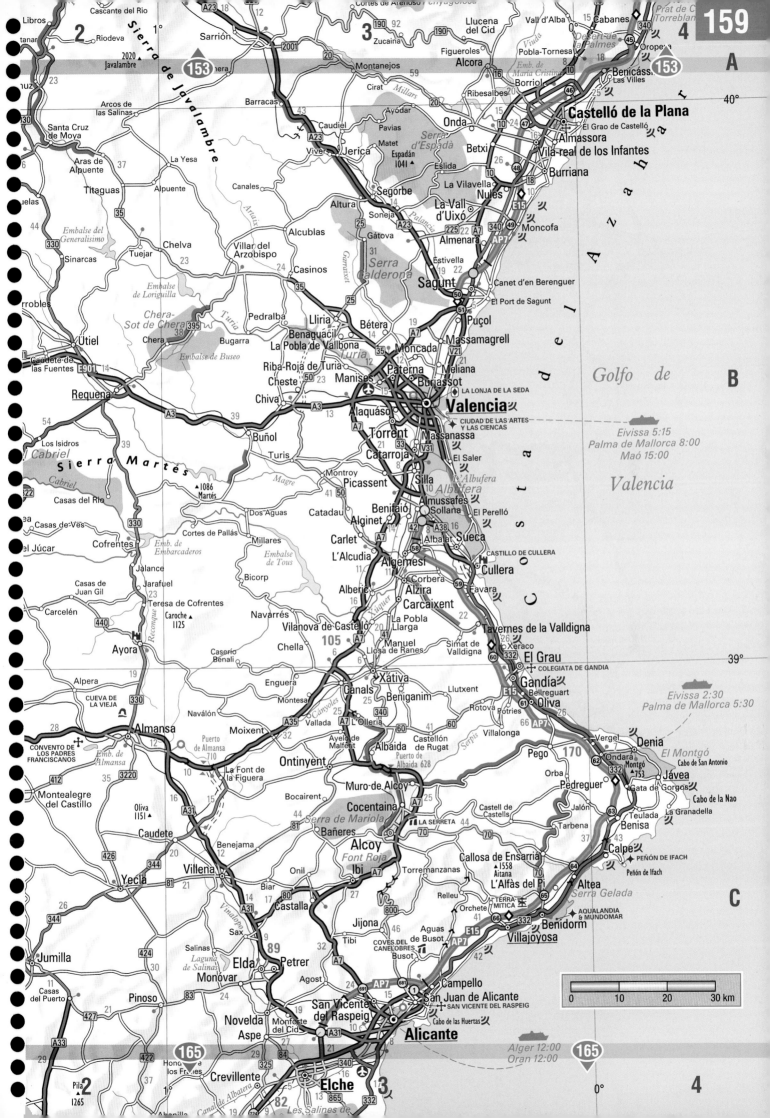

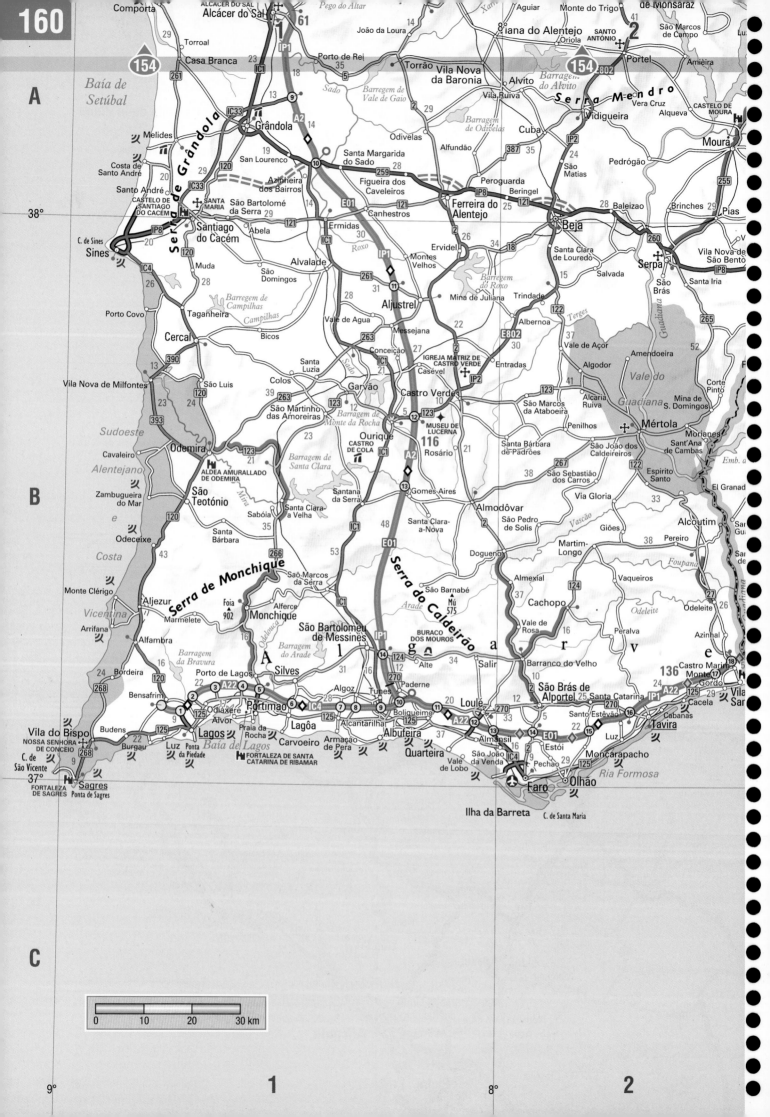

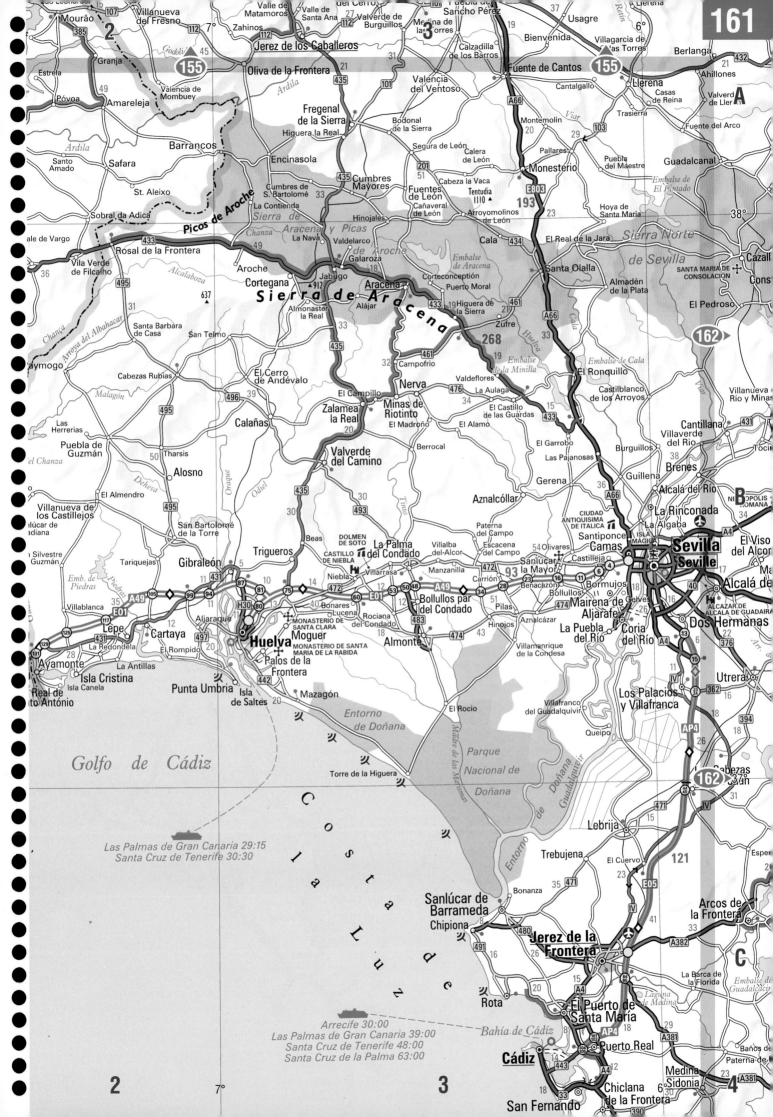

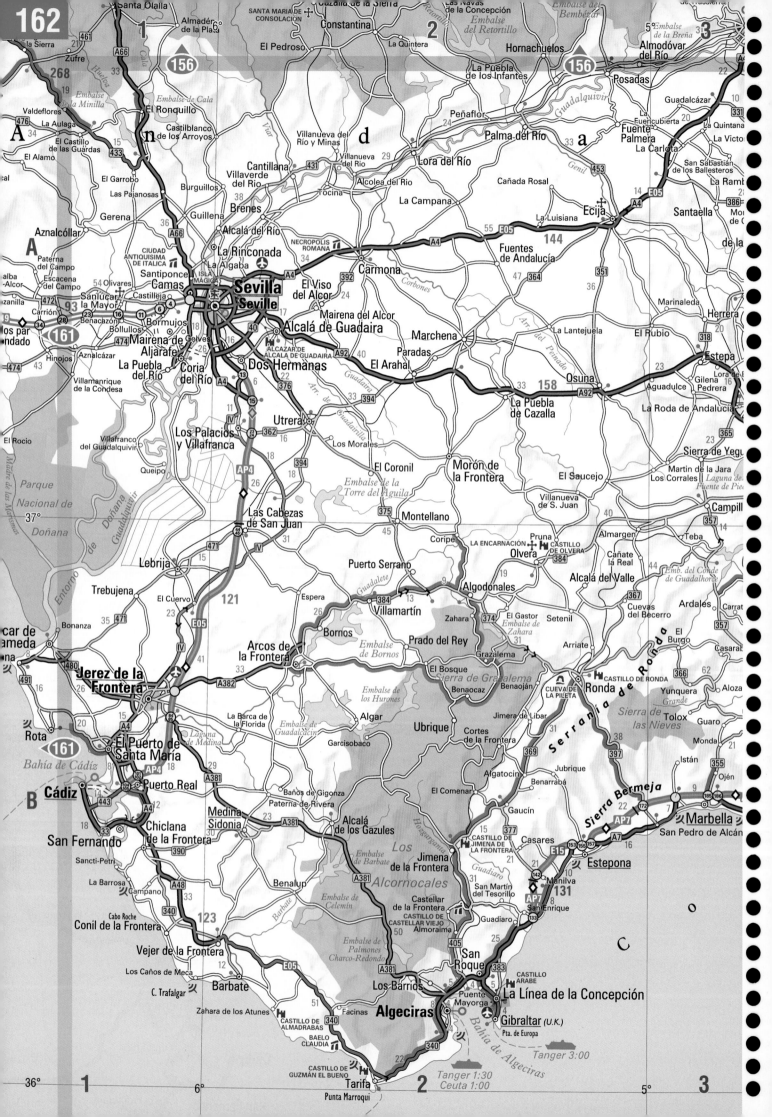

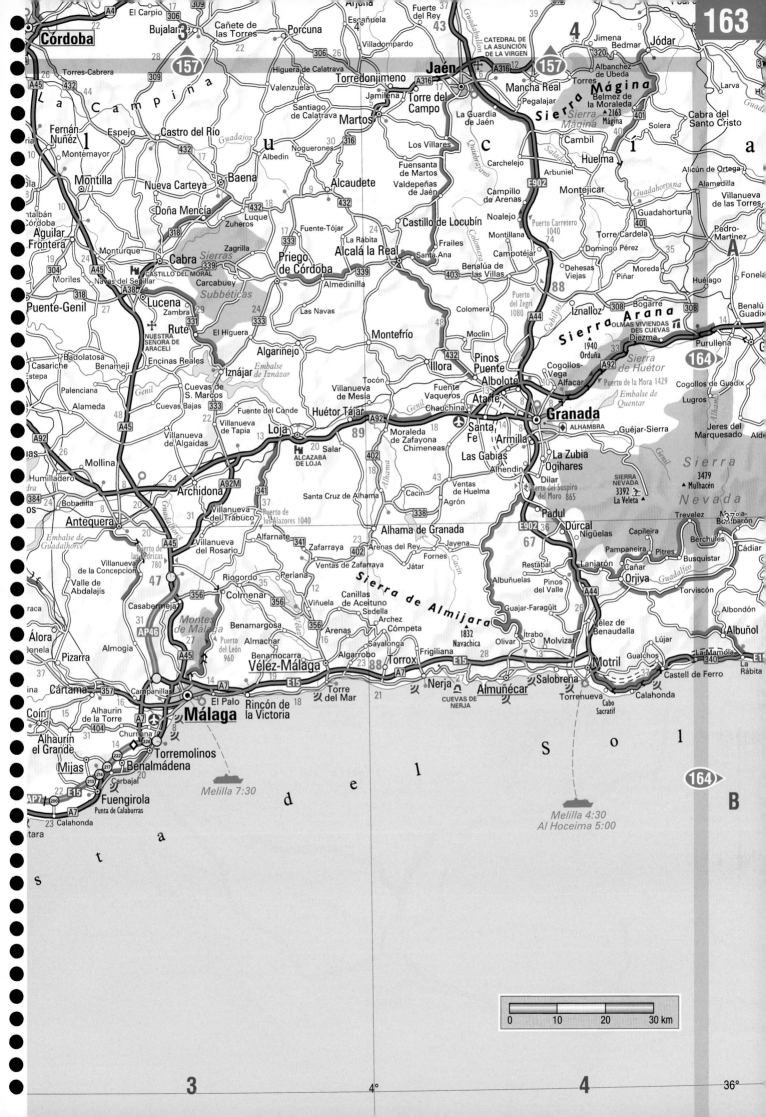

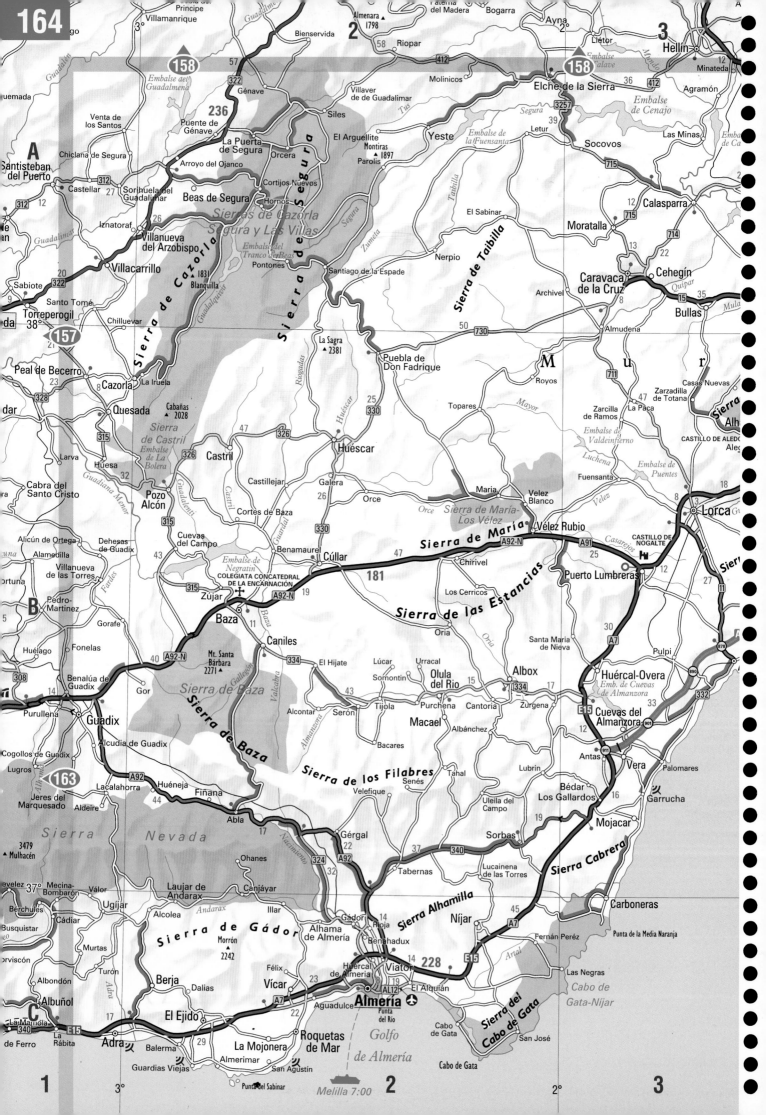

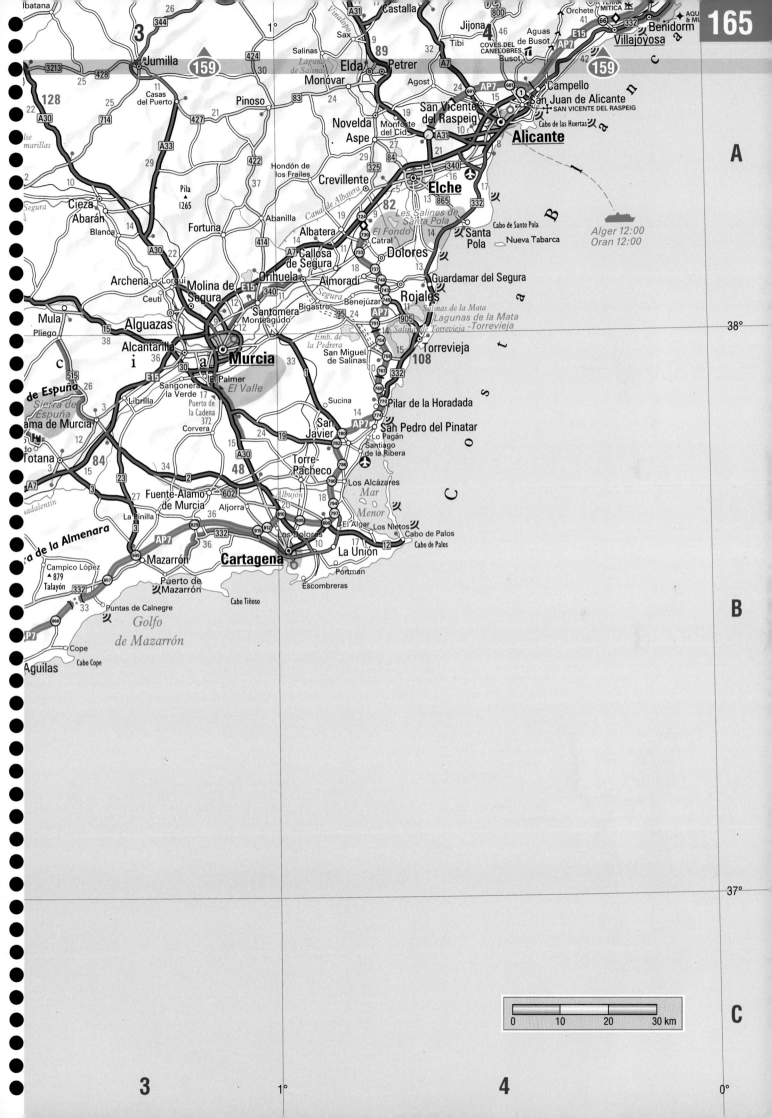

A

1

2°

2

40°

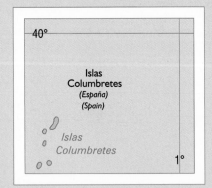

40°

Islas
Columbretes
(España)
(Spain)

*Islas
Columbretes*

1°

ISLAS
BALEARES

BALEARIC
ISLANDS

Port de Sóller
Fori
Sóller
Deia
Tunel de
Sóller
Valldemossa
Alaro
Banyalbufar
25
Estellencs
39
Esporles
11
Marratxi
Puigpunyent
12
8
MA
10
**Palma de
Mallorca**
4
Sa Dragonera
Andratx
Calviá
Can
Pastilla
Port d'Andratx
MA1
Peguera
15
13
12
S'Arenal
Barcelona 6:30
Palma
17 14
Nova
Cap Enderrocat
13
Santa Ponça
Magaluf
*Bahía
de Palma*
Cap de Cala Figuera

6

10

B

Maó 5:00

Valencia 8:00

Mallorca
Majorca

Cap I

*Eivissa 2:30
Denia 5:30*

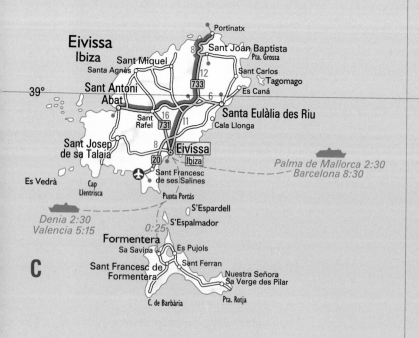

Portinatx
Eivissa
Ibiza
8
Sant Joan Baptista
Pta. Grossa
Sant Miquel
Santa Agnès
12
Sant Carlos
Tagomago
733
Sant Antoni
Abat
6
Es Caná
39°
Sant
16
Santa Eulàlia des Riu
Rafel
731
11
Cala Llonga
Sant Josep
de sa Talaia
8
Eivissa
20
Ibiza
Es Vedrà
Cap
Llentrisca
Sant Francesc
de ses Salines

*Palma de Mallorca 2:30
Barcelona 8:30*

Punta Portás
S'Espardell
*Denia 2:30
Valencia 5:15*
S'Espalmador
0:25
Formentera
Sa Savina
Es Pujols
Sant Francesc de
Formentera
Sant Ferran
Nuestra Señora
Sa Verge des Pilar
C. de Barbària
Pta. Rotja

C

1

2°

2

2   3°   3   4°   4

A

Barcelona 4:30

Capo de Cavalleria

Punta Nati   Cala Morell   Fornells

23   Es   15   Cap de Favàritx

Ciudadela   Mercadal   9

de Menorca   Ferreries   358   40°

Toro   Alaior

Cap de Formentor   Cala   Es Migjorn   20   Maó

Punta Beca   Galdana   Gran

Pollença   Port de Pollença   B. de Pollença   C. de Artrutx   Son Bou

14   Menorca   Sant   Es Castell

10   2220   Alcúdia   Cap des Pinar   Minorca   Climent   Sant Luis

12   10   Es Port d'Alcúdia   Pta. de s'Esperó

39   2200   13   B. d'Alcúdia   1:30   Punta Prima

Puig Major   40   Sa Pobla   C'an Picafort   I. de l'Aire

nalutx   1445   12   Cap Ferrutx

Selva   MA13   562

Lloseta   Muro   Morey

30   12   Cap des Freu

Inca   33   Santa   Cala Ratjada

13A   25   Margalida   Artà   9

Sta. Maria   27   Na Borja   Capdepera   Palma de Mallorca 5:00

del Camí   17   20   Sencelles   15   CUEVAS DE ARTA   Valencia 15:00

A13   Sineu   Sant Llorenç   Cap des Pinar

des Carctassar   20   Són Servera   B

35   Petra   Cala Millor

Algaida   15   18   14   Manacor   Punta de n'Amer

MONASTERIO   Porto Cristo

DE CORA   Porreres   27   CUEVAS DEL DRACH

29   Llucmajor   Cales de Mallorca

MA19   22   26   Felanitx

19   27   SAN SALVADOR   Porto Colom

Campos del Port   (MONASTERIO)

Cala d'Or

Blanc   Sa Rapita   Ses Salines   Porto Petro

Colònia de   Santanyí

Sant Jordi

Cap de ses Salines

I. des Conills

Parque Nacional

de Cabrera

Cabrera   39°

C

0   10   20   30 km

2   3°   3   4°   4

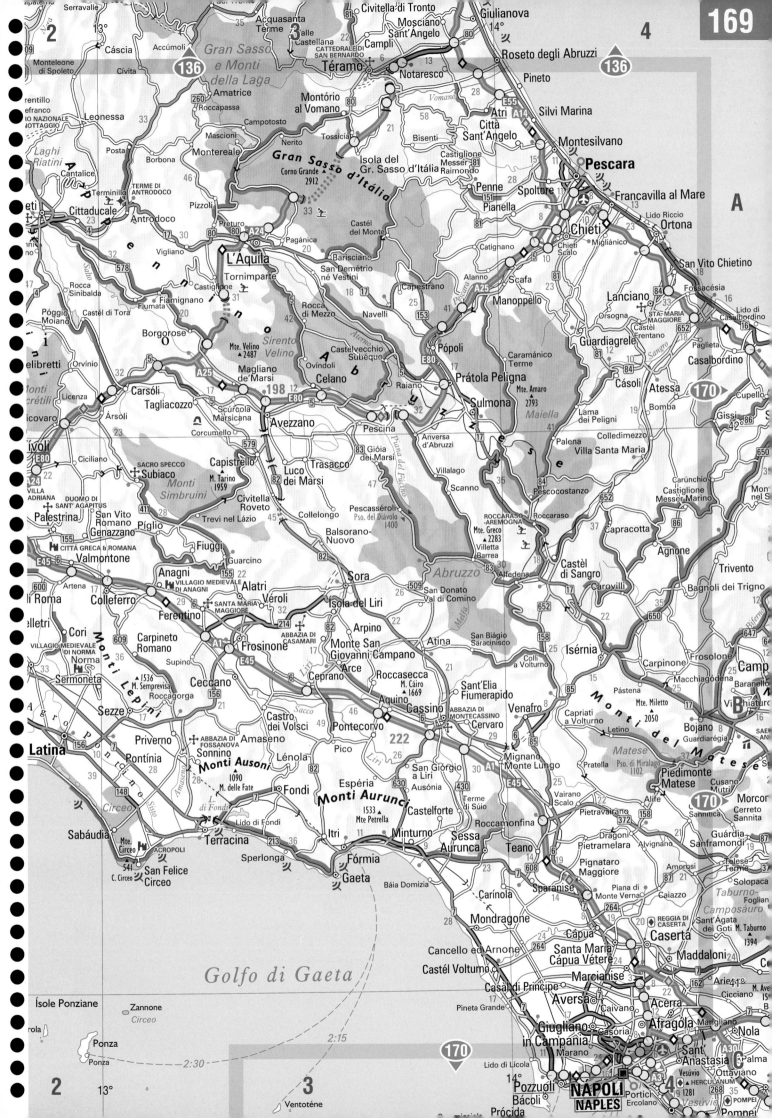

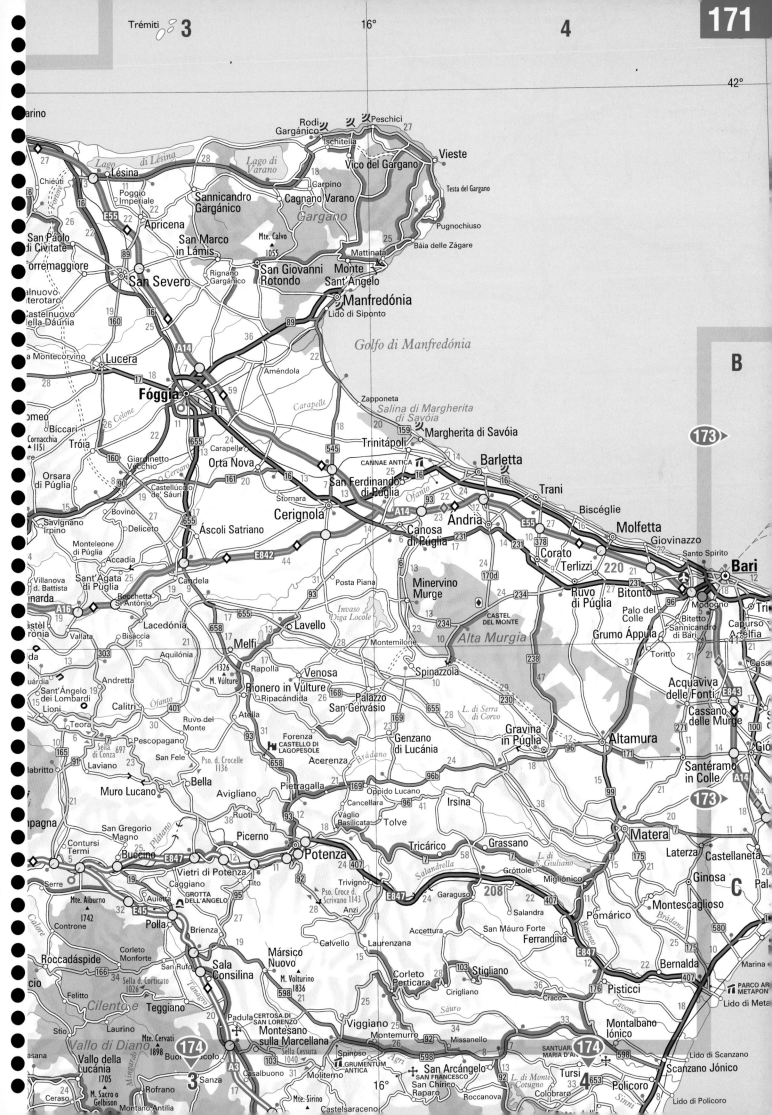

42°

16°

Rodi
Gargánico
Ischitella
Peschici   27
Vieste

Vico del Gargano

Testa del Gargano

Carpino
Cagnano Varano

Gargano

Lago di Lésina

Lago di Varano

Chiéuti   27
Lésina   3
16
26
E55   22   Apricena
Poggio Imperiale   22
San Paolo di Civitate
orremaggiore
89
Sannicandro Gargánico
San Marco in Lámis
Mte. Calvo   1055
Pugnochiuso
Báia delle Zágare

Rignano Gargánico
San Giovanni Rotondo   Monte Sant'Angelo   14   Mattinata

San Severo
19   160   16   25
89
36

Manfredónia
Lido di Siponto

alnuovo terotaro
Castelnuovo della Dáunia

a Montecorvino   Lucera
28   17   18   7   A14
655
Foggia   59
11   11
Améndola
Zapponeta   Golfo di Manfredónia

Salina di Margherita di Savóia
B

meo   Bíccari
Cornacchia   1151
Tróia
Celone   26   22   24
13   Carapelle   545   18
Carapelle
20   159
Margherita di Savóia   173

160   Giardinetto Vécchio   Orta Nova   161   20   13
Trinitápoli
CANNAE ANTICA   25   14   Barletta
Orsara di Púglia   8   90   Castellúccio de' Sáuri   655   576   San Ferdinando di Púglia   16   16
Savignano Irpino   15   655   19   Bovino   Stornara   13   Ofanto   93   22   24   Trani
Delìceto   Stornara   A14   23   Ándria   12   Biscéglie
Monteleone di Púglia   Accadía   655   Cerignola   14   Canosa di Púglia   231   17   14   E55   27   16   Molfetta
4   Sant'Ágata di Púglia   25   Áscoli Satriano   E842   44   6   6   231   24   10   378   Corato   Giovinazzo   Santo Spirito   Bari
Villanova d. Battista   Candela   9   31   Posta Piana   8   13   170d   Terlizzi   220   21   12
inarda   A16   Rocchetta S. António   93   Minervino Murge   24   234   Ruvo di Púglia   231   27   Bitonto   96   Modogno   18
stèl ronia   19   Lacedónia   658   655   17   Invaso Diga Locole   234   CASTEL DEL MONTE   10   Palo del Colle   Bitetto   Sannicandro di Bári   Capurso   elfia   41
Vallata   Bisáccia   13   Lavello   Montemilone   23   234   Alta Murgia   238   Grumo Áppula   Toritto   37   Casa
da   303   Aquilónia   1326   Rapolla   28   10   Acquaviva delle Fonti   E843   17
uárdia   Andretta   M. Vúlture   Venosa   Spinazzola   10   230   29   47   Cassano delle Murge   100   Gió
Sant'Ángelo dei Lombardi   19   Calitri   401   Rionero in Vúlture   168   Palazzo San Gervásio   655   L. di Serra di Corvo   271
Lioni   Teora   30   Ripacándida   26   169   Genzano di Lucánia   Gravina in Púglia   12   Altamura   171   11   14   Santéramo in Colle   A14
7   Pescopagano   Atella   31   Forenza   CASTELLO DI LAGOPESOLE   169   24   96   13
10   6   Sella di Conza   697   San Fele   658   Acerenza   Brádano   96b   15   13   18
abritto   165   Laviano   Pso. d. Crocelle   1136   93   Pietragalla   169   Oppido Lucano   96   41   Irsina   99   20
91   Muro Lucano   23   Bella   Avigliano   38   Cancellara   Váglio Basilicata   Tolve   38   Matera   173
pagna   21   San Gregório Magno   Ruoti   93   18   58   173
Contursi Termi   Picerno   7   Tricárico   Grassano   15   21   175   Laterza
i   San Gregório Magno   5   Buccino   E847   Potenza   407   Salandrella   L. di S. Giuliano   Castellaneta
Serre   19   Vietri di Potenza   11   24   Trivigno   Gróttole   Migliónico   Ginosa
GROTTA DELL'ANGELO   Tito   92   Pso. Croce d. Scrivano 1143   E847   Garaguso   208   22   407   Pomárico   Montescaglioso   C
Mte. Alburno   1742   E45   Caggiano   95   Anzi   24   Salandra   11   Brádano   Pal
Controne   32   Auletta   28   Accettura   San Máuro Forte   Ferrandina   12   E847   580
Polla   Brienza   Calvello   Laurenzana   Básento   Bernalda   175   Marina
Roccadáspide   19   Mársico Nuovo   15   Corleto Perticara   103   Stigliano   176   Pisticci   407
io   166   San Rufo   M. Volturino   1836   28   Ciriglian   Craco   Lido di Meta
Felitto   Sala Consilina   598   21   Sáuro   Montalbano Iónico
Cilento   Sella d. Corticato 1026   Teggiano   Agri   Viggiano   34   Missanello   7   Cavone   Scanzano
Stio   Laurino   20   Padula   CERTOSA DI SAN LORENZO   Montesano sulla Marcellana   Montemurro   92   SANTUARIO MARIA D'A   174   PARCO AR METAPON
Vallo di Diano   Mte. Cervati 1898   174   Buon   icolo   Sélla Cessuta   1040   Spinoso   92   653   Lido di Scanzano
Vallo della Lucánia   1705   A3   3   Sanza   103   Casalbuono   31   Moliterno   GRUMENTUM ANTICA   San Arcángelo   4   Tursi   Scanzano Jónico
M. Sacro o Gelbison   24   Rofrano   17   Montano Antilia   Mte. Sirino   Castelsaraceno   San Chirico Raparo   L. di Monte Cotugno   Colobrarc   Sínni   Lido di Policoro

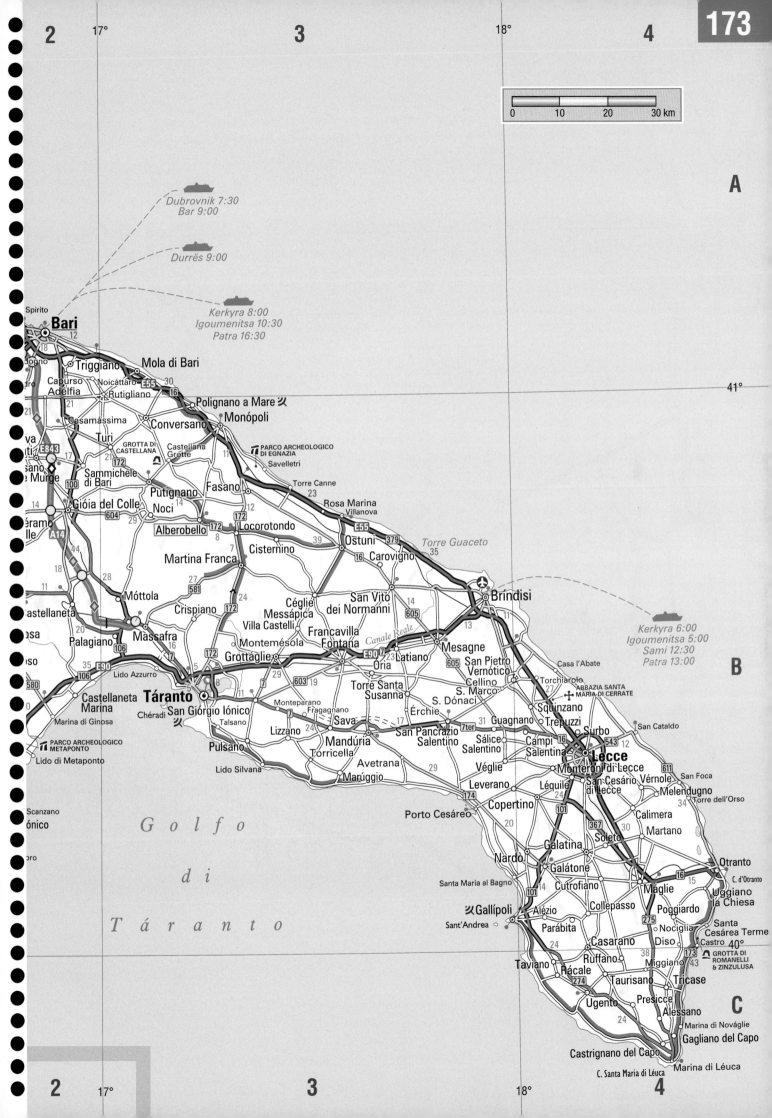

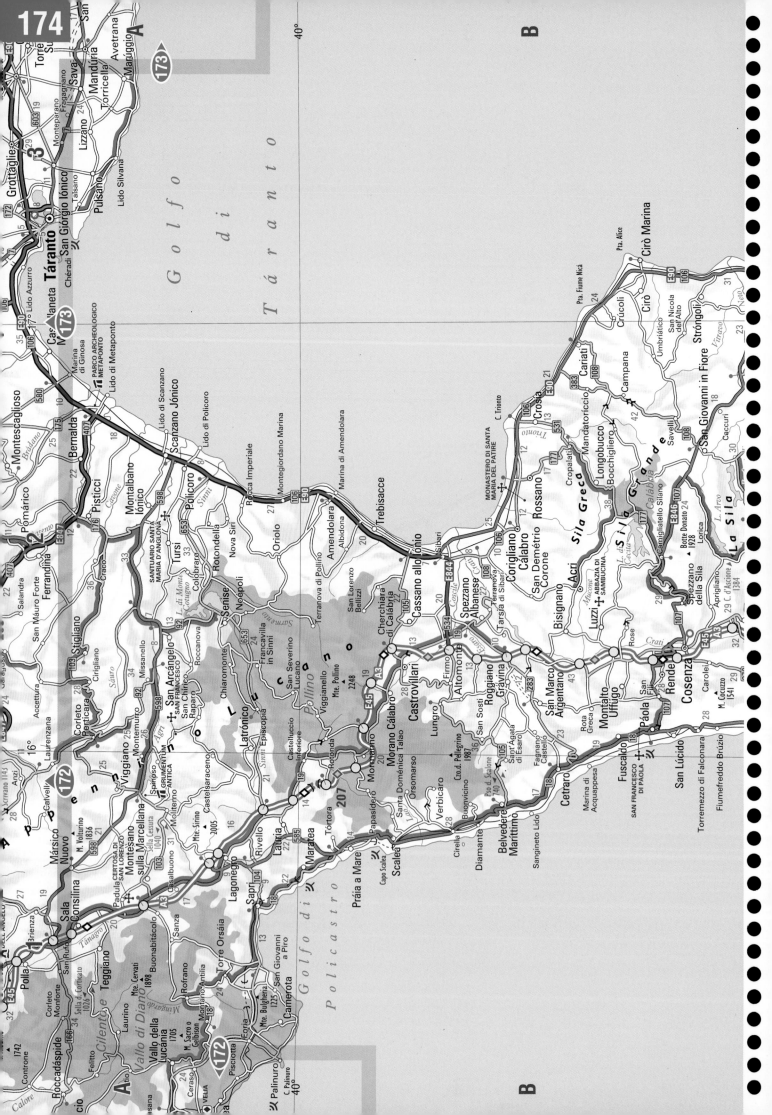

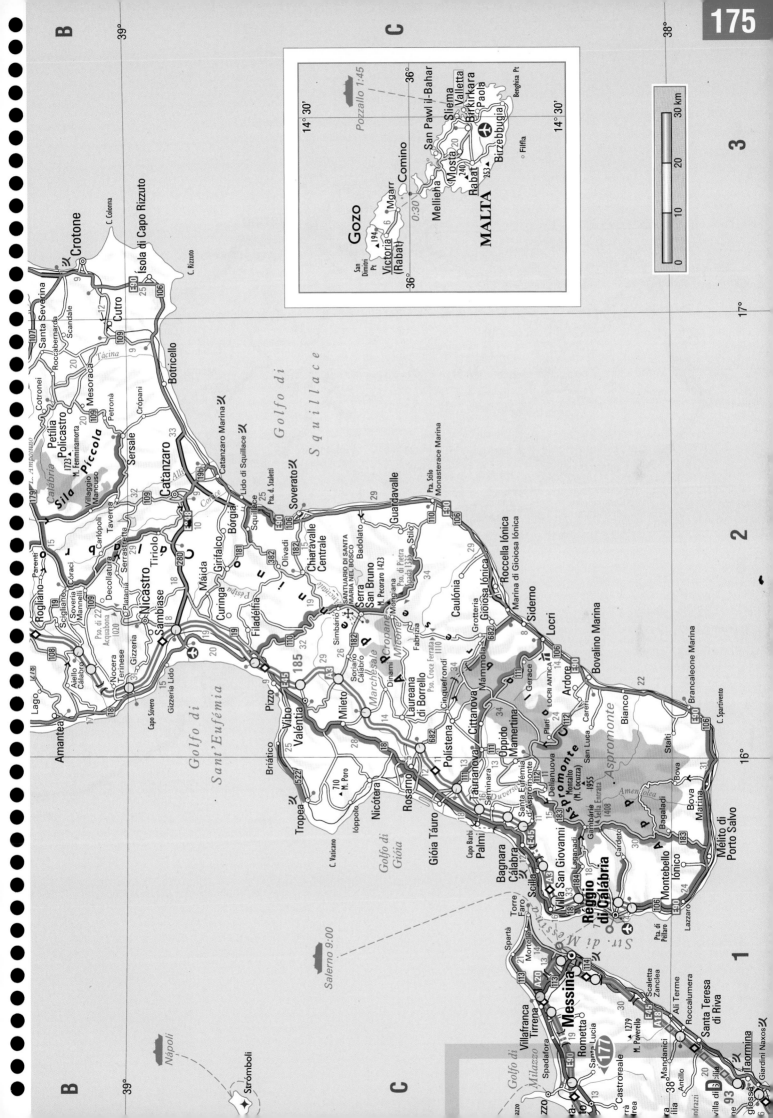

B

39°

C

Crotone
C. Colonna
Ísola di Capo Rizzuto
C. Rizzuto
Santa Severina
Roccabernarda
Scandale
Cutro
Santa Caterina
Cotronei
Mesoraca
Petronà
Crópani
Botricello
Petilia
Policastro
M. Femminamorta
Sila Piccola
1723
Sersale
Taverna
Villaggio Mancuso
Catanzaro
Catanzaro Marina
Lido di Squillace
Squillace
Bórgia
Girifalco
Máida
Curinga
Filadélfia
Olivadi
Chiaravalle Centrale
Soverato
Pra. d. Staletti
Golfo di Squillace
Pra. Stilo
Monasterace Marina
Guardavalle
Stilo
Badolato
Serra San Bruno
SANTUARIO DI SANTA MARIA NEL BOSCO
M. Pecoraro 1423
Pso. di Pietra Spada 1335
Caulónia
Roccella Iónica
Marina di Gioiosa Iónica
Gioiosa Iónica
Siderno
Locri
LOCRI ANTICA
Grotteria
Fabrizia
Mammola
Cinquefrondi
Cittanova
Polístena
Laureana di Borrello
Oppido Mamertina
Delianuova
Santa Eufemia d'Aspromonte
Taurianova
Rosarno
Gioia Táuro
Palmi
Bagnara Cálabra
Scilla
Villa San Giovanni
Réggio di Cálabria
Montebello Iónico
Mélito di Porto Salvo
Bova Marina
Bova
Bagaladi
San Luca
Platí
Careri
Aspromonte
M. Cocuzza 1955
Montalto
Gambárie 1408
Ardore
Bovalino Marina
Bianco
Brancaleone Marina
C. Spartivento
Amendolea
Staiti
Lazzaro
Pra. di Péllaro
Messina
Villafranca Tirrena
Rometta
Spadafora
Milazzo
Golfo di Milazzo
Santa Teresa di Riva
Taormina
Giardini Naxos
Alì Terme
Roccalumera
Scaletta Zanclea
Str. di Messina
Golfo di Sant'Eufémia
Pizzo
Vibo Valéntia
Mileto
Tropea
Briático
M. Poro 710
C. Vaticano
Nicótera
Golfo di Gióia
Capo Vaticano
Gizzeria Lido
Capo Súvero
Nocera Terinese
Amantea
Aiello Cálabro
Lago
Rogliano
Scigliano
Soveria Mannelli
Decollatura
Platania
Nicastro
Sambiase
Tiriolo
Serrastretta
Pso. di 22 Acquabona
Cálabria
L. Ampóllino
Sila Piccola

Golfo di Squillace

Gozo
Victoria (Rabat)
San Dimitri Pt
36°
Mgarr
Comino
Mellieha
San Pawl il-Bahar
Mosta
Valletta
Sliema
Birkirkara
Paola
Rabat
Birzebbugia
Benghisa Pt
Filfla
MALTA
14° 30'
14° 30'
36°

30 km
20
10
0

3

2

1

17°
16°
38°

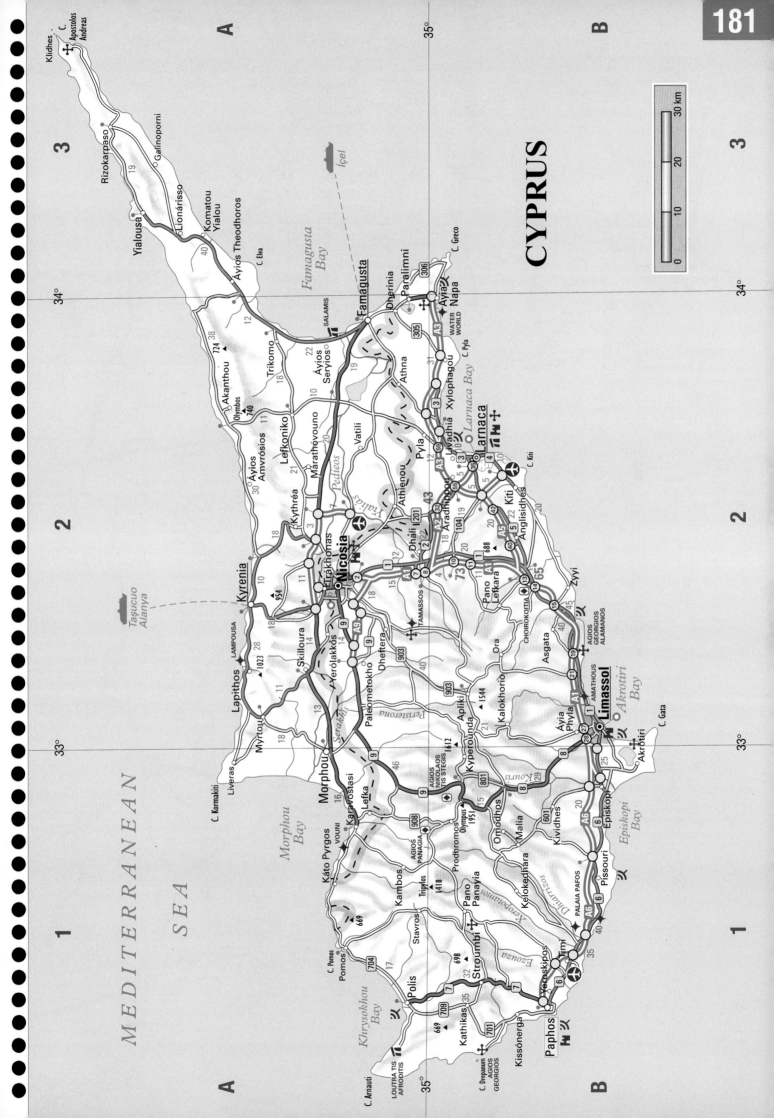

CYPRUS

A B

3 3

2 2

1 1

30 km
0 10 20

35°

34°

33°

MEDITERRANEAN SEA

C. Kormakíti
C. Arnauti
LOUTRA TIS AFRODITIS
AGIOS GEORGIOS
C. Drepanum
Kissónerga
Paphos
Kathikas
Yeroskipos
Stavros
Kambos
PALAIA PAFOS
Pano Panayía
Pólis
Khrysokhou Bay
C. Pomos
Pomos
Káto Pyrgos
Lefka
Karavóstasi
Mórphou
Liveras
Lápithos
Mórphou Bay
Myrtou
Skilloura
Verolakkós
Trikomo
Ayía Phyla
Akrotíri
Akrotíri Bay
C. Gata
Limassol
AMATHOUS
Episkopí
Episkopi Bay
Pissouri
Kolossi
Kividhes
Malia
Kelokedhara
Kívidhes
Omodhos
Prodhromos
Olympus 1951
Kyperounda
AGIOS NIKOLAOS TIS STEGIS
Paleometokho
Dheftera
Kalokhorió
Apliki
Ora
Asgata
Agios
Zyyi
AGIOS GEORGIOS ALAMANOS
Pano Lefkara
CHOIROKOITIA
Kiti
C. Kiti
Anglisidhes
Larnaca
Larnaca Bay
Kíti
Arádhippou
Athíenou
Aradhíppou
Livádhia
Pyla
C. Pyla
Xylophagoú
Athna
Dhekélia
Dhali
Dhenia
Nicosia
Trákhonas
Kythréa
Kyrenia
Táşucuo Alanya
LAMPOUSA
Vouni
Kámbos
Triplos 1418
Stroumbi
Pérvolia
Péristerona
Tamassos
Yialiás
Pedieos
Sérakhis
Agiós Panayia
Vatilí
Marathóvouno
Lefkóniko
Ayios Amvrósios
Akanthou
Olympos 740
Ayios Seryios
SALAMIS
Famagusta
Famagusta Bay
Dhérinia
Paralimni
C. Greco
Ayia Napa
WATER WORLD
C. Elea
Áyios Theodhoros
Komatou Yialou
Galinoporni
Lionárisso
Rizokarpaso
Yialousa
C. Apostolos Andreas
Klídhes
İçel

MEDITERRANEAN
SEA

Xeropótamos
Dhiárizos
Koúris

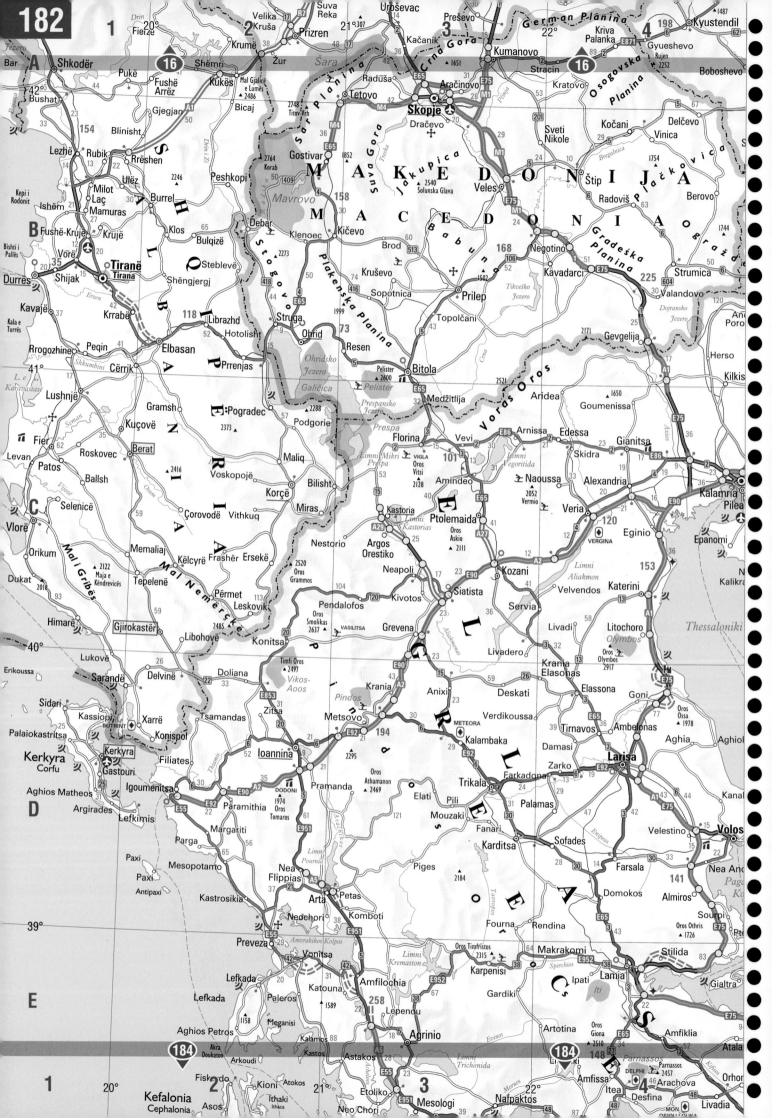

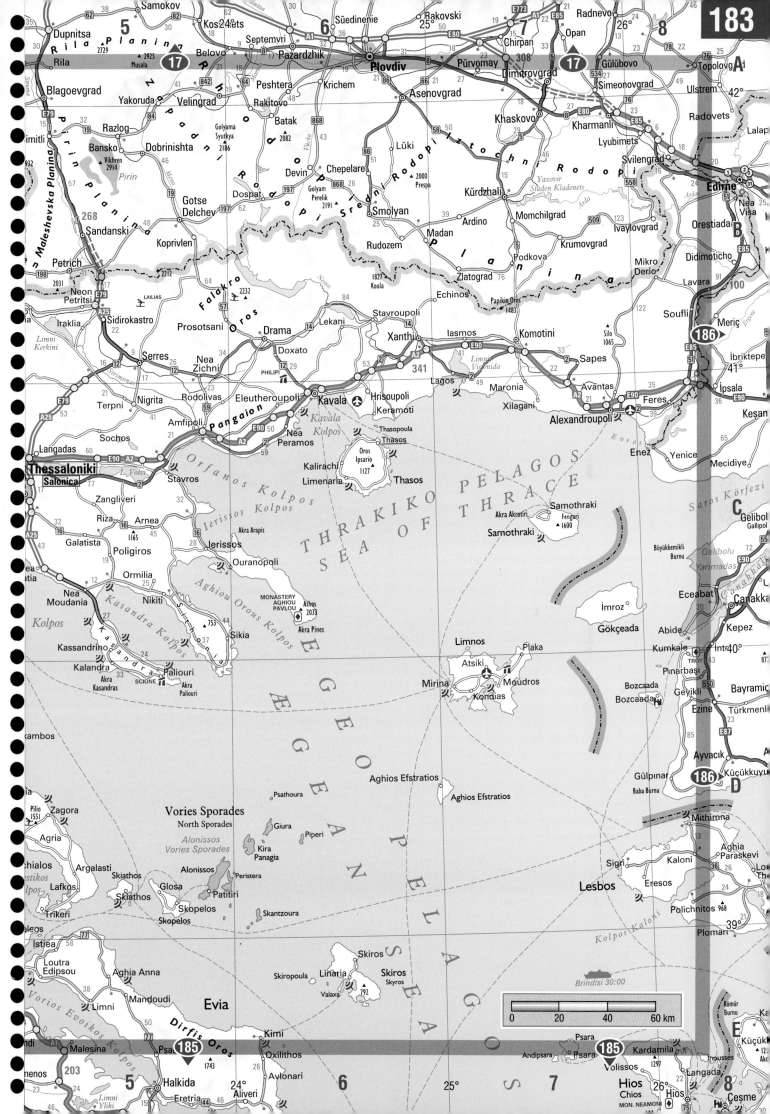

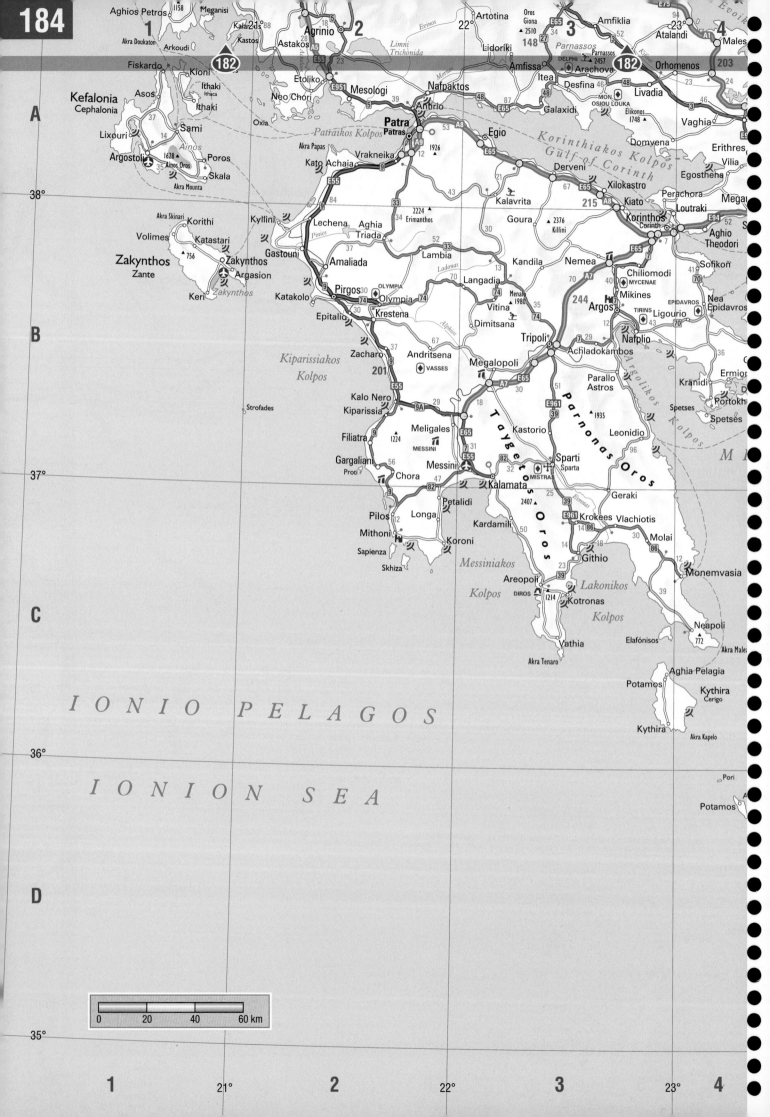

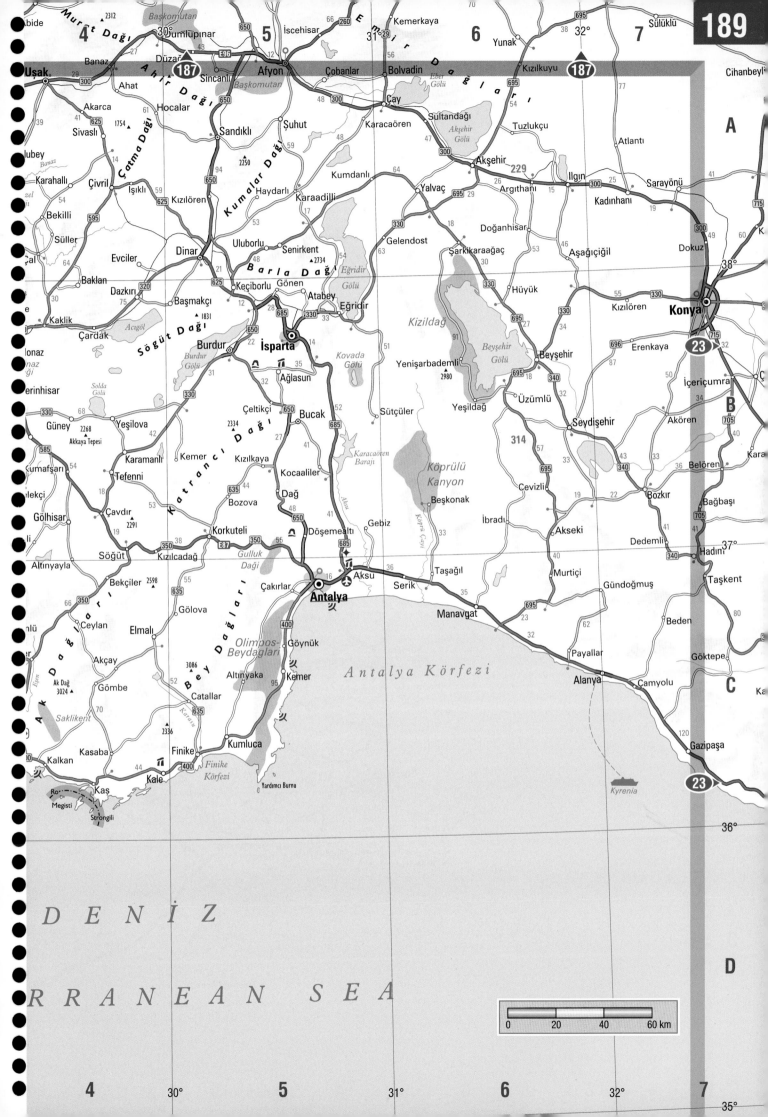

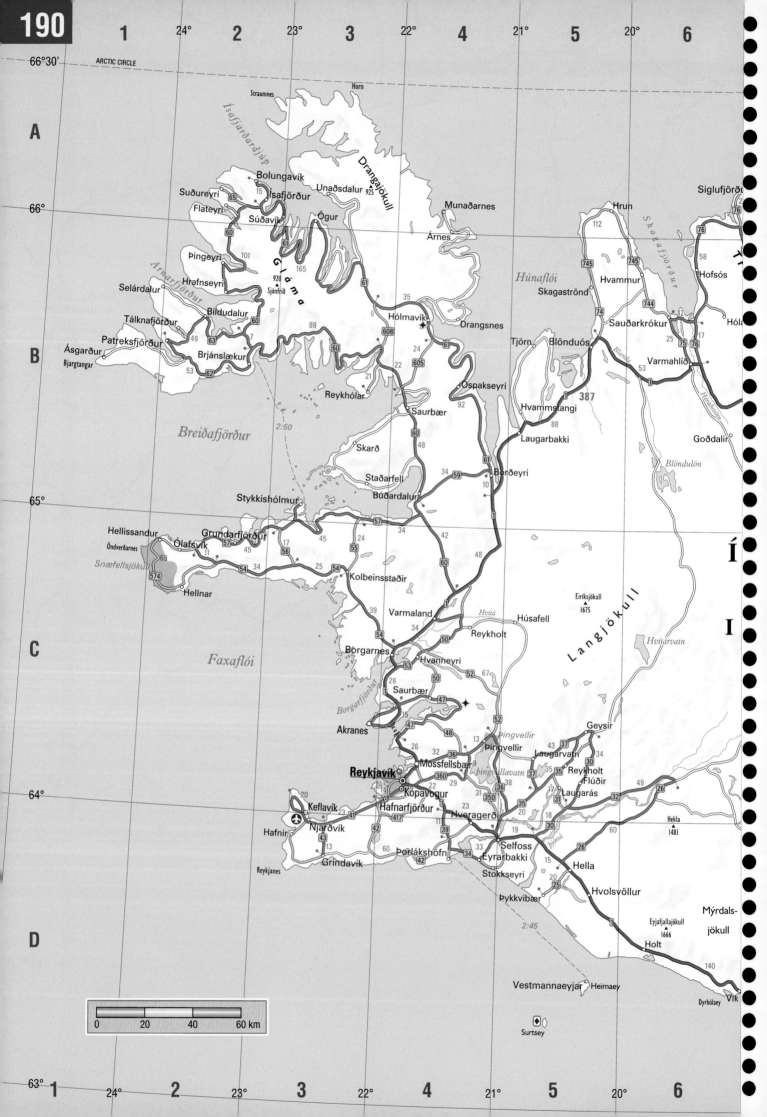

ARCTIC CIRCLE

66°30'

66°

65°

64°

63°

A
B
C
D

1 24° **2** 23° **3** 22° **4** 21° **5** 20° **6**

Straumnes
Horn
Ísafjarðardjúp
Drangajökull
Bolungavík
Suðureyri 65
Ísafjörður 15
Flateyri
Súðavík 61
Þingeyri 101
Glóma 165
Hrafnseyri 920 Sjónfríð
Selárdalur
Bíldudalur 60
Tálknafjörður 7
Patreksfjörður 49
Ásgarður
Bjargtangar
Brjánslækur
53 62
Reykhólar

Unaðsdalur 925
Ögur
Árnes
Munaðarnes
Siglufjörður
Hrun 76
112 Skagafjörður
745
Hvammur 745
Skagaströnd 74 Hofsós
744 58
Sauðárkrókur 12 Hóla
25 75 76 17
Varmahlíð
53 1
Hólmavík 35
Drangsnes
24 61
605
92 Ospakseyri
88
Hvammstangi
387
Laugarbakki

Húnaflói

Goðdalir
Blöndulón

Breiðafjörður 2:50
Saurbær 630
48
Skarð
Staðarfell
Búðardalur
57 34
Stykkishólmur

Borðeyri 61
34 59
10
1

Hellissandur
Öndverðarnes
Ólafsvík 57 17 45
11 45 56 55 24
574 54 34 25 54
Snæfellsjökull 69
Hellnar
Kolbeinsstaðir
60
42 48

Eiríksjökull 1675
Langjökull
Hvítárvatn

Í

I

Faxaflói
39
Varmaland 1
54 34
Borgarnes 50
53 Hvanneyri
28 52 67
Saurbær 50
Borgarfjörður 15 47
47 48 52
Akranes 13 Þingvellir
26 32 36 Þingvellir
Reykjavík 360 Mossfellsbær
22 29
Kópavogur 31 350
20 Keflavík 23 41 Hafnarfjörður 11
Njarðvík 42 Hveragerði
Hafnir 417 39
43
13 60 Þorlákshöfn
Grindavík 42 34 33 Selfoss
Reykjanes Eyrarbakki
Stokkseyri
Þykkvibær

Húsafell
Reykholt
Geysir
43 37
Laugarvatn 30
35 Reykholt
37 Flúðir
17 Laugarás
18 32 26
Hella 49
60 Hekla 1481
26
15
20
25 Hvolsvöllur

2:45
Eyjafjallajökull 1666
Holt
Mýrdals-jökull
140

Vestmannaeyjar Heimaey

Surtsey
Dyrhólaey Vík

0   20   40   60 km

ARCTIC CIRCLE

66°30'

Grímsey

18°

Eyjafjörður

3:30

A

66°

Raufarhöfn

85

Þistilfjörður

Fontur

Kópasker

Hlíð

Öxarfjörður

Svalbarð

Þórshöfn

177

Skjálfandi

Digranes

Bakkaflói

Ólafsfjörður

85

75

Ásbyrgi

85

Bakkafjörður

66°

Húsavík

Grenivík   Björg

Laxamýri

Jökulsá á Fjöllum

Vatnajökull

Vopnafjörður

Héraðsflói

32

Dalvík

82

Hauganes

82

864

967

83

34

46

24

85

87

1

Laugar

Vopnafjörður

Husey

Lagarfljót

Glettinganes

Akureyri

30

61

Reykjahlíð

38

Grímsstaðir

82

Sleðbrjótur

94

Bakkagerði

Hrafnagil

Mývatn

285

1

64

B

1538

Bláfjall

1

Jökulsá á Brú

Saurbær

1222

44

77

1

Egilsstaðir

23

Seyðisfjörður

84

Mýri

Móðrudalur

12

93

Neskaupstaður

S   L   A   N   D

Herðubreið

1682

Óðáðahraun

Hallormsstaður

931

32

92

92

Eskifjörður

35

1765

1460

27

Reyðarfjörður

65°

Hofsjökull

Trölladyngja

Valþjofsstaður

86

Fáskrúðsfjörður

96

C   E   L   A   N   D

Snæfell

1833

1

Stöðvarfjörður

Breiðdalsvík

Berufjörður

69

Vatnajökull

146

Djúpivogur

C

1

Þórisvatn

Tórshavn 19:00
Hirtshals 46:00

Nesjahverfi

1

Höfn   Stokksnes

Gerði

192

687

Hvannadalshnúkur

2119

64°

LAKAGÍGAR

Skaftafell

1

Skeiðarársandur

Ingólfshöfði

1

Búland

26

Kirkjubæjarklaustur

204

D

50

Langholt

1

18°   8   17°   9   16°   10   15°   11   14°   12   63°

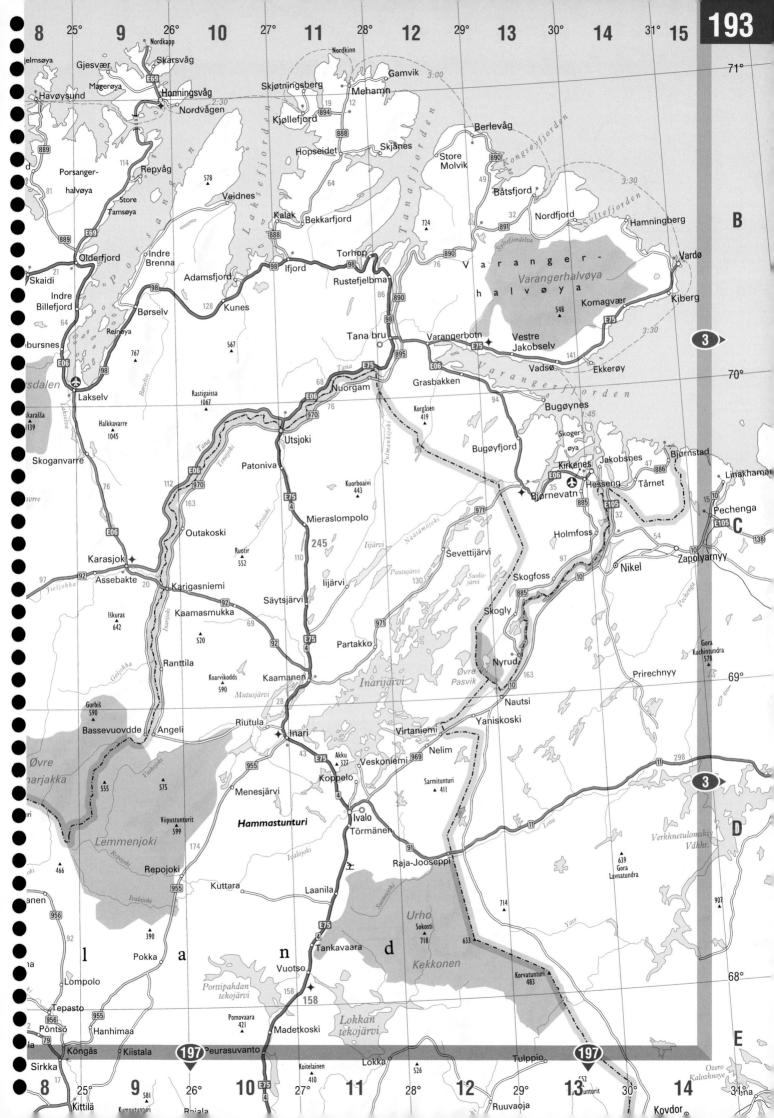

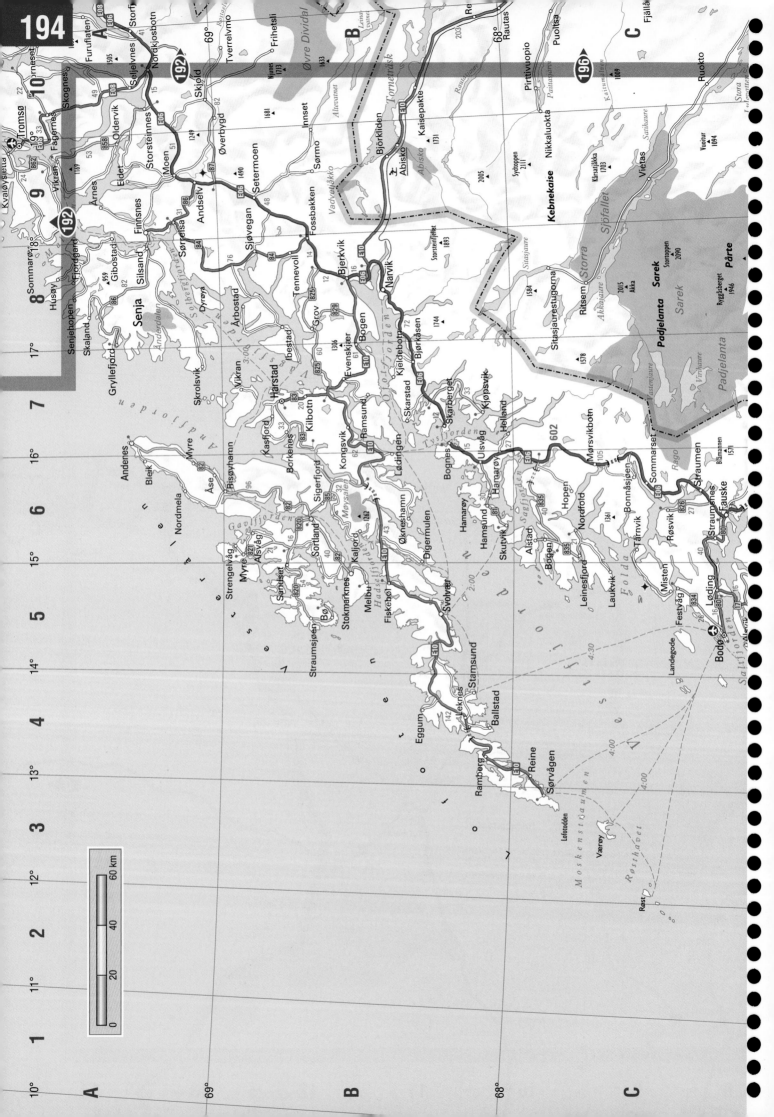

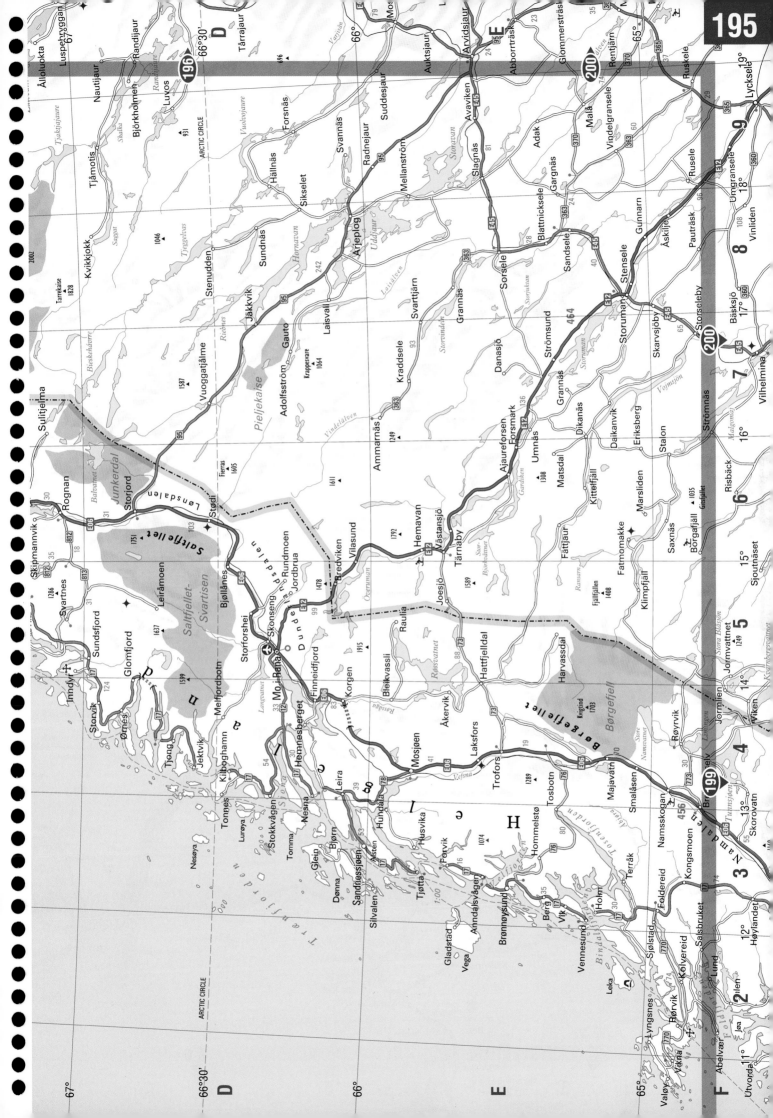

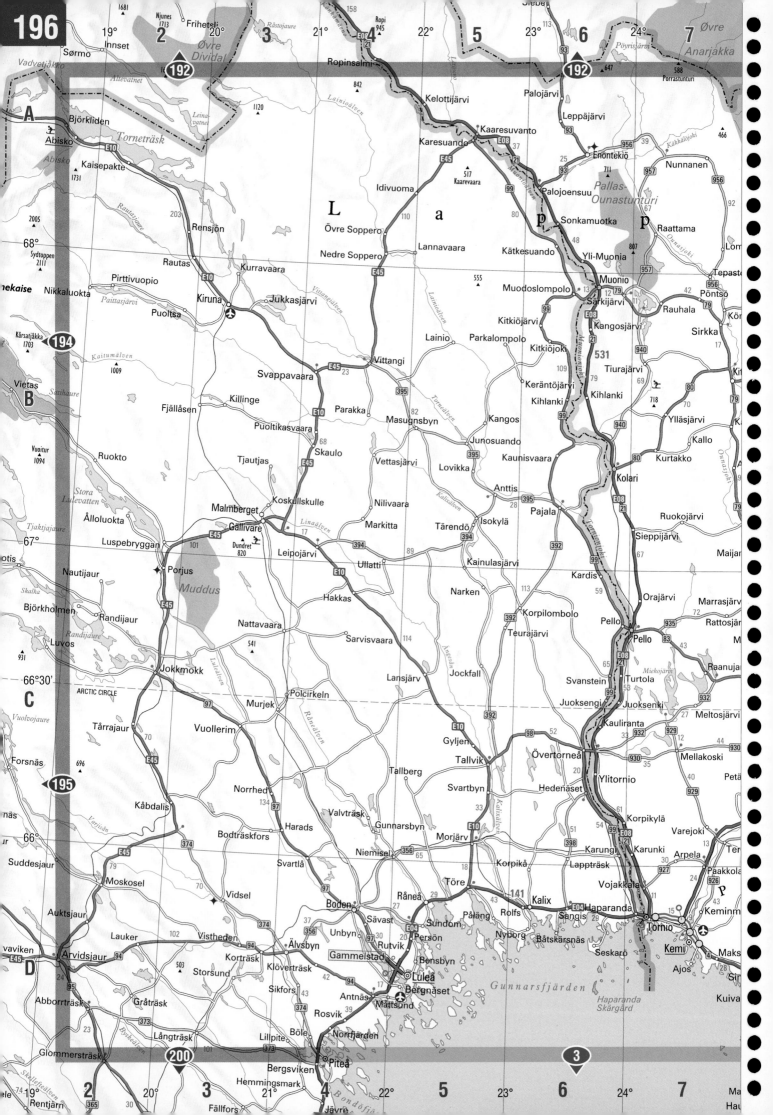

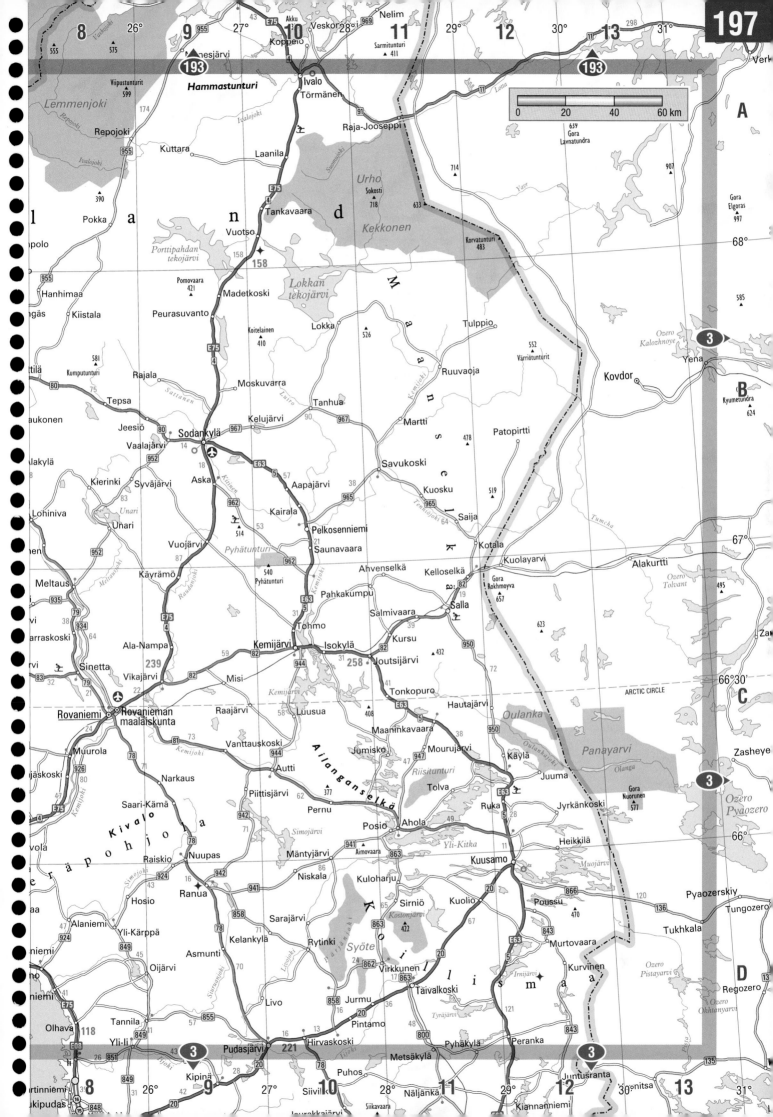

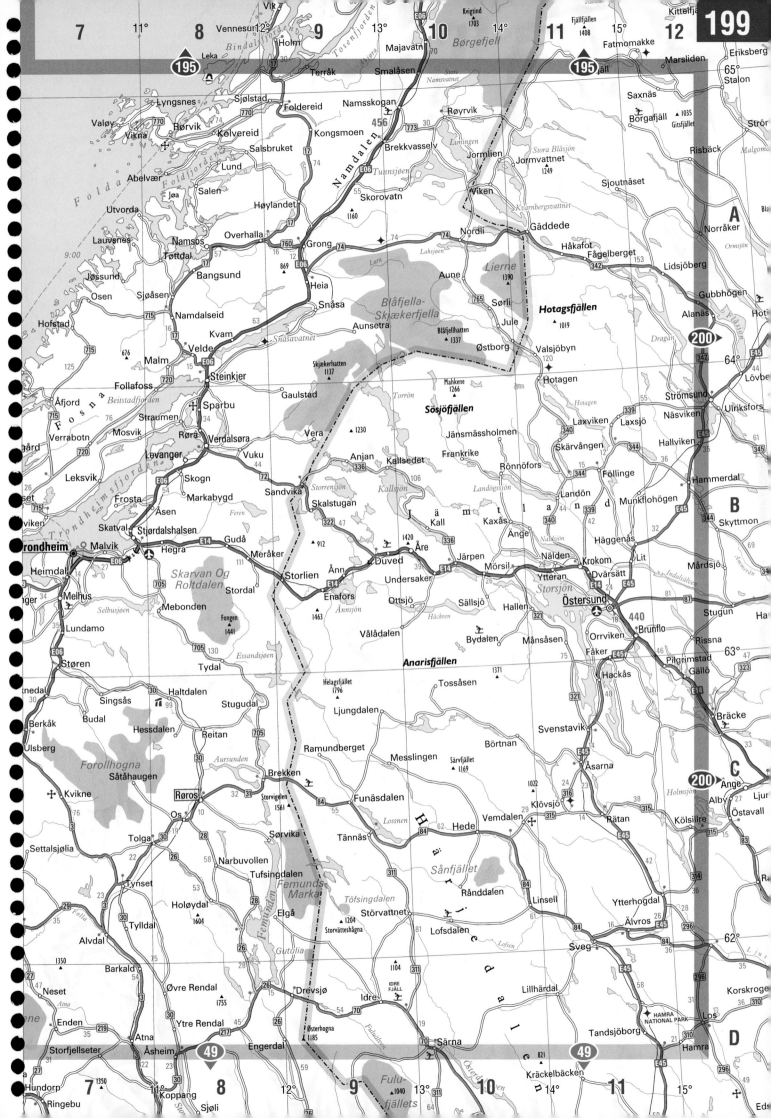

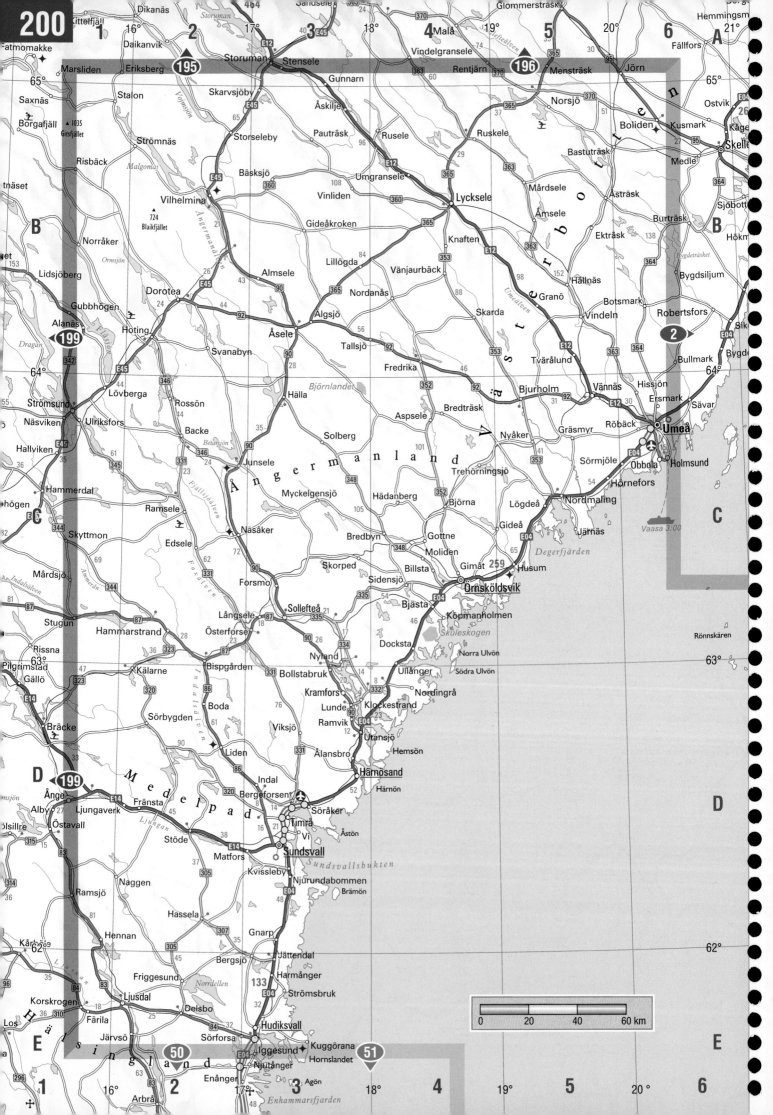

City plans • Plans de villes
Stadtpläne • Piante di città

Motorway	Autoroute	Autobahn	Autostrada
Major through route	Route principale majeur	Hauptstrecke	Strada di grande communicazione
Through route	Route principale	Schnellstrasse	Strada d'importanza regionale
Secondary road	Route secondaire		
Dual carriageway	Chaussées séparées	Nebenstrasse	Strada d'interesse locale
Other road	Autre route	Zweispurig Schnellstrasse	Strada a carreggiate doppie
Tunnel	Tunnel	Nebenstrecke	Altra strada
Limited access / pedestrian road	Rue réglementée / rue piétonne	Tunnel	Galleria stradale
One-way street	Sens unique	Beschränkter Zugang/ Fussgängerzone	Strada pedonale / a accesso limitato
Parking	Parc de stationnement	Einbahnstrasse	Senso unico
Motorway number	Numéro d'autoroute	Parkplatz	Parcheggio
National road number	Numéro de route nationale	Autobahnnummer	Numero di autostrada
European road number	Numéro de route européenne	Nationalstrassen-nummer	Numero di strada nazionale
Destination	Destination	Europäische Strassennummer	Numero di strada europea
Car ferry	Bac passant les autos	Ziel	Destinazione
Railway	Chemin de fer	Autofähre	Traghetto automobili
Rail/bus station	Gare/gare routière	Eisenbahn	Ferrovia
Underground, metro station	Station de métro	Bahnhof / Busstation	Stazione ferrovia / pullman
Cable car	Téléférique	U-Bahnstation	Metropolitano
Abbey, cathedral	Abbaye, cathédrale	Drahtseilbahn	Funivia
Church of interest	Église intéressante	Abtei, Kloster, Kathedrale	Abbazia, duomo
Synagogue	Synagogue	Interessante Kirche	Chiesa da vedere
Hospital	Hôpital	Synagoge	Sinagoga
Police station	Police	Krankenhaus	Ospedale
Post office	Bureau de poste	Polizeiwache	Polizia
Tourist information	Office de tourisme	Postamt	Ufficio postale
Place of interest	Autre curiosité	Informationsbüro	Ufficio informazioni turistiche
		Sonstige Sehenswürdigkeit	Luogo da vedere

Approach maps • Agglomérations
Carte régionale • Regionalkarte

Toll motorway – with motorway number	Autoroute à péage – avec numéro d'autoroute	Gebührenpflichtige Autobahn – mit Autobahnnummer	Autostrada a pedaggio – con numero
Toll-free motorway – with European road number	Autoroute – avec numéro de route européenne	Gebührenfreie Autobahn – Europäische Strassennummer	Autostrada – con numero di strada europea
Pre-pay motorway – vignette required	Autoroute – 'vignette'	Autobahn – 'vignette'	Autostrada – 'vignette'
Motorway services	Aire de service	Autobahnservice	Area di servizio autostradale
Motorway junction full access, restricted access	Échangeur d'autoroute accès libre, accès réglementé	Autobahnkreuz – voller/begrenzter Zugang	Raccordi autostradali – completo/parziali
Under construction	En construction	Im Bau	In construzione
Tunnel	Tunnel	Tunnel	Galleria stradale
Major route dual carriageway single carriageway	Route principale chaussées séparées chausée sans séparation	Hauptstrecke – zweispurige Schnellstrasse	Strada di grande communicazione carreggiata doppia carreggiata unica
Secondary route dual carriageway single carriageway	Route secondaire chaussées séparées chausée sans séparation	Nebenstrasse – zweispurige Schnellstrasse	Strada d'interesse locale – carreggiata doppia carreggiata unica
Other road	Autre route	Nebenstrecke	Altra strada
Car ferry	Bac passant les autos	Autofähre	Traghetto automobili
Destination	Destination	Ziel	Destinazione
Railway	Chemin de fer	Eisenbahn	Ferrovia
Railway station	Gare	Hauptbahnhof	Stazione ferrovia
Height – in metres	Altitude – en mètres	Höhe – über dem Meeresspiegel	Altezza in metri
Airport	Aéroport principal	Flughafen	Aeroporto
Airfield	Autre aéroport	Flugplatz	Aerodromo/ campo d'aviazione
City plan coverage area	Région de plan de ville	Vom Stadtplan abgedecktes Gebiet	Area della pianta della città

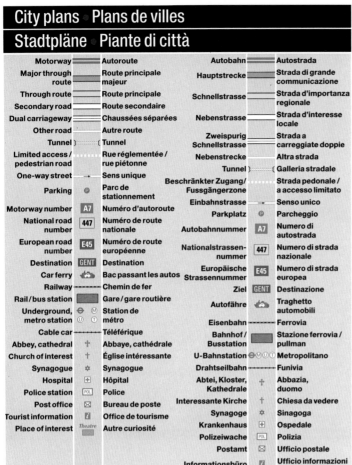

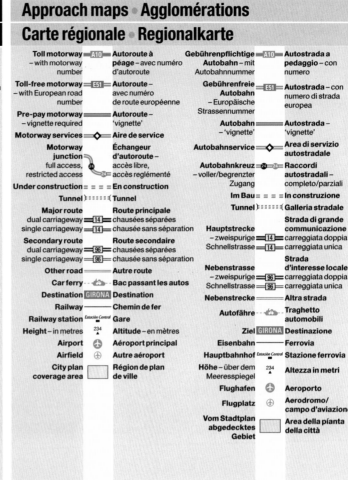

Alicante
0   km   0.5

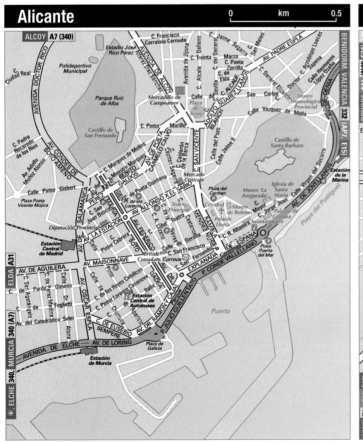

Antwerpen Antwerp
0   km   1

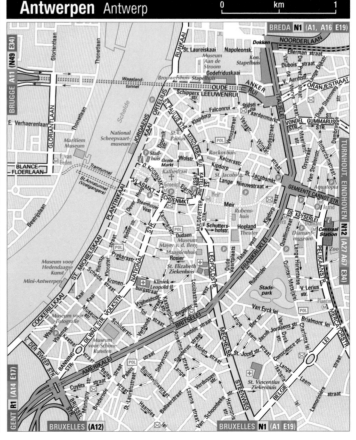

Amsterdam

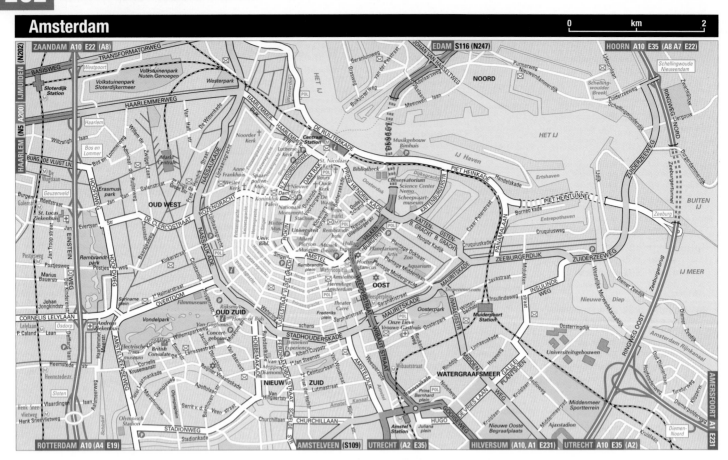

Amsterdam

Athina Athens

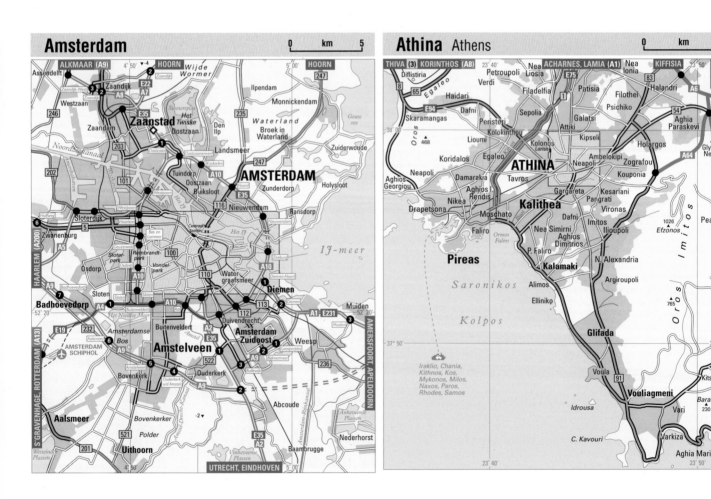

Athina Athens

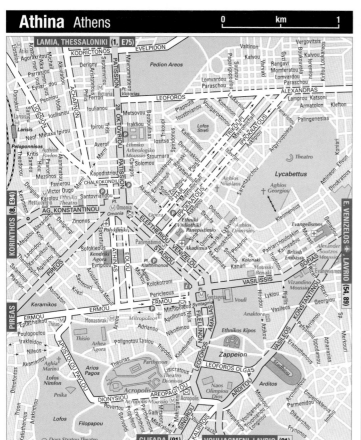

Basel

Barcelona

Barcelona

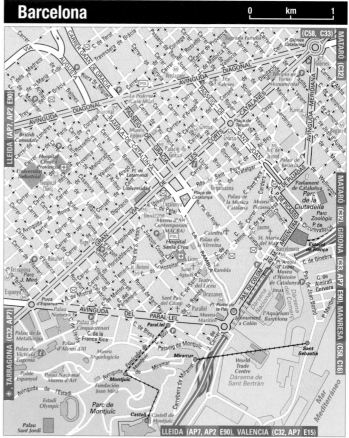

Berlin

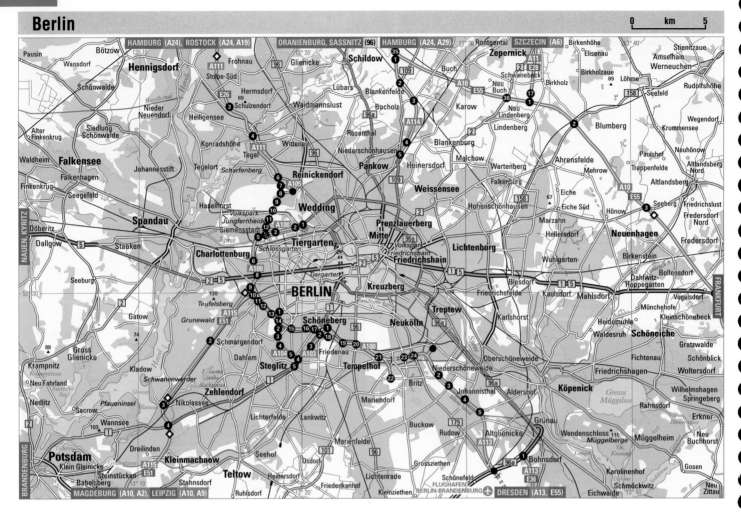

Berlin

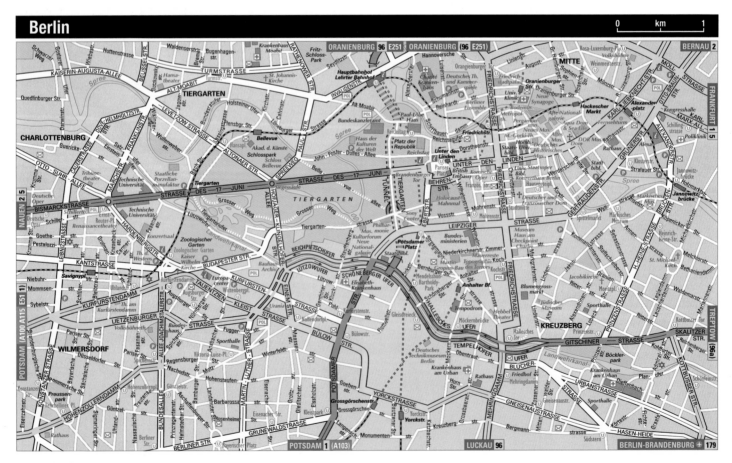

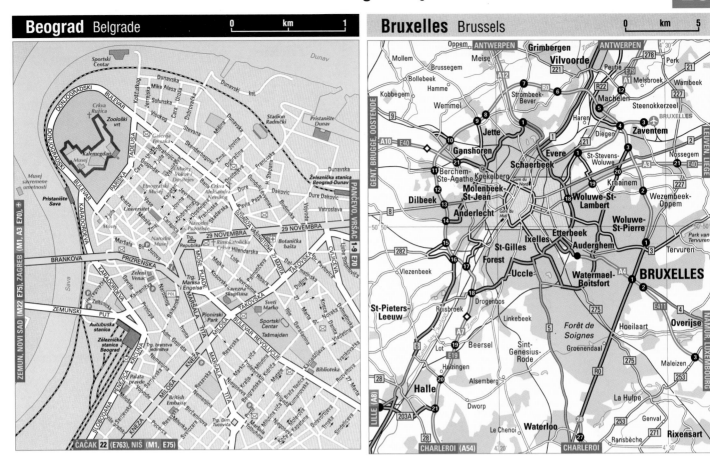

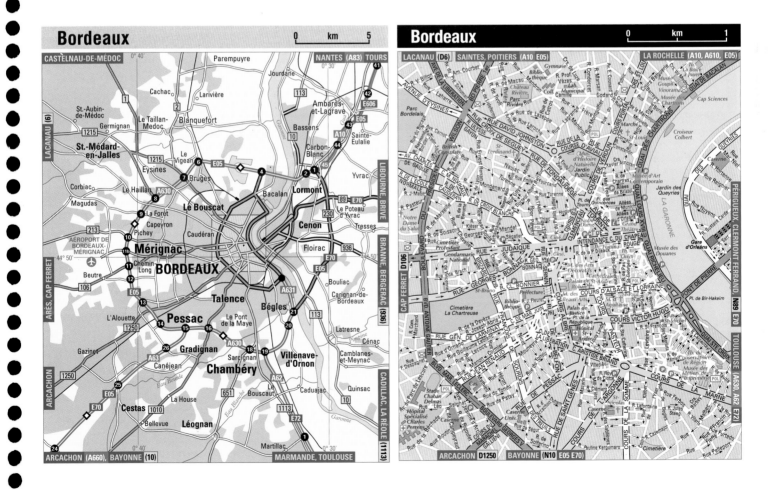

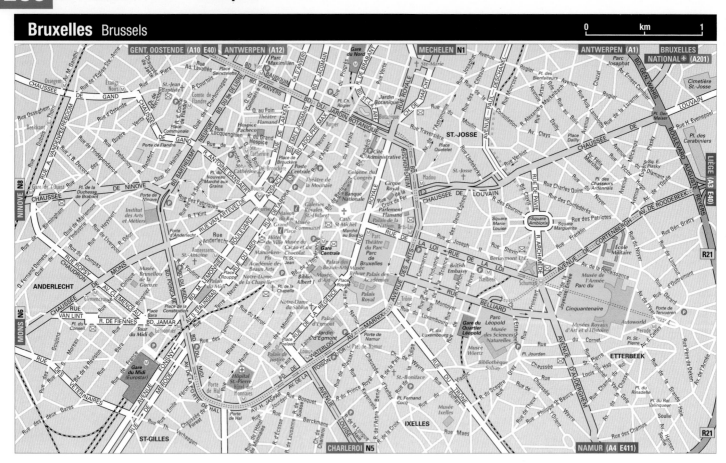

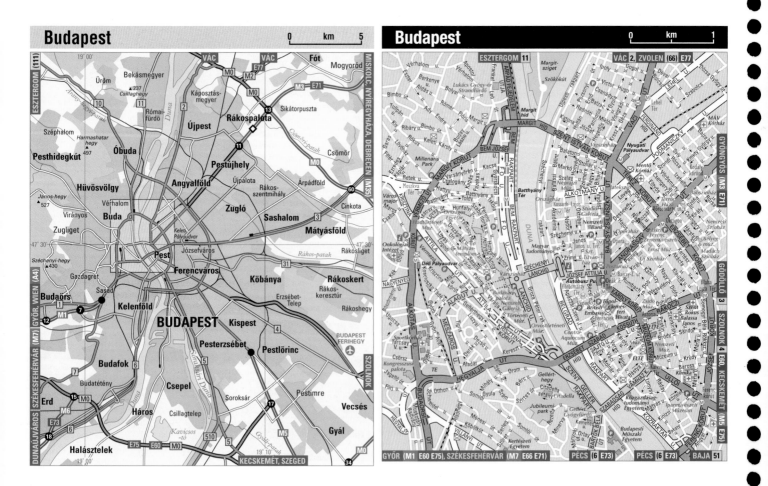

Dublin

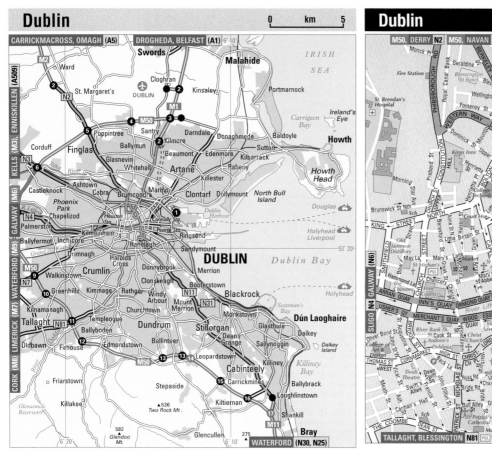

Dublin

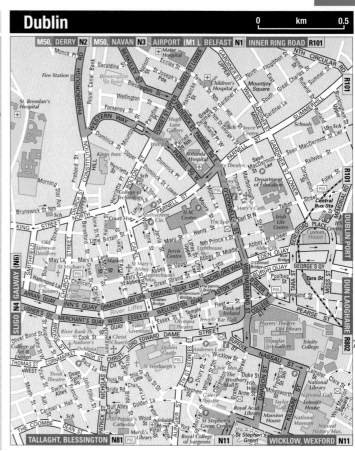

Düsseldorf

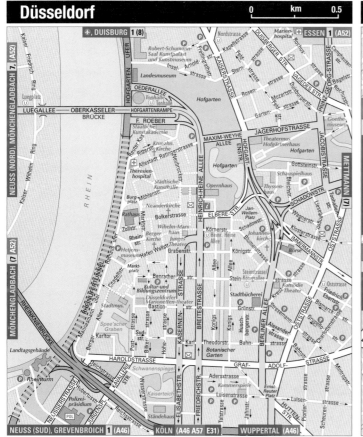

Edinburgh

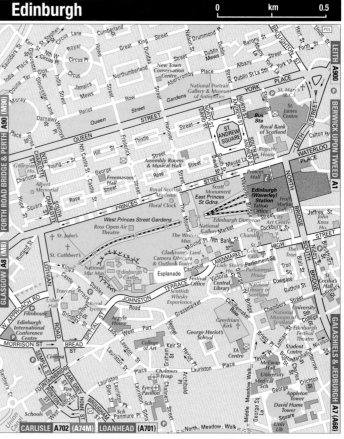

For **Cologne** see page 212
For **Copenhagen** see page 212

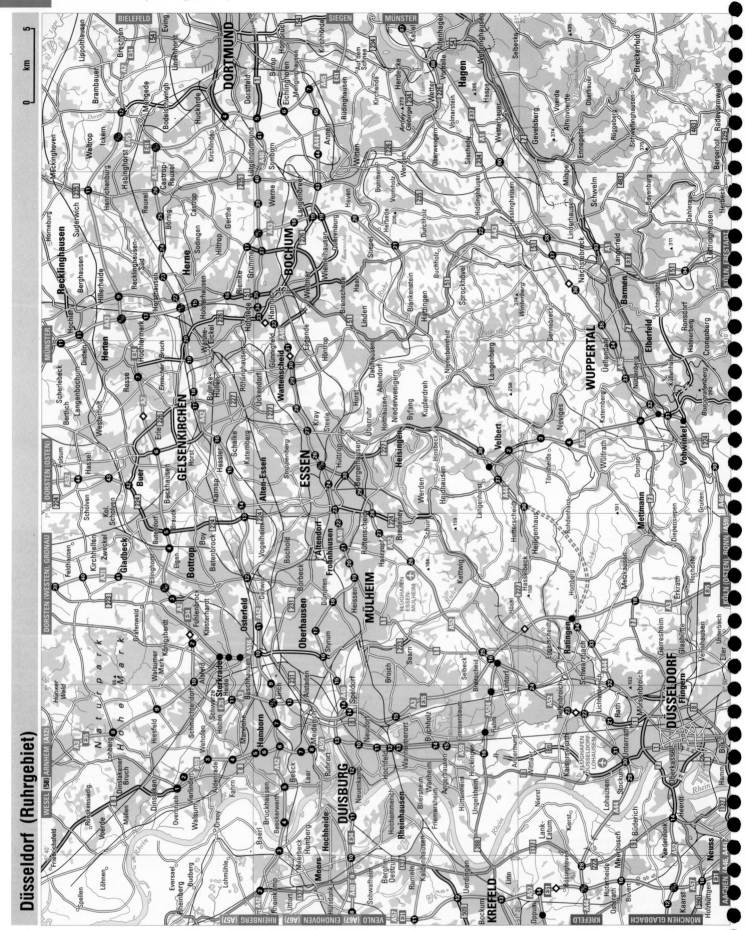

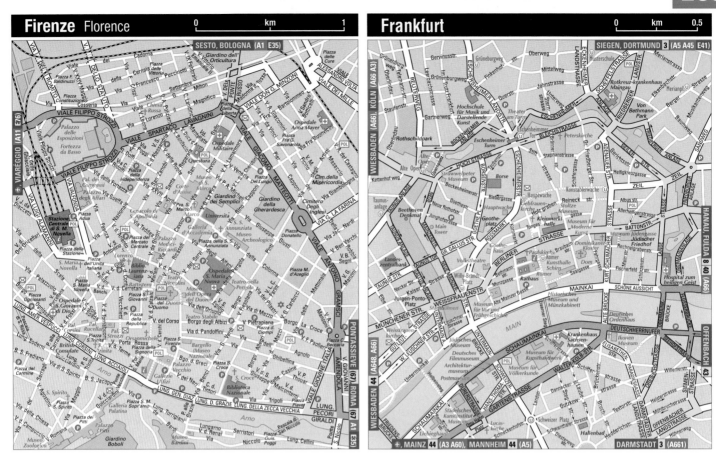

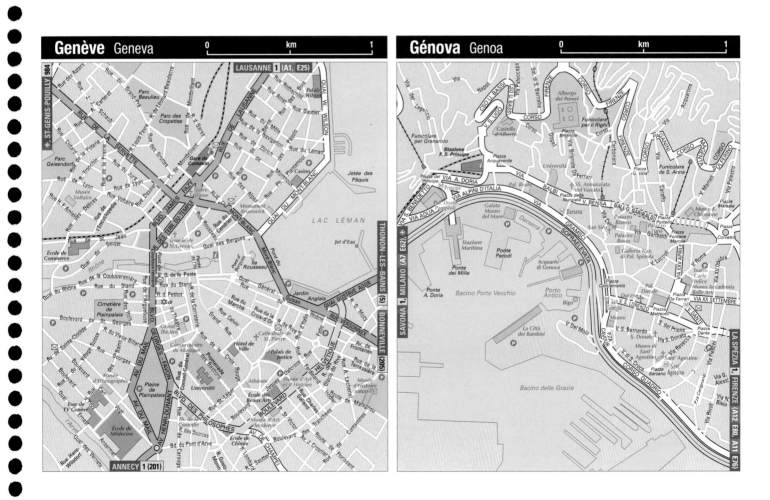

Granada

0 km 0.5

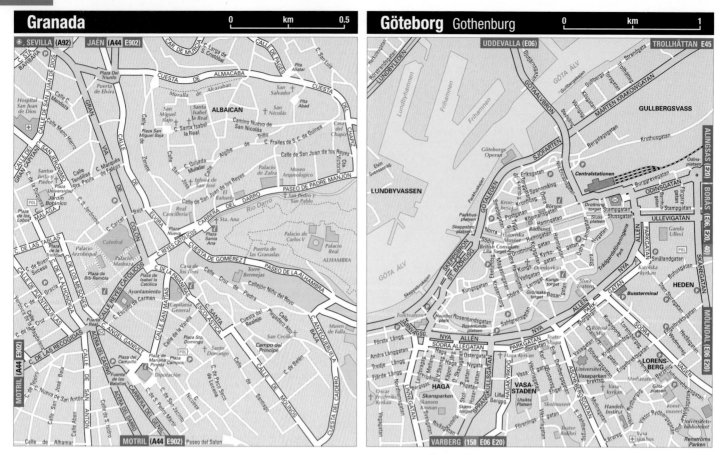

Göteborg Gothenburg

0 km 1

Hamburg

0 km 5

Hamburg

0 km 1

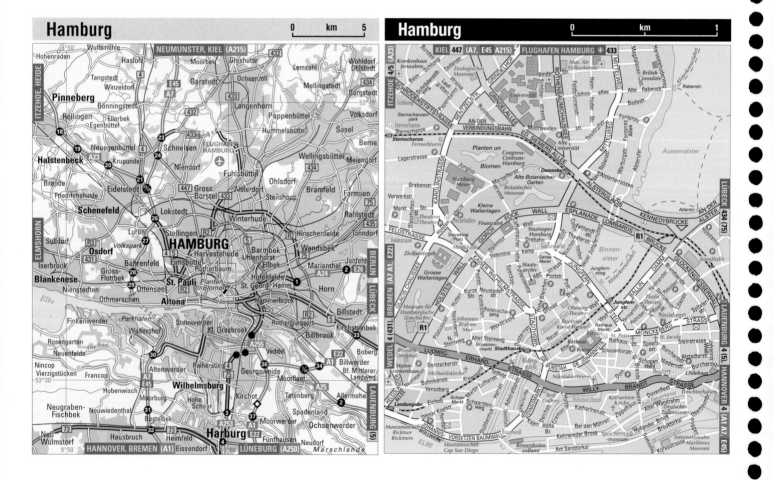

Helsinki

İstanbul

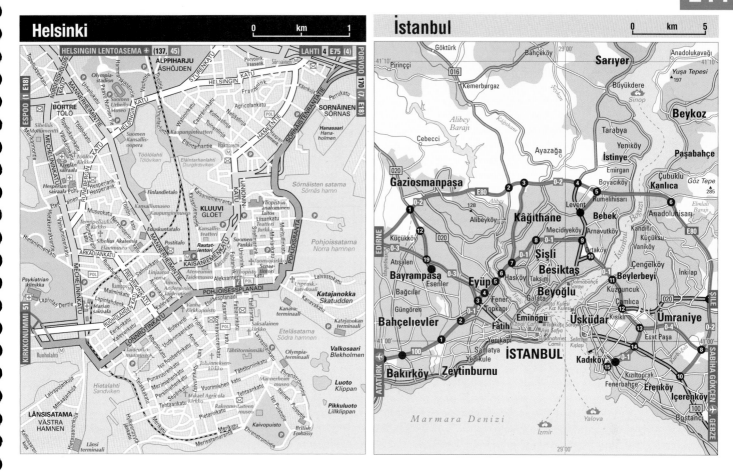

Helsinki

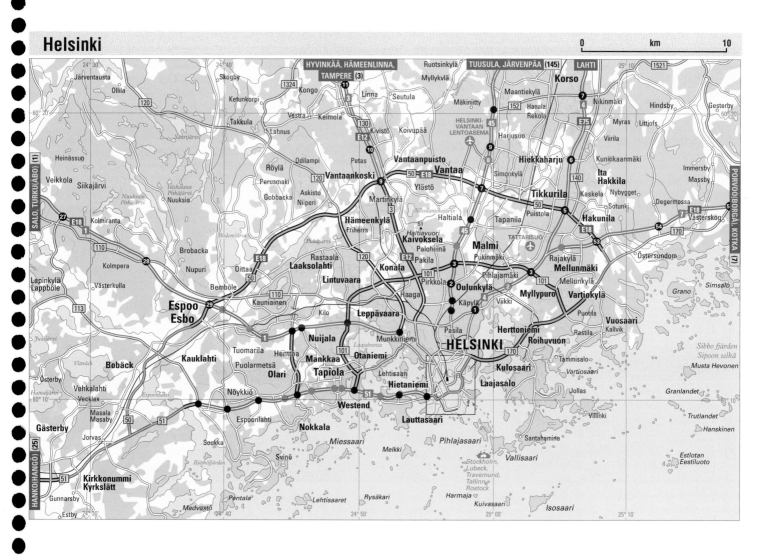

København Copenhagen

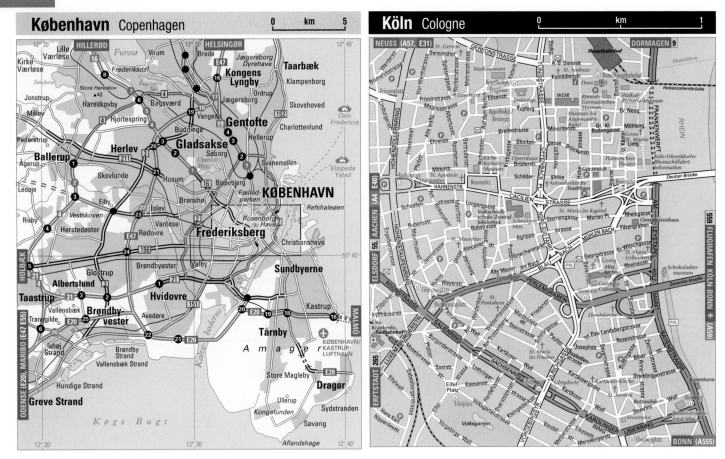

Köln Cologne

København Copenhagen

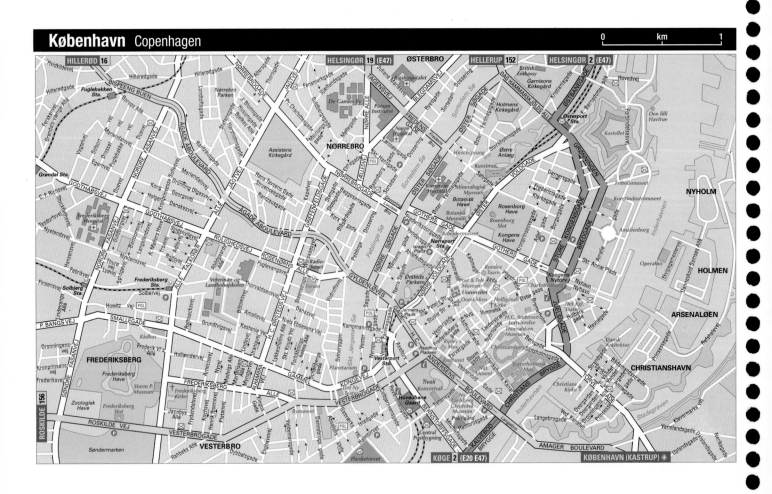

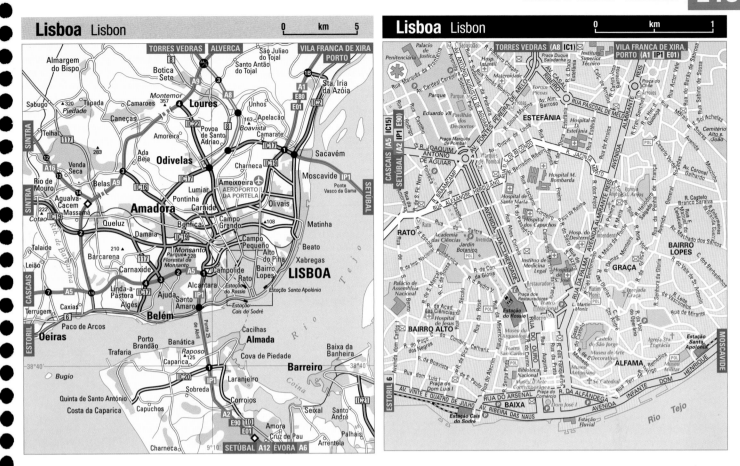

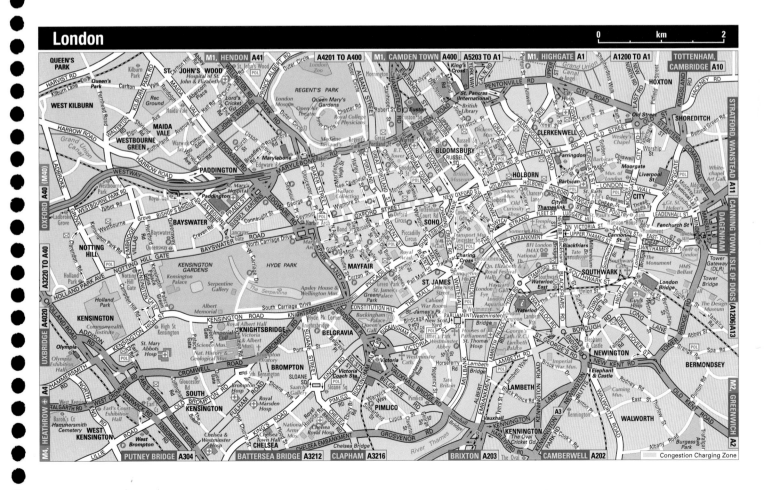

London

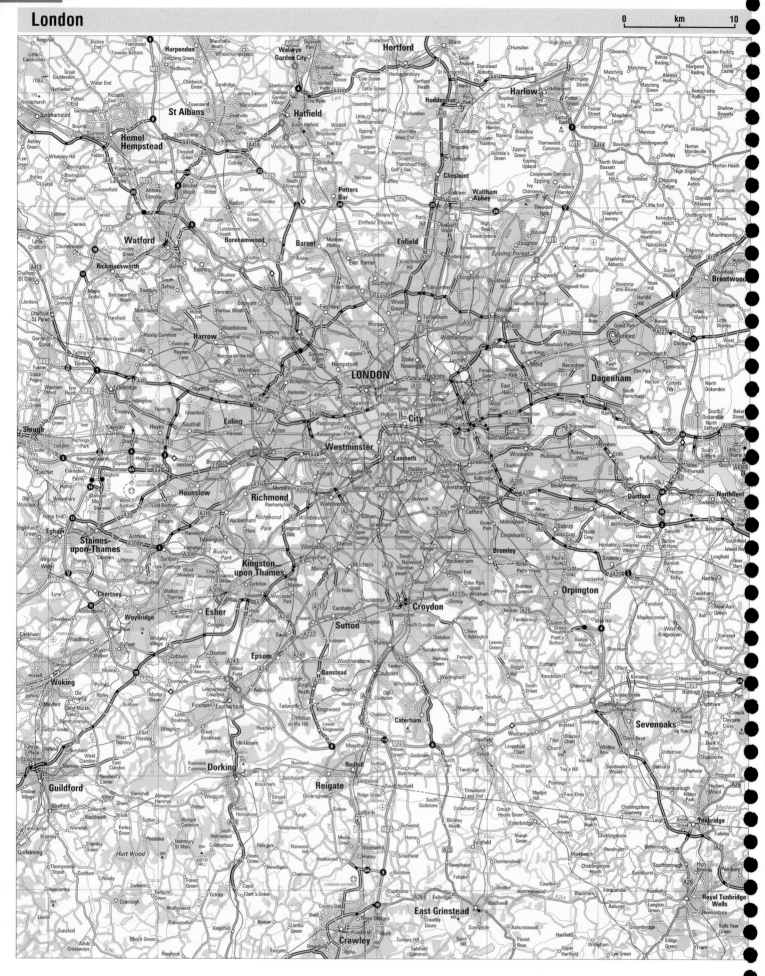

Lyon

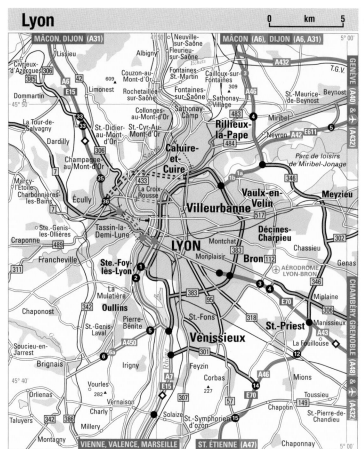

Lyon

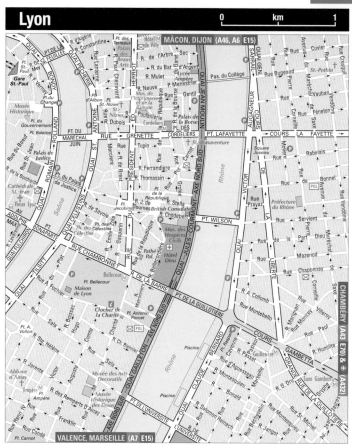

Luxembourg

Madrid

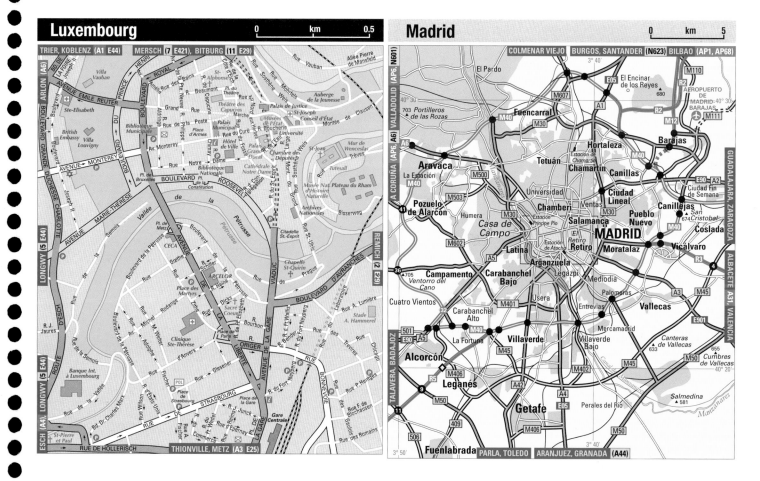

Madrid

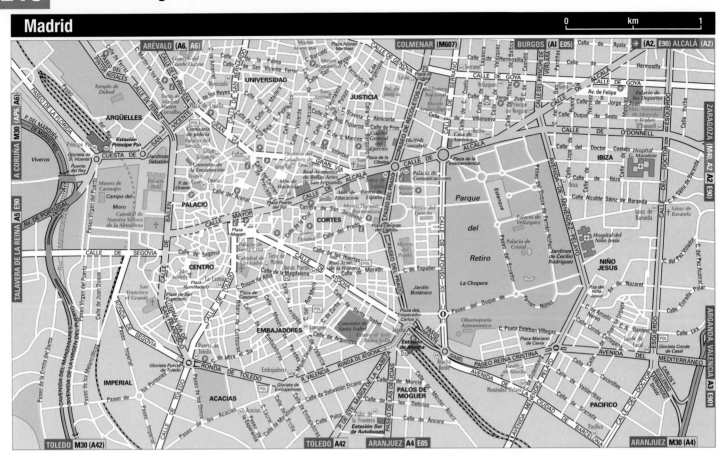

Málaga

Marseille Marseilles

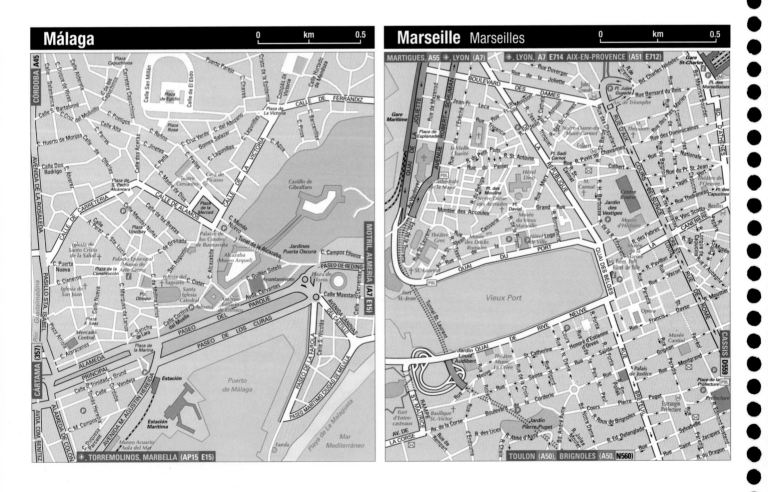

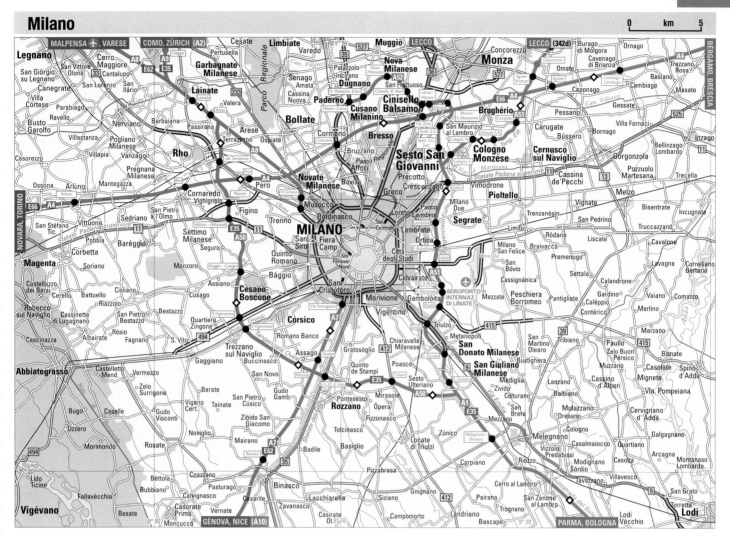

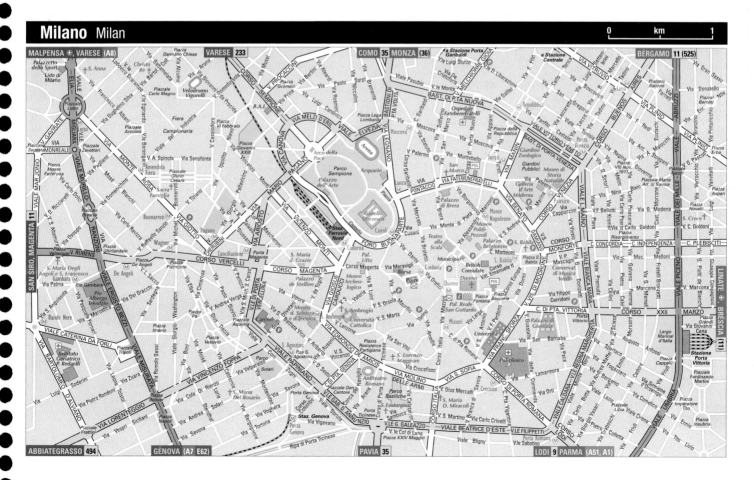

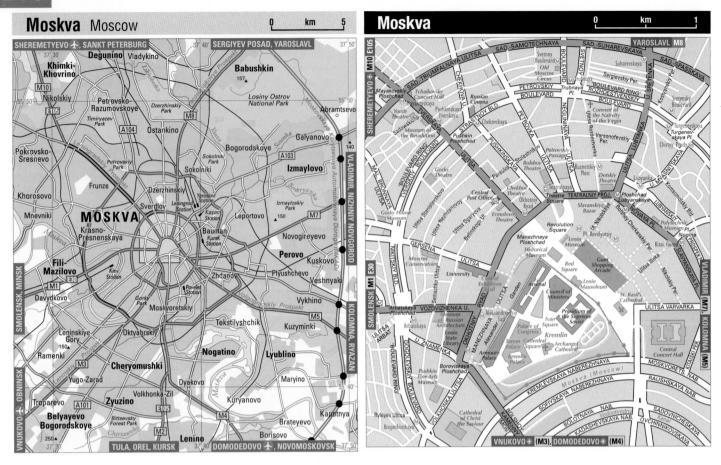

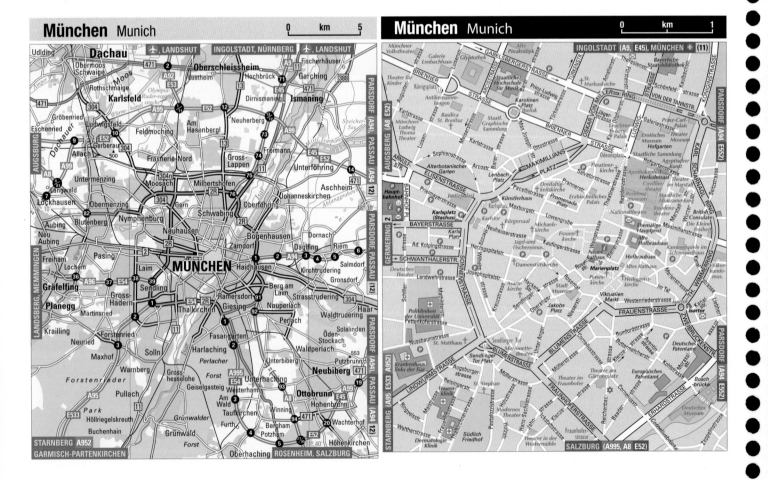

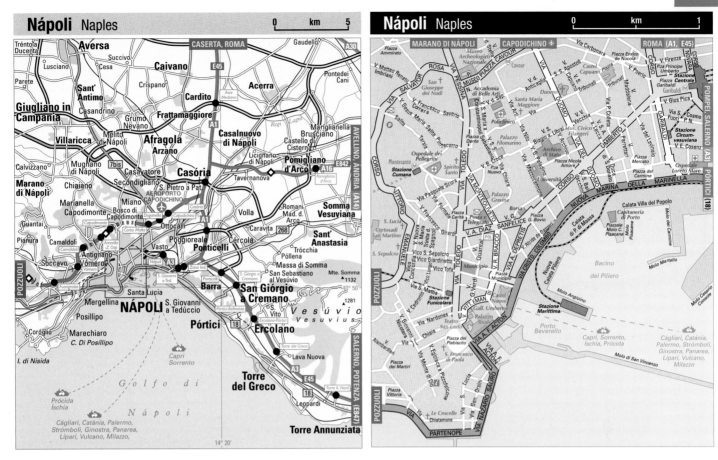

Nápoli Naples

Nápoli Naples

Oslo

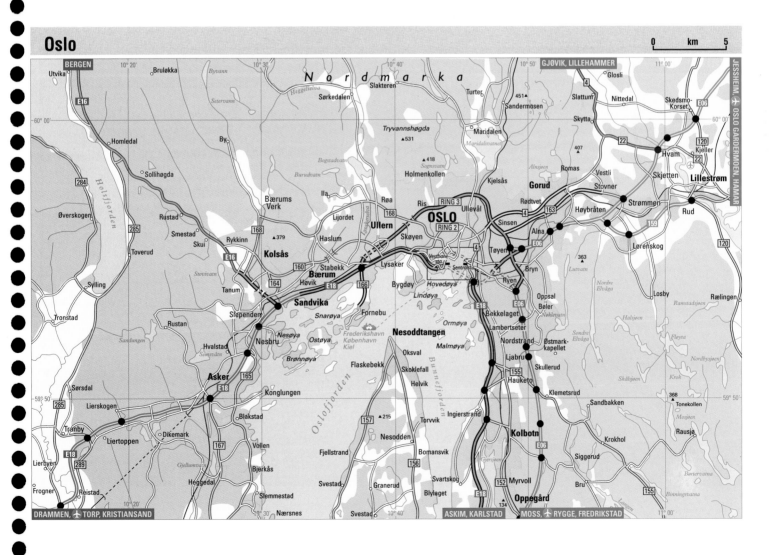

Oslo

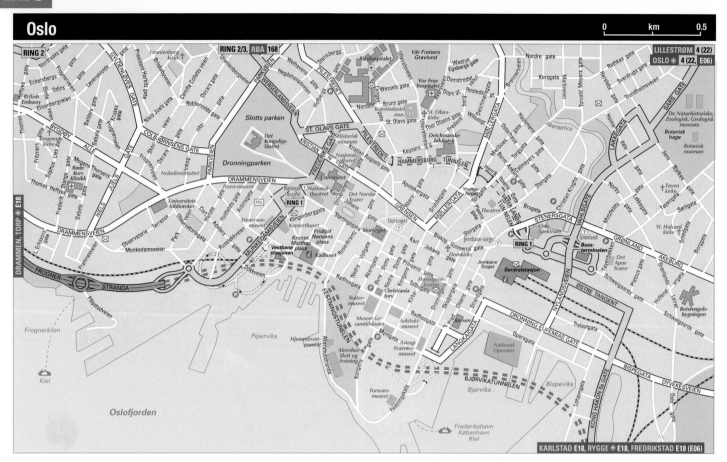

Paris

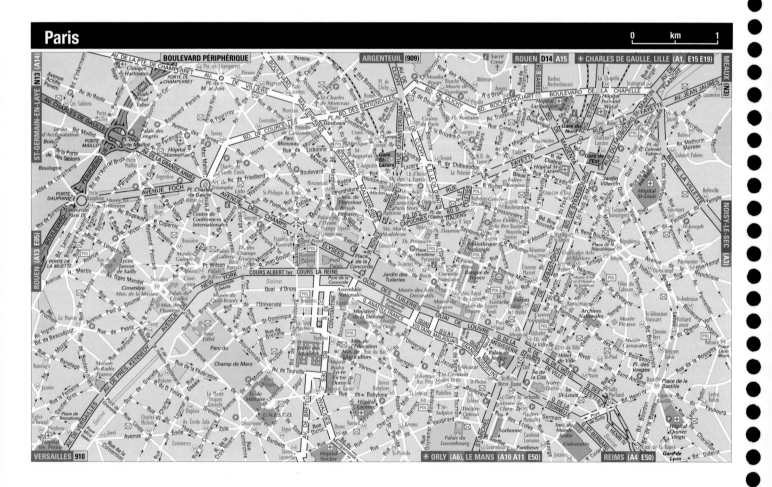

Paris

Praha Prague

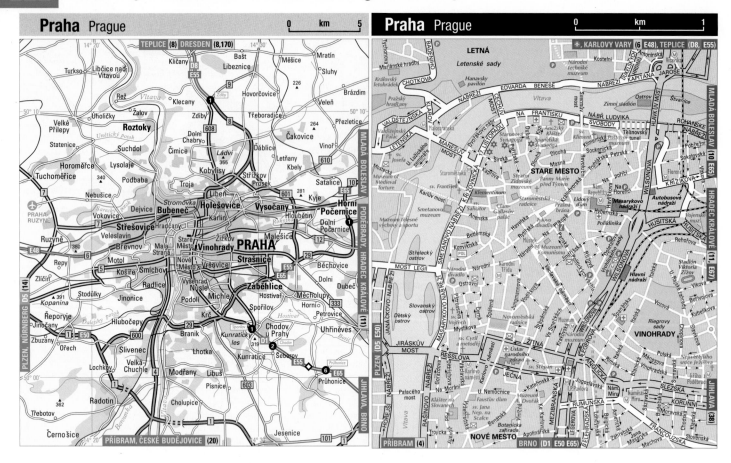

Rotterdam

Sankt-Peterburg St. Petersburg

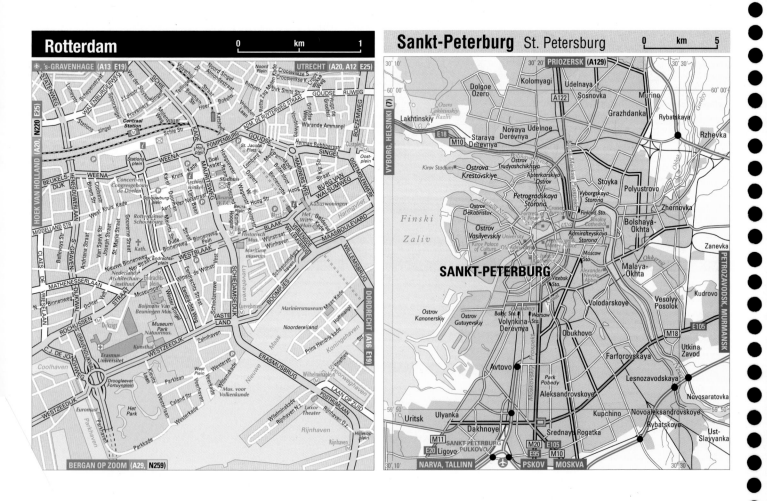

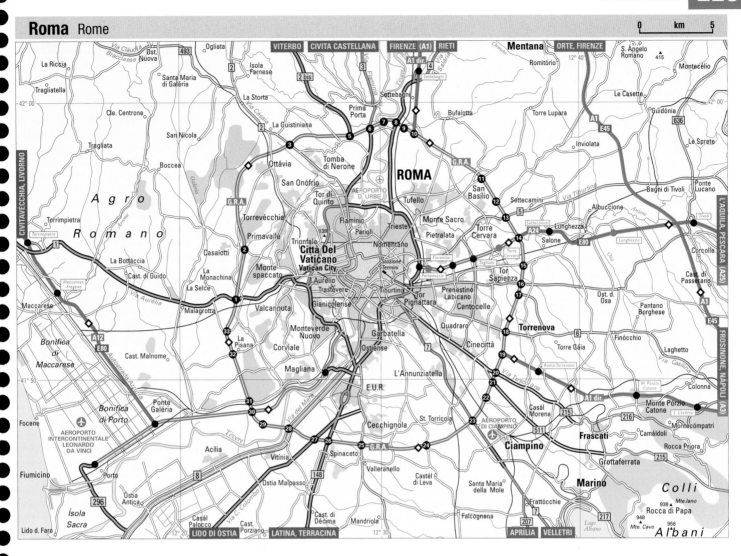

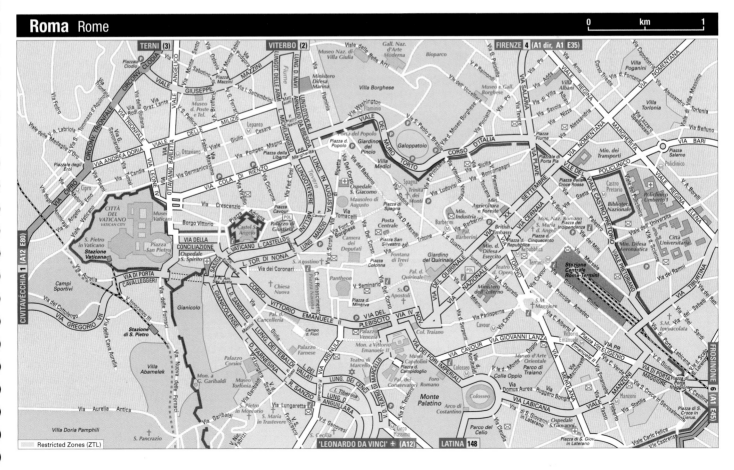

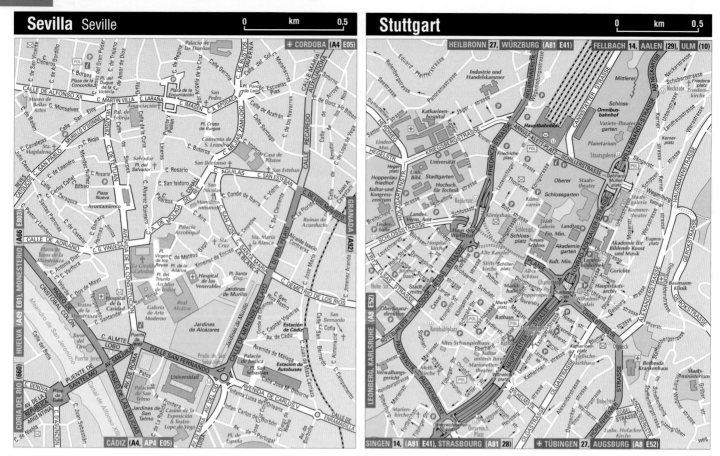

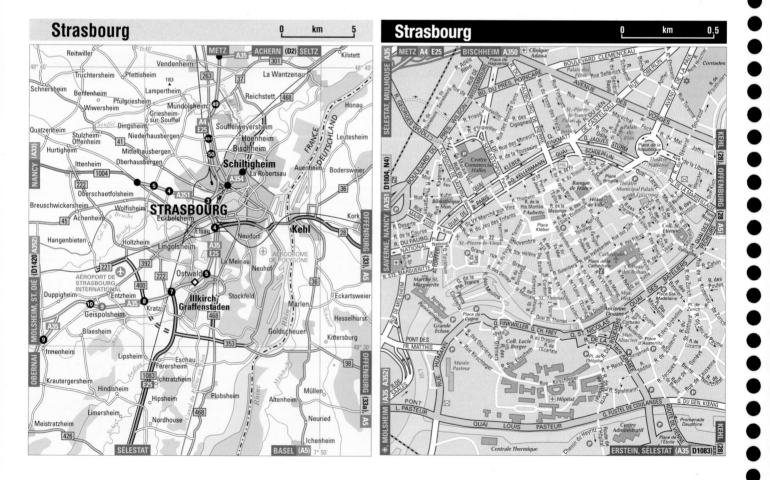

Stockholm

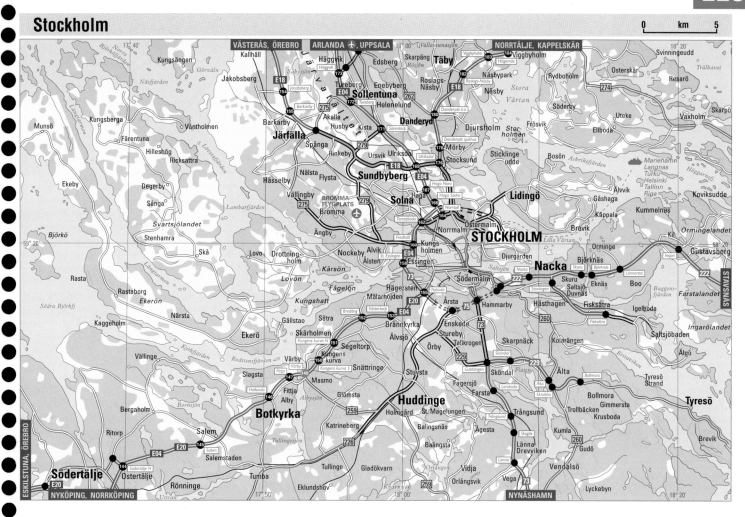

Stockholm

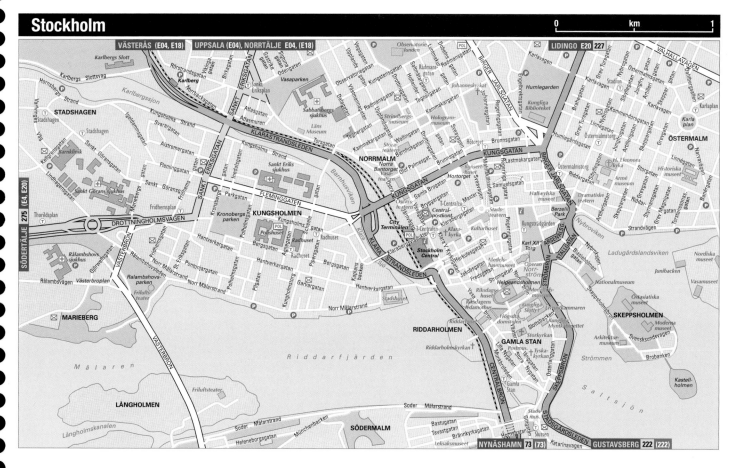

Torino Turin

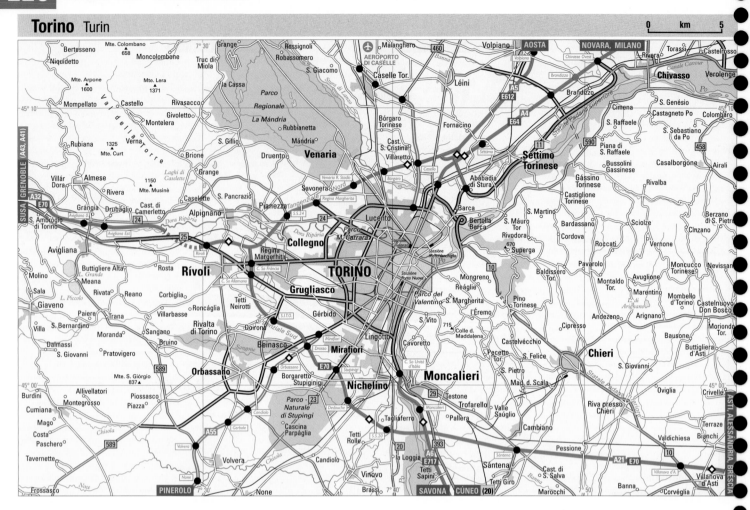

Venézia Venice

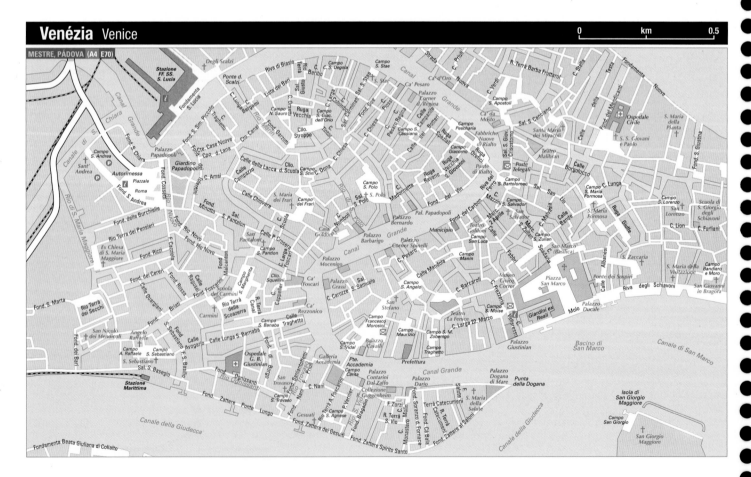

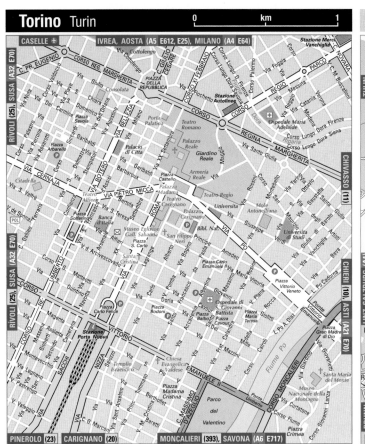

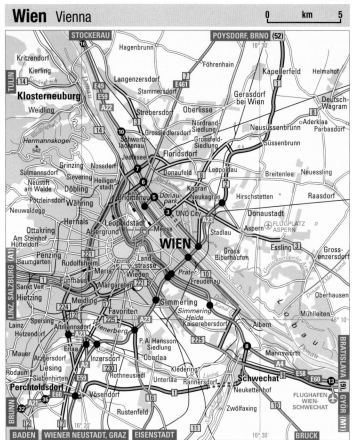

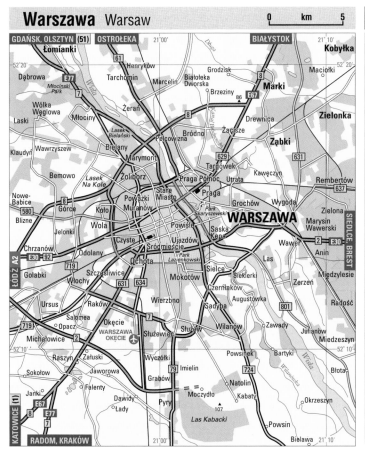

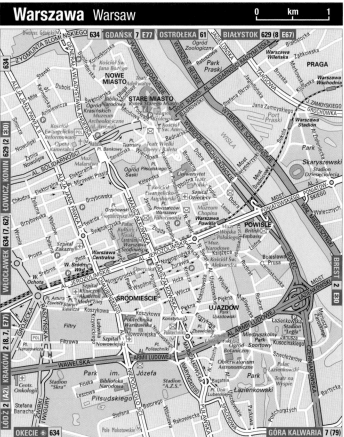

Wien Vienna

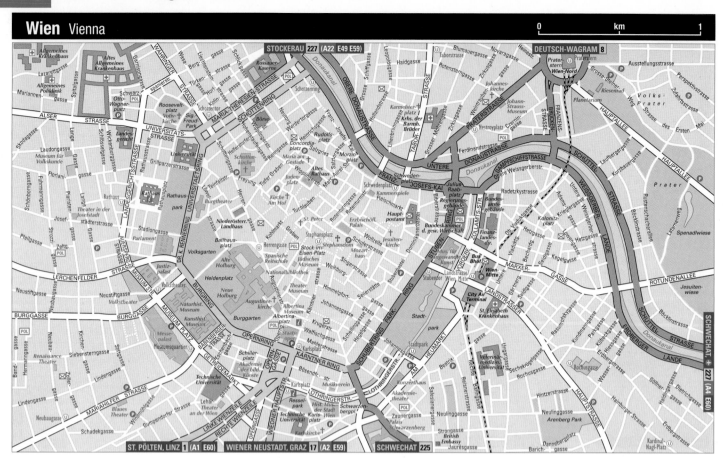

Zagreb

Zürich

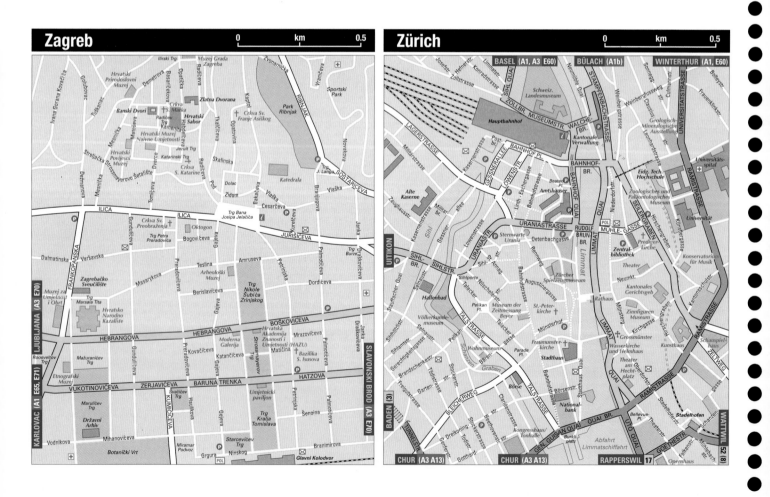

	GB	F	D	I
(A)	Austria	Autriche	Österreich	Austria
(AL)	Albania	Albanie	Albanien	Albania
(AND)	Andorra	Andorre	Andorra	Andorra
(B)	Belgium	Belgique	Belgien	Belgio
(BG)	Bulgaria	Bulgarie	Bulgarien	Bulgaria
(BIH)	Bosnia-Herzegovin	Bosnia-Herzegovine	Bosnien-Herzegowina	Bosnia-Herzogovina
(BY)	Belarus	Belarus	Weissrussland	Bielorussia
(CH)	Switzerland	Suisse	Schweiz	Svizzera
(CY)	Cyprus	Chypre	Zypern	Cipro
(CZ)	Czech Republic	République Tchèque	Tschechische Republik	Repubblica Ceca
(D)	Germany	Allemagne	Deutschland	Germania
(DK)	Denmark	Danemark	Dänemark	Danimarca
(E)	Spain	Espagne	Spanien	Spagna
(EST)	Estonia	Estonie	Estland	Estonia
(F)	France	France	Frankreich	Francia
(FIN)	Finland	Finlande	Finnland	Finlandia
(FL)	Liechtenstein	Liechtenstein	Liechtenstein	Liechtenstein
(FO)	Faeroe Islands	Îles Féroé	Färoër-Inseln	Isole Faroe
(GB)	United Kingdom	Royaume Uni	Grossbritannien und Nordirland	Regno Unito
(GBZ)	Gibraltar	Gibraltar	Gibraltar	Gibilterra
(GR)	Greece	Grèce	Greichenland	Grecia
(H)	Hungary	Hongrie	Ungarn	Ungheria
(HR)	Croatia	Croatie	Kroatien	Croazia
(I)	Italy	Italie	Italien	Italia
(IRL)	Ireland	Irlande	Irland	Irlanda
(IS)	Iceland	Islande	Island	Islanda
(KOS)	Kosovo	Kosovo	Kosovo	Kosovo
(L)	Luxembourg	Luxembourg	Luxemburg	Lussemburgo
(LT)	Lithuania	Lituanie	Litauen	Lituania
(LV)	Latvia	Lettonie	Lettland	Lettonia
(M)	Malta	Malte	Malta	Malta
(MC)	Monaco	Monaco	Monaco	Monaco
(MD)	Moldova	Moldavie	Moldawien	Moldavia
(MK)	Macedonia	Macédoine	Makedonien	Macedonia
(MNE)	Montenegro	Monténégro	Montenegro	Montenegro
(N)	Norway	Norvège	Norwegen	Norvegia
(NL)	Netherlands	Pays-Bas	Niederlande	Paesi Bassi
(P)	Portugal	Portugal	Portugal	Portogallo
(PL)	Poland	Pologne	Polen	Polonia
(RO)	Romania	Roumanie	Rumanien	Romania
(RSM)	San Marino	Saint-Marin	San Marino	San Marino
(RUS)	Russia	Russie	Russland	Russia
(S)	Sweden	Suède	Schweden	Svezia
(SK)	Slovak Republic	République Slovaque	Slowak Republik	Repubblica Slovacca
(SLO)	Slovenia	Slovénie	Slowenien	Slovenia
(SRB)	Serbia	Serbie	Serbien	Serbia
(TR)	Turkey	Turquie	Türkei	Turchia
(UA)	Ukraine	Ukraine	Ukraine	Ucraina

A

Aabenraa DK — 64 A2
Aabybro DK — 58 A2
Aach D — 107 B4
Aachen D — 80 B2
Aalborg DK — 58 A2
Aalen D — 94 C2
Aalestrup DK — 58 B2
Aalsmeer NL — 70 B1
Aalst B — 79 B4
Aalten NL — 71 C3
Aalter B — 79 A3
Äänekoski FIN — 8 A4
Aapajärvi FIN — 197 B10
Ağapınar TR — 187 C5
Aarau CH — 106 B3
Aarberg CH — 106 B2
Aarburg CH — 106 B2
Aardenburg NL — 79 A3
Aars DK — 58 B2
Aarschot B — 79 B4
Aarup DK — 59 C3
Aba H — 112 B2
Abádanes E — 152 B1
Abades E — 151 B3
Abadin E — 141 A3
Abádszalók H — 113 B4
Abaliget H — 125 A4
Abana TR — 23 A8
A Baña E — 140 B2
Abanilla E — 165 A3
Abano Terme I — 121 B4
Abarán E — 165 A3
Abasár H — 113 B4
Abbadia San Salvatore I — 135 C4
Abbaue D — 74 A2
Abbehausen D — 72 A1
Abbekäs S — 66 A2
Abbeville F — 90 A1
Abbey IRL — 28 A3
Abbeydorney IRL — 29 B2
Abbeyfeale IRL — 29 B2
Abbeyleix IRL — 30 B1
Abbey Town GB — 36 B3
Abbiategrasso I — 120 B1
Abborrträsk S — 196 D2
Abbots Bromley GB — 40 C2
Abbotsbury GB — 43 B4
Abda H — 111 B4
Abejar E — 143 C4
Abela P — 160 B1
Abelvær N — 199 A8
Abenberg D — 94 B2
Abenójar E — 157 B3
Abensberg D — 95 C3
Aberaeron GB — 39 B2
Abercarn GB — 39 C3
Aberchirder GB — 33 D4
Aberdare GB — 39 C3
Aberdaron GB — 38 B2
Aberdeen GB — 33 D4
Aberdulais GB — 39 C3
Aberdyfi GB — 39 B2
Aberfeldy GB — 35 B4
Aberffraw GB — 38 A2
Aberfoyle GB — 35 B3
Abergavenny GB — 39 C3
Abergele GB — 38 A3
Abergynolwyn GB — 38 B3
Aberporth GB — 39 B2
Abersoch GB — 38 B2
Abertillery GB — 39 C3
Abertura E — 156 A2
Aberystwyth GB — 39 B2
Abetone I — 135 A3
Abfaltersbach A — 109 C3
Abide
  Çanakkale TR — 186 B1
  Kütahya TR — 187 D4
Abiego E — 145 B3
Abild DK — 64 B1
Abingdon GB — 44 B2
Abington GB — 36 A3
Abisko S — 194 B9
Abiul P — 154 B2
Abla E — 164 B2

Ablis F — 90 C1
A Bola E — 140 B3
Abondance F — 118 A3
Abony H — 113 B4
Aboyne GB — 33 D4
Abrantes P — 154 B2
Abreiro P — 148 A2
Abreschviller F — 92 C3
Abrest F — 117 A3
Abriès F — 119 C3
Abrud RO — 17 B5
Absdorf A — 97 C3
Abtenau A — 109 B4
Abtsgmünd D — 94 C1
Abusejo E — 149 B3
Aby
  Kronoberg S — 62 A2
  Östergötland S — 56 B2
Åbyggeby S — 51 B4
Åbytorp S — 55 A6
A Cañiza E — 140 B2
A Capela E — 140 A2
Acate I — 177 B3
Accadia I — 171 B3
Accéglio I — 132 A2
Accettura I — 172 B2
Acciaroli I — 170 C3
Accous F — 145 A3
Accrington GB — 40 B1
Accúmoli I — 169 A3
Acedera E — 156 A2
Acehuche E — 155 B4
Acered E — 152 A2
Acerenza I — 172 B1
Acerno I — 170 C3
Acerra I — 170 C2
Aceuchal E — 155 C4
Acharacle GB — 34 B2
Acharnes GR — 185 A4
Achavanich GB — 32 C3
Achene B — 79 B5
Achenkirch A — 108 B2
Achensee A — 108 B2
Achenthal A — 108 B2
Achentrias GR — 185 E6
Achern D — 93 C4
Acheux-en-Amienois F — 90 A2
Achiltibuie GB — 32 C1
Achim D — 72 A2
Achladokambos GR — 184 B3
Achnasheen GB — 32 D1
Achnashellach GB — 32 D1
Achosnich GB — 34 B1
Aci Castello I — 177 B4
Aci Catena I — 177 B4
Acilia I — 168 B2
Acıpayam TR — 189 B4
Acireale I — 177 B4
Acle GB — 41 C5
A Coruña E — 140 A2
Acquacadda I — 179 C2
Acqua Doria F — 180 B1
Acquanegra sul Chiese I — 121 B3
Acquapendente I — 168 A1
Acquasanta Terme I — 136 C2
Acquasparta I — 168 A2
Acquaviva I — 135 B4
Acquaviva delle Fonti I — 171 C4
Acquaviva Picena I — 136 C2
Acquigny F — 89 A5
Ácqui Terme I — 119 C5
Acri I — 174 B2
Acs H — 112 B2
Acsa H — 112 B3
Ácsteszér H — 112 B1
Acy-en-Multien F — 90 B2
Ada SRB — 126 B2
Adak S — 195 E9
Ádalsbruk N — 48 B3
Adamas GR — 185 C5
Adamsfjord N — 193 B10
Adamuz E — 157 B3
Adana TR — 23 C8
Ádánd H — 112 C2

Adanero E — 150 B3
Adare IRL — 29 B3
Adaševci SRB — 125 B5
Adeanueva de Ebro E — 144 B2
Adelboden CH — 106 C2
Adelebsen D — 82 A1
Adélfia I — 173 A2
Adelmannsfelden D — 94 C2
Adelsheim D — 94 B1
Adelsö S — 57 A3
Ademuz E — 152 B2
Adenau D — 80 B2
Adendorf D — 72 A3
Adinkerke B — 78 A2
Adjud RO — 17 B7
Adliswil CH — 107 B3
Admont A — 110 B1
Ádneram N — 52 A2
Adolfsström S — 195 D7
Adony H — 112 B2
Adorf
  Hessen D — 81 A4
  Sachsen D — 83 B4
Adra E — 164 C1
Adradas E — 152 A1
Adrall E — 147 B2
Adrano I — 177 B3
Ádria I — 121 B5
Adrigole IRL — 29 C2
Adwick le Street GB — 40 B2
Agde F — 130 B2
Agdenes N — 198 B6
Agen F — 129 B3
Ager E — 145 C4
Agerbæk DK — 59 C1
Agerskov DK — 64 A2
Agger DK — 58 B1
Aggersund DK — 58 A2
Aggius I — 178 B3
Aggsbach Dorf A — 97 C3
Aggsbach Markt A — 97 C3
Aggtelek H — 99 C4
Aghalee GB — 27 B4
Aghia GR — 182 D4
Aghia Anna GR — 183 E5
Aghia Galini GR — 185 D5
Aghia Marina GR — 188 D1
Aghia Paraskevi GR — 186 C1
Aghia Pelagia GR — 184 C3
Aghia Triada GR — 184 B2
Aghiokambos GR — 182 D4
Aghios Efstratios GR — 183 D6
Aghios Kirikos GR — 185 B7
Aghios Matheos GR — 182 D1
Aghios Mironas GR — 185 D6
Aghios Nikolaos GR — 185 D6
Aghios Petros GR — 182 D2
Aghio Theodori GR — 184 B4
Agiçi BIH — 124 C2
Agira I — 177 B3
Aglientu I — 178 A3
Agnières F — 118 C2
Agno CH — 120 B1

Agnone I — 170 B2
Agolada E — 140 B2
Agon Coutainville F — 88 A2
Ágordo I — 121 A5
Agost E — 165 A4
Agramón E — 158 C2
Agramunt E — 147 C2
Agreda E — 144 C2
Agria GR — 183 D5
Agrigento I — 176 B2
Agrinio GR — 182 E3
Agrópoli I — 170 C2
Aguadulce
  Almería E — 164 C2
  Sevilla E — 162 A3
Agualada E — 140 A2
Agua Longa P — 148 A1
A Guarda E — 140 C2
Aguarón E — 152 A2
Aguas E — 145 B3
Aguas Belas P — 154 B2
Aguas de Busot E — 159 C3
Aguas de Moura P — 154 C2
Águas Frias P — 148 A2
Águas Santas P — 148 A1
Aguaviva E — 153 B3
Aguaviva de la Vega E — 152 A1
A Gudiña E — 141 B3
Agudo E — 156 B3
Águeda P — 148 B1
Aguessac F — 130 A2
Aguiar P — 154 C2
Aguiar da Beira P — 148 B2
Aguilafuente E — 151 A3
Aguilar de Campóo E — 142 B2
Aguilar de la Frontera E — 163 A3
Aguilas E — 164 B3
Agunnaryd S — 60 C4
Ahat TR — 187 D4
Ahaus D — 71 B3
Åheim N — 198 C2
Ahigal E — 149 B3
Ahigal de Villarino E — 149 A3
Ahillones E — 156 B2
Ahlbeck
  Mecklenburg-Vorpommern D — 66 C3
  Mecklenburg-Vorpommern D — 74 A3
Ahlen D — 81 A3
Ahlhorn D — 71 B5
Ahmetbey TR — 186 A2
Ahmetler TR — 188 A4
Ahmetli TR — 188 A2
Ahoghill GB — 27 B4
Ahola FIN — 197 C11
Ahrensbök D — 65 B3
Ahrensburg D — 72 A3
Ahrenshoop D — 66 B1
Ahun F — 116 A2
Åhus S — 63 C2
Ahvenselkä FIN — 197 C11
Aibar E — 144 B2
Aich D — 95 C4
Aicha D — 96 C1
Aichach D — 94 C3
Aidone I — 177 B3
Aiello Cálabro I — 175 B2
Aigen im Mühlkreis A — 96 C1
Aigialousa CY — 181 A3
Aigle CH — 119 A3
Aignan F — 128 C2
Aignay-le-Duc F — 104 B3
Aigre F — 115 C4
Aigrefeuille-d'Aunis F — 114 B3
Aigrefeuille-sur-Maine F — 101 B4
Aiguablava E — 147 C4
Aiguebelle F — 118 B3
Aigueperse F — 116 A3
Aigues-Mortes F — 131 B3

Aigues-Vives F — 130 B1
Aiguilles F — 119 C3
Aiguillon F — 129 B3
Ailefroide F — 118 C3
Aillant-sur-Tholon F — 104 B2
Ailly-sur-Noye F — 90 B2
Ailly-sur-Somme F — 90 B2
Aimargues F — 131 B3
Aime F — 118 B3
Ainaži LV — 8 D4
Ainet A — 109 C3
Ainhoa F — 144 A2
Ainsa E — 145 B4
Airaines F — 90 B1
Aird Asaig Tairbeart GB — 31 B2
Airdrie GB — 35 C4
Aire-sur-l'Adour F — 128 C2
Aire-sur-la-Lys F — 78 B2
Airole I — 133 B3
Airolo CH — 107 C3
Airvault F — 102 C1
Aisey-sur-Seine F — 104 B3
Aïssey F — 105 B5
Aisy-sur-Armançon F — 104 B3
Aiterhofen D — 95 C4
Aith
  Orkney GB — 33 B4
  Shetland GB — 33 A5
Aitona E — 153 A4
Aitrach D — 107 B5
Aiud RO — 17 B5
Aix-en-Othe F — 104 A2
Aix-en-Provence F — 131 B4
Aixe-sur-Vienne F — 115 C5
Aix-les-Bains F — 118 B2
Aizenay F — 114 B2
Aizkraukle LV — 8 D4
Aizpute LV — 8 D2
Ajaccio F — 180 B1
Ajain F — 116 A1
Ajaureforsen S — 195 E6
Ajdovščina SLO — 122 B2
Ajka H — 111 B4
Ajo E — 143 A3
Ajofrin E — 157 A4
Ajos FIN — 196 D7
Akanthou CY — 181 A2
Akarca TR — 189 A4
Akasztó H — 112 C3
Akçakoca TR — 187 A6
Akçaova TR — 187 A4
Akçay TR — 189 C4
Aken D — 83 A4
Åkerby S — 51 B4
Åkernes N — 52 B3
Åkersberga S — 57 A4
Åkers styckebruk S — 56 A3
Åkervik N — 195 E4
Akhisar TR — 186 D2
Akköy TR — 188 B2
Akkrum NL — 70 A2
Akören TR — 189 B7
Åkra N — 52 A2
Åkrehamn N — 52 A1
Akrotiri CY — 181 B1
Aksaray TR — 23 B8
Akşehir TR — 189 A6
Akseki TR — 189 B6
Aksla N — 46 A3
Aksu TR — 189 C5
Aktaş TR — 186 C3
Aktsyabrski BY — 13 B8
Akyazı TR — 187 B5

Alaçatı TR — 188 A1
Aládei Sardi I — 178 B3
Ala di Stura I — 119 B4
Alaejos E — 150 A2
Alagna Valsésia I — 119 B4
Alagón E — 144 C2
Alaior E — 167 B4
Alájar E — 161 B3
Alakurtti RUS — 197 C13
Alakylä FIN — 196 B7
Alameda E — 163 A3
Alameda de la Sagra E — 151 B4
Alamedilla E — 163 A4
Alamillo E — 156 B3
Alaminos E — 151 B5
Ala-Nampa FIN — 197 C9
Alanäs S — 199 A12
Alandroal P — 155 C3
Alange E — 156 B1
Alaniemi FIN — 197 D8
Alanís E — 156 B2
Alanno I — 169 A3
Alansbro S — 200 D3
Alanya TR — 189 C7
Alap H — 112 C2
Alaquáso E — 159 B3
Alaraz E — 150 B2
Alarcón E — 158 B1
Alar del Rey E — 142 B2
Alaró E — 167 B2
Alaşehir TR — 188 A3
Alássio I — 133 A4
Alatoz E — 158 B2
Alatri I — 169 B3
Alavus FIN — 8 A3
Alba
  E — 152 B2
  I — 119 C5
Alba Adriática I — 136 C2
Albacete E — 158 C2
Alba de Tormes E — 150 B2
Alba de Yeltes E — 149 B3
Alba-Iulia RO — 17 B5
Albaida E — 159 C3
Albala del Caudillo E — 156 A1
Albaladejo E — 158 C1
Albalate de Cinca E — 145 C4
Albalate del Arzobispo E — 153 A3
Albalate de las Nogueras E — 152 B1
Albalate de Zorita E — 151 B5
Alban F — 130 B1
Albánchez E — 164 B2
Albanchez de Ubeda E — 163 A4
Albano Laziale I — 168 B2
Albanyà E — 147 B3
Albaredo d'Adige I — 121 B4
Albares E — 151 B4
Albatana E — 158 C2
Albatarrec E — 153 A4
Albatera E — 165 A4
Albbruck D — 106 B3
Albedín E — 163 A3
Albelda de Iregua E — 143 B4
Albenga I — 133 A4
Albens F — 118 B2
Alberga
  Södermanland S — 56 A2
  Södermanland S — 56 B2
Albergaria-a-Nova P — 148 B1
Albergaria-a-Velha P — 148 B1
Albergaria dos Doze P — 154 B2
Alberic E — 159 B3
Albernoa P — 160 B2

Aab–Alc

Alberobello I — 173 B3
Alberoni I — 122 B1
Albersdorf D — 64 B2
Albersloh D — 81 A3
Albert F — 90 A2
Albertirsa H — 112 B3
Albertville F — 118 B3
Alberuela de Tubo E — 145 C3
Albi F — 130 B1
Albidona I — 174 B2
Albinia I — 168 A1
Albino I — 120 B2
Albinshof D — 66 C2
Albires E — 142 B1
Albisola Marina I — 133 A4
Albocácer E — 153 B4
Albolote E — 163 A4
Albondón E — 164 C1
Alborea E — 158 B2
Albox E — 164 B2
Albrechtice nad Vltavou CZ — 96 B2
Albstadt D — 107 A4
Albufeira P — 160 B1
Albuñol E — 164 C1
Albuñuelas E — 163 B4
Alburquerque E — 155 B3
Alby
  Öland S — 63 B4
  Västernorrland S — 200 D1
Alcácer do Sal P — 154 C2
Alcáçovas P — 154 C2
Alcadozo E — 158 C2
Alcafoces P — 155 B3
Alcains P — 155 B3
Alcalá de Guadaira E — 162 A2
Alcalá de Gurrea E — 144 B3
Alcalá de Henares E — 151 B4
Alcalá de la Selva E — 153 B3
Alcalá del Júcar E — 158 B2
Alcalá del Valle E — 162 B2
Alcalá del Río E — 162 A2
Alcalá de los Gazules E — 162 B2
Alcalá la Real E — 163 A4
Álcamo I — 176 B1
Alcampell E — 145 C4
Alcanadre E — 144 B1
Alcanar E — 153 B4
Alcanede P — 154 B2
Alcanena P — 154 B2
Alcañices E — 149 A3
Alcántara E — 155 B4
Alcantarilha P — 160 B1
Alcantarilla E — 165 B3
Alcañiz E — 153 A3
Alcaracejos E — 156 B3
Alcara il Fusi I — 177 A3
Alcaraz E — 158 C1
Alcaria Ruiva P — 160 B2
Alcarraz E — 153 A4
Alcaudete E — 163 A3
Alcaudete de la Jara E — 150 C3
Alcázar de San Juan E — 157 A4
Alcazarén E — 150 A3
Alcester GB — 44 A2
Alcoba E — 157 A3
Alcobaça P — 154 B1
Alcobendas E — 151 B4
Alcocer E — 152 B1
Alcochete P — 154 C2
Alcoentre P — 154 B2
Alcolea
  Almería E — 164 C2
  Córdoba E — 156 C3
Alcolea de Calatrava E — 157 B3
Alcolea de Cinca E — 145 C4

Alcolea del Pinar E 152 A1
Alcolea del Rio E. .162 A2
Alcolea de Tajo E. .150 C2
Alcollarin E 156 A2
Alconchel E. 155 C3
Alconera E. 155 C4
Alcontar E 164 B2
Alcora E 153 B3
Alcorisa E 153 B3
Alcossebre E. 153 B4
Alcoutim P. 160 B2
Alcover E 147 C2
Alcoy E 159 C3
Alcsútdoboz H 112 B2
Alcubierre E 145 C3
Alcubilla de Avellaneda E 143 C3
Alcubilla de Nogales E 141 B5
Alcubillas E. 157 B4
Alcublas E 159 B3
Alcúdia E. 167 B3
Alcudia de Guadix E 164 B1
Alcuéscar E 155 B4
Aldbrough GB. 41 B3
Aldeacentenera E 156 A2
Aldeadávila de la Ribera E 149 A3
Aldea del Cano E .155 B4
Aldea del Fresno E 151 B3
Aldea del Obispo E 149 B3
Aldea del Rey E. . .157 B4
Aldea de Trujillo E 156 A2
Aldealcorvo E 151 A4
Aldealuenga de Santa Maria E 151 A4
Aldeamayor de San Martin E. 150 A3
Aldeanueva de Barbarroya E . .150 C2
Aldeanueva del Camino E 149 B4
Aldeanueva del Codonal E. 150 A3
Aldeanueva de San Bartolomé E . . .156 A2
Aldeapozo E 144 C1
Aldeaquemada E. .157 B4
Aldea Real E 151 A3
Aldearrubia E 150 A2
Aldeaseca de la Frontera E 150 B2
Aldeasoña E 151 A3
Aldeatejada E 150 B2
Aldeavieja E 150 B3
Aldeburgh GB. . . .45 B5
Aldehuela E 152 B2
Aldehuela de Calatañazor E . .143 C4
Aldeia da Serra P .155 C3
Aldeia do Bispo P 149 B3
Aldeia do Mato P. .154 B2
Aldeia Gavinha P .154 B1
Aldeire E 164 B1
Aldenhoven D 80 B2
Aldersbach D 95 C5
Aldershot GB. 44 B3
Aldudes F 144 A2
Åled S 60 C2
Aledo E 165 B3
Alegria E 143 B4
Aleksandrovac SRB 127 C3
Aleksandrów Kujawski PL. 76 B3
Aleksandrów Łódzki PL. 86 A3
Aleksa Šantić SRB 126 B1
Ålem S 62 B4
Alençon F 89 B4
Alenquer P. 154 B1
Alenya F 146 B3
Aléria F 180 A2
Alès F 131 A3
Åles I 179 C2
Alessándria I 120 C1
Alessándria della Rocca I 176 B2
Alessano I 173 C4
Ålesund N 198 C3
Alet-les-Bains F . .146 B3
Alexandria GB 34 C3
Alexandria GR 182 C4
Alexandria RO 17 D6
Alexandroupoli GR 183 C7
Aleyrac F 131 A3
Alézio I 173 B4
Alfacar E 163 A4
Alfaiates P 149 B3
Alfajarin E 153 A3
Alfambra E 152 B2
Alfambra P 160 B1
Alfândega da Fé P 149 A3
Alfarela de Jafes P 148 A2
Alfarelos P. 148 B1
Alfarim P 154 C1
Alfarnate E. 163 B3
Alfaro E 144 B2
Alfarràs E. 145 C4
Alfaz del Pi E 159 C3
Alfedena I 169 B4
Alfeizarão P 154 B1
Alfeld Bayern D 95 B3
Alfeld Niedersachsen D . . 72 C2

Alfena P. 148 A1
Alferce P 160 B1
Alfhausen D. 71 B4
Alfonsine I. 135 A5
Alford Aberdeenshire GB. 33 D4
Alford Lincolnshire GB . .41 B4
Alforja E. 147 C1
Alfoz E 141 A3
Alfreton GB. 40 B2
Alfta S 50 A3
Alfundão P. 160 A1
Algaida E. 167 B2
Algar E 162 B2
Ålgarås S. 55 B5
Ålgård N. 52 B1
Algarinejo E. 163 A3
Algarrobo E. 163 B3
Algatocin E. 162 B2
Algeciras E 162 B2
Algemesí E 159 B3
Agés P. 154 C1
Algete E 151 B4
Alghero I 178 B2
Ålghult S 62 A3
Alginet E 159 B3
Algodor E 151 C4
Algodor P 160 B2
Algora E. 151 B5
Algoso P. 149 A3
Algoz P. 160 B1
Ålgsjö S. 200 B3
Alguaire E 145 C4
Alguazas E 165 A3
Algutsrum S 63 B4
Algyö H 126 A2
Alhama de Almería E 164 C2
Alhama de Aragón E 152 A2
Alhama de Granada E 163 B4
Alhama de Murcia E 165 B3
Alhambra E. 157 B4
Alhandra P. 154 C1
Alhaurin de la Torre E 163 B3
Alhaurin el Grande E 163 B3
Alhendin E. 163 A4
Alhóndiga E. 151 B5
Alia E 156 A2
Alia I 176 B2
Aliaga TR 186 D1
Aliaga E 153 B3
Alibunar SRB. 127 B2
Alicante E 165 A4
Alicún de Ortega E 164 B1
Alife I 170 B2
Alija del Infantado E 141 B5
Aliją P. 148 A2
Alimena I 177 B3
Alingsås S. 60 B2
Alinyà E 147 B2
Aliseda E 155 B4
Ali Terme I 177 A4
Aliveri GR 185 A5
Alixan F 117 C5
Aljaraque E 161 B2
Aljezur P 160 B1
Aljorra E 165 B3
Aljubarrota P. 154 B2
Aljucen E 155 B4
Aljustrel P 160 B1
Alken B 79 B5
Alkmaar NL. 70 B1
Alkoven A. 96 C2
Allaines F. 103 A3
Allaire F 101 B3
Allanche F 116 B2
Alland A 111 A3
Allariz E 140 B3
Allassac F 129 A4
Allauch F 131 B4
Alleen N. 52 B3
Allègre F 117 B3
Allendale Town GB 37 B4
Allendorf D 81 B4
Allentsteig A 97 C3
Allepuz E 153 B3
Allersberg D 95 B3
Allershausen D 95 C3
Alles E 142 A2
Allevard F 118 B3
Allgunnen S. 62 A3
Allihies IRL. 29 C1
Allingåbro DK 58 B3
Allmannsdorf D . . .107 B4
Allo E. 144 B1
Alloa GB. 35 B4
Allogny F 103 B4
Alloluokta S 196 B2
Allones Eure et Loire F . .90 C1
Allones Maine-et-Loire F .102 B2
Allonnes F 102 B2
Allons F 128 B2
Allos F 132 A2
Allstedt D. 82 A3
Alltwalis GB. 39 C2
Allumiere I 168 A1
Almaceda P 155 B3
Almacelles E 145 C4
Almachar E 163 B3
Almada P 154 C1
Almadén E 156 B3
Almadén de la Plata E 161 B3
Almadenejos E . . .156 B3
Almadrones E 151 B5
Almagro E 157 B4
Almajano E 144 C1
Almansa E. 159 C2

Almansil P 160 B1
Almanza E 142 B1
Almaraz E 150 C2
Almargen E 162 B2
Almarza E 143 C4
Almásfüzitö H 112 B2
Almassora E 159 B3
Almazán E 152 A1
Almazul E 152 A1
Almedina E 158 C1
Almedinilla E 163 A3
Almeida E 149 A3
Almeida P 149 B3
Almeirim P 154 B2
Almelo NL 71 B3
Almenar E 145 C4
Almenara E 159 B3
Almenar de Soria E 152 A1
Almendra P 149 B2
Almendral E 155 C4
Almendral de la Cañada E 150 B3
Almendralejo E. . . .155 C4
Almenno San Bartolomeo I . . .120 B2
Almere NL. 70 B2
Almería E 164 C2
Almerimar E 164 C2
Almese I 119 B4
Almexial P 160 B2
Älmhult S. 63 B2
Almiropotamos GR. 185 A5
Almiros GR 182 D4
Almodôvar P 160 B1
Almodóvar del Campo E 157 B3
Almodóvar del Pinar E 158 B2
Almodóvar del Río E 162 A2
Almofala P 148 B2
Almogia E 163 B3
Almoharin E 156 A1
Almonacid de la Sierra E 152 A2
Almonacid de Toledo E 157 A4
Almonaster la Real E 161 B3
Almondsbury GB . .43 A4
Almonte E 161 B3
Almoradi E 165 A4
Almoraima E 162 B2
Almorox E 150 B3
Almoster P. 154 B2
Almsele S 200 B3
Älmsta S 51 C5
Almudena E. 164 A3
Almudévar E 145 B3
Almuñécar E 163 B4
Almunge S. 51 C5
Almuradiel E 157 B4
Almussafes E 159 B3
Almvik S 62 A4
Alness GB 32 D2
Alnmouth GB. 37 A5
Alnwick GB. 37 A5
Åloppe S 51 C4
Álora E 163 B3
Alos d'Ensil F 146 B2
Alosno E 161 B2
Alozaina E 162 B3
Alpbach A 108 B2
Alpedrete de la Sierra E 151 B4
Alpedrinha P 148 B2
Alpen D 80 A2
Alpera E 159 C2
Alphen aan de Rijn NL. 70 B1
Alpiarça P 154 B2
Alpignano I 119 B4
Alpirsbach D 93 C4
Alpu TR 187 C5
Alpuente E 159 B2
Alqueva P. 160 A2
Alquézar E 145 B4
Als DK 58 B3
Alsasua E 144 B1
Alsdorf D 80 B2
Alselv DK 59 C1
Alsfeld D 81 B5
Alsike S 57 A3
Alskog S 57 C4
Alsleben D. 83 A3
Alsónémedi H 112 B3
Alsótold H 112 B3
Alsóújlak H 111 B3
Alstad N 194 C6
Alstätte D 71 B3
Alsterbro S 62 B3
Alstermo S. 62 B3
Alston GB 37 B4
Alsvåg N 194 B6
Alsvik N 194 C5
Alta N 192 C7
Älta S 57 A4
Altamura I 172 B2
Altarejos E 158 B1
Altaussee A 109 B4
Altavilla Irpina I . . .170 B2
Altavilla Silentina I 170 C3
Altdöbern D. 84 A2
Altdorf CH 107 C3
Altdorf D 95 C4
Altdorf bei Nürnberg D. 95 B3
Alte P. 160 B1
Altea E 159 C3
Altedo I 121 C4
Altena D. 81 A3
Altenau D. 82 A2
Altenberg D. 84 B1
Altenberge D 71 B4

Altenbruch D. 64 C1
Altenburg D. 83 B4
Altenfelden A. 96 C1
Altengronau D. 82 B1
Altenheim D. 93 C3
Altenhundem D. . . .81 A4
Altenkirchen Mecklenburg-Vorpommern D . .66 B2
Altenkirchen Radom D 81 B3
Altenkunstadt D . .82 B3
Altenmarkt A 110 B1
Altenmarkt D 109 A3
Altenmarkt im Pongall A 109 B4
Altensteig D. 93 C4
Altentreptow D 74 A2
Altenwalde D 64 C1
Alten-weddingen D 73 B4
Alter do Chão P. . .155 B3
Altfraunhofen D . . .95 C4
Altheim A 109 A4
Altheim D 94 B1
Althofen A 110 C1
Altınoluk TR. 186 C1
Altınova TR. 186 C1
Altıntaş TR. 187 C5
Altınyaka TR 189 C5
Altınyayla TR. 189 B4
Altkirch F 106 B2
Altlandsberg D 74 B2
Altlewin D 74 B3
Altmannstein D . . .95 C3
Altmorschen D 82 A1
Altmunster A 109 B4
Altnaharra GB. 32 C2
Alto Campoó E . . .142 A2
Altofonte I 176 A2
Altomonte I 174 B2
Alton Hampshire GB. . .44 B3
Alton Staffordshire GB .40 C2
Altopáscio I 135 B3
Altötting D. 109 A3
Altreichenau D . . .96 C1
Alt Ruppin D 74 B1
Altshausen D 107 B4
Altstätten CH 107 B4
Altura E 159 B3
Altusried D 107 B5
Alūksne LV. 8 D5
Alunda S 51 B5
Alustante E 152 B2
Alva GB 35 B4
Alvaiázere P 154 B2
Alvalade P 160 B1
Älvängen S 60 B2
Alvarenga P 148 B1
Alvares P 154 A2
Alvdal N. 199 C7
Älvdalen S. 49 A6
Alverca P 154 C1
Alversund N 46 B2
Alvesta S 62 B2
Alvignac F 129 B4
Alvignano I 170 B2
Ålvik N 46 B3
Alvik N 50 B1
Alvik S 50 B1
Alvimare F 89 A4
Alviobeira P. 154 B2
Alvito P. 160 A2
Älvkarleby S 51 B4
Älvkarleöbruk S . .51 B4
Alvor P. 160 B1
Alvorge P 154 B2
Alvøy N 46 B2
Älvros S 199 C11
Alvsbacka S 55 A4
Älvsbyn S 196 D4
Alvsered S 60 B2
Älvserod S 60 B2
Alwernia PL 86 B3
Alwinton GB. 37 A4
Alyth GB. 35 B4
Alytus LT. 13 A6
Alzénau D 93 A5
Alzey D. 93 B4
Alzira E 159 B3
Alzonne F 146 A3
Amadora P. 154 C1
Åmål S 55 A3
Amalfi I 170 C2
Amaliada GR 184 B2
Amance F 105 B5
Amancey F 105 B5
Amándola I 136 C2
Amantea I 175 B2
Amarante P 148 A1
Amareleja P 161 A2
Amares P. 148 A1
Amaseno I 169 B3
Amasra TR 187 A7
Amatrice I 169 A3
Amay P 154 B2
Ambarnyy RUS. . . .3 D13
Ambazac F 115 C5
Ambelakia GR 182 D4
Ambelonas GR . . .182 D4
Amberg D 95 B3
Ambérieu-en-Bugey F 118 B2
Ambérieux-en-Dombes F 117 A4
Ambès F 128 A2
Ambjörby S 49 B5
Ambjörnarp S 60 B3
Amble GB 37 A5
Ambleside GB 36 B4
Ambleteuse F. 78 B1
Amboise F 102 B2
Ambrières-les-Vallées F. 88 B3
Amden CH 107 B4
Amel B 80 B2
Amélia I 168 A2
Amélie-les-Bains-Palalda F 146 B3
Amelinghausen D . .72 A3
Amendoa P 154 B2

Amendoeira P 160 B2
Améndola I 171 B3
Amendolara I. 174 B2
Amer E 147 B3
A Merca E 140 B3
Amerongen NL 70 B2
Amersfoort NL. 70 B2
Amersham GB. 44 B3
Amesbury GB 44 B2
Amfiklia GR. 182 E4
Amfilochia GR. 182 E3
Amfipoli GR. 183 C5
Amfissa GR. 184 A3
Amièira P. 155 C3
Amieira P. 154 B3
Amieiro P. 148 B1
Amindeo GR. 182 C3
Åminne S. 60 B3
Amli N. 53 B4
Amlwch GB 38 A2
Ammanford GB. . . .39 C3
Ammarnäs S 195 E7
Åmmeberg S 55 B5
Amorbach D 94 B1
Amorebieta E 143 A4
Amorgos GR 185 C6
Amorosa P 148 A1
Amorosi I 170 B2
Åmot Buskerud N 48 C1
Åmot Telemark N 53 A3
Åmot S 50 B3
Åmotfors S 54 A3
Åmotsdal N 53 A4
Amou F 128 C2
Ampezzo I 122 A1
Ampfing D 95 C4
Ampflwang A 109 A4
Amplepuis F 117 B4
Amposta E 153 B4
Ampthill GB. 44 A3
Ampudia E 142 C2
Ampuero E 143 A3
Amriswil CH 107 B4
Amsele S. 200 B5
Amstelveen NL 70 B1
Amsterdam NL 70 B1
Amstetten A. 110 A1
Amtzell D. 107 B4
Amulree GB. 35 B4
Amurrio E 143 A4
Amusco E 142 B2
Anacapri I 170 C2
Anadia P 148 B1
Anadon E. 152 B2
Anafi GR 185 C6
Anagni I 169 B3
Anamur TR 23 C7
Ananyiv UA 17 B8
Anascaul IRL 29 B1
Ånäset S 2 D7
Ana-Sira N 52 B2
Anastaževo PL 76 B3
Anaya de Alba E . .150 B2
Ança P. 148 B1
Ancaster GB 40 C3
Ancede P 148 A1
Ancenis F 101 B4
Ancerville F 91 C5
Anchuras E 156 A3
Ancona I 136 B2
Ancora P 148 A1
Ancrum GB 35 C5
Ancy-le-Franc F . .104 B3
Andalo I 121 A3
Åndalsnes N 198 C4
Andance F 117 B4
Andau A. 111 B4
Andebu N 53 A6
Andeer CH. 107 C4
Andelfingen CH. . .107 B3
Andelot-Blancheville F. 105 A4
Andelot-en-Montagne F. 105 C4
Andenes N 194 A7
Andenne B 79 B5
Anderlues B. 79 B4
Andermatt CH 107 C3
Andernach D 80 B3
Andernos-les-Bains F. 128 B1
Anderslöv S 66 A2
Anderstorp S 60 B3
Andijk NL 70 B2
Andoain E 144 A1
Andocs H. 112 C1
Andolsheim F 106 A2
Andorra E 153 B3
Andorra La Vella AND. 146 B2
Andosilla E 144 B2
Andover GB 44 B2
Andratx E 166 B2
Andreapol RUS 9 D8
Andreas GB 36 B2
Andrespol PL 86 A3
Andrest F 145 A4
Andretta I 172 B1
Andrezieux-Bouthéon F. 117 B4
Ándria I 171 B4
Andrijevica MNE . .16 D3
Andritsena GR 184 B2
Andros GR 185 B5
Andrychów PL 99 B3
Andselv N 194 A9
Andújar E. 157 B3
Anduze F 131 A2
Åneby N 48 B2
Aneby S 62 A2
Añes E 143 A3
Anet F 90 C1
Anfo I 121 B3
Ang S 62 A2
Anga S 57 C4
Angaïs F 145 A3
Ånge S 199 B11
Ånge S 200 D1

Angeja P. 148 B1
Ängelholm S 61 C2
Angeli FIN 193 D9
Ängelsberg S 50 C3
Anger A 110 B2
Angera I 120 B1
Angermünde D 74 A3
Angern A. 97 C4
Angers F 102 B1
Angerville F 90 C2
Anghiari I 135 B5
Angle GB 39 C1
Anglès E 147 C3
Anglès F 130 B1
Angles F 114 B2
Anglesola E. 147 C2
Angles sur l'Anglin F. 115 B4
Anglet F 128 C1
Anglisidhes CY . . .181 B2
Anglure F 91 C3
Angoulême F 115 C4
Angoulins F 114 B2
Angsö S 56 A2
Angueira P 149 A3
Angües E. 145 B3
Anguiano E 143 B4
Anguillara Sabazia I 168 A2
Anguillara Véneta I 121 B4
Anhée B 79 B4
Anholt DK 60 C1
Aniane F 130 B2
Aniche F 78 B3
Ånimskog S. 54 B3
Anina RO 16 C4
Anixi GR 182 D3
Anizy-le-Château F 91 B3
Anjalankoski FIN. . .8 B5
Anjan S 199 B9
Anjum NL 70 A3
Ankara TR 187 C7
Ankaran SLO 122 B2
Ankarsrum S 62 A4
Ankerlia N 192 C4
Anklam D 66 C2
Ankum D 71 B4
Anlauftal A. 109 B4
Anlezy F 104 C2
Ann S 199 B9
Annaberg A 110 B2
Annaberg-Buchholz D 83 B5
Annaberg im Lammertal A. . . .109 B4
Annaburg D. 83 A5
Annahütte D 84 A1
Annalong GB. 27 B5
Annan GB 36 B3
Annecy F. 118 B3
Annelund S 60 B3
Annemasse F 118 A3
Anneberg Halland S 60 B2
Anneberg Jönköping S. . . .62 A2
Annenskiy Most RUS 9 B10
Annerstad S 60 C3
Annestown IRL 30 B1
Annevoie-Rouillon B 79 B4
Annonay F 117 B4
Annot F 132 B2
Annweiler D. 93 B3
Ano Poroia GR . . .183 B5
Ano Siros GR 185 B5
Añora E 156 B3
Anould F 106 A1
Anquela del Ducado E 152 B2
Anröchte D 81 A4
Ans DK 59 B2
Ansager DK. 59 C1
Ansbach D. 94 B2
Anse F 117 B4
Anseroeul B 79 B3
Ansfelden A. 110 A1
Ansião P 154 B2
Ansó E 144 B3
Ansoain E 144 B2
Anstruther GB 35 B5
Antalya TR. 189 C5
Antas E. 164 B3
Antegnate I 120 B2
Antequera E 163 B3
Anterselva di Mezzo I 108 C3
Antibes F. 132 B3
Antigüedad E 142 C2
Antillo I 177 B4
Antirio GR. 184 A2
Antnäs S 196 D4
Anton BG 17 D6
Antoing B 79 B3
Antonin PL. 86 A1
Antrain F. 88 B2
Antrim GB 27 B4
Antrodoco I 169 A3
Antronapiana I 119 A5
Anttis S 196 B5
Antuzede P 148 B1
Antwerp = Antwerpen B 79 A4
Antwerpen = Antwerp B 79 A4
Anversa d'Abruzzi I 169 B3
Anvin F 78 B2
Anzat-le-Luguet F 116 B3
Anzi I 172 B1
Ánzio I 168 B2
Anzola d'Emilia I. .135 A4
Anzon E 144 C2
Aosta I 119 B4
Apalhão P 155 B3
Apátfalva H 126 A2
Apatin SRB 125 B5
Apatity RUS. 3 C13

Apc H 112 B3
Apécchio I 136 B1
Apeldoorn NL 70 B2
Apen D 71 A4
Apenburg D. 73 B4
Apensen D. 72 A2
A Peroxa E. 140 B3
Apiro I 136 B2
Apliki CY 181 B2
Apolda D 82 A3
Apolonia GR 185 C5
A Pontenova E. . . .141 A3
Apostag H 112 C2
Äppelbo S 49 B6
Appennino I 136 C2
Appenzell CH 107 B4
Appiano I 108 C2
Appingedam NL . . .71 A3
Appleby-in-Westmorland GB .37 B4
Applecross GB 31 B3
Appledore GB. 42 A2
Appoigny F 104 B2
Apremont-la-Forêt F. 92 C1
Aprica I 120 A3
Apricena I 171 B3
Aprigliano I 174 B2
Aprilia I 168 B2
Apt F 131 B4
Apúlia P 148 A1
Aquiléia I 122 B2
Aquilónia I 172 B1
Aquino I 169 B3
Ar S 57 C4
Arabayona E 150 A2
Arabba I 108 C2
Araç TR 23 A7
Aracena E 161 B3
Arachova GR. 184 A3
Aračinovo MK 182 A3
Arad RO. 126 A3
Aradac SRB. 126 B2
Aradhippou CY . . .181 B2
Aragnouet F 145 B4
Aragona I 176 B2
Aramits F 144 A3
Aramon F. 131 B3
Aranda de Duero E 143 C3
Aranda de Moncayo E 152 A2
Arandeljovac SRB 127 C2
Aranjuez E 151 B4
Arantzazu E 143 B4
Aranzueque E 151 B4
Aras de Alpuente E 159 B2
Arauzo de Miel E . .143 C3
Arazede P 148 B1
Arbas F 145 B4
Árbatax I 179 C3
Arbeca E 147 C1
Arberg D 94 B2
Arbesbach A 96 C2
Arboga S 56 A1
Arbois F 105 C4
Arbon CH 107 B4
Arboréa I 179 C2
Arbório I 119 B5
Årbostad N 194 B8
Arbrå S 50 A3
Arbroath GB 35 B5
Arbúcies E 147 C3
Arbuniel E 163 A4
Arbus I 179 C2
Arcachon F 128 B1
Arce I 169 B3
Arcen NL 80 A2
Arces-Dilo F 104 A2
Arcévia I 136 B1
Arcey F 106 B1
Archanes GR. 185 D6
Archangelos GR . .188 C3
Archena E 165 A3
Archez E. 163 B4
Archiac F 115 C3
Archidona E 163 A3
Archiestown GB . . .32 D3
Archivel E. 164 A3
Arcidosso I 135 C4
Arcille I 135 C4
Arcis-sur-Aube F . .91 C4
Arc-lès-Gray F. . . .105 B4
Arco I 121 B3
Arcones E 151 A4
Arcos E 143 B3
Arcos de Jalón E. .152 A1
Arcos de la Frontera E 162 B2
Arcos de la Sierra E 152 B1
Arcos de las Salinas E 159 B2
Arcos de Valdevez P 148 A1
Arcozelo P. 148 B2
Arc-sur-Tille F 105 B4
Arcusa E 145 B4
Arcy-sur-Cure F . .104 B2
Ardagh IRL. 29 B2
Årdal N. 52 A2
Ardala S. 55 B4
Ardales E. 162 B3
Årdalstangen N . . .47 A4
Ardara I 178 B2
Ardara IRL 26 B2
Ardarroch GB 31 B3
Ardbeg GB. 34 C1
Ardcharnich GB . . .32 D1
Ardchyle GB 34 B3
Ardee IRL. 27 C4
Arden DK 58 B2
Ardentes F 103 C3
Ardenza I 134 B3
Ardersier GB 32 D2
Ardes F 116 B3

Ardessie GB 32 D1
Ardez CH 107 C5
Ardfert IRL 29 B2
Ardgay GB 32 D2
Ardglass GB 27 B5
Ardgroom IRL 29 C2
Ardhasig GB 31 B2
Ardino BG 183 B7
Ardisa E 144 B3
Ardkearagh IRL 29 C1
Ardlui GB 34 B3
Ardlussa GB 34 B2
Ardón E 142 B1
Ardooie B 78 B3
Ardore I 175 C2
Ardre S 57 C4
Ardres F 78 B1
Ardrishaig GB 34 B2
Ardrossan GB 34 C3
Are N 52 A1
Åre S 199 B10
Areia Branca P 154 B1
Aremark N 54 A2
Arenales de San
  Gregorio E 157 A4
Arenas E 163 B3
Arenas de Iguña
  E 142 A2
Arenas del Rey E 163 B4
Arenas de San Juan
  E 157 A4
Arenas de San Pedro
  E 150 B2
Arendal N 53 B4
Arendonk B 79 A5
Arengosse F 128 B2
Arentorp S 55 B3
Arenys de Mar E 147 C3
Arenys de Munt E 147 C3
Arenzano I 133 A4
Areo E 146 B2
Areopoli GR 184 C3
Ares E 140 A2
Arès F 128 B1
Ares del Maestrat
  E 153 B3
Aresvika N 198 B5
Arette F 144 A3
Aretxabaleta E 143 A4
Arevalillo E 150 B2
Arévalo E 150 A3
Arez P 155 B3
Arezzo I 135 B4
Arfeuilles F 117 A3
Argalasti GR 183 D5
Arganil P 148 B1
Argasion GR 184 B1
Argegno I 120 B2
Argelès-Gazost F 145 A3
Argelès-sur-Mer F 146 B4
Argenta I 121 C4
Argentan F 89 B3
Argentat F 116 B1
Argentera I 132 A2
Argenteuil F 90 C2
Argenthal D 93 B3
Argentiera I 178 B2
Argentona E 147 C3
Argenton-Château
  F 102 C1
Argenton-sur-Creuse
  F 103 C3
Argentré F 102 A1
Argentré-du-Plessis
  F 101 A4
Argent-sur-Sauldre
  F 103 B4
Argirades GR 182 D1
Argithani TR 189 A6
Argos GR 184 B3
Argos Orestiko
  GR 182 C3
Argostoli GR 184 A1
Argote E 143 B4
Arguedas E 144 B2
Argueil F 90 B1
Arholma S 51 C6
Århus DK 59 B3
Ariano Irpino I 170 B3
Ariano nel Polésine
  I 121 C5
Aribe E 144 B2
Aridea GR 182 C4
Arienzo I 170 B2
Arild S 61 C2
Arileod GB 34 B1
Arinagour GB 34 B1
Ariño E 153 A3
Arinthod F 118 A2
Arisaig GB 34 B2
Arisgotas E 157 A4
Aritzo I 179 C3
Ariza E 152 A1
Årjäng S 54 A3
Arjeplog S 195 D8
Arjona E 157 C3
Arjonilla E 157 C3
Arkasa GR 188 D2
Arkelstorp S 63 B2
Arklow IRL 30 B2
Arkösund S 56 B2
Ärla S 56 A2
Arlanc F 117 B3
Arlanzón E 143 B3
Arlebosc F 117 B4
Arlena di Castro I 168 A1
Arles F 131 B3
Arles-sur-Tech F 146 B3
Arló H 113 A4
Arlon B 92 B1
Armação de Pera
  P 160 B1
Armadale
  Highland GB 31 B3

Armadale continued
  West Lothian GB 35 C4
Armagh GB 27 B4
Armamar P 148 A2
Armenistis GR 185 B7
Armeno I 119 B5
Armenteros E 150 B2
Armentières F 78 B2
Armilla E 163 A4
Armiñón E 143 B4
Armoy GB 27 A4
Armuña de Tajuña
  E 151 B4
Armutlu
  Bursa TR 186 B3
  İzmir TR 188 A2
Arnac-Pompadour
  F 115 C5
Arnafjord N 46 A3
Arnage F 102 B2
Arnas F 117 A4
Arnäs S 55 B4
Arnay-le-Duc F 104 B3
Arnborg DK 59 B2
Arnea GR 183 C5
Arneberg
  Hedmark N 48 A3
  Hedmark N 49 B4
Arneburg D 73 B5
Arnedillo E 144 B1
Arnedo E 144 B1
Arneguy F 144 A2
Arnés E 153 B4
Arnes IS 190 A4
Árnes
  Akershus N 48 B3
  Troms N 194 A9
Arnfels A 110 C2
Arnhem NL 70 C2
Arnissa GR 182 C3
Arno S 56 B3
Arnold GB 40 B2
Arnoldstein A 109 C4
Arnsberg D 81 A4
Arnschwang D 95 B4
Arnsdorf D 84 A1
Arnset N 198 B6
Arnside GB 37 B4
Arnstadt D 82 B2
Arnstein D 94 B1
Arnstorf D 95 C4
Arnum DK 59 C1
Aroche E 161 B3
Árokto H 113 B4
Arolla CH 119 A4
Arolsen D 81 A5
Arona I 119 B5
Arosa
  CH 107 C4
  P 148 A1
Ærøskøbing DK 65 B3
Arøsund DK 59 C2
Arouca P 148 B1
Arøysund N 54 A1
Arpajon F 90 C2
Arpajon-sur-Cère
  F 116 C2
Arpela FIN 196 C7
Arpino I 169 B3
Arquata del Tronto
  I 136 C2
Arques F 78 B2
Arques-la-Bataille
  F 89 A5
Arquillos E 157 B4
Arraia-Maeztu E 143 B4
Arraiolos P 154 C2
Arrancourt F 92 C2
Arras F 78 B2
Arrasate E 143 A4
Arredondo E 143 A3
Arrens-Marsous F 145 B3
Arriate E 162 B2
Arrifana P 160 B1
Arrigorriaga E 143 A4
Arriondas E 142 A1
Arroba de los Montes
  E 157 A3
Arrochar GB 34 B3
Arromanches-les-Bains
  F 88 A3
Arronches P 155 B3
Arroniz E 144 B1
Arrou F 103 A3
Arroya E 142 B2
Arroya de Cuéllar
  E 150 A3
Arroyal E 142 B2
Arroyo de la Luz
  E 155 B4
Arroyo del Ojanco
  E 164 A2
Arroyo de San Servan
  E 155 C4
Arroyomolinos de
  León E 161 A3
Arroyomolinos de
  Montánchez E 156 A1
Arruda dos Vinhos
  P 154 C1
Arsac F 128 B2
Ars-en-Ré F 114 B2
Arsiè I 121 B4
Arsiero I 121 B4
Ársoli DK 59 C3
Ars-sur-Moselle F 92 B2
Årsunda S 50 B3
Artà E 167 B3
Arta GR 182 D3
Artajona E 144 B2
Artegna I 122 A2
Arteixo E 140 A2
Artemare F 118 B2
Arten I 121 A4
Artena I 169 B2

Artenay F 103 A3
Artern D 82 A3
Artés E 147 C2
Artesa de Segre E 147 C2
Arth CH 107 B3
Arthez-de-Béarn
  F 145 A3
Arthon-en-Retz F 101 B4
Arthurstown IRL 30 B2
Artieda E 144 B3
Artix F 145 A3
Artotina GR 182 E4
Artsyz UA 17 B8
Artziniega E 143 A3
Arudy F 145 A3
Arundel GB 44 C3
Arveyres F 128 B2
Arvidsjaur S 196 D2
Arvieux F 118 C3
Arvika S 54 A3
Åryd
  Blekinge S 63 B3
  Kronoberg S 62 B2
Arzachena I 178 A3
Arzano F 100 B2
Aržano HR 138 B2
Arzberg D 95 A4
Arzignano I 121 B4
Arzila P 148 B1
Arzl im Pitztal A 108 B1
Arzúa E 140 B2
As B 80 A1
AŠ CZ 83 B4
Ås N 54 A1
Åsa S 60 B2
Åsaa DK 58 A3
Aşağıçiğil TR 189 A6
Asarna S 199 C11
Åsarøy N 52 A2
Åsarp S 55 B4
Asasp F 145 A3
Åsbro S 55 A6
Åsby S 60 B2
Åsby S 62 A3
Åsbygri IS 191 A9
Ascain F 144 A2
Ascea I 172 B1
Ascha D 95 B4
Aschach an der Donau
  A 96 C2
Aschaffenburg D 93 B5
Aschbach Markt A 110 A1
Ascheberg
  Nordrhein-Westfalen
  D 81 A3
  Schleswig-Holstein
  D 65 B3
Aschendorf D 71 A4
Aschersleben D 82 A3
Asciano I 135 B4
Ascó E 153 A4
Asco F 180 A2
Áscoli Piceno I 136 C2
Áscoli Satriano I 171 B3
Ascona CH 120 A1
Ascot GB 44 B3
Ascoux F 103 A4
Åse N 194 A6
Åseda S 62 A3
Åsele S 200 B3
Åsen
  N 199 B8
  S 49 A5
Asendorf D 72 B2
Asenovgrad BG 183 A6
Åsensbruk S 54 B3
Åseral N 52 B3
Asfeld F 91 B4
Åsgårdstrand N 54 A1
Ásgarður IS 190 B1
Asgate CY 181 B2
Ash
  Kent GB 45 B5
  Surrey GB 44 B3
Ashbourne
  GB 40 B2
  IRL 30 A2
Ashburton GB 43 B3
Ashby-de-la-Zouch
  GB 40 C2
Ashchurch GB 44 B1
Åsheim N 199 D8
Ashford GB 45 B4
Ashington GB 37 A5
Ashley GB 38 B4
Ashmyany BY 13 A6
Ashton Under Lyne
  GB 40 B1
Ashwell GB 44 A3
Asiago I 121 B4
Asipovichy BY 13 B8
Aska FIN 197 B9
Askam-in-Furness
  GB 36 B3
Askeaton IRL 29 B3
Asker N 48 C2
Askersund S 55 B5
Åskilje S 200 B3
Askim N 54 A2
Askland N 53 B4
Asköping S 56 A2
Askvoll N 46 A2
Åsljunga S 61 C3
Asnæs DK 61 D1
As Neves E 140 B2
As Nogais E 141 B3
Ásola I 120 B3
Asolo I 121 B4
Asos GR 184 A1
Asotthalom H 126 A1
Aspach A 109 A4
Aspang Markt A 111 B3
Aspariegos E 149 A4

Asparn an der Zaya
  A 97 C4
Aspatria GB 36 B3
Aspberg S 55 A4
Aspe E 165 A4
Aspet F 145 A4
Aspö S 63 B3
As Pontes de García
  Rodríguez E 140 A3
Aspres-sur-Buëch
  F 132 A1
Aspsele S 200 C4
Assafora P 154 C1
Asse B 79 B4
Assebakte N 193 C9
Assel D 72 A2
Asselborn L 92 A1
Assémini I 179 C2
Assen NL 71 B3
Assenede B 79 A3
Assens
  Aarhus Amt. DK 58 B3
  Fyns Amt. DK 59 C2
Assesse B 79 B5
Assisi I 136 B1
Åsskard N 198 B5
Assling D 108 B3
Asso I 120 B2
Asson F 145 A3
Àssoro I 177 B3
Assumar P 155 B3
Åsta N 48 A3
Astaffort F 129 B3
Astakos GR 184 A2
Astorga E 141 B4
Åstorp S 61 C2
Ästräsk S 200 B5
Astudillo E 142 B2
Asten NL 80 A1
Asti I 119 C5
Astipalea GR 188 C1
Aston F 146 B2
Atabey TR 189 B5
Atalaia P 154 B3
Atalandi GR 182 E4
Atalho P 154 C2
Átány H 113 B4
Atanzón E 151 B4
Ataquines E 150 A3
Atarfe E 163 A4
Ateca E 152 A2
A Teixeira E 141 B3
Atella I 172 B1
Atessa I 169 A4
Ath B 79 B3
Athboy IRL 30 A2
Athea IRL 29 B2
Athenry IRL 28 A3
Athens = Athina
  GR 185 B4
Atherstone GB 40 C2
Athienou CY 181 A2
Athies F 90 B3
Athies-sous-Laon
  F 91 B3
Athina = Athens
  GR 185 B4
Athleague IRL 28 A3
Athlone IRL 28 A4
Athna CY 181 A2
Athy IRL 30 B2
Atienza E 151 A5
Atina I 169 B3
Atkár H 113 B3
Atlantı TR 189 A7
Atna N 199 D7
Åtorp S 55 A5
Atrå N 47 C5
Åtran S 60 B2
Atri I 169 A3
Atripalda I 170 C2
Atsiki GR 183 D7
Attendorn D 81 A3
Attichy F 90 B3
Attigliano I 168 A2
Attigny F 91 B4
Attleborough GB 41 C5
Åtvidaberg S 56 B1
Atzendorf D 73 C4
Au
  Steiermark A 110 B2
  Vorarlberg A 107 B4
  Bayern D 95 C3
  Bayern D 108 B2
Aub D 94 B2
Aubagne F 132 B1
Aubange B 92 B1
Aubel B 80 B1
Aubenas F 117 C4
Aubenton F 91 B4
Auberive F 105 B4
Aubeterre-sur-Dronne
  F 128 A3
Aubiet F 129 C3
Aubigné F 115 B3
Aubigny F 114 B2
Aubigny-au-Bac F 78 B3
Aubigny-en-Artois
  F 78 B2
Aubigny-sur-Nère
  F 103 B4
Aubin F 130 A1
Aubonne CH 105 C5
Aubrac F 116 C2
Aubusson F 116 B2
Auch F 129 C3
Auchavan GB 35 B4
Auchencairn GB 36 B3
Auchinleck GB 36 A2
Auchterarder GB 35 B4
Auchtermuchty GB 35 B4
Auchtertyre GB 31 B3
Audenge F 128 B1
Auderville F 88 A2
Audierne F 100 A1
Audincourt F 106 B1

Audlem GB 38 B4
Audruicq F 78 B2
Audun-le-Roman F 92 B1
Audun-le-Tiche F 92 B1
Aue
  Nordrhein-Westfalen
  D 81 A4
  Sachsen D 83 B4
Auerbach
  Bayern D 95 B3
  Sachsen D 83 B4
Auffach A 108 B3
Augher GB 27 B3
Aughnacloy GB 27 B4
Aughrim IRL 30 B2
Augignac F 115 C4
Augsburg D 94 C2
Augusta I 177 B4
Augusten-borg DK 64 B2
Augustfehn D 71 A4
Augustów PL 12 B5
Aukrug D 64 B2
Auktsjaur S 196 D2
Auldearn GB 32 D3
Aulendorf D 107 B4
Auletta I 172 B1
Aulla I 134 A2
Aullène F 180 B2
Aulnay F 115 B3
Aulnoye-Aymeries
  F 79 B3
Ault F 90 A1
Aultbea GB 31 B3
Aulum DK 59 B1
Aulus-les-Bains F 146 B2
Auma D 83 B3
Aumale F 90 B1
Aumetz F 92 B1
Aumont-Aubrac F 116 C3
Aunay-en-Bazois
  F 104 B2
Aunay-sur-Odon F 88 A3
Aune N 199 A10
Auneau F 90 C1
Auneuil F 90 B1
Auning DK 58 B3
Aunsetra N 199 A9
Aups F 132 B2
Aura D 82 B1
Auray F 100 B3
Aurdal N 47 B6
Aure N 198 B5
Aurich D 71 A4
Aurignac F 145 A4
Aurillac F 116 C2
Auriol F 132 B1
Auritz-Burguete
  E 144 A2
Aurlandsvangen N 47 B4
Auronzo di Cadore
  I 109 C3
Auros F 128 B2
Auroux F 117 C3
Aurskog N 48 C3
Aursmoen N 48 C3
Ausónia I 169 B3
Ausservillgraten
  A 109 C3
Austad N 52 B3
Austbygda N 47 B5
Auster Moland N 53 B4
Austre Vikebygd N 52 A1
Austrheim N 46 B1
Auterive F 146 A2
Autheuil-Authouillet
  F 89 A5
Authon F 132 A2
Authon-du-Perche
  F 102 A2
Autol E 144 B2
Autreville F 92 C1
Autrey-lès-Gray F 105 B4
Autti FIN 197 C10
Autun F 104 C3
Auty-le-Châtel F 103 B4
Auvelais B 79 B4
Auvillar F 129 B3
Auxerre F 104 B2
Auxi-le-Château F 78 B2
Auxon F 104 A2
Auxonne F 105 B4
Auxy F 104 C3
Auzances F 116 A2
Auzon F 117 B3

Avinyo E 147 C2
Åvio I 121 B3
Avioth F 92 B1
Avis P 154 B3
Avize F 91 C4
Avlonari GR 185 A5
Ávola I 177 C4
Avon F 90 C2
Avonmouth GB 43 A4
Avord F 103 B4
Avranches F 88 B2
Avril F 92 B1
Avrillé F 102 B1
Avtovac BIH 139 B4
Awans B 79 B5
Axams A 108 B2
Axat F 146 B3
Axbridge GB 43 A4
Axmarsbruk S 51 B4
Axmar S 51 B4
Axminster GB 43 B3
Axvall S 55 B4
Ay F 91 B4
Aya E 144 A1
Ayamonte E 161 B2
Ayancık TR 23 A8
Ayas TR 187 B7
Aydın TR 188 B2
Ayelo de Malferit
  E 159 C3
Ayer CH 119 A4
Ayerbe E 144 B3
Ayette F 78 B2
Ayia Napa CY 181 B3
Ayia Phyla CY 181 B2
Áyios Amvrósios
  CY 181 A2
Áyios Seryios CY 181 A2
Áyios Theodhoros
  CY 181 A3
Aykirikçi TR 187 C5
Aylesbury GB 44 B3
Ayllón E 151 A4
Aylsham GB 41 C5
Ayna E 158 C1
Ayódar E 159 B3
Ayora E 159 B2
Ayr GB 36 A2
Aysgarth GB 37 B4
Ayton GB 35 C5
Aytos BG 17 D7
Ayvacık TR 186 C1
Ayvalık TR 186 C1
Aywaille B 80 B1
Azaila E 153 A3
Azambuja P 154 B2
Azanja SRB 127 C2
Azannes-et-
  Soumazannes F 92 B1
Azanúy-Alins E 145 C4
Azaruja P 155 C3
Azay-le-Ferron F 115 B5
Azay-le-Rideau F 102 B2
Azcoitia E 143 A4
Azé F 117 A4
Azeiteiros P 155 B3
Azenhas do Mar P 154 C1
Azinhaga P 154 B2
Azinhal P 160 B2
Azinheira dos Barros
  P 160 A1
Aznalcázar E 161 B3
Aznalcóllar E 161 B3
Azóia P 154 B2
Azpeitia E 144 A1
Azuaga E 156 B2
Azuara E 153 A3
Azuqueca de Henares
  E 151 B4
Azur F 128 C1
Azzano Décimo I 122 B1

B

Baad A 107 B5
Baamonde E 140 A3
Baar CH 107 B3
Bağarasi TR 188 B2
Baarle-Nassau B 79 A4
Baarn NL 70 B2
Babadağ TR 188 B3
Babadag RO 17 C8
Babaeski TR 186 A2
Babayevo RUS 9 C9
Babenhausen
  Bayern D 107 A5
  Hessen D 93 B4
Babiak PL 76 B3
Babice PL 86 B3
Babigoszcz PL 75 A3
Babimost PL 75 B4
Babina Greda HR 125 B4
Babina Greda HR …
Babócsa H 124 A3
Bábolma H 112 B1
Baborów PL 86 B1
Baboszewo PL 77 B5
Babruysk BY 13 B8
Babsk PL 87 A4
Bač SRB 125 B5
Bacares E 164 B2
Bacău RO 17 B7
Baccarat F 92 C2
Bacharach D 93 B3
Backa S 50 B2
Bačka Palanka
  SRB 126 B1
Bačka Topola
  SRB 126 B1
Backe S 200 C1
Bäckebo S 62 B4
Bäckefors S 54 B3
Bäckhammar S 55 A5
Bački Breg SRB 125 B4
Bački-Brestovac
  SRB 126 B1
Bački Monoštor
  SRB 125 B4
Bački Petrovac
  SRB 126 B1
Bački Sokolac
  SRB 126 B1
Backnang D 94 C1
Bačko Gradište
  SRB 126 B2
Bačko Novo Selo
  SRB 125 B5
Bačko Petrovo Selo
  SRB 126 B2
Bácoli I 170 C2
Bacqueville-en-Caux
  F 89 A5
Bácsalmás H 126 A1
Bácsbokod H 125 A5
Bad Abbach D 95 C4
Badacsonytomaj
  H 111 C4
Bad Aibling D 108 B3
Badajoz E 155 C4
Badalona E 147 C3
Badalucco I 133 B3
Bad Aussee A 109 B4
Bad Bederkesa D 72 A1
Bad Bentheim D 71 B4
Bad Bergzabern D 93 B3
Bad Berka D 82 B3
Bad Berleburg D 81 A4
Bad Berneck D 95 A3
Bad Bevensen D 73 A3
Bad Bibra D 82 A3
Bad Birnbach D 95 C5
Bad Blankenburg
  D 82 B3
Bad Bleiberg A 109 C4
Bad Brambach D 83 B4
Bad Bramstedt D 64 C2
Bad Breisig D 80 B3
Bad Brückenau D 82 B1
Bad Buchau D 107 A4
Bad Camberg D 81 B4
Badderen N 192 C6
Bad Doberan D 65 B4
Bad Driburg D 81 A5
Bad Düben D 83 A4
Bad Dürkheim D 93 B4
Bad Dürrenberg D 83 A4
Bad Dürrheim D 107 A3
Bad Elster D 83 B4
Bad Ems D 81 B3
Baden
  A 111 A3
  CH 106 B3
Bádenas E 152 A2
Baden-Baden D 93 C4
Bad Endorf D 109 B3
Badenweiler D 106 B2
Baderna HR 122 B2
Bad Essen D 71 B5
Bad Fischau A 111 B3
Bad Frankenhausen
  D 82 A3
Bad Freienwalde D 74 B3
Bad Friedrichshall
  D 93 B5
Bad Füssing D 96 C1
Bad Gandersheim
  D 82 A2
Bad Gastein A 109 B4
Bad Gleichenberg
  A 110 C2
Bad Goisern A 109 B4
Bad Gottleuba D 84 B1
Bad Grund D 82 A2
Bad Hall A 110 A1
Bad Harzburg D 82 A2
Bad Herrenalb D 93 C4
Bad Hersfeld D 82 B1
Bad Hofgastein A 109 B4
Bad Homburg D 81 B4
Bad Honnef D 80 B3
Bad Hönningen D 80 B3
Badia Calavena I 121 B4
Badia Polésine I 121 B4
Bad Iburg D 71 B5
Badia Pratáglia I 135 B4
Badia Tedalda I 135 B5
Bad Innerlaterns
  A 107 B4
Bad Ischl A 109 B4
Bad Karlshafen D 81 A5
Bad Kemmeriboden
  CH 106 C2
Bądki PL 69 B3
Bad Kissingen D 82 B2
Bad Kleinen D 65 C4
Bad Kohlgrub D 108 B2
Bad König D 93 B5
Bad Königshofen
  D 82 B2
Bad Köstritz D 83 B4
Bad Kreuzen A 110 A1
Bad Kreuznach D 93 B3
Bad Krozingen D 106 B2
Bad Laasphe D 81 B4
Bad Langensalza D 82 A2
Bad Lauchstädt D 83 A3
Bad Lausick D 83 A4
Bad Lauterberg D 82 A2
Bad Leonfelden D 96 C2
Bad Liebenwerda
  D 83 A5
Bad Liebenzell D 93 C4
Bad Lippspringe D 81 A4
Bad Meinberg D 81 A4
Bad Mergentheim
  D 94 B1

Bad Mitterndorf A 109 B4
Bad Münder D 72 B2
Bad Münstereifel D 80 B2
Bad Muskau D 84 A2
Bad Nauheim D 81 B4
Bad Nenndorf D 72 B2
Bad Neuenahr-Ahrweiler D 80 B3
Bad Neustadt D 82 B2
Bad Oeynhausen D 72 B1
Badolato I 175 C2
Badolatosa E 163 A3
Bad Oldesloe D 65 C3
Badonviller F 92 C2
Bad Orb D 81 B5
Badovinci SRB 127 C1
Bad Peterstal D 93 C4
Bad Pyrmont D 72 C2
Bad Radkersburg A 110 C2
Bad Ragaz CH 107 C4
Bad Rappenau D 93 B5
Bad Reichenhall D 109 B3
Bad Saarow-Pieskow D 74 B3
Bad Sachsa D 82 A2
Bad Säckingen D 106 B2
Bad Salzdetfurth D 72 B3
Bad Salzig D 81 B3
Bad Salzuflen D 72 B1
Bad Salzungen D 82 B2
Bad Sankt Leonhard A 110 C1
Bad Sassendorf D 81 A4
Bad Schandau D 84 B2
Bad Schmiedeberg D 83 A4
Bad Schönborn D 93 B4
Bad Schussenried D 107 A4
Bad Schwalbach D 81 B4
Bad Schwartau D 65 C3
Bad Segeberg D 64 C3
Bad Soden D 81 B4
Bad Soden-Salmünster D 81 B5
Bad Sooden-Allendorf D 82 A1
Bad Sulza D 83 A3
Bad Sülze D 66 B1
Bad Tatzmannsdorf A 111 B3
Bad Tennstedt D 82 A2
Bad Tölz D 108 B2
Badules E 152 A2
Bad Urach D 94 C1
Bad Vellach A 110 C1
Bad Vilbel D 81 B4
Bad Vöslau A 111 B3
Bad Waldsee D 107 B4
Bad Wiessee D 108 B2
Bad Wildungen D 81 A5
Bad Wilsnack D 73 B4
Bad Windsheim D 94 B2
Bad Wörishafen D 108 A1
Bad Wurzach D 107 B4
Bad Zwesten D 81 A5
Bad Zwischenahn D 71 A5
Baells E 145 C4
Baena E 163 A3
Baesweiler D 80 B2
Baeza E 157 C4
Baflo NL 71 A3
Baga E 147 B2
Bagaladi I 175 C1
Bagenkop DK 65 B3
Baggetorp S 56 A2
Bagh a Chaisteil GB 31 C1
Bagheria I 176 A2
Bagn N 47 B6
Bagnacavallo I 135 A4
Bagnáia I 168 A2
Bagnara Cálabra I 175 C1
Bagnasco I 133 A4
Bagnères-de-Bigorre F 145 A4
Bagnères-de-Luchon F 145 B4
Bagni del Másino I 120 A2
Bagni di Lucca I 134 A3
Bagni di Rabbi I 121 A3
Bagni di Tivoli I 168 B2
Bagno di Romagna I 135 B4
Bagnoles-de-l'Orne F 89 B3
Bagnoli dei Trigno I 170 B2
Bagnoli di Sopra I 121 B4
Bagnoli Irpino I 170 C3
Bagnolo Mella I 120 B3
Bagnols-en-Forêt F 132 B2
Bagnols-sur-Cèze F 131 A3
Bagnorégio I 168 A2
Bagolino I 121 B3
Bagrationovsk RUS 12 A4
Bagrdan SRB 127 C3
Báguena E 152 A2
Bahabón de Esgueva E 143 C3
Bahillo E 142 B2
Báia delle Zágare I 171 B4
Báia Domizia I 169 B3
Baia Mare RO 17 B5
Baiano I 170 C2
Baião P 148 A1
Baiersbronn D 93 C4
Baiersdorf D 94 B3
Baignes-Ste Radegonde F 115 C3
Baigneux-les-Juifs F 104 B3
Baildon GB 40 B2
Bailén E 157 B4
Băileşti RO 17 C5
Baileux B 91 A4
Bailieborough IRL 27 C4
Bailleul F 78 B2
Baillonville B 79 B5
Bailó E 144 B3
Bain-de-Bretagne F 101 B4
Bains F 117 B3
Bains-les-Bains F 105 A5
Bainton GB 40 B3
Baio E 140 A2
Baiona E 140 B2
Bais F 89 B3
Baiso I 134 A3
Baiuca P 148 B2
Baja H 125 A4
Bajánsenye H 111 C3
Bajina Bašta SRB 127 D1
Bajmok SRB 126 B1
Bajna H 112 B2
Bajovo Polje MNE 139 B4
Bajša SRB 126 B1
Bak H 111 C3
Bakar HR 123 B3
Bakewell GB 40 B2
Bakio E 143 A4
Bakka N 47 C6
Bakkafjörður IS 191 A11
Bakkagerði IS 191 B12
Bække DK 59 C2
Bakken N 48 B3
Baklan TR 189 B4
Bækmarksbro DK 58 B1
Bakonybél H 111 B4
Bakonycsernye H 112 B2
Bakonyjákó H 111 B4
Bakonyszentkirály H 111 B4
Bakonyszombathely H 112 B1
Bakov nad Jizerou CZ 84 B2
Bąkowiec PL 87 A5
Baks H 113 C4
Baksa H 125 B4
Bakum D 71 B5
Bala GB 38 B3
Bâlâ TR 23 B7
Balaguer E 145 C4
Balassagyarmat H 112 A3
Balástya H 113 C4
Balatonakali H 111 C4
Balatonalmádi H 112 B2
Balatonboglár H 111 C4
Balatonbozsok H 112 C2
Balatonederics H 111 C4
Balatonfenyves H 111 C4
Balatonföldvár H 112 C1
Balatonfüred H 112 C1
Balatonfűzfő H 112 B2
Balatonkenese H 112 B2
Balatonkiliti H 112 C2
Balatonlelle H 111 C4
Balatonszabadi H 112 C2
Balatonszemes H 111 C4
Balatonszentgyörgy H 111 C4
Balazote E 158 C1
Balbeggie GB 35 B4
Balbigny F 117 B4
Balboa E 141 B4
Balbriggan IRL 30 A2
Balchik BG 17 D8
Balçova TR 188 A2
Baldock GB 44 B3
Bale HR 122 B2
Baleira E 141 A3
Baleizao P 160 A2
Balen B 79 A5
Balerma E 164 C2
Balestrand N 46 A3
Balestrate I 176 A2
Balfour GB 33 B4
Bälganet S 63 B3
Balıkesir TR 186 C2
Balıklıçeşme TR 186 B2
Bälinge S 51 C4
Balingen D 107 A3
Balingsta S 56 A3
Balintore GB 32 D3
Balizac F 128 B2
Balk NL 70 B2
Balkbrug NL 71 B3
Balla IRL 28 A2
Ballachulish GB 34 B2
Ballaghaderreen IRL 26 C2
Ballancourt-sur-Essonne F 90 C2
Ballantrae GB 36 A2
Ballao I 179 C3
Ballasalla GB 36 B2
Ballater GB 32 D3
Ballen DK 59 C3
Ballenstedt D 82 A3
Ballerias E 145 C3
Balleroy F 88 A3
Ballerup DK 61 D2
Ballesteros de Calatrava E 157 B4
Ballı TR 186 B2
Ballina IRL 26 B1
Ballinalack IRL 30 A1
Ballinamore IRL 26 B3
Ballinascarty IRL 29 C3
Ballinasloe IRL 28 A3
Ballindine IRL 28 A3
Balling DK 58 B1
Ballingarry
Limerick IRL 29 B3
Tipperary IRL 30 B1
Ballingeary IRL 29 C2
Ballinhassig IRL 29 C3
Ballinluig GB 35 B4
Ballino I 121 B3
Ballinrobe IRL 28 A2
Ballinskelligs IRL 29 C1
Ballinspittle IRL 29 C3
Ballintra IRL 26 B2
Ballivor IRL 30 A2
Ballobar E 153 A4
Ballon
F 102 A2
IRL 30 B2
Ballószög H 112 C3
Ballsh AL 182 C1
Ballstad N 194 B4
Ballum DK 64 A1
Ballybay IRL 27 B4
Ballybofey IRL 26 B3
Ballybunion IRL 29 B2
Ballycanew IRL 30 B2
Ballycarry GB 27 B5
Ballycastle
GB 27 A4
IRL 26 B1
Ballyclare GB 27 B5
Ballyconneely IRL 28 A1
Ballycotton IRL 29 C3
Ballycroy IRL 26 B1
Ballydehob IRL 29 C2
Ballyferriter IRL 29 B1
Ballygawley GB 27 B3
Ballygowan GB 27 B5
Ballyhaunis IRL 28 A3
Ballyheige IRL 29 B2
Ballyjamesduff IRL 27 C3
Ballylanders IRL 29 B3
Ballylynan IRL 30 B1
Ballymahon IRL 28 A4
Ballymena GB 27 B4
Ballymoe IRL 28 A3
Ballymoney GB 27 A4
Ballymore IRL 28 A4
Ballymote IRL 26 B2
Ballynacorra IRL 29 C3
Ballynagore IRL 30 A1
Ballynahinch GB 27 B5
Ballynure GB 27 B5
Ballyragget IRL 30 B1
Ballysadare IRL 26 B2
Ballyshannon IRL 26 B2
Ballyvaghan IRL 28 A2
Ballyvourney IRL 29 C2
Ballywalter GB 27 B5
Balmaclellan GB 36 A2
Balmaseda E 143 A3
Balmazújváros H 113 B5
Balme I 119 B4
Balmedie GB 33 D4
Balmuccia I 119 B5
Balna-paling GB 32 D2
Balneario de Panticosa E 145 B3
Balotaszállás H 126 A1
Balsa P 148 A2
Balsareny E 147 C2
Balsorano-Nuovo I 169 B3
Bålsta S 57 A3
Balsthal CH 106 B2
Balta UA 17 A8
Baltanás E 142 C2
Baltar E 140 C3
Baltasound GB 33 A6
Bălţi MD 17 B7
Baltimore IRL 29 C2
Baltinglass IRL 30 B2
Baltiysk RUS 69 A4
Baltów PL 87 A5
Balugães P 148 A1
Bælum DK 58 B3
Balve D 81 A3
Balvi LV 8 D5
Balvicar GB 34 B2
Balya TR 186 C2
Balzo I 136 C2
Bamberg D 94 B2
Bamburgh GB 37 A5
Banatska Palanka SRB 127 C3
Banatski Brestovac SRB 127 C2
Banatski Despotovac SRB 126 B2
Banatski Dvor SRB 126 B2
Banatski-Karlovac SRB 127 B3
Banatsko Arandjelovo SRB 126 A2
Banatsko-Novo Selo SRB 127 C2
Banaz TR 187 D4
Banbridge GB 27 B4
Banbury GB 44 A2
Banchory GB 33 D4
Bande
B 79 B5
E 140 B3
Bandholm DK 65 B4
Bandırma TR 186 B2
Bandol F 132 B1
Bandon IRL 29 C3
Bañeres E 159 C3
Banff GB 33 D4
Bangor
F 100 B2
Down GB 27 B5
Gwynedd GB 38 A2
IRL 26 B1
Bangsund N 199 A8
Banie PL 74 A3
Banja Koviljača SRB 127 C1
Banjaloka SLO 123 B3
Banja Luka BIH 124 C3
Banjani SRB 127 C1
Banja Vručica BIH 125 C3
Banka SK 98 C1
Bankekind S 56 B1
Bankend GB 36 A3
Bankeryd S 62 A2
Bankfoot GB 35 B4
Banloc RO 126 B3
Bannalec F 100 B2
Bannes F 91 C3
Bannockburn GB 35 B4
Bañobárez E 149 B3
Bañon E 152 B2
Banon F 132 A1
Baños E 149 B4
Baños de Gigonza E 162 B2
Baños de la Encina E 157 B4
Baños de Molgas E 140 B3
Baños de Rio Tobia E 143 B4
Baños de Valdearados E 143 C3
Bánov CZ 98 C1
Banova Jaruga HR 124 B2
Bánovce nad Bebravou SK 98 C2
Banovići BIH 139 A4
Banoviči Selo BIH 139 A4
Bánréve H 99 C4
Bansin D 66 C3
Banská Belá SK 98 C2
Banská Bystrica SK 99 C3
Banská Štiavnica SK 98 C2
Bansko BG 183 B5
Banstead GB 44 B3
Banteer IRL 29 B3
Bantheville F 91 B5
Bantry IRL 29 C2
Bantzenheim F 106 B2
Banyalbufar E 166 B2
Banyoles E 147 B3
Banyuls-sur-Mer F 146 B4
Bapaume F 90 A2
Bar
MNE 16 D3
UA 13 D7
Barabhas GB 31 A2
Barači BIH 138 A2
Baracs H 112 C2
Baracska H 112 B2
Barahona E 151 A5
Barajes de Melo E 151 B5
Barakaldo E 143 A4
Baralla E 141 B3
Barañain E 144 B2
Baranavichy BY 13 B7
Báránd H 113 B5
Baranda SRB 127 B2
Baranello I 170 B2
Baranów Sandomierski PL 87 B5
Baraqueville F 130 A1
Barasoain E 144 B2
Barbacena P 155 C3
Barbadás E 140 B3
Barbadillo E 149 B4
Barbadillo de Herreros E 143 B3
Barbadillo del Mercado E 143 B3
Barbadillo del Pez E 143 B3
Barban HR 123 B3
Barbarano Vicento I 121 B4
Barbariga HR 122 C2
Barbaros TR 186 B2
Barbastro E 145 B4
Barbate E 162 B2
Barbatona E 152 A1
Barbâtre F 114 B1
Barbazan F 145 A4
Barbeitos E 141 A3
Barbentane F 131 B3
Barberino di Mugello I 135 A4
Barbezieux-St Hilaire F 115 C3
Barbonne-Fayel F 91 C3
Barbotan-les-Thermes F 128 C2
Barby D 73 C4
Bárcabo E 145 B4
Barca de Alva P 149 A3
Barcarrota E 155 C4
Barcellona-Pozzo di Gotto I 177 A4
Barcelona E 147 C3
Barcelonette F 132 A2
Barcelos P 148 A1
Bárcena del Monasterio E 141 A4
Barcena de Pie de Concha E 142 A2
Barchfeld D 82 B2
Barcin PL 76 B2
Barcino PL 68 A1
Bárcis I 122 A1
Barco P 148 B2
Barcones E 151 A5
Barcs H 124 B3
Barcus F 144 A3
Bardejov SK 12 D4
Bårdesø DK 59 C3
Bardi I 120 C2
Bardney GB 40 B3
Bardo PL 85 B4
Bardolino I 121 B3
Bardonécchia I 118 B3
Bardoňovo SK 112 A2
Barèges F 145 B4
Barenstein D 83 B5
Barentin F 89 A4
Barenton F 88 B3
Barevo BIH 138 A3
Barfleur F 88 A2
Barga I 134 A3
Bargas E 151 C3
Barge I 119 C4
Bargemon F 132 B2
Barghe I 120 B3
Bargoed GB 39 C3
Bargrennan GB 36 A2
Bargteheide D 64 C3
Barham GB 45 B5
Bari I 173 A2
Barič Draga HR 137 A4
Barilović HR 123 B4
Bari Sardo I 179 C3
Barisciano I 169 A3
Barjac F 131 A3
Barjols F 132 B1
Barjon F 105 B3
Bårkåker N 54 A1
Barkald N 199 D7
Barkowo
Dolnośląskie PL 85 A4
Pomorskie PL 68 B2
Bârlad RO 17 B7
Bar-le-Duc F 91 C5
Barles F 132 A2
Barletta I 171 B4
Barlinek PL 75 B4
Barmouth GB 38 B2
Barmstedt D 64 C2
Barnard Castle GB 37 B5
Barnarp S 62 A2
Bärnau D 95 B4
Bärnbach A 110 B2
Barneberg D 73 B4
Barnenitz D 74 B1
Barnet GB 44 B3
Barnetby le Wold GB 40 B3
Barneveld NL 70 B2
Barneville-Carteret F 88 A2
Barnoldswick GB 40 B1
Barnowko PL 75 B3
Barnsley GB 40 B2
Barnstädt D 83 A3
Barnstaple GB 42 A2
Barnstorf D 72 B1
Barntrup D 72 C2
Baron F 90 B2
Baronissi I 170 C2
Barqueiro P 154 B2
Barquinha P 154 B2
Barr
F 93 C3
GB 36 A2
Barra P 148 B1
Barracas E 159 A3
Barraco E 150 B3
Barrado E 150 B2
Barrafranca I 177 B3
Barranco do Velho P 160 B2
Barrancos P 161 A3
Barrax E 158 B1
Barrbaar D 94 C2
Barre-des-Cevennes F 130 A2
Barreiro P 154 C1
Barreiros E 141 A3
Barrême F 132 B2
Barret-le-Bas F 132 A1
Barrhead GB 34 C3
Barrhill GB 36 A2
Barrio de Nuesra Señora E 142 B1
Barrowford GB 40 B1
Barrow-in-Furness GB 36 B3
Barrow upon Humber GB 40 B3
Barruecopardo E 149 A3
Barruelo de Santullán E 142 B2
Barruera E 145 B4
Barry GB 39 C3
Bårse DK 65 A4
Barsinghausen D 72 B2
Barssel D 71 A4
Bar-sur-Aube F 104 A3
Bar-sur-Seine F 104 A3
Barth D 66 B1
Bartholomä D 94 C1
Bartin TR 187 A7
Barton upon Humber GB 40 B3
Barúmini I 179 C2
Baruth D 74 B2
Barvaux B 80 B1
Barver D 72 B1
Barwałd PL 99 B3
Barwice PL 68 B1
Barysaw BY 13 A8
Barzana E 141 A5
Bârzava RO 16 B4
Bárzio I 120 B2
Bas E 147 B3
Bašaid SRB 126 B2
Basaluzzo I 120 C1
Basarabeasca MD 17 B8
Basauri E 143 A4
Baschi I 168 A2
Baschurch GB 38 B4
Basconcillos del Tozo E 143 B3
Bascones de Ojeda E 142 B2
Basécles B 79 B3
Basel CH 106 B2
Basélice I 170 B2
Basildon GB 45 B4
Basingstoke GB 44 B2
Baška
CZ 98 B2
HR 123 C3
Baška Voda HR 138 B2
Bäsksjö S 200 B3
Baslow GB 40 B2
Başmakçı TR 189 B5
Basovizza I 122 B2
Bassacutena I 178 A3
Bassano del Grappa I 121 B4
Bassano Romano I 168 A2
Bassecourt CH 106 B2
Bassella E 147 B2
Bassevuovdde N 193 D9
Bassou F 104 B2
Bassoues F 128 C3
Bassum D 72 B1
Båstad S 61 C2
Bastardo I 136 C1
Bastelica F 180 A2
Bastelicaccia F 180 B1
Bastia
F 180 A2
I 136 B1
Bastogne B 92 A1
Baston GB 40 C3
Bastuträsk S 200 B6
Bata H 125 A4
Batajnica SRB 127 C2
Batak BG 183 B6
Batalha P 154 B2
Bátaszék H 125 A4
Batea E 153 A4
Batelov CZ 97 B3
Bath GB 43 A4
Bathgate GB 35 C4
Batida H 126 A2
Batignano I 135 C4
Batina HR 125 B4
Bátka SK 99 C4
Batković BIH 125 C5
Batley GB 40 B2
Batnfjordsøra N 198 C4
Batočina SRB 127 C3
Bátonyterenye H 113 B3
Batrina HR 125 B3
Båtsfjord N 193 B13
Båtskärsnäs S 196 D6
Battaglia Terme I 121 B4
Bätterkinden CH 106 B2
Battice B 80 B1
Battipáglia I 170 C2
Battle GB 45 C4
Battonya H 126 A3
Batuša SRB 127 C3
Bátya H 112 C2
Bau I 179 C2
Baud F 100 B2
Baudour B 79 B3
Baugé F 102 B1
Baugy F 103 B4
Bauma CH 107 B3
Baume-les-Dames F 105 B5
Baumholder D 93 B3
Baunatal D 81 A5
Baunei I 178 B3
Bauska LV 8 D4
Bautzen D 84 A2
Bavanište SRB 127 C2
Bavay F 79 B3
Bavilliers F 106 B1
Bavorov CZ 96 B2
Bawdsey GB 45 A5
Bawinkel D 71 B4
Bawtry GB 40 B2
Bayat TR 187 D5
Bayel F 105 A3
Bayeux F 88 A3
Bayındır TR 188 A2
Bayon F 92 C2
Bayonne F 128 C1
Bayons F 132 A2
Bayramiç TR 186 C1
Bayreuth D 95 B3
Bayrischzell D 108 B3
Baza E 164 B2
Bazas F 128 B2
Baziege F 146 A2
Bazoches-les-Gallerandes F 103 A4
Bazoches-sur-Hoëne F 89 B4
Bazzano I 135 A4
Beaconsfield GB 44 B3
Beade E 140 B2
Beadnell GB 37 A5
Beaminster GB 43 B4
Bearsden GB 34 C3
Beas E 161 B3
Beasain E 144 A1
Beas de Segura E 164 A2
Beattock GB 36 A3
Beaubery F 117 A4
Beaucaire F 131 B3
Beaufort
F 118 B3
IRL 29 B2
Beaufort-en Vallée F 102 B1
Beaugency F 103 B3
Beaujeu
Alpes-de-Haute-Provence F 132 A2
Rhône F 117 A4
Beaulac F 128 B2
Beaulieu
F 103 B4
GB 44 C2
Beaulieu-sous-la-Roche F 114 B2
Beaulieu-sur-Dordogne F 129 B4
Beaulieu-sur-Mer F 133 B3
Beaulon F 104 C2
Beauly GB 32 D2
Beaumaris GB 38 A2
Beaumesnil F 89 A4
Beaumetz-lès-Loges F 78 B2
Beaumont
B 79 B4
F 129 B3
Beaumont-de-Lomagne F 129 C3
Beaumont-du-Gâtinais F 103 A4
Beaumont-en-Argonne F 91 B5
Beaumont-Hague F 88 A2
Beaumont-la-Ronce F 102 B2
Beaumont-le-Roger F 89 A4
Beaumont-sur-Oise F 90 B2
Beaumont-sur-Sarthe F 102 A2
Beaune F 105 B3
Beaune-la-Rolande F 103 A4
Beaupréau F 101 B5
Beauraing B 91 A4
Beaurepaire F 117 B5
Beaurepaire-en-Bresse F 105 C4
Beaurières F 132 A1
Beauvais F 90 B2
Beauval F 90 A2
Beauville F 129 B3
Beauvoir-sur-Mer F 114 B1
Beauvoir-sur-Niort F 114 B3
Beba Veche RO 126 A2
Bebertal D 73 B4
Bebington GB 38 A3
Bebra D 82 B1
Bebrina HR 125 B3
Beccles GB 45 A5
Becedas E 150 B2
Beceite E 153 B4
Bečej SRB 126 B2
Becerreá E 141 B3
Becerril de Campos E 142 B2
Bécherel F 101 A4
Bechhofen D 94 B2
Bechyně CZ 96 B2
Becilla de Valderaduey E 142 B1
Beckfoot GB 36 B3
Beckingham GB 40 B3
Beckum D 81 A4
Beco P 154 B2
Bécon-les-Granits F 102 B1
Bečov nad Teplou CZ 83 B4
Becsehely H 111 C3
Bedale GB 37 B5
Bedames E 143 A3
Bédar E 164 B3
Bédarieux F 130 B2
Bédarrides F 131 A3
Bedburg D 80 B2
Beddgelert GB 38 A2
Beddingestrand S 66 A2
Bédée F 101 A4
Bedegkér H 112 C2
Beden TR 189 C7
Bedford GB 44 A3
Będków PL 87 A3
Bedlington GB 37 A5
Bedlno PL 77 B4
Bedmar E 163 A4
Bédoin F 131 A4
Bedónia I 134 A2
Bedretto CH 107 C3
Bedsted DK 58 B1
Bedum NL 71 A3
Bedwas GB 39 C3
Bedworth GB 40 C2
Będzin PL 86 B3
Beekbergen NL 70 B2
Beek en Donk NL 80 A1
Beelen D 71 C5
Beelitz D 74 B1
Beer GB 43 B3
Beerfelde D 74 B3
Beerfelden D 93 B4
Beernem B 78 A3
Beeskow D 74 B3
Beetsterzwaag NL 70 A3
Beetzendorf D 73 B4
Beflelay CH 106 B2
Begaljica SRB 127 C2
Bégard F 100 A2
Begejci SRB 126 B2
Begijar E 157 C4
Begijnendijk B 79 A4
Begndal N 48 B1
Begues E 147 C2
Beguildy GB 39 B3
Begur E 147 C4
Beho B 80 B1
Behringen D 82 A2
Beilen NL 71 B3
Beilngries D 95 B3
Beine-Nauroy F 91 B4
Beinwil CH 106 B3
Beiseförth D 82 A1
Beith GB 34 C3
Beitostølen N 47 A5
Beiuş RO 16 B5
Beja P 160 A2
Béjar E 149 B4
Bekçiler TR 189 C4
Békés H 113 C5
Békéscsaba H 113 C5
Bekilli TR 189 A4
Bekkarfjord N 193 B11
Bela SK 98 B2
Bélâbre F 115 B5
Bela Crkva SRB 127 C3
Belalcázar E 156 B2
Bělá nad Radbuzou CZ 95 B4
Belanovica SRB 127 C2
Bélapátfalva H 113 A4
Bělá pod Bezdězem CZ 84 B2
Belcaire F 146 B2
Bełchatów PL 86 A3
Belchite E 153 A3
Bělčice CZ 96 B1
Belcoo GB 26 B3

Belecke D 81 A4
Beled H 111 B4
Belej HR 123 C3
Beleño E 142 A1
Bélesta F 146 B2
Belevi TR 188 A2
Belfast GB 27 B5
Belford GB 37 A5
Belfort F 106 B1
Belgentier F 132 B1
Belgern D 83 A5
Belgioioso I 120 B2
Belgodère F 180 A2
Belgooly IRL 29 C3
Belgrade = Beograd
SRB 127 C2
Belhade F 128 B2
Belica HR 124 A2
Beli Manastir HR 125 B4
Belin-Bèliet F 128 B2
Belinchón E 151 B4
Belišće HR 125 B4
Bělkovice-Lašťany
CZ 98 B1
Bella I 172 B1
Bellac F 115 B5
Bellágio I 120 B2
Bellananagh IRL 27 C3
Bellano I 120 A2
Bellária I 136 A1
Bellavary IRL 26 C1
Belleau F 90 B3
Belleek GB 26 B2
Bellegarde
Gard F 131 B3
Loiret F 103 B4
Bellegarde-en-Diois
F 132 A1
Bellegarde-en-Marche
F 116 B2
Bellegarde-sur-
Valserine F 118 A2
Belle-Isle-en-Terre
F 100 A2
Bellême F 89 B4
Bellenaves F 116 A3
Bellentre F 118 B3
Bellevaux F 118 A3
Bellevesvre F 105 C4
Belleville F 117 A4
Belleville-sur-Vie
F 114 B2
Bellevue-la-Montagne
F 117 B3
Belley F 118 B2
Bellheim D 93 B4
Bellinge DK 59 C3
Bellingham GB 37 A4
Bellinzago Novarese
I 120 B1
Bellinzona CH 120 A2
Bell-lloc d'Urgell
E 153 A4
Bello E 152 B2
Bellpuig d'Urgell
E 147 C2
Bellreguart E 159 C3
Bellsbank GB 36 A2
Belltall E 147 C2
Belluno I 121 A5
Bellver de Cerdanya
E 146 B2
Bellvis E 147 C1
Bélmez E 156 B2
Belmez de la Moraleda
E 163 A4
Belmont GB 33 A6
Belmont-de-la-Loire
F 117 A4
Belmonte
Asturias E 141 A4
Cuenca E 158 B1
P 148 B2
Belmonte de San José
E 153 B3
Belmonte de Tajo
E 151 B4
Belmont-sur-Rance
F 130 B1
Belmullet IRL 26 B1
Belobreşca RO 127 C3
Beloeil B 79 B3
Belogradchik BG 16 D5
Belokorovichi UA 13 C8
Belorado E 143 B3
Belotič SRB 127 C1
Bělotin CZ 98 B1
Belovo BG 183 A6
Belozersk RUS 9 C10
Belp CH 106 C2
Belpasso I 177 B3
Belpech F 146 A2
Belper GB 40 B2
Belsay GB 37 A5
Belsk Duzy PL 87 A4
Beltinci SLO 111 C3
Beltra IRL 26 C1
Belturbet IRL 27 B3
Beluša SK 98 B2
Belvedere Marittimo
I 174 B1
Belver de Cinca E 153 A4
Belver de los Montes
E 142 C1
Belvès F 129 B3
Belvezet F 130 A2
Belvis de la Jara
E 150 C3
Belvis de Monroy
E 150 C2
Belyy RUS 9 E8
Belz F 100 B2
Bełżec PL 13 C5
Belzig D 73 B5
Bembibre E 141 B4
Bembridge GB 44 C2
Bemmel NL 80 A1
Bemposta
Bragança P 149 A3
Santarém P 154 B2
Benabarre E 145 B4
Benacazón E 161 B3
Benaguacil E 159 B3
Benahadux E 164 C2
Benalmádena E 163 B3
Benalúa de Guadix
E 164 B1
Benalúa de las Villas
E 163 A4
Benalup E 162 B2
Benamargosa E 163 B3
Benamaurel E 164 B2
Benameji E 163 A3
Benamocarra E 163 B3
Benaocaz E 162 B2
Benaoján E 162 B2
Benarrabá E 162 B2
Benasque E 145 B4
Benátky nad Jizerou
CZ 84 B2
Benavente
E 142 B1
P 154 C2
Benavides de Órbigo
E 141 B5
Benavila P 154 B3
Bendorf D 81 B3
Benedikt SLO 110 C2
Benejama E 159 C3
Benejúzar E 165 A4
Benešov CZ 96 B2
Bénestroff F 92 C2
Benet F 114 B3
Bene Vagienna I 133 A3
Bénévent-l'Abbaye
F 116 A1
Benevento I 170 B2
Benfeld F 93 C3
Benfica P 154 B2
Bengtsfors S 54 A3
Bengtsheden S 50 B2
Beničanci HR 125 B4
Benicarló E 153 B4
Benicássim E 153 B4
Benidorm E 159 C3
Benifaió E 159 B3
Beniganim E 159 C3
Benington GB 41 B4
Benisa E 159 C4
Benkovac HR 137 A4
Benllech GB 38 A2
Benneckenstein D 82 A2
Bénodet F 100 B1
Benquerencia de la
Serena E 156 B2
Bensafrim P 160 B1
Bensbyn S 196 D5
Bensdorf D 73 B5
Benshausen D 82 B2
Bensheim D 93 B4
Bentley GB 44 B3
Bentwisch D 65 B5
Beočin SRB 126 B1
Beograd = Belgrade
SRB 127 C2
Beragh GB 27 B3
Beranga E 143 A3
Berat AL 182 C1
Bérat F 146 A2
Beratzhausen D 95 B3
Bérbaltavár H 111 B3
Berbegal E 145 C3
Berbenno di Valtellina
I 120 A2
Berberana E 143 B3
Bercedo E 143 A3
Bercel H 112 B3
Bercenay-le-Hayer
F 91 C3
Berceto I 134 A2
Berchem B 79 B3
Berchidda I 178 B3
Berching D 95 B3
Berchtesgaden D 109 B4
Bérchules E 163 B4
Bercianos de Aliste
E 149 A3
Berck F 78 B1
Berclaire d'Urgell
E 147 C1
Berdoias E 140 A1
Berducedo E 141 A4
Berdún E 144 B3
Berdychiv UA 13 D8
Bere Alston GB 42 B2
Bereguardo I 120 B2
Berehommen N 53 A3
Berehove UA 16 A5
Berek BIH 124 B3
Beremend H 125 B4
Bere Regis GB 43 B4
Berestechko UA 13 C6
Berettyóújfalu H 113 B5
Berezhany UA 13 D6
Berezivka UA 17 B9
Berezna UA 13 C9
Berg
D 95 B3
N 195 E3
S 56 B2
Berga
Sachsen-Anhalt
D 82 A3
Thüringen D 83 B4
E 147 B2
S 62 A4
Bergama TR 186 C2
Bérgamo I 120 B2
Bergara E 143 A4
Bergby S 51 B4
Berge
Brandenburg D 74 B1
Niedersachsen D 71 B4
Telemark N 53 A4
Telemark N 53 A4
Bergeforsen S 200 D3
Bergen
Mecklenburg-
Vorpommern D 66 B2
Niedersachsen D 72 B2
Bergen *continued*
Niedersachsen D 73 B3
N 46 B2
NL 70 B1
Bergen op Zoom
NL 79 A4
Bergerac F 129 B3
Bergères-lés-Vertus
F 91 C4
Bergeyk NL 79 A5
Berghausen D 93 C4
Bergheim D 80 B2
Berghem S 60 B2
Berg im Gau D 95 C3
Bergisch Gladbach
D 80 B3
Bergkamen D 81 A3
Bergkvara S 63 B4
Berglern D 95 C3
Bergnäset S 196 D5
Bergneustadt D 81 A3
Bergsäng S 49 B5
Bergshamra S 57 A4
Bergsjö S 200 E3
Bergs slussar S 56 B1
Bergsviken S 196 D4
Bergtheim D 94 B2
Bergues F 78 B2
Bergum NL 70 A2
Bergün Bravuogn
CH 107 C4
Bergwitz D 83 A4
Berhida H 112 B2
Beringel P 160 A2
Beringen B 79 A5
Berja E 164 C2
Berkåk N 199 C7
Berkeley GB 43 A4
Berkenthin D 65 C3
Berkhamsted GB 44 B3
Berkheim D 107 A5
Berkhof D 72 B2
Berkovići BIH 139 B4
Berkovitsa BG 17 D5
Berlanga E 156 B2
Berlanga de Duero
E 151 A5
Berlevåg N 193 B13
Berlikum NL 70 A2
Berlin D 74 B2
Berlstedt D 82 A3
Bermeo E 143 A4
Bermillo de Sayago
E 149 A3
Bern CH 106 C2
Bernalda I 174 A2
Bernardos E 150 A3
Bernartice
Jihočeský CZ 96 B2
Vychodočeský CZ 85 B3
Bernau
Baden-Württemberg
D 106 B3
Bayern D 109 B3
Brandenburg D 74 B2
Bernaville F 90 A2
Bernay F 89 A4
Bernburg D 83 A3
Berndorf A 111 B3
Berne D 72 A1
Bernecebarati H 112 A2
Bernhardsthal A 97 C4
Bernkastel-Kues D 92 B3
Bernolakovo SK 111 A4
Bernsdorf D 84 A2
Bernstadt D 84 A2
Bernstein A 111 B3
Bernués E 145 B3
Beromünster CH 106 B3
Beroun CZ 96 B2
Berovo MK 182 B4
Berre-l'Etang F 131 B4
Berriedale GB 32 C3
Berriew GB 39 B3
Berrocal E 161 B3
Bersenbrück D 71 B4
Bershad' UA 13 D8
Bertamiráns E 140 B2
Berthåga S 51 C4
Berthelming F 92 C2
Bertincourt F 90 A2
Bertinoro I 135 A5
Bertogne B 92 A1
Bertrix B 91 B5
Berufjörður IS 191 C11
Berville-sur-Mer F 89 A4
Berwick-upon-Tweed
GB 37 A4
Berzasca RO 16 C4
Berzence H 124 A3
Berzocana E 156 A2
Besalú E 147 B3
Besançon F 105 B5
Besenfeld D 93 C4
Besenyötelek H 113 B4
Besenyszög H 113 B4
Beshenkovichi BY 13 A8
Besigheim D 93 C5
Běšiny CZ 96 B1
Beška SRB 126 B2
Beşkonak TR 189 B6
Besle F 101 B4
Besnyö H 112 B2
Bessais-le-Fromental
F 103 C4
Bessan F 130 B2
Besse-en-Chandesse
F 116 B2
Bessèges F 131 A3
Bessé-sur-Braye
F 102 B2
Bessines-sur-Gartempe
F 115 B5
Best NL 79 A5
Bestorp S 56 B1
Betanzos E 140 A2
Betelu E 144 A2
Bétera E 159 B3
Beteta E 152 B1
Béthenville F 91 B4
Bethesda GB 38 A2
Béthune F 78 B2
Beton-Bazoches F 90 C3
Bettembourg L 92 B2
Betterdorf L 92 B2
Bettna S 56 B2
Béttola I 120 C2
Bettona I 136 B1
Bettyhill GB 32 C2
Betws-y-Coed GB 38 A3
Betxi E 159 B3
Betz F 90 B2
Betzdorf D 81 B3
Beuil F 132 A2
Beulah GB 39 B3
Beuzeville F 89 A4
Bevagna I 136 C1
Bevens-bruk S 56 A1
Beveren B 79 A4
Beverley GB 40 B3
Bevern D 81 A5
Beverstedt D 72 A1
Beverungen D 81 A5
Beverwijk NL 70 B1
Bex CH 119 A4
Bexhill GB 45 C4
Beyazköy TR 186 A2
Beychevelle F 128 A2
Beydağ TR 188 A3
Beyeğaç TR 188 B3
Beykoz TR 186 A4
Beynat F 129 A4
Beyoğlu TR 186 A4
Beypazarı TR 187 B6
Beyşehir TR 189 B6
Bezas E 152 B2
Bezau A 107 B4
Bezdan SRB 125 B4
Bèze F 105 B4
Bezenet F 116 A2
Bezhetsk RUS 9 D10
Béziers F 130 B2
Bezzecca I 121 B3
Biadki PL 85 A5
Biała
Łódzkie PL 77 C4
Opolskie PL 85 B5
Białaczów PL 87 A4
Biała Podlaska PL 13 B5
Biała Rawska PL 87 A4
Biale Błota PL 76 A2
Białobłoty PL 76 B2
Białobrzegi PL 87 A4
Białogard PL 67 C4
Białośliwie PL 76 A2
Białowąs PL 68 B1
Biały Bór PL 68 B1
Białystok PL 13 B5
Biancavilla I 177 B3
Bianco I 175 C2
Biandrate I 119 B5
Biar E 159 C3
Biarritz F 144 A2
Bias F 128 B1
Biasca CH 120 A1
Biatorbágy H 112 B2
Bibbiena I 135 B4
Bibbona I 134 B3
Biberach
Baden-Württemberg
D 93 C4
Baden-Württemberg
D 107 A4
Bibinje HR 137 A4
Bibione I 122 B2
Biblis D 93 B4
Bibury GB 44 B2
Bicaj AL 182 B2
Biccari I 171 B3
Bicester GB 44 B2
Bichl D 108 B2
Bichlbach A 108 B1
Bicorp E 159 B3
Bicos P 160 B1
Bicske H 112 B2
Bidache F 128 C1
Bidart F 144 A2
Biddinghuizen NL 70 B2
Biddulph GB 40 B1
Bideford GB 42 A2
Bidford-on-Avon
GB 44 A2
Bidjovagge N 192 C6
Bie S 56 A2
Bieber D 81 B5
Biebersdorf D 74 C2
Biedenkopf D 81 B4
Biel
CH 106 B2
E 144 B3
Bielany Wroclawskie
PL 85 A4
Bielawa PL 85 B4
Bielawy PL 77 B4
Bielefeld D 72 B1
Biella I 119 B5
Bielsa E 145 B4
Bielsk PL 77 B4
Bielsko-Biała PL 99 B3
Bielsk Podlaski PL 13 B5
Bienenbuttel D 72 A3
Bieniow PL 84 A3
Bienservida E 158 C1
Bienvenida E 156 B1
Bierdzany PL 86 B2
Bierné F 102 B1
Biersted DK 58 A2
Bierun PL 86 B3
Bierutów PL 85 A5
Bierwart B 79 B5
Bierzwina PL 75 A4
Bierzwnik PL 75 A4
Biescas E 145 B3
Biesenthal D 74 B2
Biesiekierz PL 67 B5
Bietigheim-Bissingen
D 93 C5
Bièvre B 91 B5
Bieżuń PL 77 B4
Biga TR 186 B2
Bigadiç TR 186 C3
Biganos F 128 B2
Bigas P 148 B2
Bigastro E 165 A4
Bigbury GB 42 B3
Biggar GB 36 A3
Biggin Hill GB 45 B4
Biggleswade GB 44 A3
Bignasco CH 119 A5
Biguglia F 180 A2
Bihać BIH 124 C1
Biharnagybajom
H 113 B5
Bijeljani BIH 139 B4
Bijeljina BIH 125 C5
Bijuesca E 152 A2
Bilaj HR 137 A4
Bila Tserkva UA 13 D9
Bilbao E 143 A4
Bilcza PL 87 B4
Bildudalur IS 190 B2
Bileća BIH 139 C4
Bilecik TR 187 B4
Biled RO 126 B2
Biłgoraj PL 12 C5
Bilhorod-Dnistrovskyy
UA 17 B9
Bílina CZ 84 B1
Bilisht AL 182 C2
Bilje HR 125 B4
Billdal S 60 B1
Billerbeck D 71 C4
Billericay GB 45 B4
Billesholm S 61 C2
Billingborough GB 40 C3
Billinge S 61 D3
Billingham GB 37 B5
Billinghay GB 41 B3
Billingsfors S 54 B3
Billingshurst GB 44 B3
Billom F 116 B3
Billsta S 200 C4
Billund DK 59 C2
Bilovec CZ 98 B2
Bilstein D 81 A4
Bilthoven NL 70 B2
Bilto N 192 C5
Bilzen B 80 B1
Biňa SK 112 B2
Binaced E 145 C4
Binasco I 120 B2
Binbrook GB 41 B3
Binche B 79 B4
Bindlach D 95 B3
Bindslev DK 58 A3
Binefar E 145 C4
Bingen D 93 B3
Bingham GB 40 C3
Bingley GB 40 B2
Bingsjö S 50 A2
Binic F 100 A3
Binz D 66 B2
Biograd na Moru
HR 137 B4
Bionaz I 119 B4
Bioska SRB 127 D1
Birda RO 126 B3
Birdlip GB 44 B1
Biri N 48 B2
Birkeland N 53 B4
Birkenfeld
Baden-Württemberg
D 93 C4
Rheinland-Pfalz D 92 B3
Birkenhead GB 38 A3
Birkerød DK 61 D2
Birkfeld A 110 B2
Birkirkara M 175 C3
Birmingham GB 40 C2
Birr IRL 28 A4
Birresborn D 80 B2
Birstein D 81 B5
Biržai LT 8 D4
Birzebbugia M 175 C3
Bisáccia I 172 A1
Bisacquino I 176 B2
Bisbal de Falset E 153 A4
Biscarosse F 128 B1
Biscarosse Plage
F 128 B1
Biscarrués E 144 B3
Biscéglie I 171 B4
Bischheim F 93 C3
Bischofsheim D 82 B1
Bischofshofen A 109 B4
Bischofswerda D 84 A2
Bischofswiesen D 109 B3
Bischofszell CH 107 B4
Bischwiller F 93 C3
Bisenti I 169 A3
Bishop Auckland
GB 37 B5
Bishop's Castle GB 39 B4
Bishops Lydeard
GB 43 A3
Bishop's Stortford
GB 45 B4
Bishop's Waltham
GB 44 C2
Bisignano I 174 B2
Bisingen D 93 C4
Biskupice-Oławskie
PL 85 A5
Biskupiec PL 69 B4
Bismark D 73 B4
Bismo N 198 D5
Bispgården S 200 C2
Bispingen D 72 A2
Bissen L 92 B2
Bissendorf D 71 B5
Bisserup DK 65 A4
Bistango I 119 C5
Bistarac Donje
BIH 139 A4
Bistrica BIH 124 C3
Bistrica ob Sotli
SLO 123 A4
Bistriţa RO 17 B6
Bitburg D 92 B2
Bitche F 93 B3
Bitetto I 171 B4
Bitola MK 182 B3
Bitonto I 171 B4
Bitschwiller F 106 B2
Bitterfeld D 83 A4
Bitti I 178 B3
Biville-sur-Mer F 89 A5
Bivona I 176 B2
Biwer L 92 B2
Bizeljsko SLO 123 A4
Bizovac HR 125 B4
Bjåen N 52 A3
Bjärnum S 61 C3
Bjärred S 61 D3
Bjästa S 200 C4
Bjelland
Vest-Agder N 52 B2
Vest-Agder N 52 B3
Bjelovar HR 124 B2
Bjerkreim N 52 B2
Bjerkvik N 194 B8
Bjerreby DK 65 B3
Bjerregrav DK 58 B2
Bjerringbro DK 59 B2
Bjøberg N 47 B5
Bjøllånes N 195 D5
Björbo S 50 B1
Bjordal N 46 A2
Björg IS 191 B8
Bjørkåsen N 194 B7
Björke
Gävleborg S 51 B4
Östergötland S 56 B1
Bjørkelangen N 48 C3
Björketorp S 60 B2
Björkholmen S 196 C2
Björkliden S 194 B9
Björklinge S 51 B4
Björko S 51 C6
Björkö S 60 B1
Björköby S 62 A2
Björkvik S 56 B2
Bjørn N 195 D3
Björna S 200 C4
Björneborg S 55 A5
Björnerod S 54 A2
Bjørnevatn N 193 C13
Björnlunda S 56 A3
Bjørnstad N 193 C14
Björsäter S 56 B2
Bjurberget S 49 B4
Bjurholm S 200 C5
Bjursås S 50 B2
Bjurtjärn S 55 A5
Bjuv S 61 C2
Blachownia PL 86 B2
Blackburn GB 38 A4
Blackpool GB 38 A3
Blackstad S 62 A4
Blackwater IRL 30 B2
Blackwaterfoot GB 34 C2
Blacy F 91 C4
Bladåker S 51 B5
Blaenau Ffestiniog
GB 38 B3
Blaenavon GB 39 C3
Blaengarw GB 39 C3
Blagaj
BIH 124 B2
BIH 139 B3
Blagdon GB 43 A4
Blagnac F 129 C4
Blagoevgrad BG 183 A5
Blaichach D 107 B5
Blain F 101 B4
Blainville-sur-l'Eau
F 92 C2
Blair Atholl GB 35 B4
Blairgowrie GB 35 B4
Blajan F 145 A4
Blakeney GB 39 C4
Blakstad N 53 B4
Blâmont F 92 C2
Blanca E 165 A3
Blancos E 140 C3
Blandford Forum
GB 43 B4
Blanes E 147 C3
Blangy-sur-Bresle
F 90 B1
Blankaholm S 62 A4
Blankenberge B 78 A3
Blankenburg D 82 A2
Blankenfelde D 74 B2
Blankenhain D 82 B3
Blankenheim D 80 B2
Blanquefort F 128 B2
Blansko CZ 97 B4
Blanzac F 115 C4
Blanzy F 104 C3
Blaricum NL 70 B2
Blarney IRL 29 C3
Blascomillán E 150 B2
Blascosancho E 150 B3
Błaszki PL 86 A2
Blatná CZ 96 B1
Blatné SK 111 A4
Blatnice CZ 98 C1
Blatnika BIH 139 A3
Blato HR 138 C2
Blato na Cetini
HR 138 B2
Blatten CH 119 A4
Blattnicksele S 195 E8
Blatzheim D 80 B2
Blaubeuren D 94 C1
Blaufelden D 94 B1
Blaustein D 94 C1
Blaydon GB 37 B5
Blaye F 128 A2
Blaye-les-Mines F 130 A1
Blázquez E 156 B2
Bleckede D 73 A3
Blecua E 145 B3
Bled SLO 123 A3
Bleiburg A 110 C1
Bleichenbach D 81 B5
Bleicherode D 82 A2
Bleik N 194 A6
Bleikvassli N 195 E4
Bléneau F 104 B1
Blentarp S 61 D3
Blera I 168 A2
Blérancourt F 90 B3
Bléré F 102 B2
Blesle F 116 B3
Blessington IRL 30 A2
Blet F 103 C4
Bletchley GB 44 B3
Bletterans F 105 C4
Blidö S 57 A4
Blidsberg S 60 B3
Blieskastel D 92 B3
Bligny-sur-Ouche
F 104 B3
Blikstorp S 55 B5
Blinisht AL 182 B1
Blinja HR 124 B2
Blizanówek PL 76 C3
Bliżyn PL 87 A4
Blois F 103 B3
Blokhus DK 58 A2
Blokzijl NL 70 B2
Blombacka S 55 A4
Blomberg D 72 C2
Blomskog S 54 A3
Blomstermåla S 62 B4
Blomvåg N 46 B1
Blönduós IS 190 B5
Błonie PL 77 B5
Blonville-sur-Mer F 89 A4
Blötberget S 50 B2
Blovice CZ 96 B1
Bloxham GB 44 A2
Blšany CZ 83 B5
Bludenz A 107 B4
Bludov CZ 97 B4
Blumberg D 107 B3
Blyberg S 49 A6
Blyth
Northumberland
GB 37 A5
Nottinghamshire
GB 40 B2
Blyth Bridge GB 35 C4
Blythburgh GB 45 A5
Blythe Bridge GB 40 C1
Bø
Nordland N 194 B5
Telemark N 53 A5
Boal E 141 A4
Boan MNE 139 C5
Boario Terme I 120 B3
Boat of Garten GB 32 D3
Boa Vista P 154 B2
Boğazkale TR 23 A8
Boğazlıyan TR 23 B8
Boba H 111 B4
Bobadilla
Logroño E 143 B4
Málaga E 163 A3
Bobadilla del Campo
E 150 A2
Bobadilla del Monte
E 151 B4
Bóbbio I 120 C2
Bóbbio Pellice I 119 C4
Bobigny F 90 C2
Bobingen D 94 C2
Böblingen D 93 C5
Bobolice PL 68 B1
Boboras E 140 B2
Boboshevo BG 182 A4
Bobowa PL 99 B4
Bobrová CZ 97 B4
Bobrovitsa UA 13 C9
Bobrowice PL 75 C4
Bobrówko PL 75 B4
Boca de Huérgano
E 142 B2
Bocairent E 159 C3
Bočar SRB 126 B2
Bocchigliero I 174 B2
Boceguillas E 151 A4
Bochnia PL 99 B4
Bocholt
B 80 A1
D 80 A2
Bochov CZ 83 B5
Bochum D 80 A3
Bockara S 62 A4
Bockenem D 72 B3
Bockfliess A 97 C4
Bockhorn D 71 A5
Bočna SLO 123 A3
Bocognano F 180 A2
Boconád H 113 B4
Böcs H 113 A4
Boczów PL 75 B3
Boda S 50 A2
Böda S 62 A5
Boda
Stockholm S 51 B5
Värmland S 55 A4
Västernorrland S 200 D2
Bodafors S 62 A2
Boda Glasbruk S 63 B3
Bodajk H 112 B2
Boddam
Aberdeenshire
GB 33 D5
Shetland GB 33 B5
Boddin D 73 A4
Bödefeld-Freiheit
D 81 A4
Boden S 196 D4
Bodenmais D 95 B5
Bodenteich D 73 B3
Bodenwerder D 72 C2
Bodiam GB 45 B4
Bodinnick GB 42 B2
Bodio CH 120 A1
Bodjani SRB 125 B5
Bodmin GB 42 B2
Bodø N 194 C5
Bodonal de la Sierra
E 161 A3

Bodrum TR 188 B2
Bodstedt D 66 B1
Bodträskfors S 196 C3
Bodzanów PL 77 B5
Bodzanowice PL 86 B2
Bodzechów PL 87 B5
Bodzentyn PL 87 B4
Boecillo E 150 A3
Boëge F 118 A3
Boën F 117 B3
Bogács H 113 B4
Bogadmindszent
H 125 B4
Bogajo E 149 B3
Bogarra E 158 C1
Bogarre E 163 A4
Bogatić SRB 127 C1
Bogatynia PL 84 B2
Bogda RO 126 B3
Bogdaniec PL 75 B4
Boge S 57 C4
Bogen
D 95 C4
Nordland N 194 B7
Nordland N 194 C6
S 49 B4
Bogense DK 59 C3
Bognanco Fonti I 119 A5
Bognelv N 192 B6
Bognes N 194 B7
Bogno CH 120 A2
Bognor Regis GB 44 C3
Bogoria PL 87 B5
Bograngen S 49 B4
Boguchwaly PL 69 B5
Bogumiłowice PL 86 A3
Boguslav UA 13 D9
Boguszów-Gorce
PL 85 B4
Bogyiszló H 112 C2
Bohain-en-Vermandois
F 91 B3
Böheimkirchen A 110 A2
Bohinjska Bistrica
SLO 122 A2
Böhlen D 83 A4
Böhmenkirch D 94 C1
Bohmte D 71 B5
Bohonal de Ibor E 150 C2
Böhönye H 124 A3
Bohumin CZ 98 B2
Boiro E 140 B2
Bois-d'Amont F 105 C5
Boisseron F 131 B3
Boitzenburg D 74 A2
Boixols E 147 B2
Boizenburg D 73 A3
Bojadła PL 75 C4
Bojano I 170 B2
Bojanowo PL 85 A4
Bøjden DK 64 A3
Bojkovice CZ 98 B1
Bojná SK 98 C2
Bojnice SK 98 C2
Boka SRB 126 B2
Böklund D 64 B2
Bokod H 112 B2
Böksholm S 62 A2
Boksitogorsk RUS 9 C8
Bol HR 138 B2
Bolaños de Calatrava
E 157 B4
Bolayır TR 186 B1
Bolbec F 89 A4
Bölcske H 112 C2
Bolderslev DK 64 B2
Boldog H 112 B3
Boldva H 113 A4
Böle S 196 D4
Bolea E 145 B3
Bolekhiv UA 13 D5
Bolesławiec PL 84 A3
Boleszkowice PL 74 B3
Bolewice PL 75 B5
Bólgheri I 134 B3
Bolhrad UA 17 C8
Boliden S 200 B6
Bolimów PL 77 B5
Boliqueime P 160 B1
Boljevci SRB 127 C2
Boljkovci SRB 127 C2
Bolków PL 85 B4
Bollebygd S 60 B2
Bollène F 131 A3
Bólliga E 152 B1
Bollnäs S 50 A3
Bollstabruk S 200 D3
Bollullos E 161 B3
Bollullos par del
Condado E 161 B3
Bologna I 135 A4
Bologne F 105 A4
Bolognetta I 176 B2
Bolognola I 136 C2
Bologoye RUS 9 D9
Bolótana I 178 B2
Bolsena I 168 A1
Bolshaya Vradiyevka
UA 17 B9
Bolsover GB 40 B2
Bolstad S 54 B3
Bolsward NL 70 A2
Boltaña E 145 B4
Boltenhagen D 65 C4
Boltigen CH 106 C2
Bolton GB 38 A4
Bolu TR 187 B6
Bolungavík IS 190 A2
Bolvadin TR 187 D6
Bóly H 125 B4
Bolzaneto I 133 A4
Bolzano I 108 C2
Bomba I 169 A4
Bombarral P 154 B1
Bömenzien D 73 B4
Bomlitz D 72 B2
Bømlo N 52 A1
Bøn N 48 B3
Bona F 104 B2
Bonaduz CH 107 C4
Bonanza E 161 C3
Boñar E 142 B1
Bonarbridge GB 32 D2
Bonárcado I 178 B2
Bonares E 161 B3
Bonäs S 50 A1
Bonassola I 134 A2
Bonawe GB 34 B2
Bondal N 53 A4
Bondeno I 121 C4
Bondorf D 93 C4
Bondstorp S 60 B3
Bon-Encontre F 129 B3
Bo'ness GB 35 B4
Bonete E 158 C2
Bonifacio F 180 B2
Bonigen CH 106 C2
Bonin PL 67 B5
Bonn D 80 B3
Bonnánaro I 178 B2
Bonnåsjøen N 194 C6
Bonnat F 116 A1
Bonndorf D 106 B3
Bonnétable F 102 A2
Bonnétage F 106 B1
Bonneuil-les-Eaux
F 90 B2
Bonneuil-Matours
F 115 B4
Bonneval F 103 A3
Bonneval-sur-Arc
F 119 B4
Bonneville F 118 A3
Bonnières-sur-Seine
F 90 B1
Bonnieux F 131 B4
Bönnigheim D 93 B5
Bonnyrigg GB 35 C4
Bonny-sur-Loire F 103 B4
Bono
E 145 B4
I 178 B3
Bonorva I 178 B2
Bønsnes N 48 B2
Bonyhád H 125 A4
Boom B 79 A4
Boos F 89 A5
Boostedt D 64 B3
Bootle
Cumbria GB 36 B3
Merseyside GB 38 A3
Bopfingen D 94 C2
Boppard D 81 B3
Boqueixón E 140 B2
Bor
CZ 95 B4
S 62 A2
SRB 16 C5
TR 23 C8
Boran-sur-Oise F 90 B2
Borås S 60 B2
Borba P 155 C3
Borbona I 169 A3
Borča SRB 127 C2
Borci BIH 139 B4
Borculo NL 71 B3
Bordány H 126 A1
Bordeaux F 128 B2
Bordeira P 160 B1
Bordesholm D 64 B3
Borðeyri IS 190 B4
Bordighera I 133 B3
Bording DK 59 B2
Bordón E 153 B3
Bore I 120 C2
Borehamwood GB 44 B3
Borek Strzeliński
PL 85 B5
Borek Wielkopolski
PL 76 C2
Boreland GB 36 A3
Borello I 135 A5
Borensberg S 56 B1
Borgafjäll S 199 A12
Borgarnes IS 190 C4
Borgentreich D 81 A5
Börger D 71 B4
Borger NL 71 B3
Borggård S 56 B1
Borghamn S 55 B5
Borghetta di Vara
I 134 A2
Borghetto d'Arróscia
I 133 A3
Borghetto Santo Spirito
I 133 A4
Borgholm S 62 B4
Borghorst D 71 B4
Bórgia I 175 C2
Borgloon B 79 B5
Børglum DK 58 A2
Borgo F 180 A2
Borgo alla Collina
I 135 B4
Borgo a Mozzano
I 134 B3
Borgoforte I 121 B3
Borgofranco d'Ivrea
I 119 B4
Borgomanero I 119 B5
Borgomasino I 119 B4
Borgonovo Val Tidone
I 120 B2
Borgo Pace I 135 B5
Borgorose I 169 A3
Borgo San Dalmazzo
I 133 A3
Borgo San Lorenzo
I 135 B4
Borgosésia I 119 B5
Borgo Val di Taro
I 134 A2
Borgo Valsugana
I 121 A4
Borgo Vercelli I 119 B5
Borgstena S 60 B3
Borgue GB 36 B2
Borgund N 47 A4
Borgvik S 55 A3
Borja E 144 C2
Bork D 80 A3
Borken D 80 A2
Borkenes N 194 B7
Børkop DK 59 C2
Borkowice PL 87 A4
Borkowo PL 77 B5
Borkum D 71 A3
Borlänge S 50 B2
Borlu TR 186 D3
Bormes-les-Mimosas
F 132 B2
Bórmio I 107 C5
Bormujos E 161 B3
Borna D 83 A4
Borne NL 71 B3
Bornes P 149 A2
Borne Sulinowo PL 68 B1
Bornheim D 80 B2
Bornhöved D 64 B3
Börnicke D 74 B1
Bornos E 162 B2
Borobia E 152 A2
Borodino RUS 9 E9
Borohrádek CZ 85 B4
Boronów PL 86 B2
Bórore I 178 B2
Borosźow PL 86 B2
Borota H 126 A1
Boroughbridge GB 40 A2
Borovany CZ 96 C2
Borovichi RUS 9 C8
Borovnica SLO 123 B3
Borovo HR 125 B4
Borovsk RUS 9 E10
Borovy CZ 96 B1
Borowa PL 85 A5
Borox E 151 B4
Borrby S 66 A3
Borre
DK 65 B5
N 54 A1
Borredá E 147 B2
Borrenes E 141 B4
Borriol E 159 A3
Borris
DK 59 C1
IRL 30 B2
Borris-in-Ossory
IRL 28 B4
Borrisokane IRL 28 B3
Borrisoleigh IRL 28 B4
Borrowdale GB 36 B3
Børrud N 49 C4
Borşa RO 17 B6
Borsdorf D 83 A4
Børselv N 193 B9
Borsfa H 111 C3
Borský Mikuláš
SK 98 C1
Borsodivánka H 113 B4
Borsodnádasd H 113 A4
Börte N 53 A3
Borth GB 39 B2
Bort-les-Orgues F 116 B2
Börtnan S 199 C10
Børtnes N 47 B6
Boruja Kościelne
PL 75 B5
Borup DK 61 D1
Boryslav UA 13 D5
Boryspil UA 13 C9
Boryszyn PL 75 B4
Borzęciczki PL 85 A5
Borzęcin PL 77 B5
Borzonasca I 134 A2
Borzyszkowy PL 68 A2
Borzytuchom PL 68 A2
Bosa I 178 B2
Bošáca SK 98 C1
Bosanci HR 123 B4
Bosanska Dubica
BIH 124 B2
Bosanska Gradiška
BIH 124 B3
Bosanska Kostajnica
BIH 124 B2
Bosanska Krupa
BIH 124 C2
Bosanski Brod
BIH 125 B3
Bosanski Novi
BIH 124 B2
Bosanski Petrovac
BIH 124 C2
Bosanski Šamac
BIH 125 B4
Bosansko Grahovo
BIH 138 A2
Bošany SK 98 C2
Bösárkány H 111 B4
Bosau D 65 B3
Bósca H 112 C3
Boscastle GB 42 B2
Bosco I 120 C1
Bosco Chiesanuova
I 121 B4
Bösdorf D 65 B3
Bösel D 71 A4
Bosham GB 44 C3
Bösingfeld D 72 B2
Bosjön S 49 C5
Boskoop NL 70 B1
Boskovice CZ 97 B4
Bošnjaci HR 125 B4
Bošnjane SRB 127 D3
Bossast E 145 B4
Bossolasco I 133 A4
Boštanj SLO 123 A4
Boston GB 41 C3
Bostrak N 53 A4
Böszénfa H 125 A3
Bot E 153 A4
Botajica BIH 125 C4
Bøte By DK 65 B4
Bothel GB 36 B3
Boticas P 148 A2
Botilsäter S 55 A4
Botngård N 198 B6
Botoš SRB 126 B2
Botoşani RO 17 B7
Botricello I 175 C2
Botsmark S 200 B6
Bottendorf D 81 A4
Bottesford GB 40 C3
Bottnaryd S 60 B3
Bottrop D 80 A2
Botunje SRB 127 C3
Bötzingen D 106 A2
Bouaye F 101 B4
Bouça P 149 A2
Boucau F 128 C1
Bouchain F 78 B3
Bouchoir F 90 B2
Boudreville F 105 B3
Boudry CH 106 C1
Bouesse F 103 C3
Bouguenais F 101 B4
Bouhy F 104 B2
Bouillargues F 131 B3
Bouillon B 91 B5
Bouilly F 104 A2
Bouin F 114 B2
Boulay-Moselle F 92 B2
Boulazac F 129 A3
Boule-d'Amont F 146 B3
Bouligny F 92 B1
Boulogne-sur-Gesse
F 145 A4
Boulogne-sur-Mer
F 78 B1
Bouloire F 102 B2
Bouquemaison F 78 B2
Bourbon-Lancy F 104 C2
Bourbon-l'Archambault
F 104 C2
Bourbonne-les-Bains
F 105 B4
Bourbourg F 78 B2
Bourbriac F 100 A2
Bourcefranc-le-Chapus
F 114 C2
Bourdeaux F 131 A4
Bouresse F 115 B4
Bourg F 128 A2
Bourg-Achard F 89 A4
Bourganeuf F 116 B1
Bourg-Argental F 117 B4
Bourg-de-Péage
F 117 B5
Bourg-de-Thizy F 117 A4
Bourg-de-Visa F 129 B3
Bourg-en-Bresse
F 118 A2
Bourges F 103 B4
Bourg-et-Comin F 91 B3
Bourg-Lastic F 116 B2
Bourg-Madame F 146 B2
Bourgneuf-en-Retz
F 114 A2
Bourgogne F 91 B4
Bourgoin-Jallieu
F 118 B2
Bourg-St Andéol
F 131 A3
Bourg-St Maurice
F 119 B3
Bourgtheroulde F 89 A4
Bourgueil F 102 B2
Bourmont F 105 A4
Bourne GB 40 C3
Bournemouth GB 43 B5
Bourneville F 89 A4
Bournezeau F 114 B2
Bourran F 129 B3
Bourret F 129 C4
Bourron-Marlotte F 90 C2
Bourton-on-The-Water
GB 44 B2
Boussac F 116 A2
Boussens F 145 A4
Boutersem B 79 B4
Bouttencourt F 90 B1
Bouvières F 131 A4
Bouvron F 101 B4
Bouxwiller F 93 C3
Bouzas E 140 B2
Bouzonville F 92 B2
Bova I 175 D1
Bovalino Marina I 175 C2
Bovallstrand S 54 B2
Bova Marina I 175 D1
Bovec SLO 122 A2
Bóveda E 141 B3
Bóvegno I 120 B3
Bovenau D 64 B2
Bovenden D 82 A1
Bøverdal N 198 D5
Boves F 90 B2
Bóves I 133 A3
Bovey Tracey GB 43 B3
Bovino I 171 B3
Bøvlingbjerg DK 58 B1
Bovolenta I 121 B4
Bovolone I 121 B4
Bowes GB 37 B5
Bowmore GB 34 C1
Bowness-on-
Windermere GB 36 B4
Box GB 43 A4
Boxberg
Baden-Württemberg
D 94 B1
Sachsen D 84 A2
Boxholm S 55 B6
Boxmeer NL 80 A1
Boxtel NL 79 A5
Boyabat TR 23 A8
Boyalıca TR 187 B4
Boyle IRL 26 C2
Bozan TR 187 C6
Božava HR 137 A3
Bozburun TR 188 C3
Bozcaada TR 186 C1
Bozdoğan TR 188 B3
Božepole Wielkie
PL 68 A2
Boževac SRB 127 C3
Božice CZ 97 C4
Boži Dar CZ 83 B4
Bozkır TR 189 B7
Bozouls F 130 A1
Bozova TR 189 B5
Bozüyük TR 187 C5
Bózzolo I 121 B3
Bra I 119 C4
Braås S 62 A3
Brabrand DK 59 B3
Bracadale GB 31 B2
Bracciano I 168 A2
Bracieux F 103 B3
Bräcke S 199 C12
Brackenheim D 93 B5
Brackley GB 44 A2
Bracklin IRL 27 C4
Bracknell GB 44 B3
Brackwede D 72 C1
Braco GB 35 B4
Brad RO 16 B5
Bradford GB 40 B2
Bradford on Avon
GB 43 A4
Bradina BIH 139 B4
Brådland N 52 B2
Brædstrup DK 59 C2
Brae GB 33 A5
Braemar GB 32 D3
Braemore GB 32 D1
Braga P 148 A1
Bragança P 149 A3
Brăila RO 17 C7
Braine F 91 B3
Braine-le-Comte B 79 B4
Braintree GB 45 B4
Braives B 79 B5
Brake D 72 A1
Brakel
B 79 B3
D 81 A5
Bräkne-Hoby S 63 B3
Brålanda S 54 B3
Bralin PL 86 A1
Brallo di Pregola I 120 C2
Bram F 146 A3
Bramafan F 132 B2
Bramberg am
Wildkogel A 109 B3
Bramdrupdam DK 59 C2
Bramming DK 59 C1
Brampton GB 37 B4
Bramsche D 71 B4
Branca I 136 B1
Brancaleone Marina
I 175 D2
Brancaster GB 41 C4
Brand
Nieder Östereich
A 96 C3
Vorarlberg A 107 B4
Brandbu N 48 B2
Brande DK 59 C2
Brande-Hornerkirchen
D 64 C2
Brandenberg A 108 B2
Brandenburg D 73 B5
Brand-Erbisdorf D 83 B5
Brandis D 83 A4
Brando F 180 A2
Brandomil E 140 A2
Brandon GB 45 A4
Brandshagen D 66 B2
Brandval N 49 B4
Brandýs nad Labem
CZ 84 B2
Branice PL 98 A1
Braničevo SRB 127 C3
Braniewo PL 69 A4
Branik SLO 122 B2
Brankovina SRB 127 C1
Branky CZ 98 B1
Branne F 128 B2
Brannenburg-
Degerndorf D 108 B3
Brantôme F 115 C4
Branzi I 120 A2
Bras d'Asse F 132 B2
Braskereidfoss N 48 B3
Braslaw BY 13 A7
Braşov RO 17 C6
Brasparts F 100 A2
Brassac F 130 B1
Brassac-les-Mines
F 116 B3
Brasschaat B 79 A4
Brastad S 54 B2
Břasy CZ 96 B1
Brąszewice PL 86 A2
Bratislava SK 111 A4
Brattfors S 55 A5
Brattvåg N 198 C3
Bratunac BIH 127 C1
Braubach D 81 B3
Braunau A 95 C5
Braunfels D 81 B4
Braunlage D 82 A2
Braunsbedra D 83 A3
Braunschweig D 73 B3
Bray IRL 30 A2
Bray Dunes F 78 A2
Bray-sur-Seine F 90 C3
Bray-sur-Somme F 90 B2
Brazatortas E 157 B3
Brazey-en-Plaine
F 105 B4
Brbinj HR 137 A4
Brčko BIH 125 C4
Brdani SRB 127 D2
Brdów PL 76 B3
Brea de Tajo E 151 B4
Brécey F 88 B2
Brechen D 81 B4
Brechin GB 35 B5
Brecht B 79 A4
Brecketfeld D 80 A3
Břeclav CZ 97 C4
Brecon GB 39 C3
Brécy F 103 B4
Breda
E 147 C3
NL 79 A4
Bredaryd S 60 B3
Bredbyn S 200 C4
Breddin D 73 B5
Bredebro DK 64 A1
Bredelar D 81 A4
Bredenfelde D 74 A2
Bredsjö S 50 C1
Bredstedt D 64 B1
Bredsten DK 59 C2
Bredträsk S 200 C4
Bredviken S 195 D5
Bree B 80 A1
Bregana HR 123 B4
Breganze I 121 B4
Bregenz A 107 B4
Bréhal F 88 B2
Brehna D 83 A4
Breiðdalsvík IS 191 C11
Breidenbach F 93 B3
Breil-sur-Roya F 133 B3
Breisach D 106 A2
Breitenbach
CH 106 B2
D 81 B5
Breitenberg D 96 C1
Breitenfelde D 73 A3
Breitengussbach D 94 B2
Breivikbotn N 192 B6
Brejning DK 59 C2
Brekke N 46 A2
Brekken N 199 C8
Brekkestø N 53 B4
Brekkvasselv N 199 A10
Brekstad N 198 B6
Breland N 53 B3
Bremanger N 198 D1
Bremen D 72 A1
Bremerhaven D 72 A1
Bremervörde D 72 A2
Bremgarten CH 106 B3
Bremsnes N 198 B4
Brem-sur-Mer F 114 B2
Brenderup DK 59 C2
Brenes E 162 A2
Brengova SLO 110 C2
Brenna PL 98 B2
Breno I 120 B3
Brénod F 118 A2
Brensbach D 93 B4
Brentwood GB 45 B4
Brescello I 121 C3
Bréscia I 120 B3
Breskens NL 79 A3
Bresles F 90 B2
Bresnica SRB 127 D2
Bressana I 120 B2
Bressanone I 108 C2
Bressuire F 102 C1
Brest
BY 13 B5
F 100 A1
HR 122 B2
Brestač SRB 127 C1
Brestanica SLO 123 A4
Brestova HR 123 B3
Brestovac HR 125 B3
Bretenoux F 129 B4
Breteuil
Eure F 89 B4
Oise F 90 B2
Brétigny-sur-Orge
F 90 C2
Bretten D 93 B4
Bretteville-sur-Laize
F 89 A3
Brettheim D 94 B2
Breuil-Cervinia I 119 B4
Breukelen NL 70 B2
Brevik
N 53 A5
Stockholm S 57 A4
Västra Götaland
S 55 B5
Breza BIH 139 A4
Brežice SLO 123 B4
Bréziers F 132 A2
Breznica HR 124 A2
Breznica Našička
HR 125 B4
Březnice CZ 96 B1
Brezno SK 99 C3
Brezolles F 89 B5
Březovánad Svitavou
CZ 97 B4
Brezovápod Bradlom
SK 98 C1
Brezovica
SK 99 B4
SLO 123 A3
Brezovo Polje Selo
BIH 125 C4
Briançon F 118 C3
Brianconnet F 132 B2
Briare F 103 B4
Briatexte F 129 C4
Briático I 175 C2
Briaucourt F 105 A4
Bribir HR 123 B3
Bricquebec F 88 A2
Bridgend
Argyll & Bute GB 34 C1
Bridgend GB 39 C3
Bridge of Cally GB 35 B4
Bridge of Don GB 33 D4
Bridge of Earn GB 35 B4
Bridge of Orchy
GB 34 B3
Bridgnorth GB 39 B4
Bridgwater GB 43 A4
Břidličná CZ 98 B1
Bridlington GB 41 A3
Bridport GB 43 B4
Briec F 100 A1
Brie-Comte-Robert
F 90 C2
Brienne-le-Château
F 91 C4
Brienon-sur-Armançon
F 104 B2
Brienz CH 106 C3
Brienza I 172 B1
Briesen D 74 B3
Brieskow Finkenheerd
D 74 B3
Brietlingen D 72 A3
Brieva de Cameros
E 143 B4
Briey F 92 B1
Brig CH 119 A5
Brigg GB 40 B3
Brighouse GB 40 B2
Brightlingsea GB 45 B5
Brighton GB 44 C3
Brignogan-Plage
F 100 A1
Brignoles F 132 B2
Brigstock GB 40 C3
Brihuega E 151 B5
Brijuni HR 122 C2
Brillon-en-Barrois
F 91 C5
Brilon D 81 A4
Brimnes N 46 B3
Brinches P 160 A2
Brindisi I 173 B3
Brinje HR 123 B4
Brinon-sur-Beuvron
F 104 B2
Brinon-sur-Sauldre
F 103 B4
Brinyan GB 33 B3
Brión E 140 B2
Briones E 143 B4
Brionne F 89 A4
Brioude F 117 B3
Brioux-sur-Boutonne
F 115 B3
Briouze F 89 B3
Briscous F 144 A2
Brisighella I 135 A4
Brissac-Quincé F 102 B1
Brissago CH 120 A1
Bristol GB 43 A4
Brive-la-Gaillarde
F 129 A4
Briviesca E 143 B3
Brixham GB 43 B3
Brixlegg A 108 B2
Brjánslækur IS 190 B2
Brka BIH 125 C4
Brnaze HR 138 B2
Brněnec CZ 97 B4
Brno CZ 97 B4
Bro S 57 A3
Broadclyst GB 43 B3
Broadford
GB 31 B3
IRL 28 B3
Broad Haven GB 39 C1
Broadstairs GB 45 B5
Broadstone GB 43 B4
Broadway GB 44 A2
Broager DK 64 B2
Broaryd S 60 B3
Broby S 61 C4
Brobyværk DK 59 C3
Bročanac BIH 138 B3
Brocas F 128 B2
Brock D 71 B4
Brockel D 72 A2
Brockenhurst GB 44 C2
Broczyno PL 75 A5
Brod MK 182 B3
Brodalen S 54 B2
Broddbo S 50 C3
Brodek u Přerova
CZ 98 B1
Broden-bach D 80 B3
Brodick GB 34 C2
Brod na Kupi HR 123 B3
Brodnica PL 69 B4
Brodnica Graniczna
PL 68 A3
Brodowe Łąki PL 77 A6
Brody
Lubuskie PL 75 B4
Lubuskie PL 84 A2
Mazowieckie PL 77 B5
UA 13 C6
Broglie F 89 B4
Brójce PL 75 B4
Brokind S 56 B1
Brolo I 177 A3
Brome D 73 B3
Bromley GB 45 B4
Bromölla S 63 B2
Bromont-Lamothe
F 116 B2
Brömsebro S 63 B3
Bromsgrove GB 44 A1
Bromyard GB 39 B4
Bronchales E 152 B2
Bronco E 149 B3
Brønderslev DK 58 A2
Broni I 120 B2
Brønnøysund N 195 E3
Brøns DK 59 C1
Bronte I 177 B3
Bronzani Mejdan
BIH 124 C2
Bronzolo I 121 A4
Broons F 101 A3
Broquies F 130 A1
Brora GB 32 C3
Brørup DK 59 C2
Brösarp S 63 C2
Brossac F 115 C3
Brostrud N 47 B5
Brotas P 154 C2
Brötjärna S 50 B2
Broto E 145 B3
Brottby S 57 A4
Brøttum N 48 A2
Brou F 103 A3
Brouage F 114 C2
Brough GB 37 B4
Broughshane GB 27 B4

Broughton GB 35 C4
Broughton-in-Furness GB 36 B3
Broumov CZ 85 B4
Broût-Vernet F 116 A3
Brouvelieures F 106 A1
Brouwershaven NL 79 A3
Brovary UA 13 C9
Brovst DK 58 A2
Brownhills GB 40 C2
Brozas E 155 B4
Brozzo I 120 B3
Brtnice CZ 97 B3
Brtonigla HR 122 B2
Bruay-la-Buissière F 78 B2
Bruchhausen-Vilsen D 72 B2
Bruchsal D 93 B4
Bruck D 95 B4
Brück D 74 B1
Bruck an der Grossglocknerstrasse A 109 B3
Bruck an der Leitha A 111 A3
Bruck an der Mur A 110 B2
Brückl A 110 C1
Bruckmühl D 108 B2
Brue-Auriac F 132 B1
Brüel D 65 C4
Bruen CH 107 C3
Bruère-Allichamps F 103 C4
Bruff IRL 29 B3
Bruflat N 47 B6
Brugg CH 106 B3
Brugge B 78 A3
Brüggen D 80 A2
Brühl D 80 B2
Bruinisse NL 79 A4
Brûlon F 102 B1
Brumano I 120 B2
Brumath F 93 C3
Brummen NL 70 B3
Brumov-Bylnice CZ 98 B2
Brumunddal N 48 B2
Brunau D 73 B4
Brunehamel F 91 B4
Brünen D 80 A2
Brunete E 151 B3
Brunflo S 199 B11
Brunico I 108 C2
Brunkeberg N 53 A4
Brunn D 74 A2
Brunnen CH 107 C3
Brunsbüttel D 64 C2
Brunssum NL 80 B1
Bruntál CZ 98 B1
Brušane HR 137 A4
Brusasco I 119 B5
Brusio CH 120 A3
Brusno SK 99 C3
Brusque F 130 B1
Brussels = Bruxelles B 79 B4
Brusson I 119 B4
Brüssow D 74 A3
Brusy PL 68 B2
Bruton GB 43 A4
Bruvno HR 138 A1
Bruvoll N 48 B3
Bruxelles = Brussels B 79 B4
Bruyères F 106 A1
Bruz F 101 A4
Bruzaholm S 62 A3
Brwinów PL 77 B5
Brynamman GB 39 C3
Bryncrug GB 39 B2
Bryne N 52 B1
Brynmawr GB 39 C3
Bryrup DK 59 B2
Brzeg PL 85 B5
Brzeg Dolny PL 85 A4
Brześć Kujawski PL 76 B3
Brzesko PL 99 B4
Brzeszcze PL 99 B3
Brzezie PL 68 B1
Brzeziny
Łódzkie PL 87 A3
Wielkopolskie PL 86 A2
Brzeźnica PL 84 A3
Brzeźnica Nowa PL 86 A3
Brzeżno PL 75 A4
Brzotin SK 99 C4
Brzozie Lubawskie PL 69 B4
Bua S 60 B2
Buarcos P 148 B1
Buaveg N 52 A1
Bubbio I 119 C5
Bubry F 100 B2
Buca TR 188 A2
Bucak TR 189 B5
Bučany SK 98 C1
Buccheri I 177 B3
Buccino I 172 B1
Bucelas P 154 C1
Buch
Bayern D 94 C2
Bayern D 95 C4
Buchach UA 13 D6
Bucharest = Bucureşti RO 17 C7
Buchbach D 95 C4
Buchboden A 107 B4
Buchen D 94 B1
Büchen D 73 A3
Buchenberg D 107 B5
Buchères F 104 A3
Buchholz D 72 A2
Buchloe D 108 A1
Buchlovice CZ 98 B1
Buchlyvie GB 34 B3
Bucholz D 73 A5
Buchs CH 107 B4
Buchy F 89 A5
Bückeburg D 72 B2
Buckfastleigh GB 42 B3
Buckhaven GB 35 B4
Buckie GB 33 D4
Buckingham GB 44 A3
Buckley GB 38 A3
Bückwitz D 73 B5
Bučovice CZ 97 B5
Bucsa H 113 B5
Bucureşti = Bucharest RO 17 C7
Bucy-lès-Pierrepont F 91 B3
Buczek PL 86 A3
Bud N 198 C3
Budakalasz H 112 B3
Budakeszi H 112 B2
Budal N 199 C7
Budaörs H 112 B2
Budapest H 112 B3
Búðardalur IS 190 B4
Budča SK 99 C3
Buddusò I 178 B3
Bude GB 42 B2
Budeč CZ 97 B3
Büdelsdorf D 64 B2
Budens P 160 B1
Budia E 151 B5
Budimlić-Japra BIH 124 C2
Büdingen D 81 B5
Budinšćina HR 124 A2
Budišov CZ 98 B1
Budleigh Salterton GB 43 B3
Budmerice SK 98 C1
Budoni I 178 B3
Búdrio I 135 A4
Budva MNE 16 D3
Budyně nad Ohří CZ 84 B2
Budziszewice PL 87 A3
Budzyń PL 76 B1
Bue N 52 B1
Bueña E 152 B2
Buenache de Alarcón E 158 B1
Buenache de la Sierra E 152 B2
Buenaventura E 150 B3
Buenavista de Valdavia E 142 B2
Buendia E 151 B5
Bueu E 140 B2
Buezo E 143 B3
Bugac H 112 C3
Bugarra E 159 B3
Bugeat F 116 B1
Buggerru I 179 C2
Bugojno BIH 138 A3
Bugøyfjord N 193 C13
Bugøynes N 193 C13
Bugyi H 112 B3
Buharkent TR 188 B3
Bühl
Baden-Württemberg D 93 C4
Bayern D 107 B5
Bühlertal D 93 C4
Bühlertann D 94 B1
Buia I 122 A2
Builth Wells GB 39 B3
Buin N 47 B6
Buis-les-Baronnies F 131 A4
Buitenpost NL 70 A3
Buitrago del Lozoya E 151 B4
Bujalance E 157 C3
Bujaraloz E 153 A3
Buje HR 122 B2
Bujedo E 143 B3
Bük H 111 B3
Buk PL 75 B5
Bükkösd H 125 A3
Bükkzsérc H 113 B4
Bukovci SLO 124 A1
Bukowiec PL 75 B5
Bukowina Tatrzańska PL 99 B4
Bukownica PL 86 A2
Bukowno PL 86 B3
Bülach CH 107 B3
Búland IS 191 D7
Buldan TR 188 A3
Bulgari BG 17 D7
Bulgnéville F 105 A4
Bulgurca TR 188 A2
Bülkau D 64 C1
Bulken N 46 B3
Bulkowo PL 77 B5
Bullas E 164 A3
Bulle CH 106 C2
Büllingen B 80 B2
Bullmark S 200 B6
Bulqizë AL 182 B2
Buna BIH 139 B3
Bunahowen IRL 26 B1
Bunbeg IRL 26 A2
Bunclody IRL 30 B2
Buncrana IRL 27 A3
Bunde D 71 A4
Bünde D 72 B1
Bundoran IRL 26 B2
Bunessan GB 34 B1
Bungay GB 45 A5
Bunge S 57 C5
Bunić HR 123 C4
Bunmahon IRL 30 B1
Bunnyconnellan IRL 26 B1
Buño E 140 A2
Buñol E 159 B3
Bunratty IRL 29 B3
Bunsbeek B 79 B4
Buñuel E 144 C2
Bunyola E 166 B2
Buonabitácolo I 172 B1
Buonalbergo I 170 B2
Buonconvento I 135 B4
Buonvicino I 174 B1
Burano I 122 B1
Burbach D 81 B4
Burcei I 179 C3
Burdons-sur-Rognon F 105 A4
Burdur TR 189 B5
Bureå S 2 D7
Burela E 141 A3
Büren D 81 A4
Büren an der Aare CH 106 B2
Burford GB 44 B2
Burg
Cottbus D 84 A2
Magdeburg D 73 B4
Schleswig-Holstein D 64 C2
Burgas BG 17 D7
Burgau
A 111 B3
D 94 C2
P 160 B1
Burg auf Fehmarn D 65 B4
Burgbernheim D 94 B2
Burgdorf
CH 106 B2
D 72 B3
Burgebrach D 94 B2
Bürgel D 83 B3
Burgess Hill GB 44 C3
Burghaslach D 94 B2
Burghausen D 109 A3
Burghead GB 32 D3
Burgheim D 94 C3
Burgh le Marsh GB 41 B4
Búrgio I 176 B2
Burgkirchen D 109 A3
Burgkunstadt D 82 B3
Burglengenfeld D 95 B4
Burgo P 148 B1
Burgoberbach D 94 B2
Burgohondo E 150 B3
Burgos E 143 B3
Burgsinn D 82 B1
Burgstädt D 83 B4
Burgstall D 73 B4
Burg Stargard D 74 A2
Burgsvik S 57 C4
Burgui E 144 B3
Burguillos E 162 A2
Burguillos del Cerro E 155 C4
Burguillos de Toledo E 151 C4
Burhaniye TR 186 C1
Burhave D 71 A5
Burie F 114 C3
Burjassot E 159 B3
Burk D 94 B2
Burkhardtsdorf D 83 B4
Burlada E 144 B2
Burladingen D 107 A4
Burlage D 71 A4
Burness GB 33 B4
Burnham GB 44 B3
Burnham Market GB 41 C4
Burnham-on-Crouch GB 45 B4
Burnham-on-Sea GB 43 A4
Burniston GB 40 A3
Burnley GB 40 B1
Burntisland GB 35 B4
Burón E 142 A1
Buronzo I 119 B5
Burovac SRB 127 C3
Burow D 74 A2
Burravoe GB 33 A5
Burrel AL 182 B2
Burret F 146 B2
Burriana E 159 B3
Burry Port GB 39 C2
Bürs A 107 B4
Bursa TR 186 B4
Burseryd S 60 B3
Bürstadt D 93 B4
Burton GB 37 B4
Burton Agnes GB 41 A3
Burton Bradstock GB 43 B4
Burton Latimer GB 44 A3
Burton upon Stather GB 40 B3
Burton upon Trent GB 40 C2
Burträsk S 200 B6
Burujón E 151 C3
Burwell GB 45 A4
Burwick GB 33 C4
Bury GB 40 B1
Bury St Edmunds GB 45 A4
Burzenin PL 86 A2
Busachi I 179 B2
Busalla I 134 A1
Busana I 134 A3
Busano I 119 B4
Busca I 133 A3
Busch D 73 B4
Buševec HR 124 B2
Bushat AL 182 B1
Bushey GB 44 B3
Bushmills GB 27 A4
Bušince SK 112 A3
Buskhyttan S 56 B2
Busko-Zdrój PL 87 B4
Busot E 159 C3
Busovača BIH 139 A3
Busquistar E 163 B4
Bussang F 106 B1
Busseto I 120 C3
Bussière-Badil F 115 C4
Bussière-Poitevine F 115 B4
Bussolengo I 121 B3
Bussoleno I 119 B4
Bussum NL 70 B2
Busto Arsízio I 120 B1
Büsum D 64 B1
Butera I 177 B3
Butgenbach B 80 B2
Butler's Bridge IRL 27 B3
Butryny PL 77 A5
Bütschwil CH 107 B4
Buttermere GB 36 B3
Buttevant IRL 29 B3
Buttle S 57 C4
Buttstädt D 82 A3
Butzbach D 81 B4
Bützfleth D 72 A2
Bützow D 65 C4
Buxières-les-Mines F 104 C1
Buxtehude D 72 A2
Buxton GB 40 B2
Buxy F 104 C3
Büyükçekmece TR 186 A3
Büyükkariştiran TR 186 A2
Büyükorhan TR 186 C3
Buzançais F 103 C3
Buzancy F 91 B4
Buzău RO 17 C7
Buzet HR 122 B2
Buziaş RO 126 B3
Buzsák H 111 C4
Buzy F 145 A3
By S 50 B3
Byala BG 17 D6
Byaroza BY 13 B6
Byczyna PL 86 A2
Bydalen S 199 B10
Bydgoszcz PL 76 A3
Bygdin N 47 A5
Bygdsiljum S 200 B6
Bygland N 53 B3
Byglandsfjord N 53 B3
Bygstad N 46 A2
Bykhaw BY 13 B9
Bykle N 52 A3
Bylderup-Bov DK 64 B2
Byrkjedal N 52 B2
Byrkjelo N 198 D3
Byrum DK 58 A3
Byšice CZ 84 B2
Byske S 2 D7
Býškovice CZ 98 B1
Bysław PL 76 A2
Bystré CZ 97 B4
Bystřice CZ 96 B2
Bystřice CZ 98 B2
Bystřice nad Pernštejnem CZ 97 B4
Bystřice pod Hostýnem CZ 98 B1
Bystrzyca Kłodzka PL 85 B4
Bytča SK 98 B2
Bytnica PL 75 B4
Bytom PL 86 B2
Bytom Odrzański PL 85 A3
Bytów PL 68 A2
Byxelkrok S 62 A5
Bzenec CZ 98 C1
Bzince SK 98 C1

C

Çağa TR 187 B7
Cabaços P 154 B2
Cabaj-Čápor SK 98 C2
Cabana E 140 A2
Cabanac-et-Villagrains F 128 B2
Cabañaquinta E 142 A1
Cabanas P 160 B2
Cabañas del Castillo E 156 A2
Cabañas de Yepes E 151 C4
Cabanelles E 147 B3
Cabanes E 153 B4
Cabanillas E 144 B2
Čabar HR 123 B3
Cabasse F 132 B2
Cabdella E 146 B2
Cabeceiras de Basto P 148 A1
Cabeço de Vide P 155 B3
Cabella Ligure I 120 C2
Cabeza del Buey E 156 B2
Cabeza la Vaca E 161 A3
Cabezamesada E 151 C4
Cabezarados E 157 B3
Cabezarrubias del Puerto E 157 B3
Cabezas del Villar E 150 B2
Cabezas Rubias E 161 B2
Cabezón E 142 C2
Cabezón de la Sal E 142 A2
Cabezón de Liébana E 142 A2
Cabezuela E 151 A4
Cabezuela del Valle E 149 B4
Cabo de Gata E 164 C2
Cabo de Palos E 165 B4
Cabolafuenta E 152 A1
Cabourg F 89 A3
Cabra
E 163 A3
P 148 B2
Cabrach GB 32 D3
Cabra del Santo Cristo E 163 A4
Cábras I 179 C2
Cabreiro P 140 C2
Cabreiros E 140 A3
Cabrejas E 152 B1
Cabrela P 154 C2
Cabrillas E 149 B3
Cabuna HR 125 B3
Cacabelos E 141 B4
Čačak SRB 127 D2
Cáccamo I 176 B2
Caccuri I 174 B2
Cacela P 160 B2
Cacém P 154 C1
Cáceres E 155 B4
Cachafeiro E 140 B2
Cachopo P 160 B2
Čachtice SK 98 C1
Cacin E 163 A4
Čačinci HR 125 B3
Cadafais P 154 C1
Cadalen F 129 C5
Cadalso E 149 B3
Cadaqués E 147 B4
Cadaval P 154 B1
Cadavedo E 141 A4
Čadavica BIH 138 A2
Čadca SK 98 B2
Cadeác F 145 B4
Cadelbosco di Sopra I 121 C3
Cadenazzo CH 120 A1
Cadenberge D 64 C2
Cadenet F 131 B4
Cadeuil F 114 C3
Cádiar E 164 C1
Cadillac F 128 B2
Cádiz E 162 B1
Čadjavica HR 125 B3
Cadouin F 129 B3
Cadours F 129 C4
Cadrete E 152 A3
Caen F 89 A3
Caerleon GB 39 C4
Caernarfon GB 38 A2
Caerphilly GB 39 C3
Caersws GB 39 B3
Cafede P 155 B3
Caggiano I 172 B1
Cagli I 136 B1
Cágliari I 179 C3
Čaglin HR 125 B3
Cagnano Varano I 171 B3
Cagnes-sur-Mer F 132 B3
Caher IRL 29 B4
Caherciveen IRL 29 C1
Caherdaniel IRL 29 C1
Cahors F 129 B4
Cahul MD 17 C8
Caiazzo I 170 B2
Caion E 140 A2
Cairndow GB 34 B3
Cairnryan GB 36 B1
Cairo Montenotte I 133 A4
Caister-on-Sea GB 41 C5
Caistor GB 41 B3
Caivano I 170 C2
Cajarc F 129 B4
Čajniče BIH 139 B5
Çakırlar TR 189 C5
Çakmak TR 187 C6
Čakovec HR 124 A2
Çal TR 189 A4
Cala E 161 B3
Calabritto I 172 B1
Calaceite E 153 B4
Calacuccia F 180 A2
Cala d'Or E 167 B3
Calaf E 147 C2
Calafat RO 17 C5
Calafell E 147 C2
Cala Galdana E 167 B3
Cala Gonone I 178 B3
Calahonda
Granada E 163 B4
Málaga E 163 B3
Calahorra E 144 B2
Calais F 78 B1
Cala Llonga E 166 C1
Calalzo di Cadore I 109 C3
Cala Millor E 167 B3
Calamocha E 152 B2
Calamonte E 155 C4
Cala Morell E 167 A3
Calanais GB 31 A2
Calañas E 161 B3
Calanda E 153 B3
Calangiánus I 178 B3
Călăraşi RO 17 C7
Cala Ratjada E 167 B3
Calascibetta I 177 B3
Calasetta I 179 C2
Calasparra E 164 A3
Calatafimi I 176 B1
Calatayud E 152 A2
Calatorao E 152 A2
Calau D 84 A1
Calbe D 73 C4
Calcena E 152 A2
Calcinelli I 136 B1
Calco I 120 B2
Caldarola I 136 B2
Caldaro sulla strada del Vino I 121 A4
Caldas da Rainha P 154 B1
Caldas de Boi E 145 B4
Caldas de Malavella E 147 C3
Caldas de Reis E 140 B2
Caldas de San Jorge P 148 B1
Caldas de Vizela P 148 A1
Caldaso de los Vidrios E 150 B3
Caldbeck GB 36 B3
Caldearenas E 145 B3
Caldelas P 148 A1
Calders E 147 C2
Caldes de Montbui E 147 C3
Caldicot GB 39 C4
Caldirola I 120 C2
Caledon GB 27 B4
Calella
Barcelona E 147 C3
Girona E 147 C4
Calenzana F 180 A1
Calera de León E 161 A3
Calera y Chozas E 150 C3
Caleruega E 143 C3
Caleruela E 150 C2
Cales de Mallorca E 167 B3
Calestano I 134 A3
Calfsound GB 33 B4
Calgary GB 34 B1
Calimera I 173 B4
Calitri I 172 B1
Calizzano I 133 A4
Callac F 100 A2
Callan IRL 30 B1
Callander GB 35 B3
Callas F 132 B2
Calliano
Piemonte I 119 B5
Trentino Alto Adige I 121 B4
Callington GB 42 B2
Callosa de Ensarriá E 159 C3
Callosa de Segura E 165 A4
Callús E 147 C2
Čalma SRB 127 B1
Calmbach D 93 C4
Calne GB 43 A5
Calolziocorte I 120 B2
Calonge E 147 C4
Čalovec SK 112 B1
Calpe E 159 C4
Caltabellotta I 176 B2
Caltagirone I 177 B3
Caltanissetta I 177 B3
Caltavuturo I 176 B2
Çaltılıbük TR 186 C3
Caltojar E 151 A5
Caluire-et-Cuire F 117 B4
Caluso I 119 B4
Calvello I 172 B1
Calvi F 180 A1
Calviá E 166 B2
Calvinet F 116 C2
Calvisson F 131 B3
Calvörde D 73 B4
Calw D 93 C4
Calzada de Calatrava E 157 B4
Calzada de Valdunciel E 150 A2
Calzadilla de los Barros E 155 C4
Cam GB 43 A4
Camaiore I 134 B3
Camarasa E 145 C4
Camarena E 151 B3
Camarès F 130 B1
Camaret-sur-Aigues F 131 A3
Camaret-sur-Mer F 100 A1
Camarillas E 153 B3
Camariñas E 140 A1
Camarma E 151 B4
Camarzana de Tera E 141 B4
Camas E 162 A1
Camastra I 176 B2
Cambados E 140 B2
Cambarinho P 148 B1
Camberley GB 44 B3
Cambil E 163 A4
Cambligeu F 78 B2
Cambo-les-Bains F 144 A2
Camborne GB 42 B1
Cambrai F 78 B3
Cambre E 140 A2
Cambridge GB 45 A4
Cambrils E 147 C2
Cambs D 65 C4
Camburg D 83 A3
Camden GB 44 B3
Cameleño E 142 A2
Camelford GB 42 B2
Çameli TR 189 B4
Camelle E 140 A1
Camerano I 136 B2
Camerino I 136 B2
Camerota I 172 B1
Camigliatello Silano I 174 B2
Caminha P 148 A1
Caminomorisco E 149 B3
Caminreal E 152 B2
Camisano Vicentino I 121 B4
Camlıdere TR 187 B7
Cammarata I 176 B2
Camogli I 134 A2
Camors F 100 B3
Camp IRL 29 B2
Campagna I 172 B1
Campagnano di Roma I 168 A2
Campagnático I 135 C4
Campan F 145 A4
Campana I 174 B2
Campanario E 156 B2
Campanillas E 163 B3
Campano E 162 B1
Campaspero E 151 A3
Campbeltown GB 34 C2
Campello E 165 A4
Campelos P 154 B1
Campi Bisénzio I 135 B4
Campico López E 165 B3
Campiglia Marittima I 134 B3
Campillo de Altobuey E 158 B2
Campillo de Aragón E 152 A2
Campillo de Arenas E 163 A4
Campillo de Llerena E 156 B2
Campillos E 162 A3
Câmpina RO 17 C6
Campi Salentina I 173 B4
Campli I 136 C2
Campo E 145 B4
Campobasso I 170 B2
Campobello di Licata I 176 B2
Campobello di Mazara I 176 B1
Campo da Feira E 140 A3
Campodársego I 121 B4
Campo de Bacerros E 141 B3
Campo de Caso E 142 A1
Campo de Criptana E 157 A4
Campodolcino I 120 A2
Campofelice di Roccella I 176 B2
Campofiorito I 176 B2
Campofórmido I 122 A2
Campofranco I 176 B2
Campofrio E 161 B3
Campogalliano I 121 C3
Campo Ligure I 133 A4
Campolongo I 109 C3
Campo Lugar E 156 A2
Campo Maior P 155 B3
Campomanes E 141 A5
Campomarino I 170 B3
Campo Molino I 133 A3
Campomono F 180 B1
Campo Real E 151 B4
Camporeale I 176 B2
Camporeggiano I 136 B1
Camporrells E 145 C4
Camporrobles E 158 B2
Campos P 148 A2
Camposa P 148 A1
Camposampiero I 121 B4
Camposanto I 121 C4
Campos del Port E 167 B3
Camposines E 153 A4
Campotéjar E 163 A4
Campotosto I 169 A3
Campo Túres I 108 C2
Camprodón E 147 B3
Campsegret F 129 B3
Camrose GB 39 C1
Camuñas E 157 A4
Çamyolu TR 189 C7
Çan TR 186 B2
Cana I 135 C4
Cañada del Hoyo E 158 B2
Cañadajuncosa E 158 B1
Cañada Rosal E 162 A2
Čanak HR 123 C4
Çanakkale TR 186 B1
Canale I 119 C4
Canales
Asturias E 141 B5
Castellón de la Plana E 159 B3
Canals E 159 C3
Canal San Bovo I 121 A4
Cañamares E 152 B1
Cañamero E 156 A2
Cañar E 163 B4
Cañate la Real E 162 B2
Cañaveral E 155 B4
Cañaveral de León E 161 A3
Cañaveras E 152 B1
Cañaveruelas E 151 B5
Canazei I 108 C2
Cancale F 88 B2
Cancellara I 172 B1
Cancello ed Arnone I 170 B2
Cancon F 129 B3
Canda E 141 B4
Candamil E 140 A3
Candanchu E 145 B3
Çandarlı TR 186 D1
Candas E 141 A5
Candasnos E 153 A4
Candé F 101 B4
Candela I 172 A1
Candelario E 150 B2
Candeleda E 150 B2
Cándia Lomellina I 120 B1
Candide Casamazzagno I 109 C3
Candin E 141 B4
Candosa P 148 B2
Canecas P 154 C1
Canelli I 119 C5
Canena E 157 B4
Canencia E 151 B4
Canero E 141 A4
Canet F 130 B2
Canet de Mar E 147 C3
Canet d'en Berenguer E 159 B3
Cañete E 158 A2
Cañete de las Torres E 163 A3
Canet-Plage F 146 B4
Canfranc E 145 B3
Cangas
Lugo E 141 A3
Pontevedra E 140 B2
Cangas de Narcea E 141 A4
Cangas de Onís E 142 A1
Canha P 154 C2
Canhestros P 160 A1

Canicattì I 176 B2
Canicattini Bagni
I 177 B4
Canicosa de la Sierra
E 143 C3
Caniles E 164 B2
Canillas de Aceituno
E 163 B3
Canino I 168 A1
Canisy F. 88 A2
Cañizal E 150 A2
Cañizo E 142 C1
Canjáyar E 164 C2
Çankırı TR 23 A7
Cannai I 179 C2
Cannara I 136 B1
Cánnero Riviera I . .120 A1
Cannes F 132 B3
Canneto
 Sicilia I 177 A3
 Toscana I 135 B3
Canneto sull'Oglio
 I 120 B3
Cannich GB 32 D2
Cannóbio I 120 A1
Cannock GB 40 C1
Canonbie GB 36 A4
Canosa di Púglia
 I 171 B4
Can Pastilla E 166 B2
C'an Picafort E 167 B3
Cantalapiedra E . . .150 A2
Cantalejo E 151 A4
Cantalgallo E 161 A3
Cantalice I 169 A2
Cantalpino E 150 A2
Cantalupo in Sabina
 I 168 A2
Cantanhede P 148 B1
Cantavieja E 153 B3
Čantavir SRB. 126 B1
Canterbury GB 45 B5
Cantiano I 136 B1
Cantillana E 162 A2
Cantiveros E 150 B3
Cantoria E 164 B2
Cantù I 120 B2
Canvey GB. 45 B4
Cany-Barville F. 89 A4
Canyet de Mar E . .147 C3
Caol GB 34 B2
Cáorle I 122 B1
Caorso I 120 B2
Capáccio I 172 B1
Capaci I 176 A2
Capálbio I 168 A1
Capánnori I 134 B3
Caparde BIH 139 A4
Caparroso E 144 B2
Capbreton F 128 C1
Capdenac-Gare F . .116 C2
Capdepera E 167 B3
Cap-de-Pin F 128 B2
Capel Curig GB 38 A3
Capellades E 147 C2
Capena I 168 A2
Capendu F. 146 A3
Capestang F 130 B2
Capestrano I 169 A3
Cap Ferret F. 128 B1
Capileira E 163 B4
Capinha P 148 B2
Ca'Pisani I 122 C1
Capistrello I 169 B3
Capizzi I 177 B3
Čaplje BIH 124 C2
Čapljina BIH 139 B3
Capo di Ponte I 120 A3
Caposile I 122 B1
Capoterra I 179 C2
Cappamore IRL 29 B3
Cappeln D 71 B5
Cappoquin IRL 29 B4
Capracotta I 169 B4
Capránica I 168 A2
Caprarola I 168 A2
Capretta I 135 C5
Capri I 170 C2
Capriati a Volturno
 I 170 B2
Caprino Veronese
 I 121 B3
Captieux F 128 B2
Cápua I 170 B2
Capurso I 173 A2
Capvern F 145 A4
Carabaña E 151 B4
Carabias E 151 A4
Caracal RO 17 C6
Caracenilla E 152 B1
Carággio I 133 A3
Caraman F. 146 A2
Caramánico Terme
 I 169 A4
Caranga E 141 A4
Caranguejeira P . . .154 B2
Caransebeş RO 16 C5
Carantec F 100 A2
Carapelle I 171 B3
Carasco I 134 A2
Carate Brianza I . . .120 B2
Caravaca de la Cruz
 E 164 A3
Caravággio I 120 B2
Carbajal E 163 B3
Carbajo E 155 B3
Carballeda E 140 B3
Carballeda de Avia
 E 140 B2
Carballo E 140 A2
Carbis Bay GB. 42 B1
Carbon-Blanc F 128 B2
Carbonera de Frentes
 E 143 C4
Carboneras E 164 C3
Carboneras de
 Guadazaón E 158 B2

Carbonero el Mayor
 E 151 A3
Carboneros E 157 B4
Carbónia I 179 C2
Carbonin I 108 C3
Carbonne F 146 A2
Carbost
 Highland GB 31 B2
 Highland GB 31 B2
Carcaboso E 149 B3
Carcabuey E 163 A3
Carcaixent E 159 B3
Carcans F 128 A1
Carcans-Plage F . . .128 A1
Carção P 149 A3
Carcar E 144 B2
Cárcare I 133 A4
Carcassonne F 146 A3
Carcastillo E 144 B2
Carcedo de Burgos
 E 143 B3
Carcelén E 159 B2
Carcès F 132 B2
Carchelejo E 163 A4
Çardak
 Çanakkale TR 186 B1
 Denizli TR 189 B5
Cardedeu E 147 C3
Cardeña E 157 B3
Cardenete E 158 B2
Cardeñosa E 150 B3
Cardeto I 175 C1
Cardiff GB 39 C3
Cardigan GB 39 B2
Cardona E 147 C2
Cardosos P 154 B2
Carei RO 16 B5
Carentan F. 88 A2
Carentoir F 101 B3
Careri I 175 C2
Carevdar HR 124 A2
Cargèse F 180 A1
Carhaix-Plouguer
 F. 100 A2
Caria P 148 B2
Cariati I 174 B2
Carignan F 91 B5
Carignano I 119 C4
Cariñena E 152 A2
Carini I 176 A2
Carinola I 170 B1
Carisbrooke GB 44 C2
Carlabhagh GB 31 A2
Carlepont F 90 B3
Carlet E 159 B3
Carlingford IRL 27 B4
Carlisle GB 36 B4
Carloforte I 179 C2
Carlow
 D. 65 C3
 IRL 30 B2
Carlton GB. 40 C2
Carluke GB 35 C4
Carmagnola I 119 C4
Carmarthen GB 39 C2
Carmaux F 130 A1
Carmena E 150 C3
Cármenes E 142 B1
Carmine I 133 A3
Carmona E 162 A2
Carmonita E 155 B4
Carmyllie GB 35 B5
Carnac F 100 B2
Carndonagh IRL 27 A3
Carnew IRL 30 B2
Carnforth GB 37 B4
Cárnia I 122 A2
Carno GB. 39 B3
Carnon Plage F 131 B2
Carnoustie GB. 35 B5
Carnwath GB. 35 C4
Carolei I 174 B2
Carolinensiel D 71 A4
Carolles F 88 B2
Carona I 120 A2
Caronia I 177 A3
Carovigno I 173 B3
Carovilli I 170 B2
Carpaneto Piacentino
 I 120 C2
Carpegna I 135 B5
Carpenédolo I 121 B3
Carpentras F 131 A4
Carpi I 121 C3
Carpignano Sésia
 I 119 B5
Carpineti I 134 A3
Carpineto Romano
 I 169 B3
Cărpinis RO 126 B2
Carpino I 171 B3
Carpinone I 170 B2
Carpio E 150 A2
Carquefou F 101 B4
Carqueiranne F 132 B2
Carral E 140 A2
Carranque E 151 B4
Carrapichana P 148 B2
Carrara I 134 A3
Carraroe IRL 28 A2
Carrascalejo E 156 A2
Carrascosa del Campo
 E 151 B5
Carratraca E 162 B3
Carrazeda de Ansiães
 P 148 A2
Carrazedo de
 Montenegro P. . . .148 A2
Carrbridge GB 32 D3
Carregal do Sal P . .148 B1
Carreña E 142 A2
Carrick IRL 26 B2
Carrickart IRL 26 A3
Carrickfergus GB . . .27 B5
Carrickmacross
 IRL 27 C4

Carrick-on-Shannon
 IRL 26 C2
Carrick-on-Suir IRL . .30 B1
Carrigallen IRL 27 C3
Carrión E 161 B3
Carrión de Calatrava
 E 157 A4
Carrión de los Condes
 E 142 B2
Carrizo de la Ribera
 E 141 B5
Carrizosa E 157 B5
Carro F 131 B4
Carrocera E 142 B1
Carros F 133 B3
Carrouge CH 106 C1
Carrouges F 89 B3
Carrù I 133 A3
Carryduff GB 27 B5
Carry-le-Rouet F . . .131 B4
Carsóli I 169 A3
Carsphairn GB 36 A2
Cartagena E 165 B4
Cártama E 163 B3
Cartaxo P 154 B2
Cartaya E 161 B2
Carteret F. 88 A2
Cartes E 142 A2
Carúnchio I 170 B2
Carviçães P 149 A3
Carvin F 78 B2
Carvoeira P 154 B1
Carvoeiro P 160 B1
Casabermeja E 163 B3
Casa Branca
 Portalegre P. 154 C3
 Setúbal P. 154 C2
Casacalenda I 170 B2
Casa Castalda I 136 B1
Casais E 141 B4
Casal l'Abate I 173 B4
Casalarreina E 143 B4
Casalbordino I 169 A4
Casalborgone I 119 B4
Casalbuono I 174 A1
Casalbuttano ed Uniti
 I 120 B2
Casál di Principe
 I 170 B2
Casalécchio di Reno
 I 135 A4
Casale Monferrato
 I 119 B5
Casalina I 136 C1
Casalmaggiore I . . .121 C3
Casalnuovo
 Monterotaro I . . .170 B3
Casaloldo I 121 B3
Casalpusterlengo
 I 120 B2
Casamássima I 173 B2
Casamicciola Terme
 I 170 C1
Casamozza F 180 A2
Casarabonela E 162 B3
Casarano I 173 B4
Casar de Cáceres
 E 155 B4
Casar de Palomero
 E 149 B3
Casarejos E 143 C3
Casares E 162 B2
Casares de las Hurdes
 E 149 B3
Casariche E 163 A3
Casarrubios del Monte
 E 151 B3
Casas de Don Pedro
 E 156 A2
Casas de Fernando
 Alonso E 158 B1
Casas de Haro E . . .158 B1
Casas de Juan Gil
 E 159 B2
Casas del Juan Núñez
 E 158 B2
Casas del Puerto
 E 159 C2
Casas del Rio E 159 B2
Casas de Millán E . .155 B4
Casas de Reina E . .156 B2
Casas de Ves E 159 B2
Casas-Ibáñez E 158 B2
Casasimarro E 158 B1
Casas Nuevas E 164 B3
Casasola E 150 B3
Casasola de Arión
 E 150 A2
Casasuertes E 142 A2
Casatejada E 150 C2
Casavieja E 150 B3
Casazza I 120 B2
Cascais P 154 C1
Cascante E 144 C2
Cascante del Rio
 E 152 B2
Cáscia I 169 A3
Casciana Terme I . . .134 B3
Cáscina I 134 B3
Cáseda E 144 B2
Casekow D 74 A3
Casella I 134 A2
Caselle Torinese I . .119 B4
Casemurate I 135 A5
Casenove I 136 C1
Caseres E 153 A4
Caserío Benali E . . .159 B3
Caserta I 170 B2
Casével P. 160 B1
Casillas E 150 B3
Casillas de Coria
 E 155 B4
Casina I 134 A3
Casinos E 159 B3
Čáslav CZ 97 B3
Cásola Valsénio I . .135 A4
Cásole d'Elsa I 135 B4
Cásoli I 169 A4
Casória I 170 C2

Caspe E 153 A3
Cassàde la Selva
 E 147 C3
Cassagnas F 130 A2
Cassagnes-Bégonhès
 F. 130 A1
Cassano allo Iónio
 I 174 B2
Cassano d'Adda I . .120 B2
Cassano delle Murge
 I 171 C4
Cassano Magnago
 I 120 B1
Cassano Spinola I . .120 C1
Cassel F 78 B2
Cassibile I 177 C4
Cassine I 119 C5
Cassino I 169 B3
Cassis F 132 B1
Cassolnovo I 120 B1
Cassuéjouls F 116 C2
Častá SK 98 C1
Castagnaro I 121 B4
Castagneto Carducci
 I 134 B3
Castagnola CH 120 A1
Castalla E 159 C3
Castañar de Ibor
 E 156 A2
Castanheira de Pêra
 P 154 A2
Cástano Primo I . . .120 B1
Castasegna CH 120 A2
Castéggio I 120 B2
Casteição P 148 B2
Castejón E 144 B2
Castejón de Monegros
 E 153 A3
Castejón de Sos
 E 145 B4
Castejón de Valdejasa
 E 144 C3
Castèl Baronia I . . .172 A1
Castel Bolognese
 I 135 A4
Castelbuono I 177 B3
Casteldáccia I 176 A2
Castel d'Aiano I 135 A3
Castel d'Ario I 121 B3
Casteldelfino I 132 A3
Castèl del Monte I . .169 A3
Castèl del Piano I . .135 C4
Castèl di Iúdica I . . .177 B3
Castèl di Rio I 135 A4
Castèl di Sangro I . .169 B4
Castèl di Tora I 169 A2
Castelfidardo I 136 B2
Castelfiorentino I . .135 B3
Castelforte I 169 B3
Castelfranco Emilia
 I 121 C4
Castelfranco in
 Miscano I 170 B3
Castelfranco Véneto
 I 121 B4
Castèl Frentano I . .169 A4
Casteljaloux F 128 B3
Castellabate I 170 C2
Castellammare del
 Golfo I 176 A1
Castellammare di
 Stábia I 170 C2
Castellamonte I 119 B4
Castellana Grotte
 I 173 B3
Castellane F 132 B2
Castellaneta I 173 B2
Castellaneta Marina
 I 173 B2
Castellar E 157 B4
Castellarano I 135 A3
Castellar de la Frontera
 E 162 B2
Castellar de la Ribera
 E 147 B2
Castellar del Vallés
 E 147 C3
Castellar de Santiago
 E 157 B4
Castell Arquato I . .120 C2
Castell'Azzara I 135 C4
Castellbell i Villar
 E 147 C2
Castelldans E 153 A4
Castell de Cabres
 E 153 B4
Castell de Castells
 E 159 C3
Castelldefels E 147 C2
Castell de Ferro E . .163 B4
Castelleone I 120 B2
Castellet E 147 C2
Castelletto di Brenzone
 I 121 B3
Castellfollit de la Roca
 E 147 B3
Castellfollit de
 Riubregos E 147 C2
Castellfort E 153 B3
Castellina in Chianti
 I 135 B4
Castellina Marittima
 I 134 B3
Castellóde Farfaña
 E 145 C4
Castellóde la Plana
 E 159 B3
Castello d'Empúries
 E 147 B4
Castello di Fiemme
 I 121 A4
Castelloli E 147 C2
Castellón de Rugat
 E 159 C3
Castellote E 153 B3
Castello Tesino I . . .121 A4
Castellterçol E 147 C3
Castellúccio I 121 B3

Castellúccio de'Sáuri
 I 171 B3
Castelluccio Inferiore
 I 174 B1
Castelmassa I 121 B4
Castelmáuro I 170 B2
Castelmoron-sur-Lot
 F. 129 B3
Castelnaudary F . . .146 A2
Castelnau-de-Médoc
 F. 128 A2
Castelnau-de-
 Montmirail F 129 C4
Castelnau-Magnoac
 F. 145 A4
Castelnau-Montratier
 F. 129 B4
Castelnou E 153 A3
Castelnovo ne'Monti
 I 134 A3
Castelnuovo
 Berardenga I 135 B4
Castelnuovo della
 Dáunia I 170 B3
Castelnuovo di
 Garfagnana I 134 A3
Castelnuovo di Val di
 Cécina I 135 B3
Castelnuovo Don
 Bosco I 119 B4
Castelnuovo Scrivia
 I 120 C1
Castelo Branco
 Bragança P 149 A3
 Castelo Branco P. .155 B3
Castelo de Paiva
 P 148 A1
Castelo de Vide P. . .155 B3
Castelo do Neiva
 P 148 A1
Castelo Mendo P. . .149 B3
Castelraimondo I . .136 B2
Castel San Gimignano
 I 135 B4
Castèl San Giovanni
 I 120 B2
Castèl San Pietro
 Terme I 135 A4
Castelsantángelo
 I 136 C2
Castèl Sant'Elia I . .168 A2
Castelsaraceno I . . .174 A1
Castelsardo I 178 B2
Castelserás E 153 B3
Casteltérmini I 176 B2
Castelvecchio
 Subéquo I 169 A3
Castelvetrano I 176 B1
Castèl Volturno I . . .170 B1
Castenédolo I 120 B3
Castets F 128 C1
Castiádas I 179 C3
Castiglioncello I . . .134 B3
Castiglione I 169 A3
Castiglione Chiavarese
 I 134 A2
Castiglione d'Adda
 I 120 B2
Castiglione dei Pepoli
 I 135 A4
Castiglione del Lago
 I 135 B5
Castiglione della
 Pescáia I 135 C3
Castiglione delle
 Stiviere I 121 B3
Castiglione di Sicilia
 I 177 B4
Castiglione d'Órcia
 I 135 B4
Castiglione Messer
 Marino I 170 B2
Castiglione Messer
 Raimondo I 169 A3
Castiglion Fibocchi
 I 135 B4
Castiglion Fiorentino
 I 135 B4
Castilblanco E 156 A2
Castilblanco de los
 Arroyos E 161 B4
Castil de Peones
 E 143 B3
Castilfrío de la Sierra
 E 144 C1
Castilgaleu E 145 B4
Castilisar E 144 B2
Castilleja E 161 B3
Castillejar E 164 B2
Castillejo de Martin
 Viejo E 149 B3
Castillejo de Mesleón
 E 151 A4
Castillejo de Robledo
 E 151 A4
Castillfollit de la Roca
 E 147 B3
Castillo de Bayuela
 E 150 B3
Castillo de Locubín
 E 163 A4
Castillonès F 129 B3
Castillon-la-Bataille
 F. 128 B2
Castillon-Len-
 Couserans F 146 B2
Castillonroy E 145 C4
Castilruiz E 144 C1
Castione CH 120 A2
Castions di Strada
 I 122 B2
Castirla F 180 A2
Castlebar IRL. 28 A2
Castlebellingham
 IRL 27 C4
Castleblaney IRL 27 B4
Castlebridge IRL 30 B2
Castle Cary GB 43 A4
Castlecomer IRL. 30 B1
Castlederg GB 27 B3
Castledermot IRL 30 B2

Castle Douglas GB . .36 B3
Castleford GB 40 B2
Castleisland IRL 29 B2
Castlemaine IRL 29 B2
Castlemartyr IRL 29 C3
Castlepollard IRL . . .30 A1
Castlerea IRL. 28 A3
Castleton GB 40 B2
Castletown
 Highland GB 32 C3
 Isle of Man GB. . . .36 B2
Castletown Bearhaven
 IRL 29 C2
Castletownroche
 IRL. 29 B3
Castlewellan GB 27 B5
Casto I 120 B3
Castrejón E 150 A2
Castrelo del Valle
 E 141 B3
Castres F 130 B1
Castricum NL. 70 B1
Castries F 131 B2
Castrignano del Capo
 I 173 C4
Castril E 164 B2
Castrillo de Duero
 E 151 A4
Castrillo de la Vega
 E 143 C3
Castrillo de Onielo
 E 142 C2
Castro
 E 142 A2
 I 173 B4
Castrocabón E 141 B5
Castro-Caldelas E . .141 B3
Castrocaro Terme
 I 135 A4
Castrocontrigo E . . .141 B4
Castro Daire P 148 B2
Castro dei Volsci I . .169 B3
Castro del Rio E 163 A3
Castro de Rey E 141 A3
Castrofilippo I 176 B2
Castrogonzalo E . . .142 B1
Castrojeriz E 142 B2
Castroreale I 177 A4
Castroserracin E . . .151 A4
Castro-Urdiales E . .143 A3
Castro Verde P 160 B1
Castroverde de
 Campos E 142 C1
Castroverde de Cerrato
 E 142 C2
Castuera E 156 B2
Cataduj E 159 B3
Cataéggio I 120 A2
Çatalca TR 186 A3
Catallar TR. 189 C5
Çatalzeytin TR 23 A8
Catánia I 177 B4
Catanzaro I 175 C2
Catanzaro Marina
 I 175 C2
Catarroja E 159 B3
Catarruchos P 148 B1
Catcleugh GB 37 A4
Catenanuova I 177 B3
Caterham GB. 44 B3
Cati E 153 B4
Čatići BIH 139 A4
Catignano I 169 A3
Catillon F 91 A3
Catoira E 140 B2
Caton GB 37 B4
Catral E 165 A4
Catterick GB 37 B5
Cáttolica I 136 B1
Cáttolica Eraclea
 I 176 B2
Catton GB 37 B4
Caudebec-en-Caux
 F. 89 A4
Caudete E 159 C3
Caudete de las Fuentes
 E 159 B2
Caudiel E 159 B3
Caudiès-de-
 Fenouillèdes F . .146 B3
Caudry F 91 A3
Caulkerbush GB 36 B3
Caulnes F 101 A3
Caulónia I 175 C2
Caumont-l'Evente
 F. 88 A3
Caunes-Minervois
 F. 146 A3
Cauro F 180 B1
Caussade F 129 B4
Causse-de-la-Selle
 F. 130 B2
Cauterets F 145 B3
Cava de Tirreni I . . .170 C2
Cavaglia I 119 B5
Cavaillon F 131 B4
Cavalaire-sur-Mer
 F. 132 B2
Cavaleiro P 160 B1
Cavalese I 121 A4
Cavallermaggiore
 I 119 C4
Cavallino I 122 B1
Cavárzere I 121 B5
Çavdarhisar TR 187 C4
Çavdır TR. 189 B4
Cavernães P 148 B2
Cavezzo I 121 C4
Cavignac F 128 A2

Čavle HR 123 B3
Cavo I 134 C3
Cavour I 119 C4
Cawdor GB 32 D3
Çay TR 187 D6
Cayeux-sur-Mer F . .78 B1
Çayıralan TR 23 B8
Çayırhan TR. 187 B6
Caylus F 129 B4
Cayres F 117 C3
Cazalilla E 157 C4
Cazalla de la Sierra
 E 156 C2
Cazals F. 129 B4
Cazanuecos E 142 B1
Cazaubon F. 128 C2
Cazaux F 128 B1
Cazavet F 146 A2
Cazères F 146 A2
Cazin BIH 124 C1
Cazis CH 107 C4
Čazma HR 124 B2
Cazo E 142 A1
Cazorla E 164 B2
Cazouls-lès-Béziers
 F. 130 B2
Cea
 León E 142 B1
 Orense E 140 B3
Céanuri E 143 A4
Ceauce F 88 B3
Cebolla E 150 C3
Čebovce SK. 112 A3
Cebreros E 150 B3
Čečava BIH 125 C3
Ceccano I 169 B3
Cece H 112 C2
Cecenowo PL 68 A2
Čechtice CZ. 96 B3
Čechtín CZ. 97 B3
Cécina I 134 B3
Ceclavín E 155 B4
Cedégolo I 120 A3
Cedeira E 140 A2
Cedillo E 155 B3
Cedillo del Condado
 E 151 B4
Cedrillas E 153 B3
Cedynia PL 74 B3
Cée E 140 B1
Cefalù I 177 A3
Céggia I 122 B1
Cegléd H 113 B3
Ceglédbercel H 112 B3
Céglie Messápica
 I 173 B3
Cehegín E 164 A3
Ceilhes-et-Rocozels
 F. 130 B2
Ceinos de Campos
 E 142 B1
Ceira P 148 B1
Čejč CZ 97 C4
Cekcyn PL 76 A3
Cela BIH. 124 C2
Čelákovice CZ. 84 B2
Celano I 169 A3
Celanova E 140 B3
Celbridge IRL. 30 A2
Čelebič BIH 138 B2
Celenza Valfortore
 I 170 B2
Čelić BIH 125 C4
Čelinac BIH 124 C3
Celje SLO. 123 A4
Cella E 152 B2
Celldömölk H. 111 B4
Celle D. 72 B3
Celle Ligure I 133 A4
Celles B 79 B4
Celles-sur-Belle F . .115 B3
Cellino San Marco
 I 173 B3
Celorico da Beira
 P 148 B2
Celorico de Basto
 P 148 A1
Çeltik TR 187 C6
Çeltikçi TR 189 B5
Cemaes GB 38 A2
Cembra I 121 A4
Čemerno BIH 139 B4
Cenad RO 126 A2
Cencenighe Agordino
 I 121 A4
Cenei RO 126 B2
Ceneselli I 121 B4
Cenicero E 143 B4
Cenicientos E 150 B3
Censeau F 105 C5
Čenta SRB. 126 B2
Centallo I 133 A3
Centelles E 147 C3
Cento I 121 C4
Centúripe I 177 B3
Cepeda la Mora E . .150 B2
Cépet F 129 C4
Čepin HR 125 B4
Čepinski Martinci
 HR 125 B4
Cepovan SLO 122 A2
Ceprano I 169 B3
Čeralije HR 125 B3
Cerami I 177 B3
Cerano I 120 B1
Cérans Foulletourte
 F. 102 B2
Ceraso I 172 B1
Cerbaia I 135 B4
Cerbère F 146 B4
Cercadillo E 151 A5
Cercal
 Lisboa P 154 B1
 Setúbal P. 160 B1
Čerčany CZ 96 B2
Cerceda E 151 B4
Cercedilla E 151 B3
Cercemaggiore I . . .170 B2
Cercs E 147 B2

Cercy-la-Tour F 104 C2
Cerda I 176 B2
Cerdedo E 140 B2
Cerdeira P 149 B2
Cerdon F 103 B4
Cerea I 121 B4
Ceres
GB 35 B5
I 119 B4
Cerese I 121 B3
Ceresole-Reale I 119 B4
Cereste F 132 B1
Céret F 146 B3
Cerezo de Abajo
E 151 A4
Cerezo de Riotirón
E 143 B3
Cerfontaine B 79 B4
Cergy F 90 B2
Cerignola I 171 B3
Cérilly F 103 C4
Cerisiers F 104 A2
Cerizay F 114 B3
Çerkeş TR 23 A7
Çerkezköy TR 186 A3
Cerkije SLO 123 A3
Cerknica SLO 123 B3
Cerkno SLO 122 A2
Cerkwica PL 67 B4
Cerna HR 125 B4
Černá Hora CZ 97 B4
Cernavodă RO 17 C8
Cernay F 106 B2
Cerne Abbas GB 43 B4
Cernégula E 143 B3
Cernik HR 124 B3
Cernóbbio I 120 B2
Černošin CZ 95 B4
Cernovice CZ 96 B2
Cérons F 128 B2
Cerovlje HR 123 B3
Cerovo SK 99 C3
Cerqueto I 135 C5
Cerralbo E 149 B3
Cerreto d'Esi I 136 B1
Cerreto Sannita I 170 B2
Cerrigydrudion GB 38 A3
Cërrik AL 182 B1
Cerro Muriano E 156 B3
Certaldo I 135 B4
Certosa di Pésio I 133 A3
Cerva P 148 A2
Cervaro I 169 B3
Cervatos de la Cueza
E 142 B2
Červena Řečice CZ 97 B3
Červená-Skala SK 99 C4
Cervená Voda CZ 97 A4
Cerveny Kostelec
CZ 85 B4
Cervera E 147 C2
Cervera de la Cañada
E 152 A2
Cervera del Llano
E 158 B1
Cervera del Río Alhama
E 144 B2
Cervera de Pisuerga
E 142 B2
Cervéteri I 168 B2
Cérvia I 135 A5
Cerviáde les Garriques
E 147 C1
Cervignano del Friuli
I 122 B2
Cervinara I 170 B2
Cervione F 180 A2
Cervo E 141 A3
Cervon F 104 B2
Cesana Torinese I 119 C3
Cesarica HR 137 A4
Cesarò I 177 B3
Cesena I 135 A5
Cesenático I 135 A5
Cēsis LV 8 D4
Česká Belá CZ 97 B3
Česká Kamenice
CZ 84 B2
Česká Lípa CZ 84 B2
Česká Skalice CZ 85 B4
Česká Třebová CZ 97 B4
České Budějovice
CZ 96 C2
České Velenice CZ 96 C2
Český Brod CZ 96 A2
Český Dub CZ 84 B2
Český Krumlov CZ 96 C2
Český Těšín CZ 98 B2
Češljeva Bara
SRB 127 C3
Çeşme TR 188 A1
Cessenon F 130 B2
Cesson-Sévigné
F 101 A4
Cestas F 128 B2
Čestobrodica SRB 127 D2
Cesuras E 140 A2
Cetina E 152 A2
Cetin Grad HR 123 B4
Cetinje MNE 16 D3
Cetraro I 174 B1
Ceuti E 165 A3
Ceva I 133 A4
Cevico de la Torre
E 142 C2
Cevico Navero E 142 C2
Cevins F 118 B3
Cévio CH 119 A5
Cevizli TR 189 B6
Cewice PL 68 A2
Ceylan TR 189 C4
Ceyrat F 116 B3
Ceyzériat F 118 A2
Chaam NL 79 A4
Chabanais F 115 C4
Chabeuil F 117 C5
Chabielice PL 86 A3
Chablis F 104 B2
Châbons F 118 B2
Chabówka PL 99 B3
Chabreloche F 117 B3
Chabris F 103 B3
Chagford GB 42 B3
Chagny F 105 C3
Chagoda RUS 9 C9
Chaherrero E 150 B3
Chailland F 88 B3
Chaillé-les-Marais
F 114 B2
Chailles F 103 B3
Chailley F 104 A2
Chalabre F 146 B3
Chalais F 128 A3
Chalamont F 118 B2
Châlette-sur-Loing
F 103 A4
Chalindrey F 105 B4
Challacombe GB 42 A3
Challans F 114 B2
Challes-les-Eaux
F 118 B2
Chalmazel F 117 B3
Chalmoux F 104 C2
Chalonnes-sur-Loire
F 102 B1
Châlons-en-
Champagne F 91 C4
Chalon-sur-Saône
F 105 C3
Chalupy PL 69 A3
Châlus F 115 C4
Cham
CH 106 B3
D 95 B4
Chamberet F 116 B1
Chambéry F 118 B2
Chambilly F 117 A4
Chambley F 92 B1
Chambly F 90 B2
Chambois F 89 B4
Chambon-sur-Lac
F 116 B2
Chambon-sur-Voueize
F 116 A2
Chambord F 103 B3
Chamborigaud F 131 A2
Chamboulive F 116 B1
Chamerau D 95 B4
Chamonix-Mont Blanc
F 119 B3
Chamoux-sur-Gelon
F 118 B3
Champagnac-le-Vieux
F 117 B3
Champagney F 106 B1
Champagnole F 105 C4
Champagny-Mouton
F 115 B4
Champaubert F 91 C3
Champdeniers-St Denis
F 114 B3
Champdieu F 117 B4
Champdôtre F 105 B4
Champeix F 116 B3
Champéry CH 119 A3
Champigne F 102 B1
Champignelles F 104 B2
Champigny-sur-Veude
F 102 B2
Champlitte-et-le-Prelot
F 105 B4
Champoluc I 119 B4
Champoly F 117 B3
Champorcher I 119 B4
Champrond-en-Gâtine
F 89 B5
Champs-sur-Tarentaine
F 116 B2
Champs-sur-Yonne
F 104 B2
Champtoceaux F 101 B4
Chamrousse F 118 B2
Chamusca P 154 B2
Chanac F 130 A2
Chanaleilles F 117 C3
Chandler's Ford
GB 44 C2
Chandra GR 185 D7
Chandrexa de Queixa
E 141 B3
Chañe E 150 A3
Changy F 117 A3
Chania GR 185 D5
Channes F 104 B3
Chantada E 140 B3
Chantelle F 116 A3
Chantenay-St Imbert
F 104 C2
Chanteuges F 117 B3
Chantilly F 90 B2
Chantonnay F 114 B2
Chão de Codes P 154 B2
Chaource F 104 A3
Chapa E 140 B2
Chapareillan F 118 B2
Chapel en le Frith
GB 40 B2
Chapelle Royale F 103 A3
Chapelle-St Laurent
F 102 C1
Charbonnat F 104 C3
Chard GB 43 B4
Charenton-du-Cher
F 103 C4
Charlbury GB 44 B2
Charleroi B 79 B4
Charlestown
GB 42 B2
IRL 26 C2
Charlestown of
Aberlour GB 32 D3
Charleville IRL 29 B3
Charleville-Mézières
F 91 B4
Charlieu F 117 A4
Charlottenberg S 49 C4
Charlton Kings GB 44 B1
Charly F 90 C3
Charmes F 92 C2
Charmes-sur-Rhône
F 117 C4
Charmey CH 106 C2
Charminster GB 43 B4
Charmont-en-Beauce
F 103 A4
Charny F 104 B2
Charolles F 117 A4
Chârost F 103 C4
Charquemont F 106 B1
Charrin F 104 C2
Charroux F 115 B4
Chartres F 90 C1
Charzykow PL 68 B2
Chasseneuil-sur-
Bonnieure F 115 C4
Chassigny F 105 B4
Château-Arnoux
F 132 A2
Châteaubernard
F 115 C3
Châteaubourg F 101 A4
Châteaubriant F 101 B4
Château-Chinon
F 104 B2
Château-d'Oex
CH 106 C2
Château-d'Olonne
F 114 B2
Château-du-Loir
F 102 B2
Châteaudun F 103 A3
Châteaugiron F 101 A4
Château-Gontier
F 102 B1
Château-Landon
F 103 A4
Château-la-Vallière
F 102 B2
Château-l'Evêque
F 129 A3
Châteaulin F 100 A1
Châteaumeillant
F 103 C4
Châteauneuf
Nièvre F 104 B2
Saône-et-Loire F 117 A4
Châteauneuf-de-
Randon F 117 C3
Châteauneuf-d'Ille-et-
Vilaine F 88 B2
Châteauneuf-du-Faou
F 100 A2
Châteauneuf-du-Pape
F 131 A3
Châteauneuf-en-
Thymerais F 89 B5
Châteauneuf la-Forêt
F 116 B1
Châteauneuf-le-Rouge
F 132 B1
Châteauneuf-sur-
Charente F 115 C3
Châteauneuf-sur-Cher
F 103 C4
Châteauneuf-sur-Loire
F 103 B4
Châteauneuf-sur-
Sarthe F 102 B1
Châteauponsac F 115 B5
Château-Porcien F 91 B4
Châteauredon F 132 A2
Châteaurenard
Bouches du Rhône
F 131 B3
Loiret F 104 B1
Château-Renault
F 102 B2
Châteauroux F 103 C3
Châteauroux-les-Alpes
F 118 C3
Château-Salins F 92 C2
Château-Thierry F 91 B3
Châteauvillain F 105 A3
Châtel F 119 A3
Châtelaillon-Plage
F 114 B2
Châtelaudren F 100 A3
Châtel-Censoir F 104 B2
Châtel-de-Neuvre
F 116 A3
Châtelet B 79 B4
Châtelguyon F 116 B3
Châtellerault F 115 B4
Châtel-Montagne
F 117 A3
Châtel-St Denis
CH 106 C1
Châtel-sur-Moselle
F 92 C2
Châtelus-Malvaleix
F 116 A2
Châtenois F 105 A4
Châtenois-les-Forges
F 106 B1
Chatham GB 45 B4
Châtillon I 119 B4
Châtillon-Coligny
F 103 B4
Châtillon-en-Bazois
F 104 B2
Châtillon-en-Diois
F 118 C2
Châtillon-sur
Chalaronne F 117 A4
Châtillon-sur-Indre
F 103 C3
Châtillon-sur-Loire
F 103 B4
Châtillon-sur-Marne
F 91 B3
Châtillon-sur-Seine
F 104 B3
Châtres F 91 C3
Chatteris GB 45 A4
Chatton GB 37 A5
Chauchina E 163 A4
Chaudes-Aigues
F 116 C3
Chaudrey F 91 C4
Chauffailles F 117 A4
Chaulnes F 90 B2
Chaument Gistoux
B 79 B4
Chaumergy F 105 C4
Chaumont F 105 A4
Chaumont-en-Vexin
F 90 B1
Chaumont-Porcien
F 91 B4
Chaumont-sur-Aire
F 91 C5
Chaumont-sur-Loire
F 103 B3
Chaunay F 115 B4
Chauny F 90 B3
Chaussin F 105 C4
Chauvigny F 115 B4
Chavagnes-en-Paillers
F 114 B2
Chavanges F 91 C4
Chaves P 148 A2
Chavignon F 91 B3
Chazelles-sur-Lyon
F 117 B4
Chazey-Bons F 118 B2
Cheadle
Greater Manchester
GB 40 B1
Staffordshire GB 40 C2
Cheb CZ 83 B4
Chebsara RUS 9 C11
Checa E 152 B2
Chęciny PL 87 B4
Cheddar GB 43 A4
Cheddleton GB 40 B1
Chef-Boutonne F 115 B3
Cheles E 155 C3
Chella E 159 B3
Chelles F 90 C2
Chełm PL 13 C5
Chełmno
Kujawsko-Pomorskie
PL 76 A3
Wielkopolskie PL 76 B3
Chelmsford GB 45 B4
Chelmuzhi RUS 9 A9
Chełmża PL 76 A3
Cheltenham GB 44 B1
Chelva E 159 B2
Chémery F 103 B3
Chemery-sur-Bar F 91 B4
Chemillé F 102 B1
Chemin F 105 C4
Chemnitz D 83 B4
Chénerailles F 116 A2
Cheniménil F 105 A5
Chenonceaux F 103 B3
Chenôve F 105 B3
Chepelare BG 183 B6
Chepstow GB 39 C4
Chera E 159 B3
Cherasco I 119 C4
Cherbonnières F 115 C3
Cherbourg F 88 A2
Cherchiara di Calábria
I 174 B2
Cherepovets RUS 9 C10
Chernihiv UA 13 C9
Chernivtsi UA 17 A6
Chernobyl = Chornobyl
UA 13 C9
Chernyakhovsk
RUS 12 A4
Chéroy F 104 A1
Cherven BY 13 B8
Chervonohrad UA 13 C6
Cherykaw BY 13 B9
Chesham GB 44 B3
Cheshunt GB 44 B3
Chessy-lès-Pres
F 104 A2
Cheste E 159 B3
Chester GB 38 A4
Chesterfield GB 40 B2
Chester-le-Street
GB 37 B5
Chevagnes F 104 C2
Chevanceaux F 115 C3
Chevillon F 91 C5
Chevilly F 103 A3
Chew Magna GB 43 A4
Chézery-Forens F 118 A2
Chialamberto I 119 B4
Chiampo I 121 B4
Chianale I 119 C4
Chianciano Terme
I 135 B4
Chiaramonte Gulfi
I 177 B3
Chiaramonti I 178 B2
Chiaravalle I 136 B2
Chiaravalle Centrale
I 175 C2
Chiaréggio I 120 A2
Chiari I 120 B2
Chiasso CH 120 B2
Chiávari I 134 A2
Chiavenna I 120 A2
Chiché F 102 C1
Chichester GB 44 C3
Chiclana de la Frontera
E 162 B1
Chiclana de Segura
E 164 A1
Chiddingfold GB 44 B3
Chieri I 119 B4
Chiesa in Valmalenco
I 120 A2
Chieti I 169 A4
Chieti Scalo I 169 A4
Chiéuti I 171 B3
Chigwell GB 45 B4
Chiliomodi GR 184 B3
Chillarón de Cuenca
E 152 B1
Chillarón del Rey
E 151 B5
Chilleurs-aux-Bois
F 103 A4
Chillón E 156 B3
Chilluevar E 164 B1
Chiloeches E 151 B4
Chimay B 91 A4
Chimeneas E 163 A4
Chinchilla de Monte
Aragón E 158 C2
Chinchón E 151 B4
Chingford GB 45 B4
Chinon F 102 B2
Chióggia I 122 B1
Chiomonte I 119 B3
Chipiona E 161 C3
Chippenham GB 43 A4
Chipping Campden
GB 44 A2
Chipping Norton
GB 44 B2
Chipping Ongar
GB 45 B4
Chipping Sodbury
GB 43 A4
Chirac F 130 A2
Chirbury GB 39 B3
Chirens F 118 B2
Chirivel E 164 B2
Chirk GB 38 B3
Chirnside GB 35 C5
Chişinău = Khisinev
MD 17 B8
Chişineu Criş RO 113 C5
Chissey-en-Morvan
F 104 B3
Chiusa I 108 C2
Chiusa di Pésio I 133 A3
Chiusaforte I 122 A2
Chiusa Sclafani I 176 B2
Chiusi I 135 B4
Chiva E 159 B3
Chivasso I 119 B4
Chlewiska PL 87 A4
Chludowo PL 75 B5
Chlumec nad Cidlinou
CZ 84 B3
Chlum u Třeboně
CZ 96 C2
Chmielnik PL 87 B4
Chobienia PL 85 A4
Chobienice PL 75 B4
Choceň CZ 97 A4
Choceń PL 77 B4
Chochołow PL 99 B3
Chocianów PL 85 A3
Chociw PL 86 A3
Chociwel PL 75 A4
Choczewo PL 68 A2
Chodaków PL 77 B5
Chodecz PL 77 B4
Chodov CZ 83 B4
Chodzież PL 75 B5
Chojna PL 74 B3
Chojnice PL 68 B2
Chojno
Kujawsko-Pomorskie
PL 77 B4
Wielkopolskie PL 75 B5
Chojnów PL 85 A3
Cholet F 114 A3
Chomérac F 117 C4
Chomutov CZ 83 B5
Chop UA 12 D5
Chora GR 184 B2
Chora Sfakion GR 185 D5
Chorges F 132 A2
Chorley GB 38 A4
Chornobyl = Chernobyl
UA 13 C9
Chortkiv UA 13 D6
Chorzele PL 77 A5
Chorzew PL 86 A2
Chorzów PL 86 B2
Choszczno PL 75 A4
Chotěboř CZ 97 B3
Chouilly F 91 B4
Chouto P 154 B2
Chouzy-sur-Cisse
F 103 B3
Chozas de Abajo
E 142 B1
Chrast CZ 97 B3
Chrást CZ 96 B1
Chrastava CZ 84 B2
Chřibská CZ 84 B2
Christchurch GB 44 C2
Christiansfeld DK 59 C2
Chroberz PL 87 B4
Chropyně CZ 98 B1
Chrudim CZ 97 B3
Chrzanów PL 86 B3
Chtelnica SK 98 C1
Chudovo RUS 9 C7
Chueca E 157 A4
Chulmleigh GB 42 B3
Chur CH 107 C4
Church Stretton
GB 39 B4
Churriana E 163 B3
Churwalden CH 107 C4
Chvalšiny CZ 96 C2
Chwaszczyno PL 69 A3
Chynava CZ 96 A2
Chýnov CZ 96 B2
Ciacova RO 126 B3
Ciadîr-Lunga MD 17 B8
Ciadoncha E 143 B3
Cianciana I 176 B2
Ciano d'Enza I 134 A3
Ciążen PL 76 B2
Cibakhaza H 113 C4
Ciborro P 154 C2
Cicagna I 134 A2
Cicciano I 170 C2
Ciciliano I 169 B2
Cicognolo I 120 B3
Cidadelhe P 149 B2
Cide TR 23 A7
Cidones E 143 C4
Ciechanów
Dolnośląskie PL 85 A4
Mazowieckie PL 77 B5
Ciechocinek PL 76 B3
Cielądz PL 87 A4
Ciemnik PL 75 A4
Ciempozuelos E 151 B4
Ciepielów PL 87 A5
Čierny Balog SK 99 C3
Cierp-Gaud F 145 B4
Cierpice PL 76 B3
Ciervana E 143 A3
Cierznie PL 68 B2
Cieslé PL 77 B5
Cieszyn PL 98 B2
Cieutat F 145 A4
Cieza E 165 A3
Cifer SK 98 C1
Çifteler TR 187 C6
Cifuentes E 151 B5
Cigales E 142 C2
Cigliano I 119 B5
Cihanbeyli TR 23 B7
Cillas E 152 B2
Cilleros E 149 B3
Cilleruelo de Arriba
E 143 C3
Cilleruelo de Bezana
E 143 B3
Cimalmotto CH 119 A5
Cimanes del Tejar
E 141 B5
Ciminna I 176 B2
Cimişlia MD 17 B8
Cimoláis I 122 A1
Cîmpulung RO 17 C6
Çınarcık TR 186 B4
Cinctorres E 153 B3
Cinderford GB 39 C4
Çine TR 188 B3
Činěves CZ 84 B3
Ciney B 79 B5
Cinfães P 148 A1
Cingia de Botti I 120 B3
Cingoli I 136 B2
Cinigiano I 135 C4
Cinobaňa SK 99 C3
Cinq-Mars-la-Pile
F 102 B2
Cinquefrondi I 175 C2
Cintegabelle F 146 A2
Cintruénigo E 144 B2
Ciółkowo PL 77 B4
Ciperez E 149 B3
Cirat E 153 B3
Cirella I 174 B1
Cirencester GB 44 B2
Cirey-sur-Vezouze
F 92 C2
Ciria E 152 A2
Ciriè I 119 B4
Cirigliano I 174 A2
Cirò I 174 B3
Cirò Marina I 174 B3
Ciry-le-Noble F 104 C3
Cislău RO 17 C7
Cismon del Grappa
I 121 B4
Cisneros E 142 B2
Cissac-Médoc F 128 A2
Čista CZ 96 A1
Cisterna di Latina
I 169 B2
Cistérniga E 150 A3
Cisternino I 173 B3
Cistierna E 142 B1
Čitluk BIH 139 B3
Cítov CZ 84 B2
Cittadella I 121 B4
Cittàdella Pieve I 135 C5
Cittàdel Vaticano =
Vatican City I 168 B2
Cittàdi Castello I 135 B5
Cittaducale I 169 A2
Cittanova I 175 C2
Città Sant'Angelo
I 169 A4
Ciudadela de Menorca
E 167 B3
Ciudad Real E 157 B4
Ciudad Rodrigo E 149 B3
Cividale del Friuli
I 122 A2
Cívita I 169 A3
Cívita Castellana I 168 A2
Civitanova Alta I 136 B2
Civitanova Marche
I 136 B2
Civitavécchia I 168 A1
Civitella di Romagna
I 135 A4
Civitella di Tronto
I 136 C2
Civitella Roveto I 169 B3
Civray F 115 B4
Çivril TR 189 A4
Cizur Mayor E 144 B2
Cjutadilla E 147 C2
Clabhach GB 34 B1
Clachan GB 31 B2
Clachan na Luib
GB 31 B1
Clacton-on-Sea GB 45 B5
Cladich GB 34 B2
Claggan GB 34 B2
Clairvaux-les-Lacs
F 105 C4
Clamecy F 104 B2
Claonaig GB 34 C2
Clarecastle IRL 28 B3
Claregalway IRL 28 A3
Claremorris IRL 28 A2
Clarinbridge IRL 28 A3
Clashmore
GB 32 D2
IRL 29 B4
Claudy GB 27 B3
Clausthal-Zellerfeld
D 82 A2
Cláut I 122 A1
Clay Cross GB 40 B2
Claye-Souilly F 90 C2
Cléder F 100 A1
Cleethorpes GB 41 B3
Clefmont F 105 A4
Cléguérec F 100 A2
Clelles F 118 C2
Clenze D 73 B3
Cleobury Mortimer
GB 39 B4
Cléon-d'Andran F 117 C4
Cléré-les-Pins F 102 B2
Clères F 89 A5
Clermont F 90 B2
Clermont-en-Argonne
F 91 B5
Clermont-Ferrand
F 116 B3
Clermont-l'Hérault
F 130 B2
Clerval F 105 B5
Clervaux L 92 A2
Clèry-St André F 103 B3
Cles I 121 A4
Clevedon GB 43 A4
Cleveleys GB 38 A3
Cley GB 41 C5
Clifden IRL 28 A1
Clifford GB 39 B3
Clisson F 101 B4
Clitheroe GB 40 B1
Clogh IRL 30 B1
Cloghan
Donegal IRL 26 B3
Offaly IRL 28 A4
Clogheen IRL 29 B4
Clogher GB 27 B3
Cloghjordan IRL 28 B3
Clohars-Carnoët
F 100 B2
Clonakilty IRL 29 C3
Clonaslee IRL 30 A1
Clondalkin IRL 30 A2
Clones IRL 27 B3
Clonmany IRL 27 A3
Clonmel IRL 29 B4
Clonmellon IRL 30 A1
Clonord IRL 30 A1
Clonroche IRL 30 B2
Cloone IRL 26 C3
Cloppenburg D 71 B5
Closeburn GB 36 A3
Clough GB 27 B5
Clova GB 35 B4
Clovelly GB 42 B2
Clowne GB 40 B2
Cloyes-sur-le-Loir
F 103 B3
Cloyne IRL 29 C3
Cluis F 103 C3
Cluj-Napoca RO 17 B5
Clun GB 39 B3
Clunes GB 34 B3
Cluny F 117 A4
Cluses F 118 A3
Clusone I 120 B2
Clydach GB 39 C3
Clydebank GB 34 C3
Coachford IRL 29 C3
Coagh GB 27 B4
Coalisland GB 27 B4
Coalville GB 40 C2
Coaña E 141 A4
Çobanlar TR 187 D5
Cobas E 140 A2
Cobertelade E 151 A5
Cobeta E 152 B1
Cóbh IRL 29 C3
Cobreces E 142 A2
Coburg D 82 B2
Coca E 150 A3
Cocentaina E 159 C3
Cochem D 80 B3
Cockburnspath GB 35 C5
Cockermouth GB 36 B3
Codigoro I 121 C5
Codogno I 120 B2
Codos E 152 A2
Codróipo I 122 B1
Codrongianos I 178 B2
Coelhoso P 149 A3
Coesfeld D 71 C4
Coevorden NL 71 B3
Cofrentes E 159 B2
Cogeces del Monte
E 150 A3
Coggeshall GB 45 B4
Cognac F 115 C3
Cogne I 119 B4
Cognin F 118 B2
Cogolin F 132 B2
Cogollos de Guadix
E 164 B1
Cogollos-Vega E 163 A4
Cogolludo E 151 B4
Coimbra P 148 B1
Coin E 163 B3
Coirós E 140 A2
Čoka SRB 126 B2
Col SLO 123 B3
Colares P 154 C1
Cölbe D 81 B4
Colbitz D 73 B4
Colchester GB 45 B4
Coldingham GB 35 C5
Colditz D 83 A4
Coldstream GB 35 C5
Colebrooke GB 43 B3
Colera E 146 B4
Coleraine GB 27 A4
Colfiorito I 136 B1
Cólico I 120 A2
Coligny F 118 A2
Colindres E 143 A3
Collado-Mediano
E 151 B3
Collado Villalba E 151 B4

Collagna I 134 A3
Collanzo E 142 A1
Collat F 117 B3
Coll de Nargó E . . 147 B2
Colléchio I 120 C3
Colledimezzo I . . . 169 B4
Colle di Val d'Elsa
 I 135 B4
Colleferro I 169 B3
Colle Isarco I . . . 108 C2
Collelongo I 169 B3
Collepasso I 173 B4
Collepepe I 136 C1
Collesalvetti I . . . 134 B3
Colle Sannita I . . . 170 B2
Collesano I 176 B2
Colli a Volturno I . 169 B4
Collin GB 36 A3
Collinée F 101 A3
Collingham
 Nottinghamshire
 GB 40 B2
 West Yorkshire
 GB 40 B3
Collinghorst D . . . 71 A4
Cóllio I 120 B3
Collobrières F . . . 132 B2
Collon IRL 27 C4
Collooney IRL . . . 26 B2
Colmar F 106 A2
Colmars F 132 A2
Colmenar E 163 B3
Colmenar de la Sierra
 E 151 B4
Colmenar de Oreja
 E 151 B4
Colmenar Viejo E . 151 B4
Colmonel GB 36 A2
Colne GB 40 B1
Colobraro I 174 A2
Cologna Véneta I . . 121 B4
Cologne = Köln D . . 80 B2
Cologne F 129 C3
Cologne al Serio I . 120 B2
Colombey-les-Belles
 F 92 C1
Colombey-les-deux-
 Églises F 105 A3
Colombres E 142 A2
Colomera E 163 A4
Colomers E 147 B3
Colomiers F 129 C4
Colònia de Sant Jordi
 E 167 B3
Colorno I 120 C3
Colos P 160 B1
Cölpin D 74 A2
Colpy GB 33 D4
Colsterworth GB . . 40 C3
Coltishall GB 41 C5
Colunga E 142 A1
Colwell GB 37 A4
Colwyn Bay GB . . . 38 A3
Colyford GB 43 B3
Comácchio I 121 C5
Coma-ruga E 147 C2
Combarros E 141 B4
Combeaufontaine
 F 105 B4
Comber GB 27 B5
Comblain-au-Pont
 B 80 B1
Combloux F 118 B3
Combourg F 88 B2
Combronde F 116 B3
Comeglians I 109 C3
Comillas E 142 A2
Comines F 78 B3
Cómiso I 177 C3
Comloșu Mare RO 126 B2
Commensacq F . . . 128 B2
Commentry F 116 A2
Commerau D 84 A2
Commercy F 92 C1
Como I 120 B2
Cómpeta E 163 B4
Compiègne F 90 B2
Comporta P 154 C2
Comps-sur-Artuby
 F 132 B2
Comrat MD 17 B8
Comrie GB 35 B4
Comunanza I 136 C2
Cona
 Emilia Romagna
 I 121 C4
 Veneto I 121 B5
Concarneau F 100 B2
Conceição P 160 B1
Conches-en-Ouche
 F 89 B4
Concordia Sagittária
 I 122 B1
Concordia sulla
 Sécchia I 121 C3
Concots F 129 B4
Condat F 116 B2
Condé-en-Brie F . . 91 C3
Condeixa P 148 B1
Condemios de Abajo
 E 151 A4
Condemios de Arriba
 E 151 A4
Condé-sur-l'Escaut
 F 79 B3
Conde-sur-Marne F 91 B4
Condé-sur-Noireau
 F 88 B3
Condino I 121 B3
Condom F 129 C3
Condove I 119 B4
Condrieu F 117 B4
Conegliano I 122 B1
Conflans-sur-Lanterne
 F 105 B5
Confolens F 115 B4
Conforto E 141 A3

Cong IRL 28 A2
Congleton GB 40 B1
Congosto E 141 B4
Congosto de Valdavia
 E 142 B2
Congostrina E . . . 151 A4
Conil de la Frontera
 E 162 B1
Coningsby GB 41 B3
Coniston GB 36 B3
Conlie F 102 A1
Conliège F 105 C4
Conna IRL 29 B3
Connah's Quay GB 38 A3
Connantre F 91 C3
Connaugh IRL . . . 28 B3
Connaux F 131 A3
Connel GB 34 B2
Connerré F 102 A2
Cononbridge GB . . 32 D2
Čonoplja SRB . . . 126 B1
Conques F 116 C2
Conques-sur-Orbiel
 F 146 A3
Conquista E 157 B3
Conquista de la Sierra
 E 156 A2
Consándolo I 121 C4
Consélice I 135 A4
Conselve I 121 B4
Consenvoye F 91 B5
Consett GB 37 B5
Consolacão P 154 B1
Constancia P 154 B2
Constanco E 140 A2
Constanța RO 17 C8
Constanti E 147 C2
Constantina E . . . 162 A2
Consuegra E 157 A4
Consuma I 135 B4
Contarina I 122 B1
Contay F 90 B2
Conthey CH 119 A4
Contigliano I 168 A2
Contis-Plage F . . . 128 B1
Contres F 103 B3
Contrexéville F . . . 105 A4
Controne I 172 B1
Contursi Termi I . . 172 B1
Conty F 90 B2
Conversano I 173 B3
Conwy GB 38 A3
Cookstown GB . . . 27 B4
Coole F 91 C4
Coolgreany IRL . . . 30 B2
Cooneen GB 27 B3
Cootehill IRL 27 B3
Cope E 165 B3
Copenhagen =
 København DK . . 61 D2
Copertino I 173 B4
Copparo I 121 C4
Coppenbrugge D . . 72 B2
Corabia RO 17 D6
Córaci I 175 B2
Coralići BIH 124 C1
Corato I 171 B4
Corbeil-Essonnes
 F 90 C2
Corbeny F 91 B3
Corbera E 159 B3
Corbie F 90 B2
Corbigny F 104 B2
Corbion B 91 B4
Corby GB 40 C3
Corconte E 143 A3
Corcubión E 140 B1
Corcumello I 169 A3
Cordenòns I 122 B1
Cordes-sur-Ciel F . 129 B4
Córdoba E 156 C3
Cordobilla de Lácara
 E 155 B4
Cordovado I 122 B1
Corella E 144 B2
Coreses E 150 A2
Corfe Castle GB . . 43 B4
Corga de Lobão
 P 148 B1
Cori I 169 B2
Coria E 155 B4
Coria del Rio E . . 162 A1
Corigliano Cálabro
 I 174 B2
Corinaldo I 136 B1
Corinth = Korinthos
 GR 184 B3
Cório I 119 B4
Coripe E 162 B2
Cork IRL 29 C3
Corlay F 100 A2
Corleone I 176 B2
Corleto Monforte I 172 B1
Corleto Perticara I 174 A2
Çorlu TR 186 A2
Cormainville F . . . 103 A3
Cormeilles F 89 A4
Cormery F 102 B2
Cormòns I 122 B2
Cormoz F 118 A2
Cornago E 144 B1
Cornberg D 82 A1
Cornellana E 141 A4
Corneşti MD 17 B7
Corniglio I 134 A3
Cornimont F 106 B1
Corniolo I 135 B4
Cornuda I 121 B5
Cornudella de
 Montsant E . . . 147 C1
Cornudilla E 143 B3
Cornus F 130 B2
Çorovodë AL 182 C2
Corpach GB 34 B2
Corps F 118 C2
Corps Nuds F . . . 101 B4

Corral de Almaguer
 E 157 A4
Corral de Ayllon E 151 A4
Corral de Calatrava
 E 157 B3
Corrales E 149 A4
Corral-Rubio E . . . 158 C2
Corran GB 34 B2
Corredoiras E . . . 140 A2
Corréggio I 121 C3
Corridónia I 136 B2
Corris GB 38 B3
Corrubedo E 140 B1
Córsico I 120 B2
Corsock GB 36 A3
Corte F 180 A2
Corteconceptión
 E 161 B3
Corte de Peleas E 155 C4
Cortegaca P 148 B1
Cortegada E 140 B2
Cortegana E 161 B3
Cortemaggiore I . . 120 B2
Cortemilia I 133 A4
Corte Pinto P 160 B2
Cortes E 144 C2
Cortes de Aragón
 E 153 B3
Cortes de Arenoso
 E 153 B3
Cortes de Baza E 164 B2
Cortes de la Frontera
 E 162 B2
Cortes de Pallás
 E 159 B3
Cortiçadas P 154 C2
Cortico P 148 A2
Cortijo de Arriba
 E 157 A3
Cortijos Nuevos E 164 A2
Cortina d'Ampezzo
 I 108 C3
Corton GB 41 C5
Cortona I 135 B4
Coruche P 154 C2
Corullón E 141 B4
Çorum TR 23 A8
Corvara in Badia I 108 C2
Corvera E 165 B3
Corwen GB 38 B3
Cosenza I 174 B2
Cosham GB 44 C2
Coslada E 151 B4
Cosne-Cours-sur-Loire
 F 104 B1
Cosne d'Allier F . . 103 C4
Cospeito E 140 A3
Cossato I 119 B5
Cossaye F 104 C2
Cossé-le-Vivien F . 101 B5
Cossonay CH 105 C5
Costa da Caparica
 P 154 C1
Costa de Santo André
 P 160 A1
Costalpino I 135 B4
Costa Nova P 148 B1
Costaros F 117 C3
Costeşti RO 17 C6
Costigliole d'Asti
 I 119 C5
Costigliole Saluzzo
 I 133 A3
Coswig
 Sachsen D 83 A5
 Sachsen-Anhalt D . 83 A4
Cotherstone GB . . 37 B5
Cotronei I 175 B2
Cottbus D 84 A2
Cottenham GB . . . 45 A4
Cottingham GB . . . 40 B3
Coublanc F 105 B4
Couches F 104 C3
Couço P 154 C2
Coucouron F 117 C3
Coucy-le-Château-
 Auffrique F 90 B3
Couëron F 101 B4
Couflens F 146 B2
Couhé F 115 B4
Couiza F 146 B3
Coulags GB 31 B3
Coulanges F 104 C3
Coulanges-la-Vineuse
 F 104 B2
Coulanges-sur-Yonne
 F 104 B2
Couleuvre F 104 C1
Coulmier-le-Sec F 104 B3
Coulommiers F . . . 90 C3
Coulonges-sur-l'Autize
 F 114 B3
Coulounieix-Chamiers
 F 129 A3
Coulport GB 34 B3
Coupar Angus GB . 35 B4
Coupéville F 91 C4
Couptrain F 89 B3
Coura P 140 C2
Courcelles B 79 B4
Courcelles-Chaussy
 F 92 B2
Courchevel F 118 B3
Cour-Cheverny F . 103 B3
Courçôme F 115 C4
Courçon F 114 B3
Cournon-d'Auvergne
 F 116 B3
Cournonterral F . . 130 B2
Courpière F 117 B3
Coursan F 130 B2
Courseulles-sur-Mer
 F 89 A3
Cours-la-Ville F . . 117 A4

Courson-les-Carrières
 F 104 B2
Courtalain F 103 A3
Courtenay F 104 A2
Courtomer F 89 B4
Courville
 Eure-et-Loire F . . 89 B5
 Marne F 91 B3
Coussac-Bonneval
 F 115 C5
Coutances F 88 A2
Couterne F 89 B3
Coutras F 128 A2
Couvet CH 106 C1
Couvin B 91 A4
Couzon F 104 C2
Covadonga E 142 A1
Covaleda E 143 C4
Covarrubias E . . . 143 B3
Covas P 148 A1
Cove GB 31 B3
Coventry GB 44 A2
Coverack GB 42 B1
Covigliáio I 135 A4
Covilhã P 148 B2
Cowbridge GB . . . 39 C3
Cowdenbeath GB . 35 B4
Cowes GB 44 C2
Cox F 129 C4
Cózar E 157 B4
Cozes F 114 C3
Cozzano F 180 B2
Craco I 174 A2
Cracow = Kraków
 PL 99 A3
Craibstone GB . . . 33 D4
Craighouse GB . . . 34 C2
Craignure GB . . . 34 B2
Crail GB 35 B5
Crailsheim D 94 B2
Craiova RO 17 C5
Cramlington GB . . 37 A5
Cranleigh GB 44 B3
Craon F 101 B5
Craonne F 91 B3
Craponne F 117 B4
Craponne-sur-Arzon
 F 117 B3
Crathie GB 32 D3
Crato P 154 B3
Craughwell IRL . . . 28 A3
Craven Arms GB . . 39 B4
Crawford GB 36 A3
Crawinkel D 82 B2
Crawley GB 44 B3
Creag Ghoraidh
 GB 31 B1
Crecente E 140 B2
Crèches-sur-Saône
 F 117 A4
Crécy-en-Ponthieu
 F 78 B1
Crécy-la-Chapelle
 F 90 C2
Crécy-sur-Serre F . 91 B3
Crediton GB 43 B3
Creeslough IRL . . 26 A3
Creetown GB 36 B2
Creeve GB 27 B4
Creglingen D 94 B2
Creil F 90 B2
Creissels F 130 A2
Crema I 120 B2
Cremeaux F 117 B3
Crémenes E 142 B1
Crémieu F 118 B2
Cremlingen D 73 B3
Cremona I 120 B3
Creney F 91 C4
Črenšovci SLO . . . 111 C3
Créon F 128 B2
Crepaja SRB 127 B2
Crépey F 92 C1
Crépy F 91 B3
Crépy-en-Valois F . 90 B2
Cres HR 123 C3
Crescentino I 119 B5
Crespino I 121 C4
Crespos E 150 B3
Cressage GB 39 B4
Cressensac F 129 A4
Cressia F 105 C4
Crest F 117 C5
Cresta CH 107 C4
Créteil F 90 C2
Creully F 88 A3
Creussen D 95 B3
Creutzwald F 92 B2
Creuzburg D 82 A2
Crevalcore I 121 C4
Crèvecoeur-le-Grand
 F 90 B2
Crevillente E 165 A4
Crévola d'Ossola
 I 119 A5
Crewe GB 38 A4
Crewkerne GB . . . 43 B4
Criales E 143 B3
Crianlarich GB . . . 34 B3
Criccieth GB 38 B2
Crickhowell GB . . 39 C3
Cricklade GB 44 B2
Crieff GB 35 B4
Criel-sur-Mer F . . 90 A1
Crikvenica HR . . . 123 B3
Crillon F 90 B1
Crimmitschau D . . 83 B4
Crimond GB 33 D5
Crinitz D 84 A1
Cripán E 143 B4
Criquetot-l'Esneval
 F 89 A4
Crispiano I 173 B3
Crissolo I 119 C4
Cristóbal E 149 B4
Črna SLO 110 C1
Crna Bara
 Srbija SRB 127 C1
 Vojvodina SRB . . 126 B2

Crnac HR 125 B3
Crnča SRB 127 C1
Crni Lug
 BIH 138 A2
 HR 123 B3
Crni Vrh SLO 123 B3
Crnjelovo Donje
 BIH 125 C5
Črnomelj SLO . . . 123 B4
Crocketford GB . . 36 A3
Crocq F 116 B2
Crodo I 119 A5
Croglin GB 37 B4
Crolly IRL 26 A2
Cromarty GB 32 D2
Cromer GB 41 C5
Cronat F 104 C2
Crookhaven IRL . . 29 C2
Crookstown IRL . . 29 C3
Croom IRL 29 B3
Cropalati I 174 B2
Crópani I 175 C2
Crosbost GB 31 A2
Crosby GB 38 A3
Crosia I 174 B2
Crossakiel IRL . . . 27 C3
Cross-Hands GB . . 39 C2
Crosshaven IRL . . 29 C3
Crosshill GB 36 A2
Crossmolina IRL . . 26 B1
Crotone I 175 B3
Crottendorf D . . . 83 B4
Crouy F 90 B3
Crowborough GB . 45 B4
Crowland GB 41 C3
Crowthorne GB . . 44 B3
Croyde GB 42 A2
Croydon GB 44 B3
Crozon F 100 A1
Cruas F 117 C4
Cruceni RO 126 A3
Crúcoli I 174 B3
Cruden Bay GB . . 33 D5
Crudgington GB . . 38 B4
Cruis F 132 A1
Crumlin GB 27 B4
Cruseilles F 118 A3
Crusheen IRL . . . 28 B3
Cruz de Incio E . . 141 B3
Crvenka SRB 126 B1
Crveny Kamen SK . 98 B2
Csabacsüd H 113 C4
Csabrendek H . . . 111 B4
Csákánydoroszló
 H 111 C3
Csákvár H 112 B2
Csanádapáca H . . 113 C4
Csanádpalota H . . 126 A2
Csány H 113 B3
Csanytelek H 113 C4
Csapod H 111 B3
Császár H 112 B2
Császártöltés H . . 112 C3
Csávoly H 125 A5
Csemő H 113 B3
Csengőd H 112 C3
Csépa H 113 C4
Csepreg H 111 B3
Cserkeszölö H . . . 113 C4
Csernely H 113 A4
Csesztreg H 111 C3
Csökmö H 113 B5
Csököly H 124 A3
Csokonyavisonta
 H 124 A3
Csólyospálos H . . 113 C3
Csongrád H 113 C4
Csopak H 112 C1
Csorna H 111 B4
Csorvás H 113 C4
Csurgo H 124 A3
Cuacos de Yuste
 E 150 B2
Cualedro E 140 C3
Cuanca de Campos
 E 142 B1
Cuba P 160 A2
Cubel E 152 A2
Cubelles E 147 C2
Cubillos E 143 C4
Cubillos del Sil E . 141 B4
Cubjac F 129 A3
Cubo de la Solana
 E 152 A1
Çubuk TR 23 A7
Cuckfield GB 44 B3
Cucuron F 131 B4
Cudillero E 141 A4
Cuéllar E 151 A3
Cuenca E 152 B1
Cuers F 132 B2
Cuerva E 157 A3
Cueva de Agreda
 E 144 C2
Cuevas Bajas E . . 163 A3
Cuevas del Almanzora
 E 164 B3
Cuevas del Becerro
 E 162 B2
Cuevas del Campo
 E 164 B2
Cuevas del Valle
 E 150 B2
Cuevas de San
 Clemente E . . . 143 B3
Cuevas de San Marcos
 E 163 A3
Cuges-les-Pins F . 132 B1
Cúglieri I 178 B2
Cugnaux F 129 C4
Cuijk NL 80 A1
Cuinzier F 117 A4
Cuiseaux F 105 C4
Cuisery F 105 C4
Culan F 103 C4
Culemborg NL . . . 79 A5
Cúllar E 164 B2
Cullaville GB 27 B4
Cullera E 159 B3
Cullivoe GB 33 A5

Cullompton GB . . . 43 B3
Cully CH 106 C1
Culoz F 118 B2
Cults GB 33 D4
Cumbernauld GB . 35 C4
Cumbres de San
 Bartolomé E . . . 161 A3
Cumbres Mayores
 E 161 A3
Cumiana I 119 C4
Ćumić SRB 127 C2
Cumnock GB 36 A2
Çumra TR 23 C7
Cunlhat F 117 B3
Cunski HR 123 C3
Cuntis E 140 B2
Cuorgnè I 119 B4
Cupar GB 35 B4
Cupello I 170 A2
Cupra Maríttima I . 136 B2
Cupramontana I . . 136 B2
Čuprija SRB 127 D3
Curinga I 175 C2
Currelos E 140 B3
Currie GB 35 C4
Curtea de Argeş
 RO 17 C6
Curtici RO 126 A3
Curtis E 140 A2
Curtis Santa Eulalia
 E 140 A2
Čurug SRB 126 B2
Cusano Mutri I . . . 170 B2
Cushendall GB . . . 27 A4
Cusset F 117 A3
Cussy-les-Forges
 F 104 B3
Custines F 92 C2
Cutanda E 152 B2
Cutro I 175 B2
Cutrofiano I 173 B4
Cuts F 90 B3
Cuvilly F 90 B2
Cuxhaven D 64 C1
Cvikov CZ 84 B2
Cwmbran GB 39 C3
Cybinka PL 75 B3
Czacz PL 75 B5
Czajków PL 86 A2
Czaplinek PL 75 A5
Czarlin PL 69 A3
Czarna-Dąbrówka
 PL 68 A2
Czarna Woda PL . . 68 B3
Czarnca PL 87 B3
Czarne PL 68 B1
Czarnków PL 75 B5
Czarnowo PL 76 A3
Czarnozyly PL . . . 86 A2
Czarny Bór PL . . . 85 B4
Czarny-Dunajec PL 99 B3
Czarny Las PL . . . 86 A1
Czchów PL 99 B4
Czechowice-Dziedzice
 PL 98 B2
Czempiń PL 75 B5
Czermno PL 87 A4
Czernichow PL . . . 99 B3
Czerniejewo PL . . 76 B2
Czernikowo PL . . . 76 B3
Czersk PL 68 B2
Czerwieńsk PL . . . 75 B4
Czerwionka-Leszczyny
 PL 86 B2
Częstochowa PL . . 86 B3
Czeszewo PL 76 B2
Człopa PL 75 A5
Człuchów PL 68 B2
Czołpino PL 68 A2

D

Dağ TR 189 B5
Daaden D 81 B3
Dabas H 112 B3
Dąbie PL 76 B3
Dąbki PL 67 B5
Dabo F 92 C3
Dabrowa PL 76 B2
Dąbrowa Górnicza
 PL 86 B3
Dąbrowa Tarnowska
 PL 87 B4
Dąbrowice PL . . . 77 B4
Dabrowice PL . . . 77 A5
Dachau D 108 A2
Dačice CZ 97 B3
Daday TR 23 A7
Dagali N 47 B5
Dägebüll D 64 B1
Dagmersellen CH . 106 B2
Dahlen D 83 A4
Dahlenburg D . . . 73 A3
Dahme D 83 A5
Dahn D 93 B3
Dähre D 73 B3
Daikanvik S 195 E7
Dail bho Dheas GB 31 A2
Dailly GB 36 A2
Daimiel E 157 A4
Daingean IRL . . . 30 A1
Đakovica KOS . . . 16 D4
Đakovo HR 125 B4
Dal
 Akershus N . . . 48 B3
 Telemark N . . . 47 C5
Dalaas A 107 B5
Dalabrog GB 31 B1
Dala-Floda S 50 B1
Dala-Husby S . . . 50 B2
Dala-Järna S 50 B1
Dalaman TR 188 C3
Dalarö S 57 A4
Dalbeattie GB . . . 36 B3
Dalby
 DK 59 C3
 Skåne S 61 D3
 Uppsala S 57 A3

Dalby continued
 Värmland S 49 B4
Dale
 Pembrokeshire
 GB 39 C1
 Shetland GB . . . 33 A5
 Hordaland N . . . 46 B2
 Sogn og Fjordane
 N 46 A2
Dalen
 Akershus N . . . 48 C3
 Telemark N . . . 53 A4
Daleszyce PL 87 B4
Dalhalvaig GB . . . 32 C3
Dalheim L 92 B2
Dalhem S 57 C4
Dalias E 164 C2
Dalj HR 125 B4
Dalkeith GB 35 C4
Dalkey IRL 30 A2
Dalmally GB 34 B3
Dalmellington GB . 36 A2
Dalmose DK 65 A4
Dalry
 Dumfries & Galloway
 GB 34 C3
 North Ayrshire GB . 36 A2
Dalrymple GB . . . 36 A2
Dalseter N 47 A6
Dalsjöfors S 60 B3
Dalskog S 54 B3
Dals Långed S . . . 54 B3
Dals Rostock S . . 54 B3
Dalston GB 36 B4
Dalstorp S 60 B3
Dalton-in-Furness
 GB 36 B3
Daluis F 132 A2
Dalum
 D 71 B4
 S 60 B3
Dalvik IS 191 B7
Dalwhinnie GB . . . 32 E2
Dalyan TR 188 C3
Damási GR 182 D4
Damasławek PL . . 76 B2
Damazan F 129 B3
Damgan F 101 B3
Dammarie-les-Lys
 F 90 C2
Dammartin-en-Goële
 F 90 B2
Damme D 71 B5
Damnica PL 68 A2
Dampierre F 105 B4
Dampierre-sur-Salon
 F 105 B4
Damüls A 107 B4
Damville F 89 B5
Damvillers F 92 B1
Damwoude NL . . . 70 A2
Danasjö S 195 E7
Dångebo S 63 B3
Dangers F 89 B5
Dangé-St Romain
 F 102 C2
Dangeul F 89 B4
Danilovgrad MNE . 16 D3
Danischenhagen D 64 B3
Daniszyn PL 85 A5
Danjoutin F 106 B1
Dannas S 60 B3
Dannemarie F . . . 106 B2
Dannemora S . . . 51 B4
Dannenberg D . . . 73 A4
Dánszentmiklós
 H 112 B3
Dány H 112 B3
Daoulas F 100 A1
Darabani RO 17 A7
Darány H 125 B3
Darda HR 125 B4
Dardesheim D . . . 73 C3
Darfeld D 71 B4
Darfo I 120 B3
Dargiń PL 68 A1
Dargun D 66 C1
Darlington GB . . . 37 B5
Darłowo PL 68 A1
Darmstadt D 93 B4
Darney F 105 A5
Daroca E 152 A2
Darque P 148 A1
Darragh IRL 28 B2
Dartford GB 45 B4
Dartington GB . . . 43 B3
Darton GB 40 B2
Daruvar HR 124 B3
Darvas H 113 B5
Darvel GB 36 A2
Darwen GB 38 A4
Dassel D 82 A1
Dassow D 65 C3
Datça TR 188 C2
Datteln D 80 A3
Dattenfeld D 81 B3
Daugard DK 59 C2
Daugavpils LV . . . 8 E5
Daumeray F 102 B1
Daun D 80 B2
Daventry GB 44 A2
Davle CZ 96 B2
Davor HR 124 B3
Davos CH 107 C4
Davutlar TR 188 B2
Davyd Haradok BY 13 B7
Dawlish GB 43 B3
Dax F 128 C1
Dazkırı TR 189 B4
Deal GB 45 B5
Deauville F 89 A4
Deba E 143 A4
Debar MK 182 B2
Dębe PL 77 B5
Dębica PL 87 B5
Dębnica Kaszubska
 PL 68 A2

Dębno PL 74 B3
Dębołęka PL 86 A2
Dębowa Łaka PL 69 B4
Debrc SRB 127 C1
Debrecen H 113 B5
Debrznica PL 75 B4
Debrzno PL 68 B2
Debstedt D 72 A1
Decazeville F 130 A1
Dechtice SK 98 C1
Decima I 168 B2
Decimomannu I 179 C2
Děčín CZ 84 B2
Decize F 104 C2
De Cocksdorp NL 70 A1
Decollatura I 175 B2
Decs H 125 A4
Deddington GB 44 B2
Dedeler TR 187 B5
Dedelow D 74 A2
Dedemli TR 189 B7
Dedemsvaart NL 71 B3
Dédestapolcsány
  H 113 A4
Dedovichi RUS 9 D6
Deeping St Nicholas
  GB 41 C3
Dég H 112 C2
Degaña E 141 B4
Degeberga S 61 D4
Degerby FIN 51 B7
Degerfors S 55 A5
Degerhamn S 63 B4
Degernes N 54 A2
Deggendorf D 95 C4
Deggingen D 94 C1
Dego I 133 A4
Degolados P 155 B3
De Haan B 78 A3
Dehesas de Guadix
  E 164 B1
Dehesas Viejas E 163 A4
Deia E 166 B2
Deining D 95 B3
Deinze B 79 B3
Déiva Marina I 134 A2
Dej RO 17 B5
Deje S 55 A4
De Koog NL 70 A1
Delabole GB 42 B2
Delary S 61 C3
Delbrück D 81 A4
Delčevo MK 182 B4
Delden NL 71 B3
Deleitosa E 156 A2
Delekovec HR 124 A2
Delémont CH 106 B2
Delft NL 70 B1
Delfzijl NL 71 A3
Délia I 176 B2
Delianuova I 175 C1
Deliblato SRB 127 C3
Delice TR 23 B7
Deliceto I 171 B3
Delitzsch D 83 A4
Dellach A 109 C4
Delle F 106 B2
Delme F 92 C2
Delmen-horst D 72 A1
Delnice HR 123 B3
Delsbo S 200 E2
Delvin IRL 30 A1
Delvinë AL 182 D2
Demandice SK 112 A2
Demen D 73 A4
Demidov RUS 13 A9
Demigny F 105 C3
Demirci TR 186 C3
Demirköy TR 186 A2
Demirtaş TR 186 B4
Demmin D 66 C2
Demonte I 133 A3
Demyansk RUS 9 D8
Denain F 78 B3
Denbigh GB 38 A3
Den Burg NL 70 A1
Dender-monde B 79 A4
Denekamp NL 71 B4
Den Ham NL 71 B3
Den Helder NL 70 B1
Denholm GB 35 C5
Denia E 159 C4
Denizli TR 188 B4
Denkendorf D 95 C3
Denklingen D 81 B3
Denny GB 35 B4
Den Oever NL 70 B2
Denta RO 126 B3
Déols F 103 C3
De Panne B 78 A2
Derbent TR 188 A3
Derby GB 40 C2
Derecske H 113 B5
Dereköy TR 186 A2
Derenberg D 82 A2
Derinkuyu TR 23 B8
Dermbach D 82 B2
Dermulo I 121 A4
Deronje SRB 125 B5
Derrygonnelly GB 26 B3
Derrylin GB 27 B3
Derry/Londonderry
  GB 27 B3
Dersingham GB 41 C4
Deruta I 136 C1
Dervaig GB 34 B1
Derval F 101 B4
Derveni GR 184 A3
Derventa BIH 125 C3
Dervock GB 27 A4
Desana I 119 B5
Descartes F 102 C2
Desenzano del Garda
  I 121 B3
Deset N 48 A3
Deševa BIH 139 B4
Desfina GR 184 A3
Desimirovac SRB 127 C2
Désio I 120 B2
Deskati GR 182 D3
Deskle SLO 122 A2
Desná CZ 84 B3
Dešov CZ 97 C3
Despotovac SRB 127 C3
Despotovo SRB 126 B1
Dessau D 83 A4
Deštná CZ 96 B2
Destriana E 141 B4
Désulo I 179 B3
Desvres F 78 B1
Deszk H 126 A2
Deta RO 126 B3
Detmold D 72 C1
Dětřichov CZ 98 B1
Dettelbach D 94 B2
Dettingen
  Baden-Württemberg
  D 94 C1
  Baden-Württemberg
  D 107 B4
Dettwiller F 93 C3
Detva SK 99 C3
Deurne NL 80 A1
Deutschkreutz A 111 B3
Deutschlandsberg
  A 110 C2
Deutsch Wagram
  A 111 A3
Deva RO 16 C5
Dévaványa H 113 B4
Devecikonağı TR 186 C3
Devecser H 111 B4
Develi TR 23 B8
Deventer NL 70 B3
Devil's Bridge GB 39 B3
Devin BG 183 B6
Devinska Nova Ves
  SK 111 A3
Devizes GB 43 A5
Devonport GB 42 B2
Devrek TR 187 A6
Devrekâni TR 23 A7
Đevrske HR 137 B4
De Wijk NL 71 B3
Dewsbury GB 40 B2
Deza E 152 A1
Dežanovac HR 124 B3
Dezzo I 120 B3
Dhali CY 181 A2
Dheftera CY 181 A2
Dherinia CY 181 A2
Diamante I 174 B1
Dianalund DK 61 D1
Diano d'Alba I 119 C5
Diano Marina I 133 B4
Dicomano I 135 B4
Didcot GB 44 B2
Didimoticho GR 186 A1
Die F 118 C2
Diebling F 92 B2
Dieburg D 93 B4
Diego del Carpio
  E 150 B2
Diekirch L 92 B2
Diélette F 88 A2
Diémoz F 118 B2
Dienten am Hochkönig
  A 109 B3
Diepenbeck B 79 B5
Diepholz D 71 B5
Dieppe F 89 A5
Dierberg D 74 A1
Dierdorf D 81 B3
Dieren NL 70 B3
Dierhagen D 66 B1
Diesdorf D 73 B3
Diessen D 108 B2
Diest B 79 B5
Dietenheim D 94 C2
Dietfurt D 95 B3
Dietikon CH 106 B3
Dietzenbach D 93 A4
Dieue-sur-Meuse F 92 B1
Dieulefit F 131 A4
Dieulouard F 92 C2
Dieuze F 92 C2
Diever NL 71 B3
Diez D 81 B4
Diezma E 163 A4
Differdange L 92 B1
Digermulen N 194 B6
Dignac F 115 C4
Dignano I 122 A1
Digne-les-Bains F 132 A2
Digny F 89 B5
Digoin F 104 C2
Dijon F 105 B4
Dikanäs S 195 E7
Dikili TR 186 C1
Diksmuide B 78 A2
Dilar E 163 A4
Dillenburg D 81 B4
Dillingen
  Bayern D 94 C2
  Saarland D 92 B2
Dilsen B 80 A1
Dimaro I 121 A3
Dimitrovgrad BG 183 A7
Dimitsana GR 184 B3
Dinami I 175 C2
Dinan F 101 A3
Dinant B 79 B4
Dinar TR 189 A5
Dinard F 101 A3
Dinek TR 187 C6
Dingden D 80 A2
Dingelstädt D 82 A2
Dingle
  IRL 29 B1
  S 54 B2
Dingolfing D 95 C4
Dingtuna S 56 A2
Dingwall GB 32 D2
Dinkelsbühl D 94 B2
Dinkelscherben D 94 C2
Dinklage D 71 B5
Dinslaken D 80 A2
Dinxperlo NL 80 A2
Diö S 63 B2
Diósgyör H 113 A4
Diósjeno H 112 B3
Diou F 104 C2
Dippen GB 34 C2
Dipperz D 82 B1
Dippoldiswalde D 84 B1
Dirdal N 52 B2
Dirksland NL 79 A4
Dirlewang D 108 B1
Dischingen D 94 C2
Disentis CH 107 C3
Diso I 173 B4
Diss GB 45 A5
Dissen D 71 B5
Distington GB 36 B3
Ditzingen D 93 C5
Ditzum D 71 A4
Divača SLO 122 B2
Dives-sur-Mer F 89 A3
Divín SK 99 C3
Divion F 78 B2
Divišov CZ 96 B2
Divonne les Bains
  F 118 A3
Dixmont F 104 A2
Dizy-le-Gros F 91 B4
Djúpivogur IS 191 C11
Djupvasshytta N 198 C4
Djura S 50 B1
Djurås S 50 B2
Djurmo S 50 B2
Djursdala S 62 A3
Dlouhá Loucka CZ 98 B1
Długowola PL 87 A5
Dmitrov RUS 9 D10
Dno RUS 9 D6
Doade E 141 B3
Doğanhisar TR 189 A6
Dobanovci SRB 127 C2
Dobbertin D 73 A5
Dobbiaco I 108 C3
Dobczyce PL 99 B4
Dobele LV 8 D3
Döbeln D 83 A5
Doberlug-Kirchhain
  D 83 A5
Dobern D 84 A2
Dobersberg A 97 C3
Dobiegniew PL 75 B4
Dobieszyn PL 87 A5
Doboj BIH 125 C4
Dobošnica BIH 125 C4
Doboz H 113 C5
Dobrá CZ 98 B2
Dobra
  Wielkopolskie PL 76 C3
  Zachodnio-Pomorskie
  PL 74 A3
  Zachodnio-Pomorskie
  PL 75 A4
Dobrá Niva SK 99 C3
Dobřany CZ 96 B1
Dobre PL 76 B3
Dobre Miasto PL 69 B5
Dobreta-Turnu-Severin
  RO 16 C5
Dobri H 111 C3
Dobrica SRB 126 B2
Dobrich BG 17 D7
Dobrinishta BG 183 B5
Dobříš CZ 96 B2
Dobro E 143 B3
Dobrodzień PL 86 B2
Döbrököz H 112 C2
Dobromierz PL 85 B4
Dobrosołowo PL 76 B3
Dobroszyce PL 85 A5
Dobrovnik SLO 111 C3
Dobrush BY 13 B9
Dobruška CZ 85 B4
Dobrzany PL 75 A4
Dobrzen Wielki PL 86 B1
Dobrzyca
  Wielkopolskie PL 75 A5
  Wielkopolskie PL 85 A5
  Zachodnio-Pomorskie
  PL 67 B4
Dobrzyńnad Wisłą
  PL 77 B4
Dobšiná SK 99 C4
Dobwalls GB 42 B2
Dochamps B 80 B1
Docking GB 41 C4
Docksta S 200 C4
Doddington GB 37 A4
Döderhult S 62 A4
Doesburg NL 70 B3
Doetinchem NL 71 C3
Dogliani I 133 A3
Dogueno P 160 B2
Doische B 91 A4
Dois Portos P 154 B1
Dojč SK 98 C1
Dokka N 48 B2
Dokkedal DK 58 B3
Dokkum NL 70 A2
Dokležovje SLO 111 C3
Doksy CZ 84 B2
Dokuz TR 189 A7
Dolancourt F 104 A3
Dolceácqua I 133 B3
Dol-de-Bretagne F 88 B2
Dole F 105 B4
Dølemo N 53 B4
Dolenja vas SLO 123 B3
Dolenjske Toplice
  SLO 123 B4
Dolfor GB 39 B3
Dolgarrog GB 38 A3
Dolgellau GB 38 B3
Doliana GR 182 D2
Dolianova I 179 C3
Dolice PL 75 A4
Doljani HR 138 A2
Döllach im Mölltal
  A 109 C3
Dolle D 73 B4
Dollnstein D 94 C3
Dollot F 104 A2
Döllstadt D 82 A2
Dolná Strehová
  SK 99 C3
Dolné Saliby SK 111 A4
Dolni Benešov CZ 98 B2
Dolni Bousov CZ 84 B3
Dolni Kounice CZ 97 B4
Dolni Kralovice CZ 97 B3
Dolni Újezd CZ 97 B4
Dolni Žandov CZ 95 A4
Dolný Kubín SK 99 B3
Dolo I 121 B5
Dolores E 165 A4
Dolovo SRB 127 C2
Dölsach A 109 C3
Dolsk PL 76 B2
Dolwyddelan GB 38 A3
Domaljevac BIH 125 B4
Domaniç TR 187 C4
Domaniža SK 98 B2
Domanovići BIH 139 B3
Domašov CZ 85 B5
Domaszék H 126 A1
Domaszków PL 85 B4
Domaszowice PL 86 A1
Domat-Ems CH 107 C4
Domažlice CZ 95 B4
Dombås N 198 C6
Dombasle-sur-Meurthe
  F 92 C2
Dombegyház H 126 A3
Dombóvár H 112 C2
Domène F 118 B2
Domérat F 116 A2
Domfessel F 92 C3
Domfront F 88 B3
Domfront-en-
  Champagne F 102 A2
Domingão P 154 B2
Domingo Pérez
  Granada E 163 A4
  Toledo E 150 C3
Dömitz D 73 A4
Dommartin F 91 C4
Dommartin-le-Franc
  F 91 C4
Domme F 129 B4
Dommitzsch D 83 A4
Domodóssola I 119 A5
Domokos GR 182 D4
Domoszló H 113 B4
Dompaire F 105 A5
Dompierre-du-Chemin
  F 88 B2
Dompierre-sur-Besbre
  F 104 C2
Dompierre-sur-Mer
  F 114 B2
Domrémy-la-Pucelle
  F 92 C1
Dömsöd H 112 B3
Domsure F 118 A2
Dómus de Maria I 179 D2
Domusnóvas I 179 C2
Domvena GR 184 A3
Domžale SLO 123 A3
Donado E 141 B4
Donaghadee GB 27 B5
Don Alvaro E 155 C4
Doña Mencía E 163 A3
Donaueschingen
  D 106 B3
Donauwörth D 94 C2
Don Benito E 156 B2
Doncaster GB 40 B2
Donegal IRL 26 B2
Donestebe-
  Santesteban E 144 A2
Donges F 101 B3
Dongo I 120 A2
Donington GB 41 C3
Doniños E 140 A2
Donja Bebrina HR 125 B4
Donja Brela HR 138 B2
Donja Dubica BIH 125 B4
Donja Dubrava
  HR 124 A2
Donja Kupčina
  HR 123 B4
Donja Šatornja
  SRB 127 C2
Donja Stubica HR 124 B1
Donje Brišnik BIH 138 B3
Donje Stative HR 123 B4
Donji-Andrijevci
  HR 125 B4
Donji Kazanci BIH 138 B2
Donji Koričáni
  BIH 138 A3
Donji Lapac HR 124 C1
Donji Malovan
  BIH 138 B3
Donji Miholjac HR 125 B4
Donji Mosti HR 124 A2
Donji Poloj HR 123 B4
Donji-Rujani BIH 138 B2
Donji Srb HR 138 A2
Donji Svilaj BIH 125 B4
Donji Tovarnik
  SRB 127 C1
Donji Vakuf BIH 138 A3
Donnalucata I 177 C3
Donnemarie-Dontilly
  F 90 C3
Donnersbach A 110 B1
Donnersbachwald
  A 109 B5
Donnerskirchen A 111 B3
Donorático I 134 B3
Donostia-San
  Sebastián E 144 A2
Donovaly SK 99 C3
Donzenac F 129 A4
Donzère F 131 A3
Donzy F 104 B2
Doonbeg IRL 29 B2
Doorn NL 70 B2
Dor E 140 A1
Dorchester GB 43 B4
Dørdal N 53 B5
Dordrecht NL 79 A4
Dörenthe D 71 B4
Dores GB 32 D2
Dorfen D 95 C4
Dorfgastein A 109 B4
Dorfmark D 72 B2
Dorf Mecklenburg
  D 65 C4
Dorgali I 178 B3
Dorking GB 44 B3
Dormagen D 80 A2
Dormánd H 113 B4
Dormans F 91 B3
Dornava SLO 124 A1
Dornbirn A 107 B4
Dornburg D 83 A3
Dorndorf D 82 B2
Dornecy F 104 B2
Dornes F 104 C2
Dornhan D 93 C4
Dornie GB 31 B3
Dornoch GB 32 D2
Dornum D 71 A4
Dorog H 112 B2
Dorohoi RO 17 B7
Dorotea S 200 B2
Dorotowo PL 69 B5
Dörpen D 71 B4
Dorsten D 80 A2
Dortan F 118 A2
Dortmund D 80 A3
Doruchów PL 86 A2
Dorum D 64 C1
Dörverden D 72 B2
Dörzbach D 94 B1
Dos Aguas E 159 B3
Dosbarrios E 151 C4
Döşemealtı TR 189 B5
Dos Hermanas E 162 A2
Dospat BG 183 B6
Dos-Torres E 156 B3
Dötlingen D 72 B1
Dottignies B 78 B3
Döttingen CH 106 B3
Douai F 78 B3
Douarnenez F 100 A1
Douchy F 104 B2
Douchy-les-Mines
  F 78 B3
Doucier F 105 C4
Doudeville F 89 A4
Doué-la-Fontaine
  F 102 B1
Douglas
  Isle of Man GB 36 B2
  South Lanarkshire
  GB 36 A3
Doulaincourt-Saucourt
  F 91 C5
Doulevant-le-Château
  F 91 C4
Doullens F 90 A2
Dounby GB 33 B3
Doune GB 35 B3
Dounreay GB 32 C3
Dour B 79 B3
Dourdan F 90 C2
Dourgne F 146 A3
Dournazac F 115 C4
Douro Calvo P 148 B2
Douvaine F 118 A3
Douvres-la-Délivrande
  F 89 A3
Douzy F 91 B5
Dover GB 45 B5
Dovje SLO 109 C4
Dovre N 198 D6
Downham Market
  GB 41 C4
Downhill GB 27 A4
Downpatrick GB 27 B5
Dowra IRL 26 B2
Doxato GR 183 B6
Doyet F 116 A2
Dozule F 89 A3
Drača SRB 127 C2
Dračevo
  BIH 139 C4
  MK 182 B3
Drachten NL 70 A3
Draga SLO 123 B3
Drăgăşani RO 17 C6
Dragatuš SLO 123 B4
Dragichyn BY 13 B6
Draginja SRB 127 C1
Dragocvet SRB 127 D3
Dragolovci BIH 125 C3
Dragoni I 170 B2
Dragør DK 61 D2
Dragotina HR 124 B2
Dragotinja BIH 124 B2
Dragozetići HR 123 B3
Draguignan F 132 B2
Drahnsdorf D 74 C2
Drahonice CZ 96 B2
Drahovce SK 98 C1
Drama GR 183 B6
Drammen N 54 A1
Drangedal N 53 A5
Drangsnes IS 190 B4
Dransfeld D 82 A1
Dranske D 66 B2
Draperstown GB 27 B4
Drassburg A 111 B3
Drávaszabolcs H 125 B4
Dravograd SLO 110 C2
Drawno PL 75 A4
Drawsko Pomorskie
  PL 75 A4
Drayton GB 41 C5
Drązdżewo PL 77 A6
Draženov CZ 95 B4
Draževac SRB 127 C2
Dražice HR 123 B3
Drebkau D 84 A2
Dreieich D 93 A4
Dreisen D 93 B4
Drenovci HR 125 C4
Drensteinfurt D 81 A3
Dresden D 84 A1
Dretyń PL 68 A1
Dreux F 89 B5
Dřevohostice CZ 98 B1
Drevsjø N 199 D9
Drewitz D 73 B5
Drezdenko PL 75 B4
Drežnica HR 123 B4
Drežnik-Grad HR 123 C4
Drietona SK 98 C1
Driffield GB 40 A3
Drimnin GB 34 B2
Drimoleague IRL 29 C2
Dringenberg D 81 A5
Drinić BIH 138 A2
Drinjača BIH 139 A5
Drinovci BIH 138 B3
Driopida GR 185 B5
Drivstua N 198 C6
Drlače SRB 127 C1
Drnholec CZ 97 C4
Drniš HR 138 B2
Drnje HR 124 A2
Drnovice CZ 97 B4
Dro I 121 B3
Drøbak N 54 A1
Drobin PL 77 B5
Drochia MD 17 A7
Drochtersen D 64 C2
Drogheda IRL 30 A2
Drohobych UA 13 D5
Droitwich Spa GB 44 A1
Droltowice PL 85 A5
Dromahair IRL 26 B2
Dromcolliher IRL 29 B3
Dromore
  Down GB 27 B4
  Tyrone GB 27 B3
Dromore West IRL 26 B2
Dronero I 133 A3
Dronfield GB 40 B2
Drongan GB 36 A2
Dronninglund DK 58 A3
Dronrijp NL 70 A2
Dronten NL 70 B2
Drosendorf A 97 C3
Drösing A 97 C4
Drottningholm S 57 A3
Droué F 103 A3
Drulingen F 92 C3
Drumbeg GB 32 C1
Drumcliff IRL 26 B2
Drumgask GB 32 D2
Drumkeeran IRL 26 B2
Drummore GB 36 B2
Drumnadrochit GB 32 D2
Drumquin GB 27 B3
Drumshanbo IRL 26 B2
Drumsna IRL 26 C2
Drunen NL 79 A5
Druskininkai LT 13 A5
Druten NL 80 A1
Druya BY 13 A7
Družetići SRB 127 C2
Drvar BIH 138 A2
Drvenik HR 138 B3
Drwalew PL 77 C6
Drymen GB 34 B3
Drynoch GB 31 B2
Drzewce PL 76 B2
Drzewiany PL 68 B1
Drzewica PL 87 A4
Dualchi I 178 B2
Duas Igrejas P 149 A3
Dub SRB 127 D1
Dubá CZ 84 B2
Dubăsari MD 17 B8
Duben D 74 C2
Dübendorf CH 107 B3
Dubi CZ 84 B1
Dubica HR 124 B2
Dublin IRL 30 A2
Dubna RUS 9 D10
Dubňany CZ 98 C1
Dubnica nad Váhom
  SK 98 C2
Dubnik SK 112 B2
Dubno UA 13 C6
Dubodiel SK 98 C2
Dubona SRB 127 C2
Dubovac SRB 127 C3
Dubovic BIH 124 C2
Dubranec HR 124 B1
Dubrava HR 124 B2
Dubrave BIH 125 C4
Dubravica
  HR 123 B4
  SRB 127 C3
Dubrovnik HR 139 C4
Dubrovytsya UA 13 C7
Ducey F 88 B2
Duchcov CZ 84 B1
Ducherow D 74 A2
Dučina SRB 127 C2
Duclair F 89 A4
Dudar H 112 B1
Duderstadt D 82 A2
Dudeştii Vechi RO 126 A2
Dudley GB 40 C1
Dueñas E 142 C2
Duesund N 46 B2
Dueville I 121 B4
Duffel B 79 A4
Duffield GB 40 C2
Dufftown GB 32 D3
Duga Resa HR 123 B4
Dugi Rat HR 138 B2
Dugny-sur-Meuse
  F 92 B1
Dugopolje HR 138 B2
Dugo Selo HR 124 B2
Duino I 122 B2
Duisburg D 80 A2
Dukat AL 182 C1
Dukovany CZ 97 B4
Duleek IRL 30 A2
Dülken D 80 A2
Dülmen D 80 A3
Dulovo BG 17 D7
Dulpetorpet N 49 B4
Dulverton GB 43 A3
Dumbarton GB 34 C3
Dümerek TR 187 C6
Dumfries GB 36 A3
Dumlupınar TR 187 D4
Dümpelfeld D 80 B2
Dunaalmás H 112 B2
Dunabogdány H 112 B3
Dunafalva H 125 A4
Dunaföldvár H 112 C2
Dunaharaszti H 112 B3
Dunajská Streda
  SK 111 B4
Dunakeszi H 112 B3
Dunakiliti H 111 B4
Dunakömlöd H 112 C2
Dunapataj H 112 C2
Dunaszekcsö H 125 A4
Dunaszentgyorgy
  H 112 C2
Dunatetétlen H 112 C3
Dunaújváros H 112 C2
Dunavecse H 112 C2
Dunbar GB 35 B5
Dunbeath GB 32 C3
Dunblane GB 35 B4
Dunboyne IRL 30 A2
Dundalk IRL 27 B4
Dundee GB 35 B5
Dundrennan GB 36 B3
Dundrum GB 27 B5
Dunfanaghy IRL 26 A3
Dunfermline GB 35 B4
Dungannon GB 27 B4
Dungarvan IRL 29 B4
Dungiven GB 27 B4
Dunglow IRL 26 B2
Dungourney IRL 29 C3
Duninowo PL 68 A1
Dunkeld GB 35 B4
Dunker S 56 A2
Dunkerque = Dunkirk
  F 78 A2
Dunkineely IRL 26 B2
Dunkirk = Dunkerque
  F 78 A2
Dun Laoghaire IRL 30 A2
Dunlavin IRL 30 A2
Dunleer IRL 27 C4
Dun-le-Palestel F 116 A1
Dun-les-Places F 104 B3
Dunlop GB 36 A2
Dunloy GB 27 A4
Dunmanway IRL 29 C2
Dunmore IRL 28 A3
Dunmore East IRL 30 B2
Dunmurry GB 27 B4
Dunnet GB 32 C3
Dunningen D 107 A3
Dunoon GB 34 C3
Duns GB 35 C5
Dunscore GB 36 A3
Dunsford GB 43 B3
Dunshaughlin IRL 30 A2
Dunstable GB 44 B3
Dunster GB 43 A3
Dun-sur-Auron F 103 C4
Dun-sur-Meuse F 91 B5
Dunvegan GB 31 B2
Duplek SLO 110 C2
Dupnitsa BG 17 D5
Durağan TR 23 A8
Durach D 107 B5
Durak TR 186 C3
Durana E 143 B4
Durance F 128 B3
Durango E 143 A4
Durankulak BG 17 D8
Duras F 128 B3
Durban-Corbières
  F 146 B3
Dürbheim D 107 A3
Durbuy B 79 B5
Dúrcal E 163 B4
Đurđenovac HR 125 B4
Đurđevac HR 124 A3
Đurđevik BIH 139 A4
Düren D 80 B2
Durham GB 37 B5
Đurinci SRB 127 C2
Durlach D 93 C4
Đurmanec HR 124 A1
Durness GB 32 C2
Dürnkrut A 97 C4
Dürrboden CH 107 C4
Dürrenboden CH 107 C3
Durrës AL 182 B1
Durrow IRL 30 B1
Durrus IRL 29 C2
Dursunbey TR 186 C3
Durtal F 102 B1
Durup DK 58 B1
Durusu TR 186 A3
Dusina BIH 139 B3
Dusnok H 112 C2
Dusocin PL 69 B3
Düsseldorf D 80 A2
Dusslingen D 93 C5
Duszniki PL 75 B5
Duszniki-Zdrój PL 85 B4
Dutovlje SLO 122 B2
Duvebo S 55 B5
Duved S 199 B9
Düzağac TR 187 D5
Düzce TR 187 B6
Dvärsätt S 199 B11
Dvor HR 124 B2
Dvorce CZ 98 B1
Dvorníky SK 98 C1
Dvory nad Žitavou
  SK 112 B2
Dvůr Králové nad
  Labem CZ 85 B3
Dybvad DK 58 A3
Dyce GB 33 D4
Dygowo PL 67 B4
Dykehead GB 35 B4
Dymchurch GB 45 B5

Dymer UA 13 C9
Dyrnes N 198 B4
Dywity PL 69 B5
Džanići BIH 139 B3
Dziadowa Kłoda PL 86 A1
Działdowo PL 77 A5
Działoszyce PL 87 B4
Działoszyn PL 86 A2
Dziemiany PL 68 A2
Dzierzążnia PL 77 B5
Dzierzgoń PL 69 B4
Dzierzgowo PL 77 A5
Dzierżoniów PL 85 B4
Dzisna BY 13 A8
Dziwnów PL 67 B3
Dźwierzuty PL 77 A5
Dzyarzhynsk BY 13 B7
Dzyatlava BY 13 B6

E

Ea E 143 A4
Eaglesfield GB 36 A3
Ealing GB 44 B3
Eardisley GB 39 B3
Earls Barton GB 44 A3
Earl Shilton GB 40 C2
Earlston GB 35 C5
Easington GB 41 B4
Easky IRL 26 B2
Eastbourne GB 45 C4
East Calder GB 35 C4
East Dereham GB 41 C4
Easter Skeld GB 33 A5
East Grinstead GB 45 B4
East Ilsley GB 44 B2
East Kilbride GB 36 A2
Eastleigh GB 44 C2
East Linton GB 35 C5
East Markham GB 40 B3
Easton GB 43 B4
East Wittering GB 44 C3
Eaton Socon GB 44 A3
Eaux-Bonnes F 145 B3
Eauze F 128 C3
Ebberup DK 59 C2
Ebbs A 108 B3
Ebbw Vale GB 39 C3
Ebeleben D 82 A2
Ebeltoft DK 59 B3
Ebene Reichenau A 109 C4
Eben im Pongau A 109 B4
Ebensee A 109 B4
Ebensfeld D 94 A2
Eberbach D 93 B4
Ebergötzen D 82 A2
Ebermann-Stadt D 94 B3
Ebern D 82 B2
Eberndorf A 110 C1
Ebersbach D 84 A2
Ebersberg D 108 A2
Ebersdorf
 Bayern D 82 B3
 Niedersachsen D 72 A2
Eberstein A 110 C1
Eberswalde D 74 B2
Ebnat-Kappel CH 107 B4
Éboli I 170 C3
Ebrach D 94 B2
Ebreichsdorf A 111 B3
Ebreuil F 116 A3
Ebstorf D 72 A3
Ecclefechan GB 36 A3
Eccleshall GB 40 C1
Eceabat TR 186 B1
Echallens CH 106 C1
Echauri E 144 B2
Echinos GR 183 B7
Echiré F 114 B3
Échirolles F 118 B2
Echourgnac F 128 A3
Echt NL 80 A1
Echte D 82 A2
Echternach L 92 B2
Ecija E 162 A2
Ečka SRB 126 B2
Eckartsberga D 82 A3
Eckelshausen D 81 B4
Eckental D 94 B3
Eckernförde D 64 B2
Eckerö FIN 51 B6
Eckington GB 40 B2
Éclaron F 91 C4
Écommoy F 102 B2
Écouché F 89 B3
Ecouis F 90 B1
Ecséd H 113 B3
Ecsegfalva H 113 B4
Écueillé F 103 B3
Ed S 54 B2
Eda S 49 C4
Eda glasbruk S 49 C4
Edam NL 70 B2
Edane S 55 A3
Edderton GB 32 D2
Ede NL 70 B2
Edebäck S 49 B5
Edebo S 51 B5
Edelény H 99 C4
Edelschrott A 110 B2
Edemissen D 72 B3
Edenbridge GB 45 B4
Edenderry IRL 30 A1
Edenkoben D 93 B4
Edesheim D 93 B4
Edessa GR 182 C4
Edewecht D 71 A4
Edgeworthstown IRL 30 A1
Edinburgh GB 35 C4
Edineț MD 17 A7
Edirne TR 186 A1
Edland N 52 A3
Edolo I 120 A3
Edøy N 198 B5
Edremit TR 186 C2
Edsbro S 51 C5
Edsbruk S 56 B2
Edsbyn S 50 A2
Edsele S 200 C2
Edsleskog S 54 A3
Edsvalla S 55 A4
Eekloo B 79 A3
Eemshaven NL 71 A3
Eerbeek NL 70 B3
Eersel NL 79 A5
Eferding A 96 C2
Effiat F 116 A3
Efteløt N 53 A5
Egeln D 73 C4
Eger H 113 B4
Egerbakta H 113 B4
Egernsund DK 64 B2
Egersund N 52 B2
Egerszólát H 113 B4
Egervár H 111 C3
Egg
 A 107 B4
 D 107 A5
Eggby S 55 B4
Eggedal N 47 B6
Eggenburg A 97 C3
Eggenfelden D 95 C4
Eggesin D 74 A3
Eggum N 194 B4
Egham GB 44 B3
Éghezée B 79 B4
Egiertowo PL 68 A3
Egilsstaðir IS 191 B11
Egina GR 185 B4
Eginio GR 182 C4
Egio GR 184 A3
Égletons F 116 B2
Egling D 108 B2
Eglinton GB 27 A3
Eglisau CH 107 B3
Égliseneuve-d'Entraigues F 116 B2
Eglofs D 107 B4
Egmond aan Zee NL 70 B1
Egna I 121 A4
Egosthena GR 184 A4
Egremont GB 36 B3
Egtved DK 59 C2
Eguilles F 131 B4
Eguilly-sous-Bois F 104 A3
Éguzon-Chantôme F 103 C3
Egyek H 113 B4
Egyházasrádóc H 111 B3
Ehekirchen D 94 C3
Ehingen D 94 C1
Ehra-Lessien D 73 B3
Ehrang D 92 B2
Ehrenfriedersdorf D 83 B4
Ehrenhain D 83 B4
Ehrenhausen A 110 C2
Ehringshausen D 81 B4
Ehrwald A 108 B1
Eibar E 143 A4
Eibelstadt D 94 B2
Eibenstock D 83 B4
Eibergen NL 71 B3
Eibiswald A 110 C2
Eichenbarleben D 73 B4
Eichendorf D 95 C4
Eichstätt D 95 C3
Eickelborn D 81 A4
Eide
 Hordaland N 46 B3
 Møre og Romsdal N 198 C4
Eidet N 194 A9
Eidfjord N 46 B4
Eidsberg N 54 A2
Eidsbugarden N 47 A5
Eidsdal N 198 C4
Eidsfoss N 53 A6
Eidskog N 49 B4
Eidsvåg
 Hordaland N 46 B2
 Møre og Romsdal N 198 C5
Eidsvoll N 48 B3
Eikefjord N 46 A2
Eikelandsosen N 46 B2
Eiken N 52 B3
Eikesdal N 198 C5
Eikstrand N 53 A5
Eilenburg D 83 A4
Eilsleben D 73 B4
Eina N 48 B2
Einbeck D 82 A1
Eindhoven NL 79 A5
Einsiedeln CH 107 B3
Einville-au-Jard F 92 C2
Eisenach D 82 B2
Eisenberg
 Rheinland-Pfalz D 93 B4
 Thüringen D 83 B3
Eisenerz A 110 B1
Eisenhüttenstadt D 74 B3
Eisenkappel A 110 C1
Eisenstadt A 111 B3
Eisentratten A 109 C4
Eisfeld D 82 B2
Eisleben D 82 A3
Eislingen D 94 C1
Eitensheim D 95 C3
Eiterfeld D 82 B1
Eitorf D 80 B3
Eivindvik N 46 B2
Eivissa = Ibiza E 166 C1
Eixo P 148 B1
Ejby DK 59 C2
Ejea de los Caballeros E 144 B2
Ejstrupholm DK 59 C2
Ejulve E 153 B3
Eke B 79 B3
Ekeby
 Gotland S 57 C4
 Skåne S 61 D2
 Uppsala S 51 B5
Ekeby-Almby S 56 A1
Ekenäs S 55 B4
Ekenässjön S 62 A3
Ekerö S 57 A3
Eket S 61 C3
Eketorp S 63 B4
Ekevik S 56 B2
Ekkerøy N 193 B14
Ekshärad S 49 B5
Eksingedal N 46 B2
Eksjö S 62 A2
Eksta S 57 C4
Ekträsk S 200 B5
El Alamo
 Madrid E 151 B4
 Sevilla E 161 B3
El Algar E 165 B4
El Almendro E 161 B2
El Alquián E 164 C2
Élancourt F 90 C1
El Arahal E 162 A2
El Arenal E 150 B2
El Arguellite E 164 A2
Elassona GR 182 D4
El Astillero E 143 A3
Elati GR 182 D3
Żelazno PL 85 B4
El Ballestero E 158 C1
El Barco de Ávila E 150 B2
Elbasan AL 182 B2
El Berrón E 142 A1
El Berrueco E 151 B4
Elbeuf F 89 A4
Elbingerode D 82 A2
Elbląg PL 69 A4
El Bodón E 149 B3
El Bonillo E 158 C1
El Bosque E 162 B2
El Bullaque E 157 A3
Elburg NL 70 B2
El Burgo E 162 B3
El Burgo de Ebro E 153 A3
El Burgo de Osma E 151 A4
El Burgo Ranero E 142 B1
El Buste E 144 C2
El Cabaco E 149 B3
El Callejo E 143 A3
El Campillo E 161 B3
El Campillo de la Jara E 156 A2
El Cañavete E 158 B1
El Carpio E 157 C3
El Carpio de Tajo E 150 C3
El Casar E 151 B4
El Casar de Escalona E 150 B3
El Castillo de las Guardas E 161 B3
El Centenillo E 157 B4
El Cerro E 149 B4
El Cerro de Andévalo E 161 B3
Elche E 165 A4
Elche de la Sierra E 158 C1
Elchingen D 94 C2
El Comenar E 162 B2
El Coronil E 162 A2
El Crucero E 141 A4
El Cubo de Tierra del Vino E 149 A4
El Cuervo E 162 B1
Elda E 159 C3
Eldena D 73 A4
Eldingen D 72 B3
Elefsina GR 185 A4
El Ejido E 164 C2
Elek H 113 C5
Elemir SRB 126 B2
El Escorial E 151 B3
El Espinar E 151 B3
Eleutheroupoli GR 183 C6
El Frago E 144 B3
El Franco E 141 A4
El Frasno E 152 A2
Elgå N 199 C8
El Garrobo E 161 B3
El Gastor E 162 B2
Elgin GB 32 D3
Elgoibar E 143 A4
Elgol GB 31 B2
El Gordo E 150 C2
El Grado E 145 B4
El Granado E 161 B2
El Grao de Castelló E 159 B4
El Grau E 159 C3
Elgshøa N 49 A4
El Higuera E 163 A3
El Hijate E 164 B2
El Hontanar E 152 B2
El Hoyo E 157 B4
Elie GB 35 B5
Elizondo E 144 A2
Ełk PL 12 B5
Elkhovo BG 17 D7
Ellenberg D 94 B2
Ellesmere GB 38 B4
Ellesmere Port GB 38 A4
Ellezelles B 79 B3
Ellingen D 94 B2
Ellmau A 109 B3
Ellon GB 33 D4
Ellös S 54 B2
Ellrich D 82 A2
Ellwangen D 94 C2
Elm
 CH 107 C4
Elm *continued*
 D 72 A2
Elmadağ TR 23 B7
El Madroño E 161 B3
El Maillo E 149 B3
Elmalı TR 189 C4
El Masnou E 147 C3
El Mirón E 150 B2
El Molar E 151 B4
El Molinillo E 157 A3
El Morell E 147 C2
Elmshorn D 64 C2
Elmstein D 93 B3
El Muyo E 151 A4
Elne F 146 B3
Elnesvågen N 198 C4
El Olmo E 151 A4
Elorrio E 143 A4
Elöszállás H 112 C2
Elouda GR 185 D6
Éloyes F 105 A5
El Palo E 163 B3
El Pardo E 151 B4
El Payo E 149 B3
El Pedernoso E 158 B1
El Pedroso E 162 A2
El Peral E 158 B2
El Perelló
 Tarragona E 153 B4
 Valencia E 159 B3
Elphin GB 32 C1
El Picazo E 158 B1
El Pinell de Bray E 153 A4
El Piñero E 150 A2
El Pla de Santa Maria E 147 C2
El Pobo E 153 B3
El Pobo de Dueñas E 152 B2
El Pont d'Armentera E 147 C2
El Port de la Selva E 147 B4
El Port de Llançà E 146 B4
El Port de Sagunt E 159 B3
El Prat de Llobregat E 147 C3
El Provencio E 158 B1
El Puente E 143 A3
El Puente del Arzobispo E 150 C2
El Puerto E 141 A4
El Puerto de Santa Maria E 162 B1
El Real de la Jara E 161 B3
El Real de San Vincente E 150 B3
El Robledo E 157 A3
El Rocio E 161 B3
El Rompido E 161 B2
El Ronquillo E 161 B3
El Royo E 143 C4
El Rubio E 162 A3
El Sabinar E 164 A2
El Saler E 159 B3
El Salobral E 158 C2
El Saucejo E 162 A2
Els Castells E 147 B2
Elsdorf D 80 B2
Elsenfeld D 93 B5
El Serrat AND 146 B2
Elsfleth D 72 A1
Elspeet NL 70 B2
Elst NL 70 C2
Elstead GB 44 B3
Elster D 83 A4
Elsterberg D 83 B4
Elsterwerda D 83 A5
Elstra D 84 A2
El Temple E 144 C3
El Tiemblo E 150 B3
Eltmann D 94 B2
El Toboso E 157 A5
El Tormillo E 145 C3
El Torno E 149 B4
Eltville D 93 A4
El Valle de las Casas E 142 B1
Elvas P 155 C3
Elvebakken N 192 C7
El Vellón E 151 B4
Elven F 101 B3
El Vendrell E 147 C2
Elverum N 48 B3
El Villar de Arnedo E 144 B1
Elvington GB 40 B3
El Viso E 156 B3
El Viso del Alcor E 162 A2
Elxleben D 82 A2
Ely GB 45 A4
Elzach D 106 A3
Elze D 72 B2
Emådalen S 50 A1
Embleton GB 37 A5
Embonas GR 188 C2
Embrun F 132 A2
Embún E 144 B3
Emden D 71 A4
Emecik TR 188 C2
Emet TR 186 C4
Emirdağ TR 187 C6
Emlichheim D 71 B3
Emmaboda S 63 B3
Emmaljunga S 61 C3
Emmeloord NL 70 B2
Emmen
 CH 106 B3
 NL 71 B3
Emmendingen D 106 A2
Emmer-Compascuum NL 71 B4
Emmerich D 80 A2
Emmern D 72 B2
Emöd H 113 B4
Émpoli I 135 B3
Emsbüren D 71 B4
Emsdetten D 71 B4
Emsfors S 62 A4
Emskirchen D 94 B2
Emstek D 71 B5
Emsworth GB 44 C3
Emyvale IRL 27 B4
Enafors S 199 B9
Enånger S 51 A4
Encamp AND 146 B2
Encarnaçao P 154 C1
Encinas de Abajo E 150 B2
Encinas de Esgueva E 142 C2
Encinasola E 161 A3
Encinas Reales E 163 A3
Encio E 143 B3
Enciso E 144 B1
Enden N 199 D7
Endingen D 106 A2
Endrinal E 149 B4
Endröd H 113 C4
Enebakk N 54 A2
Eneryda S 63 B2
Enese H 111 B4
Enez TR 183 C8
Enfield IRL 30 A2
Eng A 108 B2
Engelberg CH 106 C3
Engelhartszell A 96 C1
Engelskirchen D 80 B3
Engen D 107 B3
Enger N 48 B2
Engerdal N 199 D8
Engerneset N 49 A4
Enge-sande D 64 B1
Engesvang DK 59 B2
Enghien B 79 B4
Engstingen D 94 C1
Engter D 71 B5
Enguera E 159 C3
Enguidanos E 158 B2
Enkenbach D 93 B3
Enkhuizen NL 70 B2
Enklinge FIN 51 B7
Enköping S 56 A3
Enna I 177 B3
Ennezat F 116 B3
Ennigerloh D 81 A4
Enningdal N 54 B2
Ennis IRL 28 B3
Enniscorthy IRL 30 B2
Enniskean IRL 29 C3
Enniskillen GB 27 B3
Ennistimon IRL 28 B2
Enns A 110 A1
Eno FIN 9 A7
Enontekiö FIN 196 A6
Ens NL 70 B2
Enschede NL 71 B3
Ensdorf D 95 B3
Ensisheim F 106 B2
Enstaberga S 56 B2
Enstone GB 44 B2
Entlebuch CH 106 B3
Entrácque I 133 A3
Entradas P 160 B1
Entrains-sur-Nohain F 104 B2
Entrambasaguas E 143 A3
Entrambasmestas E 143 A3
Entraygues-sur-Truyère F 116 C2
Entre-os-Rios P 148 A1
Entrevaux F 132 B2
Entrin Bajo E 155 C4
Entroncamento P 154 B2
Entzheim F 93 C3
Envermeu F 89 A5
Enviken S 50 B2
Enying H 112 C2
Enzingerboden A 109 B3
Enzklösterle D 93 C4
Épagny F 90 B3
Epalinges CH 106 C1
Epannes F 114 B3
Epanomi GR 182 C4
Epe
 D 71 B4
 NL 70 B2
Épernay F 91 B3
Épernon F 90 C1
Epfig F 93 C3
Epierre F 118 B3
Épila E 152 A2
Épinac F 104 C3
Épinal F 105 A5
Episcopia I 174 A2
Episkopi CY 181 B1
Epitalio GR 184 B2
Epoisses F 104 B3
Eppenbrunn D 93 B3
Eppendorf D 83 B5
Epping GB 45 B4
Eppingen D 93 B4
Epsom GB 44 B3
Epworth GB 40 B3
Eraclea I 122 B1
Eraclea Mare I 122 B1
Erba I 120 B2
Erbach
 Baden-Württemberg D 94 C1
 Hessen D 93 B4
Erbalunga F 180 A2
Erbendorf D 95 B4
Érchie I 173 B3
Ercolano I 170 C2
Ercsi H 112 B2
Érd H 112 B2
Erdek TR 186 B2
Erdemli TR 23 C8
Erdevik SRB 126 B1
Erding D 95 C3
Erdötelek H 113 B4
Erdut HR 125 B5
Erdweg D 95 C3
Ereğli
 Konya TR 23 C8
 Zonguldak TR 187 A6
Erenkaya TR 189 B7
Eresfjord N 198 C5
Eresos GR 183 D7
Eretria GR 185 A4
Erfde D 64 B2
Erfjord N 52 A2
Erfstadt D 80 B2
Erfurt D 82 B3
Ērgli LV 8 D4
Ergoldsbach D 95 C4
Eriboll GB 32 C2
Érice I 176 A1
Ericeira P 154 C1
Eğridir TR 189 B5
Eriksberg S 195 E6
Eriksmåla S 62 B3
Eringsboda S 63 B3
Eriswil CH 106 B2
Erithres GR 185 A4
Erkelenz D 80 A2
Erkner D 74 B2
Erkrath D 80 A2
Erla E 144 B3
Erlangen D 94 B3
Erli I 133 A4
Erlsbach A 109 C3
Ermelo NL 70 B2
Ermenak TR 23 C7
Ermenonville F 90 B2
Ermezinde P 148 A1
Ermidas P 160 A1
Ermioni GR 184 B4
Ermoupoli GR 185 B5
Ermsleben D 82 A3
Erndtebrück D 81 B4
Ernée F 88 B3
Ernestinovo HR 125 B4
Ernstbrunn A 97 C4
Erolzheim D 107 A5
Erquelinnes B 79 B4
Erquy F 101 A3
Erra P 154 C2
Erratzu E 144 A2
Errindlev DK 65 B4
Erro E 144 B2
Ersa F 180 A2
Érsekcsanád H 125 A4
Ersekë AL 182 C2
Érsekvadkert H 112 B3
Ersmark S 200 C6
Erstein F 93 C3
Erstfeld CH 107 C3
Ertebølle DK 58 B2
Ertingen D 107 A4
Ervedal
 Coimbra P 148 B1
 Portalegre P 154 B3
Ervenik HR 138 A1
Ervidel P 160 B1
Ervy-le-Châtel F 104 A2
Erwitte D 81 A4
Erxleben D 73 B4
Erzsébet H 125 A4
Esbjerg DK 59 C1
Esbly F 90 C2
Escacena del Campo E 161 B3
Escairón E 140 B3
Escalada E 143 B3
Escalante E 143 A3
Escalaplano I 179 C3
Escalona E 150 B3
Escalona del Prado E 151 A3
Escalonilla E 150 C3
Escalos de Baixo P 155 B3
Escalos de Cima P 155 B3
Escamilla E 152 B1
Es Caná E 166 B1
Escañuela E 157 C3
Es Castell E 167 B4
Escatrón E 153 A3
Eschach D 107 B4
Eschau D 94 B1
Eschede D 72 B3
Eschenau D 95 B3
Eschenbach D 95 B3
Eschenz CH 107 B3
Eschershausen D 72 C2
Esch-sur-Alzette L 92 B1
Esch-sur-Sûre L 92 B1
Eschwege D 82 A2
Eschweiler D 80 B2
Escobasa de Almazán E 152 A1
Escoeuilles F 78 B1
Escombreras E 165 B4
Escos F 144 A2
Escource F 128 B1
Escragnolles F 132 B2
Escrick GB 40 B2
Escurial E 156 A2
Escurial de la Sierra E 149 B4
Esens D 71 A4
Esgos E 140 B3
Esher GB 44 B3
Eskdalemuir GB 36 A3
Eskifjörður IS 191 B12
Eskilhem S 57 C4
Eskilsäter S 55 B4
Eskilstrup DK 65 B4
Eskilstuna S 56 A2
Eskipazar TR 187 B7
Eskişehir TR 187 C5
Eslarn D 95 B4
Eslava E 144 B2
Eslida E 159 B3
Eslohe D 81 A4
Eslöv S 61 D3
Eşme TR 188 A3
Es Mercadal E 167 B4
Es Migjorn Gran E 167 B4
Espa N 48 B3
Espalion F 130 A1
Esparragalejo E 155 C4
Esparragosa del Caudillo E 156 B2
Esparragossa de la Serena E 156 B2
Esparreguera E 147 C2
Esparron F 132 B1
Espe N 46 B3
Espedal N 52 B2
Espejo
 Alava E 143 B3
 Córdoba E 163 A3
Espeland N 46 B2
Espelkamp D 72 B1
Espeluche F 131 A3
Espeluy E 157 B4
Espera E 162 B2
Esperança P 155 B3
Espéraza F 146 B3
Espéria I 169 B3
Espevær N 52 A1
Espiel E 156 B2
Espinama E 142 A2
Espiñaredo E 140 A3
Espinasses F 132 A2
Espinelves E 147 C3
Espinhal P 154 A2
Espinho P 148 A1
Espinilla E 142 A2
Espinosa de Cerrato E 143 C3
Espinosa de los Monteros E 143 A3
Espinoso del Rey E 156 A3
Espirito Santo P 160 B2
Espluga de Francolí E 147 C2
Esplús E 145 C4
Espolla E 146 B3
Espoo FIN 8 B4
Esporles E 166 B2
Es Port d'Alcúdia E 167 B3
Esposende P 148 A1
Espot E 146 B2
Es Pujols E 166 C1
Esquedas E 145 B3
Esquivias E 151 B4
Essay F 89 B4
Essen
 B 79 A4
 Niedersachsen D 71 B4
 Nordrhein-Westfalen D 80 A3
Essenbach D 95 C4
Essertaux F 90 B2
Essingen D 94 C2
Esslingen D 94 C1
Es Soleràs E 153 A4
Essoyes F 104 A3
Estacas E 140 B2
Estadilla E 145 B4
Estagel F 146 B3
Estaires F 78 B2
Estang F 128 C2
Estarreja P 148 B1
Estartit E 147 B4
Estavayer-le-Lac CH 106 C1
Este I 121 B4
Esteiro E 140 A2
Estela P 148 A1
Estella E 144 B1
Estellencs E 166 B2
Estepa E 162 A3
Estépar E 143 B3
Estepona E 162 B2
Esternay F 91 C3
Esterri d'Aneu E 146 B2
Esterwegen D 71 B4
Estissac F 104 A2
Estivadas E 140 B3
Estivareilles F 116 A2
Estivella E 159 B3
Estói P 160 B2
Estopiñán E 145 C4
Estoril P 154 C1
Estoublon F 132 B2
Estrée-Blanche F 78 B2
Estrées-St Denis F 90 B2
Estrela P 155 C3
Estremera E 151 B4
Estremoz P 155 C3
Estuna S 51 C5
Esyres F 102 B2
Esztergom H 112 B2
Etables-sur-Mer F 100 A3
Étain F 92 B1
Étalans F 105 B5
Etalle B 92 B1
Étampes F 90 C2
Etang-sur-Arroux F 104 C3
Étaples F 78 B1
Etauliers F 128 A2
Etili TR 186 C1
Etna N 48 B1
Etne N 52 A1
Etoges F 91 C3
Etoliko GR 184 A2
Eton GB 44 B3
Etréaupont F 91 B3
Étréchy F 90 C2
Étrépagny F 90 B1
Étretat F 89 A4
Étroeungt F 91 A3
Étroubles I 119 B4
Ettal D 108 B2
Ettelbruck L 92 B2
Etten NL 79 A4
Ettenheim D 106 A2
Ettington GB 44 A2
Ettlingen D 93 C4
Ettringen D 108 A1
Etuz F 105 B4
Etxarri-Aranatz E 144 B1
Etyek H 112 B2
Eu F 90 A1

Euerdorf D . . . 82 B2
Eulate E . . . 144 B1
Eupen B . . . 80 B2
Europoort NL . . . 79 A4
Euskirchen D . . . 80 B2
Eutin D . . . 65 B3
Evanger N . . . 46 B3
Évaux-les-Bains F 116 A2
Eviler
  Afyon TR . . . 189 A4
  Çanakkale TR . . 186 C1
Evenskjær N . . . 194 B7
Evenstad N . . . 48 A3
Evercreech GB . . . 43 A4
Evergem B . . . 79 A3
Everöd S . . . 61 D4
Eversberg D . . . 81 A4
Everswinkel D . . . 71 C4
Evertsberg D . . . 49 A5
Evesham GB . . . 44 A2
Évian-les-Bains F . 118 A3
Evisa F . . . 180 A1
Evje N . . . 53 B3
Evolène CH . . . 119 A4
Évora P . . . 154 C3
Evoramonte P . . . 155 C3
Evran F . . . 101 A4
Evrecy F . . . 89 A3
Évreux F . . . 89 A5
Évron F . . . 102 A1
Évry F . . . 90 C2
Ewell GB . . . 44 B3
Ewersbach D . . . 81 B4
Excideuil F . . . 115 C5
Exeter GB . . . 43 B3
Exmes F . . . 89 B4
Exminster GB . . . 43 B3
Exmouth GB . . . 43 B3
Eydehamn N . . . 53 B4
Eye
  Peterborough
    GB . . . 41 C3
  Suffolk GB . . . 45 A5
Eyemouth GB . . . 35 C5
Eyguians F . . . 132 A1
Eyguières F . . . 131 B4
Eygurande F . . . 116 B2
Eylie F . . . 145 B4
Eymet F . . . 129 B3
Eymoutiers F . . . 116 B1
Eynsham GB . . . 44 B2
Eyrarbakki IS . . . 190 D4
Eystrup D . . . 72 B2
Ezaro E . . . 140 B1
Ezcaray E . . . 143 B4
Ezcároz E . . . 144 B2
Ezine TR . . . 186 C1
Ezmoriz P . . . 148 B1

F

Fabara E . . . 153 A4
Fábbrico I . . . 121 C3
Fåberg N . . . 48 A2
Fabero E . . . 141 B4
Fábiánsebestyén
  H . . . 113 C4
Fåborg DK . . . 64 A3
Fabrègues F . . . 130 B2
Fabriano I . . . 136 B1
Fabrizia I . . . 175 C2
Facha P . . . 148 A1
Facinas E . . . 162 B2
Fačkov SK . . . 98 B2
Fadagosa P . . . 155 B3
Fadd H . . . 112 C2
Faédis I . . . 122 A2
Faenza I . . . 135 A4
Fafe P . . . 148 A1
Fagagna I . . . 122 A2
Făgăras RO . . . 17 C6
Fågelberget S . . . 199 A11
Fågelfors S . . . 62 A3
Fågelmara S . . . 63 B3
Fågelsta S . . . 55 B6
Fagerås S . . . 55 A4
Fagerheim N . . . 47 B4
Fagerhøy N . . . 48 A1
Fagerhult S . . . 62 A3
Fagerlund N . . . 48 B2
Fagernes
  Oppland N . . . 47 B6
  Troms N . . . 192 C3
Fagersanna S . . . 55 B5
Fagersta S . . . 50 B2
Fåglavik S . . . 55 B4
Fagnano Castello
  I . . . 174 B2
Fagnières F . . . 91 C4
Faido CH . . . 107 C3
Fains-Véel F . . . 91 C5
Fairford GB . . . 44 B2
Fairlie GB . . . 34 C3
Fajsz H . . . 112 C2
Fakenham GB . . . 41 C4
Fåker S . . . 199 B11
Fakse DK . . . 65 A5
Fakse Ladeplads
  DK . . . 65 A5
Falaise F . . . 89 B3
Falcade I . . . 121 A4
Falcarragh IRL . . . 26 A2
Falces E . . . 144 B2
Fălciu RO . . . 17 B8
Falconara I . . . 177 B3
Falconara Maríttima
  I . . . 136 B2
Falcone I . . . 177 A4
Faldingworth GB . . 40 B3
Falerum S . . . 56 B2
Fălești MD . . . 17 B7
Falkenberg
  Bayern D . . . 95 B4
  Bayern D . . . 95 C4
  Brandenburg D . 83 A5
  S . . . 60 C2
Falkensee D . . . 74 B2
Falkenstein
  Bayern D . . . 95 B4

Falkenstein *continued*
  Sachsen D . . . 83 B4
Falkenthal D . . . 74 B2
Falkirk GB . . . 35 B4
Falkland GB . . . 35 B4
Falköping S . . . 55 B4
Fall D . . . 108 B2
Falla S . . . 56 B1
Fallingbostel D . . . 72 B2
Falmouth GB . . . 42 B1
Falset E . . . 147 C1
Fălticeni RO . . . 17 B7
Falun S . . . 50 B2
Famagusta CY . . . 181 A2
Fammestad N . . . 46 B2
Fana N . . . 46 B2
Fanano I . . . 135 A3
Fanari GR . . . 182 D3
Fanjeaux F . . . 146 A3
Fano I . . . 136 B2
Fântânele RO . . . 126 A3
Fara in Sabina I . . 168 A2
Faramontanos de
  Tábara E . . . 149 A4
Fara Novarese I . . 119 B5
Farasdues E . . . 144 B2
Fårbo S . . . 62 A4
Fareham GB . . . 44 C2
Färentuna S . . . 57 A3
Färgelanda S . . . 54 B2
Färila S . . . 200 E1
Faringdon GB . . . 44 B2
Faringe S . . . 51 C5
Farini I . . . 120 C2
Fariza E . . . 149 A3
Färjestaden S . . . 63 B4
Farkadona GR . . . 182 D4
Farkasfa H . . . 111 C3
Färlöv S . . . 61 C4
Farmos H . . . 113 B3
Farná SK . . . 112 B2
Färnäs S . . . 50 B1
Farnborough GB . . 44 B3
Farnese I . . . 168 A1
Farnham GB . . . 44 B3
Farnroda D . . . 82 B2
Faro P . . . 160 B2
Fårö S . . . 57 C5
Fårösund S . . . 57 C5
Farra d'Alpago I . . 122 A1
Farranfore IRL . . . 29 B2
Farre DK . . . 59 B2
Farsala GR . . . 182 D4
Farsø DK . . . 58 B2
Farsund N . . . 52 B2
Farum DK . . . 61 D2
Fårup DK . . . 58 B2
Fasana I . . . 172 B1
Fasano I . . . 173 B3
Fáskrúðsfjörður
  IS . . . 191 C11
Fassberg D . . . 72 B2
Fastiv UA . . . 13 C8
Fastnäs S . . . 49 B5
Fátima P . . . 154 B2
Fatmomakke S . . . 195 E6
Fättjaur S . . . 195 E6
Faucogney-et-la-Mer
  F . . . 105 B5
Fauguerolles F . . . 128 B3
Faulenrost D . . . 74 A1
Faulquemont F . . . 92 B2
Fauquembergues F 78 B2
Fauske N . . . 194 C6
Fauville-en-Caux F . 89 A4
Fauvillers B . . . 92 B1
Fåvang N . . . 48 A2
Favara
  E . . . 159 B3
  I . . . 176 B2
Faverges F . . . 118 B3
Faverney F . . . 105 B5
Faversham GB . . . 45 B4
Favignana I . . . 176 B1
Fawley GB . . . 44 C2
Fay-aux-Loges F . . 103 B4
Fayence F . . . 132 B2
Fayet F . . . 130 B1
Fayl-Billot F . . . 105 B4
Fayón E . . . 153 A4
Fearn GB . . . 32 D3
Fécamp F . . . 89 A4
Feda N . . . 52 B2
Fedje N . . . 46 B1
Feeny IRL . . . 27 B3
Fegen S . . . 60 B3
Fegyvernek H . . . 113 B4
Fehrbellin D . . . 74 B1
Fehring A . . . 111 C3
Feichten A . . . 108 B1
Feiring N . . . 48 B3
Feistritz im Rosental
  A . . . 110 C1
Feketić SRB . . . 126 B1
Felanitx E . . . 167 B3
Feld am See A . . . 109 C4
Feldbach A . . . 110 C2
Feldberg D . . . 74 A2
Feldkirch A . . . 107 B4
Feldkirchen in Kärnten
  A . . . 109 C5
Feldkirchen-Westerham
  D . . . 108 B2
Felgueiras P . . . 148 A1
Felitto I . . . 172 B1
Félix E . . . 164 C2
Felixstowe GB . . . 45 B5
Felizzano I . . . 119 C5
Felletin F . . . 116 B2
Fellingsbro S . . . 56 A1
Felnac RO . . . 126 A3
Felnémet H . . . 113 B4
Felpéc H . . . 111 B4
Fels am Wagram A . 97 C3
Felsberg D . . . 81 A5
Felsönyék H . . . 112 C2
Felsöszentiván H . 126 A1
Felsöszentmárton
  H . . . 125 B3

Felsözsolca H . . . 113 A4
Felsted DK . . . 64 B2
Feltre I . . . 121 A4
Femsjö S . . . 60 C3
Fenagh IRL . . . 26 B3
Fene E . . . 140 A2
Fenestrelle I . . . 119 B4
Fénétrange F . . . 92 C3
Feneu F . . . 102 B1
Fengersfors S . . . 54 B3
Fenit IRL . . . 29 B2
Fensmark DK . . . 65 A4
Fenwick GB . . . 36 A2
Feolin Ferry GB . . 34 C1
Ferbane IRL . . . 28 A4
Ferdinandovac
  HR . . . 124 A3
Ferdinandshof D . . 74 A2
Fère-Champenoise
  F . . . 91 C3
Fère-en-Tardenois
  F . . . 91 B3
Ferentillo I . . . 168 A2
Ferentino I . . . 169 B3
Feres GR . . . 183 C8
Feria E . . . 155 C4
Feričanci HR . . . 125 B3
Ferizli TR . . . 187 B5
Ferla I . . . 177 B3
Ferlach A . . . 110 C1
Ferleiten A . . . 109 B3
Fermil P . . . 148 A2
Fermo I . . . 136 B2
Fermoselle E . . . 149 A3
Fermoy IRL . . . 29 B3
Fernancaballero E 157 A4
Fernán Núñez E . . 163 A3
Fernán Peréz E . . 164 C2
Fernán Ferro P . . 154 C1
Fernay-Voltaire F . 118 A3
Ferndown GB . . . 43 B5
Ferness GB . . . 32 D3
Fernhurst GB . . . 44 B3
Ferns IRL . . . 30 B2
Ferpécle CH . . . 119 A4
Ferrals-les-Corbières
  F . . . 146 A3
Ferrandina I . . . 172 B2
Ferrara I . . . 121 C4
Ferrara di Monte Baldo
  I . . . 121 B3
Ferreira E . . . 141 A3
Ferreira do Alentejo
  P . . . 160 A1
Ferreira do Zêzere
  P . . . 154 B2
Ferreras de Abajo
  E . . . 141 C4
Ferreras de Arriba
  E . . . 141 C4
Ferreries E . . . 167 B4
Ferreruela E . . . 152 A2
Ferreruela de Tabara
  E . . . 149 A3
Ferret CH . . . 119 B4
Ferrette F . . . 106 B2
Ferriere I . . . 120 C2
Ferrière-la-Grande
  F . . . 79 B3
Ferrières
  Hautes-Pyrénées
    F . . . 145 A3
  Loiret F . . . 103 A4
  Oise F . . . 90 B2
Ferrières-sur-Sichon
  F . . . 117 A3
Ferrol E . . . 140 A2
Ferryhill GB . . . 37 B5
Fertörakos H . . . 111 B3
Fertöszentmiklós
  H . . . 111 B3
Ferwerd NL . . . 70 A2
Festieux F . . . 91 B3
Festøy N . . . 198 C3
Festvåg N . . . 194 C5
Fetești RO . . . 17 C7
Fethard
  Tipperary IRL . . 29 B4
  Wexford IRL . . 30 B2
Fethiye TR . . . 188 C4
Fetsund N . . . 48 C3
Fettercairn GB . . . 35 B5
Feucht D . . . 95 B3
Feuchtwangen D . . 94 B2
Feudingen D . . . 81 B4
Feuges F . . . 91 C4
Feuquières F . . . 90 B1
Feurs F . . . 117 B4
Fevik N . . . 53 B4
Ffestiniog GB . . . 38 B3
Fiamignano I . . . 169 A3
Fiano I . . . 119 B4
Ficarazzi I . . . 176 A2
Ficarolo I . . . 121 C4
Fichtelberg D . . . 95 A3
Ficulle I . . . 135 C5
Fidenza I . . . 120 C3
Fidjeland N . . . 52 B2
Fieberbrunn A . . . 109 B3
Fier AL . . . 182 C1
Fiera di Primiero I 121 A4
Fiesch CH . . . 119 A5
Fiesso Umbertiano
  I . . . 121 C4
Figari F . . . 180 B2
Figeac F . . . 116 C2
Figeholm S . . . 62 A4
Figgjo N . . . 52 B1
Figline Valdarno I . 135 B4
Figols E . . . 145 B4
Figueira da Foz P . 148 B1
Figueira de Castelo
  Rodrigo P . . . 149 B3
Figueira dos Caveleiros
  P . . . 160 A1
Figueiredo P . . . 154 B3
Figueiredo de Alva
  P . . . 148 B2
Figueiródos Vinhos
  P . . . 154 B2

Figueres E . . . 147 B3
Figueroles E . . . 153 B3
Figueruela de Arriba
  E . . . 141 C4
Filadélfia I . . . 175 C2
Fil'akovo SK . . . 99 C3
Filderstadt D . . . 94 C1
Filey GB . . . 41 A3
Filiaşi RO . . . 17 C5
Filiates GR . . . 182 D2
Filiatra GR . . . 184 B2
Filipstad S . . . 55 A5
Filisur CH . . . 107 C4
Fillan N . . . 198 B5
Filotio GR . . . 185 B6
Filottrano I . . . 136 B2
Filskov DK . . . 59 C2
Filton GB . . . 43 A4
Filtvet N . . . 54 A1
Filzmoos A . . . 109 B4
Finale Emília I . . . 121 C4
Finale Ligure I . . . 133 A4
Fiñana E . . . 164 B2
Finby FIN . . . 51 B7
Fincham GB . . . 41 C4
Finchingfield GB . . 45 B4
Findhorn GB . . . 32 D3
Findochty GB . . . 33 D4
Finike TR . . . 189 C5
Finkenberg A . . . 108 B2
Finnea IRL . . . 27 C3
Finneidfjord N . . . 195 D4
Finnerödja S . . . 55 B5
Finnskog N . . . 49 B4
Finnsnes N . . . 194 A9
Finntorp S . . . 54 A3
Finócchio I . . . 168 B2
Finsjö S . . . 62 A4
Finsland N . . . 52 B3
Finspång S . . . 56 B1
Finsterwalde D . . . 84 A1
Finsterwolde NL . . 71 A4
Finstown GB . . . 33 B3
Fintona GB . . . 27 B3
Fionnphort GB . . . 34 B1
Fiorenzuola d'Arda
  I . . . 120 C2
Firenze = Florence
  I . . . 135 B4
Firenzuola I . . . 135 A4
Firmi F . . . 130 A1
Firminy F . . . 117 B4
Firmo I . . . 174 B2
Fischamend Markt
  A . . . 111 A3
Fischbach
  A . . . 110 B2
  D . . . 93 B3
Fischbeck D . . . 73 B5
Fischen D . . . 107 B5
Fishbourne GB . . . 44 C2
Fishguard GB . . . 39 C2
Fiskardo GR . . . 184 A1
Fiskebäckskil S . . 54 B2
Fiskebøl N . . . 194 B5
Fismes F . . . 91 B3
Fisterra E . . . 140 B1
Fitero E . . . 144 B2
Fitjar N . . . 46 C2
Fiuggi I . . . 169 B3
Fiumata I . . . 169 A3
Fiumefreddo Brúzio
  I . . . 174 B2
Fiumefreddo di Sicilia
  I . . . 177 B4
Fiumicino I . . . 168 B2
Fivemiletown GB . 27 B3
Fivizzano I . . . 134 A3
Fjälkinge S . . . 63 B2
Fjällåsen S . . . 196 B3
Fjällbacka S . . . 54 B2
Fjæra N . . . 46 C3
Fjärdhundra S . . . 56 A2
Fjellerup DK . . . 58 B3
Fjerritslev DK . . . 58 A2
Fjordgard N . . . 194 A8
Fjugesta S . . . 55 A5
Flå N . . . 47 B6
Flábygd N . . . 53 A4
Flaça E . . . 147 B3
Flace F . . . 117 A4
Fladungen D . . . 82 B2
Flaine F . . . 118 A3
Flaka FIN . . . 51 B7
Flakk N . . . 198 B6
Flåm N . . . 46 B4
Flamatt CH . . . 106 C2
Flamborough GB . 41 A3
Flammersfeld D . . 81 B3
Flassans-sur-Issole
  F . . . 132 B2
Flatdal N . . . 53 A4
Flatebø N . . . 46 B3
Flateby N . . . 48 C3
Flateland N . . . 52 A3
Flateyri IS . . . 190 A2
Flatøydegard N . . 47 B6
Flatråker N . . . 46 C2
Flattach A . . . 109 C4
Flatvarp S . . . 62 A4
Flauenskjold DK . . 58 A3
Flavigny-sur-Moselle
  F . . . 92 C2
Flavy-le-Martel F . 90 B3
Flawil CH . . . 107 B4
Flayosc F . . . 132 B2
Flechtingen D . . . 73 B4
Fleckeby D . . . 64 B2
Fleet GB . . . 44 B3
Fleetmark D . . . 73 B4
Fleetwood GB . . . 38 A3
Flehingen D . . . 93 B4
Flekke N . . . 46 A2
Flekkefjord N . . . 52 B2
Flen S . . . 56 A2
Flensburg D . . . 64 B2
Fleringe S . . . 57 C4
Flerohopp S . . . 62 B3
Flers F . . . 88 B3
Flesberg N . . . 47 C6
Fleurance F . . . 129 C3

Fleuré F . . . 115 B4
Fleurier CH . . . 105 C5
Fleurus B . . . 79 B4
Fleury
  Hérault F . . . 130 B2
  Yonne F . . . 104 B2
Fleury-les-Aubrais
  F . . . 103 B3
Fleury-sur-Andelle
  F . . . 89 A5
Fleury-sur-Orne F . 89 A3
Flieden D . . . 81 B5
Flimby GB . . . 36 B3
Flims CH . . . 107 C4
Flines-léz-Raches
  F . . . 78 B3
Flint GB . . . 38 A3
Flirey F . . . 92 C1
Flirsch A . . . 108 B1
Flisa N . . . 49 B4
Flisby S . . . 62 A3
Fliseryd S . . . 62 A4
Flix E . . . 153 A4
Flixecourt F . . . 90 A2
Flize F . . . 91 B4
Flobecq B . . . 79 B3
Floby S . . . 55 B4
Floda S . . . 60 B2
Flodden GB . . . 37 A4
Flogny-la-Chapelle
  F . . . 104 B2
Flöha D . . . 83 B5
Flonheim D . . . 93 B4
Florac F . . . 130 A2
Floreffe B . . . 79 B4
Florence = Firenze
  I . . . 135 B4
Florennes B . . . 79 B4
Florensac F . . . 130 B2
Florentin F . . . 129 C5
Florenville B . . . 91 B5
Flores de Avila E . 150 B2
Floresta I . . . 177 B3
Florești MD . . . 17 B8
Floridia I . . . 177 B4
Florina GR . . . 182 C3
Florø N . . . 46 A2
Flörsheim D . . . 93 A4
Floss D . . . 95 B4
Fluberg N . . . 48 B2
Flúðir IS . . . 190 C5
Flühli CH . . . 106 C3
Flumet F . . . 118 B3
Fluminimaggiore I 179 C2
Flums CH . . . 107 B4
Flyeryd S . . . 63 B3
Flygsfors S . . . 62 B3
Foča BIH . . . 139 B4
Foça TR . . . 186 D1
Fochabers GB . . . 32 D3
Focșani RO . . . 17 C7
Foel GB . . . 38 B3
Foeni RO . . . 126 B2
Fóggia I . . . 171 B3
Foglianise I . . . 170 B2
Föglö FIN . . . 51 B7
Fohnsdorf A . . . 110 B1
Foiano della Chiana
  I . . . 135 B4
Foix F . . . 146 B2
Fojnica
  BIH . . . 139 B3
  BIH . . . 139 B4
Fokstua N . . . 198 C6
Foldereid N . . . 199 A9
Földes H . . . 113 B5
Folégandros GR . 185 C5
Folelli F . . . 180 A2
Folgaria I . . . 121 B4
Folgosinho P . . . 148 B2
Folgoso de la Ribera
  E . . . 141 B4
Folgoso do Courel
  E . . . 141 B3
Foligno I . . . 136 C1
Folkärna S . . . 50 B3
Folkestad N . . . 198 C3
Folkestone GB . . . 45 B5
Follafoss N . . . 199 B8
Folldal N . . . 198 C6
Follebu N . . . 48 A2
Follina I . . . 121 B5
Föllinge S . . . 199 B11
Fölsbyn S . . . 54 A3
Foncebadón E . . . 141 B4
Foncine-le-Bas F . 105 C5
Fondevila E . . . 140 C2
Fondi I . . . 169 B3
Fondo I . . . 121 A4
Fonelas E . . . 164 B1
Fonfría
  Teruel E . . . 152 B2
  Zamora E . . . 149 A3
Fonn N . . . 46 A3
Fonnes N . . . 46 B1
Fonni I . . . 178 B3
Fontaine F . . . 91 C4
Fontaine de Vaucluse
  F . . . 131 B4
Fontaine-Française
  F . . . 105 B4
Fontaine-le-Dun F . 89 A4
Fontan F . . . 133 A3
Fontanarejo E . . . 157 A3
Fontane I . . . 133 A3
Fontanélice I . . . 135 A4
Fontanières F . . . 116 A2
Fontanosas E . . . 157 B3
Fonteblanda I . . . 168 A1
Fontenay-le-Comte
  F . . . 114 B3
Fontenay-Trésigny
  F . . . 90 C2
Fontevrault-l'Abbaye
  F . . . 102 B2
Fontiveros E . . . 150 B3

Fontoy F . . . 92 B1
Fontpédrouse F . . 146 B3
Font-Romeu F . . . 146 B3
Fontstown IRL . . . 30 A2
Fonyód H . . . 111 C4
Fonzaso I . . . 121 A4
Fóppolo I . . . 120 A2
Föra S . . . 62 A4
Forbach
  D . . . 93 C4
  F . . . 92 B2
Forcall E . . . 153 B3
Forcalquier F . . . 132 B1
Forcarei E . . . 140 B2
Forchheim D . . . 94 B3
Forchtenau A . . . 111 B3
Forchtenberg D . . 94 B1
Ford GB . . . 34 B2
Førde
  Hordaland N . . 52 A1
  Sogn og Fjordane
    N . . . 46 A2
Förderstedt D . . . 83 A3
Førdesfjorden N . . 52 A1
Fordham GB . . . 45 A4
Fordingbridge GB . 44 C2
Fordon PL . . . 76 A3
Fordongiánus I . . 179 C2
Forenza I . . . 172 B1
Foresta di Búrgos
  I . . . 178 B2
Forfar GB . . . 35 B5
Forges-les-Eaux F . 90 B1
Foria I . . . 172 B1
Forío I . . . 170 C1
Forjães P . . . 148 A1
Forl I . . . 135 A5
Forlì I . . . 135 A5
Forlimpopoli I . . . 135 A5
Formazza I . . . 119 A5
Formby GB . . . 38 A3
Formerie F . . . 90 B1
Fórmia I . . . 169 B3
Formigine I . . . 135 A3
Formigliana I . . . 119 B5
Formiguères F . . . 146 B3
Fornalutx E . . . 166 B2
Fornåsa S . . . 56 B1
Fornelli I . . . 178 B2
Fornells E . . . 167 A4
Fornelos de Montes
  E . . . 140 B2
Fornes E . . . 163 B4
Fornes N . . . 192 C3
Forni Avoltri I . . . 109 C3
Forni di Sopra I . . 122 A1
Forni di Sotto I . . 122 A1
Forno
  Piemonte I . . . 119 B4
  Piemonte I . . . 119 B5
Forno Alpi-Gráie I 119 B4
Forno di Zoldo I . . 121 A5
Fornos de Algodres
  P . . . 148 B2
Fornovo di Taro I . 120 C3
Foros do Arrão P . 154 B2
Forráskút H . . . 126 A1
Forres GB . . . 32 D3
Forriolo E . . . 140 B3
Fors
  Uppsala S . . . 51 B5
  Västerbotten S . 195 E6
Forsand N . . . 52 B2
Forsbacka S . . . 51 B3
Forserum S . . . 62 A2
Forshaga S . . . 55 A4
Forsheda S . . . 60 B3
Forsinard GB . . . 32 C3
Forsmo S . . . 200 C3
Forsnäs S . . . 195 D9
Forsnes N . . . 198 B5
Forssa FIN . . . 8 B3
Forssjöbruk S . . . 56 B2
Forst D . . . 84 A2
Fort Augustus GB . 32 D2
Fortanete E . . . 153 B3
Forte dei Marmi I . 134 B3
Fortezza I . . . 108 C2
Forth GB . . . 35 C4
Fort-Mahon-Plage
  F . . . 78 B1
Fortrie GB . . . 33 D4
Fortrose GB . . . 32 D2
Fortun N . . . 47 A4
Fortuna E . . . 165 A3
Fortuneswell GB . . 43 B4
Fort William GB . . 34 B2
Forvik N . . . 195 E3
Fos F . . . 145 B4
Fosdinovo I . . . 134 A3
Foss N . . . 47 B6
Fossácesia I . . . 169 A4
Fossano I . . . 133 A3
Fossato di Vico I . 136 B1
Fosse-la-Ville B . . 79 B4
Fossbakken N . . . 194 B8
Fossby N . . . 54 A2
Fossombrone I . . . 136 B1
Fos-sur-Mer F . . . 131 B3
Fot H . . . 112 B3
Fouchères F . . . 104 A3
Fouesnant F . . . 100 B1
Foug F . . . 92 C1
Fougères F . . . 88 B2
Fougerolles F . . . 105 B5
Foulain F . . . 105 A4
Fountainhall GB . . 35 C5
Fouras F . . . 114 C2
Fourchambault F . 104 B2
Fourmies F . . . 91 A4
Fourna GR . . . 182 D3
Fournels F . . . 116 C3
Fourni GR . . . 188 B1
Fournols F . . . 117 B3
Fourques F . . . 146 B3
Fourquevaux F . . . 146 A2

Fours F . . . 104 C2
Fowey GB . . . 42 B2
Foxdale GB . . . 36 B2
Foxford IRL . . . 26 C1
Foyers GB . . . 32 D2
Foynes IRL . . . 29 B2
Foz E . . . 141 A3
Foza I . . . 121 B4
Foz do Arelho P . . 154 B1
Foz do Giraldo P . 155 B3
Frabosa Soprana
  I . . . 133 A3
Frades de la Sierra
  E . . . 149 B4
Fraga E . . . 153 A4
Fragagnano I . . . 173 B3
Frailes E . . . 163 A4
Fraire F . . . 106 A1
Fraize F . . . 106 A1
Framlingham GB . . 45 A5
Frammersbach D . 94 A1
Framnes N . . . 54 A1
França P . . . 141 C4
Francaltroff F . . . 92 C2
Francavilla al Mare
  I . . . 169 A4
Francavilla di Sicilia
  I . . . 177 B4
Francavilla Fontana
  I . . . 173 B3
Francavilla in Sinni
  I . . . 174 A2
Francescas F . . . 129 B3
Franco P . . . 148 A2
Francofonte I . . . 177 B3
Francos E . . . 151 A4
Frändefors S . . . 54 B3
Franeker NL . . . 70 A2
Frangy F . . . 118 A2
Frankenau D . . . 81 A4
Frankenberg
  Hessen D . . . 81 A4
  Sachsen D . . . 83 B5
Frankenburg A . . . 109 A4
Frankenfels A . . . 110 B2
Frankenmarkt A . . 109 B4
Frankenthal D . . . 93 B4
Frankfurt
  Brandenburg D . 74 B3
  Hessen D . . . 81 B4
Frankrike S . . . 199 B10
Fränsta S . . . 200 D2
Františkovy Lázně
  CZ . . . 83 B4
Franzburg D . . . 66 B1
Frascati I . . . 168 B2
Frasdorf D . . . 109 B3
Fraserburgh GB . . 33 D4
Frashër AL . . . 182 C2
Frasne F . . . 105 C5
Frasnes-lez-Anvaing
  B . . . 79 B3
Frasseto F . . . 180 B2
Frastanz A . . . 107 B4
Fratel P . . . 155 B3
Fratta Todina I . . 135 C5
Frauenau D . . . 96 C1
Frauenfeld CH . . . 107 B3
Frauenkirchen A . . 111 B3
Frauenstein D . . . 83 B5
Frauental A . . . 110 C2
Frayssinet F . . . 129 B4
Frayssinet-le-Gélat
  F . . . 129 B4
Frechas P . . . 149 A2
Frechen D . . . 80 B2
Frechilla E . . . 142 B2
Freckenhorst D . . 71 C4
Fredeburg D . . . 81 A4
Fredelsloh D . . . 82 A1
Fredeng N . . . 48 B2
Fredensborg DK . . 61 D2
Fredericia DK . . . 59 C2
Frederiks DK . . . 59 B2
Frederikshavn DK . 58 A3
Frederikssund DK . 61 D2
Frederiksværk DK . 61 D2
Fredrika S . . . 200 B4
Fredriksberg S . . . 50 B1
Fredriksdal S . . . 62 A2
Fredrikstad N . . . 54 A1
Fregenal de la Sierra
  E . . . 161 A3
Fregene I . . . 168 B2
Freiberg D . . . 83 B5
Freiburg
  Baden-Württemberg
    D . . . 106 B2
  Niedersachsen D . 64 C2
Freienhagen D . . . 81 A5
Freienhufen D . . . 84 A1
Freiensteinau D . . 81 B5
Freihung D . . . 95 B3
Freilassing D . . . 109 B3
Freisen D . . . 92 B3
Freising D . . . 95 C3
Freistadt A . . . 96 C2
Freital D . . . 84 A1
Freixedas P . . . 149 B2
Freixo de Espada à
  Cinta P . . . 149 A3
Fréjus F . . . 132 B2
Fremdingen D . . . 94 C2
Frenštát pod
  Radhoštěm CZ . 98 B2
Freren D . . . 71 B4
Freshford IRL . . . 30 B1
Freshwater GB . . . 44 C2
Fresnay-sur-Sarthe
  F . . . 89 B4
Fresneda de la Sierra
  E . . . 152 B1
Fresneda de la Sierra
  Tiron E . . . 143 B3
Fresnedillas E . . . 151 B3
Fresnes-en-Woevre
  F . . . 92 B1

Fresne-St Mamès F 105 B4
Fresno Alhandiga E 150 B2
Fresno de la Ribera E 150 A2
Fresno de la Vega E 142 B1
Fresno de Sayago E 149 A4
Fresnoy-Folny F . . .90 B1
Fresnoy-le-Grand F 91 B3
Fressenville F 90 A1
Fresvik N 46 A3
Fréteval F 103 B3
Fretigney F 105 B4
Freudenberg
 Baden-Württemberg D 94 B1
 Nordrhein-Westfalen D 81 B3
Freudenstadt D . . .93 C4
Freux F 92 B1
Frévent F 78 B2
Freyburg D 83 A3
Freyenstein D 73 A5
Freyming-Merlebach F 92 B2
Freystadt D 95 B3
Freyung D 96 C1
Frias de Albarracin E 152 B2
Fribourg CH 106 C2
Frick CH 106 B3
Fridafors S 63 B2
Fridaythorpe GB . . .40 A3
Friedberg
 A 111 B3
 Bayern D 94 C2
 Hessen D 81 B4
Friedeburg D 71 A4
Friedewald D 82 B1
Friedland
 Brandenburg D . . .74 B3
 Mecklenburg-Vorpommern D . .74 A2
 Niedersachsen D . .82 A1
Friedrichroda D . . .82 B2
Friedrichsdorf D . . .81 B4
Friedrichshafen D 107 B4
Friedrichskoog D . .64 B1
Friedrichstadt D . . .64 B2
Friedrichswalde D . .74 A2
Friesach A 110 C1
Friesack D 73 B5
Friesenheim D 93 C3
Friesoythe D 71 A4
Friggesund S 200 E2
Frigiliana E 163 B4
Frihetsli N 192 D3
Frillesås S 60 B2
Frinnaryd S 62 A2
Frinton-on-Sea GB .45 B5
Friockheim GB 35 B5
Friol E 140 A3
Fristad S 60 B2
Fritsla S 60 B2
Fritzlar D 81 A5
Frizington GB 36 B3
Frödinge S 62 A4
Froges F 118 B2
Frohburg D 83 A4
Frohnhausen D 81 B4
Frohnleiten D 110 B2
Froissy F 90 B2
Frombork PL 69 A4
Frome GB 43 A4
Frómista E 142 B2
Fröndenberg D 81 A3
Fronsac F 128 B2
Front I 119 B4
Fronteira P 155 B3
Frontenay-Rohan-Rohan F 114 B3
Frontenhausen D . .95 C4
Frontignan F 130 B2
Fronton F 129 C4
Fröseke S 62 B3
Frosinone I 169 B3
Frosolone I 170 B2
Frosta N 199 B7
Frøstrup DK 58 A1
Frosunda S 57 A4
Frouard F 92 C2
Frövi S 56 A1
Frøyset N 46 B2
Fruges F 78 B2
Frutigen CH 106 C2
Frýdek-Mistek CZ . .98 B2
Frýdlant CZ 84 B3
Frýdlant nad Ostravicí CZ 98 B2
Frygnowo PL 77 A5
Fryšták CZ 98 B1
Fucécchio I 135 B3
Fuencaliente
 Ciudad Real E . .157 A4
 Ciudad Real E . .157 B3
Fuencemillán E . . .151 B4
Fuendejalón E 144 C2
Fuengirola E 163 B3
Fuenlabrada E 151 B4
Fuenlabrada de los Montes E 156 A3
Fuensalida E 151 B3
Fuensanta E 164 B2
Fuensanta de Martos E 163 A4
Fuente-Álamo E . .158 C2
Fuente-Álamo de Murcia E 165 B3
Fuentealbilla E 158 B2
Fuente al Olmo de Iscar E 150 A3
Fuentecén E 151 A4
Fuente Dé E 142 A2

Fuente de Cantos E 155 C4
Fuente del Arco E .156 B2
Fuente del Conde E 163 A3
Fuente del Maestre E 155 C4
Fuente de Santa Cruz E 150 A3
Fuente el Fresno E 157 A4
Fuente el Saz de Jarama E 151 B4
Fuente el Sol E . . .150 A3
Fuenteguinaldo E 149 B3
Fuentelapeña E . . .150 A2
Fuentelcésped E . .151 A4
Fuentelespino de Haro E 158 B1
Fuentelespino de Moya E 158 B2
Fuentenovilla E . . .151 B4
Fuente Obejuna E 156 B2
Fuente Palmera E 162 A2
Fuentepelayo E . . .151 A3
Fuentepinilla E . . .151 A5
Fuenterroble de Salvatierra E . . .150 B2
Fuenterrobles E . . .158 B2
Fuentes E 158 B1
Fuentesauco E . . .151 A3
Fuentesaúco E . . .150 A2
Fuentes de Andalucia E 162 A2
Fuentes de Ebro E 153 A3
Fuentes de Jiloca E 152 A2
Fuentes de la Alcarria E 151 B5
Fuentes de León E 161 A3
Fuentes de Nava E 142 B2
Fuentes de Oñoro E 149 B3
Fuentes de Ropel E 142 B1
Fuentespalda E . . .153 B4
Fuentespina E 151 A4
Fuente-Tójar E . . .163 A3
Fuente Vaqueros E 163 A4
Fuentidueña E 151 A4
Fuentidueña de Tajo E 151 B4
Fuerte del Rey E . .157 C4
Fügen A 108 B2
Fuglebjerg DK 65 A4
Fuglevik N 54 A1
Fuhrberg D 72 B2
Fulda D 82 B1
Fulgatore I 176 B1
Fully CH 119 A4
Fulnek CZ 98 B1
Fülöpszállás H 112 C3
Fulpmes A 108 B2
Fulunäs S 49 A5
Fumay F 91 B4
Fumel F 129 B3
Funäsdalen S 199 C9
Fundão P 148 B2
Funzie GB 33 A6
Furadouro P 148 B1
Fure N 46 A2
Fürstenau D 71 B4
Furstenau D 81 A5
Fürstenberg D 74 A2
Fürstenfeld A 111 B3
Fürstenfeldbruck D 108 A2
Fürstenstein D 96 C1
Fürstenwalde D . . .74 B3
Fürstenwerder D . . .74 A2
Fürstenzell D 96 C1
Furta H 113 B5
Fürth
 Bayern D 94 B2
 Hessen D 93 B4
Furth im Wald D . . .95 B4
Furtwangen D 106 A3
Furuby S 62 B3
Furudal S 50 A2
Furuflaten N 192 C4
Furulund S 61 D3
Furusjö S 60 B3
Fusa N 46 B2
Fuscaldo I 174 B2
Fusch an der Grossglocknerstrasse A 109 B3
Fushë Arrëz AL . . .182 A2
Fushë-Krujë AL . . .182 B1
Fusina I 122 B1
Fusio CH 107 C3
Füssen D 108 B1
Fustiñana E 144 B2
Futog SRB 126 B1
Futrikelv N 192 C3
Füzesabony H 113 B4
Füzesgyarmat H . .113 B5
Fužine HR 123 B3
Fyllinge S 61 C2
Fynshav DK 64 B2
Fyresdal N 53 A4

G

Gaaldorf A 110 B1
Gabaldón E 158 B2
Gabarret F 128 C2
Gabčíkovo SK 111 B4
Gabin PL 77 B4
Gabriac F 130 A1
Gaby I 119 B4
Gacé F 89 B4
Gacko BIH 139 B4
Gäddede S 199 A11

Gadebusch D 65 C4
Gadmen CH 106 C3
Gádor E 164 C2
Gádoros H 113 C4
Gael F 101 A3
Gaeta I 169 B3
Gafanhoeira P 154 C2
Gaflenz A 110 B1
Gagarin RUS 9 E9
Gaggenau D 93 C4
Gagliano Castelferrato I 177 B3
Gagliano del Capo I 173 C4
Gagnet S 50 B2
Gaibanella I 121 C4
Gaildorf D 94 B1
Gaillac F 129 C4
Gaillefontaine F . . .90 B1
Gaillon F 89 A5
Gainsborough GB . .40 B3
Gairloch GB 31 B3
Gairlochy GB 34 B3
Gáiro I 179 C3
Gaj
 HR 124 B3
 SRB 127 C3
Gaja-la-Selve F . . .146 A2
Gajanejos E 151 B5
Gajary SK 97 C4
Gajdobra SRB 126 B1
Galan F 145 A4
Galanta SK 111 A4
Galapagar E 151 B3
Galápagos E 151 B4
Galaroza E 161 B3
Galashiels GB 35 C5
Galatas GR 185 B4
Galați RO 17 C8
Galatina I 173 B4
Galatista GR 183 C5
Galátone I 173 B4
Galaxidi GR 184 A3
Galdakao E 143 A4
Galeata I 135 B4
Galende E 141 B4
Galera E 164 B2
Galéria F 180 A1
Galgamácsa H 112 B3
Galgate GB 38 A4
Galgon F 128 B2
Galices P 148 B2
Galinduste E 150 B2
Galinoporni CY . . .181 A3
Galisteo E 155 B4
Galków PL 87 A3
Gallarate I 120 B1
Gallardon F 90 C1
Gallegos de Argañán E 149 B3
Gallegos del Solmirón E 150 B2
Galleguillos de Campos E 142 B1
Galleno I 135 B3
Galliate I 120 B1
Gallicano I 134 A3
Gállio I 121 B4
Gallipoli = Gelibolu TR 186 B1
Gallipoli I 173 B3
Gällivare S 196 B3
Gallizien A 110 C1
Gallneukirchen A . .96 C2
Gällö S 199 C12
Gallocanta E 152 B2
Gällstad S 60 B3
Gallur E 144 C2
Galmisdale GB 31 C2
Galmpton GB 43 B3
Galston GB 36 A2
Galta N 52 A1
Galtelli I 178 B3
Galten DK 59 B2
Galtür A 107 C5
Galve de Sorbe E .151 A4
Galveias P 154 B2
Gálvez E 157 A3
Galway IRL 28 A2
Gamaches F 90 B1
Gámbara I 120 B3
Gambárie I 175 C1
Gambassi Terme I 135 B3
Gambatesa I 170 B2
Gambolò I 120 B1
Gaming A 110 B2
Gamla Uppsala S . .57 A4
Gamleby S 62 A4
Gamlingay GB 44 A3
Gammelgarn S 57 C4
Gammelstad S 196 D5
Gammertingen D . .107 A4
Gams CH 107 B4
Gamvik
 Finnmark N 192 B6
 Finnmark N 193 A12
Gan F 145 A3
Gáname E 149 A3
Ganda di Martello I 108 C1
Gandarela P 148 A1
Ganddal N 52 B1
Ganderkesee D 72 A1
Gandesa E 153 A4
Gandía E 159 C3
Gandino I 120 B2
Gandrup DK 58 A3
Ganges F 130 B2
Gånghester S 60 B3
Gangi I 177 B3
Gangkofen D 95 C4
Gannat F 116 A3
Gannay-sur-Loire F 104 C2
Gänserdorf A 97 C4
Ganzlin D 73 A5
Gap F 132 A2
Gara H 125 A5
Garaballa E 158 B2

Garaguso I 172 B2
Garbayuela E 156 A2
Garbhallt GB 34 B2
Garbsen D 72 B2
Garching D 109 A3
Garciaz E 156 A2
Garcihernández E 150 B2
Garcillán E 151 B3
Garcinarro E 151 B5
Garcisobaco E 162 B2
Garda I 121 B3
Gardanne F 131 B4
Gärdås S 49 B5
Gårdby S 63 B4
Gardeja PL 69 B4
Gardelegen D 73 B4
Gardermoen N 48 B3
Gardiki GR 182 E3
Garding D 64 B1
Gardone Riviera I .121 B3
Gardone Val Trómpia I 120 B3
Gárdony H 112 B2
Gardouch F 146 A2
Gårdsjö S 55 B5
Gards Köpinge S . .63 C2
Garein F 128 B2
Garelochhead GB . .34 B3
Garéoult F 132 B2
Garešnica HR 124 B2
Garéssio I 133 A4
Garforth GB 40 B2
Gargaliani GR 184 B2
Gargaligas E 156 A2
Gargallo E 153 B3
Garganta la Olla E 150 B2
Gargantiel E 156 B3
Gargellen A 107 C4
Gargilesse-Dampierre F 103 C3
Gargnano I 121 B3
Gargnäs S 195 E8
Gárgoles de Abajo E 152 B1
Gargrave GB 40 B1
Garitz D 73 C5
Garlasco I 120 B1
Garlieston GB 36 B2
Garlin F 128 C2
Garlitos E 156 B2
Garmisch-Partenkirchen D 108 B2
Garnat-sur-Engièvre F 104 C2
Garpenberg S 50 B3
Garphyttan S 55 A5
Garray E 143 C4
Garrel D 71 B5
Garriguella E 146 B4
Garrison GB 26 B2
Garrovillas E 155 B4
Garrucha E 164 B3
Gars-am-Kamp A . .97 C3
Garsås S 50 B1
Garsdale Head GB .37 B4
Gärsnäs S 63 C2
Garstang GB 38 A4
Gartow D 73 A4
Gartz D 74 A3
Gærum DK 58 A3
Garvagh GB 27 B4
Garvão P 160 B1
Garve GB 32 D2
Garwolin PL 12 C4
Garz D 66 B2
Garzyn PL 85 A4
Gąsawa PL 76 B2
Gåsborn S 49 C6
Gaschurn A 107 C5
Gascueña E 152 B1
Gasny F 90 B1
Gąsocin PL 77 B5
Gastes F 128 B1
Gastouni GR 184 B2
Gastouri GR 182 D1
Gata
 E 149 B3
 HR 138 B2
Gata de Gorgos E 159 C4
Gátaia RO 126 B3
Gatchina RUS 9 C7
Gatehouse of Fleet GB 36 B2
Gátér H 113 C3
Gateshead GB 37 B5
Gátova E 159 B3
Gattendorf A 111 A3
Gatteo a Mare I . . .136 A1
Gattinara I 119 B5
Gattorna I 134 A2
Gaucín E 162 B2
Gaulstad N 199 B9
Gaupne N 47 A4
Gautefall N 53 A4
Gauting D 108 A2
Gauto S 195 D7
Gava E 147 C3
Gavardo I 121 B3
Gavarnie F 145 B3
Gávavencsello H . .113 A5
Gavi I 120 C1
Gavião P 154 B3
Gavirate I 120 B1
Gävle S 51 B4
Gavoi I 178 B3
Gavorrano I 135 C3
Gavray F 88 B2
Gavrio GR 185 B5
Gávunda S 49 B6
Gaweinstal A 97 C4
Gaworzyce PL 85 A3
Gawroniec PL 75 A5
Gaydon GB 44 A2
Gayton GB 41 C4
Gazipaşa TR 189 C7
Gazoldo degli Ippoliti I 121 B3
Gazzuolo I 121 B3

Gdańsk PL 69 A3
Gdinj HR 138 B2
Gdov RUS 8 C5
Gdów PL 99 B4
Gdynia PL 69 A3
Gea de Albarracin E 152 B2
Geary GB 31 B2
Géaudot F 91 C4
Geaune F 128 C2
Gebesee D 82 A2
Gebiz TR 189 B5
Gebze TR 187 B4
Géderlak H 112 C2
Gedern D 81 B5
Gedinne B 91 B4
Gediz TR 187 D4
Gèdre F 145 B4
Gedser DK 65 B4
Gedsted DK 58 B2
Geel B 79 A4
Geesthacht D 72 A3
Geetbets B 79 B5
Gefell D 83 B3
Gehrden D 72 B2
Gehren D 82 B3
Geilenkirchen D . . .80 B2
Geilo N 47 B5
Geinsheim D 93 B4
Geisa D 82 B1
Geiselhöring D 95 C4
Geiselwind D 94 B2
Geisenfeld D 95 C3
Geisenhausen D . . .95 C4
Geisenheim D 93 B4
Geising D 84 B1
Geisingen D 107 B3
Geislingen D 94 C1
Geistthal A 110 B2
Geiterygghytta N . .47 B4
Geithain D 83 A4
Geithus N 48 C1
Gela I 177 B3
Geldermalsen NL . .79 A5
Geldern D 80 A2
Geldrop NL 80 A1
Geleen NL 80 B1
Gelembe TR 186 C2
Gelendost TR 189 A6
Gelibolu = Gallipoli TR 186 B1
Gelida E 147 C2
Gelnhausen D 81 B5
Gelnica SK 99 C4
Gelsa E 153 A3
Gelse H 111 C3
Gelsenkirchen D . . .80 A3
Gelsted DK 59 C2
Geltendorf D 108 A2
Gelterkinden CH . .106 B2
Gelting D 64 B2
Gelu RO 126 A3
Gelves E 162 A1
Gembloux B 79 B4
Gemeaux F 105 B4
Gémenos F 132 B1
Gemerská Poloma SK 99 C4
Gemerská Ves SK . .99 C4
Gemert NL 80 A1
Gemla S 62 B2
Gemlik TR 186 B4
Gemmenich B 80 B1
Gemona del Friuli I 122 A2
Gémozac F 114 C3
Gemund D 80 B2
Gemünden
 Bayern D 94 A1
 Hessen D 81 B4
 Rheinland-Pfalz D 93 B3
Genappe B 79 B4
Génave E 164 A2
Genazzano I 169 B2
Gençay F 115 B4
Gencsapáti H 111 B3
Gendringen NL 80 A2
Genelard F 104 C3
Genemuiden NL . . .70 B3
Generalski Stol HR 123 B4
Genevad S 61 C3
Genève = Genève CH 118 A3
Geneva = Genève CH 118 A3
Genevriéres F 105 B4
Gengenbach D 93 C4
Genillé F 103 B3
Genk B 80 B1
Genlis F 105 B4
Gennep NL 80 A1
Genner DK 64 A2
Gennes F 102 B1
Genoa = Génova I 134 A1
Genola I 133 A3
Génova = Genoa I 134 A1
Genowefa PL 76 B3
Gensingen D 93 B3
Gent = Ghent B . . .79 A3
Genthin D 73 B5
Gentioux F 116 B1
Genzano di Lucánia I 172 B2
Genzano di Roma I 168 B2
Georgenthal D 82 B2
Georgsmarienhütte D 71 B5
Gera D 83 B4
Geraardsbergen B .79 B3
Gerace I 175 C2
Geraci Sículo I 177 B3
Geraki GR 184 C3
Gérardmer F 106 A1
Geras A 97 C3
Gerberoy F 90 B1
Gerbini I 177 B3
Gerbstedt D 83 A3
Gerði IS 191 C9

Gerede TR 187 B7
Gerena E 161 B3
Geretsried D 108 B2
Gérgal E 164 B2
Gergy F 105 C3
Gerindote E 150 C3
Gerjen H 112 C2
Gerlos A 108 B3
Germay F 92 C1
Germencik TR 188 B2
Germering D 108 A2
Germersheim D 93 B4
Gernika-Lumo E . .143 A4
Gernrode D 82 A3
Gernsbach D 93 C4
Gernsheim D 93 B4
Geroda D 82 B1
Gerola Alta I 120 A2
Geroldsgrün D 83 B3
Gerolsbach D 95 C3
Gerolstein D 80 B2
Gerolzhofen D 94 B2
Gerovo HR 123 B3
Gerpinnes B 79 B4
Gerrards Cross GB 44 B3
Gersfeld D 82 B1
Gerstetten D 94 C2
Gersthofen D 94 C2
Gerstungen D 82 B2
Gerswalde D 74 A2
Gerzat F 116 B3
Gerze TR 23 A8
Gerzen D 95 C4
Gescher D 71 C4
Geseke D 81 A4
Geslau D 94 B2
Gespunsart F 91 B4
Gesté F 101 B4
Gestorf D 72 B2
Gesualda I 170 C3
Gesunda S 50 B1
Gesztely H 113 A4
Geta FIN 51 B6
Getafe E 151 B4
Getinge S 60 C2
Getxo E 143 A4
Geversdorf D 64 C2
Gevgelija MK 182 B4
Gevora del Caudillo E 155 C4
Gevrey-Chambertin F 105 B3
Gex F 118 A3
Gey D 80 B2
Geyikli TR 186 C1
Geysir IS 190 C5
Geyve TR 187 B5
Gföhl A 97 C3
Ghedi I 120 B3
Ghent = Gent B . . .79 A3
Gheorgheni RO 17 B6
Ghigo I 119 C4
Ghilarza I 178 B2
Ghisonaccia F 180 A2
Ghisoni F 180 A2
Gialtra GR 182 E4
Gianitsa GR 182 C4
Giardinetto Vécchio I 171 B3
Giardini Naxos I . .177 B4
Giarratana I 177 B3
Giarre I 177 B4
Giat F 116 B2
Giaveno I 119 B4
Giazza I 121 B4
Giba I 179 C2
Gibellina Nuova I . .176 B1
Gibostad N 194 A9
Gibraleón E 161 B3
Gibraltar GBZ 162 B2
Gic H 111 B4
Gideå S 200 C5
Gideåkroken S 200 B3
Gidle PL 86 B3
Giebelstadt D 94 B1
Gieboldehausen D .82 A2
Gielniów PL 87 A4
Gielow D 74 A1
Gien F 103 B4
Giengen D 94 C2
Giens F 132 B2
Giera RO 126 B2
Gieselwerder D 81 A5
Giessen D 81 B4
Gieten NL 71 A3
Giethoorn NL 70 B3
Giffaumont-Champaubert F . .91 C4
Gifford GB 35 C5
Gifhorn D 73 B3
Gige H 125 A3
Gijón = Xixón E . .142 A1
Gilena E 162 A3
Gilford GB 27 B4
Gillberga S 55 A3
Gilleleje DK 61 C2
Gilley F 105 B5
Gilley-sur-Loire F .104 C2
Gillingham
 Dorset GB 43 A4
 Medway GB 45 B4
Gilocourt F 90 B2
Gilserberg D 81 B5
Gilsland GB 37 B4
Gilze NL 79 A4
Gimåt S 200 C4
Gimo S 51 B5
Gimont F 129 C3
Ginasservis F 132 B1
Gingelom B 79 B5
Gingst D 66 B2
Ginosa I 171 C4
Ginzling A 108 B2
Giões P 160 B2
Gioia dei Marsi I . .169 B3
Gióia del Colle I . .173 B2
Gióia Sannitica I . .170 B2
Gióia Táuro I 175 C1

Gioiosa Iónica I . . .175 C2
Gioiosa Marea I . . .177 A3
Giosla GB 31 A2
Giovinazzo I 171 B4
Girifalco I 175 C2
Giromagny F 106 B1
Girona E 147 C3
Gironcourt-sur-Vraine F 92 C1
Gironella E 147 B3
Gironville-sous-les-Côtes F 92 C1
Girvan GB 36 A2
Gislaved S 60 B3
Gislev DK 59 C3
Gisors F 90 B1
Gissi I 170 A2
Gistad S 56 B1
Gistel B 78 A2
Gistrup DK 58 B3
Giswil CH 106 C3
Githio GR 184 C3
Giugliano in Campania I 170 C2
Giulianova I 136 C2
Giulvǎz RO 126 B2
Giurgiu RO 17 D6
Give DK 59 C2
Givet F 91 A4
Givors F 117 B4
Givry
 B 79 B4
 F 104 C3
Givry-en-Argonne F 91 C4
Givskud DK 59 C2
Giżalki PL 76 B2
Gizeux F 102 B2
Giżycko PL 12 A4
Gizzeria I 175 C2
Gizzeria Lido I 175 C2
Gjedved DK 59 C2
Gjegjan AL 182 B2
Gjendesheim N 47 A5
Gjerde N 46 B3
Gjerlev DK 58 B3
Gjermundshamn N 46 B2
Gjerrild DK 58 B3
Gjerstad N 53 B5
Gjesås N 49 B4
Gjesvær N 193 A9
Gjirokastër AL 182 C2
Gjøfjell N 54 A1
Gjøl DK 58 A2
Gjøra N 198 C6
Gjøvik N 48 B2
Gladbeck D 80 A2
Gladenbach D 81 B4
Gladstad N 195 E2
Glamis GB 35 B4
Glamoč BIH 138 A2
Glamsbjerg DK 59 C3
Gland CH 105 C5
Glandorf D 71 B4
Glanegg A 110 C1
Glanshammar S . . .56 A1
Glarus CH 107 B4
Glasgow GB 35 C3
Glashütte
 Bayern D 108 B2
 Sachsen D 84 B1
Glastonbury GB . . .43 A4
Glatzau A 110 C2
Glauchau D 83 B4
Glava S 54 A3
Glavatičevo BIH . .139 B4
Glavičice BIH 127 C1
Glavičice BIH. 127 C1
Glein
 A 110 B1
 N 195 D3
Gleinstätten A 110 C2
Gleisdorf A 110 B2
Glenamoy IRL 26 B1
Glenarm GB 27 B5
Glenavy GB 27 B4
Glenbarr GB 34 C2
Glenbeigh IRL 29 B2
Glenbrittle GB 31 B2
Glencoe GB 34 B2
Glencolumbkille IRL 26 B2
Glendalough IRL . . .30 A2
Glenealy IRL 30 B2
Glenelg GB 31 B3
Glenfinnan GB 34 B2
Glengarriff IRL 29 C2
Glenluce GB 36 B2
Glenmore IRL 30 B1
Glennamaddy IRL . .28 A3
Glenrothes GB 35 B4
Glenties IRL 26 B2
Glesborg DK 58 B3
Glesien D 83 A4
Gletsch CH 106 C3
Glewitz D 66 B1
Glifada GR 185 B4
Glimåkra S 63 B2
Glin IRL 29 B2
Glina HR 124 B2
Glinde D 72 A3
Glinojeck PL 77 B5
Glinsk IRL 28 A2
Gliwice PL 86 B2
Glödnitz A 109 C5
Głogów PL 85 A4
Głogówek PL 86 B1
Glomel F 100 A2
Glomfjord N 195 D4
Glommen S 60 C2
Glonn D 108 B2
Glorenza I 108 C1
Gloria P 154 B2
Glosa I 183 D5
Glossop GB 40 B2
Gloucester GB 39 C4

Głowaczów PL 87 A5
Główczyce PL 68 A2
Głowen D 73 B5
Głowno PL 77 C4
Głożan SRB 126 B1
Głubczyce PL 86 B1
Głuchołazy PL 85 B5
Głuchów PL 87 A4
Głuchowo PL 75 B5
Glücksburg D 64 B2
Glückstadt D 64 C2
Glumina BIH 139 A5
Glumsø DK 65 A4
Glušci SRB 127 C1
Glusk BY 13 B8
Głuszyca PL 85 B4
Glyngøre DK 58 B1
Glyn Neath GB. 39 C3
Gmünd
  Karnten A 109 C4
  Nieder Östereich
  A 96 C2
Gmund D 108 B2
Gmunden A 109 B4
Gnarp S 200 D3
Gnarrenburg D 72 A2
Gnesau A 109 C4
Gnesta S 56 A3
Gnięchowice PL 85 A4
Gniew PL 69 B3
Gniewkowo PL 76 B3
Gniezno PL 76 B2
Gnoien D 66 C1
Gnojnice BIH 139 B3
Gnojno PL 87 B4
Gnosall GB 40 C1
Gnosjö S 60 B3
Göbel TR 186 B3
Göçbeyli TR. 186 C2
Goch D 80 A2
Gochsheim D 94 A2
Göd H 112 B3
Godalming GB. 44 B3
Godby FIN 51 B6
Goðdalir IS 190 B6
Goddelsheim D 81 A4
Gódega di Sant'Urbano
  I 122 B1
Godegård S 56 B1
Godelheim D 81 A5
Goderville F 89 A4
Godiasco I 120 C2
Godič SLO 123 A3
Godkowo PL 69 A4
Godmanchester
  GB 44 A3
Gödöllő H 112 B3
Gödre H 125 A3
Godshill GB. 44 C2
Godzikowice PL 85 B5
Godziszewo PL 69 A3
Goes NL 79 A3
Goetzenbrück F 93 C3
Góglio I 119 A5
Gogolin PL 86 B2
Göhren D 66 B2
Goirle NL 79 A5
Góis P 148 B1
Góito I 121 B3
Goizueta E 144 A2
Gojna Gora SRB . . .127 D2
Gójsk PL 77 B4
Gökçedağ TR 186 C3
Gökçen TR. 188 A2
Gökçeören TR 188 A3
Gökçeyazı TR 186 C2
Göktepe TR. 188 B3
Gol N 47 B5
Gola
  HR 124 A3
  N 48 A1
Gołańcz PL 76 B2
Gölbaşı TR. 23 B7
Gölby FIN. 51 B6
Gölcük
  Kocaeli TR. 187 B4
  Niğde TR 23 B8
Golčův Jenikov CZ .97 B3
Golczewo PL 67 C3
Goldach CH 107 B4
Goldbach D 93 A5
Goldbeck D 73 B4
Goldberg D 73 A5
Goldelund D 64 B2
Goldenstedt D 72 B1
Gołębiewo PL 69 A3
Golegã P 154 B2
Goleniów PL 75 A3
Golfo Aranci I 178 B3
Gölhisar TR 189 B4
Golina PL 76 B3
Gölle H 112 C2
Göllersdorf A. 97 C4
Golling an der Salzach
  A 109 B4
Gölmarmara TR 186 D2
Golnice PL. 84 A3
Golnik SLO 123 A3
Gölova TR 189 C5
Gölpazarı TR. 187 B5
Gols A 111 B3
Golspie GB 32 D3
Golssen D 74 C2
Golub-Dobrzyń PL .77 A4
Golubinci SRB. 127 C2
Goluchów PL. 86 A1
Golymin-Ośrodek
  PL 77 B5
Golzow D 73 B5
Gomagoi I 108 C1
Gómara E 152 A1
Gömbe TR 189 C4
Gömeç TR 186 C1
Gomel = Homyel
  BY. 13 B9
Gomes Aires P 160 B1
Gómezserracin E . .150 A3
Gommern D 73 B4
Gomulin PL 86 A3

Gonäs S 50 B2
Goncelin F 118 B2
Gończyce PL. 87 A5
Gondomar
  E 140 B2
  P 148 A1
Gondrecourt-le-
  Château F 92 C1
Gondrin F 128 C3
Gönen
  Balıkesir TR 186 B2
  Isparta TR 189 B5
Gonfaron F 132 B2
Goñi E 144 B2
Goni
  GR 182 D4
  I 179 C3
Gonnesa I 179 C2
Gonnosfanádiga I . .179 C2
Gönyü H 111 B4
Gonzaga I 121 C3
Goodrich GB 39 C4
Goodwick GB 39 B1
Gooik B 79 B4
Goole GB 40 B3
Goor NL 71 B3
Göteborg =
  Gothenburg S. 60 B1
Götene S 55 B4
Gotha D 82 B2
Gothem S 57 C4
Gothenburg =
  Göteborg S 60 B1
Gotse Delchev BG 183 B5
Gottersdorf D 95 C4
Göttingen D 82 A1
Gottne S 200 C4
Götzis A. 107 B4
Gouarec F 100 A2
Gouda NL 70 B1
Goudhurst GB. 45 B4
Goumenissa GR . . .182 C4
Goura GR. 184 B3
Gourdon F 129 B4
Gourgançon F 91 C4
Gourin F 100 A2
Gournay-en-Bray F .90 B1
Gourock GB. 34 C3
Gouveia P 148 B2
Gouvy B 80 B1
Gouzeacourt F 90 A3
Gouzon F 116 A2
Govedari HR 138 C3
Govérnolo I 121 B3
Gowarczów PL. 87 A4
Gowerton GB. 39 C2
Gowidlino PL. 68 A2
Gowran IRL 30 B1
Goyatz D 74 B3
Göynük
  TR. 187 B5
  Antalya TR 189 C5
Gozdnica PL 84 A3
Gozdowo PL 77 B4
Gozee B 79 B4
Graal-Müritz D 65 B5
Grabenstätt D 109 B3
Grabhair GB 31 A2
Gråbo S 60 B2
Grabovac
  HR 138 B2
  SRB 127 C2
Grabovci SRB 127 C1
Grabow D 73 A4
Grabów PL 77 B4
Grabow nad Pilicą
  PL 87 A5
Grabów nad Prosną
  PL 86 A2
Grabowno PL 76 A2
Grabs CH 107 B4
Gračac HR 138 A1
Gračanica BIH 125 C4
Graçay F 103 B3
Grad SLO 111 C3
Gradac
  BIH 139 C4
  HR 138 B3
  MNE 139 B5
Gradačac BIH 125 C4
Gradec HR 124 B2
Gradefes E 142 B1
Grades A 110 C1
Gradil P 154 C1
Gradina
  HR 124 B3
  MNE 139 B5
Gradisca d'Isonzo
  I 122 B2
Gradište HR 125 B4
Grado
  E 141 A4
  I 122 B2
Grafenau D 96 C1
Gräfenberg D 94 B3
Gräfenhainichen D .83 A4
Grafenschlag A 97 C3
Grafenstein A 110 C1
Gräfenthal D 82 B3
Grafentonna D 82 A2
Grafenwöhr D 95 B3
Grafing D 108 A2
Grafling D 95 C4
Gräfsnäs S 54 B3
Gragnano I 170 C2
Graiguenamanagh
  IRL 30 B2
Grain GB 45 B4
Grainau D 108 B2
Graja de Iniesta E .158 B2
Grajera E 151 A4
Gram DK 59 C2
Gramais I 108 B1
Gramat F 129 B4
Gramatneusiedl A .111 A3
Grambow D 74 A3
Grammichele I 177 B3
Gramsh AL 182 C2
Gramzow D 74 A3
Gran N 48 B2
Granada E 163 A4

Granard IRL 27 C3
Grañas E 140 A3
Granátula de Calatrava
  E 157 B4
Grancey-le-Château
  F 105 B4
Grandas de Salime
  E 141 A4
Grandcamp-Maisy
  F 88 A2
Grand-Champ F 100 B3
Grand Couronne F .89 A5
Grand-Fougeray F .101 B4
Grândola P 160 A1
Grandpré F 91 B4
Grandrieu
  B 79 B4
  F 117 C3
Grandson CH 106 C1
Grandvillars F 106 B1
Grandvilliers F 90 B1
Grañén E 145 C3
Grängärde S 50 B1
Grängesberg S. 50 B1
Grange IRL. 26 B2
Grangemouth GB. . . .35 B4
Grange-over-Sands
  GB 36 B4
Granges-de-Crouhens
  F 145 B4
Granges-sur-Vologne
  F 106 A1
Gräningen D 73 B5
Granítola-Torretta
  I 176 B1
Granja
  Évora P 155 C3
  Porto P 148 A1
Granja de Moreruela
  E 142 C1
Granja de
  Torrehermosa E 156 B2
Gränna S 55 B5
Grannäs
  Västerbotten S . . .195 E7
  Västerbotten S . . .195 E8
Granö S 200 B5
Granollers E 147 C3
Granowiec PL 85 A5
Granowo PL 75 B5
Gransee D 74 A2
Gransherad N 53 A5
Grantham GB 40 C3
Grantown-on-Spey
  GB 32 D3
Grantshouse GB 35 C5
Granville F 88 B2
Granvin N 46 B3
Grærup Strand DK .59 C1
Gräsås S 60 C2
Grasbakken N 193 B12
Grasberg D 72 A2
Grasmere GB 36 B3
Gräsmyr S 200 C5
Grasö S 51 B5
Grassano I 172 B2
Grassau D 109 B3
Grasse F 132 B2
Grassington GB 40 A2
Græsted DK 61 C2
Gråsten DK 64 B2
Grästorp S 54 B3
Gratkorn A 110 B2
Gråträsk S 196 D2
Gratwein A 110 B2
Graulhet F 129 C4
Graus E 145 B4
Grávalos E 144 B2
Gravberget N 49 B4
Grave NL 80 A1
Gravedona I 120 A2
Gravelines F 78 A2
Gravellona Toce I . .119 B5
Gravendal S 50 B1
Gravens DK 59 C2
Gravesend GB 45 B4
Graveson F 131 B3
Gravina in Púglia
  I 172 B2
Gray F 105 B4
Grayrigg GB 37 B4
Grays GB 45 B4
Grayshott GB 44 B3
Graz A 110 B2
Grazalema E 162 B2
Grazzano Visconti
  I 120 C2
Greåker N 54 A2
Great Dunmow GB .45 B4
Great Malvern GB . .39 B4
Great Torrington
  GB 42 B2
Great Waltham GB .45 B4
Great Yarmouth
  GB 41 C5
Grebbestad S 54 B2
Grebenstein D 81 A5
Grębocin PL 76 A3
Greding D 95 B3
Gredstedbro DK 59 C1
Greencastle IRL 27 A3
Greenhead GB 37 B4
Greenisland GB 27 B5
Greenlaw GB 35 C5
Greenock GB 34 C3
Greenwich GB 45 B4
Grefrath D 80 A2
Greifenburg A 109 C4
Greiffenberg D 74 A2
Greifswald D 66 B2
Grein A 110 A1
Greipstad N 53 B3
Greiz D 83 B4
Grenaa DK 58 B3
Grenade F 129 C4
Grenade-sur-l'Adour
  F 128 C2

Grenchen CH 106 B2
Grendi N 53 B3
Grenivik IS 191 B7
Grenoble F 118 B2
Gréoux-les-Bains
  F 132 B1
Gresenhorst D 66 B1
Gressoney-la-Trinité
  I 119 B4
Gressoney-St.Jean
  I 119 B4
Gressthal D 82 B2
Gressvik N 54 A1
Gresten A 110 B2
Gretna GB 36 B3
Greussen D 82 A2
Greve in Chianti I . .135 B4
Greven
  Mecklenburg-
  Vorpommern D . . 73 A3
  Nordrhein-Westfalen
  D 71 B4
Grevena GR 182 C3
Grevenbroich D 80 A2
Grevenbrück D 81 A4
Grevenmacher L . . .92 B2
Grevesmühlen D 65 C4
Grevestrand DK 61 D2
Grevie S 61 C2
Greystoke GB 36 B4
Greystones IRL 30 A2
Grez-Doiceau B 79 B4
Grèzec F 129 B4
Grez-en-Bouère F .102 B1
Grezzana I 121 B4
Grgar SLO 122 A2
Grgurevci SRB 127 B1
Gries A 108 B2
Griesbach D 96 C1
Griesheim D 93 B4
Gries in Sellrain A .108 B2
Grieskirchen A 109 A4
Griffen A 110 C1
Grignan F 131 A3
Grignano I 122 B2
Grigno I 121 A4
Grignols F 128 B2
Grignon F 118 B3
Grijota E 142 B2
Grijpskerk NL 71 A3
Grillby S 56 A3
Grimaud F 132 B2
Grimbergen B 79 B4
Grimma D 83 A4
Grimmen D 66 B2
Grimmialp CH 106 C2
Grimsås S 60 B3
Grimsby GB 41 B3
Grimslöv S 62 B2
Grimstad N 53 B4
Grimstorp S 62 A2
Grindavik IS 190 D3
Grindelwald CH 106 C2
Grindheim N 52 B3
Grindsted DK 59 C1
Griñón E 151 B4
Gripenberg S 62 A2
Gripsholm S 56 A3
Grisolles F 129 C4
Grisslehamn S 51 B5
Gritley GB 33 C4
Grizebeck GB 36 B3
Grndina BIH 124 C2
Gröbming A 109 B4
Gröbzig D 83 A3
Grocka SRB 127 C2
Gröditz D 83 A5
Gródki PL 77 A5
Grodków PL 85 B5
Grodziec PL 76 B3
Grodzisk Mazowiecki
  PL 77 B5
Groenlo NL 71 B3
Groesbeek NL 80 A1
Grohote HR 138 B2
Groitzsch D 83 A4
Groix F 100 B2
Grójec PL 77 C5
Grom PL 77 A5
Gromiljca BIH 139 B4
Gromnik PL 99 B4
Gromo I 120 B2
Gronau
  Niedersachsen D . 72 B2
  Nordrhein-Westfalen
  D 71 B4
Grønbjerg DK 59 B1
Grönenbach D 107 B5
Grong N 199 A9
Grönhögen S 63 B4
Groningen
  D 73 C4
  NL 71 A3
Grønnestrand DK . . .58 A2
Grono CH 120 A2
Grönskåra S 62 A3
Grootegast NL 71 A3
Gropello Cairoli I . . .120 B1
Grorud N 48 C2
Grósio I 120 A3
Grošnica SRB 127 D2
Grossalmerode D . . .82 A1
Grossari A 109 B4
Gross Beeren D 74 B2
Gross Berkel D 72 B2
Grossbodungen D . .82 A2
Grossburgwedel D .72 B2
Grosschönau D 84 B2
Gross-Dölln D 74 A2
Grossenbrode D 65 B4
Grossenehrich D 82 A2
Grossenhain D 83 A5
Grossenkneten D . . .71 B5
Grossenlüder D 81 B5
Grossensee D 72 A3

Grossenzersdorf
  A 111 A3
Grosseto I 135 C4
Gross-Gerau D 93 B4
Grossgerungs A 96 C2
Grossglobnitz A 97 C3
Grosshabersdorf D .94 B2
Grossharras A 97 C4
Grosshartmansdorf
  D 83 B5
Grosshöchstetten
  CH 106 C2
Gross Kreutz D 74 B1
Grosskrut A 97 C4
Gross Lafferde D . . .72 B3
Gross Leuthen D 74 B3
Grosslohra D 82 A2
Grossmehring D 95 C3
Gross Muckrow D . . .74 B3
Gross Oesingen D . .72 B3
Grossostheim D 93 B5
Grosspertholz A 96 C2
Grosspetersdorf
  A 111 B3
Grosspostwitz D 84 A2
Grossraming A 110 B1
Grossräschen D 84 A2
Gross Reken D 80 A3
Grossrinderfeld D . .94 B1
Grossröhrsdorf D . . .84 A2
Gross Sarau D 65 C3
Gross Särchen D . . .84 A2
Grossschirma D 83 B5
Gross Schönebeck
  D 74 B2
Grossschweinbarth
  A 97 C4
Grosssiegharts A . . .97 C3
Grosssölk A 109 B4
Gross Umstadt D . . .93 B4
Grosswarasdorf A .111 B3
Gross Warnow D 73 A4
Gross-Weikersdorf
  A 97 C4
Gross-Welle D 73 A5
Grosswilfersdorf
  A 110 B2
Gross Wokern D 65 C5
Grostenquin F 92 C2
Grosuplje SLO 123 B3
Grotli N 198 C4
Grötlingbo S 57 C4
Grottáglie I 173 B3
Grottaminarda I 170 B3
Grottammare I 136 C2
Grotte di Castro I . .168 A1
Grotteria I 175 C2
Gróttole I 172 B2
Grou NL 70 A2
Grov N 194 B8
Grova N 53 A4
Grove E 140 B2
Grua N 48 B2
Grube D 65 B4
Grubišno Polje
  HR 124 B3
Grude BIH 138 B3
Grudusk PL 77 A5
Grudziądz PL 69 B3
Grue N 49 B4
Gruissan F 130 B2
Grullos E 141 A4
Grumo Áppula I 171 B4
Grums S 55 A4
Grünau im Almtal
  A 109 B4
Grünberg D 81 B4
Grünburg A 110 B1
Gründelhardt D 94 B1
Grundforsen S 49 A4
Grundlsee A 109 B4
Grundsund S 54 B2
Grunewald D 84 A1
Grungedal N 53 A3
Grunow D 74 B3
Grünstadt D 93 B4
Gruvberget S 50 A3
Gruyères CH 106 C2
Gruža SRB 127 D2
Grybów PL 99 B4
Grycksbo S 50 B2
Gryfice PL 67 C4
Gryfino PL 74 A3
Gryfów Śląski PL . .84 A3
Gryllefjord N 194 A8
Grymyr N 48 B2
Gryt S 56 B2
Grytgöl S 56 B1
Grythyttan S 55 A5
Grytnäs S 57 B3
Grzebienisko PL 75 B5
Grzmiąca PL 68 B1
Grzywna PL 76 A3
Gschnitz A 108 B2
Gschwend D 94 C1
Gstaad CH 106 C2
Gsteig CH 119 A4
Guadahortuna E . . .163 A4
Guadalajara E 151 B4
Guadalaviar E 152 B2
Guadalcanal E 156 B2
Guadalix de la Sierra
  E 151 B4
Guadálmez E 156 B3
Guadalupe E 156 A2
Guadamur E 151 C3
Guadarrama E 151 B3
Guadiaro E 162 B2
Guadix E 164 B1
Guagnano I 173 B3
Guagno F 180 A1
Guajar-Faragüit E .163 B4
Gualchos E 163 B4
Gualdo Tadino I 136 B1
Gualtieri I 121 C3
Guarcino I 169 B3
Guarda P 149 B2

Guardamar del Segura
  E 165 A4
Guardão P 148 B1
Guardavalle I 175 C2
Guardea I 168 A2
Guárdia I 172 B1
Guardiagrele I 169 A4
Guardiarégia I 170 B2
Guardias Viejas E 164 C2
Guárdia Sanframondi
  I 170 B2
Guardiola de Berguada
  E 147 B2
Guardo E 142 B2
Guareña E 156 B1
Guaro E 162 B3
Guarromán E 157 B4
Guasila I 179 C3
Guastalla I 121 C3
Gubbhögen S 199 A12
Gúbbio I 136 B1
Guben D 74 C3
Gubin PL 74 C3
Guðá N 199 B8
Gudavac BIH 124 C2
Guddal N 46 A2
Güderup DK 64 B2
Gudhem S 55 B4
Gudhjem DK 67 A3
Gudovac HR 124 B2
Gudow D 73 A3
Güdül TR 187 B7
Gudvangen N 46 B3
Guebwiller F 106 B2
Guéjar-Sierra E 163 A4
Guémené-Penfao
  F 101 B4
Guémené-sur-Scorff
  F 100 A2
Güenes E 143 A3
Guer F 101 B3
Guérande F 101 B3
Guéret F 116 A1
Guérigny F 104 B2
Guesa E 144 B2
Gueugnon F 104 C3
Guglionesi I 170 B2
Gühlen Glienicke
  D 74 A1
Guia P 154 B2
Guichen F 101 B4
Guidizzolo I 121 B3
Guidónia-Montecélio
  I 168 B2
Guiglia I 135 A3
Guignes F 90 C2
Guijo E 156 B3
Guijo de Coria E . . .149 B3
Guijo de Santa Bábera
  E 150 B2
Guijuelo E 150 B2
Guildford GB 44 B3
Guillaumes F 132 A2
Guillena E 162 A1
Guillestre F 118 C3
Guillos F 128 B2
Guilsfield GB 38 B3
Guilvinec F 100 B1
Guimarães P 148 A1
Guincho P 154 C1
Guînes F 78 B1
Guingamp F 100 A2
Guipavas F 100 A1
Guisborough GB 37 B5
Guiscard F 90 B3
Guiscriff F 100 A2
Guise F 91 B3
Guisona E 147 C2
Guitiriz E 140 A3
Guîtres F 128 A2
Gujan-Mestras F . . .128 B1
Gulbene LV 8 D5
Gulçayır TR 187 C6
Guldborg DK 65 B4
Gullabo S 63 B3
Gullane GB 35 B5
Gullbrå N 46 B3
Gullbrandstorp S . . .61 C2
Gulleråsen S 50 A2
Gullhaug N 53 A6
Gullringen S 62 A3
Gullspång S 55 B5
Gullstein N 198 B5
Güllük TR 188 B2
Gülnar TR 23 C7
Gülpınar TR 186 C1
Gülşehir TR 23 B8
Gulsvik N 48 B1
Gumiel de Hizán
  E 143 C3
Gummersbach D 81 A3
Gümüldür TR 188 A2
Gümüşhacıköy TR .23 A8
Gümüşova TR 187 B5
Gundelfingen D 94 C2
Gundel-fingen D . . .106 A2
Gundelsheim D 93 B5
Gunderschoffen F .93 C3
Gundertshausen
  A 109 A3
Gundinci HR 125 B4
Gündoğmuş TR 189 C7
Gunja HR 125 C4
Günlüce TR 188 C3
Gunnarn S 195 E8
Gunnarsbyn S 196 C4
Gunnarskog S 49 C4
Gunnebo S 62 A4
Gunnislake GB 42 B2
Günselsdorf A 111 B3
Guntersblum D 93 B4
Guntersdorf A 97 C4
Güntin E 140 B3
Guntramsdorf A . . .111 B3
Günyüzü TR. 187 C6
  Burdur TR 189 B4
  Denizli TR 188 B3

Günzburg D 94 C2
Gunzenhausen D . .94 B2
Güre
 Balıkesir TR 186 C1
 Uşak TR 186 D4
Gurk A 110 C1
Gurrea de Gállego
 E 144 B3
Gürsu TR 186 B4
Gušće HR 124 B2
Gusev RUS 12 A5
Gúspini I 179 C2
Gusselby S 56 A1
Güssing A 111 B3
Gusswerk A 110 B2
Gustav Adolf S 49 B5
Gustavsberg S 57 A4
Gustavsfors S 54 A3
Güstrow D 65 C5
Gusum S 56 B2
Gutcher GB 33 A5
Gutenstein A 110 B2
Gütersloh D 81 A4
Guttannen CH 106 C3
Guttaring A 110 C1
Guttau D 84 A2
Güttingen CH 107 B4
Gützkow D 66 C2
Guzów PL 77 B4
Gvardeysk RUS 12 A4
Gvarv N 53 A5
Gvozd MNE 139 C5
Gvozdansko HR . .124 B2
Gwda Wielka PL . . .68 B1
Gwennap GB 42 B1
Gy F 105 B4
Gyál H 112 B3
Gyarmat H 111 B4
Gyékényes H 124 A3
Gyé-sur-Seine F . . .104 A3
Gyljen S 196 C5
Gylling DK 59 C3
Gyoma H 113 C4
Gyömöre H 111 B4
Gyömrö H 112 B3
Gyón H 112 B3
Gyöngyfa H 125 B3
Gyöngyös H 113 B3
Gyöngyöspata H . .113 B3
Gyönk H 112 C2
Györ H 111 B4
Györszemere H . . .111 B4
Gypsera CH 106 C2
Gysinge S 51 B3
Gyttorp S 55 A5
Gyula H 113 C5
Gyulafirátót H 112 B1
Gyulaj H 112 C2

H

Haacht B 79 B4
Haag
 Nieder Östereich
 A 110 A1
 Ober Östereich A. 109 A4
 D 108 A3
Haaksbergen NL . . .71 B3
Haamstede NL 79 A3
Haan D 80 A3
Haapajärvi FIN. 3 E9
Haapsalu EST 8 C3
Haarlem NL 70 B1
Habas F 128 C2
Habay B 92 B1
Habo S 62 A2
Håbol S 54 B3
Habry CZ 97 B3
Habsheim F 106 B2
Hachenburg D 81 B3
Hacıbektaş TR 23 B8
Hacılar TR 23 B8
Hacinas E 143 C3
Hackås S 199 C11
Hacketstown IRL . . .30 B2
Hackthorpe GB 37 B4
Hadamar D 81 B4
Hädanberg S 200 C4
Haddington GB 35 C5
Hadersdorf am Kamp
 A 97 C3
Haderslev DK 59 C2
Haderup DK 59 B1
Hadım TR 23 C7
Hadleigh
 Essex GB 45 B4
 Suffolk GB 45 A4
Hadlow GB 45 B4
Hadmersleben D . . .73 B4
Hadsten DK 59 B3
Hadsund DK 58 B3
Hadžići BIH 139 B4
Hafnarfjörður IS . .190 C4
Hafnir IS 190 D3
Hafslo N 47 A4
Haganj HR 124 B2
Hagby S 63 B4
Hage D 71 A4
Hægebostad N 52 B3
Hægeland N 53 B3
Hagen
 Niedersachsen D . .72 A1
 Nordrhein-Westfalen
 D 80 A3
Hagenbach D 93 B4
Hagenow D 73 A4
Hagetmau F 128 C2
Hagfors S 49 B5
Häggenås S 199 B11
Hagondange F 92 B2
Hagsta S 51 B4
Haguenau F 93 C3
Hahnbach D 95 B3
Hahnslätten D 81 B4
Hahót H 111 C3
Haiger D 81 B4

Haigerloch D 93 C4
Hailsham GB 45 C4
Hainburg A 111 A3
Hainfeld A 110 A2
Hainichen D 83 B5
Hajdúböszörmény
 H 113 B5
Hajdúdorogo H . . .113 B5
Hajdúnánás H 113 B5
Hajdúszoboszló
 H 113 B5
Hajnáčka SK 113 A3
Hajnówka PL 13 B5
Hajós H 112 C3
Håkafot S 199 A11
Hakkas S 196 C4
Håksberg S 50 B2
Halaszi H 111 B4
Halberstadt D 82 A3
Halberton GB 43 B3
Haldem D 71 B5
Halden N 54 A2
Haldensleben D 73 B4
Halenbeck D 73 A5
Halesowen GB 40 C1
Halesworth GB 45 A5
Halfing D 109 B3
Halhjem N 46 B2
Håliden S 49 B5
Halifax GB 40 B2
Häljelöt S 56 B2
Halkida GR 185 A4
Halkirk GB 32 C3
Hall S 57 C4
Hälla S 200 C3
Hällabro S 63 B3
Hällabrottet S 56 A1
Halland GB 45 C4
Hällaryd S 63 B2
Hällaryd S 61 C3
Hällberga S 56 A2
Hällbybrunn S 56 A2
Halle
 D 79 B4
 Nordrhein-Westfalen
 D 72 B1
 Sachsen-Anhalt D . 83 A3
Hälleberga S 62 B3
Hällefors S 55 A5
Hälleforsnäs S 56 A2
Hallein A 109 B4
Hällekis S 55 B4
Hallen S 199 B11
Hällen S 51 B4
Hallenberg D 81 A4
Hällestad S 56 B1
Hällevadsholm S . . .54 B2
Hällevik S 63 B2
Hällevikstrand S . . .54 B2
Hallingby S 48 B2
Hallingeberg S 62 A4
Hallingen N 47 B6
Hall in Tirol A 108 B2
Hällnäs S 195 D9
Hällnäs S 51 B4
Hällnäs S 200 B5
Hallormsstaður
 IS 191 B11
Hallsberg S 56 A1
Hällsta S 56 A2
Hallstahammar S . . .56 A2
Hallstatt A 109 B4
Hallstavik S 51 B5
Halltorp S 63 B4
Halluin F 78 B3
Hallviken S 199 B12
Hallworthy GB 42 B2
Halmstad S 61 C2
Halsa N 198 B5
Halstead GB 45 B4
Haltdalen N 199 C8
Haltern D 80 A3
Haltwhistle GB 37 B4
Halvarsgårdarna S . .50 B2
Halver D 80 A3
Halvrimmen DK 58 A2
Ham F 90 B3
Hamar N 48 B3
Hamarhaug N 46 B2
Hamarøy N 194 B6
Hambach F 92 B3
Hambergen D 72 A1
Hambergsund S 54 B2
Hambledon GB 44 C2
Hambuhren D 72 B2
Hamburg D 72 A3
Hamdibey TR 186 C2
Hamdorf D 64 B2
Hämeenlinna FIN 8 B4
HamELN = Hamlin D 72 B2
Hamersleben D 73 B4
Hamidiye TR 187 C5
Hamilton GB 36 A2
Hamina FIN 8 B5
Hamlagrø N 46 B3
Hamlin = Hameln D 72 B2
Hamm D 81 A3
Hammar S 55 B5
Hammarland FIN . . .51 B6
Hammarö S 55 A4
Hammarstrand S . .200 C2
Hamme D 79 A4
Hammel DK 59 B2
Hammelburg D 82 B1
Hammelspring D . . .74 A2
Hammenhög S 66 A3
Hammerdal S 199 B12
Hammerfest N 192 B7
Hammershøj DK . . .58 B2
Hammerum DK 59 B2
Hamminkeln D 80 A2
Hamnavoe GB 33 A5
Hamneda S 60 C3
Hamningberg N . .193 B14
Hamoir B 80 B1
Hamont B 80 A1
Hámor H 113 A4

Hamra
 Gävleborg S 199 D12
 Gotland S 57 D4
Hamrångefjärden
 S 51 B4
Hamstreet GB 45 B4
Hamsund N 194 B6
Han TR 187 C5
Hanaskog S 61 C4
Hanau D 81 B4
Händelöp S 62 A4
Handlová SK 98 C2
Hanerau-
 Hademarschen D 64 B2
Hänger S 60 B3
Hanhimaa FIN 197 B8
Hanken S 55 B5
Hankensbüttel D . . .73 B3
Hanko FIN 8 C3
Hannover D 72 B2
Hannut B 79 B5
Han Pijesak BIH . . .139 A4
Hansnes N 192 C3
Hanstedt D 72 A3
Hanstholm DK 58 A1
Hantsavichy BY. . . .13 B7
Hanušovice CZ 85 B4
Haparanda S 196 D7
Haradok BY 13 A8
Harads S 196 C4
Häradsbäck S 63 B2
Häradsbygden S . . .50 B2
Harbo S 51 B4
Harboør DK 58 B1
Harburg
 Bayern D 94 C2
 Hamburg D 72 A2
Hårby DK 59 C3
Harc H 112 C2
Hardegarijp NL 70 A2
Hardegsen D 82 A1
Hardelot Plage F . . .78 B1
Hardenbeck D 74 A2
Hardenberg NL 71 B3
Harderwijk NL 70 B2
Hardheim D 94 B1
Hardt D 106 A3
Hareid N 198 C3
Haren
 D 71 B4
 NL 71 A3
Harestua N 48 B2
Harfleur F 89 A4
Harg S 51 B5
Hargicourt F 90 B3
Hargnies F 91 A4
Hargshamn S 51 B5
Härja S 55 B4
Harkány H 125 B4
Härkeberga S 56 A3
Harkebrügge D 71 A4
Harlech GB 38 B2
Harleston GB 45 A5
Hårlev DK 65 A5
Harlingen NL 70 A2
Harlösa S 61 D3
Harlow GB 45 B4
Harmancık TR 186 C4
Harmånger S 200 E3
Härnevi S 56 A3
Härnösand S 200 D3
Haro E 143 B4
Haroldswick GB 33 A6
Háromfa H 124 A3
Haroué F 92 C2
Harpenden GB 44 B3
Harplinge S 60 C2
Harpstedt D 72 B1
Harrogate GB 40 A2
Harrow GB 44 B3
Härryda S 60 B2
Harsefeld D 72 A2
Harsewinkel D 71 C5
Hårsova 17 C7
Harstad N 194 B7
Harsum D 72 B2
Harsvik N 199 A7
Harta H 112 C3
Hartberg A 110 B2
Hartburn GB 37 A5
Hartennes F 90 B3
Hartest GB 45 A4
Hartha D 83 A4
Hartland GB 42 B2
Hartlepool GB 37 B5
Hartmanice CZ 96 B1
Hartmannsdorf A. . .110 B2
Harvassdal N 195 E5
Harwell GB 44 B2
Harwich GB 45 B5
Harzgerode D 82 A3
Häselgehr A 108 B1
Haselünne D 71 B4
Hasköy TR 186 A1
Haslach D 106 A3
Haslach an der Mühl
 A 96 C2
Hasle DK 67 A3
Haslemere GB 44 B3
Haslev DK 65 A4
Hasloch D 94 B1
Hasparren F 144 A2
Hassela S 200 D2
Hasselfelde D 82 A2
Hasselfors S 55 A5
Hasselt
 B 79 B5
 NL 70 B3
Hassfurt D 94 A2
Hasslarp S 61 C2
Hässleholm S 61 C3
Hasslö S 63 B3
Hassloch D 93 B4
Hästbo S 51 B4
Hastersboda FIN . . .51 B7
Hästholmen S 55 B5
Hastière-Lavaux B . .79 B4
Hastigrow GB 32 C3
Hastings GB 45 C4

Hästveda S 61 C3
Hasvik N 192 B6
Hatfield
 Hertfordshire GB . . 44 B3
 South Yorkshire
 GB 40 B3
Hatherleigh GB 42 B2
Hathersage GB 40 B2
Hatlestrand N 46 B2
Hattem NL 70 B3
Hatten
 D 71 A5
 F 93 C3
Hattfjelldal N 195 E4
Hatting DK 59 C2
Hattingen D 80 A3
Hattstadt F 106 A2
Hattstedt D 64 B2
Hatvan H 112 B3
Hatvik N 46 B2
Hau D 80 A2
Haudainville F 92 B1
Hauganes IS 191 B7
Haugastøl N 47 B4
Hauge N 52 B2
Haughom N 52 B2
Haugsdal N 46 B2
Haugsdorf A 97 C4
Haukedal N 46 A3
Haukeland N 46 B2
Haukeligrend N 52 A3
Haukeliseter N 52 A3
Haukipudas FIN 3 D9
Haulerwijk NL 71 A3
Haunersdorf D 95 C4
Haus N 46 B2
Hausach D 106 A3
Hausham D 108 B2
Hausmannstätten
 A 110 C2
Hausvik N 52 B2
Hautajärvi FIN . . .197 C12
Hautefort F 129 A4
Hauterives F 117 B5
Hauteville-Lompnès
 F 118 B2
Haut-Fays B 91 A5
Hautmont F 79 B3
Hautrage B 79 B3
Hauzenberg D 96 C1
Havant GB 44 C3
Havdhem S 57 C4
Havdrup DK 61 D2
Havelange B 79 B5
Havelberg D 73 B5
Havelte NL 194 B7
Haverfordwest GB . .39 C2
Haverhill GB 45 A4
Havering GB 45 B4
Håverud N 54 B3
Havixbeck D 71 C4
Havlíčkův Brod CZ . .97 B3
Havndal DK 58 B3
Havneby DK 64 A1
Havnebyen DK 61 D1
Havnsø DK 61 D1
Havøysund N 193 A8
Havran TR 186 C2
Havsa TR 186 A1
Havstenssund S 54 B2
Havza TR 23 A8
Hawes GB 37 B4
Hawick GB 35 C5
Hawkhurst GB 45 B4
Hawkinge GB 45 B5
Haxey GB 40 B3
Hayange F 92 B2
Haydarlı TR 189 A5
Haydon Bridge GB . .37 B4
Hayle GB 42 B1
Haymana TR 187 C7
Hay-on-Wye GB 39 B3
Hayrabolu TR 186 A2
Haysyn UA 13 D8
Hayvoron UA 13 D8
Haywards Heath
 GB 44 C3
Hazebrouck F 78 B2
Hazlov CZ 83 B4
Heacham GB 41 C4
Headcorn GB 45 B4
Headford IRL 28 A2
Heanor GB 40 B2
Héas F 145 B4
Heathfield GB 45 C4
Hebden Bridge GB . .40 B1
Heberg S 60 C2
Heby S 51 C3
Hechingen D 93 C4
Hechlingen D 94 C2
Hecho E 144 B3
Hechtel B 79 A5
Hechthausen D 72 A2
Heckelberg D 74 B2
Heckington GB 41 C3
Hecklingen D 82 A3
Hed S 56 A1
Hedalen N 48 B1
Hedared S 60 B2
Heddal N 53 A5
Hédé F 101 A4
Hede S 199 C10
Hedekas S 54 B2
Hedemora S 50 B2
Hedenäset S 196 C6
Hedensted DK 59 C2
Hederslev D 82 A3
Hedesunda S 51 B4
Hedge End GB 44 C2
Hedon GB 41 B3
Heede D 71 B4
Heek D 71 B4
Heemstede NL 70 B1
Heerde NL 70 B3
Heerenveen NL 70 B2
Heerhugowaard NL 70 B1
Heerlen NL 80 B1

Heeze NL 80 A1
Heggenes N 47 A6
Hegra N 199 B8
Hegyeshalom H . . .111 B4
Hegyközség H 111 B3
Heia N 199 A9
Heide D 64 B2
Heidelberg D 93 B4
Heiden D 80 A2
Heidenau D 84 B1
Heidenheim D 94 C2
Heidenreichstein A .97 C3
Heikendorf D 64 B3
Heikkilä FIN 197 C12
Heilam GB 32 C2
Heiland N 53 B4
Heilbad Heiligenstadt
 D 82 A2
Heilbronn D 93 B5
Heiligendamn D 65 B4
Heiligendorf D 73 B3
Heiligengrabe D 73 A5
Heiligenhafen D 65 B3
Heiligenhaus D 80 A2
Heiligenkreuz A . . .111 C3
Heiligenstadt D 94 B3
Heiloo NL 70 B1
Heilsbronn D 94 B2
Heim N 198 B6
Heimburg D 82 A2
Heimdal N 199 B7
Heinerscheid L 92 A2
Heinersdorf D 74 B3
Heining D 96 C1
Heiningen D 94 C1
Heinola FIN 8 B5
Heinsberg D 80 A2
Heist-op-den-Berg
 B 79 A4
Hejde S 57 C4
Hejdeby S 57 C4
Hejls DK 59 C2
Hejnice CZ 84 B3
Hel PL. 69 A3
Helchteren B 79 A5
Heldburg D 82 B2
Heldrungen D 82 A3
Helechosa E 156 A3
Helensburgh GB . . .34 B3
Helfenberg A 96 C2
Helgen N 53 A5
Helgeroa N 53 B5
Hella
 IS 190 D5
 N 46 A3
Helland N 194 B7
Hellas S 55 B3
Helle N 52 B2
Helleland N 52 B2
Hellendoorn NL 71 B3
Hellenthal D 80 B2
Hellesøy N 46 B1
Hellesylt N 198 C3
Hellevoetsluis NL . . .79 A4
Hellin E 158 C2
Hellissandur IS . . .190 C2
Hellnar IS 190 C2
Hellum DK 58 A3
Hellvik N 52 B1
Helm-brechts D 83 B3
Helmond NL 80 A1
Helmsdale GB 32 C3
Helmsley GB 37 B5
Helmstedt D 73 B3
Hel'pa SK 99 C3
Helsa D 82 A1
Helsby GB 38 A4
Helsingborg S 61 C2
Helsinge DK 61 C2
Helsingør DK 61 C2
Helsinki FIN 8 B4
Helston GB 42 B1
Hemau D 95 B3
Hemavan S 195 E6
Hemel Hempstead
 GB 44 B3
Hemer D 81 A3
Héming F 92 C2
Hemmet DK 59 C1
Hemmingstedt D . . .64 B2
Hemmoor D 64 C2
Hemnes N 54 A2
Hemnesberget N . .195 D4
Hemse S 57 C4
Hemsedal N 47 B5
Hemslingen D 72 A2
Hemsworth GB 40 B2
Hen N 48 B2
Henån S 54 B2
Hendaye F 144 A2
Hendek TR 187 B5
Hendungen D 82 B2
Henfield GB 44 C3
Hengelo
 Gelderland NL 71 B3
 Overijssel NL 71 B3
Hengersberg D 95 C5
Hengoed GB 39 C3
Hénin-Beaumont F . .78 B2
Henley-on-Thames
 GB 44 B3
Hennan S 200 D1
Henneberg D 82 B2
Hennebont F 100 B2
Henne Strand DK . .59 C1
Hennigsdorf D 74 B2
Hennset N 198 B5
Hennstedt
 Schleswig-Holstein
 D 64 B2
 Schleswig-Holstein
 D 64 B2
Henrichemont F . . .103 B4
Henryków PL 85 B5
Henrykowo PL 69 A5
Hensås N 47 A5

Henstedt-Ulzburg
 D 64 C2
Heppenheim D 93 B4
Herad
 Buskerud N 47 B6
 Vest-Agder N 52 B2
Heradsbygd N 48 B3
Heraklion = Iraklio
 GR 185 D6
Herálec CZ 97 B4
Herand N 46 B3
Herbault F 103 B3
Herbern D 81 A3
Herbertingen D 107 A4
Herbertstown IRL . .29 B3
Herbeumont B 91 B5
Herbignac F 101 B3
Herbisse F 91 C4
Herbitzheim F 92 B3
Herbolzheim D 106 A2
Herborn D 81 B4
Herbrechtingen D . .94 C2
Herby PL 86 B2
Herceg-Novi MNE . .16 D3
Hercegovać HR . . .124 B3
Hercegszántó H . . .125 B4
Herchen D 80 B3
Heréd H 112 B3
Hereford GB 39 B4
Herefoss N 53 B4
Hereke TR 187 B4
Herencia E 157 A4
Herend H 111 B4
Herent B 79 B4
Herentals B 79 A4
Hérépian F 130 B2
Herfølge DK 61 D2
Herford D 72 B1
Herguijuela E 156 A2
Héric F 101 B4
Héricourt F 106 B1
Héricourt-en-Caux
 F 89 A4
Hérimoncourt F . . .106 B1
Heringsdorf D 65 B4
Herisau CH 107 B4
Hérisson F 103 C4
Herk-de-Stad B 79 B5
Herlufmagle DK 65 A4
Hermagor A 109 C4
Hermannsburg D . . .72 B3
Hermansverk N 46 A3
Heřmanův Městec
 CZ 97 B3
Herment F 116 B2
Hermeskeil D 92 B2
Hermisende E 141 C4
Hermonville F 91 B3
Hermsdorf D 83 B3
Hernani E 144 A2
Hernansancho E . .150 B3
Herne D 80 A3
Herne Bay GB 45 B5
Hernes N 48 B3
Herning DK 59 B1
Herøya N 53 A5
Herramelluri E 143 B3
Herräng S 51 B5
Herre N 53 A5
Herrenberg D 93 C4
Herrera E 162 A3
Herrera de Alcántara
 E 155 B3
Herrera del Duque
 E 156 A2
Herrera de los Navarros
 E 152 A2
Herrera de Pisuerga
 E 142 B2
Herreros del Suso
 E 150 B2
Herrestad S 54 B2
Herrhamra S 57 B3
Herritslev DK 65 B4
Herrljunga S 55 B4
Herrnhut D 84 A2
Herrsching D 108 A2
Herrscheid D 81 A3
Herselt B 79 A4
Herso GR 182 B4
Herstal B 80 B1
Herstmonceux GB . .45 C4
Herten D 80 A3
Hertford GB 44 B3
Hervás E 149 B4
Hervik N 52 A1
Herxheim D 93 B4
Herzberg
 Brandenburg D 74 B1
 Brandenburg D . . . 83 A5
 Niedersachsen D . .82 A2
Herzebrock D 81 A4
Herzfelde D 74 B2
Herzlake D 71 B4
Herzogenaurach D .94 B2
Herzogenbuchsee
 CH 106 B2
Herzogenburg A . . .110 A2
Herzsprung D 73 A5
Hesby N 52 A1
Hesdin F 78 B2
Hesel D 71 A4
Heskestad N 52 B2
Hessdalen N 199 C8
Hesselager DK 65 A3
Hesseng N 193 C13
Hessisch Lichtenau
 D 82 A1
Hessisch-Oldendorf
 D 72 B2
Hestra S 60 B3
Heswall GB 38 A3
Hetlevik N 46 B2
Hettange-Grande F .92 B2
Hetton-le-Hole GB . .37 B5
Hettstedt D 82 A3
Heuchin F 78 B2

Heudicourt-sous-les-
 Côtes F 92 C1
Heunezel F 105 A5
Heuqueville F 89 A4
Heves H 113 B4
Héviz H 111 C4
Hexham GB 37 B4
Heysham GB 36 B4
Heytesbury GB 43 A4
Hidas H 125 A4
Hieflau A 110 B1
Hiendelaencina E . .151 A5
Hiersac F 115 C4
High Bentham GB . . .37 B4
Highclere GB 44 B2
High Hesket GB 37 B4
Highley GB 39 B4
High Wycombe GB . .44 B3
Higuera de Arjona
 E 157 C4
Higuera de Calatrava
 E 163 A3
Higuera de la Serena
 E 156 B2
Higuera de la Sierra
 E 161 B3
Higuera de Vargas
 E 155 C4
Higuera la Real E . .161 A3
Higuers de Llerena
 E 156 B1
Higueruela E 158 C2
Hijar E 153 A3
Hilchenbach D 81 A4
Hildburghausen D . .82 B2
Hilden D 80 A2
Hilders D 82 B1
Hildesheim D 72 B2
Hilgay GB 41 C4
Hillared S 60 B3
Hille D 72 B1
Hillegom NL 70 B1
Hillerød DK 61 D2
Hillerstorp S 60 B3
Hillesheim D 80 B2
Hillesø N 194 A8
Hillmersdorf D 83 A5
Hillsborough GB 27 B4
Hillswick GB 33 A5
Hilpoltstein D 95 B3
Hiltpoltstein D 94 B3
Hilvarenbeek NL . . .79 A5
Hilversum NL 70 B2
Himarë AL 182 C1
Himbergen D 73 A3
Himesháza H 125 A4
Himmelberg A 109 C5
Himmelpforten D . . .72 A2
Himód H 111 B4
Hinckley GB 40 C2
Hindås S 60 B2
Hindelang D 108 B1
Hindelbank CH . . .106 B2
Hinderavåg N 52 A1
Hindhead GB 44 B3
Hinjosa del Valle
 E 156 B1
Hinnerup DK 59 B3
Hinneryd S 61 C3
Hinojal E 155 B4
Hinojales E 161 B3
Hinojos E 161 B3
Hinojosa del Duque
 E 156 B2
Hinojosas de Calatrava
 E 157 B3
Hinterhornbach A . .108 B1
Hinterriss A 108 B2
Hintersee
 A 109 B4
 D 74 A3
Hinterstoder A 110 B1
Hintertux A 108 B2
Hinterweidenthal D 93 B3
Hinwil CH 107 B3
Hios GR 185 A7
Hippolytushoef NL .70 B1
Hirschaid D 94 B2
Hirschau D 95 B3
Hirschfeld D 83 A5
Hirschhorn D 93 B4
Hirsingue F 106 B2
Hirson F 91 B4
Hirtshals DK 58 A2
Hirvaskoski FIN . .197 D10
Hirzenhain D 81 B5
Hisarcık TR 186 C4
Hishult S 61 C3
Hissjön S 200 C6
Hitchin GB 44 B3
Hitra N 198 B5
Hittarp S 61 C2
Hittisau A 107 B4
Hittun N 46 A1
Hitzacker D 73 A4
Hjallerup DK 58 A3
Hjällstad S 49 B5
Hjältevad S 62 A3
Hjärnarp S 61 C2
Hjartdal N 53 A4
Hjellestad N 46 B2
Hjelmeland N 52 A2
Hjelset N 198 C4
Hjerkinn N 198 C6
Hjerm DK 58 B1
Hjørdkær DK 64 A2
Hjørring DK 58 A2
Hjorted S 62 A4
Hjortkvarn S 56 B1
Hjortnäs S 50 B1
Hjortsberga S 62 B2
Hjukse N 53 A5
Hjuksebø N 53 A5
Hjulsjö S 55 A5
Hlinik nad Hronom
 SK 98 C2
Hlinsko CZ 97 B3

Hlio IS	191	A10
Hlohovec SK	98	C1
Hlubokánad Vltavou		
CZ	96	B2
Hlučín CZ	98	B2
Hlyboka UA	17	A6
Hlybokaye BY	13	A7
Hniezdne SK	99	B4
Hnilec SK	99	C4
Hnúšťa SK	99	C3
Hobol H	125	A3
Hobro DK	58	B2
Hobscheid L	92	B1
Hocalar TR	189	A4
Hochdonn D	64	B2
Hochdorf CH	106	B3
Hochfelden F	93	C3
Hochspeyer D	93	B3
Höchstadt D	94	B2
Höchstädt D	94	C2
Hochstenbach D	81	B3
Höchst im Odenwald		
D	93	B5
Höckendorf D	83	B5
Hockenheim D	93	B4
Hoddesdon GB	44	B3
Hodenhagen D	72	B2
Hodkovice CZ	84	B3
Hódmezővásárhely		
H	113	C4
Hodnet GB	38	B4
Hodonín CZ	98	C1
Hodslavice CZ	98	B2
Hoedekenskerke		
NL	79	A3
Hoegaarden B	79	B4
Hoek van Holland		
NL	79	A4
Hoenderlo NL	70	B2
Hof		
D	83	B3
N	53	A6
Hofbieber D	82	B1
Hoff GB	37	B4
Hofgeismar D	81	A5
Hofheim		
Bayern D	82	B2
Hessen D	93	A4
Hofkirchen im		
Mühlkreis A	96	C1
Höfn IS	191	C10
Hofors S	50	B3
Hofsós IS	190	B6
Hofstad N	199	A7
Höganäs S	61	C2
Högbo S	51	B3
Hogdal S	54	A2
Høgebru N	46	A4
Högfors S	50	C2
Högklint S	57	C4
Högsäter S	54	B3
Högsby S	62	A4
Högsjö S	56	A1
Hogstad S	55	B6
Högyész H	112	C2
Hohenau A	97	C4
Hohenberg A	110	B2
Hohenbucko D	83	A5
Hohenburg D	95	B3
Hohendorf D	66	B1
Hohenems A	107	B4
Hohen Neuendorf		
D	74	B2
Hohenseeden D	73	B5
Hohentauern A	110	B1
Hohentengen D	106	B3
Hohenwepel D	81	A5
Hohenwestedt D	64	B2
Hohenwutzen D	74	B3
Hohenzieritz D	74	A2
Hohn D	64	B2
Hohne D	72	B3
Hohnstorf D	73	A3
Højer D	64	B1
Højslev Stby DK	58	B2
Hok S	62	A2
Hökerum S	60	B3
Hökhuvud S	51	B5
Hokksund N	53	A5
Hökön S	63	B2
Hol N	47	B5
Hólar IS	190	B6
Holašovice CZ	96	C2
Holbæk		
Aarhus Amt. DK	58	B3
Vestsjællands Amt.		
DK	61	D1
Holbeach GB	41	C4
Holdenstedt D	73	B3
Holdhus N	46	B2
Holdorf D	71	B5
Holeby DK	65	B4
Hølen N	54	A1
Hølervasseter N	47	B6
Holešov CZ	98	B1
Holguera E	155	B4
Holíč SK	98	C1
Holice		
CZ	97	A3
SK	111	B4
Höljes S	49	B4
Hollabrunn A	97	C4
Hollandstoun GB	33	B4
Høllen N	53	B3
Hollfeld D	95	B3
Hollókő H	112	B3
Hollum NL	70	A2
Höllviksnäs S	66	A1
Holm N	195	E3
Hólmavík IS	190	B4
Holmbukt N	192	B5
Holmedal S	54	A2
Holmegil N	54	A2
Holmen N	48	B2
Holme-on-Spalding-		
Moor GB	40	B3
Holmes Chapel GB	38	A4
Holmestrand N	54	A1
Holmfirth GB	40	B2
Holmfoss N	193	C14
Holmsbu N	54	A1
Holmsjö S	63	B3
Holmsund S	200	C6
Holmsveden S	50	A3
Holmudden S	57	C5
Hölö S	57	A3
Holøydal N	199	C8
Holsbybrunn S	62	A3
Holseter N	48	A1
Holsljunga S	60	B2
Holstebro DK	59	B1
Holsted DK	59	C1
Holsworthy GB	42	B2
Holt		
D	64	B2
Norfolk GB	41	C5
Wrexham GB	38	A4
IS	190	D6
N	53	B4
Holten NL	71	B3
Holtwick D	71	B4
Holum N	52	B3
Holwerd NL	70	A2
Holycross IRL	29	B4
Holyhead GB	38	A2
Holýšov CZ	95	B5
Holywell GB	38	A3
Holywood GB	27	B5
Holzdorf D	83	A5
Holzhausen D	72	B1
Holzheim D	94	C2
Holzkirchen D	108	B2
Holzminden D	81	A5
Holzthaleben D	82	A2
Homberg		
Hessen D	81	A5
Hessen D	81	B5
Homburg D	93	B3
Hommelstø N	195	E3
Hommersåk N	52	B1
Homokmegy H	112	C3
Homokszentgyörgy		
H	124	A3
Homyel = Gomel		
BY	13	B9
Honaz TR	188	B4
Hondarribia E	144	A2
Hondón de los Frailes		
E	165	A4
Hondschoote F	78	B2
Hönebach D	82	B1
Hønefoss N	48	B2
Honfleur F	89	A4
Honiton GB	43	B3
Hönningen D	80	B2
Honningsvåg N	193	B9
Hönö S	60	B1
Honrubia E	158	B1
Hontalbilla E	151	A4
Hontheim D	92	A2
Hontianske-Nemce		
SK	98	C2
Hontoria de la Cantera		
E	143	B3
Hontoria del Pinar		
E	143	C3
Hontoria de		
Valdearados E	143	C3
Hoofddorp NL	70	B1
Hoogerheide NL	79	A4
Hoogeveen NL	71	B3
Hoogezand-Sappemeer		
NL	71	A3
Hoogkarspel NL	70	B2
Hoogkerk NL	71	A3
Hoogstede D	71	B3
Hoogstraten B	79	A4
Hook GB	44	B3
Hooksiel D	71	A5
Höör S	61	D3
Hoorn NL	70	B2
Hope GB	38	A3
Hopen N	194	C6
Hope under Dinmore		
GB	39	B4
Hopfgarten A	108	B3
Hopfgarten in		
Defereggen A	109	C3
Hopseidet N	193	B11
Hopsten D	71	B4
Hoptrup DK	59	C2
Hora Svatého		
Sebastiána CZ	83	B5
Horažďovice CZ	96	B1
Horb am Neckar D	93	C4
Horbelev DK	65	B5
Horbury GB	40	B2
Hørby DK	58	A3
Hörby S	61	D3
Horcajada de la Torre		
E	158	B1
Horcajo de los Montes		
E	156	A3
Horcajo de Santiago		
E	151	C4
Horcajo-Medianero		
E	150	B2
Horche E	151	B4
Horda S	62	A2
Hordabø N	46	B1
Hordalia N	52	A2
Hordvik N	46	B2
Hořesedly CZ	83	B5
Horezu RO	17	C6
Horgen CH	107	B3
Horgoš SRB	126	A1
Horia RO	126	A3
Hořice CZ	84	B3
Horjul SLO	123	A3
Horka D	84	A2
Hörken S	50	B1
Horki BY	13	A9
Hörle S	60	B4
Horn		
A	97	C3
D	81	A4
N	48	B2
S	62	A3
Horna E	158	C2
Hornachos E	156	B1
Hornachuelos E	162	A2
Hoya de Santa Maria		
E	161	B3
Horná Mariková		
SK	98	B2
Hornanes N	46	C2
Horná Streda SK	98	C1
Horná Štrubna SK	98	C2
Horná Súča SK	98	C1
Hornbæk		
Aarhus Amt. DK	58	B2
Frederiksværk DK	61	C2
Hornberg D	106	A3
Hornburg D	73	B3
Horncastle GB	41	B3
Horndal S	50	B3
Horndean GB	44	C2
Horne		
Fyns Amt. DK	64	A3
Ribe Amt. DK	59	C1
Hörnebo S	55	B5
Horneburg D	72	A2
Hörnefors S	200	C5
Horní Bečva CZ	98	B2
Horní Benešov CZ	98	B1
Horní Cerekev CZ	97	B3
Horní Jiřetín CZ	83	B5
Horní Lomná CZ	98	B2
Horní Maršov CZ	85	B3
Hornindal N	198	D3
Hørning DK	59	B3
Hörningsholm S	57	A3
Horní Planá CZ	96	C2
Horní Slavkov CZ	83	B4
Horní Vltavice CZ	96	C1
Hornnes N	53	B3
Horno D	84	A2
Hornos E	164	A2
Hornoy-le-Bourg F	90	B1
Hornsea GB	41	B3
Hornslet DK	59	B3
Hornstein A	111	B3
Hörnum D	64	B1
Hornum DK	58	B2
Horný Tisovnik SK	99	C3
Horodenka UA	13	D6
Horodnya UA	13	C9
Horodok		
Khmelnytskyy		
UA	13	D7
Lviv UA	13	D5
Horokhiv UA	13	C6
Horovice CZ	96	B1
Horred S	60	B2
Hörröd S	61	D4
Hörsching A	110	A1
Horsens DK	59	C2
Horsham GB	44	B3
Hørsholm DK	61	D2
Horslunde DK	65	B4
Horšovský Týn CZ	95	B4
Horst NL	80	A2
Horstel D	71	B4
Horsten D	71	A4
Horstmar D	71	B4
Hort H	113	B3
Horta P	148	A2
Horten N	54	A1
Hortezuela E	151	A5
Hortiguela E	143	B3
Hortobágy H	113	B5
Horton in Ribblesdale		
GB	37	B4
Hørve DK	61	D1
Hörvik S	63	B2
Horwich GB	38	A4
Hosanger N	46	B2
Hösbach D	93	A5
Hosena D	84	A2
Hosenfeld D	81	B5
Hosingen L	92	A2
Hosio FIN	197	D8
Hospental CH	107	C3
Hospital IRL	29	B3
Hossegor F	128	C1
Hosszúhetény H	125	A4
Hostal de Ipiés E	145	B3
Hošťálkova CZ	98	B1
Hostalric E	147	C3
Hostens F	128	B2
Hostěradice CZ	97	C4
Hostinné CZ	85	B3
Hostomice CZ	96	B2
Hostouň CZ	95	B4
Hotagen S	199	B11
Hotolisht AL	182	B2
Hotton B	79	B5
Houdain F	78	B2
Houdan F	90	C1
Houdelaincourt F	92	C1
Houeillés F	128	B3
Houffalize B	92	A1
Houghton-le-Spring		
GB	37	B5
Houlberg DK	59	B2
Houlgate F	89	A3
Hounslow GB	44	B3
Hourtin F	128	A1
Hourtin-Plage F	128	A1
Houthalen B	79	A5
Houyet B	79	B4
Hov		
DK	59	C3
N	48	B2
Hova S	55	B5
Høvåg N	53	B4
Hovborg DK	59	C1
Hovda N	47	B6
Hovden N	52	A3
Hove GB	44	C3
Hovedgård DK	59	C2
Hovelhof D	81	A4
Hoven DK	59	C1
Hovet N	47	B5
Hovingham GB	40	A3
Hovmantorp S	62	B3
Hovsta S	56	A1
Howden GB	40	B3
Howe D	72	A3
Höxter D	81	A5
Hoya D	72	B2
Hoya de Santa Maria		
E	161	B3
Hoya-Gonzalo E	158	C2
Høyanger N	46	A3
Hoyerswerda D	84	A2
Høyjord N	53	A6
Hoylake GB	38	A3
Høylandet N	199	A9
Hoym D	82	A3
Høymyr N	47	C6
Hoyocasero E	150	B3
Hoyo de Manzanares		
E	151	B4
Hoyo de Pinares		
E	150	B3
Hoyos E	149	B3
Hoyos del Espino		
E	150	B2
Hrabušice SK	99	C4
Hradec Králové CZ	85	B3
Hradec nad Moravicí		
CZ	98	B1
Hrádek CZ	97	C4
Hrádek nad Nisou		
CZ	84	B2
Hradište SK	98	C2
Hrafnagil IS	191	B7
Hrafnseyri IS	190	B2
Hranice		
Severomoravský		
CZ	98	B1
Západočeský CZ	83	B4
Hranovnica SK	99	C4
Hrasnica BIH	139	B4
Hrastnik SLO	123	A4
Hřensko CZ	84	B2
Hriňová SK	99	C3
Hrisoupoli GR	183	C6
Hrochov CZ	97	B4
Hrochův Tynec CZ	97	B3
Hrodna BY	13	B5
Hrodzyanka BY	13	B8
Hronov CZ	85	B4
Hronský Beňadik		
SK	98	C2
Hrotovice CZ	97	B4
Hrtkovci SRB	127	C1
Hrun IS	190	A5
Hrušov SK	112	A3
Hrušovany nad		
Jevišovkou CZ	97	C4
Hŕštín SK	99	B3
Hrvaćani BIH	124	C3
Hrvace HR	138	B2
Hrymayliv UA	13	D7
Huben A	109	C3
Hückel-hoven D	80	A2
Hückeswagen D	80	A3
Hucknall GB	40	B2
Hucqueliers F	78	B1
Huddersfield GB	40	B2
Huddinge S	57	A3
Huddunge S	51	B3
Hude D	72	A1
Hudiksvall S	200	E3
Huélago E	163	A4
Huélamo E	152	B2
Huelgoat F	100	A2
Huelma E	163	A4
Huelva E	161	B3
Huéneja E	164	B2
Huércal de Almeria		
E	164	C2
Huércal-Overa E	164	B3
Huerta de Abajo E	143	B3
Huerta del Rey E	143	C3
Huerta de		
Valdecarabanos		
E	151	C4
Huertahernando E	152	B1
Huesa E	164	B1
Huesca E	145	B3
Huéscar E	164	B2
Huete E	151	B5
Huétor Tájar E	163	A3
Hüfingen D	106	B3
Hufthamar N	46	B2
Hugh Town GB	42	B1
Huglfing D	108	B2
Huissen NL	70	C2
Huizen NL	70	B2
Hulín CZ	98	B1
Hüls D	80	A2
Hulsig DK	58	A3
Hulst NL	79	A4
Hult S	62	A3
Hulta S	56	B2
Hulteby S	55	A5
Hulterstad S	63	B4
Hultsfred S	62	A3
Humanes E	151	B4
Humberston GB	41	B3
Humble DK	65	B3
Humenné SK	12	D4
Humilladero E	163	A3
Humlebæk DK	61	D2
Humlum DK	58	B1
Hummelsta S	56	A2
Humpolec CZ	97	B3
Humshaugh GB	37	A4
Hundåla N	195	E3
Hundested DK	61	D1
Hundorp N	48	A1
Hundvåg N	52	A1
Hundvin N	46	B2
Hunedoara RO	17	C5
Hünfeld D	82	B1
Hungen D	81	B4
Hungerford GB	44	B2
Hunndalen N	48	B2
Hunnebostrand S	54	B2
Hunstanton GB	41	C4
Huntingdon GB	44	A3
Huntley GB	39	C4
Huntly GB	33	D4
Hünxe D	80	A2
Hurbanovo SK	112	B2
Hurdal N	48	B3
Hurezani RO	17	C5
Hurlford GB	36	A2
Hurstbourne Tarrant		
GB	44	B2
Hurstpierpoint GB	44	C3
Hürth D	80	B2
Hurum N	47	A5
Hurup DK	58	B1
Húsafell IS	190	C5
Húsavík IS	191	A8
Husbands Bosworth		
GB	44	A2
Husby		
D	64	B2
DK	59	B1
Husey IS	191	B11
Husina BIH	139	A4
Husinec CZ	96	B1
Husinish GB	31	B1
Huskvarna S	62	A2
Husnes N	46	C2
Husøy N	194	A8
Hustad N	198	C4
Hüsten D	81	A3
Hustopeče CZ	97	C4
Hustopeče nad Bečvou		
CZ	98	B1
Husum		
D	64	B2
S	200	C5
Husvika N	195	E3
Huta PL	75	B5
Hutovo BIH	139	C3
Hüttenberg A	110	C1
Hüttlingen D	94	C2
Huttoft GB	41	B4
Hutton Cranswick		
GB	40	B3
Hüttschlag A	109	B4
Huttwil CH	106	B2
Huy B	79	B5
Hüyük TR	189	B6
Hval N	48	B2
Hvåle N	47	B6
Hvaler N	54	A2
Hvalpsund DK	58	B2
Hvammstangi IS	190	B5
Hvammur IS	190	B6
Hvanneyri IS	190	C4
Hvar HR	138	B2
Hveragerði IS	190	D4
Hvidbjerg DK	58	B1
Hvide Sande DK	59	C1
Hvittingfoss N	53	A6
Hvolsvöllur IS	190	D5
Hybe SK	99	B3
Hyen N	198	D2
Hyères F	132	B2
Hyères Plage F	132	B2
Hylestad N	52	A3
Hylke DK	59	C2
Hyllestad N	46	A2
Hyllstofta S	61	C3
Hyltebruk S	60	B3
Hynnekleiv N	53	B4
Hythe		
Hampshire GB	44	C2
Kent GB	45	B5
Hyvinkää FIN	8	B4
I		
Iam RO	127	B3
Iaşi RO	17	B7
Iasmos GR	183	B7
Ibahernando E	156	A2
Ibarranguelua E	143	A4
Ibbenbüren D	71	B4
Ibeas de Juarros		
E	143	B3
Ibestad N	194	B8
Ibi E	159	C3
Ibiza = Eivissa E	166	C1
İbradı TR	189	B6
İbriktepe TR	186	A1
Ibros E	157	B4
İçel TR	23	C8
Ichenhausen D	94	C2
Ichtegem B	78	A3
Ichtershausen D	82	B2
Idanha-a-Novo P	155	B3
Idar-Oberstein D	93	B3
Idd N	54	A2
Idiazábal E	144	B1
Idivuoma S	196	A4
Idkerberget S	50	B2
Idön S	51	B5
Idre S	199	D9
Idrija SLO	123	A3
Idritsa RUS	9	D6
Idstein D	81	B4
Idvor SRB	126	B2
Iecca Mare RO	126	B2
Ielsi I	170	B2
Ieper = Ypres B	78	B2
Ierapetra GR	185	D6
Ierissos GR	183	C5
Ifjord N	193	B11
Igal H	112	C1
Igea E	144	B1
Igea Marina I	136	A1
Igelfors S	56	B1
Igersheim D	94	B1
Iggesund S	200	E3
Iglesias E	143	B3
Iglésias I	179	C2
Igls A	108	B2
Igny-Comblizy F	91	B3
Igorre E	143	A4
Igualada E	147	C2
Igüeña E	141	B4
Iguerande F	117	A4
Iharosberény H	124	A3
Ihl'any SK	99	B4
Ihlienworth D	64	C1
Ihringen D	106	A2
Ihrlerstein D	95	C3
İhsaniye TR	187	C5
Ii FIN	197	D8
Iijärvi FIN	193	C11
Iisalmi FIN	3	E10
IJmuiden NL	70	B1
IJsselmuiden NL	70	B2
IJzendijke NL	79	A3
Ikast DK	59	B2
Ikervár H	111	B3
Ilandža SRB	126	B2
Ilanz CH	107	C4
Ilava SK	98	C2
Iława PL	69	B4
il Castagno I	135	B3
Ilche E	145	C4
Ilfeld D	82	A2
Ilfracombe GB	42	A2
Ilgaz TR	23	A7
İlgın TR	189	A6
Ilhavo P	148	B1
Ilica TR	186	C2
Ilidža BIH	139	B4
Ilijaš BIH	139	B4
Ilirska Bistrica		
SLO	123	B3
Ilkeston GB	40	C2
Ilkley GB	40	B2
Illana E	151	B5
Illano E	141	A4
Illar E	164	C2
Illas E	141	A5
Illats F	128	B2
Illertissen D	94	C2
Illescas E	151	B4
Ille-sur-Têt F	146	B3
Illfurth F	106	B2
Illichivsk UA	17	B9
Illiers-Combray F	89	B5
Illkirch-Graffenstaden		
F	93	C3
Illmersdorf D	74	C2
Illmitz A	111	B3
Illora E	163	A4
Illueca E	152	A2
Ilmajoki FIN	8	A3
Ilmenau D	82	B2
Ilminster GB	43	B4
Ilok HR	126	B1
Ilomantsi FIN	9	A7
Ilow D	73	B5
Iłowa PL	84	A3
Iłowo-Osada PL	77	A5
Ilsenburg D	82	A2
Ilshofen D	94	B1
Ilz A	110	B2
Iłża PL	87	A5
Imatra FIN	9	B6
Imielin PL	86	B3
Imingen N	47	B5
Immeln S	63	B2
Immenhausen D	81	A5
Immenstadt D	107	B5
Immingham GB	41	B3
Ímola I	135	A4
Imon E	151	A5
Imotski HR	138	B3
Impéria I	133	B4
Imphy F	104	C2
İmroz TR	183	C7
Imsland N	52	A1
Imst A	108	B1
Inagh IRL	28	B2
Inari FIN	193	D10
Inca E	167	B2
Inchnadamph GB	32	C2
Incinillas E	143	B3
Indal S	200	D3
Indjija SRB	127	B2
Indre Arna N	46	B2
Indre Billefjord N	193	B9
Indre Brenna N	193	B9
İğneada TR	186	A2
Ineboln TR	23	A7
İnecik TR	186	B2
İnegöl TR	187	B4
Inerthal CH	107	B3
Infiesto E	142	A1
Ingatorp S	62	A3
Ingedal N	54	A2
Ingelheim D	93	B4
Ingelmunster B	78	B3
Ingelstad S	62	B2
Ingleton GB	37	B4
Ingolfsland N	47	C5
Ingolstadt D	95	C3
Ingrandes		
Maine-et-Loire		
F	101	B5
Vienne F	102	C2
Ingwiller F	93	C3
İnhisar TR	187	B5
Iniesta E	158	B2
Inishannon IRL	29	C3
Inishcrone IRL	26	B1
Inke H	124	A3
Inndyr N	195	C5
Innellan GB	34	C3
Innerleithen GB	35	C4
Innermessan GB	36	B2
Innertkirchen CH	106	C3
Innervillgraten A	109	C3
Innsbruck A	108	B2
Innset N	194	B9
Innvik N	198	D3
İnönü TR	187	C5
Inowłódz PL	87	A4
Inowrocław PL	76	B3
Ins CH	106	B2
Insch GB	33	D4
Insjön S	50	B2
Ińsko PL	75	A4
Instow GB	42	A2
İntepe TR	186	B1
Interlaken CH	106	C2
Intragna CH	120	A1
Introbio I	120	B2
Inverallochy GB	33	D5
Inveran		
GB	32	D2
IRL	28	A2
Inveraray GB	34	B2
Inverbervie GB	35	B5
Invergarry GB	32	D2
Invergordon GB	32	D2
Invergowrie GB	35	B4
Inverkeilor GB	35	B5
Inverkeithing GB	35	B4
Invermoriston GB	32	D2
Inverness GB	32	D2
Inveruno I	120	B1
Inverurie GB	33	D4
Ioannina GR	182	D2
Iolanda di Savoia		
I	121	C4
Ion Corvin RO	17	C7
Ióppolo I	175	C1
Ios GR	185	C6
Ipati GR	182	E4
Ipsala TR	186	B1
Ipswich GB	45	A5
Iraklia GR	183	B5
Iraklio = Heraklion		
GR	185	D6
Irdning A	110	B1
Iregszemcse H	112	C2
Irgoli I	178	B3
Irig SRB	127	B1
Ironbridge GB	39	B4
Irpin UA	13	C9
Irrel D	92	B2
Irsina I	172	B2
Irsta S	56	A2
Irthlingborough GB	44	A3
Iruela E	141	B4
Irún E	144	A2
Irurita E	144	A2
Irurzun E	144	B2
Irvine GB	36	A2
Irvinestown GB	27	B3
Isaba E	144	B3
Isabela E	157	B4
Isafjörður IS	190	A2
Isane N	198	D2
Isaszeg H	112	B3
Isbister GB	33	A5
íscar E	150	A3
Iscehisar TR	187	D5
Ischgl A	107	B5
Ischia I	170	C1
Ischia di Castro I	168	A1
Ischitella I	171	B3
Isdes F	103	B4
Ise N	54	A2
Iselle I	119	A5
Iseltwald CH	106	C2
Isen D	108	A3
Isenbüttel D	73	B3
Iseo I	120	B3
Iserlohn D	81	A3
Isérnia I	170	B2
Isfjorden N	198	C4
Ishëm AL	182	B1
Isigny-sur-Mer F	88	A2
Işıklı TR	189	A4
İskilip TR	23	A8
Isla Canela E	161	B2
Isla Cristina E	161	B2
Islares E	143	A3
Isleham GB	45	A4
Isle of Whithorn		
GB	36	B2
Ismaning D	108	A2
Isna P	154	B3
Isnestoften N	192	B6
Isny D	107	B5
Isoba E	142	A1
Isokylä		
FIN	197	C10
S	196	B5
Isola F	132	A3
Isola d'Asti I	119	C5
Isola del Gran Sasso		
d'Itália I	169	A3
Ísola della Scala I	121	B4
Ísola delle Fémmine		
I	176	A2
Isola del Liri I	169	B3
Ísola di Capo Rizzuto		
I	175	C3
Isona E	147	B2
Ispagnac F	130	A2
Isparta TR	189	B5
Isperikh BG	17	D7
İspica I	177	C3
Isselburg D	80	A2
Issigeac F	129	B3
Issogne I	119	B4
Issoire F	116	B3
Issoncourt F	91	C5
Issoudun F	103	C4
Issum D	80	A2
Is-sur-Tille F	105	B4
Issy-l'Evêque F	104	C2
Istán E	162	B3
İstanbul TR	186	A3
Istebna PL	98	B2
Istia d'Ombrone I	135	C4
Istiea GR	183	E5
Istres F	131	B3

Istvándi H 125 A3
Itea GR 184 A3
Ithaki GR 184 A1
Itoiz E 144 B2
Ítrabo E 163 B4
Itri I 169 B3
Ittireddu I 178 B2
Ittiri I 178 B2
Itzehoe D 64 C2
Ivalo FIN 193 D11
Iván H 111 B3
Ivanava BY 13 B6
Ivančice CZ 97 B4
Ivančna Gorica SLO 123 B3
Iváncsa H 112 B2
Ivanec HR 124 A2
Ivanić Grad HR 124 B2
Ivanjska BIH 124 C3
Ivanka SK 98 C2
Ivankovo HR 125 B4
Ivano-Frankivsk UA 13 D6
Ivanovice na Hané CZ 98 B1
Ivanska HR 124 B2
Ivatsevichy BY 13 B6
Ivaylovgrad BG 183 B8
Iveland N 53 B3
Ivoz Ramet B 79 B5
Ivrea I 119 B4
İvrindi TR 186 C2
Ivry-en-Montagne F 104 B3
Ivry-la-Bataille F 90 C1
Ivybridge GB 42 B3
Iwaniska PL 87 B5
Iwiny PL 85 A3
Iwuy F 78 B3
Ixworth GB 45 A4
Izarra E 143 B4
Izbica Kujawska PL 76 B3
Izbište SRB 127 B3
Izeda P 149 A3
Izegem B 78 B3
Izernore F 118 A2
Izmayil UA 17 C8
İzmir TR 188 A2
İzmit = Kocaeli TR 187 B4
Iznájar E 163 A3
Iznalloz E 163 A4
Iznatoraf E 164 A1
İznik TR 187 B4
Izola SLO 122 B2
Izsák H 112 C3
Izsófalva H 99 C4
Izyaslav UA 13 C7

J

Jabalquinto E 157 B4
Jablanac HR 123 C3
Jablanica BIH 139 B3
Jablonec nad Jizerou CZ 84 B3
Jablonec nad Nisou CZ 84 B3
Jablonica SK 98 C1
Jablonka PL 99 B3
Jabłonna PL 77 B5
Jablonnénad Orlicí CZ 97 A4
Jablonne Podještědí CZ 84 B2
Jablonov nad Turňou SK 99 C4
Jabłonowo Pomorskie PL 69 B4
Jablúnka CZ 98 B1
Jablunkov CZ 98 B2
Jabučje SRB 127 C2
Jabugo E 161 B3
Jabuka SRB 127 C2
Jabukovac HR 124 B2
Jaca E 145 B3
Jáchymov CZ 83 B4
Jacobidrebber D 72 B1
Jade D 71 A5
Jäderfors S 50 B3
Jädraås S 50 B3
Jadraque E 151 B5
Jaén E 163 A4
Jagare BIH 124 C3
Jagel D 64 B2
Jagenbach A 96 C3
Jægerspris DK 61 D1
Jagodina SRB 127 D3
Jagodnjak HR 125 B4
Jagodzin PL 84 A3
Jagstheim D 94 B2
Jagstzell D 94 B2
Jahodna SK 111 A4
Jajce BIH 138 A3
Ják H 111 B3
Jakabszálbs H 112 C3
Jäkkvik S 195 D8
Jakobsnes N 193 C14
Jakovlje HR 124 B1
Jakšic HR 125 B3
Jakubany SK 99 B4
Jalance E 159 B2
Jalasjärvi FIN 8 A3
Jalhay B 80 B1
Jaligny-sur-Besbre F 117 A3
Jallais F 102 B1
Jalón E 159 C3
Jâlons F 91 C4
Jamena SRB 125 C5
Jamilena E 163 A4
Jämjö S 63 B3
Jamnička Kiselica HR 124 B1
Jamno PL 67 B5
Jamoigne B 92 B1
Jämsä FIN 8 B4
Jämshög S 63 B2
Jamu Mare RO 126 B3
Janakkala FIN 8 B4
Jandelsbrunn D 96 C1
Jänickendorf D 74 B2
Janikowo PL 76 B3
Janja BIH 125 C5
Janjina HR 138 C3
Janki
Łódzkie PL 86 A3
Mazowieckie PL 77 B5
Jankov CZ 96 B2
Jankowo Dolne PL 76 B2
Jánoshalma H 126 A1
Jánosháza H 111 B4
Jánoshida H 113 B4
Jánossomorja H 111 B4
Janovice nad Uhlavou CZ 96 B1
Janów PL 86 B3
Janowiec Wielkopolski PL 76 B2
Janowo PL 77 A5
Jänsmässholmen S 199 B10
Janville F 103 A3
Janzé F 101 B4
Jarabá SK 99 C3
Jaraczewo PL 76 C2
Jarafuel E 159 B2
Jaraicejo E 156 A2
Jaraíz de la Vera E 150 B2
Jarak SRB 127 C1
Jarandilla de la Vera E 150 B2
Jaray E 152 A1
Järbo S 50 B3
Jard-sur-Mer F 114 B2
Jaren N 48 B2
Jargeau F 103 B4
Jarkovac SRB 126 B2
Järlåsa S 51 C4
Jarmen D 66 C2
Järna S 57 A3
Jarnac F 115 C3
Järnäs S 200 C5
Järnforsen S 62 A3
Jarny F 92 B1
Jarocin PL 76 C2
Jaroměř CZ 85 B3
Jaroměřice nad Rokytnou CZ 97 B3
Jaroslav CZ 97 A4
Jaroslavice CZ 97 C4
Jarosław PL 12 C5
Jaroslawiec PL 68 A1
Jarošov nad Nežarkou CZ 96 B3
Järpås S 55 B3
Järpen S 199 B10
Jarrow GB 37 B5
Järso FIN 51 B6
Järvenpää FIN 8 B4
Jarvornik CZ 85 B4
Järvsö S 200 E2
Jarzé F 102 B1
Jaša Tomic SRB 126 B2
Jasenak HR 123 B4
Jasenica BIH 124 C2
Jasenice HR 137 A4
Jasenovac HR 124 B2
Jasenovo SRB 127 C3
Jasień PL 84 A3
Jasienica PL 84 A2
Jasło PL 12 D4
Jásova SK 112 B2
Jasseron F 118 A2
Jastarnia PL 69 A3
Jastrebarsko HR 123 B4
Jastrowie PL 68 B1
Jastrzębia-Góra PL 68 A3
Jastrzębie Zdrój PL 98 B2
Jászals-Lószentgyörgy H 113 B4
Jászapáti H 113 B4
Jászárokszállás H 113 B3
Jászberény H 113 B3
Jászdózsa H 113 B4
Jászfényszaru H 113 B3
Jászjakóhalma H 113 B4
Jászkarajenö H 113 B4
Jászkisér H 113 B4
Jászladány H 113 B4
Jászszentlászló H 113 C3
Jásztelek H 113 B4
Játar E 163 B4
Jättendal S 200 E3
Jatznick D 74 A2
Jaun CH 106 C2
Jausiers F 132 A2
Jávea E 159 C4
Jävenitz D 73 B4
Javerlhac F 115 C4
Javier E 144 B2
Javorani BIH 124 C3
Javorina SK 99 B4
Javron F 89 B3
Jawor PL 85 A4
Jaworzno PL 86 B3
Jaworzyna Śl. PL 85 B4
Jayena E 163 B4
Jažow PL 84 A2
Jebel RO 126 B3
Jebjerg DK 58 B2
Jedburgh GB 35 C5
Jedlinsk PL 87 A5
Jedlnia PL 87 A5
Jedlnia Letnisko PL 87 A5
Jednorożec PL 77 A6
Jedovnice CZ 97 B4
Jędrychow PL 69 B4
Jędrzejów PL 87 B4
Jedwabno PL 77 A5
Jeesiö FIN 197 B9
Jegłownik PL 69 A4
Jegun F 129 C3
Jēkabpils LV 8 D4
Jektevik N 46 C2
Jektvik N 195 D4
Jelcz-Laskowice PL 85 A5
Jelenec SK 98 C2
Jelenia Góra PL 85 B3
Jelgava LV 8 D3
Jelka SK 111 A4
Jelling DK 59 C2
Jels DK 59 C2
Jelsa
HR 138 B2
N 52 A2
Jelšava SK 99 C4
Jemgum D 71 A4
Jemnice CZ 97 B3
Jena D 82 B3
Jenaz CH 107 C4
Jenbach A 108 B2
Jenikow PL 75 A4
Jennersdorf A 111 C3
Jenny S 62 A4
Jerchel D 73 B4
Jeres del Marquesado E 164 B1
Jerez de la Frontera E 162 B1
Jerez de los Caballeros E 155 C4
Jerica E 159 B3
Jerichow D 73 B5
Jerka PL 75 B5
Jermenovci SRB 126 B3
Jerslev DK 58 A3
Jerte E 150 B2
Jerup DK 58 A3
Jerxheim D 73 B3
Jerzmanowice PL 87 B3
Jerzu I 179 C3
Jerzwałd PL 69 B4
Jesberg D 81 B5
Jesenice
Středočeský CZ 83 B5
Středočeský CZ 96 B2
SLO 109 C5
Jeseník CZ 85 B5
Jesenké SK 99 C4
Jesi I 136 B2
Jésolo I 122 B1
Jessen D 83 A4
Jessenitz D 73 A4
Jessheim N 48 B3
Jessnitz D 83 A4
Jesteburg D 72 A2
Jeumont F 79 B4
Jeven-stedt D 64 B2
Jever D 71 A4
Jevičko CZ 97 B4
Jevišovice CZ 97 C3
Jevnaker N 48 B2
Jezerane HR 123 B4
Jezero
BIH 138 A3
HR 123 B4
Jezów PL 87 A3
Jičín CZ 84 B3
Jičíněves CZ 84 B3
Jihlava CZ 97 B3
Jijona E 159 C3
Jilemnice CZ 84 B3
Jilové CZ 84 B2
Jilovéu Prahy CZ 96 B2
Jimbolia RO 126 B2
Jimena E 163 A4
Jimena de la Frontera E 162 B2
Jimera de Libar E 162 B2
Jimramov CZ 97 B4
Jince CZ 96 B1
Jindřichovice CZ 83 B4
Jindřichův Hradec CZ 96 B3
Jirkov CZ 83 B5
Jistebnice CZ 96 B2
Joachimsthal D 74 B2
João da Loura P 154 C2
Jobbágyi H 112 B3
Jochberg A 109 B3
Jockfall S 196 C5
Jódar E 163 A4
Jodoigne B 79 B4
Joensuu FIN 9 A6
Joesjö S 195 E5
Joeuf F 92 B1
Jõgeva EST 8 C5
Johanngeorgenstadt D 83 B4
Johannishus S 63 B3
Johanniskirchen D 95 C4
Johansfors S 63 B3
John o'Groats GB 32 C3
Johnshaven GB 35 B5
Johnstone GB 34 C3
Johnstown IRL 30 B1
Jõhvi EST 8 C5
Joigny F 104 B2
Joinville F 91 C5
Jokkmokk S 196 C2
Jöllenbeck D 72 B1
Jomala FIN 51 B6
Jönåker S 56 B2
Jonava LT 13 A6
Jonchery-sur-Vesle F 91 B3
Jondal N 46 B3
Jondalen N 53 A5
Joniškis LT 8 D3
Jönköping S 62 A2
Jonkowo PL 69 B5
Jønnbu N 53 A5
Jonsberg S 56 B2
Jonsered S 60 B2
Jonstorp S 61 C2
Jonzac F 114 C3
Jorba E 147 C2
Jordanów PL 99 B3
Jordanowo PL 75 B4
Jordanów Śląski PL 85 B4
Jordbro S 57 A4
Jordbrua N 195 D5
Jördenstorf D 66 C1
Jordet N 49 A4
Jordøse DK 59 C3
Jork D 72 A2
Jörlanda S 60 B1
Jormlien S 199 A10
Jormvattnet S 199 A11
Jörn S 200 A6
Jørpeland N 52 A2
Jorquera E 158 B2
Jošan HR 123 C4
Jošavka BIH 124 C3
Josipdol HR 123 B4
Josipovac HR 125 B4
Jössefors S 54 A3
Josselin F 101 B3
Jøssund N 199 A7
Jostedal N 47 A4
Jósvafő H 99 C4
Jou P 148 A2
Jouarre F 90 C3
Joué-lès-Tours F 102 B2
Joué-sur-Erdre F 101 B4
Joure NL 70 B2
Joutseno FIN 9 B6
Joutsijärvi FIN 197 C10
Joux-la-Ville F 104 B2
Jouy F 90 C1
Jouy-le-Châtel F 90 C3
Jouy-le-Potier F 103 B3
Joyeuse F 131 A3
Joze F 116 B3
Juankoski FIN 8 A6
Juan-les-Pins F 132 B3
Jübek D 64 B2
Jubera E 144 B1
Jubrique E 162 B2
Jüchsen D 82 B2
Judaberg N 52 A1
Judenburg A 110 B1
Juelsminde DK 59 C3
Jugon-les-Lacs F 101 A3
Juillac F 129 A4
Juillan F 145 A4
Juist D 71 A4
Jukkasjärvi S 196 B3
Jule N 199 A10
Julianadorp NL 70 B1
Julianstown IRL 30 A2
Jülich D 80 B2
Jullouville F 88 B2
Jumeaux F 117 B3
Jumièges F 89 A4
Jumilhac-le-Grand F 115 C5
Jumilla E 159 C2
Jumisko FIN 197 C11
Juncosa E 153 A4
Juneda E 147 C1
Jung S 55 B4
Jungingen D 93 C5
Junglingster L 92 B2
Juniville F 91 B4
Junosuando S 196 B5
Junqueira P 149 A2
Junsele S 200 C2
Juoksengi S 196 C6
Juoksenki FIN 196 C6
Juprelle B 80 B1
Jurata PL 69 A3
Jurbarkas LT 12 A5
Jurjevo HR 123 C3
Jūrmala LV 8 D3
Jurmu FIN 197 D10
Juromenha P 155 C3
Jursla S 56 B2
Jussac F 116 C2
Jussey F 105 B4
Jussy F 90 B3
Juta H 125 A3
Jüterbog D 74 C2
Juuka FIN 3 E11
Juuma FIN 197 C12
Juvigny-le-Terte F 88 B2
Juvigny-sous-Andaine F 89 B3
Juzennecourt F 105 A3
Jyderup DK 61 D1
Jyrkänkoski FIN 197 C12
Jyväskylä FIN 8 A4

K

Kaamanen FIN 193 C11
Kaamasmukka FIN 193 C10
Kaaresuvanto FIN 192 D6
Kaarssen D 73 A4
Kaatscheuvel NL 79 A5
Kaba H 113 B5
Kåbdalis S 196 C3
Kačarevo SRB 127 C2
Kács H 113 B4
Kadan CZ 83 B5
Kadarkút H 125 A3
Kadınhanı TR 189 A7
Kaduy RUS 9 C10
Kåfalla S 56 A1
Kåfjord N 192 C7
Kåfjordbotn N 192 C4
Kågeröd S 61 D3
Kahl D 93 A5
Kahla D 82 B3
Kainach bei Voitsberg A 110 B2
Kaindorf A 110 B2
Kainulasjärvi S 196 C5
Kairala FIN 197 B10
Kaisepakte S 192 D3
Kaisersesch D 80 B3
Kaiserslautern D 93 B3
Kaisheim D 94 C2
Kajaani FIN 3 D10
Kajárpéc H 111 B4
Kajdacs H 112 C2
Kakanj BIH 139 A4
Kakasd H 125 A4
Kaklik TR 189 B4
Kakolewo PL 85 A4
Kál H 113 B4
Kalajoki FIN 3 D8
Kalak N 193 B11
Kalamata GR 184 B3
Kalambaka GR 182 D3
Kalamria GR 182 C4
Kalandra GR 183 D5
Kälarne S 200 D2
Kalavrita GR 184 A3
Kalbe D 73 B4
Kalce SLO 123 B3
Káld H 111 B4
Kale
Antalya TR 189 C4
Denizli TR 188 B3
Kalecik TR 23 A7
Kalefeld D 82 A2
Kalesija BIH 139 A4
Kalety PL 86 B2
Kalevala RUS 3 D12
Kalhovd N 47 B5
Kali HR 137 A4
Kalimnos GR 188 C2
Kaliningrad RUS 69 A5
Kalinkavichy BY 13 B8
Kalinovac HR 124 A3
Kalinovik BIH 139 B4
Kalinovo SK 99 C3
Kalirachi GR 183 C6
Kaliska
Pomorskie PL 68 A3
Pomorskie PL 68 B3
Kalisko PL 86 A3
Kalisz PL 86 A2
Kalisz Pomorski PL 75 A4
Kaljord N 194 B6
Kalkan TR 189 C4
Kalkar D 80 A2
Kalkım TR 186 C2
Kall
D 80 B2
S 199 B10
Källby S 55 B4
Kållered S 60 B2
Kållerstad S 60 B3
Kallinge S 63 B3
Kallmünz D 95 B3
Kallo FIN 196 B7
Kallsedet S 199 B9
Källvik S 56 B3
Kalmar S 63 B4
Kalmthout B 79 A4
Kalná SK 112 A2
Kalocsa H 112 C2
Kalokhorio CY 181 B2
Kalo Nero GR 184 B2
Kaloni GR 186 C1
Káloz H 112 C2
Kals A 109 B3
Kalsdorf A 110 C2
Kaltbrunn CH 107 B4
Kaltenbach A 108 B2
Kaltenkirchen D 64 C2
Kaltennordheim D 82 B2
Kalundborg DK 61 D1
Kalush UA 13 D6
Kalv S 60 B3
Kalvåg N 198 D1
Kalvehave DK 65 A5
Kalwang A 110 B1
Kalwaria-Zebrzydowska PL 99 B3
Kalyazin RUS 9 D10
Kam H 111 B3
Kaman TR 23 B7
Kamares GR 185 C5
Kambos CY 181 A1
Kamen D 81 A3
Kamenice CZ 97 B3
Kamenice nad Lipou CZ 96 B3
Kameničná SK 112 B2
Kamenný Most SK 112 B2
Kamenny Ujezd CZ 96 C2
Kamenska HR 124 B3
Kamensko HR 138 B2
Kamenz D 84 A2
Kamičak BIH 124 C2
Kamień PL 87 A4
Kamieniec Zabk PL 85 B4
Kamienka SK 99 B4
Kamień Krajeński PL 76 A2
Kamienna Góra PL 85 B4
Kamień Pomorski PL 67 C3
Kamieńsk PL 86 A3
Kamiros Skala GR 188 C2
Kamnik SLO 123 A3
Kampen NL 70 B2
Kampinos PL 77 B5
Kamp-Lintfort D 80 A2
Kampor HR 123 C3
Kamyanets-Podil's'kyy UA 13 D7
Kamyanka-Buz'ka UA 13 C6
Kamýk nad Vltavou CZ 96 B2
Kanal SLO 122 A2
Kanalia GR 182 D4
Kandalaksha RUS 3 C13
Kandanos GR 185 D4
Kandel D 93 B4
Kandern D 106 B2
Kandersteg CH 106 C2
Kandila GR 184 B3
Kandıra TR 187 A5
Kandyty PL 69 A5
Kanfanar HR 122 B2
Kangasala FIN 8 B4
Kangos S 196 B5
Kangosjärvi FIN 196 B6
Kaniów PL 75 C3
Kanjiža SRB 126 A2
Kankaanpää FIN 8 B3
Kannus FIN 3 E8
Kanturk IRL 29 B3
Kapaklı TR 186 A2
Kapellen
A 110 B2
B 79 A4
Kapellskär S 57 A5
Kapfenberg A 110 B2
Kapfenstein A 110 C2
Kaplice CZ 96 C2
Kapljuh BIH 124 C2
Kápolna H 113 B4
Kápolnásnyék H 112 B2
Kaposfö H 125 A3
Kaposfüred H 125 A3
Kaposszekcsö H 125 A4
Kaposvár H 125 A3
Kapp N 48 B2
Kappel D 93 C3
Kappeln D 64 B2
Kappelshamn S 57 C4
Kappl A 107 B5
Kappstad S 55 A4
Kaprun A 109 B3
Kaptol HR 125 B3
Kapuvár H 111 B4
Karaadilli TR 189 A5
Karabiğa TR 186 B2
Karabük TR 187 A7
Karaburun TR 186 D1
Karacabey TR 186 B3
Karacaköy TR 186 A3
Karacaören TR 189 A5
Karacasu TR 188 B3
Karácsond H 113 B4
Karád H 112 C1
Karahallı TR 189 A4
Karaisalı TR 23 C8
Karaman
Balıkesir TR 186 C3
Karaman TR 23 C7
Karamanlı TR 189 B4
Karamürsel TR 187 B4
Karan SRB 127 D1
Karancslapujto H 113 A3
Karaova TR 188 B2
Karapınar TR 23 C7
Karasjok N 193 C9
Karasu TR 187 A5
Karataş
Adana TR 23 C8
Manisa TR 188 A3
Karatoprak TR 188 B2
Karavostasi CY 181 A1
Karbenning S 50 B3
Kårberg S 55 B5
Kårböle S 199 D12
Karby
D 64 B2
DK 58 B1
Kårby S 62 A4
Karby S 57 A4
Karcag H 113 B4
Karczów PL 86 B1
Karczowiska PL 85 A4
Kardamena GR 188 C2
Kardamila GR 185 A7
Kardamili GR 184 C3
Kardašova Rečice CZ 96 B2
Kardis S 196 C6
Karditsa GR 182 D3
Kärdla EST 8 C3
Kardoskút H 113 C4
Karesuando S 192 D6
Kargı TR 23 A8
Kargopol RUS 9 B11
Kargowa PL 75 B4
Karigasniemi FIN 193 C9
Karise DK 65 A5
Karistos GR 185 A5
Karkkila FIN 8 B4
Karlholmsbruk S 51 B4
Karlino PL 67 B4
Karlobag HR 137 A4
Karlovac HR 123 B4
Karlovasi GR 188 B1
Karlovčic SRB 127 C2
Karlovice CZ 85 B5
Karlovo BG 17 D6
Karlovy Vary CZ 83 B4
Karłowice PL 86 B1
Karlsborg S 55 B5
Karlshamn S 63 B2
Karlshöfen D 72 A2
Karlshus N 54 A1
Karlskoga S 55 A5
Karlskrona S 63 B3
Karlsrud N 47 B5
Karlsruhe D 93 B4
Karlstad S 55 A4
Karlstadt D 94 B1
Karlstetten A 110 A2
Karlstift A 96 C2
Karlstorp S 62 A3
Karmacs H 111 C4
Karmin PL 85 A5
Kärna S 60 B1
Karnobat BG 17 D7
Karojba HR 122 B2
Karow D 73 A5
Karpacz PL 85 B3
Karpathos GR 188 D2
Karpenisi GR 182 E3
Karpuzlu TR 188 B2
Kärrbo S 56 A2
Karrebaeksminde DK 65 A4
Karshult S 60 B3
Karsin PL 68 B2
Kårsta S 57 A4
Karstädt D 73 A4
Kartal TR 186 B4
Kartitsch A 109 C3
Kartuzy PL 68 A3
Karungi S 196 C6
Karunki FIN 196 C7
Karup DK 59 B2
Karviná CZ 98 B2
Kås DK 58 A2
Kaş TR 189 C4
Kasaba TR 189 C4
Kašava CZ 98 B1
Kåseberga S 66 A3
Kasejovice CZ 96 B1
Kasfjord N 194 B7
Kashin RUS 9 D10
Kašina HR 124 B2
Kasina-Wielka PL 99 B4
Kaskinen FIN 8 A2
Kašperské Hory CZ 96 B1
Kassandrino GR 183 C5
Kassel D 81 A5
Kassiopi GR 182 D1
Kastamonu TR 23 A7
Kastav HR 123 B3
Kasteli GR 185 D4
Kastellaun D 93 A3
Kastelli GR 185 D6
Kaštel-Stari HR 138 B2
Kaštel Zegarski HR 138 A1
Kasterlee B 79 A4
Kastl D 95 B3
Kastlösa S 63 B4
Kastorf D 65 C3
Kastoria GR 182 C3
Kastorio GR 184 B3
Kastraki GR 185 C6
Kastrosikia GR 182 D2
Kastsyukovichy BY 13 B10
Kaszaper H 113 C4
Katakolo GR 184 B2
Katapola GR 185 C6
Katastari GR 184 B1
Katerbow D 74 B1
Katerini GR 182 C4
Kathikas CY 181 B1
Kätkesuando S 196 A6
Katlenburg-Lindau D 82 A2
Kato Achaia GR 184 A2
Káto Pyrgos CY 181 A1
Katouna GR 182 E3
Katovice CZ 96 B1
Katowice PL 86 B3
Katrineberg S 50 A3
Katrineholm S 56 B2
Kattarp S 61 C2
Kattavia GR 188 D2
Katthammarsvik S 57 C4
Kattilstorp S 55 B4
Katwijk NL 70 B1
Katymár H 125 A5
Kąty Wrocławskie PL 85 A4
Katzenelnbogen D 81 B3
Katzhütte D 82 B3
Kaub D 93 A3
Kaufbeuren D 108 B1
Kauhajoki FIN 8 A3
Kauhava FIN 8 A3
Kaukonen FIN 196 B7
Kauliranta FIN 196 C6
Kaulsdorf D 82 B3
Kaunas LT 13 A5
Kaunisvaara S 196 B6
Kaupanger N 47 A4
Kautokeino N 192 C7
Kautzen A 97 C3
Kavadarci MK 182 B4
Kavajë AL 182 B1
Kavakköy TR 186 B1
Kavaklı TR 186 A2
Kavaklıdere TR 188 B3
Kavala GR 183 C6
Kavarna BG 17 D8
Kävlinge S 61 D3
Kawcze PL 68 A1
Kaxås S 199 B10
Kaxholmen S 62 A2
Käylä FIN 197 C12
Kaymakçı TR 188 A3
Kaymaz TR 187 C6
Kaynarca TR 187 A5
Käyrämö FIN 197 C9
Kayseri TR 23 B8
Kaysersberg F 106 A2
Kazanlük BG 17 D6
Kazár H 113 A3
Kazimierza Wielka PL 87 B4
Kazincbarcika H 113 A4
Kaźmierz PL 75 B5
Kcynia PL 76 A2
Kdyně CZ 95 B5
Kea GR 185 B5
Keadew IRL 26 B2
Keady GB 27 B4
Kecel H 112 C3
Keçiborlu TR 189 B5
Kecskemét H 113 C3
Kėdainiai LT 13 A5
Kędzierzyn-Koźle PL 86 B2
Keel IRL 28 A1
Keenagh IRL 28 A4
Keerbergen B 79 A4
Kefalos GR 188 C1
Kefken TR 187 A5
Keflavík IS 190 C3
Kegworth GB 40 C2
Kehl D 93 C3
Kehrigk D 74 B2
Keighley GB 40 B2
Keila EST 8 C4
Keillmore GB 34 C2
Keiss GB 32 C3
Keith GB 33 D4
Kelankylä FIN 197 D10
Kelberg D 80 B2
Kelbra D 82 A3
Kelč CZ 98 B1
Kelchsau A 108 B3
Këlcyrë AL 182 C2

Kel–Koz 247

Keld GB 37 B4
Kelebia H 126 A1
Kelekçi TR 188 B4
Kelemér H 99 C4
Keles TR 186 C4
Kelheim D 95 C3
Kell D 92 B2
Kellas GB 32 D3
Kellinghusen D 64 C2
Kelloselkä FIN 197 C11
Kells
GB 27 B4
IRL 27 C4
Kelmis B 80 B2
Kelokedhara CY 181 B1
Kelottijärvi FIN 192 D6
Kelsall GB 38 A4
Kelso GB 35 C5
Kelsterbach D 93 A4
Keltneyburn GB 35 B3
Kelujärvi FIN 197 B10
Kemaliye TR 188 A3
Kemalpaşa TR 188 A2
Kematen A 108 B2
Kemberg D 83 A4
Kemer
Antalya TR 189 C5
Burdur TR 189 B5
Muğla TR 189 C4
Kemerkaya TR 187 D6
Kemeten A 111 B3
Kemi FIN 196 D7
Kemijärvi FIN 197 C10
Keminmaa FIN 196 D7
Kemnath D 95 B3
Kemnay GB 33 D4
Kemnitz
Brandenburg D 74 B1
Mecklenburg-Vorpommern D 66 B2
Kempen D 80 A2
Kempsey GB 39 B4
Kempten D 107 B5
Kemptthal CH 107 B3
Kendal GB 37 B4
Kenderes H 113 B4
Kengyel H 113 B4
Kenilworth GB 44 A2
Kenmare IRL 29 C2
Kenmore GB 35 B4
Kennacraig GB 34 C2
Kenyeri H 111 B4
Kenzingen D 106 A2
Kepez TR 186 B1
Kępice PL 68 A1
Kępno PL 86 A2
Kepsut TR 186 C3
Keramoti GR 183 C6
Keräntöjärvi S 196 B6
Keratea GR 185 B4
Kerava FIN 8 B4
Kerecsend H 113 B4
Kerekegyhaza H 112 C3
Kerepestarcsa H 112 B3
Keri GR 184 B1
Kérien F 100 A2
Kerkafalva H 111 C3
Kerken D 80 A2
Kerkrade NL 80 B2
Kerkyra GR 182 D1
Kerlouan F 100 A1
Kernascléden F 100 A2
Kernhof A 110 B2
Kerns CH 106 C3
Kerpen D 80 B2
Kerrysdale GB 31 B3
Kerta H 111 B4
Kerteminde DK 59 C3
Kerzers CH 106 C2
Keşan TR 186 B1
Kesgrave GB 45 A5
Kesh GB 26 B3
Keskin TR 23 B7
Kesselfall A 109 B3
Kestenga RUS 3 D12
Keswick GB 36 B3
Keszthely H 111 C4
Kétegyháza H 113 C5
Kéthely H 111 C4
Kętrzyn PL 12 A4
Kettering GB 44 A3
Kettlewell GB 40 A1
Kęty PL 99 B3
Ketzin D 74 B1
Keula D 82 A2
Keuruu FIN 8 A4
Kevelaer D 80 A2
Kevermes H 113 C5
Kevi SRB 126 B1
Keyingham GB 41 B3
Keynsham GB 43 A4
Kežmarok SK 99 B4
Kharmanli BG 183 B7
Khaskovo BG 183 B7
Khimki RUS 9 E10
Khisinev = Chişinău
MD 17 B8
Khmelnik UA 13 D7
Khmelnytskyy UA 13 D7
Khodoriv UA 13 D6
Kholm RUS 9 D7
Khotyn UA 13 D7
Khoyniki BY 13 C8
Khust UA 17 A5
Khvoynaya RUS 9 C9
Kiato GR 184 A3
Kibæk DK 59 B1
Kiberg N 193 B14
Kicasalih TR 186 A1
Kičevo MK 182 B2
Kidderminster GB 39 B4
Kidlington GB 44 B2
Kidsgrove GB 40 B1
Kidwelly GB 39 C2
Kiefersfelden D 108 B3
Kiel D 64 B3
Kielce PL 87 B4
Kiełczygłów PL 86 A3
Kielder GB 37 A4
Kiełpino PL 68 A3
Kielpiny PL 77 A4
Kierinki FIN 197 B8
Kiernozia PL 77 B4
Kierspe D 81 A3
Kietrz PL 86 B2
Kietz D 74 B3
Kiev = Kyyiv UA 13 C9
Kiezmark PL 69 A3
Kiffisia GR 185 A4
Kifino Selo BIH 139 B4
Kihlanki
FIN 196 B6
S 196 B6
Kiistala FIN 197 B8
Kije PL 87 B4
Kijevo HR 138 B2
Kikallen N 46 B2
Kikinda SRB 126 B2
Kil
N 53 B5
Örebro S 55 A6
Värmland S 55 A4
Kila S 55 A3
Kilafors S 50 A3
Kilbaha IRL 29 B2
Kilbeggan IRL 30 A1
Kilberry GB 34 C2
Kilbirnie GB 34 C3
Kilboghamn N 195 D4
Kilbotn N 194 B7
Kilb Rabenstein A 110 A2
Kilchattan GB 34 C2
Kilchoan GB 34 B1
Kilcock IRL 30 A2
Kilconnell IRL 28 A3
Kilcormac IRL 28 A4
Kilcreggan GB 34 C3
Kilcullen IRL 30 A2
Kilcurry IRL 27 B4
Kildare IRL 30 A2
Kildinstroy RUS 3 B13
Kildonan GB 32 C3
Kildorrery IRL 29 B3
Kilegrend N 53 A4
Kilen N 53 A4
Kilgarvan IRL 29 C2
Kiliya UA 17 C8
Kilkee IRL 29 B2
Kilkeel GB 27 B4
Kilkelly IRL 26 C2
Kilkenny IRL 30 B1
Kilkieran IRL 28 A2
Kilkinlea IRL 29 B2
Kilkis GR 182 B4
Killadysert IRL 29 B2
Killala IRL 26 B1
Killaloe IRL 28 B3
Killarney IRL 29 B2
Killashandra IRL 27 B3
Killashee IRL 28 A4
Killearn GB 34 B3
Killeberg S 61 C4
Killeigh IRL 30 A1
Killenaule IRL 29 B4
Killimor IRL 28 A3
Killin GB 34 B3
Killinaboy IRL 28 B2
Killinge S 196 B3
Killinick IRL 30 B2
Killorglin IRL 29 B2
Killucan IRL 30 A1
Killybegs IRL 26 B2
Killyleagh GB 27 B5
Kilmacrenan IRL 26 A3
Kilmacthomas IRL 30 B1
Kilmaine IRL 28 A2
Kilmallock IRL 29 B3
Kilmarnock GB 36 A2
Kilmartin GB 34 B2
Kilmaurs GB 36 A2
Kilmeadan IRL 30 B1
Kilmeedy IRL 29 B3
Kilmelford GB 34 B2
Kilmore Quay IRL 30 B2
Kilmuir GB 32 D2
Kilnaleck IRL 27 C3
Kilninver GB 34 B2
Kilpisjärvi FIN 192 C4
Kilrea GB 27 B4
Kilrush IRL 29 B2
Kilsmo S 56 A1
Kilsyth GB 35 C3
Kiltoom IRL 28 A3
Kilwinning GB 36 A2
Kimasozero RUS 3 D12
Kimi GR 185 A5
Kimolos GR 185 C5
Kimovsk RUS 9 E10
Kimratshofen D 107 B5
Kimry RUS 9 D10
Kimstad S 56 B1
Kinbrace GB 32 C3
Kincardine GB 35 B4
Kincraig GB 32 D3
Kindberg A 110 B2
Kindelbruck D 82 A3
Kingarrow IRL 26 B2
Kingisepp RUS 9 C6
Kingsbridge GB 43 B3
Kingsclere GB 44 B2
Kingscourt IRL 27 C4
King's Lynn GB 41 C4
Kingsteignton GB 43 B3
Kingston
Greater London
GB 44 B3
Moray GB 32 D3
Kingston Bagpuize
GB 44 B2
Kingston upon Hull
GB 40 B3
Kingswear GB 43 B3
Kingswood GB 43 A4
Kington GB 39 B3
Kingussie GB 32 D2
Kınık
Antalya TR 188 C4
İzmir TR 186 C2
Kinloch
Highland GB 31 B2
Kinloch *continued*
Highland GB 32 C2
Kinlochbervie GB 32 C1
Kinlochewe GB 32 D1
Kinlochleven GB 34 B3
Kinlochmoidart GB 34 B2
Kinloch Rannoch
GB 35 B3
Kinloss GB 32 D3
Kinlough IRL 26 B2
Kinn N 48 B2
Kinna S 60 B2
Kinnared S 60 B3
Kinnarp S 55 B4
Kinnegad IRL 30 A1
Kinne-Kleva S 55 B4
Kinnitty IRL 28 A4
Kinrooi B 80 A1
Kinross GB 35 B4
Kinsale IRL 29 C3
Kinsarvik N 46 B3
Kintarvie GB 31 A2
Kintore GB 33 D4
Kinvarra IRL 28 A3
Kioni GR 184 A1
Kiparissia GR 184 B2
Kipfenburg D 95 C3
Kippen GB 35 B3
Kiraz TR 188 A3
Kirazlı TR 186 B1
Kirberg D 81 B4
Kirchbach in
Steiermark A 110 C2
Kirchberg
CH 106 B2
Baden-Württemberg
D 94 B1
Rheinland-Pfalz D 93 B3
Kirchberg am Wechsel
A 110 B2
Kirchberg an der
Pielach A 110 A2
Kirchberg in Tirol
A 109 B3
Kirchbichl A 108 B3
Kirchdorf
Bayern D 96 C1
Mecklenburg-Vorpommern D 65 C4
Niedersachsen D 72 B1
Kirchdorf an der Krems
A 109 B5
Kirchdorf in Tirol
A 109 B3
Kirchenlamitz D 83 B3
Kirchenthumbach
D 95 B3
Kirchhain D 81 B4
Kirchheim
Baden-Württemberg
D 94 C1
Bayern D 108 A1
Hessen D 81 B5
Kirchheimbolanden
D 93 B4
Kirchhundem D 81 A4
Kirchlintein D 72 B2
Kirchschlag A 111 B3
Kirchweidach D 109 A3
Kirchzarten D 106 B2
Kircubbin GB 27 B5
Kireç TR 186 C3
Kırıkkale TR 23 B7
Kirillov RUS 9 C11
Kirishi RUS 9 C8
Kırka TR 187 C5
Kırkağaç TR 186 C2
Kirkbean GB 36 B3
Kirkbride GB 36 B3
Kirkby GB 38 A4
Kirkby Lonsdale
GB 37 B4
Kirkby Malzeard
GB 40 A2
Kirkbymoorside
GB 37 B6
Kirkby Stephen GB 37 B4
Kirkcaldy GB 35 B4
Kirkcolm GB 36 B1
Kirkconnel GB 36 A2
Kirkcowan GB 36 B2
Kirkcudbright GB 36 B2
Kirkehamn N 52 B2
Kirke Hyllinge DK 61 D1
Kirkenær N 49 B4
Kirkenes N 193 C14
Kirkham GB 38 A4
Kirkintilloch GB 35 C3
Kirkjubæjarklaustur
IS 191 D7
Kirkkonummi FIN 8 B4
Kırklareli TR 186 A2
Kirkmichael GB 35 B4
Kirk Michael GB 36 B2
Kirkoswald GB 36 A2
Kirkpatrick Fleming
GB 36 A3
Kirkton of Glenisla
GB 35 B4
Kirkwall GB 33 C4
Kirkwhelpington
GB 37 A5
Kirn D 93 B3
Kirovsk RUS 3 C13
Kirriemuir GB 35 B5
Kırşehir TR 23 B8
Kirton GB 41 C3
Kirton in Lindsey
GB 40 B3
Kirtorf D 81 B5
Kiruna S 196 B3
Kisa S 62 A3
Kisač SRB 126 B1
Kisbér H 112 B2
Kiseljak BIH 139 B4
Kisielice PL 69 B4
Kisköre H 113 B4
Kiskőrös H 112 C3
Kiskunfélegyháza
H 113 C3
Kiskunhalas H 112 C3
Kiskunlacháza H 112 B2
Kiskunmajsa H 113 C3
Kisláng H 112 C2
Kisslegg D 107 B4
Kissolt H 112 C3
Kissónerga CY 181 B1
Kist D 94 B1
Kistanje HR 138 B1
Kistelek H 113 C3
Kisterenye H 113 A3
Kisújszállás H 113 B4
Kisvárda H 16 A5
Kisvejke H 112 C2
Kiszkowo PL 76 B2
Kiszombor H 126 A2
Kitee FIN 9 A7
Kithnos GR 185 B5
Kiti CY 181 B2
Kitkiöjärvi S 196 B6
Kitkiöjoki S 196 B6
Kittelfjäll S 195 E6
Kittendorf D 74 A1
Kittilä FIN 196 B7
Kittlitz D 84 A2
Kittsee A 111 A4
Kitzbühel A 109 B3
Kitzingen D 94 B2
Kiuruvesi FIN 3 E10
Kivertsi UA 13 C6
Kividhes CY 181 B1
Kivik S 63 C2
Kivotos GR 182 C3
Kıyıköy TR 186 A3
Kızılcabölük TR 188 B4
Kızılcadağ TR 189 B4
Kızılcahamam TR 23 A7
Kızılırmak TR 23 A7
Kızılkaya TR 189 B5
Kızılkuyu TR 187 D6
Kızılören
Afyon TR 189 A5
Konya TR 189 B7
Kjeldebotn N 194 B7
Kjellerup DK 59 B2
Kjellmyra N 49 B4
Kjøllefjord N 193 B11
Kjopmannskjaer N 54 A1
Kjøpsvik N 194 B7
Kl'ačno SK 98 C2
Kladanj BIH 139 A4
Kläden D 73 B4
Klädesholmen S 60 B1
Kladnice HR 138 B2
Kladno CZ 84 B2
Kladruby CZ 95 B4
Klagenfurt A 110 C1
Klågerup S 61 D3
Klagstorp S 66 A2
Klaipėda LT 8 E2
Klaistow D 74 B1
Klaksvík FO 4 A3
Klana HR 123 B3
Klanac HR 123 C4
Klanjec HR 123 A4
Klardorf D 95 B4
Klarup DK 58 A3
Klašnice BIH 124 C3
Klässbol S 55 A3
Klášterec nad Ohří
CZ 83 B5
Klášter pod Znievom
SK 98 C2
Klatovy CZ 96 B1
Klaus an der
Pyhrnbahn A 110 B1
Klazienaveen NL 71 B3
Kłecko PL 76 B2
Kleczew PL 76 B3
Klein Plasten D 74 A1
Klein Sankt Paul
A 110 C1
Kleinsölk A 109 B4
Kleinzell A 110 B2
Klejtrup DK 58 B2
Klek SRB 126 B2
Klemensker DK 67 A3
Klenak SRB 127 C1
Klenci pod Cerchovem
CZ 95 B4
Klenica PL 75 C4
Klenje SRB 127 C1
Klenoec MK 182 B2
Klenovec SK 99 C3
Klenovica HR 123 B3
Klenovnik HR 124 A2
Kleppe N 52 B1
Kleppestø N 46 B2
Kleptow D 74 A2
Kleszewo PL 77 B6
Kleve D 80 A2
Klevshult S 60 B4
Klewki PL 77 A5
Kličevac SRB 127 C3
Kliening A 110 C1
Klietz D 73 B5
Klikuszowa PL 99 B3
Klimkovice CZ 98 B2
Klimontów PL 87 B5
Klimovichi BY 13 B9
Klimpfjäll S 195 E5
Klin RUS 9 D10
Klinča Sela HR 123 B4
Klingenbach A 111 B3
Klingenberg D 93 B5
Klingenmunster D 93 B4
Klingenthal D 83 B4
Klinken D 73 A4
Klintehamn S 57 C4
Kliny PL 87 A4
Kliplev DK 64 B2
Klippan S 61 C3
Klis HR 138 B2
Klitmøller DK 58 A1
Klitten S 49 A6
Klixbüll D 64 B1
Kljajićevo SRB 126 B1
Ključ BIH 138 A2
Klobouky CZ 97 C4
Kłobuck PL 86 B2
Klockestrand S 200 D3
Kłodawa
Lubuskie PL 75 B4
Wielkopolskie PL 76 B3
Kłodzko PL 85 B4
Kløfta N 48 B3
Klokkarvik N 46 B2
Klokkerholm DK 58 A3
Klokočov SK 98 B2
Kłomnice PL 86 B3
Klonowa PL 86 A2
Kloosterzande NL 79 A4
Kłopot PL 74 B3
Klos AL 182 B2
Kloštar Ivanić HR 124 B2
Kloster
D 66 B2
DK 59 B1
Klösterle A 107 B5
Klostermansfeld D 82 A3
Klosterneuburg A 97 C4
Klosters CH 107 C4
Kloten CH 107 B3
Klötze D 73 B4
Klöverträsk S 196 D4
Klövsjö S 199 C11
Kluczbork PL 86 B2
Kluczewo PL 75 A5
Kluisbergen B 79 B3
Klundert NL 79 A4
Klutz D 65 C4
Klwów PL 87 A4
Klyetsk BY 13 B7
Knaben N 52 B2
Knaften S 200 B4
Knapstad N 54 A2
Knäred S 61 C3
Knaresborough GB 40 A2
Knarvik N 46 B2
Knebel DK 59 B3
Knebworth GB 44 B3
Knesebeck D 73 B3
Knesselare B 78 A3
Knežak SLO 123 B3
Kneževi Vinogradi
HR 125 B4
Kneževo HR 125 B4
Knić SRB 127 D2
Knighton GB 39 B3
Knin HR 138 A2
Knislinge S 61 C4
Knittelfeld A 110 B1
Knivsta S 57 A3
Knock IRL 28 A3
Knocktopher IRL 30 B1
Knokke-Heist B 78 A3
Knowle GB 44 A2
Knurów PL 86 B2
Knutby S 51 C5
Knutsford GB 38 A4
Kobarid SLO 122 A2
København =
Copenhagen DK 61 D2
Kobenz A 110 B1
Kobersdorf A 111 B3
Kobiernice PL 99 B3
Kobierzyce PL 85 B4
Kobilje SLO 111 C3
Kobiór PL 86 B2
Koblenz
CH 106 B3
D 81 B3
Kobryn BY 13 B6
Kobylanka PL 75 A3
Kobylin PL 85 A5
Kobylniki PL 77 B5
Kocaali TR 187 A5
Kocaaliler TR 189 B5
Kocaeli = İzmit
TR 187 B4
Kočani MK 182 B4
Koçarlı TR 188 B2
Koceljevo SRB 127 C1
Kočerin BIH 138 B3
Kočevje SLO 123 B3
Kočevska Reka
SLO 123 B3
Kochel am see D 108 B2
Kocs H 112 B2
Kocsér H 113 B3
Kocsola H 112 C2
Koczala PL 68 B2
Kodal N 53 A6
Kode S 60 B1
Kodersdorf D 84 A2
Kodrab PL 86 A3
Koekelare B 78 A2
Kofçaz TR 186 A2
Köflach A 110 B2
Køge DK 61 D2
Kohlberg D 95 B4
Kohtla-Järve EST 8 C5
Köinge S 60 B2
Kojetín CZ 98 B1
Kökar FIN 51 C7
Kokava SK 99 C3
Kokkola FIN 3 E8
Kokori BIH 124 C3
Kokoski PL 69 A3
Koksijde B 78 A2
Kola
BIH 124 C3
RUS 3 B13
Köla S 54 A3
Kołacin PL 87 A3
Kolari FIN 196 B6
Kolárovo SK 112 B1
Kolašin MNE 16 D3
Kolbäck S 56 A2
Kolbacz PL 75 A3
Kolbeinsstaðir IS 190 C3
Kolbermoor D 108 B3
Kolbnitz A 109 C4
Kolbotn N 54 A1
Kolbu N 48 B2
Kolby Kås DK 59 C3
Kolczewo PL 67 C3
Kolczyglowy PL 68 A2
Kolding DK 59 C2
Kölesd H 112 C2
Kolgrov N 46 A1
Kolín CZ 97 A3
Kolind DK 59 B3
Kolinec CZ 96 B1
Koljane HR 138 B2
Kølkær DK 59 B2
Kölleda D 82 A3
Kollum NL 70 A3
Köln = Cologne D 80 B2
Koło PL 76 B3
Kołobrzeg PL 67 B4
Kolochau D 83 A5
Kolomyya UA 13 D6
Kolonowskie PL 86 B2
Koloveč CZ 95 B5
Kolpino RUS 9 C7
Kolrep D 73 A5
Kölsillre S 199 C12
Kolsko PL 75 C4
Kolsva S 56 A1
Kolta SK 112 A2
Kolunič BIH 138 A2
Koluszki PL 87 A3
Kolut SRB 125 B4
Kolvereid N 199 A8
Kølvrå DK 59 B2
Komadi H 113 B5
Komagvær N 193 B14
Komarica BIH 125 C3
Komárno SK 112 B2
Komárom H 112 B2
Komatou Yialou
CY 181 A3
Komboti GR 182 D3
Komen SLO 122 B2
Komin HR 138 B3
Komiža HR 138 B2
Komjáti H 99 C4
Komjatice SK 112 A2
Komletinci HR 125 B4
Komló H 125 A4
Kömlo H 113 B4
Komoča SK 112 B2
Komorniki PL 75 B5
Komorzno PL 86 A2
Komotini GR 183 B7
Konak SRB 126 B2
Konakovo RUS 9 D10
Konarzyny PL 68 B2
Kondias GR 183 D7
Kondopaga RUS 9 A9
Kondorfa H 111 C3
Kondoros H 113 C4
Konevo RUS 9 A11
Køng DK 65 A4
Konga S 63 B3
Köngäs FIN 196 B7
Kongerslev DK 58 B3
Kongsberg N 53 A5
Kongshamn N 53 B4
Kongsmark DK 64 A1
Kongsmoen N 199 A9
Kongsvik N 194 B7
Kongsvinger N 48 B3
Konice CZ 97 B4
Konie PL 77 C5
Koniecpol PL 86 B3
Königsberg D 82 B2
Königsbronn D 94 C2
Königsbrück D 84 A1
Königsbrunn D 94 C2
Königsdorf D 108 B2
Königsee D 82 B3
Königshorst D 74 B1
Königslutter D 73 B3
Königssee D 109 B3
Königstein
Hessen D 81 B4
Sachsen D 84 B2
Königstetten A 97 C4
Königswartha D 84 A2
Konigswiesen A 96 C2
Königswinter D 80 B3
Königs Wusterhausen
D 74 B2
Konin PL 76 B3
Konispol AL 182 D2
Konitsa GR 182 C2
Köniz CH 106 C2
Konjevići BIH 139 A5
Konjevrate HR 138 B2
Konjic BIH 139 B3
Konjščina HR 124 A2
Könnern D 83 A3
Konnerud N 53 A6
Konopiska PL 86 B2
Konotop PL 75 C4
Końskie PL 87 A4
Konsmo N 52 B3
Konstancin-Jeziorna
PL 77 B6
Konstantynów Łódzki
PL 86 A3
Konstanz D 107 B4
Kontich B 79 A4
Kontiolahti FIN 9 A6
Konya TR 189 B7
Konz D 92 B2
Kópasker IS 191 A9
Kópavogur IS 190 C4
Kopčany SK 98 C1
Koper SLO 122 B2
Kopervik N 52 A1
Kópháza H 111 B3
Kopice PL 85 B5
Kopidlno CZ 84 B3
Köping S 56 A1
Köpingebro S 66 A2
Köpingsvik S 62 B4
Köpmanholmen
S 200 C4
Koppang N 48 A3
Koppangen N 192 C4
Kopparberg S 50 C1
Koppelo FIN 193 D11
Koppom S 54 A3
Koprivlen BG 183 B5
Koprivna BIH 125 C4
Koprivnica HR 124 A2
Kopřivnice CZ 98 B2
Köprübaşı TR 186 D3
Koprzywnica PL 87 B5
Kopstal L 92 B2
Kopychyntsi UA 13 D6
Kopytkowo PL 69 B3
Korbach D 81 A4
Körbecke D 81 A4
Korçë AL 182 C2
Korčula HR 138 C3
Korczyców PL 75 B3
Korenita SRB 127 C1
Korets UA 13 C7
Korfantów PL 85 B5
Körfez TR 187 B4
Korgen N 195 D4
Korinth DK 64 A3
Korinthos = Corinth
GR 184 B3
Korita
BIH 138 A2
HR 139 C3
Korithi GR 184 B1
Korkuteli TR 189 B5
Körmend H 111 B3
Korne PL 68 A2
Korneuburg A 97 C4
Kornevo RUS 69 A5
Kórnik PL 76 B2
Kornsjø N 54 B2
Környe H 112 B2
Koromačno HR 123 C3
Koroni GR 184 C2
Koronos GR 185 B6
Koronowo PL 76 A2
Körösladány H 113 C5
Köröstarcsa H 113 C5
Korosten UA 13 C8
Korostyshev UA 13 C8
Korpikå S 196 D6
Korpikylä FIN 196 C6
Korpilombolo S 196 C6
Korsberga
Jönköping S 62 A3
Skaraborg S 55 B5
Korshavn N 54 A1
Korskrogen S 200 E1
Korsnäs S 50 B2
Korsør DK 65 A4
Korsun
Shevchenkovskiy
UA 13 D9
Korträsk S 196 D3
Kortrijk B 78 B3
Korucu TR 186 C2
Koryčany CZ 98 B1
Korzeńsko PL 85 A4
Korzybie PL 68 A1
Kos GR 188 C2
Kosakowo PL 69 A3
Kosanica MNE 139 B5
Kösching D 95 C3
Kościan PL 75 B5
Kościelec PL 76 B3
Kościerzyna PL 68 A2
Koserow D 66 B2
Košetice CZ 97 B3
Košice SK 12 D4
Kosjerić SRB 127 D1
Koška HR 125 B4
Koskullskulle S 196 B3
Kosovska Mitrovica
KOS 16 D4
Kosta S 62 B3
Kostajnica HR 124 B2
Kostajnik SRB 127 C1
Kostanjevica SLO 123 B4
Kostelec nad Černými
Lesy CZ 96 B2
Kostelec na Hané
CZ 97 B5
Kostice CZ 84 B1
Kostkowo PL 68 A3
Kostojevići SRB 127 C1
Kostolac SRB 127 C3
Kostomłoty PL 85 A4
Kostopil UA 13 C7
Kostów PL 86 A2
Kostrzyn
Lubuskie PL 74 B3
Wielkopolskie PL 76 B2
Koszalin PL 67 B5
Koszęcin PL 86 B2
Kőszeg H 111 B3
Koszwaly PL 69 A3
Koszyce PL 87 B4
Kot SLO 123 B4
Kotala FIN 197 B11
Kötelek H 113 B4
Köthen D 83 A3
Kotka FIN 8 B5
Kotomierz PL 76 A3
Kotor MNE 16 D3
Kotoriba HR 124 A2
Kotorsko BIH 125 C4
Kotor Varoš BIH 124 C3
Kotovsk UA 17 B8
Kotronas GR 184 C3
Kötschach A 109 C3
Kötzting D 95 B4
Koudum NL 70 B2
Kouřim CZ 96 A2
Kout na Šumave
CZ 95 B5
Kouvola FIN 8 B5
Kovačevac SRB 127 C2
Kovačica SRB 126 B2
Kovdor RUS 197 B13
Kovel' UA 13 C6
Kovilj SRB 126 B2
Kovin SRB 127 C2
Kowal PL 77 B4
Kowalewo Pomorskie
PL 69 B3
Kowalów PL 75 B3
Kowary PL 85 B3
Köyceğiz TR 188 C3
Kozani GR 182 C3

Kozarac
  BIH 124 C2
  HR 124 B1
Kozárovce SK 98 C2
Kozelets UA. 13 C9
Kozica HR 138 B3
Kozieglowy PL. 86 B3
Kozienice PL. 87 A5
Kozina SLO 122 B2
Kozje SLO 123 A4
Kozlu TR 187 A6
Kozluk BIH. 139 A5
Kozmin PL. 85 A5
Kożminek PL. 86 A2
Kozolupy CZ 96 B1
Kożuchów PL 84 A3
Kožuhe BIH 125 C4
Kozyatyn UA 13 D8
Kozyürük TR 186 A1
Kräckelbräken S 49 A6
Krackow D 74 A3
Kraddsele S. 195 E7
Krag PL 68 A1
Kragenæs DK 65 B4
Kragerø N 53 B5
Kragi PL 68 B1
Kragujevac SRB . . .127 C2
Kraiburg D 109 A3
Krajenka PL. 68 B1
Krajišnik SRB 126 B2
Krajková CZ. 83 B4
Krajné SK. 98 C1
Krajnik Dolny PL. . . .74 A3
Krakača BIH. 124 B1
Kräklingbo S 57 C4
Kraków = Cracow
  PL. 99 A3
Krakow am See D . .73 A5
Králíky CZ 85 B4
Kraljevica HR 123 B3
Kraljevo SRB. 16 D4
Kral'ovany SK 99 B3
Král'ov Brod SK . . .111 A4
Kralovice CZ 96 B1
Kralupy nad Vltavou
  CZ 84 B2
Králův Dvůr CZ. 96 B2
Kramfors S 200 D3
Kramsach A. 108 B2
Kramsk PL. 76 B3
Kråmvik N 53 A4
Kranenburg D 80 A2
Krania GR 182 D3
Krania Elasonas
  GR. 182 D4
Kranichfeld D 82 B3
Kranidi GR. 184 B4
Kranj SLO 123 A3
Kranjska Gora
  SLO 109 C4
Krapanj HR 138 B1
Krapina HR 124 A1
Krapje HR 124 B2
Krapkowice PL. 86 B1
Kraselov CZ. 96 B1
Krašič HR 123 B4
Kråslava LV 8 E5
Kraslice CZ 83 B4
Krasna PL 87 A4
Krasna Lipa CZ 84 B2
Krasne PL 77 B5
Kraśnik PL. 12 C5
Krašnja SLO 123 A3
Krásno SK 98 B2
Krásnohorské
  Podhradie SK 99 C4
Krasno Polje HR . . .123 C4
Krasnozavodsk
  RUS 9 D11
Krasnystaw PL 13 C5
Krasnyy RUS. 13 A9
Krasnyy Kholm
  RUS 9 C10
Krasocin PL. 87 B4
Kraszewice PL. 86 A2
Kraszkowice PL. . . .86 A2
Kratigos GR. 186 C1
Kratovo MK 182 A4
Kraubath A 110 B1
Krausnick D. 74 B2
Krautheim D 94 B1
Kravaře CZ. 84 B2
Kravaře CZ 98 B2
Kravarsko HR 124 B2
Kraznějov CZ. 96 B1
Krčedin SRB 126 B2
Kŭrdzhali BG. 183 B7
Krefeld D 80 A2
Kregme DK 61 D2
Krembz D. 73 A4
Kremenets UA. 13 C6
Kremmen D 74 B2
Kremna SRB 127 D1
Kremnica SK 98 C2
Krempe D. 64 C2
Krems A. 97 C3
Kremsbrücke A . . .109 C4
Kremsmünster A . .110 A1
Křemže CZ. 96 C2
Křenov CZ. 97 B4
Krepa PL. 76 C2
Krepa Krajeńska
  PL. 75 A5
Krepsko PL. 68 B1
Kreševo BIH 139 B4
Kressbronn D 107 B4
Krestena GR 184 B2
Kretinga LT 8 E2
Krettsy RUS. 9 C8
Kreuth D 108 B2
Kreuzau D 80 B2
Kreuzlingen CH. . . .107 B4
Kreuztal D 81 B3
Krewelin D 74 B2
Krezluk BIH. 138 A3
Krichem BG. 183 A6
Krieglach A 110 B2

Kriegsfeld D 93 B3
Kriens CH. 106 B3
Krimml A 108 B2
Krimpen aan de IJssel
  NL. 79 A4
Křinec CZ. 84 B3
Kristdala S. 62 A4
Kristiansand N 53 B4
Kristianstad S. 61 C4
Kristiinankaupunki
  FIN 8 A2
Kristinefors S 49 B4
Kristinehamn S 55 A5
Kriváň SK. 99 C3
Kriva Palanka MK .182 A4
Křivoklát CZ. 96 A1
Křiž HR. 124 B2
Křižanov CZ. 97 B4
Križevci HR 124 A2
Krk HR 123 B3
Krka SLO 123 B3
Krnjača SRB 127 C2
Krnjak HR 123 B4
Krnjeuša BIH 124 C2
Krnov CZ. 98 A1
Krobia PL. 85 A4
Kroczyce PL. 86 B3
Krøderen N 48 B1
Krokees GR. 184 C3
Krokek S. 56 B2
Krokom S. 199 B11
Krokowa PL. 68 A3
Krokstad-elva N . . .53 A5
Kroksund N 54 A2
Kroměříž CZ. 98 B1
Krommenie NL. 70 B1
Krompachy SK 99 C4
Kronach D. 82 B3
Kronshagen D. 64 B3
Kronshtadt RUS 9 C6
Kröpelin D 65 B4
Kropp D 64 B2
Kroppenstedt D 73 C4
Kropstädt D 74 C1
Krościenko nad
  Dunajcem PL 99 B4
Kröslin D 66 B2
Krośnice PL. 85 A5
Krośniewice PL. 77 B4
Krosno PL. 12 D4
Krosno Odrzańskie
  PL. 75 B4
Krostitz D. 83 A4
Krotoszyn PL. 85 A5
Krottendorf A. 110 B2
Krouna CZ. 97 B4
Krowiarki PL. 86 B2
Krrabë AL. 182 B1
Kršan HR 123 B3
Krško SLO 123 B4
Krstac MNE 139 B4
Krstur SRB 126 A2
Křtiny CZ. 97 B4
Kruft D 80 B3
Kruishoutem B 79 B3
Krujë AL. 182 B1
Krulyewshchyna
  BY 13 A7
Krumbach
  A 111 B3
  D 94 C2
Krumovgrad BG . . .183 B7
Krün D 108 B2
Krupá CZ 84 B1
Krupina SK 99 C3
Krupa na Vrbasu
  BIH. 124 C3
Krupanj SRB 127 C1
Krupina SK 99 C3
Krupka CZ 84 B1
Krupki BY. 13 A8
Krusá DK. 64 B2
Kruščica BIH 139 A3
Kruševac SRB 16 D4
Kruševo MK. 182 B3
Kruszwica PL. 76 B3
Kruszyn PL 77 B4
Krychaw BY. 13 B9
Krynica PL. 99 B4
Krynica Morska PL .69 A4
Krzęcin PL. 75 A4
Krzelów PL. 85 A4
Krzepice PL. 86 B2
Krzepielów PL. 85 A4
Krzeszowice PL. . . .86 B3
Krzeszyce PL. 75 B4
Krzynowlaga Mała
  PL. 77 A5
Krzywiń PL. 75 C5
Krzyżanowice PL. . .98 B2
Krzyżowa PL 99 B3
Krzyż Wielkopolski
  PL. 75 B5
Ksiaz Wielkopolski
  PL. 87 B4
Książ Wielkopolski
  PL. 76 B2
Ktębowiec PL. 75 A5
Kübekháza H 126 A2
Küblis CH 107 C4
Kuchary PL. 86 A1
Kuchl A 109 B4
Kucice PL. 77 B5
Kuciste HR 138 C3
Kuçovë AL. 182 C1
Küçükbahçe TR. . .188 A1
Küçükköy TR. 186 C1
Küçükkuyu TR. . . .186 C1
Kucura SRB. 126 B1
Kuczbork-Osada
  PL. 77 A5
Kuddby S. 56 B2
Kudowa-Zdrój PL. . .85 B4
Kufstein A 108 B3
Kuggeboda S 63 B3
Kuggörana S. 200 E3
Kühbach D 95 C3
Kühmo FIN 3 D11
Kühnsdorf A 110 C1

Kuhstedt D 72 A1
Kuinre NL. 70 B2
Kuivaniemi FIN. . .197 D8
Kuivastu EST. 8 C3
Kukës AL 182 A2
Kuklin PL. 77 A5
Kukljica HR 137 A4
Kukujevci SRB 127 B1
Kula
  Srbija SRB. 127 C3
  Vojvodina SRB. . .126 B1
  TR. 188 A3
Kuldīga LV. 8 D7
Kulen Vakuf BIH . .124 C2
Kulina BIH 125 C4
Kullsdedt D. 82 A2
Kulmain D 95 B3
Kulmbach D. 82 B3
Kuloharju FIN 197 D11
Kulu TR 23 B7
Kumachevo RUS. . .69 A5
Kumafşarı TR 189 B4
Kumane SRB 126 B2
Kumanovo MK. . . .182 A3
Kumdanlı TR 189 A5
Kumkale TR. 186 C1
Kumla S. 56 A1
Kumlakyrkby S. 50 C3
Kumlinge FIN 51 B7
Kumluca TR. 189 C5
Kumrovec HR 123 A4
Kunadacs H. 112 C3
Kunágota H 113 C5
Kunbaja H 126 A1
Kunda EST. 8 C5
Kundl A 108 B2
Kunes N 193 B10
Kunfehértó H. 126 A1
Kungälv S 60 B1
Kungsängen S 57 A3
Kungsäter S 60 B2
Kungsbacka S. 60 B2
Kungsgården S. . . .50 B3
Kungshamn S. 54 B2
Kungs-Husby S. . . .56 A3
Kungsör S 56 A2
Kunhegyes H 113 B4
Kunmadaras H 113 B4
Kunovice CZ. 98 B1
Kunów PL 87 B5
Kunowo
  Wielkopolskie PL . .76 C2
  Zachodnio-Pomorskie
  PL. 74 A3
Kunštát CZ. 97 B4
Kunszállás H 113 C3
Kunszentmárton
  H 113 C4
Kunszentmiklós
  H 112 B3
Kunžak CZ. 97 B3
Künzelsau D 94 B1
Kuolayarvi RUS. . .197 C12
Kuolio FIN. 197 D11
Kuopio FIN 8 A5
Kuosku FIN 197 B11
Kup
  H 111 B4
  PL 86 B1
Kupferzell D. 94 B1
Kupinec HR 123 B4
Kupinečki Kraljevac
  HR 124 B1
Kupinovo SRB. 127 C2
Kupirovo HR 138 A2
Kupjak HR 123 B3
Kupres BIH 138 B3
Küps D 82 B3
Kurd H 112 C2
Küre TR 23 A7
Kuressaare EST. . . .8 C3
Kurikka FIN 8 A3
Kurилovec SRB . . .124 A2
Kuřím CZ 97 B4
Kuřivody CZ 84 B2
Kurki PL 77 A5
Kurort Oberwiesenthal
  D 83 B4
Kurort Schmalkalden
  D 82 B2
Kurort Stolberg D . .82 A2
Kurort Wippra D . . .82 A3
Kurów PL. 12 C5
Kurowice PL. 86 A3
Kurravaara S 196 B3
Kursu FIN 197 C11
Kuršumlija SRB
  SRB. 16 D4
Kurşunlu
  Bursa TR 187 B4
  Çankırı TR 23 A7
Kurtakko FIN. 196 B7
Kürten D 80 A3
Kurucaşile TR 187 A7
Kurvinen FIN 197 D12
Kurzelów PL. 87 B3
Kusadak SRB 127 C2
Kuşadası TR 188 B2
Kusel D 93 B3
Kusey D 73 B4
Küsnacht CH. 106 B3
Küssaberg D 106 B3
Küstelberg D 81 A4
Kütahya TR 187 C4
Kutenholz D. 72 A2
Kutina HR 124 B2
Kutjevo HR 125 B3
Kutná Hora CZ. 97 B3
Kутtara FIN. 193 D10
Küttingen CH. 106 B3
Kúty SK. 98 C1
Kuusamo FIN 197 D12
Kuusankoski FIN . .8 B5
Kuvshinovo RUS . . .9 D9
Kuyucak TR. 188 B3
Kuzmin SRB 127 B1
Kuźnia Raciborska
  PL. 86 B2
Kuźnica Czarnkowska
  PL. 75 B5

Kuźnica Żelichowska
  PL. 75 B5
Kvalsund N 192 B7
Kvaløysletta N. . . .192 C2
Kvalsund N. 192 B7
Kvam
  Nord-Trøndelag
  N 199 A8
  Oppland N 198 D6
Kvamsøy N 46 A3
Kvænangsbotn N .192 C6
Kvanndal N 46 B3
Kvänum S 55 B4
Kværndrup DK 59 C3
Kvås N 52 B3
Kvasice CZ. 98 B1
Kvelde N 53 A5
Kvenna N. 198 C5
Kville S. 54 B2
Kvillsfors S 62 A3
Kvinesdal N 52 B2
Kvinlog N 52 B2
Kvinnherad N 46 C2
Kvissel DK. 58 A3
Kvissleby S. 200 D3
Kviteseid N 53 A4
Kvitsøy N 52 A1
Kwakowo PL 68 A2
Kwidzyn PL. 69 B3
Kwilcz PL. 75 B5
Kyjov CZ 98 C1
Kyleakin GB. 31 B3
Kyle of Lochalsh
  GB. 31 B3
Kylerhea GB. 31 B3
Kylestrome GB 32 C1
Kyllburg D 92 A2
Kyllini GR 184 B2
Kynšperk nad Ohří
  CZ 83 B4
Kyperounda CY. . .181 B1
Kyrenia CY. 181 A2
Kyritz D 73 B5
Kyrkhult S 63 B2
Kyrksæterøra N. . .198 B6
Kysucké Nové Mesto
  SK 98 B2
Kythira GR. 184 C3
Kythréa CY 181 A2
Kyustendil BG. 16 D5
Kyyiv = Kiev UA. . . .13 C9
Kyyjärvi FIN. 8 A4

L

Laa an der Thaya A .97 C4
La Adrada E. 150 B3
Laage D. 65 C5
La Alameda E 157 B4
La Alberca E 149 B3
La Alberca de Záncara
  E 158 B1
La Albergueria de
  Argañán E. 149 B3
La Albuera E 155 C4
La Aldea del Portillo del
  Busto E 143 B3
La Algaba E 162 A1
La Aliseda de Tormes
  E 150 B2
La Almarcha E. . . .158 B1
La Almolda E 153 A3
La Almunia de Doña
  Godina E 152 A2
Laanila FIN 193 D11
La Antillas E 161 B2
La Arena E 141 A4
Laatzen D. 72 B2
La Aulaga E 161 B3
La Balme-de-Sillingy
  F. 118 B3
Laban IRL. 28 A3
La Bañeza E 141 B5
La Barca de la Florida
  E 162 B2
La Barre-de-Monts
  F. 114 B1
La Barre-en-Ouche
  F. 89 B4
La Barrosa E 162 B1
La Barthe-de-Neste
  F. 145 A4
La Bassée F. 78 B2
La Bastide-de-Sérou
  F. 146 A2
La Bastide-des-
  Jourdans F. 132 B1
Labastide-Murat F .129 B4
La Bastide-Puylaurent
  F. 117 C4
Labastide-Rouairoux
  F. 130 B1
Labastide-St Pierre
  F. 129 C4
La Bathie F 118 B3
La Baule-Escoublac
  F. 101 B3
La Bazoche-Gouet
  F. 102 A2
La Bégude-de-Mazenc
  F. 131 A3
Labenne F 128 C1
La Bernerie-en-Retz
  F. 114 A1
Labin HR 123 B3
La Bisbal d'Empordà
  E 147 C4
Łabiszyn PL. 76 B2
Lablachère F 131 A3

Kużnica Żelichowska
  PL. 75 B5
Kvalsund N 192 B7
Kvam
  Nord-Trøndelag
  N 199 A8
  Oppland N 198 D6
Kvamsøy N 46 A3
Kvænangsbotn N .192 C6
Kvanndal N 46 B3
Kvänum S 55 B4
Kværndrup DK 59 C3
Kvås N 52 B3
Kvasice CZ. 98 B1
Kvelde N 53 A5
Kvenna N. 198 C5
Kville S. 54 B2
Kvillsfors S 62 A3
Kvinesdal N 52 B2
Kvinlog N 52 B2
Kvinnherad N 46 C2
Kvissel DK. 58 A3
Kvissleby S. 200 D3
Kviteseid N 53 A4
Kvitsøy N 52 A1
Kwakowo PL 68 A2
Kwidzyn PL. 69 B3
Kwilcz PL. 75 B5
Kyjov CZ 98 C1
Kyleakin GB. 31 B3
Kyle of Lochalsh
  GB. 31 B3
Kylerhea GB. 31 B3
Kylestrome GB 32 C1
Kyllburg D 92 A2
Kyllini GR 184 B2
Kynšperk nad Ohří
  CZ 83 B4
Kyperounda CY. . .181 B1
Kyrenia CY. 181 A2
Kyritz D 73 B5
Kyrkhult S 63 B2
Kyrksæterøra N. . .198 B6
Kysucké Nové Mesto
  SK 98 B2
Kythira GR. 184 C3
Kythréa CY 181 A2
Kyustendil BG. 16 D5
Kyyiv = Kiev UA. . . .13 C9
Kyyjärvi FIN. 8 A4

Lábod H 124 A3
Laboe D. 64 B3
La Boissière F. 89 A4
La Bóveda de Toro
  E 150 A2
La Bourboule F . . .116 B2
Labouheyre F 128 B2
La Brède F 128 B2
La Bresse F 106 A1
La Bridoire F 118 B2
La Brillanne F 132 B1
Labrit F 128 B2
Labros E 152 A2
La Bruffière F 114 A2
La Boissière F 130 B1
Labruguière F 130 B1
Labrujo P. 148 A1
L'Absie F 114 B3
La Bussière F 103 B4
Laç AL 182 B1
La Caillère F 114 B3
Lacalahorra E 164 B1
La Caletta
  Cágliari I 179 C2
  Núoro I. 178 B3
La Calmette F 131 B3
La Calzada de Oropesa
  E 150 C2
La Campana E 162 A2
La Cañada E 150 B3
Lacanau F 128 B1
Lacanau-Océan F .128 A1
Lacanche F 104 B3
La Canourgue F . . .130 A2
La Capelle F 91 B3
La Cardanchosa
  E 156 B2
La Caridad E 141 A4
La Carlota E 162 A3
La Carolina E 157 B4
Lacaune F 130 B1
La Cava E 153 B4
La Cavalerie F 130 A2
Laceby GB. 41 B3
Lacedónia I 172 A1
La Celle-en-Moravan
  F. 104 B3
La Celle-St Avant
  F. 102 B2
La Cerca E 143 B3
La Chaise-Dieu F .117 B3
La Chaize-Giraud
  F. 114 B2
La Chaize-le-Vicomte
  F. 114 B2
La Chambre F 118 B3
La Chapelaude F . .116 A2
La Chapelle-d'Angillon
  F. 103 B4
La Chapelle-en-
  Aalgaudémar F. .118 C3
La Chapelle-en-Vercors
  F. 118 C2
La Chapelle-Glain
  F. 101 B4
La Chapelle-la-Reine
  F. 90 C2
La Chapelle-Laurent
  F. 116 B3
La Chapelle-St Luc
  F. 91 C4
La Chapelle-sur-Erdre
  F. 101 B4
La Chapelle-
  Vicomtesse F . . .103 B3
La Charce F 132 A1
La Charité-sur-Loire
  F. 104 B2
La Chartre-sur-le-Loir
  F. 102 B2
La Châtaigneraie
  F. 114 B3
La Châtre F 103 C3
La Chaussée-sur-
  Marne F 91 C4
La Chaux-de-Fonds
  CH. 106 B1
Lachen CH. 107 B3
Lachendorf D 72 B3
La Cheppe F 91 B4
La Chèze F 101 A3
Lachowice PL. 99 B3
La Ciotat F 132 B1
Łąck PL 77 B4
Läckeby S. 62 B4
Läckö S 55 B4
La Clayette F 117 A4
La Clusaz F 118 B3
Lacock GB. 43 A4
La Codosera E 155 B3
La Concha E 143 A3
La Condamine-
  Châtelard F. 132 A2
Láconi I. 179 C3
La Contienda E . . .161 A3
La Coquille F 115 C4
La Coronada E 156 B2
La Côte-St André
  F. 118 B2
La Cotinière F 114 C2
La Courtine F 116 B2
Lacq F 145 A3
La Crau F 132 B2
La Crèche F 115 B3
La Croix F 102 B2
Lacroix-Barrez F . .116 C2
Lacroix-St Ouen F . .90 B2
Lacroix-sur-Meuse
  F. 92 C1
La Croix-Valmer F .132 B2
La Cumbre E 156 A2
Lad H 125 A3
Ladbergen D 71 B4
Ladek-Zdrój PL 85 B4

Ladelund D 64 B2
Ladendorf A. 97 C4
Ladignac-le-Long
  F. 115 C5
Ladíspoli I 168 B2
Ladoeiro P. 155 B3
Ladon F 103 B4
La Douze F 129 A3
Ladushkin RUS. . . .69 A5
Ladybank GB. 35 B4
Laer D 71 B4
La Espina E 141 A4
La Estrella E 156 A2
La Farga de Moles
  E 146 B2
La Fatarella E 153 A4
La Felipa E 158 B2
La Fère F 90 B3
La Ferrière
  Indre-et-Loire F . .102 B2
  Vendée F 114 B2
La Ferrière-en-
  Parthenay F 115 B3
La Ferté-Alais F . . .90 C2
La Ferté-Bernard
  F. 102 A2
La Ferté-Frênel F. .89 B4
La Ferté-Gaucher
  F. 90 C3
La Ferté-Imbault
  F. 103 B3
La Ferté-Macé F . .89 B4
La Ferté-Milon F . . .90 B3
La Ferté-sous-Jouarre
  F. 90 C3
La Ferté-St-Aubin
  F. 103 B3
La Ferté-St-Cyr F . .103 B3
La Ferté-Vidame F .89 B4
La Ferté Villeneuil
  F. 103 B3
La Feuillie F 90 B1
La Flèche F 102 B1
La Flotte F 114 B2
La Fouillade F 130 A1
La Fregeneda E . . .149 B3
La Fresneda E 153 B4
La Fuencubierta E .162 A3
La Fuente de San
  Esteban E 149 B3
La Fulioala E 147 C2
La Gacilly F 101 B3
La Galera E 153 B4
Lagan S 60 C3
Laganadi I 175 C1
Lagarde F 146 A2
La Garde-Freinet
  F. 132 B2
Lagares
  Coimbra P 148 B2
  Porto P. 148 A1
La Garnache F 114 B2
Lagaro I 135 A4
La Garriga E 147 C3
La Garrovilla E 155 C4
Lagartera E 150 C2
La Gaubretière F . .114 B2
Lågbol S 51 B5
Lage D 72 C1
Lägerdorf D 64 C2
Lagg GB. 34 C2
Laggan GB. 32 D2
Laggartorp S 55 A5
La Gineta E 158 B1
Lagnieu F 118 B2
Lagny-sur-Marne F .90 C2
Lago
  Calábria I 175 B2
  Veneto I 121 B5
Lagôa P. 160 B1
Lagoaça P 149 A3
Lagonegro I 174 A1
Lagos
  GR 183 B7
  P. 160 B1
Lagosanto I 121 C5
Łagów
  Lubuskie PL. 75 B4
  Świętokrzyskie PL. .87 B5
La Granadella
  Alicante E 159 C4
  Lleida E 153 A4
La Grand-Combe
  F. 131 A3
La Grande-Croix
  F. 117 B4
La Grande-Motte
  F. 131 B3
La Granja d'Escarp
  E 153 A4
La Granjuela E 156 B2
Lagrasse F 146 A3
La Grave F 118 B3
La Gravelle F 101 A4
Laguardia E 143 B4
La Guardia E 151 C4
La Guardia de Jaén
  E 163 A4
Laguarres E 145 B4
Laguenne F 116 B1
La Guerche-de-
  Bretagne F 101 B4
La Guerche-sur-
  l'Aubois F 104 C1
La Guérinière F . . .114 B1
Laguiole F 116 C2
Laguna de Duera
  E 150 A3
Laguna del
  Marquesado E . .152 B2
Laguna de Negrillos
  E 142 B1

Lagundo I 108 C2
Lagunilla E 149 B3
La Haba E 156 B2
Laharie F 128 B1
La-Haye-du-Puits F .88 A2
La Haye-Pesnel F .88 B2
Lahden D 71 B4
La Herlière F 78 B2
La Hermida E 142 A2
La Herrera E 158 C1
Laheycourt F 91 C5
La Higuera E 158 C2
La Hiniesta E 149 A4
Lahnstein D 81 B3
Laholm S 61 C3
La Horcajada E . . .150 B2
La Horra E 143 C3
Lahr D 93 C3
Lahti FIN 8 B4
La Hulpe B 79 B4
La Hutte F 89 B4
Laichingen D 94 C1
L'Aigle F. 89 B4
La Iglesuela E 150 B3
La Iglesuela del Cid
  E 153 B3
Laignes F 104 B3
Laiguéglia I 133 B4
L'Aiguillon-sur-Mer
  F. 114 B2
Laimbach am Ostrong
  A. 97 C3
Laina E 152 A1
Lainio S 196 B5
Lairg GB. 32 C2
La Iruela E 164 B2
Laissac F 130 A1
Laisvall S. 195 D8
Láives I 121 A4
La Javie F 132 A2
Lajkovac SRB 127 C2
La Jonchère-St
  Maurice F 116 A1
La Jonquera E 146 B3
Lajoskomárom H .112 C2
Lajosmizse H. 112 B3
Lak H 99 C4
Lakenheath GB 45 A4
Lakitelek H 113 C4
Lakki GR 185 D4
Lakolk DK 64 A1
Łąkorz PL. 69 B4
Lakšárska Nová Ves
  SK 98 C1
Lakselv N 193 B8
Laksfors N 195 E4
Laktaši BIH 124 C3
La Lantejuela E . . .162 A2
Lalapaşa TR. 186 A1
L'Albagès E 153 A4
Lalbenque F 129 B4
L'Alcúdia E 159 B3
L'Aldea E 153 B4
Lalín E 140 B2
Lalinde F 129 B3
La Línea de la
  Concepción E . . .162 B2
Lalizolle F 116 A3
La Llacuna E 147 C2
Lalley F 118 C2
Lalling D 95 C5
Lalm N 198 D6
La Londe-les-Maures
  F. 132 B2
La Loupe F 89 B5
La Louvière B 79 B4
L'Alpe-d'Huez F . . .118 B3
La Luisiana E 162 A2
Laluque F 128 C1
Lam D 95 B5
La Machine F 104 C2
la Maddalena I 178 A3
Lama dei Peligni I .169 A4
Lamadrid E 142 A2
Lamagistère F 129 B3
La Mailleraye-sur-Seine
  F. 89 A4
La Malène F 130 A2
Lama Mocogno I . .135 A3
La Mamola E 163 B4
La Manresana dels
  Prats E 147 C2
Lamarche F 105 A4
Lamarche-sur-Saône
  F. 105 B4
Lamargelle F 105 B3
Lamarosa P. 154 B2
Lamarque F 128 A2
Lamas E 148 B1
La Masadera E . . .145 C3
Lamas de Moaro
  P 140 B2
Lamastre F 117 C4
La Mata E 150 C2
La Mata de Ledesma
  E 149 A4
La Mata de
  Monteagudo E . .142 B1
Lambach A 109 A4
Lamballe F 101 A3
Lamberhurst GB. . .45 B4
Lambesc F 131 B4
Lambia GR. 184 B2
Lambley GB. 37 B4
Lambourn GB 44 B2
Lamego P 148 A2
La Meilleraye-de-
  Bretagne F. 101 B4
La Ménitré F 102 B1
L'Ametlla de Mar
  E 153 B4
Lamia GR. 182 E4
Lammhult S. 62 A2
La Mojonera E 164 C2
La Mole F. 132 B2
La Molina E 147 B2
La Monnerie-le-Montel
  F. 117 B3
La Morera E 155 C4

La Mothe-Achard
  F. 114 B2
Lamothe-Cassel F 129 B4
Lamothe-Montravel
  F. 128 B3
La Mothe-St Héray
  F. 115 B3
Lamotte-Beuvron
  F. 103 B4
La Motte-Chalançon
  F. 131 A4
La Motte-du-Caire
  F. 132 A2
La Motte-Servolex
  F. 118 B2
Lampertheim D . . . 93 B4
Lampeter GB 39 B2
L'Ampolla E 153 B4
Lamprechtshausen
  A. 109 B3
Lamsfeld D 74 C3
Lamspringe D . . . 72 C3
Lamstedt D 72 A2
La Mudarra E . . . 142 C2
La Muela E 152 A2
La Mure F 118 C2
Lamure-sur-Azergues
  F. 117 A4
Lana I 108 C2
Lanaja E 145 C3
Lanarce F 117 C3
Lanark GB 36 A3
La Nava E 161 B3
La Nava de Ricomalillo
  E 156 A3
La Nava de Santiago
  E 155 B4
Lancaster GB . . . 37 B4
Lanchester GB . . . 37 B5
Lanciano I 169 A4
Lancing GB 44 C3
Lançon-Provence
  F. 131 B4
Lancova Vas SLO .124 A1
Landau
  Bayern D 95 C4
  Rheinland-Pfalz D . 93 B4
Landeck A 108 B1
Landen B 79 B5
Landerneau F . . . 100 A1
Landeryd S 60 B3
Landesbergen D . . 72 B2
Landete E 158 B2
Landévant F . . . 100 B2
Landévennec F . . 100 A1
Landivisiau F . . . 100 A1
Landivy F 88 B2
Landl A 108 B3
Landön S 199 B11
Landos F 117 C3
Landouzy-le-Ville F 91 B4
Landquart CH . . . 107 C4
Landrecies F . . . 91 A3
Landreville F . . . 104 A3
Landriano I 120 B2
Landsberg D . . . 108 A1
Lands-berg D . . . 83 A4
Landsbro S 62 A2
Landscheid D . . . 92 B2
Landshut D 95 C4
Landskrona S . . . 61 D2
Landstuhl D 93 B3
Lanesborough IRL .28 A4
Lanester F 100 B2
Lanestosa E . . . 143 A3
La Neuve-Lyre F . .89 B4
La Neuveville CH . .106 B2
Langå DK 59 B2
Langada GR . . . 185 A7
Langadas GR . . . 183 C5
Langa de Duero E 151 A4
Langadia GR . . . 184 B3
Langangen N . . . 53 A5
Långared S 60 B2
Långaröd S 61 D3
Långared S 60 B3
Långås S 60 C2
Långasjö S 63 B3
Langau A 97 C3
Langeac F 117 B3
Langeais F 102 B2
Langedijk NL . . . 70 B1
Langeln D 73 C3
Langelsheim D . . 72 C3
Langemark-Poelkapelle
  B 78 B2
Langen
  Hessen D. . . . 93 B4
  Niedersachsen D. .72 A1
Langenau D 94 C2
Langenberg D . . . 81 A4
Langenburg D . . . 94 B1
Längenfeld A . . . 108 B1
Langenfeld D . . . 80 A2
Langenhorn D . . . 64 B1
Langenlois A . . . 97 C3
Langenlonsheim D 93 B3
Langennaudorf D . 83 A5
Langenneufnach D 94 C2
Langenthal CH . . 106 B2
Langenzenn D . . . 94 B2
Langeoog D 71 A4
Langeskov DK . . . 59 C3
Langesund N . . . 53 A5
Langewiesen D . . 82 B2
Långflon S 49 A4
Langförden D . . . 71 B5
Langhagen D . . . 73 A4
Länghem S 60 B3
Langhirano I . . . 120 C3
Langholm GB . . . 36 A4
Langholt IS . . . 191 D7
Långlöt S 62 B4
Langnau CH . . . 106 C2
Langø DK 65 B4
Langogne F . . . 117 C3
Langon F 128 B2
Langquaid D . . . 95 C4
Långrädna S . . . 56 B2

Langreo E 142 A1
Langres F 105 B4
Långsele S 200 C3
Långserud S . . . 54 A3
Langset N 48 B3
Långshyttan S . . . 50 B3
Langstrand N . . . 192 B7
Långträsk S . . . 196 D3
Langueux F . . . 101 A3
Languidic F . . . 100 B2
Längvik S 57 A4
Langwarden D . . . 71 A5
Langwathby GB . . 37 B4
Langwedel D . . . 72 B2
Langweid D 94 C2
Langwies CH . . . 107 C4
Lanheses P 148 A1
Laniçta PL 77 B4
Lanildut F 100 A1
Lanjarón E 163 B4
Lanmeur F 100 A2
Lanna
  Jönköping S. . . . 60 B3
  Örebro S. . . . 55 A5
Lännaholm S . . . 51 C4
Lannavaara S . . . 196 A4
Lannéanou F . . . 100 A2
Lannemezan F . . . 145 A4
Lanneuville-sur-Meuse
  F. 91 B5
Lannilis F 100 A1
Lannion F 100 A2
La Nocle-Maulaix
  F. 104 C2
Lanouaille F . . . 115 C5
Lansjärv S 196 C5
Lanškroun CZ . . . 97 B4
Lanslebourg-Mont-
  Cenis F 119 B3
Lanta F 129 C4
Lantadilla E . . . 142 B2
Lanton F 128 B1
Lantosque F . . . 133 B3
La Nuez de Arriba
  E 143 B3
Lanusei I 179 C3
Lanúvio I 168 B2
Lanvollon F . . . 100 A3
Lánycsók H . . . 125 A4
Lanz D 73 A4
Lanza E 140 A2
Lanzada E 140 A2
Lanzahita E . . . 150 B3
Lanžhot CZ 97 C4
Lanzo Torinese I . .119 B4
Laole SRB 127 C3
Laon F 91 B3
Laons F 89 B5
La Paca E 164 B3
La Pacaudière F . .117 A3
Lapalisse F . . . 117 A3
La Palma d'Ebre
  E 153 A4
La Palma del Condado
  E 161 B3
La Palme F . . . 146 B4
La Palmyre F . . . 114 C2
La Parra E 155 C4
Łapczyna Wola PL. .87 B3
La Pedraja de Portillo
  E 150 A3
La Peraleja E . . . 152 B1
La Petit-Pierre F . .93 C3
La Pinilla E . . . 165 B3
Lapithos CY . . . 181 A2
La Plagne F . . . 118 B3
La Plaza E 141 A4
Laplume F 129 B3
La Pobla de Lillet
  E 147 B2
La Pobla de Vallbona
  E 159 B3
La Pobla Llarga E .159 B3
La Pola de Gordón
  E 142 B1
la Porta F 180 A2
La Pouëze F . . . 102 B1
Lapoutroie F . . . 106 A2
La Póveda de Soria
  E 143 B4
Lapovo SRB . . . 127 C3
Läppe S 56 A1
Lappeenranta FIN . .8 B6
Lappoluobbal N . .192 C7
La Preste F . . . 146 B3
La Primaube F . . 130 A1
Lapseki TR 186 B1
Lapua FIN 8 A3
La Puebla de Almoradie
  E 157 A4
La Puebla de Cazalla
  E 162 A2
La Puebla de los
  Infantes E . . . 162 A2
La Puebla del Río
  E 162 A1
La Puebla de
  Montalbán E. . .150 C3
La Puebla de Roda
  E 145 B4
La Puebla de Valdavia
  E 142 B2
La Puebla de Valverde
  E 152 B2
La Pueblanueva E 150 C3
La Puerta de Segura
  E 164 A2
La Punt CH . . . 107 C4
L'Áquila I 169 A3
La Quintana E . . 162 A3
La Quintera E . . . 162 A2
La Rábita
  Granada E. . . .164 C1
  Jaén E. . . . 163 A3
Laracha E 140 A2
Laragh IRL 30 A2

Laragne-Montéglin
  F. 132 A1
La Rambla E . . . 163 A3
l'Arboç E 147 C2
L'Arbresle F . . . 117 B4
Lärbro S. 57 C4
Larceveau F . . . 144 A2
Larche
  Alpes-de-Haute-
    Provence F . . .132 A2
  Corrèze F . . . 129 A4
Las Navillas E . . . 157 A3
Las Negras E . . . 164 C3
La Solana E . . . 157 B4
La Souterraine F . .116 A1
Las Pajanosas E . .161 B3
Laspaules E . . . 145 B4
Las Pedroñas E . .158 B1
La Spézia I . . . 134 A2
Las Planes d'Hostoles
  E 147 B3
Las Rozas
  Cantabria E . . .142 B2
  Madrid E . . . 151 B4
Lassan D 66 C2
Lassay-les-Châteaux
  F. 89 B3
Lasseube F . . . 145 A3
Lassigny F 90 B2
La Storta I . . . 168 B2
Lastovo HR . . . 138 C2
Lastras de Cuéllar
  E 151 A3
Lästringe S . . . 56 B3
Lastrup D 71 B4
Las Uces E 149 A3
La Suze-sur-Sarthe
  F. 102 B2
Las Veguillas E . .149 B4
Las Ventas con Peña
  Aguilera E . . . 157 A3
Las Ventas de San
  Julián E 150 B2
Las Villes E . . . 153 B4
Latasa E 144 B2
Látera E 168 A1
Laterza I 171 C4
La Teste F 128 B1
Lathen D 71 B4
Latheron GB . . . 32 C3
La Thuile I . . . 119 B3
Latiano I 173 B3
Latina I 169 B2
Latisana I 122 B2
Látky SK 99 C3
La Toba E 152 B2
La Toledana E . . 157 A3
La Torre de Cabdella
  E 146 B1
La Torre de Esteban
  Hambrán E . . . 151 B3
La Torre del l'Espanyol
  E 153 A4
La Torresaviñán
  E 152 B1
La Tour d'Aigues
  F. 132 B1
La Tour de Peilz
  CH 106 C1
La Tour-du-Pin F . .118 B2
La Tranche-sur-Mer
  F. 114 B2
La Tremblade F . .114 C2
La Trimouille F . . 115 B5
La Trinité F . . . 100 B2
La Trinité-Porhoët
  F. 101 A3
Latrónico I . . . 174 A2
Latronquière F . . 116 C2
Latterbach CH . . 106 C2
La Turballe F . . . 101 B3
Laubach D 81 B4
Laubert F 117 C3
Laucha D 83 A3
Lauchhammer D . .84 A1
Lauchheim D . . . 94 C2
Lauda-Königshofen
  D 94 B1
Laudal N 52 B3
Lauder GB 35 C5
Lauenau D 72 B2
Lauenburg D . . . 73 A3
Lauf D 95 B3
Laufach D 94 A1
Laufen
  CH 106 B2
  D 109 B3
Lauffen D 93 B5
Laugar IS 191 B8
Laugarás IS . . . 190 C5
Laugarbakki IS . .190 B5
Laugarvatn IS . . 190 C5
Laugharne GB . . . 39 C2
Lauingen D 94 C2
Laujar de Andarax
  E 164 C2
Laukaa FIN 8 A4
Lauker S 196 D2
Laukvik N 194 C5
Launceston GB . . 42 B2
La Unión E . . . 165 B4
Launois-sur-Vence
  F. 91 B4
Laupheim D 94 C1
Lauragh IRL . . . 29 C2
Laureana di Borrello
  I 175 C2
Laurencekirk GB . .35 B5
Laurencetown IRL. .28 A3
Laurenzana I . . . 172 B1
Lauria I 174 A1
Laurière F 116 A1
Laurieston GB . . . 36 B2
Laurino I 172 B1
Lausanne CH . . . 106 C1
Laussonne F . . . 117 C4
Lauta D 84 A2
Lautenthal D . . . 82 A2
Lauterach A . . . 107 B4
Lauterbach D . . . 81 B5

Lauterbrunnen
  CH 106 C2
Lauterecken D . . . 93 B3
Lauterhofen D . . . 95 B3
Lautrec F 130 B1
Lauvsnes N . . . 199 A7
Lauvvik N 52 B2
Las Navas de la
  Concepción E. . .156 C2
Las Navas del Marqués
  E 150 B3
Lauzerte F 129 B4
Lauzès F 129 B4
Lauzun F 129 B3
Lavagna I 134 A2
Laval F 102 A1
La Vall d'Uixó E . .159 B3
Lavamünd A . . . 110 C1
Lavara GR 186 A1
Lavardac F 129 B3
Lavarone I 121 B4
Lavau F 104 B1
Lavaur F 129 C4
La Vecilla de Curueño
  E 142 B1
La Vega
  Asturias E . . . 141 A5
  Asturias E . . . 142 A1
  Cantabria E . . .142 A2
Lavelanet F . . . 146 B2
La Velilla E . . . 151 A4
La Velles E 150 A2
Lavello I 172 A1
Lavelsloh D 72 B1
Lavenham GB . . . 45 A4
Laveno I 120 B1
La Ventosa E . . . 152 B1
Lavezzola I . . . 135 A4
Laviano I 172 B1
La Victoria E . . . 162 A3
La Vid E 151 A4
Lavik N 46 A2
La Vilavella E . . . 159 B3
La Vilella Baixa E .147 C1
La Villa de Don
  Fadrique E . . . 157 A4
Lavilledieu F . . . 131 A3
La Villedieu F . . 115 B3
La Ville Dieu-du-Temple
  F. 129 B4
Lavinio-Lido di Enea
  I 168 B2
Lav is I 121 A4
Lavit F 129 C3
Lavoncourt F . . . 105 B4
Lavos P 148 B1
La Voulte-sur-Rhône
  F. 117 C4
Lavoûte-Chilhac
  F. 117 B3
Lavradio P . . . 154 C1
Lavre P 154 C2
Lavrio GR 185 B5
Le Wantzenau F . .93 C3
Lawers GB 35 B3
Ławy PL 75 B3
Laxå S 55 B5
Laxamýri IS . . . 191 B8
Laxe E 140 A2
Laxey GB 36 B2
Laxford Bridge GB .32 C1
Laxhall S 55 B4
Laxsjö S . . . 199 B11
Laxtjarn S 49 B6
Laxvik S 61 C2
Laxviken S . . 199 B11
La Yesa E 159 B3
Laza E 141 B3
Lazarevac SRB . . 127 C2
Lazarevo SRB . . 126 B2
Lazise I 121 B3
Łaziska Grn. PL. . .86 B2
Lazkao E 144 A1
Lázně Bělohrad
  CZ 84 B3
Lázně Bohdaneč
  CZ 97 A3
Lázně Kynžvart CZ .95 A4
Lazonby GB 37 B4
La Zubia E . . . 163 A4
Lazzaro I 175 D1
Lea GB 40 B3
Leadburn GB . . . 35 C4
Leadhills GB . . . 36 A3
Leap IRL 29 C2
Leatherhead GB . .44 B3
Łeba PL 68 A2
Lebach D 92 B2
Le Barp F 128 B2
Le Bar-sur-Loup F 132 B2
Le Béage F . . . 117 C4
Le Beausset F . . 132 B1
Le Bekke B 79 A4
Le Bessat F . . . 117 B4
Le Bleymard F . . 130 A2
Le Blanc F 115 B5
Le Boullay-Mivoye
  F. 89 B5
Le Boulou F . . . 146 B3
Le Bourg F . . . 129 B4
Le Bourg-d'Oisans
  F. 118 B3
Le Bourget-du-Lac
  F. 118 B2
Le Bourgneuf-la-Forêt
  F. 101 A5
Le Bousquet d'Orb
  F. 130 B2
Le Brassus CH . . 105 C5
Le Breuil F . . . 117 A3
Le Breuil-en-Auge
  F. 89 A4
Le Brusquet F . . 132 A2
Le Bry CH . . . 106 C2
Le Bugue F . . . 129 B3
Le Buisson F . . . 129 B3

Lebus D 74 B3
Lebusa D 83 A5
Leca da Palmeira
  P 148 A1
Lecce I 173 B4
Lecco I 120 B2
Lécera E 153 A3
Lećevica HR . . . 138 B2
Lech A 107 B5
Le Chambon-
  Feugerolles F . .117 B4
Le Chambon-sur-
  Lignon F . . . 117 B4
Le Château d'Oléron
  F. 114 C2
Le Châtelard F . . 118 B3
Le Châtelet F . . . 103 C4
Le Chatelet-en-Brie
  F. 90 C2
Lechbruck D . . . 108 B1
Lechena GR . . . 184 B2
Le Chesne F . . . 91 B4
Le Cheylard F . . 117 C4
Lechlade GB . . . 44 B2
Lechovice CZ . . . 97 C4
Leciñena E . . . 145 C3
Leck D 64 B1
Le Collet-de-Deze
  F. 131 A2
Le Conquet F . . 100 A1
Le Creusot F . . . 104 C3
Le Croisic F . . . 101 B3
Le Crotoy F . . . 78 B1
Lectoure F . . . 129 C3
Le Lardin-St Lazare
  F. 129 A4
Le Lauzet-Ubaye
  F. 132 A2
Le Lavandou F . .132 B2
Le Lion-d'Angers
  F. 102 B1
Le Locle CH . . . 106 B1
Le Loroux-Bottereau
  F. 101 B4
Le Louroux-Béconnais
  F. 101 B5
Lelów PL 86 B3
Le Luc F 132 B2
Le Lude F 102 B2
Lelystad NL . . . 70 B2
Lem
  Ringkøbing DK . .59 B1
  Viborg Amt. DK . .58 B1
Le Malzieu-Ville F .116 C3
Le Mans F . . . 102 A2
Le Mas-d'Azil F . .146 A2
Le Massegros F . 130 A2
Le Mayet-de-Montagne
  F. 117 A3
Le May-sur-Evre F 101 B5
Lembach F . . . 93 B3
Lemberg F . . . 93 B3
Lembèye F . . . 145 A3
Lemelerveld NL . . 71 B3
Le Mêle-sur-Sarthe
  F. 89 B4
Le Ménil F . . . 105 A5
Le Merlerault F . .89 B4
Le Mesnil-sur-Oger
  F. 91 C4
Lemförde D . . . 71 B5
Lemgo D 72 B1
Le Miroir F . . . 105 C4
Lemland FIN . . . 51 B7
Lemmer NL . . . 70 B2
Le Molay-Littry F .88 A3
Le Monastier-sur-
  Gazeille F . . . 117 C3
Le Monêtier-les-Bains
  F. 118 C3
Le Mont-Dore F . 116 B2
Le Montet F . . . 116 A3
Le Mont-St Michel
  F. 88 B2
Lempdes F . . . 116 B3
Le Muret F . . . 128 B2
Le Muy F 132 B2
Lemvig DK . . . 58 B1
Lemwerder D . . . 72 A1
Lena N 48 B2
Lenart SLO . . . 110 C2
Lenartovce SK . . 99 C4
Lenauheim RO . . 126 B2
Lencloître F . . . 102 C2
Lend A 109 B4
Lendalfoot GB . . . 36 A2
Lendava SLO . . . 111 C3
Lendery RUS . . . 3 E12
Lendinara I . . . 121 B4
Lendorf A 109 C4
Lendum DK . . . 58 A3
Le Neubourg F . .89 A4
Lengefeld D . . . 83 B5
Lengerich
  Niedersachsen D. .71 B4
  Nordrhein-Westfalen
    D 71 B4
Lengyeltóti H . . 111 C4
Lenhovda S . . . 62 B3
Lenk CH 106 C2
Lennartsfors S . . 54 A2
Lennestadt D . . . 81 A4
Lennoxtown GB . .35 C3
Leno I 120 B3
Lénola I 169 B3
Le Nouvion-en-
  Thiérache F . . . 91 A3
Lens
  B 79 B3
  F. 78 B2
Lensahn D . . . 65 B3
Lens Lestang F . .117 B5
Lensvik N . . . 198 B6

Lentellais E 141 B3
Lentföhrden D 64 C2
Lenti H 111 C3
Lentini I 177 B3
Lenungshammar S 54 A3
Lenzburg CH 106 B3
Lenzen D 73 A4
Lenzerheide CH . .107 C4
Leoben A 110 B2
Leogang A 109 B3
Leominster GB 39 B4
León E 142 B1
Léon F 128 C1
Leonberg D 93 C5
Léoncel F 118 C2
Leonding A 96 C2
Leonessa I 169 A2
Leonforte I 177 B3
Leonidio GR 184 B3
Leopoldsburg B 79 A5
Leopoldsdorf im
  Marchfeld A 111 A3
Leopoldshagen D . .74 A2
Leova MD 17 B8
Le Palais F 100 B2
Le Parcq F 78 B2
Lepe E 161 B2
Le Péage-de-
  Roussillon F 117 B4
Le Pellerin F 101 B4
Lepenou GR 182 E3
Le Perthus F 146 B3
Le Pertuis F 117 B4
Le Petit-Bornand
  . . . . .118 B3
Lephin GB 31 B2
L'Épine F 132 A1
Le Poët F 132 A1
Lepoglava HR 124 A2
Le Poiré-sur-Vie F 114 B2
Le Pont CH 105 C5
Le Pont-de-Montvert
  . . . . .130 A2
Le Porge F 128 B1
Le Porge-Océan F 128 B1
Le Portel F 78 B1
Le Pouldu F 100 B2
Le Pouliguen F 101 B3
Leppäjärvi FIN . . .192 D7
Leppävirta FIN 8 A5
Leppin D 73 B4
le Prese I 120 A3
Lepsény H 112 C2
Le Puy-en-Velay F 117 B3
Le Puy-Ste Réparade
  F 131 B4
Le Quesnoy F 79 B3
Léquile I 173 B4
Le Rayol F 132 B2
Lercara Friddi I . . .176 B2
Lerdal S 54 B2
Leré F 103 B4
Lérici I 134 A2
Lerin E 144 B2
Lerma E 143 B3
Lerm-et-Musset F .128 B2
Lermoos A 108 B1
Le Roeulx B 79 B4
Le Rouget F 116 C2
Lérouville F 92 C1
Le Rozier F 130 A2
Lerum S 60 B2
Le Russey F 106 B1
Lervik N 54 A1
Lerwick GB 33 A5
Lés E 145 B4
Les Abrets F 118 B2
Les Aix-d'Angillon
  F 103 B4
Lesaka E 144 A2
Les Ancizes-Comps
  F 116 B2
Les Andelys F 90 B1
Les Arcs
  Savoie F 119 B3
  Var F 132 B2
Les-Aubiers F 102 C1
Les Baux-de-Provence
  F 131 B3
Les Bézards F 103 B4
Les Bois CH 106 B1
Les Bordes F 103 B4
Les Borges Blanques
  E 147 C1
Les Borges del Camp
  E 147 C2
Les Brunettes F . . .104 C2
Lesbury GB 37 A5
Les Cabannes F . . .146 B2
L'Escala E 147 B4
Lescar F 145 A3
L'Escarène F 133 B3
Lesce SLO 123 A3
Lescheraines F . . .118 B3
Lesconil F 100 B1
Les Contamines-
  Montjoie F 118 B3
les Coves de Vinroma
  E 153 B4
Les Déserts F 118 B2
Les Deux-Alpes F .118 B3
Les Diablerets CH 119 A4
Lesdins F 90 B3
Les Echelles F 118 B2
Le Sel-de-Bretagne
  F 101 B4
Le Sentier CH 105 C5
Les Escaldes
  AND 146 B2
Les Essarts F 114 B2
Les Estables F 117 C4
Les Eyzies-de-Tayac
  F 129 B4
Les Gets F 118 A3
Les Grandes-Ventes
  F 89 A5
Les Haudères CH .119 A4

Les Herbiers F 114 B2
Les Hôpitaux-Neufs
  F 105 C5
Lesična SLO 123 A4
Lésina I 171 B3
Lesjaskog S 198 C5
Lesjöfors S 49 C6
Leskovac SRB 16 D4
Leskova Dolina
  SLO 123 B3
Leskovec
  CZ 98 B1
  SLO 123 B4
Leskovice
  CZ 97 B3
  SLO 123 B4
Leskovik AL 182 C2
Leslie GB 35 B4
Les Lucs-sur-Boulogne
  F 114 B2
Les Mages F 131 A3
Lesmahagow GB . . .36 A3
Les Mazures F 91 B4
Les Mées F 132 A1
Lesmont F 91 C4
Les Mureaux F 90 C1
Leśna PL 84 A3
Lesneven F 100 A1
Leśnica PL 86 B2
Leśnica SRB 127 C1
Leśniów Wielkopolski
  PL 75 C4
Lesnoye RUS 9 C9
Les Omergues F . .132 A1
Les Ormes-sur-Voulzie
  F 90 C3
Les Orres F 132 A2
Le Souquet F 128 C1
Lesparre-Médoc
  F 128 A2
Lespezzia E 91 B3
l'Espérance F 91 B3
l'Esperou F 130 A2
Les Pieux F 88 A2
Lesponne F 145 A4
Les Ponts-de-Cé
  F 102 B1
Les Ponts-de-Martel
  CH 106 C1
Les Praz F 119 B3
L'Espunyola E 147 B2
Les Riceys F 104 B3
Les Roches F 117 B4
Les Rosaires F 101 A3
Les Rosiers F 102 B1
Les Rousses F 105 C5
Les Sables-d'Olonne
  F 114 B2
Lessach A 109 B4
Lessay F 88 A2
Lessebo S 62 B3
Les Settons F 104 B3
Lessines B 79 B3
L'Estany E 147 C3
Les Ternes F 116 B2
Lesterps F 115 B4
Les Thilliers-en-Vexin
  F 90 B1
Les Touches F 101 B4
Les Trois Moûtiers
  F 102 B2
Les Vans F 131 A3
Les Verrières CH . .105 C5
Les Vignes F 130 A2
Leswalt GB 36 B1
Leszno
  Mazowieckie PL . .77 B5
  Wielkopolskie PL . .85 A4
Leszno Górne PL . . .84 A3
Letchworth GB 44 B3
Le Teil F 131 A3
Le Teilleul F 88 B3
Le Temple-de-Bretagne
  F 101 B4
Letenye H 111 C3
Le Theil F 89 B4
Le Thillot F 106 B1
Letino I 170 B2
Letohrad CZ 97 A4
Le Touquet-Paris-Plage
  F 78 B1
Le Touvet F 118 B2
Letovice CZ 97 B4
Le Translay F 90 B1
Le Tréport F 90 A1
Letschin D 74 B3
Letterfrack IRL 28 A2
Letterkenny IRL . . .26 B2
Lettermacaward
  IRL 26 B2
Lettoch GB 32 D3
Letur E 164 A2
Letux E 153 A3
Letzlingen D 73 B4
Leucate F 146 B4
Leuchars GB 35 B5
Leuglay F 105 B3
Leuk CH 119 A4
Leukerbad CH 119 A4
Leumrabhagh GB . .31 A2
Leuna D 83 A4
Leusden NL 70 B2
Leutenberg D 82 B3
Leuterschach D . . .108 B1
Leutershausen D . .94 B2
Leutkirch D 107 B5
Leuven B 79 B4
Leuze-en-Hainaut
  B 79 B3
Le Val F 132 B2
Le Val-André F 101 A3
Le Val-d'Ajol F 105 B5
Levan AL 182 C1
Levanger N 199 B8
Levanjska Varoš
  HR 125 B4
Lévanto I 134 A2
Levaré F 88 B3
Levata I 120 B3
Leveld N 47 B5
Leven
  East Yorkshire
    GB 41 B3

Leven continued
  Fife GB 35 B5
Leverano I 173 B3
Le Verdon-sur-Mer
  F 114 C2
Leverkusen D 80 A2
Levern D 72 B1
Levet F 103 C4
Levice SK 112 A2
Lévico Terme I 121 A4
Levie F 180 B2
Levier F 105 C5
Le Vigan F 130 B2
le Ville I 135 B5
Levinovac HR 124 B3
Le Vivier-sur-Mer F 88 B2
Levoča SK 99 B4
Levroux F 103 C3
Lewes GB 45 C4
Lewin Brzeski PL . .85 B5
Lewisham GB 44 B3
Leyburn GB 37 B5
Leyland GB 38 A4
Leysdown-on-Sea
  GB 45 B4
Leysin CH 119 A4
Lezajsk PL 12 C5
Lézardrieux F 100 A2
Lézat-sur-Léze F . .146 A2
Lezay F 115 B3
Lezhë AL 182 B1
Lézignan-Corbières
  F 130 B1
Lezignan-la-Cèbe
  F 130 B2
Ležimir SRB 126 B1
Lézinnes F 104 B3
Lezoux F 117 B3
Lezuza E 158 C1
Lhenice CZ 96 C2
Lherm F 146 A2
Lhommaizé F 115 B4
L'Hospitalet F 146 B2
L'Hospitalet de l'Infant
  E 147 D1
L'Hospitalet de
  Llobregat E 147 C3
L'Hospitalet-du-Larzac
  F 130 B2
Lhuître F 91 C4
Liancourt F 90 B2
Liart F 91 B4
Liatorp S 63 B2
Liatrie GB 32 D2
Liban F 84 B3
Libceves CZ 84 B1
Libéchov CZ 84 B2
Liber E 141 B3
Liberec CZ 84 B3
Libiąż PL 86 B3
Libina CZ 98 B1
Libochovice CZ 84 B2
Libohovë AL 182 C2
Libourne F 128 B2
Libramont B 92 B1
Librazhd AL 182 B2
Librilla E 165 B3
Libros E 152 B2
Licata I 176 B2
Licciana Nardi I . . .134 A3
Licenza I 169 A2
Liceros E 151 A4
Lich D 81 B4
Lichères-près-
  Aigremont F 104 B2
Lichfield GB 40 C2
Lichtenau
  A 97 C3
  D 81 A4
Lichtenberg D 83 B3
Lichtenfels D 82 B3
Lichtensteig CH . . .107 B4
Lichtenstein D 83 B4
Lichtenvoorde NL . .71 C3
Lichtervelde B 78 A3
Lička Jesenica
  HR 123 B4
Lickershamn S 57 C4
Lički Osik HR 123 C4
Ličko Lešće HR . . .123 C4
Licodía Eubéa I . . .177 B3
Licques F 78 B1
Lida BY 13 B6
Lidar N 47 A6
Lidečko CZ 98 B2
Liden S 200 D2
Lidhult S 60 C3
Lidköping S 55 B4
Lido I 122 B1
Lido Azzurro I 173 B3
Lido degli Estensi
  I 122 C1
Lido degli Scacchi
  I 122 C1
Lido della Nazioni
  I 122 C1
Lido di Camaiore I 134 B3
Lido di Casalbordino
  I 169 A4
Lido di Castél Fusano
  I 168 B2
Lido di Cincinnato
  I 168 B2
Lido di Classe I . . .135 A5
Lido di Fermo I . . .136 B2
Lido di Fondi I 169 B3
Lido di Jésolo I . . .122 B1
Lido di Lícola I 170 C2
Lido di Metaponto
  I 174 A2
Lido di Óstia I 168 B2
Lido di Policoro I . .174 A2
Lido di Pompósa I .122 C1
Lido di Savio I 135 A5
Lido di Scanzano
  I 174 A2
Lido di Siponto I . .171 B3
Lido di Squillace I .175 C2

Lido di Volano I . . .122 C1
Lido Riccio I 169 A4
Lidoriki GR 184 A3
Lido Silvana I 173 B3
Lidsjöberg S 199 A12
Lidzbark PL 77 A4
Lidzbark Warmiński
  PL 69 A5
Liebenau
  A 96 C2
  D 72 B2
Liebenwalde D 74 B2
Lieberose D 74 C3
Liebling RO 126 B3
Lieboch A 110 C2
Liège B 80 B1
Lieksa FIN 3 E12
Lienen D 71 B4
Lienz A 109 C3
Liepāja LV 8 D2
Lier B 79 A4
Lierbyen N 54 A1
Liernais F 104 B3
Liesing A 109 C3
Liestal CH 106 B2
Liétor E 158 C2
Lieurac F 146 B2
Lieurey F 89 A4
Liévin F 78 B2
Liezen A 110 B1
Liffol-le-Grand F . . .92 C1
Lifford IRL 27 B3
Liffré F 101 A4
Ligardes F 129 B3
Lignano Sabbiadoro
  I 122 B2
Ligne F 101 B4
Lignières F 103 C4
Ligny-en-Barrois F .92 C1
Ligny-le-Châtel F . .104 B2
Ligoła Polska PL . .85 A5
Ligourio GR 184 B4
Ligowo P 77 B4
Ligueil F 102 B2
Likavka SK 99 B3
Likenäs S 49 B5
Likhoslavl RUS 9 D9
Lild Strand DK 58 A1
L'Île-Bouchard F . .102 B2
l'Île-Rousse F 180 A1
Lilienfeld A 110 A2
Lilienthal D 72 A1
Lilla Edet S 54 B3
Lilla Tjärby S 61 C3
Lille
  B 79 A4
  F 78 B3
Lillebonne F 89 A4
Lilleby GB 37 B6
Lillehammer N 48 A2
Lillerød DK 61 D2
Lillers F 78 B2
Lillesand N 53 B4
Lillestrøm N 48 C3
Lillhärdal S 199 D11
Lillkyrka S 56 A3
Lillo E 157 A4
Lillögda S 200 B3
Lillpite S 196 D4
Lima S 49 B5
Limanowa PL 99 B4
Limassol CY 181 B2
Limavady GB 27 A4
Limbach-Oberfrohna
  D 83 B4
Limbaži LV 8 D4
Limbourg B 80 B1
Limburg D 81 B4
Lime DK 58 B3
Limedsforsen S . . .49 B5
Limenaria GR 183 C6
Limenas Chersonisou
  GR 185 D6
Limerick IRL 29 B3
Lisia Góra PL 87 B5
Limésy F 89 A4
Limmared S 60 B3
Limni GR 183 E5
Limoges F 115 C5
Limogne-en-Quercy
  F 129 B4
Limoise F 104 C2
Limone Piemonte
  I 133 A3
Limone sul Garda
  I 121 B3
Limons F 117 B3
Limours F 90 C2
Limoux F 146 A3
Linares E 157 B4
Linares de Mora E 153 B3
Linares de Riofrio
  E 149 B4
Linaria GR 183 E6
Linas de Broto E . .145 B3
Lincoln GB 40 B3
Lind DK 59 B1
Lindås N 46 B2
Lindau D 107 B4
Lindberget N 48 A3
Lindelse DK 65 B3
Lindenberg D 74 B3
Lindenberg im Allgäu
  D 107 B4
Lindern D 71 B4
Linderöd S 61 D3
Lindesberg S 56 A1
Lindesnäs S 50 B1
Lindesnes N 52 C3
Lindholmen S 57 A4
Lindknud DK 59 C2
Lindlar D 80 A3
Lindö S 56 B2
Lindome S 60 B2
Lindos GR 188 C3
Lindow D 74 B1
Lindsdal S 62 B4
Lindshammar S 62 A3
Lindstedt D 73 B4
Lindved DK 59 C2

Linë CZ 96 B1
Lingbo S 50 A3
Lingen D 71 B4
Linghed S 50 B2
Linghem S 56 B1
Linguaglossa I 177 B4
Linia PL 68 A2
Linie PL 74 A3
Liniewo PL 68 A3
Linkenheim D 93 B4
Linköping S 56 B1
Linksness GB 33 C3
Linlithgow GB 35 C4
Linneryd S 63 B3
Linnes Hammarby
  S 51 C4
Linnich D 80 B2
Linsell S 199 C10
Linslade GB 44 B3
Linthal CH 107 C4
Linyola E 147 C1
Linz
  A 96 C2
  D 80 B3
Liomseter N 47 A6
Lionárisso CY 181 A3
Lioni I 172 B1
Lion-sur-Mer F 89 A3
Lipany SK 99 B4
Lipar SRB 126 B1
Lipari I 177 A3
Lipcani MD 17 A7
Liperi FIN 9 A6
Liphook GB 44 B3
Lipiany PL 75 A3
Lipik HR 124 B3
Lipka PL 68 B2
Lipki Wielkie PL . . .75 B4
Lipnica PL 68 B2
Lipnica Murowana
  PL 99 B4
Lipník nad Bečvou
  CZ 98 B1
Lipno
  Kujawsko-Pomorskie
    PL 77 B4
  Łódzkie PL 86 A2
Liposthey F 128 B2
Lipovac HR 125 B5
Lipovec CZ 97 B4
Lipovljani HR 124 B2
Lipowiec PL 77 A6
Lipowina PL 69 A4
Lippborg D 81 A4
Lippó H 125 B4
Lippoldsberg D 81 A5
Lippstadt D 81 A4
Lipsko PL 87 A5
Liptál CZ 98 B1
Liptovská-Lúžna
  SK 99 C3
Liptovská Osada
  SK 99 C3
Liptovská-Teplička
  SK 99 C4
Liptovský Hrádok
  SK 99 B3
Liptovský Milkuláš
  SK 99 B3
Lipusz PL 68 A2
Lipůvka CZ 97 B4
Liré F 101 B4
Lisac BIH 139 A3
Lisbellaw GB 27 B3
Lisboa = Lisbon P 154 C1
Lisbon = Lisboa P 154 C1
Lisburn GB 27 B4
Liscannor IRL 28 B2
Lisdoonvarna IRL . .28 A2
Lisewo PL 69 B3
Lisięcice PL 86 B1
Lisieux F 89 A4
Lisjö S 56 A2
Liskeard GB 42 B2
L'Isle CH 105 C5
L'Isle-Adam F 90 B2
L'Isle-de-Noé F . . .129 C3
L'Isle-en-Dodon F 145 A4
L'Isle-Jourdain
  Gers F 129 C4
  Vienne F 115 B4
L'Isle-sur-la-Sorgue
  F 131 B4
L'Isle-sur-le-Doubs
  F 105 B5
L'Isle-sur-Serein
  F 104 B3
Lisle-sur-Tarn F . . .129 C4
Lismore IRL 29 B4
Lisnaskea GB 27 B3
Lišov CZ 96 B2
Lisów
  Lubuskie PL 74 B3
  Śląskie PL 86 B2
Lisse NL 70 B1
Lissycasey IRL 28 B2
List D 64 A1
Listerby S 63 B3
Listowel IRL 29 B2
Listrac-Médoc F . . .128 A2
Liszki PL 99 A3
Liszkowo PL 76 A2
Lit S 199 B11
Litava SK 99 C3
Litcham GB 41 C4
Lit-et-Mixe F 128 B1
Litija SLO 123 A3
Litke H 112 A3
Litlabø N 52 A1
Litochoro GR 182 C4
Litoměřice CZ 84 B2
Litomyšl CZ 97 B4
Litovel CZ 98 B1
Litschau A 96 C3
Littlehampton GB . .44 C3
Littleport GB 45 A4
Littleton IRL 29 B4

Little Walsingham
  GB 41 C4
Litvinov CZ 83 B5
Livadero GR 182 C3
Livadhia CY 181 B2
Livadi GR 182 C3
Livadia GR 184 A3
Livarot F 89 B4
Liveras CY 181 A1
Livernon F 129 B4
Liverovici MNE . . .139 C5
Liverpool GB 38 A4
Livigno I 107 C5
Livingston GB 35 C4
Livno BIH 138 B2
Livold SLO 123 B3
Livorno I 134 B3
Livorno Ferraris I .119 B5
Livron-sur-Drôme
  F 117 C4
Lixhem F 92 C3
Lixouri GR 184 A1
Lizy-sur-Ourcq F . . .90 B3
Lizzano I 173 B3
Lizzano in Belvedere
  I 135 A3
Ljig SRB 127 C2
Ljørdalen N 49 A5
Ljosland N 52 B3
Ljubija BIH 124 C2
Ljubinje BIH 139 C4
Ljubljana SLO 123 A3
Ljubno ob Savinji
  SLO 123 A3
Ljubovija SRB 127 C1
Ljubuški BIH 138 B3
Ljugarn S 57 C4
Ljung S 60 B3
Ljunga S 56 B2
Ljungaverk S 200 D2
Ljungby S 60 C3
Ljungbyhed S 61 C3
Ljungbyholm S 63 B4
Ljungdalen S 199 C9
Ljungsarp S 60 B3
Ljungsbro S 56 B1
Ljungskile S 54 B2
Ljusdal S 200 E2
Ljusfallshammar S .56 B1
Ljusne S 51 A4
Ljusterö S 57 A4
Ljutomer SLO 111 C3
Lluki BG 183 B6
Lladurs E 147 B2
Llafranc F 147 C4
Llagostera E 147 C3
Llanaelhaiarn GB . .38 B2
Llanarth GB 39 B2
Llanbedr GB 38 B2
Llanbedrog GB 38 B2
Llanberis GB 38 A2
Llanbister GB 39 B3
Llanbrynmair GB . .39 B3
Llançà E 146 B4
Llandeilo GB 39 C3
Llandissilio GB 39 C2
Llandovery GB 39 C3
Llandrillo GB 38 B3
Llandrindod Wells
  GB 39 B3
Llandudec F 100 A1
Llandudno GB 38 A3
Llandysul GB 39 B2
Llanelli GB 39 C2
Llanerchymedd GB 38 A2
Llanes E 142 A2
Llanfair Caereinion
  GB 38 B3
Llanfairfechan GB . 38 A3
Llanfyllin GB 38 B3
Llangadog GB 39 C3
Llangefni GB 38 A2
Llangollen GB 38 B3
Llangrannog GB . . .39 B2
Llangurig GB 39 B3
Llanidloes GB 39 B3
Llanilar GB 39 B2
Llanrhystud GB 39 B2
Llanrwst GB 38 A3
Llansannan GB 38 A3
Llansawel GB 39 B2
Llanstephan GB . . .39 C2
Llanteno E 143 A3
Llanthony GB 39 C3
Llantrisant GB 39 C3
Llantwit-Major GB . 39 C3
Llanuwchllyn GB . .38 B3
Llanwddyn GB 38 B3
Llanwrda GB 39 C3
Llanwrtyd Wells
  GB 39 B3
Llanybydder GB . . .39 B2
Llanymynech GB . .38 B3
Llavorsi E 146 B2
Lleida E 153 A4
Llera E 156 B1
Llerena E 156 B1
Lles E 146 B2
Llessui E 146 B2
Llinars E 147 B2
Lliria E 159 B3
Llivia E 146 B2
Llodio E 143 A4
Lloret de Mar E . . .147 C3
Llosa de Ranes E .159 B3
Lloseta E 167 B2
Llucena del Cid E .153 B3
Llucmajor E 167 B2
Llutxent E 159 C3
Llwyngwril GB 38 B2
Llysen GB 39 B3
Lnáře CZ 96 B1
Lniano PL 76 A3
Lo B 78 B3
Loanhead GB 35 C4
Loano I 133 A4
Loarre E 145 B3
Löbau D 84 A2

Löbejün D 83 A3
Löberöd S 61 D3
Łobez PL 75 A4
Löbnitz D 66 B1
Lobón E 155 C4
Loburg D 73 B5
Łobżenica PL 76 A2
Locana I 119 B4
Locarno CH 120 A1
Loccum D 72 B2
Loče SLO 123 A4
Lochailort GB 34 B2
Lochaline GB 34 B2
Lochans GB 36 B1
Locharbriggs GB . . .36 A3
Lochau A 107 B4
Loch Baghasdail
  GB 31 B1
Lochcarron GB 31 B3
Lochearnhead GB . .34 B3
Lochem NL 71 B3
Loches F 102 B2
Lochgelly GB 35 B4
Lochgilphead GB . . .34 B2
Lochgoilhead GB . . .34 B3
Lochinver GB 32 C1
Loch nam Madadh
  GB 31 B1
Lochranza GB 34 C2
Ločika SRB 127 D3
Lockenhaus A 111 B3
Lockerbie GB 36 A3
Löcknitz D 74 A3
Locmaria F 100 B2
Locmariaquer F . . .100 B3
Locminé F 100 B3
Locorotondo I 173 B3
Locquirec F 100 A2
Locri I 175 C2
Locronan F 100 A1
Loctudy F 100 B1
Lodares de Osma
  E 151 A5
Lodé I 178 B3
Lodeinoye Pole RUS 9 B8
Lodève F 130 B2
Lodi I 120 B2
Løding N 194 C5
Lødingen N 194 B6
Lodosa E 144 B1
Lödöse S 54 B3
Łódź PL 86 A3
Loeches E 151 B4
Løfallstrand N 46 B3
Lofer A 109 B3
Lofsdalen S 199 C10
Loftahammar S 62 A4
Lofthus N 46 B3
Loftus GB 37 B6
Loga N 52 B2
Logatec SLO 123 B3
Lögdeå S 200 C5
Lograto I 120 B3
Logroño E 143 B4
Logrosán E 156 A2
Løgstør DK 58 B2
Løgumgårde DK . . .64 A1
Løgumkloster DK . .64 A1
Lohals DK 65 A3
Lohiniva FIN 197 B8
Lohja FIN 8 B4
Löhlbach D 81 A4
Lohmen
  Mecklenburg-
    Vorpommern D . .65 C5
  Sachsen D 84 B2
Löhnberg D 81 B4
Lohne D 71 B5
Löhne D 72 B1
Lohr D 94 B1
Lohra D 81 B4
Lohsa D 84 A2
Loiano I 135 A4
Loimaa FIN 8 B3
Lóiri I 178 B3
Loitz D 66 C2
Loivos F 148 A2
Loivos do Monte
  P 148 A2
Loja E 163 A3
Lojanice SRB 127 C1
Lojsta S 57 C4
Løjt Kirkeby DK 64 A2
Lok SK 112 A2
Lokca SK 99 B3
Løken N 54 A2
Lokeren B 79 A3
Loket CZ 83 B4
Lokka FIN 197 B10
Løkken
  DK 58 A2
  N 198 B6
Loknya RUS 9 D7
Lökosháza H 113 C5
Lokve SRB 126 B3
Lollar D 81 B4
L'Olleria E 159 C3
Lölling-Graben A . .110 C1
Lom
  BG 17 D5
  N 198 D5
  SK 99 C3
Lombez F 146 A1
Lomello I 120 B1
Łomianki PL 77 B5
Lomma S 61 D3
Lommaryd S 62 A2
Lommatzsch D 83 A5
Lommel B 79 A5
Lommersum D 80 B2
Lomnice CZ 97 B4
Lomnice nad Lužnici
  CZ 96 B2
Lomnice-nad Popelkou
  CZ 84 B3
Łompolo FIN 196 A7
Lomsjö S 200 B2
Łomża PL 12 B5
Lönashult S 63 B2
Lønborg DK 59 C1
Londerzeel B 79 A4

Londinières F 89 A5
London GB 44 B3
Lonevåg N 46 B2
Longa GR 184 C2
Longare I 121 B4
Longares E 152 A2
Longarone I 122 A1
Longastrino I 135 A5
Long Bennington
GB 40 C3
Longbenton GB . . .37 A5
Longchamp-sur-Aujon
F 105 A3
Longchaumois F . .118 A2
Long Eaton GB 40 C2
Longeau F 105 B4
Longecourt-en-Plaine
F 105 A3
Longeville-les-St Avold
F 92 B2
Longeville-sur-Mer
F 114 B2
Longford IRL 28 A4
Longframlington
GB 37 A5
Longhope GB 33 C3
Longhorsley GB . . .37 A5
Longhoughton GB .37 A5
Longi I 177 A3
Long Melford GB . . .45 A4
Longny-au-Perche
F 89 B4
Longobucco I 174 B2
Long Preston GB . . .40 A1
Longré F 115 B3
Longroiva P 149 B2
Long Sutton GB 41 C4
Longtown
Cumbria GB 36 A4
Herefordshire GB . .39 C4
Longueau F 90 B2
Longué-Jumelles
F 102 B1
Longuyon F 92 B1
Longvic F 105 B4
Longvilly B 92 A1
Longwy F 92 B1
Lonigo I 121 B4
Löningen D 71 B4
Lonja HR 124 B2
Lönneberga S 62 A3
Lönsboda S 63 B2
Lønset N 198 C6
Lons-le-Saunier F .105 C4
Lønstrup DK 58 A2
Looe GB 42 B2
Loone-Plage F 78 A2
Loon op Zand NL . . .79 A5
Loosdorf A 110 A2
Lo Pagán E 165 B4
Lopar HR 123 C3
Lopare BIH 125 C4
Lopera E 157 C3
Lopigna F 180 A1
Loppersum NL 71 A3
Łopuszna PL 99 B4
Łopuszno PL 87 B4
Lor F 91 B4
Lora N 198 C5
Lora de Estepa E . .162 A3
Lora del Río E 162 A2
Loranca del Campo
E 151 B5
Lörby S 63 B2
Lorca E 164 B3
Lorch D 93 A4
Lørenfallet N 48 B3
Lørenskog N 48 C2
Loreo I 122 B1
Loreto I 136 B2
Lorgues F 132 B2
Lorica I 174 B2
Lorient F 100 B2
Lorignac F 114 C3
Loriol-sur-Drôme
F 117 C4
Lormes F 104 B2
Loro Ciuffenna I . .135 B4
Lorqui E 165 A3
Lörrach D 106 B2
Lorrez-le-Bocage
F 103 A4
Lorris F 103 B4
Lorup D 71 B4
Łoś PL 77 C5
Los S 199 D12
Losacino E 149 A3
Los Alcázares E . . .165 B4
Los Arcos E 144 B1
Losar de la Vera E .150 B2
Los Barios de Luna
E 141 B5
Los Barrios E 162 B2
Los Caños de Meca
E 162 B1
Los Cerricos E 164 B2
Los Corrales E 162 A2
Los Corrales de Buelna
E 142 A2
Los Dolores E 165 B3
Losenstein A 110 B1
Los Gallardos E . . .164 B3
Losheim
Nordrhein-Westfalen
D 80 B2
Saarland D 92 B2
Los Hinojosos E . . .158 B1
Los Isidros E 159 B2
Los Molinos E 151 B3
Los Morales E 162 A2
Los Navalmorales
E 156 A3
Los Navalucillos
E 156 A3
Losne F 105 B4
Los Nietos E 165 B4
Løsning DK 59 C2

Los Palacios y
Villafranca E 162 A2
Los Pozuelos de
Calatrava E 157 B3
Los Rábanos E 143 C4
Los Santos E 149 B4
Los Santos de la
Humosa E 151 B4
Los Santos de
Maimona E 155 C4
Lossburg D 93 C4
Losse F 128 B2
Losser NL 71 B4
Lossiemouth GB . . .32 D3
Lössnitz D 83 B4
Loštice CZ 97 B4
Los Tijos E 142 A2
Lostwithiel GB 42 B2
Los Villares E 163 A4
Los Yébenes E . . .157 A4
Løten N 48 B3
Lotorp S 56 B1
Lottefors S 50 A3
Löttorp S 62 A5
Lotyń PL 68 B1
Lotzorai I 179 C3
Louargat F 100 A2
Loudéac F 101 A3
Loudun F 102 B2
Loué F 102 B1
Loughborough GB .40 C2
Loughbrickland GB 27 B4
Loughrea IRL 28 A3
Louhans F 105 C4
Louisburgh IRL 28 A2
Loukhi RUS 3 C13
Loulay F 114 B3
Loulé P 160 B1
Louny CZ 84 B1
Lourdes F 145 A3
Lourenzá E 141 A3
Loures P 154 C1
Loures-Barousse
F 145 A4
Lourical P 154 A2
Lourinhã P 154 B1
Lourmarin F 131 B4
Loury F 103 B4
Lousa
Bragança P 149 A2
Castelo Branco P. 155 B3
Lousã P 148 B1
Lousa P 154 C1
Lousada
E 140 B3
P 148 A1
Louth GB 41 B3
Loutra Edipsou
GR 183 E5
Loutraki GR 184 B3
Loutropoli Thermis
GR 186 C1
Louverné F 102 A1
Louvie-Juzon F . . .145 A3
Louviers F 89 A5
Louvigné-du-Désert
F 88 B2
Louvois F 91 B4
Lova I 121 B5
Lovasberény H . . .112 B2
Lövåsen S 49 C5
Lovászpatona H . .111 B4
Lövberga S 200 C1
Lovech BG 17 D6
Lövenich D 80 A2
Lovere I 120 B3
Lövestad S 61 D3
Loviisa FIN 8 B5
Lovikka S 196 B5
Lovinobaña SK 99 C3
Loviste HR 138 B3
Lovnäs S 49 A5
Lövö H 111 B3
Lovosice CZ 84 B2
Lovozero RUS 3 C14
Lovran HR 123 B3
Lovreć HR 138 B2
Lovrenc na Pohorju
SLO 110 C2
Lovrin RO 126 B2
Lövstabruk S 51 B4
Löwenberg D 74 B2
Löwenberg D 94 B1
Lowestoft GB 41 C5
Lowick GB 37 A5
Łowicz PL 77 B4
Loxstedt D 72 A1
Loyew BY 13 C9
Łoż SLO 123 B3
Loza CZ 96 B1
Łozina PL 85 A5
Loznica SRB 127 C1
Loznicko Polje
SRB 127 C1
Lozorno SK 111 A4
Lozovik SRB 127 C3
Lozoya E 151 B4
Lozoyuela E 151 B4
Lozzo di Cadore I .109 C3
Luanco E 141 A5
Luarca E 141 A4
Lubaczów PL 13 C5
Lubań PL 84 A3
Lubanie PL 76 B3
Lubanów PL 86 A3
Lubars D 73 B5
Lubasz PL 75 B5
Lubawa PL 69 B4
Lubawka PL 85 B4
Lübbecke D 72 B1
Lübben D 74 C2
Lübbenau D 84 A1
Lübczyna PL 74 A3
Lübeck D 65 C3
Lubenec CZ 83 B5
Lubersac F 115 C5
Lübesse D 73 A4
Lubia E 152 A1
Lubian E 141 B4

Lubiatowo PL 75 A4
Lubichowo PL 69 B3
Lubicz Dolny PL . . .76 A3
Lubień PL 99 B3
Lubienia PL 87 A5
Lubień Kujawski
PL 77 B4
Lubieszewo PL 75 A4
Lubin
Dolnośląskie PL . . .85 A4
Zachodnio-Pomorskie
PL 67 C3
Lublin PL 12 C5
Lubliniec PL 86 B2
Lubmin D 66 B2
Lubniewice PL 75 B4
Lubochnia PL 87 A4
Lubomierz
Dolnośląskie PL . . .84 A3
Małopolskie PL 99 B4
Lubomino PL 69 A5
Luboń PL 76 B1
L'ubotin SK 99 B4
Lubowidz PL 77 A4
Łubowo
Wielkopolskie PL . 76 B2
Zachodnio-Pomorskie
PL 68 B1
Lubraniec PL 76 B3
Lubrin E 164 B2
Lubrza PL 85 B5
Lubsko PL 84 A2
Lübtheen D 73 A4
Lubuczewo PL 68 A2
Luby CZ 83 B4
Lübz D 73 A5
Luc F 117 C3
Lucainena de las
Torres E 164 B2
Lucan IRL 30 A2
Lučani SRB 127 D2
Lúcar E 164 B2
Luçay-le-Mâle F . . .103 B3
Lucca I 134 B3
Lucciana F 180 A2
Lucé F 90 C1
Luče SLO 123 A3
Lucena
Córdoba E 163 A3
Huelva E 161 B3
Lucena-les-Aix F . 104 C2
Lucenay-l'Evéque
F 104 B3
Luc-en-Diois F 118 C2
Lučenec SK 99 C3
Luceni E 144 C2
Lucens CH 106 C1
Lucera I 171 B3
Luceram F 133 B3
Lüchow D 73 B4
Luciana E 157 B3
Lucignano I 135 B4
Lucija SLO 122 B2
Lucka D 83 A4
Luckau D 84 A1
Luckenwalde D 74 B2
Lückstedt D 73 B4
Luco dei Marsi I . .169 B3
Luçon F 114 B2
Luc-sur-Mer F 89 A3
Ludanice SK 98 C2
Ludbreg HR 124 A2
Lüdenscheid D 81 A3
Lüdersdorf D 65 C3
Ludgershall GB 44 B2
Ludgo S 56 B3
Lüdinghausen D . . .80 A3
Ludlow GB 39 B4
Ludomy PL 75 B5
Ludvika S 50 B2
Ludweiler Warndt
D 92 B2
Ludwigsburg D 94 C1
Ludwigsfelde D 74 B2
Ludwigslust D 73 A4
Ludwigstadt D 82 B3
Ludza LV 8 D5
Luesia E 144 B2
Luftkurort Arendsee
D 73 B4
Lug
BIH 139 C4
HR 125 B4
Luga RUS 9 C6
Lugagnano Val d'Arda
I 120 C2
Lugano CH 120 A1
Lugau D 83 B4
Lugnas S 55 B4
Lúgnola I 168 A2
Lugny F 105 C3
Lugo
E 140 A3
I 135 A4
Lugoj RO 16 C4
Lugones E 141 A5
Lugros E 163 A4
Luhačovice CZ 98 B1
Luhe D 95 B4
Luino I 120 B1
Luintra E 140 B3
Lujar E 163 B4
Luka nad Jihlavou
CZ 97 B3
Lukavac BIH 125 C4
Lukavika BIH 125 C4
Lukovë AL 182 D1
Lukovica SLO 123 A3
Lukovit BG 17 D6
Lukovo HR 123 C3
Lukovo Šugorje
HR 137 A4
Łukowica PL 99 B4
Łuków PL 12 C5
Łukowice Brzeskie
PL 85 B5
Łukta PL 69 B5
Lula I 178 B3

Luleå S 196 D5
Lüleburgaz TR 186 A2
Lumbarda HR 138 C3
Lumbier E 144 B2
Lumbrales E 149 B3
Lumbreras E 143 B4
Lumbres F 78 B2
Lumezzane I 120 B3
Lummelunda S 57 C4
Lummen B 79 B5
Lumparland FIN . . .51 B7
Lumpiaque E 152 A2
Lumsås DK 61 D1
Lumsden GB 33 D4
Lumsheden S 50 B3
Lun HR 123 C3
Luna E 144 B3
Lunamatrona I 179 C2
Lunano I 136 B1
Lunas F 130 B2
Lund
N 199 A8
Skåne S 61 D3
Västra Götaland
S 54 A3
Lundamo N 199 B7
Lunde
DK 59 C1
Sogn og Fjordane
N 46 A3
Sogn og Fjordane
N 46 A3
Telemark N 53 A5
S 200 D3
Lundebyvollen N . . .49 B4
Lunden D 64 B2
Lunderseter N 49 B4
Lunderskov DK 59 C2
Lundsberg S 55 A5
Lüneburg D 72 A3
Lunel F 131 B3
Lünen D 81 A3
Lunéville F 92 C2
Lungern CH 106 C3
Lungro I 174 B2
Lunz am See A 110 B2
Luogosanto I 178 A3
Łupawa PL 68 A2
Lupión E 157 B4
Lupoglav HR 123 B3
Luppa D 83 A4
Luque E 163 A3
Lurago d'Erba I . . .120 B2
Lúras I 178 B3
Lurcy-Lévis F 104 C1
Lure F 105 B5
Lurgan GB 27 B4
Luri F 180 A2
Lury-sur-Arnon F .103 B4
Lušci Palanka BIH 124 C2
Lusévera I 122 A2
Lushnjë AL 182 C1
Lusignan F 115 B4
Lusigny-sur-Barse
F 104 A3
Lusnić BIH 138 B2
Luso P 148 B1
Lúsówko PL 75 B5
Luspebryggan S . .196 B2
Luss GB 34 B3
Lussac F 128 B2
Lussac-les-Châteaux
F 115 B4
Lussac-les-Eglises
F 115 B5
Lussan F 131 A3
Lüssow D 65 C5
Lustenau A 107 B4
Luštěnice CZ 84 B2
Luster N 47 A4
Lutago I 108 C2
Lutherstadt Wittenberg
D 83 A4
Lütjenburg D 65 B3
Lutnes N 49 A4
Lutocin PL 77 B4
Lutomiersk PL 86 A3
Luton GB 44 B3
Lutry CH 106 C1
Lutsk UA 13 C6
Lutter am Barenberge
D 72 C3
Lutterworth GB 40 C2
Lututów PL 86 A2
Lützen D 83 A4
Lutzow D 73 A4
Luusua FIN 197 C10
Luvos S 196 C1
Luxembourg L 92 B2
Luxeuil-les-Bains
F 105 B5
Luxey F 128 B2
Luz
Évora P 155 C3
Faro P 160 B1
Faro P 160 B2
Luzarches F 90 B2
Luže CZ 97 B4
Luzech F 129 B4
Luzern CH 106 B3
Luzino PL 68 A3
Luz-St Sauveur F .145 B3
Luzy F 104 C2
Luzzi I 174 B2
L'viv UA 13 D6
Lwówek PL 75 B5
Lwówek Śląski PL . .84 A3
Lyakhavichy BY . . .13 B7
Lybster GB 32 C3
Lychen D 74 A2
Lychkova RUS 9 D8
Lyckeby S 63 B3
Lycksele S 200 B4
Lydd GB 45 C4
Lydford GB 42 B2
Lydney GB 39 C4
Lyepyel BY 13 A8

Lygna N 48 B2
Lykkja N 47 B5
Lykling N 52 A1
Lyme Regis GB 43 B4
Lymington GB 44 C2
Lympne GB 45 B5
Lyndhurst GB 44 C2
Lyneham GB 43 A5
Lyness GB 33 C3
Lyngdal
Buskerud N 47 C6
Vest-Agder N 52 B3
Lyngør N 53 B5
Lyngsa DK 58 A3
Lyngseidet N 192 C4
Lyngsnes N 199 A8
Lynmouth GB 42 A3
Lynton GB 42 A3
Lyntupy BY 13 A7
Lyon F 117 B4
Lyons-la-Forêt F . . .90 B1
Lyozna BY 13 A9
Lyrestad S 55 B5
Lysánad Labem
CZ 84 B2
Lysápod Makytou
SK 98 B2
Lysebotn N 52 A2
Lysekil S 54 B2
Lysice CZ 97 B4
Lysomice PL 76 A3
Lysøysund N 198 B6
Lyss CH 106 B2
Lystrup DK 59 B3
Lysvik S 49 B5
Łyszkowice PL 77 C4
Lytham St Anne's
GB 38 A3
Lyuban RUS 9 C7
Lyubertsy RUS . . .9 E10
Lyubimets BG 183 B8
Lyuboml' UA 13 C6
Lyubytino RUS 9 C8

M

Maaninkavaara
FIN 197 C11
Maarheeze NL 80 A1
Maaseik B 80 A1
Maastricht NL 80 B1
Mablethorpe GB . . .41 B4
Mably F 117 A4
Macael E 164 B2
Maçanet de Cabrenys
E 146 B3
Mação P 154 B2
Macau F 128 A2
Maccagno-Agra I . .120 A1
Maccarese I 168 B2
Macchiagódena I . .170 B2
Macclesfield GB . . .40 B1
Macduff GB 33 D4
Maceda E 140 B3
Macedo de Cavaleiros
P 149 A3
Maceira
Guarda P 148 B2
Leiria P 154 B2
Macelj HR 124 A1
Macerata I 136 B2
Macerata Féltria I .136 B1
Machault F 91 B4
Machecoul F 114 B2
Mchowo PL 77 A5
Machrihanish GB . .34 C2
Machynlleth GB . . .39 B3
Macieira P 148 A1
Maciejowice PL 87 A5
Macinaggio F 180 A2
Mackenrode D 82 A2
Mačkovci SLO 111 C3
Macomer I 178 B2
Macon B 91 A4
Mâcon F 117 A4
Macotera E 150 B2
Macroom IRL 29 C3
Macungaga I 119 B4
Madan BG 183 B6
Madängsholm S . . .55 B4
Madaras H 126 A1
Maddaloni I 170 B2
Made NL 79 A4
Madeley GB 38 B4
Maderuelo E 151 A4
Madetkoski FIN . . .197 B9
Madley GB 39 B4
Madocsa H 112 C2
Madona LV 8 D5
Madonna di Campíglio
I 121 A3
Madrid E 151 B4
Madridejos E 157 A4
Madrigal de las Altas
Torres E 150 A2
Madrigal de la Vera
E 150 B2
Madrigalejo E 156 A2
Madrigalejo de Monte
E 143 B3
Madrigueras E 158 B2
Madroñera E 156 A2
Maël-Carhaix F . . .100 A2
Maella E 153 A4
Maello E 150 B3
Maesteg GB 39 C3
Mafra P 154 C1
Magacela E 156 B2
Magallon E 144 C2
Magaluf E 166 B2
Magán E 151 C4
Magaña E 144 C1
Magasa I 121 B3
Magaz E 142 C2
Magdeburg D 73 B4
Magenta I 120 B1
Magescq F 128 C1
Maghera GB 27 B4

Magherafelt GB . . .27 B4
Maghull GB 38 A4
Magilligan GB 27 A4
Magione I 135 B5
Magioto P 154 C1
Maglaj BIH 125 C4
Maglehem S 63 C2
Magliano de'Marsi
I 169 A3
Magliano in Toscana
I 168 A1
Magliano Sabina I .168 A2
Maglić SRB 126 B1
Máglie I 173 B4
Maglód H 112 B3
Magnac-Bourg F . .115 C5
Magnac-Laval F . . .115 B5
Magnières F 92 C2
Magnor N 49 C4
Magnuszew PL 87 A5
Magny-Cours F . . .104 C2
Magny-en-Vexin F . .90 B1
Mágocs H 125 A4
Maguilla E 156 B2
Maguiresbridge GB 27 B3
Magyarbóly H 125 B4
Magyarkeszi H 112 C2
Magyarszék H 125 A4
Mahide E 141 C4
Mahilyow BY 13 B9
Mahmudiye TR . . .187 C5
Mahora E 158 B2
Mahovo HR 124 B2
Mähring D 95 B4
Maia
E 144 A2
P 148 A1
Maiaelrayo E 151 A4
Maials E 153 A4
Maîche F 106 B1
Máida I 175 C2
Maiden Bradley GB 43 A4
Maidenhead GB . . .44 B3
Maiden Newton GB 43 B4
Maidstone GB 45 B4
Maienfeld CH 107 B4
Maignelay Montigny
F 90 B2
Maijanen FIN 197 B8
Maillezais F 114 B3
Mailly-le-Camp F . . .91 C4
Mailly-le-Château
F 104 B2
Mainar E 152 A2
Mainbernheim D . . .94 B2
Mainburg D 95 C3
Mainhardt D 94 B1
Maintal D 81 B4
Maintenon F 90 C1
Mainvilliers F 90 C1
Mainz D 93 A4
Maiorca P 148 B1
Mairena de Aljarafe
E 162 A2
Mairena del Alcor
E 162 A2
Maisach D 108 A2
Maishofen A 109 B3
Maison-Rouge F . . .90 C3
Maissau A 97 C3
Maisse F 90 C2
Maizières-lès-Vic F 92 C2
Maja HR 124 B2
Majadahonda E . . .151 B4
Majadas E 150 C2
Majavatn N 195 E4
Majs H 125 B4
Majšperk SLO 123 A4
Makarska HR 138 B3
Makkum NL 70 A2
Maklár H 113 B4
Makó H 126 A2
Makoszyce PL 85 B5
Makov SK 98 B2
Makowarsko PL . . .76 A2
Maków Mazowiecki
PL 77 B6
Maków Podhalański
PL 99 B3
Makrakomi GR . . .182 E4
Maksniemi FIN . . .196 D7
Malå S 195 E9
Mala Krsna SRB . .126 A1
Malacky SK 97 C5
Maladzyechna BY . .13 A7
Málaga E 163 B3
Malagón E 157 A4
Malaguilla E 151 B4
Malahide IRL 30 A2
Mala Kladuša BIH .124 B1
Mala Krsna SRB . .127 C3
Malalbergo I 121 C4
Malá Lehota SK . . .98 C2
Malanów PL 76 C3
Mala Pijace SRB . .126 A1
Mala Subotica HR .124 A2
Malaucène F 131 A4
Malaunay F 89 A5
Malaya Vishera RUS 9 C8
Malborghetto I 109 C4
Malbork PL 69 A4
Malborn D 92 B2
Malbuisson F 105 C5
Malcésine I 121 B3
Malchin D 74 A1
Malching D 96 C1
Malchow D 73 A5
Malcocinado E 156 B2
Malczyce PL 85 A4
Maldegem B 79 A3
Malden NL 80 A1
Maldyty PL 69 B4
Malè I 121 A3
Malemort F 129 A4
Malente D 65 B3
Maletto I 177 B3
Malexander S 56 B1
Malgrat de Mar E . .147 C3
Malhadas P 149 A3
Malia
CY 181 B3
GR 185 D6
Malicorne-sur-Sarthe
F 102 B1
Malijai F 132 A2
Malildjoš SRB 126 B1
Malilla S 62 A3
Malin IRL 27 A3
Málinec SK 99 C3
Malingsbo S 50 C2
Maliniec PL 76 B3
Malinska HR 123 B3
Maliq AL 182 C2
Maljevac HR 123 B4
Malkara TR 186 B1
Małki PL 69 B4
Malko Tŭrnovo BG .17 D7
Mallaig GB 34 A2
Mallaranny IRL 28 A2
Mallemort F 131 B4
Mallén E 144 C2
Malléon F 146 A2
Mallersdorf-Pfaffenberg
D 95 C4
Málles Venosta I . .108 C1
Malling DK 59 B3
Mallnitz A 109 C4
Mallow IRL 29 B3
Mallwyd GB 38 B3
Malm N 199 A8
Malmbäck S 62 A2
Malmberget S 196 B3
Malmby S 56 A3
Malmédy B 80 B2
Malmesbury GB . . .43 A4
Malmköping S 56 A2
Malmö S 61 D3
Malmön S 54 B2
Malmslätt S 56 B1
Malnate I 120 B1
Malo I 121 B4
Małogoszcz PL 87 B4
Maloja CH 120 A2
Małomice PL 84 A3
Måløy N 198 D2
Malpartida E 155 B4
Malpartida de la Serena
E 156 B2
Malpartida de Plasencia
E 150 C1
Malpas
E 145 B4
GB 38 A4
Malpica P 155 B3
Malpica de Bergantiños
E 140 A2
Malpica de Tajo E .150 C3
Malsch D 93 C4
Malšice CZ 96 B2
Malta A 109 C4
Maltat F 104 C2
Maltby GB 40 B2
Malung S 49 B5
Malungsfors S 49 B5
Maluszów PL 75 B4
Maluszyn PL 87 B3
Malva E 142 C1
Malvaglia CH 120 A1
Malveira P 154 C1
Malvik N 199 B7
Malyn UA 13 C8
Mamarrosa P 148 B1
Mamer L 92 B2
Mamers F 89 B4
Mamirolle F 105 B5
Mammendorf D . . .108 A2
Mámmola I 175 C2
Mamoiada I 178 B3
Mamonovo RUS . . .69 A4
Mamuras AL 182 B1
Maňa SK 112 A2
Manacor E 167 B3
Manavgat TR 189 C6
Mancera de Abajo
E 150 B2
Mancha Real E . . .163 A4
Manchester GB 40 B1
Manching D 95 C3
Manchita E 156 B1
Manciano I 168 A1
Manciet F 128 C2
Mandal N 52 B3
Mandanici I 177 A4
Mándas I 179 C3
Mandatoríccio I . . .174 B2
Mandayona E 151 B5
Mandelieu-la-Napoule
F 132 B2
Mandello del Lário
I 120 B2
Manderfeld B 80 B2
Manderscheid D . . .80 B2
Mandino Selo BIH .138 B3
Mandoudi GR 183 E5
Mandra GR 185 A4
Mandraki GR 188 C2
Mandúria I 173 B3
Mane
Alpes-de-Haute-
Provence F 132 B1
Haute-Garonne F .145 A4
Manérbio I 120 B3
Mañeru E 144 B2
Manetin CZ 96 B1
Manfredónia I 171 B3
Mangalia RO 17 D8
Manganeses de la
Lampreana E . . .149 A4
Manganeses de la
Polvorosa E 141 B5

Mangen N 48 C3
Manger N 46 B2
Mangiennes F 92 B1
Mangotsfield GB 43 A4
Mångsbodarna S 49 A5
Mangualde P 148 B2
Maniago I 122 A1
Manilva E 162 B2
Manisa TR 186 D2
Manises E 159 B3
Mank A 110 A2
Månkarbo S 51 B4
Manlleu E 147 C3
Manna DK 58 A2
Männedorf CH 107 B3
Mannersdorf am
  Leithagebirge A .111 B3
Mannheim D 93 B4
Manningtree GB . .45 B5
Manoppello I 169 A4
Manorbier GB 39 C2
Manorhamilton IRL 26 B2
Manosque F 132 B1
Manowo PL 67 B5
Manresa E 147 C2
Månsarp S 62 A2
Månsåsen S 199 B11
Manschnow D 74 B3
Mansfeld D 82 A3
Mansfield GB 40 B2
Mansilla de Burgos
  E 143 B3
Mansilla de las Mulas
  E 142 B1
Manskog S 55 A3
Mansle F 115 C4
Manso F 180 A1
Manteigas P 148 B2
Mantel D 95 B4
Mantes-la-Jolie F . .90 C1
Mantes-la-Ville F . .90 C1
Manthelan F 102 B2
Mantorp S 56 B1
Mántova I 121 B3
Mänttä FIN 8 A4
Mäntyjärvi FIN . .197 C10
Manuel E 159 B3
Manyas TR 186 B2
Manzanal de Arriba
  E 141 B4
Manzanares E 157 A4
Manzanares el Real
  E 151 B4
Manzaneda
  León E 141 B4
  Orense E 141 B3
Manzanedo E 143 B3
Manzaneque E 157 A4
Manzanera E 153 B3
Manzanilla E 161 B3
Manzat F 116 B2
Manziana I 168 A2
Manziat F 117 A4
Maó E 167 B4
Maoča BIH 125 C4
Maqueda E 150 B3
Mara E 152 A2
Maramaraereğlisi
  TR 186 B2
Maraña E 142 A1
Maranchón E 152 A1
Maranello I 135 A3
Marano I 170 C2
Marano Lagunare
  I 122 B2
Marans F 114 B2
Maratea I 174 B1
Marateca P 154 C2
Marathokambos
  GR 188 B1
Marathonas GR . .185 A4
Marathóvouno
  CY 181 A2
Marazion GB 42 B1
Marbach
  Baden-Württemberg
  D 94 C1
  Hessen D 82 B1
  F 92 C2
Marbäck S 60 B3
Mårbacka S 55 A4
Marbella E 162 B3
Marboz F 118 A2
Marburg D 81 B4
Marcali H 111 C4
Marčana HR 122 C2
Marcaria I 121 B3
Marcelová SK 112 B2
Marcenat F 116 B2
March GB 41 C4
Marchamalo E 151 B4
Marchaux F 105 B5
Marche-en-Famenne
  B 79 B5
Marchegg A 111 A3
Marchena E 162 A2
Marchenoir F 103 B3
Marcheprime F 128 B2
Marciac F 128 C3
Marciana Marina I 134 C3
Marcianise I 170 B2
Marcigny F 117 A4
Marcilla E 144 B2
Marcillac-la-Croisille
  F 116 B2
Marcillac-Vallon F .130 A1
Marcillat-en-Combraille
  F 116 A2
Marcille-sur-Seine
  F 91 C3
Marcilloles F 118 B2
Marcilly-le-Hayer F .91 C3
Marcinkowice PL . . .75 A5
Marciszów PL 85 B4
Marck F 78 B1
Marckolsheim F . . .106 A2

Marco de Canevezes
  P 148 A1
Mårdsele S 200 B5
Mårdsjö S 200 C1
Mareham le Fen
  GB 41 B3
Marek S 62 A3
Marennes F 114 C2
Maresquel F 78 B1
Mareuil F 115 C4
Mareuil-en-Brie F . .91 C3
Mareuil-sur-Arnon
  F 103 C4
Mareuil-sur-Lay F .114 B2
Mareuil-sur-Ourcq
  F 90 B3
Margam GB 39 C3
Margariti GR 182 D2
Margate GB 45 B5
Margaux F 128 A2
Margerie-Hancourt
  F 91 C4
Margès F 117 B5
Margherita di Savóia
  I 171 B4
Margita SRB 126 B3
Margone I 119 B4
Margonin PL 76 B2
Margut F 91 B5
Maria E 164 B2
Mariager DK 58 B2
Mariana E 152 B1
Maria Neustift A . .110 B1
Mariannelund S . . .62 A3
Mariánópoli I 176 B2
Mariánské Lázně
  CZ 95 B4
Mariapfarr A 109 B4
Maria Saal A 110 C1
Mariazell A 110 B2
Maribo DK 65 B4
Maribor SLO 110 C2
Marieberg S 56 A1
Mariefred S 56 A3
Mariehamn FIN . . .51 B6
Marieholm S 61 D3
Mariembourg B 79 B4
Marienbaum D 80 A2
Marienberg D 83 B5
Marienheide D 81 A3
Marienthal D 73 B3
Mariestad S 55 B4
Marieux F 90 A2
Marigliano I 170 C2
Marignane F 131 B4
Marigny
  Jura F 105 C4
  Manche F 88 A2
Marigny-le-Châtel
  F 91 C3
Marija Bistrica HR 124 A2
Marijampolė LT 13 A5
Marin E 140 B2
Marina del Cantone
  I 170 C2
Marina di Acquappesa
  I 174 B1
Marina di Alberese
  I 168 A1
Marina di Amendolara
  I 174 B2
Marina di Árbus I . .179 C2
Marina di Campo I 134 C3
Marina di Carrara
  I 134 A3
Marina di Castagneto-
  Donorático I . . .134 B3
Marina di Cécina I 134 B3
Marina di Gáiro I . .179 C3
Marina di Ginosa I 173 B2
Marina di Gioiosa
  Iónica I 175 C2
Marina di Grosseto
  I 135 C3
Marina di Léuca I .173 C4
Marina di Massa I .134 A3
Marina di Nováglie
  I 173 C4
Marina di Pisa I . . .134 B3
Marina di Ragusa
  I 177 C3
Marina di Ravenna
  I 135 A5
Marina di Torre Grande
  I 179 C2
Marinaleda E 162 A3
Marina Romea I . . .135 A5
Marine de Sisco F .180 A2
Marinella I 176 B1
Marinella di Sarzana
  I 134 A3
Marineo I 176 B2
Marines F 90 B1
Maringues F 116 B3
Marinha das Ondas
  P 154 A2
Marinha Grande P 154 B2
Marinhas P 148 A1
Marino I 168 B2
Marjaliza E 157 A4
Markabygd N 199 B8
Markaryd S 61 C3
Markdorf D 107 B4
Markelo NL 71 B3
Market Deeping GB 40 C3
Market Drayton GB 38 B4
Market Harborough
  GB 40 C3
Markethill GB 27 B4
Market Rasen GB . .40 B3
Market Warsop GB .40 B2
Market Weighton
  GB 40 B3
Markgröningen D . .93 C5
Markhausen D 71 B4
Marki PL 77 B6
Markina-Xemein E 143 A4
Markinch GB 35 B4

Märkische Buchholz
  D 74 B2
Markitta S 196 B4
Markkleeberg D . . .83 A4
Marklohe D 72 B2
Marknesse NL 70 B2
Markneukirchen D .83 B4
Markopoulo GR . . .185 B4
Markovac
  Srbija SRB 127 C3
  Vojvodina SRB . .126 B3
Markowice PL 86 B2
Markranstädt D . . .83 A4
Marksuhl D 82 B2
Markt Allhau A 111 B3
Markt Bibart D 94 B2
Markt Erlbach D . . .94 B2
Marktheidenfeld D .94 B1
Markt Indersdorf D .95 C3
Marktl D 95 C4
Marktleuthen D 83 B3
Marktoberdorf D . .108 B1
Marktredwitz D 95 A4
Markt Rettenbach
  D 108 B1
Markt Schwaben
  D 108 A2
Markt-Übelbach A .110 B2
Markušica HR 125 B4
Markušovce SK . . .99 C4
Marl D 80 A3
Marlborough
  Devon GB 42 B3
  Wiltshire GB 44 B2
Marle F 91 B3
Marlieux F 117 A5
Marlow
  D 66 B1
  GB 44 B3
Marma S 51 B4
Marmagne F 104 C3
Marmande F 128 B3
Marmara TR 186 B2
Marmaris TR 188 C3
Marmelete P 160 B1
Marmolejo E 157 B3
Marmoutier F 93 C3
Marnay F 105 B4
Marne D 64 C2
Marnheim D 93 B4
Marniz D 73 A4
Maroldsweisach D .82 B2
Marolles-les-Braults
  F 89 B4
Maromme F 89 A5
Marone I 120 B3
Maronia GR 183 C7
Maroslele H 126 A2
Maróstica I 121 B4
Marotta I 136 B2
Marpisa GR 185 B6
Marquion F 78 B3
Marquise F 78 B1
Marradi I 135 A4
Marrasjärvi FIN . . .197 C8
Marraskoski FIN . .197 C8
Marratxi E 166 B2
Marrúbiu I 179 C2
Marrum NL 70 A2
Marrupe E 150 B3
Marsac F 129 C5
Marsac-en-Livradois
  F 117 B3
Marságlia I 120 C2
Marsala I 176 B1
Marsberg D 81 A4
Marsciano I 135 C5
Marseillan F 130 B2
Marseille = Marseilles
  F 131 B4
Marseille en Beauvaisis
  F 90 B1
Marseilles = Marseille
  F 131 B4
Mársico Nuovo I . .172 B1
Marske-by-the-Sea
  GB 37 B5
Mars-la-Tours F . . .92 B1
Marslev DK 65 B3
Marssac-sur-Tarn
  F 129 C4
Märsta S 57 A3
Marstal DK 65 B3
Marstrand S 60 B1
Marta I 168 A1
Martano I 173 B4
Martel F 129 B4
Martelange B 92 B1
Martfeld D 72 B2
Martfű H 113 B4
Martham GB 41 C5
Marthon F 115 C4
Martiago E 149 B3
Martigné-Briand F 102 B1
Martigné-Ferchaud
  F 101 B4
Martigne-sur-Mayenne
  F 102 A1
Martigny CH 119 A4
Martigny-les-Bains
  F 105 A4
Martigues F 131 B4
Martim-Longo P . .160 B2
Martin SK 98 B2
Martina CH 108 C1
Martina Franca I . .173 B3
Martinamor E 150 B2
Martin de la Jara
  E 162 A3
Martinengo I 120 B2
Martín Muñoz de las
  Posadas E 150 A3
Martinsberg A 97 C3
Martinšćica HR . . .123 C3
Martinshöhe D 93 B3
Martinsicuro I 136 C2
Martinszell D 107 B5
Mártis I 178 B2
Martofte DK 59 C3
Martonvásár H 112 B2

Martorell E 147 C2
Martos E 163 A4
Martres Tolosane
  F 146 A1
Martti FIN 197 B11
Marugán E 150 B3
Marúggio I 173 B3
Marvão P 155 B3
Marvejols F 130 A2
Marville F 92 B1
Marwałd PL 77 A4
Marykirk GB 35 B5
Marypark GB 32 D3
Maryport GB 36 B3
Marytavy GB 42 B2
Marzabotto I 135 A4
Marzahna D 74 C1
Marzahne D 73 B5
Marzamemi I 177 C4
Marzocca I 136 B2
Masa E 143 B3
Mas-Cabardès F . .146 A3
Máscali I 177 B4
Mascaraque E 157 A4
Mascarenhas P . . .149 A2
Mascioni I 169 A3
Mas de Barberáns
  E 153 B4
Mas de las Matas
  E 153 B3
Masegoso E 158 C1
Masegoso de Tajuña
  E 151 B5
Masera I 119 A5
Masevaux F 106 B1
Masfjorden N 46 B2
Masham GB 37 B5
Masi N 192 C7
Maside E 140 B2
Maslacq F 144 A3
Maslinica HR 138 B2
Maşloc RO 126 B3
Maslovare BIH 138 A3
Masone I 133 A4
Massa I 134 A3
Massa Fiscáglia I .121 C5
Massafra I 173 B3
Massa Lombarda
  I 135 A4
Massa Lubrense I 170 C2
Massamagrell E . . .159 B3
Massa Maríttima I .135 B3
Massa Martana I . .136 C1
Massanassa E 159 B3
Massarosa I 134 B3
Massat F 146 B2
Massay F 103 B3
Massbach D 82 B2
Masseret F 116 B1
Masseube F 145 A4
Massiac F 116 B3
Massignac F 115 C4
Massing D 95 C4
Massmechelen B . .80 B1
Masterud N 49 B4
Mästocka S 61 C3
Masty BY 13 B6
Masúa I 179 C2
Masueco E 149 A3
Masugnsbyn S . . .196 B5
Mašun SLO 123 B3
Maszewo
  Lubuskie PL 75 B3
  Zachodnio-Pomorskie
  PL 75 A4
Mata de Alcántara
  E 155 B4
Matala GR 185 E5
Matalebreras E . . .144 C1
Matallana de Torio
  E 142 B1
Matamala E 151 A5
Mataporquera E . .142 B2
Matapozuelos E . . .150 A3
Mataró E 147 C3
Matarocco I 176 B1
Matélica I 136 B2
Matera I 172 B2
Mátészalka H 16 B5
Matet E 159 B3
Matfors S 200 D3
Matha F 115 C3
Mathay F 106 B1
Matignon F 101 A3
Matilla de los Caños
  del Rio E 149 B4
Matlock GB 40 B2
Matosinhos P 148 A1
Matour F 117 A4
Mátrafüred H 113 B3
Mátraterenye H . . .113 A3
Matre
  Hordaland N 46 B2
  Hordaland N 52 A1
Matrei am Brenner
  A 108 B2
Matrei in Osttirol
  A 109 B3
Matrice I 170 B2
Matsdal S 195 E6
Mattarello I 121 A4
Mattersburg A 111 B3
Mattighofen A 109 A4
Mattinata I 171 B4
Mattos P 154 B2
Mattsee A 109 B4
Måttsund S 196 D5
Matulji HR 123 B3
Maubert-Fontaine
  F 91 B4
Maubeuge F 79 B3
Maubourguet F . . .145 A4
Mauchline GB 36 A2
Maud GB 33 D4
Mauer-kirchen A . .109 A4
Mauern D 95 C3
Mauguio F 131 B3
Maulbronn D 93 C4
Maule F 90 C1

Mauléon F 114 B3
Mauléon-Barousse
  F 145 B4
Mauléon-Licharre
  F 144 A3
Maulévrier F 114 A3
Maum IRL 28 A2
Maurach A 108 B2
Maure-de-Bretagne
  F 101 B4
Maureilhan F 130 B2
Mãureni RO 126 B3
Mauriac F 116 B2
Mauron F 101 A3
Maurs F 116 C2
Maury F 146 B3
Maussane-les-Alpilles
  F 131 B3
Mautern A 97 C3
Mauterndorf A 109 B4
Mautern im Steiermark
  A 110 B1
Mauthausen A 110 A1
Mauthen A 109 C3
Mauvezin F 129 C3
Mauzé-sur-le-Mignon
  F 114 B3
Maxent F 101 B3
Maxey-sur-Vaise F .92 C1
Maxial P 154 B1
Maxieira P 154 B2
Maxwellheugh GB .35 C5
Mayalde E 149 A4
Maybole GB 36 A2
Mayen D 80 B3
Mayenne F 88 B3
Mayet F 102 B2
Mayorga E 142 B1
Mayres F 117 C4
Mayrhofen A 108 B2
Mazagón E 161 B3
Mazaleón E 153 A4
Mazamet F 130 B1
Mazan F 131 A4
Mazara del Vallo I .176 B1
Mazarambroz E . . .157 A3
Mazarete E 152 B1
Mazaricos E 140 B2
Mazarrón E 165 B3
Mažeikiai LT 8 D3
Mazères F 146 A2
Mazères-sur-Salat
  F 145 A4
Mazières-en-Gâtine
  F 115 B3
Mazin HR 138 A1
Mazuelo E 143 B3
Mazyr BY 13 B8
Mazzarino I 177 B3
Mazzarrà Sant'Andrea
  I 177 A4
Mazzo di Valtellina
  I 120 A3
Mdzewo PL 77 B5
Mealabost GB 31 A2
Mealhada P 148 B1
Méan B 79 B5
Meana Sardo I 179 C3
Meaulne F 103 C4
Meaux F 90 C2
Mebonden N 199 B8
Mecerreyes E 143 B3
Mechelen B 79 A4
Mechernich D 80 B2
Mechowo PL 75 A4
Mechterstädt D 82 B2
Mecikal PL 68 B2
Mecina-Bombarón
  E 164 C1
Mecitözü TR 23 A8
Meckenbeuren D . .107 B4
Meckenheim
  Rheinland-Pfalz
  D 80 B3
  Rheinland-Pfalz D .93 B4
Meckesheim D 93 B4
Mecseknádasd H .125 A4
Meda
  I 120 B2
  P 149 B2
Medak HR 137 A4
Mede I 120 B1
Medebach D 81 A4
Medelim P 155 A3
Medemblik NL 70 B2
Medena Selista
  BIH 138 A2
Medesano I 120 C3
Medevi S 55 B5
Medgidia RO 17 C8
Medgyesháza H . .113 C5
Medhamn S 55 A4
Media RO 17 B6
Medicina I 135 A4
Medinaceli E 152 A1
Medina de las Torres
  E 155 C4
Medina del Campo
  E 150 A3
Medina de Pomar
  E 143 B3
Medina de Rioseco
  E 142 C1
Medina Sidonia E .162 B2
Medinilla E 150 B2
Medja SRB 126 B2
Medjedja BIH 139 B5
Medulin HR 122 C2
Meduno I 122 A1
Medveda SRB 127 C3
Medvedov SK 111 B4
Medvezhyegorsk
  RUS 9 A9
Medvide HR 137 A4
Medvode SLO 123 A3
Medzev SK 99 C4
Medžitlija MK 182 C3

Meerane D 83 B4
Meerle B 79 A4
Meersburg D 107 B4
Meeuwen B 79 A5
Megalo Horio GR . .188 C2
Megalopoli GR 184 B3
Megara GR 185 A4
Megève F 118 B3
Meggenhofen A . . .109 A4
Megra RUS 9 B10
Megyaszó H 113 A5
Mehamn N 193 A11
Mehedeby S 51 B4
Méhkerék H 113 C5
Mera
  Coruña E 140 A2
  Coruña E 140 A3
Meråker N 199 B8
Merano I 108 C2
Merate I 120 B2
Mercadillo E 143 A3
Mercatale I 135 B5
Mercatino Conca I 136 B1
Mercato San Severino
  I 170 C2
Mercato Saraceno
  I 135 B5
Merching D 108 A1
Merchtem B 79 B4
Merdrignac F 101 A3
Merdžanići BIH . . .139 B3
Meré E 142 A2
Mere GB 43 A4
Meréville F 90 C2
Merfeld D 80 A3
Méribel F 118 B3
Méribel Motraret
  F 118 B3
Meriç TR 186 A1
Mérida E 155 C4
Mérignac F 128 B2
Měřín CZ 97 B3
Mering D 94 C2
Merkendorf D 94 B2
Merklín CZ 96 B1
Merksplas B 79 A4
Merlánea S 56 A2
Mern DK 65 A5
Mernye H 111 C4
Mersch L 92 B2
Merseburg D 83 A3
Mers-les-Bains F . .90 A1
Merthyr Tydfil GB . .39 C3
Mertingen D 94 C2
Mértola P 160 B2
Méru F 90 B2
Merufe P 140 B2
Mervans F 105 C4
Merville F 78 B2
Méry-sur-Seine F . .91 C3
Merzen D 71 B4
Merzifon TR 23 A8
Merzig D 92 B2
Mesagne I 173 B3
Mesão Frio P 148 A2
Mesas de Ibor E . .156 A2
Meschede D 81 A4
Meschers-sur-Gironde
  F 114 C3
Meslay-du-Maine
  F 102 B1
Mesna N 48 A2
Mesnalien N 48 A2
Mesocco CH 120 A2
Mésola I 122 C1
Mesologi GR 184 A2
Mesopotamo GR . .182 D2
Mesoraca I 175 B2
Messac F 101 B4
Messancy B 92 B1
Messdorf D 73 B4
Messei F 88 B3
Messejana P 160 B1
Messelt N 48 A3
Messina I 177 A4
Messingen D 71 B4
Messini GR 184 B3
Messkirch D 107 B4
Messlingen S 199 C9
Messstetten D 107 A3
Mesta GR 185 A6
Mestanza E 157 B3
Městec Králové CZ .84 B3
Mestlin D 73 A4
Město Albrechtice
  CZ 85 B5
Město Libavá CZ . .98 B1
Město Touškov CZ .96 B1
Mestre I 122 B1
Mesvres F 104 C3
Mesztegnyő H 111 C4
Meta I 170 C2
Metajna HR 137 A4
Metelen D 71 B4
Methana GR 185 B4
Methlick GB 33 D4
Methven GB 35 B4
Methwold GB 41 C4
Metković HR 139 B3
Metlika SLO 123 B4
Metnitz D 110 C1
Metsäkylä FIN . . .197 D11
Metslawier NL 70 A3
Metsovo GR 182 D3
Metten D 95 C4
Mettendorf D 92 B2
Mettet B 79 B4
Mettingen D 71 B4
Mettlach D 92 B2
Mettlen CH 106 C2
Mettmann D 80 A2
Metz F 92 B2
Metzervisse F 92 B2
Metzingen D 94 C1
Meulan F 90 B1
Meung-sur-Loire
  F 103 B3
Meuselwitz D 83 A4
Meuzac F 115 C5
Mevagissey GB 42 B2

Mens F 118 C2
Menslage D 71 B4
Mensträsk S 200 A5
Mentana I 168 A2
Menton F 133 B3
Méntrida E 151 B3
Méobecq F 115 B5
Méounes-les-Montrieux
  F 132 B1
Meppel NL 70 B3
Meppen D 71 B4
Mequinenza E 153 A4
Mer F 103 B3

Mexborough GB 40 B2
Meximieux F 118 B2
Mey GB 32 C3
Meyenburg D 73 A5
Meyerhöfen D 71 B5
Meylan F 118 B2
Meymac F 116 B2
Meyrargues F 132 B1
Meyrueis F 130 A2
Meyssac F 129 A4
Meysse F 117 C4
Meyzieu F 117 B4
Mèze F 130 B2
Mézériat F 117 A5
Mežica SLO 110 C1
Mézidon-Canon F 89 A3
Mézières-en-Brenne F 115 B5
Mézières-sur-Issoire F 115 B4
Mézilhac F 117 C4
Mézilles F 104 B2
Mézin F 128 B3
Mezőberény H 113 C5
Mezőcsát H 113 B4
Mezőfalva H 112 C2
Mezőhegyes H 126 A2
Mezőkeresztes H 113 B4
Mezőkomárom H 112 C2
Mezőkövácsháza H 113 C4
Mezőkövesd H 113 B4
Mezőörs H 111 B4
Mézos F 128 B1
Mezőszilas H 112 C2
Mezőtúr H 113 B4
Mezquita de Jarque E 153 B3
Mezzano
Emilia Romagna I 135 A5
Trentino Alto Adige I 121 A4
Mezzojuso I 176 B2
Mezzoldo I 120 A2
Mezzolombardo I 121 A4
Mgarr M 175 C3
Miajadas E 156 A2
Miały PL 75 B5
Mianowice PL 68 A2
Miasteczko Krajeńskie PL 76 A2
Miasteczko Śl. PL 86 B2
Miastko PL 68 A1
Michalovce SK 12 D4
Michałowice PL 87 B3
Michelau D 94 B2
Michelbach D 94 B2
Micheldorf A 110 B1
Michelhausen A 110 A2
Michelsneukirchen D 95 B4
Michelstadt D 93 B5
Michendorf D 74 B2
Mickleover GB 40 C2
Midbea GB 33 B4
Middelburg NL 79 A3
Middelfart DK 59 C2
Middelharnis NL 79 A4
Middelkerke B 78 A2
Middelstum NL 71 A3
Middlesbrough GB 37 B5
Middleton Cheney GB 44 A2
Middleton-in-Teesdale GB 37 B4
Middletown GB 27 B4
Middlewich GB 38 A4
Middlezoy GB 43 A4
Midhurst GB 44 C3
Midleton IRL 29 C3
Midlum D 64 C1
Midsomer Norton GB 43 A4
Midtgulen N 198 D2
Midtskogberget N 49 A4
Midwolda NL 71 A4
Mid Yell GB 33 A5
Miechów PL 87 B4
Miedes de Aragón E 152 A2
Miedes de Atienza E 151 A4
Międzybodzie Bielskie PL 99 B3
Międzybórz PL 85 A5
Międzychód PL 75 B4
Międzylesie PL 85 B4
Międzyrzec Podlaski PL 12 C5
Międzyrzecz PL 75 B4
Międzywodzie PL 67 B3
Międzyzdroje PL 67 C3
Miejska Górka PL 85 A4
Miélan F 145 A4
Mielec PL 87 B5
Mielęcin PL 75 A3
Mielno
Warmińsko-Mazurskie PL 77 A5
Zachodnio-Pomorskie PL 67 B5
Miengo E 143 A3
Mieraslompolo FIN 193 C11
Miercurea Ciuc RO 17 B6
Mieres
Asturias E 141 A5
Girona E 147 B3
Mieroszów PL 85 B4
Mierzyn PL 86 A3
Miesau D 93 B3
Miesbach D 108 B2
Mieścisko PL 76 B2
Mieste D 73 B4
Miesterhorst D 73 B4
Mieszków PL 76 B2
Mieszkowice PL 74 B3
Mietków PL 85 B4
Migennes F 104 B2
Miggiano I 173 C4
Migliánico I 169 A4
Migliarino I 121 C4
Migliónico I 172 B2
Mignano Monte Lungo I 169 B3
Migné F 115 B5
Miguel Esteban E 157 A4
Miguelturra E 157 B4
Mihajlovac SRB 127 C2
Mihàld H 111 C4
Mihalgazi TR 187 B5
Mihalıççık TR 187 C6
Mihályi H 111 B4
Mihla D 82 A2
Mihohnić HR 123 B3
Miholjsko HR 123 B4
Mihovljan HR 124 A1
Mijares E 150 B3
Mijas E 163 B3
Mike H 124 A3
Mikines GR 184 B3
Mikkeli FIN 8 B5
Mikkelvik N 192 B3
Mikleuš HR 125 B3
Mikołajki Pomorskie PL 69 B4
Mikolów PL 86 B2
Mikonos GR 185 B6
Mikorzyn PL 86 A2
Mikro Derio GR 183 B8
Mikstat PL 86 A1
Mikulášovice CZ 84 B2
Mikulov CZ 97 C4
Mikulovice CZ 85 B5
Milagro E 144 B2
Miłakowo PL 69 A5
Milan = Milano I 120 B2
Miland N 47 C5
Milano = Milan I 120 B2
Milano Marittima I 135 A5
Milas TR 188 B2
Milazzo I 177 A4
Mildenhall GB 45 A4
Milejewo PL 69 A4
Milelín CZ 85 B3
Miletić SRB 125 B5
Miletićevo SRB 126 B3
Mileto I 175 C2
Milevsko CZ 96 B2
Milford IRL 26 A3
Milford Haven GB 39 C1
Milford on Sea GB 44 C2
Milhão P 149 A3
Milići BIH 139 A5
Miličin CZ 96 B2
Milicz PL 85 A5
Milín CZ 96 B2
Militello in Val di Catánia I 177 B3
Miljevina BIH 139 B4
Milkowice PL 85 A4
Millançay F 103 B3
Millares E 159 B3
Millas F 146 B3
Millau F 130 A2
Millesimo I 133 A4
Millevaches F 116 B2
Millom GB 36 B3
Millport GB 34 C3
Millstatt A 109 C4
Millstreet
Cork IRL 29 B2
Waterford IRL 29 B4
Milltown
Galway IRL 28 A3
Kerry IRL 29 B1
Milltown Malbay IRL 28 B2
Milly-la-Forêt F 90 C2
Milmarcos E 152 A2
Milmersdorf D 74 A2
Milna HR 138 B2
Milnthorpe GB 37 B4
Milogórze PL 69 A5
Miłomłyn PL 69 B4
Milos GR 185 C5
Miloševo SRB 127 C3
Miłosław PL 76 B2
Milot AL 182 B1
Milówka PL 99 B3
Miltach D 95 B4
Miltenberg D 94 B1
Milton Keynes GB 44 A3
Miltzow D 66 B2
Milverton GB 43 A3
Milzyn PL 76 B3
Mimice HR 138 B2
Mimizan F 128 B1
Mimizan-Plage F 128 B1
Mimoň CZ 84 B2
Mina de Juliana P 160 B1
Mina de São Domingos P 160 B2
Minas de Riotinto E 161 B3
Minateda E 158 C2
Minaya E 158 B1
Minde P 154 B2
Mindelheim D 108 A1
Mindelstetten D 95 C3
Minden D 72 B1
Mindszent H 113 C4
Minehead GB 43 A3
Mineo I 177 B3
Minerbe I 121 B4
Minérbio I 121 C4
Minervino Murge I 171 B4
Minglanilla E 158 B2
Mingorria E 150 B3
Minnesund N 48 B3
Miño E 140 A2
Miño de San Esteban E 151 A4
Minsen D 71 A4
Minsk BY 13 B7
Mińsk Mazowiecki PL 12 B4
Minsterley GB 39 B4
Mintlaw GB 33 D4
Minturno I 169 B3
Mionica
BIH 125 C4
SRB 127 C2
Mios F 128 B2
Mira
E 158 B2
I 121 B5
P 148 B1
Mirabel E 155 B4
Mirabel-aux-Baronnies F 131 A4
Mirabella Eclano I 170 B3
Mirabella Imbáccari I 177 B3
Mirabello I 121 C4
Miradoux F 129 B3
Miraflores de la Sierra E 151 B4
Miralrio E 151 B5
Miramar P 148 A1
Miramare I 136 A1
Miramas F 131 B3
Mirambeau F 114 C3
Miramont-de-Guyenne F 129 B3
Miranda de Arga E 144 B2
Miranda de Ebro E 143 B4
Miranda do Corvo P 148 B1
Miranda do Douro P 149 A3
Mirande F 129 C3
Mirandela P 149 A2
Mirandilla E 155 C4
Mirándola I 121 C4
Miranje HR 137 A4
Mirano I 121 B5
Miras AL 182 C2
Miravet E 153 A4
Miré F 102 B1
Mirebeau F 102 C2
Mirebeau-sur-Bèze F 105 B4
Mirecourt F 105 A5
Mirepoix F 146 A2
Mires GR 185 D5
Miribel F 117 B4
Miričina BIH 125 C4
Mirina GR 183 D7
Mirna SLO 123 B4
Miroslav CZ 97 C4
Mirosławice PL 85 B4
Mirosławiec PL 75 A5
Mirošov CZ 96 B1
Mirotice CZ 96 B2
Mirovice CZ 96 B2
Mirow D 74 A1
Mirsk PL 84 B3
Mirzec PL 87 A5
Misi FIN 197 C9
Misilmeri I 176 A2
Miske H 112 C3
Miskolc H 113 A4
Mislinja SLO 110 C2
Missanello I 174 A2
Missillac F 101 B3
Mistelbach
A 97 C4
D 95 B3
Misten N 194 C5
Misterbianco I 177 B4
Misterhult S 62 A4
Mistretta I 177 B3
Misurina I 109 C3
Mitchelstown IRL 29 B3
Mithimna GR 186 C1
Mithoni GR 184 C2
Mitilini GR 186 C1
Mitilinii GR 188 B1
Mittelberg
Tirol A 108 C1
Vorarlberg A 107 B5
Mittenwald D 108 B2
Mittenwalde D 74 B2
Mitterback A 110 B2
Mitterdorf im Mürztal A 110 B2
Mitter-Kleinarl A 109 B4
Mittersheim F 92 C2
Mittersill A 109 B3
Mitterskirchen D 95 C4
Mitterteich D 95 B4
Mitton F 128 B2
Mittweida D 83 B4
Mitwitz D 82 B3
Mizhhir'ya UA 13 D5
Mjällby S 63 B2
Mjåvatn N 53 B4
Mjöbäck S 60 B2
Mjölby S 56 B1
Mjølfjell N 46 B3
Mjøndalen N 53 A6
Mjørlund N 48 B2
Mladá Boleslav CZ 84 B2
Mladá Vožice CZ 96 B2
Mladé Buky CZ 85 B3
Mladenovac SRB 127 C2
Mladenovo SRB 126 B1
Mladikovine BIH 139 A3
Mława PL 77 A5
Mlinište BIH 138 A2
Młodzieszyn PL 77 B5
Młogoszyn PL 77 B4
Młynary PL 69 A4
Mnichóvice CZ 96 B2
Mnichovo Hradiště CZ 84 B2
Mniów PL 87 A4
Mnisek nad Hnilcom SK 99 C4
Mníšek pod Brdy CZ 96 B2
Mniszek PL 87 A4
Mniszków PL 87 A4
Mo
Hedmark N 48 B3
Hordaland N 46 B2
Mo *continued*
Møre og Romsdal N 198 C5
Telemark N 53 A3
Gävleborg S 51 A3
Västra Götaland S 54 B2
Moaña E 140 B2
Moate IRL 28 A4
Mocejón E 151 C4
Močenok SK 111 A4
Mochales E 152 A1
Mochowo PL 77 B4
Mochy PL 75 B5
Mockern D 73 B4
Mockfjärd S 50 B1
Möckmühl D 94 B1
Mockrehna D 83 A4
Moclin E 163 A4
Mocsa H 112 B2
Möcsény H 125 A4
Modane F 118 B3
Modbury GB 42 B3
Módena I 121 C3
Módica I 177 C3
Modigliana I 135 A4
Modlin PL 77 B5
Mödling A 111 A3
Modliszewice PL 87 A4
Modliszewko PL 76 B2
Modogno I 171 B4
Modra SK 98 C1
Modran BIH 125 C3
Modriča BIH 125 C4
Möðrudalur IS 191 B10
Modrý Kamen SK 99 C3
Moëlan-sur-Mer F 100 B2
Moelfre GB 38 A2
Moelv N 48 B2
Moen N 194 A9
Moena I 121 A4
Moerbeke B 79 A3
Moers D 80 A2
Móes P 148 B2
Moffat GB 36 A3
Mogadouro P 149 A3
Mogata S 56 B2
Móggio Udinese I 122 A2
Mogielnica PL 87 A4
Mogilany PL 99 B3
Mogilno PL 76 B2
Mogliano I 136 B2
Mogliano Véneto I 122 B1
Mogor E 140 B2
Mógoro I 179 C2
Moguer E 161 B3
Mohács H 125 B4
Moheda S 62 A2
Mohedas E 149 B3
Mohedas de la Jara E 156 A2
Mohelnice CZ 97 B4
Mohill IRL 26 C3
Möhlin CH 106 B2
Moholm S 55 B5
Mohorn D 83 A5
Mohyliv-Podil's'kyy UA 13 D7
Moi N 52 B2
Moià E 147 C3
Móie I 136 B2
Moimenta da Beira P 148 B2
Mo i Rana N 195 D5
Moirans F 118 B2
Moirans-en-Montagne F 118 A2
Moisaküla EST 8 C4
Moisdon-la-Rivière F 101 B4
Moissac F 129 B4
Moita
Coimbra P 148 B1
Guarda P 149 B2
Santarém P 154 B2
Setúbal P 154 C1
Moita dos Ferreiros P 154 B1
Moixent E 159 C3
Mojacar E 164 B3
Mojados E 150 A3
Mojmírovce SK 112 A2
Mojtin SK 98 C2
Möklinta S 50 B3
Mokošica HR 139 C4
Mokronog SLO 123 A4
Mokro Polje HR 138 A2
Mokrzyska PL 99 A4
Møkster N 46 B2
Mol
B 79 A5
SRB 126 B2
Mola di Bari I 173 A3
Molai GR 184 C3
Molare I 133 A4
Molaretto I 119 B4
Molas F 145 A4
Molassano I 134 A1
Molbergen D 71 B4
Mold GB 38 A3
Molde N 198 C4
Møldrup DK 58 B2
Moledo do Minho P 148 A1
Molfetta I 171 B4
Molfsee D 64 B3
Moliden S 200 C4
Molières F 129 B4
Molina de Aragón E 152 B2
Molina de Segura E 165 A3
Molinar E 143 A3
Molinaseca E 141 B4
Molinella I 121 C4
Molinet F 104 C2
Molinicos E 158 C1
Molini di Tures I 108 C2
Molinos de Duero E 143 C4
Molins de Rei E 147 C3
Moliterno I 174 A1
Molkom S 55 A4
Möllbrücke A 109 C4
Mölle S 61 C2
Molledo E 142 A2
Möllenbeck D 74 A2
Mollerussa E 147 C1
Mollet de Perelada E 146 B3
Mollina E 163 A3
Mölln D 73 A3
Molló E 146 B3
Mollösund S 54 B2
Mölltorp S 55 B5
Mölnbo S 56 A3
Mölndal S 60 B2
Mölnlycke S 60 B2
Molompize F 116 B3
Moloy F 105 B3
Molsheim F 93 C3
Moltzow D 73 A5
Molve HR 124 A3
Molveno I 121 A3
Molvizar E 163 B4
Molzbichl A 109 C4
Mombaróccio I 136 B1
Mombeltrán E 150 B2
Mombris D 93 A5
Mombuey E 141 B4
Momchilgrad BG 183 B7
Mommark DK 64 B3
Momo I 119 B5
Monaghan IRL 27 B4
Monar Lodge GB 32 D2
Monasterace Marina I 175 C2
Monasterevin IRL 30 A1
Monasterio de Rodilla E 143 B3
Monastir I 179 C3
Monbahus F 129 B3
Monbazillac F 129 B3
Moncada E 159 B3
Moncalieri I 119 B4
Moncalvo I 119 B5
Monção P 140 B2
Moncarapacho P 160 B2
Moncel-sur-Seille F 92 C2
Monchegorsk RUS 3 C13
Mönchengladbach = Munchen-Gladbach D 80 A2
Mónchio della Corti I 134 A3
Monchique P 160 B1
Monclar-de-Quercy F 129 C4
Moncofa E 159 B3
Moncontour F 101 A3
Moncoutant F 114 B3
Monda E 162 B3
Mondariz E 140 B2
Mondavio I 136 B1
Mondéjar E 151 B4
Mondello I 176 A2
Mondim de Basto P 148 A2
Mondolfo I 136 B2
Mondoñedo E 141 A3
Mondorf-les-Bains L 92 B2
Mondoubleau F 102 B2
Mondovì I 133 A3
Mondragon F 131 A3
Mondragone I 170 B1
Mondsee A 109 B4
Monéglia I 134 A2
Monegrillo E 153 A3
Monein F 145 A3
Monemvasia GR 184 C4
Mónesi I 133 A3
Monesiglio I 133 A4
Monesterio E 161 A3
Monestier-de-Clermont F 118 C2
Monestiés F 130 A1
Monéteau F 104 B2
Moneygall IRL 28 B4
Moneymore GB 27 B4
Monfalcone I 122 B2
Monfero E 140 A2
Monflanquin F 129 B3
Monflorite E 145 B3
Monforte P 155 B3
Monforte da Beira
E 155 B3
P 155 B3
Monforte d'Alba I 133 A3
Monforte del Cid E 165 A4
Monforte de Lemos E 140 B3
Monforte de Moyuela E 152 A2
Monghidoro I 135 A4
Mongiana I 175 C2
Monguelfo I 108 C3
Monheim D 94 C2
Moniaive GB 36 A3
Monifieth GB 35 B5
Monikie GB 35 B5
Monistrol-d'Allier F 117 C3
Monistrol de Montserrat E 147 C2
Monistrol-sur-Loire F 117 B4
Mönkebude D 74 A2
Monkton GB 36 A2
Monmouth GB 39 C4
Monnaie F 102 B2
Monnerville F 90 C2
Monnickendam NL 70 B2
Monolithos GR 188 C2
Monópoli I 173 B3
Monor H 112 B3
Monóvar E 159 C3
Monpazier F 129 B3
Monreal
D 80 B3
E 144 B2
Monreal del Campo E 152 B2
Monreale I 176 A2
Monroy E 155 B4
Monroyo E 153 B3
Mons B 79 B3
Monsaraz P 155 C3
Monschau D 80 B2
Monségur F 128 B3
Monsélice I 121 B4
Mønshaug N 46 B3
Monster NL 70 B1
Mönsterås S 62 A4
Monsummano Terme I 135 B3
Montabaur D 81 B3
Montafia I 119 C5
Montagnac F 130 B2
Montagnana I 121 B4
Montaigu F 114 B2
Montaigu-de-Quercy F 129 B4
Montaiguët-en-Forez F 117 A3
Montaigut F 116 A2
Montaigut-sur-Save F 129 C4
Montainville F 90 C1
Montalbán E 153 B3
Montalbán de Córdoba E 163 A3
Montalbano Elicona I 177 A4
Montalbano Iónico I 174 A2
Montalbo E 158 B1
Montalcino I 135 B4
Montaldo di Cósola I 120 C2
Montalegre P 148 A2
Montalieu-Vercieu F 118 B2
Montalivet-les-Bains F 114 C2
Montallegro I 176 B2
Montalto delle Marche I 136 C2
Montalto di Castro I 168 A1
Montalto Pavese I 120 C2
Montalto Uffugo I 174 B2
Montalvão P 155 B3
Montamarta E 149 A4
Montana BG 17 D5
Montana-Vermala CH 119 A4
Montánchez E 156 A1
Montanejos E 153 B3
Montano Antilia I 172 B1
Montans F 129 C4
Montargil P 154 B2
Montargis F 103 B4
Montastruc-la-Conseillère F 129 C4
Montauban F 129 B4
Montauban-de-Bretagne F 101 A3
Montbard F 104 B3
Montbarrey F 105 B4
Montbazens F 130 A1
Montbazon F 102 B2
Montbéliard F 106 B1
Montbenoit F 105 C5
Montbeugny F 104 C2
Montblanc E 147 C2
Montbozon F 105 B5
Montbrison F 117 B4
Montbron F 115 C4
Montbrun-les-Bains F 131 A4
Montceau-les-Mines F 104 C3
Montcenis F 104 C3
Montchanin F 104 C3
Montcornet F 91 B4
Montcuq F 129 B4
Montdardier F 130 B2
Mont-de-Marsan F 128 C2
Montdidier F 90 B2
Monteagudo E 165 A3
Monteagudo de las Vicarias E 152 A1
Montealegre E 142 C2
Montealegre del Castillo E 159 C2
Montebello Iónico I 175 D1
Montebello Vicentino I 121 B4
Montebelluna I 121 B5
Montebourg F 88 A2
Montebruno I 134 A2
Monte-Carlo MC 133 B3
Montecarotto I 136 B2
Montecassiano I 136 B2
Montecastrilli I 168 A2
Montecatini Terme I 135 B3
Montécchio I 136 B1
Montécchio Emilia I 121 C3
Montécchio Maggiore I 121 B4
Montech F 129 C4
Montechiaro d'Asti I 119 B5
Monte Clara P 155 B3
Monte Clérigo P 160 B1
Montecórice I 170 C2
Montecorvino Rovella I 170 C2
Monte da Pedra P 155 B3
Monte de Goula P 155 B3
Montederramo E 141 B3
Montedoro I 176 B2
Monte do Trigo P 155 C3
Montefalco I 136 C1
Montefalcone di Val Fortore I 170 B3
Montefalcone nel Sánnio I 170 B2
Montefano I 136 B2
Montefiascone I 168 A2
Montefiorino I 134 A3
Montefortino I 136 C2
Montefranco I 168 A2
Montefrío E 163 A4
Montegiordano Marina I 174 A2
Montegiórgio I 136 B2
Monte Gordo P 160 B2
Montegranaro I 136 B2
Montehermoso E 149 B3
Montejicar E 163 A4
Montejo de la Sierra E 151 A4
Montejo de Tiermes E 151 A4
Monte Juntos P 155 C3
Montel-de-Gelat F 116 B2
Monteleone di Púglia I 171 B3
Monteleone di Spoleto I 169 A2
Monteleone d'Orvieto I 135 C5
Montelepre I 176 A2
Montelibretti I 168 A2
Montelier F 117 C5
Montélimar F 131 A3
Montella
E 146 B2
I 170 C3
Montellano E 162 A2
Montelupo Fiorentino I 135 B4
Montemaggiore Belsito I 176 B2
Montemagno I 119 C5
Montemayor E 163 A3
Montemayor de Pinilla E 150 A3
Montemésola I 173 B3
Montemilleto I 170 B2
Montemilone I 172 A1
Montemolin E 161 A3
Montemónaco I 136 C2
Montemor-o-Novo P 154 C2
Montemor-o-Velho P 148 B1
Montemurro I 174 A1
Montendre F 128 A2
Montenegro de Cameros E 143 B4
Montenero di Bisáccia I 170 B2
Monteneuf F 101 B3
Monteparano I 173 B3
Montepescali I 135 C4
Montepiano I 135 A4
Monte Porzio I 136 B2
Montepulciano I 135 B4
Monte Real P 154 B2
Montereale I 169 A3
Montereale Valcellina I 122 A1
Montereau-Faut-Yonne F 90 C2
Monte Redondo P 154 B2
Monterénzio I 135 A4
Monte Romano I 168 A1
Monteroni d'Arbia I 135 B4
Monteroni di Lecce I 173 B4
Monterosso al Mare I 134 A2
Monterosso Almo I 177 B3
Monterosso Grana I 133 A3
Monterotondo I 168 A2
Monterotondo Maríttimo I 135 B3
Monterrey E 141 C3
Monterroso E 140 B3
Monterrubio de la Serena E 156 B2
Monterubbiano I 136 B2
Montesa E 159 C3
Montesalgueiro E 140 A2
Monte San Giovanni Campano I 169 B3
Montesano sulla Marcellana I 174 A1
Monte San Savino I 135 B4
Monte Sant'Angelo I 171 B3
Montesárchio I 170 B2
Montescaglioso I 171 C4
Montesclaros E 150 B3
Montesilvano I 169 A4
Montespértoli I 135 B4
Montesquieu-Volvestre F 146 A2
Montesquiou F 129 C3
Montestruc-sur-Gers F 129 C3
Montes Velhos P 160 B1
Montevarchi I 135 B4
Montéveglio I 135 A4
Monte Vilar P 154 B1
Montfaucon F 101 B4
Montfaucon-d'Argonne F 91 B5
Montfaucon-en-Velay F 117 B4
Montferrat
Isère F 118 B2
Var F 132 B2
Montfort-en-Chalosse F 128 C2

Montfort-l'Amaury F 90 C1
Montfort-le-Gesnois F 102 A2
Montfort-sur-Meu F 101 A4
Montfort-sur-Risle F 89 A4
Montgai E 147 C1
Montgaillard F 145 A4
Montgenèvre F 118 C3
Montgiscard F 146 A2
Montgomery GB 39 B3
Montguyon F 128 A2
Monthermé F 91 B4
Monthey CH 119 A3
Monthois F 91 B4
Monthureux-sur-Saône F 105 A4
Monti I 178 B3
Monticelli d'Ongina I 120 B2
Montichiari I 120 B3
Monticiano I 135 B4
Montiel E 158 C1
Montier-en-Der F 91 C4
Montieri I 135 B4
Montiglio I 119 B5
Montignac F 129 A4
Montigny-le-Roi F 105 B4
Montigny-lès-Metz F 92 B2
Montigny-sur-Aube F 105 B3
Montijo
E 155 C4
P 154 C2
Montilla E 163 A3
Montillana E 163 A4
Montilly F 104 C2
Montivilliers F 89 A4
Montjaux F 130 A1
Montjean-sur-Loire F 102 B1
Montlhéry F 90 C2
Montlieu-la-Garde F 128 A2
Mont-Louis F 146 B3
Montlouis-sur-Loire F 102 B2
Montluçon F 116 A2
Montluel F 117 B5
Montmarault F 116 A2
Montmartin-sur-Mer F 88 B2
Montmédy F 92 B1
Montmélian F 118 B3
Montmeyan F 132 B2
Montmeyran F 117 C4
Montmirail
Marne F 91 C3
Sarthe F 102 A2
Montmiral F 118 B2
Montmirat F 131 B3
Montmirey-le-Château F 105 B4
Montmoreau-St Cybard F 115 C4
Montmorency F 90 C2
Montmorillon F 115 B4
Montmort-Lucy F 91 C3
Montoir-de-Bretagne F 101 B3
Montoire-sur-le-Loir F 102 B2
Montoito P 155 C3
Montolieu F 146 A3
Montório al Vomano I 169 A3
Montoro E 157 B3
Montpellier F 131 B2
Montpezat-de-Quercy F 129 B4
Montpezat-sous-Bouzon F 117 C4
Montpon-Ménestérol F 128 A3
Montpont-en-Bresse F 105 C4
Montréal
Aude F 146 A3
Gers F 128 C3
Montredon-Labessonnié F 130 B1
Montréjeau F 145 A4
Montrésor F 103 B3
Montresta I 178 B2
Montret F 105 C4
Montreuil
Pas de Calais F 78 B1
Seine St Denis F 90 C2
Montreuil-aux-Lions F 90 B3
Montreuil-Bellay F 102 B1
Montreux CH 106 C1
Montrevault F 101 B4
Montrevel-en-Bresse F 118 A2
Montrichard F 103 B3
Montricoux F 129 B4
Mont-roig del Camp E 147 C1
Montrond-les-Bains F 117 B4
Montrose GB 35 B5
Montroy E 159 B3
Montsalvy F 116 C2
Montsauche-les-Settons F 104 B3
Montseny E 147 C3
Montsoreau F 102 B2
Mont-sous-Vaudrey F 105 C4
Monts-sur-Guesnes F 102 C2
Mont-St Aignan F 89 A5
Mont-St Vincent F 104 C3
Montsûrs F 102 A1
Montuenga E 150 A3
Montuïri E 167 B3
Monturque E 163 A3
Monza I 120 B2
Monzón E 145 C4
Monzón de Campos E 142 B2
Moorbad Lobenstein D 83 B3
Moordorf D 71 A4
Moorslede B 78 B3
Moos D 107 B3
Moosburg D 95 C3
Moosburg im Kärnten A 110 C1
Mór H 112 B2
Mora E 157 A4
Móra P 154 C2
Mora S 50 A1
Moraby S 50 B2
Mòra d'Ebre E 153 A4
Mora de Rubielos E 153 B3
Moradillo de Roa E 151 A4
Morąg PL 69 B4
Mórahalom H 126 A1
Moraime E 140 A1
Morais P 149 A3
Mòra la Nova E 153 A4
Moral de Calatrava E 157 B4
Moraleda de Zafayona E 163 A4
Moraleja E 149 B3
Moraleja del Vino E 150 A2
Morales del Vino E 150 A2
Morales de Toro E 150 A2
Morales de Valverde E 141 C5
Moralina E 149 A3
Morano Cálabro I 174 B2
Mörarp S 61 C2
Morasverdes E 149 B3
Morata de Jalón E 152 A2
Morata de Jiloca E 152 A2
Morata de Tajuña E 151 B4
Moratalla E 164 A3
Moravče SLO 123 A3
Moravec CZ 97 B4
Moraviţa RO 126 B3
Morávka CZ 98 B2
Moravská Třebová CZ 97 B4
Moravské Budějovice CZ 97 B3
Moravské Lieskové SK 98 C1
Moravske Toplice SLO 111 C3
Moravský-Beroun CZ 98 B1
Moravský Krumlov CZ 97 B4
Moravský Svätý Ján SK 98 C1
Morawica PL 87 B4
Morawin PL 86 A2
Morbach D 92 B3
Morbegno I 120 A2
Morbier F 105 C5
Mörbisch am See A 111 B3
Mörbylånga S 63 B4
Morcenx F 128 B2
Morciano di Romagna I 136 B1
Morcone I 170 B2
Morcuera E 151 A4
Mordelles F 101 A4
Mordoğan TR 188 A1
Moréac F 100 B3
Morebattle GB 35 C5
Morecambe GB 36 B4
Moreda
Granada E 163 A4
Oviedo E 142 A1
Morée F 103 B3
Moreles de Rey E 141 B5
Morella E 153 B3
Moreruela de los Infanzones E 149 A4
Morés E 152 A2
Móres I 178 B2
Morestel F 118 B2
Moretonhampstead GB 43 B3
Moreton-in-Marsh GB 44 B2
Moret-sur-Loing F 90 C2
Moretta I 119 C4
Moreuil F 90 B2
Morez F 105 C5
Mörfelden D 93 B4
Morgat F 100 A1
Morges CH 105 C5
Morgex I 119 B4
Morgongåva S 51 C3
Morhange F 92 C2
Morhet B 92 B1
Mori I 121 B3
Morialmé B 79 B4
Morianes P 160 B2
Moriani Plage F 180 A2
Mórichida H 111 B4
Moriles E 163 A3
Morille E 150 B2
Moringen D 82 A1
Morjärv S 196 C5
Morkarla S 51 B4
Mørke DK 59 B3
Mørkøv DK 61 D1
Morkovice-Slížany CZ 98 B1
Morlaàs F 145 A3
Morlaix F 100 A2
Morley F 91 C5
Mörlunda S 62 A3
Mormanno I 174 B1
Mormant F 90 C2
Mornant F 117 B4
Mornay-Berry F 103 B4
Morón de Almazán E 152 A1
Morón de la Frontera E 162 A2
Morović SRB 125 B5
Morozzo I 133 A3
Morpeth GB 37 A5
Morphou CY 181 A1
Mörrum S 63 B2
Morsbach D 81 B3
Mörsch D 93 C4
Mörsil S 199 B10
Morsum D 64 B1
Mørsvikbotn N 194 C6
Mortagne-au-Perche F 89 B4
Mortagne-sur-Gironde F 114 C3
Mortagne-sur-Sèvre F 114 B3
Mortágua P 148 B1
Mortain F 88 B3
Mortara I 120 B1
Morteau F 105 B5
Mortegliano I 122 B2
Mortelle I 177 A4
Mortemart F 115 B4
Mortimer's Cross GB 39 B4
Mortrée F 89 B4
Mörtschach A 109 C3
Mortsel B 79 A4
Morud DK 59 C3
Morwenstow GB 42 B2
Moryń PL 74 B3
Morzeszczyn PL 69 B3
Morzewo PL 69 B4
Morzine F 118 A3
Mosbach D 93 B5
Mosbjerg DK 58 A3
Mosby N 53 B3
Mosca P 149 A3
Moscavide P 154 C1
Moščenica HR 124 B2
Mošćenice HR 123 B3
Moščenicka Draga HR 123 B3
Mosciano Sant'Ángelo I 136 C2
Mościsko PL 85 B4
Moscow = Moskva RUS 9 E10
Mosina PL 75 B5
Mosjøen N 195 E4
Moskog N 46 A3
Moskorzew PL 87 B3
Moskosel S 196 D2
Moskuvarra FIN 197 B9
Moskva = Moscow RUS 9 E10
Moslavina Podravska HR 125 B3
Moşniţa Nouă RO 126 B3
Moso in Passiria I 108 C2
Mosonmagyaróvár H 111 B4
Mošorin SRB 126 B2
Mošovce SK 98 C2
Mosqueruela E 153 B3
Moss N 54 A1
Mossfellsbær IS 190 C4
Mössingen D 93 C5
Møsstrand N 47 C5
Most CZ 83 B5
Mosta M 175 C3
Mostar BIH 139 B3
Mosterhamn N 52 A1
Mostki PL 75 B4
Most na Soči SLO 122 A2
Móstoles E 151 B4
Mostová SK 111 A4
Mostowo PL 68 A1
Mostuéjouls F 130 A2
Mosty PL 75 A3
Mostys'ka UA 13 D5
Mosvik N 199 B7
Mota del Cuervo E 158 B1
Mota del Marqués E 150 A2
Motala S 55 B6
Motherwell GB 35 C4
Möthlow D 74 B1
Motilla del Palancar E 158 B2
Motnik SLO 123 A3
Motovun HR 122 B2
Motril E 163 B4
Motta I 121 B4
Motta di Livenza I 122 B1
Motta Montecorvino I 170 B3
Motta Visconti I 120 B1
Mottisfont GB 44 B2
Móttola I 173 B3
Mou DK 58 B3
Mouchard F 105 C4
Moudon CH 106 C1
Moudros GR 183 D7
Mougins F 132 B2
Mouilleron en-Pareds F 114 B3
Mouliherne F 102 B2
Moulinet F 133 B3
Moulins F 104 C2
Moulins-Engilbert F 104 C2
Moulins-la-Marche F 89 B4
Moulismes F 115 B4
Moult F 89 A3
Mountain Ash GB 39 C3
Mount Bellew Bridge IRL 28 A3
Mountfield GB 27 B3
Mountmellick IRL 30 A1
Mountrath IRL 30 A1
Mountsorrel GB 40 C2
Moura P 160 A2
Mourão P 155 C3
Mourenx F 145 A3
Mouriés F 131 B3
Mourmelon-le-Grand F 91 B4
Mouronho P 148 B1
Mourujärvi FIN 197 C11
Mouscron B 78 B3
Mousehole GB 42 B1
Moussac F 131 B3
Moussey F 92 C2
Mousteru F 100 A2
Moustey F 128 B2
Moustiers-Ste Marie F 132 B2
Mouthe F 105 C5
Mouthier-Haute-Pierre F 105 B5
Mouthoumet F 146 B3
Moutier CH 106 B2
Moûtiers F 118 B3
Moutiers-les-Mauxfaits F 114 B2
Mouy F 90 B2
Mouzaki GR 182 D3
Mouzon F 91 B5
Møvik N 46 B2
Moville IRL 27 A3
Moy
Highland GB 32 D2
Tyrone GB 27 B4
Moycullen IRL 28 A2
Moyenmoutier F 92 C2
Moyenvic F 92 C2
Mózar E 141 C5
Mozhaysk RUS 9 E10
Mozirje SLO 123 A3
Mözs H 112 C2
Mozzanica I 120 B2
Mramorak SRB 127 C2
Mrčajevci SRB 127 D2
Mrkonjić Grad BIH 138 A3
Mrkopalj HR 123 B3
Mrocza PL 76 A2
Mroczeń PL 86 A1
Mroczno PL 69 B4
Mrzezyno PL 67 B4
Mšec CZ 84 B1
Mšeno CZ 84 B2
Mstów PL 86 B3
Mstsislaw BY 13 A9
Mszana Dolna PL 99 B4
Mszczonów PL 77 C5
Muć HR 138 B2
Múccia I 136 B2
Much D 80 B3
Mücheln D 83 A3
Much Marcle GB 39 C4
Muchów PL 85 A4
Much Wenlock GB 39 B4
Mucientes E 142 C2
Muckross IRL 29 B2
Mucur TR 23 B8
Muda P 160 B1
Mudanya TR 186 B3
Mudau D 93 B5
Müden D 72 B3
Mudersbach D 81 B3
Mudurnu TR 187 B6
Muel E 152 A2
Muelas del Pan E 149 A4
Muess D 73 A4
Muff IRL 27 A3
Mugardos E 140 A2
Muge P 154 B2
Mügeln
Sachsen D 83 A5
Sachsen-Anhalt D 83 A5
Múggia I 122 B2
Mugnano I 135 B5
Mugron F 128 C2
Mugueimes E 140 C3
Muhi H 113 B4
Mühlacker D 93 C4
Mühlbach am Hochkönig A 109 B4
Mühlberg
Brandenburg D 83 A5
Thüringen D 82 B2
Mühldorf
A 109 C4
D 95 C4
Muhleberg CH 106 C2
Mühleim D 107 A3
Muhlen-Eichsen D 65 C4
Mühlhausen
Bayern D 94 B2
Thüringen D 82 A2
Mühltroff D 83 B3
Muhos FIN 3 D10
Muhr A 109 B4
Muine Bheag IRL 30 B2
Muirkirk GB 36 A2
Muir of Ord GB 32 D2
Muirteira P 154 B1
Mukacheve UA 12 D5
Muker GB 37 B4
Mula E 165 A3
Muğla TR 188 B3
Mulben GB 32 D3
Mulegns CH 107 C4
Mules I 108 C2
Mülheim D 80 A2
Mulhouse F 106 B2
Muljava SLO 123 B3
Mullanys Cross IRL 26 B2
Müllheim D 106 B2
Mullhyttan S 55 A5
Mullinavat IRL 30 B1
Mullingar IRL 30 A1
Mullion GB 42 B1
Müllrose D 74 B3
Mullsjö S 60 B3
Mulseryd S 60 B3
Munaðarnes IS 190 A4
Munana E 150 B2
Muñás E 141 A4
Münchberg D 83 B3
Müncheberg D 74 B3
München = Munich D 108 A2
Munchen-Gladbach = Mönchengladbach D 80 A2
Münchhausen D 81 B4
Mundaka E 143 A4
Münden D 82 A1
Munderfing A 109 A4
Munderkingen D 107 A4
Mundesley GB 41 C5
Munera E 158 B1
Mungia E 143 A4
Munich = München D 108 A2
Muñico E 150 B2
Muniesa E 153 A3
Munka-Ljungby S 61 C2
Munkebo DK 59 C3
Munkedal S 54 B2
Munkflohögen S 199 B11
Munkfors S 49 C5
Munktorp S 56 A2
Münnerstadt D 82 B2
Muñopepe E 150 B3
Muñotello E 150 B2
Münsingen
CH 106 C2
D 94 C1
Munsö S 57 A3
Münster
CH 106 C3
Hessen D 93 B4
Munster D 72 B3
Münster D 71 C4
Munster F 106 A2
Muntibar E 143 A4
Münzkirchen A 96 C1
Muodoslompolo S 196 B6
Muonio FIN 196 B6
Muotathal CH 107 C3
Muradiye TR 186 D2
Murakeresztúr H 124 A2
Murán SK 99 C4
Murano I 122 B1
Muras E 140 A3
Murat F 116 B2
Muratlı TR 186 A2
Murato F 180 A2
Murat-sur-Vèbre F 130 B1
Murau A 109 B5
Muravera I 179 C3
Murazzano I 133 A4
Murça P 148 A2
Murchante E 144 B2
Murchin D 66 C2
Murcia E 165 B3
Murczyn PL 76 B2
Mur-de-Barrez F 116 C2
Mur-de-Bretagne F 100 A2
Mur-de-Sologne F 103 B3
Mureck A 110 C2
Mürefte TR 186 B2
Muret F 146 A2
Murg CH 107 B4
Murguia E 143 B4
Muri CH 106 B3
Murias de Paredes E 141 B4
Muriedas E 143 A3
Muriel Viejo E 143 C4
Murillo de Rio Leza E 143 B4
Murillo el Fruto E 144 B2
Murjek S 196 C3
Murlaggan GB 34 B2
Murmansk RUS 3 B13
Murmashi RUS 3 B13
Murnau D 108 B2
Muro
E 167 B3
F 180 A1
Muro de Alcoy E 159 C3
Murol F 116 B2
Muro Lucano I 172 B1
Muron F 114 B3
Muros E 140 B1
Muros de Nalón E 141 A4
Murowana Goślina PL 76 B2
Mürren CH 106 C2
Murrhardt D 94 C1
Murska Sobota SLO 111 C3
Mursko Središće HR 111 C3
Murtas E 164 C1
Murten CH 106 C2
Murter HR 137 B4
Murtiçi TR 189 C6
Murtosa P 148 B1
Murtovaara FIN 197 D12
Murvica HR 137 A4
Murviel-lès-Béziers F 130 B2
Mürzsteg A 110 B2
Murzynowo PL 75 B4
Mürzzuschlag A 110 B2
Musculdy F 144 A3
Muskö S 57 A4
Mušov CZ 97 C4
Musselburgh GB 35 C4
Musselkanaal NL 71 B4
Mussidan F 129 A3
Mussomeli I 176 B2
Musson B 92 B1
Mussy-sur-Seine F 104 B3
Mustafakemalpaşa TR 186 B3
Muszaki PL 77 A5
Muszyna PL 99 B4
Mut TR 23 C7
Muta SLO 110 C2
Muthill GB 35 B4
Mutné SK 99 B3
Mutriku E 143 A4
Muttalip TR 187 C5
Mutterbergalm A 108 B2
Muurola FIN 197 C8
Muxía E 140 A1
Muxilka-Ugarte E 143 A4
Muzillac F 101 B3
Mužla SK 112 B2
Muzzano del Turgnano I 122 B2
Mybster GB 32 C3
Myckelgensjö S 200 C3
Myennes F 104 B1
Myjava SK 98 C1
Myking N 46 B2
Mykland N 53 B4
Myra N 53 B5
Myrdal N 46 B4
Myre
Nordland N 194 A6
Nordland N 194 B6
Myresjö S 62 A2
Mýri IS 191 B8
Myrtou CY 181 A2
Mysen N 54 A2
Mysłakowice PL 85 B3
Myślenice PL 99 B3
Myślibórz PL 75 B3
Mysłowice PL 86 B3
Myszków PL 86 B3
Mytishchi RUS 9 E10
Mýtna SK 99 C3
Mýtne Ludany SK 112 A2
Mýto CZ 96 B1

N

Nå N 46 B3
Naaldwijk NL 79 A4
Naantali FIN 8 B2
Naas IRL 30 A2
Nabais P 148 B2
Nabbelund S 62 A5
Nabburg D 95 B4
Načeradec CZ 96 B2
Náchod CZ 85 B4
Nacław PL 68 A1
Nadarzyce PL 75 A5
Nadarzyn PL 77 B5
Nádasd H 111 C3
Nădlac RO 126 A2
Nádudvar H 113 B5
Nadvirna UA 13 D6
Näfels CH 107 B4
Nafpaktos GR 184 A2
Nafplio GR 184 B3
Nagel D 95 B3
Nagele NL 70 B2
Naggen S 200 D2
Nagłowice PL 87 B4
Nagold D 93 C4
Nagore E 144 B2
Nagyatád H 124 A3
Nagybajom H 124 A3
Nagybaracska H 125 A4
Nagybátony H 113 B3
Nagyberény H 112 C2
Nagybörzsöny H 112 B2
Nagycenk H 111 B3
Nagycserkesz H 113 B5
Nagydorog H 112 C2
Nagyfüged H 113 B4
Nagyhersány H 125 B4
Nagyigmánd H 112 B2
Nagyiván H 113 B4
Nagykanizsa H 111 C3
Nagykáta H 113 B3
Nagykonyi H 112 C2
Nagykörös H 113 B3
Nagykörü H 113 B4
Nagylóc H 112 A3
Nagymágocs H 113 C4
Nagymányok H 125 A4
Nagymaros H 112 B2
Nagyoroszi H 112 A3
Nagyrábé H 113 B5
Nagyréde H 113 B3
Nagyszékely H 112 C2
Nagyszénás H 113 C4
Nagyszokoly H 112 C2
Nagytöke H 113 C4
Nagyvázsony H 111 C4
Nagyvenyim H 112 C2
Naharros E 152 B1
Nahe D 64 C3
Naila D 83 B3
Nailloux F 146 A2
Nailsworth GB 43 A4
Naintré F 115 B4
Nairn GB 32 D3
Najac F 129 B4
Nájera E 143 B4
Nak H 112 C2
Nakksjø N 53 A5
Nakło nad Notecią PL 76 A2
Nakskov DK 65 B4
Nalda E 143 B4
Nälden S 199 B11
Nálepkovo SK 99 C4
Nalliers F 114 B2
Nallıhan TR 187 B6
Nalzen F 146 B2
Nalžouské Hory CZ 96 B1
Namdalseid N 199 A8
Náměšť nad Oslavou CZ 97 B4
Námestovo SK 99 B3
Namnå N 49 B4
Namsos N 199 A8
Namsskogan N 199 A10
Namur B 79 B4
Namysłów PL 86 A1
Nançay F 103 B4
Nanclares de la Oca E 143 B4
Nancy F 92 C2
Nangis F 90 C3
Nannestad N 48 B3
Nant F 130 A2
Nanterre F 90 C2
Nantes F 101 B4
Nanteuil-le-Haudouin F 90 B2
Nantiat F 115 B5
Nantua F 118 A2
Nantwich GB 38 A4
Naoussa
Cyclades GR 185 B6
Imathia GR 182 C4
Napajedla CZ 98 B1
Napiwoda PL 77 A5
Naples = Nápoli I 170 C2
Nápoli = Naples I 170 C2
Nar S 57 C4
Nara N 46 A1
Naraval E 141 A4
Narberth GB 39 C2
Nærbø N 52 B1
Narbonne F 130 B1
Narbonne-Plage F 130 B2
Narbuvollen N 199 C8
Narcao I 179 C2
Nardò I 173 B4
Narkaus FIN 197 C9
Narken S 196 C5
Narmo N 48 B3
Narni I 168 A2
Naro I 176 B2
Naro Fominsk RUS 9 E10
Narón E 140 A2
Narros del Castillo E 150 B2
Narta HR 124 B2
Naruszewo PL 77 B5
Narva EST 8 C6
Narvik N 194 B8
Narzole I 133 A3
Näs FIN 51 B7
Nås S 50 B1
Näs S 57 C4
Näsåker S 200 C2
Năsăud RO 17 B6
Nasavrky CZ 97 B3
Nasbinals F 116 C3
Næsbjerg DK 59 C1
Näshull S 62 A3
Našice HR 125 B4
Nasielsk PL 77 B5
Naso I 177 A3
Nassau D 81 B3
Nassenfels D 95 C3
Nassenheide D 74 B2
Nassereith A 108 B1
Nässjö S 62 A2
Nastätten D 81 B3
Næstved DK 65 A4
Näsum S 63 B2
Näsviken S 199 B12
Natalinci SRB 127 C2
Naters CH 119 A5
Nater-Stetten D 108 A2
Nattavaara S 196 C3
Natters A 108 B2
Nattheim D 94 C2
Nättraby S 63 B3
Naturno I 108 C1
Naucelle F 130 A1
Nauders A 108 C1
Nauen D 74 B1
Naul IRL 30 A2
Naumburg D 83 A3
Naundorf D 83 B5
Naunhof D 83 A4
Naustdal N 46 A2
Nautijaur S 196 C2
Nautsi RUS 193 D13
Nava E 142 A1
Navacerrada E 151 B3
Navaconcejo E 149 B4
Nava de Arévalo E 150 B3
Nava de la Asunción E 150 A3
Nava del Rey E 150 A2
Navafriá E 151 A4
Navahermosa E 157 A3
Navahrudak BY 13 B6
Naval E 145 B4
Navalacruz E 150 B3
Navalcán E 150 B2
Navalcarnero E 151 B3
Navaleno E 143 C3
Navalmanzano E 151 A3
Navalmoral E 150 B3
Navalmoral de la Mata E 150 C2
Navalón E 159 C3
Navalonguilla E 150 B2
Navalperal de Pinares E 150 B3
Navalpino E 157 A3
Navaltalgordo E 150 B3
Navaltoril E 156 A3
Navaluenga E 150 B3
Navalvillar de Pela E 156 A2
Navan IRL 30 A2
Navaperal de Tormes E 150 B2
Navapolatsk BY 13 A8
Navarclés E 147 C2
Navarredonda de Gredos E 150 B2
Navarrenx F 144 A3
Navarrés E 159 B3
Navarrete E 143 B4
Navarrevisca E 150 B3
Navás E 147 C2
Navascués E 144 B2
Navas del Madroño E 155 B4
Navas del Rey E 151 B3

Navas del Sepillar E 163 A3
Navas de Oro E . . .150 A3
Navas de San Juan E 157 B4
Navasfrias E 149 B3
Nave I 120 B3
Nave de Haver P . .149 B3
Nävekvarn S 56 B2
Navelli I 169 A3
Navenby GB 40 B3
Näverkärret S 56 A1
Naverstad S 54 B2
Navés E 147 C2
Navezuelas E 156 A2
Navia E 141 A4
Navia de Suarna E 141 B4
Navilly F 105 C4
Năvodari RO 17 C8
Naxos GR 185 B6
Nay F 145 A3
Nazaré P 154 B1
Nazarje SLO 123 A3
Nazilli TR 188 B3
Nazza D 82 A2
Nea Anchialos GR 182 D4
Nea Epidavros GR 184 B4
Nea Flippias GR .182 D2
Nea Kalikratia GR 183 C5
Nea Makri GR . . .185 A4
Nea Moudania GR 183 C5
Neap GB 33 A5
Nea Peramos .183 C6
Neapoli
Kozani GR 182 C3
Kriti GR 185 D6
Lakonia GR 184 C4
Nea Stira GR . . .185 A5
Neath GB 39 C3
Nea Visa GR . . .186 A1
Nea Zichni GR . .183 B5
Nebljusi HR . . .124 C1
Neblo SLO . . .122 A2
Nebolchy RUS . . .9 C8
Nebra D 82 A3
Nebreda E . . .143 C3
Nechanice CZ . . .84 B3
Neckargemünd D .93 B4
Neckarsulm D . . .94 B1
Neda E 140 A2
Neded SK 112 A1
Nedelišče HR 124 A2
Nederweert NL . . .80 A1
Nedreberg N 48 B3
Nedre Gärdsjö S . .50 B2
Nedre Soppero S . .196 A4
Nedstrand N 52 A1
Nedvĕdice CZ 97 B4
Nędza PL 86 B2
Neede NL 71 B3
Needham Market GB 45 A5
Needingworth GB . .44 A3
Neermoor D 71 A4
Neeroeteren B 80 A1
Neerpelt B 79 A5
Neesen D 72 B1
Neetze D 73 A3
Nefyn GB 38 B2
Negotin SRB . . .16 C5
Negotino MK 182 B4
Negrar I 121 B3
Negredo E 151 A4
Negreira E 140 B2
Nègrepelisse F . .129 B4
Negru Vodă RO . .17 D8
Negueira de Muñiz E 141 A4
Neheim D 81 A3
Neila E 143 B4
Néive I 119 C5
Nejdek CZ 83 B4
Nekla PL 76 B2
Neksø DK 67 A4
Nelas P 148 B2
Nelaug N 53 B4
Nelidovo RUS 9 D8
Nelim FIN 193 D12
Nellingen D 94 C1
Nelson GB 40 B1
Neman RUS . . .12 A5
Nemea GR 184 B3
Nemesgörzsöny H 111 B4
Nemeskér H 111 B3
Nemesnádudvar H 125 A5
Nemesszalók H . . .111 B4
Németkér H 112 C2
Nemours F 103 A4
Nemška Loka SLO 123 B4
Nemšová SK 98 C2
Nenagh IRL . . .28 B3
Nenince SK . . .112 A3
Nenita GR . . .185 A7
Nenzing A 107 B4
Neochori GR 182 D3
Neo Chori GR . . .184 A2
Neon Petritsi GR .183 B5
Nepi I 168 A2
Nepomuk CZ 96 B1
Nérac F 129 B3
Neratovice CZ 84 B2
Nerchau D 83 A4
Néré F 115 C3
Neresheim D 94 C2
Nereto I 136 C2
Nerezine HR . . .123 C3
Nereźišća HR . . .138 B2
Neringa LT 12 A4
Néris-les-Bains F . .116 A2
Nerito I 169 A3
Nerja E 163 B4
Néronde F 117 B4
Nérondes F 103 C4
Nerpio E 164 A2

Nersingen D 94 C2
Nerva E 161 B3
Nervesa della Battáglia I 121 B5
Nervi I 134 A2
Nes
Buskerud N 48 B1
Hedmark N 48 B2
NL 70 A2
Sogn og Fjordane N 46 A3
Sør-Trøndelag N .198 B6
Nesbyen N 47 B6
Neset N 199 D7
Nesflaten N 52 A2
Nesjahverfi IS . .191 C10
Neskaupstaður IS 191 B12
Nesland N 53 A3
Neslandsvatn N . .53 B5
Nesle F 90 B2
Nesna N 195 D4
Nesoddtangen N . .48 C2
Nesovice CZ 98 B1
Nesselwang D . . .108 B1
Nesslau CH . . .107 B4
Nessmersiel D . . .71 A4
Nesso I 120 B2
Nesterov UA 13 C5
Nestorio GR 182 C3
Nesttun N 46 B2
Nesvady SK 112 B2
Nesvatnstemmen N 53 B4
Nether Stowey GB . .43 A3
Netland N 52 B2
Netolice CZ 96 B2
Netphen D 81 B4
Netstal CH . . .107 B4
Nettancourt F . . .91 C4
Nettetal D 80 A2
Nettlingen D 72 B3
Nettuno I 168 B2
Neualbenreuth D .95 B4
Neubeckum D 81 A4
Neubrandenburg D 74 A2
Neubruchhausen D 72 B1
Neubukow D 65 B4
Neuburg D 94 C3
Neuchâtel CH . .106 C1
Neudau A 111 B3
Neudietendorf D . .82 B2
Neudorf D 93 B4
Neuenbürg D 93 C4
Neuenburg D . . .71 A4
Neuendorf D . . .66 B2
Neuenhagen D . . .74 B2
Neuenhaus D . . .71 B3
Neuenkirchen
Niedersachsen D . .71 B5
Niedersachsen D . .72 A2
Nordrhein-Westfalen D 71 B4
Nordrhein-Westfalen D 81 B3
Neuenrade D 81 A3
Neuenwalde D . . .64 C1
Neuerburg D . . .92 A2
Neufahrn
Bayern D 95 C3
Bayern D 95 C4
Neuf-Brisach F . .106 A2
Neufchâteau
B 92 B1
F 92 C1
Neufchâtel-en-Bray F 90 B1
Neufchâtel-sur-Aisne F 91 B4
Neuflize F 91 B4
Neugersdorf D . . .84 B2
Neuhardenberg D .74 B3
Neuharlingersiel D .71 A4
Neuhaus
Bayern D 95 B3
Bayern D 96 C1
Niedersachsen D . .64 C2
Niedersachsen D . .73 A3
Niedersachsen D . .81 A5
Neuhaus a Rennweg D 82 B3
Neuhausen
CH 107 B3
D 83 B5
Neuhausen ob Eck D 107 B3
Neuhof
Bayern D 94 B2
Hessen D 82 B1
Neuhofen an der Krems A 110 A1
Neuillé-Pont-Pierre F 102 B2
Neuilly-en-Thelle F .90 B2
Neuilly-le-Réal F .104 C2
Neuilly-l'Évêque F 105 B4
Neuilly-St Front F . .90 B3
Neu-Isenburg D . .93 A4
Neukalen D 66 C1
Neu Kaliss D . . .73 A4
Neukirch D 84 A2
Neukirchen
A 109 A4
Hessen D 81 B5
Schleswig-Holstein D 64 B1
Neukirchen am Grossvenediger A 109 B3
Neukirchen bei Heiligen Blut D 95 B4
Neukloster D . . .65 C4
Neulengbach A . .110 A2
Neulise F 117 B4
Neum BIH 139 C3
Neumagen D 92 B2
Neumarkt D 95 B3

Neumarkt am Wallersee A 109 B4
Neumarkt im Hausruckkreis A 109 A4
Neumarkt im Mühlkreis A 96 C2
Neumarkt im Steiermark A 110 B1
Neumarkt Sankt Veit D 95 C4
Neumünster D . . .64 B2
Neunburg vorm Wald D 95 B4
Neung-sur-Beuvron F 103 B3
Neunkirch
Luzern CH 106 B3
Schaffhausen CH 107 B3
Neunkirchen
A 111 B3
Nordrhein-Westfalen D 80 B3
Saarland D . . .92 B2
Neunkirchen am Brand D 94 B3
Neuötting D 95 C4
Neupetershain D . .84 A3
Neuravensburg D .107 B4
Neureut D 93 B4
Neuruppin D 74 B1
Neusäss D 94 C2
Neusiedl A 111 B3
Neuss D 80 A2
Neussargues-Moissac F 116 B2
Neustadt
Bayern D 94 B2
Bayern D 95 B4
Bayern D 95 C3
Brandenburg D . 73 B5
Hessen D 81 B5
Niedersachsen D . .72 B2
Rheinland-Pfalz D .93 B4
Sachsen D 84 A2
Schleswig-Holstein D 65 B3
Thüringen D 82 B3
Thüringen D 83 B3
Neustadt-Glewe D . 73 A4
Neustift im Stubaital A 108 B2
Neustrelitz D 74 A2
Neutal A 111 B3
Neutrebbin D 74 B3
Neu-Ulm D 94 C2
Neuves-Maisons F .92 C2
Neuvic
Corrèze F 116 B2
Dordogne F 129 A3
Neuville-aux-Bois F 103 A4
Neuville-de-Poitou F 115 B4
Neuville-les-Dames F 117 A5
Neuville-sur-Saône F 117 B4
Neuvy-le-Roi F . .102 B2
Neuvy-Santour F . .104 A2
Neuvy-St Sépulchre F 103 C3
Neuvy-sur-Barangeon F 103 B4
Neuwied D 80 B3
Neuzelle D 74 B3
Névache F 118 B3
Neveklov CZ 96 B2
Nevel RUS . . .9 D6
Neverfjord N . . .192 B7
Nevers F 104 C2
Nevesinje BIH . .139 B4
Névez F 100 B2
Nevlunghavn N . .53 B5
Nevşehir TR 23 B8
New Abbey GB . .36 B3
New Aberdour GB .33 D4
New Alresford GB . .44 B2
Newark-on-Trent GB 40 B3
Newbiggin-by-the-Sea GB 37 A5
Newbliss IRL . . .27 B3
Newborough GB . .38 A2
Newbridge IRL . . .30 A2
Newbridge on Wye GB 39 B3
Newburgh
Aberdeenshire GB 33 D4
Fife GB 35 B4
Newbury GB . . .44 B2
Newby Bridge GB .36 B4
Newcastle GB . . .27 B5
Newcastle Emlyn GB 39 B2
Newcastleton GB .37 A4
Newcastle-under-Lyme GB 40 B1
Newcastle upon Tyne GB 37 B5
Newcastle West IRL 29 B2
Newchurch GB . . .39 B3
New Costessey GB 41 C5
New Cumnock GB . .36 A2
Newent GB 39 C4
New Galloway GB . .36 A2
Newham GB 45 B4
Newhaven GB . . .45 C4
Newington GB . . .45 B5
Newinn IRL . . .29 B4
Newlyn GB 42 B1
Newmachar GB . .33 D4
Newmarket
Suffolk GB . . .45 A4
Western Isles GB . 31 A2
IRL 29 B2
Newmarket-on-Fergus IRL 28 B3
New Mills GB 40 B2

New Milton GB 44 C2
New Pitsligo GB . . .33 D4
Newport
Isle of Wight GB . 44 C2
Newport GB 39 C4
Pembrokeshire GB 39 B2
Telford & Wrekin GB 38 B4
Mayo IRL 28 A2
Tipperary IRL . . .29 B3
Newport-on-Tay GB 35 B5
Newport Pagnell GB 44 A3
Newquay GB . . .42 B1
New Quay GB . . .39 B2
New Radnor GB . .39 B3
New Romney GB . .45 C4
New Ross IRL . . .30 B2
Newry GB 27 B4
New Scone GB . . .35 B4
Newton Abbot GB . .43 B3
Newton Arlosh GB . .36 B3
Newton Aycliffe GB 37 B5
Newton Ferrers GB 42 B2
Newtonhill GB . . .33 D4
Newtonmore GB . .32 D2
Newton Stewart GB 36 B2
Newtown
Herefordshire GB 39 B4
Powys GB . . .39 B3
Newtownabbey GB 27 B5
Newtownards GB .27 B5
Newtownbutler GB .27 B3
Newtown Cunningham IRL 27 B3
Newtown Hamilton GB 27 B4
Newtownmountkennedy IRL 30 A2
Newtown St Boswells GB 35 C5
Newtown Sands IRL 29 B2
Newtownstewart GB 27 B3
Nexon F 115 C5
Neyland GB . . .39 C2
Nibbiano I 120 C2
Nibe DK 58 B2
Nicastro I 175 C2
Niccone I 135 B5
Nice F 133 B3
Nickelsdorf A 111 B4
Nicolosi I 177 B4
Nicosia
CY 181 A2
I 177 B3
Nicótera I 175 C1
Nidda D 81 B5
Niğde TR 23 C8
Nidzica PL 77 A5
Niebla E 161 B3
Nieborów PL 77 B5
Niebüll D 64 B1
Niechanowo PL . . .76 B2
Niechorze PL 67 B4
Niedalino PL 67 B5
Niederaula D 82 B1
Niederbipp CH . . .106 B2
Niederbronn-les-Bains F 93 C3
Niederfischbach D .81 B3
Niedergörsdorf D . .74 C1
Niederkrüchten D . .80 A2
Niederndorf A . . .108 B3
Nieder-Olm D 93 B4
Niedersachswerfen D 82 A2
Niederstetten D . . .94 B1
Niederurnen CH . .107 B4
Niederwölz A 110 B1
Niedoradz PL 85 A3
Niedorp PL 99 B4
Niegosławice PL . .85 A3
Nieheim D 81 A5
Niemcza PL 85 B4
Niemegk D 74 B1
Niemisel S 196 C5
Niemodlin PL 85 B5
Nienburg
Niedersachsen D . .72 B2
Sachsen-Anhalt D .83 A3
Niepołomice PL . . .99 A4
Nierstein D 93 B4
Niesky D 84 A2
Niestronno PL 76 B2
Nieświń PL 87 A4
Nieszawa PL 76 B3
Nieul-le-Dolent F .114 B2
Nieul-sur-Mer F . .114 B2
Nieuw-Amsterdam NL 71 B3
Nieuw-Buinen NL .71 B3
Nieuwegein NL . . .70 B2
Nieuwe Niedorp 70 B1
Nieuwe-Pekela NL . .71 A3
Nieuwerkerken B . .79 B5
Nieuwe-schans NL .71 A4
Nieuwolda NL 71 A3
Nieuwpoort B . . .78 A2
Nieuw-Weerdinge NL 71 B3
Nigrita GR . . .183 C5
Nigüelas E 163 B4
Níjar E 164 C2
Nijemci HR 125 B5
Nijkerk NL 70 B2
Nijlen B 79 A4
Nijmegen NL 80 A1
Nijverdal NL 71 B3
Nikel RUS . . .193 C14
Nikinci SRB 127 C1
Nikiti GR 183 C5
Nikitsch A 111 B3
Nikkala S 196 C6
Nikla H 111 C4
Niklasdorf A 110 B2
Niksar TR . . .23 A8
Nikšić MNE . . .139 C4

Nilivaara S 196 B4
Nîmes F 131 B3
Nimis I 122 A2
Nimtofte DK 58 B3
Nin HR 137 A4
Nindorf D 64 B2
Ninemilehouse IRL .30 B1
Ninove B 79 B4
Niort F 114 B3
Niš SRB 16 C4
Nisa P 155 B3
Niscemi I 177 B3
Niskala FIN . . .197 D10
Nissafors S 60 B3
Nissan-lez-Ensérune F 130 B2
Nissedal N 53 A4
Nissumby DK 58 B1
Nisterud N 53 A5
Niton GB 44 C2
Nitra SK 98 C2
Nitrianske-Pravno SK 98 C2
Nitrianske Rudno SK 98 C2
Nitry F 104 B2
Nittedal N 48 B2
Nittenau D 95 B4
Nittendorf D 95 B3
Nivala FIN 3 E9
Nivelles B 79 B4
Nivnice CZ 98 C1
Nizbor CZ 96 B1
Nižná SK 99 B3
Nižná Boca SK . . .99 C3
Nižne Repaše SK . .99 B4
Nizza Monferrato I 119 C5
Njarðvík IS 190 D3
Njegoševo SRB . .126 B1
Njivice HR . . .123 B3
Njurundabommen S 200 D3
Njutånger S . . .200 E3
Noailles F 90 B2
Noain E 144 B2
Noale I 121 B5
Noalejo E 163 A4
Noblejas E 151 C4
Noceda E 141 B4
Nocera Inferiore I .170 C2
Nocera Terinese I .175 B2
Nocera Umbra I . .136 B1
Noceto I 120 C3
Noci I 173 B3
Nociglia I 173 B4
Nodeland N 53 B3
Nödinge S 60 B2
Nods F 105 B5
Noé F 146 A2
Noépoli I 174 A2
Noeux-les-Mines F .78 B2
Noez E 157 A3
Nogales E 155 C4
Nogara I 121 B4
Nogarejas E 141 B4
Nogaro F 128 C2
Nogent F 105 A4
Nogent l'Artaud F .90 C3
Nogent-le-Roi F . .90 C1
Nogent-le-Rotrou F 89 B4
Nogent-sur-Seine F 91 C3
Nogent-sur-Vernisson F 103 B4
Nogersund S . . .63 B2
Noguera E 152 B2
Nogueras E 163 A3
Nohfelden D 92 B3
Nohn D 80 B2
Noia E 140 B2
Noicáttaro I 173 A2
Noirétable F 117 B3
Noirmoutier-en-l'Île F 114 A1
Noja E 143 A3
Nojewo PL 75 B5
Nokia FIN 8 B3
Nol S 60 B2
Nola I 170 C2
Nolay F 104 C3
Noli I 133 A4
Nolnyra S 51 B4
Nombela E 150 B3
Nomeny F 92 C2
Nomexy F 92 C2
Nonancourt F . . .89 B5
Nonant-le-Pin F . . .89 B4
Nonántola I 121 C4
Nonaspe E 153 A4
None I 119 C4
Nontron F 115 C4
Nonza F 180 A2
Noordhorn NL . . .71 A3
Noordwijk NL 70 B1
Noordwijkerhout NL 70 B1
Noordwolde NL . . .70 B3
Noppikoski S 50 A1
Nora S 55 A6
Nørager DK 58 B2
Norberg S 50 B2
Norboda S 51 B5
Nórcia I 136 C2
Nordagutu N 53 A5
Nordanås S 200 B4
Nordausques F . . .78 B2
Nordborg DK 64 C2
Norddal N 198 C4
Nordeide N 46 A3

Nordhalben D . . .82 B3
Nordhausen D . . .82 A2
Nordheim vor der Rhön D 82 B2
Nordholz D 64 C1
Nordhorn D 71 B4
Nordingrå S 200 D4
Nordkjosbotn N . .192 C3
Nordli N 199 A10
Nördlingen D 94 C2
Nordmaling S . . .200 C5
Nordmark S 49 C6
Nordmela N . . .194 A6
Nord-Odal N 48 B3
Nordre Osen N . .48 A3
Nordsinni N 48 B1
Nørdstedalsseter 198 D4
Nordstemmen D . .72 B2
Nordvågen N . . .193 B10
Nordwalde D . . .71 B4
Noreña E 142 A1
Noresund N 48 B1
Norg NL 71 A3
Norheimsund N . .46 B3
Norie S 63 B2
Norma I 169 B2
Nornäs S 49 A5
Norråker S 200 B1
Norrala S 51 A3
Norra Vi S 62 A3
Norrby S 200 B3
Nørre Aaby DK . .59 C2
Nørre Alslev DK . .65 B4
Nørre Lyndelse DK 59 C3
Nørre Nebel DK . .59 C1
Nørrent-Fontes F .78 B2
Nørre Snede DK . .59 C2
Nørresundby DK . .58 A2
Nørre Vorupør DK . .58 B1
Norrfjärden S . . .196 D4
Norrhult Klavreström S 62 A3
Norrköping S 56 B2
Norrskedika S . . .51 B5
Norrsundet S . . .51 B4
Norrtälje S 57 A4
Nors DK 58 A1
Norsbron S 55 A4
Norsholm S 56 B1
Norsjö S 200 B5
Nörten-Hardenberg D 82 A1
Northallerton GB . .37 B5
Northampton GB . .44 A3
North Berwick GB . .35 B5
North Charlton GB .37 A5
Northeim D 82 A2
Northfleet GB . . .45 B4
North Frodingham GB 40 B3
North Kessock GB 32 D2
Northleach GB . . .44 B2
North Molton GB . .42 A3
North Petherton GB 43 A3
North Somercotes GB 41 B4
North Tawton GB . .42 B3
North Thoresby 41 B3
North Walsham GB 41 C5
Northwich GB . . .38 A4
Norton GB . . .40 A3
Nortorf D 64 B2
Nort-sur-Erdre F .101 B4
Nörvenich D 80 B2
Norwich GB 41 C5
Nøsen N 47 B5
Nossa Senhora do Cabo P 154 C1
Nossebro S 55 B3
Nössemark S 54 A2
Nossen D 83 A5
Notaresco I 169 A3
Noto I 177 C4
Notodden N 53 A5
Nottingham GB . .40 C2
Nottuln D 71 C4
Nouan-le-Fuzelier F 103 B4
Nouans-les-Fontaines F 103 B3
Nougaroulet F . .129 C3
Nouvion F 78 B1
Nouzonville F . . .91 B4
Nová SK 111 C3
Nová Baňa SK . .98 C2
Nová Bystrica SK .99 B3
Nová Bystřice CZ .97 B3
Nova Crnja SRB .126 B2
Nova Gorica SLO .122 B2
Nova Gradiška HR 124 B3
Nováky SK 98 C2
Novalaise F . . .118 B2
Novales E 145 B3
Nova Levante I . .108 C2
Novalja HR 137 A3
Nová Paka CZ . . .84 B3
Nova Pazova SRB 127 C2
Nová Pec CZ 96 C1
Novara I 120 B1
Novara di Sicília I .177 A4
Nova Siri I 174 A2
Nové Mezzola I . . .120 A2
Nova Topola BIH .124 B3
Novaya Ladoga RUS 9 B8
Nova Zagora BG . .17 D6
Nové Hrady CZ . .96 C2
Novelda E 165 A4
Novellara I 121 C3
Nové Město na Moravĕ CZ 97 B4

Nové Mĕsto pod Smrkem CZ 84 B3
Nové Mitrovice CZ .96 B1
Noventa di Piave I 122 B1
Noventa Vicentina I 121 B4
Novés E 151 B3
Noves F 131 B3
Nové Sady SK . . .98 C1
Novés de Segre E 147 B2
Nové Strašeci CZ .84 B1
Nové Zámky SK . .112 B2
Novgorod RUS . . .9 C7
Novi di Módena I .121 C3
Novigrad
Istarska HR 122 B2
Zadarsko-Kninska HR 137 A4
Novigrad Podravski HR 124 A2
Novi Kneževac SRB 126 A2
Novi Ligure I . . .120 C1
Noville B 92 A1
Novi Marof HR . . .124 A2
Novion-Porcien F .91 B4
Novi Pazar
BG 17 D7
SRB 16 D4
Novi Sad SRB . .126 B1
Novi Slankamen SRB 126 B2
Novi Travnik BIH .139 A3
Novi Vinodolski HR 123 B3
Novohrad-Volynskyy UA 13 C7
Novo Mesto SLO .123 B4
Novo Miloševo SRB 126 B2
Novorzhev RUS . . .9 D6
Novo Selo BIH . . .125 B3
Novoselytsya UA . .17 A7
Novosokolniki RUS .9 D6
Novoveská Huta SK 99 C4
Novovolynsk UA . .13 C6
Novska HR 124 B2
Nový Bor CZ 84 B2
Nový Bydžov CZ . .84 B3
Novy-Chevrières F .91 B4
Nowy Dwór Mazowiecki PL 77 B5
Nový-Hrozenkov CZ 98 B2
Nový Jičín CZ 98 B2
Nový Knín CZ . . .96 B2
Nowa Cerekwia PL .86 B1
Nowa Dęba PL . . .87 B5
Nowa Karczma PL . 68 A3
Nowa Kościoł PL . .85 A3
Nowa Ruda PL . . .85 B4
Nowa Słupia PL . . .87 B5
Nowa Sól PL 85 A3
Nowa Wieś PL . . .69 B4
Nowa-Wieś Wielka PL 76 B3
Nowe PL 69 B3
Nowe Brzesko PL . .87 B4
Nowe Grudze PL . .77 B4
Nowe Kiejkuty PL . .77 A6
Nowe Miasteczko PL 85 A3
Nowe Miasto
Mazowieckie PL . .77 B5
Mazowieckie PL . .87 A4
Nowe Miasto Lubawskie PL . .69 B4
Nowe Miasto nad Wartą PL 76 B2
Nowe Skalmierzyce PL 86 A2
Nowe Warpno PL . .74 A3
Nowica PL 69 A4
Nowogard PL 75 A4
Nowogród Bobrzanski PL 84 A3
Nowogrodziec PL . .84 A3
Nowosolna PL . . .86 A3
Nowy Dwór Gdański PL 69 A4
Nowy Korczyn PL . .87 B4
Nowy Sącz PL . . .99 B4
Nowy Staw PL . . .69 A4
Nowy Targ PL . . .99 B4
Nowy Tomyśl PL . .75 B5
Nowy Wiśnicz PL . .99 B4
Noyalo F 101 B3
Noyal-Pontivy F . .100 A3
Noyant F 102 B2
Noyelles-sur-Mer F 78 B1
Noyen-sur-Sarthe F 102 B1
Noyers F 104 B2
Noyers-sur-Cher F 103 B3
Noyers-sur-Jabron F 132 A1
Noyon F 90 B2
Nozay F 101 B4
Nuaillé F 102 B1
Nuaillé-d'Aunis F .114 B3
Nuars F 104 B2
Nubledo E 141 A5
Nuéno E 145 B3
Nuestra Señora Sa Verge des Pilar E 166 C1
Nueva E 142 A2
Nueva Carteya E .163 A3
Nuevalos E 152 A2
Nuits F 104 B3
Nuits-St Georges F 105 B3
Nule I 178 B3
Nules E 159 B3

Nulvi I 178 B2
Numana I 136 B2
Numansdorp NL . . .79 A4
Nümbrecht D 81 B3
Nunchritz D 83 A5
Nuneaton GB 40 C2
Nunnanen FIN 196 A7
N Unnaryd S 60 B3
Nuñomoral E 149 B3
Nunspeet NL 70 B2
Nuorgam FIN . . .193 B11
Núoro I 178 B3
Nurallao I 179 C3
Nuremberg = Nürnberg
D 94 B3
Nurmes FIN 3 E11
Nürnberg = Nuremberg
D 94 B3
Nurri I 179 C3
Nürtingen D 94 C1
Nus I 119 B4
Nusnäs S 50 B1
Nusplingen D 107 A3
Nuštar HR 125 B4
Nuupas FIN 197 C9
Nyåker S 200 C5
Nyáregyháza H 112 B3
Nyarlörinc H 113 C3
Nyasvizh BY 13 B7
Nybble S 55 A5
Nybergsund N 49 A4
Nybøl DK 64 B2
Nyborg
DK 59 C3
S 196 D6
Nybro S 62 B3
Nybster GB 32 C3
Nyby DK 65 B5
Nye S 62 A3
Nyékládháza H 113 B4
Nyergesujfalu H 112 B2
Nyhammar S 50 B1
Nyhyttan S 55 A5
Nyírád H 111 B4
Nyírbátor H 16 B5
Nyíregyháza H 16 B4
Nyker DK 67 A3
Nykil S 56 B1
Nykirke N 48 B2
Nykøbing
Falster DK 65 B4
Vestsjællands Amt.
DK 61 D1
Nykøbing Mors DK .58 B1
Nyköping S 56 B3
Nykroppa S 55 A5
Nykvarn S 56 A3
Nykyrke S 55 B5
Nyland S 200 C3
Nylars DK 67 A3
Nymburk CZ 84 B3
Nynäshamn S 57 B3
Nyon CH 118 A3
Nyons F 131 A4
Nýřany CZ 96 B1
Nýrsko CZ 95 B5
Nyrud N 193 C13
Nysa PL 85 B5
Nysäter S 55 A3
Nyseter N 198 C5
Nyskoga S 49 B4
Nysted DK 65 B4
Nystrand N 53 A5
Nyúl H 111 B4
Nyvoll N 192 B7

O

Oadby GB 40 C2
Oakengates GB 38 B4
Oakham GB 40 C3
Oanes N 52 B2
Obalj BIH 139 B4
Oban GB 34 B2
O Barco E 141 B4
Obbola S 200 C6
Obdach A 110 B1
Obejo E 156 B3
Oberammergau D 108 B2
Oberasbach D 94 B2
Oberau D 108 B2
Oberaudorf D 108 B3
Oberbruck F 106 B1
Oberdiessbach
CH 106 C2
Oberdorf CH 106 B2
Oberdrauburg A . . .109 C3
Oberelsbach D 82 B2
Obere Stanz A 110 B2
Ober Grafendorf
A 110 A2
Obergünzburg D . .108 B1
Obergurgl A 108 C2
Oberhausen D 80 A2
Oberhof D 82 B2
Oberkirch D 93 C4
Oberkirchen D 81 A4
Oberkochen D 94 C2
Obermassfeld-
Grimmenthal D . .82 B2
Ober-Morlen D 81 B4
Obermünchen D . . .95 C3
Obernai F 93 C3
Obernberg A 96 C1
Obernburg D 93 B5
Oberndorf D 93 C4
Oberndorf bei Salzburg
A 109 B3
Obernkirchen D 72 B2
Oberort A 110 B2
Oberpullendorf A . .111 B3
Oberriet CH 107 B4
Oberröblingen D . . .82 A3
Oberrot D 94 B1
Oberstaufen D 107 B5
Oberstdorf D 107 B5

Obertauern A 109 B4
Obertilliach A 109 C3
Obertraubling D . . .95 C4
Obertraun A 109 B4
Obertrubach D 95 B3
Obertrum A 109 B4
Oberursel D 81 B4
Obervellach A 109 C4
Oberviechtach D . . .95 B4
Oberwart A 111 B3
Oberwesel D 93 A3
Oberwinter D 80 B3
Oberwölz Stadt A . .110 B1
Oberzell D 96 C1
Óbice PL 87 B4
Óbidos P 154 B1
Obing D 109 B3
Objat F 129 A4
Objazda PL 68 A2
Öblarn A 109 B5
Obninsk RUS 9 E10
O Bolo E 141 B3
Oborniki PL 75 B5
Oborniki Śląskie
PL 85 A4
Obornjača SRB . . .126 B1
Obrenovac SRB . . .127 C2
Obrež SRB 127 C1
Obrigheim D 93 B5
Obrov SLO 123 B3
Obrovac
HR 137 A4
SRB 126 B1
Obrovac Sinjski
HR 138 B2
Obruk TR 23 B7
Obrzycko PL 75 B5
Obudovac BIH 125 C4
Ocaña E 151 C4
O Carballiño E 140 B2
Occhiobello I 121 C4
Occimiano I 119 B5
Očevlja BIH 139 A4
Ochagavia E 144 B2
Ochiltree GB 36 A2
Ochla PL 84 A3
Ochotnica-Dolna
PL 99 B4
Ochotnica-Górna
PL 99 B4
Ochsenfurt D 94 B2
Ochsenhausen D .107 A4
Ochtendung D 80 B3
Ochtrup D 71 B4
Ocieka PL 87 B5
Ockelbo S 50 B3
Öckerö S 60 B1
Ocniţa MD 17 A7
O Corgo E 141 B3
Očová SK 99 C3
Ócsa H 112 B3
Öcseny H 125 A4
Öcsöd H 113 C4
Octeville F 88 A2
Ocypel PL 69 B3
Ödåkra S 61 C2
Odby DK 58 B1
Odda N 46 B3
Odder DK 59 C3
Ödeborg S 54 B2
Odeceixe P 160 B1
Odechów PL 87 A5
Odeleite P 160 B2
Odemira P 160 B1
Ödemiş TR 188 A2
Odensbacken S 56 A1
Odense DK 59 C3
Odensjö
Jönköping S 62 A2
Kronoberg S 60 C3
Oderberg D 74 B3
Oderzo I 122 B1
Odesa = Odessa
UA 17 B9
Ödeshög S 55 B5
Odessa = Odesa
UA 17 B9
Odiáxere P 160 B1
Odie GB 33 B4
Odiham GB 44 B3
Odintsovo RUS 9 E10
Odivelas P 160 A1
Odolanów PL 85 A5
Odón E 152 B2
Odorheiu Secuiesc
RO 17 B6
Odrowaz PL 87 A4
Odry CZ 98 B1
Odrzywół PL 87 A4
Ødsted DK 59 C2
Odžaci SRB 126 B1
Odžak BIH 125 B4
Oebisfelde D 73 B3
Oederan D 83 B5
Oeding D 71 C3
Oegstgeest NL 70 B1
Oelde D 81 A4
Oelsnitz D 83 B4
Oer-Erkenschwick
D 80 A3
Oerlinghausen D . .72 C1
Oettingen D 94 C2
Oetz A 108 B1
Oeventrop D 81 A4
Offanengo I 120 B2
Offenbach D 81 B4
Offenburg D 93 C4
Offida I 136 C2
Offingen D 94 C2
Offranville F 89 A5
Ofir P 148 A1
Ofte N 53 A4
Ofterschwang D . . .107 B5
Oggiono I 120 B2
Ogihares E 163 A4
Ogliastro Cilento I .170 C3
Ogliastro Marina I .170 C2
Ogmore-by-Sea GB 39 C3
Ogna N 52 B1
Ogre LV 8 D4

Ogrodzieniec PL . . .86 B3
Ogulin HR 123 B4
Ögur IS 190 A3
Ohanes E 164 B2
Ohey B 79 B5
Ohlstadt D 108 B2
Ohrdruf D 73 B3
Ohrdruf D 82 B2
Ohrid MK 182 B2
Öhringen D 94 B1
Oia E 140 B2
Oiã P 148 B1
Oiartzun E 144 A2
Oijärvi FIN 197 D8
Oilgate IRL 30 B2
Oimbra E 148 A2
Oiselay-et-Grachoux
F 105 B4
Oisemont F 90 B1
Oisterwijk NL 79 A5
Öja S 57 C4
Öje S 49 B5
Ojén E 162 B3
Ojrzeń PL 77 B5
Ojuelos Altos E . . .156 B2
Okalewo PL 77 A4
Okány H 113 C5
Okehampton GB . . .42 B2
Oklaj HR 138 B2
Økneshamn N 194 B6
Okoč SK 111 B4
Okoličné SK 99 B3
Okonek PL 68 B1
Okonin PL 69 B3
Okřísky CZ 97 B3
Oksa PL 87 B4
Oksbøl DK 59 C1
Oksby DK 59 C1
Øksfjord N 192 B6
Øksna N 48 B3
Okučani HR 124 B3
Okulovka RUS 9 C8
Ólafsfjörður IS 191 A7
Ólafsvík IS 190 C2
ÓLagnö S 57 A4
Olague E 144 B2
Oland N 53 B4
Olargues F 130 B1
Oława PL 85 B5
Olazagutia E 144 B1
Olbernhau D 83 B5
Ólbia I 178 B3
Olching D 108 A2
Oldbury GB 43 A4
Oldcastle IRL 27 C3
Old Deer GB 33 D4
Oldeberkoop NL . . .70 B3
Oldeboorn NL 70 A2
Olden N 198 D3
Oldenbrok D 71 A5
Oldenburg
Niedersachsen D . 71 A5
Schleswig-Holstein
D 65 B3
Oldenzaal NL 71 B3
Olderdalen N 192 C4
Olderfjord N 193 B9
Oldersum D 71 A4
Oldervik N 192 C2
Oldham GB 40 B1
Oldisleben D 82 A3
Oldmeldrum GB . . .33 D4
Olea E 142 B2
Oleby S 49 B5
Olechów PL 87 A5
Oledo P 155 B3
Oléggio I 120 B1
Oleiros
Coruña E 140 A2
Coruña E 140 B1
P 154 B3
Oleksandriya UA . . .13 C7
Olen B 79 A4
Ølen N 52 A1
Olenegorsk RUS . . .3 B13
Olenino RUS 9 D8
Olesa de Montserrat
E 147 C2
Oleśnica PL 85 A5
Olešnice CZ 97 B4
Olesno PL 86 B2
Oletta F 180 A2
Olette F 146 B3
Olevsk UA 13 C7
Olfen D 80 A3
Olgiate Comasco
I 120 B1
Olginate I 120 B2
Ølgod DK 59 C1
Olgrinmore GB 32 C3
Olhão P 160 B2
Olhava FIN 197 D8
Olhavo P 154 B1
Oliana E 147 B2
Olias del Rey E 151 C4
Oliena I 178 B3
Oliete E 153 B3
Olimbos GR 188 D2
Olite E 144 B2
Oliva E 159 C3
Oliva de la Frontera
E 155 C4
Oliva de Mérida E .156 B1
Oliva de Plasencia
E 149 B3
Olivadi I 175 C2
Olival P 154 B2
Olivar E 163 B4
Olivares E 161 B3
Olivares de Duero
E 142 C2
Olivares de Júcar
E 158 B1
Oliveira de Azeméis
P 148 B1
Oliveira de Frades
P 148 B1
Oliveira do Conde
P 148 B2

Oliveira do Douro
P 148 A1
Oliveira do Hospital
P 148 B2
Olivenza E 155 C3
Olivet F 103 B3
Olivone CH 107 C3
Öljehult S 63 B3
Olkusz PL 86 B3
Ollerton GB 40 B2
Ollerup DK 65 A3
Olliergues F 117 B3
Ölme S 55 A4
Olmedilla de Alarcón
E 158 B1
Olmedillo de Roa
E 143 C3
Olmedo
E 150 A3
I 178 B2
Olmeto F 180 B1
Olmillos de Castro
E 149 A3
Olmos de Ojeda E 142 B2
Olney GB 44 A3
Olocau del Rey E .153 B3
Olofström S 63 B2
Olomouc CZ 98 B1
Olonets RUS 9 B8
Olonne-sur-Mer F .114 B2
Olonzac F 130 B1
Oloron-Ste Marie
F 145 A3
Olost E 147 C3
Olot E 147 B3
Olovo BIH 139 A4
Olpe D 81 A3
Olsberg D 81 A4
Olsene B 79 B3
Olserud S 55 A4
Olshammar S 55 B5
Olshanka UA 13 D9
Olszanica PL 85 A3
Olsztyn
Śląskie PL 86 B3
Warmińsko-Mazurskie
PL 69 B5
Olsztynek PL 77 A5
Olszyna PL 84 A3
Olszyny PL 77 A6
Oltedal N 52 B2
Olten CH 106 B2
Olteniţa RO 17 C7
Olula del Rio E 164 B2
Ølve N 46 B2
Olvega E 144 C2
Olvera E 162 B2
Olympia GR 184 B2
Olzai I 178 B3
Omagh GB 27 B3
Omalos GR 185 D4
Omegna I 119 B5
Omiš HR 138 B2
Omišalj HR 123 B3
Ommen NL 71 B3
Omodhos CY 181 B1
Omoljica SRB 127 C2
On B 79 B5
Oña E 143 B3
Onano I 168 A1
O Näsberg S 49 B5
Oñati E 143 A4
Onda E 159 B3
Ondara E 159 C4
Ondarroa E 143 A4
Onesse-et-Laharie
F 128 B1
Oneşti RO 17 B7
Onhaye B 79 B4
Onich GB 34 B2
Onil E 159 C3
Onís E 142 A2
Önnestad S 61 C4
Onsala S 60 B2
Ontinyent E 159 C3
Ontur E 158 C2
Onzain F 103 B3
Onzonilla E 142 B1
Oostburg NL 79 A3
Oostende B 78 A2
Oosterend NL 70 A2
Oosterhout NL 79 A4
Oosterwolde NL . . .71 B3
Oosterzele B 79 B3
Oosthuizen NL 70 B2
Oostkamp B 78 A3
Oostmalle B 79 A4
Oost-Vlieland NL . . .70 A2
Oostvoorne NL 79 A4
Ootmarsum NL 71 B3
Opalenica PL 75 B5
O Páramo E 140 B3
Oparany CZ 96 B2
Opatija HR 123 B3
Opatów
Śląskie PL 86 B2
Świętokrzyskie PL . 87 B5
Wielkopolskie PL . .86 A2
Opatówek PL 86 A2
Opatowiec PL 87 B4
Opava CZ 98 B1
O Pedrouzo E 140 B2
Opeinde NL 70 A3
Oper Thalkirchdorf
D 107 B5
Opglabbeerk B 80 A1
Opicina I 122 B2
O Pino E 140 B2
Oplotnica SLO 123 A4
Opmeer NL 70 B1
Opochka RUS 9 D6
Opočno CZ 85 B4
Opoczno PL 87 A4
Opole PL 86 B1
Oporów PL 77 B4
O Porriño E 140 B2
Opovo SRB 127 B2
Oppach D 84 A2

Oppdal N 198 C6
Oppeby
Östergötland S 56 B1
Södermanland S . . 56 B2
Oppedal N 46 A2
Oppegård N 54 A1
Oppenau D 93 C4
Oppenberg A 110 B1
Oppenheim D 93 B4
Óppido Lucano I . .172 B1
Óppido Mamertina
I 175 C1
Opponitz A 110 B1
Oppstad N 48 B3
Oprtalj HR 122 B2
Opsaheden S 49 B5
Opusztaszer H 113 C4
Opuzen HR 138 B3
Ora
CY 181 B2
I 121 A4
Orada P 155 C3
Oradea RO 16 B4
Oradour-sur-Glane
F 115 C5
Oradour-sur-Vayres
F 115 C4
Oragonja SLO 122 B2
Orah BIH 139 C4
Orahova BIH 138 A3
Orahovica HR 125 B3
Orahovo BIH 124 B3
Oraison F 132 B1
Orajärvi FIN 196 C7
Orange F 131 A3
Orani I 178 B3
Oranienbaum D 83 A4
Oranienburg D 74 B2
Oranmore IRL 28 A3
Orašac SRB 127 C2
Orašje BIH 125 B4
Oravská Lesná SK . 99 B3
Oravská Polhora
SK 99 B3
Oravské Veselé SK 99 B3
Oravsky-Podzámok
SK 99 B3
Orba E 159 C3
Orbacém P 148 A1
Orbais F 91 C3
Ørbæk DK 59 C3
Orbassano I 119 B4
Orbe CH 105 C5
Orbec F 89 A4
Orbetello I 168 A1
Orbetello Scalo I . .168 A1
Ørbigny F 103 B3
Ørby DK 59 B3
Ørbyhus S 51 B4
Orce E 164 B2
Orcera E 164 A2
Orchamps-Vennes
F 105 B5
Orches F 102 C2
Orchete E 159 C3
Orchies F 78 B3
Orchowo PL 76 B3
Orcières F 118 C3
Ordes E 140 A2
Ordhead GB 33 D4
Ordino AND 146 B2
Ordizia E 144 A1
Orduña E 143 B4
Ore S 50 A2
Orea E 152 B2
Orebić HR 138 C3
Örebro S 56 A1
Öregcsertő H 112 C3
Öregrund S 51 B5
Orehoved DK 65 B4
Orellana de la Sierra
E 156 A2
Orellana la Vieja
E 156 A2
Ören TR 188 B2
Örencik TR 187 C4
Orestiada GR 186 A1
Organyà E 147 B2
Orgaz E 157 A4
Orgelet F 105 C4
Ørgenvika N 48 B1
Orgères-en-Beauce
F 103 A3
Orgibet F 145 B4
Orgnac-l'Aven F . . .131 A3
Orgon F 131 B4
Orgósolo I 178 B3
Orhaneli TR 186 C3
Orhangazi TR 187 B4
Orhei MD 17 B8
Orhomenos GR . . .184 A3
Oria E 164 B2
Ória I 173 B3
Origny-Ste Benoite
F 91 B3
Orihuela E 165 A4
Orihuela del Tremedal
E 152 B2
Orikum AL 182 C1
Oriola P 154 C3
Oriolo I 174 A2
Oriovac HR 125 B3
Orissaare EST 8 C3
Oristano I 179 C2
Öriszentpéter H . . .111 C3
Ørje N 54 A2
Orjiva E 163 B4
Orkanger N 198 B6
Örkelljunga S 61 C3
Örkény H 112 B3
Orlamünde D 82 B3
Orléans F 103 B3
Orlová CZ 98 B2
Orlovat SRB 126 B2
Ormea I 133 A3
Ormelet N 54 A1
Ormemyr N 53 A5
Ormília GR 183 C5
Ormos GR 185 B5
Ormož SLO 124 A2
Ormskirk GB 38 A4

Ornans F 105 B5
Ornäs S 50 B2
Ørnes N 195 D4
Orneta PL 69 A5
Ørnhøj DK 59 B1
Örnsköldsvik S . . .200 C4
Orolik HR 125 B4
Orom SRB 126 B1
Oron-la-Ville CH . .106 C1
Oronsko PL 87 A4
Oropa I 119 B4
Oropesa
Castellón de la Plana
E 153 B4
Toledo E 150 C2
O Rosal E 140 C2
Orosei I 178 B3
Orosháza H 113 C4
Oroslavje HR 124 B1
Oroszlány H 112 B2
Oroszlo H 125 A4
Orotelli I 178 B3
Orozko E 143 A4
Orphir GB 33 C3
Orpington GB 45 B4
Orreaga-Roncesvalles
E 144 A2
Orrefors S 62 B3
Orrviken S 199 B11
Orsa S 50 A1
Orsara di Púglia I .171 B3
Orsay F 90 C2
Orscholz D 92 B2
Orsennes F 103 C3
Orserum S 55 B5
Orsha BY 13 A9
Orsières CH 119 A4
Örsjö S 63 B3
Ørslev DK 65 A4
Örslösa S 55 B3
Orsogna I 169 A4
Orsomarso I 174 B1
Orşova RO 16 C5
Ørsta N 198 C3
Ørsted DK 58 B3
Örsundsbro S 56 A3
Ortaca TR 188 C3
Ortakent TR 188 B2
Ortaklar TR 188 B2
Ortaköy TR 23 B8
Orta Nova I 171 B3
Orte I 168 A2
Ortenburg D 96 C1
Orth A 111 A3
Orthez F 128 C2
Ortigueira E 140 A3
Ortilla E 145 B3
Ortisei I 108 C2
Orţişoara RO 126 B3
Ortnevik N 46 A3
Orton GB 37 B4
Ortona I 169 A4
Ortrand D 84 A1
Orubica HR 124 B3
Ørum DK 58 B2
Orune I 178 B3
Orusco E 151 B4
Orvalho P 155 A3
Orvault F 101 B4
Ørvella N 53 A5
Orvieto I 168 A2
Orvínio I 169 A2
Oryakhovo BG 17 D5
Orzesze PL 86 B2
Orzinuovi I 120 B2
Orzivécchi I 120 B2
Orzyny PL 77 A6
Os
Hedmark N 48 B3
Hedmark N 199 C8
Osann-Monzel D . . .92 B2
Osbruk S 62 A2
Øsby DK 59 C2
Osby S 61 C3
Oščadnica SK 98 B2
Oschatz D 83 A5
Oschersleben D . . .73 B4
Óschiri I 178 B3
Ościłowo PL 77 B5
Osdorf D 64 B3
Osečina SRB 127 C1
Osečná CZ 84 B2
Oseja de Sajambre
E 142 A1
Osek CZ 84 B1
Osen N 199 A7
Osera de Ebro E . .153 A3
Osidda I 178 B3
Osie PL 69 B3
Osiecza
Pomorskie PL . . .68 B3
Wielkopolskie PL . . 75 C5
Osieczno PL 75 A4
Osiek
Kujawsko-Pomorskie
PL 76 B3
Kujawsko-Pomorskie
PL 77 A4
Pomorskie PL 69 B3
Świętokrzyskie PL . 87 B5
Osiek nad Notecią
PL 76 A2
Osielsko PL 76 A3
Osijek HR 125 B4
Osilnica SLO 123 B3
Ósilo I 178 B2
Ósimo I 136 B2
Osinja BIH 125 B3
Osintorf BY 13 A9
Osipaonica SRB . .127 C3
Osjaków PL 86 A2
Oskamull GB 34 B1
Oskarshamn S 62 A4
Oskarström S 60 C2
Oslany SK 98 C2
Oslavany CZ 97 B4
Ošlje HR 139 C3
Oslo N 48 C2
Øsløs DK 58 A1

Osmancık TR 23 A8
Osmaneli TR 187 B4
Osmo S 57 B3
Osmolin PL 77 B4
Osnabrück D 71 B5
Óšno Lubuskie PL .75 B3
Osoblaha CZ 85 B5
Osor HR 123 C3
Osorno E 142 B2
Øsøyra N 46 A2
Øsøyri N 46 B2
Øspakseyri IS 190 B4
Os Peares E 140 B3
Ospedaletti I 133 B3
Ospitaletto I 120 B3
Oss NL 80 A1
Ossa de Montiel E 158 C1
Ossi I 178 B2
Ossjøen N 47 B5
Ossun F 145 A3
Ostanå S 61 C4
Ostanvik S 50 A2
Ostashkov RUS 9 D8
Östavall S 200 D1
Ostbevern D 71 B4
Østborg N 199 A10
Østby N 49 A4
Osted D 61 D1
Ostenfeld D 64 B2
Oster UA 13 C9
Øster Assels DK . . .58 B1
Osterburg D 73 B4
Osterburken D 94 B1
Österbybruk S 51 B4
Østerbyhavn DK . . .58 A4
Österbymo S 62 A3
Ostercappeln D 71 B5
Österfärnebo S 51 B3
Osterfeld D 83 A3
Österforse S 200 C3
Osterhever D 64 B1
Osterhofen D 95 C5
Osterholz-Scharmbeck
D 72 A1
Øster Hornum DK . .58 B2
Øster Hurup DK . . .58 B3
Øster Jølby DK 58 B1
Øster-marie DK 67 A4
Österlövsta S 51 B4
Østermiething A . .109 A3
Osterode am Harz
D 82 A2
Ostersiel D 64 B1
Östersund S 199 B11
Øster Tørslev DK . .58 B3
Östervåla S 51 B4
Östervallskog S 54 A2
Øster Vrå DK 58 A3
Osterwieck D 73 C3
Osterzell D 108 B1
Ostffyasszonyfa
H 111 B4
Östfora S 51 C4
Östhammar S 51 B5
Ostheim F 106 A2
Ostheim vor der Rhön
D 82 B2
Osthofen D 93 B4
Ostiano I 120 B3
Ostíglia I 121 B4
Ostiz E 144 B2
Östmark S 49 B4
Ostnor S 50 A1
Ostojićevo SRB . . .126 B2
Ostra I 136 B2
Ostra Amtervik S . . .55 A4
Östraby S 61 D3
Ostrach D 107 B4
Östra Husby S 56 B2
Östra Ljungby S 61 C3
Östra Ryd S 56 B2
Ostrau D 83 A5
Ostrava CZ 98 B2
Østre Halsen N 53 A6
Ostrhauderfehn D . .71 A4
Ostritz D 84 A2
Ostróda PL 69 B4
Ostroh UA 13 C7
Ostrołęka PL 12 B4
Ostropole PL 68 B1
Ostrosko PL 75 B5
Ostrov
CZ 83 B4
RUS 8 D6
Ostrov nad Oslavou
CZ 97 B3
Ostrówek PL 86 A2
Ostrowiec PL 68 A1
Ostrowiec-
Świętokrzyski PL . 87 B5
Ostrowite PL 77 A4
Ostrów Mazowiecka
PL 12 B4
Ostrowo PL 76 B3
Ostrów Wielkopolski
PL 86 A1
Ostrožac BIH 139 B3
Ostrzeszów PL 86 A1
Ostseebad
Kühlungsborn D . 65 B4
Ostuni I 173 B3
Osuna E 162 A2
Osvětimany CZ 98 B1
Oswestry GB 38 B3
Oświęcim PL 86 B3
Osztopán H 111 C4
Oteiza E 144 B2
Otelec RO 126 B2
Oteo E 143 A3
Oterbekk N 54 A1
Otero de Herreros
E 151 B3
Otero de O Bodas
E 141 C4
Othem S 57 C4
Otley GB 40 B2
Otmuchów PL 85 B5
Otočac HR 123 C4

Otok		Øyeren N 49 B4	Palazzo San Gervásio	Parades de Rubiales	Patterdale GB 36 B4	Pély H. 113 B4
Splitsko-Dalmatinska		Oyfiell N. 53 A4	I. 172 B1	E. 150 A2	Patti I. 177 A3	Pembroke GB 39 C2
HR 138 B2		Øygårdslia N 53 B4	Palazzuolo sul Senio	Paradinas de San Juan	Páty H 112 B2	Pembroke Dock
Vukovarsko-Srijemska		Oykel Bridge GB . . .32 D2	I. 135 A4	E. 150 B2	Pau F 145 A3	GB. 39 C2
HR 125 B4		Øymark N. 54 A2	Paldiski EST 8 C4	Paradiso di Cevadale	Pauillac F 128 A2	Peñacerrada E 143 B4
Otoka BIH 124 C2		Oyonnax F 118 A2	Pale BIH 139 B4	I. 108 C1	Paularo I. 109 C4	Penacova P 148 B1
Otranto I. 173 B4		Øyslebø N 52 B3	Palekastro GR. 185 D7	Paradyż PL. 87 A4	Paulhaguet F 117 B3	Peña de Cabra E . .149 B4
Otrić HR. 138 A2		Øystese N 46 B3	Palena I. 169 A4	Parainen FIN 8 B3	Paulhan F 130 B2	Peñafiel E 151 A3
Otrícoli I. 168 A2		Oyten D 72 A2	Palencia E 142 B2	Parakhino Paddubye	Paulilátino I 178 B2	Peñafiel P 148 A1
Otrokovice CZ. 98 B1		Øyuvsbu N. 52 A3	Palenciana E 163 A3	RUS. 9 C8	Pauliström S 62 A3	Peñaflor E 162 A2
Otta N. 198 D6		Ozaeta E 143 B4	Paleochora GR 185 D4	Parakka S. 196 B4	Paullo I. 120 B2	Peñalba de Santiago
Ottana I 178 B3		Ozalj HR. 123 B4	Paleometokho CY 181 B1	Paralimni CY 181 A2	Paulstown IRL 30 B1	E 141 B4
Ottaviano I. 170 C2		Ožbalt SLO 110 C2	Palermo I. 176 A2	Parallo Astros GR 184 B3	Pausa D. 83 B3	Peñalsordo E. 156 B2
Ottenby S. 63 B4		Ózd H 113 A4	Paleros GR 182 E2	Paramé F. 88 B2	Pauträsk S 200 B3	Penalva do Castelo
Ottendorf-Okrilla D 84 A1		Ožd'any SK. 99 C3	Palestrina I 169 B2	Paramithia GR. 182 D2	Pavia	P 148 B2
Ottenhöfen D. 93 C4		Ozieri I 178 B3	Pálfa H 112 C2	Páramo del Sil E . .141 B4	I. 120 B2	Penamacôr P. 149 B2
Ottenschlag A. 97 C3		Ozimek PL. 86 B2	Palfau A 110 B1	Parandaça P 148 A2	P. 154 C2	Peñaparda E 149 B3
Ottensheim A. 96 C2		Ozimica BIH. 139 A4	Palhaça P 148 B1	Paravadella E 141 A3	Pavias E. 159 B3	Peñaranda de
Otterbach D. 93 B3		Ozora H. 112 C2	Palheiros da Tocha	Paray-le-Monial F .104 C3	Pavilly F. 89 A4	Bracamonte E. . .150 B2
Otterbäcken S. 55 B5		Ozorków PL. 77 C4	P. 148 B1	Parceiros P 154 B2	Pavullo nel Frignano	Peñaranda de Duero
Otterberg D. 93 B3		Ozzano Monferrato	Palheiros de Quiaios	Parcey F. 105 B4	I. 135 A3	E 143 C3
Otterburn GB. 37 A4		I. 119 B5	P. 148 B1	Parchim D 73 A4	Pawłowice E. 86 A1	Peñarroya de Tastavins
Otter Ferry GB. 34 B2			Paliaopoli GR 185 B5	Parchim PL. 77 A6	Pawłowice PL. 98 B2	E 153 B4
Otterndorf D. 64 C1			Palić SRB. 126 A1	Parcice PL. 86 A2	Paxi GR 182 D2	Peñarroya-
Ottersburg D 72 A2			Palidoro I 168 B2	Pardilla E 151 A4	Payallar TR 189 C6	Pueblonuevo E. .156 B2
Ottersweier D. 93 C4			Palinuro I 172 B1	Pardubice CZ 97 A3	Payerne CH 106 C1	Peñarrubia E 141 B3
Otterup DK. 59 C3		**P**	Paliouri GR 183 D5	Paredes	Paymogo E 161 B2	Peñascosa E 158 C1
Ottery St Mary GB. . .43 B3			Paliseul B. 91 B5	E 151 B5	Payrac F. 129 B4	Peñas de San Pedro
Ottignies B. 79 B4		Paakkola FIN 196 D7	Pallanza I. 119 B5	E 148 A1	Pazardzhik BG. . . .183 A6	E 158 C2
Ottmarsheim F 106 B2		Paal B. 79 A5	Pallares E 155 B4	Paredes de Coura	Pazaryeri TR 187 B4	Persan F. 90 B2
Ottobeuren D. 107 B5		Pabianice PL. 86 A3	Pallaruelo de Monegros	P 140 C2	Pazin HR 122 B2	Persberg S. 55 A5
Öttömös H. 126 A1		Pacanów PL. 87 B5	E 145 C3	Paredes de Nava	Paziols F 146 B3	Persenbeug A 110 A2
Ottone I. 120 C2		Paceco I 176 B1	Pallas Green IRL . . .29 B3	E 142 B2	Pčelić HR. 124 B3	Pershore GB. 44 A1
Ottsjö S 199 B10		Pachino I. 177 C4	Pallerols E. 146 B2	Paredes de Siguenza	Peal de Becerro E 164 B1	Persón S 196 D5
Ottweiler D. 92 B3		Pačir SRB 126 B1	Palling D 109 A3	E 151 A5	Peasedown St	Perstorp S. 61 C3
Ötvešti RO. 126 B3		Pack A 110 B2	Palluau F 114 B2	Pareja E 151 B5	John GB. 43 A4	Perth GB 35 B4
Ötvöskónyi H 124 A3		Paços de Ferreira	Palma P 154 C2	Parennes F 102 A1	Peasmarsh GB 45 C4	Pertisau A 108 B2
Otwock PL. 12 B4		P 148 A1	Palma Campánia	Parenti I 175 B2	Peć KOS. 16 D4	Pertoča SLO 111 C3
Ouanne F. 104 B2		Pacov CZ 96 B3	I. 170 C2	Parentis-en-Born	Penede GB 39 C2	Pertuis F 131 B4
Ouarville F. 90 C1		Pacsa H 111 C4	Palma del Rio E. . .162 A2	F. 128 B1	Penela P. 154 A2	Perućac SRB. 127 D1
Oucques F 103 B3		Pacy-sur-Eure F 89 A5	Palma de Mallorca	Parey D 73 B4	Pénestin F 101 B3	Perúgia I 136 B1
Oud-Beijerland NL .79 A4		Paczków PL. 85 B5	E 166 B2	Parfino RUS. 9 D7	Penhas Juntas P . .149 A2	Perušić HR 123 C4
Ouddorp NL. 79 A3		Padany RUS 3 E13	Palma di Montechiaro	Parga GR 182 D2	Peniche P. 154 B1	Péruwelz B. 79 B3
Oudemirdum NL. . . .70 B2		Padborg DK. 64 B2	I. 176 B2	Pargny-sur-Saulx F 91 C4	Penicuik GB. 35 C4	Pervomaysk UA. . . .13 D9
Oudenaarde B. 79 B3		Padej SRB. 126 B2	Palmádula I 178 B2	Pari-Gagné F. 117 A4	Penig D 83 B4	Perwez B 79 B4
Oudenbosch NL 79 A4		Padene HR. 138 A2	Palmanova I 122 B2	Parigné-l'Évêque	Penilhos P. 160 B2	Pesadas de Burgos
Oudenburg B. 78 A3		Paderborn D 81 A4	Palma Nova E 166 B2	F. 102 B2	Peninsola i	E 143 B3
Oude-Pekela NL 71 A4		Paderne D 160 B1	Palmela P 154 C2	Parikkala FIN 9 B6	Peñiscola E 153 B4	Pesaguero E 142 A2
Oude-Tonge NL 79 A4		Padiham GB 40 B1	Palmerola E 147 B3	Paris F 90 C2	Penistone GB 40 B2	Pésaro I 136 B1
Oudewater NL. 70 B1		Padina SRB 126 B2	Palmi I 175 C1	Parisot F 129 B4	Penkridge GB 40 C1	Pescantina I 121 B3
Oud Gastel NL. 79 A4		Padinska Skela	Pálmonostora H . . .113 C3	Parkalompolo S . . .196 B5	Penkun D 74 A3	Pescara I. 169 A4
Oudon F. 101 B4		SRB. 127 C2	Palo del Colle I 171 B4	Parkano FIN. 8 A3	Penmarch F. 100 B1	Pescasséroli I 169 B3
Oughterard IRL 28 A2		Padornelo P. 148 A1	Palojärvi FIN 192 D7	Parknasilla IRL 29 C2	Pennabilli I. 135 B5	Peschici I 171 B4
Ouguela P 155 B3		Pádova I. 121 B4	Palojoensuu FIN . .196 A6	Parla E 151 B4	Penne I 169 A3	Peschiera del Garda
Ouhrum F 89 A3		Padragkút H 111 B4	Palomares E 165 B4	Parlavá E 147 B4	Penne-d'Agenais	I. 121 B3
Ouistreham F 89 A3		Padria I. 178 B2	Palomares del Campo	Parma I. 120 C3	F. 129 B3	Péscia I 135 B3
Oulainen FIN 3 D9		Padrón E 140 B2	E 158 B1	Parndorf A 111 B3	Pennes I 108 C2	Pescina I 169 A3
Oulchy-le-Château		Padru I 178 B3	Palomas E 156 B1	Párnica SK. 99 B3	Pennyghael GB 34 B1	Pescocostanzo I . .169 B4
F. 91 B3		Padstow GB. 42 B2	Palombara Sabina	Parnu EST 8 C4	Penrhyndeudraeth	Pescopagano I 172 B1
Oullins F 117 B4		Padul E 163 A4	I. 168 A2	Parolis E. 164 A2	GB. 38 B2	Pesco Sannita I. . . .170 B2
Oulmes F 114 B3		Padula I. 172 B1	Palos de la Frontera	Paros GR 185 B6	Penrith GB. 37 B4	Peshkopi AL. 182 B2
Oulton GB. 41 C5		Páduli I 170 B2	E 161 B3	Parrillas E 150 B2	Penryn GB. 42 B1	Peshtera BG 183 A6
Oulton Broad GB. . . .41 C5		Paesana I. 119 C4	Palotaboszok H. . . .125 A4	Parsberg D. 95 B3	Pentraeth GB. 38 A2	Pesmes F 105 B4
Oulu FIN. 3 D9		Paese I. 121 B5	Palotás H. 112 B3	Parstein D 74 B3	Pentrefoelas GB 38 B3	Pešnica SLO 110 C2
Oulx I 119 B3		Pag HR. 137 A4	Pals E. 147 C4	Partakko FIN 193 C11	Penygroes	Peso da Régua P . .148 A2
Oundle GB. 40 C3		Pagani I. 170 C2	Pålsboda S 56 A1	Partanna I 176 B1	Carmarthenshire	Pesquera de Duero
Ouranópoli GR 183 C6		Pagánica I. 169 A3	Paluzza I 109 C4	Parthenay F 102 C1	GB. 39 C2	E 142 C2
Ourém P. 154 B2		Pagánico I. 135 C4	Pamhagen A 111 B3	Partinico I 176 A2	Gwynedd GB. 38 A2	Pessac F 128 B2
Ourense E. 140 B3		Paglieta I 169 A4	Pamiers F 146 A2	Partizani SRB 127 C2	Penzance GB. 42 B1	Pestovo RUS. 9 C9
Ourique P. 160 B1		Pagny-sur-Moselle	Pamiętowo PL. 76 A2	Partizánske SK 98 C2	Penzberg D 108 B2	Petäjäskoski FIN . .197 C8
Ourol E. 140 A3		F. 92 C2	Pampaneira E 163 B4	Partney GB. 41 B4	Penzlin D. 74 A2	Petalidi GR 184 C2
Ouroux-en-Morvan		Páhi H 112 C3	Pamparato I. 133 A3	Påryd S 63 B4	Pepinster B 80 B1	Pétange L. 92 B1
F. 104 B2		Pahkakumpu	Pampilhosa	Parzymiechy PL. 86 A2	Peqin AL. 182 B1	Petas GR 182 D3
Ouroux-sur-Loire		FIN. 197 C11	Aveiro P. 148 B1	Paşcani RO 17 B7	Pér H 111 B4	Peteranec HR 124 A2
F. 103 B4		Pahl D 108 B2	Coimbra P 148 B2	Pasewalk D. 74 A2	Pera Boa P. 148 B2	Peterborough GB . . .41 C3
Ovada I. 133 A4		Paide EST 8 C4	Pampliega E 143 B3	Pašina Voda MNE 139 B5	Perachora GR 184 A3	Peterculter GB. 33 D4
Ovar P 148 B1		Paignton GB 43 B3	Pamplona E 144 B2	Påskallavik S. 62 A4	Perafita I. 148 A1	Peterhead GB. 33 D5
Ovelgönne D 72 A1		Pailhès F 146 A2	Pampow D. 73 A4	Paslek PL. 69 A4	Peraleda de la Mata	Peterlee GB. 37 B5
Overath D 80 B3		Paimboeuf F 101 B3	Pamukçu TR 186 C2	Pašman HR 137 B4	E 150 C2	Petersfield GB. 44 B3
Overbister GB 33 B4		Paimpol F 100 A2	Pamukkale TR 188 B4	Passage East IRL . .30 B2	Peraleda del Zaucejo	Petershagen
Øverbygd N. 192 D3		Paimpont F 101 A3	Pamukova TR 187 B5	Passail A 110 B2	E 156 B2	Brandenburg D . . .74 B2
Overdinkel NL 71 B4		Painswick GB 43 A4	Panagyurishte BG. .17 D6	Passais F 88 B3	Peraleda de San	Brandenburg D . . .74 B3
Överenhörna S 56 A3		Painten D 95 C3	Pancalieri I. 119 C4	Passau D 96 C1	Román E. 156 A2	Nordrhein-Westfalen
Överhalla N. 199 A8		Paisley GB. 34 C3	Pančevo SRB 127 C2	Passegueiro P. 148 B1	Perales de Alfambra	D 72 B1
Overijse B 79 B4		Pajala S 196 B6	Pancey F 91 C5	Passignano sul	E 152 B2	Petershausen D 95 C3
Over-jerstal DK. 59 C2		Pajares E 141 A5	Pancorvo E 143 B3	Trasimeno I. 135 B5	Perales del Puerto	Peterswell IRL 28 A3
Overlade DK 58 B2		Pajares de los Oteros	Pancrudo E 152 B2	Passo di Tréia I . . .136 B2	E 149 B3	Pétervására H 113 A4
Överö FIN 51 B7		E 142 B1	Pandino I. 120 B2	Passopisciaro I 177 B4	Perales de Tajuña	Petília Policastro 175 B2
Overpelt B. 79 A5		Pajęczno PL. 86 A2	Pandrup DK. 58 A2	Passow D. 74 A3	E 151 B4	Petín E 141 B3
Overton GB 38 B4		Páka H 111 C3	Panenský-Týnec	Passy F 118 B3	Peralta E 144 B2	Pétipsy CZ. 83 B5
Övertorneå S. 196 C6		Pakość PL. 76 B3	CZ. 84 B1	Pega P 149 B2	Peralta de la Sal E 145 C4	Petkus D 74 C2
Överum S. 62 A4		Pakosławice PL. 85 B5	Panes E 142 A2	Pegau D. 83 A4	Peralva P. 160 B2	Petlovac HR. 125 B4
Ovídiopol UA. 17 B9		Pakoštane HR 137 B4	Panevėžys LT 8 E4	Peggau A 110 B2	Peralveche E. 152 B1	Petäjävesi SRB 127 C1
Oviedo E 141 A5		Pakrac HR 124 B3	Pangbourne GB 44 B2	Pegli I. 133 A4	Perama GR 185 D5	Petöfiszallás H 113 C3
Oviglio I 119 C5		Paks H 112 C2	Panissières F 117 B4	Pegnitz D. 95 B3	Peranka FIN. 197 D12	Petra E 167 B3
Ovindoli I. 169 A3		Palacios de la Sierra	Panki PL. 86 B2	Pego E 159 C3	Perbál H 112 B2	Petralia Sottana I . .177 B3
Ovodda I 178 B3		E 143 C3	Pannes F 103 A4	Pegões-Estação	Perchtoldsdorf A . . .111 A3	Petrčane HR 137 A4
Øvre Årdal N 47 A4		Palaciòs de la	Panningen NL 80 A1	P 154 C2	Percy F. 88 B2	Petrella Tifernina I 170 B2
Øvrebygd N. 52 B2		Valduerna E 141 B5	Pannonhalma H 111 B4	Pegões Velhos P. .154 C2	Perdasdefogu I 179 C3	Petrer E 159 C3
Øvre Rendal N. 199 D8		Palacios del Sil E .141 B4	Pano Lefkara CY . . .181 B2	Pegów PL. 85 A4	Perdiguera E 145 C3	Petreto-Bicchisano
Øvre Sirdal N 52 B2		Palacios de Sanabria	Pano Panayia CY . .181 B1	Pegswood GB. 37 A5	Peredo P 149 A3	F. 180 B1
Övre Soppero S. . . .196 A4		E 141 B4	Panormos GR 185 B6	Peguera E 166 B2	Pereiro	Petrich BG 183 B5
Övre Ullerud S. 55 A4		Palaciosrubios E. . .150 A2	Panschwitz-Kuckau	Paterna del Campo	Faro P 160 B2	Petrijevci HR 125 B4
Ovruch UA. 13 C8		Palafrugell E 147 C4	D. 84 A2	E 161 B3	Guarda P 149 B2	Petrinja HR 124 B2
Ovtrup DK. 59 C1		Palagiano I 173 B3	Pansdorf D 65 C3	Paterna del Madera	Santarém P 154 B2	Petrodvorets RUS. . .9 C6
Owińska PL. 76 B1		Palagonia I. 177 B3	Pantano de Cíjara	E 158 C1	Pereiro de Aguiar	Pétrola E 158 C2
Oxaback S. 60 B2		Paláia I. 135 B3	E 156 A3	Paterna de Rivera	E 140 B3	Petronà I 175 B2
Oxberg S. 49 A6		Palaiokastritsa	Panticosa E 145 B3	E 162 B2	Perelada E 147 B4	Petronell A. 111 A3
Oxelösund S 56 B3		GR. 182 D1	Pantin F 90 C2	Paternion A 109 C4	Perelejos de las	Petroşani RO. 17 C5
Oxenholme GB. 37 B4		Palaiseau F 90 C2	Pantoja E 151 B4	Paternò I 177 B3	Truchas E 152 B2	Petrovac SRB 127 C3
Oxford GB. 44 B2		Palamas GR. 182 D4	Pantón E 140 B3	Paternópoli I 170 C3	Perello E 153 B4	Petrovaradin SRB 126 B1
Oxie S 61 D3		Palamós E. 147 C4	Panxon E. 140 B2	Patersdorf D 95 B4	Perenna E 149 A3	Petrovice
Oxilithos GR 185 A5		Pälång S 196 D5	Páola I 174 B2	Paterswolde NL. 71 A3	Pererúela E 149 A4	BIH 139 A4
Oxted GB. 45 B4		Palanga LT 8 E2	Paola I. 175 C3	Patitíri GR 183 D5	Peréruela E 149 A3	CZ. 84 B1
Oyaca TR 187 C7		Palanzano I 134 A3	Pápa H 111 B4	Patmos GR 188 B1	Pérfugas I 178 B2	Petrovo RUS. 69 A5
Øye N. 47 A5		Palárikovo SK 112 A2	Papasidero I 174 B1	Patna GB. 36 A2	Perg A. 110 A1	Petrozavodsk RUS . .9 B9
Øyenkilen N. 54 A1		Palas de Rei E. 140 B3	Pápateszér H. 111 B4	Patnow PL. 76 B3	Pérgine Valsugana	Pettenbach A. 109 B5
Øyer N 48 A2		Palata I. 170 B2	Papenburg D 71 A4	Patoniva FIN 193 C11	I. 121 A4	Pettigo IRL 26 B3
		Palau I 178 A3	Papenhain D. 94 C2	Patopirtti FIN 197 B12	Pérgola I 136 B1	Petworth GB. 44 C3
		Palavas-les-Flots	Paphos CY. 181 B1	Patos AL. 182 C1	Pergusa I 177 B3	Peuerbach A 96 C1
		F. 131 B2	Pappenheim D. 94 C2	Patra = Patras GR 184 A2	Periam RO 126 A2	Peuntenansa E 142 A2
		Palazuelos de la Sierra	Paprotnia PL. 77 B5	Patras = Patra GR 184 A2	Periana E 163 B3	Peurasuvanto FIN 197 B9
		E 143 B3	Parábita I 173 B4	Patreksfjörður IS. . .190 B2	Périers F 88 A2	Pevensey Bay GB. . .45 C4
		Palazzo Adriano I . .176 B2	Paráčin SRB 127 D3	Patricksvell IRL 29 B3	Périgueux F 129 A3	Peveragno I 133 A3
		Palazzo del Pero I 135 B4	Parád H 113 B4	Patrimonio F 180 A2	Perino I 120 C2	Pewsey GB. 44 B2
		Palazzolo Acréide	Parada	Patrington GB. 41 B3	Pello	Pewsum D 71 A4
		I 177 B3	Bragança P 149 A3	Pattada I. 178 B3	FIN 196 C7	Peyrat-le-Château
		Palazzolo sull Oglio	Viseu P 148 B1	Pattensen	S. 196 C6	F. 116 B1
Øye N 47 A5		I. 120 B2	Paradas E. 162 A2	Niedersachsen D. .72 A3	Peloche E 156 A2	Peyrehorade F. 128 C1
Øyer N 48 A2			Paradela E 140 B3	Niedersachsen D. . 72 B2	Pelplin PL. 69 B3	

Peyriac-Minervois
F. 146 A3
Peyrins F. 117 B5
Peyrissac F 116 B1
Peyrolles-en-Provence
F. 132 B1
Peyruis F. 132 A1
Pézarches F. 90 C2
Pézenas F 130 B2
Pezinok SK 111 A4
Pezuls F 129 B3
Pfaffenhausen D. .108 A1
Pfaffenhofen
 Bayern D 94 C2
 Bayern D 95 C3
Pfaffenhoffen F 93 C3
Pfäffikon CH 107 B3
Pfarrkirchen D. 95 C4
Pfeffenhausen D. . . .95 C3
Pfetterhouse F 106 B2
Pforzheim D. 93 C4
Pfreimd D. 95 B4
Pfronten D. 108 B1
Pfullendorf D. 107 B4
Pfullingen D. 94 C1
Pfunds A 108 C1
Pfungstadt D. 93 B4
Pfyn CH 107 B3
Phalsbourg F. 92 C3
Philippeville B 79 B4
Philippsreut D. 96 C1
Philippsthal D 82 B1
Piacenza I. 120 B2
Piacenza d'Adige
 I. 121 B4
Piádena I 120 B3
Piana F. 180 A1
Piana Crixia I. 133 A4
Piana degli Albanesi
 I. 176 B2
Piana di Monte Verna
 I. 170 B2
Piancastagnáio I. .135 C4
Piandelagotti I. . . .134 A3
Pianella
 Abruzzi I. 169 A4
 Toscana I. 135 B4
Pianello Val Tidone
 I. 120 C2
Pianoro I 135 A4
Pians A. 108 B1
Pias E. 141 B4
Pias P. 160 A2
Piaseczno PL. 77 B6
Piasek PL. 74 B3
Piaski PL 69 A4
Piastów PL. 77 B5
Piaszcyna PL. 68 A2
Piątek PL 77 B4
Piatra Neamţ RO. . .17 B7
Piazza al Sérchio
 I. 134 A3
Piazza Armerina I .177 B3
Piazza Brembana
 I. 120 B2
Piazze I. 135 C4
Piazzola sul Brenta
 I. 121 B4
Picassent E 159 B3
Piccione I. 136 B1
Picerno I 172 B1
Picher D. 73 A4
Pickering GB 40 A3
Pico I 169 B3
Picón E 157 A3
Picquigny F. 90 B2
Piechowice PL. 84 B3
Piecnik PL 75 A5
Piedicavallo I. 119 B4
Piedicroce F. 180 A2
Piedimonte Etneo
 I. 177 B4
Piedimonte Matese
 I. 170 B2
Piedimulera I. 119 A5
Piedipaterno I. 136 C1
Piedrabuena E. . . .157 A3
Piedraescrita E. . . .156 A3
Piedrafita E 142 A1
Piedrahita E. 150 B2
Piedralaves E. 150 B3
Piedras Albas E. . .155 B4
Piedras Blancas E .141 A5
Piegaro I 135 C5
Piekary Śl. PL 86 B2
Piekoszów PL. 87 B4
Pieksämäki FIN 8 A5
Pielenhofen D. 95 B3
Pielgrzymka PL. 85 A3
Pieniężno PL. 69 A5
Pieńsk PL. 84 A3
Pienza I. 135 B4
Piera E. 147 C2
Pieranie PL 76 B3
Pierowall GB 33 B4
Pierre-Buffière F . .115 C5
Pierrecourt F 105 B4
Pierre-de-Bresse
 F. 105 C4
Pierrefeu-du-Var
 F. 132 B2
Pierrefitte-Nestalas
 F. 145 B3
Pierrefitte-sur-Aire
 F. 92 C1
Pierrefonds F 90 B2
Pierrefontaine-les-
 Varans F. 105 B5
Pierrefort F 116 C2
Pierrelatte F 131 A3
Pierrepont
 Aisne F 91 B3
 Meurthe-et-Moselle
 F. 92 B1
Piesendorf A 109 B3
Pieštany SK. 98 C1
Pieszkowo PL. 69 A5

Pieszyce PL. 85 B4
Pietarsaari FIN 3 E8
Pietragalla I 172 B1
Pietra Ligure I 133 A4
Pietralunga I 136 B1
Pietramelara I 170 B2
Pietraperzia I 177 B3
Pietrasanta I 134 B3
Pietravairano I. 170 B2
Pieve del Cáiro I . .120 B1
Pieve di Bono I . . .121 B3
Pieve di Cadore I. .122 A1
Pieve di Cento I . . .121 C4
Pieve di Soligo I . .121 B5
Pieve di Teco I. . . .133 A3
Pievepélago I. 134 A3
Pieve Santo Stefano
 I. 135 B5
Pieve Torina I. 136 B2
Piges GR 182 D3
Piglio I 169 B3
Pigna I 133 B3
Pignataro Maggiore
 I. 170 B2
Piiittisjärvi FIN 197 C9
Pijnacker NL 70 B1
Pikalevo RUS 9 C9
Piła PL 75 A5
Pilar de la Horadada
 E 165 B4
Pilas E 161 B3
Pilastri I 121 C4
Piława Górna PL 85 B4
Piławki PL 69 B4
Pilchowice PL. 86 B2
Pilea GR. 183 C5
Pilgrimstad S. 199 C12
Pili
 Dodekanisa GR . .188 C2
 Trikala GR 182 D3
Pilica PL. 86 B3
Pilis H. 112 B3
Piliscaba H 112 B2
Pilisszántó H. 112 B2
Pilisvörösvár H . . .112 B2
Pilos GR. 184 C2
Pilsting D 95 C4
Pilszcz PL 98 A1
Pilterud N. 48 C2
Pilu RO. 113 C5
Pina de Ebro E . . .153 A3
Piñar E 163 A4
Pınarbaşı TR 186 C1
Pınarhisar TR 186 A2
Pinas F 145 A4
Pincehely H 112 C2
Pinchbeck GB 41 C3
Pińczów PL. 87 B4
Pineda de la Sierra
 E 143 B3
Pineda de Mar E . .147 C3
Pinerella I. 135 A5
Pinerolo I. 119 C4
Pineta Grande I. . . .170 C1
Pineto I. 169 A4
Piney F. 91 C4
Pinggau A 111 B3
Pinhal Novo P 154 C2
Pinhão P 148 A2
Pinheiro
 Aveiro P. 148 A1
 Aveiro P. 148 B1
Pinheiro Grande
 P 154 B2
Pinhel P 149 B2
Pinhoe GB. 43 B3
Pinilla E 158 C2
Pinilla de Toro E . .150 A2
Pinkafeld A. 111 B3
Pinneberg D 72 A2
Pinnow D. 74 C3
Pino F. 180 A2
Pino del Rio E 142 B2
Pino de Val E 140 B2
Pinofranqueado E .149 B3
Pinols F. 117 B3
Piñor E. 140 B2
Pinos del Valle E . .163 B4
Pinoso E 159 C2
Pinos Puente E . . .163 A4
Pinsk BY 13 B7
Pintamo FIN. 197 D10
Pinto E 151 B4
Pinzano al Tagliamento
 I. 122 A1
Pinzio P 149 B2
Pinzolo I. 121 A3
Pióbbico I 136 B1
Piombino I. 134 C3
Pionki PL. 87 A5
Pionsat F 116 A2
Pióraco I 136 B1
Piornal E 150 B2
Piotrkowice PL. 87 B4
Piotrków-Kujawski
 PL. 76 B3
Piotrków Trybunalski
 PL. 86 A3
Piotrowo PL. 75 B5
Piove di Sacco I . . .121 B5
Piovene I 121 B4
Piperskärr S 62 A4
Pípriac F 101 B4
Piraeus = Pireas
 GR 185 B4
Piran SLO 122 B2
Pireas = Piraeus
 GR 185 B4
Piré-sur-Seiche F .101 A4
Pirgi GR. 185 A6
Pirgos
 Ilia GR. 184 B2
 Kriti GR 185 D6
Piriac-sur-Mer F . .101 B3
Piringsdorf A 111 B3
Pirmasens D 93 B3
Pirna D. 84 B1
Pirnmill GB 34 C2
Pirot SRB. 16 D5

Pirovac HR 137 B4
Pirttivuopio S. 196 B2
Pisa I 134 B3
Pisany F. 114 C3
Pisarovina HR 124 B1
Pischelsdorf in der
 Steiermark A. 110 B2
Pischia RO. 126 B3
Pisciotta I. 172 B1
Pisek CZ 96 B2
Pisogne I 120 B3
Pissos F 128 B2
Pissouri CY 181 B1
Pisticci I. 174 A2
Pistóia I 135 B3
Piteå S 196 D4
Piteşti RO. 17 C6
Pithiviers F 103 A4
Pitigliano I. 168 A1
Pitkyaranta RUS. 9 B7
Pitlochry GB 35 B4
Pitomača HR 124 B3
Pitres E 163 B4
Pittentrail GB 32 D2
Pitvaros H 126 A2
Pivka SLO 123 B3
Pivnice SRB. 126 B1
Piwniczna PL. 99 B4
Pizarra E 163 B3
Pizzano I 121 A3
Pizzighettone I 120 B2
Pizzo I 175 C2
Pizzoli I 169 A3
Pizzolungo I. 176 A1
Pjätteryd S. 61 C4
Plabennec F 100 A1
Placencia E 143 A4
Plaffeien CH 106 C2
Plaisance
 Gers F 128 C3
 Haute-Garonne F. .129 C4
 Tarn F 130 B1
Plaka GR 183 D7
Plan E. 145 B4
Planá CZ 95 B4
Planánad Lužnici
 CZ 96 B2
Plaňany CZ 96 A3
Planchez F. 104 B3
Plancoët F 101 A3
Plancy-l'Abbaye F .91 C3
Plan-de-Baix F. . . .118 C2
Plandište SRB. 126 B3
Plan-d'Orgon F . . .131 B3
Plánice CZ. 96 B1
Planina
 SLO 123 A4
 SLO 123 B3
Plankenfels D 95 B3
Plasencia E 149 B3
Plasenzuela E 156 A1
Plaški HR 123 B4
Plassen
 Buskerud N 47 B4
 Hedmark N 49 A4
Plášt'ovce SK 112 A3
Plasy CZ 96 B1
Platamona Lido I . .178 B2
Platania I 175 B2
Platanos GR 185 D4
Platí I 175 C2
Platičevo SRB. 127 C1
Platja d'Aro E 147 C4
Plattling D. 95 C4
Plau D 73 A5
Plaue
 Brandenburg D . . .73 B5
 Thüringen D. 82 B2
Plauen D 83 B4
Plavecký Mikuláš
 SK 98 C1
Plavinas LV 8 D4
Plavna SRB. 99 B4
Plavnica SK 99 B4
Plavno HR 138 A2
Playben F. 100 A2
Pléaux F 116 B2
Pleine-Fougères F .88 B2
Pleinfeld D. 94 B2
Pleinting D. 95 C5
Plélan-le-Grand F . .101 B3
Plémet F 101 A3
Pléneuf-Val-André
 F. 101 A3
Plentzia E. 143 A4
Plérin F 101 A3
Pleševic SK 99 C4
Plessa D. 83 A5
Plessé F 101 B4
Plestin-les-Grèves
 F. 100 A2
Pleszew PL 76 C2
Pleternica HR 125 B3
Plettenberg D 81 A3
Pleubian F 100 A2
Pleumartin F 115 B4
Pleumeur-Bodou
 F. 100 A2
Pleurs F 91 C3
Pleven BG 17 D6
Plevnik-Drienové
 SK 98 B2
Pleyber-Christ F . .100 A2
Pliego E. 165 B3
Pliešovce SK. 99 C3
Plitvička Jezera
 HR 123 C4
Plitvički Ljeskovac
 HR 123 C4
Ploaghe I 178 B2
Ploče HR 138 B3
Plochingen D. 94 C1
Płock PL 77 B4
Ploemeur F 100 B2
Ploërmel F. 101 B3
Ploeuc-sur-Lié F . .101 A3
Plogastel St Germain
 F. 100 B1
Plogoff F 100 A1
Ploieşti RO 17 C7

Plomari GR 186 D1
Plombières-les-Bains
 F. 105 B5
Plomin HR 123 B3
Plön D 65 B3
Plonéour-Lanvern
 F. 100 B1
Plonia PL 74 A3
Płoniawy PL. 77 B6
Płońsk PL. 77 B5
Płoskinia PL. 69 A4
Ploskovice CZ. 84 B2
Płośnica PL. 77 B5
Plössberg D. 95 B4
Płoty PL. 67 C4
Plouagat F 100 A2
Plouaret F 100 A2
Plouarzel F 100 A1
Plouay F. 100 B2
Ploubalay F 101 A3
Ploubazlanec F. . . .100 A1
Ploudalmézeau F . .100 A1
Ploudiry F 100 A1
Plouescat F 100 A1
Plouézec F. 100 A2
Plougasnou F 100 A2
Plougastel-Daoulas
 F. 100 A1
Plougonven F 100 A2
Plougonver F 100 A2
Plougrescant F. . . .100 A1
Plouguenast F. 101 A3
Plouguerneau F . . .100 A1
Plouha F 100 A2
Plouhinec F 100 A1
Plouigneau F 100 A2
Ploumanac'h F 100 A1
Plounévez-Quintin
 F. 100 A2
Plouray F 100 A2
Plouzévédé F 100 A1
Plovdiv BG. 183 A6
Plozévet F 100 B1
Plumbridge GB 27 B3
Pluméliau F 100 B3
Plumlov CZ. 97 B5
Plungė LT. 8 E2
Pluty PL 69 A5
Pluvigner F 100 B3
Plužine
 BIH 139 B4
 MNE 139 B4
Pluznica PL. 69 B3
Plymouth GB 42 B2
Plymstock GB 42 B2
Plytnica PL. 68 B1
Plyusa RUS 9 C6
Plzeň CZ. 96 B1
Pniewy PL 75 B5
Pobes E 143 B4
Poběžovice CZ 95 B4
Pobiedziska PL 76 B2
Pobierowo PL. 67 B3
Pobla de Segur E .145 B4
Pobladura del Valle
 E 142 B1
Pobla-Tornesa E . .153 B4
Pobra de Trives E .141 B3
Pobra do Brollón
 E 141 B3
Pobra do Caramiñal
 E 140 B2
Pobudje BIH 139 A5
Počátky CZ. 97 B3
Poceirão P 154 C2
Pociecha PL. 87 A4
Pockau D. 83 B5
Pocking D. 96 C1
Pocklington GB. 40 B3
Podbořany CZ. 83 B5
Podbrdo SLO. 122 A2
Podbrezová SK. 99 C3
Podčetrtek SLO. . . .123 A4
Poddębice PL. 76 C3
Poděbrady CZ. 84 B3
Podence P 149 A3
Podenzana I. 128 C2
Podenzano I 120 C2
Podersdorf am See
 A. 111 B3
Podgaje PL 68 B1
Podgora HR. 138 B3
Podgóra PL. 87 A5
Podgorač HR 125 B4
Podgorica MNE 16 D3
Podgorie AL. 182 C2
Podgrad SLO. 123 B3
Podhájska SK 112 A2
Podkova BG 183 B7
Podlapača HR 123 C4
Podlejki PL. 69 B5
Podlužany SK 98 C2
Podnovlje BIH 125 C4
Podolie SK. 98 C1
Podolínec SK. 99 B4
Podolsk RUS 9 E10
Podporozhy RUS . . .9 B9
Podromanija BIH. . .139 B4
Podturen HR 111 C3
Podvín CZ. 97 C4
Podwilk PL. 99 B3
Poetto I 179 C3
Poggendorf D 66 B2
Poggiardo I 173 B4
Poggibonsi I 135 B4
Póggio a Caiano I .135 B4
Poggio Imperiale I .171 B3
Póggio Mirteto I. . .168 A2
Póggio Moiano I . .169 A2
Póggio Renatico I .121 C4
Póggio Rusco I. . . .121 C4
Pöggstall A 97 C3
Pogny F. 91 C4
Pogorzela PL. 85 A5
Pogorzelice PL. 68 A2
Pogradec AL 182 C2
Pogrodzie PL. 69 A4
Pohorelá SK 99 C4
Pohořelice CZ. 97 C4
Pohronská Polhora
 SK 99 C3

Poiares P. 148 B1
Poio E 140 B2
Poirino F 119 C4
Poisson F 117 A4
Poissons F 91 C5
Poissy F. 90 C2
Poitiers F. 115 B4
Poix-de-Picardie F .90 B1
Poix-Terron F. 91 B4
Pokka FIN 197 A8
Pokój PL. 86 B1
Pokupsko HR 124 B1
Pol E. 141 A3
Pola RUS 9 D7
Pol a Charra GB . . .31 B1
Pola de Allande E .141 A4
Pola de Laviana E .142 A1
Pola de Lena E . . .141 A5
Pola de Siero E . . .142 A1
Pola de Somiedo
 E 141 A4
Polaincourt-et-
 Clairefontaine F .105 B5
Połajewo PL. 75 B5
Polán E 151 C3
Polanica-Zdrój PL. . .85 B4
Połaniec PL. 87 B5
Polanów PL. 68 A1
Polatı TR 187 C7
Polatsk BY 13 A8
Polch D 80 B3
Polcirkeln S. 196 C4
Pólczno PL 68 A2
Połczyn-Zdrój PL. . . .67 C5
Polegate GB 45 C4
Poleñino E 145 C3
Polesella I 121 C4
Polessk RUS 12 A4
Polgár H 113 B5
Polgárdi H 112 B2
Polhov Gradec
 SLO 123 A3
Police D. 74 A3
Police nad Metují
 CZ 85 B4
Polichnitos GR 186 C1
Polička CZ. 97 B4
Poličnik HR 137 A4
Policoro I 174 A2
Policzna PL. 87 A5
Poligiros GR 183 C5
Polignano a Mare
 I. 173 B3
Poligny F 105 C4
Polis CY 181 A1
Polistena I 175 C2
Polizzi Generosa I .176 B3
Poljana SRB. 127 C3
Poljanak HR 123 C4
Poljčane SLO. 123 A4
Polje BIH 125 C3
Poljice
 BIH 138 A2
 BIH 139 A4
Polkowice PL. 85 A4
Polla I 172 B1
Pollas E 150 A2
Pöllau A 110 B2
Polleben D. 82 A3
Pollença E 167 B3
Pollenfeld D. 95 C3
Pollfoss N 198 D4
Póllica I 170 C3
Polminhac F 116 C2
Polná CZ. 97 B3
Polna RUS. 8 C6
Polne PL. 75 A5
Polomka SK. 99 C3
Polonne UA 13 C7
Polperro GB. 42 B2
Polruan GB 42 B2
Pöls A. 110 B1
Polska Cerekiew
 PL. 86 B2
Poltár SK 99 C3
Põltsamaa EST 8 C4
Polyarny RUS 3 B30
Polyarnyye Zori
 RUS 3 C13
Polzela SLO. 123 A4
Pomarance I 135 B3
Pomarez F 128 C2
Pomárico I 172 B2
Pomáz H 112 B3
Pombal P 154 B2
Pomeroy GB 27 B4
Pomézia I 168 B2
Pommard F. 105 B3
Pommelsbrunn D . . .95 B3
Pomonte I 134 C3
Pomorie BG. 17 D7
Pomos CY 181 A1
Pompei I. 170 C2
Pompey F 92 C2
Pomposa I. 122 C1
Poncin F 118 A2
Pondorf D 95 C3
Ponferrada E 141 B4
Poniec PL. 85 A4
Ponikva SLO 123 A4
Poniky SK 99 C3
Pons F. 114 C3
Ponsacco I 134 B3
Pont I 119 B4
Pont-a-Celles B 79 B4
Pontacq F. 145 A3
Pontailler-sur-Saône
 F. 105 B4
Pont-à-Marcq F 78 B3
Pont-à-Mousson F .92 C2
Pontão P. 154 B2
Pontardawe GB 39 C3
Pontarddulais GB . . .39 C2
Pontarion F 116 B1
Pontarlier F 105 C5
Pontassieve I 135 B4
Pontaubault F. 88 B2
Pont-Audemer F . . .89 A4
Pontaumur F 116 B2
Pont-Aven F. 100 B2

Pont Canavese I . .119 B4
Pontcharra F 118 B3
Pontcharra-sur-Turdine
 F. 117 B4
Pontchâteau F. . . .101 B3
Pont-Croix F 100 A1
Pont-d'Ain F 118 A2
Pont-de-Beauvoisin
 F. 118 B2
Pont-de-Buis-lès-
 Quimerch F. 100 A1
Pont-de-Chéruy F .118 B2
Pont de Dore F . . .117 B3
Pont-de-Labeaume
 F. 117 C4
Pont-de-l'Arche F .89 A5
Pont de Molins E. .147 B3
Pont-de-Roide F . .106 B1
Pont-de-Salars F . .130 A1
Pont-d'Espagne F .145 B3
Pont de Suert E . . .145 B4
Pont-de-Vaux F . . .117 A4
Pont-de-Veyle F. . .117 A4
Pont d'Ouilly F 89 B3
Pont-du-Château
 F. 116 B3
Pont-du-Navoy F. .105 C4
Ponte a Moriano I .134 B3
Ponte Arche I. 121 A3
Ponteareas E 140 B2
Pontebba I 109 C4
Ponte Cáffaro I . . .121 B3
Pontecagnano I. . .170 C2
Ponte-Caldelas E .140 B2
Pontecesures E . . .140 B2
Pontecorvo I. 169 B3
Ponte da Barca P .148 A1
Pontedássio I 133 B4
Pontedécimo I. . . .133 A4
Ponte de Lima P . .148 A1
Ponte dell'Ólio I. . .120 C2
Pontedera I 134 B3
Ponte de Sor P . . .154 B2
Pontedeume E. . . .140 A2
Ponte di Barbarano
 I. 121 B4
Ponte di Legno I . .121 A3
Ponte di Nava I . . .133 A4
Ponte di Piave I . . .122 B1
Ponte Felcino I . . .136 B1
Pontefract GB 40 B2
Ponte Gardena I . .108 C2
Pontegenil E. 135 B3
Pontelagoscuro I . .121 C4
Ponteland GB 37 A5
Pontelandolfo I . . .170 B2
Ponte-Leccia F . . .180 A2
Pontelongo I 121 B5
Ponte nelle Alpi I. .122 A1
Pont-en-Royans F 118 B2
Pontenure I 120 C2
Pontenx-les-Forges
 F. 128 B1
Ponterwyd GB 39 B3
Ponte San Giovanni
 I. 136 B1
Ponte San Pietro I .120 B2
Pontevedra E. 140 B2
Pontevico I. 120 B3
Pont Farcy F 88 B2
Pontfaverger-
 Moronvillers F . . .91 B4
Pontgibaud F 116 B2
Ponticino I 135 B4
Pontigny F 104 B2
Pontijou F 103 B3
Pontínia I 169 B3
Pontinvrea I 133 A4
Pontivy F 100 A3
Pont-l'Abbé F 100 B1
Pont-l'Évêque F . . .89 A4
Pontlevoy F 103 B3
Pontoise F 90 B2
Pontones E 164 A2
Pontonx-sur-l'Abour
 F. 128 C2
Pontoon IRL 26 C1
Pontorson F 88 B2
Pontrémoli I. 134 A2
Pont-Remy F 90 A1
Pontresina CH 107 C4
Pontrhydfendigaid
 GB 39 B3
Pontrieux F 100 A2
Ponts E 147 C2
Ponts-aux-Dames
 F. 90 C2
Pont Scorff F 100 B2
Pöntsö FIN. 196 B7
Pont-Ste Maxence
 F. 90 B2
Pont-St Esprit F. . .131 A3
Pont-St Mamet F . .129 B3
Pont-St Martin
 F. 101 B4
 I. 119 B4
Pont-St Vincent F . .92 C2
Pont-sur-Yonne F .104 A2
Pontvallain F 102 B2
Ponza I 169 C2
Poo E 142 A2
Poole GB 43 B5
Poolewe GB 31 B3
Poperinge B. 78 B2
Pópoli I. 169 A3
Popovac SRB 127 D3
Popovača HR 124 B2
Popow PL. 77 B4
Poppel B 79 A5
Poppenhausen
 Bayern D. 82 B2
 Hessen D. 82 B1
Poppi I 135 B4
Poprad SK. 99 B4
Popučke SRB 127 C1
Pópulo P 148 A2
Populónia I 134 C3

Pörböly H. 125 A4
Porcuna E 163 A3
Pordenone I. 122 B1
Pordic F. 100 A3
Poręba PL. 86 B3
Poreč HR 122 B2
Pori FIN 8 B2
Porjus S. 196 C2
Porkhov RUS. 9 D6
Porlezza I. 120 A2
Porlock GB 43 A3
Pornassio I. 133 A3
Pörnbach D. 95 C3
Pornic F. 101 B3
Pornichet F 101 B3
Porodin SRB. 127 C3
Poronin PL. 99 B3
Poros
 Attiki GR 185 B4
 Kefalonia GR. . . .184 A1
Poroszló H. 113 B4
Porozina HR 123 B3
Porquerolles F. . . .132 C2
Porrentruy CH. 106 B2
Porreres E 167 B3
Porretta Terme I . .135 A3
Porsgrunn N 53 A5
Porspoder F 100 A1
Port-a-Binson F. 91 B3
Portacloy IRL 26 B1
Portadown GB. 27 B4
Portaferry GB 27 B5
Portaje E 155 B4
Portalegre P. 155 B3
Portarlington IRL. . .30 A1
Port Askaig GB 34 C1
Portavadie GB. 34 C2
Portavogie GB. 27 B5
Portbail F. 88 A2
Port Bannatyne GB 34 C2
Portbou F 146 B4
Port-Camargue F .131 B3
Port Charlotte GB . .34 C1
Port d'Andratx E . .166 B2
Port-de-Bouc F . . .131 B3
Port-de-Lanne F . .128 C1
Port de Pollença
 E 167 B3
Port-des-Barques
 F. 114 C2
Port de Sóller E . .166 B2
Portegrandi I 122 B1
Portel P 155 C3
Portela P 148 B1
Port Ellen GB. 34 C1
Portelo P 141 C4
Portemouro E 140 B2
Port-en-Bessin F. . .88 A3
Port'Ercole I 168 A1
Port Erin GB 36 B2
Portes-lès-Valence
 F. 117 C4
Portets F 128 B2
Port Eynon GB 39 C2
Portezuelo E 155 B4
Port Glasgow GB . .34 C3
Portglenone GB . . .27 B4
Porthcawl GB 39 C3
Port Henderson GB 31 B3
Porthleven GB. 42 B1
Porthmadog GB . . .38 B2
Porticcio F 180 B1
Portici I 170 C2
Portico di Romagna
 I. 135 A4
Portilla de la Reina
 E 142 A2
Portillo E 150 A3
Portimao P. 160 B1
Portinatx E. 166 B1
Portinho da Arrabida
 P 154 C1
Port Isaac GB 42 B2
Portishead GB. 43 A4
Port-Joinville F . . .114 B1
Portknockie GB. . . .33 D4
Port-la-Nouvelle F 130 B2
Portlaoise IRL 30 A1
Portlethen GB 33 D4
Port Logan GB. 36 B2
Port Louis F 100 B2
Portmagee IRL 29 C1
Portmahomack GB 32 D3
Portman E 165 B4
Port Manech F 100 B2
Portnacroish GB . . .34 B2
Portnahaven GB . . .34 C1
Port Nan Giuran
 GB 31 A2
Port-Navalo F 100 B3
Port Nis GB 31 A2
Porto
 F. 180 A1
 P 148 A1
Porto-Alto P 154 C2
Porto Azzurro I . . .134 C3
Portocannone I . . .170 B3
Porto Cerésio I . . .120 B1
Porto Cervo I 178 A3
Porto Cesáreo I . .173 B3
Porto Colom E. . . .167 B3
Porto Covo P. 160 B1
Porto Cristo E 167 B3
Porto d'Áscoli I. . .136 C2
Porto de Lagos P .160 B1
Porto de Mos P . . .154 B2
Porto de Rei P . . .154 C2
Porto do Son E . . .140 B2
Porto Empédocle
 I. 176 B2
Portoferráio I 134 C3
Portofino I 134 A2
Porto Garibaldi I . .122 C1
Portogruaro I 122 B1
Portokhelion GR . .184 B4
Portomaggiore I . .121 C4
Portomarin E. 140 B3
Porton GB 44 B2
Portonovo E 140 B2

Portopalo di Capo Passero I 177 C4
Porto Petro E 167 B3
Porto Pino I 179 D2
Porto Potenza Picena I 136 B2
Portør N 53 B5
Porto Recanati I 136 B2
Porto San Giórgio I 136 B2
Porto Sant'Elpidio I 136 B2
Porto Santo Stéfano I 168 A1
Portoscuso I 179 C2
Porto Tolle I 122 C1
Porto Tórres I 178 B2
Porto-Vecchio F 180 B2
Portovénere I 134 A2
Portpatrick GB 36 B1
Portreath GB 42 B1
Portree GB 31 B2
Portroe IRL 28 B3
Portrush GB 27 A4
Port St Mary GB 36 B2
Portsall F 100 A1
Portsmouth GB 44 C2
Portsoy GB 33 D4
Port-Ste Marie F 129 B3
Portstewart GB 27 A4
Port-St-Louis-du-Rhône F 131 B3
Port-sur-Saône F . . .105 B5
Port Talbot GB 39 C3
Portugalete E 143 A4
Portumna IRL 28 A3
Port-Vendres F 146 B4
Port William GB 36 B2
Porvoo FIN 8 B4
Porzuna E 157 A3
Posada
  Oviedo E 141 A5
  Oviedo E 142 A2
  I 178 B3
Posada de Valdeón E 142 A2
Posadas E 162 A2
Poschiavo CH 120 A3
Posedarje HR 137 A4
Posio FIN 197 C11
Positano I 170 C2
Possagno I 121 B4
Posseck D 83 B4
Possesse F 91 C4
Pössneck D 83 B3
Posta I 169 A3
Postal I 108 C2
Posta Piana I 172 A1
Postbauer-Heng D . .95 B3
Posterholt NL 80 A2
Postioma I 121 B5
Postíra HR 138 B2
Postojna SLO 123 B3
Postoloprty CZ 84 B1
Postomino PL 68 A1
Posušje BIH 138 B3
Potamos
  Attiki GR 184 C3
  Attiki GR 184 D4
Potegowo PL 68 A2
Potenza I 172 B1
Potenza Picena I . . .136 B2
Potes E 142 A2
Potigny F 89 B3
Potočari BIH 127 C1
Potoci
  BIH 138 A2
  BIH 139 B3
Potony H 125 B3
Potries E 159 C3
Potsdam D 74 B2
Potštát CZ 98 B1
Pottenbrunn A 110 A2
Pottendorf A 111 B3
Pottenstein
  A 111 B3
  D 95 B3
Potters Bar GB 44 B3
Pöttmes D 94 C3
Pöttsching A 111 B3
Potworów PL 87 A4
Pouancé F 101 B4
Pougues-les-Eaux F 104 B2
Pouilly-en-Auxois F 104 B3
Pouilly-sous Charlieu F 117 A4
Pouilly-sur-Loire F 104 B1
Poujol-sur-Orb F . .130 B2
Poullaouen F 100 A2
Poulton-le-Fylde GB 38 A4
Poundstock GB 42 B2
Pourcy F 91 B3
Pourrain F 104 B2
Poussu FIN 197 D12
Pouyastruc F 145 A4
Pouy-de-Touges F 146 A2
Pouzauges F 114 B3
Pova de Santa Iria P 154 C1
Považská Bystrica SK 98 B2
Povedilla E 158 C1
Povenets RUS 9 A9
Povlja HR 138 B2
Povljana HR 137 A4
Póvoa
  Beja P 161 A2
  Santarém P 154 B2
Póvoa de Lanhosa P 148 A1
Póvoa de Varzim P 148 A1
Póvoa e Meadas P 155 B3
Powidz PL 76 B2

Poyales del Hoyo E 150 B2
Poynton GB 40 B1
Poyntz Pass GB 27 B4
Poysdorf A 97 C4
Poza de la Sal E 143 B3
Pozán de Vero E 145 B4
Pozanti TR 23 C8
Požarevac SRB 127 C3
Požega
  HR 125 B3
  SRB 127 D2
Poznań PL 76 B1
Pozo Alcón E 164 B2
Pozoantiguo E 150 A2
Pozoblanco E 156 B3
Pozo Cañada E 158 C2
Pozo de Guadalajara E 151 B4
Pozo de la Serna E 157 B4
Pozohondo E 158 C2
Pozondón E 152 B2
Pozrzadło Wielkie PL 75 A4
Pozuel del Campo E 152 B2
Pozuelo de Alarcón E 151 B4
Pozuelo de Calatrava E 157 B4
Pozuelo del Páramo E 142 B1
Pozuelo de Zarzón E 149 B3
Pozzallo I 177 C3
Pozzomaggiore I 178 B2
Pozzo San Nicola I 178 B2
Pozzuoli I 170 C2
Pozzuolo I 135 B4
Prabuty PL 69 B4
Prača BIH 139 B4
Prachatice CZ 96 B1
Prada E 141 B3
Pradelle F 118 C2
Pradelles F 117 C3
Prades
  E 147 C1
  F 146 B3
Pradła PL 86 B3
Prado
  E 142 A1
  P 148 A1
Prado del Rey E 162 B2
Pradoluengo E 143 B3
Pragelato I 119 B3
Pragersko SLO 123 A4
Prägraten A 109 B3
Prague = Praha CZ .84 B2
Praha = Prague CZ .84 B2
Prahecq F 115 B3
Praia F 154 B1
Práia a Mare I 174 B1
Praia da Rocha P . . .160 B1
Praia da Viera P 154 B2
Praia de Mira P 148 B1
Praiano I 170 C2
Pralboino I 120 B3
Pralognan-la-Vanoise F 118 B3
Pramanda GR 182 D3
Pranjani SRB 127 C2
Prapatnica HR 138 B2
Præstø DK 65 A5
Praszka PL 86 A2
Prat F 146 A1
Prata I 135 C4
Prata di Pordenone I 122 B1
Pratau D 83 A4
Prat de Compte E . . .153 B4
Pratdip E 147 C1
Pratella I 170 B2
Prato I 135 B4
Prátola Peligna I 169 A3
Pratola Serra I 170 C2
Prats-de-Mollo-la-Preste F 146 B3
Prauthoy F 105 B4
Pravia E 141 A4
Praxmar A 108 B2
Prayssac F 129 B4
Prazzo I 132 A3
Prebold SLO 123 A4
Préchac F 128 B2
Précy-sur-Thil F 104 B3
Předín CZ 97 B3
Predappio I 135 A4
Predazzo I 121 A4
Predejane SLO 123 B3
Predlitz A 109 B4
Predmeja SLO 122 B2
Predoï I 108 B2
Pré-en-Pail F 89 B3
Prees GB 38 B4
Preetz D 64 B3
Préfailles F 101 B3
Pregarten A 96 C2
Pregrada HR 123 A4
Preignan F 129 C3
Preili LV 8 D5
Preitenegg A 110 C1
Prekaja BIH 138 A2
Preko HR 137 A4
Preljina SRB 127 D2
Prelog HR 124 A2
Preloščica HR 124 B2
Přelouč CZ 97 A3
Prem SLO 123 B3
Premantura HR 122 C2
Prémery F 104 B2
Prémia I 119 A5
Premià de Mar E . . .147 C3
Premnitz D 73 B5
Prémont F 91 A3
Prenzlau D 74 A2
Preodac BIH 138 A2

Přerov CZ 98 B1
Prerow D 66 B1
Presencio E 143 B3
Presicce I 173 C4
Presly F 103 B4
Pressac F 115 B4
Pressath D 95 B3
Pressbaum A 111 A3
Prestatyn GB 38 A3
Prestebakke N 54 B2
Presteigne GB 39 B3
Přeštice CZ 96 B1
Preston
  Lancashire GB . . .38 A4
  Scottish Borders GB 35 C5
Prestonpans GB 35 C5
Prestwick GB 36 A2
Prettin D 83 A4
Preturo I 169 A3
Pretzchendorf D 83 B5
Pretzier D 73 B4
Pretzsch D 83 A4
Preuilly-sur-Claise F 115 B4
Prevalje SLO 110 C1
Prevenchères F 131 A2
Préveranges F 116 A2
Preveza GR 182 E2
Prevršac HR 124 B2
Prezid HR 123 B3
Priaranza del Bierzo E 141 B4
Priay F 118 A2
Pribeta SK 112 B2
Priboj
  BIH 125 C4
  SRB 16 D3
Přibor CZ 98 B2
Příbram CZ 96 B2
Pribylina SK 99 B3
Přibyslav CZ 97 B3
Priego E 152 B1
Priego de Córdoba E 163 A3
Priekule LV 8 D2
Prien D 109 B3
Prienai LT 13 A5
Prievidza SK 98 C2
Prigradica HR 138 C2
Prigrevica SRB 125 B5
Prijeboj HR 123 C4
Prijedor BIH 124 C2
Prijepolje SRB 16 D3
Prilep MK 182 B3
Priluka BIH 138 B2
Primda CZ 95 B4
Primel-Trégastel F 100 A2
Primišlje HR 123 B4
Primorsk
  Kaliningrad RUS . .69 A5
  Severo-Zapadnyy RUS 9 B6
Primošten HR 138 B1
Primstal D 92 B2
Princes Risborough GB 44 B3
Princetown GB 42 B2
Principina a Mare I 135 C4
Priolo Gargallo I 177 B4
Prioro E 142 B2
Priozersk RUS 9 B7
Pirrechnyy RUS .193 C14
Prisoje BIH 138 B3
Priština KOS 16 D4
Pritzerbe D 73 B5
Pritzier D 73 A4
Pritzwalk D 73 A5
Privas F 117 C4
Priverno I 169 B3
Privlaka
  Vukovarsko-Srijemska HR . . .125 B4
  Zadarska HR 137 A4
Prizna HR 123 C3
Prizren KOS 16 D4
Prizzi I 176 B2
Prnjavor
  BIH 125 C3
  HR 124 B1
  SRB 127 C1
Proaza E 141 A4
Probištip . . . .—
Probstzella D 82 B3
Probus GB 42 B2
Prócchio I 134 C3
Prochowice PL 85 A4
Prócida I 170 C2
Prodhromos CY 181 B1
Prodo I 135 C5
Proença-a-Nova P . .154 B3
Proença-a-Velha P 155 A3
Profondeville B 79 B4
Prokuplje SRB 16 D4
Promachonas GR . . .183 B5
Pronsfeld D 80 B2
Propriano F 180 B1
Prosec CZ 97 B4
Prösen D 83 A5
Prosenjakovci SLO 111 C3
Prosotsani GR 183 B5
Prostějov CZ 98 B1
Prószków PL 86 B1
Proszowice PL 87 B4
Protić BIH 138 A2
Protivanov CZ 97 B4
Protivín CZ 96 B2
Prötzel D 74 B2
Provins F 90 C3
Prozor BIH 139 B3
Prrenjas AL 182 B2
Prudhoe GB 37 B5
Prudnik PL 85 B5
Pruggern A 109 B4
Prügy H 113 A5
Prüm D 80 B2

Pruna E 162 B2
Prunelli-di-Fiumorbo F 180 A2
Prunetta I 135 A3
Pruniers F 103 C4
Prusice PL 85 A4
Pruské SK 98 B2
Pruszce PL 76 A3
Pruszcz Gdański PL 69 A3
Pruszków PL 77 B5
Prutz A 108 B1
Pružany BY 13 B6
Pružina SK 98 B2
Pürvomay BG 183 A7
Pryzlęg PL 75 B4
Przasnysz PL 77 A5
Przechlewo PL 68 B2
Przecław PL 87 B5
Przedbórz PL 87 A3
Przedecz PL 76 B3
Przejęslav PL 84 A3
Przemków PL 85 A3
Przemocze PL 75 A3
Przemyśl PL 12 D5
Przerąb PL 87 A3
Przewodnik PL 69 B3
Przewodowo Parcele PL 77 B5
Przewóz PL 84 A2
Przezmark PL 69 B4
Przodkowo PL 68 A3
Przybiernów PL 75 A3
Przyborowice PL 77 B5
Przybyszew PL 87 A4
Przybyszów PL 86 A3
Przylęg PL 75 B4
Przysucha PL 87 A4
Przytoczna PL 75 B4
Przytyk PL 87 A4
Przywidz PL 68 A3
Psachna GR 185 A4
Psara GR 185 A6
Psary PL 76 C3
Pskov RUS 9 D6
Pszczew PL 75 B4
Pszczółki PL 69 A3
Pszczyna PL 98 B2
Pszów PL 86 B2
Pteleos GR 182 D4
Ptolemaida GR 182 C3
Ptuj SLO 124 A1
Ptusza PL 68 B1
Puch A 109 B4
Puchberg am Schneeberg A . . .110 B2
Puchevillers F 90 A2
Puchheim D 108 A2
Púchov SK 98 B2
Puck PL 69 A3
Puçol E 159 B3
Puconci SLO 111 C3
Pudasjärvi FIN 197 D10
Puderbach D 81 B3
Pudozh RUS 9 B10
Puebla de Albortón E 153 A3
Puebla de Alcocer E 156 B2
Puebla de Beleña E 151 B4
Puebla de Don Fadrique E 164 B2
Puebla de Don Rodrigo E 156 A3
Puebla de Guzmán E 161 B2
Puebla de la Calzada E 155 C4
Puebla de la Reina E 156 B1
Puebla de Lillo E . . .142 A1
Puebla del Maestre E 161 A3
Puebla del Principe E 158 C1
Puebla de Obando E 155 B4
Puebla de Sanabria E 141 B4
Puebla de Sancho Pérez E 155 C4
Puente Almuhey E 142 B2
Puente de Domingo Flórez E 141 B4
Puente de Génave E 164 A2
Puente del Congosto E 150 B2
Puente de Montañana E 145 B4
Puente Duero E 150 A3
Puente-Genil E 162 A3
Puente la Reina E . .144 B2
Puente la Reina de Jaca E 144 B3
Puentelarra E 143 B3
Puente Mayorga E . .162 B2
Puente Viesgo E . . .143 A3
Puertas
  Asturias E 142 A2
  Salamanca E 149 A3
Puerto de Mazarrón E 165 B3
Puerto de Santa Cruz E 156 A2
Puerto de San Vicente E 156 A2
Puerto-Lápice E 157 A4
Puertollano E 157 B3
Puerto Lumbreras E 164 B3
Puerto Moral E 161 B3
Puerto Real E 162 B1
Puerto Rey E 156 A2
Puerto Seguro E 149 B3
Puerto Serrano E . . .162 B2

Puget-Sur-Argens F 132 B2
Puget-Théniers F . . .132 B2
Puget-ville F 132 B2
Pugnochiuso I 171 B4
Puigcerdà E 146 B2
Puigpunyent E 166 B2
Puig Reig E 147 C2
Puillon F 128 C2
Puimichel F 132 B2
Puimoisson F 132 B2
Puiseaux F 103 A4
Puisieux F 90 A2
Puisserguier F 130 B2
Puivert F 146 B3
Pujols F 128 B2
Pujçerdà SK 98 C2
Pukanec SK 98 C2
Pukavik S 63 B2
Pukë AL 182 A1
Pula
  HR 122 C2
  I 179 C2
Puławy PL 12 C4
Pulborough GB 44 C3
Pulfero I 122 A2
Pulgar E 157 A3
Pulheim D 80 A2
Pulkau A 97 C3
Pulpi E 164 B3
Pulsano I 173 B3
Pulsnitz D 84 A2
Pułtusk PL 77 B6
Pumpsaint GB 39 B3
Punat HR 123 B3
Punta Marina I 135 A5
Punta Prima E 167 B4
Punta Sabbioni I . . .122 B1
Puntas de Calnegre E 165 B3
Punta Umbria E 161 B3
Puolanka FIN 3 D10
Puoltikasvaara S . . .196 B4
Puoltsa S 196 B2
Puračić BIH 125 C4
Purbach am Neusiedler See A 111 B3
Purchena E 164 B2
Purfleet GB 45 B4
Purgstall A 110 A2
Purkersdorf A 111 A3
Purmerend NL 70 B1
Purullena E 164 B1
Pushkin RUS 9 C7
Pushkino RUS 9 D10
Püspökladány H 113 B5
Pusté Ulany SK 111 A4
Pustoshka RUS 9 D6
Puszcza Mariańska PL 77 C5
Puszczykowo PL 76 B1
Pusztamagyaród H 111 C3
Pusztamonostor H 113 B3
Pusztaszabolcs H . .112 B2
Pusztavám H 112 B2
Putanges-Pont-Ecrepin F 89 B3
Putbus D 66 B2
Putignano I 173 B3
Putlitz D 73 A5
Putnok H 99 C4
Putte B 79 A4
Puttelange-aux-Lacs F 92 B2
Putten NL 70 B2
Puttgarden D 65 B4
Püttlingen D 92 B2
Putzu Idu I 179 B2
Puy-Guillaume F 117 B3
Puylaroque F 129 B4
Puylaurens F 146 A3
Puy-l'Évêque F 129 B4
Puymirol F 129 B3
Puyôo F 128 C2
Puyrolland F 114 B3
Pwllheli GB 38 B2
Pyetrikaw BY 13 B8
Pyhäjärvi FIN 3 E9
Pyhäkylä FIN 197 D11
Pyla CY 181 A2
Pyla-sur-Mer F 128 B1
Pyrzyce PL 75 A3
Pysely CZ 96 B2
Pýskowice PL 86 B2
Pytalovo RUS 8 D5
Pyzdry PL 76 B2

Quakenbrück D 71 B4
Quargnento I 119 C5
Quarré-les-Tombes F 104 B2
Quarteira P 160 B1
Quartu Sant'Élena I 179 C3
Quatre-Champs F . . .91 B4
Quedlinburg D 82 A3
Queensferry
  Edinburgh GB . . .35 C4
  Flintshire GB 38 A3
Queige F 118 B3
Queipo E 161 B3
Queixans E 146 B2
Quelaines-St-Gault F 102 B1
Queljada P 148 A1
Quemada E 143 C3
Queralbs E 147 B3
Quercianella I 134 B3
Querfurt D 82 A3
Quérigut F 146 B3
Quero
  E 157 A4
  I 121 B4
Querqueville F 88 A2
Quesada E 164 B1

Questembert F 101 B3
Quettehou F 88 A2
Quevauvillers F 90 B2
Quevy B 79 B4
Quiaios P 148 B1
Quiberon F 100 B2
Quiberville F 89 A4
Quickborn D 64 C2
Quiévrain B 79 B3
Quillan F 146 B3
Quillebeuf F 89 A4
Quimper F 100 A1
Quimperlé F 100 B2
Quincampoix F 89 A5
Quincoces de Yuso E 143 B3
Quincy F 103 B4
Quinéville F 88 A2
Quingey F 105 B4
Quinson F 132 B2
Quinssaines F 116 A2
Quinta-Grande P . . .154 C2
Quintana de la Serena E 156 B2
Quintana del Castillo E 141 B4
Quintana del Marco E 141 B5
Quintana del Puenta E 142 B2
Quintanar de la Orden E 157 A4
Quintanar de la Sierra E 143 C3
Quintanar del Rey E 158 B2
Quintanilla de la Mata E 143 C3
Quintanilla del Coco E 143 C3
Quintanilla de Onésimo E 150 A3
Quintanilla de Somoza E 141 B4
Quintas de Valdelucio E 142 B2
Quintela P 148 B2
Quintin F 100 A3
Quinto E 153 A3
Quinzano d'Oglio I 120 B3
Quiroga E 141 B3
Quismondo E 150 B3
Quissac F 131 B2
Quistello I 121 B3

R

Raab A 96 C1
Raabs an der Thaya A 97 C3
Raahe FIN 3 D9
Raajärvi FIN 197 C9
Raalte NL 71 B3
Raamsdonksveer NL 79 A4
Raanujarvi FIN 196 C7
Raattama FIN 196 A7
Rab HR 123 C3
Rabac HR 123 B3
Rábade E 140 A3
Rábafüzes H 111 C3
Rábahidvég H 111 B3
Rabanales E 149 A3
Rábapatona H 111 B4
Rabapordány H 111 B4
Rabastens F 129 C4
Rabastens-de-Bigorre F 145 A4
Rabat = Victoria M 175 C3
Rabat M 175 C3
Rabča SK 99 B3
Rabe SRB 126 A2
Rabi CZ 96 B1
Rabino PL 67 C4
Rabka PL 99 B3
Rabrovo SRB 127 C3
Rača SRB 127 C3
Rácale I 173 C4
Rácalmás H 112 B2
Racalmuto I 176 B2
Racconigi I 119 C4
Rače SLO 123 A4
Rachecourt-sur-Marne F 91 C4
Raciąż PL 77 B5
Racibórz PL 86 B2
Račinovci HR 125 C4
Ráckeve H 112 B2
Racławice PL 87 B4
Racławice Śląskie PL 86 B1
Racot PL 75 B5
Rada SLO 123 A4

Radlje ob Dravi SLO 110 C2
Radłów PL 87 B4
Radmer an der Stube A 110 B1
Radnejaur S 195 E9
Radnice CZ 96 B1
Radohova BIH 138 A3
Radojevo SRB 126 B2
Radolfzell D 107 B3
Radom PL 87 A5
Radomice PL 77 B4
Radomin PL 77 A4
Radomsko PL 86 A3
Radomyshl UA 13 C8
Radomyśl Wielki PL 87 B5
Radošina SK 98 C1
Radošovce SK 98 C1
Radoszewice PL 86 A2
Radoszyce PL 87 A4
Radotin CZ 96 B2
Radovets BG 186 A1
Radoviš MK 182 B4
Radovljica SLO 123 A3
Radowo Wielkie PL . .75 A4
Radstadt A 109 B4
Radstock GB 43 A4
Raduc HR 137 A4
Raduša MK 182 A3
Radviliškis LT 8 E3
Radzanów
  Mazowieckie PL . .77 B5
  Mazowieckie PL . .87 A4
Radziejów PL 76 B3
Radziejowice PL 77 B5
Radzovce SK 113 A3
Radzyń Chełmiński PL 69 B3
Raeren B 80 B2
Raesfeld D 80 A2
Raffadali I 176 B2
Rafina GR 185 A4
Rafsbotn N 192 B7
Ragachev BY 13 B9
Ragály H 99 C4
Rägeleje DK 61 C2
Raglan GB 39 C4
Ragnitz A 110 C2
Ragusa I 177 C3
Rahden D 72 B1
Råholt N 48 B3
Raiano I 169 A3
Raigada E 141 B3
Rain D 94 C2
Rainbach im Mühlkreis A 96 C2
Rainham GB 45 B4
Rairiz de Veiga E . . .140 B3
Raisdorf D 64 B3
Raisio FIN 8 B3
Raiskio FIN 197 D9
Raiva
  Aveiro P 148 A1
  Coimbra P 148 B1
Raja-Jooseppi FIN 193 D12
Rajala FIN 197 B9
Rajcza PL 99 B3
Rajec SK 98 B2
Rájec-Jestřebí CZ . . .97 B4
Rajecké Teplice SK .98 B2
Rajevo Selo HR 125 C4
Rajhrad CZ 97 B4
Rajić HR 124 B3
Rajka H 111 B4
Rakaca H 99 C4
Rakamaz H 113 A5
Rakek SLO 123 B3
Rakhiv UA 17 A6
Rakitna SLO 123 B3
Rakitovo BG 183 B6
Rakkestad N 54 A2
Rákóczifalva H 113 B4
Rakoniewice PL 75 B5
Rakoszyce PL 85 A4
Raková SK 98 B2
Rakovac BIH 125 B3
Rakovica HR 123 C4
Rakovník CZ 96 A1
Rakow D 66 B2
Raków PL 87 B5
Rakvere EST 8 C5
Ralja SRB 127 C2
Rälla S 62 B4
Ramacastañas E 150 B2
Ramacca I 177 B3
Ramales de la Victoria E 143 A3
Ramberg N 194 B4
Rambervillers F 92 C2
Rambouillet F 90 C1
Rambucourt F 92 C1
Ramdala S 63 B3
Ramerupt F 91 C4
Ramingstein A 109 B4
Ramírás E 140 B2
Ramiswil CH 106 B2
Ramkvilla S 62 A2
Ramme DK 58 B1
Rämmen S 49 B6
Ramnäs S 56 A2
Ramnes N 54 A1
Râmnicu Vâlcea RO 17 C6
Ramonville-St Agne F 129 C4
Rampside GB 36 B3
Ramsau D 109 B3
Ramsbeck D 81 A4
Ramsberg S 56 A1
Ramsele S 200 C2
Ramsey
  Cambridgeshire GB 44 A3
  Isle of Man GB . . .36 A2
Ramseycleuch GB . .36 A3

Ramsgate GB 45 B5
Ramsjö S 200 D1
Ramstein-Meisenbach D 93 B3
Ramsund N 194 B7
Ramundberget S . 199 C9
Ramvik S 200 D3
Ranalt A 108 B2
Rånäs S 51 C5
Rance B 91 A4
Ránchio I 135 B5
Randaberg N 52 A1
Randalstown GB . . 27 B4
Randan F 117 A3
Randazzo I 177 B3
Rånddalen S . . . 199 C10
Randegg A 110 A1
Randers DK 58 B3
Randijaur S 196 C2
Randin E 140 C3
Randsverk N . . 198 D6
Råneå S 196 D5
Rånes F 89 B3
Rångedala S 60 B3
Ranis D 82 B3
Rankweil A 107 B4
Rännäväg S 60 B3
Ränneslöv S 61 C3
Rannoch Station GB 34 B3
Ranovac SRB . . . 127 C3
Ransäter S 55 A4
Ransbach-Baumbach D 81 B3
Ransta S 56 A2
Ranttila FIN 193 C9
Ranua FIN 197 D9
Ranum DK 58 B2
Ranvalhal P 154 B1
Raon-l'Étape F . . 92 C2
Ráossi I 121 B4
Rapallo I 134 A2
Rapla EST 8 C4
Rapness GB 33 B4
Rapolano Terme I . 135 B4
Rapolla I 172 B1
Raposa P 154 B2
Rapperswil CH . . 107 B3
Raša HR 123 B3
Rasal E 145 B3
Rascafria E 151 B4
Rasdorf D 82 B1
Raseiniai LT 13 A5
Rašica SLO 123 B3
Rasines E 143 A3
Rasquera E 153 A4
Rássina I 135 B4
Rastatt D 93 C4
Rastede D 71 A4
Rastenberg D . . . 82 A3
Rastošnica BIH . . 125 C4
Rastovac MNE . . . 139 C4
Rasueros E 150 A2
Rasy PL 86 A3
Raszków PL 86 A1
Rätan S 199 C11
Ratece SLO 109 C4
Ratekau D 65 C3
Ratež SLO 123 B4
Rathangan IRL . . . 30 A2
Rathcoole IRL . . . 30 A2
Rathcormack IRL . . 29 B3
Rathdrum IRL . . . 30 B2
Rathebur D 74 A2
Rathenow D 73 B5
Rathfriland GB . . . 27 B4
Rathkeale IRL . . . 29 B3
Rathmelton IRL . . . 27 A3
Rathmolyon IRL . . 30 A2
Rathmore IRL . . . 29 B2
Rathmullan IRL . . . 27 A3
Rathnew IRL 30 B2
Rathvilly IRL 30 B2
Ratibořské Hory CZ 96 B2
Ratingen D 80 A2
Ratková SK 99 C4
Ratkovo SRB . . . 126 B1
Ratne UA 13 C6
Rattelsdorf D 94 A2
Ratten A 110 B2
Rattosjärvi FIN . . 196 C7
Rattray GB 35 B4
Rättvik S 50 B2
Ratvika N 199 B7
Ratzeburg D 65 C3
Rätzlingen D 73 B4
Raucourt-et-Flaba F 91 B4
Raudeberg N . . . 198 D2
Raufarhöfn IS . . 191 A10
Raufoss N 48 B2
Rauhala FIN . . . 196 B7
Rauland N 53 A4
Raulhac F 116 C2
Raulia N 195 E5
Rauma FIN 8 B2
Raundal N 46 B3
Raunds GB 44 A3
Rauris A 109 B4
Rautas S 196 B2
Rautavaara FIN . . 3 E11
Rauville-la-Bigot F . . 88 A2
Rauzan F 128 B2
Ravanusa I 176 B2
Rava-Rus'ka UA . . 13 C5
Ravča HR 138 B3
Ravels B 79 A4
Rävemåla S 63 B3
Ravenglass GB . . 36 B3
Ravenna I 135 A5
Ravensburg D . . . 107 B4
Rävlanda S 60 B2
Ravna Gora HR . . 123 B3
Ravne na Koroškem SLO 110 C1

Ravnje SRB 127 C1
Ravno BIH 139 C3
Ravno Selo SRB . . 126 B1
Rawa Mazowiecka PL 87 A4
Rawicz PL 85 A4
Rawtenstall GB . . 40 B1
Rayleigh GB 45 B4
Ražana SRB 127 C1
Ražanac HR 137 A4
Razboj BIH 124 B3
Razes F 115 B5
Razgrad BG 17 D7
Razkrižje SLO . . . 111 C3
Razlog BG 183 B5
Razo E 140 A2
Reading GB 44 B3
Réalmont F 130 B1
Rebais F 90 C3
Reboly RUS 3 E12
Rebordelo P 149 A2
Recanati I 136 B2
Recas E 151 B4
Recco I 134 A2
Recess IRL 28 A2
Recey-sur-Ource F 105 B3
Recezinhos P . . . 148 A1
Rechnitz A 111 B3
Rechytsa BY 13 B9
Recke D 71 B4
Recklinghausen D . 80 A3
Recoaro Terme I . 121 B4
Recogne B 92 B1
Recoules-Prévinquières F . 130 A1
Recsk H 113 B4
Recz PL 75 A4
Reda PL 69 A3
Redalen N 48 B2
Redange L 92 B1
Redcar GB 37 B5
Redditch GB 44 A2
Redefin D 73 A4
Redhill GB 44 B3
Redics H 111 C3
Redkino RUS 9 D10
Redland GB 33 B3
Redlin D 73 A5
Redon F 101 B3
Redondela E 140 B2
Redondo E 155 C3
Red Point GB . . . 31 B3
Redruth GB 42 B1
Redzikowo PL . . . 68 A2
Reepham GB 41 C5
Rees D 80 A2
Reeth GB 37 B5
Reetz D 73 A4
Reftele S 60 B3
Regalbuto I 177 B3
Regen D 95 C5
Regensburg D . . . 95 B4
Regenstauf D . . . 95 B4
Reggello I 135 B4
Réggio di Calábria I 175 C1
Reggiolo I 121 C3
Réggio nell'Emília I 121 C3
Reghin RO 17 B6
Régil E 144 A1
Regna S 56 B1
Regniéville F 92 C1
Regny F 117 B4
Rego da Leirosa P 154 A2
Regöly H 112 C2
Regueiro E 140 B2
Reguengo
  Portalegre P . . . 155 B3
  Santarém P 154 B2
Reguengos de Monsaraz P . . . 155 C3
Rehau D 83 B4
Rehburg D 72 B2
Rehden D 72 B1
Rehna D 65 C4
Reichelsheim D . . 93 B4
Reichelshofen D . . 94 B2
Reichenau A . . . 110 B2
Reichenbach
  Sachsen D 83 B4
  Sachsen D 84 A2
Reichenfels A . . . 110 B1
Reichensachsen D . 82 A2
Reichertshofen D . 95 C3
Reichshoffen F . . 93 C3
Reiden CH 106 B2
Reigada
  E 141 A4
  P 149 B3
Reigate GB 44 B3
Reillanne F 132 B1
Reillo E 158 B2
Reims F 91 B4
Reinach CH 106 B3
Reinbek D 72 A3
Reinberg D 66 B2
Reine N 194 C4
Reinfeld D 65 C3
Reinheim D 93 B4
Reinli N 47 B6
Reinosa E 142 A2
Reinstorf D 65 C4
Reinsvoll N 48 B2
Reisach A 109 C4
Reiss GB 32 C3
Reitan N 199 C8
Reit im Winkl D . . 109 B3

Remels D 71 A4
Remetea Mare RO 126 B3
Remich L 92 B2
Rémilly F 92 B2
Remiremont F . . . 105 A5
Remolinos E 144 C2
Remoulins F 131 B3
Remscheid D 80 A3
Rémuzat F 131 A4
Rena N 48 A3
Renaison F 117 A3
Renazé F 101 B4
Renchen D 93 C4
Rencurel F 118 B2
Rende I 174 B2
Rendina GR 182 D3
Rendsburg D 64 B2
Renedo E 150 A3
Renens CH 105 C5
Renfrew GB 34 C3
Rengsjö S 50 A3
Reni UA 17 C8
Rennebu N 198 C6
Rennerod D 81 B4
Rennertshofen D . 94 C3
Rennes F 101 A4
Rennes-les-Bains F 146 B3
Rennweg A 109 B4
Rens DK 64 B2
Rensjön S 196 A2
Rentería E 144 A2
Rentjärn S 200 A4
Répcelak H 111 B4
Repojoki FIN . . . 193 D9
Repvåg N 193 B9
Requena E 159 B2
Rerik D 65 B4
Resana I 121 B4
Resarö S 57 A4
Reschen = Résia I . 108 C1
Resen MK 182 B3
Resende P 148 A2
Résia = Reschen I . 108 C1
Reşiţa
  RO 16 C4
  RO 126 B3
Resko PL 67 C4
Resnik SRB 127 C2
Ressons-sur-Matz F 90 B2
Restábal E 163 B4
Resuttano I 177 B3
Retamal E 155 C4
Retford GB 40 B3
Rethel F 91 B4
Rethem D 72 B2
Rethimno GR . . . 185 D5
Retie B 79 A5
Retiers F 101 B4
Retortillo E 149 B3
Retortillo de Soria E 151 A4
Retournac F 117 B4
Rétság H 112 B3
Rettenegg A . . . 110 B2
Retuerta del Bullaque E 157 A3
Retz A 97 C3
Retzbach D 94 B1
Reuden D 73 B5
Reuilly F 103 B4
Reus E 147 C2
Reusel NL 79 A5
Reuterstadt Stavenhagen D . 74 A1
Reuth D 95 B4
Reutlingen D . . . 94 C1
Reutte A 108 B1
Reuver NL 80 A2
Revel F 146 A2
Revello I 119 C4
Revenga E 151 B3
Revest-du-Bion F . 132 A1
Révfülöp H 111 C4
Revigny-sur-Ornain F 91 C4
Revin F 91 B4
Řevnice CZ 96 B2
Řevničov CZ 84 B1
Revo I 121 A4
Revsnes N 47 A4
Revúca SK 99 C4
Rewa PL 69 A3
Rewal PL 67 B4
Rexbo S 50 B2
Reyðarfjörður IS 191 B11
Reyero E 142 B1
Reykhólar IS . . . 190 B3
Reykholt
  Árnessýsla IS . . 190 C5
  Borgarfjarðarsýsla IS 190 C4
Reykjahlið IS . . . 191 B9
Reykjavík IS 190 C4
Rezé F 101 B4
Rēzekne LV 8 D5
Rezovo BG 17 E8
Rezzato I 120 B3
Rezzoáglio I 134 A2
Rhade D 72 A2
Rhaunen D 93 B3
Rhayader GB . . . 39 B3
Rheda-Wiedenbrück D 81 A4
Rhede
  Niedersachsen D . 71 A4
  Nordrhein-Westfalen D 80 A2
Rheinau D 93 C3
Rheinbach D 80 B2
Rheinberg D 80 A2
Rheine D 71 B3
Rheinfelden D . . 106 B2
Rheinsberg D . . . 74 A1
Rhêmes-Notre-Dame I 119 B4
Rhenen NL 70 C2
Rhens D 81 B3

Rheydt D 80 A2
Rhiconich GB . . . 32 C2
Rhinow D 73 B5
Rhiw GB 38 B2
Rho I 120 B2
Rhoden D 81 A5
Rhodes GR 188 C3
Rhondda GB 39 C3
Rhosllanerchrugog GB 38 A3
Rhosneigr GB . . . 38 A2
Rhossili GB 39 C2
Rhubodach GB . . 34 C2
Rhuddlan GB . . . 38 A3
Rhyl GB 38 A3
Rhynie GB 33 D4
Riala S 57 A4
Riallé F 101 B4
Riaño E 142 B1
Riano I 168 A2
Rians F 132 B1
Rianxo E 140 B2
Riaza E 151 A4
Riba E 143 A3
Ribadavia E 140 B2
Ribadeo E 141 A3
Riba de Saelices E 152 B1
Ribadesella E . . . 142 A1
Ribaflecha E 143 B4
Ribaforada E . . . 144 C2
Ribare SRB 127 C3
Ribarroja d'Ebre E 153 A4
Riba-Roja de Turia E 159 B3
Ribe DK 59 C1
Ribeauvillé F . . . 106 A2
Ribécourt-Dreslincourt F 90 B2
Ribeira da Pena P 148 A2
Ribeira de Piquin E 141 A3
Ribemont F 91 B3
Ribera I 176 B2
Ribérac F 129 A3
Ribera de Cardós E 146 B2
Ribera del Fresno E 156 B1
Ribesalbes E . . . 159 A3
Ribes de Freser E 147 B3
Ribiers F 132 A1
Ribnica
  BIH 139 A4
  SLO 123 B3
Ribnica na Potorju SLO 110 C2
Ribnik HR 123 B4
Ribniţa MD 17 B8
Ribnitz-Damgarten D 66 B1
Ribolla I 135 C4
Řicany
  CZ 97 B4
  CZ 96 B2
Riccia I 170 B2
Riccione I 136 A1
Ricco Del Golfo I . 134 A2
Richebourg F . . . 105 A4
Richelieu F 102 B2
Richisau CH . . . 107 B3
Richmond
  Greater London GB 44 B3
  North Yorkshire GB 37 B5
Richtenberg D . . . 66 B1
Richterswil CH . . 107 B3
Rickling D 64 B3
Rickmansworth GB 44 B3
Ricla E 152 A2
Riddarhyttan S . . 50 C2
Ridderkerk NL . . . 79 A4
Riddes CH 119 A4
Ridjica SRB 125 B5
Ried A 109 A4
Riedenburg D . . . 95 C3
Ried im Oberinntal A 108 B1
Riedlingen D . . . 107 A4
Riedstadt D 93 B4
Riegersburg A . . 110 C2
Riego de la Vega E 141 B5
Riego del Camino E 149 A4
Riello E 141 B5
Riemst B 80 B1
Rienne B 91 B4
Riénsena E 142 A2
Riesa D 83 A5
Riese Pio X I . . . 121 B4
Riesi I 177 B3
Riestedt D 82 A3
Rietberg D 81 A4
Rieti I 169 A2
Rietschen D 84 A2
Rieumes F 146 A2
Rieupeyroux F . . 130 A1
Rieux-Volvestre F 146 A2
Riez F 132 B2
Rīga LV 8 D4
Riggisberg CH . . 106 C2
Rignac F 130 A1
Rignano Gargánico I 171 B3
Rigolato I 109 C3
Rigutino I 135 B4
Riihimäki FIN . . . 8 B4
Rijeka HR 123 B3
Rijen NL 79 A4
Rijkevorsel B . . . 79 A4
Rijssen NL 71 B3
Rila BG 183 A5
Rilić BIH 138 B3
Rilievo I 176 B1
Rillé F 102 B2
Rillo de Gallo E . . 152 B2
Rimavská Baňa SK . 99 C3

Rimavská Seč SK . .99 C4
Rímavská Sobota SK 99 C4
Rimbo S 57 A4
Rimforsa S 56 B1
Rímini I 136 A1
Rîmnicu Sărat RO . 17 C7
Rimogne F 91 B4
Rimpar D 94 B1
Rimske Toplice SLO 123 A4
Rincón de la Victoria E 163 B3
Rincón de Soto E . 144 B2
Rindal N 198 B6
Rinde N 46 A3
Ringarum S 56 B2
Ringaskiddy IRL . . 29 C3
Ringe DK 59 C3
Ringebu N 48 A2
Ringkøbing DK . . 59 B1
Ringsaker N 48 B2
Ringsted DK 61 D1
Ringwood GB . . . 44 C2
Rinkaby S 63 C2
Rinkabyholm S . . 63 B4
Rinlo E 141 A3
Rinn A 108 B2
Rinteln D 72 B2
Rio E 140 B3
Riobo E 140 B2
Riodeva E 152 B2
Rio do Coures P . 154 B2
Rio Douro P 148 A2
Riofrio E 150 B3
Rio Frio P 154 C2
Riofrio de Aliste E 149 A3
Rio frio de Riaza E 151 A4
Riogordo E 163 B3
Rioja E 164 C2
Riola I 135 A4
Riola Sardo I . . . 179 C2
Riolobos E 155 B4
Riom F 116 B3
Riomaggiore I . . . 134 A2
Rio Maior P 154 B2
Rio Marina I 134 C3
Riom-ès-Montagnes F 116 B2
Rion-des-Landes F 128 C2
Rionegro del Puente E 141 B4
Rionero in Vúlture I 172 B1
Riopar E 158 C1
Riós E 141 C3
Rioseco E 142 A1
Rioseco de Tapia E 141 B5
Rio Tinto P 148 A1
Riotord F 117 B4
Riotorto E 141 A3
Rioz F 105 B5
Ripac BIH 124 C1
Ripacándida I . . . 172 B1
Ripanj SRB 127 C2
Ripatransone I . . 136 C2
Ripley GB 40 B2
Ripoll E 147 B3
Ripon GB 40 A2
Riposto I 177 B4
Ripsa S 56 B2
Risan MNE 16 D3
Risbäck S 200 B1
Risca GB 39 C3
Rischenau D 81 A5
Riscle F 128 C2
Risebo S 56 B2
Risnes N 46 A2
Rišňovce SK 98 C1
Risør N 53 B5
Risøyhamn N . . . 194 B6
Rissna S 199 B12
Ritsem S 194 C8
Ritterhude D 72 A1
Riutula FIN . . . 193 D10
Riva del Garda I . 121 B3
Riva Ligure I . . . 133 B3
Rivanazzano I . . 120 C2
Rivarolo Canavese I 119 B4
Rivarolo Mantovano I 121 B3
Rive-de-Gier F . . 117 B4
Rivedoux-Plage F 114 B2
Rivello I 174 A1
Rivergaro I 120 C2
Rives F 118 B2
Rivesaltes F 146 B3
Rivignano I 122 B2
Rivne UA 13 C7
Rivoli I 119 B4
Rivolta d'Adda I . 120 B2
Rixheim F 106 B2
Rixo S 54 B2
Riza GR 183 C5
Rizokarpaso CY . 181 A3
Rjukan N 47 C5
Rø DK 67 A3
Rö S 57 A4
Roa
  E 143 C3
  N 48 B2
Roade GB 44 A3
Roager DK 59 C1
Roaldkvam N . . . 52 A2
Roanne F 117 A4
Röbäck S 200 C6
Robakowo PL . . . 69 B3
Röbbio I 120 B1
Röbel D 73 A5
Roberton GB . . . 35 C5
Robertsfors S . . 200 B6
Robertville B . . . 80 B2
Robin Hood's Bay GB 37 B6
Robleda E 149 B3

Robledillo de Trujillo E 156 A2
Robledo
  Albacete E 158 C1
  Orense E 141 B4
Robledo de Chavela E 151 B3
Robledo del Buey E 156 A3
Robledo del Mazo E 156 A3
Robledollano E . . 156 A2
Robles de la Valcueva E 142 B1
Robliza de Cojos E 149 B4
Robres E 145 C3
Robres del Castillo E 144 B1
Rocafort de Queralt E 147 C2
Rocamadour F . . 129 B4
Roccabernarda I . 175 B2
Roccabianca I . . . 120 B3
Rocca di Mezzo I . 169 A3
Rocca di Papa I . 168 B2
Roccagorga I . . . 169 B3
Rocca Imperiale I 174 A2
Roccalbegna I . . 135 C4
Roccalumera I . . 177 B4
Roccamena I . . . 176 B2
Roccamonfina I . . 170 B1
Roccanova I 174 A2
Roccapalumba I . 176 B2
Roccapassa I . . . 169 A3
Rocca Priora I . . 136 B2
Roccaraso I 169 B4
Rocca San Casciano I 135 A4
Roccasecca I . . . 169 B3
Rocca Sinibalda I 169 A2
Roccastrada I . . . 135 B4
Roccatederighi I . 135 B4
Roccella Iónica I . 175 C2
Rocchetta
  Sant'António I . . 172 A1
Rocester GB 40 C2
Rochdale GB . . . 40 B1
Rochechouart F . 115 C4
Rochefort
  B 79 B5
  F 114 C3
Rochefort-en-Terre F 101 B3
Rochefort-Montagne F 116 B2
Rochefort-sur-Nenon F 105 B4
Roche-lez-Beaupré F 105 B5
Rochemaure F . . 131 A3
Rocheservière F . 114 B2
Rochester
  Medway GB 45 B4
  Northumberland GB 37 A4
Rochlitz D 83 A4
Rociana del Condado E 161 B3
Rockenhausen D . 93 B3
Rockhammar S . . 56 A1
Rockneby S 62 B4
Ročko Polje HR . . 123 B3
Ročov CZ 84 B1
Rodach D 82 B2
Roda de Bara E . 147 C2
Roda de Ter E . . 147 C3
Rodalben D 93 B3
Rødberg N 47 B5
Rødby DK 65 B4
Rødbyhavn DK . . 65 B4
Rødding
  Sønderjyllands Amt. DK 59 C2
  Viborg Amt. DK . . 58 B1
Rödeby S 63 B3
Rodeiro E 140 B3
Rødekro DK 64 A2
Roden NL 71 A3
Rödental D 82 B3
Rodenkirchen D . 72 A1
Rödermark D . . . 93 B4
Rodewisch D . . . 83 B4
Rodez F 130 A1
Rodi Gargánico I . 171 B3
Roding D 95 B4
Rödjebro S 51 B4
Rødkærsbro DK . . 59 B2
Rodolivos GR . . . 183 C5
Rodoñá E 147 C2
Rødvig DK 65 A5
Roermond NL . . . 80 A1
Roesbrugge B . . 78 B2
Roeschwoog F . . 93 C4
Roeselare B 78 B3
Roetgen D 80 B2
Roffiac F 116 B3
Röfors S 55 B5
Rofrano I 172 B1
Rogač HR 138 B2
Rogačica SRB . . . 127 C1
Rogatec SLO . . . 123 A4
Rogatica BIH . . . 139 B5
Rogatyn UA 13 D6
Rogätz D 73 B4
Roggendorf D . . . 65 C4
Roggiano Gravina I 174 B2
Roghadal GB . . . 31 B2
Rogliano
  F 180 A2
  I 175 B2
Rogne N 47 A6

Rognes F 131 B4
Rogny-les-7-Ecluses F 103 B4
Rogowo PL 76 B2
Rogoznica HR . . . 138 B1
Rogoźnica PL . . . 85 A4
Rogoźno PL 76 B1
Rohan F 101 A3
Röhlingen D 94 C2
Rohožník SK 98 C1
Rohr D 82 B2
Rohrbach A 96 C1
Rohrbach-lès-Bitche F 92 B3
Rohrberg D 73 B4
Rohr im Gebirge A 110 B2
Röhrnbach D . . . 96 C1
Roisel F 90 B3
Roja LV 8 D3
Rojales E 165 A4
Röjeråsen S 50 B1
Rojewo PL 76 B3
Rokiciny PL 87 A3
Rokietnica PL . . . 75 B5
Rokiškis LT 8 E4
Rokitki PL 85 A3
Rokycany CZ . . . 96 B1
Rolampont F . . . 105 B4
Rold DK 58 B2
Røldal N 52 A2
Rolde NL 71 B3
Rolfs S 196 D6
Rollag N 47 B6
Rollán E 149 B4
Rolle CH 105 C5
Roma = Rome I . . 168 B2
Roma S 57 C4
Romagnano Sésia I 119 B5
Romagné F 88 B2
Romakloster S . . 57 C4
Roman RO 17 B7
Romana I 178 B2
Romanèche-Thorins F 117 A4
Romano di Lombardia I 120 B2
Romanshorn CH . 107 B4
Romans-sur-Isère F 118 B2
Rombas F 92 B2
Rome = Roma I . . 168 B2
Romeán E 141 B3
Romenay F 105 C4
Romeral E 157 A4
Römerstein D . . . 94 C1
Rometta I 177 A4
Romford GB 45 B4
Romhány H 112 B3
Römhild D 82 B2
Romilly-sur-Seine F 91 C3
Romont CH 106 C1
Romorantin-Lanthenay F 103 B3
Romrod D 81 B5
Romsey GB 44 C2
Rømskog N 54 A2
Rønbjerg DK . . . 58 B1
Roncal E 144 B3
Ronce-les-Bains F 114 C2
Ronchamp F . . . 106 B1
Ronchi dei Legionari I 122 B2
Ronciglione I . . . 168 A2
Ronco Canavese I 119 B4
Ronco Scrivia I . . 120 C1
Ronda E 162 B2
Rønde DK 59 B3
Rone S 57 C4
Ronehamn S . . . 57 C4
Rong N 46 B1
Rönnäng S 60 B1
Rønne DK 67 A3
Ronneburg D . . . 83 B4
Ronneby S 63 B3
Rönneshytta S . . 55 B6
Rönninge S 57 A3
Rönnöfors S . . . 199 B10
Ronse B 79 B3
Roosendaal NL . . 79 A4
Roosky IRL 26 C3
Ropczyce PL . . . 87 B5
Ropeid N 52 A2
Ropinsalmi FIN . 192 D5
Ropuerelos del Páramo E 141 B5
Roquebilière F . . 133 A3
Roquebrun F . . . 130 B2
Roquecourbe F . . 130 B1
Roquefort F 128 B2
Roquemaure F . . 131 A3
Roquesteron F . . 132 B3
Roquetas de Mar E 164 C2
Roquetes E 153 B4
Roquevaire F . . . 132 B1
Røra N 199 B8
Rörbäcksnäs S . . 49 A4
Rørbæk DK 58 B2
Rore BIH 138 A2
Röro S 60 B1
Røros N 199 C8
Rorschach CH . . 107 B4
Rørvig DK 61 D1
Rørvik N 199 A8
Rörvik S 62 A2
Rosà I 121 B4
Rosal de la Frontera E 161 B2
Rosalina Mare I . . 122 B1
Rosans F 132 A1
Rosário P 160 B1
Rosarno I 175 C1

Rosbach D 81 B3
Rosche D 73 B3
Rościszewo PL 77 B4
Roscoff F 100 A2
Roscommon IRL 28 A3
Roscrea IRL 28 B4
Rosdorf D 82 A1
Rose I 174 B2
Rosegg A 109 C5
Rosehall GB 32 D2
Rosehearty GB 33 D4
Rosel GB 88 A1
Rosell E 153 B4
Roselló E 153 A4
Rosendal N 46 C3
Rosenfeld D 93 C4
Rosenfors S 62 A3
Rosenheim D 108 B3
Rosenow D 74 A2
Rosenthal D 81 A4
Rosersberg S 57 A3
Roses E 147 B4
Roseto degli Abruzzi
  I 169 A4
Roseto Valfortore
  I 170 B3
Rosheim F 93 C3
Rosia I 135 B4
Rosice CZ 97 B4
Rosières-en-Santerre
  F 90 B2
Rosignano Marittimo
  I 134 B3
Rosignano Solvay
  I 134 B3
Roşiori-de-Vede
  RO 17 C6
Roskhill GB 31 B2
Roskilde DK 61 D2
Roskovec AL 182 C1
Röslau D 83 B3
Roslev DK 58 B1
Rosmaninhal P 155 B3
Rosnowo PL 67 B5
Rosolini I 177 C3
Rosova MNE 139 B5
Rosoy F 104 A2
Rosporden F 100 B2
Rosquete P 154 B2
Rosrath D 80 B3
Rossa CH 120 A2
Rossano I 174 B2
Rossas
  Aveiro P 148 B1
  Braga P 148 A1
Rossdorf D 82 B2
Rossett GB 38 A4
Rosshaupten D 108 B1
Rossiglione I 133 A4
Rossignol B 92 B1
Rossla D 82 A3
Rosslare IRL 30 B2
Rosslare Harbour
  IRL 30 B2
Rosslau D 83 A4
Rosslea GB 27 B3
Rossleben D 82 A3
Rossön S 200 C2
Ross-on-Wye GB 39 C4
Rossoszyca PL 86 A2
Rosswein D 83 A5
Röstånga S 61 C3
Roštár SK 99 C4
Rostock D 65 B5
Rostrenen F 100 A2
Røsvik N 194 C6
Rosvik S 196 D4
Rosyth GB 35 B4
Röszke H 126 A2
Rot S 49 A6
Rota E 161 C3
Rota Greca I 174 B2
Rot am See D 94 B2
Rotberget N 49 B4
Rotella I 136 C2
Rotenburg
  Hessen D 82 B1
  Niedersachsen D . . .72 A2
Roth
  Bayern D 94 B3
  Rheinland-Pfalz D . .81 B3
Rothbury GB 37 A5
Rothemühl D 74 A2
Röthenbach D 95 B3
Rothenburg D 84 A2
Rothenburg ob der
  Tauber D 94 B2
Rothéneuf F 88 B2
Rothenklempenow
  D 74 A3
Rothenstein D 94 C3
Rotherham GB 40 B2
Rothes GB 32 D3
Rothesay GB 34 C2
Rothwell GB 44 A3
Rotnes N 48 B2
Rotonda I 174 B2
Rotondella I 174 A2
Rotova E 159 C3
Rott
  Bayern D 108 B1
  Bayern D 108 B3
Rottach-Egern D 108 B2
Röttenbach D 94 B3
Rottenbuch D 108 B1
Rottenburg
  Baden-Württemberg
  D 93 C4
  Bayern D 95 C3
Rottenmann A 110 B1
Rotterdam NL 79 A4
Rotthalmünster D . . .96 C1
Rottingdean GB 44 C3
Röttingen D 94 B1
Rottleberode D 82 A2
Rottne S 62 A2
Rottneros S 55 A4
Rottofreno I 120 B2
Rottweil D 107 A3
Rötz D 95 B4

Roubaix F 78 B3
Roudnice nad Labem
  CZ 84 B2
Roudouallec F 100 A2
Rouen F 89 A5
Rouffach F 106 B2
Rougé F 101 B4
Rougemont F 105 B5
Rougemont le-Château
  F 106 B1
Rouillac F 115 C3
Rouillé F 115 B4
Roujan F 130 B2
Roulans F 105 B5
Roundwood IRL 30 A1
Rousínov CZ 97 B4
Roussac F 115 B5
Roussennac F 130 A1
Rousses F 130 A2
Roussillon F 117 B4
Rouvroy-sur-Audry
  F 91 B4
Rouy F 104 B2
Rovaniemen
  maalaiskunta
  FIN 197 C8
Rovaniemi FIN 197 C8
Rovato I 120 B2
Rovensko pod
  Troskami CZ 84 B3
Roverbella I 121 B3
Rovereto I 121 B4
Rövershagen D 65 B5
Roverud N 49 B4
Rovigo I 121 B4
Rovinj HR 122 B2
Rovišce HR 124 B2
Rów PL 74 B3
Rowy PL 68 A2
Royal Leamington Spa
  GB 44 A2
Royal Tunbridge Wells
  GB 45 B4
Royan F 114 C2
Royat F 116 B3
Roybon F 118 B2
Roybridge GB 34 B3
Roye F 90 B2
Royère-de-Vassivière
  F 116 B1
Røykenvik N 48 B2
Royos E 164 B2
Rørvik N 199 A10
Royston GB 44 A3
Rozadas E 141 A4
Rozalén del Monte
  E 151 C5
Rózańsko PL 75 B3
Rozay-en-Brie F 90 C2
Roždalovice CZ 84 B3
Rozdilna UA 17 B9
Rozental PL 69 B4
Rozhyshche UA 13 C6
Rożmitál pod
  Třemšínem CZ 96 B1
Rožňava SK 99 C4
Rožnov pod
  Radhoštěm CZ 98 B2
Rozoy-sur-Serre F . . .91 B4
Rozprza PL 86 A3
Roztoky CZ 84 B2
Rozvadov CZ 95 B4
Rozzano I 120 B2
Rrëshen AL 182 B1
Rrogozhine AL 182 B1
Ruanes E 156 A2
Rubbestadneset
  N 46 C2
Rubi E 147 C3
Rubiá E 141 B4
Rubiacedo de Abajo
  E 143 B3
Rubielos Bajos E . . .158 B1
Rubielos de Mora
  E 153 B3
Rubiera I 121 C3
Rubik AL 182 B1
Rucandio E 143 B3
Rud
  Akershus N 48 B3
  Buskerud N 48 B2
Ruda
  PL 86 A2
  S 62 A4
Rudabánya H 99 C4
Ruda Maleniecka
  PL 87 A4
Ruda Pilczycka PL . . .87 A4
Ruda Śl. PL 86 B2
Ruddervorde B 78 A3
Ruden A 110 C1
Rudersberg D 94 C1
Rudersdorf A 111 B3
Rüdersdorf D 74 B2
Ruderting D 96 C1
Rüdesheim D 93 B3
Rudkøbing DK 65 B3
Rudmanns A 97 C3
Rudna
  CZ 96 A2
  PL 85 A4
Rudnik SRB 127 C2
Rudniki
  Opolskie PL 86 A2
  Śląskie PL 86 B3
Rudno
  Dolnośląskie PL . . .85 A4
  Pomorskie PL 69 B3
Rudnya RUS 13 A9
Rudolstadt D 82 B3
Rudowica PL 84 A3
Rudozem BG 183 B6
Rudskoga S 55 A5
Rudston GB 40 A3
Ruds Vedby DK 61 D1
Rudy PL 86 B2
Rue F 78 B1
Rueda E 150 A3
Rueda de Jalón E . . .152 A2

Ruelle-sur-Touvre
  F 115 C4
Ruerrero E 143 B3
Ruffano I 173 C4
Ruffec F 115 B4
Rugby GB 44 A2
Rugeley GB 40 C2
Ruggstrop S 62 B4
Rugles F 89 B4
Rugozero RUS 3 D13
Rühen D 73 B3
Ruhla D 82 B2
Ruhland D 84 A1
Ruhle D 71 B4
Ruhpolding D 109 B3
Ruhstorf D 96 C1
Ruidera E 158 C1
Ruillé-sur-le-Loir
  F 102 B2
Ruinen NL 71 B3
Ruiselede B 78 A3
Ruka FIN 197 C12
Rulles B 92 B1
Rülzheim D 93 B4
Rum H 111 B3
Ruma SRB 127 B1
Rumboci BIH 138 B3
Rumenka SRB 126 B1
Rumia PL 69 A3
Rumigny F 91 B4
Rumilly F 118 B2
Rumma S 56 B2
Rumney GB 39 C3
Rumont F 91 C5
Runa P 154 B1
Runcorn GB 38 A4
Rundmoen N 195 D5
Rungsted DK 61 D2
Runhällen S 51 B3
Runowo PL 69 A5
Runtuna S 56 B3
Rupa HR 123 B3
Ruppichteroth D 80 B3
Rupt-sur-Moselle
  F 106 B1
Rus E 157 B4
Ruse BG 17 D7
Ruše SLO 110 C2
Rusele S 200 B4
Ruševo HR 125 B4
Rush IRL 30 A2
Rushden GB 44 A3
Rusiec PL 86 A2
Rusinowo
  Zachodnio-Pomorskie
  PL 67 C4
  Zachodnio-Pomorskie
  PL 75 A5
Ruskele S 200 B4
Ruski Krstur SRB . .126 B1
Ruskington GB 40 B3
Rusovce SK 111 A4
Rüsselsheim D 93 B4
Russelv N 192 C4
Russi I 135 A5
Rust A 111 B3
Rustefjelbma N . . .193 B12
Rustrel F 131 B4
Ruszki PL 77 B5
Ruszów PL 84 A3
Rute E 163 A3
Rüthen D 81 A4
Rutherglen GB 35 C3
Ruthin GB 38 A3
Ruthven GB 32 D2
Ruthwell GB 36 B3
Rüti CH 107 B3
Rutigliano I 173 A3
Rutledal N 46 A2
Ruurlo NL 71 B3
Ruuvaoja FIN 197 B11
Ruvo del Monte I . . .172 B1
Ruvo di Púglia I 171 B4
Ruynes-en-Margeride
  F 116 C3
Ružic HR 138 B2
Ružomberok SK 99 B3
Ruzsa H 126 A1
Ry DK 59 B2
Rybany SK 98 C2
Rybina PL 69 A4
Rybnik PL 86 B2
Rychliki PL 69 B4
Rychlocice PL 86 A2
Rychnov nad Kněžnou
  CZ 85 B4
Rychnowo PL 77 A5
Rychtal PL 86 A1
Rychwał PL 76 B3
Ryczów PL 87 A3
Ryczywół PL 87 A5
Ryczywół PL 75 B5
Ryd S 63 B2
Rydaholm S 62 B2
Rydal S 60 B2
Rydbo S 57 A4
Rydboholm S 60 B2
Ryde GB 44 C2
Rydöbruk S 60 C3
Rydsgård S 66 A2
Rydsnäs S 62 A3
Rydultowy PL 86 B2
Rydzyna PL 85 A4
Rye GB 45 C4
Ryjewo PL 69 B3
Rymań PL 67 C4
Rýmařov CZ 98 B1
Rynarzewo PL 76 A2
Ryomgård DK 59 B3
Rypefjord N 192 B7
Rypin PL 77 A4

Rysjedalsvika N 46 A2
Ryssby S 60 C4
Rytel PL 68 B2
Rytinki FIN 197 D10
Rytro PL 99 B4
Rzeczenica PL 68 B2
Rzeczniów PL 87 A5
Rzeczyca PL 87 A4
Rzęgnowo PL 77 A5
Rzejowice PL 87 A3
Rzemień PL 87 B5
Rzepin PL 75 B3
Rzesznikowo PL 67 C4
Rzeszów PL 12 C4
Rzgów PL 86 A3
Rzhev RUS 9 D9

S

Saal
  Bayern D 82 B2
  Bayern D 95 C3
Saalbach A 109 B3
Saalburg D 83 B3
Saales F 92 C3
Saalfeld D 82 B3
Saalfelden am
  Steinernen Meer
  A 109 B3
Saanen CH 106 C2
Saarbrücken D 92 B2
Saarburg D 92 B2
Saarijärvi FIN 8 A4
Saari-Kämä FIN . . .197 C9
Saarlouis D 92 B2
Saas-Fee CH 119 A4
Šabac SRB 127 C1
Sabadell E 147 C3
Sabáudia I 169 B3
Sabbioneta I 121 C3
Sabero E 142 B1
Sabiñánigo E 145 B3
Sabiote E 157 B4
Sables-d'Or-les-Pins
  F 101 A3
Sablé-sur-Sarthe
  F 102 B1
Sabóia P 160 B1
Saborsko HR 123 B4
Sabrosa P 148 A2
Sabugal P 149 B2
Sabuncu TR 187 C5
Sacecorbo E 152 B1
Saceda del Rio E . . .151 B5
Sacedón E 151 B5
Săcele RO 17 C6
Saceruela E 156 B3
Sachsenburg D 109 C4
Sachsenhagen D 72 B2
Sacile I 122 B1
Sacramenia E 151 A4
Sada E 140 A2
Sádaba E 144 B2
Saddell GB 34 C2
Sadernes E 147 B3
Sadki PL 76 A2
Sadkowice PL 87 A4
Sadlinki PL 69 B3
Sadów PL 75 B3
Sadská CZ 84 B2
Saelices E 151 C5
Saelices de Mayorga
  E 142 B1
Saerbeck D 71 B4
Saeul B 92 B1
Safaalan TR 186 A3
Safara P 161 A2
Säffle S 55 A4
Saffron Walden GB . .45 A4
Safranbolu TR 187 A7
Sagard D 66 B2
S'Agaro E 147 C4
Sągmyra S 50 B2
Sagone F 180 A1
Sagres P 160 C1
Ságújfalu H 113 A3
Sagunt E 159 B3
Sagvåg N 52 A1
Ságvár H 112 C2
Sagy F 105 C4
Sahagún E 142 B1
Šahy SK 112 A2
Saignelégier CH . . .106 B1
Saignes F 116 B2
Saija FIN 197 B11
Saillagouse F 146 B3
Saillans F 118 C2
Sains Richaumont
  F 91 B3
St Abb's GB 35 C5
St Affrique F 130 B1
St Agnan F 104 C2
St Agnant F 114 C3
St Agnes GB 42 B1
St Agrève F 117 B4
St Aignan F 103 B3
St Aignan-sur-Roë
  F 101 B4
St Albans GB 44 B3
St Alban-sur-Limagnole
  F 117 C3
St Amand-en-Puisaye
  F 104 B2
St Amand-les-Eaux
  F 79 B3
St Amand-Longpré
  F 103 B3
St Amand-Montrond
  F 103 C4
St Amans F 117 C3
St Amans-Soult F . .130 B1

St Amant-Roche-Savine
  F 117 B3
St Amarin F 106 B1
St Ambroix F 131 A3
St Amé F 106 A1
St Amour F 118 A2
St André-de-Corcy
  F 117 B4
St André-de-Cubzac
  F 128 B2
St André-de-l'Eure
  F 89 B5
St André-de-
  Roquepertuis F .131 A3
St André-de-Sangonis
  F 130 B2
St Andre-de-Valborgne
  F 130 A2
St André-les-Alpes
  F 132 B2
St Andrews GB 35 B5
St Angel F 116 B2
St Anthème F 117 B3
St Antoine F 180 A2
St Antoine-de-Ficalba
  F 129 B3
St Antönien CH 107 C4
St Antonin-Noble-Val
  F 129 B4
St Août F 103 C3
St Armant-Tallende
  F 116 B3
St Arnoult F 90 C1
St Asaph GB 38 A3
St Astier F 129 A3
St Athan GB 39 C3
St Aubin
  CH 106 C1
  F 105 B4
  GB 88 A1
St Aubin-d'Aubigne
  F 101 A4
St Aubin-du-Cormier
  F 101 A4
St Aubin-sur-Aire F .92 C1
St Aubin-sur-Mer F .89 A4
St Aulaye F 128 A3
St Austell GB 42 B2
St Avit F 116 B2
St Avold F 92 B2
St Aygulf F 132 B2
St Bauzille-de-Putois
  F 130 B2
St Béat F 145 B4
St Beauzély F 130 A1
St Bees GB 36 B3
St Benim-d'Azy F .104 C2
St Benoît-du-Sault
  F 115 B5
St Benoit-en-Woëvre
  F 92 C1
St Berthevin F 102 A1
St Blaise-la-Roche
  F 92 C3
St Blazey GB 42 B2
St Blin F 105 A4
St Bonnet F 118 C3
St Bonnet Briance
  F 115 C5
St Bonnet-de-Joux
  F 104 C3
St Bonnet-le-Château
  F 117 B4
St Bonnet-le-Froid
  F 117 B4
St Brévin-les-Pins
  F 101 B3
St Briac-sur-Mer F 101 A3
St Brice-en-Coglès
  F 88 B2
St Brieuc F 101 A3
St Bris-le-Vineux
  F 104 B2
St Broladre F 88 B2
St Calais F 102 B2
St Cannat F 131 B4
St Cast-le-Guildo
  F 101 A3
St Céré F 129 B4
St Cergue CH 118 A3
St Cergues F 118 A3
St Cernin F 116 B2
St Chamant F 116 B1
St Chamas F 131 B4
St Chamond F 117 B4
St Chély-d'Apcher
  F 116 C3
St Chély-d'Aubrac
  F 116 C2
St Chinian F 130 B1
St Christol F 131 A4
St Christol-lès-Alès
  F 131 A3
St Christoly-Médoc
  F 114 C3
St Christophe-du-
  Ligneron F 114 B2
St Christophe-en-
  Brionnais F 117 A4
St Ciers-sur-Gironde
  F 128 A2
St Clair-sur-Epte F .90 B1
St Clar F 129 C3
St Claud F 115 C4
St Claude F 118 A2
St Clears GB 39 C2
St Columb Major
  GB 42 B2
St Come-d'Olt F . . .130 A1
St Cosme-en-Vairais
  F 89 B4
St Cyprien
  Dordogne F 129 B4
  Pyrénées-Orientales
  F 146 B4
St Cyr-sur-Loire F .102 B2
St Cyr-sur-Mer F . .132 B1
St Cyr-sur-Methon
  F 117 A4

St David's GB 39 C1
St Denis F 90 C2
St Denis-d'Oléron
  F 114 B2
St Denis d'Orques
  F 102 A1
St Didier F 117 A4
St Didier-en-Velay
  F 117 B4
St Dié F 92 C2
St Dier-d'Auvergne
  F 117 B3
St Dizier F 91 C4
St Dizier-Leyrenne
  F 116 A1
Ste Adresse F 89 A4
Ste Anne F 89 B4
Ste Anne-d'Auray
  F 100 B3
Ste Croix CH 105 C5
Ste Croix-Volvestre
  F 146 A2
Ste Engrâce F 144 A3
Ste Enimie F 130 A2
St Efflam F 100 A2
Ste Foy-de-Peyrolières
  F 146 A2
Ste Foy-la-Grande
  F 128 B3
Ste Foy l'Argentiere
  F 117 B4
Ste Gauburge-Ste
  Colombe F 89 B4
Ste Gemme la Plaine
  F 114 B2
Ste Geneviève F 90 B2
Ste Hélène F 128 B2
Ste Hélène-sur-Isère
  F 118 B3
Ste Hermine F 114 B2
Ste Jalle F 131 A4
Ste Livrade-sur-Lot
  F 129 B3
Ste Marie-aux-Mines
  F 106 A2
Ste Marie-du-Mont
  F 88 A2
Ste Maure-de-Touraine
  F 102 B2
Ste Maxime F 132 B2
Ste Ménéhould F . . .91 B4
Ste Mère-Église F . .88 A2
St Emiland F 104 C3
St Émilion F 128 B2
St Enoder GB 42 B2
Ste Ode B 92 A1
Saintes F 114 C3
Ste Savine F 91 C4
Ste Sévère-sur-Indre
  F 103 C4
Ste Sigolène F 117 B4
St Esteben F 144 A2
St Estèphe F 128 A2
Ste Suzanne F 102 A1
St Étienne F 117 B4
St Étienne-de-Baigorry
  F 144 A2
St Étienne-de-Cuines
  F 118 B3
St Étienne-de-Fursac
  F 116 A1
St Étienne-de-Montluc
  F 101 B4
St Étienne-de-St Geoirs
  F 118 B2
St Étienne-de-Tinée
  F 132 A2
St Étienne-du-Bois
  F 118 A2
St Étienne-du-Rouvray
  F 89 A5
St Étienne-les-Orgues
  F 132 A1
Ste Tulle F 132 B1
St Fargeau F 104 B2
St Félicien F 117 B4
St Felix-de-Sorgues
  F 130 B1
St Félix-Lauragais
  F 146 A2
Saintfield GB 27 B5
St Fillans GB 35 B3
St Firmin F 118 C3
St Florent F 180 A2
St Florentin F 104 B2
St Florent-le-Vieil
  F 101 B4
St Florent-sur-Cher
  F 103 C4
St Flour F 116 B3
St Flovier F 103 C3
St Fort-sur-le-Né
  F 115 C3
St Fulgent F 114 B2
St Galmier F 117 B4
St Gaudens F 145 A4
St Gaultier F 115 B5
St Gély-du-Fesc F . .130 B2
St Genest-Malifaux
  F 117 B4
St Gengoux-le-National
  F 104 C3
St Geniez F 132 A2
St Geniez-d'Olt F . .130 A1
St Genis-de-Saintonge
  F 114 C3
St Genis-Pouilly F .118 A3
St Genix-sur-Guiers
  F 118 B2
St Georges Buttavent
  F 88 B3
St Georges-d'Aurac
  F 117 B3
St Georges-de-
  Commiers F 118 B2

St Georges-de-Didonne
  F 114 C3
St Georges-de-
  Luzençon F 130 A1
St Georges-de Mons
  F 116 B2
St Georges-de-Reneins
  F 117 A4
St Georges d'Oléron
  F 114 C2
St Georges-en-Couzan
  F 117 B3
St Georges-lès-
  Baillargeaux F . .115 B4
St Georges-sur-Loire
  F 102 B1
St Georges-sur-Meuse
  B 79 B5
St Geours-de-Maremne
  F 128 C1
St Gérand-de-Vaux
  F 117 A3
St Gérand-le-Puy
  F 117 A3
St Germain F 105 B5
St Germain-Chassenay
  F 104 C2
St Germain-de-Calberte
  F 130 A2
St Germain-de-
  Confolens F 115 B4
St Germain-des-Joux
  F 118 A2
St Germain-des-Fossés
  F 117 A3
St Germain-du-Bois
  F 105 C4
St Germain-du-Plain
  F 105 C4
St Germain-du-Puy
  F 103 B4
St Germain-en-Laye
  F 90 C2
St Germain-Laval
  F 117 B4
St Germain-Lembron
  F 116 B3
St Germain-les-Belles
  F 116 B1
St Germain-Lespinasse
  F 117 A3
St Germain-l'Herm
  F 117 B3
St Gervais-d'Auvergne
  F 116 A2
St Gervais-les-Bains
  F 118 B3
St Gervais-sur-Mare
  F 130 B2
St Gildas-de-Rhuys
  F 100 B3
St Gildas-des-Bois
  F 101 B3
St Gilles
  Gard F 131 B3
  Ille-et-Vilaine F . .101 A4
St Gilles-Croix-de-Vie
  F 114 B2
St Gingolph F 119 A3
St Girons
  Ariège F 146 B2
  Landes F 128 C1
St Girons-Plage F .128 C1
St Gobain F 91 B3
St Gorgon-Main F .105 B5
St Guénolé F 100 B1
St Harmon GB 39 B3
St Helens GB 38 A4
St Helier GB 88 A1
St Herblain F 101 B4
St Hilaire
  Allier F 104 C2
  Aude F 146 A3
St Hilaire-de-Riez
  F 114 B2
St Hilaire-des-Loges
  F 114 B3
St Hilaire-de-
  Villefranche F . .114 C3
St Hilaire-du-Harcouët
  F 88 B2
St Hilaire-du-Rosier
  F 118 B2
St Hippolyte
  Aveyron F 116 C2
  Doubs F 106 B1
St Hippolyte-du-Fort
  F 130 B2
St Honoré-les-Bains
  F 104 C2
St Hubert B 92 A1
St Imier CH 106 B2
St Issey GB 42 B2
St Ives
  Cambridgeshire
  GB 44 A3
  Cornwall GB 42 B1
St Izaire F 130 B1
St Jacques-de-la-Lande
  F 101 A4
St Jacut-de-la-Mer
  F 101 A3
St James F 88 B2
St Jaume d'Enveja
  E 153 B4
St Jean-Brévelay
  F 101 B3
St Jean-d'Angély
  F 114 C3
St Jean-de-Belleville
  F 118 B3
St Jean-de-Bournay
  F 118 B2
St Jean-de-Braye
  F 103 B3
St Jean-de-Côle F .115 C4
St Jean-de-Daye F .88 A2

St Jean de Losne
F 105 B4
St Jean-de-Luz F . 144 A2
St Jean-de-Maurienne
F 118 B3
St Jean-de-Monts
F 114 B1
St Jean-d'Illac F . 128 B2
St Jean-du-Bruel
F 130 A2
St Jean-du-Gard F 131 A2
St Jean-en-Royans
F 118 B2
St Jean-la-Riviere
F 133 B3
St Jean-Pied-de-Port
F 144 A2
St Jean-Poutge F .129 C3
St Jeoire F 118 A3
St Joachim F 101 B3
St Johnstown IRL . 27 B3
St Jorioz F 118 B3
St Joris Winge B . 79 B4
St Jouin-de-Marnes
F 102 C1
St Juéry F 130 B1
St Julien F 118 A2
St Julien-Chapteuil
F 117 B4
St Julien-de-Vouvantes
F 101 B4
St Julien-du-Sault
F 104 A2
St Julien-du-Verdon
F 132 B2
St Julien-en-Born
F 128 B1
St Julien-en-Genevois
F 118 A3
St Julien-l'Ars F . 115 B4
St Julien la-Vêtre
F 117 B3
St Julien-Mont-Denis
F 118 B3
St Julien-sur-
Reyssouze F . . . 118 A2
St Junien F 115 C4
St Just
F 131 A3
GB 42 B1
St Just-en-Chaussée
F 90 B2
St Just-en-Chevalet
F 117 B3
St Justin F 128 C2
St Just-St Rambert
F 117 B4
St Keverne GB. . . 42 B1
St Lary-Soulan F . 145 B4
St Laurent-d'Aigouze
F 131 B3
St Laurent-de-
Chamousset F . 117 B4
St Laurent-de-Condel
F 89 A3
St Laurent-de-la-
Cabrerisse F . . .146 A3
St Laurent-de-la-
Salanque F 146 B3
St Laurent-des-Autels
F 101 B4
St Laurent-du-Pont
F 118 B2
St Laurent-en-Caux
F 89 A4
St Laurent-en-
Grandvaux F . . 105 C4
St Laurent-Médoc
F 128 A2
St Laurent-sur-Gorre
F 115 C4
St Laurent-sur-Mer
F 88 A3
St Laurent-sur-Sèvre
F 114 B3
St Leger B 92 B1
St Léger-de-Vignes
F 104 C2
St Léger-sous-Beuvray
F 104 C3
St Léger-sur-Dheune
F 104 C3
St Léonard-de-Noblat
F 116 B1
St Leonards GB. . 45 C4
St Lô F 88 A2
St Lon-les-Mines
F 128 C1
St Louis F 106 B2
St Loup F 117 A3
St Loup-de-la-Salle
F 105 C3
St Loup-sur-Semouse
F 105 B5
St Lunaire F 101 A3
St Lupicin F 118 A2
St Lyphard F 101 B3
St Lys F 146 A2
St Macaire F 128 B2
St Maclou F 89 A4
St Maixent-l'École
F 115 B3
St Malo F 88 B1
St Mamet-la-Salvetat
F 116 C2
St Mandrier-sur-Mer
F 132 B1
St Marcel
Drôme F. 117 C4
Saône-et-Loire F . 105 C3
St Marcellin F . . . 118 B2
St Marcellin sur Loire
F 117 B4
St Marcet F 145 A4
St Mards-en-Othe
F 104 A2

St Margaret's-at-Cliffe
GB 45 B5
St Margaret's Hope
GB 33 C4
St Mars-la-Jaille F 101 B4
St Martin-d'Ablois
F 91 C3
St Martin-d'Auxigny
F 103 B4
St Martin-de-Belleville
F 118 B3
St Martin-de-Bossenay
F 91 C3
St Martin-de-Crau
F 131 B3
St Martin-de-Londres
F 130 B2
St Martin-d'Entraunes
F 132 A2
St Martin-de-
Queyrières F . . 118 C3
St Martin-de-Ré F .114 B2
St Martin des Besaces
F 88 A3
St Martin-d'Estreaux
F 117 A3
St Martin-de-Valamas
F 117 C4
St Martin-d'Hères
F 118 B2
St Martin-du-Frêne
F 118 A2
St Martin-en-Bresse
F 105 C4
St Martin-en-Haut
F 117 B4
St Martin-la-Méanne
F 116 B1
St Martin-Osmonville
F 90 B1
St Martin-sur-Ouanne
F 104 B2
St Martin-Valmeroux
F 116 B2
St Martin-Vésubie
F 133 A3
St Martory F 145 A4
St Mary's GB 33 C4
St Mathieu F 115 C4
St Mathieu-de-Tréviers
F 131 B2
St Maurice CH . . . 119 A3
St Maurice-Navacelles
F 130 B2
St Maurice-sur-Moselle
F 106 B1
St Mawes GB. . . . 42 B1
St Maximin-la-Ste
Baume F 132 B1
St Méard-de-Gurçon
F 128 B3
St Médard-de-
Guizières F . . .128 A2
St Médard-en-Jalles
F 128 B2
St Méen-le-Grand
F 101 A3
St Menges F 91 B4
St Merløse DK . . . 61 D1
St Mésto CZ. . . . 85 B4
St M'Hervé F . . . 101 A4
St Michel
Aisne F 91 B4
Gers F 145 A4
St Michel-Chef-Chef
F 101 B3
St Michel-de-Castelnau
F 128 B2
St Michel-de-Maurienne
F 118 B3
St Michel-en-Grève
F 100 A2
St Michel-enl'Herm
F 114 B2
St Michel-Mont-Mercure
F 114 B3
St Mihiel F 92 C1
St Monance GB . . 35 B5
St Montant F 131 A3
St Moritz CH 107 C4
St Nazaire F 101 B3
St Nazaire-en-Royans
F 118 B2
St Nazaire-le-Désert
F 131 A4
St Nectaire F 116 B2
St Neots GB. . . . 44 A3
St Nicolas-de-Port
F 92 C2
St Nicolas-de-Redon
F 101 B3
St Nicolas-du-Pélem
F 100 A2
St Niklaas B 79 A4
St Omer F 78 B2
St Pair-sur-Mer F . 88 B2
St Palais F 144 A2
St Palais-sur-Mer
F 114 C2
St Pardoux-la-Rivière
F 115 C4
St Paul-Cap-de-Joux
F 129 C4
St Paul-de-Fenouillet
F 146 B3
St Paul-de-Varax
F 118 A2
St Paulien F 117 B3
St Paul-le-Jeune F 131 A3
St Paul-lès-Dax F .128 C1
St Paul-Trois-Châteaux
F 131 A3
St Pé-de-Bigorre
F 145 A3
St Pée-sur-Nivelle
F 144 A2
St Péravy-la-Colombe
F 103 B3
St Péray F 117 C4
St Père-en-Retz F .101 B3

St Peter Port GB . .88 A1
St Petersburg = Sankt-
Peterburg RUS . . .9 C7
St Philbert-de-Grand-
Lieu F 114 A2
St Pierre F 130 B1
St Pierre-d'Albigny
F 118 B3
St Pierre-d'Allevard
F 118 B3
St Pierre-de-Chartreuse
F 118 B2
St Pierre-de-Chignac
F 129 A3
St Pierre-de-la-Fage
F 130 B2
St Pierre-d'Entremont
F 118 B2
St Pierre-d'Oléron
F 114 C2
St Pierre-Eglise F . 88 A2
St Pierre-en-Port F .89 A4
St Pierre-le-Moûtier
F 104 C2
St Pierre Montlimart
F 101 B4
St Pierre-Quiberon
F 100 B2
St Pierre-sur-Dives
F 89 A3
St Pierreville F . . 117 C4
St Pieters-Leeuw B 79 B4
St Plancard F . . . 145 A4
St Poix F 101 B4
St Pol-de-Léon F . 100 A2
St Polgues F 117 B3
St Pol-sur-Ternoise
F 78 B2
St Pons-de-Thomières
F 130 B1
St Porchaire F . . . 114 C3
St Pourçain-sur-Sioule
F 116 A3
St Priest F 117 B4
St Privat F 116 B2
St Quay-Portrieux
F 100 A3
St Quentin F 90 B3
St Quentin-la-Poterie
F 131 A3
St Quentin-les-Anges
F 102 B1
St Rambert-d'Albon
F 117 B4
St Rambert-en-Bugey
F 118 B2
St Raphaël F 132 B2
St Rémy-de-Provence
F 131 B3
St Rémy-du-Val F .89 B4
St Remy-en-Bouzemont
F 91 C4
St Renan F 100 A1
St Révérien F . . . 104 B2
St Riquier F 90 A1
St Romain-de-Colbosc
F 89 A4
St Rome-de-Cernon
F 130 A1
St Rome-de-Tarn
F 130 A1
St Sadurni-d'Anoia
E 147 C2
St Saëns F 89 A5
St Sampson GB. . . 88 A1
St Samson-la-Poterie
F 90 B1
St Saturnin-de-Lenne
F 130 A2
St Saturnin-lès-Apt
F 131 B4
St Sauflieu F 90 B2
St Saulge F 104 B2
St Sauveur
Finistère F 100 A2
Haute-Saône F . . 105 B5
St Sauveur-de-
Montagut F . . .117 C4
St Sauveur-en-Puisaye
F 104 B2
St Sauveur-en-Rue
F 117 B4
St Sauveur-Lendelin
F 88 A2
St Sauveur-le-Vicomte
F 88 A2
St Sauveur-sur-Tinée
F 132 A3
St Savin
Gironde F 128 A2
Vienne F 115 B4
St Savinien F 114 C3
St Savournin F . . 131 B4
St Seine-l'Abbaye
F 105 B3
St Sernin-sur-Rance
F 130 B1
St Sevan-sur-Mer F 88 B1
St Sever F 128 C2
St Sever-Calvados
F 88 B2
St Sorlin-d'Arves
F 118 B3
St Soupplets F . . . 90 B2
St Sulpice F 129 C4
St Sulpice-Laurière
F 116 A1
St Sulpice-les-Feuilles
F 115 B5
St Symphorien F .128 B2
St Symphoriende-Lay
F 117 B4
St Symphorien d'Ozon
F 117 B4
St Symphoriensur-
Coise F 117 B4
St Teath GB 42 B2
St Thégonnec F . .100 A2
St Thiébault F . . . 105 A4

St Trivier-de-Courtes
F 118 A2
St Trivier sur-Moignans
F 117 A4
St Trojan-les-Bains
F 114 C2
St Tropez F 132 B2
St Truiden B 79 B5
St Vaast-la-Hougue
F 88 A2
St Valérien F 104 A2
St Valery-en-Caux
F 89 A4
St Valéry-sur-Somme
F 78 B1
St Vallier
Drôme F 117 B4
Saône-et-Loire F . 104 C3
St Vallier-de-Thiey
F 132 B2
St Vaury F 102 C1
St Venant F 78 B2
St Véran F 119 C3
St Vincent I 119 B3
St Vincent-de-Tyrosse
F 128 C1
St Vit F 105 B4
St Vith B 80 B2
St Vivien-de-Médoc
F 114 C2
St Yan F 117 A4
St Ybars F 146 A2
St Yorre F 117 A3
St Yrieix-la-Perche
F 115 C5
Saissac F 146 A3
Saja E 142 A2
Sajan SRB 126 B2
Šajkaš SRB 126 B2
Sajókaza H. 99 C4
Sajószentpéter H .113 A4
Sajóvámos H. . . 113 A4
Sakarya TR 187 B5
Sakskøbing DK . . 65 B4
Sakule SRB 126 B2
Sala S 50 C3
Sala Baganza I . . 120 C3
Sala Consilina I . 172 B1
Salakovac SRB . 127 C3
Salamanca E . . . 150 B2
Salamina GR . . . 185 B4
Salandra I 172 B2
Salaparuta I 176 B1
Salar E 163 A3
Salardú E 145 B4
Salas E 141 A4
Salas de los Infantes
E 143 B3
Salau F 146 B2
Salavaux CH . . . 106 C2
Salbertrand I . . . 119 B3
Salbohed S 50 C3
Salbris F 103 B4
Salbu N 46 A2
Salce E 141 B4
Salching D 95 C4
Salcombe GB . . . 43 B3
Saldaña E 142 B2
Saldus LV 8 D3
Sale I 120 C1
Saleby S 55 B4
Salem D 107 B4
Salemi I 176 B1
Salen
Argyll & Bute GB . 34 B2
Highland GB . . . 34 B2
N 199 A8
Sälen S 49 A5
Salernes F 132 B2
Salerno I 170 C2
Salers F 116 B2
Salford GB 40 B1
Salgótarján H . . . 113 A3
Salgueiro P 155 B3
Salhus N 46 B2
Sali HR. 137 B4
Sálice Salentino I .173 B3
Salientes E 141 B4
Salies-de-Béarn F 144 A3
Salies-du-Salat F .145 A4
Salignac-Eyvigues
F 129 B4
Saligney-sur-Roudon
F 104 C2
Salihli TR 188 A3
Salihorsk BY . . . 13 B7
Salinas
Alicante E 159 C3
Huesca E 145 A4
Salinas de Medinaceli
E 152 A1
Salinas de Pisuerga
E 142 B2
Salindres F 131 A3
Saline di Volterra
I 135 B3
Salins-les-Bains F 105 C4
Salir P 160 B1
Salisbury GB . . . 44 B2
Salla
A 110 B1
FIN 197 C11
Sallachy GB. . . . 32 C2
Sallanches F . . . 118 B3
Sallent E 147 C2
Sallent de Gállego
E 145 B3
Salles F 128 B2
Salles-Curan F . . 130 A1
Salles-sur-l'Hers
F 146 A2
Sallins IRL 30 A2
Sällsjö S 199 B10
Salmerón E 152 B1
Salmiech F 130 A1
Salmivaara FIN . 197 C11
Salmoral E 150 B2

Salo FIN 8 B3
Salò I 121 B3
Salobreña E 163 B4
Salon-de-Provence
F 131 B4
Salonica = Thessaloniki
GR 182 C4
Salonta RO 16 B4
Salorino E 155 B3
Salornay-sur-Guye
F 104 C3
Salorno I 121 A4
Salou E 147 C2
Šalovci SLO 111 C3
Salsbruket N . . . 199 A8
Salses-le-Chateau
F 146 B3
Salsomaggiore Terme
I 120 C2
Salt E 147 C3
Saltaire GB 40 B2
Saltara I 136 B1
Saltash GB. 42 B2
Saltburn-by-the-Sea
GB 37 B6
Saltcoats GB . . . 34 C3
Saltfleet GB 41 B4
Salto P 148 A2
Saltrød N 53 B4
Saltsjöbaden S . . 57 A4
Saltvik
FIN 51 B7
S 62 A4
Saludécio I 136 B1
Salussola I 119 B5
Saluzzo I 119 C4
Salvacañete E . . 152 B2
Salvada P 160 B2
Salvagnac F . . . 129 C4
Salvaleon E 155 C4
Salvaterra de Magos
P 154 B2
Salvaterra do Extremo
P 155 B4
Salvatierra
Avila E 143 B4
Badajoz E 155 C4
Salvatierra de Santiago
E 156 A1
Salviac F 129 B4
Salzburg A 109 B4
Salzgitter D 72 B3
Salzgitter Bad D . 72 B3
Salzhausen D . . . 72 A3
Salzhemmendorf D 72 B2
Salzkotten D 81 A4
Salzmünde D . . . 83 A3
Salzwedel D 73 B4
Samadet F 128 C2
Samandıra TR . . 186 B4
Samassi I 179 C2
Samatan F 146 A1
Sambiase I 175 C2
Sambir UA 13 D5
Samborowo PL . . 69 B4
Sambuca di Sicília
I 176 B2
Samedan CH . . . 107 C4
Samer F 78 B1
Sami GR. 184 A1
Şamlı TR 186 C2
Sammichele di Bari
I 173 B2
Samnaun CH . . . 107 C5
Samobor HR . . . 123 B4
Samoëns F 118 A3
Samokov BG . . . 17 D5
Samora Correia P .154 C2
Šamorín SK . . . 111 A4
Samos
E 141 B3
GR 188 B1
Samoš SRB 126 B2
Samothraki GR . .183 C7
Samper de Calanda
E 153 A3
Sampéyre I 133 A3
Sampieri I 177 C3
Sampigny F 92 C1
Samplawa PL. . . 69 B4
Samproniano I . . 168 A1
Samtens D 66 B2
Samugheo I 179 C2
San Adrián E . . . 144 B2
San Agustin E . . 164 C2
San Agustin de
Guadalix E . . . 151 B4
San Alberto I . . . 135 A5
San Amaro E . . . 140 B2
Sânandrei RO . . 126 B3
San Andrès del
Rabanedo E . . 142 B1
San Antanio di Santadi
I 179 C2
San Antolín de Ibias
E 141 A4
San Arcángelo I . 174 A2
Sanary-sur-Mer F 132 B1
San Asensio E . . 143 B4
San Bartolomé las
Abiertas E . . . 150 C3
San Bartolomé la
Torre E 161 B2
San Bartolomé
Pinares E 150 B3
San Bartolomeo in
Galdo I 170 B3
San Benedetto del
Tronto I 136 C2
San Benedetto in Alpe
I 135 B4
San Benedetto Po
I 121 B3
San Benito E . . . 156 B3
San Benito de la
Contienda E . . 155 C3
San Biágio Plátani
I 176 B2

San Biágio Saracinisco
I 169 B3
San Bonifacio I . . 121 B4
San Calixto E . . . 156 C2
San Cándido I . . . 109 C3
San Carlo
CH 119 A5
I 176 B2
San Carlos del Valle
E 157 B4
San Casciano dei Bagni
I 135 C4
San Casciano in Val di
Pesa I 135 B4
San Cataldo
Puglia I 173 B4
Sicilia I 176 B2
San Cebrián de Castro
E 149 A4
Sancergues F . . . 104 B1
Sancerre F 103 B4
San Cesário di Lecce
I 173 B4
Sancey-le-Long F .105 B5
Sanchiorian E . . .150 B3
San Chirico Raparo
I 174 A2
Sanchonuño E . . 151 A3
San Cibrao das Viñas
E 140 B3
San Cipirello I . . . 176 B2
San Ciprián E . . . 141 A3
San Clemente E . 158 B1
San Clodio E . . . 141 B3
Sancoins F 104 C1
San Colombano al
Lambro I 120 B2
San Costanzo I . . 136 B2
San Crisóbal de
Entreviñas E . . 142 B1
San Cristóbal de la
Polantera E . . . 141 B5
San Cristóbal de la
Vega E 150 A3
San Cristovo E . . 141 C3
Sancti-Petri E . . . 162 B1
Sancti-Spiritus E .149 B3
Sand
Hedmark N 48 B3
Rogaland N . . . 52 A2
Sanda S 57 C4
San Damiano d'Asti
I 119 C5
San Damiano Macra
I 133 A3
Sandane N 198 D3
San Daniele del Friuli
I 122 A2
Sandanski BG . . . 183 B5
Sandared S 60 B2
Sandarne S 51 A4
Sandau D 73 B5
Sandbach
D 96 C1
GB 38 A4
Sandbank GB . . . 34 C3
Sandbanks GB . . 43 B5
Sandbukt N 192 C5
Sandby DK 65 B4
Sande
D 71 A5
Sogn og Fjordane
N 46 A2
Vestfold N 54 A1
Sandefjord N . . . 54 A1
Sandeid N 52 A1
San Demétrio Corone
I 174 B2
San Demétrio né
Vestini I 169 A3
Sandersleben D . .82 A3
Sanderstølen N . . 47 B6
Sandes N 53 B3
Sandesneben D . . 65 C3
Sandhead GB . . . 36 B2
Sandhem S 60 B3
Sandhorst D 71 A4
Sandhurst GB . . . 44 B3
Sandıklı TR 189 A5
Sandillon F 103 B4
Sandl A 96 C2
Sandnes GB 52 B1
Sandness GB . . . 33 A5
Sandnessjøen N . 195 D3
Sando E 149 B3
Sandomierz PL . . 87 B5
San Dónaci I . . . 173 B3
San Donàdi Piave
I 122 B1
San Donato Val di
Comino I 169 B3
Sándorfalva H . . . 126 A2
Sandøy N 198 C4
Sandrigo I 121 B4
Sandsele S 195 E8
Sandset N 194 B5
Sandsjöfors S . . . 62 A2
Sandstad N 198 B6
Sandvatn N 52 B2
Sandvig-Allinge DK 67 A3
Sandvika
Akershus N 48 C2
Hedmark N 48 B3
Nord-Trøndelag
N 199 B9
Sandviken S 51 B3
Sandwich GB. . . . 45 B5
Sandy GB. 44 A3
San Emiliano E . . 141 B5
San Enrique E . . 162 B2
San Esteban E . . 141 A4
San Esteban de
Gormaz E 151 A4
San Esteban de la
Sierra E 149 B4
San Esteban de Litera
E 145 C4

San Esteban del Molar
E 142 C1
San Esteban del Valle
E 150 B3
San Esteban de
Valdueza E . . . 141 B4
San Fele I 172 B1
San Felice Círceo
I 169 B3
San Felices E . . . 143 B3
San Felices de los
Gallégos E . . . 149 B3
San Felice sul Panaro
I 121 C4
San Ferdinando di
Púglia I 171 B4
San Fernando E . 162 B1
San Fernando de
Henares E . . . 151 B4
San Fili I 174 B2
San Foca I 173 B4
San Fratello I . . . 177 B3
Sangatte F 78 B1
San Gavino Monreale
I 179 C2
San Gémini Fonte
I 168 A2
Sangerhausen D . .82 A3
San Germano
Vercellese I . . . 119 B5
San Giácomo
Trentino Alto Adige
I 108 C2
Umbria I 136 C1
San Gimignano I . 135 B4
San Ginésio I . . . 136 B2
Sanginetto Lido I . 174 B1
San Giórgio a Liri
I 169 B3
San Giorgio della
Richinvelda I . . . 122 A1
San Giórgio del Sánnio
I 170 B2
San Giórgio di
Lomellina I 120 B1
San Giórgio di Nogaro
I 122 B2
San Giorgio di Piano
I 121 C4
San Giórgio Iónico
I 173 B3
San Giovanni a Piro
I 172 B1
San Giovanni Bianco
I 120 B2
San Giovanni di Sinis
I 179 C2
San Giovanni in Croce
I 120 B3
San Giovanni in Fiore
I 174 B2
San Giovanni in
Persiceto I 121 C4
San Giovanni Reatino
I 169 A2
San Giovanni Rotondo
I 171 B3
San Giovanni Suérgiu
I 179 C2
San Giovanni Valdarno
I 135 B4
Sangis S 196 D6
San Giuliano Terme
I 134 B3
San Giustino I . . . 135 B5
San Godenzo I . . 135 B4
Sangonera la Verde
E 165 B3
San Gregorio Magno
I 172 B1
Sangüesa E 144 B2
Sanguinet F 128 B1
San Guiseppe Jato
I 176 B2
Sanica BIH. 124 C2
Sanitz D 65 B5
San Javier E . . . 165 B4
San Jorge P 154 B2
San José E 164 C2
San Juan E 143 B3
San Juan de Alicante
E 165 A4
San Juan de la Nava
E 150 B3
San Justo de la Vega
E 141 B4
Sankt Aegyd am
Neuwalde A. . . . 110 B2
Sankt Andrä A . . 110 C1
Sankt Andreasberg
D 82 A2
Sankt Anna S . . . 56 B2
Sankt Anna am Aigen
A. 110 C2
Sankt Anton am
Arlberg A 107 B5
Sankt Anton an der
Jessnitz A 110 B2
Sankt Augustin D . 80 B3
Sankt Blasien D . 106 B3
Sankt Englmar D . 95 B4
Sankt Gallen
A 110 B1
CH 107 B4
Sankt Gallenkirch
A 107 B5
Sankt Georgen
A 96 C2
D 106 A3
Sankt Georgen am
Reith A 110 B1
Sankt Georgen ob
Judenburg A. . . 110 B1
Sankt Georgen ob
Murau A. 109 B5
Sankt Gilgen A . . 109 B4
Sankt Goar D . . . 81 B3
Sankt Goarshausen
D 81 B3
Sankt Ingbert D . . 92 B3

Sankt Jacob A 109 C5
Sankt Jakob in
  Defereggen A . . .109 C3
Sankt Johann am
  Tauern A. 110 B1
Sankt Johann am
  Wesen A 109 A4
Sankt Johann im
  Pongau A. 109 B4
Sankt Johann in Tirol
  A. 109 B3
Sankt Katharein an der
  Laming A. 110 B2
Sankt Kathrein am
  Hauenstein A . .110 B2
Sankt Lambrecht
  A. 110 B1
Sankt Leonhard am
  Forst A. 110 A2
Sankt Leonhard im
  Pitztal A. 108 B1
Sankt Lorenzen A .109 C3
Sankt Marein
  Steiermark A . . 110 B2
  Steiermark A . . 110 B2
Sankt Margarethen im
  Lavanttal A. . . .110 C1
Sankt Margrethen
  CH 107 B4
Sankt Michael A. .110 B2
Sankt Michael im
  Burgenland A . . .111 B3
Sankt Michael im
  Lungau A. 109 B4
Sankt Michaelisdonn
  D. 64 C2
Sankt Niklaus CH .119 A4
Sankt Nikolai im
  Sölktal A 109 B5
Sankt Olof S 63 C2
Sankt Oswald D. . . .96 C1
Sankt Paul
  A. 110 C1
  F. 132 A2
Sankt Peter D 106 A3
Sankt Peter am
  Kammersberg A .110 B1
Sankt-Peterburg = St
  Petersburg RUS. . .9 C7
Sankt Peter-Ording
  D. 64 B1
Sankt Pölten A. . . .110 A2
Sankt Radegund
  A. 110 B2
Sankt Ruprecht an der
  Raab A 110 B2
Sankt Salvator A . .110 C1
Sankt Stefan A. . . .110 C1
Sankt Stefan an der
  Gail A 109 C4
Sankt Stefan im
  Rosental A. 110 C2
Sankt Valentin A . .110 A1
Sankt Veit an der Glan
  A. 110 C1
Sankt Veit an der
  Gölsen A 110 A2
Sankt Veit in
  Defereggen A . . .109 C3
Sankt Wendel D. . . .92 B3
Sankt Wolfgang
  A. 109 B4
  D. 108 A3
San Lazzaro di Sávena
  I. 135 A4
San Leo I. 135 B5
San Leonardo de
  Yagüe E 143 C4
San Leonardo in
  Passiria I. 108 C2
San Lorenzo al Mare
  I. 133 B3
San Lorenzo a Merse
  I. 135 B4
San Lorenzo Bellizzi
  I. 174 B2
San Lorenzo de
  Calatrava E. . . .157 B4
San Lorenzo de El
  Escorial E 151 B3
San Lorenzo de la
  Parrilla E 158 B1
San Lorenzo di Sebato
  I. 108 C2
San Lorenzo in Campo
  I. 136 B1
San Lorenzo Nuovo
  I. 168 A1
San Lourenco P . .160 A1
San Luca I 175 C2
Sanlúcar de Barrameda
  E 161 C3
Sanlúcar de Guadiana
  E 160 B2
Sanlúcar la Mayor
  E 161 B3
San Lúcido I 174 B2
Sanluri I 179 C2
San Marcello I 136 B2
San Marcello Pistoiese
  I. 135 A3
San Marcial E 149 A4
San Marco I 170 C2
San Marco Argentano
  I. 174 B2
San Marco dei Cavoti
  I. 170 B2
San Marco in Lámis
  I. 171 B3
San Marino RSM .136 B1
San Martin de
  Castañeda E. . . .141 B4
San Martin de la Vega
  E 151 B4
San Martin de la Vega
  del Alberche E . .150 B2
San Martin del Tesorillo
  E 162 B2
San Martin de Luiña
  E 141 A4

San Martin de
  Montalbán E . . .157 A3
San Martin de Oscos
  E 141 A4
San Martin de Pusa
  E 150 C3
San Martin de Unx
  E 144 B2
San Martin de
  Valdeiglesias E . .150 B3
San Martino di
  Campagna I. . . .122 A1
San Martino di
  Castrozza I. 121 A4
San-Martino-di-Lota
  F. 180 A2
San Martino in Pénsilis
  I. 170 B3
San Mateo de Gallego
  E 144 C3
San Máuro Forte I .172 B2
San Michele all'Adige
  I. 121 A4
San Michele di
  Ganzaria I. 177 B3
San Michele Mondov i
  I. 133 A3
San Miguel de Aguayo
  E 142 A2
San Miguel de Bernuy
  E 151 A4
San Miguel del Arroyo
  E 150 A3
San Miguel de Salinas
  E 165 B4
Sânmihaiu Roman
  RO. 126 B3
San Millán de la
  Cogolla E 143 B4
San Miniato I 135 B3
San Muñoz E 149 B3
Sänna S 55 B5
Sannazzaro
  de'Burgondi I . . .120 B1
Sanne D. 73 B4
Sannicandro di Bari
  I. 171 B4
Sannicandro
  Gargánico I 171 B3
San Nicola del'Alto
  I. 174 B2
San Nicolás del Puerto
  E 156 C2
Sânnicolau Mare
  RO. 126 A2
San Nicolò I 121 C4
San Nicolò Gerrei
  I. 179 C3
Sannidal N. 53 B5
Sanniki PL. 77 B4
Sanok PL. 12 D5
San Pablo de los
  Montes E. 157 A3
San Pancrázio
  Salentino I 173 B3
San Pantaleo I . . .178 A3
San Páolo di Civitate
  I. 171 B3
San Pawl il-Bahar
  M 175 C3
San Pedro
  Albacete E. 158 C1
  Oviedo E 141 A4
San Pedro de
  Alcántara E 162 B3
San Pedro de Ceque
  E 141 B4
San Pedro del Arroyo
  E 150 B3
San Pedro de Latarce
  E 142 C1
San Pedro del Pinatar
  E 165 B4
San Pedro del Romeral
  E 143 A3
San Pedro de Merida
  E 156 B1
San Pedro de
  Valderaduey E . .142 B2
San Pedro Manrique
  E 144 B1
San Pellegrino Terme
  I. 120 B2
San Piero a Sieve
  I. 135 B4
San Piero in Bagno
  I. 135 B4
San Piero Patti I . .177 A3
San Pietro I 177 B3
San Pietro in Casale
  I. 121 C4
San Pietro in Gu I .121 B4
San Pietro in Palazzi
  I. 134 B3
San Pietro in Volta
  I. 122 B1
San Pietro Vara I . .134 A2
San Pietro Vernótico
  I. 173 B3
San Polo d'Enza I .121 C3
Sanquhar GB. 36 A3
San Quírico d'Orcia
  I. 135 B4
San Rafael del Rio
  E 153 B4
San Remo I 133 B3
San Román de
  Cameros E 143 B4
San Roman de Hernija
  E 150 A2
San Román de la Cuba
  E 142 B2
San Roman de los
  Montes E. 150 B3
San Romao P. 155 C3
San Roque E 162 B2
San Roque de Riomera
  E 143 A3
San Rufo I 172 B1

San Sabastián de los
  Ballesteros E . . .162 A3
San Salvador de
  Cantamuda E . . .142 B2
San Salvo I 170 A2
San Salvo Marina
  I. 170 A2
San Sebastián de los
  Reyes E. 151 B4
San Sebastiano Curone
  I. 120 C2
San Secondo
  Parmense I. 120 C3
Sansepolcro I 135 B5
San Serverino Marche
  I. 136 B2
San Severino Lucano
  I. 174 A2
San Severo I 171 B3
San Silvestre de
  Guzmán E 161 B2
Sanski Most BIH . .124 C2
San Sosti I 174 B2
San Stéfano di Cadore
  I. 109 C3
San Stino di Livenza
  I. 122 B1
Santa Agnès I 166 B1
Santa Amalia E . . .156 A1
Santa Ana
  Cáceres E. 156 A2
  Jaén E 163 A4
Santa Ana de Pusa
  E 150 C3
Santa Barbara E . .153 B4
Santa Bárbara P . .160 B1
Santa Barbara de Casa
  E 161 B2
Santa Bárbara de
  Padrões P. 160 B2
Santacara E 144 B2
Santa Catarina I . .160 B2
Santa Caterina di
  Pittinuri I. 178 B2
Santa Caterina
  Villarmosa I. . . .177 B3
Santa Cesárea Terme
  I. 173 B4
Santa Clara-a-Nova
  P. 160 B1
Santa Clara-a-Velha
  P. 160 B1
Santa Clara de Louredo
  P. 160 B2
Santa Coloma de
  Farners E 147 C3
Santa Coloma de
  Gramenet E 147 C3
Santa Coloma de
  Queralt E 147 C2
Santa Colomba de
  Curueño E. 142 B1
Santa Colomba de
  Somoza E. 141 B4
Santa Comba E . . .140 A2
Santa Comba Dão
  P. 148 B1
Santa Comba de
  Rossas P. 149 A3
Santa Cristina I . . .120 B2
Santa Cristina de la
  Polvorosa E 141 B5
Santa Croce Camerina
  I. 177 C3
Santa Croce di
  Magliano I. 170 B2
Santa Cruz
  E 140 A2
  P. 154 B1
Santa Cruz de Alhama
  E 163 A4
Santa Cruz de
  Campezo E 143 B4
Santa Cruz de Grio
  E 152 A2
Santa Cruz de la
  Salceda E 151 A4
Santa Cruz de la Sierra
  E 156 A2
Santa Cruz de la Zarza
  E 151 C4
Santa Cruz del Retamar
  E 151 B3
Santa Cruz del Valle
  E 150 B2
Santa Cruz de Moya
  E 159 B2
Santa Cruz de Mudela
  E 157 B4
Santa Cruz de
  Paniagua E 149 B3
Santadi I. 179 C2
Santa Doménica Talao
  I. 174 B1
Santa Doménica
  Vittória I. 177 B3
Santa Elena E 157 A4
Santa Elena de Jamuz
  E 141 B5
Santaella E 162 A3
Santa Eufemia E . .156 B3
Santa Eufémia
  d'Aspromonte I .175 C1
Santa Eulalia E . . .152 B2
Santa Eulália P . . .155 C3
Santa Eulalia de Oscos
  E 141 A3
Santa Eulàlia des Riu
  E 166 C1
Santa Fe E 163 A4
Santa Fiora I 135 C4
Sant'Ágata dei Goti
  I. 170 B2
Sant'Ágata di Ésaro
  I. 174 B1
Sant'Ágata di Puglia
  I. 171 B3
Sant'Agata Feltria
  I. 135 B5

Sant'Ágata Militello
  I. 177 A3
Santa Gertrude I . .108 C1
Santa Giustina I. . .121 A5
San Agust ide
  Lluçanès I 147 B3
Santa Iria P 160 B2
Santa Leocadia P .148 A1
Santa Lucia del Mela
  I. 177 A4
Santa Lucia-de-Porto-
  Vecchio F 180 B2
Santa Luzia P 160 B1
Santa Maddalena
  I. 108 C3
Santa Magdalena de
  Polpis E. 153 B4
Santa Margalida E 167 B3
Santa Margarida
  P. 154 B2
Santa Margarida do
  Sado P. 160 A1
Santa Margaridao de
  Montbui E. 147 C2
Santa Margherita
  I. 179 D2
Santa Margherita di
  Belice I 176 B2
Santa Margherita
  Ligure I 134 A2
Santa Maria
  CH 108 C1
  E 144 B1
Santa Maria al Bagno
  I. 173 B3
Santa Maria Cápua
  Vétere I 170 B2
Santa Maria da Feira
  P. 148 B1
Santa Maria de Cayón
  E 143 A3
Santa Maria de Corco
  E 147 B3
Santa Maria de Huerta
  E 152 A1
Santa Maria de la
  Alameda E 151 B3
Santa Maria de las
  Hoyas E 143 C3
Santa Maria del Camí
  E 167 B2
Santa Maria del Campo
  E 143 B3
Santa Maria del Campo
  Rus E. 158 B1
Santa Maria della Versa
  I. 120 C2
Santa Maria del
  Páramo E 142 B1
Santa Maria del Taro
  I. 134 A2
Santa Maria de
  Mercadillo E . . .143 C3
Santa Maria de Nieva
  E 164 B3
Santa Maria de
  Trassierra E 156 C3
Santa Maria di Licodia
  I. 177 B3
Santa Maria-di-
  Rispéscia I. 168 A1
Santa Maria la Palma
  I. 178 B2
Santa Maria la Real de
  Nieva E 150 A3
Santa Maria Maggiore
  I. 119 A5
Santa Maria
  Ribarredonda E .143 B3
Santa Marina del Rey
  E 141 B5
Santa Marinella I. .168 A1
Santa Marta
  Albacete E. 158 C1
  Badajoz E 155 C4
Santa Marta de
  Magasca E 156 A1
Santa Marta de
  Penaguião P. . . .148 A2
Santa Marta de Tormes
  E 150 B2
Santana
  Évora P 154 C2
  Setúbal P 154 C1
Sântana RO 126 A3
Santana da Serra
  P. 160 B1
Santana do Mato
  P. 154 C2
Sant'Ana de Cambas
  P. 160 B2
Sant'Anastasia I . .170 C2
Santander E 143 A3
Sant'Andrea Frius
  I. 179 C3
Sant'Ángelo dei
  Lombardi I 172 B1
Sant'Angelo in Vado
  I. 136 B1
Sant'Angelo Lodigiano
  I. 120 B2
Santa Ninfa I 176 B1
Sant'Antíoco I 179 C2
Sant Antoni Abat
  E 166 C1
Sant Antoni de Calonge
  E 147 C4
Sant'Antonio-di-Gallura
  I. 178 B3
Santanyí E 167 B3
Santa Olalla
  Huelva E 161 B3
  Toledo E. 150 B3
Santa Pau E 147 B3
Santa Pola E 165 A4
Santa Ponça E 166 B2
Santarcángelo di
  Romagna I. 136 A1
Santarém P 154 B2

Santa Severa
  F. 180 A2
  I. 168 A1
Santa Severina I . .175 B2
Santas Martas E . .142 B1
Santa Sofia I 135 B4
Santa Suzana
  Évora P 155 C3
  Setúbal P 154 C2
Santa Teresa di Riva
  I. 177 B4
Santa Teresa Gallura
  I. 178 A3
Santa Uxia E 140 B2
Santa Valburga I . .108 C1
Santa Vittória in
  Matenano I. 136 B2
Sant Boi de Llobregat
  E 147 C3
Sant Carles de la
  Rápita E 153 B4
Sant Carlos E 166 B1
Sant'Caterina I . . .135 C4
Sant Celoni E 147 C3
Sant Climent E . . .167 B4
Santed E 152 A2
Sant'Egídio alla Vibrata
  I. 136 C2
Sant'Elia a Pianisi
  I. 170 B2
Sant'Elia Fiumerapido
  I. 169 B3
Santelices E 143 A3
San Telmo E 161 B3
Sant'Elpidio a Mare
  I. 136 B2
Santéramo in Colle
  I. 171 C4
Santervas de la Vega
  E 142 B2
Sant Feliu E 147 C3
Sant Feliu de Codines
  E 147 C3
Sant Feliu de Guixols
  E 147 C4
Sant Feliu Sasserra
  E 147 C3
Sant Ferran E 166 C1
Sant Francesc de
  Formentera E . . .166 C1
Sant Francesc de ses
  Salines E. 166 C1
Santhià I. 119 B5
Sant Hilari Sacalm
  E 147 C3
Sant Hipólit de
  Voltregá E 147 B3
Santiago de Alcántara
  E 155 B3
Santiago de Calatrava
  E 163 A3
Santiago de
  Compostela E . . .140 B2
Santiago de la Espade
  E 164 A2
Santiago de la Puebla
  E 150 B2
Santiago de la Ribera
  E 165 B4
Santiago del Campo
  E 155 B4
Santiago de Litem
  P. 154 B2
Santiago do Cacém
  P. 160 B1
Santiago do Escoural
  P. 154 C2
Santiago Maior P. .155 C3
Santibáñez de Béjar
  E 150 B2
Santibáñez de la Peña
  E 142 B2
Santibáñez de Murias
  E 142 A1
Santibáñez de
  Vidriales E. 141 B4
Santibáñez el Alto
  E 149 B3
Santibáñez el Bajo
  E 149 B3
Santillana E 142 A2
Santiponce E 162 A1
San Tirso de Abres
  E 141 A3
Santisteban del Puerto
  E 157 B4
Santiuste de San Juan
  Bautiste E 150 A3
Santiz E 149 A4
Sant Jaume dels
  Domenys E 147 C2
Sant Joan Baptista
  E 166 B1
Sant Joan de les
  Abadesses E 147 B3
Sant Jordi E 153 B4
Sant Josep de sa Talaia
  E 166 C1
Sant Juliáde Loria
  AND. 146 B2
Sant'Ilario d'Enza
  I. 121 C3
Sant Llorençde
  Morunys E 147 B2
Sant Llorençes
  Carctassar E 167 B3
Sant Llorenç Savall
  E 147 C3
Sant Luis E 167 B4
Sant Mart ide Llemaná
  E 147 B3
Sant Marti de Maldá
  E 147 C2
Sant Marti Sarroca
  E 147 C2
Sant Mateu E 153 B4
Sant Miquel E 166 B1
Santo Aleixo P . . .161 A2
Santo Amado P . . .161 A2
Santo Amaro P . . .155 C3

Santo André P 160 A1
Santo Domingo E .155 C3
Santo Domingo de la
  Calzada E 143 B4
Santo Domingo de
  Silos E. 143 C3
Santo Estêvão
  Faro P 160 B2
  Santarém P 154 C2
Santok PL 75 B4
Santomera E 165 A3
Santoña E 143 A3
Santo Tirso P. 148 A1
Santotis E 142 A2
Santo Tomé E 164 A1
Santovenia
  Burgos E 143 B3
  Zamora E. 142 C1
Sant Pau de Seguries
  E 147 B3
Santpedor E 147 C2
Sant Pere de
  Riudebitles E . . .147 C2
Sant Pere Pescador
  E 147 B4
Sant Pere Sallavinera
  E 147 C2
Sant Quirze de Besora
  E 147 B3
Sant Rafel E 166 C1
Sant Ramon E 147 C2
Santu Lussurgiu I .178 B2
Santutzi E 143 A3
Sant Vincençde
  Castellet E 147 C2
San Valentino alla Muta
  I. 108 C1
San Venanzo I 135 C5
San Vicente de
  Alcántara E 155 B3
San Vicente de Arana
  E 144 B1
San Vicente de la
  Barquera E 142 A2
San Vicente de la
  Sonsierra E 143 B4
San Vicente de Toranzo
  E 143 A3
San Vietro E 149 A3
San Vigilio I. 108 C2
San Vincente del
  Raspeig E 165 A4
San Vincenzo I . . .134 B3
San Vito I 179 C3
San Vito al Tagliamento
  I. 122 B1
San Vito Chietino
  I. 169 A4
San Vito dei Normanni
  I. 173 B3
San Vito di Cadore
  I. 108 C3
San Vito lo Capo I 176 A1
San Vito Romano
  I. 169 B2
Sanxenxo E 140 B2
Sanza I 172 B1
São Aleixo P 155 C3
São Barnabé P . . .160 B1
São Bartoloméda Serra
  P. 160 A1
São Bartolomeu de
  Messines P. 160 B1
São Bento P. 140 C2
São Brás P 160 B2
São Brás de Alportel
  P. 160 B2
São Braz do
  Reguedoura P. . .154 C2
São Cristóvão P . .154 C2
São Domingos P. .160 B1
São Geraldo P 154 C2
São Jacinto P 148 B1
São João da Madeira
  P. 148 B1
São João da Pesqueira
  P. 148 A2
São João da Ribeira
  P. 154 B2
São João da Serra
  P. 148 B1
São João da Venda
  P. 160 B2
São João dos
  Caldeireiros P. . .160 B2
São Julião P 155 B3
São Leonardo P . .155 C3
São Luis P 160 B1
São Manços P 155 C3
São Marcos da
  Ataboeira P. 160 B2
São Marcos da Serra
  P. 160 B1
São Marcos de Campo
  P. 155 C3
São Martinho da
  Cortiça P. 148 B1
São Martinho das
  Amoreiras P. 160 B1
São Martinho do Porto
  P. 154 B1
São Matias
  Beja P 160 A2
  Évora P 154 C2
São Miguel d'Acha
  P. 155 A3
São Miguel de
  Machede P. 155 C3

São Pedro da Torre
  P. 140 C2
São Pedro de Cadeira
  P. 154 B1
São Pedro de Muel
  P. 154 B1
São Pedro de Solis
  P. 160 B2
São Pedro do Sul
  P. 148 B1
Saorge F 133 B3
São Romão P. 154 C2
São Sebastião dos
  Carros P. 160 B2
São Teotónio P. . . .160 B1
São Torcato P 148 A1
Sapataria P 154 C1
Sapes GR. 183 B7
Sapiãos P. 148 A2
Sa Pobla E 167 B3
Sappada I. 109 C3
Sappen N. 192 C5
Sapri I. 174 A1
Sarajärvi FIN 197 D10
Sarajevo BIH 139 B4
Saramon F. 129 C3
Sarandë AL 182 D2
Saranovo SRB. . . .127 C2
Saraorci SRB. 127 C3
Sa Rapita E 167 B3
Saray TR 186 A2
Saraycık TR. 187 C4
Sarayköy TR 188 B3
Saraylar TR 186 B2
Sarayönü TR 189 A7
Sárbia PL 75 B5
Sarbinowo
  Zachodnio-Pomorskie
  PL 67 B4
  Zachodnio-Pomorskie
  PL 74 B3
Sárbogárd H. 112 C2
Sarcelles F. 90 B2
Sarche I. 121 A3
Sardara I 179 C2
Sardoal P. 154 B2
Sardón de Duero
  E 150 A3
Sare F. 144 A2
S'Arenal E 166 B2
Šarengrad HR 125 B5
Sarentino I 108 C2
Sarezzo I 120 B3
Sargans CH 107 B4
Sári H. 112 B3
Saribeyler TR 186 C2
Sarıcakaya TR . . .187 B5
Sari-d'Orcino F . . .180 A1
Sarıgöl TR 188 A3
Sarıkaya TR 23 B8
Sarıköy TR 186 B2
Sarilhos Grandes
  P. 154 C2
Sariñena E. 145 C3
Saruba TR 187 C7
Sárisáp H. 112 B2
Sariyer TR 186 A4
Sarkad H 113 C5
Särkesztes H 112 B2
Sárkeresztúr H . . .112 B2
Särkijärvi FIN. 196 B6
Şarkikaraağaç TR 189 A6
Şarköy TR 186 B2
Sarlat-la-Canéda
  F. 129 B4
Sarliac-sur-l'Isle F 129 A3
Sármellék H. 111 C4
Särna S 199 D10
Sarnadas P 155 B3
Sarnano I 136 B2
Sarnen CH 106 C3
Sarnesfield GB . . .39 B4
Sárnico I 120 B2
Sarno I 170 C2
Sarnonico I 121 A4
Sarnow D. 74 A2
Sarny UA 13 C7
Särö S 60 B1
Saronno I 120 B2
Šárosd H. 112 B2
Sárovce SK 112 A2
Sarpoil F 117 B3
Sarpsborg N 54 A2
Sarracin E 143 B3
Sarral E 147 C2
Sarralbe F 92 B3
Sarrancolin F. 145 B4
Sarras F 117 B4
Sarre I 119 B4
Sarreaus E 140 B3
Sarrebourg F. 92 C3
Sarreguemines F . .92 B3
Sárrétudvari H. . . .113 B5
Sarre-Union F 92 C3
Sarria E 141 B3
Sarriáde Ter E 147 B3
Sarrión E 153 B3
Sarroca de Lleida
  E 153 A4
Sarroch I. 179 C3
Sarron F. 128 C2
Sársina I 135 B5
Særslev DK. 59 C3
Sarstedt D 72 B2
Sárszentlőrinc H . .112 C2
Sárszentmihaly H .112 B2
Sárszentmiklós
  H. 112 C2
Sarteano I 135 C4
Sartène F. 180 B1
Sartilly F. 88 B2
Sartirana Lomellina
  I. 120 B1
Saruhanlı TR 186 D2
Sárvár H. 111 B3
Sarvisvaara S 196 C4
Sarzana I 134 A2

Sarzeau F 101 B3
Sarzedas P 155 B3
Sasalli TR 188 A1
Sasamón E 142 B2
Sa Savina E 166 C1
Sásd H 125 A4
Sasino PL 68 A2
Sássari I 178 B2
Sassello I 133 A4
Sassenberg D 71 C5
Sassetta I 134 B3
Sassnitz D 66 B2
Sassocorvaro I 136 B1
Sasso d'Ombrone I 135 C4
Sassoferrato I 136 B1
Sassoleone I 135 A4
Sasso Marconi I 135 A4
Sassuolo I 135 A3
Sástago E 153 A3
Šaštinske Stráže SK 98 C1
Sas van Gent NL 79 A3
Såtåhaugen N 199 C7
Satão P 148 B2
Såtenäs S 55 B3
Säter S 50 B2
Sätila S 60 B2
Satillieu F 117 B4
Satnica Đakovačka HR 125 B4
Sátoraljaújhely H 16 A4
Satow D 65 C4
Sätra-brunn S 50 C3
Sætre N 54 A1
Satrup D 64 B2
Satteins A 107 B4
Satu Mare RO 17 B5
Saturnia I 168 A1
Saucats F 128 B2
Saucelle E 149 A3
Sauda N 52 A2
Sauðarkrókur IS 190 B6
Saudasjøen N 52 A2
Sauerlach D 108 B2
Saugues F 117 C3
Sauherad N 53 A5
Saujon F 114 C3
Sauland N 53 A4
Saulces Monclin F 91 B4
Saulgau D 107 A4
Saulgrub D 108 B2
Saulieu F 104 B3
Saulnot F 106 B1
Sault F 131 A4
Sault-Brénaz F 118 B2
Sault-de-Navailles F 128 C2
Saulx F 105 B5
Saulxures-sur-Moselotte F 106 B1
Saulzais-le-Potier F 103 C4
Saumos F 128 B1
Saumur F 102 B1
Saunavaara FIN 197 B10
Saundersfoot GB 39 C2
Saurat F 146 B2
Saurbær
Borgarfjarðarsýsla IS 190 C4
Dalasýsla IS 190 B4
Eyjafjarðarsýsla IS 191 B7
Sáuris I 109 C3
Sausset-les-Pins F 131 B4
Sauteyrargues F 131 B2
Sauvagnat F 116 B2
Sauve F 131 B2
Sauveterre-de-Béarn F 144 A3
Sauveterre-de-Guyenne F 128 B2
Sauviat-sur-Vige F 116 B1
Sauxillanges F 117 B3
Sauzet
Drôme F 117 C4
Lot F 129 B4
Sauzé-Vaussais F 115 B4
Sauzon F 100 B2
Sava I 173 B3
Sävar S 200 C6
Sævareid N 46 B2
Savarsin RO 16 B5
Sävast S 196 D4
Savaştepe TR 186 C2
Savci SLO 111 C3
Säve S 60 B1
Savelletri I 173 B3
Savelli I 174 B2
Savenay F 101 B4
Saverdun F 146 A2
Saverne F 93 C3
Savières F 91 C3
Savigliano I 119 C4
Savignac-les-Eglises F 129 A3
Savignano Irpino I 171 B3
Savignano sul Rubicone I 136 A1
Savigny-sur-Braye F 102 B2
Saviñán E 152 A2
Savines-le-lac F 132 A2
Savino Selo SRB 126 B1
Savio I 135 A5
Sävja S 51 C4
Šavnik MNE 139 C5
Savognin CH 107 C4
Savona I 133 A4
Savonlinna FIN 9 B6
Savournon F 132 A1
Sævråsvåg N 46 B2
Sävsjö S 62 A2
Savsjön S 50 C1
Sävsjöström S 62 A3
Savudrija HR 122 B2
Savukoski FIN 197 B11
Sawbridgeworth GB 45 B4
Sawtry GB 44 A3
Sax E 159 C3
Saxdalen S 50 B1
Saxilby GB 40 B3
Saxmundham GB 45 A5
Saxnäs S 195 F6
Saxthorpe GB 41 C5
Sayalonga E 163 B3
Sayatón E 151 B5
Sayda D 83 B5
Säytsjärvi FIN 193 C11
Śazava CZ 97 B3
Sázava CZ 96 B2
Scaër F 100 A2
Scafa I 169 A4
Scalasaig GB 34 B1
Scalby GB 40 A3
Scalea I 174 B1
Scaletta Zanclea I 177 A4
Scalloway GB 33 A5
Scamblesby GB 41 B3
Scandale I 175 B2
Scandiano I 121 C3
Scandicci I 135 B4
Scandolara Ravara I 120 B3
Scanno I 169 B3
Scansano I 168 A1
Scanzano Jónico I 174 A2
Scarborough GB 40 A3
Scardovari I 122 C1
Scardoy GB 32 D2
Scarperia I 135 B4
Scarriff IRL 28 B3
Scey-sur-Saône et St Albin F 105 B4
Schachendorf A 111 B3
Schaffhausen CH 107 B3
Schafstädt D 83 A3
Schafstedt D 64 B2
Schäftlarn D 108 B2
Schagen NL 70 B1
Schalkau D 82 B3
Schangnau CH 106 C2
Schapbach D 93 C4
Scharbeutz D 65 B3
Schärding A 96 C1
Scharnitz A 108 B2
Scharrel D 71 A4
Schattendorf A 111 B3
Scheemda NL 71 A3
Scheessel D 72 A2
Schéggia I 136 B1
Scheibbs A 110 A2
Scheibenberg D 83 B4
Scheidegg D 107 B4
Scheifling A 110 B1
Scheinfeld D 94 B2
Schelklingen D 94 C1
Schenefeld
Schleswig-Holstein D 64 B2
Schleswig-Holstein D 72 A2
Schenklengsfeld D 82 B1
Scherfede D 81 A5
Schermbeck D 80 A2
Scherpenzeel NL 70 B2
Schesslitz D 94 B3
Scheveningen NL 70 B1
Schiedam NL 79 A4
Schieder-Schwalenberg D 72 C2
Schierling D 95 C4
Schiers CH 107 C4
Schildau D 83 A4
Schillingen D 92 B2
Schillingsfürst D 94 B2
Schilpário I 120 A3
Schiltach D 93 C4
Schiltigheim F 93 C3
Schio I 121 B4
Schirmeck F 92 C3
Schirnding D 83 B4
Schkeuditz D 83 A4
Schkölen D 83 A3
Schlabendorf D 84 A1
Schladen D 73 B3
Schladming A 109 B4
Schlangen D 81 A4
Schleiden D 80 B2
Schleiz D 83 B3
Schleswig D 64 B2
Schleusingen D 82 B2
Schlieben D 83 A5
Schliengen D 106 B2
Schliersee D 108 B2
Schlitz D 81 B5
Schloss Neuhans D 81 A4
Schlossvippach D 82 A3
Schlotheim D 82 A2
Schluchsee D 106 B3
Schlüchtern D 81 B5
Schmallenberg D 81 A4
Schmelz D 92 B2
Schmidmühlen D 95 B3
Schmiedeberg D 84 B1
Schmiedefeld D 82 B2
Schmirn A 108 B2
Schmölln
Brandenburg D 74 A3
Sachsen D 83 B4
Schnaittach D 95 B3
Schneeberg D 83 B4
Schneizlreuth D 109 B3
Schneverdingen D 72 A2
Schöder A 109 B5
Schoenburg B 80 B2
Schollene D 73 B5
Schöllkrippen D 81 B5
Schomberg D 107 A3
Schönach D 95 C4
Schönau
Baden-Württemberg D 106 B2
Bayern D 95 C4
Schönbeck D 74 A2
Schönberg
Bayern D 96 C1
Mecklenburg-Vorpommern D 65 C3
Schleswig-Holstein D 65 B3
Schönebeck D 73 B4
Schöneck D 83 B4
Schönecken- D 80 B2
Schönermark D 74 A2
Schönewalde D 83 A5
Schongau D 108 B1
Schöngrabern A 97 C4
Schönhagen D 81 A5
Schönhausen D 73 B5
Schöningen D 73 B3
Schönkirchen D 64 B3
Schönsee D 95 B4
Schöntal D 94 B1
Schönthal D 95 B4
Schonungen D 94 A2
Schönwalde D 65 B3
Schoondijke NL 79 A3
Schoonebeek NL 71 B3
Schoonhoven NL 79 A4
Schopfheim D 106 B2
Schöppenstedt D 73 B3
Schörfling A 109 B4
Schorndorf D 94 C1
Schortens D 71 A4
Schotten D 81 B5
Schramberg D 106 A3
Schraplau D 83 A3
Schrattenberg A 97 C4
Schrecksbach D 81 B5
Schrems A 96 C3
Schrobenhausen D 95 C3
Schröcken A 107 B5
Schrozberg D 94 B1
Schruns A 107 B4
Schüpfheim CH 106 C3
Schüttorf D 71 B4
Schwaan D 65 C5
Schwabach D 94 B3
Schwäbisch Gmünd D 94 C1
Schwäbisch Hall D 94 B1
Schwabmünchen D 108 A1
Schwadorf A 111 A3
Schwagstorf D 71 B4
Schwaigern D 93 B5
Schwalmstadt D 81 B5
Schwanberg A 110 C2
Schwanden CH 107 C4
Schwandorf D 95 B4
Schwanebeck D 73 C4
Schwanenstadt A 109 A4
Schwanewede D 72 A1
Schwanfeld D 94 B2
Schwangau D 108 B1
Schwarmstedt D 72 B2
Schwarza D 82 B2
Schwarzach im Pongau A 109 B4
Schwarzau im Gebirge A 110 B2
Schwarzenau A 97 C3
Schwarzenbach D 83 B3
Schwarzenbach am Wald D 83 B3
Schwarzenbek D 72 A3
Schwarzenberg D 83 B4
Schwarzenburg CH 106 C2
Schwarzenfeld D 95 B4
Schwarz-heide D 84 A1
Schwaz A 108 B2
Schwechat A 111 A3
Schwedt D 74 A3
Schwei D 71 A5
Schweich D 92 B2
Schweighausen D 106 A2
Schweinfurt D 94 A2
Schweinitz D 83 A5
Schweinrich D 74 A1
Schwelm D 80 A3
Schwemsal D 83 A4
Schwendt A 109 B3
Schwenningen D 107 A3
Schwepnitz D 84 A1
Schwerin D 73 A4
Schwerte D 81 A3
Schweskau D 73 B4
Schwetzingen D 93 B4
Schwyz CH 107 B3
Sciacca I 176 B2
Scicli I 177 C3
Ściechów PL 75 B3
Scigliano I 175 B2
Scilla I 175 C1
Ścinawa PL 85 A4
Scionzier F 118 A3
Scoglitti I 177 C3
Scole GB 45 A5
Sconser GB 31 B2
Scopello
Piemonte I 119 B5
Sicilia I 176 A1
Scordia I 177 B3
Scorzè I 121 B5
Scotch Corner GB 37 B5
Scotter GB 40 B3
Scourie GB 32 C1
Scousburgh GB 33 B5
Scrabster GB 32 C3
Screeb IRL 28 A2
Scremerston GB 37 A5
Scritto I 136 B1
Scunthorpe GB 40 B3
Scuol CH 107 C5
Scúrcola Marsicana I 169 A3
Seaford GB 45 C4
Seaham GB 37 B5
Seahouses GB 37 A5
Seascale GB 36 B3
Seaton GB 43 B3
Sebazac-Concourès F 130 A1
Seben TR 187 B6
Sebersdorf A 110 B2
Sebezh RUS 8 D6
Sebnitz D 84 B2
Seborga I 133 B3
Seby S 63 B4
Seč
Vychodočeský CZ 97 B3
Západočeský CZ 96 B1
Sečanj SRB 126 B2
Secemin PL 87 B3
Séchault F 91 B4
Seckau A 110 B1
Seclin F 78 B3
Secondigny F 114 B3
Seda P 155 B3
Sedan F 91 B4
Sedano E 143 B3
Sedbergh GB 37 B4
Sedella E 163 B3
Séderon F 131 A4
Sedgefield GB 37 B5
Sedico I 121 A5
Sédilo I 178 B2
Sédini I 178 B2
Sedlarica HR 124 B3
Sedlčany CZ 96 B2
Sedlec-Prčice CZ 96 B2
Sedlice CZ 96 B1
Sędziejowice PL 86 A3
Sędziszów PL 87 B4
Sędziszów Małapolski PL 87 B5
Seebach F 93 C3
Seeboden A 109 C4
Seefeld
Brandenburg D 74 B2
Niedersachsen D 71 A5
Seefeld in Tirol A 108 B2
Seeg D 108 B1
Seehausen
Sachsen-Anhalt D 73 B4
Sachsen-Anhalt D 73 B4
Seeheim-Jugenheim D 93 B4
Seelbach D 93 C3
Seelow D 74 B3
Seelze D 72 B2
Seerhausen D 83 A5
Sées F 89 B4
Seesen D 82 A2
Seeshaupt D 108 B2
Seewalchen A 109 B4
Seferihisar TR 188 A1
Sefkerin SRB 127 B2
Segård N 48 B2
Segerstad S 55 A4
Segesd H 124 A3
Seglinge FIN 51 B7
Segmon S 55 A4
Segonzac F 115 C3
Segorbe E 159 B3
Segovia E 151 B3
Segré F 101 B5
Segura
E 144 B1
P 155 B3
Segura de León E 161 A3
Segura de los Baños E 152 B3
Ségur-les-Villas F 116 B2
Segurrilla E 150 B3
Sehnde D 72 B2
Seia P 148 B2
Seiches-sur-le-Loir F 102 B1
Seifhennersdorf D 84 B2
Seignelay F 104 B2
Seijo E 140 C2
Seilhac F 116 B1
Seilles B 79 B5
Seim N 46 B2
Seinäjoki FIN 8 A3
Seissan F 145 A4
Seitenstetten Markt A 110 A1
Seixal P 154 C1
Seiz A 110 B1
Seizthal A 110 B1
Sejerslev DK 58 B1
Seksna RUS 9 C11
Selárdalur IS 190 B1
Selárgius I 179 C3
Selb D 83 B4
Selby GB 40 B2
Selca HR 138 B2
Selce HR 123 B3
Selçuk TR 188 B2
Selde DK 58 B2
Selenča SRB 126 B1
Selendi
Manisa TR 186 D2
Manisa TR 186 D3
Selenicë AL 182 C1
Sélestat F 106 A2
Seleuš SRB 126 B2
Selevac SRB 127 C2
Selfoss IS 190 D5
Selgua E 145 C4
Selice SK 112 A1
Seligenstadt D 93 A4
Seligenthal D 82 B2
Selimiye TR 188 B2
Selizharovo RUS 9 D8
Selja S 50 A1
Selje N 198 C2
Seljelvnes N 192 C3
Seljord N 53 A4
Selkirk GB 35 C5
Sellano I 136 C1
Selles-St Denis F 103 B3
Selles-sur-Cher F 103 B3
Sellières F 105 C4
Sellin D 66 B2
Sellye H 125 B3
Selm D 80 A3
Selnica ob Dravi SLO 110 C2
Selongey F 105 B4
Selonnet F 132 A2
Selow D 65 C4
Selsey GB 44 C3
Selsingen D 72 A2
Selters D 81 B3
Seltz F 93 C4
Selva E 167 B2
Selva di Cadore I 108 C3
Selva di Val Gardena I 108 C2
Selvik
Sogn og Fjordane N 46 A2
Vestfold N 54 A1
Selvino I 120 B2
Selyatyn UA 17 B6
Sem N 54 A1
Semeljci HR 125 B4
Semič SLO 123 B4
Semide
F 91 B4
P 148 B1
Semily CZ 84 B3
Seminara I 175 C1
Semlac RO 126 A2
Semlacu Mare RO 126 B3
Semmen-stedt D 73 B3
Šempeter SLO 123 A4
Semriach A 110 B2
Semur-en-Auxois F 104 B3
Sena E 145 C3
Sena de Luna E 141 B5
Senarpont F 90 B1
Sénas F 131 B4
Senćanski Trešnjevac SRB 126 B1
Sencelles E 167 B2
Senčur SLO 123 A3
Senden
Bayern D 94 C2
Nordrhein-Westfalen D 80 A3
Sendenhorst D 81 A3
Sendim P 149 A3
Senec SK 111 A4
Seneffe B 79 B4
Séneghe I 178 B2
Senés E 164 B2
Senez F 132 B2
Senftenberg D 84 A1
Sengouagnet F 145 B4
Sengwarden D 71 A5
Senica SK 98 C1
Senice na Hané CZ 98 B1
Senigállia I 136 B2
Senirkent TR 189 A5
Sénis I 179 C2
Senise I 174 A2
Senj HR 123 C3
Senje SRB 127 D3
Senjehopen N 194 A8
Senjski Rudnik SRB 127 D3
Senlis F 90 B2
Sennan S 60 C2
Sennecey-le-Grand F 105 C3
Sennen GB 42 B1
Senno BY 13 A8
Sénnori I 178 B2
Sennwald CH 107 B4
Sennybridge GB 39 C3
Senohrad SK 99 C3
Senonches F 89 B5
Senones F 92 C2
Senorb ì I 179 C3
Senovo SLO 123 A4
Senožeče SLO 123 B3
Senožeti SLO 123 A3
Sens F 104 A2
Sens-de-Bretagne F 101 A4
Senta SRB 126 B2
Senterada E 145 B4
Sentilj SLO 110 C2
Šentjernej SLO 123 B4
Šentjur SLO 123 A4
Senumstad N 53 B4
Seoane E 141 B3
Seon CH 106 B3
Sépeaux F 104 B2
Sépey CH 119 A4
Sepino I 170 B2
Sępólno Krajeńskie PL 76 A2
Seppenrade D 80 A3
Seppois F 106 B2
Septemvri BG 183 A6
Septeuil F 90 C1
Sepúlveda E 151 A4
Sequals I 122 A1
Sequeros E 149 B3
Seraincourt F 91 B4
Seraing B 80 B1
Seravezza I 134 B3
Sered' SK 98 C1
Seredka RUS 8 C6
Şereflikoçhisar TR 23 B7
Seregélyes H 112 B2
Seregno I 120 B2
Sérent F 101 B3
Serfaus A 108 B1
Sergiyev Posad RUS 9 D11
Seriate I 120 B2
Sérifontaine F 90 B1
Serifos GR 185 B5
Sérignan F 130 B2
Serik TR 189 C6
Serina I 120 B2
Serinhisar TR 188 B4
Sermaises F 90 C2
Sermaize-les-Bains F 91 C4
Sérmide I 121 C4
Sermoneta I 169 B2
Sernache de Bonjardim P 154 B2
Sernancelhe P 148 B2
Serock PL 77 B6
Serón E 164 B2
Serón de Najima E 152 A1
Serooskerke NL 79 A3
Seròs E 153 A4
Serpa P 160 B2
Serracapriola I 171 B3
Serrada E 150 A3
Serra de Outes E 140 B2
Serradifalco I 176 B2
Serradilla E 155 B4
Serradilla del Arroyo E 149 B3
Serradilla del Llano E 149 B3
Serramanna I 179 C2
Serramazzoni I 135 A3
Serranillos E 150 B3
Serrapetrona I 136 B2
Serra San Bruno I 175 C2
Serra San Quírico I 136 B2
Serrastretta I 175 B2
Serravalle
Piemonte I 119 B5
Umbria I 136 C2
Serravalle di Chienti I 136 B1
Serravalle Scrívia I 120 C1
Serre I 172 B1
Serrejón E 150 C2
Serres
F 132 A1
GR 183 B5
Serrières F 117 B4
Serrières-de-Briord F 118 B2
Sersale I 175 B2
Sertã P 154 B2
Sertig Dörfli CH 107 C4
Servance F 106 B1
Serverette F 117 C3
Servia GR 182 C4
Servian F 130 B2
Serviers F 131 A3
Servigliano I 136 B2
Serzedelo P 148 A1
Seseña Nuevo E 151 B4
Sesimbra P 154 C1
Seskarö S 196 D6
Seskinore GB 27 B3
Sesma E 144 B1
Sessa Aurunca I 170 B1
Ses Salines E 167 B3
Sesta Godano I 134 A2
Šestanovac HR 138 B2
Sestao E 143 A4
Sestino I 135 B5
Sesto I 109 C3
Sesto Calende I 120 B1
Sesto Fiorentino I 135 B4
Séstola I 135 A3
Sesto San Giovanni I 120 B2
Sestriere I 119 C3
Sestri Levante I 134 A2
Sestroretsk RUS 9 B7
Sestu I 179 C3
Sesvete HR 124 B2
Setcases E 146 B3
Sète F 130 B2
Setenil E 162 B2
Setermoen N 194 B9
Šetonje SRB 127 C3
Setskog N 54 A2
Settalsjølia N 199 C7
Séttimo Torinese I 119 B4
Settimo Vittone I 119 B4
Settle GB 40 A1
Setúbal P 154 C2
Seubersdort D 95 B3
Seùi I 179 C3
Seùlo I 179 C3
Seurre F 105 C4
Sevel DK 58 B1
Sevenoaks GB 45 B4
Sévérac-le-Château F 130 A2
Sever do Vouga P 148 B1
Severin HR 123 B4
Severomorsk RUS 3 B13
Séveso I 120 B2
Ševětin CZ 96 B2
Sevettijärvi FIN 193 C12
Sévigny F 91 B4
Sevilla = Seville E 162 A2
Sevilla la Nueva E 151 B3
Seville = Sevilla E 162 A2
Sevilleja de la Jara E 156 A3
Sevlievo BG 17 D6
Sevnica SLO 123 A4
Sevojno SRB 127 D1
Sevrier F 118 B3
Sexdrega S 60 B3
Seyches F 129 B3
Seyda D 83 A4
Seydişehir TR 189 B6
Seyðisfjörður IS 191 B12
Seyitgazi TR 187 C5
Seyitömer TR 187 C4
Seymen TR 186 A2
Seyne F 132 A2
Seynes F 131 A3
Seyssel F 118 B2
Sežana SLO 122 B2
Sézanne F 91 C3
Sezulfe P 149 A2
Sezze I 169 B3
Sfântu Gheorghe RO 17 C6
Sforzacosta I 136 B2
Sgarasta Mhor GB 31 B1
's-Gravendeel NL 79 A4
's-Gravenhage = The Hague NL 70 B1
's-Gravenzande NL 79 A4
Shaftesbury GB 43 A4
Shaldon GB 43 B3
Shalskiy RUS 9 B9
Shanagolden IRL 29 B2
Shanklin GB 44 C2
Shap GB 37 B4
Sharpness GB 43 A4
Shawbury GB 38 B4
's-Heerenberg NL 80 A2
Sheerness GB 45 B4
Sheffield GB 40 B2
Shefford GB 44 A3
Shëmri AL 182 A2
Shenfield GB 45 B4
Shëngjergj AL 182 B2
Shepetivka UA 13 C7
Shepshed GB 40 C2
Shepton Mallet GB 43 A4
Sherborne GB 43 B4
Shercock IRL 27 C4
Sheringham GB 41 C5
's-Hertogenbosch NL 79 A5
Shiel Bridge GB 32 D1
Shieldaig GB 31 B3
Shijak AL 182 B1
Shillelagh IRL 30 B2
Shimsk RUS 9 C7
Shipston-on-Stour GB 44 A2
Shklow BY 13 A9
Shkodër AL 182 A1
Shoeburyness GB 45 B4
Shoreham-by-Sea GB 44 C3
Shotley Gate GB 45 B5
Shrewsbury GB 38 B4
Shugozero RUS 9 C9
Shumen BG 17 D7
Siabost GB 31 A2
Siamanna I 179 C2
Sianów PL 67 B5
Siatista GR 182 C3
Siauges-St Romain F 117 B3
Šiauliai LT 8 E3
Sibari I 174 B2
Sibbhult S 63 B2
Šibenik HR 138 B1
Sibinj HR 125 B3
Sibiu RO 17 C6
Sibnica SRB 127 C2
Sibsey GB 41 B4
Siculiana I 176 B2
Šid SRB 125 B5
Sidari GR 182 D1
Siddeburen NL 71 A3
Sidensjö S 200 C4
Siderno I 175 C2
Sidirokastro GR 183 B5
Sidmouth GB 43 B3
Sidzina PL 99 B3
Siebe N 192 D7
Siebenlehn D 83 A5
Siedlce PL 12 B5
Siedlice PL 75 A4
Siedlinghausen D 81 A4
Siedlisko PL 75 B5
Siegburg D 80 B3
Siegen D 81 B4
Siegenburg D 95 C3
Sieghartskirchen A 111 A3
Siegsdorf D 109 B3
Siekierki PL 74 B3
Sielpia PL 87 A4
Siemiany PL 69 B4
Siena I 135 B4
Sieniawka PL 84 B2
Sienno PL 87 A5
Sieppijärvi FIN 196 B7
Sieradz PL 86 A2
Sieraków
Śląskie PL 86 B2
Wielkopolskie PL 75 B5
Sierakowice PL 68 A2
Sierck-les-Bains F 92 B2
Sierentz F 106 B2
Sierning A 110 A1
Sierpc PL 77 B4
Sierra de Fuentes E 155 B4
Sierra de Luna E 144 B3
Sierra de Yeguas E 162 A3
Sierre CH 119 A4
Siestrzeń PL 77 B5
Sietamo E 145 B3
Siewierz PL 86 B3
Sigdal N 48 B1
Sigean F 130 B1
Sigerfjord N 194 B6
Sighetu-Marmatiei RO 17 B5
Sighişoara RO 17 B6
Sigillo I 136 B1
Siglufjörður IS 191 A7
Sigmaringen D 107 A4
Signa I 135 B4
Signes F 132 B1
Signy-l'Abbaye F 91 B4
Signy-le-Petit F 91 B4
Sigogne F 115 C3
Sigri GR 183 D7
Sigtuna S 57 A3
Sigueiro E 140 B2
Sigüenza E 151 A5
Sigües E 144 B2
Sigulda LV 8 D4
Siilinjärvi FIN 8 A5
Sikenica SK 112 A2
Sikfors S 196 D4

Sikia GR. 183 C5
Sikinos GR 185 C6
Sikkilsdalseter N. . .47 A6
Siklós H. 125 B4
Sikórz PL. 77 B4
Sikselet S. 195 D8
Silandro I. 108 C1
Silánus I 178 B2
Silbaš SRB. 126 B1
Silbersted D. 64 B2
Şile TR 187 A4
Siles E 164 A2
Silgueiros P. 148 B2
Silifke TR. 23 C7
Siliqua I 179 C2
Silistra BG. 17 C7
Silivri TR. 186 A3
Siljan N 53 A5
Siljansnäs S 50 B1
Silkeborg DK. 59 B2
Silla E 159 B3
Sillamäe EST. 8 C5
Silleda E. 140 B2
Sillé-le-Guillaume
  F. 102 A1
Sillenstede D. 71 A4
Sillerud S 54 A3
Sillian A 109 C3
Silloth GB 36 B3
Silno PL. 68 B2
Silnowo PL. 68 B1
Silo HR. 123 B3
Sils E 147 C3
Silsand N 194 A8
Silte S. 57 C4
Šilute LT. 12 A4
Silvalen N 195 E3
Silvaplana CH 107 C4
Silvares P. 148 B2
Silvberg S 50 B2
Silverdalen S. 62 A3
Silvermines IRL. 28 B3
Silverstone GB 44 A2
Silverton GB 43 B3
Silves P 160 B1
Silvi Marina I 169 A4
Simandre F 105 C3
Šimanovci SRB 127 C2
Simard F 105 C4
Simat de Valldigna
  E 159 B3
Simav TR 186 B3
Simbach
  Bayern D 95 C4
  Bayern D 95 C5
Simbário I 175 C2
Simeonovgrad BG 183 A7
Simeria RO 17 C5
Simi GR 188 C2
Simićevo SRB 127 C3
Simitli BG. 183 B5
Simlångsdalen S. . . .60 C3
Simmerath D. 80 B2
Simmerberg D 107 B4
Simmern D. 93 B3
Simo FIN 197 D8
Šimonovce SK. 99 C4
Simonsbath GB. 43 A3
Simonstorp S 56 B2
Simontornya H 112 C2
Simplon CH 119 A5
Simrishamn S 63 C2
Sinaia RO. 17 C6
Sinalunga I 135 B4
Sinarcas E 159 B2
Sincan TR 187 C7
Sincanlı TR 187 D5
Sindal DK 58 A3
Sindelfingen D 93 C5
Sindia I 178 B2
Sındırgı TR 186 C3
Sinekli TR 186 A3
Sines P 160 B1
Sinetta FIN 197 C8
Sineu E 167 B3
Singen D 107 B3
Singleton GB 44 C3
Singsås N 199 C7
Siniscóla I 178 B3
Sinj HR. 138 B2
Sinlabajos E 150 A3
Sinn D 81 B4
Sinnai I 179 C3
Sinnes N 52 B2
Sinop TR 23 A8
Sins CH 106 B3
Sinsheim D 93 B4
Sint Annaland NL . . .79 A4
Sint Annaparochie
  NL 70 A2
Sint Athonis NL. 80 A1
Sint Nicolaasga NL 70 B2
Sint Oedenrode NL 79 A5
Sintra P 154 C1
Sinzheim D. 93 C4
Sinzig D. 80 B3
Siófok H. 112 C2
Sion CH 119 A4
Sion Mills GB. 27 B3
Siorac-en-Périgord
  F. 129 B3
Šipanska Luka HR 139 C3
Šipovo BIH. 138 A3
Sira N 52 B2
Siracusa I. 177 B4
Siret RO. 17 B7
Sirevåg N. 52 B2
Sirig SRB. 126 B1
Sirkka FIN 196 B7
Sirmione I 121 B3
Sirniö FIN. 197 D11
Sirok H. 113 B4
Široki Brijeg BIH . . 139 B3
Sirolo I 136 B2
Siruela E 156 B2
Sisak HR 124 B2
Sisante E 158 B1
Šišljavić HR. 123 B4
Sissach CH 106 B2

Sissonne F 91 B3
Sistelo P. 140 C2
Sisteron F 132 A1
Sistiana I 122 B2
Sistranda N 198 B5
Sitasjaurestugorna
  S 194 C8
Sitges E 147 C2
Sitia GR 185 D7
Sittard NL. 80 A1
Sittensen D 72 A2
Sittingbourne GB . . .45 B4
Sitzenroda D 83 A4
Sivac SRB. 126 B1
Sivaslı TR. 189 A4
Siverić HR. 138 B2
Sivrihisar TR. 187 C6
Sixt-Fer-á-Cheval
  F. 119 A3
Siziano I 120 B2
Sizun F. 100 A1
Sjenica SRB. 16 D3
Sjoa N. 198 D6
Sjøåsen N 199 A8
Sjöbo S 61 D3
Sjøenden
  Hedmark N 48 A3
  Hedmark N 48 B3
Sjøholt N 198 C3
Sjøli N 48 A3
Sjølstad N 199 A9
Sjölunda S 56 A1
Sjømarken S 60 B2
Sjørring DK. 58 B1
Sjötofta S. 60 B3
Sjötorp S 55 B4
Sjoutnäset S 199 A11
Sjøvegan N 194 B8
Sjuntorp S 54 B3
Skåbu N 47 A6
Skafså N 53 A4
Skaftafell IS 191 D9
Skagaströnd IS 190 B5
Skagen DK 58 A3
Skagersvik S 55 B5
Skaiå N. 53 B3
Skaidi N 193 B8
Skala GR 184 A1
Skala PL. 87 B3
Skaland N 194 A8
Skala Oropou GR .185 A4
Skala-Podilska UA .13 D7
Skalat UA. 13 D6
Skalbmierz PL. 87 B4
Skålevik N 53 B4
Skalica SK 98 C1
Skalité SK. 98 B2
Skällinge S 60 B2
Skalná CZ 83 B4
Skals DK 58 B2
Skælskør DK. 65 A4
Skalstugan S 199 B9
Skanderborg DK 59 B2
Skånes-Fagerhult
  S 61 C3
Skåne-Tranås S 61 D3
Skånevik N 52 A1
Skänninge S 55 B6
Skanör med Falsterbo
  S. 66 A1
Skåpafors S 54 A3
Skępe PL. 75 B4
Skara S 55 B4
Skærbæk DK 64 A1
Skarberget N 194 B7
Skärblacka S 56 B1
Skarð IS 190 B3
Skarda S 200 B4
Skare N 46 C3
Skåre S 55 A4
Skärhamn S 60 B1
Skarnes N 48 B3
Skärplinge S 51 B4
Skarp Salling DK. . . .58 B2
Skarrild DK 59 C1
Skarstad N. 194 B7
Skärstad S 62 A2
Skarsvåg N 193 A9
Skarszewy PL. 69 A3
Skårup DK 65 A3
Skärvången S 199 B11
Skarvsjöby S. 195 F8
Skaryszew PL. 87 A5
Skarżysko-Kamienna
  PL. 87 A4
Skarżysko Ksiazece
  PL. 87 A4
Skatøy N 53 B5
Skattkärr S 55 A4
Skattungbyn S 50 A1
Skatval N 199 B7
Skaulo S 196 B4
Skave DK 59 B1
Skawina PL 99 B3
Skebobruk S 51 C5
Skebokvarn S 56 A2
Skedala S 61 C2
Skedevi S. 56 B1
Skedsmokorset N . .48 B3
Skee S 54 B2
Skegness GB. 41 B4
Skei N 46 A3
Skela SRB 127 C2
Skelani BIH 127 C1
Skellefteå S 2 D7
Skelleftehamn S 2 D7
Skelmersdale GB . . .38 A4
Skelmorlie GB 34 C3
Skelund DK 58 B3
Skender Vakuf
  BIH. 138 A3
Skene S 60 B2
Skępe PL. 77 B4
Skepplanda S 60 B2
Skeppshult S 60 B3
Skerries IRL. 30 A2
Ski N 54 A1
Skiathos GR 183 D5
Skibbereen IRL. 29 C2

Skibotn N 192 C4
Skidra GR 182 C4
Skien N 53 A5
Skierniewice PL. 77 C5
Skillingaryd S 60 B4
Skillinge S 63 C2
Skilloura CY. 181 A2
Skinnardai S 57 A4
Skinnskatteberg S .50 C2
Skipmannvik N 195 C6
Skipness GB 34 C2
Skipsea GB 41 B3
Skipton GB 40 B1
Skiptvet N 54 A2
Skiros GR 183 E6
Skivarp S 66 A2
Skive DK 58 B2
Skjånes N 193 B12
Skjærhalden N 54 A2
Skjeberg N. 54 A2
Skjeggedal N 46 B3
Skjelanger N 46 B1
Skjeljavik N 46 C2
Skjern DK. 59 C1
Skjervøy N. 192 B4
Skjold
  Rogaland N 52 A1
  Troms N 192 C3
Skjoldastraumen N 52 A1
Skjolden N 47 A4
Skjønhaug N 54 A2
Skjøtningsberg
  N 193 A11
Škocjan SLO 123 B4
Skoczów PL. 98 B2
Skodborg DK. 59 C2
Škofja Loka SLO . .123 A3
Škofljica SLO. 123 B3
Skog S 51 A3
Skoganvarre N 193 C9
Skogen S 54 A3
Skogfoss N 193 C13
Skoghall S 55 A4
Skogly N 193 C13
Skogn N 199 B8
Skognes N 192 C3
Skogstorp
  Halland S 60 C2
  Södermanland S . . .56 A2
Skoki PL. 76 B2
Skokloster S 57 A3
Sköldinge S 56 A2
Skole UA. 13 D5
Skollenborg N 53 A5
Sköllersta S 56 A1
Skomlin PL. 86 A2
Skonseng N 195 D5
Skopelos GR. 183 D5
Skopje MK. 182 A3
Skoppum N 54 A1
Skórcz PL. 69 B3
Skorogoszcz PL. 86 B1
Skoroszów PL. 85 A5
Skorovatn N 199 A10
Skorped S 200 C3
Skørping DK 58 B2
Skotfoss N 53 A5
Skotniki PL. 87 A3
Skotselv N. 48 C1
Skotterud N 49 C4
Skottorp S 61 C2
Skovby DK 64 B2
Skövde S 55 B4
Skovsgård DK. 58 A2
Skrad HR 123 B3
Skradin HR 138 B1
Skråmestø N 46 B1
Škrdlovice CZ 97 B3
Skrea S 60 C2
Skreia N 48 B2
Skrolsvik N 194 A7
Skruv S 63 B3
Skrwilno PL. 77 A4
Skrydstrup DK. 59 C2
Skucani BIH. 138 B2
Skudeneshavn N. . .52 A1
Skui N 48 C2
Skulsk PL. 76 B3
Skultorp S 55 B4
Skultuna S. 56 A2
Skuodas LT. 8 D2
Skurup S 66 A2
Skute N 48 B2
Skuteč CZ. 97 B3
Skutskär S 51 B4
Skutvik N 194 B6
Skvyra UA 13 D8
Skwierzyna PL. 75 B4
Skýcov SK 98 C2
Skyllberg S 55 B5
Skyttmon S 200 C1
Skyttorp S 51 B4
Sládkovičovo SK. . .111 A4
Slagelse DK. 61 D1
Slagharen NL. 71 B3
Slagnäs S 195 E9
Slaidburn GB. 40 B1
Slane IRL. 30 A2
Slangerup DK. 61 D2
Slano HR 139 C3
Slantsy RUS. 8 C6
Slaný CZ 84 B2
Šlapanice CZ. 97 B4
Slåstad N 48 B3
Slatina
  BIH 139 B3
  HR 125 B3
  RO 17 C6
Slatiňany CZ 97 B3
Slatinice CZ. 98 B1
Slättberg S 50 A1
Slattum N. 48 C2
Slavičín CZ. 98 B1
Slavkov CZ 98 C1
Slavkovica SRB. . . .127 C2
Slavkov u Brna CZ . .97 B4
Slavonice CZ 97 C3

Slavonski Brod
  HR. 125 B4
Slavonski Kobas
  HR. 125 B3
Slavošovce SK. 99 C4
Slavskoye RUS. 69 A5
Slavuta UA. 13 C7
Sława
  Lubuskie PL. 85 A4
  Zachodnio-Pomorskie
  PL. 67 C4
Slawharad BY 13 B9
Sławków PL. 86 B3
Sławno
  Wielkopolskie PL . .76 B2
  Zachodnio-Pomorskie
  PL. 68 A1
Sławoborze PL. 67 C4
Sl'ažany SK. 98 C2
Sleaford GB 40 C3
Sleðbrjótur IS 191 B11
Sledmere GB 40 A3
Sleights GB 37 B6
Slemmestad N 54 A1
Ślesin PL 76 B3
Sliač SK 99 C3
Sliema M 175 C3
Sligo IRL 26 B2
Slite S. 57 C4
Slitu N 54 A2
Sliven BG. 17 D7
Śliwice PL 68 B3
Slobozia RO 17 C7
Slochteren NL 71 A3
Slöinge S 60 C2
Słomniki PL. 87 B4
Slonim BY 13 B6
Słońsk PL. 75 B3
Slootdorp NL. 70 B1
Slottsbron S 55 A4
Slövåg N. 46 A2
Slovenj Gradec
  SLO 110 C2
Slovenska Bistrica
  SLO 123 A4
Slovenská L'upča
  SK 99 C3
Slovenská-Ves SK. .99 B4
Slovenské Darmoty
  SK 112 A3
Slovenske Konjice
  SLO 123 A4
Słubice PL. 74 B3
Sluderno I 108 C1
Sluis NL. 78 A3
Šluknov CZ. 84 A2
Slunj HR. 123 B4
Słupca PL. 76 B2
Słupia PL. 87 A3
Słupiec PL. 85 B4
Słupsk PL 68 A2
Slutsk BY 13 B7
Småländsstenar S ..60 B3
Smalåsen N 195 E4
Smardzewo PL. 75 B4
Smarhon BY 13 A7
Šmarje SLO. 123 B4
Šmarjeta SLO. 123 B4
Šmartno SLO. 123 A3
Smečno CZ 84 B2
Smedby S 63 B4
Smědec CZ 96 C2
Smederevo SRB . . .127 C2
Smederevska Palanka
  SRB 127 C2
Smedjebacken S . . .50 B2
Smęgorzów PL. 87 B5
Smeland N. 53 B4
Smidary CZ. 84 B3
Śmigiel PL. 75 B5
Smilde NL 71 B3
Smiřice CZ. 85 B3
Smithfield GB 36 B4
Śmitowo PL. 75 A5
Smögen S 54 B2
Smogulec PL. 76 A2
Smoldzino PL. 68 A2
Smolenice SK 98 C1
Smolensk RUS. 13 A10
Smolník SK. 99 C4
Smolyan BG 183 B6
Smuka SLO 123 B3
Smygehamn S 66 A2
Smykow PL. 87 A4
Snainton GB. 40 A3
Snaith GB 40 B2
Snaptun DK. 59 C3
Snarby N 192 C3
Snarum N. 48 B1
Snåsa N 199 A9
Snedsted DK 58 B1
Sneek NL 70 A2
Sneem IRL. 29 C2
Snejbjerg DK 59 B1
Snillfjord N 198 B6
Snøde DK. 65 A3
Snøfjord N 193 B8
Snogebaek DK 67 A4
Snyatyn UA. 13 D6
Soave I 121 B4
Sober E 140 B3
Sobernheim D 93 B3
Soběslav CZ 96 B2
Sobota
  Dolnośląskie PL. . .85 A3
  Łódzkie PL. 77 B4
Sobótište SK. 98 C1
Sobótka CZ. 84 B1
Sobótka
  Dolnośląskie PL. . .85 B4
  Wielkopolskie PL. . .86 A1
Sobra HR. 139 C3
Sobrado
  Coruña E 140 A2
  Lugo E 141 B3
Sobral da Adica P 161 A2
Sobral de Monte
  Agraço P. 154 C1

Sobreira Formosa
  P 154 B3
Søby DK. 64 B3
Soca SLO. 122 A2
Sochaczew PL. 77 B5
Sochos GR 183 C5
Socodor RO. 113 C5
Socol RO. 127 C3
Socovos E. 164 A3
Socuéllamos E 158 B1
Sodankylä FIN 197 B9
Söderåkra S. 63 B4
Söderala S 51 A3
Söderås S 50 B2
Söderbärke S. 50 B2
Söderby-Karl S. 51 C5
Söderfors S 51 B4
Söderhamn S 51 A4
Söderköping S 56 B2
Söderö S 56 B1
Södingberg A. 110 B2
Södra Finnö S 56 B2
Södra Ny S. 55 A4
Södra Råda S 55 A5
Södra Sandby S 61 D3
Södra Vi S 62 A3
Sodražica SLO 123 B3
Sodupe E 143 A3
Soengas P. 148 A1
Soest
  D. 81 A4
  NL. 70 B2
Sofades GR 182 D4
Sofia = Sofiya BG . .17 D5
Sofikon GR 184 B4
Sofiya = Sofia BG . .17 D5
Sofronea RO 126 A3
Sögel D. 71 B4
Sogliano al Rubicone
  I 135 A5
Sogndalsfjøra N . . .46 A4
Søgne N 53 B3
Söğütköy TR 188 C3
Soham GB. 45 A4
Sohland D. 84 A2
Sohren D 93 B3
Søndeled N 53 B5
Sønderborg DK. 64 B2
Sønderby DK 64 B2
Sønder Felding DK.59 C1
Sønderho DK. 59 C1
Sønder Hygum DK .59 C1
Sønder Omme DK.59 C1
Sondershausen D. .82 A2
Søndersø DK 59 C3
Søndervig DK 59 B1
Søndre Enningdal
  Kappel N. 54 B2
Sóndrio I 120 A2
Soneja E 159 B3
Son en Breugel NL .80 A1
Songe N 53 B5
Songeons F. 90 B1
Sonkamuotka FIN 196 A6
Sonkovo RUS. 9 D10
Sönnarslöv S. 61 D4
Sonneberg D. 82 B3
Sonnefeld D 82 B3
Sonnewalde D 84 A1
Sonnino I 169 B3
Sonogno CH 120 A1
Sonsbeck D 80 A2
Sonseca E 157 A4
Son Servera E 167 B3
Sonstorp S 56 B1
Sonta SRB. 125 B5
Sontheim D 94 C2
Sonthofen D 107 B5
Sontra D. 82 A1
Sopelana E 143 A4
Sopje HR 125 B3
Soporňa SK 111 A4
Sopot
  PL. 69 A3
  SRB 127 C2
Sopotnica MK 182 B3
Sopron H 111 B3
Šor SRB 127 C1
Sora I 169 B3
Soragna I 120 C3
Söråker S 200 D3
Sorano I 168 A1
Sorbara I 121 C4
Sorbas E 164 B2
Sórbolo I 121 C3
Sørbygden S 200 D2
Sordal N. 52 B3
Sordale GB 32 C3
Sore F 128 B2
Sörenberg CH 106 C3
Soresina I 120 B2
Sorèze F 146 A3
Sörforsa S 200 E3
Sorges F 115 C4
Sórgono I 179 B3
Sorgues F 131 A3
Sorgun TR 23 B8
Soria E 143 C4
Soriano Cálabro I .175 C2
Soriano nel Cimino
  I 168 A2
Sorihuela del
  Guadalimar E 164 A1
Sorisdale GB 34 B1
Sørkjosen N. 192 C4
Sørli N 199 A10
Sormás H. 111 C3
Sörmjöle S. 200 C6
Sørmo N. 194 B9
Sornac F 116 B2
Sorø DK 61 D1
Soroca MD. 17 A8
Sørreisa N 194 A9
Sorrento I 170 C2
Sorsele S 195 E8
Sörsjön S. 49 A5
Sorso I 178 B2
Sort E. 146 B2
Sortavala RUS. 9 B7
Sortino I 177 B3
Sortland N 194 B6
Sørum N. 48 B2
Sørumsand N 48 C3
Sorunda S. 57 A3
Sørvågen N 194 C3
Sørvær N 192 B6
Sorvik S 50 B2
Sørvika N 199 C8
Sos F 128 B3
Sösdala S 61 C3
Sos del Rey Católico
  E 144 B2
Sošice HR 123 B4
Sosnica PL. 75 A5
Sośnicowice PL. 86 B2
Sośno PL 76 A2
Sosnovyy Bor RUS. .9 C6
Sosnowiec PL. 86 B3
Sospel F 133 B3
Šoštanj SLO 123 A4
Sotaseter N 198 D4
Sotillo de Adrada
  E 150 B3
Sotillo de la Ribera
  E 143 C3
Sotin HR 125 B5
Sotkamo FIN 3 D11
Sotobañado y Priorato
  E 142 B2
Soto de la Marina
  E 143 A3
Soto del Barco E . .141 A4
Soto de los Infantes
  E 141 A4
Soto de Real E 151 B4
Soto de Ribera E . .141 A5
Sotoserrano E 149 B3
Soto y Amio E 141 B5
Sotresgudo E 142 B2
Sotrondio E 142 A1
Sotta F 180 B2
Sottomarina I. 122 B1
Sottrum D 72 A2
Sottunga FIN 51 B7
Sotuelamos E 158 B1
Souain F 91 B4
Soual F. 146 A3
Soucy F 104 A2
Souda GR 185 D5
Soudron F 91 C4
Souesmes F 103 B4
Soufflenheim F 93 C3
Soufli GR 186 A1
Souillac F. 129 B4
Souilly F 91 B5
Soulac-sur-Mer F . .114 C2
Soulaines-Dhuys F 91 C4
Soulatgé F 146 B3
Soultz-Haut-Rhin
  F 106 B2
Soultz-sous-Forêts
  F 93 C3
Soumagne B 80 B1
Soumoulou F 145 A3
Souppes-sur-Loing
  F 103 A4
Souprosse F 128 C2
Sourdeval F 88 B3
Soure P 154 A2
Sournia F 146 B3
Souro Pires P 149 B2
Sourpi GR 182 D4
Sours F. 90 C1
Sousceyrac F 116 C2
Sousel P. 155 C3
Soustons F 128 C1
Söğüt
  Bilecik TR 187 B5
  Burdur TR 189 B4
Soutelo de Montes
  E 140 B2
Southam GB 44 A2
Southampton GB . . .44 C2
Southborough GB. . .45 B4
South Brent GB 42 B3
South Cave GB 40 B3
Southend GB. 34 C2
Southend-on-Sea
  GB 45 B4
South Hayling GB. . .44 C3
South Molton GB. . .42 A3
South Ockendon
  GB 45 B4
South Petherton
  GB 43 B4
Southport GB. 38 A3
South Shields GB. . .37 B5
South Tawton GB. . .42 B3
Southwell GB 40 B3
Southwold GB. 45 A5
South Woodham
  Ferrers GB. 45 B4
Söğütlu TR. 187 B5
Souto P 148 B2
Soutochao E 141 C3
Souto da Carpalhosa
  P 154 B2
Souvigny F 104 C2
Souzay-Champigny
  F 102 B1
Soverato I 175 C2
Soveria Mannelli I 175 B2
Sövestad S 66 A2
Sovetsk RUS. 12 A4
Sovići BIH 138 B3
Sovicille I. 135 B4
Søvik N 198 C3
Sowerby GB 37 B5
Soyaux F 115 C4
Søyland N 52 B1
Sozopol BG 17 D7
Spa B. 80 B1
Spadafora I 177 A4

Sik–Spa 265

Švermov CZ 84 B2
Sveti Ivan Zabno
HR 124 B2
Sveti Ivan Zelina
HR 124 B2
Sveti Nikole MK 182 B3
Sveti Rok HR 137 A4
Světlá nad Sázavou
CZ 97 B3
Světlyy RUS 69 A5
Svetvinčenat HR . . .122 B2
Švica HR 123 C4
Svidník SK 12 D4
Švihov CZ 96 B1
Svilajnac SRB 127 C3
Svilengrad BG 183 B8
Svindal N 54 A2
Svinhult S 62 A3
Svinna SK 98 C2
Svinninge
DK 61 D1
S 57 A4
Sviritsa RUS 9 B8
Svishtov BG 17 D6
Svislach BY 13 B6
Svit SK 99 B4
Svitavy CZ 97 B4
Svodin SK 112 B2
Svolvær N 194 B5
Svortemyr N 46 A2
Svortland N 52 A1
Svratka CZ 97 B4
Svrčinovec SK 98 B2
Svullrya N 49 B4
Svyetlahorsk BY 13 B8
Swadlincote GB 40 C2
Swaffham GB 41 C4
Swanage GB 43 B5
Swanley GB 45 B4
Swanlinbar IRL 26 B3
Swansea GB 39 C3
Swarzędz PL 76 B2
Swatragh GB 27 B4
Świątki PL 69 B5
Świdnica
Dolnośląskie PL . . .85 B4
Lubuskie PL 84 A3
Świdnik PL 12 C5
Świdwin PL 67 C4
Świebodzice PL 85 B4
Świebodzin PL 75 B4
Świecie PL 76 A3
Świedziebnia PL 77 A4
Świeradów Zdrój
PL 84 B3
Świerki PL 85 B4
Świerzawa PL 85 A3
Świerzno PL 67 C3
Święta PL 74 A3
Święta Anna PL 86 B3
Świętno PL 75 B5
Swifterbant NL 70 B2
Swindon GB 44 B2
Swineshead GB 41 C3
Swinford IRL 26 C2
Świnoujście PL 66 C3
Swinton GB 35 C5
Swobnica PL 74 A3
Swords IRL 30 A2
Swornegacie PL 68 B2
Sya S 56 B1
Syasstroy RUS 9 B8
Sycewice PL 68 A1
Sychevka RUS 9 E9
Syców PL 86 A1
Sycowice PL 75 B4
Sydnes N 52 A1
Syftland N 46 B2
Syke D 72 B1
Sykkylven N 198 C3
Sylling N 48 C2
Sylte N 198 C4
Symbister GB 33 A5
Symington GB 36 A3
Symonds Yat GB 39 C4
Sypniewo
Kujawsko-Pomorskie
PL 76 A2
Wielkopolskie PL . . .68 B1
Syserum S 62 A4
Sysslebäck S 49 B4
Syväjärvi FIN 197 B8
Szabadbattyán H. . .112 B2
Szabadegyháza H . .112 B2
Szabadszállás H . . .112 C3
Szadek PL 86 A2
Szajol H 113 B4
Szakály H 112 C2
Szakcs H 112 C2
Szakmár H 112 C3
Szalánta H 125 B4
Szałas PL 87 A4
Szalkszentmárton
H 112 C3
Szalonna H 99 C4
Szamocin PL 76 A2
Szamotuły PL 75 B5
Szany H 111 B4
Szarvas H 113 C4
Szarvaskö H 113 B4
Szászvár H. 125 A4
Százhalombatta
H 112 B2
Szczawa PL 99 B4
Szczawnica PL 99 B4
Szczecin PL 74 A3
Szczecinek PL 68 B1
Szczekociny PL 87 B3
Szczercow PL 86 A3
Szczucin PL 87 B5
Szczuczarz PL 75 A5
Szczuki PL 77 B5
Szczurowa PL 87 B4
Szczyrk PL 99 B3
Szczytna PL 85 B4
Szczytno PL 77 A5
Szczyty PL 86 A2
Szécsény H 112 A3
Szederkény H 125 B4
Szedres H 112 C2

Szeged H 126 A2
Szeghalom H 113 B5
Szegvár H 113 C4
Székesfehérvár
H 112 B2
Székkutas H 113 C4
Szekszárd H 125 A4
Szemplino Czarne
PL 77 A5
Szemud PL 68 A3
Szendehely H 112 B3
Szendrö H 99 C4
Szentendre H. 112 B3
Szentes H 113 C4
Szentgotthárd H . . .111 C3
Szentlászló H 125 A3
Szentlörinc H 125 A3
Szentmártonkáta
H 113 B3
Szenyér H 111 C4
Szeremle H 125 A4
Szerencs H 113 A5
Szerep H 113 B5
Szigetszentmiklós
H 112 B3
Szigetvár H 125 A3
Szikáncs H 113 A4
Szikszó H. 113 A4
Szil H 111 B4
Szilvásvárad H 113 A4
Szklarska Poreba
PL 84 B3
Szlichtyngowa PL . . .85 A4
Szob H 112 B2
Szolnok H 113 B4
Szombathely H 111 B3
Szorosad H 112 C2
Szpetal Graniczny
PL 77 B4
Szprotawa PL 84 A3
Szreńsk PL 77 A5
Sztum PL 69 B4
Sztutowo PL 69 A4
Szubin PL 76 A2
Szücsi H. 113 B3
Szulmierz PL 77 B5
Szulok PL 124 A3
Szumanie PL 77 B4
Szwecja PL 75 A5
Szydłów
Łódzkie PL 86 A3
Świętokrzyskie PL . .87 B5
Szydłowiec PL 87 A4
Szydlowo PL 77 A5
Szydłowo PL 75 A5
Szymanów PL 77 B5
Szynkielów PL 86 A2

T

Taastrup DK 61 D2
Tab H 112 C2
Tabanera la Luenga
E 151 A3
Tabaqueros E 158 B2
Tábara E 149 A4
Tabenera de Cerrato
E 142 B2
Taberg S 62 A2
Tabernas E 164 B2
Tabiano Bagni I 120 C3
Taboada E 140 B3
Taboadela E 140 B3
Tábor CZ 96 B2
Táborfalva H 112 B3
Taborište HR 124 B2
Tábua P 148 B1
Tabuaco P 148 A2
Tabuenca E 152 A2
Tabuyo del Monte
E 141 B4
Täby S 57 A4
Tác H 112 B2
Tachov CZ 95 B4
Tadcaster GB 40 B2
Tadley GB 44 B2
Tafalla E 144 B2
Tafjord N 198 C4
Taganheira P 160 B1
Tågarp S 61 D2
Taggia I 133 B3
Tagliacozzo I 169 A3
Táglio di Po I 121 B5
Tagnon F 91 B4
Tahal E 164 B2
Tahitótfalu H 112 B3
Tahtaköprü TR 187 C4
Tailfingen D 107 A4
Taillis F 101 A4
Tain GB 32 D2
Tain-l'Hermitage
F 117 B4
Taipadas P 154 C2
Taivalkoski FIN 197 D11
Takene S 55 A4
Takovo SRB 127 C2
Taksony H 112 B3
Tal E 140 B2
Talachyn BY 13 A8
Talamello I 135 B5
Talamone I 168 A1
Talant F 105 B3
Talarrubias E 156 A2
Talaván E 155 B4
Talavera de la Reina
E 150 C3
Talavera la Real E . .155 C4
Talayuela E 150 C2
Talayuelas E 159 B2
Talgarth GB 39 C3
Talgje N 52 A1
Talhadas P 148 B1
Táliga E 155 C3
Talinat F 116 B3
Tálknafjörður IS 190 B2
Talla I 135 B4
Talladale GB 31 B3
Tallaght IRL 30 A2
Tallard F 132 A2

Tällberg S 50 B1
Tallberg S 196 C5
Tallinn EST 8 C4
Talloires F 118 B3
Tallow IRL 29 B3
Tallsjö S 200 B4
Tallvik S 196 C5
Talmay F 105 B4
Talmont-St Hilaire
F 114 B2
Talmont-sur-Gironde
F 114 C3
Talne UA 13 D9
Talsano I 173 B3
Talsi LV. 8 D3
Talvik N 192 B6
Talybont GB 39 B3
Tal-Y-Llyn GB 38 B3
Tamajón E 151 B4
Tamame E 149 A4
Tamames E 149 B3
Tamarit de Mar E . .147 C2
Tamarite de Litera
E 145 C4
Tamariu E. 147 C4
Tamási H 112 C2
Tambach-Dietharz
D 82 B2
Tameza E 141 A4
Tammisaari FIN 8 B3
Tampere FIN 8 B3
Tamsweg A 109 B4
Tamurejo E 156 B3
Tamworth GB 40 C2
Tana bru N 193 B12
Tañabueyes E 143 B3
Tanakajd H 111 B3
Tananger N 52 B1
Tanaunella I 178 B3
Tancarville F 89 A4
Tandsjöborg S 199 D11
Tånga S 61 C2
Tangelic H 112 C2
Tangen N 48 B3
Tangerhütte D 73 B4
Tangermünde D 73 B4
Tanhua FIN 197 B10
Taninges F 118 A3
Tankavaara FIN 197 A10
Tann D 82 B2
Tanna D 83 B3
Tannadice GB 35 B5
Tannåker S. 60 C3
Tännäs S 199 C9
Tannay
Ardennes F 91 B4
Nièvre F 104 B2
Tännesberg D 95 B4
Tannheim A 108 B1
Tannila FIN. 197 D8
Tanowo PL 74 A3
Tanum S 54 B2
Tanumshede S 54 B2
Tanus F 130 A1
Tanvald CZ 84 B3
Taormina I 177 B4
Tapa EST 8 C4
Tápióbicske H 112 B3
Tápiógyörgye H 113 B3
Tápióság H 112 B3
Tápiószecsö H 112 B3
Tápiószele H 113 B3
Tápiószentmárton
H 113 B3
Tapolca H 111 C4
Tapolcafö H 111 B4
Tar HR 122 B2
Tarabo S. 60 B2
Taradell E. 147 C3
Tarakli TR. 187 B5
Taramundi E 141 A3
Tarancón E 151 B4
Táranto I 173 B3
Tarare F 117 B4
Tarascon F 131 B3
Tarascon-sur-Ariège
F 146 B2
Tarashcha UA 13 D9
Tarazona E 144 C2
Tarazona de la Mancha
E 158 B2
Tarbena E 159 C3
Tarbert
GB 34 C2
IRL 29 B2
Tarbes F 145 A4
Tarbet GB 34 B3
Tarbolton GB 36 A2
Tarcento I 122 A2
Tarčin BIH 139 B4
Tarczyn PL 77 C5
Tardajos E 143 B3
Tardelcuende E 151 A5
Tardets-Sorholus
F 144 A3
Tardienta E 145 C3
Tärendö S 196 B5
Targon F 128 B2
Târgovişte RO 17 C6
Târgu-Jiu RO. 17 C5
Târgu Mureş RO 17 B6
Târgu Ocna RO. 17 B7
Târgu Secuiesc
RO. 17 C7
Telč CZ 97 B3
Tarifa E. 162 B2
Tariquejas E 161 B2
Tárján H 112 B2
Tárkany H 112 B2
Tarland GB. 33 D4
Tarlów PL. 87 A5
Tarm DK 59 C1
Tärnaby S 195 E6
Tarnalelesz H. 113 A4
Tarnaörs H 113 B4

Tårnåveni RO 17 B6
Tårnet N 193 C14
Tarnobrzeg PL. 87 B5
Tarnos F 128 C1
Tarnów
Lubuskie PL. 75 B3
Małopolskie PL. 87 B4
Tarnowo Podgórne
PL. 75 B5
Tarnowskie Góry
PL. 86 B2
Tärnsjö S. 51 B3
Tärnvik N 194 C6
Tarouca P. 148 A2
Tarp D. 64 B2
Tarquínia I 168 A1
Tarquínia Lido I 168 A1
Tarragona E 147 C2
Tàrrajaur S. 196 C2
Tàrrega E 147 C2
Tarrenz A 108 B1
Tårs
Nordjyllands DK 58 A3
Storstrøms DK 65 B4
Tarsia I 174 B2
Tarsus TR 23 C8
Tartas F 128 C2
Tartu EST. 8 C5
Tarves GB 33 D4
Tarvísio I 109 C4
Taşağıl TR 189 C6
Täsch CH 119 A4
Taşköprü TR 23 A8
Tasov CZ. 97 B4
Tasovčići BIH. 139 B3
Taşucuo TR 23 C7
Tát H 112 B2
Tata H. 112 B2
Tatabánya H 112 B2
Tataháza H 126 A1
Tatarbunary UA 17 C8
Tatárszentgyörgy
H 112 B3
Tatranská-Lomnica
SK 99 B4
Tau N 52 A1
Tauberbischofsheim
D 94 B1
Taucha D 83 A4
Taufkirchen D 95 C4
Taufkirchen an der
Pram A 96 C1
Taulé F 100 A2
Taulignan F 131 A3
Taulov DK 59 C2
Taunton GB 43 A3
Taunusstein D 81 B4
Tauragė LT 12 A5
Taurianova I. 175 C2
Taurisano I 173 C4
Tauste E 144 C2
Tauves F 116 B2
Tavankut SRB 126 A1
Tavannes CH 106 B2
Tavarnelle val di Pesa
I 135 B4
Tavas TR 188 B4
Tavaux F 105 B4
Tävelsås S 62 B2
Taverna I 175 B2
Taverne CH 120 A1
Tavernelle I 135 B5
Tavernes de la
Valldigna E 159 B3
Tavérnola Bergamasca
I 120 B3
Taverny F 90 B2
Tavescan E 146 B2
Taviano I 173 C4
Tavira P. 160 B2
Tavistock GB 42 B2
Tavşanlı TR 187 C4
Tayinloan GB. 34 C2
Taynuilt GB 34 B2
Tayport GB 35 B5
Tázlár H 112 C3
Tazones E 142 A1
Tczew PL. 69 A3
Tczów PL 87 A5
Teangue GB 31 B3
Teano I 170 B2
Teba E 162 B3
Tebay GB 37 B4
Techendorf A 109 C4
Tecklenburg D 71 B4
Tecko-matorp S 61 D3
Tecuci RO 17 C7
Tefenni TR 189 B4
Tegelsmora S 51 B4
Tegernsee D 108 B2
Teggiano I 172 B1
Tegoleto I 135 B4
Teichel D 82 B3
Teignmouth GB 43 B3
Teillay F 101 B4
Teillet F 130 B1
Teisendorf D 109 B3
Teistungen D 82 A2
Teixeiro E 140 A2
Tejada de Tiétar E . .150 B2
Tejado E 152 A1
Tejares E 150 B2
Tejn DK 67 A3
Teke TR. 187 A4
Tekirdağ TR 186 B2
Tekovské-Lužany
SK 112 A2
Telavåg N. 46 B1
Telč CZ 97 B3
Telese Terme I 170 B2
Telford GB 38 B4
Telfs A 108 B2
Telgárt SK 99 C4
Telgte D 71 C4
Tellingstedt D 64 B2
Telšiai LT 8 E3
Telti I 178 B3
Teltow D 74 B2
Tembleque E 157 A4
Temelín CZ. 96 B2

Temerin SRB 126 B1
Temiño E 143 B3
Témpio Pausánia
I 178 B3
Templederry IRL 28 B3
Templemore IRL 28 B4
Temple Sowerby
GB 37 B4
Templin D. 74 A2
Temse B 79 A4
Tenay F 118 B2
Tenbury Wells GB . . .39 B4
Tenby GB 39 C2
Tence F 117 B4
Tende F 133 A3
Tenhult S 62 A2
Tenja HR 125 B4
Tennenbronn D 106 A3
Tenneville B 92 A1
Tennevoll N 194 B8
Tensta S 51 B4
Tenterden GB 45 B4
Teo E 140 B2
Teora I 172 B1
Tepasto FIN 196 B7
Tepelenë AL 182 C2
Teplá CZ 95 B4
Teplice CZ 84 B1
Teplička nad Váhom
SK 98 B2
Tepsa FIN 197 B8
Tera E 143 C4
Téramo I 169 A3
Ter Apel NL 71 B4
Tasovčići BIH. 139 B3
Terchová SK 99 B3
Terebovlya UA 13 D6
Teremia Mare RO . .126 B2
Terena P 155 C3
Teresa de Cofrentes
E 159 B2
Terešov CZ 96 B1
Terezín CZ 84 B2
Terezino Polje HR . .124 B3
Tergnier F 90 B3
Teriberka RUS 3 B14
Terlizzi I 171 B4
Termas de Monfortinho
P 155 A4
Terme di Súio I 169 B3
Terme di Valdieri I . .133 A3
Termens E 145 C4
Termes F 116 C3
Términi Imerese I . .176 B2
Terminillo I 169 A2
Térmoli I 170 B3
Termonfeckin IRL . . .27 C4
Ternberg A 110 B1
Terndrup DK 58 B3
Terneuzen NL 79 A3
Terni I 168 A2
Ternitz A 111 B3
Ternopil UA 13 D6
Terpni GR 183 C5
Terracina I 169 B3
Terråk N 195 E3
Terralba I 179 C2
Terranova di Pollino
I 174 B2
Terranova di Sibari
I 174 B2
Terras do Bouro
P 148 A1
Terrasini I 176 A2
Terrassa E 147 C3
Terrasson-la-Villedieu
F 129 A4
Terrazos E 143 B3
Terriente E 152 B2
Terrugem P 155 C3
Tertenía I 179 C3
Teruel E 152 B2
Tervola FIN 196 C7
Tervuren B 79 B4
Terzaga E 152 B2
Tešanj BIH 125 C3
Tesáske-Mlyňany
SK 98 C2
Teslić BIH 125 C3
Tessin D 66 B1
Tessy-sur-Vire F 88 B2
Tét H 111 B4
Tetbury GB 43 A4
Teterchen F 92 B2
Teterow D 65 C5
Teteven BG 17 D6
Tetiyev UA 13 D8
Tetovo MK 182 A2
Tettau D 82 B3
Tettnang D 107 B4
Teublitz D. 95 B4
Teuchern D 83 A4
Teulada
E 159 C4
I 179 D2
Teupitz D. 74 B2
Teurajärvi S 196 C5
Tielt B 78 A3
Tienen B 79 B4
Tengen D 106 B3
Teviothead GB. 36 A4
Tewkesbury GB. 39 C4
Thale D. 82 A3
Thalfang D 92 B2
Thalgau A 109 B4
Thalkirch CH 107 C4
Thalmässing D 95 B3
Thalwil CH 107 B3
Thame GB 44 B3
Thann F 106 B2
Thannhausen D 94 C2
Thaon-les-Vosges
F 105 A5
Tharandt D. 83 B5
Tharsis E 161 B2
Thasos GR 183 C6
Thatcham GB 44 B2
Thaxted GB 45 B4
Thaynges CH 107 B3
Theale GB 44 B2
The Barony GB 33 B3

Thebes = Thiva
GR 185 A4
Theding-hausen D .72 B2
Theessen D 73 B5
The Hague = 's-
Gravenhage NL . . .70 B1
Themar D. 82 B2
Thénezay F 102 C1
Thenon F 129 A4
Theologos GR 183 C6
Therouanne F 78 B2
Thessaloniki = Salonica
GR 182 C4
Thetford GB 45 A4
Theux B 80 B1
Thézar-les-Corbières
F 146 A3
Thèze F 145 A3
Thiberville F 89 A4
Thibie F 91 C4
Thiélbemont-Farémont
F 91 C4
Thiendorf D 84 A1
Thiene I 121 B4
Thierrens CH 106 C1
Thiers F 117 B3
Thiesi I 178 B2
Thiessow D 66 B2
Thiezac F 116 B2
Þingeyri IS 190 B2
Þingvellir IS 190 C4
Thionville F 92 B2
Thira GR 185 C6
Thiron-Gardais F 89 B4
Thirsk GB 37 B5
Thisted DK. 58 B1
Thiva = Thebes
GR 185 A4
Thivars F 90 C1
Thiviers F 115 C4
Thizy F 117 A4
Tholen NL 79 A4
Tholey D 92 B3
Thomas Street IRL . .28 A3
Thomastown IRL 30 B1
Thônes F 118 B3
Thonnance-les-
Joinville F 91 C5
Thonon-les-Bains
F 118 A3
Thorame-Basse F . .132 A2
Thorame-Haute F . .132 A2
Thorens-Glières F . .118 A3
Thorigny-sur-Oreuse
F 91 C3
Thörl A 110 B2
Þorlákshöfn IS 190 D4
Thornaby on Tees
GB 37 B5
Thornbury GB 43 A4
Thorne GB 40 B3
Thornhill
Dumfries & Galloway
GB 36 A3
Stirling GB 35 B3
Thornthwaite GB 36 B3
Thornton-le-Dale
GB 40 A3
Þórshöfn IS 191 A10
Thouarcé F 102 B1
Thouars F 102 C1
Thrapston GB 44 A3
Threlkeld GB. 36 B3
Thrumster GB 32 C3
Thueyts F 117 C4
Thuin B 79 B4
Thuir F 146 B3
Thumau D 95 A3
Thun CH 106 C2
Thuret F 116 B3
Thurey F 105 C4
Thüringen A 107 B4
Thurins F 117 B4
Thürkow D 65 C5
Thurles IRL 29 B4
Thurø By DK 65 A3
Thurmaston GB 40 C2
Thursby GB 36 B3
Thurso GB 32 C3
Thury-Harcourt F 89 B3
Thusis CH 107 C4
Thyborøn DK. 58 B1
Þykkvibær IS 190 D5
Thyregod DK 59 C2
Tibi E 159 C3
Tibro S. 55 B5
Tidaholm S 55 B4
Tidan S. 55 B5
Tidersrum S 62 A3
Tiedra E 150 A2
Tiefenbach D 95 B4
Tiefencastel CH 107 C4
Tiefenort D 82 B2
Tiefensee D 74 B2
Tiel NL 79 A5
Tielmes E 151 B4
Tielt B 78 A3
Tienen B 79 B4
Tiengen D 106 B3
Tierga E 152 A2
Tiermas E 144 B2
Tierp S 51 B4
Tierrantona E 145 B4
Tighina MD 17 B8
Tighnabruaich GB . . .34 C2
Tignes F 119 B3
Tigy F 103 B4
Tihany H 112 C1
Tijnje NL 70 A2
Tijola E 164 B2
Tikhvin RUS. 9 C8
Tilburg NL 79 A5
Til Châtel F 105 B4
Tilh F 128 C2
Tillac F 145 A4
Tillberga S 56 A2
Tille F 90 B2
Tillicoultry GB 35 B4
Tilloy Bellay F 91 B4

Tilly F 115 B5
Tilly-sur-Seulles F . . .88 A3
Tim DK 59 B1
Timau I 109 C4
Timbaki GR 185 D5
Timi CY 181 B1
Timişoara RO 126 B3
Timmele S 60 B3
Timmendorfer Strand
D 65 C3
Timmernabben S 62 B4
Timmersdala S 55 B4
Timoleague IRL 29 C3
Timolin IRL 30 B2
Timrå S. 200 D3
Timsfors S 61 C3
Timsgearraidh GB . . .31 A1
Tinajas E 152 B1
Tinalhas P 155 B3
Tinchebray F 88 B3
Tincques F 78 B2
Tineo E. 141 A4
Tinglev DK 64 B2
Tingsryd S 63 B2
Tingstäde S 57 C4
Tingvoll N 198 C5
Tinlot B. 79 B5
Tinnoset N 53 A5
Tinos GR 185 B6
Tintagel GB 42 B2
Tinténiac F 101 A4
Tintern GB 39 C4
Tintigny B 92 B1
Tione di Trento I 121 A3
Tipperary IRL 29 B3
Tiptree GB 45 B4
Tirana = Tiranë
AL 182 B1
Tiranë= Tirana AL . .182 B1
Tirano I 120 A3
Tiraspol MD 17 B8
Tire TR 188 A2
Tires I 108 C2
Tiriez E 158 C1
Tirig E. 153 B4
Tiriolo I 175 C2
Tirnavos GR 182 D4
Tirrénia I 134 B3
Tirschenreuth D 95 B4
Tirstrup DK. 59 B3
Tirteafuera E 157 B3
Tisno HR 137 B4
Tišnov CZ 97 B4
Tisovec SK 99 C3
Tisselskog S 54 B3
Tistedal N 54 A2
Tistrup DK 59 C1
Tisvildeleje DK 61 C2
Tiszabö H. 113 B4
Tiszacsege H. 113 B5
Tiszadorogma H . . .113 B4
Tiszaföldvár H 113 C4
Tiszafüred H 113 B4
Tiszajenö H 113 B4
Tiszakécske H 113 C4
Tiszakeszi H 113 B4
Tiszakürt H 113 C4
Tiszalök H 113 A5
Tiszalúc H 113 A5
Tiszanána H 113 B4
Tiszaörs H 113 B4
Tiszaroff H 113 B4
Tiszasüly H 113 B4
Tiszasziget H 126 A2
Tiszaszőlős H 113 B4
Tiszaújváros H 113 B5
Tiszavasvári H 113 B5
Titaguas E 159 B2
Titel SRB 126 B2
Titisee-Neustadt
D 106 B3
Tito I 172 B1
Titova Korenica
HR 123 C4
Titran N 198 B5
Tittling D 96 C1
Tittmoning D 109 A3
Titz D 80 A2
Tiurajärvi FIN 196 B7
Tived S. 55 B5
Tiverton GB 43 B3
Tivisa E 153 A4
Tivoli I 168 B2
Tizsadob H. 113 A5
Tjällmo S 56 B1
Tjåmotis S 195 D9
Tjæreborg DK 59 C1
Tjautjas S 196 B3
Tjøme N 54 A1
Tjong N 195 D4
Tjonnefoss N. 53 B4
Tjörn IS 190 B5
Tjörnarp S 61 D3
Tjøtta N 195 E3
Tkon HR 137 B4
Tleń PL 68 B3
Tlmače SK 98 C2
Tłuchowo PL 77 B4
Tlumačov CZ 98 B1
Tóalmás H 112 B3
Toano I 134 A3
Toba D 82 A2
Tobarra E 158 C2
Tobercurry IRL 26 B2
Tobermore GB 27 B4
Tobermory GB 34 B1
Toberonochy GB 34 B2
Tobha Mor GB 31 B1
Tobo S 51 B4
Tocane-St Apre F . .129 A3
Tocha P 148 B1
Tocina E 162 A2
Töcksfors S 54 A2
Tocón E 163 A4
Todal N 198 C5
Todi I 136 C1

Todmorden GB 40 B1
Todorici BIH. 138 A3
Todtmoos D 106 B3
Todtnau D 106 B2
Toén E 140 B3
Tofta
 Gotland S. 57 C4
 Skaraborg S. 55 B4
Toftbyn S. 50 B2
Tofte N 54 A1
Töftedal S 54 B2
Tofterup DK. 59 C1
Toftlund DK 59 C2
Tófú H 125 A4
Tohmo FIN. 197 C10
Tokaj H. 113 A5
Tokarnia PL 87 B4
Tokary PL. 76 C3
Tokod H 112 B2
Tököl H 112 B2
Tolastadh bho Thuath
 GB 31 A2
Toledo E. 151 C3
Tolentino I 136 B2
Tolfa I 168 A1
Tolg S. 62 A2
Tolga N. 199 C8
Tolkmicko PL. 69 A4
Tollarp S. 61 D3
Tollered S. 60 B2
Tølløse DK. 61 D1
Tolmachevo RUS. 9 C6
Tolmezzo I 122 A2
Tolmin SLO 122 A2
Tolna H. 112 C2
Tolnanémedi H 112 C2
Tolob GB 33 B5
Tolosa
 E 144 A1
 P 155 B3
Tolox E. 162 B3
Tolpuddle GB. 43 B4
Tolva
 E 145 B4
 FIN 197 C11
Tolve I 172 B2
Tomar P 154 B2
Tomaševac SRB . . .126 B2
Tomašica BIH 124 C2
Tomášikovo SK. . . .111 A4
Tomašouka BY 13 C5
Tomášovce SK 99 C3
Tomaszów Mazowiecki
 PL. 87 A4
Tomatin GB 32 D3
Tombeboeuf F. 129 B3
Tomdoun GB. 32 D1
Tomelilla S. 66 A2
Tomellosa E. 151 B5
Tomelloso E. 157 A4
Tomiño E 140 C2
Tomintoul GB 32 D3
Tomislavgrad BIH 138 B3
Tomisław P. 84 A3
Tomisławice PL. 76 B3
Tomnavoulin GB. . . .32 D3
Tompa H. 126 A1
Tompaládony H. . . .111 B3
Tomra N 198 C3
Tomter N 54 A1
Tona E 147 C3
Tonara I 179 B3
Tonbridge GB 45 B4
Tondela P. 148 B1
Tønder DK. 64 B1
Tongeren B 79 B5
Tongue GB. 32 C2
Tönisvorst D 80 A2
Tønjum N. 47 A4
Tonkopuro FIN . .197 C11
Tonnay-Boutonne
 F. 114 C3
Tonnay-Charente
 F. 114 C3
Tonneins F. 129 B3
Tonnerre F 104 B2
Tonnes N 195 D4
Tönning D 64 B1
Tonsåsen N 47 B6
Tonstad N 52 B2
Toomyvara IRL 28 B3
Toormore IRL. 29 C2
Topares E. 164 B2
Topas E 150 A2
Topľa SRB 127 C2
Toplița RO 17 B6
Topola SRB 127 C2
Topolčani MK. 182 B3
Topol'čany SK 98 C2
Topol'čianky SK 98 C2
Topolje HR. 124 B2
Topólka PL. 76 B3
Topol'niky SK 111 B4
Topolovățu Mare
 RO 126 B3
Toponár H 125 A3
Toporów PL. 75 B4
Topsham GB 43 B3
Topusko HR. 124 B1
Toques E 140 B3
Torà E 147 C2
Toral de los Guzmanes
 E 142 B1
Toral de los Vados
 E 141 B4
Torbalı TR 188 A2
Torbjörntorp S. 55 B4
Torbole I. 121 B3
Torchiarolo I 173 B4
Torcross GB. 43 B3
Torcy-le-Petit F 89 A5
Torda SRB 126 B2
Tørdal N. 53 A4
Tordehumos E. 142 C1
Tordera E. 147 C3
Tordesillas E. 150 A2
Tordesilos E 152 B2

Töre S 196 D5
Töreboda S 55 B5
Toreby DK. 65 B4
Torekov S. 61 C2
Torella dei Lombardi
 I. 170 C3
Torelló E. 147 B3
Toreno E 141 B4
Torfou F. 114 A2
Torgau D 83 A5
Torgelow D 74 A3
Torgueda P 148 A2
Torhamn S 63 B3
Torhop N 193 B11
Torhout B 78 A3
Torigni-sur-Vire F . .88 A3
Torija E. 151 B4
Toril E. 152 B2
Torino = Turin I . . .119 B4
Toritto I. 171 C4
Torkovichi RUS. 9 C7
Torla E 145 B3
Tormac RO. 126 B3
Törmänen FIN . . .193 D11
Tormestorp S. 61 C3
Tórmini I 121 B3
Tornada P 154 B1
Tornal'a SK 99 C4
Tornavacas E 150 B2
Tornby DK. 58 A2
Tornesch D 72 A2
Torness GB 32 D2
Torniella I 135 B4
Tornimparte I 169 A3
Torning DK. 59 B2
Tornio FIN 196 D7
Tornjoš SRB 126 B1
Tornos E 152 B2
Toro E 150 A2
Törökszentmiklós
 H 113 B4
Toropets RUS 9 D7
Torpa S. 61 C3
Torpè I 178 B3
Torphins GB 33 D4
Torpo N 47 B5
Torpoint GB. 42 B2
Torpsbruk S 62 A2
Torquay GB 43 B3
Torquemada E 142 B2
Torralba de Burgo
 E 151 A5
Torralba de Calatrava
 E 157 A4
Torrão P 154 C2
Torre Annunziata
 I. 170 C2
Torreblacos E 143 C4
Torreblanca E 153 B4
Torreblascopedro
 E 157 B4
Torrecaballeros E . .151 A3
Torrecampo E 156 B3
Torre Canne I 173 B3
Torre Cardela E . . .163 A4
Torrecilla E 152 B1
Torrecilla de la Jara
 E 156 A3
Torrecilla de la Orden
 E 150 A2
Torrecilla del Pinar
 E 151 A3
Torrecilla en Cameros
 E 143 B4
Torrecillas de la Tiesa
 E 156 A2
Torre das Vargens
 P 154 B3
Torre de Coelheiros
 P 154 C3
Torre de Dom Chama
 P 149 A2
Torre de Juan Abad
 E 157 B4
Torre de la Higuera
 E 161 B3
Torre del Bierzo E 141 B4
Torre del Burgo E .151 B4
Torre del Campo
 E 163 A4
Torre del Greco I . .170 C2
Torre del Lago Puccini
 I. 134 B3
Torre dell'Orso I . . .173 B4
Torre del Mar E . . .163 B3
Torredembarra E . .147 C2
Torre de Miguel
 Sesmero E 155 C4
Torre de Moncorvo
 P 149 A2
Torre de Santa Maria
 E 156 A1
Torredonjimeno E 163 A4
Torre do Terranho
 P 148 B2
Torre Faro I 177 A4
Torregrosa E 147 C1
Torreira P 148 B1
Torrejoncillo E 155 B4
Torrejón de Ardoz
 E 151 B4
Torrejón de la Calzada
 E 151 B4
Torrejón del Rey
 E 151 B4
Torrejon el Rubio
 E 156 A1
Torrelaguna E 151 B4
Torrelapaja E 152 A2
Torre la Ribera E . .145 B4
Torrelavega E 142 A2
Torrelobatón E 150 A2
Torrelodones E 151 B4
Torre los Negros
 E 152 B2
Torremaggiore I . . .171 B3
Torremanzanas E .159 C3
Torremayor E. 155 C4
Torremezzo di
 Falconara I 174 B2

Torremocha E 156 A1
Torremolinos E 163 B3
Torrenieri I 135 B4
Torrenostra E 153 B4
Torrenova I 168 B2
Torrent E 159 B3
Torrente de Cinca
 E. 153 A4
Torrenueva
 Ciudad Real E. . .157 B4
 Granada E 163 B4
Torreorgaz E 155 B4
Torre Orsáia I. 172 B1
Torre-Pacheco E . .165 B4
Torre Péllice I 119 C4
Torreperogil E 157 B4
Torres E 163 A4
Torresandino E 143 C3
Torre Santa Susanna
 I 173 B3
Torres-Cabrera E . .163 A3
Torres de la Alameda
 E 151 B4
Torres Novas P . . .154 B2
Torres Vedras P. . .154 B1
Torrevieja E 165 B4
Torricella I 173 B3
Torri del Benaco I .121 B3
Torridon GB. 31 B3
Torriglia I 134 A2
Torrijos E 151 C3
Tørring DK. 59 C2
Torrita di Siena I . .135 B4
Torroal P 154 C2
Torroella de Montgrí
 E 147 B4
Torrox E 163 B4
Torrskog S 54 A3
Torsåker S 50 B3
Torsang S 50 B2
Torsås S. 63 B4
Torsby S 49 B4
Torsetra N 48 B2
Torshälla S. 56 A2
Tórshavn FO 4 A3
Torslanda S 60 B1
Torsnes N 46 B3
Törtel H 113 B3
Törtoles E 150 B2
Tórtoles de Esgueva
 E 142 C2
Tortol i I 179 C3
Tortona I 120 C1
Tórtora I 174 B1
Tortoreto Lido I . . .136 C2
Tortorici I 177 A3
Tortosa E 153 B4
Tortosendo P. 148 B2
Tortuera E 152 B2
Tortuero E 151 B4
Toruń PL 76 A3
Torup S 60 C3
Tor Vaiánica I. 168 B2
Torver GB. 36 B3
Tørvikbygde N. 46 B3
Torviscón E 163 B4
Torzhok RUS 9 D9
Torzym PL. 75 B4
Tosbotn N 195 E3
Toscelanor-Maderno
 I 121 B3
Tosno RUS. 9 C7
Tossa de Mar E . . .147 C3
Tossåsen S 199 C10
Tosse F 128 C1
Tösse S 54 B3
Tossicia I 169 A3
Tosya TR 23 A8
Tószeg H 113 B4
Toszek PL. 86 B2
Totana E 165 B3
Totebo S. 62 A4
Tôtes F 89 A5
Tótkomlós H 113 C4
Totland N 198 D2
Tøtlandsvik N 52 A2
Totnes GB 43 B3
Tótszerdahely H . .124 A2
Tøttdal N 199 A8
Totton GB 44 C2
Touça P 149 A2
Toucy F 104 B2

Tovdal N. 53 B4
Towcester GB 44 A3
Town Yetholm GB . .35 C5
Tråastølen N 47 B4
Trabada E 141 A3
Trabadelo E. 141 B4
Trabanca E 149 A3
Trabazos E. 149 A3
Traben-Trarbach D .92 B3
Trabia I. 176 B2
Tradate I 120 B1
Trädet S 60 B3
Trafaria P 154 C1
Tragacete E 152 B2
Tragwein A. 96 C2
Traiguera E 153 B4
Trainel F. 91 C3
Traisen A 110 A2
Traismauer A 97 C3
Traitsching D. 95 B4
Trákhonas CY 181 A2
Tralee IRL. 29 B2
Tramacastilla de Tena
 E 145 B3
Tramagal P. 154 B2
Tramariglio I 178 B2
Tramatza I 179 B2
Tramelan CH 106 B2
Tramonti di Sopra
 I 122 A1
Tramore IRL. 30 B1
Tramòpot F 92 C1
Trana I 119 B4
Tranås S. 55 B5
Tranbjerg DK. 59 B3
Tranby N 54 A1
Trancoso P 148 B2
Tranebjerg DK. 59 C3
Tranekær DK 65 B3
Tranemo S. 60 B3
Tranent GB. 35 C5
Tranevåg N 52 B2
Trängslet S 49 A5
Tranhult S 60 B3
Trani I 171 B4
Trans-en-Provence
 F. 132 B2
Transtrand S 49 A5
Tranum DK. 58 A2
Tranvik N 57 A4
Trápani I 176 A1
Trappes F. 90 C2
Traryd S 61 C3
Trasacco I 169 B3
Trasierra E 156 B1
Träslövsläge S 60 B2
Trasmiras E 140 B3
Traspinedo E. 150 A3
Trate SLO 110 C2
Trauchgau D 108 B1
Traun A. 110 A1
Traunreut D 109 B3
Traunstein D 109 B3
Traunwalchen D . .109 B3
Tråvad S. 55 B4
Travemünde D 65 C3
Traversétolo I 120 C3
Travnik
 BIH 139 A3
 SLO 123 B3
Travo
 F. 180 B2
 I 120 C2
Trawsfynydd GB . . .38 B3
Trbovlje SLO 123 A4
Trbušani SRB 127 D2
Trebatsch D 74 B3
Trebbin D. 74 B2
Třebechovice pod
 Orebem CZ 85 B3
Trebel D 73 B4
Třebenice CZ. 84 B1
Trébeurden F. 100 A2
Třebíč CZ. 97 B3
Trebinje BIH. 139 C4
Trebisacce I 174 B2
Trebitz D 83 A4
Trebnje SLO. 123 B4
Třeboň CZ 96 B2
Třebovice CZ. 97 B4
Trebsen D 83 A4
Trebujena E 161 C3
Trecastagni I 177 B4
Trecate I. 120 B1
Trecenta I 121 B4
Tredegar GB 39 C3
Tredózio I. 135 A4
Treffen A. 109 C4
Treffort F 118 A2
Treffurt D. 82 A2
Trefnant GB. 38 A3
Tregaron GB 39 B3
Trégastel-Plage F .100 A2
Tregnago I 121 B4
Tregony GB. 42 B2
Tréguier F. 100 A2
Trégunc F 100 B2
Treharris GB. 39 C3
Trehörningsjö S . .200 C4
Tréia I 136 B2
Treignac F. 116 B1
Treignat F 116 A2
Treignes B 91 A4
Treis-Karden D 80 B3
Trekanten S 63 B4
Trélazé F 102 B1
Trelech GB. 39 C2
Trélissac F 129 A3
Trelleborg S 66 A2
Trélon F 91 A4
Trélou-sur-Marne F .91 B3
Tremblay-le-Vicomte
 F. 89 B5
Tremés P 154 B2
Tremezzo I 120 B2
Třemošná CZ. 96 B1
Tremp E 145 B4

Trenčianska Stankovce
 SK 98 C1
Trenčianska Turná
 SK 98 C2
Trenčianske Teplá
 SK 98 C2
Trenčianske Teplice
 SK 98 C2
Trenčín SK. 98 C2
Trendelburg D 81 A5
Trengereid N 46 B2
Trensacq F. 128 B2
Trent D 66 B2
Trento I 121 A4
Treorchy GB. 39 C3
Trept F 118 B2
Trepuzzi I 173 B4
Trescore Balneário
 I 120 B2
Tresenda I 120 A3
Tresfjord N. 198 C4
Tresigallo I. 121 C4
Trešnjevica SRB . .127 D3
Tresnurághes I . . .178 B2
Trespaderne E. . . .143 B3
Třešt CZ. 97 B3
Trestina I 135 B5
Tretower GB 39 C3
Trets F 132 B1
Tretten N 48 A2
Treuchtlingen D 94 C2
Treuen D 83 B4
Treuenbrietzen D . .74 B1
Treungen N 53 A4
Trevelez E 163 B4
Trevi I 136 C1
Treviana E 143 B3
Treviglio I 120 B2
Trevignano Romano
 I 168 A2
Trevi nel Lázio I . . .169 B3
Treviso I 122 B1
Trévoux F 117 B4
Trézelles F 117 A3
Trezzo sull'Adda I .120 B2
Trhová Kamenice
 CZ 97 B3
Trhové Sviny CZ. . .96 C2
Triacastela E 141 B3
Triaize F 114 B2
Trianda GR 188 C3
Triaucourt-en-Argonne
 F. 91 C5
Tribanj Krušcica
 HR 137 A4
Triberg D 106 A3
Tribsees D 66 B1
Tribuče SLO. 123 B4
Tricárico I 172 B2
Tricase I 173 C4
Tricésimo I. 122 A2
Trieben A 110 B1
Triebes D. 83 B4
Triepkendorf D 74 A2
Trier D 92 B2
Trieste I 122 B2
Trie-sur-Baïse F . .145 A4
Triggiano I 173 A2
Triglitz D 73 A5
Trignac F. 101 B3
Trigueros E 161 B3
Trigueros del Valle
 E 142 C2
Trikala GR 182 D3
Trikeri GR 183 D5
Trikomo CY 181 A2
Trilj HR. 138 B2
Trillo E 152 B1
Trilport F. 90 C2
Trim IRL 30 A2
Trimdon GB. 37 B5
Trindade
 Beja P 160 B2
 Bragança P 149 A2
Třinec CZ. 98 B2
Tring GB 44 B3
Trinità d'Agultu I . .178 A2
Trinitápoli I 171 B4
Trino I 119 B5
Trinta P 148 B2
Triora I 133 B3
Tripoli GR 184 B3
Triponzo I 136 C1
Triptis D 83 B3
Triste E 144 B3
Trittau D. 72 A3
Trivento I 170 B2
Trivero I 119 B5
Trivigno I 172 B1
Trn BIH 124 C3
Trnava
 HR 125 B4
 SK. 98 C1
Trnovec SK 112 A1
Trnovo BIH. 139 B4
Trnovska vas
 SLO 110 C2
Troarn F. 89 A3
Trochtelfingen D . . .94 C1
Trödje S. 51 B4
Troense DK. 65 A3
Trofa P 148 A1
Trofaiach A. 110 B2
Trofors N 195 E4
Trogir HR. 138 B2
Troia I 171 B3
Tróia P 154 C2
Troina I 177 B3
Troisdorf D 80 B3
Trois-Ponts B 80 B1
Troisvierges L 92 A2
Trojane SLO. 123 A3
Troldhede DK. 59 C1
Trollhättan S 54 B3
Trolog BIH 138 B2
Tromello I 120 B1
Tromøy N. 53 B4
Tromsø N 192 C3

Trondheim N 199 B7
Tronget F. 116 A3
Trönninge S. 61 C2
Trönningeby S. 60 B2
Trönö S 51 A3
Tronzano-Vercellese
 I. 119 B5
Trôo F. 102 B2
Troon GB 36 A2
Tropea I 175 C1
Tropy Sztumskie
 PL. 69 B4
Trosa S. 57 B3
Trösken S 50 B3
Trosly-Breuil F 90 B3
Trossingen D. 107 A3
Trostberg D. 109 A3
Trouville-sur-Mer F 89 A4
Trowbridge GB. 43 A4
Troyes F. 104 A3
Trpanj HR. 138 B3
Trpinja HR 125 B4
Trsće HR 123 B3
Třsice CZ. 98 B1
Trstená SK 99 B3
Trstenci BIH. 125 B3
Trsteno HR 139 C3
Trstice SK 111 A4
Trstin SK 98 C1
Trubia E 141 A5
Trubjela MNE. 139 C4
Truchas E 141 B4
Trujillanos E 155 C4
Trujillo E 156 A2
Trumieje PL 69 B4
Trun
 CH 107 C3
 F. 89 B4
Truro GB 42 B1
Trusetal D 82 B2
Truskavets' UA 13 D5
Trustrup DK. 59 B3
Trutnov CZ. 85 B3
Truze PL 86 A1
Tryszczyn PL. 76 A2
Trzcianka PL 75 A5
Trzciel PL. 75 B4
Trzcińsko Zdrój PL .74 B3
Trzebiatów PL. 67 B4
Trzebiel PL. 84 A2
Trzebielino PL. 68 A2
Trzebień PL. 84 A3
Trzebiez PL 74 A3
Trzebinia PL. 86 B3
Trzebnica PL 85 A5
Trzebnice PL 85 A4
Trzeciewiec PL 76 A3
Trzemeszno PL 76 B2
Trzemeszno-Lubuskie
 PL. 75 B4
Trzetrzewina PL. . . .99 B4
Tržič SLO 123 A3
Tsamandas GR . . .182 D2
Tschagguns A 107 B4
Tschernitz D 84 A2
Tsebrykove UA 17 B9
Tsyelyakhany BY. . .13 B6
Tua P 148 A2
Tuam IRL 28 A3
Tubbergen NL 71 B3
Tubilla del Lago E 143 C3
Tübingen D 93 C5
Tubize B. 79 B4
Tučapy CZ 96 B2
Tučepi HR 138 B3
Tuchan F 146 B3
Tüchen D 73 A5
Tuchola PL 76 A2
Tuchomie PL. 68 A2
Tuchów PL. 99 B5
Tuczno PL 75 A5
Tuddal N. 53 A4
Tudela E. 144 B2
Tudela de Duero
 E 150 A3
Tudweiliog GB. 38 B2
Tuejar E 159 B2
Tuffé F 102 A2
Tufsingdalen N . . .199 C8
Tuhaň CZ. 84 B2
Tui E 140 B2
Tukhkala RUS . .197 D13
Tukums LV 8 D3
Tula I 178 B2
Tulcea RO 17 C8
Tul'chyn UA 13 D8
Tulette F 131 A3
Tuliszków PL. 76 B3
Tulla IRL 28 B3
Tullamore IRL 30 A1
Tulle F 116 B1
Tullins F 118 B2
Tulln A 97 C4
Tullow IRL 30 B2
Tułowice PL. 85 B5
Tulppio FIN 197 B12
Tulsk IRL 28 A3
Tumba S. 57 A3
Tummel Bridge GB .35 B3
Tun S 55 B3
Tuna
 Kalmar S. 62 A4
 Uppsala S 51 B5
Tuna Hästberg S. . .50 B2
Tunçbilek TR 187 C4
Tunes P 160 B1
Tungelsta S 57 A4
Tunnerstad S. 55 B5
Tunnhovd N 47 B5
Tunstall GB 45 A5
Tuohikotti FIN 8 B5
Tuoro sul Trasimeno
 I 135 B5
Tupadły PL 76 B3
Tupanari BIH 139 A4
Tupik RUS 9 E8
Tuplice PL 84 A2
Tura H. 112 B3
Turanj HR. 137 A4

Turany SK 99 B3
Turbe BIH. 139 A3
Turbenthal CH 107 B3
Turcia E 141 B5
Turčianske Teplice
 SK 98 C2
Turcifal P 154 B1
Turckheim F. 106 A2
Turda RO 17 B5
Turégano E 151 A4
Turek PL. 76 B3
Türgovishte BG. . . .17 D7
Turgutlu TR 188 A2
Turi I 173 B3
Turin = Torino I . . .119 B4
Turis E 159 B3
Türje H 111 C4
Turka UA 12 D5
Túrkeve H 113 B4
Türkheim D 108 A1
Türkmenli TR. 186 C1
Turku FIN 8 B3
Turleque E 157 A4
Turňa nad Bodvou
 SK 99 C4
Turnberry GB. 36 A2
Turnhout B. 79 A4
Türnitz A. 110 B2
Turnov CZ 84 B3
Turnu RO 126 A3
Turnu Măgurele
 RO 17 D6
Turón E 164 C1
Turoszów PL 84 B2
Turowo PL. 77 A5
Turquel P 154 B1
Turri I 179 C2
Turries F. 132 A2
Turriff GB. 33 D4
Tursi I 174 A2
Turtmann CH 119 A4
Turtola FIN. 196 C6
Turze PL. 86 A1
Turzovka SK 98 B2
Tusa I 177 B3
Tuscánia I 168 A1
Tuse DK 61 D1
Tušilovic HR 123 B4
Tuszyn PL. 86 A3
Tutow D 66 C2
Tutrakan BG. 17 C7
Tuttlingen D 107 B3
Tutzing D 108 B2
Tuzla
 BIH 125 C4
 TR. 23 C8
Tuzlukçu TR. 189 A6
Tvååker S 60 B2
Tväralund S 200 B5
Tvärskog S 63 B4
Tvedestrand N 53 B4
Tveit
 Hordaland N 47 B4
 Rogaland N 52 A2
Tver RUS 9 D9
Tverrelvmo N. 192 D3
Tversted DK. 58 A3
Tving S. 63 B3
Tvrdošin SK. 99 B3
Tvrdošovce SK . . .112 A2
Twardogóra PL. 85 A5
Twatt GB 33 B3
Twello NL. 70 B3
Twimberg A 110 C1
Twist D 71 B4
Twistringen D 72 B1
Tworóg PL. 86 B2
Twyford
 Hampshire GB . . .44 B2
 Wokingham GB . .44 B3
Tyachiv UA. 17 A5
Tychówka PL 67 C5
Tychowo PL. 67 C5
Tychy PL 86 B2
Tydal N. 199 B8
Týec nad Labem
 CZ 97 A3
Tynemouth GB 37 A5
Tyngsjö S 49 B5
Týništěnad Orlicí
 CZ 85 B4
Týn nad Vltavou
 CZ 96 B2
Tynset N. 199 C7
Tyresö S. 57 A4
Tyringe S 61 C3
Tyrislöt S 56 B2
Tyristrand N. 48 B2
Tyrrellspass IRL . . .30 A1
Tysnes N 46 B2
Tysse N 46 B2
Tyssebotn N 46 B2
Tyssedal N. 46 B3
Tystberga S. 56 B3
Tysvær N 52 A1
Tywyn GB. 39 B2
Tzermiado GR 185 D6
Tzummarum NL. . . .70 A2

U

Ub SRB 127 C2
Ubby DK. 61 D1
Úbeda E. 157 B4
Überlingen D. 107 B4
Ubidea E 143 A4
Ubli HR. 138 C2
Ubrique E 162 B2
Ucero E 143 C3
Uchaud F. 131 B3

Uchte D 72 B1
Uckerath D. 80 B3
Uckfield GB 45 C4
Ucklum S. 54 B2
Uclés E. 151 C5
Ucria I. 177 A3
Udbina HR 137 A4
Uddebo S. 60 B3
Uddeholm S. 49 B5
Uddevalla S. 54 B2
Uddheden S. 49 C4
Uden NL. 80 A1
Uder D 82 A2
Udiča SK 98 B2
Udine I. 122 A2
Udvar H 125 B4
Ueckermünde D . . .74 A3
Uelsen D 71 B3
Uelzen D 73 B3
Uetendorf CH 106 C2
Uetersen D. 72 A2
Uetze D 72 B3
Uffculme GB 43 B3
Uffenheim D 94 B2
Ugarana E 143 A4
Ugento I. 173 C4
Ugerlde DK 61 D1
Uggerby DK 58 A3
Uggerslev DK 59 C3
Uggiano la Chiesa
I. 173 B4
Ugijar E 164 C1
Ugine F 118 B3
Uglejevik BIH 125 C5
Uglenes N 46 B2
Uglich RUS 9 D11
Ugljane HR 138 B2
Ugod H. 111 B4
Uherské Hradiště
CZ 98 B1
Uherský Brod CZ . .98 B1
Uherský Ostroh
CZ 98 C1
Uhingen D 94 C1
Uhlířské-Janovice
CZ 96 B3
Uhřiněves CZ 96 A2
Uhyst D 84 A2
Uig GB 31 B2
Uitgeest NL 70 B1
Uithoorn NL 70 B1
Uithuizen NL 71 A3
Uithuizermeeden
NL 71 A3
Uivar RO 126 B2
Ujazd
Łódzkie PL 87 A3
Opolskie PL 86 B2
Ujezd u Brna CZ . . .97 B4
Ujhartyán H 112 B3
Ujkigyós H 113 C5
Ujpetre H 125 B4
Ujście PL 75 A5
Ujsolt H 112 C3
Ujszász H. 113 B4
Ujszentmargita H .113 B5
Ujué E 144 B2
Ukanc SLO. 122 A2
Ukmergė LT 13 A6
Ukna S. 56 B2
Ula TR 188 B3
Ulaş TR 186 A2
Ulássai I. 179 C3
Ulbjerg DK 58 B2
Ulbster GB 32 C3
Ulceby GB 40 B3
Ulcinj MNE. 16 E3
Uldum DK 59 C2
Ulefoss N. 53 A5
Uleila del Campo
E 164 B2
Ulëz AL. 182 B1
Uljma SRB 127 B3
Ullånger S 200 C4
Ullapool GB 32 D1
Ullared S 60 B2
Ullatti S 196 B4
Ullatun N 52 A2
Ulldecona E 153 B4
Ulldemolins E 147 C1
Ullerslev DK. 59 C3
Ullervad S 55 B4
Üllés H 126 A1
Üllő H 112 B3
Ulm D. 94 C1
Ulme P 154 B2
Ulmen D. 80 B2
Ulnes N 47 B6
Ulog BIH 139 B4
Ulricehamn S. 60 B3
Ulrichstein D 81 B5
Ulrika S 56 B1
Ulriksfors S 200 C1
Ulrum NL 71 A3
Ulsberg N. 198 C6
Ulsta GB. 33 A5
Ulsted DK. 58 A3
Ulsteinvik N. 198 C2
Ulstrup
Vestsjællands Amt.
DK 59 C3
Viborg Amt. DK . .59 B2
Ulsvåg N 194 B6
Ulubey TR 188 A4
Uluborlu TR 189 A5
Ulukışla TR 23 C8
Ulverston GB. 36 B3
Ulvik N 46 B3
Umag HR 122 B2
Uman UA 13 D9
Umba RUS 3 C14
Umbértide I. 135 B5
Umbriático I. 174 B2
Umčari SRB. 127 C2
Umeå S 200 C6
Umgransele S. 200 B4
Umhausen A 108 B1
Umka SRB. 127 C2

Umljanovic HR . . .138 B2
Umnäs S 195 E7
Umurbey TR 186 B1
Unaðsdalur IS 190 A3
Unapool GB. 32 C1
Unari FIN 197 B8
Uncastillo E. 144 B2
Undenäs S. 55 B5
Undersaker S 199 B10
Undredal N 46 B4
Unešić HR 138 B2
Úněšov CZ. 96 B1
Ungheni MD. 17 B7
Unhais da Serra P .148 B2
Unhošt CZ. 84 B2
Unichowo PL. 68 A2
Uničov CZ. 98 B1
Uniejów PL. 76 C3
Unisław PL. 76 A3
Unkel D 80 B3
Unken A 109 B3
Unna D 81 A3
Unnaryd S 60 C3
Unquera E 142 A2
Unterach A. 109 B4
Unterägeri CH 107 B3
Unterammergau D 108 B2
Unterhaching D. . .108 A2
Unteriberg CH 107 B3
Unterkochen D 94 C2
Unter Langkampfen
A. 108 B3
Unterlaussa A 110 B1
Unterlüss D 72 B3
Untermünkheim D .94 B1
Unterschächen
CH 107 C3
Unterschleissheim
D 95 C3
Unterschwaningen
D 94 B2
Untersiemau D 82 B2
Unter-steinbach D .94 B2
Unterweissenbach
A. 96 C2
Unterzell D. 95 B4
Upavon GB 44 B2
Upice CZ. 85 B4
Upiłka PL 68 B2
Upphärad S 54 B3
Uppingham GB 40 C3
Upplanda-Väsby S .57 A3
Uppsala S. 51 C4
Uppsjøhytta N 48 A1
Upton-upon-Severn
GB 39 B4
Ur F 146 B2
Uras I. 179 C2
Uraz PL. 85 A4
Urbánia I. 136 B1
Urbino I. 136 B1
Urçay F 103 C4
Urda E 157 A4
Urdax E 144 A2
Urdilde E 140 B2
Urdos F 145 B3
Urk NL. 70 B2
Úrkút H. 111 B4
Urla TR. 188 A1
Urlingford IRL 30 B1
Urnäsch CH. 107 B4
Urnes N 47 A4
Uroševac KOS. 16 D4
Urracal E 164 B2
Urries E 144 B2
Urroz E. 144 B2
Ursensollen D 95 B3
Urshult S 63 B2
Uršna Sela SLO. . .123 B4
Urszulewo PL. 77 B4
Ury F 90 C2
Urziceni RO. 17 C7
Urzulei I. 178 B3
Uşak TR. 187 D4
Usedom D 66 C2
Useldange L. 92 B1
Uséllus I. 179 C2
Ushakovo RUS 69 A5
Usingen D 81 B4
Usini I. 178 B2
Usk GB. 39 C4
Uskedal N 46 C2
Üsküdar TR. 186 A4
Uslar D 82 A1
Úsov CZ. 97 B5
Usquert NL. 71 A3
Ussássai I. 179 C3
Ussé F 102 B2
Usséglio I. 119 B4
Ussel
Cantal F 116 B2
Corrèze F. 116 B2
Usson-du-Poitou
F. 115 B4
Usson-en-Forez F .117 B3
Usson-les-Bains
F. 146 B3
Ustaoset N 47 B5
Ustaritz F. 144 A2
Uštěk CZ 84 B2
Uster CH 107 B3
Ústí CZ. 98 B1
Ustikolina BIH 139 B4
Ústí nad Labem CZ .84 B2
Ústí nad Orlicí CZ. .97 B4
Ustiprača BIH 139 B5
Ustka PL. 68 A1
Ust Luga RUS 8 C6
Ustroń PL. 98 B2
Ustronie Morskie
PL. 67 B4
Ustyuzhna RUS. . . .9 C10
Uszód H. 112 C2
Utåker H 52 A1
Utansjö S 200 D3
Utebo E 152 A3
Utena LT. 13 A6
Utery CZ. 95 B5

Uthaug N 198 B6
Utiel E 159 B2
Utne N 46 B3
Utö S 57 B4
Utrecht NL. 70 B2
Utrera E 162 A2
Utrillas E 153 B3
Utsjoki FIN 193 C11
Utstein kloster N . . .52 A1
Uttendorf A 109 B3
Uttenweiler D. 107 A4
Utterslev DK 65 B4
Uttoxeter GB 40 C2
Utvälinge S 61 C2
Utvorda N 199 A7
Uusikaarlepyy FIN . .3 E8
Uusikaupunki FIN . . .8 B2
Uvaly CZ. 96 A2
Uvdal N 47 B5
Uza F 128 B1
Uzdin SRB. 126 B2
Uzdowo PL. 77 A5
Uzein F. 145 A3
Uzel F. 100 A3
Uzerche F 116 B1
Uzès F 131 A3
Uzhhorod UA. 12 D5
Uzhok UA. 12 D5
Užice SRB. 127 D1
Uznach CH. 107 B3
Üzümlü
Konya TR. 189 B6
Muğla TR 188 C4
Uzunköprü TR. . . .186 A1

V

Vaalajärvi FIN 197 B9
Vaas F 102 B2
Vaasa FIN. 8 A2
Vaasen NL. 70 B2
Vabre F. 130 B1
Vác H 112 B3
Vacha D 82 B2
Váchartyán H 112 B3
Väckelsång S 63 B2
Vacqueyras F 131 A3
Vad S. 50 B2
Vada I 134 B3
Väddö S 51 C5
Väderstad S 55 B5
Vadheim N. 46 A2
Vadillo de la Sierra
E 150 B2
Vadillos E. 152 B1
Vadla N. 52 A2
Vado I 135 A4
Vado Lìgure I. 133 A4
Vadsø N. 193 B13
Vadstena S 55 B5
Vadum DK 58 A2
Vaduz FL. 107 B4
Vafos N 53 B5
Våg H 111 B4
Vågåmo N 198 D6
Væggerløse DK. . . .65 B4
Vaggeryd S 62 A2
Vaghia GR 184 A4
Vàglia I. 135 B4
Vàglio Basilicata I .172 B1
Vagney F 106 A1
Vagnhärad S 57 B3
Vagnsunda S 57 A4
Vaiano I. 135 B4
Vaiges F 102 A1
Vaihingen D 93 C4
Vaillant F 105 B4
Vailly-sur-Aisne F . .91 B3
Vailly-sur Sauldre
F. 103 B4
Vairano Scalo I . . .170 B2
Vaison-la-Romaine
F. 131 A4
Vaite F 105 B4
Väjern S 54 B2
Vajszló H 125 B3
Vaksdal N. 46 B2
Vál H. 112 B2
Valaam RUS. 9 B7
Valada P. 154 B2
Váladalen S 199 B10
Valadares P 148 A1
Valado P. 154 B1
Valandovo MK. . . .182 B4
Valašská SK. 99 B3
Valaská Belá SK. . .98 C2
Valašská Dubová
SK. 99 B3
Valašská Polanka
CZ 98 B1
Valašské Klobouky
CZ 98 B2
Valašské Meziříčí
CZ 98 B1
Valberg F 132 A2
Vålberg S 55 A4
Valbo S. 51 B4
Valbom P 148 A1
Valbondione I 120 A3
Valbonnais F 118 C2
Valbuena de Duero
E 142 C2
Vălcani RO. 126 B2
Valdagno I. 121 B4
Valdahon F 105 B5
Valdaracete E 151 B4
Valday RUS 9 D8
Valdealgorfa E. . . .153 B3
Valdecaballeros E 156 A2
Valdecabras E 152 B1
Valdecarros E 150 B2
Valdeconcha E 151 B5
Valdeflores E 161 B3
Valdeganga E 158 B2
Valdelacasa E. 150 B2

Valdelacasa de Tajo
E. 156 A2
Valdelarco E 161 B3
Valdelosa E 149 A4
Valdeltormo E 153 B4
Valdemanco de Esteras
E 156 B3
Valdemarsvik S 56 B2
Valdemorillo E. . . .151 B3
Valdemoro E 151 B4
Valdemoro Sierra
E. 152 B2
Valdenoceda E 143 B3
Valdeobispo E 149 B3
Valdeolivas E 152 B1
Valdepeñas E 157 B4
Valdepeñas de Jaén
E. 163 A4
Valdepiélago E 142 B1
Valdepolo E 142 B1
Valderas E 142 B1
Valdérice I 176 A1
Valderrobres E 153 B4
Valderrueda E 142 B2
Val de San Lorenzo
E 141 B4
Val de Santo Domingo
E 150 B3
Val d'Esquières F .132 B2
Valdestillas E 150 A3
Valdetorres E 156 B1
Valdetorres de Jarama
E 151 B4
Valdeverdeja E 150 C2
Valdevimbre E 142 B1
Valdieri I. 133 A3
Valdilecha E 151 B4
Val-d'Isère F 119 B3
Valdobbiàdene I . . .121 B4
Valdocondes E 143 C3
Valdoviño E 140 A2
Valea lui Mihai RO . .16 B5
Vale de Açor
Beja P 160 B2
Portalegre P . . .154 B3
Vale de Agua P . . .160 B1
Vale de Cambra P .148 B1
Vale de Lobo P . . .160 B1
Vale de Prazeres
P 148 B2
Vale de Reis P 154 C2
Vale de Rosa P . . .160 B2
Vale de Santarém
P 154 B2
Vale de Vargo P . . .160 B2
Vale do Peso P . . .155 B3
Valega P. 148 B1
Valéggio sul Mincio
I 121 B3
Valeiro P. 154 C2
Valença P. 140 B2
Valençay F 103 B3
Valence
Charente F. 115 C4
Drôme F. 117 C4
Valence d'Agen F .129 B3
Valence d'Albigeois
F. 130 A1
Valence-sur-Baise
F. 129 C3
Valencia E 159 B3
Valencia de Alcántara
E 155 B3
Valencia de Don Juan
E 142 B1
Valencia de las Torres
E 156 B1
Valencia del Ventoso
E 161 A3
Valencia de Mombuey
E 161 A2
Valenciennes F 79 B3
Valensole F 132 B1
Valentano I. 168 A1
Valentigney F 106 B1
Valentine F 145 A4
Valenza I 120 B1
Valenzuela E 163 A3
Valenzuela de
Calatrava E 157 B4
Våler
Hedmark N 48 B3
Østfold N 54 A1
Valera de Abajo E .158 B1
Valeria E 158 B1
Valestrand N 52 A1
Valestrandsfossen
N 46 B2
Valevåg N. 52 A1
Valfabbrica I 136 B1
Valflaunes F. 131 B2
Valga EST. 8 D5
Valgorge F 131 A3
Valgrisenche I 119 B4
Valguarnera Caropepe
I. 177 B3
Valhelhas P. 148 B2
Valjevo SRB. 127 C1
Valka LV. 8 D4
Valkeakoski FIN 8 B4
Valkenburg NL. 80 B1
Valkenswaard NL . .79 A5
Valkó H. 112 B3
Valla S. 56 A2
Valladares E 140 B2
Valladolid E. 150 A3
Vallákra S. 61 D2
Vallata I 172 A1
Vallberga S 61 C3
Vall d'Alba E 153 B3
Valldemossa E 166 B2
Valle N 52 A3
Valle Castellana I. .136 C2
Valle de Abdalajís
E 163 B3
Valle de Cabuérniga
E 142 A2

Valle de la Serena
E 156 B2
Valle de Matamoros
E 155 C4
Valle de Santa Ana
E 155 C4
Valledolmo I. 176 B2
Valledoria I. 178 B2
Vallelado E. 150 A3
Vallelunga Pratameno
I 176 B2
Valle Mosso I. 119 B5
Vallen
Asturias E 142 A1
Asturias E 142 A1
Vallendar D 81 B3
Vallentuna S 57 A4
Valleraugue F 130 A2
Vallermosa I. 179 C2
Vallet F. 101 B4
Valletta M. 175 C3
Valley GB. 38 A2
Vallfogona de Riucorb
E 147 C2
Valli del Pasúbio I 121 B4
Vallo della Lucánia
I. 172 B1
Valloire F 118 B3
Vallombrosa I 135 B4
Vallon-Pont-d'Arc
F. 131 A3
Vallorbe CH 105 C5
Vallouise F 118 C3
Valls E 147 C2
Vallset N. 48 B3
Vallsta S. 50 A3
Vallstena S. 57 C4
Valmadrid E 153 A3
Valmiera LV 8 D4
Valmojado E 151 B3
Valmont F 89 A4
Valmontone I 169 B2
Valö S. 51 B5
Valognes F 88 A2
Valonga P. 148 B1
Valongo P. 148 A1
Válor E. 164 C1
Valoria la Buena
E 142 C2
Valøy N. 199 A7
Valpaços P. 148 A2
Valpelline I. 119 B4
Valpiana I. 135 B3
Valpovo HR 125 B4
Valras-Plage F 130 B2
Valréas F 131 A3
Vals CH 107 C4
Valsavarenche I. . .119 B4
Valsequillo E 156 B2
Valsjöbyn S 199 A11
Vals-les-Bains F . . .117 C4
Valsonne F 117 B4
Valstagna I 121 B4
Valtablado del Rio
E 152 B1
Val Thorens F 118 B3
Valtice CZ 97 C4
Valtiendas E 151 A4
Valtierra E 144 B2
Valtopina I. 136 B1
Valtorta I 120 B2
Valtournenche I. . .119 B4
Valverde E 144 C2
Valverde de Burguillos
E 155 C4
Valverde de Júcar
E 158 B1
Valverde de la Vera
E 150 B2
Valverde de la Virgen
E 142 B1
Valverde del Camino
E 161 B3
Valverde del Fresno
E 149 B3
Valverde de Llerena
E 156 B2
Valverde de Mérida
E 156 B1
Valvträsk S 196 C4
Vamberk CZ. 85 B4
Vamdrup DK 59 C2
Våmhus S 50 A1
Vamlingbo S 57 D4
Vamos GR 185 D5
Vámosmikola H. . . .112 B2
Vámosszabadi H. . .111 B4
Vanault-les-Dames
F 91 C4
Vandel DK 59 C2
Vandenesse F 104 C2
Vandenesse-en-Auxois
F 104 B3
Vandóies I. 108 C2
Väne-Åsaka S 54 B3
Vänersborg S 54 B3
Vänersnäs S 54 B3
Vang N 47 A5
Vänge S 51 C4
Vangsnes N. 46 A3
Vänjaurbäck S. . . .200 B4
Vänjaurbäck S . . .200 B4
Vännacka S 54 A3
Vannareid N 192 B3
Vännäs S 200 C5
Vannes F 101 B3
Vannsätter S 51 A3
Vannvåg N 192 B3
Vansbro S 49 B6
Vanse N 52 B2
Vantaa FIN. 8 B4
Vanttauskoski
FIN. 197 C9
Vanviken N 199 B7
Vanyarc H 112 B3
Vaour F 129 B4
Vapnyarka UA 13 D8
Vaprio d'Adda I. . .120 B2

Vaqueiros P. 160 B2
Vara S. 55 B3
Varacieux F 118 B2
Varades F. 101 B4
Varages F. 132 B1
Varaldsøy N. 46 B2
Varallo I. 119 B5
Varangerbotn N. . .193 B12
Varano de'Melegari
I. 120 C3
Varaždin HR. 124 A2
Varaždinske Toplice
HR 124 A2
Varazze I 133 A4
Varberg S. 60 B2
Vardal N 48 B2
Varde DK 59 C1
Vårdö FIN 51 B7
Varde D 71 A5
Varėna LT. 13 A6
Vårenes N 52 A1
Varengeville-sur-Mer
F. 89 A4
Varenna I 120 A2
Varennes-en-Argonne
F. 91 B5
Varennes-le-Grand
F. 105 C3
Varennes-St Sauveur
F. 105 C4
Varennes-sur-Allier
F 117 A3
Varennes-sur-Amance
F. 105 B4
Vareš BIH 139 A4
Varese I 120 B1
Varese Lìgure I . . .134 A2
Vârfurile RO. 16 B5
Vårgårda S. 60 A2
Vargas
E 143 A3
P 154 B2
Vargön S 54 B3
Varhaug N 52 B1
Variaşu Mic RO. . .126 A3
Varilhes F. 146 A2
Varin SK 98 B2
Väring S 55 B4
Váriz P. 149 A3
Varkaus FIN. 8 A5
Varmahlíð IS 190 B6
Varmaland IS. 190 C4
Värmlands Bro S. . .55 A4
Värmskog S 55 A3
Varna
BG 17 D7
SRB 127 C1
Värnamo S. 60 B4
Varnhem S 55 B4
Varnsdorf CZ. 84 B2
Värö S. 60 B2
Varoška Rijeka
BIH 124 B1
Valpjófsstaður IS 191 B11
Városlöd H 111 B4
Várpalota H 112 B2
Varreddes F 90 C2
Vars F 118 C3
Varsi I 120 C2
Varssevald NL 71 C3
Vårsta S. 57 A3
Vartdal N 198 C3
Vartofta S 55 B4
Várvölgy H. 111 C4
Varzi I 120 C2
Varzjelas P 148 B1
Varzo I 119 A5
Varzy F 104 B2
Vasad H 112 B3
Väse S 55 A4
Vašica SRB 125 B5
Vasilevichi BY 13 B8
Väskinde S 57 C4
Vaskút H 125 A4
Vaslui RO. 17 B7
Vassbotn N 53 B4
Vassenden N. 47 A6
Vassieux-en-Vercors
F 118 C2
Vassmolösa S 63 B4
Vassy F 88 B3
Västanvik S 50 B1
Västeräs S 56 A2
Västerby S 50 B2
Västerfärnebo S. . .50 C3
Västergarn S 57 C4
Västerhaninge S . . .57 A4
Västervik S 62 A4
Västra Ämtervik S. .55 A4
Västra-Bodarne S . .60 B2
Västra Karup S 61 C2
Vasvár H 111 B3
Vasylkiv UA 13 C9
Vatan F 103 B3
Vätö S. 57 C4
Vatland N 52 B3
Vatnås N 48 C1
Vatne N 53 B3
Vatnestrøm N. 53 B4
Vätö S 51 C5
Vatra-Dornei RO . .17 B6
Vatry F 91 C4
Vattholma S 51 B4
Vättis CH 107 C4
Vauchamps F 91 C3
Vauchassis F 104 A2
Vaucouleurs F. 92 C1

Vaudoy-en-Brie F .90 C3
Vaulen N 52 B1
Vaulruz CH. 106 C1
Vaulx Vraucourt F . .90 A2
Vaumas F. 104 C2
Vausseroux F 115 B3
Vauvenargues F . .132 B1
Vauvert F 131 B3
Vauvillers F 105 B5
Vaux-sur-Sure B . . .92 B1
Vawkavysk BY. 13 B6
Vaxholm S 57 A4
Växjö S. 62 B2
Våxtorp S. 61 C3
Vayrac F 129 B4
Važec SK 99 B3
Veberöd S 61 D3
Vechelde D 72 B3
Vechta D 71 B5
Vecinos E. 149 B4
Vecsés H 112 B3
Vedavågen N 52 A1
Veddige S 60 B2
Vedersø DK 59 B1
Vedeseta I 120 B2
Vedevåg S 56 A1
Vedra E 140 B2
Vedum S 55 B3
Veendam NL 71 A3
Veenendaal NL 70 B2
Vega
Asturias E 142 A1
Asturias E 142 A1
Vega de Espinareda
E 141 B4
Vega de Infanzones
E 142 B1
Vegadeo E 141 A3
Vega de Pas E 143 A3
Vega de Valcarce
E 141 B4
Vega de Valdetronco
E 150 A2
Vegårshei N 53 B4
Vegas de Coria E .149 B3
Vegas del Condado
E 142 B1
Vegby S 60 B3
Vegger DK 58 B2
Veggli N 47 B6
Veghel NL. 80 A1
Veglast D 66 B1
Véglie I. 173 B3
Veguillas E. 151 B4
Vegusdal N 53 B4
Veidholmen N 198 B4
Veidnes N. 193 B10
Veikåker N 48 B1
Veinge S 61 C3
Vejbystrand S 61 C2
Vejen DK 59 C2
Vejer de la Frontera
E 162 B2
Vejle DK 59 C2
Vejprty CZ 83 B5
Velada E. 150 B3
Vela Luka HR. 138 C2
Velayos E 150 B3
Velbert D 80 A3
Velburg D 95 B3
Velde N. 199 A8
Velden
Bayern D 95 B3
Bayern D 95 C4
Velden am Worther See
A. 109 C5
Velefique F 164 B2
Velen D. 80 A2
Velenje SLO. 123 A4
Veles MK 182 B3
Velesevec HR 124 B2
Velešin CZ. 96 C2
Velestino GR 182 D4
Velez Blanco E . . .164 B2
Vélez de Benaudalla
E 163 B4
Vélez-Málaga E . . .163 B3
Vélez Rubio E 164 B2
Veliki Radinci
SRB 127 B1
Velika HR 125 B3
Velika Gorica HR . .124 B2
Velika Grdevac
HR 124 B3
Velika Greda SRB .126 B3
Velika Ilova BIH . . .125 C3
Velika Kladuša
BIH 124 B1
Velika Kopanica
HR 125 B4
Velika Krsna SRB .127 C2
Velika Obarska
BIH 125 C5
Velika Pisanica
HR 124 B3
Velika Plana SRB . .127 C3
Velika Zdenci HR . .124 B3
Velike Lašče SLO. .123 B3
Velike Središte
SRB 126 B3
Veliki Gaj SRB . . .126 B3
Veliki Popović
SRB 127 C3
Velikiye Luki RUS . . .9 D7
Veliko Gradište
SRB 127 C3
Veliko Orašje
SRB 127 C3
Veliko Selo SRB . .127 C3
Veliko Türnovo BG .17 D6
Velilla del Río Carrió
E 142 B2
Velilla de San Antonio
E 151 B4
Veli Lošinj HR 137 A3
Velingrad BG 183 A5
Velizh RUS. 9 E7

Veljun HR 123 B4
Velká Biteš CZ. 97 B4
Velka Hled'scbe CZ 95 B4
Velká Lomnica SK . .99 B4
Velkánad Veličkou
CZ 98 C1
Velké Bystřice CZ . .98 B1
Velké Heraltice CZ. .98 B1
Velké Karlovice CZ 98 B2
Vel'ke'Kostol'any
SK 98 C1
Vel'ké Leváre SK . .97 C5
Velké Losiny CZ . . .98 A1
Velké Meziříčí CZ. .97 B4
Velké Pavlovice
CZ 97 C4
Vel'ké Rovné SK . . .98 B3
Vel'ké Uherce SK. . .98 C1
Vel'ké Zálužie SK. .98 C1
Vel'ký Blahovo SK. .99 C4
Velky Bor CZ 96 B5
Vel'ký Cetin SK . . .112 A2
Vel'ký Krtiš SK 112 A3
Vel'ký Meder SK . .111 B4
Velky Ujezd CZ 98 B1
Vellahn D 73 A3
Vellberg D 94 B1
Velles F 103 C3
Velletri I 168 B2
Vellinge S 66 A2
Vellisca E 151 B5
Velliza S 150 A3
Vellmar D 81 A5
Velp NL 70 B2
Velten D 74 B2
Velvary CZ 84 B2
Velvendos GR 182 C4
Vemb DK 59 B1
Vemdalen S 199 C10
Veme N 48 B2
Véménd H 125 A4
Vemmedrup DK. . . .61 D2
Vena S 62 A3
Venaco F 180 A2
Venafro I 169 B4
Venarey-les-Laumes
F 104 B3
Venaría I 119 B4
Venasca I 133 A3
Venčane SRB. 127 C2
Vence F 132 B3
Venda Nova
Coimbra P 154 A2
Leiria P 154 B2
Vendas Novas P . .154 C2
Vendays-Montalivet
F 114 C2
Vendel S 51 B4
Vendelso S 57 A4
Vendeuil F 91 B3
Vendeuvre-sur-Barse
F 104 A3
Vendoeuvres F . . .115 B5
Vendôme F 103 B3
Venelles F 131 B4
Veness GB 33 B4
Venézia = Venice
I 122 B1
Venialbo E 150 A2
Venice = Venézia
I 122 B1
Vénissieux F 117 B4
Venjan S 49 B5
Venlo NL 80 A2
Vennesla N 53 B3
Vennesund N 195 E3
Vennezey F 92 C2
Venn Green GB 42 B2
Venosa I 172 B1
Venray NL 80 A1
Vent A 108 C1
Venta de Baños E .142 C2
Venta del Moro E . .158 B2
Venta de los Santos
E 157 B4
Venta las Ranas E 142 A1
Ventanueva E 141 A4
Ventas de Huelma
E 163 A4
Ventas de Zafarraya
E 163 B3
Ventavon F 132 A1
Ventimiglia I 133 B3
Ventnor GB 44 C2
Ventosa de la Sierra
E 143 C4
Ventosilla E 143 C4
Ventspils LV 8 D2
Venturina I 134 B3
Venzolasca F 180 A2
Venzone I 122 A2
Vép H 111 B3
Vera
E 164 B3
N 199 B9
Vera Cruz P 160 A2
Vera de Bidasoa
E 144 A2
Vera de Moncayo
E 144 C2
Verbánia I 119 B5
Verberie F 90 B2
Verbicaro I 174 B1
Verbier CH 119 A4
Vercelli I 119 B5
Vercel-Villedieu-le-
Camp F 105 B5
Verchen D 66 C1
Vercheny F 118 C2
Verclause F 131 A4
Verdalsøra N 199 B8
Verden D 72 B2
Verdens Ende N . . .54 A1
Verdikoussa GR . .182 D3
Verdille F 115 C3
Verdú E 147 C2
Verdun F 92 B1

Verdun-sur-Garonne
F 129 C4
Verdun-sur-le-Doubs
F 105 C4
Veresegyház H . . .112 B3
Verfeil F 129 C4
Vergato I 135 A4
Vergel E 159 C4
Vergeletto CH 120 A1
Verges E 147 B4
Vergiate I 120 B1
Vergt F 129 A3
Veria GR 182 C4
Verin E 141 C3
Veringenstadt D . .107 A4
Verl D 81 A4
Verma N 198 C5
Vermand F 90 B3
Vermelha P 154 B1
Vermenton F 104 B2
Vernago I 108 C1
Vernante I 133 A3
Vernantes F 102 B2
Vernár SK 99 C4
Vernasca I 120 C2
Vernayaz CH 119 A4
Vernazza I 134 A2
Vern-d'Anjou F . . .102 B1
Verneřice CZ 84 B2
Vernet F 146 A2
Vernet-les-Bains
F 146 B3
Verneuil F 91 B3
Verneuil-sur-Avre
F 89 B4
Vernier CH 118 A3
Vérnio I 135 A4
Vérnole I 173 B4
Vernon F 90 B1
Verny F 92 B2
Veróce H 112 B3
Verolanuova I 120 B3
Véroli I 169 B3
Verona I 121 B4
Verpelét H 113 B4
Verrabotn N 199 B7
Verrès I 119 B4
Verrey-sous-Salmaise
F 104 B3
Verrières F 115 B4
Versailles F 90 C2
Versam CH 107 C4
Verseg H 112 B3
Versmold D 71 B5
Versoix CH 118 A3
Verteillac F 115 C4
Vértesacsa H 112 B2
Vertou F 101 B4
Vertus F 91 C3
Verviers B 80 B1
Vervins F 91 B3
Verwood GB 43 B5
Veryan GB 42 B2
Veržej SLO 111 C3
Verzuolo I 133 A3
Verzy F 91 B4
Vescovato F 180 A2
Vése H 124 A3
Veselinad Lužnicí
CZ 96 B2
Veselinad Moravou
CZ 98 C1
Veseliy BG 17 D7
Vésime I 119 C5
Veskoniemi FIN. .193 D11
Vesoul F 105 B5
Vespolate I 120 B1
Vessigebro S 60 C2
Vestbygd N 52 B2
Vestenanova I 121 B4
Vester Husby S 56 B2
Vester Nebel DK . . .59 C2
Vester Torup DK. . .58 A2
Vester Vedsted DK .59 C1
Vestervig DK 58 B1
Vestfossen N 53 A5
Vestmannaeyjar
IS 190 D5
Vestmarka N 48 C3
Vestnes N 198 C4
Vestone I 120 B3
Vestre Gausdal N . .48 A2
Vestre Jakobselv
N 193 B13
Vestre Slidre N 47 A5
Vesyegonsk RUS . .9 C10
Veszprém H 112 B1
Veszprémvarsány
H 112 B1
Vésztő H 113 C5
Vetlanda S 62 A3
Vetovo HR 125 B3
Vetralla I 168 A2
Vigneulles-lès-
Hattonchâtel F . .92 C1
Vétroz CH 119 A4
Vetschau D 84 A2
Vettasjärvi S 196 B4
Vetto I 134 A3
Vetulónia I 135 C3
Veules-les-Roses F 89 A4
Veulettes-sur-Mer
F 89 A4
Veum N 53 A4
Veurne B 78 A2
Veverská Bityška
CZ 97 B4
Vevey CH 106 C1
Vevi GR 182 C3
Vevring N 46 A2
Vex CH 119 A4
Veynes F 132 A1
Veyre-Monton F . .116 B3
Veyrier F 118 B3
Vézelay F 104 B2
Vézelise F 92 C2
Vézenobres F 131 A3
Vezins F 102 B1

Vézins-de-Lévézou
F 130 A1
Vezirhan TR 187 B5
Vezirköprü TR 23 A8
Vezza di Óglio I . . .120 A3
Vezzani F 180 A2
Vezzano I 121 A4
Vezzano sul Cróstolo
I 121 C3
Vi S 200 D3
Viadana I 121 C3
Via Gloria P 160 B2
Viana P 143 B4
Viana do Alentejo
P 154 C2
Viana do Bolo E . .141 B3
Viana do Castelo
P 148 A1
Vianden L 92 B2
Viannos GR 185 D6
Viaréggio I 134 B3
Viator F 164 C2
Vibble S 57 C4
Viborg DK 58 B2
Vibo Valéntia I . . .175 C2
Vibraye F 102 A2
Vic F 147 C3
Vicar E 164 C2
Vicarello I 134 B3
Vicari I 176 B2
Vícchio I 135 B4
Vicdessos F 146 B2
Vic-en-Bigorre F . .145 A4
Vicenza I 121 B4
Vic-Fézensac F . . .129 C3
Vichy F 117 A3
Vickan S 60 B2
Vickerstown GB . . .36 B3
Vic-le-Comte F . . .116 B3
Vico F 180 A1
Vico del Gargano
I 171 B3
Vico Equense I . . .170 C2
Vicopisano I 134 B3
Vicosoprano CH . .120 A2
Vicovaro I 169 A2
Vic-sur-Aisne F 90 B3
Vic-sur-Cère F . . .116 C2
Victoria = Rabat
M 175 C3
Vidago P 148 A2
Vidauban F 132 B2
Vide P 148 B2
Videbæk DK. 59 B1
Videm SLO. 123 B3
Videseter N 198 D4
Vidigueira P 160 A2
Vidin BG. 16 D5
Vidlin GB 33 A5
Vidsel S 196 D3
Vidzy BY. 13 A7
Viechtach D 95 B4
Vieille-Brioude F . .117 B3
Vieira P 154 B2
Vieira do Minho P .148 A1
Vieiros P 155 C3
Vielha E 145 B4
Vielle-Aure F 145 B4
Viellespesse F . . .116 B3
Viellevigne F 114 B2
Vielmur-sur-Agout
F 130 B1
Vielsalm B 80 B1
Viels Maison F 91 C3
Vienenburg D 73 C3
Vienna = Wien A . .111 A3
Vienne F 117 B4
Vieritz D 73 B5
Viernheim D 93 B4
Vierraden D 74 A3
Viersen D 80 A2
Vierville-sur-Mer F .88 A3
Vierzon F 103 B4
Vieste I 171 B4
Vietas S 194 C9
Vieteren B 78 B2
Vietri di Potenza I .172 B1
Vietri sul Mare I . .170 C2
Vieux-Boucau-les-
Bains F 128 C1
Vif F 118 B2
Vig DK 61 D1
Vigásio I 121 B3
Vigaun A. 109 B4
Vigeland N 52 B3
Vigeois F 116 B1
Vigévano I 120 B1
Viggianello I 174 B2
Viggiano I 174 A1
Vigliano I 169 A3
Vigmostad N 52 B3
Vignale I 119 B5
Vignanello I 168 A2
Vignole Borbera I . .120 C1
Vignory F 105 A4
Vignoux-sur Barangeon
F 103 B4
Vigo E 140 B2
Vigo di Fassa I . . .121 A4
Vigone I 119 C4
Vigrestad N 52 B1
Vihiers F 102 B1
Viitasaari FIN 8 A4
Viiconejos E 151 B4
Vik IS 190 D6
Vik
Nordland N 195 E3
Rogaland N 52 B1
Sogn og Fjordane
N 46 A3
S 63 C2
Vika S 50 B2
Vikajärvi FIN 197 C9
Vikane N. 54 A1
Vikarbyn S 50 B2
Vike N 46 B2
Vikedal N 52 A1

Vikeland N 53 B3
Viken
Jämtland S. . . .199 A10
Skåne S. 61 C2
Viker N. 48 B2
Vikersund N. 48 C1
Vikeså N. 52 B2
Vikevåg N. 52 A1
Vikingstad S 56 B1
Vikmanshyttan S. .50 B2
Vikna N. 199 A7
Vikøy N. 46 B3
Vikran
Troms N 192 C2
Troms N 194 B7
Viksjö S 200 D3
Viksøyri N 46 A3
Viksta S 51 B4
Vila Boim P 155 C3
Vila Chã de Ourique
P 154 B2
Viladamat E 147 B4
Vila de Cruces E . .140 B2
Vila de Rei P 154 B2
Vila do Bispo P . . .160 B1
Vila do Conde P . .148 A1
Viladrau E 147 C3
Vila Flor P 149 A2
Vila Franca das Navas
P 149 B2
Vilafranca del Maestrat
E 153 B3
Vilafranca del Penedès
E 147 C2
Vila Franca de Xira
P 154 C1
Vila Fresca P 154 C1
Vilagarcía de Arousa
E 140 B2
Vilajuiga E 147 B4
Vilamarín E 140 B3
Vilamartín de
Valdeorras E . . .141 B3
Vila Nogueira P . .154 C1
Vilanova de Castelló
E 159 B3
Vila Nova da Baronia
P 154 C2
Vila Nova de Cerveira
P 140 C2
Vila Nova de Famalicão
P 148 A1
Vila Nova de Foz Côa
P 149 A2
Vila Nova de Gaia
P 148 A1
Vila Nova de Milfontes
P 160 B1
Vila Nova de Paiva
P 148 B2
Vila Nova de São Bento
P 161 B2
Vilanova de Sau E 147 C3
Vilanova i la Geltrú
E 147 C2
Vilapedre E 140 A3
Vila Pouca de Aguiar
P 148 A2
Vila Praja de Ancora
P 148 A1
Vilarandelo P 148 A2
Vilar de Santos E. .140 B3
Vilardevós E 141 C3
Vila Real P 148 A2
Vila-real de los Infantes
E 159 B3
Vila Real de Santo
António P 160 B2
Vilar Formosa P . .149 B3
Vila-Rodona E 147 C2
Vila Ruiva P 160 A2
Vilasantar E 140 A2
Vilaseca E 147 C2
Vila Seca P 148 B1
Vilassar de Mar E .147 C3
Vilasund S 195 D5
Vila Velha de Ródão
P 155 B3
Vila Verde
Braga P 148 A1
Lisboa P 154 C1
Vila Verde de Filcalho
P 161 B2
Vila Viçosa P 155 C3
Vilches E 157 B4
Vildbjerg DK 59 B1
Vilémov CZ 97 B3
Vileyka BY 13 A7
Vilhelmina S 200 B3
Vilia GR 184 A4
Viljandi EST. 8 C4
Villabáñez E 150 A3
Villablanca E 161 B2
Villablino E 141 B4
Villabona E 144 A1
Villabragima E . . .142 C1
Villabuena del Puente
E 150 A2
Villacadima E 151 A4
Villacañas E 157 A4
Villacarriedo E . . .143 A3
Villacarrillo E 164 A1
Villa Castelli I 173 B3
Villacastín E 150 B3
Villach A 109 C4
Villacidro I 179 C2
Villaconejos E . . .151 B4
Villaconejos de
Trabaque E 152 B1
Villa Cova de Lixa
P 148 A1
Villada E 142 B2
Villadangos del
Páramo E 141 B5
Villadecanes E . . .141 B4
Villa del Prado E . .151 B3
Villa del Río E 157 C3
Villadepera E 149 A3
Villa de Peralonso
E 149 A3

Villa di Chiavenna
I 120 A2
Villadiego E 142 B2
Villadompardo E . .163 A3
Villadóssola I 119 A5
Villaeles de Valdavia
E 142 B2
Villaescusa de Haro
E 158 B1
Villafáfila E 142 C1
Villafeliche I 152 A2
Villaflores E 150 A2
Villafrades de Campos
E 142 B2
Villafranca
Ávila E 150 B2
Navarra E 144 B2
Villafranca de Córdoba
E 150 A3
Villafranca del Bierzo
E 141 B4
Villafranca de los
Barros E 155 C4
Villafranca de los
Caballeros E . . .157 A4
Villafranca di Verona
I 121 B3
Villafranca in Lunigiana
I 134 A2
Villafranca-Montes de
Oca E 143 B3
Villafranca Tirrena
I 177 A4
Villafranco del Campo
E 152 B2
Villafranco del
Guadalquivir E .161 B3
Villafrati I 176 B2
Villafrechós E 142 C1
Villafruela E 143 C3
Villagarcia de las
Torres E 156 B1
Villaggio Mancuso
I 175 B2
Villagonzalo E . . .156 B1
Villagotón E 141 B4
Villagrains F 128 B2
Villaharta E 156 B3
Villahermosa E . . .158 C1
Villaherreros E . . .142 B2
Villahoz E 143 B3
Villaines-la-Juhel F 89 B3
Villajoyosa E 159 C3
Villalago I 169 B3
Villalba
I 176 B2
Villalba de Calatrava
E 157 B4
Villalba de Guardo
E 142 B2
Villalba del Alcor
E 161 B3
Villalba de la Sierra
E 152 B1
Villalba de los Alcores
E 142 C2
Villalba de los Barros
E 155 C4
Villalba del Rey E .151 B5
Villalcampo E 149 A3
Villalcázar de Sirga
E 142 B2
Villalengua E 152 A2
Villalgordo del Júcar
E 158 B1
Villalgordo del
Marquesado E . .158 B1
Villalmóndar E . . .143 B3
Villalón de Campos
E 142 B1
Villalonga E 159 C3
Villalonso E 150 A2
Villalpando E 142 C1
Villaluenga E 151 B4
Villalumbroso E . .142 B2
Villálvaro E 143 C3
Villamalea E 158 B2
Villamanán E 142 B1
Villamanin E 142 B1
Villamanrique E . .157 B5
Villamanrique de la
Condesa E 161 B3
Villamanta E 151 B3
Villamantilla E . . .151 B3
Villamar I 179 C2
Villamartin E 162 B2
Villamartín de Campos
E 142 B2
Villamartín de Don
Sancho E 142 B1
Villamassárgia I . .179 C2
Villamayor E 142 A1
Villamayor de Calatrava
E 157 B3
Villamayor de Campos
E 142 C1
Villamayor de Santiago
E 157 A5
Villambard F 129 A3
Villamejil E 141 B4
Villamesías E 156 A2
Villaminaya E 157 A4
Villa Minozzo I . . .134 A3
Villamor de los
Escuderos E . . .150 A2
Villamoronta E . . .142 B2
Villamuelas E 151 C4
Villamuriel de Cerrato
E 142 C2
Villandraut F 128 B2
Villanova I 173 B3
Villanova d'Asti I . .119 C4
Villanova del Battista
I 171 B3
Villanova Mondovi i
I 133 A3
Villanova Monteleone
I 178 B2
Villante E 143 B3

Villantério I 120 B2
Villanubla E 142 C2
Villanueva de Alcardete
E 157 A4
Villanueva de Alcorón
E 152 B1
Villanueva de Algaidas
E 163 A3
Villanueva de Argaña
E 143 B3
Villanueva de Bogas
E 157 A4
Villanueva de Córdoba
E 156 B3
Villanueva de Gállego
E 144 C3
Villanueva del Aceral
E 150 A3
Villanueva de la
Concepcion E . .163 B3
Villanueva de la Fuente
E 158 C1
Villanueva de la Jara
E 158 B2
Villanueva de la Reina
E 157 B4
Villanueva del
Arzobispo E . . .164 A2
Villanueva de la Serena
E 156 B2
Villanueva de la Sierra
E 149 B3
Villanueva de las
Manzanas E . . .142 B1
Villanueva de las Peras
E 141 C5
Villanueva de las
Torres E 164 B1
Villanueva de la Vera
E 150 B2
Villanueva del Campo
E 142 C1
Villanueva del Duque
E 156 B3
Villanueva del Fresno
E 155 C3
Villanueva del Huerva
E 152 A2
Villanueva de los
Castillejos E . . .161 B2
Villanueva de los
Infantes E 157 B5
Villanueva del Rey
E 156 B2
Villanueva del Rio
E 162 A2
Villanueva del Río y
Minas E 162 A2
Villanueva del Rosario
E 163 B3
Villanueva del Trabuco
E 163 A3
Villanueva de Mesía
E 163 A4
Villanueva de Nía
E 142 B2
Villanueva de Oscos
E 141 A4
Villanueva de San
Carlos E 157 B4
Villanueva de San Juan
E 162 A2
Villanueva de Tapia
E 163 A3
Villanueva de
Valdegovia E . . .143 B3
Villány H. 125 B4
Villaputzu I 179 C3
Villaquejida E 142 B1
Villaquilambre E . .142 B1
Villaquiran de los
Infantes E 142 B2
Villaralto E 156 B3
Villarcayo E 143 B3
Villard-de-Lans F . .118 B2
Villar de Barrio E . .140 B3
Villar de Cañas E . .158 B1
Villar de Chinchilla
E 158 C2
Villar de Ciervo E .149 B3
Villardeciervos E . .141 C4
Villar de Domingo
Garcia E 152 B1
Villardefrades E . .142 C1
Villar del Arzobispo
E 159 B3
Villar del Buey E . .149 A3
Villar del Cobo E . .152 B2
Villar del Humo E . .158 B2
Villar de los Navarros
E 152 A2
Villar del Pedroso
E 156 A2
Villar del Rey E . . .155 B4
Villar del Río E . . .143 B4
Villar del Saz de
Navalón E 152 B1
Villar de Rena E. . .156 A2
Villarejo E 151 A4
Villarejo de Fuentes
E 158 B1
Villarejo de Orbigo
E 141 B5
Villarejo de Salvanes
E 151 B4
Villarejo-Periesteban
E 158 B1
Villares del Saz E .158 B1
Villargordo del Cabriel
E 158 B2
Villarino E 149 A3
Villarino de Conso
E 141 B3
Villarluengo E 153 B3
Villarobledo E 143 B3
Villarosa I 177 B3
Villar Perosa I 119 C4
Villarramiel E 142 B2
Villarrasa E 161 B3

Villarreal de San Carlos
E 150 C1
Villarrin de Campos
E 142 C1
Villarrobledo E . . .158 B1
Villarroya de la Sierra
E 152 A2
Villarroya de los
Pinares E 153 B3
Villarrubia de los Ojos
E 157 A4
Villarrubia de Santiago
E 151 C4
Villarrubio E 151 C5
Villars-les-Dombes
F 117 A5
Villarta de los Montes
E 156 A3
Villarta de San Juan
E 157 A4
Villasana de Mena
E 143 A3
Villasandino E 142 B2
Villa San Giovanni
I 175 C1
Villa Santa Maria I 169 B4
Villasante E 143 A3
Villa Santina I 122 A1
Villasarracino E . . .142 B2
Villasayas E 151 A5
Villasdardo E 149 A3
Villaseca de Henares
E 151 B5
Villaseca de Laciana
E 141 B4
Villaseca de la Sagra
E 151 C4
Villaseco de los
Gamitos E 149 A3
Villaseco de los Reyes
E 149 A3
Villasequilla de Yepes
E 151 C4
Villasimius I 179 C3
Villasmundo I 177 B4
Villasor I 179 C2
Villastar E 152 B2
Villastellone I 119 C4
Villatobas E 151 C4
Villatorp E 150 B2
Villatoya E 158 B2
Villavaliente E 158 B2
Villavelayo E 143 B4
Villavella E 141 B3
Villaver de de
Guadalimar E . .158 C1
Villaverde del Rio
E 162 A2
Villaviciosa de
Córdoba E 156 B3
Villaviciosa de Odón
E 151 B4
Villavieja de Yeltes
E 149 B3
Villayón E 141 A4
Villé F 93 C3
Villebois-Lavalette
F 115 C4
Villecerf F 90 C2
Villecomtal F 130 A1
Villedieu-les-Poêles
F 88 B2
Villedieu-sur-Indre
F 103 C3
Ville-di-Pietrabugno
F 180 A2
Villedômain F 103 B3
Villefagnan F 115 B4
Villefontaine F . . .118 B2
Villefort F 131 A2
Villefranche-
d'Albigeois F . . .130 B1
Villefranche-d'Allier
F 116 A2
Villefranche-de-
Lauragais F 146 A2
Villefranche-de-
Lonchat F 128 B3
Villefranche-de-Panat
F 130 A1
Villefranche-de-
Rouergue F 130 A1
Villefranche-du-
Périgord F 129 B4
Villefranche-sur-Cher
F 103 B3
Villefranche-sur-Mer
F 133 B3
Villefranche-sur-Saône
F 117 A4
Villegenon F 103 B4
Villel E 152 B2
Villemaur-sur-Vanne
F 104 A2
Villemontais F 117 B3
Villemur-sur-Tarn
F 129 C4
Villena E 159 C3
Villenauxe-la-Grande
F 91 C3
Villenave-d'Ornon
F 128 B2
Villeneuve
CH 119 A3
F 129 B5
Villeneuve-d'Ascq
F 78 B3
Villeneuve-de-Berg
F 131 A3
Villeneuve-de-Marsan
F 128 C2
Villeneuve-de-Rivière
F 145 A4
Villeneuve-la-Guyard
F 90 C3
Villeneuve-
l'Archevêque F . .104 A2

Villeneuve-le-Comte F 90 C2
Villeneuve-lès-Avignon F 131 B3
Villeneuve-les-Corbières F 146 B3
Villeneuve-St Georges F 90 C2
Villeneuve-sur-Allier F 104 C2
Villeneuve-sur-Lot F 129 B3
Villeneuve-sur-Yonne F 104 A2
Villeréal F 129 B3
Villerias E 142 C2
Villeromain F 103 B3
Villers-Bocage
Calvados F 88 A3
Somme F 90 B2
Villers-Bretonneux F 90 B2
Villers-Carbonnel F 90 B2
Villers-Cotterêts F 90 B3
Villersexel F 105 B5
Villers-Farlay F 105 C4
Villers-le-Gambon B 79 B4
Villers-le-Lac F 106 B1
Villers-sur-Mer F 89 A3
Villerupt F 92 B1
Villerville F 89 A4
Villeseneux F 91 C4
Ville-sous-la-Ferté F 105 A3
Ville-sur-Illon F 105 A5
Ville-sur-Tourbe F 91 B4
Villetrun F 103 B3
Villetta Barrea I 169 B3
Villeurbanne F 117 B4
Villeveyrac F 130 B2
Villevocance F 117 B4
Villiers-St Benoit F 104 B2
Villiers-St Georges F 91 C3
Villingen D 106 A3
Villmar D 81 B4
Villoldo E 142 B2
Villon F 104 B3
Villoria E 150 B2
Vilnes N 46 A1
Vilnius LT 13 A6
Vils
A 108 B1
DK 58 B1
Vilsbiburg D 95 C4
Vilseck D 95 B3
Vilshofen D 96 C1
Vilshult S 63 B2
Vilusi MNE 139 C4
Vilvestre E 149 A3
Vilvoorde B 79 B4
Vimeiro P 154 B1
Vimercate I 120 B2
Vimianzo E 140 A1
Vimieiro P 154 C3
Vimioso P 149 A3
Vimmerby S 62 A3
Vimoutiers F 89 B4
Vimperk CZ 96 B1
Vimy F 78 B2
Vinadi CH 108 C1
Vinadio I 133 A3
Vinaixa E 147 C1
Vinarós E 153 B4
Vinäs S 50 B1
Vinay F 118 B2
Vinberg S 60 C2
Vinca F 146 B3
Vinča SRB 127 C2
Vinchiaturo I 170 B2
Vinci I 135 B3
Vindeby DK 65 A3
Vindelgransele S 195 E9
Vindeln S 200 B5
Vinderup DK 58 B1
Vindsvik N 52 A2
Vinets F 91 C4
Vineuil F 103 B3
Vinga RO 126 A3
Vingåker S 56 A1
Vingnes N 48 A2
Vingrau F 146 B3
Vingrom N 48 A2
Vinhais P 149 A3
Vinica
HR 124 A2
MK 182 B4
SK 112 A3
SLO 123 B4
Viniegra de Arriba E 143 B4
Vinje
Hordaland N 46 B3
Sør-Trøndelag N 198 B6
Telemark N 53 A3
Vinkovci HR 125 B4
Vinliden S 200 B3
Vinninga S 55 B4
Vinnytsya UA 13 D8
Vinon F 103 B4
Vinon-sur-Verdon F 132 B1
Vinslöv S 61 C3
Vinstra N 48 A1
Vintjärn S 50 B3
Vintrosa S 55 A5
Viñuela E 163 B3
Viñuela de Sayago E 149 A4
Viñuelas E 151 B4
Vinuesa E 143 C4
Vinzelberg D 73 B4
Viöl D 64 B2
Viola I 133 A3
Violay F 117 B4
Vipava SLO 122 B2
Vipiteno I 108 C2
Vipperow D 74 A1
Vir
BIH 138 B3
HR 137 A4
Vira CH 120 A1
Vire F 88 B3
Vireda S 62 A2
Vireux F 91 A4
Virgen A 109 B3
Virgen de la Cabeza E 157 B3
Virginia IRL 27 C3
Virieu F 118 B2
Virieu-le-Grand F 118 B2
Virje HR 124 A2
Virkkunen FIN 197 D10
Virklund DK 59 B2
Virovitica HR 124 B3
Virsbo S 50 C3
Virserum S 62 A3
Virtaniemi FIN 193 D12
Virton B 92 B1
Virtsu EST 8 C3
Viry F 118 A3
Vis HR 138 B2
Visbek D 71 B5
Visby
DK 64 A1
S 57 C4
Visé B 80 B1
Višegrad BIH 139 B5
Viserba I 136 A1
Viseu P 148 B2
Visiedo E 152 B2
Viskafors S 60 B2
Visland N 52 B2
Vislanda S 62 B2
Visnes N 52 A1
Višnja Gora SLO 123 B3
Višnjan HR 122 B2
Višnové CZ 97 C4
Visnums-Kil S 55 A5
Viso del Marqués E 157 B4
Visoko
BIH 139 B4
SLO 123 A3
Visone I 119 C5
Visp CH 119 A4
Vissefjärda S 63 B3
Visselhövede D 72 B2
Vissenbjerg DK 59 C3
Visso I 136 C2
Vistabella del Maestrat E 153 B3
Vistheden S 196 D3
Vita I 176 B1
Vitanje SLO 123 A4
Vitebsk = Vitsyebsk BY 13 A9
Viterbo I 168 A2
Vitez BIH 139 A3
Vithkuq AL 182 C2
Vitigudino E 149 A3
Vitina
BIH 138 B3
GR 184 B3
Vitis A 97 C3
Vitkov CZ 98 B1
Vitoria-Gasteiz E 143 B4
Vitré F 101 A4
Vitrey-sur-Mance F 105 B4
Vitry-en-Artois F 78 B2
Vitry-le-François F 91 C4
Vitry-sur-Seine F 90 C2
Vitsand S 49 B4
Vitsyebsk = Vitebsk BY 13 A9
Vittangi S 196 B4
Vittaryd S 60 C3
Vitteaux F 104 B3
Vittel F 105 A4
Vittinge S 51 C4
Vittória I 177 C3
Vittório Véneto I 122 B1
Vittsjö S 61 C3
Viù I 119 B4
Viul N 48 B2
Vivario F 180 A2
Viveiro E 140 A3
Vivel del Rio Martin E 152 B3
Viver E 159 B3
Viverols F 117 B3
Viveros E 158 C1
Viviers F 131 A3
Vivonne F 115 B4
Vivy F 102 B1
Vize TR 186 A2
Vizille F 118 B2
Viziňada HR 122 B2
Viziru RO 17 C7
Vizovice CZ 98 B1
Vizvár H 124 A3
Vizzavona F 180 A2
Vizzini I 177 B3
Vlachiotis GR 184 C3
Vlachovice CZ 98 B1
Vlachovo SK 99 C4
Vláchovo Březi CZ 96 B1
Vladimirci SRB 127 C1
Vladimirovac SRB 127 B2
Vladislav CZ 97 B3
Vlagtwedde NL 71 A4
Vlajkovac SRB 127 B3
Vlasenica BIH 139 A4
Vlašim CZ 96 B2
Vlatkovići BIH 138 A3
Vledder NL 70 B3
Vlissingen NL 79 A3
Vlkolínec SK 99 B3
Vlorë AL 182 C1
Vlotho D 72 B1
Vnanje Gorice SLO 123 B3
Vobarno I 121 B3
Voćin HR 124 B3
Vöcklabruck A 109 A4
Vöcklamarkt A 109 B4
Vodanj SRB 127 C2
Voderady SK 98 C1
Vodice
Istarska HR 123 B3
Šibenska HR 137 B4
SLO 123 A3
Vodňany CZ 96 B2
Vodnjan HR 122 C2
Vodskov DK 58 A3
Voe GB 33 A5
Voersá DK 58 A3
Voghera I 120 C2
Vogogna I 119 A5
Vogošća BIH 139 B4
Vogué F 131 A3
Vohburg D 95 C3
Vohenstrauss D 95 B4
Vöhl D 81 A4
Vöhrenbach D 106 A3
Vöhringen D 94 C2
Void-Vacon F 92 C1
Voiron F 118 B2
Voise F 90 C1
Voisey F 105 B4
Voiteg RO 126 B3
Voiteur F 105 C4
Voitsberg A 110 B2
Vojakkala FIN 196 D7
Vojens DK 59 C2
Vojka SRB 127 C2
Vojlovica SRB 127 C2
Vojnić HR 123 B4
Vojnice SK 112 B2
Vojnik SLO 123 A4
Vojvoda Stepa SRB 126 B2
Volada GR 188 D2
Volargne I 121 B3
Volary CZ 96 C1
Volče SLO 122 A2
Volda N 198 C3
Volendam NL 70 B2
Volga RUS 9 C11
Volimes GR 184 B1
Volissos GR 185 A6
Volkach D 94 B2
Völkermarkt A 110 C1
Volkhov RUS 9 C8
Völklingen D 92 B2
Volkmarsen D 81 A5
Voll N 198 C4
Vollenhove NL 70 B2
Vollore-Montagne F 117 B3
Vollsjö S 61 D3
Volodymyr-Volyns'kyy UA 13 C6
Volokolamsk RUS 9 D9
Volos GR 182 D4
Volosovo RUS 9 C6
Volovets UA 13 D5
Voltággio I 120 C1
Volta Mantovana I 121 B3
Volterra I 135 B3
Voltri I 133 A4
Volturara Áppula I 170 B3
Volturara Irpina I 170 C2
Volvic F 116 B3
Volx F 132 B1
Volyně CZ 96 B1
Vonitsa GR 182 E2
Vönöck H 111 B4
Vonsild DK 59 C2
Voorschoten NL 70 B1
Vopnafjörður IS 191 B11
Vorau A 110 B2
Vorbasse DK 59 C2
Vorchdorf A 109 B4
Vorden
D 71 B5
NL 71 B3
Vordernberg A 110 B1
Vordingborg DK 65 A4
Vorë AL 182 B1
Voreppe F 118 B2
Vorey F 117 B3
Vorgod DK 59 B1
Vormsund N 48 B3
Võru EST 8 D5
Voskopojë AL 182 C2
Voss N 46 B3
Votice CZ 96 B2
Voué F 91 C4
Vouillé F 115 B4
Voulx F 90 C2
Voussac F 116 A3
Vouvray F 102 B2
Vouvry CH 119 A3
Vouzela P 148 B1
Vouziers F 91 B4
Voves F 103 A3
Voxna S 50 A2
Voy GB 33 B3
Voynitsa RUS 3 D12
Voznesenye RUS 9 B9
Vrå
DK 58 A2
S 60 C3
Vráble SK 98 C2
Vračenovići MNE 139 C4
Vračev Gaj SRB 127 C3
Vraćevsnica SRB 127 C2
Vrådal N 53 A4
Vrakneika GR 184 A2
Vrana HR 123 C3
Vranduk BIH 139 A3
Vrångö S 60 B1
Vrani RO 127 B3
Vranić SRB 127 C2
Vraniči BIH 139 B4
Vranja HR 123 B3
Vranjak BIH 125 C4
Vranje SRB 16 D4
Vranovice CZ 97 C4
Vranov nad Dyje CZ 97 C3
Vransko SLO 123 A3
Vrapčići BIH 139 B3
Vratimov CZ 98 B2
Vratsa BG 17 D5
Vrbanja HR 125 C4
Vrbanjci BIH 124 C3
Vrbas SRB 126 B1
Vrbaška BIH 124 B3
Vrbnik
Primorsko-Goranska HR 123 B3
Zadarsko-Kninska HR 138 A2
Vrbno pod Pradědem CZ 85 B5
Vrboska HR 138 B2
Vrbov SK 99 B4
Vrbovce SK 98 C1
Vrbové SK 98 C1
Vrbovec HR 124 B2
Vrbovski SRB 127 C2
Vrbovsko HR 123 B4
Vrchlabí CZ 84 B3
Vrčin SRB 127 C2
Vrdy CZ 97 B3
Vrebac HR 137 A4
Vreden D 71 B3
Vreoci SRB 127 C2
Vretstorp S 55 A5
Vrginmost HR 124 B1
Vrgorac HR 138 B3
Vrhnika SLO 123 B3
Vrhovine HR 123 C4
Vrhpolie SRB 127 C1
Vriezenveen NL 71 B3
Vrigne-aux-Bois F 91 B4
Vrigstad S 62 A2
Vrlika HR 138 B2
Vrnograč BIH 124 B1
Vron F 78 B1
Vroomshoop NL 71 B3
Vroutek CZ 83 B5
Vrpolje HR 125 B4
Vršac SRB 126 B3
Vrsar HR 122 B2
Vrsi HR 137 A4
Vrtoče BIH 124 C2
Vrútky SK 98 B2
Všeruby CZ 95 B4
Všestary CZ 85 B3
Vsetín CZ 98 B1
Vučkovica SRB 127 D2
Vught NL 79 A5
Vuillafans F 105 B5
Vukovar HR 125 B5
Vuku N 199 B8
Vulcan RO 17 C5
Vulcănești MD 17 C8
Vuoggatjålme S 195 D7
Vuojärvi FIN 197 B9
Vuolijoki FIN 3 D10
Vuollerim S 196 C3
Vuotso FIN 197 A10
Vuzenica SLO 110 C2
Vyartsilya RUS 9 A7
Vyborg RUS 9 B6
Výčapy CZ 97 B3
Výčapy-Opatovce SK 98 C2
Východna SK 99 B3
Vydrany SK 111 A4
Vyerkhnyadzvinsk BY 13 A7
Vyhne SK 98 C2
Vy-lès Lure F 105 B5
Vylkove UA 17 C8
Vynohradiv UA 17 A5
Vyshniy Volochek RUS 9 D9
Vyškov CZ 97 B5
Vysokánad Kysucou SK 98 B2
Vysoké Mýto CZ 97 B4
Vysokovsk RUS 9 D10
Vyšší Brod CZ 96 C2
Vytegra RUS 9 B10

W

Waabs D 64 B2
Waalwijk NL 79 A5
Waarschoot B 79 A3
Wabern D 81 A5
Wąbrzeźno PL 69 B3
Wąchock PL 87 A5
Wachow D 74 B1
Wachów PL 86 B2
Wächtersbach D 81 B5
Wackersdorf D 95 B4
Waddington GB 40 B3
Wadebridge GB 42 B2
Wadelsdorf D 84 A2
Wädenswil CH 107 B3
Wadern D 92 B2
Wadersloh D 81 A4
Wadlew PL 86 A3
Wadowice PL 99 B3
Wagenfeld D 72 B1
Wageningen NL 70 C2
Waghäusel D 93 B4
Waging D 109 B3
Wagrain A 109 B4
Wagrowiec PL 76 B2
Wahlsdorf D 74 C2
Wahlstedt D 64 C3
Wahrenholz D 73 B3
Waiblingen D 94 C1
Waidhaus D 95 B4
Waidhofen an der Thaya A 97 C3
Waidhofen an der Ybbs A 110 B1
Waimes B 80 B2
Wainfleet All Saints GB 41 B4
Waizenkirchen A 96 C1
Wakefield GB 40 B2
Wałbrzych PL 85 B4
Walchensee D 108 B2
Walchsee A 109 B3
Wałcz PL 75 A5
Wald CH 107 B3
Waldaschaff D 94 B1
Waldbach A 110 B2
Waldböckelheim D 93 B3
Waldbröl D 81 B3
Waldeck D 81 A5
Waldenburg D 83 B4
Waldfischbach-Burgalben D 93 B3
Waldheim D 83 A5
Waldkappel D 82 A1
Waldkirch D 106 A2
Waldkirchen D 96 C1
Waldkirchen am Wesen A 96 C1
Waldkraiburg D 109 A3
Wald-Michelbach D 93 B4
Waldmohr D 93 B3
Waldmünchen D 95 B4
Waldring A 109 B3
Waldsassen D 95 A4
Waldshut D 106 B3
Waldstatt CH 107 B4
Waldwisse F 92 B2
Walenstadt CH 107 B4
Walentynów PL 87 A5
Walichnowy PL 86 A2
Walincourt F 90 A3
Walkenried D 82 A2
Walkeringham GB 40 B3
Wallasey GB 38 A3
Walldürn D 94 B1
Wallenfells D 82 B3
Wallenhorst D 71 B5
Wallers F 78 B3
Wallersdorf D 95 C4
Wallerstein D 94 C2
Wallingford GB 44 B2
Wallitz D 74 A1
Walls GB 33 A5
Wallsbüll D 64 B2
Walmer GB 45 B5
Walsall GB 40 C2
Walshoutem B 79 B5
Walsrode D 72 B2
Waltenhofen D 107 B5
Waltershausen D 82 B2
Waltham Abbey GB 45 B4
Waltham on the Wolds GB 40 C3
Walton-on-Thames GB 44 B3
Walton-on-the-Naze GB 45 B5
Wamba E 142 C2
Wanderup D 64 B2
Wandlitz D 74 B2
Wanfried D 82 A2
Wangen im Allgäu D 107 B4
Wangerooge D 71 A4
Wangersen D 72 A2
Wängi CH 107 B3
Wanna D 64 C1
Wansford GB 40 C3
Wantage GB 44 B2
Wanzleben D 73 B4
Waplewo PL 77 A5
Wapnica PL 75 A4
Wapno PL 76 B2
Warburg D 81 A5
Wardenburg D 71 A5
Ware GB 44 B3
Waregem B 79 B3
Wareham GB 43 B4
Waremme B 79 B5
Waren D 74 A1
Warendorf D 71 C4
Warga NL 70 A2
Warin D 65 C4
Wark GB 37 A4
Warka PL 87 A5
Warkworth GB 37 A5
Warlubie PL 69 B3
Warminster GB 43 A4
Warnemünde D 65 B5
Warnow D 65 C4
Warnsveld NL 70 B3
Warrenpoint GB 27 B4
Warrington GB 38 A4
Warsaw = Warszawa PL 77 B6
Warsingsfehn D 71 A4
Warsow D 73 A4
Warstein D 81 A4
Warszawa = Warsaw PL 77 B6
Warta PL 86 A2
Wartberg A 110 B1
Warth A 107 B5
Warwick GB 44 A2
Warza D 82 B2
Wasbister GB 33 B3
Washington GB 37 B5
Wąsosz PL 85 A4
Wasselonne F 93 C3
Wassen CH 107 C3
Wassenaar NL 70 B1
Wasserauen CH 107 B4
Wasserburg D 108 A3
Wassertrüdingen D 94 B2
Wassy F 91 C4
Wasungen D 82 B2
Watchet GB 43 A3
Waterford IRL 30 B1
Watergrasshill IRL 29 B3
Waterloo B 79 B4
Waterville IRL 29 C1
Watford GB 44 B3
Wathlingen D 72 B3
Watten
F 78 B2
GB 32 C3
Wattens A 108 B2
Watton GB 41 C4
Wattwil CH 107 B4
Waunfawr GB 38 A2
Wavignies F 90 B2
Wavre B 79 B4
Wearhead GB 37 B4
Węchadłow PL 87 B4
Wedel D 72 A2
Wedemark D 72 B2
Weedon Bec GB 44 A2
Weener D 71 A4
Weert NL 80 A1
Weesp NL 70 B2
Weeze D 80 A2
Weferlingen D 73 B4
Wegeleben D 82 A3
Weggis CH 106 B3
Węgierska-Górka PL 99 B3
Węgliniec PL 84 A3
Węgorzyno PL 75 A4
Węgrzynice PL 75 B4
Wegscheid D 96 C1
Wehdel D 72 A1
Wehr D 106 B2
Weibersbrunn D 94 B1
Weichering D 95 C3
Weida D 83 B4
Weiden D 95 B4
Weidenberg D 95 B3
Weidenhain D 83 A4
Weidenstetten D 94 C1
Weierbach D 93 B3
Weikersheim D 94 B1
Weil D 108 A1
Weil am Rhein D 106 B2
Weilburg D 81 B4
Weil der Stadt D 93 C4
Weilerswist D 80 B2
Weilheim
Baden-Württemberg D 94 C1
Bayern D 108 B2
Weilmünster D 81 B4
Weiltensfeld A 110 C1
Weimar D 82 B3
Weinberg D 94 B2
Weinfelden CH 107 B4
Weingarten
Baden-Württemberg D 93 B4
Baden-Württemberg D 107 B4
Weinheim D 93 B4
Weinstadt D 94 C1
Weismain D 82 B3
Weissbriach A 109 C4
Weissenbach A 108 B1
Weissenberg D 84 A2
Weissenbrunn D 82 B3
Weissenburg D 94 B2
Weissenfels D 83 A3
Weissenhorn D 94 C2
Weissenkirchen A 97 C3
Weissensee D 82 A3
Weissenstadt D 83 B3
Weisskirchen im Steiermark A 110 B1
Weisstannen CH 107 C4
Weisswasser D 84 A2
Weitendorf D 65 C5
Weitersfeld A 97 C3
Weitersfelden A 96 C2
Weitnau D 107 B5
Wéitra A 96 C2
Weiz A 110 B2
Wejherowo PL 68 A3
Welkenraedt B 80 B1
Wellaune D 83 A4
Wellin B 91 A5
Wellingborough GB 44 A3
Wellington
Somerset GB 43 B3
Telford & Wrekin GB 38 B4
Wellingtonbridge IRL 30 B2
Wells GB 43 A4
Wells-next-the-Sea GB 41 C4
Wels A 109 A5
Welschenrohr CH 106 B2
Welshpool GB 38 B3
Welver D 81 A3
Welwyn Garden City GB 44 B3
Welzheim D 94 C1
Welzow D 84 A2
Wem GB 38 B4
Wembury GB 42 B2
Wemding D 94 C2
Wenden D 81 B3
Wendisch Rietz D 74 B3
Wendlingen D 94 C1
Weng A 109 A4
Weng bei Admont A 110 B1
Wengen CH 106 C2
Wenigzell A 110 B2
Wennigsen D 72 B2
Wenns A 108 B1
Wenzenbach D 95 B4
Weppersdorf A 111 B3
Werben D 73 B4
Werbig D 74 C2
Werdau D 83 B4
Werder D 74 B1
Werdohl D 81 A3
Werfen A 109 B4
Werkendam NL 79 A4
Werl D 81 A3
Werlte D 71 B4
Wermelskirchen D 80 A3
Wermsdorf D 83 A4
Wernberg Köblitz D 95 B4
Werne D 81 A3
Werneck D 94 B2
Werneuchen D 74 B2
Wernigerode D 82 A2
Wertach D 108 B1
Wertheim D 94 B1
Wertingen D 94 C2
Weseke D 80 A2
Wesel D 80 A2
Wesenberg D 74 A1
Wesendorf D 73 B3
Wesołowo PL 77 A5
Wesselburen D 64 B1
Wesseling D 80 B2
West Bridgford GB 40 C2
West Bromwich GB 40 C2
Westbury
Shropshire GB 38 B4
Wiltshire GB 43 A4
Westbury-on-Severn GB 39 C4
Westendorf A 108 B3
Westensee D 64 B2
Westerbork NL 71 B3
Westerburg D 81 B3
Westerhaar NL 71 B3
Westerholt D 71 A4
Westerkappeln D 71 B4
Westerland D 64 B1
Westerlo B 79 A4
Westerstede D 71 A4
West Haddon GB 44 A2
Westheim D 94 B2
Westhill GB 33 D4
Westkapelle
B 78 A3
NL 79 A3
West Kilbride GB 34 C3
West Linton GB 35 C4
West Lulworth GB 43 B4
West Mersea GB 45 B4
Westminster GB 44 B3
Weston GB 40 C1
Weston-super-Mare GB 43 A4
Westport IRL 28 A2
Westruther GB 35 C5
West-Terschelling NL 70 A2
Westward Ho! GB 42 A2
West Woodburn GB 37 A4
Wetheral GB 37 B4
Wetherby GB 40 B2
Wetter
Hessen D 81 B4
Nordrhein-Westfalen D 80 A3
Wetteren B 79 A3
Wettin D 83 A3
Wettringen D 71 B4
Wetzikon CH 107 B3
Wetzlar D 81 B4
Wewelsfleth D 64 C2
Wexford IRL 30 B2
Weybridge GB 44 B3
Weyerbusch D 81 B3
Weyer Markt A 110 B1
Weyersheim F 93 C3
Weyhe D 72 B1
Weyhill GB 44 B2
Weymouth GB 43 B4
Weyregg A 109 B4
Węzyska PL 75 B3
Whalton GB 37 A5
Whauphill GB 36 B2
Wheatley GB 44 B2
Whickham GB 37 B5
Whipsnade GB 44 B3
Whitburn GB 35 C4
Whitby GB 37 B6
Whitchurch
Hampshire GB 44 B2
Herefordshire GB 39 C4
Shropshire GB 38 B4
White Bridge GB 32 D2
Whitegate IRL 29 C3
Whitehaven GB 36 B3
Whitehead GB 27 B5
Whithorn GB 36 B2
Whitley Bay GB 37 A5
Whitstable GB 45 B5
Whittington GB 38 B4
Whittlesey GB 41 C3
Wiązów PL 85 B5
Wick GB 32 C3
Wickede D 81 A3
Wickford GB 45 B4
Wickham GB 44 C2
Wickham Market GB 45 A5
Wicklow IRL 30 B2
Wicko PL 68 A2
Widawa PL 86 A2
Widdrington GB 37 A5
Widecombe in the Moor GB 42 B3
Widemouth GB 42 B2
Widnes GB 38 A4
Widuchowo PL 74 A3
Więcbork PL 76 A2
Wiefelstede D 71 A5
Wiehe D 82 A3
Wiehl D 81 B3
Wiek D 66 B2
Większyce PL 86 B1
Wielbark PL 77 A5
Wiele PL 68 B2
Wieleń PL 75 B5
Wielgie
Kujawsko-Pomorskie PL 77 B4
Łódzkie PL 86 A2
Mazowieckie PL 87 A5
Wielgomłyny PL 87 A3
Wielichowo PL 75 B5
Wieliczka PL 99 B4
Wielka Łąka PL 76 A3
Wielowies PL 86 B2
Wieluń PL 86 A2
Wien = Vienna A 111 A3
Wiener Neustadt A 111 B3
Wiepke D 73 B4
Wierden NL 71 B3
Wieren D 73 B3
Wieruszów PL 86 A2

Wierzbica
 Mazowieckie PL. . . 77 B6
 Mazowieckie PL. . . 87 A5
Wierzbie PL. 86 A2
Wierzbięcin PL. 75 A4
Wierzchowo PL. 75 A5
Wierzchucino PL. . . .68 A3
Wierzchy PL. 86 A2
Wies A. 110 C2
Wiesau D. 95 B4
Wiesbaden D. 93 A4
Wieselburg A. 110 A2
Wiesen CH. 107 C4
Wiesenburg D. 73 B5
Wiesenfelden D. 95 B4
Wiesensteig D. 94 C1
Wiesentheid D. 94 B2
Wiesloch D. 93 B4
Wiesmath A. 111 B3
Wiesmoor D. 71 A4
Wietmarschen D. . . .71 B4
Wietze D. 72 B2
Wigan GB. 38 A4
Wiggen CH. 106 C2
Wigston GB. 40 C2
Wigton GB. 36 B3
Wigtown GB. 36 B2
Wijchen NL. 80 A1
Wijhe NL. 70 B3
Wijk bij Duurstede
 NL. 70 C2
Wil CH. 107 B4
Wilamowice PL. 99 B3
Wilczęta PL. 69 A4
Wilczkowice PL. 77 B4
Wilczna PL. 76 B3
Wilczyn PL. 76 B3
Wildalpen A. 110 B1
Wildbad D. 93 C4
Wildberg
 Baden-Württemberg
 D. 93 C4
 Brandenburg D. . . .74 B1
Wildegg CH. 106 B3
Wildendürnbach A. .97 C4
Wildeshausen D. . . .72 B1
Wildon A. 110 C2
Wilfersdorf A. 97 C4
Wilhelmsburg
 A. 110 A2
 D. 74 A2
Wilhelmsdorf D. . . .107 B4
Wilhelmshaven D. . .71 A5
Wilków PL. 77 B5
Willebadessen D. . . .81 A5
Willebroek B. 79 A4
Willgottheim F. 93 C3
Willhermsdorf D. . . .94 B2
Willich D. 80 A2
Willingen D. 81 A4
Willington GB. 37 B5
Willisau CH. 106 B3
Wilmslow GB. 40 B1
Wilsdruff D. 83 A5
Wilster D. 64 C2
Wilsum D. 71 B3
Wilton GB. 44 B2
Wiltz L. 92 B1
Wimborne Minster
 GB. 43 B5
Wimereux F. 78 B1
Wimmenau F. 93 C3
Wimmis CH. 106 C2
Wincanton GB. 43 A4
Winchcombe GB. . . .44 B2
Winchelsea GB. 45 C4
Winchester GB. 44 B2
Windermere GB. 36 B4
Windischeschenbach
 D. 95 B4
Windischgarsten
 A. 110 B1
Windorf D. 96 C1
Windsbach D. 94 B2
Windsor GB. 44 B3
Wingene B. 78 A3
Wingham GB. 45 B5
Winkleigh GB. 42 B3
Winklern A. 109 C3
Winnenden D. 94 C1
Winnica PL. 77 B5
Winnigstedt D. 73 B3
Winnweiler D. 93 B3
Winschoten NL. 71 A4
Winsen
 Niedersachsen D. . .72 A3
 Niedersachsen D. . .72 B2
Winsford GB. 38 A4
Wińsko PL. 85 A4
Winslow GB. 44 B3
Winsum
 Friesland NL. 70 A2
 Groningen NL. 71 A3
Winterberg D. 81 A4
Winterfeld D. 73 B4
Winterswijk NL. 71 C3
Winterthur CH. 107 B3
Wintzenheim F. 106 A2
Winzer D. 95 C5
Wipperdorf D. 82 A2
Wipperfürth D. 80 A3
Wirksworth GB. 40 B2
Wisbech GB. 41 C4
Wischhafen D. 64 C2
Wishaw GB. 35 C4
Wisła PL. 98 B2
Wisła Wielka PL. . . .98 B2
Wiślica PL. 87 B4
Wismar D. 65 C4
Wiśniewo PL. 77 A5
Wiśniowa PL. 99 B4
Wissant F. 78 A1
Wissembourg F. 93 B3
Wissen D. 81 B3
Witanowice PL. 99 B3
Witham GB. 45 B4
Withern GB. 41 B4
Withernsea GB 41 B4
Witkowo PL. 76 B2
Witmarsum NL. 70 A2
Witney GB. 44 B2
Witnica PL. 75 B3
Witonia PL. 77 B4
Wittdün D. 64 B1
Wittelsheim F. 106 B2
Witten D. 80 A3
Wittenberge D. 73 A4
Wittenburg D. 73 A4
Wittenheim F. 106 B2
Wittichenau D. 84 A2
Wittighausen D. 94 B1
Wittingen D. 73 B3
Wittislingen D. 94 C2
Wittlich D. 92 B2
Wittmannsdorf A. . .110 C2
Wittmund D. 71 A4
Wittorf D. 72 A2
Wittstock D. 73 A5
Witzenhausen D. . . .82 A1
Wiveliscombe GB . . .43 A3
Wivenhoe GB. 45 B4
Władysławowo PL. . .69 A3
Wleń PL. 84 A3
Włocławek PL. 77 B4
Włodawa PL. 13 C5
Włodzimierzów PL. . .87 A3
Włoszczowa PL. 84 A3
Włostów PL. 87 B5
Włoszakowice PL. . . .75 C5
Włoszczowa PL. 87 B3
Wöbbelin D. 73 A4
Woburn GB. 44 B3
Wodzisław PL. 87 B4
Wodzisław Śląski
 PL. 98 B2
Woerden NL. 70 B1
Woerth F. 93 C3
Wohlen CH. 106 B3
Woippy F. 92 B2
Wojcieszow PL. 85 B3
Wojkowice Kościelne
 PL. 86 B3
Wojnicz PL. 99 B4
Woking GB. 44 B3
Wokingham GB. 44 B3
Wola Jachowa PL. . .87 B4
Wola Niechcicka
 PL. 86 A3
Wolbórz PL. 87 A3
Wolbrom PL. 87 B3
Wołczyn PL. 86 A2
Woldegk D. 74 A2
Wolfach D. 93 C4
Wolfegg D. 107 B4
Wolfen D. 83 A4
Wolfenbüttel D. 73 B3
Wolfersheim D. 81 B4
Wolfhagen D. 81 A5
Wolfratshausen D. .108 B2
Wolfsberg A. 110 C1
Wolfsburg D. 73 B3
Wolf's Castle GB. . . .39 C2
Wolfshagen D. 74 A2
Wolfstein D. 93 B3
Wolfurt A. 107 B4
Wolgast D. 66 B2
Wolhusen CH. 106 B3
Wolin PL. 67 C3
Wolka PL. 87 A4
Wolkenstein D. 83 B5
Wölkersdorf A. 97 C4
Wöllersdorf A. 111 B3
Wollin D. 73 B5
Wöllstadt D. 81 B4
Wolmirstedt D. 73 B4
Wolnzach D. 95 C3
Wołów PL. 85 A4
Wolsztyn PL. 75 B5
Wolvega NL. 70 B2
Wolverhampton
 GB. 40 C1
Wolverton GB. 44 A3
Wombwell GB. 40 B2
Woodbridge GB. 45 A5
Woodhall Spa GB . . .41 B3
Woodstock GB. 44 B2
Wookey Hole GB. . . .43 A4
Wool GB. 43 B4
Woolacombe GB. . . .42 A2
Wooler GB. 37 A4
Woolwich GB. 45 B4
Wooperton GB. 37 A5
Worb CH. 106 C2
Worbis D. 82 A2
Worcester GB. 39 B4
Wördern A. 97 C4
Wörgl A. 108 B3
Workington GB. 36 B3
Worksop GB. 40 B2
Workum NL. 70 B2
Wörlitz D. 83 A4
Wormer NL. 70 B1
Wormhout F. 78 B2
Wormit GB. 35 B5
Worms D. 93 B4
Worpswede D. 72 A1
Wörrstadt D. 93 B4
Wörschach A. 110 B1
Worsley GB. 38 A4
Wörth
 Bayern D. 93 B5
 Bayern D. 95 B4
 Bayern D. 95 C4
 Rheinland-Pfalz D. .93 B4
Worthing GB. 44 C3
Woudsend NL. 70 B2
Woumen B. 78 A2
Woźniki PL. 86 B3
Wragby GB. 41 B3
Wrangle GB. 41 B4
Wręczyca Wlk. PL. . .86 B2
Wredenhagen D. 73 A5
Wremen D. 72 A1
Wrentham GB. 45 A5
Wrexham GB. 38 A3
Wriedel D. 72 A3
Wriezen D. 74 B3
Wrist D. 64 C2
Wróblewo
 Mazowieckie PL. . .77 B5
 Wielkopolskie PL. .75 B5
Wrocki PL. 69 B4
Wrocław PL. 85 A5
Wronki PL. 75 B5
Wroxham GB. 41 C5
Września PL. 76 B2
Wrzosowo PL. 67 B4
Wschowa PL. 85 A4
Wulfen D. 80 A3
Wülfen D. 83 A3
Wulkau D. 73 B5
Wünnenberg D. 81 A4
Wünsdorf D. 74 B2
Wunsiedel D. 95 A4
Wunstorf D. 72 B2
Wuppertal D. 80 A3
Wurmannsquick D. . .95 C4
Würselen D. 80 B2
Wurzbach D. 82 B3
Würzburg D. 94 B1
Wurzen D. 83 A4
Wust D. 74 B1
Wusterhausen D. . . .73 B5
Wusterwitz D. 73 B5
Wustrau-Altfriesack
 D. 74 B1
Wustrow D. 66 B1
Wuustwezel B. 79 A4
Wye GB. 45 B4
Wyględów PL. 87 A5
Wyk D. 64 B1
Wykroty PL. 84 A3
Wylye GB. 43 A5
Wymiarki PL. 84 A3
Wymondham GB. . . .41 C5
Wyrzysk PL. 76 A2
Wyśmierzyce PL. . . .87 A4
Wysoka
 Dolnośląskie PL. . .85 A3
 Wielkopolskie PL. .76 A2
Wyszanów PL. 86 A2
Wyszogród PL. 77 B5

X

Xanten D. 80 A2
Xanthi GR. 183 B6
Xarrë AL. 182 D2
Xátiva E. 159 C3
Xeraco E. 159 B3
Xert E. 153 B4
Xerta E. 153 B4
Xertigny F. 105 A5
Xilagani GR. 183 C7
Xilokastro GR. 184 A3
Xinzo de Limia E. . .140 B3
Xixón = Gijón E. . . .142 A1
Xove E. 140 A3
Xubia E. 140 A3
Xunqueira de Ambia
 E. 140 B3
Xunqueira de
 Espadañedo E. . .140 B3
Xylophagou CY. 181 B2

Y

Yablanitsa BG. 17 D6
Yağcılar TR. 186 C3
Yahyalı TR. 23 B8
Yakoruda BG. 183 A5
Yalova TR. 187 B4
Yalvaç TR. 189 A6
Yambol BG. 17 D7
Yampil UA. 13 D8
Yaniskoski RUS .193 D12
Yantarnyy RUS. 69 A4
Yarbasan TR. 186 D3
Yarcombe GB. 43 B3
Yaremcha UA. 13 D6
Yarm GB. 37 B5
Yarmouth GB. 44 C2
Yarrow GB. 35 C4
Yasinya UA. 17 A6
Yatağan TR. 188 B3
Yate GB. 43 A4
Yatton GB. 43 A4
Yavoriv UA. 13 D5
Yaxley GB. 41 C3
Yazıca TR. 187 B6
Yazıköy TR. 188 C2
Ybbs A. 110 A2
Ybbsitz A. 110 B1
Ydby DK. 58 B1
Yddal N. 46 B2
Ydes F. 116 B2
Yealmpton GB. 42 B3
Yebra de Basa E. . .145 B3
Yecla E. 159 C2
Yecla de Yeltes E. . .149 B3
Yelsk BY. 13 C8
Yelverton GB. 42 B2
Yena RUS. 197 B14
Yenice
 Ankara TR. 23 B7
 Aydın TR. 188 B3
 Çanakkale TR. . . .186 C2
 Edirne TR. 183 C8
Yenifoça TR. 186 D1
Yenihisar TR. 188 B2
Yeniköy Plaji TR. . .186 B3
Yenipazar TR. 188 B3
Yenişarbademli
 TR. 189 B6
Yenişehir TR. 187 B4
Yenne F. 118 B2
Yeovil GB. 43 B4
Yepes E. 151 C4
Yerköy TR. 23 B8
Yerólakkos CY. 181 A2
Yeroskípou CY. 181 B1
Yerseke NL. 79 A4
Yerville F. 89 A4
Yeşildağ TR. 189 B6
Yeşilhisar TR. 23 B8
Yeşilköy TR. 186 B3
Yeşilova TR. 189 B4
Yeşilyurt TR. 188 A3
Yeste E. 164 A2
Yezerishche BY. 9 E6
Y Felinheli GB. 38 A2
Ygos-St Saturnin
 F. 128 C2
Ygrande F. 104 C1
Yialousa CY. 181 A3
Yiğilca TR. 187 B6
Yli-Ii FIN. 197 D8
Yli-Kärppä FIN. 197 D8
Yli-Muonia FIN. 196 A6
Ylitornio FIN. 196 C6
Ylivieska FIN. 3 D9
Ylläsjärvi FIN. 196 B7
Ymonville F. 103 A3
Yngsjö S. 63 C2
York GB. 40 B2
Youghal IRL. 29 C4
Yoğuntaş TR. 186 A2
Yozgat TR. 23 B8
Ypres = Ieper B. . . .78 B2
Yport F. 89 A4
Ypsonas CY. 181 B1
Yssingeaux F. 117 B4
Ystad S. 66 A2
Ystalyfera GB. 39 C3
Ystebrød N. 52 B1
Ystradgynlais GB. . .39 C3
Ytre Arna N. 46 B2
Ytre Enebakk N. 54 A2
Ytre Rendal N. 199 D8
Ytteran S. 199 B11
Ytterhogdal S. 199 C11
Yttermalung S. 49 B5
Yunak TR. 187 D6
Yuncos E. 151 B4
Yunquera E. 162 B3
Yunquera de Henares
 E. 151 B4
Yushkozero RUS. . .3 D13
Yverdon-les-Bains
 CH. 106 C1
Yvetot F. 89 A4
Yvignac F. 101 A3
Yvoir B. 79 B4
Yvonand CH. 106 C1
Yxnerum S. 56 B2
Yzeure F. 104 C2

Z

Zaamslag NL. 79 A3
Zaanstad NL. 70 B1
Žabalj SRB. 126 B2
Zabar H. 113 A4
Žabari SRB. 127 C3
Zabiče SLO. 123 B3
Zabierzów PL. 87 B3
Ząbki PL. 77 B6
Ząbkowice Śląskie
 PL. 85 B4
Zablaće HR. 138 B1
Žabljak MNE. 139 B5
Žabno PL. 87 B4
Žabno HR. 124 A1
Žabokreky SK. 98 C2
Zabor PL. 75 C4
Żabowo PL. 75 A4
Zabrdje BIH. 125 C4
Zábřeh CZ. 97 B4
Zabrežje SRB. 127 C2
Ząbrowo PL. 67 C4
Zabrze PL. 86 B2
Zabrzeź PL. 99 B4
Zacharo GR. 184 B2
Zadar HR. 137 A4
Zadzim PL. 86 A2
Zafarraya E. 163 B3
Zafferana Etnea I. . .177 B4
Zafra E. 155 C4
Žaga SLO. 122 A2
Zagajica SRB. 127 C3
Żagań PL. 84 A3
Zaglav HR. 137 B4
Zaglavak SRB. 127 D1
Zagnańsk PL. 87 B4
Zagora GR. 183 D5
Zagorc SLO. 110 C2
Zagoričani BIH. 138 B3
Zagorje SLO. 123 A4
Zagórów PL. 76 B2
Zagradje SRB. 127 C2
Zagreb HR. 124 B1
Zagrilla E. 163 A3
Zagvozd HR. 138 B3
Zagwiździe PL. 86 B1
Zagyvarekas H. 113 B4
Zagyvaróna H. 113 A3
Zahara E. 162 B2
Zahara de los Atunes
 E. 162 B2
Zahínos E. 155 C4
Zahna D. 83 A4
Záhoří CZ. 96 B2
Zahrádka CZ. 97 B3
Zahrensdorf D. 73 A3
Zaidín E. 153 A4
Zaječar SRB. 16 D5
Zákamenné SK. 99 B3
Zákány H. 124 A2
Zákányszék H. 126 A1
Zaklíczyn PL. 99 B4
Zakopane PL. 99 B3
Zakroczym PL. 77 B5
Zakrzew PL. 87 A5
Zakrzewo PL. 76 B3
Zakupy CZ. 84 B2
Zakynthos GR. 184 B1
Zalaapáti H. 111 C4
Zalabaksa H. 111 C3
Zalaegerszeg H. . . .111 C3
Zalakomár H. 111 C4
Zalak7ppány H. 111 C3
Zalalövő H. 111 C3
Zalamea de la Serena
 E. 156 B2
Zalamea la Real E. .161 B3
Zalaszentgrót H. . . .111 C4
Zalaszentiván H. . . .111 C3
Zalău RO. 17 B5
Zalavár H. 111 C4
Zalcsie E. 86 A3
Zaldibar E. 143 A4
Žalec SLO. 123 A4
Zalesie PL. 77 A5
Zalewo PL. 69 B4
Zalishchyky UA. 13 D6
Zalla E. 143 A3
Zaltbommel NL. 79 A5
Zamárdi H. 112 C1
Zamarte PL. 68 B2
Zamberk CZ. 85 B4
Zambra E. 163 A3
Zambugueira do Mar
 P. 160 B1
Zámoly H. 112 B2
Zamora E. 149 A4
Zamość PL. 13 C5
Zamoście PL. 86 A3
Zams A. 108 B1
Zandhoven B. 79 A4
Žandov CZ. 84 B2
Zandvoort NL. 70 B1
Zangliveri GR. 183 C5
Zánka H. 111 C4
Zaorejas E. 152 B1
Zaovine SRB. 127 D1
Zapadnaya Dvina
 RUS. 9 D8
Zapfend D. 94 A2
Zapole PL. 86 A2
Zapolyarnyy
 RUS. 193 C14
Zapponeta I. 171 B3
Zaprešić HR. 124 B1
Zaragoza E. 153 A3
Zarasai LT. 13 A7
Zarautz E. 144 A1
Zarcilla de Ramos
 E. 164 B3
Zaręby PL. 77 A6
Żarki PL. 86 B3
Żarko GR. 182 D4
Zarnow PL. 87 A4
Zarnowiec PL. 68 A3
Zaroišice CZ. 97 B4
Żarów PL. 85 B4
Zarren B. 78 A2
Zarrentin D. 73 A3
Żary PL. 84 A3
Zarza Capilla E. 156 B2
Zarza de Alange E. .156 B1
Zarza de Granadilla
 E. 149 B3
Zarza de Tajo E. . . .151 B4
Zarza la Mayor E. . .155 B4
Zarzadilla de Totana
 E. 164 B3
Zarzuela del Monte
 E. 150 B3
Zarzuela del Pinar
 E. 151 A3
Zas E. 140 A2
Zásmuky CZ. 96 B3
Žatec CZ. 83 B5
Zaton HR. 139 C4
Zatonie D. 84 A3
Zator PL. 99 A3
Zauchwitz D. 74 B2
Zavala BIH. 139 C3
Zavalje BIH. 124 C1
Zavattarello I. 120 C2
Zavidovići BIH. 139 A4
Zavlaka SRB. 127 C1
Zawady PL. 77 C5
Zawadzkie PL. 86 B2
Zawdy PL. 86 A2
Zawidów PL. 84 A3
Zawidz PL. 77 B4
Zawiercie PL. 86 B3
Zawoja PL. 99 B3
Zawonia PL. 85 A5
Žažina HR. 124 B2
Zázrivá SK. 99 B3
Zbarazh UA. 13 D6
Zbąszyń PL. 75 B4
Zbąszynek PL. 75 B4
Zbehy SK. 98 C2
Zbiersk PL. 76 C3
Zbiroh CZ. 96 B1
Zblewo PL. 69 B3
Zbójno PL. 77 A4
Zbrachlin PL. 76 A3
Zbraslav CZ. 96 B2
Zbraslavice CZ. 97 B3
Ždala HR. 124 A3
Ždánice CZ. 98 B1
Žďár nad Sázavou
 CZ. 97 B3
Zdbice PL. 75 A5
Zdenci HR. 125 B3
Ždiar SK. 99 B4
Zdice CZ. 96 B1
Zdirec nad Doubravou
 CZ. 97 B3
Zdolbuniv UA. 13 C7
Zdounky CZ. 98 B1
Zdrelo SRB. 127 C3
Zduńska Wola PL. . .86 A2
Zduny
 Łódzkie PL. 77 B4
 Wielkopolskie PL. .85 A5
Żdżary PL. 87 A4
Zdziechowice
 Opolskie PL. 86 A2
 Wielkopolskie PL. .76 B2
Zdziszowice PL. 86 B2
Zebera E. 143 A4
Žebrák CZ. 96 B1
Zebreira P. 155 B3
Zebrzydowa PL. 84 A3
Zalamea la Real E. .161 B3
Zechlin D. 74 A1
Zechlinerhütte D. . .74 A1
Zederhaus A. 109 B4
Žednik SRB. 126 B1
Zeebrugge B. 78 A3
Zegrze PL. 77 B6
Zehdenick D. 74 B2
Zehren D. 83 A5
Zeil D. 94 A2
Zeilarn D. 95 C4
Zeist NL. 70 B2
Zeithain D. 83 A5
Zeitz D. 83 A4
Želatava CZ. 97 B3
Żelazno PL. 68 A2
Zele B. 79 A4
Zelenoborskiy RUS .3 C13
Zelenogorsk RUS. . . .9 B6
Zelenograd RUS. . . .9 D10
Zelenogradsk RUS .12 A4
Železná Ruda CZ. . . .96 B1
Železnice CZ. 84 B3
Železnik SRB. 127 C2
Železniki SLO. 123 A3
Železný Brod CZ. . . .84 B3
Zelhem NL. 71 B3
Želiezovce SK. 112 A2
Želkowo PL. 68 A2
Zell
 CH. 106 B2
 Baden-Württemberg
 D. 93 C4
 Baden-Württemberg
 D. 106 B2
 Rheinland-Pfalz D. .92 A3
Zella-Mehlis D. 82 B2
Zell am See A. 109 B3
Zell am Ziller A. . . .108 B2
Zell an der Pram A. .96 C1
Zell bei Zellhof A. . .96 C2
Zellerndorf A. 97 C3
Zellingen D. 94 B1
Želovce SK. 112 A3
Zelów PL. 86 A3
Zeltweg A. 110 B1
Zelzate B. 79 A3
Zemberovce SK. 98 C2
Zembrzyce PL. 99 B3
Zemianske-Kostoľany
 SK. 98 C2
Zemitz D. 66 C2
Zemné SK. 112 B1
Zemst B. 79 B4
Zemun SRB. 127 C2
Zemunik Donji HR .137 A4
Zenica BIH. 139 A3
Zennor GB. 42 B1
Žepa BIH. 139 B5
Žepče BIH. 139 A4
Zepponami I. 168 A2
Zerbst D. 73 C5
Zerf D. 92 B2
Zerind RO. 113 C5
Żerków PL. 76 B2
Zermatt CH. 119 A4
Zernez CH. 107 C5
Zerpen-schleuse D .74 B2
Zestoa E. 144 A1
Zetel D. 71 A4
Zeulenroda D. 83 B3
Zeven D. 72 A2
Zevenaar NL. 70 C3
Zevenbergen NL. . . .79 A4
Zévio I. 121 B4
Zeytinbaği TR. 186 B3
Zeytindağ TR. 186 D2
Zgierz PL. 86 A3
Zgorzelec PL. 84 A3
Zgošča BIH. 139 A4
Zhabinka BY. 13 B6
Zharkovskiy RUS. . . .9 E8
Zhashkiv UA. 13 D9
Zhlobin BY. 13 B9
Zhmerynka UA. 13 D8
Zhodzina BY. 13 A8
Zhytomyr UA. 13 C8
Žiar nad Hronom
 SK. 98 C2
Zicavo F. 180 B2
Zickhusen D. 65 C4
Zidani Most SLO. . .123 A4
Ziddorf D. 73 A5
Ziębice PL. 85 B5
Ziegendorf D. 73 A4
Ziegenrück D. 83 B3
Zieleniec
 Dolnośląskie PL. . .85 B4
 Warmińsko-Mazurskie
 PL. 77 A6
Zachodnio-Pomorskie
 PL. 75 A4
Zielona D. 75 A4
Zielona Góra PL. . . .75 C4
Zieluń-Osada PL. . . .77 A4
Ziemetshausen D. . .94 C2
Zierenberg D. 81 A5
Zierikzee NL. 79 A3
Ziersdorf A. 97 C3
Zierzow D. 73 A4
Ziesar D. 73 B5
Ziesendorf D. 65 C5
Ziethen D. 74 B2
Žihle CZ. 96 A1
Žilina SK. 98 B2
Ziltendorf D. 74 B3
Zimandu Nou RO .126 A3
Zimna Woda PL. 77 A5
Zimnicea RO. 17 D6
Zinal CH. 119 A4
Zinasco I. 120 B2
Zingst D. 66 B1
Zinkgruvan S. 55 B6
Zinkovy CZ. 96 B1
Zinnowitz D. 66 B2
Zirc H. 112 B1
Žiri SLO. 123 A3
Zirl A. 108 B2
Zirndorf D. 94 B2
Žirovnice CZ. 97 B3
Zistersdorf A. 97 C4
Žitište SRB. 126 B2
Zitsa GR. 182 D2
Zittau D. 84 B2
Živaja HR. 124 B2
Živinice BIH. 139 A4
Zlatar HR. 124 A2
Zlatar Bistrica HR .124 A2
Zlate Hory CZ. 85 B5
Zlaté Klasy SK. 111 A4
Zlaté Moravce SK. . .98 C2
Zlatná na Ostrove
 SK. 112 B1
Zlatníky SK. 98 C2
Zlatograd BG. 183 B7
Žlebič SLO. 123 B3
Zlín CZ. 98 B1
Złocieniec PL. 75 A5
Złoczew PL. 86 A2
Zlonice CZ. 84 B2
Złotniki Kujawskie
 PL. 76 B3
Złotoryja PL. 85 A3
Złotów PL. 68 B2
Złoty Stok PL. 85 B4
Zlutice CZ. 83 B5
Zmajevac HR. 124 C2
Zmajevo SRB. 126 B1
Żmigród PL. 85 A4
Zmijavci HR. 138 B3
Žminj HR. 122 B2
Żnin PL. 76 B2
Znojmo CZ. 97 C4
Zöblitz D. 83 B5
Zocca I. 135 A3
Zoetermeer NL. 70 B1
Zofingen CH. 106 B2
Zogno I. 120 B2
Zohor SK. 111 A3
Zolling D. 95 C3
Zolochiv UA. 13 D6
Zomba H. 112 C2
Zomergem B. 79 A3
Zoñán E. 141 A3
Zonguldak TR. 187 A6
Zonhoven B. 79 B5
Zonza F. 180 B2
Zörbig D. 83 A4
Zorita E. 156 A2
Żory PL. 98 A2
Zossen D. 74 B2
Zottegem B. 79 B3
Zoutkamp NL. 71 A3
Zovi Do BIH. 139 B4
Zreče SLO. 123 A4
Zrenjanin SRB. 126 B2
Žrnovica HR. 138 B2
Zručnad Sazavou
 CZ. 97 B3
Zsadány H. 113 C5
Zsámbék H. 112 B2
Zsámbok H. 112 B3
Zsana H. 126 A1
Zschopau D. 83 B5
Zuberec SK. 99 B3
Zubieta E. 144 A2
Zubiri E. 144 B2
Zubtsov RUS. 9 D9
Zucaina E. 153 B3
Zudar D. 66 B2
Zuera E. 144 C3
Zufre E. 161 B3
Zug CH. 107 B3
Zuheros E. 163 A3
Zuidhorn NL. 71 A3
Zuidlaren NL. 71 A3
Zuidwolde NL. 71 B3
Zújar E. 164 B2
Žukowo PL. 69 A3
Žuljana HR. 138 C3
Žulová CZ. 85 B5
Zülpich D. 80 B2
Zumaia E. 144 A1
Zumárraga E. 143 A4
Zundert NL. 79 A4
Županja HR. 125 B4
Zurgena E. 164 B2
Zürich CH. 107 B3
Żuromin PL. 77 A4
Zurzach CH. 106 B3
Zusmarshausen D .94 C2
Zusow D. 65 C4
Züssow D. 66 C2
Žuta Lokva HR. 123 C4
Zutphen NL. 70 B3
Žužemberk SLO. . . .123 B3
Zvenyhorodka UA. .13 D9
Zvikovské Podhradi
 CZ. 96 B2
Zvolen SK. 99 C3
Zvolenská Slatina
 SK. 99 C3
Zvornik BIH. 139 A5
Zwartsluis NL. 70 B3
Zweibrücken D. 93 B3
Zweisimmen CH. . .106 C2
Zwettl A. 97 C3
Zwettl an der Rodl
 A. 96 C2
Zwickau D. 83 B4
Zwiefalten D. 107 A4
Zwieryn PL. 75 B4
Zwierzno PL. 69 A4
Zwiesel D. 96 B1
Zwieselstein A. 108 C2
Zwoleń PL. 87 A5
Zwolle NL. 70 B3
Zwönitz D. 83 B4
Żychlin PL. 77 B4
Zydowo
 Wielkopolskie PL. .76 B2
 Zachodnio-Pomorskie
 PL. 68 A1
Żyrardów PL. 77 B5
Żytno PL. 86 B3
Żywiec PL. 99 B3
Zyyi CY. 181 B2